Mobil 1998
TRAVEL GUIDE®

Great Lakes

ILLINOIS • INDIANA
MICHIGAN • OHIO • WISCONSIN

ONTARIO

Fodor's Travel Publications, Inc.

Guide Staff

General Manager: Diane E. Connolly

Editorial/Inspection Coordinators: Sara D. Hauber, Doug Weinstein

Inspection Assistant: Brenda Piszczek

Editorial Assistants: Korrie Klier, Julie Raio, Kathleen Rose, Kristin Schiller, Elizabeth Schwar

Creative Director: Fabrizio La Rocca

Cover Design: John Olenyik

Cover Photograph: Phil Schermeister/Photographers/Aspen

Acknowledgments

We gratefully acknowledge the help of our more than 100 field representatives for their efficient and perceptive inspection of every lodging and dining establishment listed; the establishments' proprietors for their coorperation in showing their facilities and providing information about them; the many users of previous editions of the *Mobil Travel Guide* who have taken the time to share their experiences; and for their time and information, the thousands of chambers of commerce, convention and visitors bureaus, city, state, and provincial tourism offices, and government agencies who assisted in our research.

Mobil

Copyright

Published in 1998 by Fodor's Travel Publications, Inc.
201 E. 50th St.
New York, NY 10022

Great Lakes
ISBN 0-679-03500-1
ISSN 0076-9789

Printed in the United States of America
10 9 8 7 6 5 4 3 2 1

Contents

Great Lakes

Maps

Larger, more detailed maps are available at many Mobil service stations

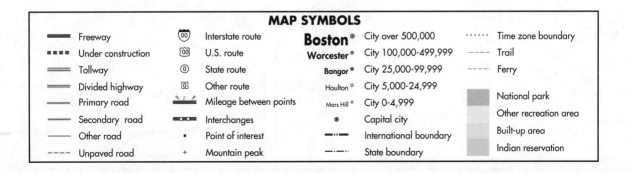

MAP SYMBOLS

Freeway	⬡ Interstate route	**Boston**⊛ City over 500,000
Under construction	⬡ U.S. route	**Worcester**⊛ City 100,000-499,999
Tollway	⊚ State route	**Bangor**⊛ City 25,000-99,999
Divided highway	▢ Other route	Houlton ○ City 5,000-24,999
Primary road	Mileage between points	Mars Hill ○ City 0-4,999
Secondary road	Interchanges	⊛ Capital city
Other road	▪ Point of interest	International boundary
Unpaved road	+ Mountain peak	State boundary

- ⋯⋯ Time zone boundary
- ---- Trail
- ---- Ferry
- National park
- Other recreation area
- Built-up area
- Indian reservation

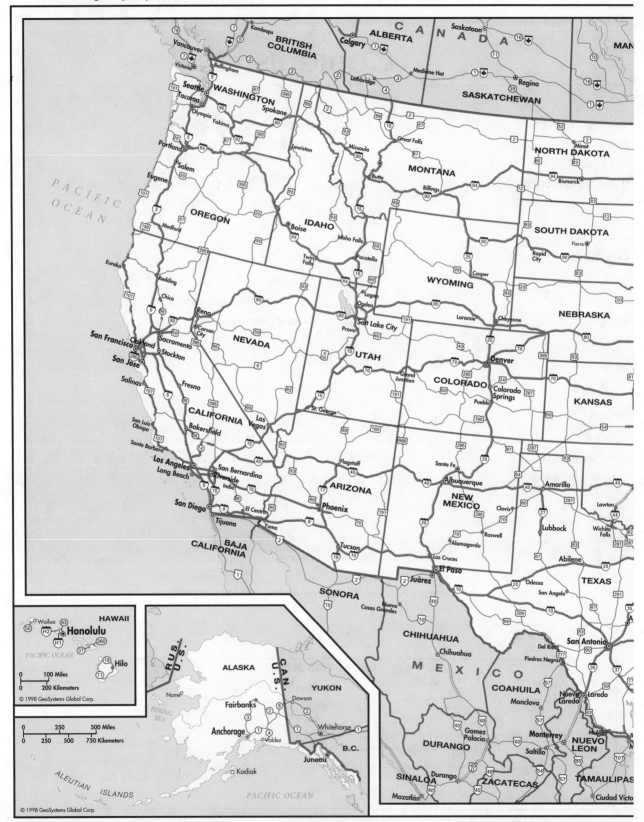

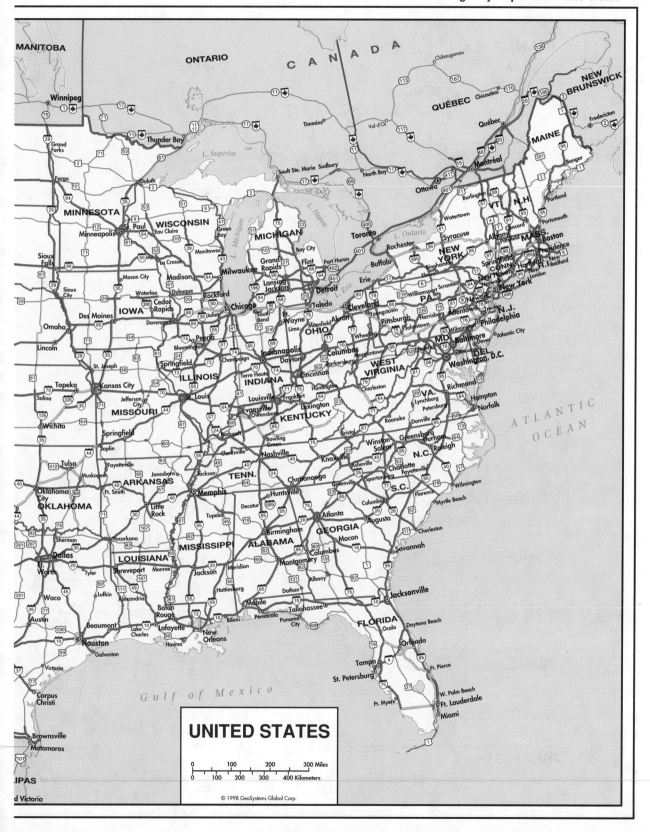

UNITED STATES

0   100   200   300 Miles
0   100   200   300   400 Kilometers

© 1998 GeoSystems Global Corp.

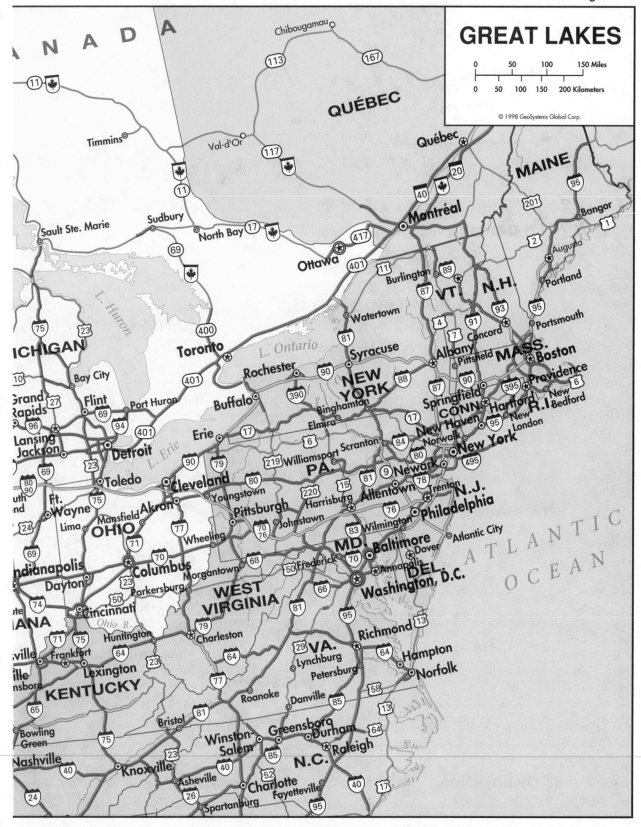

GREAT LAKES

© 1998 GeoSystems Global Corp.

MANITOBA

Winnipeg ⊛

L. of the Woods

ONTARIO

NORTH DAKOTA

Bismarck ⊛

L. Superior

Thunder Bay ⊛

187
4:35

Duluth ⊛

292
6:24

MINNESOTA

156
3:05

WISCONSIN

SOUTH DAKOTA

Pierre ⊛

St. Paul

Minneapolis ⊛

278
5:58

Green Bay ⊛

MICH

306
6:27

Mississippi

268
5:21

Madison ⊛

79
1:33

Milwaukee ⊛

116
2:19

Grand Rapids

1:

384
7:39

247
4:55

361
7:17

R.

150
2:58

146

89

234
4:39

IOWA

Chicago ⊛

NEBRASKA

Des Moines ⊛

136
2:42

171
3:25

Davenport ⊛

168
3:22

188
3:43

INDIAN

Omaha ⊛

Lincoln ⊛

Platte R.

188
3:44

194
3:50

140
2:46

135
2:40

Bloomington ⊛

178
3:31

Missouri R.

Springfield ⊛

63
1:14

216
4:15

Indianapolis ⊛

KANSAS

Topeka ⊛

63
1:16

Kansas City ⊛

406
8:05

343
6:50

ILLINOIS

97
1:56

238
4:46

112
2:14

252
5:02

St. Louis ⊛

264
5:16

Louisville

MISSOURI

Wichita ⊛

Arkansas

Springfield ⊙

307
6:05

175
3:30

OKLAHOMA

Tulsa ⊙

R.

ARKANSAS

Nas ⊛

TENN

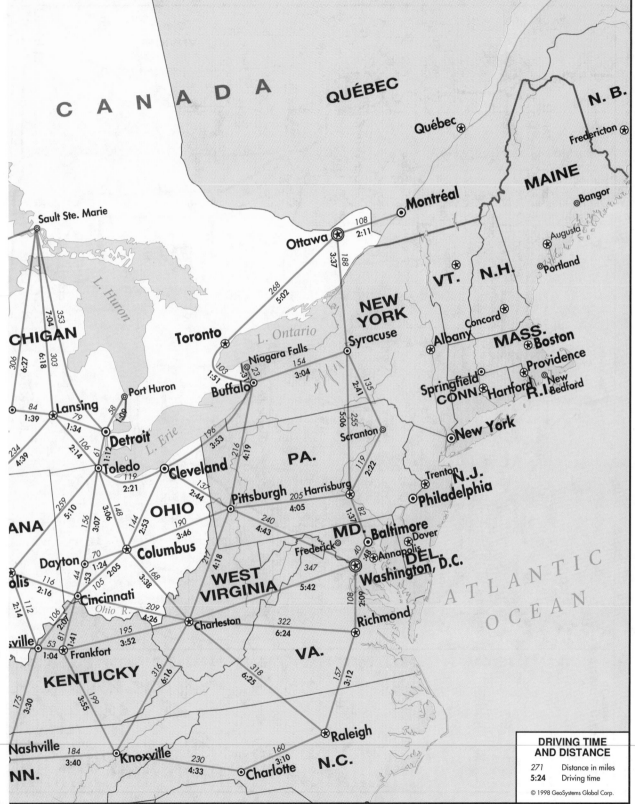

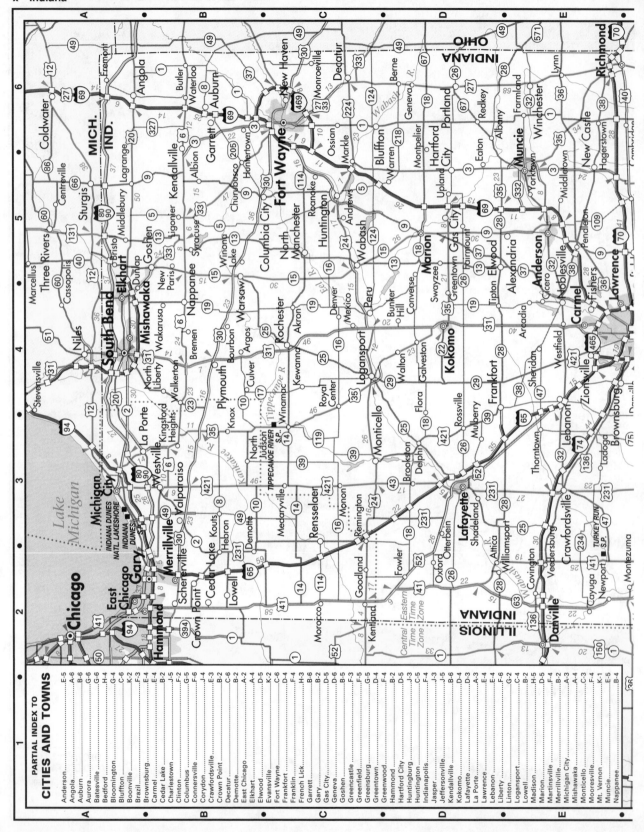

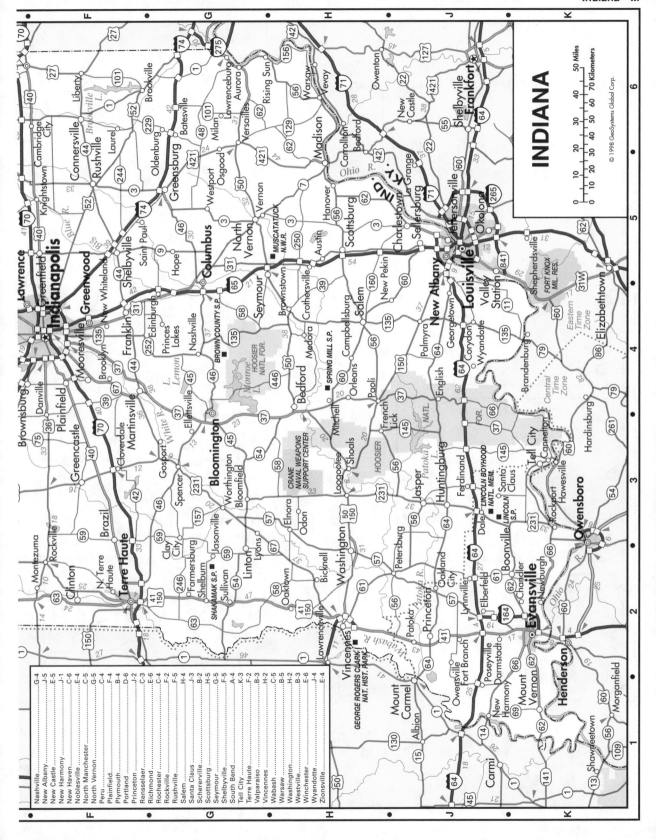

INDIANA

© 1998 GeoSystems Global Corp.

50 Miles
70 Kilometers

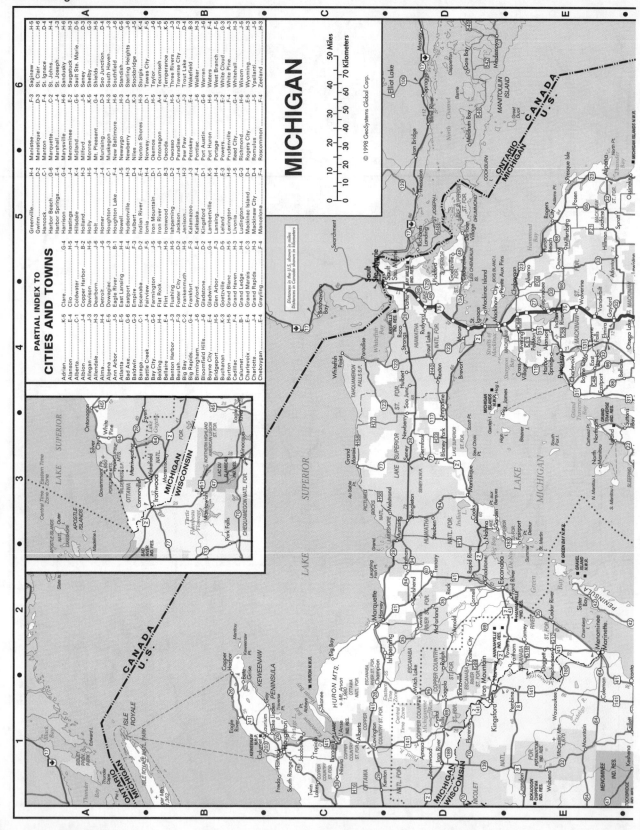

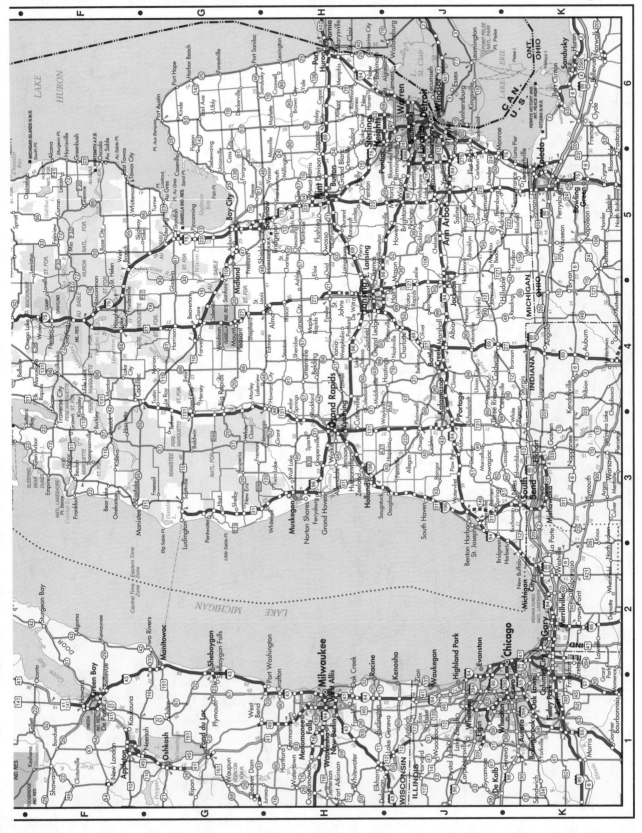

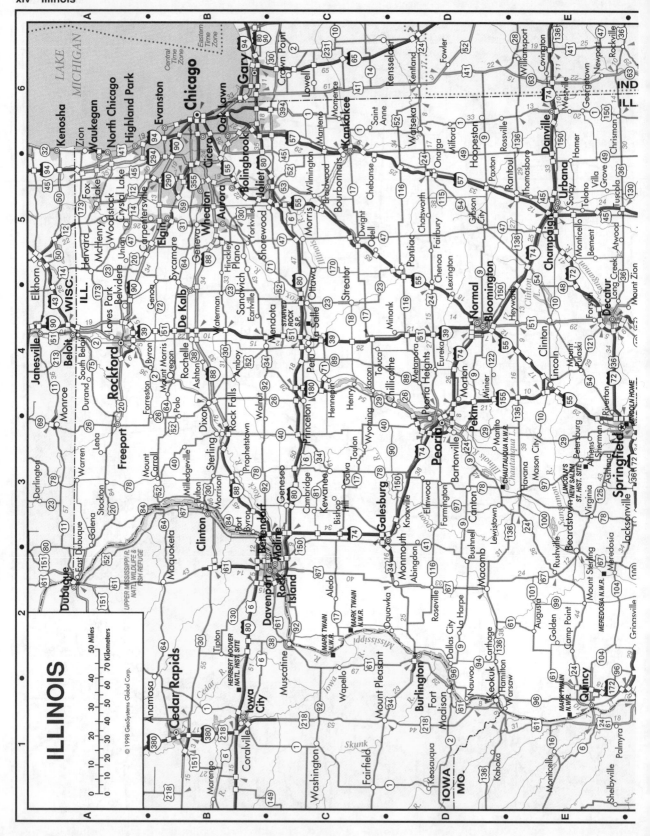

ILLINOIS

© 1998 GeoSystems Global Corp.

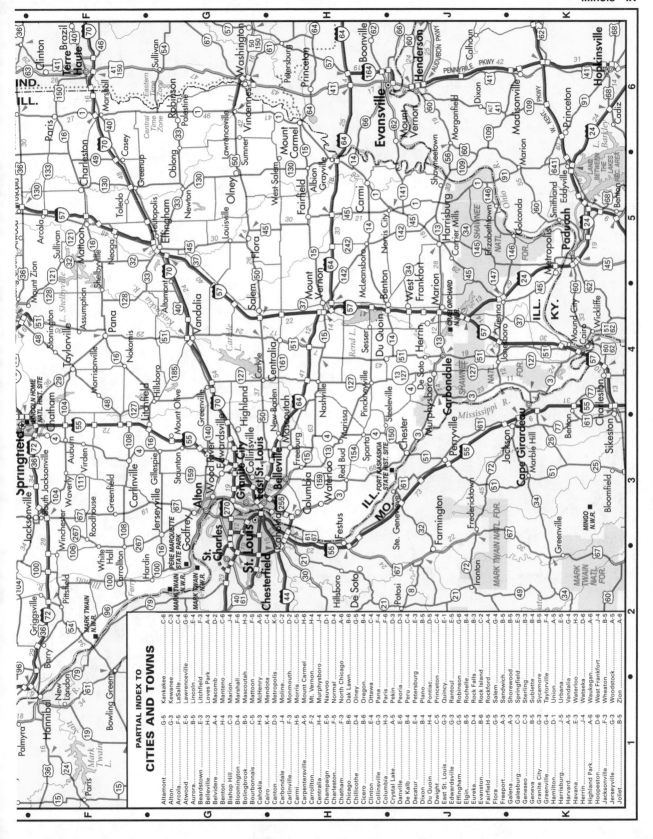

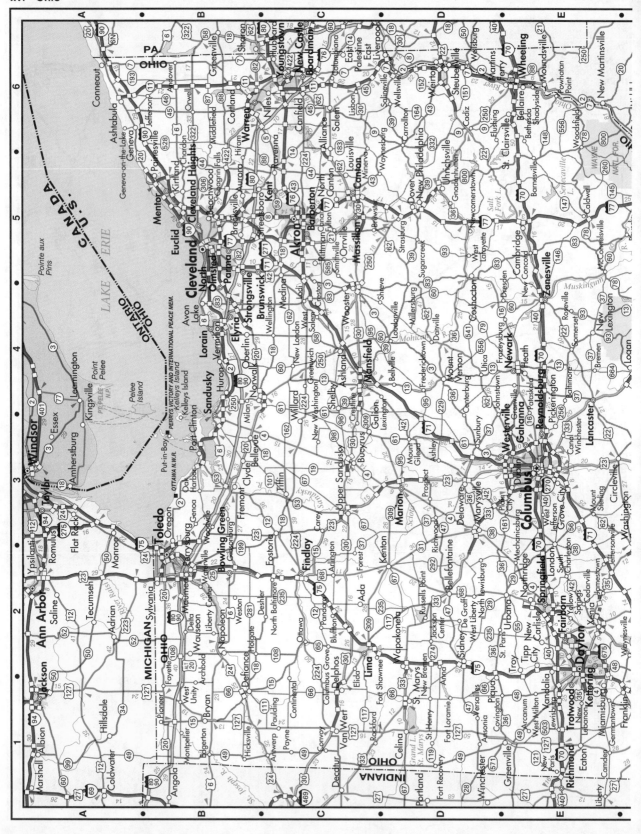

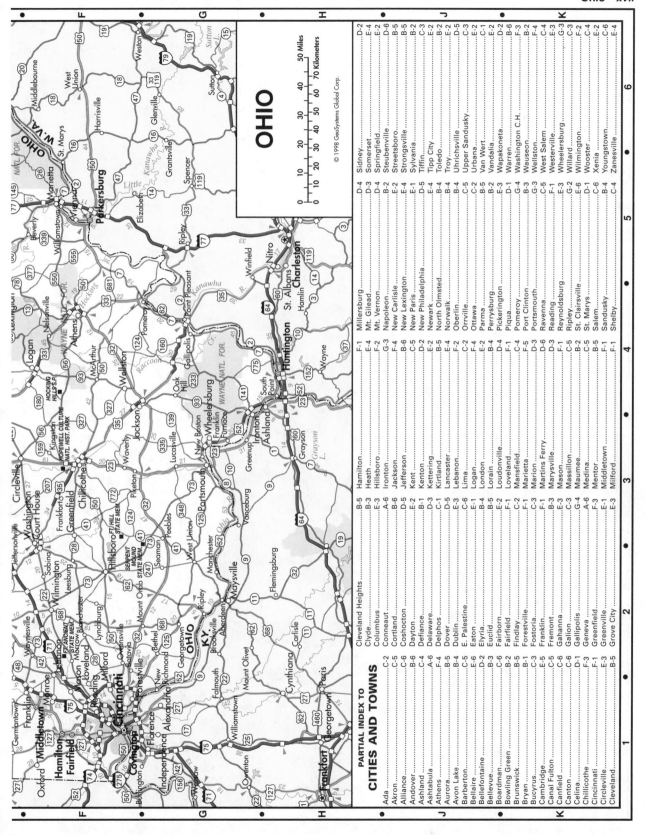

OHIO

© 1998 GeoSystems Global Corp.

Scale: 0 10 20 30 40 50 Miles / 0 10 20 30 40 50 60 70 Kilometers

PARTIAL INDEX TO
CITIES AND TOWNS

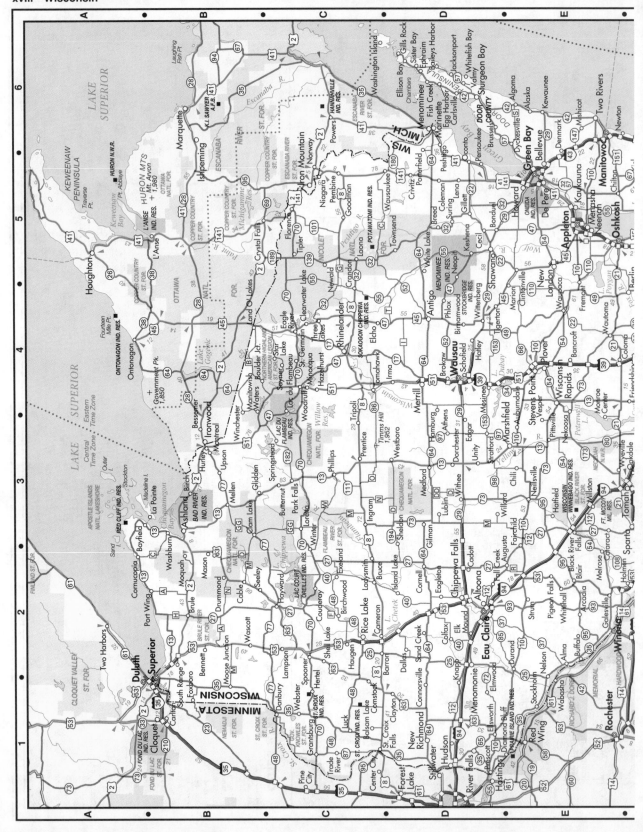

WISCONSIN

© 1998 GeoSystems Global Corp.

Scale:
0 10 20 30 40 50 Miles
0 10 20 30 40 50 60 70 Kilometers

PARTIAL INDEX TO CITIES AND TOWNS

Place	Grid	Place	Grid	Place	Grid
Algoma	E-6	Hales Corners	C-4	Menomonee Falls	G-5
Alma	E-2	Hayward	C-2	Menomonie	D-2
Antigo	D-4	Hudson	D-1	Merrill	D-4
Appleton	E-5	Hurley	A-4	Milwaukee	G-6
Ashland	B-3	Janesville	G-4	Mineral Point	G-3
Baileys Harbor	D-6	Kaukauna	E-5	Minocqua	C-4
Baraboo	F-4	Kenosha	G-6	Mt. Horeb	G-4
Bayfield	A-3	Lac du Flambeau	C-4	Neenah	E-5
Beaver Dam	F-5	La Crosse	E-2	New Glarus	G-4
Beloit	H-4	Ladysmith	C-2	New London	E-5
Black River Falls	E-3	Lake Geneva	G-5	Oconomowoc	G-5
Boulder Junction	B-4	Land O' Lakes	B-4	Oconto	D-5
Burlington	G-5	Lyndon Station	F-3	Oshkosh	E-5
Cable	B-2	Madison	G-4	Park Falls	C-3
Cedarburg	F-5	Manitowish Waters	B-3	Peshtigo	D-6
Chippewa Falls	D-2	Manitowoc	E-6	Platteville	G-3
Cornell	D-2	Marinette	D-6	Plymouth	E-5
Crandon	C-4	Marshfield	E-3	Port Washington	F-6
Delavan	G-5	Mauston	F-3	Portage	F-4
DePere	E-5	Medford	D-3	Prairie du Chien	G-2
Dodgeville	G-3	Menasha	E-5	Prairie du Sac	F-4
Durand	D-2			Racine	G-6
Eagle River	C-4			Reedsburg	F-3
East Troy	G-5			Rhinelander	C-4
Egg Harbor	D-6			Rice Lake	C-2
Elkhart Lake	E-5			Richland Center	F-3
Elkhorn	G-5			Ripon	F-5
Ellison Bay	D-6			River Falls	D-1
Ephraim	D-6			St. Croix Falls	C-1
Fish Creek	D-6			St. Germain	C-4
Fond du Lac	F-5			Sauk City	G-4
Fontana	G-5			Sayner	C-4
Fort Atkinson	G-5			Shawano	D-5
Galesville	E-2			Sheboygan	E-5
Gillett	D-5			Sister Bay	D-6
Green Bay	E-5			Sparta	E-2
Green Lake	F-4			Spooner	C-2
				Spring Green	F-3
				Stevens Point	E-4
				Stoughton	G-4
				Sturgeon Bay	D-6
				Superior	B-2
				Three Lakes	C-4
				Tomah	F-3
				Tomahawk	C-4
				Two Rivers	E-6
				Washington Island	C-6
				Watertown	G-5
				Waukesha	G-5
				Waupaca	E-4
				Waupun	F-5
				Wausau	D-4
				Wausaukee	D-5
				Wautoma	E-4
				Wauwatosa	G-5
				West Allis	G-5
				West Bend	F-5
				Whitehall	E-2
				Whitewater	G-5
				Wisconsin Dells	F-4
				Wisconsin Rapids	E-4
				Woodruff	C-4

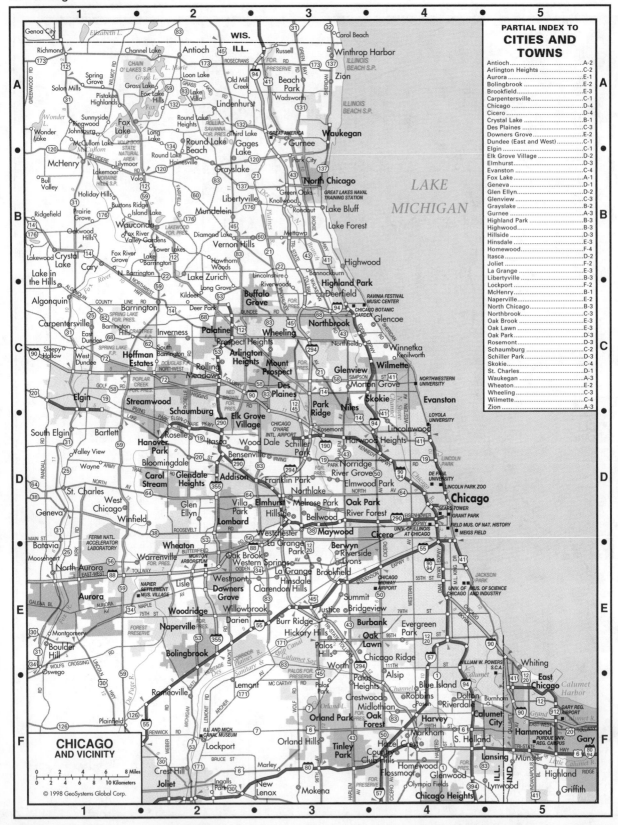

CHICAGO
AND VICINITY

0   2   4   6   8 Miles
0 2 4 6 8 10 Kilometers

© 1998 GeoSystems Global Corp.

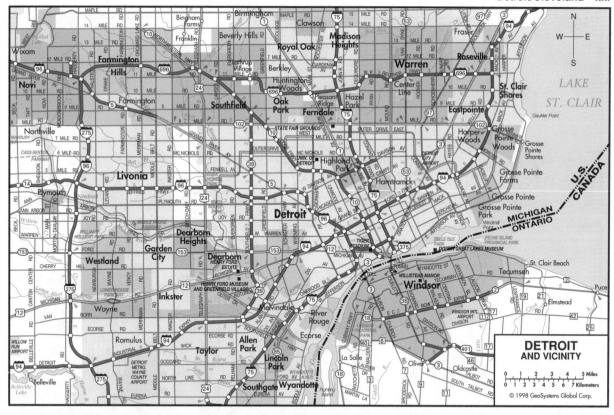

DETROIT
AND VICINITY

0 1 2 3 4 5 Miles
0 1 2 3 4 5 6 7 Kilometers

© 1998 GeoSystems Global Corp.

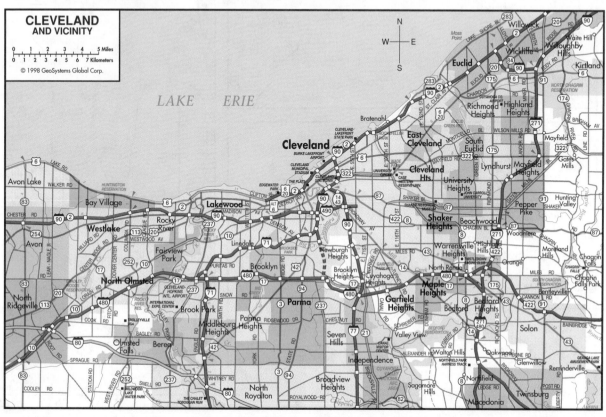

CLEVELAND
AND VICINITY

0 1 2 3 4 5 Miles
0 1 2 3 4 5 6 7 Kilometers

© 1998 GeoSystems Global Corp.

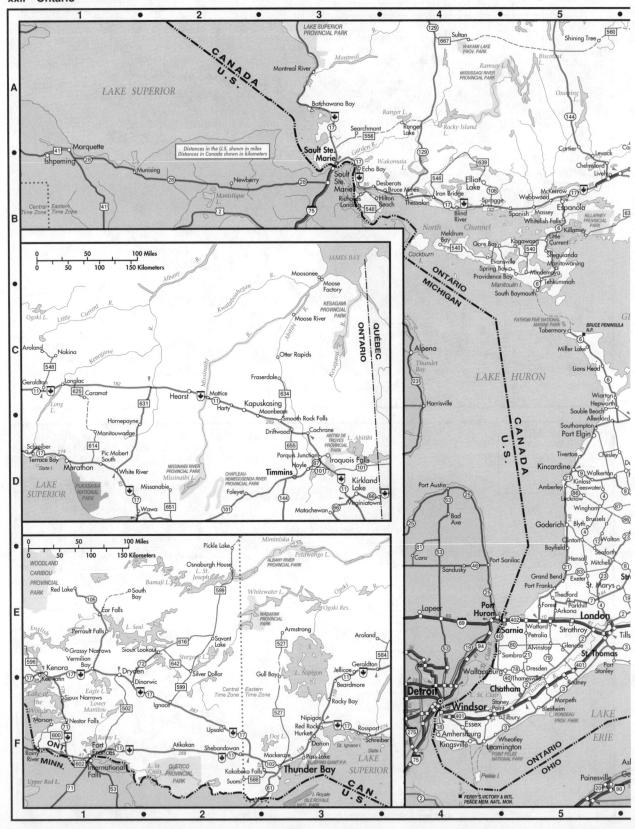

Distances in the U.S. shown in miles
Distances in Canada shown in kilometers

0   50   100 Miles
0   50   100   150 Kilometers

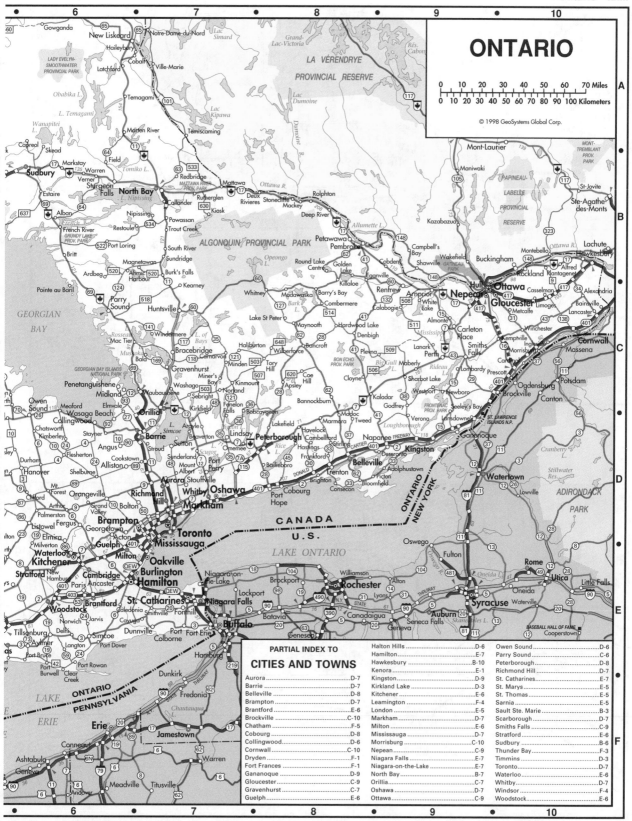

ONTARIO

0 10 20 30 40 50 60 70 Miles
0 10 20 30 40 50 60 70 80 90 100 Kilometers

© 1998 GeoSystems Global Corp.

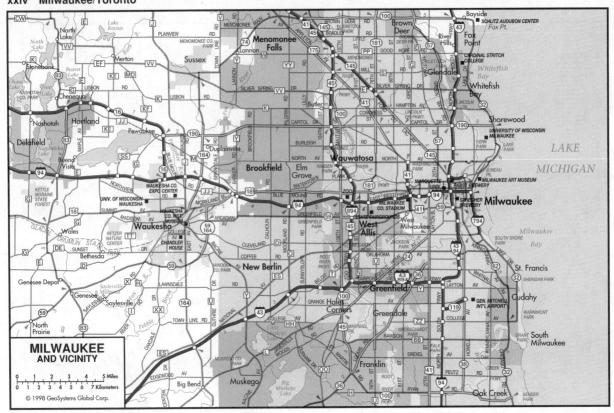

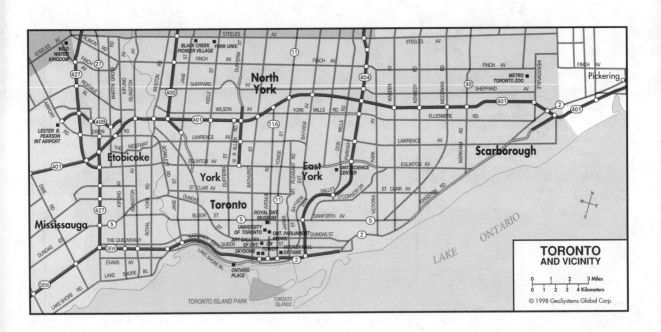

Before a long trip,
it's always smart to stop at Mobil.

On its ten-year, billion-mile mission, the International Space Station won't make pit stops, and its air system can't ever break down. So the grease for its fans and motors isn't a detail. It had to pass nearly as many tests as astronauts do, and in the end a Mobil synthetic won the job. What excites us is that we didn't create this grease for outer space. You can buy the same stuff (Mobilith SHC® 220) for your bicycle, bus or paper mill. Which, to us, shows the value of how we do research, trying to make things better than necessary. Nobody asked us to develop synthetic lubes, but we pursued it because that's how real innovation works. You aim to exceed present-day expectations so that when the future arrives, you're already there. To learn more, visit www.mobil.com.

Mobil® The energy
to make a difference

Back when racing began, our decals were a lot easier to read.

When J. Frank Duryea's race car streamed across the finish line at a breathtaking 5 mph, Mobil helped get it there. Of course, Mobil Motor Oil has protected somewhat more sophisticated engines since then. In fact, Mobil 1 is the official oil of Team Penske, the most successful team in Indy history. So whether you work in racing or race to work, call 1-800-ASK-MOBIL and find out more about any of our advanced oils. After all, we've found there's really only one place to promote our name. Under the hood.

A Word to Our Readers

Whether you're going on an extended family vacation, a weekend getaway, or a business trip, you need good, solid information on where to stay and eat and what to see and do. It would be nice if you could take a corps of well-seasoned travelers with you to suggest lodgings and activities, or ask a local restaurant critic for advice on dining spots, but since these options are rarely practical, the *Mobil Travel Guide* is the next best thing. It puts a huge database of information at your disposal and provides the value judgments and advice you need to use that information to its fullest.

Published by Fodor's Travel Publications, Inc., in collaboration with Mobil Corporation, the sponsor since 1958, these books contain the most comprehensive, up-to-date information possible on each region. In fact, listings are revised and ratings reviewed annually, based on inspection reports from our field representatives, evaluation by senior staff, and comments from more than 100,000 readers. These incredible data are then used to develop the *Mobil Travel Guide*'s impartial quality ratings, indicated by stars, which Americans have trusted for decades.

Space limitations make it impossible for us to include every fine hotel and restaurant, so we have picked a representative group, all above-average for their type. There's no charge to any establishment for inclusion, and only places that meet our standards are chosen. Because travelers' needs differ, we make every effort to select a variety of establishments and provide the information to decide what's right for you. If you're looking for a lodging at a certain price or location, or even one that offers 24-hour room service, you'll find the answers you need at your fingertips. Take a minute to read the next section, How to Use This Book; it'll make finding the information you want a breeze.

Also look at Making the Most of Your Trip, the section that follows. It's full of tips from savvy travelers that can help you save money, stay safe, and get around more easily—the keys to making any trip a success.

Of course, the passage of time means that some establishments will close, change hands, remodel, improve, or go downhill. Though every effort has been made to ensure the accuracy of all information when it was printed, change is inevitable. Always call and confirm that a place is open and that it has the features you want. Whatever your experiences at any of the establishments we list—and we hope they're terrific—or if you have general comments about our guide, we'd love to hear from you. Use the convenient postage-paid card near the end of this book, or drop us a line at the *Mobil Travel Guide,* Fodor's Travel Publications, Inc., 4709 W. Golf Road, Suite 803, Skokie, IL 60076.

So pack this book in your suitcase or toss it next to you on the front seat. If it gets dog-eared, so much the better. We here at the *Mobil Travel Guide* wish you a safe and successful trip.

Bon voyage and happy driving,

THE EDITORS

Welcome

For 40 years, the *Mobil Travel Guide* has provided travelers in North America with reliable advice on finding good value, quality service, and the attractions that give a destination its special character. During this time, our teams of culinary and hospitality experts have worked hard to develop objective and exacting standards. In so doing, they seek to fully meet the desires and expectations of a broad range of customers.

At Mobil, we demonstrate the energy to make a difference through a commitment to excellence that allows us to bring the best service and products to the people we serve. We believe that the ability to respond to and anticipate customers' needs is what distinguishes good companies from truly great ones.

It is our hope, whether your travels are for business or leisure, over a long distance or a short one, that this book will be your companion, dependably guiding you to quality and value in lodging and dining.

Finally, I ask that you help us improve the guides. Please take the time to fill out the customer feedback form at the back of this book or contact us on the Internet at www.mobil.com/travel.

Lucio A. Noto

Lucio A. Noto
Chairman and
Chief Executive Officer
Mobil Corporation

How to Use This Book

The *Mobil Travel Guide* is easy to use. Each state chapter begins with a general introduction that both provides a general geographical and historical orientation to the state and covers basic statewide tourist information, from state recreation areas to seat-belt laws. The balance of each chapter is devoted to the travel destinations within the state—cities and towns, state and national parks, and tourist regions—which, like the states themselves, are arranged alphabetically.

What follows is an explanation of the wealth of information you'll find within those travel destinations—information on the area, on things to see and do there, and on where to stay and eat.

Maps and Map Coordinates

The first thing you'll notice is that next to each destination is a set of map coordinates. These refer to the appropriate state map in the front of this book. In addition, there are maps of selected larger cities in the front section as well as maps of key neighborhoods within the sections on the cities themselves.

Destination Information

Because many travel destinations are so close to other cities and towns where visitors might find additional attractions, accommodations, and restaurants, cross-references to those places are included whenever possible. Also listed are addresses and phone numbers for travel-information resources—usually the local chamber of commerce or office of tourism—as well as pertinent vital statistics and a brief introduction to the area.

What to See and Do

More than 11,000 museums, art galleries, amusement parks, universities, historic sites and houses, plantations, churches, state parks, ski areas, and other attractions are described in the *Mobil Travel Guide*. A white star on a black background ★ signals that the attraction is one of the best in the state. Since municipal parks, public tennis courts, swimming pools, and small educational institutions are common to most towns, they are generally excluded.

Following the attraction's description are the months and days it's open, address/location and phone number, and admission costs (see the inside front cover for an explanation of the cost symbols). Note that directions are given from the center of the town under which the attraction is listed, which may not necessarily be the town in which the attraction is located. Zip codes are listed only if they differ from those given for the town.

Events

Events—categorized as annual, seasonal, or special—are highlighted. An annual event is one that's held every year for a period of usually no longer than a week to 10 days; festivals and fairs are typical entries. A seasonal event is one that may or may not be annual and that is held for a number of weeks or months in the year, such as horse racing, summer theater, concert or opera festivals, and professional sports. Special event listings occur infrequently and mark a certain date or event, such as a centennial or other commemorative celebration.

Major Cities

Additional information on airports and transportation, suburbs, and neighborhoods, including a list of restaurants by neighborhood, may be included for large cities.

Lodging and Restaurant Listings

ORGANIZATION

For both lodgings and restaurants, when a property is in a town that does not have its own heading, the listing appears under the town nearest its location with the address and town in parentheses immediately after the establishment name. In large cities, lodgings located within 5 miles of major, commercial airports are listed under a separate "Airport" heading, following the city listings.

LODGING CLASSIFICATIONS

Each property is classified by type according to the characteristics below. Because the following features and services are found at most motels, lodges, motor hotels, and hotels, they are not shown in those listings:

- Year-round operation with a single rate structure unless otherwise quoted
- European plan (meals not included in room rate)
- Bathroom with tub and/or shower in each room
- Air-conditioned/heated, often with individual room control
- Cots
- Daily maid service
- Phones in rooms
- Elevators

Motels and Lodges. Accommodations are in low-rise structures with rooms easily accessible to parking (usually free). Properties have outdoor room entry and small, functional lobbies. Service is often limited, and dining may not be offered in lower-rated motels and lodges. Shops and businesses are found only in higher-rated properties, as are bellhops, room service, and restaurants serving three meals daily.

Lodges differ from motels primarily in their emphasis on outdoor recreational activities and in location. They are often found in resort and rural areas rather than in major cities or along highways.

Motor Hotels. Offering the convenience of motels along with many of the features of hotels, motor hotels range from low-rise structures offering limited services to multistory buildings with a wide range of services and facilities. Multiple building entrances, elevators, inside hallways, and parking areas (generally free) near access doors are some of the features of a motor hotel. Lobbies offer sitting areas and 24-hour desk and switchboard services. Often bellhop and valet services as well as restaurants serving three meals a day are found. Expanded recreational facilities and more than one restaurant are available in higher-rated properties.

The distinction between motor hotels and hotels in metropolitan areas is minor.

Hotels. To be categorized as a hotel, an establishment must have most of the following facilities and services: multiple floors, a restaurant and/or coffee shop, elevators, room service, bellhops, a spacious lobby, and recreational facilities. In addition, the following features and services not shown in listings are also found:

- Valet service (one-day laundry/cleaning service)
- Room service during hours restaurant is open
- Bellhops
- Some oversize beds

Resorts. These specialize in stays of three days or more and usually offer American Plan and/or housekeeping accommodations. Their emphasis is on recreational facilities, and a social

director is often available. Food services are of primary importance, and guests must be able to eat three meals a day on the premises, either in restaurants or by having access to an on-site grocery store and preparing their own meals.

Inns. Frequently thought of as a small hotel, an inn is a place of homelike comfort and warm hospitality. It is often a structure of historic significance, with an equally interesting setting. Meals are a special occasion, and refreshments are frequently served in late afternoon. Rooms are usually individually decorated, often with antiques or furnishings representative of the locale. Phones, bathrooms, and TVs may not be available in every room.

Guest Ranches. Like resorts, guest ranches specialize in stays of three days or more. Guest ranches also offer meal plans and extensive outdoor activities. Horseback riding is usually a feature; there are stables and trails on the ranch property, and trail rides and daily instruction are part of the program. Many guest ranches are working ranches, ranging from casual to rustic, and guests are encouraged to participate in ranch life. Eating is often family-style and may also include cookouts. Western saddles are assumed; phone ahead to inquire about English saddle availability.

Cottage Colonies. These are housekeeping cottages and cabins that are usually found in recreational areas. Any dining or recreational facilities are noted in our listing.

DINING CLASSIFICATIONS

Restaurants. Most dining establishments fall into this category. All have a full kitchen and offer table service and a complete menu. Parking on or near the premises, in a lot or garage, is assumed. When a property offers valet or other special parking features, or when only street parking is available, it is noted in the listing.

Unrated Dining Spots. These places, listed after Restaurants in many cities, are chosen for their unique atmosphere, specialized menu, or local flavor. They include delis, ice-cream parlors, cafeterias, tearooms, and pizzerias. Because they may not have a full kitchen or table service, they are not given a *Mobil Travel Guide* rating. Often they offer extraordinary value and quick service.

QUALITY RATINGS

The *Mobil Travel Guide* has been rating lodgings and restaurants on a national basis since the first edition was published in 1958. For years the guide was the only source of such ratings, and it remains among the few guidebooks to rate restaurants across the country.

All listed establishments were inspected by experienced field representatives or evaluated by a senior staff member. Ratings are based upon their detailed inspection reports of the individual properties, on written evaluations of staff members who stay and dine anonymously, and on an extensive review of comments from our readers.

You'll find a key to the rating categories, ★ through ★★★★★, on the inside front cover. All establishments in the book are recommended. Even a ★ place is above average, usually providing a basic, informal experience. Rating categories reflect both the features the property offers and its quality in relation to similar establishments.

For example, lodging ratings take into account the number and quality of facilities and services, the luxury of appointments, and the attitude and professionalism of staff and management. A ★ establishment provides a comfortable night's lodging. A ★★ property offers more than a facility that rates one star, and the decor is well planned and integrated. Establishments that rate ★★★ are professionally managed and staffed and often beautifully appointed; the lodging experience is truly excellent and the range of facilities is extensive. Properties that have been given ★★★★ not only offer many services but also have their own style and personality; they are luxurious, creatively decorated, and superbly maintained. The ★★★★★ properties are among the best in the United States, superb in every respect and entirely memorable, year in and year out.

Restaurant evaluations reflect the quality of the food and the ingredients, preparation, and presentation as well as service levels and the property's decor and ambience. A restaurant that has fairly simple goals for menu and decor but that achieves those goals superbly might receive the same number of stars as a restaurant with somewhat loftier ambitions but whose execution falls somewhat short of the mark. In general, ★ indicates a restaurant that's a good choice in its area, usually fairly simple and perhaps catering to a clientele of locals and families; ★★ denotes restaurants that are more highly recommended in their area; ★★★ restaurants are of national caliber, with professional and attentive service and a skilled chef in the kitchen; ★★★★ reflects superb dining choices, where remarkable food is served in equally remarkable surroundings; and ★★★★★ represents that rarefied group of the best restaurants in the country, where in addition to near perfection in every detail, there's that special something extra that makes for an unforgettable dining experience. A list of the four-star and five-star establishments in this region is located just before the state listings.

Each rating is reviewed annually and each establishment must work to maintain its rating (or improve it). Every effort is made to assure that ratings are fair and accurate; the designated ratings are published purely as an aid to travelers.

In general, properties that are very new or have recently undergone major management changes are considered difficult to assess fairly and are often listed without ratings.

Good Value Check Mark. In all locales, you'll find a wide range of lodging and dining establishments with a ✓ in front of a star rating. This indicates an unusually good value at economical prices as follows:

In Major Cities and Resort Areas

Lodging: average $105–$125 per night for singles; average $115–$140 per night for doubles

Restaurants: average $25 for a complete lunch; average $40 for a complete dinner, exclusive of beverages and gratuities

Local Area Listings

Lodging: average $50–$60 per night for singles; average $60–$75 per night for doubles

Restaurants: average $12 for a complete lunch; average $20 for a complete dinner, exclusive of beverages and gratuities

LODGINGS

Each listing gives the name, address, directions (when there is no street address), neighborhood and/or directions from downtown (in major cities), phone number (local and 800), fax number, number and type of rooms available, room rates, and seasons open (if not year-round). Also included are details on recreational and dining facilities on property or nearby, the presence of a luxury level, and credit-card information. A key to the symbols at the end of each listing is on the inside front cover. (Note that Mobil Corporation credit cards cannot be used for payment of meals and room charges.)

All prices quoted in the *Mobil Travel Guide* publications are expected to be in effect at the time of publication and during the entire year; however, prices cannot be guaranteed. In some localities there may be short-term price variations because of special events or holidays. Whenever possible, these price changes are noted. Certain resorts have complicated rate structures that vary with the time of year; always confirm listed rates when you make your plans.

RESTAURANTS

Listings give the name, address, directions (when there is no street address), neighborhood and/or directions from downtown (in major cities), phone number, hours and days of operation (if not open daily year-round), reservation policy, cuisine (if other than American), price range for each meal served, children's meals (if offered), specialties, and credit card information. Additionally, special features such as chef ownership, ambience, and entertainment are noted. By carefully reading the detailed restaurant information and comparing prices, you can easily determine whether the restaurant is formal and elegant or informal and comfortable for families.

TERMS AND ABBREVIATIONS IN LISTINGS

The following terms and abbreviations are used consistently throughout the listings:

A la carte entrees With a price, refers to the cost of entrees/main dishes only that are not accompanied by side dishes.

AP American plan (lodging plus all meals).

Bar Liquor, wine, and beer are served in a bar or cocktail lounge and usually with meals unless otherwise indicated (e.g., "wine, beer").

Business center The property has a designated area accessible to all guests with business services.

Business servs avail The property can perform/arrange at least two of the following services for a guest: audiovisual equipment rental, binding, computer rental, faxing, messenger services, modem availability, notary service, obtaining office supplies, photocopying, shipping, and typing.

Cable Standard cable service; "premium" indicates that HBO, Disney, Showtime, or similar services are available.

Ck-in, ck-out Check-in time, check-out time.

Coin lndry Self-service laundry.

Complete meal Soup and/or salad, entree, and dessert, plus nonalcoholic beverage.

Continental bkfst Usually coffee and a roll or doughnut.

Cr cds: A, American Express; C, Carte Blanche; D, Diners Club; DS, Discover; ER, enRoute; JCB, Japanese Credit Bureau; MC, MasterCard; V, Visa.

D Followed by a price, indicates room rate for a "double"—two people in one room in one or two beds (the charge may be higher for two double beds).

Downhill/x-country ski Downhill and/or cross-country skiing within 20 miles of property.

Each addl Extra charge for each additional person beyond the stated number of persons at a reduced price.

Early-bird dinner A meal served at specified hours, typically around 4:30–6:30 pm.

Exc Except.

Exercise equipt Two or more pieces of exercise equipment on the premises.

Exercise rm Both exercise equipment and room, with an instructor on the premises.

Fax Facsimile machines available to all guests.

Golf privileges Privileges at a course within 10 miles

Hols Holidays

In-rm modem link Every guest room has a connection for a modem that's separate from the phone line.

Kit. or kits. A kitchen or kitchenette that contains stove or microwave, sink, and refrigerator and that is either part of the room or a separate room. If the kitchen is not fully equipped, the listing will indicate "no equipt" or "some equipt".

Luxury level A special section of a hotel, covering at least an entire floor, that offers increased luxury accommodations. Management must provide no less than three of these four services: separate check-in and check-out, concierge, private lounge, and private elevator service (key access). Complimentary breakfast and snacks are commonly offered.

MAP Modified American plan (lodging plus two meals).

Movies Prerecorded videos are available for rental.

No cr cds accepted No credit cards are accepted.

No elvtr In hotels with more than two stories, it's assumed there are elevators; only their absence is noted.

No phones Phones, too, are assumed; only their absence is noted.

Parking There is a parking lot on the premises.

Private club A cocktail lounge or bar available to members and their guests. In motels and hotels where these clubs exist, registered guests can usually use the club as guests of the management; the same is frequently true of restaurants.

Prix fixe A full meal for a stated price; usually one price is quoted.

Res Reservations.

S Followed by a price, indicates room rate for a "single," i.e., one person.

Semi-a la carte Meals include vegetable, salad, soup, appetizer, or other accompaniments to the main dish.

Serv bar A service bar, where drinks are prepared for dining patrons only.

Serv charge Service charge is the amount added to the restaurant check in lieu of a tip.

Table d'hôte A full meal for a stated price, dependent upon entree selection; no a la carte options are available.

Tennis privileges Privileges at tennis courts within 5 miles.

TV Indicates color television; B/W indicates black-and-white television.

Under certain age free Children under that age are not charged for if staying in room with a parent.

Valet parking An attendant is available to park and retrieve a car.

VCR VCRs in all guest rooms.

VCR avail VCRs are available for hookup in guest rooms.

Special Information for Travelers with Disabilities

The *Mobil Travel Guide* symbol D shown in accommodation and restaurant listings indicates establishments that are at least partially accessible to people with mobility problems.

The *Mobil Travel Guide* criteria for accessibility are unique to our publication. Please do not confuse them with the universal symbol for wheelchair accessibility. When the D symbol appears following a listing, the establishment is equipped with facilities to accommodate people using wheelchairs or crutches or otherwise needing easy access to doorways and rest rooms. Travelers with severe mobility problems or with hearing or visual impairments may or may not find facilities they need. Always phone ahead to make sure that an establishment can meet your needs.

All lodgings bearing our D symbol have the following facilities:

- ISA-designated parking near access ramps
- Level or ramped entryways to building
- Swinging building entryway doors minimum 3'0"
- Public rest rooms on main level with space to operate a wheelchair; handrails at commode areas
- Elevators equipped with grab bars and lowered control buttons
- Restaurants with accessible doorways; rest rooms with space to operate wheelchair; handrails at commode areas

- Minimum 3′0″ width entryway to guest rooms
- Low-pile carpet in rooms
- Telephone at bedside and in bathroom
- Bed placed at wheelchair height
- Minimum 3′0″ width doorway to bathroom
- Bath with open sink—no cabinet; room to operate wheelchair
- Handrails at commode areas; tub handrails
- Wheelchair accessible peephole in room entry door
- Wheelchair accessible closet rods and shelves

All restaurants bearing our D symbol offer the following facilities:

- ISA-designated parking beside access ramps
- Level or ramped front entryways to building
- Tables to accommodate wheelchairs
- Main-floor rest rooms; minimum 3′0″ width entryway

- Rest rooms with space to operate wheelchair; handrails at commode areas

In general, the newest properties are apt to impose the fewest barriers.

To get the kind of service you need and have a right to expect, do not hesitate when making a reservation to question the management in detail about the availability of accessible rooms, parking, entrances, restaurants, lounges, or any other facilities that are important to you, and confirm what is meant by "accessible." Some guests with mobility impairments report that lodging establishments' housekeeping and maintenance departments are most helpful in describing barriers. Also inquire about any special equipment, transportation, or services you may need.

Making the Most of Your Trip

A few diehard souls might fondly remember the trip where the car broke down and they were stranded for a week, or the vacation that cost twice what it was supposed to. For most travelers, though, the best trips are those that are safe, smooth, and within their budget. To help you make your trip the best it can be, we've assembled a few tips and resources.

Saving Money

ON LODGING

After you've seen the published rates, it's time to look for discounts. Many hotels and motels offer them—for senior citizens, business travelers, families, you name it. It never hurts to ask—politely, that is. Sometimes, especially in late afternoon, desk clerks are instructed to fill beds, and you might be offered a lower rate, or a nicer room, to entice you to stay. Look for bargains on stays over multiple nights, in the off-season, and on weekdays or weekends (depending on location). Many hotels in major metropolitan areas, for example, have special weekend package plans, which offer considerable savings on rooms and may include breakfast, cocktails, and meal discounts. Prices change frequently throughout the year, so phone ahead.

Another way to save money is to choose accommodations that give you more than just a standard room. Rooms with kitchen facilities enable you to cook some meals for yourself, reducing restaurant costs. A suite might save money for two couples traveling together. Even hotel luxury levels can provide good value, as many include breakfast or cocktails in the price of the room.

State and city sales taxes as well as special room taxes can increase your room rates as much as 25% per day. We are unable to bring this specific information into the listings, but we strongly urge that you ask about these taxes when placing reservations in order to understand the total price to you.

Watch out for telephone-usage charges that hotels frequently impose on long-distance calls, credit-card calls, and other phone calls—even those that go unanswered. Before phoning from your room, read the information given to you at check-in, and then be sure to read your bill carefully before checking out. You won't be expected to pay for charges that weren't spelled out. (On the other hand, it's not unusual for a hotel to bill you for your calls after you return home.) Consider using public telephones in hotel lobbies; the savings may outweigh the inconvenience.

ON DINING

There are several ways to get a less-expensive meal at a more-expensive restaurant. Early-bird dinners are popular in many parts of the country and offer considerable savings. If you're interested in sampling a ★★★★ or ★★★★★ establishment, consider going at lunchtime. While the prices then are probably relatively high, they may be half of those at dinner and come with the same ambience, service, and cuisine.

PARK PASSES

While many national parks, monuments, seashores, historic sites, and recreation areas may be used free of charge, others charge an entrance fee (ranging from $1 to $5 per person to $5 to $15 per carload) and/or a "use fee" for special services and facilities. If you plan to make several visits to federal recreation areas, consider one of the following National Park Service money-saving programs:

Park Pass. This is an annual entrance permit to a specific unit in the National Park Service system that normally charges an entrance fee. The pass admits the permit holder and any accompanying passengers in a private noncommercial vehicle or, in the case of walk-in facilities, the holder's spouse, children, and parents. It is valid for entrance fees only. A Park Pass may be purchased in person or by mail from the National Park Service unit at which the pass will be honored. The cost is $15 to $20, depending upon the area.

Golden Eagle Passport. This pass, available to people who are between 17 and 61, entitles the purchaser and accompanying passengers in a private noncommercial vehicle to enter any outdoor NPS unit that charges an entrance fee and admits the purchaser and family to most walk-in fee-charging areas. Like the Park Pass, it is good for one year and does not cover use fees. It may be purchased from the National Park Service, Office of Public Inquiries, Room 1013, US Department of the Interior, 18th and C Sts NW, Washington, DC 20240, phone 202/208–4747; at any of the 10 regional offices throughout the country; and at any NPS area that charges a fee. The cost is $50.

Golden Age Passport. Available to citizens and permanent residents of the United States 62 years or older, this is a lifetime entrance permit to fee-charging recreation areas. The fee exemption extends to those accompanying the permit holder in a private noncommercial vehicle or, in the case of walk-in facilities, to the holder's spouse and children. The passport also entitles the holder to a 50% discount on use fees charged in park areas but not to fees charged by concessionaires. Golden Age Passports must be obtained in person. The applicant must show proof of age, i.e., a driver's license, birth certificate, or signed affidavit attesting to age (Medicare cards are not acceptable proof). Passports are available at most park service units where they're used, at National Park Service headquarters (see above), at park system regional offices, at National Forest Supervisors' offices, and at most Ranger Station offices. The cost is $10.

Golden Access Passport. Issued to citizens and permanent residents of the United States who are physically disabled or visually impaired, this passport is a free lifetime entrance permit to fee-charging recreation areas. The fee exemption extends to those accompanying the permit holder in a private noncommercial vehicle or, in the case of walk-in facilities, to the holder's spouse and children. The passport also entitles the holder to a 50% discount on use fees charged in park areas but not to fees charged by concessionaires. Golden Access Passports must be obtained in person. Proof of eligibility to receive federal benefits is required (under programs such as Disability Retirement, Compensation for Military Service-Connected Disability, Coal Mine Safety and Health Act, etc.), or an affidavit must be signed attesting to eligibility. These passports are available at the same outlets as Golden Age Passports.

FOR SENIOR CITIZENS
Look for the senior-citizen discount symbol in the lodging and restaurant listings. Always call ahead to confirm that the discount is being offered, and be sure to carry proof of age. At places not listed in the book, it never hurts to ask if a senior-citizen discount is offered. Two organizations provide additional information for mature travelers: the American Association of Retired Persons (AARP), 601 E St NW, Washington, DC 20049, phone 202/434–2277, and the National Council of Senior Citizens, 8403 Cosville, Ste 1200, Silver Springs, MD 20910, phone 301/528-8800.

Tipping

Tipping is an expression of appreciation for good service, and often service workers rely on tips as a significant part of their income. However, you never need to tip if service is poor.

IN HOTELS
Doormen in major city hotels are usually given $1 for getting you a cab. Bellhops expect $1 per bag, usually $2 if you have only one bag. Concierges are tipped according to the service they perform. It's not mandatory to tip when you've asked for suggestions on sightseeing or restaurants or help in making reservations for dining. However, when a concierge books you a table at a restaurant known to be difficult to get into, a gratuity of $5 is appropriate. For obtaining theater or sporting event tickets, $5–$10 is expected. Maids, often overlooked by guests, may be tipped $1–$2 per day of stay.

AT RESTAURANTS
Coffee shop and counter service wait staff are usually given 8%–10% of the bill. In full-service restaurants, tip 15% of the bill, before sales tax. In fine restaurants, where the staff is large and shares the gratuity, 18%–20% for the waiter is appropriate. In most cases, tip the maitre d' only if service has been extraordinary and only on the way out; $20 is the minimum in upscale properties in major metropolitan areas. If there is a wine steward, tip him or her at least $5 a bottle, more if the wine was decanted or if the bottle was very expensive. If your busboy has been unusually attentive, $2 pressed into his hand on departure is a nice gesture. An increasing number of restaurants automatically add a service charge to the bill in lieu of a gratuity. Before tipping, carefully review your check.

AT AIRPORTS
Curbside luggage handlers expect $1 per bag. Car-rental shuttle drivers who help with your luggage appreciate a $1 or $2 tip.

Staying Safe

The best way to deal with emergencies is to be prepared enough to avoid them. However, unforeseen situations do happen, and you can prepare for them.

IN YOUR CAR
Before your trip, make sure your car has been serviced and is in good working order. Change the oil, check the battery and belts, and make sure tires are inflated properly (this can also improve gas mileage). Other inspections recommended by the car's manufacturer should be made, too.

Next, be sure you have the tools and equipment to deal with a routine breakdown: jack, spare tire, lug wrench, repair kit, emergency tools, jumper cables, spare fan belt, auto fuses, flares and/or reflectors, flashlights, first-aid kit, and, in winter, a windshield scraper and shovel.

Bring all appropriate and up-to-date documentation—licenses, registration, and insurance cards—and know what's covered by your insurance. Also bring an extra set of keys, just in case.

En route, always buckle up!

If your car does break down, get out of traffic as soon as possible—pull well off the road. Raise the hood and turn on your emergency flashers or tie a white cloth to the roadside door handle or antenna. Stay near your car. Use flares or reflectors to keep your car from being hit.

IN YOUR LODGING

Chances are slim that you will encounter a hotel or motel fire. The ▨ in a listing indicates that there were smoke detectors and/or sprinkler systems in the rooms we inspected. Once you've checked in, make sure that any smoke detector in your room is working properly. Ascertain the locations of fire extinguishers and at least two fire exits. Never use an elevator in a fire.

For personal security, use the peephole in your room's door.

PROTECTING AGAINST THEFT

To guard against theft wherever you go, don't bring any more of value than you need. If you do bring valuables, leave them at your hotel rather than in your car, and if you have something very expensive, lock it in a safe. Many hotels have one in each room; others will store your valuables in the hotel's safe. And of course, don't carry more money than you need; use traveler's checks and credit cards, or visit cash machines.

For Travelers with Disabilities

A number of publications can provide assistance. Fodor's *Great American Vacations for Travelers with Disabilities* ($19.50) covers 38 top U.S. travel destinations, including parks, cities, and popular tourist regions. It's available from bookstores or by calling 800/533–6478. The most complete listing of published material for travelers with disabilities is available from *The Disability Bookshop,* Twin Peaks Press, Box 129, Vancouver, WA 98666, phone 360/694–2462. A comprehensive guidebook to the national parks is *Easy Access to National Parks: The Sierra Club Guide for People with Disabilities* ($16), distributed by Random House.

The Reference Section of the National Library Service for the Blind and Physically Handicapped (Library of Congress, Washington, DC 20542, phone 202/707–9275 or 202/707–5100) provides information and resources for persons with mobility problems and hearing and vision impairments, as well as information about the NLS talking-book program (or visit your local library).

Traveling to Canada

Citizens of the United States do not need visas to enter Canada, but proof of citizenship—passport, birth certificate, or voter registration card—is required. A driver's license is not acceptable. Naturalized citizens will need their naturalization certificates or their U.S. passport to reenter the United States. Children under 18 who are traveling on their own should carry a letter from a parent or guardian giving them permission to travel in Canada.

Travelers entering Canada in automobiles licensed in the United States may tour the provinces for up to three months without fee. Drivers are advised to carry their motor vehicle registration card and, if the car is not registered in the driver's name, a letter from the registered owner authorizing use of the vehicle. If the car is rented, carry a copy of the rental contract stipulating use in Canada. For your protection, ask your car insurer for a Canadian Non-resident Interprovince Motor Vehicle Liability Insurance Card. This card ensures that your insurance company will meet minimum insurance requirements in Canada.

The use of seat belts by drivers and passengers is compulsory in all provinces. A permit is required for the use of citizens' band radios. Rabies vaccination certificates are required for dogs or cats.

No handguns may be brought into Canada. If you plan to hunt, sporting rifles and shotguns plus 200 rounds of ammunition per person will be admitted duty-free. Hunting and fishing licenses must be obtained from the appropriate province. Each province has its own regulations concerning the transportation of firearms.

The Canadian dollar's rate of exchange with the U.S. dollar varies; contact your local bank for the latest figures. Since customs regulations can change, it's recommended that you contact the Canadian consulate or embassy in your area. Offices are located in Atlanta, Boston, Buffalo, Chicago, Dallas, Detroit, Los Angeles, Minneapolis, New York City, Seattle, and Washington, DC. For the most current and detailed listing of regulations and sources, ask for the annually revised brochure "Canada: Travel Information," which is available upon request.

Important Toll-Free Numbers
and On-Line Information

HOTELS AND MOTELS

Adam's Mark 800/444–2326
Web www.adamsmark.com
Best Western .... 800/528–1234, TDD 800/528–2222
Web www.bestwestern.com
Budgetel Inns 800/428–3438
Web www.budgetel.com
Budget Host 800/283–4678
Clarion 800/252–7466
Web www.clarioninn.com
Comfort 800/228–5150
Web www.comfortinn.com
Courtyard by Marriott 800/321–2211
Web www.courtyard.com
Days Inn 800/325–2525
Web www.travelweb.com/daysinn.html
Doubletree 800/528–0444
Web www.doubletreehotels.com
Drury Inns 800/325–8300
Web www.drury-inn.com
Econo Lodge 800/446–6900
Web www.hotelchoice.com
Embassy Suites 800/362–2779
Web www.embassy-suites.com
Exel Inns of America 800/356–8013
Fairfield Inn by Marriott 800/228–2800
Web www.marriott.com
Fairmont Hotels 800/527–4727
Forte 800/225–5843
Four Seasons 800/332–3442
Web www.fourseasons.com
Friendship Inns 800/453–4511
Web www.hotelchoice.com
Hampton Inn 800/426–7866
Web www.hampton-inn.com
Hilton .... 800/445–8667, TDD 800/368–1133
Web www.hilton.com
Holiday Inn .... 800/465–4329, TDD 800/238–5544
Web www.holiday-inn.com
Howard Johnson .... 800/654–4656, TDD 800/654–8442
Web www.hojo.com
Hyatt & Resorts 800/233–1234
Web www.hyatt.com
Inns of America 800/826–0778
Inter-Continental 800/327–0200
Web www.interconti.com
La Quinta .... 800/531–5900, TDD 800/426–3101
Web www.laquinta.com
Loews 800/235–6397
Web www.loewshotels.com
Marriott 800/228–9290
Web www.marriott.com
Master Hosts Inns 800/251–1962

Meridien 800/225–5843
Motel 6 .... 800/466–8356
Nikko International 800/645–5687
Web www.hotelnikko.com
Omni 800/843–6664
Web www.omnirosen.com
Park Inn 800/437–7275
Web www.p-inns.com/parkinn.html
Quality Inn 800/228–5151
Web www.qualityinn.com
Radisson 800/333–3333
Web www.radisson.com
Ramada .... 800/228–2828, TDD 800/228–3232
Web www.ramada.com/ramada.html
Red Carpet/Scottish Inns 800/251–1962
Red Lion 800/547–8010
Web www.travelweb.com/travelweb/rl/common/redlion.html
Red Roof Inn 800/843–7663
Web www.redroof.com
Renaissance 800/468–3571
Web www.niagara.com/nf.renaissance
Residence Inn by Marriott 800/331–3131
Web www.marriott.com
Ritz-Carlton 800/241–3333
Web www.ritzcarlton.com
Rodeway 800/228–2000
Web www.rodeway.com
Sheraton 800/325–3535
Web www.sheraton.com
Shilo Inn 800/222–2244
Signature Inns 800/822–5252
Web www.signature-inns.com
Sleep Inn 800/221–2222
Web www.sleepinn.com
Super 8 .... 800/848–8888
Web www.super8motels.com/super8.html
Susse Chalet 800/258–1980
Web www.sussechalet.com
Travelodge/Viscount 800/255–3050
Web www.travelodge.com
Vagabond 800/522–1555
Westin Hotels & Resorts 800/937-8461
Web www.westin.com
Wyndham Hotels & Resorts 800/822–4200
Web www.travelweb.com

AIRLINES

Air Canada 800/776–3000
Web www.aircanada.ca
Alaska 800/426–0333
Web www.alaska-air.com/home.html
Aloha 800/367–5250
American 800/433–7300
Web www.americanair.com/aahome/aahome.html

America West..800/235–9292
Web www.americawest.com
British Airways 800/247–9297
Web www.british-airways.com
Canadian 800/426–7000
Web www.cdair.ca
Continental...800/525–0280
Web www.flycontinental.com
Delta...800/221–1212
Web www.delta-air.com
Hawaiian...800/367–5320
IslandAir...800/323–3345
Mesa...800/637–2247
Northwest...800/225–2525
Web www.nwa.com
SkyWest..800/453–9417
Southwest 800/435–9792
Web www.iflyswa.com
TWA..800/221–2000
Web www.twa.com
United 800/241–6522
Web www.ual.com
USAir...800/428–4322
Web www.usair.com

TRAINS

Amtrak 800/872–7245
Web www.amtrak.com

BUSES

Greyhound..800/231–2222
Web www.greyhound.com

CAR RENTALS

Advantage...800/777–5500
Alamo 800/327–9633
Web www.goalamo.com
Allstate...800/634–6186
Avis...800/331–1212
Web www.avis.com
Budget..800/527–0700
Web www.budgetrentacar.com
Dollar 800/800–4000
Web www.dollarcar.com
Enterprise...800/325–8007
Web www.pickenterprise.com
Hertz 800/654–3131
Web www.hertz.com
National 800/328–4567
Web www.nationalcar.com
Payless 800/237–2804
Rent-A-Wreck 800/535–1391
Web www.rent-a-wreck.com
Sears 800/527–0770
Thrifty...800/367–2277
Web www.thrifty.com
Ugly Duckling 800/843–3825
U-Save 800/272–8728
Value...800/327–2501
Web www.go-value.com

Four-Star and Five-Star Establishments
in the Great Lakes

ILLINOIS

★★★★★ Restaurants
Charlie Trotter's, *Chicago*
Everest, *Chicago*
Le Français, *Wheeling*

★★★★ Lodgings
Fairmont, *Chicago*
Four Seasons, *Chicago*
Oak Brook Hills, *Oak Brook*
Omni Chicago Hotel, *Chicago*
Renaissance, *Chicago*
The Ritz-Carlton, *Chicago*
Westin River North Chicago, *Chicago*

★★★★ Restaurants
Ambria, *Chicago*
Arun's, *Chicago*
Carlos', *Highland Park*

Ritz-Carlton Dining Room (The Ritz-Carlton), *Chicago*
Seasons (Four Seasons), *Chicago*
Spiaggia, *Chicago*
Trio, *Evanston*

MICHIGAN

★★★★ Lodgings
Amway Grand Plaza, *Grand Rapids*
The Ritz-Carlton, Dearborn, *Dearborn*
Townsend, *Birmingham*

★★★★ Restaurant
The Lark, *Bloomfield Hills*

OHIO

★★★★★ Restaurant
Maisonette, *Cincinnati*

★★★★ Lodging
The Ritz-Carlton, Cleveland, *Cleveland*

★★★★ Restaurants
L'Auberge, *Dayton*
Orchid's (Omni Netherland Plaza), *Cincinnati*

WISCONSIN

★★★★ Lodgings
The American Club, *Sheboygan*
Canoe Bay Inn & Cottages, *Rice Lake*

★★★★ Restaurants
Grenadier's, *Milwaukee*
Sanford, *Milwaukee*

Illinois

Population: 11,430,602
Land area: 55,646 square miles
Elevation: 279-1,235 feet
Highest point: Charles Mound (Jo Daviess County)
Entered Union: December 3, 1818 (21st state)
Capital: Springfield
Motto: State Sovereignty-National Union
Nickname: Land of Lincoln
State flower: Violet
State bird: Cardinal
State tree: White oak
State fair: August 8-17, 1998, in Springfield
Time zone: Central
Web: www.enjoyillinois.com

Ilinois extends from Chicago, on the shores of Lake Michigan, to the vast woodlands of Shawnee National Forest. It is a major transportation center, and its resources include wheat, corn, soybeans and livestock, minerals, coal, oil and an immense diversity of manufactured goods. The growth of this industrial-agricultural giant has been remarkable. In a century and a half it has evolved from a frontier to a vast empire of cities, farms, mines and mills. There are nearly 1 million factory workers; more than 90 percent of its land is cultivated, producing more than 40 different crops with an annual value of $4.2 billion. Livestock value averages more than $1 billion annually.

The state takes its name from the confederated tribes who called themselves the Iliniwek ("superior men") and inhabited the valley of the Illinois River. In 1673, the first known white men entered the land of the Iliniwek. Father Jacques Marquette and Louis Jolliet paddled down the Mississippi, returned up the Illinois and carried their canoes across the portage where Chicago now stands. Five years later, Robert Cavelier de La Salle established Fort Crève Coeur, near Peoria Lake. French interest then shifted to the area around Cahokia and Kaskaskia. Fort de Chartres was built in 1720, and trappers and traders soon followed. The district was designated Illinois, the first official use of the name.

French rule ended when the British seized Fort de Chartres in 1765, but the British stayed in Illinois only briefly. The region was important to the American cause and was won by George Rogers Clark in 1778-1779. For a while Illinois was claimed as a county by Virginia, but it was ceded to the federal government; in 1787 it became part of the Northwest Territory. This territory was variously subdivided; Illinois, first part of Indiana Territory, became Illinois Territory in 1809, with Ninian Edwards as its first governor. Nine years later it was admitted as the twenty-first state.

Through the early years of the 19th century, the Sauk (or Sac) and Fox struggled to retain their lands. They were moved across the Mississippi by a treaty that touched off the Black Hawk War of 1832. The defeat of the Sauk and Fox, and a later treaty forcing the Potawatomi to cede their lands, virtually removed Native Americans from the state. Settlers then surged into the fertile country.

A young backwoods lawyer named Abraham Lincoln returned from the Black Hawk War and entered politics. As leader of the Sangamon County delegation in the state legislature, he was successful in moving the capital from Vandalia to Springfield. Lincoln supported projects for waterway improvements, which resulted in canals and interstate railroads. The new transportation system helped build commercial centers and contributed to the state's eventual industrialization. The Civil War sparked broad industrialization and rapid growth, which together with vast agricultural riches have carried the state through many economic crises.

Illinois stretches 385 miles from north to south. As a vacation area, it offers lakes and rivers with excellent fishing, beautiful parks and recreation areas, historic and archeological sites, landmark buildings, prairie lands and canyons. The attractions in Chicago and the surrounding area are endless, as are the hundreds of festivals and events sponsored by cities and towns year-round throughout the state.

When to Go/Climate

Illinois weather can be extreme and unpredictable. Winters can bring heavy snows; summers are often hot, hazy and humid. Summer thunderstorms are frequent and magnificent. Tornadoes have been recorded anytime from spring through fall.

AVERAGE HIGH/LOW TEMPERATURES (°F)

CHICAGO

Jan 29/13	**May** 70/48	**Sept** 75/54
Feb 34/17	**June** 80/58	**Oct** 63/42
Mar 46/29	**July** 84/63	**Nov** 48/32
Apr 59/39	**Aug** 82/62	**Dec** 34/19

SPRINGFIELD

Jan 33/16	**May** 75/52	**Sept** 79/56
Feb 37/20	**June** 84/62	**Oct** 67/44
Mar 50/32	**July** 87/66	**Nov** 52/34
Apr 64/43	**Aug** 84/63	**Dec** 37/22

Parks and Recreation Finder

Directions to and information about the parks and recreation areas below are given under their respective town/city sections. Please refer to those sections for details.

Key to abbreviations: I.P. = Interstate Park; N.B.C. = National Battlefield & Cemetery; N.B.P. = National Battlefield Park; N.F. = National Forest; N.G. = National Grassland; N.H. = National Historical Park; N.H.S. = National Historic Site; N.M. = National Monument; N.Mem. = National Memorial; N.M.P. = National Military Park; N.P. = National Park; N.Pres. = National Preserve; N.R. = National Recreational Area; N.R.R. = National Recreational River; N.S. = National Seashore; N.S.T. = National Scenic Trail; N.V.M. = National Volcanic Monument; S.B. = State Beach; S.C.P. = State Conservation Park; S.G. = State Garden; S.H.A. = State Historic Area; S.H.P. = State Historic Park; S.N.A. = State Natural Area; S.P. = State Park; S.R. = State Reserve; S.R.A. = State Recreation Area; S.Res.P. = State Resort Park; S.R.P. = State Rustic Park.

NATIONAL PARK AND RECREATION AREAS

Place Name	Listed Under
Lincoln Home N.H.S.	SPRINGFIELD
Shawnee N.F.	CARBONDALE

STATE RECREATION AREAS

Place Name	Listed Under
Argyle Lake S.P.	MACOMB
Castle Rock S.P.	OREGON
Chain O'Lakes S.P.	ANTIOCH
Ferne Clyffe S.P.	MARION
Fort Kaskaskia State Historic Site	same
Fox Ridge S.P.	CHARLESTON
Gebhard Woods S.P.	MORRIS
Giant City S.P.	CARBONDALE
Horseshoe Lake State Conservation Area	CAIRO
Illinois Beach S.P.	same
Johnson Sauk Trail S.P.	KEWANEE
Jubilee College S.P.	PEORIA
Kankakee River S.P.	KANKAKEE
Kickapoo S.P.	DANVILLE
Lincoln Trail S.P.	MARSHALL
Lincoln's New Salem State Historic Site	PETERSBURG
Lowden Memorial S.P.	OREGON
Matthiessen S.P.	PERU
Moraine Hills S.P.	McHENRY
Nauvoo S.P.	NAUVOO
Père Marquette S.P.	same
Ramsey Lake S.P.	VANDALIA
Rock Cut S.P.	ROCKFORD
Starved Rock S.P.	same
Stephen A. Forbes S.P.	SALEM
Wayne Fitzgerrell S.R.A.	BENTON
White Pines Forest S.P.	OREGON

Water-related activities, hiking, riding, various other sports, picnicking and visitor centers, as well as camping, are available in many of these areas. Camping is permitted in more than 60 areas: ($6-$11/site/nite) only by permit from the park ranger, obtainable for overnight or a maximum of 14 nights. Pets on leash only. State parks are open daily, weather permitting, except Jan 1 & Dec 25. For full information about state parks, tent camping and other facilities, contact the Department of Natural Resources, Division of Land Management & Education, 600 N Grand Ave W, Springfield 62706; 217/782-6752.

SKI AREAS

Place Name	Listed Under
Chestnut Mt Resort	GALENA
Wilmot Mt Ski Area	ANTIOCH

FISHING & HUNTING

Lakes, streams and rivers provide fishing to suit every freshwater angler. The Illinois shoreline of Lake Michigan is 63 miles long. Nonresident season fishing license $24.50; 10-day license $13; 1-day Lake Michigan $2.50. Licenses and further information may be obtained from the Department of Natural Resources, License Section, 524 S 2nd St, PO Box 19459, Springfield 62794-9459, phone 217/782-2965, or department vendors throughout the state.

Many areas of the state provide good hunting, with Canada geese, ducks, quail, rabbits and squirrels plentiful. (Deer & turkey hunting by permit only.) Nonresident season hunting license $50.75; 5-day license $28.75. Additional stamps required for waterfowl ($10.50), pheasant and fur-bearing game ($5.50). The Department of Natural Resources maintains shooting areas at numerous places throughout the state. For more information concerning fishing and hunting in Illinois, contact the Department of Natural Resources, 524 S 2nd St, Springfield 62701; 217/782-

7454. Other licenses may be obtained from department vendors throughout the state.

Driving Information

Safety belts are mandatory for all persons in front seat of vehicle. Children under 7 years must be in an approved passenger restraint anywhere in vehicle: ages 5 or 6 may use a regulation safety belt; age 4 and under must use an approved safety seat. For further information phone 312/283-2400.

INTERSTATE HIGHWAY SYSTEM

The following alphabetical listing of Illinois towns in *Mobil Travel Guide* shows that these cities are within 10 miles of the indicated Interstate highways. A highway map, however, should be checked for the nearest exit.

Highway Number	Cities/Towns within 10 miles
INTERSTATE 39	Peru, Rockford.
INTERSTATE 55	Bloomington, Brookfield, Chicago, Cicero, Collinsville, Downers Grove, Edwardsville, Hinsdale, Joliet, La Grange, Lincoln, Lockport, Naperville, Oak Lawn, Springfield.
INTERSTATE 57	Arcola, Benton, Cairo, Champaign/Urbana, Charleston, Chicago, Effingham, Homewood, Kankakee, Marion, Mattoon, Mt Vernon, Oak Lawn, Salem.
INTERSTATE 64	Belleville, Collinsville, Mt Vernon.
INTERSTATE 70	Altamont, Collinsville, Edwardsville, Effingham, Greenville, Marshall, Vandalia.
INTERSTATE 72	Champaign/Urbana, Decatur, Springfield.
INTERSTATE 74	Bloomington, Champaign/Urbana, Danville, Galesburg, Moline, Peoria.
INTERSTATE 80	Chicago, Homewood, Joliet, Lockport, Moline, Morris, Ottawa, Peru, Rock Island.
INTERSTATE 88	Aurora, Brookfield, Chicago, Chicago O'Hare Airport Area, Cicero, De Kalb, Dixon, Downers Grove, Elmhurst, Geneva, Glen Ellyn, Hillside, Hinsdale, Itasca, La Grange, Moline, Naperville, Oak Brook, Oak Park, St Charles, Wheaton.
INTERSTATE 90	Arlington Heights, Chicago, Chicago O'Hare Airport Area, Cicero, Elgin, Elmhurst, Hillside, Itasca, Oak Park, Rockford, Schaumburg, Union.
INTERSTATE 94	Chicago, Chicago O'Hare Airport Area, Evanston, Glenview, Grayslake, Gurnee, Highland Park, Highwood, Libertyville, Northbrook, Skokie, Waukegan, Wheeling, Wilmette.
INTERSTATE 290	Arlington Heights, Chicago, Chicago O'Hare Airport Area, Cicero, Elmhurst, Glen Ellyn, Hillside, Itasca, Libertyville, Northbrook, Oak Brook, Oak Park, Schaumburg.
INTERSTATE 294	Arlington Heights, Chicago, Chicago O'Hare Airport Area, Cicero, Elmhurst, Evanston, Glen Ellyn, Glenview, Highland Park, Highwood, Hillside, Itasca, Libertyville, Northbrook, Oak Brook, Oak Park, Skokie, Wheeling, Wilmette.
INTERSTATE 355	(North-South Tollway): Chicago O'Hare Airport Area, Downers Grove, Elmhurst, Glen Ellyn, Hillside, Hinsdale, Itasca, La Grange, Lockport, Naperville, Oak Brook, Schaumburg, Wheaton.

Additional Visitor Information

For specific information about Illinois attractions, activities and travel counseling, contact the Illinois Bureau of Tourism, phone 800/2-CONNECT or 800/406-6418 (TTY).

Locations of Illinois tourist information centers (Apr-Oct): off I-80 (eastbound) near Rapid City; off I-57 near Monee; off I-24 (westbound) near Metropolis; off I-57 near Whittington; off I-57 (northbound) near Anna; off I-64 (eastbound) near New Baden; off I-70 (eastbound) near Highland; off I-70 (westbound) near Marshall; off I-74 (westbound) near Oakwood; off I-80 (eastbound) near South Holland; off I-90 (southbound) near South Beloit.

Altamont (G-5)

(See also Effingham, Vandalia)

Pop 2,296 **Elev** 619 ft **Area code** 618 **Zip** 62411
Information Altamont Chamber of Commerce, PO Box 141; 618/483-5714.

Motel

✔★ **SUPER 8.** *Rte 2, Box 296, 1/4 mi S on IL 128, 1 blk S of I-70 exit 82.* 618/483-6300; FAX 618/483-3323. 25 rms, 2 story. S $40.88; D $50.88; each addl $4; under 12 free. Crib $6. Pet accepted; $8. TV; cable (premium). Playground. Restaurant adj 6 am-9 pm. Ck-out 11 am. Coin lndry. Cr cds: A, C, D, DS, MC, V.

D ✔ ≈ ⚓ SC

Restaurant

✔★ **GILBERT'S.** *1/4 mi S of I-70 exit 82.* 618/483-6288. Hrs: 6 am-9 pm; Fri, Sat to 10 pm (summer). Semi-a la carte: bkfst $1.50-$3.80, lunch $1.75-$5.25, dinner $3.95-$8.75. Child's meals. Specializes in steak, chicken, pork tenderloin. Pennsylvania Dutch-style building. Cr cds: DS, MC, V.

D SC

Alton (G-3)

(See also Cahokia, Collinsville, Edwardsville)

Founded 1817 **Pop** 32,905 **Elev** 500 ft **Area code** 618 **Zip** 62002 **E-mail** altoncvb@ezl.com
Information Greater Alton/Twin Rivers Convention & Visitor's Bureau, 200 Piasa St; 618/465-6676 or 800/258-6645.

Alton is located on the bluffs just above the confluence of the Mississippi and Missouri rivers. It has three historic districts, four square blocks of antique stores and many opulent houses, the former residences of steamboat captains, industrialists and railroad barons. Here, in 1837, Elijah Lovejoy, the abolitionist editor, died protecting his press from a pro-slavery mob. In the Alton Cemetery is a 93-foot monument to Lovejoy. A sandbar in the river was the scene of the projected Lincoln-Shields duel of 1842, which was settled without bloodshed. The final Lincoln-Douglas debate was held in Alton on October 15, 1858. Alton was the home of Robert Wadlow, the tallest man in history; a life-size 9-foot statue of Wadlow is on College Ave.

What to See and Do

Brussels Ferry. Ferry boat navigates across the Illinois River at the confluence of the Mississippi River. (Daily) 20 mi W on Great River Rd (IL 100), near Grafton. Phone 618/786-3636.   **Free.**

Confederate Soldiers' Cemetery. Monument lists names of soldiers who died in Illinois' first state prison, which was a prisoner-of-war camp during the Civil War. Rozier St, W of State St.

Père Marquette State Park (see). Approx 23 mi W on IL 100.

Piasa Bird Painting Reproduction. According to Native American legend, a monster bird frequented these bluffs and preyed on all who came near. When Marquette sailed down the Mississippi in 1673, he spotted "high rocks with hideous monsters painted on them" at this spot. The paintings, destroyed by quarrying in the 19th century, were reproduced in 1934. These reproductions in turn were destroyed by the construction of the Great River Road. They were again reproduced on a bluff farther up the river. On the bluffs NW of town, best seen from the river and IL 100.

Raging Rivers Waterpark. 20 acres include Tree House Harbor, an interactive family play area; Lazy River float ride; body flumes; giant wave pool; and white water rapids ride. (Memorial Day wkend-Labor Day wkend) 15 mi NW on IL 100 to Grafton, at 100 Palisades Pkwy. Phone 800/548-7573.   ¢¢¢¢

Village of Elsah. Many buildings are more than 100 yrs old. Museum (Apr-Nov, Thurs-Sun afternoons). 11 mi W on Great River Rd (IL 100). Phone 618/374-1059.   **Free.**

Motel

★ ★ **HOLIDAY INN.** *3800 Homer Adams Pkwy. 618/462-1220; FAX 618/462-0906.* 137 rms, 4 story. S $72.90-$82.50; D $82.90-$92.50; each addl $10; under 18 free. Crib free. Pet accepted. TV; cable (premium), VCR (movies). Indoor pool; whirlpool. Restaurant 6 am-2 pm, 5-10 pm; Sun from 7 am. Rm serv. Bar 11-1 am; Sun noon-10 pm; entertainment. Ck-out noon. Meeting rms. Business servs avail. In-rm modem link. Bellhops. Free airport, RR station transportation. Exercise equipt; weight machine, stair machine, sauna. Game rm. Balconies. Cr cds: A, C, D, DS, JCB, MC, V.

D ✇ ≋ ✈ ⊠ ⊛ SC

Lodge

★ **PERE MARQUETTE LODGE & CONFERENCE CENTER.** *(IL 100, Grafton 62037) 3 mi N. 618/786-2331; FAX 618/786-3498.* 72 rms, 2 story. S $62; D $72; each addl $10; under 17 free. Crib free. TV; cable, VCR avail (movies). Indoor pool; whirlpool. Complimentary coffee in rms. Restaurant 6:30 am-9 pm; wkends to 10 pm. Bar 4 pm-1 am. Ck-out noon. Meeting rms. Business servs avail. Lighted tennis. Sauna. Playground. Game rm. Rec rm. Lawn games. Some balconies. Picnic tables, grills. On Mississippi River. Cr cds: A, C, D, DS, MC, V.

D ⚡ ⚞ ≋ ⚐ ⊠ ⊛

Inn

★ **HOMERIDGE.** *(1470 N State St, Jerseyville 62052) 1 mi N on IL 267. 618/498-3442.* 5 rms, 3 story. No rm phones. S, D $75-$85. Complimentary full bkfst. Ck-out noon, ck-in 2 pm. Pool. Game rm. Lawn games. Built in 1867; Italianate Victorian decor. Previous home of Senator Theodore S. Chapman. Totally nonsmoking. Cr cds: A, MC, V.

≋ ⊠ ⊛

Restaurant

★ ★ **TONY'S.** *312 Piasa St. 618/462-8384.* Hrs: 4:30-10:30 pm; Fri, Sat to 11:30 pm; Sun to 10 pm. Closed some major hols. Res accepted. Italian menu. Bar. Semi-a la carte: dinner $8.95-$32. Child's meals. Specializes in pepperloin steak, pasta, pizzas. Valet parking. Outdoor dining. Six dining rms. Cr cds: A, C, D, DS, MC, V.

D SC ⊸

Antioch (A-2 see Chicago map)

(For accommodations see Gurnee, Waukegan)

Settled 1836 **Pop** 6,105 **Elev** 772 ft **Area code** 847 **Zip** 60002
Information Chamber of Commerce, 884 Main St; 847/395-2233.

What to See and Do

Chain O'Lakes Area. Yr-round recreational facilities, including fishing, ice-fishing, boating, cross-country skiing and snowmobiling trails.

Chain O'Lakes State Park. Encompasses 6,063 acres. Fishing, hunting; boating (ramp, rentals, motors). Hiking, bridle trails (rentals). Cross-country skiing, snowmobiling. Picnicking, concession. Camping. Standard hrs, fees. (Daily) 6 mi W on IL 173 in Spring Grove. Phone 847/587-5512. **Free.**

Hiram Butrick Sawmill. Replica of the water-powered sawmill (1839) around which the community grew. Tours (by appt). 790 Cunningham Dr at Gage Brothers Park on Sequoit Creek. Phone 847/395-2160.   **Free.**

Wilmot Mt Ski Area. 3 mi N on IL 83, then W on WI County C; 1 mi S of Wilmot, WI, near Illinois state line (see LAKE GENEVA, WI).

Motel

★ ★ **BEST WESTERN REGENCY INN.** *350 IL 173. 847/395-3606.* 68 rms, 3 story, 24 suites. May-Sept: S, D $74-$104; suites $94-$114; under 18 free; lower rates rest of yr. Crib $7. Pet accepted, some restrictions; $25 deposit. TV; cable (premium), VCR avail. Complimentary continental bkfst. Restaurant nearby. Bar 3 pm-1 am. Ck-out 11 am. Meeting rms. Business servs avail. In-rm modem link. Health club privileges. Indoor pool; whirlpool. Refrigerator, wet bar in suites. Cr cds: A, C, D, DS, ER, MC, V.

D ✇ ≋ ⊠ ⊛ SC

Arcola (F-5)

(See also Champaign/Urbana, Decatur, Mattoon)

Pop 2,678 **Elev** 678 ft **Area code** 217 **Zip** 61910
Information Arcola Chamber of Commerce, 135 N Oak, PO Box 274; 217/268-4530 or 800/336-5456.

Arcola is located in Illinois' Amish Country, where it is not unusual to see horse-drawn carriages traveling the highways.

What to See and Do

Rockome Gardens. Native rocks inlaid in concrete to form fences, arches, ornamental designs; landscaped gardens, ponds; petting zoo; train and buggy rides; lookout tower, treehouse; Amish-style restaurant, shops; replica of Amish house. Re-creation of Illinois frontier village on 15 acres, including craft guild shop, blacksmith shop, old country store, calico shop, bakery, furniture and candle shops; antique museum; special wkend events. (Memorial Day-Oct, daily; mid-Apr-Memorial Day, days vary) 5 mi

W on IL 133. Phone 217/268-4106. Admission includes all attractions exc buggy ride. ¢¢¢

Motel

★ ★ **COMFORT INN.** *610 E Springfield. 217/268-4000; FAX 217/268-4001.* 40 rms, 2 story. Apr-Nov: S $35-$45; D $38-$49; each addl $7; wkend, hol rates; lower rates rest of yr. Crib $7. TV; cable (premium). Complimentary continental bkfst. Restaurant opp 6 am-11 pm. Ck-out 11 am. Business servs avail. Some refrigerators. Cr cds: A, D, DS, MC, V.

D ⊠ SC

Restaurants

✔★ **DUTCH KITCHEN.** *127 E Main. 217/268-3518.* Hrs: 7:30 am-7 pm. Closed 2 wks Jan. Amish, Amer menu. Semi-a la carte: bkfst $1.95-$5, lunch, dinner $5.25-$7.50. Child's meals. Specializes in shoofly pie, Dutch sausage, apple butter. Salad bar. Family-owned. No cr cds accepted.

★ ★ **FRENCH EMBASSY.** *112 W Springfield Rd, jct IL133 & IL 45; enter through bowling alley. 217/268-4949.* Hrs: 5-9 pm. Closed Sun, Mon; major hols. Res accepted. French menu. Bar. Semi-a la carte: dinner $10.50-$21. Specializes in seasonal dishes, French sauces. Own baking. Two intimate dining areas adj bowling alley. Cr cds: A, DS, MC, V.

D ⬓

★ **ROCKOME FAMILY STYLE.** *125 N County Rd 425E, 5 mi W on IL 133, on the grounds of Rockome Gardens. 217/268-4106.* E-mail amishcm@aol.com; web www.rockome.com. Hrs: 11 am-7 pm; hrs vary mid-Apr-mid-May. Closed Mon, Tues mid-Sept-Oct; also Nov-mid-Apr. Complete meals: lunch, dinner $10.80. Child's meals. Specializes in Amish cooking, shoofly pie, chicken. Own baking. Season open is the same as Rockome Gardens. Cr cds: DS, MC, V.

D

Arlington Heights

(C-2 see Chicago map)

(See also Chicago O'Hare Airport Area, Wheeling)

Settled 1836 **Pop** 75,460 **Elev** 700 ft **Area code** 847
Information Chamber of Commerce, 180 N Arlington Heights Rd, PO Box 6, 60006; 847/253-1703.

What to See and Do

Historical Museum. Complex consists of 1882 house, 1907 house, a coach house and a reconstructed log cabin. (Sat-Sun; closed major hols) Also here is a country store (Thurs-Sun). 500 N Vail Ave. Phone 847/255-1225. Museum ¢

Long Grove Village. Restored 19th-century village with more than 100 antique shops, boutiques and restaurants. (Daily) 1 mi N, at jct IL 53, 83 in Long Grove. Phone 847/634-0888. **Free.**

Motels

★ ★ ★ **COURTYARD BY MARRIOTT.** *100 W Algonquin Rd (IL 62) (60005). 847/437-3344; FAX 847/437-3367.* 147 rms, 3 story. S $82-$102; D $92-$112; suites $125; under 12 free. Crib free. TV; cable (premium), VCR avail. Indoor pool; whirlpool. Complimentary coffee in rms. Restaurant 6:30-10:30 am, 5:30-10 pm; Sat, Sun 7 am-1 pm. Rm serv. Bar 4-11 pm; closed Sun. Ck-out 1 pm. Coin lndry. Meeting rms. Business servs avail. In-rm modem link. Valet serv. Sundries. Exercise equipt;

weights, treadmill. Refrigerator, microwave in suites. Some private patios, balconies. Cr cds: A, C, D, DS, MC, V.

D ⩰ 🏃 ⛷ 🐾 SC

★ ★ **HILTON GARDEN INN.** *(900 W Lake Cook Rd, Buffalo Grove 60089)* 1/2 mi E on Lake Cook Rd. 847/215-8883; FAX 847/215-9304. 156 rms, 2 story. S, D $89-$99; wkend rates. Crib free. TV; cable (premium). Indoor pool; whirlpool. Coffee in rms. Restaurant 6:30 am-1:30 pm. Bar 5-10 pm. Ck-out 11 am. Coin lndry. Meeting rms. Business servs avail. In-rm modem link. Valet serv. Sundries. Airport transportation. Lighted tennis. Exercise equipt; weight machine, bicycles. Some balconies, patios. Cr cds: A, C, D, DS, JCB, MC, V.

D ⛷ ⩰ 🏃 ⛷ 🐾 SC

★ **HOLIDAY INN EXPRESS.** *2120 S Arlington Heights Rd (60005). 847/593-9400; FAX 847/593-3632.* 125 rms, 3 story. S, D $99; under 18 free. TV; cable (premium), VCR avail. Complimentary continental bkfst. Restaurant opp open 24 hrs. Ck-out noon. Meeting rms. Business servs avail. In-rm modem link. Valet serv. Some refrigerators. Balconies. Cr cds: A, C, D, DS, ER, JCB, MC, V.

D ⛷ 🐾 SC

★ ★ **LA QUINTA.** *1415 W Dundee Rd (IL 68) (60004), E off IL 53. 847/253-8777; FAX 847/818-9167.* 123 rms, 4 story. S $78-$88; D $84-$91; suites $114; under 18 free. Crib free. Pet accepted, some restrictions. TV; cable (premium), VCR avail. Heated pool. Complimentary continental bkfst. Complimentary coffee in rms. Restaurant adj 11-1 am. Ck-out noon. Meeting rms. Business servs avail. In-rm modem link. Valet serv. Sundries. Cr cds: A, C, D, DS, MC, V.

D 🐾 ⩰ ⛷ 🐾 SC

Motor Hotel

★ ★ **AMERISUITES.** *2111 S Arlington Heights Rd (60005), 1 mi N of I-90, exit Arlington Heights Rd N. 847/956-1400; FAX 847/956-0804.* 113 suites, 6 story. S $96; D $106; each addl $10; under 12 free; wkend packages. Crib free. Pet accepted. TV; cable (premium). Complimentary buffet bkfst. Complimentary coffee in rms. Restaurant open 24 hrs. Ck-out noon. Meeting rms. Business center. Valet serv Mon-Fri. Exercise equipt; weight machine, treadmill. Health club privileges. Whirlpool. Refrigerators. Some theme suites. Cr cds: A, C, D, DS, MC, V.

D 🐾 🏃 ⛷ 🐾 SC 🚶

Hotels

★ ★ **ARLINGTON PARK HILTON CONFERENCE CENTER.** *3400 W Euclid Ave (60005). 847/394-2000; FAX 847/394-2095.* 420 rms, 13 story. S $105-$195; D $125-$215; each addl $15; suites $250-$675; family, wkend rates. Crib free. Pet accepted, some restrictions. TV; cable (premium). Indoor pool; whirlpool. Complimentary coffee in rms. Restaurant 6:30 am-10 pm. Bar 11-2 am; Sun from noon. Ck-out 11 am. Convention facilities. Business center. In-rm modem link. Gift shop. Tennis. Exercise rm; instructor, weight machines, bicycles, sauna. Massage. Some bathrm phones. Luxury level. Cr cds: A, C, D, DS, ER, JCB, MC, V.

D 🐾 ⛷ ⩰ 🏃 ⛷ 🐾 SC 🚶

★ ★ ★ **RADISSON.** *75 W Algonquin Rd (60005). 847/364-7600; FAX 847/364-7665.* 201 rms, 6 story. S, D $109-$149; each addl $10; suites $195-$350; under 18 free; wkend rates. Crib free. Pet accepted, some restrictions. TV; cable (premium), VCR avail. Indoor pool; whirlpool. Coffee in rms. Restaurant (see SAGE'S SAGES). Bar 11-1 am; entertainment Tues-Sat. Ck-out noon. Meeting rms. Business servs avail. In-rm modem link. Gift shop. Free airporttransportation. Exercise equipt; weight machine, bicycles, sauna. Bathrm phone, refrigerator in suites. Cr cds: A, C, D, DS, ER, JCB, MC, V.

D 🐾 ⩰ 🏃 ⛷ 🐾 SC

Restaurants

★ ★ ★ **LE TITI DE PARIS.** *1015 W Dundee Rd. 847/506-0222.* Hrs: 11:30 am-3 pm, 5:30-10 pm; Sat from 5:30 pm. Closed Sun, Mon; July 4, Thanksgiving, Dec 24, 25. Res accepted. French menu. Serv bar. Wine list. A la carte entrees: lunch $11.50-$18, dinner $19.75-$26.50. Prix fixe: dinner $43. Child's meals. Specialties: pigeon with roasted sweet garlic; lobster with warm champagne chive sauce; Norwegian salmon with cider sauce & apples. Own pastries. Menu changes seasonally. Cr cds: A, C, D, DS, JCB, MC, V.

D

★ ★ **PALM COURT.** *1912 N Arlington Heights Rd (60004). 847/870-7770.* Hrs: 11 am-midnight; Fri to 1 am; Sat 5 pm-1 am; Sun noon-10 pm. Closed July 4, Dec 25. Res accepted. Continental menu. Bar. Semi-a la carte: lunch $5.95-$9.95, dinner $9.95-$19.95. Specialties: Dover sole, veal Oscar, rack of lamb. Pianist (dinner) exc Sun. Parking. Cr cds: A, C, D, DS, MC, V.

D

★ ★ **RETRO BISTRO.** *(1746 W Golf Rd, Mt Prospect 60056) 847/439-2424.* Hrs: 11:30 am-3 pm, 5:30-10:30 pm; Sat from 5 pm. Closed Sun; some major hols. Res accepted. Continental menu. Bar. A la carte entrees: lunch $6-$10.50, dinner $12-$16.50. Child's meals. Specializes in Ahi tuna, pork tenderloin, ostrich medallions. Own pastries. Contemporary bistro. Cr cds: A, C, D, MC, V.

D

★ ★ ★ **SAGE'S SAGES.** *(See Radisson Hotel) 847/593-6200.* Hrs: 6:30 am-11 pm; Sun to 9 pm. Res accepted. Bar 11-1 am. Buffet: bkfst $7.50. Semi-a la carte: lunch $5.95-$12, dinner $10.95-$23.95. Specializes in prime aged beef, fresh grilled seafood, veal. Own pastries. Entertainment Tues-Sat. Valet parking (dinner). Three dining areas. Cr cds: A, C, D, DS, JCB, MC, V.

D

Aurora (B-5)

(See also Geneva, Joliet, Naperville, St Charles)

Settled 1834 **Pop** 99,581 **Elev** 676 ft **Area code** 630 **E-mail** aurora-tourism@ci.aurora.il.us **Web** www.ci.aurora.il.us/tourism

Information Aurora Area Convention & Tourism Council, PO Box 907, 60507; 630/897-5581 or 800/477-4369.

Pottawattomie chief Waubonsie and his tribesmen inhabited this area on the Fox River when, in the 1830s, pioneers arrived from the East. Water power and fertile lands attracted more settlers, and the two villages united as Aurora. Today, the city prospers due to its location along a high-tech corridor.

What to See and Do

Aurora Historical Museum. In restored Ginsberg Bldg, the museum contains displays of 19th-century life, collection of Mastodon bones, history center and research library and public art displays. (Apr-Dec, Wed, Sat & Sun afternoons) 20 W Downer Pl. Phone 630/897-9029. ¢¢

Blackberry Historical Farm Village. An 1840s working farm; children's animal farm; craft demonstrations; wagon rides, pony rides; children's discovery barn, train. (May-Labor Day, daily; after Labor Day-Oct, Fri-Sun) W on I-88 (East-West Tollway) to Orchard Rd, S to Galena Blvd, then W to Barnes Rd. Phone 630/892-1550. ¢¢¢

Fermi National Accelerator Laboratory. World's highest energy particle accelerator is on a 6,800-acre site. Also on grounds are hiking trails and a buffalo herd. Obtain brochures for self-guided tours in the atrium of the 15-story Wilson Hall (daily). Art & cultural events, films in auditorium. 2 mi

N on IL 31, 2½ mi E on Butterfield Rd (IL 56), then N on Kirk Rd, at Pine St in Batavia. Phone 630/840-3351. **Free.**

Paramount Arts Centre (1931). This theater was designed by Rapp and Rapp to compete with the opulent movie palaces of the area; restored to its original appearance, it offers a variety of productions throughout the yr. 23 E Galena Blvd, along river. Guided backstage tours, phone 630/896-7676. (Daily) Box office 630/896-6666. Tours ¢

Schingoethe Center for Native American Cultures. Private collection, thousands of Native American artifacts; jewelry, textiles, pottery, baskets. (Sun-Tues, Thurs, Fri; closed major hols) 347 S Gladstone Ave. Phone 630/844-5402. **Free.**

SciTech-Science and Technology Interactive Center. In former post office, this center provides more than 150 hands-on learning exhibits using motion, light, structures and sound. (Wed-Sun) 18 W Benton. Phone 630/859-3434. ¢¢

Motels

✔★ ★ **BEST WESTERN FOX VALLEY INN.** *2450 N Farnsworth (60505). 630/851-2000; FAX 630/851-8885.* 108 rms, 2 story. S $52-$64; D $58-$70; each addl $5; under 12 free. Crib $5. TV; cable (premium). Pool. Restaurant adj 6 am-11 am. Bar; entertainment Fri & Sat, dancing exc Sun. Ck-out noon. Meeting rms. Business servs avail. Sundries. Exercise equipt; weights, bicycles. Cr cds: A, C, D, DS, MC, V.

D

★ **COMFORT INN.** *4005 Gabrielle Lane (60504). 630/820-3400.* 51 rms, 2 story. S $66-$76; D $73-$83; each addl $7; under 18 free. Crib free. TV; cable (premium). Complimentary continental bkfst. Restaurant nearby. Ck-out 11 am. Meeting rm. Business servs avail. Cr cds: A, C, D, DS, ER, JCB, MC, V.

D

★ ★ **COMFORT SUITES.** *111 N Broadway (60505). 630/896-2800; FAX 630/896-2887.* 82 suites, 3 story. S $79-$159; D $79-$199; under 18 free; wkend rates; higher rates Dec 31. Crib free. TV; cable (premium), VCR (movies). Indoor pool; whirlpool, poolside serv. Complimentary continental bkfst. Complimentary coffee in rms. Restaurant adj 11-1 am. Ck-out 11 am. Coin lndry. Meeting rms. Business center. In-rm modem link. Sundries. Gift shop. X-country ski 2 mi. Exercise equipt; stair machine, ski machine. Game rm. Refrigerators. Cr cds: A, C, D, DS, ER, JCB, MC, V.

D

Belleville (H-3)

Founded 1814 **Pop** 42,785 **Elev** 529 ft **Area code** 618
Information Belleville Tourism, Inc, 216 East A St, 62220; 618/233-6769 or 800/677-9255.

Named Belleville (beautiful city) by its early French settlers, the city today is largely populated by people of German extraction. Belleville, the governmental, financial and medical center of southern Illinois, is the headquarters of Scott Air Force Base.

What to See and Do

National Shrine of Our Lady of the Snows. Unique architecture and imaginative landscaping on 200 acres; features a replica of the Lourdes Grotto in France. Visitor center, restaurant, lodging, gift shop. (Daily) 9500 W IL 15. Phone 618/397-6700. **Free.**

Motor Hotels

★ **HYATT LODGE.** *2120 W Main St (62223). 618/234-9400; FAX 618/234-6142.* 80 rms, 2 story. Mid-May-mid-Sept: S $61-$67; D

$69-$81; each addl $6; suites $85-$125; under 16 free; lower rates rest of yr. Crib free. TV; cable (premium), VCR avail (movies). Pool. Complimentary continental bkfst..Restaurant 7 am-midnight. Bar 11:30-1 am; wkends to 2 am. Ck-out noon. Meeting rms. In-rm modem link. Valet serv. Gift shop. Refrigerators, microwaves. Cr cds: A, C, D, DS, MC, V.

✔★ **TOWN HOUSE.** *400 S Illinois (62220). 618/233-7881; FAX 618/233-7885.* 55 rms, 2 story. S $39.45; D $42.45; each addl $5; under 12 free. Crib free. Pet accepted, some restrictions. TV; cable (premium). Restaurant 6 am-9 pm. Rm serv from 8 am. Bar 5 pm-2 am; entertainment. Whirlpool. Ck-out noon. Meeting rms. Business servs avail. In-rm modem link. Health club privileges. Refrigerators, microwaves avail. Cr cds: A, C, D, DS, MC, V.

Inn

✔★ **SWANS COURT.** *421 Court St (62220). 618/233-0779.* 4 rms, 2 share bath. S $45-$80; D $65-$80; wkly rates. TV in common rm. Complimentary full bkfst. Restaurant nearby. In-rm modem link. Luggage handling. Free guest lndry. Built in 1883; some original furnishing, period antiques. Totally nonsmoking. Cr cds: A, DS, MC, V.

Restaurant

★ **FISCHER'S.** *2100 W Main St (62223). 618/233-1131; FAX 618/233-1135.* Hrs: 7 am-midnight. Closed July 4, Dec 24 evening. Res accepted. Continental menu. Bar 10-2 am. Semi-a la carte: lunch $4.95-$8.95, dinner $5.95-$17.50. Child's meals. Specializes in seafood, veal, steak. Contemporary restaurant with a touch of elegance. Family-owned. Cr cds: A, C, D, DS, MC, V.

Benton (H-4)

Pop 7,216 **Elev** 470 ft **Area code** 618 **Zip** 62812
Information Benton Area Chamber of Commerce, 500 W Main St, PO Box 574; 618/438-2121.

What to See and Do

Rend Lake. Created from the Big Muddy and Casey Fork rivers, the Y-shaped Rend Lake covers 19,000 acres adjacent to 21,000 acres of public land with 6 recreation areas. Two beaches; fishing for bass, crappie and catfish; hunting, trap range; boating (launches, marina). Hiking, biking & horseback riding trails. Golf course. Restaurant. Five campgrounds, amphitheaters, programs. Visitor center at the main dam. (Apr-Oct) Fee for some activities. 5 mi N via I-57, exit IL 154. Phone 618/724-2493. On the E shore, off I-57 exit 77, is

Wayne Fitzgerrell State Recreation Area. Approx one-third of the 3,300 acres is used for hunting and dog field trial grounds. Swimming, waterskiing; fishing, hunting; boating (ramps, dock). Hiking, bridle trails. Picnicking (shelters); playground, grocery, restaurant. Camping, tent & trailer sites (dump station, hookups); cabins. Standard hrs, fees. Phone 618/629-2320.

Southern Illinois Arts & Crafts Marketplace. Houses Illinois Artisan shops & galleries. Special events, demonstrations. (Daily; closed Jan 1, Easter, Thanksgiving, Dec 25) 6 mi N on I-57 then W on IL 154. Phone 618/629-2220. **Free.**

Annual Event

Rend Lake Water Festival. Mid-May.

Motel

✔★ **DAYS INN.** *711 W Main. 618/439-3183.* 55 rms, 2 story. S $39.88; D $48.88; each addl $5; suite $90-$95; under 12 free; higher rates special events. Crib avail. Pet accepted. TV; cable, VCR avail (movies). Restaurant 6 am-10 pm. Bar 3-10 pm; entertainment. Ck-out noon. Meeting rms. Business servs avail. Refrigerators, microwaves avail. Picnic tables. Cr cds: A, C, D, DS, MC, V.

Resort

★ ★ **REND LAKE.** *(11712 E Windy Ln, Whittington 62897)* 5 mi N on I-57 to IL 154 (exit 77), in Wayne Fitzgerrell State Park. 618/629-2211; FAX 618/629-2584; res: 800/633-3341. Web dnr.state.il.us/parks/parkinfo/rendlake.htm. 90 units, 20 rms in lodge, 22 cottages. Mar-mid-Nov: S, D $57-$75; each addl $9; cottages $65; under 12 free; 2-day min wkends, hols; lower rates rest of yr. Crib $3. TV. Pool; wading pool. Playground. Dining rm 8 am-9 pm. Ck-out 11 am. Meeting rms. Business servs avail. Lighted tennis. 18-hole golf privileges; greens fee $32, pro. Some refrigerators. On Rend Lake. Operated by state park. Cr cds: A, D, DS, MC, V.

Bishop Hill (C-3)

(For accommodations see Galesburg, Kewanee)

Settled 1846 **Pop** 131 **Elev** 780 ft **Area code** 309 **Zip** 61419

What to See and Do

★ **Bishop Hill State Historic Site.** Settled in 1846 by Swedish immigrants seeking religious freedom, the communal-utopian colony was led by Erik Jansson until his assassination in 1850. In 1861, the communally-owned property was divided and the colony dissolved. Descendants of the settlers still live in the community. The state-owned Colony Hotel and Colony Church still stand, as do 15 of the original 21 buildings. (Daily; closed Jan 1, Thanksgiving, Dec 25; hrs vary, phone ahead) 2 mi N on country rd 39. Phone 309/927-3345. **Free.** Among the restorations are

Steeple Building (1854). This three-story Greek-revival edifice is of handmade brick covered with plaster. The clock, in its wooden steeple, was designed with only one hand. The Heritage Museum houses displays of the community's history. The Bishop Hill Heritage collection of late 19th-century Bishop Hill memorabilia is here; slide show daily in season. (Apr-Dec, daily; closed Thanksgiving, Dec 25) Phone 309/927-3899. ¢

Colony Church (1848). This gambrel-roofed building houses a collection of Bishop Hill artifacts. Second floor features restored sanctuary with original walnut pews.

Colony Blacksmith Shop. Traditional craftsmen selling and demonstrating crafts. Phone 309/927-3390.

Bishop Hill Museum. Houses collection of paintings by Olof Krans, whose primitive folk art depicts the Bishop Hill colony of his childhood.

Colony Store (1853). Restored general store with original shelving and counters. (Daily; closed Thanksgiving, Dec 25) Phone 309/927-3596.

Village tours. The Bishop Hill Heritage Assn conducts tours of the village (all yr, by appt). Phone 309/927-3899. ¢¢

Annual Events

Concert Series. Sun afternoon concerts. June.

Bishop Hill Jordbruksdagarna. Agricultural celebration features harvesting demonstrations, children's games, "colony stew," hayrack rides. Late Sept.

Julmarknad. Christmas market with decorated shops; Swedish foods; "Juletomte" (Christmas elf) and "Julbok" (Christmas goat) roam the village. Thanksgiving wkend & 1st wkend Dec.

Lucia Nights. Festival of lights. "Lucias" with candle crowns serve coffee and sweets to guests; choral programs, carolers, sleigh rides. Mid-Dec.

Bloomington (D-4)

(See also Peoria)

Founded 1843 **Pop** 51,972 **Elev** 829 ft **Area code** 309
Information Bloomington-Normal Convention & Visitors Bureau, 210 S East St, PO Box 1586; 309/829-1641 or 800/433-8226.

Bloomington, the McLean County seat, took its name from the original settlement of Blooming Grove. Two McLean County residents, Abe Brokaw and John Deere, initiated production of iron plows to till prairie soil.

The Illinois Republican party was formed here in 1856 at the Anti-Nebraska convention, at which Abraham Lincoln made the famous "lost speech" spelling out the principles that were to elect him president. Bloomington was also the home of Adlai E. Stevenson, vice president under Grover Cleveland. His grandson, Illinois Governor Adlai E. Stevenson II, twice Democratic candidate for president and US Ambassador to the United Nations, is buried here. Along with agriculture, the founding of Illinois Wesleyan University and the selection of North Bloomington (now the twin city of Normal) as the site for Illinois State University helped determine the town's economic future.

What to See and Do

Funk Prairie Home (1863). Built by LaFayette Funk with lumber and timber felled in Funk's Grove, the large Italianate house with wrap-around porches features elaborately decorated parlor with Chickering piano, Italian marble fireplace, gold valance boards above windows. Guided tours (allow 1¼ hrs; reservations advised) include adj Gem and Mineral Museum. (Mar-Dec, Tues-Sat; closed hols) S on I-55 exit 154 to Shirley, then 1¼ mi. Phone 309/827-6792. **Free.**

Illinois State University (1857). (22,000 students) The first state university in Illinois. Tours arranged. 1 mi S of jct US 51, I-55 in Normal. Phone 309/438-2181. On campus is

Adlai E. Stevenson Memorial Room. Contains personal memorabilia, photographs. (Mon-Fri) Phone 309/438-5669. **Free.**

Illinois Wesleyan University (1850). (1,800 students) North side residential area on US 51, I-55 Business & IL 9. Liberal arts college. E University St. Phone 309/556-3034. On campus are

Evelyn Chapel. The design of this chapel, focal point of the central campus, is derived from early Moravian architecture in America. The brick exterior is laid in the Flemish bond pattern, and the interior has custom-made woodwork with graceful scalloped surfaces, which add to the acoustical brilliance of the building.

Sheean Library. Contains the papers of former US Congressman Leslie Arends and the Gernon Collection of 19th- and 20th-century literature. Also on display is a collection of Native American pottery of Major John Wesley Powell, former faculty member of Wesleyan and credited with the first exploration of the Colorado River and the Grand Canyon. **Free.**

Miller Park Zoo. Big cats, river otters in natural settings; sea lions; tropical rain forest; children's zoo. (Daily) On Morris Ave, ½ mi N of I-55 Business. Phone 309/823-4250. ¢

Other activities in Miller Park include swimming, fishing, boating, picnicking, tennis and miniature golf (some fees). There is a playground and a steam locomotive display. Band concerts are held in season.

Old Courthouse Museum. Maintained by McLean County Historical Society, housed in 1903 courthouse. Exhibits include area history, farming, an authentic courtroom, hands-on displays and a research library. Museum store. (Daily exc Sun; closed most major hols) 200 N Main St. Phone 309/827-0428. ¢

Seasonal Events

The American Passion Play. Scottish Rite Temple, 110 E Mulberry St. A cast of more than 300; presented annually since 1924. Phone 309/829-3903. Sat & Sun, late Mar-mid-May.

Illinois Shakespeare Festival. Ewing Manor, Emerson & Towanda Sts. Shakespearean performances preceded by madrigal music and entertainment. Phone 309/438-2535. July-early Aug.

Motels

✔★ ★ **BEST INNS OF AMERICA.** *1905 W Market St (61701), 1 blk E of I-55/74 exit 160A. 309/827-5333; FAX 309/827-5333, ext. 113.* 107 rms, 2 story. S $35-$41; D $43-$50; each addl $7; under 18 free. Crib free. Pet accepted. TV; cable (premium). Pool. Complimentary continental bkfst. Restaurant adj 10 am-midnight. Ck-out 1 pm. Business servs avail. In-rm modem link. Cr cds: A, C, D, DS, MC, V.

D ✔ ≋ ⊠ 🐾 SC

★ ★ **BEST WESTERN EASTLAND SUITES HOTEL AND CONFERENCE CENTER.** *1801 Eastland Dr (61704), near Bloomington-Normal Airport. 309/662-0000; FAX 309/663-6668.* 88 kit. suites, 2 story. S $60-$125; D $105-$250; under 18 free; wkly rates; higher rates graduation. Crib free. TV; cable (premium). Indoor pool. Complimentary continental bkfst. Complimentary coffee in rms. Restaurant nearby. Ck-out noon. Coin lndry. Meeting rms. Business center. Bellhops. Free airport, RR station, bus depot transportation. Exercise equipt; weight machine, bicycle, sauna. Balconies. Picnic tables, grills. Cr cds: A, C, D, DS, MC, V.

D ≋ ✈ 🍴 🐾 🚶 🏊

★ **BEST WESTERN UNIVERSITY INN.** *(6 Traders Circle, Normal 61761) Off Main St (US 51), ¼ mi S of I-55 exit 165A. 309/454-4070; FAX 309/888-4505.* 102 rms, 2 story. S $55-$61; D $61-$68; each addl $7; kit. units $61; under 12 free. Crib free. Pet accepted. TV; cable (premium). Sauna. Heated pool. Complimentary continental bkfst. Restaurant nearby. Ck-out 11 am. Meeting rms. Business servs avail. Valet serv. Free airport, RR station, bus depot transportation. Cr cds: A, C, D, DS, MC, V.

D ✔ ≋ ⊠ 🐾 SC

✔★ ★ **FAIRFIELD INN BY MARRIOTT.** *(202 N Landmark Dr, Normal 61761) Jct Veterans Pkwy & College Ave. 309/454-6600; FAX 309/454-6600, ext. 709.* 128 rms, 3 story. S $45-$56; D $52-$62; each addl $7; under 18 free. Crib free. TV; cable (premium). Heated pool. Complimentary continental bkfst. Restaurant nearby. Ck-out noon. Meeting rms. Business servs avail. In-rm modem link. Cr cds: A, C, D, DS, MC, V.

D ≋ ⊠ 🐾 SC

★ ★ **HAMPTON INN.** *604-½ I.A.A. Dr (61701), Empire St (IL 9) to I.A.A. Dr. 309/662-2800; FAX 309/662-2811.* 108 rms, 3 story. S $64-$68; D $70-$72; under 18 free; higher rates special events. Crib free. TV; cable (premium). Heated pool. Complimentary continental bkfst. Restaurant adj open 24 hrs. Ck-out noon. Meeting rm. Business servs avail. In-rm modem link. Sundries. Free airport, RR station, bus depot transportation. Health club privileges. Cr cds: A, C, D, DS, JCB, MC, V.

D ≋ ⊠ 🐾 SC

★ ★ **RAMADA INN.** *1219 Holiday Dr (61704), Veterans Pkwy & Empire St (IL 9). 309/662-5311; FAX 309/663-1732.* 209 rms, 2 story. S $49-$68; D $58-$77; under 18 free. Crib free. Pet accepted. TV; cable (premium). Indoor pool; whirlpool. Restaurant 6:30 am-1 pm, 5:30-9 pm. Rm serv. Bar 4:30 pm-midnight. Ck-out noon. Coin lndry. Meeting rms. Business servs avail. Bellhops. Sundries. Free airport, RR station, bus depot transportation. Exercise equipt; stair machine, treadmill, sauna. Miniature golf. Game rm. Cr cds: A, C, D, DS, JCB, MC, V.

D ✔ ≋ 🚶 🐾 🏊 SC

Motor Hotel

★ ★ **HOLIDAY INN.** *(8 Traders Circle, Normal 61761) Near jct US 55, IL 51. 309/452-8300; FAX 309/454-6722.* 160 rms, 5 story. S $64-$74; D $78-$83; each addl $9; under 18 free. Crib free. Pet accepted. TV; cable (premium), VCR avail (movies). Indoor pool; whirlpool. Complimentary coffee in lobby. Restaurant 6:30 am-2 pm, 5-10 pm. Rm serv. Bar 3 pm-midnight. Ck-out noon. Meeting rms. Business center. Bellhops. Valet serv. Free airport, RR station, bus depot transportation. Exercise equipt; weights, bicycles, sauna. Game rm. Cr cds: A, C, D, DS, MC, V.

Hotel

★ ★ ★ **JUMER'S CHATEAU.** *1601 Jumer Dr (61704), off Veterans Pkwy, near Bloomington-Normal Airport. 309/662-2020; FAX 309/662-2020, ext. 617.* 180 rms, 5 story, 26 suites. S $85-$100; D $94-$103; each addl $9; suites $107-$154; under 18 free; wkend rates; golf plans. Crib free. Pet accepted. TV; cable (premium). Indoor pool; whirlpool. Coffee in lobby. Restaurant 6:30 am-10 pm; Fri, Sat to 11 pm; Sun 7 am-10 pm. Bar 11:30-1 am; Sun noon-midnight; entertainment exc Sun. Ck-out noon. Meeting rms. Business servs avail. Gift shop. Free airport, RR station, bus depot transportation. Exercise equipt; weight machine, stair machine, sauna. Game rm. Rec rm. Refrigerator, minibar in suites. French decor. Library, antiques. Cr cds: A, C, D, DS, JCB, MC, V.

Restaurants

✔★ ★ **CENTRAL STATION CAFE.** *220 E Front St (61701), Downtown Bloomington. 309/828-2323.* Hrs: 11 am-midnight; Closed Mon (Memorial Day-Labor Day); some major hols. Continental, Amer menu. Bar. Semi-a la carte: lunch $3.95-$6.95, dinner $6.95-$15.95. Specializes in mesquite grilled fresh seafood, prime rib, barbecued ribs. Entertainment Thurs-Sat. In former fire station (1902). Cr cds: A, C, D, MC, V.

★ ★ **JIM'S STEAK HOUSE.** *2307 E Washington St (61704). 309/663-4142.* Hrs: 11-1 am; Sat & Sun from 4 pm. Closed Dec. 25. Res accepted. Bar. Semi-a la carte: lunch $4.25-$8.95, dinner $9.50-$25.95. Specializes in dry-aged steak, prime rib, fresh fish. Pianist Thurs-Sat. Rustic decor. Cr cds: A, C, D, DS, MC, V.

Brookfield (E-3 see Chicago map)

(See also Cicero, La Grange)

Pop 18,876 **Elev** 620 ft **Area code** 708 **Zip** 60513
Information Chamber of Commerce, 3724 Grand Blvd; 708/485-1434.

What to See and Do

Brookfield Zoo (Chicago Zoological Park). One of the finest zoos in the country, it has barless, naturally landscaped enclosures housing more than 2,000 exotic and familiar animals. Exhibits include The Fragile Kingdom, an introduction to Asia and Africa with emphasis on how the regions' animals—including large cats—relate to each other and to their environment; Tropic World, a simulated rain forest; Africa!, five-acre savannah exhibit; Seven Seas Panorama (dolphin shows several times daily; fee); Children's Zoo (animal demonstrations June-Aug, daily; fee); and Motor Safari Tours (early spring-late fall; fee); free winter shuttle; picnic areas, concessions. Special events throughout the yr, including National Pig Day (early Mar), Teddy Bear Picnic (early Aug), Boo! at the Zoo (Oct) and Holiday Magic Festival (Dec evenings). Parking (fee). (Daily) 31st St & 1st Ave. Phone 708/485-0263. ¢¢

Motel

★ **COLONY.** *9232 W Ogden Ave (IL 34). 708/485-0300.* 36 rms, 1-2 story, 6 kits. S $31.95; D $31.95-$33.95; each addl $3; kit. units $51.95-$53.95. TV. Complimentary coffee. Restaurant nearby. Ck-out 11 am. Cr cds: A, C, D, DS, MC, V.

Cahokia (H-3)

(For accommodations see Belleville, Collinsville, Edwardsville)

Founded 1699 **Pop** 17,550 **Elev** 411 ft **Area code** 618 **Zip** 62206
Information Cahokia Area Chamber of Commerce, 905 Falling Springs Rd; 618/332-1900.

Cahokia, the oldest town in Illinois, was once the center of a vast French missionary area that included what is now Chicago, more than 260 miles northeast. The first church in Illinois was built here by Father St Cosme in 1699, and a trading post developed around the mission. Cahokia came under the British flag in 1765 and under the American flag in 1778.

What to See and Do

Cahokia Courthouse State Historic Site. Believed to be the oldest house (ca 1735) in the state. Former house of François Saucier, son of the builder of Fort de Chartres. Sold in 1793, it was used as a territorial courthouse and jail until 1814. Museum display of courtroom and period lifestyle; interpretive program. (Tues-Sat) 107 Elm St, just off IL 3. Phone 618/332-1782. **Free.**

Cahokia Mounds State Historic Site. This site preserves the central section of the only prehistoric city north of Mexico. Archaeological finds indicate that the Cahokia site was first inhabited around A.D. 700. Eventually a very complex community developed; the city of Cahokia covered six sq mi and had a population of tens of thousands. The earthen mounds, used primarily for ceremonial activities of the living, originally numbered more than 100. Only 68 are currently preserved. Monks Mound, the great platform mound named for Trappist monks who once lived near it (1809-1813), is the largest mound north of Mexico and also the largest prehistoric earthen construction in the New World. Its base covers 14 acres, and it rises in 4 terraces to a height of 100 ft. Two other types of mounds, conical and ridgetop, are also found here. Archaeological excavations have partially uncovered remains of four circular sun calendars, which once consisted of large, evenly spaced log posts probably used to predict the changing seasons. One has been reconstructed in the original location. The 2,000-acre site has a resident archaeologist. Activities include hiking and picnicking. Self-guided tours avail. A museum displays artifacts from the nearby mounds and village areas (Mar-Nov, daily; rest of yr, Wed-Sun; closed major hols). I-255 exit 24, W on Collinsville Rd. For further information contact Public Relations, PO Box 681, Collinsville 62234; 618/346-5160. **Free.**

Historic Holy Family Mission Log Church. Completed in 1799; restored in 1949; the original walnut logs stand upright in Canadian fashion. The old cemetery is behind the church. (June-Aug, daily) At jct IL 3, 157. Phone 618/337-4548. **Donation.**

Cairo (K-4)

(For accommodations see Carbondale)

Settled 1837 **Pop** 4,846 **Elev** 314 ft **Area code** 618 **Zip** 62914
Information Chamber of Commerce, 220 8th St; 618/734-2737.

Farther south than Richmond, Virginia, Cairo (CARE-o), a city of magnolia trees, is located at the confluence of the Ohio and Mississippi rivers.

Settlement was attempted in 1818 by a St Louis merchant, who named the site Cairo because he thought it resembled the Egyptian capital. Cairo and the southern tip of Illinois are still locally referred to as "Little Egypt." Dominating rail and river traffic, spearheading the thrust of free territory into the South and harboring citizens with Southern sympathies, strategic Cairo was immediately fortified after the outbreak of the Civil War. Cairo served as headquarters, fortress, supply depot and hospital for Grant's Army of the Tennessee. After the Civil War, the town had the highest per capita commercial valuation in the United States, and citizens, rich with war profits, lavished money on both public and private building projects that, according to the National Register of Historic Places, remain as "individual works of architectural brilliance."

Bridges at Cairo connect three states: Illinois, Missouri and Kentucky. Local legend has it that a penny tossed into the confluence of the rivers at Point Cairo will bring one back again. The levee, rising from the river delta, and the streets along it retain the flavor of the steamboat era.

What to See and Do

Custom House Museum. 19th-century Federal building contains artifacts and replicas from Cairo's past. (Mon-Fri) 1400 Washington Ave.   **Free.**

Fort Defiance State Park. Splendid view of the confluence of Ohio and Mississippi rivers on 39 acres; site of Civil War fort. On US 51 at S edge of town.

Horseshoe Lake State Conservation Area. Large flocks of Canada geese migrate to these 10,336 acres in winter. Fishing, hunting; boating (ramp; 10 hp motor limit mid-Mar-mid-Nov). Hiking. Picnicking, concession. Camping. Standard hrs, fees. 7 mi NW on IL 3. Phone 618/776-5689.

Magnolia Manor (1869). Italianate/Victorian mansion (14 rms), built for wealthy flour merchant, contains period furnishings, items of local historical interest. View of Mississippi and Ohio rivers from tower. (Daily; closed some major hols) 2700 Washington Ave. Phone 618/734-0201.   ¢¢

Carbondale (J-4)

(See also Cairo, Du Quoin, Marion)

Founded 1852 **Pop** 27,033 **Elev** 415 ft **Area code** 618 **Zip** 62901
Information Convention and Tourism Bureau, 1245 E Main St, suite A32; 618/529-4451 or 800/526-1500.

Carbondale is surrounded by lakes and rivers, including Crab Orchard and Little Grassy lakes and the Big Muddy River. Railroad yards, Southern Illinois University and surrounding coal fields give the community a unique personality.

What to See and Do

Bald Knob. View of three states from this high point in the Illinois Ozarks. 16 mi S on US 51 to Cobden, then 4 mi W to Alto Pass.

Giant City State Park. Picturesque rock formations and a prehistoric "stone fort" on 3,694 acres. Fishing, hunting. Hiking, riding trails. Picnicking, concession, lodge, dining rm. Camping, cabins, horse campground. Standard hrs, fees. (Daily) 10 mi S on US 51, then E on unnumbered road, in Makanda. Phone 618/457-4836.   **Free.**

⭐ **Shawnee National Forest.** Approx 266,000 acres, bordered on E by Ohio River, on W by Mississippi River; unusual rock formations, varied wildlife. Swimming; fishing, hunting; boating. Hiking, bridle trails. Picnicking. Camping on first-come basis. Fees may be charged at recreation sites. S, W & E of town, via I-57, I-24, US 51, IL 13/127, 148. Contact Forest Supervisor, 901 S Commercial St, Harrisburg 62946; 618/253-7114.   ¢¢

Southern Illinois University (1869). (24,000 students) S on Illinois Ave, US 51. Phone 618/453-2121. On campus is

University Museum. Exhibits southern Illinois history, nationally known artists, local collections; changing exhibits. Gift shop. (Tues-Sun, by appt; closed hols & university recesses) N end of Faner Hall. Phone 618/453-5388.   **Free.**

Motels

✔★ **BEST INNS OF AMERICA.** *1345 E Main St, jct University Mall & Frontage Rd. 618/529-4801.* 86 rms, 2 story. S $38.88; D $49.88; each addl $6; under 18 free; higher rates special university events. Crib free. Pet accepted. TV; cable. Pool. Complimentary continental bkfst. Restaurant adj 3 pm-midnight. Ck-out 1 pm. Cr cds: A, C, D, DS, MC, V.

 D ✔ ≈ ⇴ 🐾 SC

★ **SUPER 8.** *1180 E Main St, 1½ mi E on IL 13. 618/457-8822; FAX 618/457-4186.* 63 rms, 3 story. No elvtr. S $36.88-$42.88; D $39.88-$55.88; under 12 free. Crib free. Pet accepted. TV; cable. Restaurant adj 6 am-midnight. Ck-out 11 am. Cr cds: A, C, D, DS, MC, V.

D ✔ ⇴ ⇴ 🐾 SC

Cottage Colony

★ **GIANT CITY LODGE.** *(336 S Church Rd, Makanda 62958) 12 mi S on Giant City Rd. 618/457-4921.* 34 cottages. S, D $45-$80; each addl $5. Closed mid-Dec-Jan. Crib $5. TV. Pool. Dining rm 8 am-8:30 pm; Sun to 8 pm. Bar to 9 pm. Meeting rms. Gift shop. Microwaves; some wet bars. In Giant City State Park. Cr cds: A, D, MC, V.

 D ✔ ⇆ ≈ 🐾

Restaurants

★ **MARY LOU'S GRILL.** *114 S Illinois Ave. 618/457-5084.* Hrs: 7 am-2 pm. Closed Sun, Mon; most major hols. Semi-a la carte: bkfst $1.95-$5, lunch $3-$4.75. Specializes in cream pies, biscuits & gravy. Family-owned. Cr cds: MC, V.

⊐

✔★ **TRES HOMBRES.** *119 N Washington St. 618/457-3308.* Hrs: 11 am-10 pm. Closed most major hols. Res accepted. Mexican menu. Bar. Semi-a la carte: lunch $3-$7, dinner $5-$10. Specializes in fajitas. Entertainment Thurs. Southwestern atmosphere. Extensive beer selection. Cr cds: A, D, DS, MC, V.

 D ⊐

Unrated Dining Spot

BOOBY'S. *406 S Illinois Ave. 618/549-3366.* Hrs: 11 am-10 pm; Fri, Sat to midnight. Closed some major hols. Bar. Deli menu. Semi-a la carte: lunch, dinner $2.79-$5.99. Specializes in submarine sandwiches, deli fare. Beer garden. Cr cds: MC, V.

D

Centralia (H-4)

(See also Edwardsville, Mt Vernon, Salem)

Founded 1853 **Pop** 14,274 **Elev** 499 ft **Area code** 618 **Zip** 62801
Information Chamber of Commerce, 130 S Locust St; 618/532-6789.

Centralia, named for the Illinois Central Railroad, and its neighbors, Central City and Wamac, form a continuous urban area that is the trading center and labor pool for four counties in south-central Illinois.

What to See and Do

Centralia Carillon. This 160-ft tower houses 65 bells. Concerts; tours (by appt). 114 N Elm at Noleman. Phone 618/533-4381.   **Free.**

Fairview Park. Site of Engine 2500. One of the largest steam locomotives ever built (225 tons), the engine was donated to the city by the Illinois Central Railroad. Swimming. Picnicking, playgrounds. (Daily) W on IL 161, at W Broadway.

Lakes.

Raccoon Lake. Fishing, boating (ramp). 3 mi E on IL 161, then 1/2 mi N on Country Club Rd. (Apr-Oct) **Lake Centralia.** Swimming, fishing, boating. Picnicking. 8 mi NE on Green Street Rd.

Motel

 ★ **CENTRALIA.** *215 S Poplar. 618/532-7357; FAX 618/533-4304.* 57 rms, 1-2 story. S $35; D $39-$50; each addl $5; under 12 free. Crib $5. TV; cable. Complimentary coffee in lobby. Restaurant nearby. Ck-out 11 am. Business servs avail. Cr cds: A, C, D, DS, MC, V.

 SC

Restaurant

★ ★ **CENTRALIA HOUSE.** *111 N Oak St. 618/532-9754.* Hrs: 4-11 pm. Closed Sun; major hols. Res accepted. Cajun, Amer menu. Bar. Semi-a la carte: dinner $18-$25. Specializes in shrimp, pepper steak. Turn-of-the-century elegance. Cr cds: A, C, D, DS, JCB, MC, V.

Champaign/Urbana

(E-5)

(See also Arcola, Danville)

Settled Urbana, 1822 **Pop** Champaign, 63,502; Urbana, 36,344 **Elev** Champaign, 742 ft; Urbana, 727 ft **Area code** 217 **Zip** Urbana, 61801 **E-mail** kimp@cucvb.org
Information Convention & Visitors Bureau, 1817 S Neil St, Ste 201, PO Box 1607, Champaign 61820-1607; 217/351-4133 or 800/369-6151.

Champaign and Urbana, separately incorporated, are united as the home of the University of Illinois. Champaign started as West Urbana when the Illinois Central Railroad ran its line two miles west of Urbana, the county seat. Defying annexation by Urbana in 1855, the new community was incorporated in 1860 as Champaign and prospered as a trade center. Today the two communities are geographically one; Champaign continues as a commercial and industrial center, with the larger part of the university falling within the boundaries of Urbana.

Urbana became the seat of Champaign County in 1833, but its anticipated growth was interrupted when the railroad bypassed it. In 1867, the Industrial University was opened in Urbana. Now the University of Illinois, it extends into the other "twin city," Champaign. Lincoln Square, the second downtown covered mall in the US, is a forerunner in the revitalization of downtown districts.

What to See and Do

Champaign County Historical Museum. Located in the Edwardian Wilber mansion (1907); many original items. (Wed-Fri & Sun; closed some major hols) 709 W University Ave, Champaign. Phone 217/356-1010. ¢

Lake of the Woods County Preserve. Swimming, boating (rentals); fishing. Golf (phone 217/586-2183). Picnicking, playground. Also Early American Museum and botanical gardens (Memorial Day-Labor Day, daily; after Labor Day-early Oct, wkends). Visitor center. Park (daily). 10 mi W on I-74, then 1/4 mi N on IL 47, in Mahomet. Phone 217/586-3360 (park) or 217/586-2612 (museum). **Free.**

University of Illinois (1867). (35,815 students) Included among the 200 major buildings on campus are the main library, the third-largest academic library in the US (daily); the undergraduate library, which was built under-

ground to prevent throwing a shadow on the Morrow Plots, the oldest experimental plot of land still in use; Mumford House, the oldest building on campus (1870); Altgeld Hall with a carillon that plays tunes periodically throughout the day; Krannert Center for the Performing Arts, which presents ballet and opera productions; the 69,200-seat Memorial Stadium; and the domed Assembly Hall, which hosts basketball games and concerts. Campus walking tour avail. Wright St. Information desk at Illini Union, Wright & Green Sts; phone 217/333-4666. Campus Visitors Center, Levis Faculty Center, 919 W Illinois (Mon-Fri); phone 217/333-1345. Also on campus are

Krannert Art Museum. (Tues-Sat; also Sun afternoons) Peabody St, between 4th & 6th Sts. Phone 217/333-1860. **Free.**

World Heritage Museum. (Academic yr, Mon-Fri, also Sun afternoons) Lincoln Hall, Wright St. Phone 217/333-2360. **Free.**

Museum of Natural History. (Mon-Sat, also Sun afternoons) Green St, adj Illini Union. Phone 217/333-2517. **Free.**

William M. Staerkel Planetarium. Second-largest planetarium in Illinois projects 5,000 visible stars on a 50-ft dome. Multimedia shows, lectures. (Thurs-Sat) 2400 W Bradley Ave, in Parkland College Cultural Center, Champaign. Phone 217/351-2200. ¢¢

Motels

(Rates may be higher for special university wkends)

★ ★ **BEST WESTERN CUNNINGHAM PLACE.** *(1907 Cunningham Ave, Urbana 61801)* 217/367-8331; FAX 217/384-3370. 105 rms, 2 story, 48 suites. S $59-$65; D $69-$78; each addl $7; suites $85-$120; under 18 free. Crib free. Pet accepted, some restrictions. TV; cable (premium). VCR avail. Indoor pool. Complimentary full bkfst. Bar 5-10 pm, closed Sat, Sun. Ck-out noon. Meeting rms. Business servs avail. Bellhops. Valet serv. Free airport transportation. Exercise equipt; weight machines, bicycles, sauna. Some refrigerators, microwaves. Private patios, balconies. Cr cds: A, C, D, DS, JCB, MC, V.

D ★ ≈ ⊀ ⊠ ⊠ SC

★ ★ **BEST WESTERN LINCOLN LODGE.** *(403 W University Ave, Urbana 61801)* 1/2 mi W on US 45/150 (IL 10), 1 mi S of I-74 Lincoln Ave exit. 217/367-1111; FAX 217/367-8233. 31 rms, 1-2 story. S $48.95; D $54.95; each addl $6; under 12 free. Crib free. TV; cable (premium). Pool. Ck-out noon. Business servs avail. Cr cds: A, C, D, DS, MC, V.

≈ ⊠ ⊠ SC

★ ★ **BEST WESTERN PARADISE INN.** *(1001 N Dunlap, Savoy 61874)* 3 1/2 mi S, near University of Illinois-Willard Airport. 217/356-1824; FAX 217/356-1824, ext. 190. 62 rms, 1-2 story. S $43-$49; D $53-$63; each addl $4; under 12 free. Crib $4. Pet accepted, some restrictions; $2/day. TV; cable (premium). Heated pool; wading pool. Playground. Complimentary continental bkfst. Complimentary coffee in rms. Restaurant nearby. Ck-out 11 am. Coin lndry. Meeting rm. Business servs avail. In-rm modem link. Free airport transportation. Cr cds: A, C, D, DS, MC, V.

★ ≈ ⊀ ⊠ ⊠ SC

★ ★ **COMFORT INN.** *(305 W Marketview Dr, Champaign 61821)* 1/2 mi N of jct I-74 & N Neil St exit. 217/352-4055; FAX 217/352-4055, ext. 329. 67 rms, 2 story. Mar-Oct: S $54.99; D $60.99; each addl $6; suites $64.99-$70.99; under 18 free; lower rates rest of yr. Crib free. Pet accepted, some restrictions. TV; cable (premium). Indoor pool; whirlpool. Complimentary continental bkfst. Restaurant nearby. Ck-out 11 am. Meeting rm. Business servs avail. Refrigerators in suites; microwaves avail. Cr cds: A, C, D, DS, ER, JCB, MC, V.

D ★ ≈ ⊠ ⊠ SC

★ ★ **LA QUINTA.** *(1900 Center Dr, Champaign 61820)* 1 blk N of I-74 Neil St exit. 217/356-4000; FAX 217/352-7783. 120 rms, 2 story. S $50-$57; D $57-$64; each addl $7; under 18 free. Crib free. Pet accepted, some restrictions. TV; cable (premium). Heated pool. Complimentary continental bkfst. Restaurant adj open 24 hrs. Ck-out noon. Coin lndry. Meeting rms. In-rm modem link. Valet serv. Cr cds: A, DS, MC, V.

⊡ ⬛ ⬛ ⬛ ⬛ SC

✔★ **RED ROOF INN.** *(212 W Anthony Dr, Champaign 61820)* 217/352-0101; FAX 217/352-1891. 112 rms, 2 story. June-Oct: S $31.99-$47.99; D $39.99-$54.99; each addl $7-$9; under 18 free; lower rates rest of yr. Crib avail. Pet accepted. TV; cable. Complimentary coffee in lobby. Restaurant nearby. Ck-out noon. Business servs avail. Picnic table. Cr cds: A, C, D, DS, MC, V.

⊡ ⬛ SC

★ **SUPER 8.** *(202 Marketview Dr, Champaign 61820)* I-74, Neil St exit N. 217/359-2388. 61 rms, 2 story. S $44-$49; D $49-$59; each addl $5; under 12 free. Crib free. Pet accepted; $10 deposit. TV; cable (premium). Complimentary coffee. Restaurant nearby. Ck-out 11 am. Coin lndry. Business servs avail. Cr cds: A, C, D, DS, MC, V.

⊡ ⬛ ⬛ SC

Motor Hotel

★★ **RADISSON SUITE.** *(101 Trade Center Dr, Champaign 61820)* 217/398-3400; FAX 217/398-6147. 199 suites, 4-5 story. S $95-$125; D $105-$135; each addl $10; under 18 free. Crib free. TV; cable (premium), VCR avail. Indoor pool; whirlpool. Complimentary full bkfst. Complimentary coffee in rms. Restaurant adj 11-1 am. Ck-out noon. Coin lndry. Meeting rms. Business center. In-rm modem link. Bellhops. Sundries. Free airport, RR station, bus depot, U of I transportation. Exercise equipt; bicycle, ski machine. Health club privileges. Refrigerators, wet bars; microwaves avail. Cr cds: A, C, D, DS, ER, JCB, MC, V.

⊡ ⬛ ⬛ ⬛ ⬛ SC ⬛

Hotels

★★ **CHANCELLOR.** *(1501 S Neil St, Champaign 61820)* 2 mi S of I-74 Neil St exit. 217/352-7891; FAX 217/352-8108. 225 rms, 4-7 story. S $61-$71; D $69-$79; each addl $8; suites $100-$200; under 18 free. Crib free. Pet accepted. TV; cable. 2 pools; 1 indoor; wading pool, whirlpools. Supervised child's activities. Complimentary continental bkfst. Restaurant 6 am-11 pm; to 2 am wkends. Bar 4 pm-1 am, closed Sun. Ck-out 1 pm. Meeting rms. Business servs avail. In-rm modem link. Gift shop. Free airport, RR, bus transportation. Game rm. Exercise equipt; weight machines, stair machines, saunas. Microwaves avail. Dinner theater. Cr cds: A, C, D, DS, MC, V.

⊡ ⬛ ⬛ ⬛ ⬛ ⬛ SC

★★★ **JUMER'S CASTLE LODGE.** *(209 S Broadway, Urbana 61801)* Lincoln Square, 1½ mi S of I-74 Lincoln exit. 217/384-8800; FAX 217/384-9001; res: 800/285-8637. 130 rms, 4 story. S $82-$127; D $92-$127; each addl $10; suites $107-$154; under 18 free; wkend rates. Crib free. Pet accepted, some restrictions; $25 deposit. TV; cable (premium). Saunas. Indoor pool; whirlpool. Complimentary coffee in lobby. Restaurant 6:30 am-10 pm; Fri, Sat to 11 pm. Rm serv. Bar 4 pm-1 am; entertainment. Ck-out noon. Meeting rms. Business servs avail. In-rm modem link. Shopping arcade. Free airport transportation. Some fireplaces. Cr cds: A, C, D, DS, ER, JCB, MC, V.

⊡ ⬛ ⬛ ⬛ ⬛ ⬛ SC

★★ **UNIVERSITY INN.** *(302 E John St, Champaign 61820)* 1½ mi SE, on campus, S of I-74 Neil St exit. 217/384-2100; FAX 217/384-2298; res: 800/322-8282. Web www.stadiumview.com. 203 rms, 21 story. S $61-$67; D $69-$72; each addl $8; suites $200-$300; monthly rates. Crib free. TV; cable. Pool privileges. Complimentary continental bkfst. Restaurant 7 am-2 pm, 5:30-10 pm. Bar 2 pm-1 am; closed Sun. Ck-out 1 pm. Meeting rms. Free covered parking. Free airport transportation. Some refrigerators. Cr cds: A, C, D, DS, MC, V.

⊡ ⬛ ⬛ SC

Restaurants

✔★ **HOUSE OF HUNAN.** *(403 N Mattis St, Champaign 61821)* In Country Fair shopping center. 217/398-3388. Hrs: 11 am-10 pm; Sat, Sun from noon. Res accepted. Chinese menu. Bar. Semi-a la carte: lunch $3.95-$7.95; dinner $7.50-$15.95. Complete meals: dinner $11-$13.50. Specializes in orange beef, seafood combination, Cantonese lobster. Cr cds: A, C, D, DS, MC, V.

⊡ ⬛

★ **NED KELLY'S.** *(1601 N Cunningham Ave, Urbana 61801)* 217/344-8201. Hrs: 11 am-10 pm; Fri, Sat to 11 pm; Sun to 9 pm. Closed Dec 25. Res accepted. Bar. Semi-a la carte: lunch $6-$10, dinner $8-$18. Child's meals. Specializes in steak, prime rib, pasta. Multi-level dining with Australian theme. Cr cds: A, C, D, DS, MC, V.

⊡ ⬛

★★ **TIMPONE'S.** *(710 S Goodwin Ave, Urbana 61801)* 7 blks S of University Ave. 217/344-7619. Hrs: 11 am-10 pm; Fri, Sat to 11 pm. Closed Sun; most major hols. Res accepted. Contemporary Italian, Amer menu. Bar. Semi-a la carte: lunch $3.75-$9.95, dinner $8.95-$19.95. Specializes in fresh seafood, pasta, pizza. Own desserts. Cr cds: MC, V.

Charleston (F-5)

(For accommodations see Arcola, Mattoon)

Pop 20,398 **Elev** 686 ft **Area code** 217 **Zip** 61920 **E-mail** cacc@advant.com

Information Charleston Area Chamber of Commerce, 501 Jackson St, PO Box 77; 217/345-7041.

One of the great Lincoln/Douglas debates was held here on September 18, 1858. As an itinerate lawyer riding the circuit, Abraham Lincoln practiced law in the area. His father, Thomas Lincoln, and stepmother once lived in a cabin eight miles south of Charleston.

What to See and Do

Coles County Courthouse (1898). Courthouse sits on Charleston Square, where Lincoln practiced law in an earlier courthouse, and where Charleston Riot took place; riot involved 300 men in armed conflict during the Civil War.

Eastern Illinois University (1895). (10,000 students) Tarble Arts Center on 9th St houses visual arts exhibits; changing displays. (Daily exc Mon; closed major hols) (See ANNUAL EVENTS) Phone 217/581-2787. **Free.**

Fox Ridge State Park. A rugged area of 1,500 acres with Ridge Lake maintained by Illinois Natural History Survey. Fishing (permit from survey required); boating (no motors). Hiking. Picnicking. Camping (standard fees). 7 mi S on IL 130. Phone 217/345-6416.

Lincoln Log Cabin State Historic Site. This 86-acre site contains the Thomas Lincoln Log Cabin, reconstructed on the original foundation as it was when Abraham Lincoln's father built it in 1840; a reconstructed 1840s farm surrounds the cabin. Nearby, in Shiloh Cemetery, are the graves of Thomas Lincoln and Sarah Bush Lincoln, the president's stepmother. Interpretive program offered June-Aug. Picnicking. (Daily; closed Jan 1, Thanksgiving, Dec 25) (See ANNUAL EVENTS) 8 mi S on 4th St Rd. Phone 217/345-6489. **Free.**

Moore Home State Historic Site. Before leaving for his inauguration, Lincoln ate his last meal here with his stepmother and her daughter, Mrs. Matilda Moore. (June-Aug, limited hrs) 7 mi S on 4th St Rd. Phone 217/345-6489. **Free.**

Annual Events

Coles County Fair. Fairgrounds, on Madison Ave. July-early Aug.

Celebration: A Festival of the Arts. Eastern Illinois University. College of Fine Arts hosts a festival of the arts with exhibits including paintings, crafts, pottery and sculpture; plays, music, dancing; foods from around the world; children's activities. Late Aug.

Harvest Frolic and Trades Fair. Lincoln Log Cabin State Historic Site. Festival based on central Illinois' agricultural history; exhibits, entertainment. First wkend Oct.

Motel

✔★ **ECONO LODGE.** *810 W Lincoln Hwy. 217/345-7689; FAX 217/345-7697.* 52 rms, 2 story. S $38-$79; D $42-$85; under 12 free. Crib $5. Pet accepted; $10 deposit. TV; cable (premium), VCR avail. Complimentary continental bkfst. Restaurant nearby. Ck-out 11 am. Business servs avail. Refrigerators, microwaves avail. Cr cds: A, C, D, DS, JCB, MC, V.

[D] [⚡] [SC]

Motor Hotel

✔★ ★ **BEST WESTERN WORTHINGTON INN.** *920 W Lincoln Hwy, 3 mi W on IL 16 exit I-57. 217/348-8161; FAX 217/348-8165.* Web www.bestwestern.com/thisco/bw/14144/14144_b.html. 67 rms, 1-2 story. S, D $59-$74; each addl $3; suites $114-$124; under 12 free; wkly rates. Crib free. Pet accepted, some restrictions. TV; cable, VCR avail. Complimentary coffee in lobby. Restaurants 6:30 am-2 pm, 5-9 pm (also see TAPESTRIES). Ck-out 11 am. Meeting rms. Business servs avail. Free airport transportation. Health club privileges. Heated pool. Some refrigerators, microwaves. Cr cds: A, D, DS, MC, V.

[D] [⚡] [≋] [SC]

Restaurant

✔★ **TAPESTRIES.** *(See Best Western Worthington Inn Motor Hotel) 217/348-8165.* Hrs: 6:30 am-2 pm; Sun brunch from 10:30 am. Res accepted. Semi-a la carte: bkfst $3-$7, lunch $4.50-$7. Sun brunch $8.25. Child's meals. Specializes in taco salad, classic burgers, stir-fried chicken. Casual dining in fine-dining atmosphere. Totally nonsmoking. Cr cds: A, C, D, DS, MC, V.

[D] [SC]

Chicago (B-6)

Settled 1803 **Pop** 2,783,726 **Elev** 596 ft **Area code** 312, 773 **E-mail** tourism@ci.chi.il.us **Web** www.ci.chi.il.us/tourism

Information Chicago Office of Tourism, Chicago Cultural Center, 78 E Washington St, 60602; 312/744-2400 or 800/226-6632.

Suburbs *North:* Evanston, Glenview, Gurnee, Highland Park, Highwood, Northbrook, Skokie, Wilmette; *Northwest:* Arlington Heights, Itasca, Schaumburg, Wheeling; *West:* Brookfield, Cicero, Downers Grove, Elmhurst, Geneva, Glen Ellyn, Hillside, Hinsdale, La Grange, Naperville, Oak Brook, Oak Park, St Charles, Wheaton; *South:* Homewood, Oak Lawn. (See individual alphabetical listings.)

"I have struck a city—a real city—and they call it Chicago," wrote Rudyard Kipling. For poet Carl Sandburg, it was the "City of the Big Shoulders"; for writer A.J. Liebling, a New Yorker, it was the "Second City." Songwriters have dubbed it a "toddlin' town," and "my kind of town." Boosters say it's a "city that works"; pedestrians acknowledge that it's a windy city. But over and above all the words and slogans is the city itself and the people who helped make it what it is today.

The people of Chicago represent a varied ethnic and racial mix. From the Native Americans who gave the city its name— *Checagou*—to the restless Easterners who traveled west in search of land and opportunity, to the hundreds of thousands of venturesome immigrants from Europe, Asia and Latin America who brought with them the foods and customs of the Old World, and to the Southern blacks and Appalachians who came in hope of finding better jobs and housing—all have contributed to the city's strength, vitality and the cosmopolitan ambience that makes Chicago a distinctive and unique experience for the visitor.

Chicago's past is equally distinctive—built on adversity and contradiction. The first permanent settler was a black man, Jean Baptist Point du Sable. The city's worst tragedy, the Great Fire of 1871, was the basis for its physical and cultural renaissance. In the heart of one of the poorest ethnic neighborhoods, two young women of means, Jane Addams and Ellen Gates Starr, created Hull House, a social service institution that has been copied throughout the world. A city of neat frame cottages and bulky stone mansions, it produced the geniuses of the Chicago School of Architecture (Louis Sullivan, Daniel Burnham, Dankmar Adler, William LeBaron Jenney, John Willborn Root), whose innovative tradition was carried on by Frank Lloyd Wright and Ludwig Mies van der Rohe. Even its most famous crooks provide a study in contrasts: Al Capone, the prohibition gangster, and Samuel Insull, the financial finagler whose stock manipulations left thousands of small investors penniless in the late twenties.

Chicago's early merchants resisted the intrusion of the railroad, yet the city became the rail center of the nation. Although Chicago no longer boasts a stockyard, its widely diversified economy makes it one of the most stable cities in the country. Metropolitan Chicago has more than 12,000 factories with a $20-billion annual payroll and ranks first in the United States in the production of canned and frozen foods, metal products, machinery, railroad equipment, letter press printing, office equipment, musical instruments, telephones, housewares, candy and lampshades. It has the world's busiest airport, largest grain exchange and biggest mail-order business. It is a great educational center (58 institutions of higher learning); one of the world's largest convention and trade-show cities; a showplace, marketplace, shopping and financial center; a city of skyscrapers, museums, parks, and churches, with more than 2,700 places of worship.

Although a city of the prairie, Chicago turns its best face toward Lake Michigan, where a green fringe of parks forms an arc from Evanston to the Indiana border. The Loop is a city within a city, with many corporate headquarters, banks, stores and other enterprises. To the far south are the docks along the Calumet River, used by ocean vessels since the opening of the St Lawrence Seaway and servicing a belt of factories, steel mills and warehouses. Behind these lies a maze of industrial and shopping areas, schools and houses.

Although Louis Jolliet mapped the area as early as 1673, and du Sable and a compatriot, Antoine Ouilmette, had established a trading post by 1796, the real growth of the city did not begin until the 19th century and the advent of the Industrial Revolution.

In 1803, the fledging US government took possession of the area and sent a small military contingent from Detroit to select the site for a fort. Fort Dearborn was built at a strategic spot on the mouth of the Chicago River; on the opposite bank, a settlement slowly grew. Fort and settlement were abandoned when the British threatened them during the War of 1812. On their way to Fort Wayne, soldiers and settlers were attacked and killed or held captive by Native Americans who had been armed by the British. The fort was rebuilt in 1816; a few survivors returned, new settlers arrived, but there was little activity until Chicago was selected as the terminal site of the proposed Illinois and Michigan Canal. This started a land boom.

Twenty thousand Easterners swept through on their way to the riches of the West. Merchants opened stores; land speculation was rampant. Although 1837—the year Chicago was incorporated as a city—was marked by financial panic, the pace of expansion and building did not falter. In 1841, grain destined for world ports began to pour into the city; almost immediately, Chicago became the largest grain market in the world. In the wake of the grain came herds of hogs and cattle for the Chicago slaughterhouses. Tanneries, packing plants, mills and factories soon sprang up.

The Illinois and Michigan Canal, completed in 1848, quadrupled imports and exports. The railroads fanned out from the city, transporting merchandise throughout the nation and bringing new produce to Chicago.

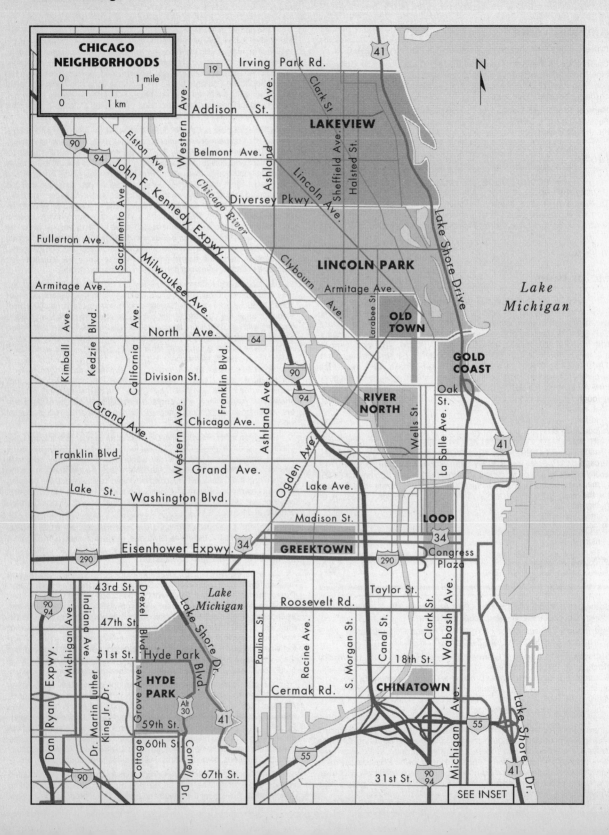

CHICAGO
NEIGHBORHOODS

0   1 mile
0   1 km

Irving Park Rd.

LAKEVIEW

Addison   St.   Ave.

Belmont Ave.

Diversey Pkwy.

Western   Ave.

Ashland   Ave.

Clark St.

Sheffield Ave.

Halsted St.

Lincoln Ave.

Elston   Ave.

John F. Kennedy Expwy.

Milwaukee   Ave.

Chicago River

Fullerton Ave.

Sacramento Ave.

Armitage Ave.

LINCOLN PARK

Clybourn   Ave.

Armitage Ave.

Larabee St.

OLD
TOWN

GOLD
COAST

Lake
Michigan

Kimball   Ave.

Kedzie   Blvd.

California   Ave.

North   Ave.

Franklin Blvd.

Division St.

Ashland Ave.

RIVER
NORTH

Oak
St.

Wells   St.

La Salle Ave.

Grand   Ave.

Chicago Ave.

Ogden Ave.

Franklin Blvd.

Western   Ave.

Grand   Ave.

Lake   St.

Washington Blvd.

Lake Ave.

Madison St.

LOOP

Eisenhower Expwy.

GREEKTOWN

Congress
Plaza

Taylor St.

43rd St.

47th St.

51st St.

Drexel   Blvd.

Lake Shore Dr.

Lake
Michigan

Roosevelt Rd.

Paulina   St.

Racine   Ave.

S. Morgan St.

Canal St.

Clark St.

18th St.

Wabash   Ave.

Indiana   Ave.

Michigan   Ave.

Dan Ryan Expwy.

Dr. Martin Luther King Jr. Dr.

Hyde Park

HYDE
PARK

Cottage Grove Ave.

Cornell   Dr.

59th St.

60th St.

67th St.

Cermak Rd.

CHINATOWN

Michigan   Ave.

Lake Shore Dr.

31st St.

SEE INSET

During the slump that followed the panic of 1857, Chicago built a huge wooden shed (the Wigwam) at the southeast corner of Wacker and Lake to house the Republican National Convention. Abraham Lincoln was nominated Republican candidate for president here in 1860. The Civil War doubled grain shipments from Chicago. In 1865, the mile-square Union Stock Yards were established. Chicago was riotously prosperous; its population skyrocketed. Then, on October 8, 1871, fire erupted in a cow barn and roared through the city, destroying 15,768 buildings, killing almost 300 people and leaving a third of the population homeless. But temporary and permanent rebuilding started at once, and Chicago emerged from the ashes to take advantage of the rise of industrialization. The labor unrest of the period produced the Haymarket bombing and the Pullman and other strikes. The 1890s were noteworthy for cultural achievements: orchestras, libraries, universities and the new urban architectural form for which the term "skyscraper" was coined. The Columbian Exposition of 1893, a magnificent success, was followed by depression and municipal corruption.

Chicago's fantastic rate of growth continued into the 20th century. Industries boomed during World War I, and in the 1920s the city prospered as never before—unruffled by dizzying financial speculation and notorious gang warfare, an outgrowth of Prohibition. The stock market crash of 1929 brought down the shakier financial pyramids; the repeal of Prohibition virtually ended the rackets; and a more sober Chicago produced the Century of Progress Exposition in 1933. Chicago's granaries and steel mills helped carry the country through World War II. The past several decades have seen a reduction of manufacturing jobs in the area, and an increase of jobs in the service industries and employment in the fields of finance, law, advertising and insurance. Among the city projects for the 1990s are the relocation of a section of Lake Shore Drive resulting in uninterrupted grounds linking the Field Museum, John G. Shedd Aquarium and Adler Planetarium; expansion of McCormick Place convention complex and a third major city airport.

THE VISITOR'S CHICAGO

Although in the eyes of some, Chicago evokes the image of an industrial giant, it is a city in which the arts flourish. Chicagoans are proud of their world-famous symphony orchestra, which Igor Stravinsky declared second to none; their Lyric Opera; and their award-winning classical music station, WFMT. Author Studs Terkel and poet Gwendolyn Brooks not only live in Chicago but make it an integral part of their creative work. Since 1912, Chicago has been the home of *Poetry* magazine. Chicago's theater community is vibrant, with more than 100 off-Loop theaters presenting quality drama. The collections at the Art Institute, the Museum of Contemporary Art, the Terra Museum of American Art and the many galleries along Michigan Ave and in the River North area are among the best in the country.

Other museums are equally renowned: the Museum of Science and Industry, the Field Museum of Natural History, the Chicago Children's Museum at Navy Pier and the various specialty museums that reflect the ethnic and civic interests of the city.

The zoos, the planetarium and aquarium, as well as the many parks and beaches along the lakefront, afford pleasure for visitors of any age. The attractions of the city are many, and sightseeing tours can be taken by boat, bus, car, bicycle or foot.

Buses and rapid transit lines are integrated into one system—the most extensive in the nation—with interchangeable transfers. Elevated lines run through the Loop. Subway trains run under State and Dearborn streets and go onto elevated structures both to the north and south. Rapid transit lines also serve the West Side as well as O'Hare and Midway airports.

Driving and parking in Chicago are no more difficult than in any other major city. There are indoor and outdoor parking areas near and in the Loop; some provide shuttle bus service to the Loop or to the Merchandise Mart. Conducted tours are provided by diverse tour companies.

The attractions decribed under CHICAGO are arranged topically, and most contain neighborhood designations following their addresses. The Loop is considered the center of the city, with State St running north and south, and Madison St east and west, as the bases. The attractions contain the following designations: The Loop, Near North, North, Near South,

South and West. The eastern border of the city is Lake Michigan. In addition, some attractions in outlying areas are listed.

Transportation

Airports: *O'Hare Intl Airport,* Mannheim Rd & Kennedy Expy, 19 mi NW of Loop (see CHICAGO O'HARE AIRPORT AREA), phone 312/686-2200; *Chicago Midway Airport,* 5700 S Cicero Ave (approx 8 mi S of Loop), phone 312/767-0500.

Car Rental Agencies: See IMPORTANT TOLL-FREE NUMBERS.

Public Transportation: Chicago Transit Authority/Regional Transit Authority, phone 312/836-7000.

Rail Passenger Service: Amtrak 800/872-7245.

What to See and Do

HISTORIC LANDMARKS AND BUILDINGS

Auditorium Building (1889). Landmark structure designed by Louis Sullivan and Dankmar Adler. Interior is noted for its intricate system of iron framing, breathtaking ornamentation and near-perfect acoustics. Now houses Roosevelt University. 430 S Michigan Ave, in the Loop.

Carson Pirie Scott (1899). Landmark department store building is considered architect Louis Sullivan's masterpiece. Extraordinary cast iron ornamentation on 1st and 2nd floors frames the display windows like paintings. (Mon-Sat & selected Sun; closed some major hols) State & Madison Sts, in the Loop. Phone 312/641-4000.

Chicago Board of Trade (1929). World's leading commodity futures exchange. Viewing galleries, visitor center and exhibits on 5th floor (Mon-Fri; closed hols). 141 W Jackson Blvd, at La Salle St, in the Loop. Phone 312/435-3590. **Free.**

Chicago Cultural Center. Chicago landmark with Tiffany glass domes, mosaics, marble walls and stairs; houses visitor information center. Free programs and changing exhibits sponsored by the Chicago Department of Cultural Affairs. (Daily; closed hols) 78 E Washington St, at Michigan Ave, in the Loop. Phone 312/346-3278. **Free.** Also here is

   Museum of Broadcast Communications. Collection of antique radios and televisions; archives of vintage and current radio and television series and events; Radio Hall of Fame; special screenings in Kraft TeleCenter. (Daily; closed hols) Phone 312/629-6000. **Free.**

Chicago Mercantile Exchange (1983). The world's leading financial futures exchange. A collection of international markets ranging from pork bellies and lumber to currencies, interest rates and stock index products. Visitors gallery on 4th floor. (Mon-Fri; closed hols; group tours arranged with advance notice) 30 S Wacker Dr, in the Loop. Phone 312/930-8249. **Free.**

Chicago *Tribune* Tower (1925). Essentially, this is a *moderne* building (36 story) with a Gothic-detailed base and crown; it does exactly what publisher Joseph Medill intended: it "thames" the Chicago river. The tower's once strong foundation has been loosening in recent yrs, and structural engineers have noted that the edifice has been slowly sinking at the rate of almost a foot a year due to seepage from a sublevel bog just W along the riverbank. Bits and pieces of historic structures from around the world are embedded in the exterior walls of the lower floors. 435 N Michigan Ave, Near North Side. Phone 312/222-3994.

Civic Opera Building (1929). On the lower levels, under 45 floors of commercial office space, are the richly art-deco, 3,600-seat Civic Opera House, home of the Lyric Opera of Chicago; and the 900-seat Civic Theatre. 20 N Wacker Dr, in the Loop. Phone 312/372-7800.

Jane Addams' Hull House. Two original Hull House buildings, restored Hull Mansion (1856) and dining hall (1905), which formed the nucleus of the 13-building settlement complex founded in 1889 by Jane Addams and Ellen Gates Starr, social welfare pioneers. Exhibits and presentations on the history of Hull House, the surrounding neighborhood, ethnic groups and women's history. (Mon-Fri, also Sun afternoons; closed hols) 800 S Halsted St, on campus of University of Illinois at Chicago, West Side. Phone 312/413-5353. **Free.**

John Hancock Center (1969). World's tallest office-residential skyscraper (100 stories); 1/4-mi high. The observatory, at 1,030 ft, offers an excellent view of the city, the Chicago lakefront and four states. (Daily; cashier located on 94th floor) Parking garage in building (fee). 875 N Michigan Ave, Near North Side. Phone 312/751-3681. Observatory ¢¢

Marina City (1959-1967). Condominium and commercial building complex with marina and boat storage. Includes two 550-ft-tall cylindrical buildings; home of the "House of Blues." Designed by Bertrand Goldberg Associates, this is one of the most unusual downtown living-working complexes in the United States. 300 N State St, N side of Chicago River, Near North Side. Phone 312/661-0046.

Marshall Field's (1902, 1907). Landmark for more than a century; one of the most famous stores in the country. A traditional Chicago meeting place is under its clock, which projects over the sidewalk. On one side is an inner court rising 13 stories, on the other is a 6-story rotunda topped by a Tiffany dome made of 1.6 million pieces of glass. (Daily; closed Thanksgiving, Dec 25) 111 N State St, in the Loop. Phone 312/781-4882.

McCormick Place Convention Complex. Nation's largest exposition and meeting complex. Exhibits, special shows, Arie Crown Theatre and restaurant facilities. E 23rd St & S Lake Shore Dr, South Side. Phone 312/791-7000.

Merchandise Mart (1930). The world's largest commercial building; restaurants and shopping avail. Apparel Center adj. Wells St at Chicago River, Near North Side. Phone 312/527-7600.

Monadnock Building (1889-1891). Highest wall-bearing building in Chicago was, at the time of its construction, the tallest and largest office building in the world. It is now considered one of the masterworks of the Chicago school of architecture. Designed by Burnham & Root; south addition by Holabird & Roche (1893). 53 W Jackson Blvd, in the Loop.

Navy Pier. This landmark extends more than 1/2-mi into the lake. Recently renovated, the pier features a 150-ft-high Ferris wheel, carousel, children's museum, four-masted schooner, shops, restaurants and arcades. 600 E Grand Ave, Near North Side. The Skyline Stage offers a variety of music in the summertime; phone 312/595-PIER for information.

North Pier Chicago. Three-blk-long warehouse (1905) converted into festival marketplace with more than 50 shops; restaurants, bars, nightclubs, video arcades, miniature golf. Parking (fee). (Daily; closed Jan 1, Thanksgiving, Dec 25) 435 E Illinois St, 4 blks E of N Michigan Ave, Near North Side. Phone 312/836-4300. **Free.**

Orchestra Hall (1904). Historic Orchestra Hall is home of the Chicago Symphony Orchestra and stage for the Civic Orchestra of Chicago, chamber music groups, Allied Arts musical attractions and children's programs. 220 S Michigan Ave, in the Loop. For ticket information phone 312/294-3000.

Prairie Ave Historic District. Area where millionaires lived during the 1800s. Prairie Ave, between 18th & Cullerton Sts, South Side. The **Clarke House** (ca 1835), the oldest house still standing in the city, has been restored and now stands at a site near its original location. The **Glessner House** (1886), 1800 S Prairie Ave, is owned and maintained by the Chicago Architecture Foundation. Designed by architect Henry Hobson Richardson, the house has 35 rms, many of which are restored with original furnishings; interior courtyard. Two-hr guided tour of both houses (Wed, Fri-Sun). Other houses on the cobblestone street are **Kimball House** (1890), 1801 S Prairie Ave, replica of a French château, **Coleman House** (ca 1885), 1811 S Prairie Ave, and **Keith House** (ca 1870), 1900 S Prairie Ave. Architectural tours. Phone 312/922-3432. One-house tour ¢¢;   Two-house tour ¢¢¢

Richard J. Daley Center and Plaza. This 31-story, 648-ft building houses county and city courts and administrative offices. In the plaza is the Chicago Picasso sculpture; across Washington St is the Chicago Miro sculpture. Randolph & Clark Sts, in the Loop.

Robie House (1909). Designed by Frank Lloyd Wright, this may be the ultimate example of the prairie house. Tours (one daily, noon; closed major hols). 5757 S Woodlawn Ave, near the University of Chicago campus, South Side. Phone 312/702-8374. ¢¢

★ **Sears Tower** (1974). This 110-story office building, designed by Skidmore, Owings & Merrill, is the Northern Hemisphere's tallest, rising 1,454 ft over the city. Skydeck observation area on 103rd floor (daily) with optional "Chicago Experience" multimedia presentation. *Universe,* a motorized, kinetic mobile by Alexander Calder, is located in the Wacker Dr lobby. More than 30 shops and restaurants are in the building. Skydeck entrance on Jackson Blvd, between Franklin & Wacker. 233 S Wacker Dr, in the Loop. Phone 312/875-9696. Skydeck ¢¢¢

The Newberry Library (1887). Houses more than 1.4 million volumes and several million manuscripts. Internationally famous collections on the Renaissance, Native Americans, the Chicago Renaissance, the American West, local and family history, music history, history of printing, calligraphy, cartography, others. Exhibits open to the public. Admission to reading rms by registration. (Tues-Sat; closed major hols) Tours (Thurs, Sat). 60 W Walton St, Near North Side. Phone 312/255-3510. **Free.**

The Rookery (1886). Oldest remaining steel-skeleton skyscraper in the world. Designed by Burnham & Root, the remarkable glass-encased lobby was remodeled in 1905 by Frank Lloyd Wright. 209 S La Salle St, in the Loop.

United States Post Office (1933). Largest in the world under one roof. Individuals may join 1 1/2-hr guided group tours (Mon-Fri, 2 tours daily; no tours hols & Dec). No cameras. Res required. 433 W Van Buren St, in the Loop. Phone 312/765-3009. **Free.**

Water Tower (1869). Fanciful, Gothic-revival tower that survived the Great Chicago Fire of 1871. Now houses Chicago Office of Tourism Visitor Information Center (phone 312/744-2400). 806 N Michigan Ave, Near North Side.

Wrigley Building (1924). One of the most beloved buildings in the city, the white terra cotta Spanish-Renaissance-style tower is actually two structures connected by bridges. Headquarters of the chewing gum empire; illuminated nightly. 400 N Michigan Ave, Near North Side.

MUSEUMS

Adler Planetarium (1930). Bronze sundial by sculptor Henry Moore in entry plaza. Two-part Sky Show in Universe and Sky theaters, Zeiss VI projector and horizon projection system; Sat & Sun morning children's shows. Exhibits on modern astronomy and astronomical techniques; Race to the Moon exhibit features videotape of first manned landing on the moon; 2.6-oz moon rock; early scientific instruments; displays on the *Voyager,* satellites; navigation and the use of telescopes (including the telescope William Herschel used to discover Uranus); computerized observing station linked with Apache Point observatory in New Mexico; solar telescope. Museum (daily; closed Thanksgiving, Dec 25). 1300 S Lake Shore Dr, on a peninsula in Lake Michigan, Near South Side. Phone 312/922-STAR (recorded schedule) or 312/322-0304. ¢¢

Balzekas Museum of Lithuanian Culture. Antiques, art, children's museum, memorabilia and literature spanning 1,000 yrs of Lithuanian history. Exhibits include amber, armor and antique weapons, rare maps, textiles, dolls, stamps, coins; research library. (Daily; closed Jan 1, Thanksgiving, Dec 25) Free admission Mon. 6500 S Pulaski Rd, South Side. Phone 773/582-6500. ¢¢

Chicago Fire Academy. Built on site where the Great Fire of 1871 is believed to have started. One-hr guided tour of facilities for training firefighters; films. Tours (Mon-Fri, twice daily). 558 W DeKoven St, West Side. Phone 312/747-8151. **Free.**

Chicago Historical Society. Changing exhibits focus on the history and development of Chicago. Selected aspects of Illinois and US history include galleries devoted to costumes, decorative arts and architecture. Pioneer craft demonstrations; hands-on gallery. (Daily; closed Jan 1, Thanksgiving, Dec 25) Free admission Mon. Clark St at North Ave, Near North Side. Phone 312/642-4600. ¢¢

DuSable Museum of African-American History. African and African-American art objects; displays of black history in Africa and the United States. Extensive collection includes paintings, sculpture, artifacts, textiles, books and photographs. (Daily; closed some major hols) Free admission Thurs. 740 E 56th Pl, South Side. Phone 773/947-0600. ¢¢

★ **Field Museum.** (1920). One of the largest natural history museums in the world. Includes world culture, history, animal and gem exhibits. Egyptian tomb complex with burial shaft, chamber and mummies. Touchable displays in the Place for Wonder; Traveling the Pacific features exhibits on Pacific natural history and cultures. Special exhibits, films, lectures, demonstrations and performances; cafeteria, concession. (Daily; closed Jan 1, Thanksgiving, Dec 25) List of touchables for visually impaired avail. Free admission Wed. Roosevelt Rd, at Lake Shore Dr, Near South Side. Phone 312/922-9410. ¢¢

John G. Shedd Aquarium (1929). The world's largest indoor aquarium features more than 6,000 freshwater and marine animals displayed in 200 naturalistic habitats; divers hand-feed fish, sharks, eels and turtles several times daily in 90,000-gallon Coral Reef Exhibit. The Oceanarium re-creates a Northwest Pacific ecosystem with whales, dolphins, sea otters and seals. A colony of penguins inhabit a Falkland Islands exhibit. (Daily; closed Jan 1, Dec 25) Free admission Thurs. 1200 S Lake Shore Dr, at Roosevelt Rd, Near South Side. Phone 312/939-2438. ¢¢¢

Museum of Contemporary Art. Changing exhibits of contemporary art; paintings, sculpture, video, performance, films, lectures. (Daily exc Mon; closed Jan 1, Thanksgiving, Dec 25) Free admission 1st Tues of each month. 220 E Chicago Ave, Near North Side. Phone 312/280-2660 or -5161 (recording). ¢¢

Museum of Holography/Chicago. Permanent collection of holograms (three-dimensional images made with lasers) featuring pieces from the US and many European and Asian countries. (Wed-Sun, afternoons; closed most hols) 1134 W Washington Blvd, West Side. Phone 312/226-1007. ¢¢

★ **Museum of Science and Industry.** More than 2,000 exhibit units use visitor interaction to illustrate scientific principles and industrial concepts. Among the many displays are the "Idea Factory," Apollo 8 spacecraft, miniature circus with 22,000 hand-carved pieces, chick incubator, coal mine, captured German U-boat, 16-ft-tall, walk-through human heart model. (Daily; closed Dec 25) Free admission Thurs. 57th St & Lake Shore Dr, South Side. Phone 773/684-1414. ¢¢¢ Also here is

    Crown Space Center. This 35,000-sq-ft space center houses the latest in space exhibitions; 334-seat Omnimax Theater in a 76-ft diameter projection dome. Omnimax ¢¢¢

Nature Museum of the Chicago Academy of Sciences. Exhibits explore science through nature and the environment. Water works exhibit and research laboratory, Children's Gallery, hands-on activites and changing exhibits. (Daily) Free admission Tues. North Pier, 435 E Illinois St, third level, Near North Side. Phone 312/871-2668. ¢¢

Oriental Institute Museum. Outstanding collection of archaeological material illustrating the art, architecture, religion and literature from the ancient Near East. Lectures, workshops, free films (Sun; limited hrs). Museum (daily exc Mon; closed Jan 1, Thanksgiving, Dec 25). 1155 E 58th St, on University of Chicago campus, South Side. Phone 773/702-9521. **Free.**

Peace Museum. Exhibits focusing on the role of the arts, the sciences, labor, women, minorities and religious institutions on issues of war and peace; on the contributions of individual peacemakers. (Tues-Sat; schedule varies, phone ahead) 314 W Institute Pl, Near North Side. Phone 312/440-1860. ¢¢

Polish Museum of America. Polish culture, folklore, immigration; art gallery, archives and library; Paderewski and Kosciuszko rms. (Daily; closed Jan 1, Good Friday, Dec 25) 984 N Milwaukee Ave, Near North Side. Phone 773/384-3352. **Free.**

Spertus Museum. Permanent collection of ceremonial objects from many parts of the world; sculpture, graphic arts and paintings; ethnic materials spanning centuries; changing exhibits in fine arts; documentary films and photographs. Rosenbaum Artifact Center has hands-on exhibits on ancient Near East archaeology. (Daily exc Sat; closed some hols & Jewish hols) Free admission Fri. 618 S Michigan Ave, in the Loop. Phone 312/322-1747. ¢¢

Terra Museum of American Art. Collection of 18th-, 19th- and 20th-century paintings by American artists. (Daily exc Mon; closed some major hols) Free admission Tues. 666 N Michigan Ave, Near North Side. Phone 312/664-3939. ¢¢

★ **The Art Institute of Chicago** (1879). World-renowned collection of American and European paintings, sculpture, prints and drawings, classical art, Asian art, European and American decorative arts; textiles; primitive art; photography; architectural drawings and fragments; stained-glass windows by Marc Chagall; 68 Thorne miniature rms; reconstructed Chicago Stock Exchange Trading Rm, Arthur Rubloff's paperweight collection

and Kraft Education Center. The School of the Art Institute and the Goodman Theatre are also located here; gift shop, garden restaurant (summer), cafeteria and dining rm (all yr). (Daily; closed Dec 25) Free admission Tues. Michigan Ave & Adams St, in Grant Park, in the Loop. For details about gallery talks and special lectures phone 312/443-3600. ¢¢¢

CHURCHES AND SYNAGOGUES

Chicago Loop Synagogue (1957). The eastern wall of this building is a unique example of contemporary stained glass, depicting ancient Hebraic symbols whirling through the cosmos. (Mon-Fri) 16 S Clark St, in the Loop. Phone 312/346-7370.

Chicago Temple (First Methodist Episcopal Church,1923). 568 ft from street level to the tip of its Gothic tower—highest church spire in the world. Tours (Mon-Fri; no tours hols). 77 W Washington St, in the Loop. Phone 312/236-4548 for tour schedules.

Fourth Presbyterian Church. Completed in 1914, this beautiful church is a fine example of Gothic design. One of its architects, Ralph A. Cram, was a leader of the Gothic revival in the United States. (Daily) 866 N Michigan Ave, Near North Side. Phone 312/787-4570.

Holy Name Cathedral (Roman Catholic). Neo-Gothic architecture. (Daily) Guided tours, res required. 735 N State St, Near North Side. Phone 312/787-8040.

Our Lady of Sorrows Basilica (1890-1902). Worth seeing are the Shrine Altar of the Seven Holy Founders of the Servites (main altar of Carrara marble) and the beautiful English Baroque steeple, chapels, paintings and other architectural ornamentations (daily). Tours (by res). 3121 W Jackson Blvd, West Side. Phone 312/638-5800.

Rockefeller Memorial Chapel. Designed by Bertram Grosvenor Goodhue Assocs; noted for its Gothic construction, vaulted ceiling, 8,600 pipe organ and 72-bell carillon. Guided tours by appt. 5850 S Woodlawn Ave, on University of Chicago campus, Near North Side. Phone 312/702-8374.

OUTDOOR ART AND PLAZAS

Batcolumn (1977). This 100-ft-tall, 20-ton welded steel sculpture resembles a baseball bat, set in a concrete base. Designed by artist Claes Oldenburg. 600 W Madison St, outside the Harold Washington Social Security Administration Bldg plaza, in the Loop.

Flamingo (1974). Sculptor Alexander Calder's stabile is 53 ft high and weighs 50 tons. Federal Center Plaza, Adams & Dearborn Sts, in the Loop.

Miro's Chicago (1981). The structure, made of steel, wire mesh, concrete, bronze and ceramic tile, is 39 ft tall. The Brunswick Bldg, 69 W Washington, in the Loop.

The Four Seasons (1974). This 3,000-sq-ft mosaic designed by Marc Chagall contains more than 250 different shades and hues of marble, stone, granite and glass. First National Plaza, Monroe & Dearborn Sts, in the Loop.

Untitled (1967). Created by Pablo Picasso, the structure is 50 ft high and weighs 162 tons. Richard J. Daley Plaza, Washington & Dearborn Sts, in the Loop.

Untitled Sounding Sculpture (1975). Unique "sounding sculpture" set in reflecting pool. Designed by Harry Bertoia. Amoco Bldg, 200 E Randolph, in the Loop.

SHOPPING

★ **Michigan Avenue.** Michigan Ave, between the Chicago River on the S and Oak St on the N, is one of the world's great shopping areas, with representative branches of many national and international specialty and department stores. Near North Side. Also on the "Magnificent Mile" are

    Nike Town. Since opening in 1993 the 5-story sports store has become a tourist attraction in its own right. Exhibits include the Nike Museum, a video theater, display of athletic gear worn by Michael Jordan and a basketball court with a 28-ft likeness of the basketball star. (Daily; closed some major hols) 669 N Michigan Ave. Phone 312/642-6363.

    Chicago Place. Eight-story vertical mall with more than 50 stores and 7 restaurants. (Daily; closed Jan 1, Easter, Dec 25) 700 N Michigan Ave. Phone 312/642-4811.

Water Tower Place. Atrium mall with more than 125 shops, 11 restaurants and 7 movie theaters; and the Ritz-Carlton Hotel. (Daily; closed some hols) 835 N Michigan Ave. Phone 312/440-3165.

900 N Michigan Shops. More than 60 shops and restaurants around marble atrium. (Daily; closed some hols) Phone 312/915-3916.

North Pier Chicago. Festival marketplace in converted 19th-century warehouses. Near North Side.

Oak Street. The block between Michigan Ave and N Rush St is lined with small shops that specialize in high fashion and the avant-garde from around the world. Near North Side.

State Street. Besides many specialty stores, shopping on State St includes the famous Marshall Field's department store, Carson Pirie Scott department store and some of the world's most renowned architecture. Renovations have returned State St to its 1920s glamour, with period lamp posts, ornamental subway kiosks, landscaped planters and multicolored sidewalks. A self-guided tour of 20 historically significant State St buildings is avail. Phone 312/35-STATE. In the Loop.

Wabash Avenue. This unique street, always in the shadow of elevated train tracks, is known for its many specialty stores—books, music, musical instruments, records, mens clothing, tobacco, etc—as well as being the center of the wholesale and retail jewelry trade. S of the river to Congress Ave, in the Loop.

PARKS AND ZOOS

Brookfield Zoo (see BROOKFIELD).

Chicago Botanic Garden (see NORTHBROOK).

Garfield Park and Conservatory. Outdoor formal gardens. Conservatory has eight houses and propagating houses on more than five acres. Permanent exhibits. Four major shows annually at Horticultural Hall and Show House. (Daily) 300 N Central Park Blvd, West Side. Phone 312/746-5100. **Free.**

Grant Park. Chicago's downtown park. Contains the James C. Petrillo Music Shell. (See ANNUAL and SEASONAL EVENTS) Stretching from Randolph St to McFetridge Dr, in the Loop. Also in Grant Park is

  Buckingham Fountain. Carved of pink Georgia marble; formal gardens nearby. The waters rise 135 ft; color display and water spectacle (May-Oct 1, daily). Foot of Congress St.

Lincoln Park. Largest in Chicago, stretches almost the entire length of the N end of the city along the lake. Contains statues of Lincoln, Hans Christian Andersen, Shakespeare and others; 9-hole golf course, driving range, miniature golf, bike and jogging paths, obstacle course, protected beaches. Near North Side. In park are

  Lincoln Park Zoological Gardens. The zoo is situated on 35 acres and houses more than 1,600 animals, including many exotic and endangered species; one of the largest collections in the United States. The Regenstein Small Mammal and Reptile House is a glass-domed facility housing over 200 animals, including endangered species. A well-known gorilla collection is housed in a spectacular naturalistic habitat and thousands of migrant and resident birds are sheltered in a wooded area. Also here is a 5-acre farm-in-the-zoo and a children's zoo with Discovery Center. Guided tours, zoo films and lectures, talks at the animal habitats. (Daily) W entrance, Webster Ave & Stockton Dr; E entrance, Cannon Dr off Fullerton Ave. Phone 312/742-2000. **Free.**

  Lincoln Park Conservatory. Has 4 glass buildings, 18 propagating houses and 3 acres of cold frames; formal and rock gardens; extensive collection of orchids. Four major flower shows annually at Show House. (Daily) Stockton Dr near Fullerton. Phone 312/742-7736. **Free.**

Six Flags Great America (see GURNEE).

ENTERTAINMENT AND CONVENTION FACILITIES
Convention, cultural and recreation centers.

  Civic Opera Building. Civic Center for the Performing Arts, 20 N Wacker Dr, 312/346-0270.

  Petrillo Music Shell. Columbus Dr & Jackson Blvd in Grant Park, 312/294-2420. (See ANNUAL and SEASONAL EVENTS)

  McCormick Place. E 23rd St & S Lake Shore Dr, 312/791-7000.

  Orchestra Hall. 220 S Michigan Ave, 312/435-6666.

  Rosemont Convention Center. 5555 N River Rd, Rosemont; 708/692-2220.

  Rosemont Horizon. Off Northwest Tollway (I-90), Lee St exit, at 6920 Mannheim Rd in Rosemont; 708/635-6600 (recording). (See CHICAGO O'HARE AIRPORT AREA)

  Soldier Field Stadium. Lake Shore Dr & E McFetridge Dr, 312/294-2200.

  United Center. 1901 W Madison St, 312/455-4000.

Performing arts—City.

  Chicago Symphony Orchestra. Orchestra Hall, 220 S Michigan Ave, 312/435-6666.

  Chicago Cultural Center. 78 E Washington St, 312/341-1521.

  Lyric Opera of Chicago. Civic Opera House, 20 N Wacker Dr, 312/332-2244.

Performing arts—Outlying Areas.

  Marriott's Lincolnshire Resort Theater. Lincolnshire, 847/634-0200 (see WHEELING).

  North Shore Center for the Performing Arts. 847/679-9501 (see SKOKIE).

  Pheasant Run Dinner Theatre. W on IL 64, in St Charles, 630/584-6300.

  Ravinia Festival. 312/728-4642 (see HIGHLAND PARK).

Theaters.

  Apollo. 2540 N Lincoln Ave, 773/935-6100.

  Arie Crown. McCormick Place, E 23rd St & S Lake Shore Dr, 312/791-6000.

  Auditorium. 50 E Congress Pkwy, 312/902-1500.

  Chicago Theatre. 175 N State St, 312/443-1130.

  Briar Street. 3133 N Halsted St, 773/348-4000.

  Civic Opera House. Civic Center for Performing Arts, 20 N Wacker Dr, 312/322-2244.

  Goodman. 200 S Columbus Dr, at the Art Institute, 312/443-3800.

  Mayfair. Featuring *Shear Madness,* 636 S Michigan Ave, 312/786-9120.

  Royal George. 1641 N Halsted St, 312/988-9000.

  Second City. 1616 N Wells St, 312/337-3992; and 1608 N Wells St, 312/642-8189.

  Shubert. 22 W Monroe St, 312/902-1500.

  Steppenwolf. 1650 N Halsted St, 312/335-1650.

  Theatre Bldg. 1225 W Belmont Ave, 773/327-5252.

  Victory Gardens. 2257 N Lincoln Ave, 773/871-3000.

EDUCATION

DePaul University. (16,700 students) The N campus, with its blend of modern and Gothic architecture, is an integral part of Chicago's historic Lincoln Park neighborhood. The Blue Demons, DePaul's basketball team, play their home games at the Rosemont Horizon in Rosemont (see). Tours (by appt). Lincoln Park campus, Fullerton & Halsted St, Near North Side; Loop campus, 25 E Jackson Blvd. Phone 312/362-8300.

Illinois Institute of Technology (1892). (6,000 students) Campus designed by Mies van der Rohe. 3300 S Federal St, South Side. Phone 312/567-3000.

Loyola University (1870). (14,300 students) Martin d'Arcy Renaissance & Medieval Art Gallery (daily exc Sat; closed hols, semester breaks), phone 312/508-2679. Fine Arts Gallery of the Edward Crown Center; exhibits (Mon-Fri; closed hols), phone 312/508-2820. Lake Shore campus, 6525 N Sheridan Rd. Downtown campus, 820 N Michigan Ave, North Side. Phone 312/915-6000.

Northwestern University Chicago Campus (1920). (5,400 students) Schools of Medicine, Law, Dentistry and University College. Lake Shore Dr & Chicago Ave, Near North Side. Phone 312/503-8649. (See EVANSTON)

Roosevelt University (1945). (6,400 students) Auditorium Bldg designed by Louis Sullivan and engineered by Dankmar Adler in 1889. Entrance at 430 S Michigan Ave, in the Loop. Phone 312/341-3500.

University of Chicago (1892). (7,800 students) It was on this campus that Enrico Fermi produced the first sustained nuclear reaction. The University of Chicago also has had one of the highest number of Nobel Prize winners of any institution. The campus includes the Oriental Institute, the Robie House, the Rockefeller Memorial Chapel and the David and Alfred Smart Museum of Art, on Greenwood Ave (daily exc Mon; free; phone 312/702-0200). Guided 1-hr campus tours leave from 1212 E 59th St. 5801 S Ellis Ave, South Side. For tour schedule phone 312/702-8374.

University of Illinois at Chicago (1965). (24,000 students) Comprehensive urban university. On campus is Jane Addams' Hull House. Near I-94 & I-290, West Side. Phone 312/996-7000.

TOURS

☆ **Architectural tours.** View the city's architecture by bus, boat, bike or on foot. Sponsored by the Chicago Architecture Foundation; approx 50 different architectural tours of the city's neighborhoods and suburbs. (Days vary; no tours Jan 1, Easter, July 4, Thanksgiving, Dec 25) Phone 312/922-TOUR (recording) or contact Chicago Architecture Foundation, 224 S Michigan Ave, 60604; 312/922-3424. Among tours offered are

Graceland Cemetery Tour. View burial sites and monuments of Chicago's famous historical figures. Headstones of businessmen Marshall Field and Philip Armour, detective Allan Pinkerton, heavyweight boxing champions Jack Johnson and Robert Fitzsimmons, baseball's National League founder William Hulbert. Cemetery at Clark St & Irving Park Rd on North Side. (Sept-Oct, Sun) Contact Chicago Architecture Foundation; 312/922-3432 or 312/922-TOUR. ¢¢¢

Chicago Highlights Bus Tour. This 4-hr bus tour covers the Loop, the Gold Coast, Hyde Park, three historic districts and three university campuses; includes interior of Frank Lloyd Wright's Robie House. (Mar-Nov, Sat; rest of yr, 1st & 3rd Sat of month) 224 S Michigan Ave. Res required, phone 312/922-3432. ¢¢¢¢¢

Loop Walking Tours. Each tour 2 hrs long. *Early Skyscrapers* traces origins of Chicago School of Architecture and skyscrapers built 1880-1940. Includes the Monadnock & the Rookery. *Modern & Beyond* reviews important newer buildings, including the Federal Center, IBM Bldg and the James R. Thompson Center; also public murals and sculptures by Calder, Chagall, Miro, Picasso, Henry Moore and Dubuffet. (Mar-Nov, daily; rest of yr, Fri-Mon) Depart from Tour Center, 224 S Michigan Ave. Phone 312/922-3432. ¢¢¢

Chicago River Boat Tour. This 1½-hr tour covers N and S branches of the Chicago River with views of the city's celebrated riverfront architecture; historic 19th-century railroad bridges and warehouses, 20th-century bridgehouses and magnificent Loop skyscrapers. (May-Sept, daily; Oct, Tues, Thurs, Sat & Sun; no tours Labor Day) 455 E Illinois. Res required, phone 312/942-3432. ¢¢¢¢¢

Sightseeing boat tours.

Mercury, the Skyline Cruiseline. Offers 1-hr, 1½-hr and 2-hr lake and river cruises; also Sun brunch, dinner & luncheon cruises. (Late Apr-Sept) Wacker Dr & Michigan Ave (S side of Michigan Ave Bridge). For information phone 312/332-1353. ¢¢¢-¢¢¢¢

Shoreline Marine Company. 30-min tour of lakefront. (May-Sept, daily) Departures from Shedd Aquarium, afternoons, & Buckingham Fountain, evenings. Phone 312/222-9328. ¢¢¢

Wendella. One-, 1½- and 2-hr lake and river cruises. (Apr-mid-Oct, daily) 400 N Michigan Ave, at the Wrigley Bldg (NW side of Michigan Ave Bridge). Phone 312/337-1446. ¢¢¢-¢¢¢¢

Spirit of Chicago. Lunch, brunch, dinner and moonlight cruises; entertainment. (Apr-Oct, daily) Navy Pier. Phone 312/836-7899. ¢¢¢¢

Sightseeing bus tours.

American Sightseeing Tours. Depart from Palmer House Hotel, 17 E Monroe St. 312/251-3100.

Gray Line Tours. Phone 312/427-3107. Tours depart from 17 E Monroe St.

Chicago Motor Coach Co. Double-decker tours depart from Sears Tower at Jackson & Wacker; Field Museum; Michigan & Pearson and Michigan & Wacker. Phone 312/666-1000.

Untouchable Tours. Guided tour of gangster hot spots of 1920s and '30s. Departs from Here's Chicago. Tour with dinner and revue also avail. (Daily; res strongly recommended) Phone 312/881-1195. ¢¢¢¢

☆ **Walking tours of Pullman Historic District.** Built in 1880-1884 to house the workers of George M. Pullman's Palace Car Co, the original town was a complete model community with many civic and recreational facilities. Unlike most historic districts, nine-tenths of the original buildings still stand. The 1½-hr tours start at the Historic Pullman Center, 614 E 113th St. Tours (May-Oct, 1st Sun of month; 2 departures). Phone 773/785-8181. ¢¢

SPORTS

Professional sports

American League baseball (Chicago White Sox). Comiskey Park, 333 W 35th St. Phone 312/674-1000.

National League baseball (Chicago Cubs). Wrigley Field, 1060 W Addison St. Phone 773/404-2827.

NBA (Chicago Bulls). United Center, 1901 W Madison St. Phone 312/455-4000.

NFL (Chicago Bears). Soldier Field, 1600 S Waldron. Phone 847/295-6600.

NHL (Chicago Blackhawks). United Center, 1901 W Madison St. Phone 312/455-7000.

Horse racing

Balmoral Park Race Track. 25 mi S on 1-94 to IL 394, continue S to Elmscourt Lane in Crete. Harness racing. (All yr, days vary) Phone 312/568-5700 or 708/672-7544.

Hawthorn Race Course. Approx 7 mi W (see CICERO).

Maywood Park Race Track. 8600 W North Ave, in Maywood, I-290, exit 1st Ave N. Parimutuel harness racing. Nightly exc Sun. Also TV simulcast Thoroughbred racing (daily) and summer harness racing (nightly exc Sun). For schedule, fees phone 708/343-4800.

Sportsman's Park Race Track. Approx 7 mi W (see CICERO).

Annual Events

Chicago Auto Show. McCormick Place. Hundreds of foreign and domestic cars are displayed. 2nd wkend Feb.

St Patrick's Day Parade. City parade Sat before hol; South Side parade Sun before hol. Wkend closest Mar 17.

Taste of Chicago. Grant Park. Selected Chicago restaurants offer sample-size specialties. Late June-early July.

Grant Park July 3 Concert. At Petrillo Music Shell. Lakefront blazes with cannon flashes as the symphony welcomes Independence Day with the *1812 Overture;* fireworks. July 3.

Chicago to Mackinac Races. On Lake Michigan. 3rd wkend July.

Venetian Night. Monroe St Harbor. Venetian aquatic parade, fireworks. Late July.

Air & Water Show. North Ave Beach. Dazzling display of air/sea virtuosity by Blue Angels and Golden Knights Parachute teams. Late Aug.

Jazz Festival. Grant Park. Late Aug-early Sept.

Chicago International Film Festival. New international films shown throughout city. Phone 312/644-3400 or 312/644-3456 (24-hr hotline). 3 wks Oct.

Seasonal Events

Ravinia Festival (see HIGHLAND PARK). Early June-mid-Sept.

Grant Park concerts. James C. Petrillo Music Shell. Free concerts. Wed & Fri-Sun. Phone 312/742-7638. Late June-Aug.

Additional Visitor Information

Contact the Chicago Office of Tourism, Chicago Cultural Center, 78 E Washington St, 60602; 312/744-2400 or 800/226-6632. The Office of Tourism distributes an events calendar, maps and museum guides, hotel and restaurant guides plus other information concerning the Chicago area. (Mon-Sat, also Sun afternoons)

The historic Water Tower, southeast corner of Chicago and Michigan Ave, houses a visitor information center that provides brochures and information on points of interest and transportation. (Daily)

There are five Illinois Travel Information Centers, located at 310 S Michigan Ave, at Sears Tower, at the James R. Thompson Center, 100 W Randolph St, and at Midway & O'Hare Airports. (Mon-Fri).

Chicago magazine is helpful for anyone visiting Chicago; available at most newsstands. Also *Key-This Week in Chicago and Where,* at major hotels, provides up-to-date information. For additional information see any of the daily newspapers; special sections to look at are: *Friday* in the Friday *Chicago Tribune;* the *Arts & Entertainment* section in the Sunday *Chicago Tribune;* and the *Weekend Plus* section of the Friday *Chicago Sun-Times.* A free weekly newspaper, *The Reader,* provides information on local events, art and entertainment.

When available, half-price, day-of-performance tickets are offered at a slight service charge at the HOT TIX ticket booth, Chicago Place at 700 N Michigan Ave or 108 N State St (Daily). There is also a booth at 1616 Sherman Ave in Evanston and one in the Oak Park Visitor Center, 158 Forest Ave in Oak Park. (Tues-Sat; Sun tickets sold on Sat) For available tickets phone 312/977-1755.

Chicago O'Hare Airport Area

For additional attractions and accommodations, see CHICAGO O'HARE AIRPORT AREA, which follows CHICAGO.

City Neighborhoods

Many of the restaurants, unrated dining establishments and some lodgings listed under Chicago include neighborhoods as well as exact street addresses. Geographic descriptions of these areas are given, followed by a table of restaurants arranged by neighborhood.

Chinatown: South of 18th St, west of Clark St, north of Cermak Rd and east of the Chicago River.

Gold Coast: South of North Ave, west of the lake, north of Oak St and east of LaSalle St.

Greektown: West of the Loop on Halsted St between Van Buren St on the south and Madison St on the north and east of Ashland Ave.

Hyde Park: South of the Loop; south of 47th St, west of the lake, north of the Midway Plaisance (60th St) and east of Cottage Grove Ave.

Lakeview: Includes New Town and Wrigleyville; south of Irving Park Rd, west of the lake, north of Diversey Pkwy and east of Ashland Ave.

Lincoln Park: Includes Old Town and DePaul; south of Diversey Pkwy, west of the lake, north of North Ave and east of Clybourn Ave.

Loop: Area within the "loop" of the elevated train tracks; south of Lake St, west of Wabash Ave, north of Congress Pkwy and east of Wells St. **North of the Loop:** North of Lake St. **South of the Loop:** South of Congress Pkwy.

Old Town: Wells St between Division St on the south and North Ave on the north; also area of Lincoln Park south of Armitage Ave, west of Clark St, north of North Ave and east of Larrabee St.

River North: North of the Merchandise Mart and Chicago River, west of Wells St, south of Division St and east of the river's North Branch.

CHICAGO RESTAURANTS BY NEIGHBORHOOD AREAS
(For full description, see alphabetical listings under Restaurants)

CHINATOWN
Emperor's Choice. 2238 S Wentworth Ave

GOLD COAST
Biggs. 1150 N Dearborn St
Brasserie Bellevue (Sutton Place Hotel). 21 E Bellevue Place
Pump Room (Omni Ambassador East Hotel). 1301 N State Parkway
Salpicón. 1252 N Wells St

GREEKTOWN
Greek Islands. 200 S Halsted St
Parthenon. 314 S Halsted St
Santorini. 800 W Adams St

LAKEVIEW
Ann Sather. 929 W Belmont Ave
Arco De Cuchilleros. 3445 N Halsted St
Bella Vista. 1001 W Belmont Ave
Erwin. 2995 N Halsted St
Mia Francesca. 3311 N Clark St
N.N. Smokehouse. 1465 W Irving Park
Schulien's. 2100 W Irving Park Rd

LINCOLN PARK
Ambria (Belden-Stratford Hotel). 2300 N Lincoln Park West
Blue Mesa. 1729 N Halsted St
Café Ba Ba Reeba. 2024 N Halsted St
Chapulin. 1962 N Halsted St
Charlie Trotter's. 816 W Armitage Ave
Emilio's Tapas. 444 W Fullerton St
Geja's. 340 W Armitage Ave
Pockets. 2618 N Clark St
Relish. 2044 N Halsted St
Sole Mio. 917 W Armitage Ave
Un Grand Cafe (Belden-Stratford Hotel). 2300 Lincoln Park West
Vinci. 1732 N Halsted St

THE LOOP
Berghoff. 17 W Adams St
The Big Downtown (Palmer House Hilton Hotel). 124 Wabash Ave
Everest. 440 S La Salle St
La Strada. 155 N Michigan Ave
Nick's Fishmarket. 1 First National Plaza
Russian Tea Cafe. 63 E Adams St
Trattoria No. 10. 10 N Dearborn St
Vivere. 71 W Monroe St

NORTH OF THE LOOP
Arun's. 4156 N Kedzie Ave
Avanzare. 161 E Huron St
Bice. 158 E Ontario St
Bistro 110. 110 E Pearson St
Blackhawk Lodge. 41 E Superior St
Boulevard (Inter-Continental Hotel). 505 N Michigan Ave
Cape Cod Room (The Drake Hotel). 140 E Walton Place
Cielo (Omni Chicago Hotel). 676 N Michigan Ave
Como Inn. 546 N Milwaukee Ave
Con Fusion. 1616 N Damen Ave
Cuisines (Renaissance Hotel). 1 W Wacker Dr
Eli's The Place For Steak. 215 E Chicago Ave
Entre Nous (Fairmont Hotel). 200 N Columbus Dr
Gibsons Steakhouse. 1028 N Rush St
Grappa. 200 E Chestnut St
Hatsuhana. 160 E Ontario St
House Of Hunan. 535 N Michigan Ave
Il Toscanaccio. 636 N St Clair St
Iron Mike's Grille (Tremont Hotel). 100 E Chestnut St
Lawry's The Prime Rib. 100 E Ontario St
Le Bouchon. 1958 N Damen Ave
Les Nomades. 222 E Ontario St

Lutz's Continental Cafe & Pastry Shop. 2458 W Montrose Ave
Marché. 833 W Randolph St
Morton's. 1050 N State St
Nix (Regal Knickerbocker Hotel). 163 E Walton Pl
Palm (Swissôtel Hotel). 323 E Wacker Dr
Papagus (Embassy Suites Hotel). 620 N State St
Park Avenue Cafe (Doubletree Guest Suites Hotel). 198 E Delaware Pl
Pizzeria Uno. 29 E Ohio St
Ritz-Carlton Dining Room (The Ritz-Carlton Hotel). 160 E Pearson St
Riva. 700 E Grand Ave
The Saloon. 200 E Chestnut
Sayat Nova. 157 E Ohio St
Seasons (Four Seasons Hotel). 120 E Delaware Place
Shaw's Crab House. 21 E Hubbard St
Signature Room At The 95th. 875 N Michigan Ave
Spiaggia. 980 N Michigan Ave
Spruce. 238 E Ontario St
Streeterville Grille & Bar. 301 E North Water St
Su Casa. 49 E Ontario St
Szechwan East. 340 E Ohio St
Tucci Benucch. 900 N Michigan Ave
Tucci Milan. 6 W Hubbard St
Vivo. 838 W Randolph
Zinfandel. 59 W Grand Ave

SOUTH OF THE LOOP
Buckingham's (Hilton & Towers Hotel). 720 S Michigan Ave
Prairie (Hyatt On Printers Row Hotel). 500 S Dearborn St
Printer's Row. 550 S Dearborn St
Tuscany. 1014 W Taylor St

RIVER NORTH
Ben Pao. 52 W Illinois St
Big Bowl Cafe. 159 1/2 W Erie St
Brasserie Jo. 59 W Hubbard St
Celebrity Cafe (Westin River North Chicago Hotel). 320 N Dearborn St
Centro. 710 N Wells St
Chicago Chop House. 60 W Ontario St
Club Gene & Georgetti. 500 N Franklin St
Coco Pazzo. 300 W Hubbard St
Ed Debevic's. 640 N Wells St
Frontera Grill. 445 N Clark St
Gordon. 500 N Clark St
Hard Rock Cafe. 63 W Ontario St
Harry Caray's. 33 W Kinzie St
Hat Dance. 325 W Huron St
Kiki's Bistro. 900 N Franklin
Klay Oven. 414 N Orleans St
Maggiano's. 516 N Clark St
Mango. 712 N Clark St
Michael Jordan's. 500 N La Salle St
Planet Hollywood. 633 N Wells St
Redfish. 400 N State St
Scoozi. 410 W Huron
Spago. 520 N Dearborn St
Topolobampo. 445 N Clark St
Trattoria Parma. 400 N Clark St

Note: When a listing is located in a town that does not have its own city heading, it will appear under the city nearest to its location. In these cases, the address and town appear in parenthesis immediately following the name of the establishment.

Motels

★ ★ HAMPTON INN. (6540 S Cicero Ave, Bedford Park 60638) 2 blk S of Midway Airport. 708/496-1900; FAX 708/496-1997. Web www.hamptoninn.com. 171 rms, 5 story. S $89; D $99; under 18 free. Crib free. TV; cable (premium). Complimentary continental bkfst. Restaurant nearby. Rm serv. Ck-out noon. Meeting rms. Business servs avail. In-rm modem link. Valet serv. Free airport transportation. Exercise equipt; treadmill, stair machine. Cr cds: A, C, D, DS, MC, V.

D 🏋 ✈ 🚳 🔥 SC

★ ★ SLEEP INN. (6650 S Cicero Ave, Bedford Park 60638) W on I-55, S on Cicero Ave, near Midway Airport. 708/594-0001; FAX 708/594-0058. 120 rms, 118 with shower only, 3 story. S $79-$85; D $85; each addl $6; under 18 free. Crib free. TV; cable (premium). Complimentary continental bkfst. Ck-out noon. Meeting rms. Business servs avail. In-rm modem link. Free airport transportation. Exercise equipt; bicycle, treadmill. Whirlpool. Cr cds: A, C, D, DS, JCB, MC, V.

D 🏋 ✈ 🚳 🔥 SC

Motor Hotels

★ BEST WESTERN RIVER NORTH. 125 W Ohio St (60610), west of N Michigan Ave, River North. 312/467-0800; FAX 312/467-1665. 148 rms, 7 story. S $105-$129; D $117-$141; each addl $8; suites $150-$170; under 18 free; wkend rates; higher rates special events. Crib free. TV; cable (premium), VCR avail. Indoor pool. Complimentary coffee in rms. Restaurant 6:30 am-11 pm; Sat, Sun to 1 am. Rm serv. Ck-out noon. Meeting rm. Business servs avail. In-rm modem link. Bellhops. Free parking. Exercise equipt; weights, bicycles, sauna. Some refrigerators. Cr cds: A, C, D, DS, MC, V.

🏊 🏋 🚳 🔥 SC

✔ ★ COMFORT INN. 601 W Diversey Pkwy (60614), Lincoln Park. 773/348-2810; FAX 773/348-1912. 74 rms, 5 story. S $78-$115; D $88-$125; each addl $10; suites $205-$215; under 18 free. TV; cable (premium). Complimentary continental bkfst. Ck-out noon. Meeting rm. Business servs avail. Saunas. Health club privileges. Some in-rm whirlpools. Cr cds: A, C, D, DS, ER, JCB, MC, V.

🚳 🔥 SC

★ ★ HOLIDAY INN-MIDWAY AIRPORT. 7353 S Cicero Ave (IL 50) (60629), near Midway Airport, south of the Loop. 773/581-5300; FAX 773/581-8421. 161 rms, 5 story. S $84; D $94; each addl $10; under 18 free; wkend rates. Crib free. TV; cable (premium). Pool. Complimentary full bkfst. Restaurant 6 am-10 pm. Rm serv. Bar 5 pm-1 am; entertainment wkends. Ck-out noon. Meeting rms. Business servs avail. Bellhops. Free airport transportation. Exercise equipt; treadmill, weight machine. Cr cds: A, C, D, DS, JCB, MC, V.

D 🏊 🏋 ✈ 🚳 🔥 SC

★ RAMADA INN LAKE SHORE. 4900 S Lake Shore Dr (60615), Hyde Park. 773/288-5800; FAX 773/288-5745. 182 rms, 2-4 story. S $89; D $94; each addl $10; suites $155; under 19 free; wkend rates. Crib free. Pet accepted, some restrictions. TV; cable (premium). Pool; poolside serv. Restaurant 6:30 am-10 pm. Rm serv. Bar 11-1 am. Ck-out 11 am. Meeting rms. Business center. Bellhops. Valet serv. Many rms with view of Lake Michigan. Cr cds: A, C, D, DS, MC, V.

D 🐾 🏊 🚳 🔥 SC ⛷

Hotels

★ ★ AMBASSADOR WEST. 1300 N State Pkwy (60610), at Goethe St, Gold Coast. 312/787-3700; FAX 312/640-2967. 219 rms, 12 story. S, D $199-$229; each addl $20; suites $239-$1,200; under 18 free; wkend rates; package plans. Crib free. Valet parking $23.50. TV; cable (premium), VCR avail. Restaurant 6:30 am-10:30 pm. Rm serv. Bar from 4:30 pm. Ck-out noon. Meeting rms. Business servs avail. Barber, beauty shop. Exercise equipt; weight machine, bicycles. Minibars; wet bars in suites; microwaves avail. Cr cds: A, C, D, DS, JCB, MC, V.

D 🏋 🚳 🔥 SC

★ ★ BELDEN-STRATFORD. 2300 Lincoln Park West (60614), Lincoln Park. 773/281-2900; FAX 773/880-2039; res: 800/800-8301. 50 kit. units in 16 story landmark bldg. S, D $125-$205; wkly, wkend rates. Crib $10. Valet parking $18. TV; cable, VCR avail. Complimentary coffee in rms. Restaurants (see AMBRIA and UN GRAND CAFE). Bar 6-11 pm.

Ck-out noon. Coin lndry. Business servs avail. In-rm modem link. Barber, beauty shop. Exercise equipt; weight machines, treadmill. Microwaves. Views of park, Lake Michigan and skyline. Cr cds: A, C, D, DS, MC, V.

★ ★ BEST WESTERN INN. *162 E Ohio St (60611), north of the Loop.* 312/787-3100; FAX 312/573-3140. 358 rms, 22 story. S, D $129-$169; suites $235-$425; under 17 free; package plans. Valet parking $16. TV; cable. Restaurant 6:30 am-10:30 pm; Fri, Sat to midnight. Bar 11-2 am. Ck-out noon. Guest lndry. Meeting rms. Gift shop. Airport transportation. Indoor tennis privileges. Health club privileges. Sun deck on top floor. Cr cds: A, C, D, DS, JCB, MC, V.

✔★ CITY SUITES. *933 W Belmont Ave (60657), Lakeview.* 773/404-3400; res: 800/248-9108; FAX 773/404-3405. Web www.city inns.com. 45 rms, 4 story. 29 suites. S $85; D $95; each addl $10; suites $99; under 12 free; wkly rates. Crib free. Pet accepted, some restrictions; $200 deposit. Garage parking $7. TV; cable (premium), VCR avail. Complimentary continental bkfst. Restaurant adj 7 am-10 pm. Ck-out noon. Coin lndry. Health club privileges. Refrigerator in suites. Microwaves avail. Cr cds: A, C, D, DS, ER, MC, V.

★ ★ CLARIDGE. *1244 N Dearborn Pkwy (60610), Gold Coast.* 312/787-4980; FAX 312/266-0978; res: 800/245-1258. E-mail claridge-ho tel@att.net; web www.claridge.com. 168 rms, 14 story. S $119-$175; D $135-$190; each addl $15; suites $250-$450; under 18 free; wkend packages. Crib free. Pet accepted, some restrictions. Valet parking $20.25. TV. Complimentary continental bkfst. Restaurant 6:30 am-10:30 pm. Bar noon-2 am. Ck-out noon. Meeting rms. Business servs avail. Concierge. Airport transportation. Health club privileges. Minibars. Fireplace in some suites. Library. In historic residential area. Cr cds: A, C, D, DS, JCB, MC, V.

★ ★ COURTYARD BY MARRIOTT. *30 E Hubbard St (60611), north of the Loop.* 312/329-2500; FAX 312/329-0293. 334 rms, 15 story. S, D $115-$209; suites $199-$249; under 18 free; wkly, wkend rates. Crib free. Garage parking, in/out $22. TV; cable (premium). Indoor pool; whirlpool. Complimentary coffee in rms. Restaurant 6:30 am-11 pm. Bar 4 pm-midnight. Ck-out 1 pm. Coin lndry. Meeting rms. Business servs avail. In-rm modem link. Gift shop. Exercise equipt; weight machine, bicycles. Health club privileges. Refrigerators; microwaves avail. Cr cds: A, C, D, DS, MC, V.

✔★ ★ DAYS INN LAKE SHORE DRIVE. *644 N Lake Shore Dr (60611), at Ontario St, opp Lake Michigan, north of the Loop.* 312/943-9200; FAX 312/255-4411. 578 rms, 33 story. S $89-$189; D $99-$199; each addl $15; suites $275-$800; under 17 free; wkend rates. Crib free. Garage, in/out $18. TV; cable. Pool. Restaurant 6:30 am-10 pm; Fri, Sat to 11 pm. Bar 11 am-midnight. Ck-out noon. Coin lndry. Meeting rms. Business center. In-rm modem link. Gift shop. Airport transportation. Exercise equipt; weight machine, bicycle. Some refrigerators. Panoramic view. Overlooks lake. Cr cds: A, C, D, DS, ER, JCB, MC, V.

★ ★ DOUBLETREE GUEST SUITES. *198 E Delaware Place (60611), north of the Loop.* 312/664-1100; FAX 312/664-9881. Web www.doubletreehotels.com/chicago. 345 suites, 30 story. S, D $129-$265; each addl $25; under 18 free; wkend rates. Crib free. Valet parking, in/out $23.50. TV; cable (premium), VCR avail. Indoor pool; whirlpool. Coffee in rms. Restaurants 6:30-2 am. Rm serv 24 hrs. Ck-out noon. Coin lndry. Meeting rms. Business center. In-rm modem link. Concierge. Gift shop. Exercise equipt; weight machine, stair machine, sauna. Game rm. Refrigerators, microwaves, minibars. Cr cds: A, C, D, DS, MC, V.

★ ★ THE DRAKE. *140 E Walton Place (60611), at Lake Shore Dr & N Michigan Ave, north of the Loop.* 312/787-2200; FAX 312/787-1431; res: 800/553-7253. Web www.hilton.com. 535 rms, 10 story. S, D $265-$335; suites $365-$2,150; family, wkend rates. Crib free. Valet park-

ing $23.25/night; in/out privileges. TV; cable (premium), VCR avail. Restaurant 6:30 am-11 pm (also see CAPE COD ROOM). Rm serv 24 hrs. Bar 11-2 am; piano bar. Ck-out noon. Convention facilities. Business center. In-rm modem link. Concierge. Shopping arcade. Barber. Exercise equipt; rower, stair machine. Health club privileges. Minibars; microwaves avail; wet bar in some suites. Overlooks Lake Michigan. Luxury level. Cr cds: A, C, D, DS, ER, JCB, MC, V.

★ ★ EMBASSY SUITES. *600 N State St (60610), north of the Loop.* 312/943-3800; FAX 312/943-7629. 358 suites, 11 story. S, D $249-$279; under 12 free. Crib free. Garage, in/out $22. TV; cable (premium), VCR avail. Indoor pool; whirlpool. Complimentary full bkfst. Complimentary coffee in rms. Restaurant (see PAPAGUS). Bar. Ck-out noon. Meeting rms. Business center. In-rm modem link. Concierge. Gift shop. Exercise equipt; weights, bicycles, sauna. Health club privileges. Refrigerators, microwaves, minibars, wet bars. Cr cds: A, C, D, DS, JCB, MC, V.

★ ★ EXECUTIVE PLAZA. *71 E Wacker Dr (60601), on the south bank of the Chicago River, north of the Loop.* 312/346-7100; FAX 312/346-1721. 417 rms, 39 story. S $159-$199; D $179-$219; each addl $20; suites $295-$850; under 18 free; wkend rates; package plans. Garage, in/out $20. TV; cable. Coffee in rms. Restaurant 6:30 am-11 pm. Bar to 2 am. Ck-out noon. Meeting rms. Business center. Concierge. Gift shop. Exercise equipt; weight machine, treadmill. Health club privileges. Bathrm phones, minibars. Some wet bars in suites. Cr cds: A, C, D, DS, MC, V.

★ ★ ★ FAIRMONT. *200 N Columbus Dr (60601), north of the Loop.* 312/565-8000; FAX 312/856-1032; res: 800/527-4727. E-mail chi fairmont@aol.com; web www.fairmont.com. An international collection of art and antiques grace the interior of this neo-classical pink granite tower. Guest rooms are exceptionally spacious with windows that open on dramatic lake and city views. 692 rms, 42 story. S, D $199-$329; each addl $35; suites $500-$3,600; under 18 free. Crib free. Valet parking, in/out $26. TV; cable (premium), VCR avail. Pool privileges. Restaurants (see ENTRE NOUS). Rm serv 24 hrs. Bar 11-2 am; entertainment Tues-Sat. Ck-out 1 pm. Convention facilities. Business center. In-rm modem link. Concierge. Health club privileges. Bathrm phones, minibars. Cr cds: A, C, D, DS, ER, JCB, MC, V.

★ ★ ★ FOUR SEASONS. *120 E Delaware Place (60611), at 900 N Michigan Ave complex, north of the Loop.* 312/280-8800; FAX 312/280-1748. E-mail fourtff@aol.com; web www.fourseasonsregent.com. From the spacious English country manor-style lobby of this sparkling hotel, it's easy to forget that you're on the seventh floor of a 66-story skyscraper, just above a chic shopping mall on Chicago's fashionable North Michigan Avenue. Many of the guest rooms, which begin on floor 30, have spectacular views of the city and/or Lake Michigan and all the necessities and comforts for work or relaxation. 343 rms, 66 story bldg, guest rms on floors 30-46, 157 suites. S $325-$445; D $365-$485; each addl $30; suites $690-$995; wkend rates; special packages. Crib free. Pet accepted. Self-park adj, in/out $15.25. TV; cable (premium), VCR avail (movies). Indoor pool; whirlpool. Restaurant (see SEASONS). Rm serv 24 hrs. Bar 11:30-1 am; entertainment. Ck-out noon. Convention facilities. Business center. In-rm modem link. Concierge. Shopping access to 900 North Michigan Mall. Barber, beauty shop. Extensive exercise rm; instructor, weight machine, stair machine, sauna, steam rm. Massage. Bathrm phones, minibars; some wet bars. Lake 3 blks. Cr cds: A, C, D, DS, ER, JCB, MC, V.

★ ★ ★ HILTON & TOWERS. *720 S Michigan Ave (60605), opp Grant Park, south of the Loop.* 312/922-4400; FAX 312/922-5240. Web www.hilton.com. 1,543 rms, 25 story. S $165-$185; D $190-$210; each addl $25; suites from $250; wkend rates. Garage $19; valet parking $21. TV; cable (premium). Indoor pool; whirlpools. Complimentary coffee in rms. Restaurants 5:30-1:30 am (also see BUCKINGHAM'S). Rm serv 24 hrs. Bars to 2 am; entertainment. Ck-out 11 am. Convention facilities. Business center. Concierge. Shopping arcade. Barber, beauty shop. Exercise rm; instructor, weights, bicycles, sauna. Massage. Mini-bars. Luxury level. Cr cds: A, C, D, DS, ER, JCB, MC, V.

★ ★ ★ **HOLIDAY INN-CITY CENTRE.** *300 E Ohio St (60611), north of the Loop.* 312/787-6100; FAX 312/787-6238. 500 rms, 26 story. S, D $165-$240; each addl $20; suites $400-$700; under 18 free; wkend plan. Crib free. Garage adj $17.50. TV; cable (premium), VCR avail. Pool; whirlpools, lifeguard. Restaurant 6:30 am-11 pm. Bars 11:30-2 am. Ck-out noon. Coin lndry. Meeting rms. Business center. In-rm modem link. Tennis privileges. Exercise rm; instructor, weights, bicycles, sauna, steam rm. Massage. Sauna in suites. Cr cds: A, C, D, DS, JCB, MC, V.

★ ★ **HOLIDAY INN-MART PLAZA.** *350 N Orleans St (60654), atop Apparel Center, adj Merchandise Mart, River North.* 312/836-5000; FAX 312/222-9508. 526 rms, 23 story; guest rms on floors 16-23. S $119-$219; D $134-$244; each addl $16; suites $325-$525; under 18 free; wkend rates; package plans. Crib free. Pet accepted, some restrictions. Garage $13/day. TV. Indoor pool. Restaurant 6:30 am-2 pm, 5-10:30 pm. Bars noon-2 am. Ck-out noon. Coin lndry. Convention facilities. Shopping arcade. Barber, beauty shop. Airport transportation. Exercise equipt; bicycles, treadmill. Refrigerator in suites. Cr cds: A, C, D, DS, JCB, MC, V.

★ ★ **HYATT AT UNIVERSITY VILLAGE.** *625 S Ashland Ave (60607), at Rush-Presbyterian-St Luke's Medical Center, west of the Loop.* 312/243-7200; FAX 312/243-1289. Web www.hyatt.com. 114 rms, 4 story. S $120-$195; D $120-$220; each addl $25; suites $185-$560; under 18 free; wkend, wkly, monthly rates. Crib free. TV; cable (premium), VCR avail. Pool privileges. Restaurant 6:30 am-10 pm. Rm serv. Bar 11 am-midnight. Ck-out noon. Meeting rms. Business center. Valet serv. Valet parking. Tennis privileges. Exercise equipt; weight machine, bicycles. Health club privileges. Some refrigerators; microwaves avail. Near University of Illinois Chicago campus. Cr cds: A, C, D, DS, MC, V.

★ ★ **HYATT ON PRINTERS ROW.** *500 S Dearborn St (60605), Printer's Row, south of the Loop.* 312/986-1234; FAX 312/939-2468. Web www.hyatt.com. 161 rms, 7-12 story. S $165-$205; D $185-$230; each addl $25; suites $450-$1,000; wkend rates. Crib free. Valet parking $24; self-park $16. TV; cable (premium), VCR avail. Restaurant 6:30 am-11 pm (also see PRAIRIE). Bar 11-1 am. Ck-out noon. Meeting rms. Business servs avail. Airport transportation. Exercise equipt; bicycles, treadmill. Massage. Health club privileges. Bathrm phones, minibars. Financial district nearby. Cr cds: A, C, D, DS, ER, JCB, MC, V.

★ ★ ★ **HYATT REGENCY.** *151 E Wacker Dr (60601), opp Chicago River, north of the Loop.* 312/565-1234; FAX 312/565-2966. 2,019 rms, 34 story (East Tower), 36 story (West Tower). S $119-$289; D $119-$309; each addl $25; suites $565-$3,500; under 18 free; package plans. Crib free. Garage, in/out $24. TV; cable (premium), VCR avail (movies). Restaurant open 6 am-midnight. Rm serv 24 hrs. Bar 11-2 am; entertainment. Ck-out noon. Convention facilities. Business center. In-rm modem link. Concierge. Shopping arcade. Barber, beauty shop. Health club privileges. Minibars; some in-rm steam baths, whirlpools. Bathrm phone, refrigerator in suites. Luxury level. Cr cds: A, C, D, DS, ER, JCB, MC, V.

★ ★ ★ **INTER-CONTINENTAL.** *505 N Michigan Ave (60611), just north of the Chicago River, at Grand Ave, north of the Loop.* 312/944-4100; FAX 312/944-1320; res: 800/327-0200. 845 rms, 2 bldgs, 26 & 42 story, 42 suites. S, D $179-$319; each addl $25; suites from $375; under 14 free. Crib free. Covered parking $25/day. TV; cable, VCR avail. Indoor pool; poolside serv. Coffee in rms. Restaurants 6:30 am-11 pm. Rm serv 24 hrs. Afternoon tea 2-5 pm. Bar 11-1 am; entertainment Thurs-Sun. Ck-out noon. Convention facilities. Business center. In-rm modem link. Concierge. Gift shop. Exercise rm; instructor, weight machines, bicycles, sauna. Massage. Minibars, bathrm phones; microwaves avail. Two buildings, one of which was originally constructed (1929) as the Medinah Athletic Club. Cr cds: A, C, D, DS, ER, JCB, MC, V.

★ ★ **LENOX SUITES.** *616 N Rush St (60611), north of the Loop.* 312/337-1000; FAX 312/337-7217; res: 800/445-3669. 324 kit. units, 17 story. S $149-$209; D $159-$219; each addl $10; under 16 free; wkend, monthly rates. Crib free. Valet parking $17.50. TV; cable (premium), VCR avail. Complimentary continental bkfst. Restaurants 6 am-11 pm. Rm serv. Bar 11-2 am. Ck-out 11 am. Coin lndry. Meeting rms. Business servs avail. In-rm modem link. Concierge. Exercise equipt; treadmill, bicycle. Health club privileges. Microwaves. Cr cds: A, C, D, DS, JCB, MC, V.

★ ★ ★ **MARRIOTT.** *540 N Michigan Ave (60611), at Ohio St, north of the Loop.* 312/836-0100; FAX 312/836-6139. 1,172 rms, 46 story. S $159-$249; D $189-$299; suites $590-$1,150; under 18 free; wkend rates. Crib free. Pet accepted. Valet parking $23.25. TV; cable (premium), VCR avail. Indoor pool; whirlpool, poolside serv. Coffee in rms. Restaurant 6:30 am-midnight. Bar 11-2 am. Ck-out noon. Convention facilities. Business center. In-rm modem link. Concierge. Shopping arcade. Barber, beauty shop. Exercise rm; instructor, weight machines, bicycles, sauna. Massage. Basketball courts. Game rm. Bathrm phone in suites; microwaves avail. Luxury level. Cr cds: A, C, D, DS, ER, JCB, MC, V.

★ ★ **MIDLAND.** *172 W Adams St (60603), the Loop.* 312/332-1200; FAX 312/332-5909; res: 800/621-2360. 257 rms, 10 story. S, D $175-$225; each addl $20; suites from $450; under 18 free; wkend rates. Crib free. TV; cable (premium). Complimentary full bkfst. Restaurant 6:30 am-11 pm. Bar 11 am-midnight. Ck-out noon. Convention facilities. Business servs avail. Gift shop. Airport transportation. Exercise equipt; weight machine, bicycles. Massage. Health club privileges. Some refrigerators, microwaves. Cr cds: A, C, D, DS, JCB, MC, V.

★ **MOTEL 6.** *162 E Ontario St (60611), north of the Loop.* 312/787-3580; FAX 312/787-1299. 191 rms, 15 story. June-Aug: S $89; D $99; each addl $10; suites $99-$109; under 17 free; wkend rates; higher rates: New Years Eve, special events; lower rates rest of yr. Crib free. Valet parking $16. TV; cable. Restaurant 11:30 am-9:30 pm. No rm serv. Ck-out noon. Meeting rms. Health club privileges. Cr cds: A, C, D, DS, MC, V.

★ ★ **OMNI AMBASSADOR EAST.** *1301 N State Parkway (60610), at Goethe St, Gold Coast.* 312/787-7200; FAX 312/787-4760. 275 rms, 17 story. S $170-$180; D $200-$210; each addl $20; suites $200-$400; under 17 free; wkend rates. Crib free. Valet parking $23.50. TV; cable (premium). Restaurant (see PUMP ROOM). Bar 11-1 am. Ck-out noon. Meeting rms. Business servs avail. Concierge. Barber, beauty shop. Airport transportation. Health club privileges. Minibars; microwaves avail. Cr cds: A, C, D, DS, JCB, MC, V.

★ ★ ★ **OMNI CHICAGO HOTEL.** *676 N Michigan Ave (60611), north of the Loop.* 312/944-6664; FAX 312/266-3015; res: 800/THE-OMNI. Web ww.omnihotels.com. This hotel, with its marble floors, vaulted ceilings and art-deco touches of dark wood, occupies the first 25 floors of the 40-story City Place building, an office and retail complex. 347 rms, 25 story. S $275; D $295; suites $320-$2,000; under 12 free. Crib free. Parking in/out $24. TV; cable (premium), VCR avail. Indoor pool; whirlpool. Coffee in rms. Restaurant (see CIELO). Rm serv 24 hrs. Bar 11 am-midnight; entertainment. Ck-out noon. Meeting rms. Business center. In-rm modem link. Concierge. Exercise equipt; weight machine, bicycles, sauna. Minibars, wet bars; microwaves avail. Sun deck. Cr cds: A, C, D, DS, JCB, MC, V.

★ ★ **PALMER HOUSE HILTON.** *17 E Monroe St (60603), at State St, the Loop.* 312/726-7500; FAX 312/263-2556. 1,639 rms, 23 story. S $175-$300; D $200-$325; each addl $25; suites from $650; family, wkend rates. Crib free. Pet accepted. Garage $15, valet $21.25. TV; cable (premium), VCR avail. Indoor pool; whirlpool. Complimentary coffee in rms. Restaurants 6:30-2 am. Bars 11:30-2 am; entertainment. Ck-out noon. Convention facilities. Business center. In-rm modem link. Concierge. Shopping arcade. Barber, beauty shop. Airport transportation. Exercise rm; instructor, weights, bicycles, sauna, steam rm. Massage. Minibars. Refrigerator in suites. Luxury level. Cr cds: A, C, D, DS, ER, JCB, MC, V.

D ✦ ≈ ✗ ⊿ ⋀ SC ✦

★ ✦ **PARK BROMPTON INN.** *528 W Brompton Ave (60657), in Lakeview.* 773/404-3499; res: 800/727-5108; FAX 773/404-3495. Web www.cityinns.com. 52 rms, 4 story, 22 kit. suites. S $85; D $95; each addl $10; suites $99; under 12 free; wkend rates (2-day min). Crib free. Pet accepted, some restrictions; $200 deposit. Garage parking $7. TV; cable (premium). Complimentary continental bkfst. Restaurant nearby. Ck-out noon. No bellhops. Coin lndry. Health club privileges. Refrigerator, microwave, wet bar in suites. Cr cds: A, C, D, DS, ER, MC, V.

✦ ⊠ SC

★ ★ ★ **RADISSON.** *160 E Huron (60611), north of the Loop.* 312/787-2900; FAX 312/787-5158. E-mail radchgo@ix.netcom.com. 341 rms, 40 story, 96 suites. Apr-Dec: S $139-$199; D $134-$209; each addl $15; suites $179-$259; under 17 free; wkend rates; lower rates rest of yr. Crib free. Pet accepted, some restrictions. Valet parking $21. TV; cable (premium), VCR avail. Pool; poolside serv. Complimentary coffee in rms. Restaurant 6 am-11 pm. Rm serv 24 hrs. Bar noon-midnight. Ck-out noon. Convention facilities. Business center. In-rm modem link. Concierge. Gift shop. Barber. Exercise equipt; weight machine, bicycle. Minibars; some refrigerators; microwaves avail. Cr cds: A, C, D, DS, ER, JCB, MC, V.

D ✦ ≈ ✗ ⊿ ⋀ SC ✦

★ ★ **RAMADA CONGRESS.** *520 S Michigan Ave (60605), south of the Loop.* 312/427-3800; FAX 312/427-7264. 840 rms, 8-14 story. S $75-$135; D $85-$155; each addl $20; suites $300-$700; under 17 free; higher rates Taste of Chicago. Crib free. Valet parking $17; garage $17. TV; cable, VCR avail. Complimentary coffee in rms. Restaurant 6:30 am-10:30 pm. Bar 5 pm-1 am. Ck-out noon. Convention facilities. Business servs avail. Concierge. Shopping arcade. Barber. Coin lndry. Exercise equipt; treadmill, stair machine. Cr cds: A, C, D, DS, ER, JCB, MC, V.

✗ ⊿ ⋀ SC

★ ★ **RAPHAEL.** *201 E Delaware Place (60611), north of the Loop.* 312/943-5000; FAX 312/943-9483; res: 800/821-5343. 172 rms, 17 story, 72 suites. S, D $150-$200; each addl $20; under 12 free; suites $170-$250; wkend rates. Crib free. Valet parking, in/out $22.50. TV; cable (premium), VCR avail. Restaurant 6:30-11 am, 11:30 am-2 pm, 5-10 pm; Sun 5-9 pm. Rm serv. Bar 11-1:30 am; entertainment Fri, Sat. Ck-out 1 pm. Meeting rms. Health club privileges. Minibars. Cr cds: A, C, D, DS, MC, V.

D ⊠ ⋀ SC

★ ★ ★ **REGAL KNICKERBOCKER.** *163 E Walton Place (60611), north of the Loop.* 312/751-8100; FAX 312/751-9205; res: 800/621-8140. Web www.regalhotels.com/chicago. 305 rms, 14 story. S $145-$225, D $165-$245; each addl $20; suites $250-$1,000; under 18 free; wkend rates. Crib free. Valet parking, in/out $23.50. TV; cable (premium) VCR avail. Pool privileges. Restaurant (see NIX). Rm serv 24 hrs. Bar 11-2 am. Ck-out noon. Meeting rms. Business servs avail. In-rm modem link. Concierge. Indoor tennis privileges. Exercise equipt; weights, treadmill. Health club privileges. Minibars; some refrigerators. Luxury level. Cr cds: A, C, D, DS, JCB, MC, V.

D ✦ ≈ ✗ ⊿ ⋀ SC

★ ★ ★ **RENAISSANCE.** *1 W Wacker Dr (60601), on the Chicago River, north of the Loop.* 312/372-7200; FAX 312/372-0093. Web www.renaissancehotels.com. The interior of this white-stone-and-glass lodging evokes a grand 19th-century hotel with its multiple fountains, crystal chandeliers, marble accents and grand staircase. All guest rooms have sitting areas and many offer dramatic river views. 553 units, 27 story. S $270-$350; D $290-$370; each addl $20; suites $500-$900; under 18 free; wkend plans. Crib free. Pet accepted, some restrictions. Garage; valet parking in/out $26. TV; cable (premium), VCR avail. Indoor pool;

whirlpool, poolside serv. Restaurants 6 am-midnight (also see CUISINES). Rm serv 24 hrs. Bar 11-2 am; pianist, jazz trio. Ck-out 1 pm. Convention facilities. Business center. In-rm modem link. Concierge. Shopping arcade. Tennis privileges. Exercise rm; instructor, weight machine, bicycles, sauna. Massage. Minibars; bathrm phone in suites. Luxury level. Cr cds: A, C, D, DS, ER, JCB, MC, V.

D ✦ 🏃 ≈ ✗ ⊿ ⋀ SC 🏃

★ ★ **RESIDENCE INN BY MARRIOTT.** *201 E Walton Place (60611), north of the Loop.* 312/943-9800; FAX 312/943-8579. 221 kit. suites, 19 story. Suites $169-$325; wkend, wkly, monthly rates. Crib free. Pet accepted, some restrictions; $5. Valet parking, in/out $22. TV; cable (premium). Pool privileges. Complimentary continental bkfst; afternoon refreshments. Complimentary coffee in rms. Restaurant adj 6:30 am-10 pm. Ck-out noon. Coin lndry. Meeting rms. Business servs avail. In-rm modem link. Exercise equipt; weight machine, bicycles. Health club privileges. Microwaves. One blk from Oak St beach. Cr cds: A, C, D, DS, JCB, MC, V.

D ✦ ✗ ⊿ ⋀ SC

★ ★ ★ ★ **THE RITZ-CARLTON.** *160 E Pearson St (60611), at Water Tower Place, north of the Loop.* 312/266-1000; FAX 312/266-1194; res: 800/621-6906 (exc IL). Magnificent flower arrangements, a fountain, wicker and palms set the tone in the two-story greenhouse lobby here. The guest rooms upstairs are spacious with mahogany furniture, cherry-wood armoires and wingback chairs. 429 rms, 31 story, 84 suites. S, D $315-$395; each addl $30; suites $415-$1,050; under 12 free; wkend rates, special packages. Crib free. Pet accepted. Parking in/out $25.50/day. TV; cable (premium), VCR avail. Heated pool $10; whirlpool. Restaurant 6:30-1 am (also see RITZ-CARLTON DINING ROOM). Rm serv 24 hrs. Bar from 11 am; Fri, Sat to 2 am. Ck-out 1 pm. Convention facilities. Business center. In-rm modem link. Concierge. Tennis privileges. Exercise rm; instructor, weights, bicycles, sauna, steam rm. Massage. Bathrm phones, minibars; refrigerators avail. Kennels avail. Cr cds: A, C, D, DS, ER, JCB, MC, V.

D ✦ ✦ ≈ ✗ ⊿ ⋀ 🏃

★ ★ **THE SENECA.** *200 E Chestnut St (60611), north of the Loop.* 312/787-8900; FAX 312/988-4438; res: 800/800-6261. 122 rms, 17 story, 85 kit. suites. S $149-$245; D $169-$265; each addl $20; under 12 free; wkend, hol rates. Crib $10. Valet parking $22. TV; cable (premium), VCR avail. Complimentary coffee in rms. Restaurants 7:30 am-10:30 pm. Bar from 11:30 am. Ck-out noon. Coin lndry. Meeting rms. Business servs avail. In-rm modem link. Concierge. Beauty shop. Exercise equipt; weights, bicycle. Refrigerators. Cr cds: A, C, D, DS, MC, V.

D ✗ ⊿ ⋀ SC

★ ★ ★ **SHERATON CHICAGO HOTEL & TOWERS.** *301 E North Water St (60611), Columbus Dr at Chicago River, north of the Loop.* 312/464-1000; FAX 312/464-9140. Web www.sheraton.com. 1,204 rms, 34 story, 54 suites. S $199-$269; D $219-$289; each addl $25; suites $350-$3500; under 17 free. Pet accepted, some restrictions. Garage, in/out $24. TV; cable (premium), VCR avail. Indoor pool. Complimentary coffee in rms. Restaurant 6-1 am. Rm serv 24 hrs. Bar 11-1:30 am; pianist. Ck-out noon. Convention facilities. Business center. In-rm modem link. Concierge. Gift shop. Tennis privileges. Exercise equipt; weight machines, bicycles, sauna. Massage. Minibars. On Chicago River, near Navy Pier. Views of Lake Michigan and skyline. Luxury level. Cr cds: A, C, D, DS, ER, JCB, MC, V.

D ✦ 🏃 ≈ ✗ ⊿ ⋀ SC 🏃

★ ★ **SUMMERFIELD SUITES.** *166 E Superior St (60611), north of the Loop.* 312/787-6000; FAX 312/787-4331. 120 suites, 29 story, 100 kit. suites. Mar-Dec: S, D $149-$259; each addl $25; under 16 free; wkend, hol rates; lower rates rest of yr. Crib free. Garage parking $17; valet $27. TV; cable (premium), VCR (movies). Heated pool. Complimentary full bkfst. Complimentary coffee in rms. Restaurant 11 am-10 pm. No rm serv. Bar from 5 pm. Ck-out noon. Coin lndry. Meeting rms. Business servs avail. In-rm modem link. Concierge. Barber. Exercise equipt; weights, bicycle. Health club privileges. Refrigerators, microwaves. Cr cds: A, C, D, DS, JCB, MC, V.

[D] [≈] [✗] [≥] [�] [SC]

↩★ SURF. *555 W Surf St (60657), Lakeview.* 773/528-8400; res: 800/787-3108; FAX 773/528-8483. Web www.cityinns.com. 55 rms, 4 story. S $79-$89; D $99-$129; each addl $10; suites $99-$129; under 12 free; wkends (2-day min). Crib free. Pet accepted; $200 deposit. Garage parking $8. TV; cable. Complimentary continental bkfst. Restaurant nearby. No rm serv. Ck-out 11 am. In-rm modem link. No bellhops. Concierge. Health club privileges. Cr cds: A, C, D, DS, ER, JCB, MC, V.

[✦] [≥] [⚒] [SC]

★★★ SUTTON PLACE. *21 E Bellevue Place (60611), Gold Coast.* 312/266-2100; FAX 312/266-2103; res: 800/606-8188. E-mail info@chi.suttonplace.com; web www.travelweb.com/sutton.html. 246 rms, 22 story, 40 suites. S $245-$270; D $260-$285; each addl $25; suites $315-$725; under 16 free; wkend rates. Crib free. Pet accepted, some restrictions; $200 refundable. Valet parking $24. TV; cable (premium), VCR (movies). Restaurant (see BRASSERIE BELLEVUE). Rm serv 24 hrs. Bar 11:30-1 am; Fri, Sat to 2 am. Ck-out noon. Meeting rms. Business center. In-rm modem link. Concierge. Airport transportation. Exercise equipt; stair machine, treadmill. Health club privileges. Bathrm phones, minibars. Penthouse suites with garden terrace. Cr cds: A, C, D, DS, JCB, MC, V.

[D] [✦] [✗] [≥] [⚒] [SC] [⚫]

★★★ SWISSÔTEL. *323 E Wacker Dr (60601), off Chicago River East, at Michigan Ave, south of the Loop.* 312/565-0565; FAX 312/565-0540; res: 800/644-7263. 630 rms, 43 story. S $309-$349; D $329-$369; each addl $20; suites $395-$2,500; under 14 free. Covered parking, in/out $26. TV; cable (premium), VCR avail. Indoor pool; whirlpool. Restaurant 6 am-10:30 pm. Rm serv 24 hrs. Bar 11-2 am. Ck-out 1 pm. Convention facilities. Business center. In-rm modem link. Concierge. Gift shop. Exercise rm; instructor, weight machines, bicycles, sauna. Massage. Bathrm phones, minibars. Panoramic views of city and Lake Michigan. Cr cds: A, C, D, DS, ER, JCB, MC, V.

[D] [≈] [✗] [≥] [⚒] [SC] [⚫]

★★★ TREMONT. *100 E Chestnut St (60611), north of the Loop.* 312/751-1900; FAX 312/751-8691; res: 800/621-8133. 129 rms, 16 story. S, D $225-$245; suites $345-$925; under 18 free; wkend rates. Crib free. Pet accepted, some restrictions. Parking $23. TV; cable (premium), VCR (movies). Coffee in rms. Restaurant 6:30 am-11 pm. Rm serv 24 hrs. Bar 11-midnight. Ck-out noon. Meeting rms. Business servs avail. In-rm modem link. Concierge. Bathrm phones, minibars; microwaves avail. Cr cds: A, C, D, DS, JCB, MC, V.

[D] [✦] [≥] [⚫]

★★★ WESTIN. *909 N Michigan Ave (60611), at Delaware Place, north of the Loop.* 312/943-7200; FAX 312/649-7447. Web www.westin.com. 740 rms, 27 story. S, D $269-$329; each addl $20; suites $350-$1,500; under 18 free; package plans. Crib free. Pet accepted, some restrictions. Valet parking, in/out $25. TV; cable (premium). Restaurant 6:30 am-10 pm. Rm serv 24 hrs. Bar 11-1:30 am. Ck-out noon. Convention facilities. Business center. In-rm modem link. Concierge. Gift shop. Exercise equipt; weights, bicycles, sauna. Massage. Minibars; many bathrm phones; microwaves avail. Luxury level. Cr cds: A, C, D, DS, ER, JCB, MC, V.

[D] [✦] [✗] [≥] [⚒] [SC] [⚫]

★★★★ WESTIN RIVER NORTH CHICAGO. *320 N Dearborn St (60610), River North.* 312/744-1900; FAX 312/527-2650. The polished granite, black lacquer and mahogany interior of this hotel has an understated elegance. Floor-to-ceiling windows look out on a rock garden. Guest rooms are furnished in either contemporary or traditional style. 422 rms, 20 story. S $275-$315; D $270-$310; each addl $25; suites $450-$2,500 under 18 free; special packages. Crib free. Pet accepted, some restrictions. Valet parking $26 in/out. TV; cable (premium), VCR avail. Coffee in rms. Restaurant 6:30 am-11 pm (also see CELEBRITY CAFE). Rm serv 24 hrs. Bar 11-1:30 am; pianist 6 days. Ck-out noon. Convention facilities. Business center. In-rm modem link. Concierge. Exercise rm; instructor,

weights, bicycles, sauna. Massage. Bathrm phones, minibars. Cr cds: A, C, D, DS, ER, JCB, MC, V.

[D] [✦] [✗] [≥] [⚒] [SC] [⚫]

★★★ WHITEHALL. *105 E Delaware (60611), north of the Loop.* 312/944-6300; FAX 312/944-8552; res: 800/948-4255. E-mail chiwhitehall@worldnet.att.net; web www.preferredhotels.com/preferred.html. 221 rms, 21 story. S, D $285-$385; each addl $25; suites $550-$2,000; under 12 free; wkly, wkend rates. Crib free. Valet parking $24.50. Restaurant 6:30 am-10 pm. Rm serv 24 hrs. Bar from 11 am. Ck-out noon. Meeting rms. Business servs avail. In-rm modem link. Concierge. Exercise equipt; weight machines, treadmills. Health club privileges. Minibars. Luxury level. Cr cds: A, C, D, DS, JCB, MC, V.

[D] [✗] [≥] [⚒] [SC]

Inn

★★ GOLD COAST GUEST HOUSE. *113 W Elm St (60610), Gold Coast.* 312/337-0361; FAX 312/337-0362. Web www.bbchicago.com. 4 rms, 2 with shower only, 3 story. Apr-Dec: S, D $119-$165; wkly rates; lower rates rest of yr. TV; VCR avail. Complimentary continental bkfst. Restaurant nearby. Ck-out noon. Business servs avail. Indoor tennis privileges. Health club privileges. Renovated brick townhome built in 1873. Cr cds: A, DS, MC, V.

[⚫] [≥] [⚒]

Restaurants

★★★★ AMBRIA. *(See Belden-Stratford Hotel)* 773/472-5959. The mood is retro-elegance at this restaurant housed in a turn-of-the-century hotel and decorated with dark wood and Art Nouveau fixtures. French, continental menu. Specializes in fresh seafood, seasonal offerings. Menu changes seasonally; daily specialties. Own baking. Hrs: 6-9:30 pm; Fri, Sat to 10:30 pm. Closed Sun; major hols. Res accepted. Bar. Wine list. A la carte entrees: dinner $22-$30. Prix fixe: dinner $48 & $64. Valet parking. Chef-owned. Cr cds: A, C, D, DS, JCB, MC, V.

[D]

↩★ ANN SATHER. *929 W Belmont Ave, Lakeview.* 312/348-2378. Web www.gwebb.com/a/ann.html. Hrs: 7 am-10 pm; Fri, Sat to 11 pm. Swedish, Amer menu. Bar. A la carte entrees: bkfst $3.75-$6.75, lunch & dinner $4.25-$6.95. Complete meals: lunch, dinner $6.95-$10.95. Specializes in Swedish pancakes, beefsteak, fresh fish. Bkfst menu avail all day. Opened 1945. Cr cds: A, MC, V.

[D] [SC] [↩]

★★★★ ARUN'S. *4156 N Kedzie Ave, north of the Loop.* 773/539-1909. This bi-level dining room has lots of natural wood, complemented by Thai art and a small art gallery—world's apart from the typical storefront ethnic restaurant. Seafood is a must; daily specials supplement the extensive basic menu. Thai menu; special "chef-designed" menus. Specialties: phad Thai, three-flavored red snapper, spicy roast eggplant. Hrs: 5-10 pm; Sun to 9 pm. Closed Mon; major hols. Res accepted. Bar. A la carte entrees: dinner $11.95-$24.95. Cr cds: A, C, D, DS, MC, V.

★★★ AVANZARE. *161 E Huron St, north of the Loop.* 312/337-8056. Hrs: 11:30 am-2 pm, 5:30-9:30 pm; Fri to 10:30 pm; Sat 5-10:30 pm; Sun 5-9 pm. Closed major hols. Res accepted. Italian menu. Bar. A la carte entrees: lunch $11-$17, dinner $13-$26. Specialties: grilled prime veal chop with wild mushroom lasagna, seared salmon with artichokes & tomatoes, pappardelle with shrimp & calamari. Own pasta. Outdoor dining. Contemporary decor with Frank Lloyd Wright accents; Virginio Ferrari sculptures. Cr cds: A, C, D, DS, JCB, MC, V.

[D] [↩]

★★ BELLA VISTA. *1001 W Belmont Ave, Lakeview.* 773/404-0111. Hrs: 11:30 am-2:30 pm, 5-11 pm; Fri to midnight; Sat 5 pm-midnight; Sun 5-9 pm. Closed Thanksgiving, Dec 25. Res accepted. Contemporary Italian menu. Bar. A la carte entrees: lunch $6-$10.50, dinner $9-$17.95. Specialties: fire-roasted calamari with lemon rosemary sauce, grilled salmon with angel hair pasta. Valet parking (dinner). Contemporary, eclectic decor. In renovated bank building (1929). Cr cds: A, D, DS, MC, V.

D ⊿

✔★ ★ **BEN PAO.** *52 W Illinois St (60610), River North.* 312/222-1888. Hrs: 11:30 am-2 pm, 5-10 pm; Fri to 11 pm; Sat 5-11 pm; Sun 4-9 pm. Closed most major hols. Res accepted. Chinese menu. Bar. A la carte entrees: lunch $7.95-$10.95, dinner $8.95-$16.95. Child's meals. Specializes in grilled satays, black peppered scallops, seven-flavored chicken. Own desserts. Valet parking. Outdoor dining. Dramatic Chinese decor with waterfall columns. Cr cds: A, C, D, DS, JCB, MC, V.

D

★ **BERGHOFF.** *17 W Adams St, the Loop.* 312/427-3170. Web www.Berghoff.chicago.com. Hrs: 11 am-9 pm; Fri to 9:30 pm; Sat to 10 pm. Closed Sun; major hols. Res accepted. German, Amer menu. Semi-a la carte: lunch $6.50-$11, dinner $9-$17. Child's meals. Specialties: Wienerschnitzel, chicken Dijon, sauerbraten. In 1881 building. Family-owned since 1898. Cr cds: A, MC, V.

D ⊿

★ ★ **BICE.** *158 E Ontario St, north of the Loop.* 312/664-1474. Hrs: 11:30 am-10:30 pm; Fri, Sat to 11:30 pm. Closed Jan 1, Dec 25. Res accepted. Northern Italian menu. Bar. A la carte entrees: lunch $11-$20, dinner $14-$25. Own pastries, desserts, pasta. Valet parking (dinner). Outdoor dining. Contemporary Italian decor. Cr cds: A, C, D, MC, V.

⊿

★ ★ **THE BIG DOWNTOWN.** *(See Palmer House Hilton Hotel)* 312/917-7399. Hrs: 11-2 am. Res accepted (dinner). Bar. Semi-a la carte: lunch $8-$16, dinner $10-$22. Specialties: barbecue ribs, rotisserie chicken, banana tiramisu. Own baking. Blues & jazz Fri, Sat. 1940s-style diner with jazz memorabilia, miniature replica of the Chicago El. Cr cds: A, C, D, DS, ER, JCB, MC, V.

D ⊿

★ ★ ★ **BIGGS.** *1150 N Dearborn St (60610), Gold Coast.* 312/787-0900. Hrs: 5-10 pm. Closed some major hols. Res accepted. Continental menu. Bar. Wine cellar. A la carte entrees: dinner $17.95-$32.95. Specialties: beef Wellington, rack of lamb, caviar. Valet parking. Outdoor dining. Formal dining in mansion built 1874. Original oil paintings. Cr cds: A, C, D, DS, MC, V.

⊿

★ ★ **BISTRO 110.** *110 E Pearson St, north of the Loop.* 312/266-3110. Hrs: 11:30 am-11 pm; Fri, Sat to midnight; Sun brunch 11 am-4 pm. Closed some major hols. Res accepted. French, Amer menu. Bar. A la carte entrees: lunch $7.95-$15.95, dinner $10.95-$24.95. Sun Jazz brunch $6.95-$14.95. Specializes in chicken prepared in wood-burning oven, fish. Valet parking. Outdoor dining. French bistro atmosphere. Cr cds: A, C, D, DS, MC, V.

D ⊿

★ ★ **BLACKHAWK LODGE.** *41 E Superior St, north of the Loop.* 312/280-4080. Hrs: 11:30 am-3 pm, 5-10 pm; Fri, Sat to 11 pm; Bluegrass Sun brunch 11 am-3 pm. Closed some major hols. Res accepted. Bar. Semi-a la carte: lunch $7.95-$15.95, dinner $12.95-$22.95. Sun brunch $7.95-$14.95. Specializes in fresh fish, smoked tenderloin of beef, seasonal game. Valet parking. Outdoor dining on screened porch. Lodge atmosphere; eclectic artifacts. Cr cds: A, C, D, DS, MC, V.

D ⊿

✔★ **BLUE MESA.** *1729 N Halsted St (60614), Lincoln Park.* 312/944-5990. Hrs: 11:30 am-2:30 pm, 5-10:30 pm; Fri to 11:30 pm; Sat 11:30 am-midnight; Sun 4-10 pm; Sun brunch 11 am-2:30 pm. Closed Thanksgiving, Dec 25. Res accepted. Southwestern menu. Bar. Semi-a la carte: lunch, dinner $6.95-$13.95. Sun brunch $6.95-$12.95. Child's meals. Specialties: blue corn chicken enchilada, stuffed sopaipilla, fajitas. Valet parking. Outdoor dining. Cr cds: A, C, D, DS, MC, V.

D

★ ★ ★ **BOULEVARD.** *(See Inter-Continental Hotel)* 312/321-8888. Hrs: 6:30-10:30 am, 11:30 am-2 pm, 6-10 pm; Sat from 6 pm. Closed Sun; some major hols. Res accepted (lunch, dinner). Mediterranean menu. Bar. Wine cellar. Complete meal: bkfst $10-$15. A la carte entrees: lunch $8-$18, dinner $11-$30. Child's meals. Specialties: cornmeal-crust pizza, paella Valencia, tapas. Own baking, pasta. Jazz Wed-Sat. Formal dining in elegant atmosphere with ornate ceiling, artwork. Cr cds: A, C, D, DS, JCB, MC, V.

D ⊿ ♥

★ ★ **BRASSERIE BELLEVUE.** *(See Sutton Place Hotel)* 312/266-9212. E-mail info@chi.suttonplace.com; web www.travelweb.com/sutton.html. Hrs: 7 am-11 pm; Sun brunch 11 am-2:30 pm. Res accepted. Contemporary American, Bistro menu. Bar. Semi-a la carte: bkfst $7.95-$10.95, lunch $7.95-$15.95, dinner $9-$26.95. Sun brunch $13.95. Valet parking. Outdoor dining. Modern decor with Art Deco accent. Cr cds: A, C, D, DS, JCB, MC, V.

D ⊿

★ ★ ★ **BRASSERIE JO.** *59 W Hubbard St (60610), River North.* 312/595-0800. Hrs: 11:30 am-midnight; Fri to 1 am; Sat 5 pm-1 am; Sun from 4 pm. Closed Thanksgiving, Dec 24, 25. Res accepted. French menu. Bar. Wine cellar. Semi-a la carte: lunch $7.95-$15.95, dinner $9.50-$19.95. Specialties: smoked salmon, onion tart Uncle Hansi, Brasserie steak pomme frites. Own baking, pasta. Valet parking. Outdoor dining. Authentic French brasserie decor; casual European elegance. Cr cds: A, C, D, DS, JCB, MC, V.

D ⊿

★ ★ ★ **BUCKINGHAM'S.** *(See Hilton & Towers Hotel)* 312/294-6600. Web www.hilton.com. Hrs: 5:30-10 pm; Sun brunch 10 am-2 pm. Res accepted. Bar. Wine list. A la carte entrees: dinner $16.50-$26.95. Sun brunch $37.95. Prix fixe: dinner $33.95. Child's meals. Specialties: Australian lamb chops, Buckingham's porterhouse, Maryland crab cakes. Own baking. Valet parking. Elegant decor; cherrywood pillars, Italian marble; artwork. Cr cds: A, C, D, DS, ER, JCB, MC, V.

D ⊿

★ ★ **CAPE COD ROOM.** *(See The Drake Hotel)* 312/787-2200. Web www.hilton.com. Hrs: noon-11 pm. Closed Dec 25. Res accepted. International seafood menu. Bar. Semi-a la carte: lunch, dinner $19-$37. Specialties: Maryland crab cakes, turbot, bookbinder's soup. Own baking. Valet parking. Nautical decor. View of Lake Michigan. Cr cds: A, C, D, DS, ER, JCB, MC, V.

D ⊿

★ ★ ★ **CELEBRITY CAFE.** *(See Westin River North Chicago Hotel)* 312/836-5499. Hrs: 6:30-11 am, 11:30 am-10:30 pm; Fri, Sat to 11 pm; Sun brunch 10 am-2 pm. Res accepted. Bar from 11 am. A la carte entrees: bkfst $7-$13, lunch $6-$14, dinner $14-$25. Sun brunch $39. Child's meals. Specialties: sea bass wrapped in crispy potato, grilled 16-oz prime sirloin steak, grilled salmon with honey-mustard glaze. Menu changes seasonally. Own pastries. Valet parking. Overlooks Chicago River. Cr cds: A, C, D, DS, ER, JCB, MC, V.

D ⊿

★ **CENTRO.** *710 N Wells St, River North.* 312/988-7775. Hrs: 11 am-11 pm; Fri, Sat to 11:30 pm; Sun 4-10 pm. Closed Easter, Dec 25. Res accepted. Italian menu. Bar. A la carte entrees: lunch $6-$12, dinner $7.50-$25. Specialties: pappardelle, chicken Vesuvio, baked cavatelli. Valet parking. Outdoor dining. Bistro atmosphere. Cr cds: A, C, D, DS, MC, V.

D ⊿

✔★ ★ ★ **CHAPULIN.** *1962 N Halsted St (60614), Lincoln Park.* 773/665-8677. Hrs: 5-10:30 pm; Fri, Sat to 11:30 pm. Closed Mon; major hols. Res accepted. Mexican menu. Bar. Semi-a la carte: dinner $10-$19. Specialties: molcajete with grilled chicken, grilled pork loin in anchiote, red snapper Vera Cruz. Valet parking. Mexican decor with vibrant colors, original artwork by local artist Oscar Romero. Cr cds: A, C, D, DS, MC, V.

D

★ ★ ★ ★ **CHARLIE TROTTER'S.** *816 W Armitage Ave, Lincoln Park.* 773/248-6228. A young culinary wizard named Charlie Trotter puts his magic to work in a contemporary restaurant offering two six-course dinner menus, one of them a vegetable tasting menu. There are three dining rooms, plus a chic table for four set up in the busy kitchen. American menu with French and Asian influences. Specialties: hand-harvested sea scallop, organic beef strip loin, artichoke & goat cheese terrine. Two dégustation menus available nightly. Own baking. Hrs: 5:30-10 pm. Closed Sun, Mon; major hols. Res required. Bar. Wine cellars. A la carte entrees: dinner $32-$40. Table d'hôte (dégustation menu): dinner $70-$90. Valet parking. Chef-owned. Jacket. Totally nonsmoking. Cr cds: A, C, D, JCB, MC, V.

D

★ ★ **CHICAGO CHOP HOUSE.** *60 W Ontario St (60610), River North.* 312/787-7100. Hrs: 11:30 am-11 pm; Fri to 11:30 pm; Sat 4-11:30 pm; Sun 4-11 pm. Closed some major hols. Res accepted. Bar. Semi-a la carte: lunch $5.95-$18.95, dinner $15.95-$28.95. Specializes in prime rib, NY strip steak, lamb chops. Valet parking. Entertainment. Turn-of-the-century Chicago decor. Cr cds: A, C, D, DS, JCB, MC, V.

D

★ ★ ★ **CIELO.** *(See Omni Chicago Hotel)* 312/944-7676. Hrs: 6:30 am-10 pm; Fri, Sat to 11 pm; Sun brunch 10:30 am-2 pm. Res accepted. Mediterranean menu. Bar to midnight. Wine list. A la carte entrees: bkfst $4.95-$11.95, lunch $8.25-$12.50, dinner $8.50-$30. Sun brunch $24.95. Specialties: soft shell crabs, wood-burned pizza. Pianist, vocalist Tues-Sat. Valet parking. Elegant, stylish dining with view of city. Original art. Cr cds: A, C, D, DS, JCB, MC, V.

D

★ ★ **CLUB GENE & GEORGETTI.** *500 N Franklin St (60610), River North.* 312/527-3718. Hrs: 11:30 am-midnight. Closed Sun; major hols; also 1st wk July. Res accepted. Italian, Amer menu. Bar. Semi-a la carte: lunch $7-$18, dinner $12.50-$23.50. Specialties: prime strip steak, filet mignon, chicken Vesuvio. Valet parking. Chicago saloon atmosphere. Family-owned. Cr cds: A, C, D, MC, V.

D

★ ★ ★ **COCO PAZZO.** *300 W Hubbard St, River North.* 312/836-0900. Hrs: 11:30 am-2:30 pm, 5:30-10:30 pm; Fri to 11 pm; Sat 5:30-11 pm; Sun 5-10 pm. Closed major hols. Res accepted. Italian menu. Serv bar. Semi-a la carte: lunch $10.95-$16, dinner $12-$27. Specializes in Tuscan dishes, cacciucco, bistecca alla Florentina. Own baking. Valet parking. Outdoor dining. Contemporary decor. Cr cds: A, C, D, MC, V.

D

★ ★ **COMO INN.** *546 N Milwaukee Ave, north of the Loop.* 312/421-5222. Hrs: 11:30 am-11 pm; Fri, Sat to midnight; Sun noon-11 pm. Closed some major hols. Res accepted. Northern Italian menu. Bar. A la carte entrees: lunch $5.95-$12.95, dinner $12.95-$22.95. Child's meals. Specialties: chicken Vesuvio, veal al limone, veal Marsala. Pianist (dinner). Valet parking. Italian decor; antiques. Family-owned. Cr cds: A, C, D, DS, MC, V.

D

★ ★ **CON FUSION.** *1616 N Damen Ave (60647), in Bucktown, north of the Loop.* 773/772-7100. Hrs: 11:30 am-2 pm, 5:30-10 pm; Fri to 11 pm; Sat 5:30-11 pm; Sun 5:30-9 pm. Closed major hols. Res accepted. Fusion menu. Bar. A la carte entrees: lunch $8-$9, dinner $14-$23. Specialties: tuna tartar with ginger wasabi dressing, sautéed breast of duck in black peppercorn sauce, roasted loin of ostrich. Own baking. Valet parking. Outdoor dining. Minimalist decor with black and white furnishings. Cr cds: A, D, MC, V.

D

★ ★ ★ **CUISINES.** *(See Renaissance Hotel)* 312/372-4459. Hrs: 11:30 am-2 pm, 5:30-10:30 pm. Closed major hols. Res accepted. Mediterranean menu. Bar. Wine cellar. Semi-a la carte: lunch $6.95-$16.95, dinner $6.95-$24.95. Specialities: veal medallions with wild mushrooms, crabmeat & Shiitake mushrooms in phyllo with smoked tomato coulis,

seared snapper with artichokes. Valet parking. Intimate dining in Mediterranean atmosphere. Cr cds: A, C, D, DS, ER, JCB, MC, V.

D

★ ★ **ELI'S THE PLACE FOR STEAK.** *215 E Chicago Ave, north of the Loop.* 312/642-1393. Hrs: 11 am-3 pm, 5-10:30 pm; Fri to 11 pm; Sat, Sun from 5 pm. Closed major hols. Res accepted. Bar to midnight. Semi-a la carte: lunch $8.95-$12.95, dinner $19.95-$32.95. Specializes in steak, liver. Own cheesecake. Piano bar. Valet parking. Club-like atmosphere; original artwork of Chicago scenes. Cr cds: A, C, D, DS, MC, V.

D

★ **EMILIO'S TAPAS.** *444 W Fullerton St (60614), Lincoln Park.* 773/327-5100. Hrs: 11:30 am-10 pm; Fri, Sat to 11 pm. Closed major hols. Res accepted. Spanish tapas menu. Bar. A la carte entrees: lunch $3.50-$7.95, dinner $3.50-$16.95. Specialties: garlic potato salad, baked goat cheese, paella de mariscos. Own pastries. Valet parking. Outdoor dining. Casual Spanish garden atmosphere; overlooks courtyard. Cr cds: A, D, MC, V.

D

★ **EMPEROR'S CHOICE.** *2238 S Wentworth Ave, Chinatown.* 312/225-8800. Hrs: 11:45-12:30 am; Sun to 11:30 pm. Cantonese seafood menu. Serv bar. A la carte entrees: lunch, dinner $6.95-$19.95. Semi-a la carte (Mon-Fri): lunch $5.95-$9.95. Prix fixe: dinner for two $38-$58. Specialties: whole steamed oysters with black bean sauce, lobster, poached shrimp in shell with soy dip. Chinese artifacts including Ching dynasty emperor's robe; ink drawings of emperors from each dynasty. Cr cds: A, DS, MC, V.

D

★ ★ **ENTRE NOUS.** *(See Fairmont Hotel)* 312/565-7997. Hrs: 5:30-10:30 pm; Sat to 11 pm. Closed Sun. Res accepted. Continental menu. Bar. Extensive wine list. Semi-a la carte: dinner $18-$27. Prix fixe: dinner $29. Specializes in regional Amer cuisine, seasonal dishes. Pianist. Valet parking. Elegant dining. Cr cds: A, C, D, DS, ER, JCB, MC, V.

D

★ ★ **ERWIN.** *2995 N Halsted St (60657), Lakeview.* 773/528-7200. Hrs: 5:30-10 pm; Fri, Sat to 11 pm; Sun 5-9:30 pm. Sun brunch 10:30 am-2:30 pm. Closed Mon; most major hols. Res accepted. Bar. Semi-a la carte: dinner $12.95-$16.95. Sun brunch $3.95-$9.95. Specializes in smoked trout appetizers, wood-grilled pork tenderloin, fresh seafood. Valet parking. Casual bistro atmosphere. Cr cds: A, C, D, DS, MC, V.

D

★ ★ ★ ★ ★ **EVEREST.** *440 S La Salle St, 40th floor of Midwest Stock Exchange, the Loop.* 312/663-8920. Chef/owner Jean Joho has brought fine Alsatian cuisine and a broad array of appropriate wines to this 40th-floor, art deco-ish aerie with African safari murals in a downtown Chicago financial skycraper. Creative French menu with Alsatian influence. Specialties: marbre of cold bouillabaisse, seafood and shellfish; Maine lobster with Alsace gewurztraminer and ginger; poached tenderloin of beef, pot au feu style, with horseradish cream. Hrs: 5:30-9:30 pm (last sitting); Fri, Sat to 10 pm (last sitting). Closed Sun, Mon; major hols. Res required. Serv bar. Extensive wine list; specializes in wines from Alsace. A la carte entrees: dinner $23-$35. Prix fixe: 8-course dinner $79. Free valet parking. Chef-owned. Jacket. Cr cds: A, C, D, DS, JCB, MC, V.

D

★ ★ ★ **FRONTERA GRILL.** *445 N Clark St, River North.* 312/661-1434. Hrs: 11:30 am-2:30 pm, 5-10 pm; Fri to 11 pm; Sat 5-11 pm; Sat brunch 10:30 am-2:30 pm. Closed Sun, Mon. Mexican menu. Bar. A la carte entrees: lunch $8-$12, dinner $9-$18.95. Sat brunch $5.95-$9.50. Specialties: grilled fresh fish, duck breast adobo, carne asada. Valet parking. Outdoor dining. Regional Mexican cuisine; casual dining. Cr cds: A, C, D, DS, MC, V.

D

★ **GEJA'S.** *340 W Armitage Ave, Lincoln Park.* 773/281-9101. Hrs: 5-10:30 pm; Fri to midnight; Sat to 12:30 am; Sun 4:30-10 pm.

Closed some major hols. Res accepted Sun-Thurs. Fondue menu. Bar. Complete meals: dinner $18.50-$29.95. Specializes in cheese, meat, seafood & dessert fondues. Flamenco and classical guitarist nightly. Variety of wines, sold by the glass. Cr cds: A, C, D, DS, MC, V.

★ ★ **GIBSONS STEAKHOUSE.** *1028 N Rush St (60611), north of the Loop.* 312/266-8999. Hrs: 3 pm-1 am; Sun 4 pm-midnight. Closed major hols. Bar 3 pm-2 am. Wine list. Semi-a la carte: dinner $10-$32. Specializes in prime-aged steak, Chicago-cut steak, fresh seafood. Pianist in bar nightly. Valet parking. Art deco decor. Cr cds: A, C, D, DS, MC, V.

★ ★ ★ **GORDON.** *500 N Clark St, River North.* 312/467-9780. Hrs: noon-2 pm, 5:30-9:30 pm; Mon from 5:30 pm; Fri to 11:30 pm; Sat 5:30 pm-midnight; Sun 5-9:30 pm. Closed major hols. Res accepted. Bar. Wine list. A la carte entrees: lunch $8-$15, dinner $14-$29. Pre-theatre menu (3 courses): $29. Specialties: original artichoke fritter, flourless chocolate cake. Menu changes seasonally. Own pastries, ice cream. Pianist nightly, jazz trio Sat (winter). Valet parking. Jacket (dinner). Cr cds: A, C, D, DS, JCB, MC, V.

★ ★ **GRAPPA.** *200 E Chestnut St (60611), north of the Loop.* 312/337-4500. Hrs: 11:30 am-2:30 pm, 5-10 pm; Fri, Sat to 11 pm. Closed most major hols. Res accepted. Italian menu. Bar. Semi-a la carte: lunch $7.95-$12.95, dinner $11.95-$24.95. Specialties: grilled tuna, rabbit, seafood stew. Valet parking. Sophisticated trattoria-style decor; open cooking area. Cr cds: A, C, D, DS, JCB, MC, V.

✔★ ★ **GREEK ISLANDS.** *200 S Halsted St, Greektown.* 312/782-9855. Hrs: 11 am-midnight; Fri, Sat to 1 am. Closed Thanksgiving, Dec 25. Res accepted Sun-Thurs. Greek, Amer menu. Bar. A la carte entrees: lunch $5-$8.50, dinner $5.95-$15.95. Complete meals: lunch, dinner $9.95-$16.95. Specialties: lamb with artichoke, broiled red snapper, saganaki. Valet parking. Greek decor; 5 dining areas. Family-owned. Cr cds: A, C, D, DS, MC, V.

★ ★ **HARRY CARAY'S.** *33 W Kinzie St, at Dearborn St, River North.* 312/828-0966. Web www.harrycarays.com. Hrs: 11:30 am-3 pm, 5-10:30 pm; Fri to 11 pm; Sat 5-11 pm; Sun 4-10 pm. Closed Dec 25. Res accepted. Italian, Amer menu. Bar. A la carte entrees: lunch, dinner $8.95-$39.95. Specializes in chicken Vesuvio, lamb chop oreganato, steak. Valet parking. Baseball memorabilia. Cr cds: A, C, D, DS, MC, V.

✔★ ★ **HAT DANCE.** *325 W Huron St, River North.* 312/649-0066. Hrs: 11:30 am-2 pm, 5:30-10 pm; Fri to 11:30 pm; Sat 11:30 am-3:30 pm, 5-11:30 pm; Sun 5-9 pm. Closed most major hols. Res accepted. Nouvelle Mexican menu. Bar. A la carte entrees: lunch $6-$10.95, dinner $7.95-$15.95. Specialties: corn pudding, marinated pork chops, wood-roasted chicken. Valet parking evenings. Outdoor snack bar. Unique decor with Aztec accents. Cr cds: A, C, D, DS, MC, V.

★ ★ **HATSUHANA.** *160 E Ontario St, north of the Loop.* 312/280-8808. Hrs: 11:45 am-2 pm, 5:30-10 pm; Sat from 5 pm. Closed Sun; some major hols. Res accepted. Japanese menu. Serv bar. A la carte entrees: lunch $9-$19, dinner $10-$24. Complete meals: dinner $14-$26. Specialties: tempura, Hatsuhana and sushi specials. Sushi bar. Traditional Japanese decor. Cr cds: A, C, D, JCB, MC, V.

★ **HOUSE OF HUNAN.** *535 N Michigan Ave, north of the Loop.* 312/329-9494. Hrs: 11:30 am-10:30 pm. Closed Thanksgiving. Res accepted. Chinese menu. Bar. Semi-a la carte: lunch $6.95-$9.50, dinner $8.95-$19.95. Specialties: spicy beef & scallops, Neptune delight, empress chicken. Chinese decor. Cr cds: A, C, D, DS, JCB, MC, V.

★ ★ **IL TOSCANACCIO.** *636 N St Clair St (60611), north of the Loop.* 312/664-2777. Hrs: 7:30-10 am, 11:30 am-2:30 pm; 5:30-10:30 pm; Fri to 11 pm; Sat 5:30-11 pm; Sun 5-10 pm; Sat, Sun brunch 11:30 am-3 pm. Res accepted. Italian menu. Bar. A la carte entrees: bkfst $1.50-$2.50, lunch $11.50-$15, dinner $11-$17. Sat, Sun brunch $8-$12. Specialties: rigatoni Toscanaccio, grilled portabello mushroom with roasted peppers, salmon filet sautéed with shrimp. Own pasta. Valet parking (dinner). Outdoor dining. Casual, rustic Italian atmosphere with murals, wrought-iron fixtures. Cr cds: A, D, MC, V.

★ ★ **IRON MIKE'S GRILLE.** (See Tremont Hotel) 312/587-8989. Hrs: 7 am-11 pm; Sun brunch 11 am-3 pm. Res accepted. Bar. Buffet: bkfst $8.95. A la carte entrees: lunch $10-$15, dinner $30-$45. Sun brunch $10-$15. Specialties: duck cigar, Iron Mike's 20-oz pork chop, paddle steak. Own baking. Pianist exc Mon. Valet parking. Outdoor dining. Sports club atmosphere; tribute to former Chicago Bears coach. Cr cds: A, C, D, DS, ER, JCB, MC, V.

✔★ ★ **KIKI'S BISTRO.** *900 N Franklin (60610), River North.* 312/335-5454. Hrs: 11:30 am-10 pm; Fri to 11 pm; Sat 5-11 pm. Closed Sun; major hols. Res accepted. French Provençale menu. Bar. Semi-a la carte: lunch $7-$14.50, dinner $12-$17. Specialties: roasted chicken, sautéed duck breast with leg confit, sautéed calves liver with pearl onions. Own desserts, ice cream. Rustic, country-French decor with unfinished woodwork, brick walls. Cr cds: A, C, D, DS, MC, V.

★ ★ **KLAY OVEN.** *414 N Orleans St, River North.* 312/527-3999. Hrs: 11:30 am-2:30 pm, 5:30-10:30 pm. Closed major hols. Res accepted. Indian menu. Bar. A la carte entrees: lunch buffet $7.95, dinner $6.95-$25.95. Specialties: sikandari champa, tandoori batera, jheenga bemisaal. Tableside preparation in elegant surroundings. Modern Indian art display. Cr cds: A, D, MC, V.

★ ★ ★ **LA STRADA.** *155 N Michigan Ave, opp Grant Park, at Randolph St, the Loop.* 312/565-2200. Hrs: 11:30 am-10 pm; Fri to 11 pm, Sat 5-11 pm; early-bird dinner 5-6:30 pm. Closed Sun; some major hols. Res accepted. Northern Italian menu. Bar. Wine cellar. A la carte entrees: lunch $11-$15, dinner $11-$29. Specialties: zuppe de pesce, red snapper, veal scaloppini. Own baking, desserts. Pianist from 5 pm. Valet parking. Tableside cooking. Cr cds: A, C, D, DS, MC, V.

★ ★ ★ **LAWRY'S THE PRIME RIB.** *100 E Ontario St, north of the Loop.* 312/787-5000. Hrs: 11:30 am-2 pm, 5-11 pm; Fri, Sat to midnight; Sun 3-10 pm. Closed July 4, Dec 25. Res accepted. Bar. Wine list. Semi-a la carte: lunch $5.75-$10.95, dinner $19.95-$29.95. Child's meals. Specializes in prime rib, English trifle. Own baking. Valet parking (dinner). In 1896 McCormick mansion. Chicago counterpart of famous California restaurant. Cr cds: A, C, D, DS, JCB, MC, V.

✔★ **LE BOUCHON.** *1958 N Damen Ave (60647), in Bucktown, north of the Loop.* 773/862-6600. Hrs: 5:30-11 pm; Fri, Sat 5 pm-midnight. Closed Sun; major hols. Res accepted. French menu. Bar. Semi-a la carte: dinner $11-$14.95. Specialties: roast duck for two, Jean Claude onion tart, maravis au choclat. Own pastries, desserts. French bistro decor with lace curtains, pressed-tin ceiling. Cr cds: A, C, D, DS, MC, V.

★ ★ ★ **LES NOMADES.** *222 E Ontario St (60611), north of the Loop.* 312/649-9010. Hrs: 5-9:30 pm; Fri, Sat to 10:30 pm. Closed Sun, Mon; most major hols. Res accepted. French menu. Bar. Wine list. A la carte entrees: dinner $18-$26. Specialties: grilled razor clams, cochon de lait braised in white wine and Dijon mustard. Own baking, pasta. Valet parking. Contemporary French decor; polished woods, tile murals, zinc bar. Jacket. Totally nonsmoking. Cr cds: A, C, D, MC, V.

★ ★ **MAGGIANO'S.** *516 N Clark St (60610), River North.* *312/644-7700.* Hrs: 11:30 am-2 pm, 5-10 pm; Fri to 11 pm; Sat 11:30 am-11 pm; Sun noon-10 pm. Closed Thanksgiving, Dec 25. Res accepted. Southern Italian menu. Bar. A la carte entrees: lunch $7.95-$14.95, dinner $9.95-$29.95. Specialties: Maggiano's salad, country-style rigatoni, roasted chicken with rosemary. Own baking. Valet parking. Outdoor dining. 1940s, family-style decor with wood columns and bistro-style seating. Cr cds: A, C, D, DS, MC, V.

D

★ ★ **MANGO.** *712 N Clark St (60610), River North. 312/337-5440.* Hrs: 11:30 am-2 pm, 5-11 pm; Fri to midnight; Sat 5 pm-midnight; Sun 4-9 pm. Closed most major hols. Res accepted. Contemporary Amer menu. Bar. A la carte entrees: lunch $8-$13, dinner $9-$17. Specialties: duck mango with proscuitto, Mediterranean fish soup, Wright's flourless chocolate cake. Own baking. Lively atmosphere with vibrant colors, artwork. Cr cds: A, C, D, DS, MC, V.

D

★ ★ **MARCHÉ.** *833 Randolph St, north of the Loop. 312/226-8399.* Hrs: 11:30 am-2 pm, 5:30-10 pm; Thurs to 11 pm; Fri to midnight; Sat 5:30 pm-midnight; Sun from 5:30 pm. Closed major hols. Res accepted. French menu. Bar. Wine list. A la carte entrees: lunch $8-$15, dinner $13-$29. Specialties: spit-roasted chicken with pommes frites, spit-roasted rabbit with lavender sauce, yellowfin tuna. Own baking, desserts. Valet parking. Contemporary decor with custom-crafted furnishings, open kitchens. Cr cds: A, C, D, MC, V.

D

✔★ ★ **MIA FRANCESCA.** *3311 N Clark St, in Lakeview. 773/281-3310.* Hrs: 5-10:30 pm; Fri, Sat to 11 pm; Sun to 10:30 pm. Closed major hols. Italian menu. Bar. A la carte entrees: dinner $7.95-$18.95. Child's meals. Specialities: linguine Sugo di scampi, skatewing al Balsamic, penne Siciliana. Valet parking. Marble colonnades; photographs of Rome. Cr cds: A, MC, V.

D

★ ★ ★ **MORTON'S.** *1050 N State St, north of the Loop. 312/266-4820.* Hrs: 5:30-11 pm; Sun 5-10 pm. Closed major hols. Res accepted. Bar. Wine cellar. A la carte entrees: dinner $17-$30. Specialties: Maine lobster, prime dry-aged porterhouse steak, Sicilian veal chops. Valet parking. Menu on blackboard. English club atmosphere, decor. Cr cds: A, C, D, DS, JCB, MC, V.

D

✔★ **N.N. SMOKEHOUSE.** *1465 W Irving Park (60613), Lakeview. 773/868-4700.* Hrs: 11:30 am-10 pm; Fri to 11 pm; Sat noon-11 pm; Sun noon-9 pm. Closed Mon; most major hols. Wine, beer. Semi-a la carte: lunch $4.75-$9.50, dinner $5.85-$14.75. Child's meals. Specialties: spare ribs, Memphis pulled pork, Mississippi fried catfish. Own baking. Casual southern smokehouse atmosphere. Cr cds: C, D, DS, MC, V.

D ♥

★ ★ **NICK'S FISHMARKET.** *1 First National Plaza, Dearborn & Monroe Sts, the Loop. 312/621-0200.* E-mail nicks@earthlink.net; web www.harmonnickolas.com. Hrs: 11:30 am-3 pm, 5:30-11 pm; Fri to midnight; Sat 5:30 pm-midnight. Closed Sun; major hols. Res accepted. Bar 11-2 am. A la carte entrees: lunch $8.50-$55, dinner $14-$55. Specializes in fresh seafood, live Maine lobster, veal. Pianist exc Mon (dinner). Valet parking. Braille menu. Cr cds: A, C, D, DS, JCB, MC, V.

D

★ ★ **NIX.** *(See Regal Knickerbocker Hotel) 312/751-8100.* Hrs: 6 am-10:30 pm; Sun brunch 9 am-2 pm. Res accepted. Bar. A la carte entrees: bkfst $6-$10.50, lunch $8-$9, dinner $14-$26. Sun brunch $15.95. Child's meals. Specialties: fajita egg rolls, southwestern Peking duck, grilled lamb chop in wonton shell. Own desserts. Valet parking. Outdoor dining. Crisp, contemporary decor; casual dining. Cr cds: A, C, D, DS, JCB, MC, V.

D

★ ★ **PALM.** *(See Swissôtel Hotel) 312/616-1000.* Hrs: 11:30 am-11 pm. Res accepted. Bar. A la carte entrees: lunch $14-$32. Specializes in prime aged beef, jumbo Nova Scotia lobsters, fresh seafood. Own desserts. Valet parking. Outdoor dining. Casual, energetic atmosphere; caricatures of celebrities and regular customers line walls. Family-owned. Cr cds: A, C, D, MC, V.

D

✔★ ★ **PAPAGUS.** *(See Embassy Suites Hotel) 312/642-8450.* Hrs: 11:30 am-10 pm; Fri to midnight; Sat noon-midnight; Sun noon-10 pm. Res accepted. Greek menu. Bar. A la carte entrees: lunch $8-$15, dinner $7.75-$24.95. Specializes in braised lamb with orzo, Greek chicken, seafood. Valet parking. Outdoor dining. Rustic, country taverna atmosphere. Cr cds: A, C, D, DS, JCB, MC, V.

D

★ ★ ★ **PARK AVENUE CAFE.** *(See Doubletree Guest Suites) 312/944-4414.* Hrs: 5-11 pm; Sun to 10 pm; Sun brunch 10:30 am-2 pm. Closed Jan 1, Dec 25. Res accepted. Contemporary Amer menu. Bar. Wine list. A la carte entrees: dinner $18.50-$29.75. Tasting menu: dinner $52. Sun brunch $30. Specialties: brioche-crusted cod with wild mushrooms, pot au feu of squab, hot and cold foie gras. Own baking, pasta. Valet parking. Warm atmosphere with antique barber poles and American folk art. Cr cds: A, C, D, DS, JCB, MC, V.

D

✔★ **PARTHENON.** *314 S Halsted St (60661), Greektown. 312/726-2407.* Hrs: 11-1 am; Sat to 2 am. Closed Thanksgiving, Dec 25. Greek, Amer menu. Bar. A la carte entrees: lunch $4.95-$9.95, dinner $5.95-$10. Child's meals. Specializes in broiled whole fresh fish, saganaki, lamb. Free valet parking. Ancient Greek decor. Family-owned. Cr cds: A, C, D, DS, MC, V.

D

★ ★ ★ **PRAIRIE.** *(See Hyatt On Printers Row Hotel) 312/663-1143.* Hrs: 6:30-10 am, 11:30 am-2 pm, 5:30-10 pm; Fri to 11 pm; Sat 7 am-2 pm, 5:30-11 pm; Sun 7-10:30 am, 5:30-10 pm; Sun brunch (winter) 10 am-2 pm. Res accepted. Bar. A la carte entrees: bkfst $5-$7, lunch, dinner $14-$26. Sun brunch $9-$16. Specialties: grilled baby Coho salmon with bacon, leeks and black walnuts; grilled sturgeon with vegetables and wild rice; grilled buffalo steak. Own pastries. Seasonal menu. Valet parking. Decor in the style of Frank Lloyd Wright; oak trim, architectural photographs and drawings. Cr cds: A, C, D, DS, ER, JCB, MC, V.

D

★ ★ ★ **PRINTER'S ROW.** *550 S Dearborn St, south of the Loop. 312/461-0780.* Hrs: 11:30 am-2:30 pm, 5-10 pm; Fri to 11 pm; Sat 5-11 pm. Closed Sun; major hols. Res accepted. Continental menu. Bar. Wine list. A la carte entrees: lunch $8.75-$12.95, dinner $14.95-$21.95. Specializes in fresh seafood, duck, seasonal game. Own pastries, desserts. In old printing building (1897). Cr cds: A, C, D, DS, MC, V.

D

★ ★ ★ **PUMP ROOM.** *(See Omni Ambassador East Hotel) 312/266-0360.* Hrs: 7 am-2:30 pm, 6-11:45 pm; Sun 7-11 am, 5-9:45 pm; Sun brunch 11 am-2:30 pm. Res accepted. Bar. Wine list. A la carte entrees: bkfst $6-$10.50. A la carte entrees: lunch $10.50-$15.95, dinner $17.50-$30.50. Sun brunch $25.95. Specializes in seared salmon, prime rib, lamb chops. Own pastries, sorbet. Pianist. Valet parking. Famous dining rm; was once haunt of stars, celebrities; celebrity photographs. Cr cds: A, C, D, DS, MC, V.

✔★ **REDFISH.** *400 N State St (60610), River North. 312/467-0325.* Hrs: 11:30 am-10 pm; Fri to 11 pm; Sat noon-11 pm; Sun noon-10 pm. Closed most major hols. Res accepted. Cajun/Creole menu. Bar to midnight. Semi-a la carte: lunch $10-$18, dinner $15-$18. Child's meals. Specialties: redfish, jambalaya. Jazz & blues Thurs-Sat. Valet parking. Outdoor dining. Louisiana roadhouse with Mardi Gras decor; masks, voodoo doll displays. Cr cds: A, C, D, DS, JCB, MC, V.

D

★ ★ **RELISH.** *2044 N Halsted St, Lincoln Park. 312/868-9034.* Hrs: 5:15-10 pm; Fri, Sat to 11 pm; Sun to 9 pm. Res accepted. Continental menu. Bar. A la carte entrees: dinner $9.50-$16.75. Specialties: shrimp-stuffed brook trout, wild mushroom and goat cheese picnic, herb-stuffed chicken. Valet parking. Outdoor dining. California atmosphere. Original paintings by local artists. Chef-owned. Cr cds: A, C, D, MC, V.

[D]

★ ★ ★ ★ **RITZ-CARLTON DINING ROOM.** *(See The Ritz-Carlton Hotel) 312/227-5866.* Burled wood paneling, crystal chandeliers and forest-green banquettes lend elegance to this split-level dining room classic. French-inspired menu. Specialties: lobster with couscous, New Zealand venison steak in pepper crust, Colorado rack of lamb glazed with thyme and honey. Own pastries. Hrs: 6-11 pm; Sun to 10:30 pm; Sun brunch 10:30 am-2:30 pm. Res accepted. Bar. A la carte entrees: dinner $26-$37. Sun brunch $42. Pianist. Valet parking. Menu changes daily. Cr cds: A, C, D, DS, ER, JCB, MC, V.

[D] [↵]

★ ★ ★ **RIVA.** *700 E Grand Ave (60611), at Navy Pier, north of the Loop. 312/644-7482.* Hrs: 11:30 am-3 pm, 5-11 pm; Fri, Sat to midnight; Sun noon-9 pm. Res accepted. Continental menu. Bar. Wine list. A la carte entrees: lunch $12.95-$26.95, dinner $14.95-$31.95. Specialties: filet of tuna, cedar plank fish, Chilean sea bass. Own baking, pasta. Valet parking. Semi-formal atmosphere with striking views of Lake Michigan and Chicago skyline. Cr cds: A, DS, MC, V.

[D] [↵]

★ ★ **RUSSIAN TEA CAFE.** *63 E Adams St (60604), the Loop. 312/360-0000.* Hrs: 11 am-11 pm; Mon to 4 pm; Fri to midnight; Sat noon-midnight; Sun 1-9 pm. Closed Jan 1, Memorial Day. Res accepted. Russian, Ukrainian menu. Bar. Semi-a la carte: lunch $7-$13, dinner $18-$27. Specializes in borscht, shashlik, wild game. Traditional caviar service. Russian dolls on display. Cr cds: A, C, D, DS, JCB, MC, V.

[D] [↵]

★ ★ **THE SALOON.** *200 E Chestnut (60611), north of the Loop. 312/280-5454.* Hrs: 11 am-11 pm. Closed some major hols. Res accepted. Bar. Semi-a la carte: lunch $5.95-$11.95, dinner $14.95-$27.95. Specializes in steak, prime rib, fresh seafood. Modern steakhouse atmosphere. Cr cds: A, C, D, DS, MC, V.

[D] [↵]

★ ★ **SALPICÓN.** *1252 N Wells St (60610), Gold Coast. 312/988-7811.* E-mail seviche@msn.com; web www.salpicon.com. Hrs: 5-10 pm; Fri, Sat to 11 pm; early-bird dinner to 6:30 pm; Sun brunch 11 am-2:30 pm. Closed Tues; Jan 1, Thanksgiving, Dec 25. Res accepted. Mexican menu. Bar. Semi-a la carte: dinner $12.95-$21.95. Complete meal: dinner $19.95. Tasting menu: $37. Sun brunch $8.95-$15.95. Specialties: shrimp with garlic sauce, beef tenderloin with wild mushrooms, lamb loin chops with garlic pasilla chile sauce. Own desserts. Valet parking. Outdoor dining. Casual yet elegant atmosphere with vibrant colors, original artwork. Totally nonsmoking. Cr cds: A, C, D, DS, MC, V.

[D]

★ ★ **SANTORINI.** *800 W Adams St, Greektown. 312/829-8820.* Hrs: 11 am-midnight; Fri, Sat to 1 am. Closed Thanksgiving, Dec 25. Res accepted. Greek menu. Bar. A la carte entrees: lunch $6.50-$13.95, dinner $9.95-$22.95. Specializes in fresh seafood, grilled lamb chops, Greek-style chicken. Valet parking. Simulated Greek town. Cr cds: A, D, MC, V.

[D] [↵]

★ **SAYAT NOVA.** *157 E Ohio St (60611), north of the Loop. 312/644-9159.* Hrs: 11:30 am-10:30 pm; Sat noon-11 pm; Sun 3-10 pm. Closed major hols. Res accepted. Armenian menu. Bar. Semi-a la carte: lunch $6.95-$11.95, dinner $9.90-$16.95. Specializes in lamb chops, charbroiled kebab, cous cous. Family-owned. Cr cds: A, C, D, DS, MC, V.

[↵]

★ **SCHULIEN'S.** *2100 W Irving Park Rd, Lakeview. 773/478-2100.* Hrs: 11:30 am-midnight; Fri to 1 am; Sat 4 pm-1 am; Sun 4-10 pm.

Closed Mon. German, Amer menu. Bar. Semi-a la carte: lunch $5.95-$11, dinner $10.95-$21.95. Specialties: barbecued ribs, Wienerschnitzel, planked whitefish. Magician (dinner). Parking. Authentic Chicago saloon decor. Established 1886. Family-owned. Cr cds: A, C, D, DS, MC, V.

[↵]

★ ★ **SCOOZI.** *410 W Huron (60610), River North. 312/943-5900.* Hrs: 11:30 am-2 pm, 5-9:30 pm; Fri to 10:30 pm; Sat 5-10:30 pm; Sun 4-9 pm. Closed Thanksgiving, Dec 25. Res accepted. Italian menu. Bar. A la carte entrees: lunch $7-$15, dinner $7-$21. Specializes in woodburning-oven pizza, antipasti, homemade pasta. Own pasta, desserts. Valet parking. Outdoor dining. Casual atmosphere with loft-style ceilings, woodburning oven and antipasti bar. Cr cds: A, C, D, DS, JCB, MC, V.

[D] [↵]

★ ★ ★ **SEASONS.** *(See Four Seasons Hotel) 312/649-2349.* Walnut paneling and old porcelains grace this refined dining room. Specialties: potato-crusted Atlantic salmon with dill-mustard gnocchi, rack of lamb with garlic-roasted artichoke, Nantucket stew of lobster, crab & sunchokes. Menu changes seasonally. Own baking. Hrs: 6:30-9:30 am, 11:30 am-2 pm, 6-10 pm; Sun brunch 10:30 am-1:30 pm. Res accepted. Bar 11:30-1 am. A la carte entrees: bkfst $9.50-$15, lunch $12-$22, dinner $24-$36. Prix fixe: 3-course lunch $21.50, 5-course dinner $62. Sun brunch $45. Child's meals. Pianist, jazz trio Sat. Valet parking $15; validated self-parking $5. Jacket. Cr cds: A, C, D, DS, ER, JCB, MC, V.

[D] [↵] [♥]

★ ★ **SHAW'S CRAB HOUSE.** *21 E Hubbard St, north of the Loop. 312/527-2722.* Hrs: 11:30 am-10 pm; Fri, Sat to 11 pm; Sun from 5 pm. Closed Thanksgiving, Dec 25. Res accepted. A la carte entrees: lunch $7.95-$14.95, dinner $13.95-$23.95. Specializes in grilled fish, crab cakes, oysters. Entertainment Tues, Thurs 7-10 pm. Valet parking. Decor re-creates look and atmosphere of 1940s seafood house. Cr cds: A, C, D, DS, MC, V.

[D] [↵]

★ ★ **SIGNATURE ROOM AT THE 95th.** *875 N Michigan Ave (60611), in John Hancock Center, north of the Loop. 312/787-9596.* Hrs: 11 am-2 pm, 5-11 pm; Sat 11 am-2:30 pm, 5:30-11 pm; Sun brunch 10:30 am-2 pm. Closed Jan 1, Dec 25. Res accepted. Bar 11-12:30 am; Fri, Sat to 1:30 am. Semi-a la carte: lunch $5.95-$7.25. Buffet: lunch $8.75. A la carte entrees: dinner $21-$29.95. Specializes in seafood, lamb, beef. Pianist Fri, Sun; jazz trio Sat. Magnificent views of city and lake from 95th floor. Cr cds: A, C, D, DS, JCB, MC, V.

[D] [↵]

✔★ **SOLE MIO.** *917 W Armitage Ave, Lincoln Park. 773/477-5858.* Hrs: 11:30 am-2 pm, 5:30-10 pm; Fri, Sat 5:30-11 pm; Sun from 5:30 pm. Closed major hols. Res accepted. Italian, French menu. Bar. A la carte entrees: lunch, dinner $8.95-$16.95. Specialties: pappardelle verdi al prosciutto, grilled beef tenderloin, mushroom ravioli in gargonzola sauce. Valet parking (dinner). Cr cds: A, D, MC, V.

[↵]

★ ★ **SPAGO.** *520 N Dearborn St (60610), River North. 312/527-3700.* Hrs: 11:30 am-2:30 pm, 5:30-10 pm; Fri 11:30 am-2:30 pm, 5 pm-midnight; Sat 5 pm-midnight. Closed some major hols. Res accepted. Bar. A la carte entrees: lunch $11.50-$16.75, dinner $18.75-$28.50. Specializes in pasta, seafood, pizza with duck sausage. Own baking. Valet parking. Contemporary decor with light woods, vibrant colors. Cr cds: A, D, DS, MC, V.

[D]

★ ★ ★ ★ **SPIAGGIA.** *980 N Michigan Ave, on 2nd level of One Magnificent Mile building, north of the Loop. 312/280-2750.* Elegant, modern decor—complete with two-story atrium, arches and Italian marble colonnades—adds to the luxurious dining experience at Spiaggia. There are breathtaking views of Lake Michigan through 34-foot-high windows. Elaborate filled pasta dishes, delightful desserts and remarkable wines add adventure. Italian menu. Specialties: wood-roasted veal chops, skewered boneless quail, scallops with porcini mushrooms. Own pastries, pasta. Hrs: 11:30 am-2 pm, 5:30-9:30 pm; Fri, Sat to 10:30 pm; Sun 5:30-9 pm.

Closed major hols. Res accepted. Bar to 11 pm; Fri, Sat to midnight; Sun to 10 pm. Extensive wine list. A la carte entrees: lunch $8.95-$17.95, dinner $16.95-$32.95. Pianist (dinner). Seasonal menu. Parking. Jacket (dinner). Cr cds: A, C, D, DS, JCB, MC, V.

★ ★ ★ **SPRUCE.** *238 E Ontario St (60611), north of the Loop.* 312/642-3757. Hrs: 11:30 am-2 pm, 5:30-10 pm; Fri to 11 pm; Sat 5:30-11 pm. Closed Sun; major hols. Res accepted. Contemporary Amer menu. Bar 11:30 am-10 pm; Fri, Sat to 11 pm. Wine cellar. A la carte entrees: lunch $9-$19, dinner $17-$24. Tasting menu: lunch $15-$17, dinner $45. Specializes in seasonal dishes, chef's tasting menu. Own baking. Valet parking. Contemporary decor with light woods, large floral arrangements; below street level with windows looking out to sidewalk. Cr cds: A, D, DS, MC, V.

★ ★ **STREETERVILLE GRILLE & BAR.** *301 E North Water St (60611), north of the Loop.* 312/670-0788. Hrs: 11:30 am-10 pm; Sat 5-10:30 pm; Sun brunch 10 am-2 pm. Closed Jan 1, Dec 25. Res accepted. Serv bar. Semi-a la carte: lunch $8-$17. A la carte entrees: dinner $18-$30. Specializes in steak, prime rib, pasta. Valet parking. Outdoor dining. Cr cds: A, C, D, DS, ER, JCB, MC, V.

✔★ **SU CASA.** *49 E Ontario St, north of the Loop.* 312/943-4041. Hrs: 11:30 am-11 pm; Fri, Sat to midnight. Closed Thanksgiving, Dec 25. Res accepted. Mexican menu. Bar. Semi-a la carte: lunch, dinner $4.95-$12.95. Specialties: chicken poblano, shrimp a la Veracruzana, pan-fried red snapper. Valet parking. Outdoor dining. 16th-century Mexican decor; Mexican artifacts. Cr cds: A, C, D, DS, MC, V.

★ ★ **SZECHWAN EAST.** *340 E Ohio St (60611), north of the Loop.* 312/255-9200. Hrs: 11:30 am-2 pm, 5-10 pm; Sun brunch to 2 pm. Closed Thanksgiving. Res accepted. Chinese menu. Bar to 1 am. Buffet: lunch $8.95. A la carte entrees: dinner $7.95-$23.95. Sun brunch $15.95. Specialties: Governor's chicken, steamed black sea bass with ginger and scallions, orange beef. Valet parking. Outdoor dining. Chinese decor with large golden Buddha, etched glass. Cr cds: A, C, D, DS, JCB, MC, V.

★ ★ ★ **TOPOLOBAMPO.** *445 N Clark St, River North.* 312/661-1434. Regional Mexican menu. Specializes in gourmet cuisine featuring complex sauces, exotic wild game. Own pastries. Hrs: 11:30 am-2 pm, 5:30-9:30 pm; Fri, Sat 5:30-10:30 pm. Closed Sun, Mon. Res accepted. Bar. Wine list. A la carte entrees: lunch $8-$14, dinner $15.50-$22. Valet parking. Outdoor dining. Intimate dining. Cr cds: A, C, D, DS, MC, V.

★ ★ ★ **TRATTORIA NO. 10.** *10 N Dearborn St, the Loop.* 312/984-1718. Hrs: 11:30 am-2 pm, 5:30-9 pm; Fri to 10 pm; Sat 5:30-10 pm. Closed Sun; major hols. Res accepted. Italian menu. Bar. Wine list. A la carte entrees: lunch, dinner $10.95-$22.95. Specialties: ravioli, rack of lamb, veal chop. Own pastries. Valet parking. Dining in grotto-style trattoria. Cr cds: A, C, D, DS, MC, V.

★ ★ **TRATTORIA PARMA.** *400 N Clark St (60610), River North.* 312/245-9933. E-mail parma@vinci-group.com. Hrs: 11:30 am-2 pm, 5:30-10:30 pm; Sat 5:30-11 pm; Sun 4-9:30 pm. Closed some major hols. Res accepted. Italian menu. Bar. A la carte entrees: lunch $5.95-$11.95, dinner $9.95-$15.95. Specialties: stuffed rigatoni with tomato cream sauce, grilled pork chop with ricotto whipped potatoes. Valet parking (dinner). Outdoor dining. Murals of Venice, artwork. Cr cds: A, D, MC, V.

✔★ **TUCCI BENUCCH.** *900 N Michigan Ave, 5th floor, north of the Loop.* 312/266-2500. Hrs: 11:30 am-10 pm; Fri, Sat to 11 pm; Sun noon-9 pm. Closed Thanksgiving, Dec 25. Northern Italian menu. Bar. A la carte entrees: lunch, dinner $8.95-$13.95. Child's meals. Specializes in pasta, thin-crust pizza, salads. Own desserts. Replica of Italian country villa. Totally nonsmoking. Cr cds: A, C, D, DS, MC, V.

✔★ **TUCCI MILAN.** *6 W Hubbard St, north of the Loop.* 312/222-0044. Hrs: 11:30 am-10 pm; Fri to 11 pm; Sat noon-11 pm; Sun 5-9 pm. Res accepted. Northern Italian menu. Bar. A la carte entrees: lunch, dinner $6.95-$19. Specializes in fresh pastas, rotisserie items, organic vegetable dishes. Valet parking (dinner). Original art. Cr cds: A, C, D, DS, MC, V.

★ ★ **TUSCANY.** *1014 W Taylor St (60607), south of the Loop.* 312/829-1990. Hrs: 11 am-3:30 pm, 5-11 pm; Sat 5 pm-midnight; Sun 2-9:30 pm. Closed most major hols. Res accepted. Northern Italian menu. Bar. Semi-a la carte: lunch $8.95-$15, dinner $8.75-$30. Specialties: grilled baby octopus, ravioli pera, New Zealand lamb. Valet parking. Storefront windows, wood-burning pizza oven. Cr cds: A, C, D, DS, MC, V.

★ ★ **UN GRAND CAFE.** *(See Belden-Stratford Hotel)* 773/348-8886. Hrs: 6-10:30 pm; Fri, Sat to 11:30 pm; Sun 5-9:30 pm. Closed major hols. Res accepted. Serv bar. A la carte entrees: dinner $14-$19. Specializes in fresh grilled seafood, steak frites, salads. Valet parking. Outdoor dining. French bistro decor. Cr cds: A, C, D, DS, JCB, MC, V.

✔★ **VINCI.** *1732 N Halsted St (60614), Lincoln Park.* 312/266-1199. Web www.vinci-group.com. Hrs: 5:30-10:30 pm; Fri, Sat to 11:30 pm; Sun 3:30-9:30 pm; Sun brunch 10 am-2:30 pm. Closed most major hols. Res accepted. Italian menu. Bar. A la carte entrees: dinner $6.95-$17.95. Child's meals. Specialties: polenta con funghi, grilled duck breast, linguine della Nonna. Valet parking (dinner). Warm, rustic atmosphere. Cr cds: A, C, D, MC, V.

★ ★ **VIVERE.** *71 W Monroe St, main floor of the Italian Village complex, the Loop.* 312/332-4040. Hrs: 11:30 am-2:30 pm, 5-10 pm; Fri to 11 pm; Sat 5-11 pm. Closed Sun; major hols. Res accepted. Regional Italian menu. Bar. Extensive wine list. A la carte entrees: lunch $11-$21, dinner $16-$31. Specialties: tortelli di pecorino dolce, pesce del giorno come volete, medaglione di vitello. Valet parking. One of 3 restaurants in the Italian Village complex. Elegant dining in a contemporary Baroque setting; marble mosaic flooring. Family-owned. Cr cds: A, C, D, DS, JCB, MC, V.

★ ★ **VIVO.** *838 W Randolph, north of the Loop.* 312/733-3379. Hrs: 11:30 am-2:30 pm, 5:30-10 pm; Thurs to 11 pm; Fri to midnight; Sat, Sun 5:30 pm-midnight. Closed some major hols. Res accepted. Southern Italian menu. Bar. A la carte entrees: lunch $6-$14, dinner $10-$26. Specialties: black linguine with crabmeat, baked whole snapper, risotto with white asparagus. Own baking, pasta. Valet parking. Outdoor dining. Dramatic, contemporary decor with unique artwork and lighting. Cr cds: A, C, D, MC, V.

★ ★ **ZINFANDEL.** *59 W Grand Ave (60610), north of the Loop.* 312/527-1818. Hrs: 11:30 am-2:30 pm, 5:30-10 pm; Fri, Sat to 11 pm. Sat brunch from 10:30 am. Closed Sun, Mon; major hols. Res accepted. Bar. Wine list. Semi-a la carte: lunch $7-$11, dinner $16-$18.95. Sat brunch $4.75-$10.50. Specializes in regional American cuisine. Menu changes monthly with emphasis on different regions. Valet parking. Eclectic art. Cr cds: A, C, D, MC, V.

Unrated Dining Spots

ARCO DE CUCHILLEROS. *3445 N Halsted St, Lakeview. 773/296-6046.* Hrs: 4 pm-11 pm; Fri, Sat to midnight; Sun noon-10 pm; Sun brunch to 3 pm. Closed Mon; most major hols. Spanish tapas menu. Bar. A la carte entrees: lunch, dinner $1.95-$5.95. Specialties: fish cheeks sauteed with garlic & white wine, mussels in white wine & cream sauce, boiled potatoes in fresh garlic mayonnaise. Patio dining. Casual atmosphere. Cr cds: A, C, D, MC, V.

BIG BOWL CAFE. *159½ W Erie St, River North. 312/787-8297.* Hrs: 11:30 am-10 pm; Fri, Sat to 11 pm. Closed Sun; Thanksgiving, Dec 25. Wine, beer. Semi-a la carte: lunch, dinner $1.95-$6.95. Specializes in Asian cuisine. Casual, informal atmosphere. Cr cds: A, C, D, DS, MC, V.

CAFÉ BA BA REEBA. *2024 N Halsted St, Lincoln Park. 773/935-5000.* Hrs: 11:30 am-2:30 pm, 5:30-11 pm; Mon from 5:30 pm; Fri, Sat to midnight; Sun noon-10 pm. Closed some major hols. Spanish tapas menu. Bar. A la carte entrees: lunch, dinner $1.95-$7.95. Specialties: baked goat cheese, grilled squid with lemon, garlic and olive oil. Valet parking. Authentic Spanish tapas bar. Cr cds: A, C, D, DS, MC, V.

ED DEBEVIC'S. *640 N Wells St, River North. 312/664-1707.* Hrs: 11 am-10 pm; Fri & Sat to midnight. Closed Thanksgiving, Dec 24-25. Bar. Semi-a la carte: lunch, dinner $1.50-$6.95. Specializes in chili, hamburgers, meat loaf, salads. Own desserts. Valet parking. Replica of 1950s diner. No cr cds accepted.

HARD ROCK CAFE. *63 W Ontario St, River North. 312/943-2252.* Hrs: 11:30 am-11 pm; Fri to midnight; Sat 11 am-midnight; Sun to 10 pm. Closed Thanksgiving, Dec 25. Bar to 12:30 am; Fri, Sat to 1:30 am; Sun to midnight. Semi-a la carte: lunch, dinner $5.95-$11.95. Specializes in lime barbecue chicken, watermelon ribs, hamburgers. Valet parking. Rock memorabilia. Cr cds: A, D, MC, V.

LUTZ'S CONTINENTAL CAFE & PASTRY SHOP. *2458 W Montrose Ave, north of the Loop. 773/478-7785.* Hrs: 11 am-10 pm. Closed Mon; major hols. Wine, beer. A la carte entrees: lunch, dinner $5.50-$10.50. Specializes in light lunches, whipped cream tortes, hand-dipped truffles. Own candy, ice cream. Outdoor dining. Bakeshop. Continental café atmosphere. Family-owned. Cr cds: MC, V.

MICHAEL JORDAN'S. *500 N La Salle St, River North. 312/644-3865.* Hrs: 11 am-10 pm; Fri, Sat to 11:30 pm. Res accepted (lunch). Bar. Semi-a la carte: lunch $4.95-$12.95, dinner $11.95-$26.95. Specialties: Michael's "Nothin But Net" burger, Juanita's macaroni & cheese, steak. Valet parking. High-ceilinged bar (1st floor) featuring large video wall. Dining rm (2nd floor), Michael Jordan memorabilia displayed; artwork; casual dining. Cr cds: A, C, D, DS, JCB, MC, V.

PIZZERIA UNO. *29 E Ohio St, north of the Loop. 312/321-1000.* Hrs: 11:30-1 am; Sat to 2 am; Sun to midnight. Closed Thanksgiving, Dec 25. Bar. Limited menu. Lunch, dinner $2.95-$8. Specialty: deep-dish pizza. Cr cds: A, D, DS, MC, V.

PLANET HOLLYWOOD. *633 N Wells St, River North. 312/266-7827.* Hrs: 11 am-midnight; Fri, Sat to 1 am. Italian, Mexican, Amer menu. Bar to 1:45 am. Semi-a la carte: lunch, dinner $6.95-$17.95. Specialties: turkey burgers, vegetable pizza, pasta. Faux palm trees and searchlights evoke the glamour of Hollywood. Authentic Hollywood memorabilia displayed. Gift shop. Cr cds: A, D, DS, MC, V.

POCKETS. *2618 N Clark St, Lincoln Park. 773/404-7587.* Hrs: 11 am-11 pm; Fri, Sat to midnight; Sun to 10 pm. Closed Thanksgiving, Dec 24-25. A la carte entrees: lunch, dinner $3.50-$6.25. Specialties: chipati sandwiches, calzone, pizza. No cr cds accepted.

Chicago O'Hare Airport Area (D-3 see Chicago map)

(See also Arlington Heights, Chicago, Elmhurst, Itasca, Schaumburg)

Information Des Plaines Chamber of Commerce, 1401 Oakton St, 60018; 847/824-4200.

Known as the "world's busiest airport," O'Hare is surrounded by an array of hotels, restaurants and entertainment facilities—a city unto itself, crossing municipal boundaries.

Services and Information

Information: 312/686-2200.

Lost and Found: 312/686-2200.

Weather: 312/976-2300.

Cash Machines: Terminals 1, 2, 3.

Airlines: Aer Lingus, Aeroflot, Air Canada, Air France, Air India, Air Jamaica, Alitalia, America West, American, ATA, Austrian, British Airways, Canadian Arlns Intl, Casino Express, China Eastern, Continental, Delta, El Al, Japan Arlns, KLM, Korean Air, Kuwait Airways, LOT, Lufthansa, Mexicana, Northwest, Reno Air, Royal Jordanian, SABENA, SAS, Swissair, Taesa, TAROM, TWA, United, United Express, USAir.

What to See and Do

Cernan Earth and Space Center. Unique domed theater providing "wrap-around" multimedia programs on astronomy, geography and other topics; free exhibits on space exploration; gift shop. Show (Thurs-Sat evenings, matinee Sat; no shows most hols). 4 mi S via River Rd, at 2000 N 5th Ave in River Grove, on campus of Triton College. Phone 708/583-3100. ¢¢¢

Rosemont Horizon. Auditorium with an 18,500 seating capacity hosts concerts, sports and other events. Box office (daily exc Sun). Off Northwest Tollway (I-90) Lee St exit, at 6920 Mannheim Rd in Rosemont. For schedule and ticket prices phone 847/635-6601 (recording). To charge reservations phone Ticketmaster at 312/559-1212.

Motels

★ ★ **COURTYARD BY MARRIOTT.** *(2950 S River Rd, Des Plaines 60018)* 2 mi N of I-90 exit River Rd. 847/824-7000; FAX 847/824-4574. 180 rms, 5 story. S, D $149; suites from $159; under 12 free; wkend rates. Crib free. TV; cable (premium). Indoor pool; whirlpool. Complimentary coffee in rms. Restaurant 6:30 am-2 pm, 5-10 pm. Rm serv from 5 pm. Bar 4 pm-midnight. Ck-out 1 pm. Coin lndry. Meeting rms. Business servs avail. In-rm modem link. Valet serv. Sundries. Gift shop. Free airport transportation. Exercise equipt; weights, bicycles. Refrigerator in suites. Some balconies. Cr cds: A, C, D, DS, MC, V.

★ ★ **EXEL INN.** *(2881 Touhy Ave (IL 72), Elk Grove Village 60007)* 847/803-9400; FAX 847/803-9771. 123 rms, 3 story. S $52.99-$60.99; D $62.99-$64.99; under 18 free. Crib avail. Pet accepted, some restrictions. TV; cable. Complimentary continental bkfst. Coffee in rms. Restaurant nearby. Ck-out noon. Coin lndry. Business servs avail. In-rm modem link. Free airport transportation. Exercise equipt; bicycle, treadmill. Refrigerators avail. Cr cds: A, C, D, DS, MC, V.

D ★ 🛪 🏊 🏌 SC

★ ★ **HAMPTON INN.** (100 Busse Rd, Elk Grove Village 60007) 1¹/₂ mi N on US 12/45 to Higgins Rd (IL 72), then 4 mi W to jct Busse Rd (IL 83). 847/593-8600; FAX 847/593-8607. 125 rms, 4 story. S $79-$85; D $89; under 18 free; wkend rates. Crib free. TV; cable (premium). Complimentary continental bkfst. Restaurant nearby. Ck-out noon. Meeting rm. Business servs avail. In-rm modem link. Free airport transportation. Health club privileges. Cr cds: A, C, D, DS, JCB, MC, V.

D 🏌 🏊 SC

★ **HOWARD JOHNSON LODGE.** (8201 W Higgins Rd, Chicago 60631) 773/693-2323; FAX 773/693-3771. 110 rms, 2 story. May-Aug: S, D $99-$109; under 12 free; lower rates rest of yr. Crib free. TV; cable (premium). Ck-out noon. Coin lndry. Business servs avail. Free airport transportation. Cr cds: A, C, D, DS, ER, JCB, MC, V.

D 🛪 🏊 🏌 SC

✓★ ★ **LA QUINTA.** (1900 Oakton St, Elk Grove Village 60007) 2 mi NW on I-90 to Elmhurst Rd, then N to Oakton St. 847/439-6767; FAX 847/439-5464. 142 rms, 4 story. S $79-$84; D $84-$91; each addl $7; under 18 free. Crib free. Pet accepted, some restrictions. TV; cable (premium). Heated pool. Complimentary continental bkfst. Restaurant opp 7 am-11 pm. Ck-out noon. Meeting rms. Business servs avail. In-rm modem link. Valet serv. Free airport transportation. Health club privileges. Some refrigerators. Cr cds: A, C, D, DS, MC, V.

D 🏊 🛪 🏌 SC

★ ★ **RESIDENCE INN BY MARRIOTT.** (9450 W Lawrence, Schiller Park 60176) 847/725-2210; FAX 847/725-2211. 169 kit. suites, 3-6 story. 1-bedrm $129-$179; 2-bedrm $149-$179; 3-bedrm $450; monthly rates. Crib free. Pet accepted; $100. TV; cable (premium). Pool, whirlpool. Complimentary continental bkfst. Coffee in rms. Restaurant adj. Ck-out noon. Coin lndry. Meeting rms. Business center. In-rm modem link. Valet serv. Free airport transportation. Health club privileges. Refrigerators, microwaves. Balconies. Picnic tables, grills. Cr cds: A, C, D, DS, JCB, MC, V.

D 🏊 🛪 🏌 SC

Motor Hotels

✓★ ★ **BEST WESTERN MIDWAY.** (1600 Oakton St, Elk Grove Village 60007) 2 mi NW on I-90 to Elmhurst Rd, then N to Oakton St, then W. 847/981-0010; FAX 847/364-7365. 165 rms, 3 story. S $75-$95; D $88-$105; each addl $10; suites from $150; under 12 free. Crib free. TV; cable (premium). Pool; whirlpool. Complimentary coffee in rms. Restaurant 6 am-2 pm, 5-10 pm. Rm serv. Bar 4 pm-midnight. Ck-out noon. Meeting rms. Business servs avail. In-rm modem link. Symposium theater. Bellhops. Free airport transportation. Sauna. Game rm. Some refrigerators. Cr cds: A, C, D, DS, JCB, MC, V.

D 🏊 🏌 SC

★ ★ **COMFORT INN.** (2175 E Touhy Ave, Des Plaines 60018) Touhy Ave & River Rd. 847/635-1300; FAX 847/635-7572. 148 rms, 3 story. S $94-$104; D $104-$114; each addl $10; suites $120-$130; under 18 free. Crib free. TV; cable (premium). Complimentary continental bkfst. Coffee in rms. Restaurant adj 5:30-2 am. Bar 11-1 am. Ck-out 1 pm. Meeting rms. Business servs avail. Valet serv. Free airport transportation. Exercise equipt; weight machine, bicycle. Whirlpool. Cr cds: A, C, D, DS, ER, JCB, MC, V.

D 🛪 🏌 SC

Hotels

★ ★ **HOLIDAY INN.** (5440 N River Rd, Rosemont 60018) on US 45, 1 mi E of O'Hare Intl Airport. 847/671-6350; FAX 847/671-5406. 507 rms, 14 story. S $159; D $169; each addl $10; suites $175-$200; under 18 free; wkend package. Crib free. Pet accepted. TV; cable (premium). 2 pools, 1 indoor; whirlpool. Restaurant 6:30 am-midnight. Bars 11-2 am; wkends to 4 am; entertainment exc Sun. Ck-out noon. Coin lndry. Meeting rms. Business center. In-rm modem link. Free airport transportation. Exercise equipt; weight machine, stair machine, sauna. Game rm. Refrigerators avail. Minibars. Cr cds: A, C, D, DS, MC, V.

D 🏊 🛪 🏌 SC

★ ★ ★ **HOTEL SOFITEL.** (5550 N River Rd, Rosemont 60018) 2 blks S of I-90 exit River Rd S. 847/678-4488; FAX 847/678-4244. 304 rms, 10 story. S $205-$215; D $225-$235; each addl $10; suites $305-$325; under 18 free. Crib free. Pet accepted, some restrictions. Valet parking $12. TV; cable (premium). Indoor pool. Restaurants 6:30-12:30 am. Rm serv 24 hrs. Bar 11-1 am. Ck-out noon. Convention facilities. Business center. In-rm modem link. Concierge. Gift shop. Free airport transportation. Exercise equipt; weights, bicycles, sauna. Bathrm phones, minibars; refrigerators avail. Traditional European-style hotel. Cr cds: A, C, D, DS, ER, JCB, MC, V.

D 🏊 🛪 🏌 SC

★ ★ ★ **HYATT REGENCY.** (9300 W Bryn Mawr Ave, Rosemont 60018) River Rd (US 45) at Kennedy Expy exit River Rd S. 847/696-1234; FAX 847/698-0139. 1,100 rms, 10 story. S $189-$225; D $194-$250; each addl $25; suites $300-$800. Crib free. Parking $13. TV; cable (premium). Indoor pool. Restaurants 6 am-midnight. Rm serv 24 hrs. Bars noon-2 am. Ck-out noon. Convention facilities. Business center. In-rm modem link. Free airport transportation. Exercise equipt; weights, bicycles, sauna, steam rm. Massage. Wet bar in suites. Many balconies. 12-story atrium lobby. Luxury level. Cr cds: A, C, D, DS, ER, JCB, MC, V.

D 🏊 🛪 🏌 SC

★ ★ **MARRIOTT.** (8535 W Higgins Rd, Chicago 60631) on IL 72, 1¹/₂ mi E of O'Hare Intl Airport at Kennedy Expy, Cumberland Ave N exit. 773/693-4444; FAX 773/714-4297. 681 rms, 12 story. S, D $149-$204; suites $179-$450; under 18 free; wkend plans. Crib free. Pet accepted. TV; cable (premium). 2 pools, 1 indoor/outdoor; wading pool, whirlpool, poolside serv. Restaurants 6:30 am-10 pm. Rm serv to midnight. Bars 11:30-1:30 am. Ck-out noon. Coin lndry. Convention facilities. Business center. In-rm modem link. Concierge. Gift shop. Valet parking. Free airport transportation. Exercise equipt; weights, bicycles. Refrigerators, microwaves avail. Private patios, balconies. Luxury level. Cr cds: A, C, D, DS, ER, JCB, MC, V.

D 🏊 🛪 🏌 SC

★ ★ ★ **MARRIOTT SUITES.** (6155 N River Rd, Rosemont 60018) I-190E exit River Rd N. 847/696-4400; FAX 847/696-2122. 256 suites, 11 story. S $189; D $199; wkend rates. Crib free. Pet accepted. TV; cable (premium), VCR avail. Indoor pool; whirlpool. Coffee in rms. Restaurant 6:30 am-10:30 pm. Bar 11:30 am-midnight. Ck-out 1 pm. Meeting rms. Business servs avail. In-rm modem link. Gift shop. Free airport transportation. Exercise equipt; bicycles, stair machine, sauna. Health club privileges. Refrigerators, wet bars; microwaves avail. Cr cds: A, C, D, DS, ER, JCB, MC, V.

D 🏊 🛪 🏌 SC

★ ★ **RAMADA PLAZA HOTEL O'HARE.** (6600 N Mannheim Rd, Rosemont 60018) 2 mi N of O'Hare Intl Airport, just N of jct US 12/45, IL 72, N of Kennedy Expy (I-90) Mannheim Rd exit. 847/827-5131; FAX 847/827-5659. 723 rms, 2-9 story. S, D $119-$151; each addl $10; suites $175-$485; studio rms $145; under 18 free; wkend rates. Crib free. Parking. TV; cable (premium). Indoor/outdoor pool; whirlpool, poolside serv. Restaurants 6 am-11 pm. Bars 11-2 am. Ck-out noon. Convention facilities. Business center. In-rm modem link. Gift shop. Free airport transportation. Tennis. Lighted 9-hole par-3 golf, putting green. Exercise equipt; weight machine, stair machine, sauna. Game rm. Lawn games. Refrigerator in some suites. Many private patios, balconies. Cr cds: A, C, D, DS, ER, JCB, MC, V.

D 🏊 🛪 🏌 SC

★ ★ ★ **ROSEMONT SUITES O'HARE.** (5500 N River Rd, Rosemont 60018) 2 blks S of Kennedy Expy (I-90). 847/678-4000; FAX 847/928-7659; 800 888/476-7366. 294 suites, 8 story. S, D $177-$215; under 17 free; wkend rates. Crib free. TV; cable (premium). Indoor pool;

whirlpool. Complimentary full bkfst. Restaurant 11 am-11 pm. Rm serv 6-1 am. Bar to 1 am. Ck-out noon. Meeting rms. Business center. In-rm modem link. Gift shop. Free airport, RR station transportation. Exercise equipt; weight machine, bicycles, sauna. Health club privileges. Refrigerators, microwaves, minibars, wet bars. Opp Rosemont Convention Center. Cr cds: A, C, D, DS, ER, JCB, MC, V.

★ ★ ★ **SHERATON GATEWAY SUITES.** (6501 N Mannheim Rd, Rosemont 60018) 1/2 mi N of I-190 exit Mannheim Rd N. 847/699-6300; FAX 847/699-0391. Web www.sheraton.com/sheraton/html/properties/hotel_and_resorts/040.html. 297 suites, 11 story. Sept-Dec: S, D $200-$245; each addl $10; under 18 free; wkend rates; lower rates rest of yr. Crib free. Pet accepted. TV; cable (premium), VCR avail. Indoor pool; whirlpool. Complimentary coffee in rms. Restaurant 11 am-2 pm, 5-10 pm. Rm serv 24 hrs. Bar 11-2 am. Ck-out noon. Convention facilities. Business center. In-rm modem link. Gift shop. Free airport transportation. Exercise equipt; treadmills, stair machine, sauna. Health club privileges. Refrigerators; some microwaves. Cr cds: A, C, D, DS, ER, JCB, MC, V.

★ ★ **SHERATON SUITES.** (121 NW Point Blvd, Elk Grove Village 60007) 847/290-1600; FAX 847/290-1129. 255 rms, 7 story. Apr-June & mid-Sept-mid-Nov: S, D $159-$169; under 18 free; wkend rates; lower rates rest of yr. Crib free. Pet accepted, some restrictions; $50. TV; cable (premium), VCR avail. 2 pools, 1 indoor; whirlpool. Complimentary coffee in rms. Restaurant 6:30 am-10 pm. Bar 11:30 am-midnight. Ck-out 1 pm. Coin lndry. Meeting rms. Business servs avail. In-rm modem link. Gift shop. Free airport transportation. Exercise equipt; treadmills, rower, sauna. Game rm. Refrigerators; some microwaves. Cr cds: A, C, D, DS, ER, JCB, MC, V.

★ ★ ★ **THE WESTIN-O'HARE.** (6100 River Rd, Rosemont 60018) I-90E exit River Rd N. 847/698-6000; FAX 847/698-4591. 525 rms, 12 story. S $189-$245; D $209-$265; each addl $20; suites $220-$1,000; under 18 free; wkend rates. Valet parking $10. TV; cable (premium). Indoor pool; whirlpool, poolside serv. Restaurant 6 am-11 pm. Rm serv 24 hrs. Bar 2 pm to midnight. Ck-out 1 pm. Convention facilities. Business center. Gift shop. Free airport transportation. Exercise rm; instructor, weights, bicycles, sauna. Minibars; some bathrm phones. Luxury level. Cr cds: A, C, D, DS, ER, JCB, MC, V.

Restaurants

★ ★ **BLACK RAM.** (1414 Oakton St, Des Plaines 60018) 1 mi N of I-90 (Kennedy Expy) River Rd (US 45) exit N. 847/824-1227. Hrs: 11 am-11 pm; Sat from 4 pm; Sun 1-10 pm. Closed most major hols. Res accepted. Bar. Semi-a la carte: lunch $8-$15, dinner $15-$25. Specializes in steak, veal, fresh seafood. Own pastries. Entertainment Fri, Sat. Parking. Family-owned. Cr cds: A, C, D, DS, MC, V.

★ ★ ★ **CAFE LA CAVE.** (2777 Mannheim Rd, Des Plaines 60018) 1 mi N on Mannheim Rd, N of jct US 12/45, 1 blk N of jct IL 72. 847/827-7818. Hrs: 11:30 am-11:30 pm; Sat from 5 pm; Sun 5-9:30 pm. Closed some major hols. Res accepted. French, continental menu. Bar. Wine list. Semi-a la carte: lunch $6-$14.95, dinner $18.95-$33.95. Specialties: steak Diane prepared tableside, Dover sole, medallions of lobster. Valet parking. Cr cds: A, C, D, DS, JCB, MC, V.

★ ★ **CARLUCCI RIVERWAY.** (6111 N River Rd, Rosemont 60018) 2 1/2 mi E off I-90 River Rd exit. 847/518-0990. E-mail carlucci@enteract.com; web www.enteract.com/~carlucci. Hrs: 11 am-2:30 pm; Fri to 11 pm; Sat 5-11 pm; Sun 4:30-9 pm. Closed major hols. Res accepted. Tuscan, Italian menu. Bar to 1 am. A la carte entrees: lunch $7.95-$12.95, dinner $10.95-$22.95. Specializes in fresh pasta, seafood,

rotisserie items. Own pastries. Valet parking. Outdoor dining. Tuscan decor; traditional trattoria setting; frescos. Cr cds: A, C, D, DS, MC, V.

★ ★ ★ **NICK'S FISHMARKET.** (10275 W Higgins Rd, Rosemont 60018) jct Mannheim & Higgins Rds. 847/298-8200. E-mail nicksfish@earthlink.net. Hrs: 6-10 pm; Fri, Sat to 11 pm. Closed most major hols. Res accepted. Continental menu. Bar to 2 am. Wine list. A la carte entrees: dinner $14-$55. Specializes in fresh seafood, steak, veal. Own pastries. Jazz combo Fri, Sat. Valet parking. Braille, Japanese menu. 3 large saltwater aquariums. Cr cds: A, C, D, DS, JCB, MC, V.

★ ★ **ROSEWOOD.** (9421 W Higgins Rd, Rosemont 60018) E of airport, at River Rd. 847/696-9494. Hrs: 11 am-11 pm; Sat from 4 pm; Sun 4-9 pm. Closed most major hols. Res accepted. Bar. Semi-a la carte: lunch $10-$14, dinner $25-$30. Specializes in steak, fresh seafood, pasta. Pianist Wed-Sat. Valet parking. Intimate atmosphere. Rosewood millwork throughout. Cr cds: A, C, D, DS, MC, V.

★ **SAYAT NOVA.** (20 W Golf Rd, Des Plaines 60016) On IL 58. 847/296-1776. Hrs: 11:30 am-2 pm, 4-10:30 pm; Sat 4-11:30 pm; Sun 4-10 pm. Closed Mon; most major hols. Res accepted. Middle Eastern menu. Serv bar. Semi-a la carte: lunch $6-$10, dinner $10-$15. Specializes in shish kebab, sautéed chicken, lamb chops. Own desserts. Parking. Middle Eastern decor. Cr cds: A, C, D, DS, MC, V.

★ ★ ★ **WALTER'S.** (28 Main, Park Ridge 60068) 3 1/2 mi NE of O'Hare Airport; 1 1/2 mi N of Kennedy Expy Cumberland exit N. 847/825-2240. Hrs: 11:30 am-2 pm, 5:30-9 pm; Sat from 5:30 pm. Closed Sun, Mon; major hols. Res accepted. Serv bar. Wine list. A la carte entrees: lunch, dinner $4.95-$26.95. Specializes in grilled seafood, rack of lamb, steak. Own baking, pasta. Parking. In 1890s building; atrium dining; 30-ft skylight. Seasonal menu. Cr cds: A, C, D, DS, JCB, MC, V.

Cicero (B-6)

(For accommodations see Chicago)

Founded 1867 **Pop** 67,436 **Elev** 606 ft **Area code** 708 **Zip** 60650
Information Chamber of Commerce, 4937 W 25th St, Rm 209; 708/863-6000.

Cicero, named after the Roman orator, is second only to Chicago as a manufacturing center; nearly 200 industrial plants are located here. In addition, many fine ethnic bakeries and restaurants can be found along Cermak Road.

What to See and Do

Horse racing.

Hawthorne Race Course. Thoroughbred racing (Oct-Dec) and harness racing (Jan-Feb) on a one-mi track. (Daily) 3501 S Laramie Ave. For schedule phone 708/780-3700. Grandstand ¢¢

Sportsman's Park Race Track. Thoroughbred racing (Feb-May). Harness racing (May-Oct). 3301 S Laramie Ave. Phone 312/242-1121. (Daily) Grandstand **Free.**

Collinsville (G-3)

(See also Belleville, Cahokia, Edwardsville)

Pop 22,446 **Elev** 550 ft **Area code** 618 **Zip** 62234

Information Chamber of Commerce, 221 W Main St, phone 618/344-2884; or the Convention & Tourism Bureau, 1 Gateway Dr, phone 618/345-4999.

What to See and Do

Horse racing. Fairmount Park. Thoroughbred (mid-Apr-Oct) and harness racing (Oct-early Apr). (Daily) 2 mi W on US 40 at jct I-255. Phone 618/345-4300. Grandstand ¢

Annual Event

Italian Fest. Main St, downtown. Entertainment, food, bocce ball tournament, 10K run. Usually mid-late Sept.

Motels

✓★ **BEST WESTERN BO-JON INN.** *Jct I-55/70 exit 15B & IL 159. 618/345-5720; FAX 618/345-5721.* 40 rms, 2 story. Apr-early Sept: S, D $50-$60; each addl $5; lower rates rest of yr. Pet accepted, some restrictions. TV; cable (premium), VCR avail (movies). Pool. Complimentary continental bkfst. Restaurant nearby. Ck-out 11 am. Business servs avail. In-rm modem link. Picnic tables, grills. Cr cds: A, C, D, DS, MC, V.

✓★ **BEST WESTERN HERITAGE INN.** *2003 Mall Rd. 618/345-5660; FAX 618/345-8135.* 80 rms, 2 story. May-Sept: S $55-$69; D $62-$75; each addl $10; suite $120; under 12 free; lower rates rest of yr. Crib free. TV; cable (premium), VCR avail (movies). Complimentary continental bkfst. Rm serv 24 hrs. Ck-out noon. Meeting rm. Business servs avail. Coin lndry. Exercise equipt; weight machine, bicycle. Indoor pool; whirlpool. Refrigerators, microwaves avail. Cr cds: A, C, D, DS, MC, V.

★★ **DRURY INN.** *602 N Bluff, just N of jct IL 157 & I-55/70. 618/345-7700.* 123 rms, 4 story. S $50-$80; D $62-$90; each addl $10; under 18 free. Crib free. TV; cable (premium). Indoor pool. Complimentary continental bkfst. Restaurant adj 6 am-11 pm. Ck-out noon. In-rm modem link. Health club privileges. Cr cds: A, C, D, DS, MC, V.

✓★ **HOWARD JOHNSON.** *301 N Bluff Rd, I-55/70 exit 11. 618/345-1530; FAX 618/345-1321.* 87 rms, 2 story. June-Aug: S $40-$50; D $55-$65; each addl $5; under 10 free; lower rates rest of yr. Crib free. Pet accepted, some restrictions. TV; cable (premium). Pool; wading pool. Restaurant adj 10 am-10 pm. Bar noon-1 am; Sat to 2 am. Ck-out noon. Coin lndry. Business servs avail. Private patios. Cr cds: A, C, D, DS, MC, V.

Motor Hotel

★★★ **HOLIDAY INN.** *1000 Eastport Plaza Dr, on I-55/70, at IL 157 exit 11. 618/345-2800; FAX 618/345-9804.* 231 rms, 5 story. S $85.95-$119; D $95.95-$129; each addl $10; suites $89.95-$500. Crib free. TV; cable (premium), Indoor pool; whirlpool. Complimentary continental bkfst. Restaurant 6:15 am-10:30 pm; wknd hrs vary. Bar 3 pm-midnight, Fri, Sat to 1 am. Ck-out noon. Coin lndry. Meeting rms. Business servs avail. In-rm modem link. Exercise equipt; bicycles, stair machine, sauna. Game rm. Microwaves avail. Cr cds: A, C, D, DS, ER, JCB, MC, V.

Inn

✓★ **MAGGIE'S.** *2102 N Keebler Rd. 618/344-8283.* 5 rms, 3 story. No rm phones. S $35-$75; D $45-$85; each addl $10. Pet accepted, some restrictions. TV; cable, VCR (movies). Complimentary full bkfst. Ck-out noon, ck-in 4-6 pm. Indoor pool; whirlpool. Built in 1900; former boarding house. Totally nonsmoking. No cr cds accepted.

Danville (E-6)

(See also Champaign/Urbana)

Founded 1827 **Pop** 33,828 **Elev** 597 ft **Area code** 217 **Zip** 61832

Information Danville Area Convention & Visitors Bureau, 100 W Main St, Rm 146, PO Box 992, 61834; 217/442-2096 or 800/383-4386.

The site of Danville is mentioned in old French records as Piankeshaw, "center of more Native American trails than any spot within a six-day journey." Named for Dan Beckwith, its first settler, it has been under the flags of France, Great Britain and the United States and was the scene of a battle between Spanish forces and the Kickapoo. It has approximately 150 industries and is the center of a wide trade area.

What to See and Do

Forest Glen Preserve. Nature preserve, wildlife refuge. Observation tower overlooks Vermilion River. Picnicking. Camping (fee). Pioneer homestead, trails, arboretum. (Daily) 10 mi SE, in Westville. Phone 217/662-2142. **Free.**

Kickapoo State Park. Several lakes on 2,843 acres. Fishing, hunting; boating (ramp, electric motors); canoe trail, rentals. Hiking. Horseback riding (rentals). Picnicking, concession. Camping. Standard hrs, fees. (Daily) 4 mi W on I-74, exit 210. Phone 217/442-4915. **Free.**

Vermilion County Museum. House built in 1855 by William Fithian, physician and statesman; Lincoln stayed here Sept 21, 1858; period furnishings, natural history rm, art gallery; carriage house, herb garden. (Daily exc Mon; closed Thanksgiving, Dec 25) 116 N Gilbert St. Phone 217/442-2922. ¢

Annual Events

Balloon Classic Illinois. Vermilion County Airport. June.

National Sweet Corn Festival. 15 mi N in Hoopeston. Forty tons of corn-on-the-cob, tractor pulls, antique auto show, horse show, National Sweetheart Pageant. Phone 217/283-7873. Labor Day wknd.

Motels

✓★ **COMFORT INN.** *383 Lynch Drive, I-74 & Lynch Dr exit 220. 217/443-8004.* 56 rms, 2 story, 14 suites. S $43.99-$51.99; D $48.99-$58.99; each addl $5; suites $52.99-$70.99; under 18 free; higher rates special events. Crib free. Pet accepted. TV; cable (premium). Indoor pool; whirlpool. Complimentary continental bkfst. Ck-out 11 am. Business servs avail. In-rm modem link. Game rm. Cr cds: A, C, D, DS, ER, MC, V.

★★ **FAIRFIELD INN BY MARRIOTT.** *389 Lynch Rd, I-74 exit 220. 217/443-3388.* 56 rms, 3 story. S $54.99; D $59.99; each addl $6; under 18 free; higher rates special events. Crib free. TV; cable (premium). Indoor pool; whirlpool. Complimentary continental bkfst. Restaurant nearby. Ck-out noon. Meeting rms. Business servs avail. Game rm. Cr cds: A, D, DS, MC, V.

[D] [≈] [⊁] [♨] [SC]

★★ **RAMADA INN.** *388 Eastgate Dr, I-74 exit 220. 217/446-2400; FAX 217/446-3878.* 131 rms, 2 story. S $60-$64; D $62-$68; each addl $6; suites $98; under 18 free; wknd rates. Crib free. Pet accepted, some restrictions. TV; cable (premium). Pool. Complimentary continental bkfst. Complimentary coffee in rms. Restaurant 6 am-9 pm. Rm serv. Bar 11-1 am, Sun 1-11 pm. Ck-out noon. Coin lndry. Meeting rms. Business servs avail. Valet serv. Sundries. Free local airport transportation. Exercise equipt; weight machine, bicycles. Minibar in suites. Cr cds: A, C, D, DS, JCB, MC, V.

[D] [✔] [≈] [⊀] [⊁] [♨] [SC]

Motor Hotel

★ **DAYS INN.** *77 N Gilbert St. 217/443-6600; FAX 217/443-2345.* 93 rms, 6 story. S $60-$75; D $70-$85; under 18 free; each addl $10. Crib free. TV; cable (premium). Pool. Complimentary coffee in lobby. Restaurant 6:30 am-1:30 pm, 5-9 pm; Sun to 1:30 pm. Rm serv. Bar 3 pm-2 am; entertainment Tues-Sat. Ck-out 11 am. Meeting rms. Exercise equipt; treadmill, bicycle. Microwaves avail. Cr cds: A, C, D, DS, JCB, MC, V.

[D] [≈] [⊀] [⊁] [♨] [SC]

Inn

★ **THE BOOKWALTER HOUSE.** *1701 N Logan Ave. 217/443-5511; res: 800/397-7039; FAX 217/431-4966.* 4 rms, 2 share bath, 2 story, 2 suites. S, D $75; each addl $10; suites $95-$105; under 12 free; wkly rates. Crib free. TV in some rms; VCR avail (movies). Complimentary full bkfst. Ck-out 11 am, ck-in 4 pm. Business servs avail. In-rm modem link. Luggage handling. Lawn games. Fireplace in suites. Picnic tables. Built in 1922; Tudor Revival style. Cr cds: A, MC, V.

[⊁] [♨]

Decatur (E-4)

(See also Lincoln, Springfield)

Founded 1829 **Pop** 83,885 **Elev** 670 ft **Area code** 217 **E-mail** decatur@midwest.net **Web** www.decaturcvb.com

Information Decatur Area Convention & Visitors Bureau, 202 E North St, 62523; 217/423-7000 or 800/331-4479.

In 1830, 21-year-old Abraham Lincoln drove through what would later become Decatur with his family to settle on the Sangamon River, a few miles west. He worked as a farmer and railsplitter and made his first political speech in what is now Decatur's Lincoln Square. Today, agri-business, manufacturing, Richland Community College and Millikin University provide a varied economy.

What to See and Do

Birks Museum. Decorative arts museum with more than 1,000 pieces of china, crystal and pottery; some from 15th and 16th centuries. (Sept-May, Sun-Thurs; summer by appt only) 1184 W Main St, in Gorin Hall, on campus of Millikin University. Phone 217/424-6337. **Free.**

Children's Museum. Featuring hands-on exhibits of the arts, science & technology. (Tues-Sat, also Sun afternoons; closed major hols) 55 S Country Club Dr. Phone 217/423-KIDS. ¢¢

Fairview Park. Approx 180 acres. Swimming pool; tennis. Biking trail. Picnicking, playground, baseball diamonds, horseshoe pits. (Daily) Jct US 36, IL 48. For further details on recreational facilities in the city's 1,967 acres of municipal parks, contact the Decatur Park District, 620 E Riverside, 62521; 217/422-5911. **Free.**

Friends Creek Regional Park. Nature trails; picnicking, playground. Camping (showers, dump station; fee). Amphitheater. (May-Oct, daily) 16 mi NE via I-72, Argenta exit. Phone 217/423-7708.

Lake Decatur. Shoreline drive; boating, fishing. SE edge of town, on the Sangamon River.

Macon County Historical Society Museum. Exhibit Center with displays of local artifacts; 1890s Victorian farmhouse exhibit; also Prairie Village with 1860s schoolhouse, 1850s printing shop, 1880s log cabin, blacksmith shop, 1890s train depot and Macon County's first courthouse, where Lincoln once practiced law. (Tues-Sun afternoons; closed major hols) 5580 North Fork Rd. Phone 217/422-4919. ¢

Millikin Place. Housing development (1909) laid out and landscaped by Walter Burley Griffin, who designed Australia's capital, Canberra, in an international competition. Street features prairie-school entrance, naturalized landscaping and houses by Marion Mahony, Griffin's wife, and Frank Lloyd Wright, for whom both Griffin and Mahony worked at the famous Oak Park Studio. Numbers 1 and 3 Millikin Place are by Mahony; 2 Millikin Place attributed to Wright. (Houses private) Entrance adj to 125 N Pine St.

Rock Springs Center for Environmental Discovery. Approx 1,320 acres with hiking & self-guided interpretive trails; picnic area, shelter, rest rms. Visitor's Center with scheduled events and programs throughout yr. (Daily; closed Easter, Thanksgiving, Dec 25) S on IL 48, W 2 mi on Rock Spring Rd. 1495 Brozio Lane. Phone 217/423-7708. **Free.**

Scovill Park and Zoo. Picnicking, playground. Zoo has over 500 animals. ZO & O Express Train takes visitors around zoo. Oriental garden. (May-Oct, daily) E shore of Lake Decatur, S of US 36. Phone 217/421-7435. Zoo ¢

Motels

✔★★ **BUDGETEL INN.** *5100 Hickory Point (Frontage Rd) (62526), I-72 exit 141B. 217/875-5800; FAX 217/875-7537.* 105 rms, 2 story. S $39.95-$42.95; D $43.95-$46.95; each addl $7; under 18 free. Crib free. Pet accepted. TV; cable, VCR avail. Complimentary continental bkfst. Complimentary coffee in rms. Restaurant nearby. Ck-out noon. Meeting rms. Business servs avail. In-rm modem link. Some refrigerators, microwaves. Cr cds: A, C, D, DS, MC, V.

[D] [✔] [⊁] [♨] [SC]

★ **FAIRFIELD INN BY MARRIOTT.** *1417 Hickory Point Dr (62522), 6 mi N on IL 51, I-72 exit 38. 217/875-3337.* 63 rms, 3 story. S, D $55.95; suites $66.95; under 18 free; wknd rates. Crib free. TV; cable (premium). Indoor pool; whirlpool. Complimentary continental bkfst. Restaurant nearby. Ck-out noon. Business servs avail. Game rm. Refrigerator, microwave in suites. Cr cds: A, D, DS, MC, V.

[D] [≈] [⊁] [♨] [SC]

Motor Hotel

★★★ **HOLIDAY INN SELECT CONFERENCE HOTEL.** *Wyckles Rd (62522), 3 mi W on US 36. 217/422-8800; FAX 217/422-9155.* 383 rms, 2-4 story. S, D $85-$95; each addl $10; suites $110-$250; under 19 free. Crib free. Pet accepted; $25 deposit. TV; cable, VCR avail. Indoor pool; wading pool, whirlpool. Playground. Restaurants 6 am-11 pm; Fri, Sat to 1 am. Rm serv. Bar noon-1 am, Sun to 10 pm; entertainment exc Sun. Ck-out noon. Convention facilities. Business center. In-rm modem link. Bellhops. Gift shop. Free airport transportation. Lighted tennis. Exercise equipt; bicycles, treadmill, sauna. Holidome. Game rm. Picnic tables, fishing pond. Cr cds: A, C, D, DS, JCB, MC, V.

[D] [✔] [⊁] [⚓] [⊀] [⊁] [♨] [SC] [⊀]

De Kalb (B-4)

(See also Aurora, Geneva, Oregon, St Charles)

Pop 34,925 **Elev** 880 ft **Area code** 815 **Zip** 60115
Information Chamber of Commerce, 122 N 1st St, Suite E; 815/756-6306.

De Kalb is known as the "barb city" since barbed wire was invented here in 1873 by Joseph Glidden. The first county farm bureau was also established in De Kalb. De Kalb is home to Northern Illinois University.

What to See and Do

Ellwood House Museum. Victorian mansion built by Isaac Ellwood, early manufacturer of barbed wire; restored interiors 1880-1915; carriage house with horse-drawn vehicles, barbed wire and farm implements; 1890s playhouse; extensive grounds and gardens. Guided tours. (Mar-early Dec, daily exc Mon, afternoons; closed some major hols) Entrance at rear, off Augusta Ave. 509 N 1st St. Phone 815/756-4609. ¢¢

Northern Illinois University (1895). (22,000 students) Anthropology museum in Stevens Bldg has Native American and Southeast Asian displays (free). Art galleries in several locations; displays change frequently. One-hr guided tour of campus leaves Office of Admissions, Williston Hall, once a day (daily exc Sun; no tours hols). W Lincoln Hwy (IL 38). Phone 815/753-0446. Also self-guided walking tour booklets. Phone 815/753-1157 (Campus Assistance Center).

Annual Event

Corn Fest. Downtown business district. Three-day street festival. Phone 815/748-CORN. Last full wkend Aug.

Seasonal Event

Stage Coach Theater. 2 mi N on IL 23, then ½ mi E on Barber Greene Rd. Summer community theater. Reservations suggested. Phone 815/758-1940 for current show and dates. Mid-June-mid-Sept.

Motels

✔★ **HoJo INN.** *1321 W Lincoln Hwy. 815/756-1451; FAX 815/756-7260.* 60 rms, 2 story. S $39-$50; D $45-$56; under 12 free; wkly, monthly rates. Crib free. TV; cable (premium), VCR avail. Complimentary continental bkfst. Ck-out noon. Business servs avail. Cr cds: A, C, D, DS, JCB, MC, V.

D ⊠ ⊠ 🔥 SC

★★ **SUPER 8.** *800 Fairview Dr. 815/748-4688.* 44 rms, 2 story. S $45-$60; D $55-$70; each addl $7; suites $95-$110; under 12 free; higher rates NIU graduation, Cornfest. Crib $5. TV; cable (premium). Indoor pool; whirlpool. Complimentary continental bkfst. Ck-out 11 am. Coin lndry. Meeting rm. Business servs avail. Cr cds: A, C, D, DS, MC, V.

D ⊠ ⊠ 🔥 SC

★★ **UNIVERSITY INN.** *1212 W Lincoln Hwy, ¾ mi W on IL 38. 815/758-8661; FAX 815/758-2603.* 114 rms, 2 story. S, D $40; each addl $5; under 18 free. Crib free. Pet accepted, some restrictions. TV; cable (premium). Heated pool. Complimentary continental bkfst. Ck-out noon. Coin lndry. Meeting rms. Business servs avail. Near Northern Illinois Univ campus. Cr cds: A, C, D, DS, MC, V.

D ✔ ⊠ ⊠ 🔥 SC

Restaurant

★★ **MATTHEW BOONE'S.** *122 S First St. 815/758-1776.* Hrs: 11:30 am-2 pm, 5-9 pm; Fri, Sat to 10 pm; Sun brunch 11 am-2 pm. Summer hrs vary. Res accepted. Bar. Semi-a la carte: lunch $3.95-$7.50, dinner $4.95-$11.95. Buffet (Fri, Sat): dinner $10.95. Sun brunch $6.95.

Child's meals. Specializes in steak, prime rib, fresh seafood. Dinner theater (seasonal). Art deco decor. Cr cds: A, C, D, DS, MC, V.

Des Plaines

(see Chicago O'Hare Airport Area)

Dixon (B-4)

(See also Oregon)

Settled 1830 **Pop** 15,144 **Elev** 659 ft **Area code** 815 **Zip** 61021
Information Dixon Area Chamber of Commerce, 74 Galena Ave; 815/284-3361.

At the southernmost point of the Black Hawk Trail, Dixon sits on the banks of the Rock River. Established as a trading post and tavern by John Dixon, it now is a center for light industry. The 40th president of the United States, Ronald Reagan, was born in nearby Tampico and grew up in Dixon.

What to See and Do

John Deere Historic Site. Site where first self-scouring steel plow was made in 1837; reconstructed blacksmith shop (demonstrations Wed-Sun); restored house and gardens; two-acre natural prairie. (Apr-Oct, daily) 8393 S Main; 6 mi NE on IL 2 in Grand Detour. Phone 815/652-4551. ¢¢

Lincoln Statue Park. Park includes the site of Ft Dixon, around which the town was built, and a statue of Lincoln as a young captain in the Black Hawk War in 1832. A plaque on the statue summarizes Lincoln's military career; at the base of the statue is a bas-relief of John Dixon. Along N bank of river between Galena & Peoria Aves. **Free.** Also in the park is

Old Settlers' Memorial Log Cabin. Built in 1894 and dedicated to the area's early settlers; period furnishings. (Memorial Day-Labor Day, Sat & Sun; rest of yr, by appt) Phone 815/284-3577. **Free.**

Ronald Reagan's Boyhood Home. Two-story, three-bedrm house with 1920s furnishings; memorabilia connected with the former president's childhood and acting and political careers. Visitor center adj. (Mar-Dec, daily; rest of yr, Sat & Sun) 816 S Hennepin. Phone 815/288-3404. **Free.**

Annual Event

Petunia Festival. Carnival, parade, arts & crafts, bicycle race, tennis tournament, beer garden, fireworks. Wk of July 4th.

Motel

★★ **BEST WESTERN BRANDYWINE LODGE.** *443 IL 2, 3 mi W. 815/284-1890; FAX 815/284-1174.* 91 rms, 2 story. S $55-$58; D $62-$65; each addl $7; suites $60-$160; under 12 free. Crib free. Heated pool; whirlpool. TV; cable, VCR avail (movies). Restaurant 6:30 am-9 pm; Sun to 2 pm. Rm serv. Bar 11 am-9 pm. Ck-out noon. Meeting rms. Business servs avail. Exercise equipt; bicycles, treadmill. Cr cds: A, C, D, DS, MC, V.

D ⊠ 🏋 ⊠ 🔥 SC

Inn

★★ **HILLENDALE.** *(600 W Lincolnway (US 30), Morrison 61270) 815/772-3454; FAX 815/772-7023; res: 800/349-7702.* 10 rms (3 with shower only), 3 story. S, D $55-$150; each addl $5. Children over 12 yrs only. Some TV; cable (premium), VCR avail (movies). Complimentary full bkfst. Restaurant nearby. Ck-out 11 am, ck-in 3 pm. X-country ski 3 mi. Built in 1891; antiques. Totally nonsmoking. Cr cds: A, C, D, DS, MC, V.

 ⊠ ⊠

Downers Grove

(E-2 see Chicago map)

(See also Hinsdale, Oak Brook)

Settled 1832 **Pop** 46,858 **Elev** 725 ft **Area code** 708 **Zip** 60515
Information Visitors Bureau, 5202 Washington St, Suite 2; 800/934-0615.

What to See and Do

Historical Museum. Victorian house (1892) contains 10 rms of period furnishings, antiques and artifacts; changing exhibits. (Wed, Sun) 831 Maple Ave. Phone 708/963-1309. **Free.**

Morton Arboretum. On 1,500 acres. Native trees and woody plants collected from around the world and grown for use in landscapes, research and education; wetlands; nature trails; prairie restoration. Visitor center. Restaurant. Library (daily exc Sun; closed hols). Grounds (daily). W on I-88 to jct IL 53, then 1 mi N, in Lisle. Phone 708/719-2400. Per vehicle ¢¢¢

Motels

★ ★ **COMFORT INN.** 3010 Finley Rd. 630/515-1500; FAX 630/515-1595. 121 rms, 3 story. S, D $64-$71; each addl $5; under 18 free. Crib free. TV; cable (premium). Heated pool. Complimentary continental bkfst. Restaurant nearby. Ck-out noon. Meeting rm. Business servs avail. In-rm modem link. Valet serv. Health club privileges. Cr cds: A, C, D, DS, ER, JCB, MC, V.

D ≈ ⊠ ⋀ SC

★ ★ **HOLIDAY INN EXPRESS.** 3031 Finley Rd, I-355 exit Butterfield Rd. 630/810-9500; FAX 630/810-0059. 123 rms, 3 story. S $74; D $81; each addl $6; suites $84-$94; under 18 free. Crib free. TV; cable (premium). Complimentary continental bkfst. Restaurant nearby. Ck-out noon. Meeting rms. Business servs avail. In-rm modem link. Health club priviliges. Cr cds: A, C, D, DS, MC, V.

D ⊠ SC

✔★ **RED ROOF INN.** 1113 Butterfield Rd, off I-88, Highland Ave exit. 630/963-4205; FAX 630/963-4425. 135 rms, 2 story. S $45.99; D $51.99-$58.99; under 18 free. Crib free. Pet accepted. TV; cable (premium). Complimentary coffee in lobby. Restaurant nearby. Ck-out 11 am. Meeting rm. Business servs avail. In-rm modem link. Cr cds: A, C, D, DS, MC, V.

D ✤ ⊠ ⋀ SC

Hotels

★ ★ ★ **EMBASSY SUITES.** (707 E Butterfield Rd, Lombard 60148) Off I-88, Highland Ave exit E on Butterfield ¼ mi. 630/969-7500; FAX 630/969-8776. 262 suites, 10 story. S, D $159; each addl $20; under 18 free; wkend rates. Crib free. TV; cable (premium). Indoor pool; whirlpool. Coffee in rm. Complimentary full bkfst. Restaurant 11:30 am-11 pm. Bar. Ck-out noon. Meeting rms. Business servs avail. In-rm modem link. Gift shop. Exercise equipt; weight machine, stair machine, sauna. Refrigerators. Cr cds: A, C, D, DS, MC, V.

D ≈ ⊀ ⊠ ⋀ SC

★ ★ ★ **MARRIOTT SUITES.** 1500 Opus Place, off I-88, Highland Ave exit to Butterfield Rd, then S on Finley Rd. 630/852-1500; FAX 630/852-6527. 254 suites, 7 story. S $109-$125; D $109-$139; wkend rates. Crib free. Pet accepted. TV; cable (premium); VCR avail (movies $6). Indoor/outdoor pool; whirlpool. Coffee in rms. Restaurant 7 am-10 pm. Bar from 11:30 am. Ck-out noon. Meeting rms. Business servs avail. In-rm modem link. Gift shop. Exercise equipt; weight machine, stair machine, sauna. Refrigerators. Balconies. Cr cds: A, C, D, DS, ER, JCB, MC, V.

D ✤ ≈ ⊀ ⊠ ⊠

★ ★ ★ **RADISSON SUITE.** 2111 Butterfield Rd, half-mi W of I-355. 630/971-2000; FAX 630/971-1021. 247 suites, 7 story. Suites $156; under 12 free; wkend packages. Crib free. TV; cable (premium); VCR avail. Indoor pool; whirlpool. Coffee in rm. Complimentary full bkfst. Restaurant 11 am-11 pm. Bar noon-1 am; Fri, Sat to 2 am. Ck-out noon. Convention facilities. Business servs avail. In-rm modem link. Local RR station, bus depot transportation. Exercise equipt; weight machine, treadmills. Refrigerators. Luxury level. Cr cds: A, C, D, DS, JCB, MC, V.

D ≈ ⊀ ⊠ ⋀ SC

Restaurants

★ **COPPERFIELD'S.** 1341 Butterfield Rd, I-355 exit Butterfield Rd, half-mi E. 630/852-2424. Hrs: 10:30-1 am; Mon to 11 pm; Fri, Sat to 2 am; Sun 10 am-11 pm. Bar. Semi-a la carte: lunch $3.50-$6.50, dinner $8.50-$15. Sun brunch $9.95. Child's meals. Specializes in beef, seafood, chicken. Cr cds: A, C, D, DS, MC, V.

D

✔★ **GOLDEN DUCK.** 500 W. Ogden Ave. 630/968-8887. Hrs: 11 am-9 pm; Sun to 8 pm. Closed Mon. Res accepted. Bohemian, Amer menu. Bar. Semi-a la carte: lunch $4.95-$7.50, dinner $5.50-$7.50. Child's meals. Specializes in roast duck, cordon bleu, breaded pork loin. Salad bar. Own pastries. Cr cds: A, MC, V.

D

Dundee <small>(C-1 see Chicago map)</small>

(See also Elgin)

Pop 3,550 (est) **Elev** 750 ft **Area code** 847 **Zip** 60118

Two Pottowatomie villages were nearby when settlers first arrived in 1835. A Scotsman won a lottery and was permitted to name the settlement after his home town in Scotland, Dundee.

What to See and Do

Haeger Factory Outlet. Pottery manufacturing; old and modern methods demonstrated during guided tour (Mon-Fri, 2 tours daily). Ceramic Museum. Factory outlet store (daily; closed some hols). Van Buren St, 2 blks S of IL 72. Phone 847/426-3441. **Free.**

Racing Rapids Action Park. Features water slides, tube slide, go-carts, bumper boats, lazy river and children's pool area. (June-Aug & Labor Day wkend, daily) IL 25 & IL 72. Phone 847/426-5525. ¢¢¢¢

Santa's Village Theme Park. More than 30 rides; live shows and petting zoo. Picnic areas. Also Polar Dome Ice Arena for skating (late Sept-Mar, Sat, Sun & hols; fee). (June-Aug, daily; Mother's Day-Memorial Day & Sept, wkends only) At jct IL 25, 72. Phone 847/426-6751. Admission includes all rides. ¢¢¢¢

Inn

★ ★ **VICTORIAN ROSE GARDEN.** (314 Washington St, Algonquin 60102) 847/854-9667; FAX 847/854-3236; 800 888/854-9667. 5 rms (2 share bath, 4 with shower only), 2 story. No rm phones. S, D $55-$135; each addl $10. TV in sitting rm. Complimentary full bkfst. Restaurant nearby. Ck-out 11 am, ck-in 4 pm. Built in 1886; furnished with a baby grand piano. Totally nonsmoking. Cr cds: A, MC, V.

⊠

Restaurants

✔★ **CHA CHA CHA.** 16 E Main St (IL 72). 847/428-4774. Hrs: 11:30 am-10 pm; Fri, Sat to 11 pm; Sun noon-9 pm. Closed Thanksgiving, Dec 25. Res accepted. Mexican menu. Bar. Semi-a la carte: lunch $5.25-

$8.55, dinner $6.25-$11.95. Specialties: chicken, beef & seafood fajitas. Mexican village decor. Cr cds: A, MC, V.

★ ★ **DURAN'S OF DUNDEE.** *(8 S River St, East Dundee) E on Main St (IL 72),* 1/2 blk S. 847/428-0033. Hrs: 11 am-2:30 pm, 5-9 pm; Fri to 10 pm; Sat 5-10 pm; Sun 4-8 pm. Closed some major hols. Res accepted. Semi-a la carte: lunch $3.95-$8.95, dinner $7.95-$23.95. Child's meals. Specializes in filet mignon, broiled fish, veal. Own cheesecakes. Dining in restored house. Cr cds: A, C, D, DS, MC, V.

★ ★ **MILK PAIL.** *14N 630 IL 25 (Milk Pail Village), 3 mi SE on IL 25;* 1/2 mi N of Northwest Tollway (I-90), IL 25 exit. 847/742-5040. Hrs: 11 am-9 pm; Sat from 9 am; Sun 10 am-9 pm. Closed Dec 25. Res accepted. Bar. Semi-a la carte: bkfst $1.75-$8.75, lunch $5.75-$10.95, dinner $8.95-$19.95. Sun buffet $12.95. Child's meals. Specializes in turkey, chicken, trout. Country atmosphere. Cr cds: A, C, D, DS, MC, V.

Du Quoin (H-4)

(For accommodations see Benton, Carbondale, Marion)

Pop 6,697 **Elev** 468 ft **Area code** 618 **Zip** 62832

Du Quoin, in the fertile agricultural and mining region southeast of St Louis, is a shipping point for coal, grain, livestock and fruit.

Annual Event

Du Quoin State Fair. Farm, house, art and livestock shows; concerts; auto, harness racing; World Trotting Derby. For details contact PO Box 408; 618/542-9373. Late Aug-Labor Day.

Inn

✔★ **OXBOW.** *(US 13/IL 127S, Pinckneyville 62274) 1.3 mi S on US 13 & IL 127.* 618/357-9839; res: 800/929-6888. 6 rms, 2 story. No rm phones. S, D $50-$65; each addl $15; under 6 free; wkly rates. Complimentary full bkfst. Ck-out 11 am, ck-in noon. Indoor pool. Built in 1929. Totally nonsmoking. Cr cds: MC, V.

Restaurant

✔★ ★ **TO PERFECTION.** *1*1/2 *mi S on US 51 at jct IL 14.* 618/542-2002. Hrs: 11 am-2 pm, 4-9 pm; Fri to 10 pm; Sat 4-10 pm. Closed Sun. Bar. Semi-a la carte: lunch $3.95-$6.95, dinner $8.95-$14.95. Specializes in prime rib, fresh seafood, hand-cut steak. Cr cds: MC, V.

Edwardsville (G-3)

(See also Alton, Belleville, Cahokia, Collinsville)

Pop 14,579 **Elev** 552 ft **Area code** 618 **Zip** 62025
Information Edwardsville/Glen Carbon Chamber of Commerce, 200 University Park Dr, Ste 260; 618/656-7600.

What to See and Do

Madison County Historical Museum. Ten-rm house (1836) contains period rms, history and genealogy reference library, pioneer and Native American artifacts; seasonal exhibits. (Wed-Fri, Sun; closed hols) 715 N Main St. Phone 618/656-7562. **Free.**

Southern Illinois University at Edwardsville (1957). (11,800 students) Louis Sullivan Architectural Ornament collection on 2nd flr of Lovejoy Library (daily). Campus tours (Mon-Fri, by appt). Phone 618/692-2000.

Motel

★ **COMFORT INN.** *3080 S IL 157.* 618/656-4900; FAX 618/656-0998. 71 rms, 3 story. S $65-$70; D $70-$85; each addl $5; under 18 free; higher rates special events. Crib free. Pet accepted. TV; cable (premium). Complimentary continental bkfst. Coffee in rms. Ck-out noon. Meeting rms. Business servs avail. Indoor pool. Game rm. Cr cds: A, C, D, DS, MC, V.

Restaurant

★ ★ **RUSTY'S.** *1201 N Main St.* 618/656-1113; FAX 618/656-1114. Hrs: 11 am-1:30 pm, 5-9 pm; Fri, Sat 5-11 pm; Sun brunch 11 am-2 pm. Closed most major hols. Res accepted. Italian, Amer menu. Bar. Semi-a la carte: lunch $4.50-$9.50, dinner $9.50-$24.50. Buffet: lunch $5.95. Sun brunch $7.25. Child's meals. Specializes in seafood, prime rib, veal. Entertainment Fri, Sat. Former trading post built 1819. Cr cds: A, C, D, DS, MC, V.

Effingham (G-5)

(See also Altamont, Mattoon)

Settled 1853 **Pop** 11,851 **Elev** 592 ft **Area code** 217 **Zip** 62401 **E-mail** chamber@effingham.net **Web** www.effingham.net/chamber
Information Greater Effingham Chamber of Commerce & Industry, 508 W Fayette, PO Box 643; 217/342-4147.

This town is a regional center and seat of Effingham County. Industry includes housing and furniture components, graphic arts and refrigeration. Outdoor recreation is popular here, with Lake Sara offering fishing, boating and golfing opportunities.

Motels

★ **BEST INNS OF AMERICA.** *1209 N Keller Dr, off I-57/70 exit 160.* 217/347-5141. 83 rms, 2 story. Mid-May-Oct: S $36.88-$43; D $39-$46; each addl $7; under 18 free; lower rates rest of yr. Crib free. Pet accepted, some restrictions. TV; cable. Pool. Complimentary continental bkfst. Restaurant adj open 24 hrs. Ck-out 1 pm. Cr cds: A, C, D, DS, MC, V.

★ **BEST WESTERN RAINTREE INN.** *Fayette Ave, I-57 & I-70 exit 159.* 217/342-4121. 65 rms, 2 story. May-Oct: S $39.95-$52; D $48-$59; each addl $5; under 12 free; higher rates special events; lower rates rest of yr. Crib $1. Pet accepted, some restrictions. TV; cable (premium). Complimentary continental bkfst. Restaurant nearby. Ck-out 11 am. Business servs avail. Pool. Some balconies. Cr cds: A, C, D, DS, MC, V.

★ **BUDGETEL.** *1103 Ave of Mid America.* 217/342-2525; FAX 217/347-7341. 122 rms, 4 story, 14 suites. S $46.95-$52.95; D $52.95-$55.95; suites $58.99-$65.99; under 18 free; wkly rates; higher rates special events. Crib free. Pet accepted, some restrictions. TV; cable. Complimentary continental bkfst. Complimentary coffee in rms.

Restaurant adj 6 am-10 pm. Ck-out noon. Meeting rms. Business servs avail. Coin lndry. Health club privileges. Indoor pool. Cr cds: A, C, D, DS, MC, V.

⊡ 🐾 ≈ ✕ 🔥 SC

★ ★ **COMFORT SUITES.** *1310 W Fayette, 3 bks E off I-57 & I-70 exit 159.* 217/342-3151; FAX 217/342-3555. 65 rms, 3 story. S $59-$65; D $65-$75; each addl $6; under 18 free; higher rates special events. Crib avail. Pet accepted. TV; cable (premium). Complimentary continental bkfst. Restaurant adj 6-2 am. Ck-out 11 am. Business center. In-rm modem link. Coin lndry. Health club privileges. Indoor pool. Refrigerators, microwaves avail. Cr cds: A, C, D, DS, MC, V.

⊡ 🐾 ≈ ✕ 🔥 SC 🚶

✔ ★ **DAYS INN.** *W Fayette Rd, 2 blks E of I-57 & I-70, exit 159.* 217/342-9271. 122 rms, 2 story. Apr-mid-Sept: S $38.88; D $49.95; each addl $5; under 13 free; lower rates rest of yr. Crib free. Pet accepted. TV; cable. Pool. Complimentary continental bkfst. Restaurant adj 6-2 am. Bar 11-1 am. Ck-out noon. Health club privileges. Microwaves avail. Cr cds: A, C, D, DS, MC, V.

🐾 ≈ ✕ 🔥 SC

✔ ★ ★ **HAMPTON INN.** *1509 Hampton Dr.* 217/342-4499; FAX 217/347-2828. 60 rms, 2 story. S $49-$59; D $54-$64; suites $79; under 18 free; higher rates special events. Crib avail. Pet accepted. TV; cable (premium). Complimentary continental bkfst. Restaurant nearby. Ck-out noon. Business servs avail. In-rm modem link. Health club privileges. Indoor pool. Refrigerators, microwaves avail. Cr cds: A, D, DS, MC, V.

⊡ 🐾 ≈ ✕ 🔥 SC

★ ★ **HOLIDAY INN.** *1600 W Fayette Ave.* 217/342-4161. 135 rms, 2 story. S $45-$60; D $50-$65; each addl $5; suites $95; under 17 free. Crib free. Pet accepted. TV; cable. Pool. Restaurant 6 am-9 pm; Fri, Sat to 10 pm. Rm serv. Bar 3 pm-1 am, Sun to 10 pm. Ck-out noon. Meeting rms. Business servs avail. Airport, RR station, bus depot transportation. Health club privileges. Cr cds: A, C, D, DS, JCB, MC, V.

⊡ 🐾 ≈ ✕ 🔥 SC

★ ★ **RAMADA KELLER.** *At jct IL 32/33 & I-57/70, exit 160.* 217/342-2131; FAX 217/347-8757. 169 rms, 2 story, 8 condo units. S $52-$89; D $60-$89; each addl $7; suites $89-$129; condos $109-$129; under 18 free. Crib free. Pet accepted, some restrictions. TV; cable. 2 pools, 1 indoor; whirlpool. Playground. Complimentary continental bkfst. Restaurant 6 am-10 pm. Rm serv. Bar noon-midnight; entertainment. Ck-out noon. Meeting rms. Valet serv. Gift shop. Free RR station, bus depot transportation. Exercise equipt; weights, bicycles, sauna, steam rm. Bowling alley. Miniature golf. Game rm. Some in-rm whirlpools. Balconies. Cr cds: A, C, D, DS, MC, V.

⊡ 🐾 ≈ ✕ ✕ 🔥 SC

✔ ★ **SUPER 8.** *1400 Thelma Keller Ave.* 217/342-6888; FAX 217/347-2863. 49 rms, 2 story. S $42.88-$56.88; D $48.88-$60.88; each addl $5; under 12 free. Crib free. Pet accepted, some restrictions. TV; cable. Complimentary coffee in lobby. Ck-out 11 am. Cr cds: A, C, D, DS, MC, V.

≈ 🔥 SC

Restaurants

✔ ★ **CHINA BUFFET.** *1500 W Fayette Ave.* 217/342-3188. Hrs: 11 am-10 pm; Fri, Sat to 11 pm. Res accepted. Chinese menu. Semi-a la carte: lunch $4.15-$6.25, dinner $4.95-$12.99. Child's meals. Specialties: General Tso's chicken, sweet & sour pork, shrimp lo mein. Own baking. Chinese decor; photos of Great Wall of China. Cr cds: MC, V.

✔ ★ **EL RANCHERITO.** *1313 Keller Dr, 3 blks N of I-57.* 217/342-4753. Hrs: 11 am-10 pm; Fri, Sat to 11 pm. Closed Thanksgiving. Res accepted. Mexican menu. Serv bar. Semi-a la carte: lunch $2.99-

$5.79, dinner $4.99-$9.99. Child's meals. Specializes in fajitas, chimichangas, burritos Mexicanos. Own baking. Authentic Mexican decor; waitstaff are native Spanish speakers. Cr cds: A, MC, V.

SC 🔌

★ **NIEMERG'S STEAK HOUSE.** *1410 W Fayette Ave.* 217/342-3921. Hrs: 6-2 am; Sun to midnight. Closed Dec 25. Res accepted (lunch, dinner). Bar 11-1 am. Semi-a la carte: bkfst $1.90-$4.95, lunch $2.95-$7.65, dinner $4-$12.75. Child's meals. Specializes in fried chicken, steak, seafood. Own baking, pasta. Casual, family-style dining. Cr cds: A, D, MC, V.

⊡ 🔌

Elgin (B-5)

(See also Dundee, Union)

Founded 1835 **Pop** 77,010 **Elev** 752 ft **Area code** 847 **E-mail** dramsay@interaccess.com **Web** www.enjoyelgin.com

Information Elgin Area Convention and Visitors Bureau, 77 Riverside Dr, 60120; 847/695-7540 or 800/217-5362.

It was here that the famous Elgin watch was produced. It was also here that the process of packing milk for long transport, or "condensing" it, was invented right after the Civil War by a young man named Gail Borden. Located in the heart of the Fox River Valley, Elgin has many interesting turn-of-the-century houses. The scenic Fox River divides the town and is used primarily for canoeing, fishing and cycling on the Fox River Bicycle Trail.

What to See and Do

Elgin Area Historical Society Museum. In Old Main, a mid-19th-century school building once known as Elgin Academy, the museum contains artifacts of area history. (Wed-Sat, also by appt) 360 Park St, between College St & Academy Place. Phone 847/742-4248. ¢

Forest preserves.

Burnidge. On 484 acres. Hiking. Cross-country skiing, snowmobiling, toboggan slide. Picnicking. Coombs Rd. Phone 847/695-8410.

Tyler Creek. On 50 acres. Hiking trails, ball diamonds. Picnicking on bluff. IL 31. Phone 847/741-5082.

Voyageurs Landing. On 16 acres. Boat ramp. Picnic shelter. Frontage Rd via IL 31. Phone 847/741-0106.

Blackhawk. On 186 acres. Historical burial mound. Fishing, boating (ramp), canoeing. Hiking, bicycle, bridle trails. Picnicking (shelter). S on IL 31 at the Fox River, in South Elgin. Phone 847/741-7883.

Fox River Trolley Museum. Historic and antique railway equipment displays; oldest interurban railcar in America. Optional 3-mi ride along the scenic Fox River on interurban railcars and trolleys of the early 1900s. (See ANNUAL EVENTS) (July-Aug, Sat & Sun; mid-May-June & Sept-Oct, Sun; also Memorial Day, July 4, Labor Day) S on IL 31 in South Elgin. Phone 847/697-4676. Museum **Free**; Train ride ¢¢

Grand Victoria Riverboat Casino. Cruises sail every 2 hrs. Reservations required. (Daily) 250 S Grove Ave. Phone 847/888-1000. **Free.**

Lord's Park. On 120 acres; includes zoo, tennis courts, pool, lagoons, playgrounds and picnic areas. Grand Blvd. Phone 847/931-6120. Also here is

Elgin Public Museum. Stuffed birds, fish, animals; local and regional history, anthropology, and natural history; discovery rm. (Apr-Oct, daily exc Mon; rest of yr, wkends) 225 Grand Blvd. Phone 847/741-6655. ¢

Annual Events

Trolley Fest. Fox River Trolley Museum. Features once-a-yr operation of historic and antique rail equipment; also model trolley displays. Last wkend June.

Historic Cemetery Walk. Historical Society conducts tours of Bluff City Cemetery. Actors in period costumes stand at grave-sites and tell stories of past lives. Phone 847/742-4248. Last Sun Sept.

Touching on Traditions. Lords Park pavilion. Display honors over 50 countries whose people who have made their homes in Elgin. Costumes, decorations, objects of traditional importance. Phone 847/741-6655. Sat after Thanksgiving-1st Sat Jan.

Seasonal Event

Elgin Symphony Orchestra. Phone 847/622-0300. Oct-Apr.

Motel

⍽★ ★ **DAYS INN.** *1585 Dundee Ave (60120), jct IL 25, Northwest Tollway (I-90).* 847/695-2100; FAX 847/697-9114. 96 rms, 2 story. S $54-$65; D $70-$79; each addl $6; under 18 free. Crib free. TV; cable (premium). Pool, whirlpool. Complimentary continental bkfst. Restaurant nearby. Ck-out 11 am. Meeting rms. Business servs avail. Sundries. Private patios, balconies. Cr cds: A, C, D, DS, MC, V.

⍽⍽⍽⍽ SC

Motor Hotel

★ ★ **HOLIDAY INN.** *345 W River Rd (60123).* 847/695-5000; FAX 847/695-6556. 203 rms, 5 story. S $68; D $76; each addl $8; suites $125-$185; under 18 free; wkend rates. Crib free. TV; cable (premium). Sauna. Heated pool, whirlpool. Coffee in rms. Restaurant 6 am-2 pm, 5-10 pm; Sat from 7 am. Rm serv. Bar 4 pm-midnight; wkends to 1 am. Ck-out noon. Coin lndry. Meeting rms. Business servs avail. In-rm modem link. Valet serv. Holidome. Game rm. Cr cds: A, C, D, DS, ER, JCB, MC, V.

D ⍽⍽⍽⍽ SC

Elk Grove Village

(see Itasca)

Elmhurst (D-3 see Chicago map)

(See also Chicago O'Hare Airport Area, Hillside, Oak Brook)

Settled 1843 **Pop** 42,029 **Elev** 680 ft **Area code** 630 **Zip** 60126
Information Chamber of Commerce & Industry, 105 Maple Ave, PO Box 752; 630/834-6060.

What to See and Do

Elmhurst Historical Museum. Housed in 1892 building; changing exhibits on suburbanization and local history. Research and genealogy collections. Self-guided architectural walking tours. (Daily exc Mon, afternoons; also by appt; closed hols) 120 E Park Ave. Phone 630/833-1457.   **Free.**

Lizzadro Museum of Lapidary Art. Large collection of jade and other hardstone carvings, including displays of minerals, animal dioramas, fossils and gemstones. (Tues-Sat, also Sun afternoons; closed major hols) 220 Cottage Hill Ave, in Wilder Park. Phone 630/833-1616.   ¢¢

Motel

★ ★ **HOLIDAY INN.** *624 N York Rd.* 630/279-1100; FAX 630/279-4038. 229 rms, 4 story. S $80-$90; D $90-$100; suites $150; under 17 free; wkend rates. Crib free. Pet accepted, some restrictions. TV; cable (premium). Indoor pool; whirlpool. Restaurant 7 am-2 pm, 5-10 pm. Rm serv. Bar 11 am-midnight. Ck-out 11 am. Coin lndry. Meeting rms. Business servs avail. In-rm modem link. Valet serv. Free O'Hare Airport transportation. Putting green. Exercise equipt; weight machine, bicycle, sauna. Game rm. Balconies. Cr cds: A, C, D, DS, JCB, MC, V.

D ⍽⍽⍽⍽⍽ SC

Motor Hotel

★ ★ **COURTYARD BY MARRIOTT.** *370 N IL 83 at IL 64 (North Ave).* 630/941-9444; FAX 630/941-3539. 140 units, 7 story, 14 suites. S $89; D $99; each addl $10; suites $99-$129; under 16 free. Crib free. TV; cable (premium), VCR. Indoor pool; whirlpool. Coffee in rms. Restaurant nearby 10 am-10 pm. Bar 4-10 pm, closed Sun. Ck-out 1 pm. Coin lndry. Meeting rms. Business servs avail. In-rm modem link. Valet serv. Exercise equipt; weight machine, treadmill, sauna. Health club privileges. Cr cds: A, C, D, DS, MC, V.

D ⍽⍽⍽⍽ SC

Restaurant

★ **CAFE LAS BELLAS ARTES.** *112 W Park Ave.* 630/530-7725. Hrs: 11 am-2:30 pm, 5:30-10 pm; Fri to 11 pm; Sat 2:30-10 pm; Sun brunch 10 am-2 pm. Closed Mon; some major hols; 2 wks late Aug. Res accepted. Eclectic menu. Bar. Semi-a la carte: lunch $7.50-$15, dinner $15-$25. Prix fixe: lunch $15, dinner $35. Sun brunch $6-$15. Specializes in seafood, fowl, beef tenderloin. European-style decor. Cr cds: A, MC, V.

D

Evanston (B-6)

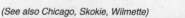

(See also Chicago, Skokie, Wilmette)

Settled 1853 **Pop** 73,233 **Elev** 600 ft **Area code** 847 **E-mail** evchamber@aol.com
Information Chamber of Commerce, One Rotary Center, 1560 Sherman Ave, Suite 860, 60201; 847/328-1500.

Located on the shores of Lake Michigan and adjoining the northern limits of Chicago, Evanston boasts five institutions of higher learning. In 1674, Marquette landed in the natural harbor of what was later the village of Gross Point, important as a lake port. In 1853 the village was renamed Evanston in honor of John Evans, one of the founders of Northwestern University.

What to See and Do

Charles Gates Dawes House (1895). The 28-rm house of General Charles G. Dawes, Nobel Peace Prize winner (1926) and vice president under Calvin Coolidge. National landmark with original furnishings and artifacts in restored rms; local history exhibits; large research collection. Gift shop. Tours. (Tues-Sat afternoons; closed hols) 225 Greenwood St, off Sheridan Rd. Phone 847/475-3410.   ¢¢

Frances E. Willard Home/National Woman's Christian Temperance Union. House where Frances E. Willard, founder of the world-wide WCTU, lived with her family; authentically preserved house contains many souvenirs of her career. Administration building on grounds houses Willard Memorial Alcohol Research Library. (Mon-Fri by appt; closed 1 wk July-Aug, hols) 1730 Chicago Ave. Phone 847/864-1397. **Donation.**

Grosse Point Lighthouse (1873). Constructed after a Lake Michigan wreck near Evanston cost 300 lives. Historical center housed in former fog signal house. Lighthouse film and tower tour (June-Sept, Sat-Sun; closed hol wkends). Sheridan Rd & Central St. Phone 847/328-6961. ¢

Ladd Arboretum. International Friendship Garden; Cherry Tree Lane. (Daily) McCormick Blvd between Emerson & Green Bay Rds. Phone 847/864-5181. **Free.** Also here is

Evanston Ecology Center. Home of Evanston Environmental Assn. Nature education and activities. Environmental educational programs; greenhouse; library. (Daily exc Sun) 2024 McCormick Blvd. Phone 847/864-5181. **Free.**

Merrick Rose Garden. Seasonal displays; 1,200 rose bushes, 65 varieties. Lake Ave & Oak St. **Free.**

Mitchell Indian Museum. Collection of more than 3,000 items of Native American art and artifacts; baskets, pottery, jewelry, Navajo rugs, beadwork, clothing, weapons, tools, stoneware. (Daily exc Mon; closed school hols) Kendall College, 2408 Orrington Ave, 1 blk W of Sheridan Rd. Phone 847/866-1395. ¢

Northwestern University (founded 1851, opened 1855). (11,700 students) Undergraduate and graduate schools in Evanston, professional schools in Chicago; John Evans Center, 1800 Sheridan Rd, has information (Mon-Fri). Dearborn Observatory (1888), 2131 Sheridan Rd, has free public viewing (Apr-Oct, Fri; two viewings, reservation only, phone 847/491-7650); Lindheimer Astronomical Research Center (Apr-Oct, Sat; no viewing). Other places of interest are the Shakespeare Garden, University Library, Norris University Center, Alice Millar Religious Center, Theatre and Interpretation Center, Mary and Leigh Block Gallery (daily exc Mon), Pick-Staiger Concert Hall (many free performances), Dyche Stadium (football), Welsh-Ryan Arena (basketball). Guided walking tours of the lakefront campus leave 1801 Hinman Ave (academic yr, one departure daily exc Sun; July-Aug, two departures Mon-Fri; res, phone 847/491-7271). Clark St at Sheridan Rd. Phone 847/491-3741.

Annual Event

Custer's Fair. Jct Main St & Chicago Ave. Festival featuring over 400 artists and crafters. Phone 847/328-2204. Wkend late June.

Motor Hotel

★ ★ **HOLIDAY INN.** *1501 Sherman Ave (60201). 847/491-6400; FAX 847/328-3090.* 159 rms, 12 story. S, D $114-$124; each addl $10; suites $159-$209; under 18 free. TV; cable (premium), VCR avail. Heated pool; wading pool. Complimentary coffee in rms. Restaurant 6:30 am-2 pm, 5-10 pm. Rm serv. Bar 4 pm-1 am. Ck-out noon. Coin lndry. Meeting rms. Business servs avail. In-rm modem link. Bellhops. Valet serv. Exercise equipt; weights, treadmill, sauna. Health club privileges. Microwaves avail. Cr cds: A, D, DS, JCB, MC, V.

D ≈ ✕ ✕ ✕ SC

Hotel

★ ★ **OMNI ORRINGTON.** *1710 Orrington Ave (60201). 847/866-8700; FAX 847/866-8724.* 277 rms, 9 story. S $135-$165; D $135-$185; each addl $20; suites $200-$450; studio rms $115; under 18 free; wkend rates; higher rates NU graduation (2-day min). Crib free. Valet, covered parking $12. TV; cable, VCR avail. Restaurant 6:30 am-11 pm. Bar 11 am-midnight. Convention facilities. Business servs avail. In-rm modem link. Gift shop. Health club privileges. Cr cds: A, C, D, DS, ER, JCB, MC, V.

D ✕ ✕ SC

Inn

★ **MARGARITA EUROPEAN INN.** *1566 Oak Ave (60201). 847/869-2273.* 42 rms, 18 share bath, 6 story, 11 suites. No A/C. Apr-Dec: S $90-$120; D $100-$130; each addl $10; suites $125-$150; higher rates university graduation; lower rates rest of yr. Crib $10. TV in some rms.

Complimentary continental bkfst. Restaurant 11:30 am-2 pm, 5:30-9 pm; Fri, Sat 5:30-10 pm. Ck-out 11 am, ck-in 2 pm. Business servs avail. In-rm modem link. Valet serv. Built in 1912; originally used as a woman's club. Antique furniture, rooftop garden. Cr cds: A, C, D, MC, V.

D SC

Restaurants

★ ★ **THE DINING ROOM AT KENDALL COLLEGE.** *2408 Orrington Ave (60201). 847/866-1399.* E-mail grandpre@interaccess.com. Hrs: noon-1:30 pm, 6-8 pm; Sat 6-8:30 pm. Closed Sun; major hols. Res required. Complete meal: lunch $14.95. A la carte entrees: dinner $14.95-$17.95. Specializes in regional Amer and French cuisine. Own baking. Open kitchen. Kitchen and dining rm staffed by Culinary School of Kendall College students. Totally nonsmoking. Cr cds: A, DS, MC, V.

D

★ **JILLY'S CAFE.** *2614 Green Bay Rd (60201-1422). 847/869-7636.* Hrs: 11:30 am-2 pm, 5-9 pm; Fri, Sat to 10 pm; Sun 5-8 pm; Sun brunch 10:30 am-2 pm. Closed Mon; some major hols. Res accepted. Wine. Semi-a la carte: lunch $5-$8, dinner $9-$16. Sun brunch $16.50. Menu changes quarterly. Specializes in fresh fish, seasonal game. Own pastries. Cr cds: A, C, D, MC, V.

★ **KUNI'S.** *511 Main St (60202). 847/328-2004.* Hrs: 11:30 am-2 pm, 5-10 pm; Sun from 5 pm. Closed Tues; Jan 1, Thanksgiving, Dec 25. Japanese menu. Sushi bar. A la carte entrees: lunch $5.75-$10, dinner $10-$24. Specializes in sushi, sashimi, tempura, beef & chicken teriyaki. Cr cds: A, MC, V.

D

✓★ **LAS PALMAS.** *1642 Maple St (60201). 847/328-2555.* Hrs: 11 am-10 pm; Fri, Sat to 11 pm; Sun from 1 pm. Closed Thanksgiving, Dec 25. Res accepted. Mexican menu. Bar. Semi-a la carte: lunch $3.50-$6.25, dinner $5.95-$12.95. Specializes in steak & chicken fajitas, grilled jumbo shrimp with garlic sauce. Harpist Thurs, Sat. Parking. Outdoor dining. Mexican decor. Cr cds: A, C, D, DS, MC, V.

D

✓★ **LINDO MEXICO.** *1934 Maple St (60201). 847/475-3435.* Hrs: 11:30 am-10 pm; Fri, Sat to midnight; Sun 4-10 pm. Closed Jan 1, Thanksgiving, Dec 25. Res accepted. Mexican menu. Serv bar. Semi-a la carte: lunch $4.95-$8.95, dinner $7.95-$13.95. Specializes in fajitas, enchiladas suizas. Parking. Mexican decor. Cr cds: A, C, D, DS, MC, V.

D SC ↵

✓★ **LUCKY PLATTER.** *514 Main St (60202), ¹/₂ blk E of Chicago Ave. 847/869-4064.* Hrs: 7 am-10 pm. Continental menu. Semi-a la carte: bkfst $3.95-$7.95, lunch, dinner $6-$15. Specializes in grilled fish, vegetarian entrees, chef-made pizzas. Own baking. Street parking. Informal, traditional, family-style dining area; knick-knacks and local art throughout. Totally nonsmoking. Cr cds: MC, V.

★ ★ **NEW JAPAN RESTAURANT.** *1322-24 Chicago Ave (60201). 847/475-5980.* Hrs: 11:30 am-2:15 pm, 5-9:15 pm; Fri, Sat to 10:15 pm; Sun 4:30-8:45 pm. Closed Mon; major hols. Res accepted. Japanese menu; also French menu (dinner). Serv bar. A la carte entrees: lunch $5.95-$6.95. Complete meals: dinner $11.50-$18.50. Specializes in sushi, tempura, sukiyaki. Cr cds: A, C, D, MC, V.

D

★ ★ ★ **OCEANIQUE.** *505 Main St. 847/864-3435.* Hrs: 5:30-9:30 pm; Fri, Sat to 10 pm. Closed Sun; major hols. Res accepted. French, Amer menu. Extensive wine list. Semi-a la carte: dinner $13.95-$28.95. Complete meals: dinner $28.95. Specializes in fresh fish, sirloin steak, rack of lamb. Own pastries, desserts. In historic building (1929). Southern European decor. Cr cds: A, D, DS, MC, V.

D ↵

★ ★ **PETE MILLER'S STEAKHOUSE.** *1557 Sherman Ave (60201). 847/328-0399.* Hrs: 11:30 am-2 pm, 5-10 pm; Fri to 11 pm; Sat 5-11 pm; Sun 4:30-10 pm; Sun brunch 10 am-noon. Closed July 4, Thanksgiving, Dec 25. Res accepted. Bar to 12:30 am, Sun to 11:30 pm. Semi-a la carte: lunch $5.95-$18, dinner $15-$30. Sun brunch $17.95. Specialties: prime-aged steak. Salad bar (lunch). Jazz nightly. Valet parking Thurs-Sat. Separate billiard rm. Cr cds: A, C, MC, V.

✔ ★ **SIAM SQUARE.** *622 Davis St (60201). 847/475-0860.* Hrs: 11:30 am-10 pm; Fri, Sat to 10:30 pm; Sun to 9 pm. Closed Thanksgiving, Dec 25. Res accepted. Wine, beer. Thai menu. A la carte entrees: lunch, dinner $5.25-$9.95; buffet: lunch $6.95-$9.95. Complete meal: dinner $8.95-$13.95. Specializes in fresh spring rolls with plum sauce, seafood & duck, seasonal Thai dishes. Outdoor dining. 18th-century Thai decor. Cr cds: A, C, D, DS, MC, V.

D ⬛

★ ★ ★ **TRIO.** *1625 Hinman Ave (60201). 847/733-8746.* A signature of Trio is its unusual presentation of food—artistically arranged on slabs of marble and mirror, in huge deep bowls, in bamboo baskets, in a lacquer box, as well as on decorative plates. Continental menu. Own baking. Hrs: 5:30-9:30 pm; Sat 5-10:30 pm; Sun 5-9 pm. Closed Mon; some major hols. Res recommended. Serv bar. Wine cellar. Complete meal: dinner $60-$75. Jacket. Totally nonsmoking. Cr cds: A, C, D, DS, JCB, MC, V.

D

★ ★ **VA PENSIERO.** *1566 Oak Ave (60201), in The Margarita European Inn, 1 blk E of Ridge Ave. 847/475-7779.* Hrs: 11:30 am-2 pm, 5:30-9 pm; Fri to 10 pm; Sat 5:30-10 pm. Closed Sun; some major hols. Res accepted. Italian menu. Bar. Semi-a la carte: lunch $7-$12, dinner $15.50-$21.50. Specialities: arrosta di salmone senape, gamberi con salsa di pistacchi, ravioli di carciofi. Own pastries. Outdoor dining. Cr cds: A, C, D, DS, MC, V.

D ⬛

Unrated Dining Spots

CARMEN'S. *1012 Church St. 847/328-0031.* Hrs: 11 am-11 pm; Fri to midnight; Sat 4 pm-midnight; Sun 4-11 pm. Closed some major hols. Res accepted. Bar. A la carte entrees: lunch, dinner $4-$20. Specializes in stuffed pizza, pasta, Italian beef sandwiches. Parking. Cr cds: A, MC, V.

D

MERLE'S #1 BARBECUE. *1727 Benson St (60201). 847/475-7766.* Hrs: 11:30 am-10:30 pm; Fri, Sat to 11:30 pm; Sun noon-10 pm. Closed Thanksgiving, Dec 25. Southwestern menu. Bar. Semi-a la carte: lunch $4.50-$7.95, dinner $8.95-$13.95. Child's meals. Specializes in pulled pork, baby back ribs, chicken barbecue. Cr cds: A, D, MC, V.

Fort Kaskaskia State Historic Site (J-3)

(For accommodations see Carbondale)

(6 mi NW of Chester, near Ellis Grove, off IL 3)

This 275-acre park includes the earthworks of the old fort, built in 1733, rebuilt in 1736 by the French and, finally, destroyed to prevent British occupation after the Treaty of Paris. As a result of post-Revolutionary War anarchy (1784), the ruins of the fort, while in the hands of the Connecticut renegade John Dodge, were the scene of murders and revelry. Nearby is the Garrison Hill Cemetery where 3,800 old settlers' remains rest, removed from the original graveyard when floodwaters threatened to wash them away. The Pierre Menard mansion, at the base of the bluffs along the Mississippi, was built in 1802 in the style of a French colonial house. The home has been called the "Mt Vernon of the West." Some original furnishings have been reclaimed and reinstalled by the state; tours (daily). The park provides hiking, picnicking, tent & trailer camping (dump station; hookups; standard fees). For information contact Site Manager, 4372 Park Rd, Ellis Grove 62241; 618/859-3741 or 618/859-3031 (Menard Mansion).

Freeport (A-3)

(See also Rockford)

Settled 1838 **Pop** 25,840 **Elev** 780 ft **Area code** 815 **Zip** 61032 **E-mail** stephcvb@mwci.net

Information Stephenson County Convention & Visitors Bureau, 2047 AYP Rd; 815/233-1357 or 800/369-2955.

According to legend, Freeport is named for the generosity of its pioneer settler, William Baker, who was chided by his wife for running a "free port" for everyone coming along the trail. It was the scene of the second Lincoln-Douglas debate; the site is marked by a memorial boulder and a life-size statue of Lincoln and Douglas in debate. Freeport, an agricultural and industrial center, is the seat of Stephenson County.

What to See and Do

Freeport Arts Center. Collection includes Oriental and Native American art; European painting and sculpture; Egyptian, Greek and American antiquities; contemporary exhibits. (Daily exc Mon, afternoons; closed hols) 121 N Harlem Ave. Phone 815/235-9755. ¢

Krape Park. Merry-go-round (mid-May-mid-Sept), garden, waterfall, duck pond. Boat rentals, tennis courts, miniature golf. Picnicking, playground, concession (mid-May-mid-Sept). (Daily) Park Blvd. Phone 815/235-6114. **Free.**

Silvercreek and Stephenson Railroad. Trips on a 1912, 36-ton steam locomotive with 3 antique cabooses and a flat car. Also historical museum. (Memorial Day-Labor Day, periodic wkends) Walnut & Lamm Rds. Phone 815/232-2306. ¢¢

Stephenson County Historical Museum. In the 1857 Oscar Taylor house, museum features 19th-century furnishings and changing exhibits. On grounds with arboretum are 1840 log cabin, turn-of-the-century schoolhouse, blacksmith shop and farm museum. (May-Oct, Wed-Sun; rest of yr, Fri-Sun, afternoons; closed hols). 1440 S Carroll Ave. Phone 815/232-8419. ¢

Annual Event

Stephenson County Fair. 7 days mid-Aug.

Motel

★ ★ **GUEST HOUSE INN.** *1300 E South St. 815/235-3121; FAX 815/235-4946.* 85 rms, 2 story. S $61; D $67; each addl $6; under 19 free. Crib free. Pet accepted. TV; cable (premium). Heated pool; poolside serv. Complimentary coffee in rms. Restaurant 6 am-2 pm, 5-10 pm. Rm serv. Bar 4 pm-1 am. Ck-out noon. Meeting rms. Business servs avail. Exercise equipt; stair machine, weight machine. Game rm. Cr cds: A, C, D, DS, JCB, MC, V.

D 🐾 ≈ 🏋 🚫 🛠 **SC**

Restaurant

✔ ★ **BELTLINE CAFE.** *325 W South St. 815/232-5512.* Hrs: 5:30 am-2 pm. Closed Easter, Thanksgiving, Dec 25. Semi-a la carte: bkfst

$2.25-$4.75, lunch $2.25-$5.25. Specializes in homemade soups and pies. Built 1890. No cr cds accepted.

SC

Galena (A-3)

(See also Platteville, WI)

Founded 1826 **Pop** 3,647 **Elev** 609 ft **Area code** 815 **Zip** 61036
Information Galena/Jo Daviess County Convention & Visitors Bureau, 720 Park Ave; 800/747-9377.

A quiet town of historical and architectural interest set on terraces cut by the old Fever River, Galena was once a major crossroads for French exploration of the New World and the commercial and cultural capital of the Northwest Territory. Deposits of lead were discovered in the region by the mid-18th century; when the town was laid out, it was named for the ore. By 1845, the area was producing nearly all the nation's lead, and Galena was the richest and most important city in the state. With wealth came opulence; the grand mansions standing today were built on fortunes acquired from the lead and steamboat business. However, the mining of lead peaked just before the outbreak of the Civil War. After the war, the city's importance declined rapidly. Although Galena's sympathies were divided at the outbreak of the Civil War, two companies were formed to support the Union. Ulysses S. Grant, who had recently come to Galena from St Louis, accompanied local troops to Springfield as drillmaster.

The town has changed little since the middle of the last century. To walk the streets of Galena today is to take a step back in time. The 19th-century architecture varies from federal to Greek revival and from Italianate to Queen Anne. Ninety percent of the town's buildings are listed on the National Register of Historic Places. A favorite destination of weekend travelers from surrounding areas, especially Chicago, Galena is also a mecca for antique hunters and specialty shoppers.

What to See and Do

Belvedere Mansion & Gardens (1857). Italianate/"steamboat Gothic" mansion (22 rms) restored and furnished with antiques, including pieces used on set of *Gone With the Wind*. (Memorial Day-Oct, daily) Combination ticket with Dowling House. 1008 Park Ave. Phone 815/777-0747. ¢¢

Dowling House (ca 1826). Restored stone house, oldest in Galena, is authentically furnished as a trading post with primitive living quarters. Guided tours. (May-Dec, daily; rest of year, limited hrs) Combination ticket with Belvedere Mansion & Gardens. 220 N Diagonal St. Phone 815/777-1250. ¢¢

Galena-Jo Daviess County History Museum. Located in 1858 Italianate house, museum displays Civil War artifacts, decorative arts; *A Ripple in Time,* a color slide tape presentation on way of life of the town's earliest settlers; original Peace in Union, Thomas Nast's version of the surrender at Appomattox. (Daily; closed Jan 1, Thanksgiving, Dec 25) 211 S Bench St. Phone 815/777-9129. ¢¢

Grace Episcopal Church (1848). Gothic-revival church was later remodeled by William LeBaron Jenney, father of the skyscraper. Contains Belgian stained-glass windows; eagle lecturn carved by early Galena craftsman; one-manual organ in use since 1838—brought from New York City to New Orleans and then by steamboat to Galena. (Sun; also by appt) Hill & Prospect Sts. Phone 815/777-2590. **Donation.**

Grant Hills Antique Auto Museum. Display of more than 35 antique and classic automobiles; changing exhibits. (Mid-May-Oct, daily; rest of yr, wkends; closed Jan 1, Thanksgiving, Dec 25) 1 mi E on US 20. Phone 815/777-2115. ¢¢

Old Market House State Historic Site. (1845-1846). Once hub of city life, this Greek-revival building and forecourt were originally used as city market. Historical and architectural exhibits; interpretive program. (Thurs-Mon; closed Jan 1, Thanksgiving, Dec 25) Market Square, N Commerce St. Phone 815/777-2570. **Free.**

Sightseeing. Several trolley tours are available. For information contact the Convention and Visitors Bureau.

Silver Eagle **Casino Cruises.** Departs from Frenteress Lake Marina, near East Dubuque. (Daily; winter months operates dockside; closed Christmas eve) 11 mi W on IL 20. For schedule, reservations phone 815/777-2648 or 800/SILVER-1.

Skiing. Chestnut Mt Resort. Quad, 2 triple chairlifts, 5 rope tows; patrol, school, rentals; snowmaking; restaurants, cafeteria, bars; lodge. Longest run 3,500 ft; vertical drop 475 ft. (Mid-Nov-mid-Mar, daily) 8700 W Chestnut Rd, 8 mi SE. Phone 815/777-1320 or 800/397-1320. ¢¢¢¢

Ulysses S. Grant Home State Historic Site. Italianate house was given to General Grant upon his return from the Civil War (1865); original furnishings and Grant family items. Interpretive program. Picnicking. (Apr-Dec, daily; rest of yr, Thurs-Mon; closed Jan 1, Thanksgiving, Dec 25) 500 Bouthillier St. Phone 815/777-0248. ¢

Vinegar Hill Lead Mine & Museum. Guided tour of old mine showing early mining techniques. (June-Aug, daily; May & Sept-Oct, wkends) 6 mi N on IL 84, then E on Furlong Rd, to 8885 N Three Pines Rd. Phone 815/777-0855. ¢

Annual Events

June Tour of Historic Homes. Five houses open to public. 2nd wkend June.

Stagecoach Trail Festival. A celebration of pioneer and Native American history. 4th wkend June.

Antique Town Rod Run. Recreation Park. Pre-1949 vehicles. July.

Galena Arts Festival. 3rd wkend July.

Fall Tour of Homes. Last full wkend Sept.

Ladies' Getaway. Entertainment and demonstrations especially for women. Mid-Sept.

Galena Country Fair. Grant City Park. Exhibits, entertainment, country food. Columbus Day wkend.

Motels

★ ★ **BEST WESTERN QUIET HOUSE SUITES.** *9923 W US 20.* 815/777-2577; FAX 815/777-0584. 42 suites, 3 story. S $91-$180; D $91-$190; each addl $10; higher rates: special events, wkends. Pet accepted, some restrictions; $15. TV; cable (premium). Indoor/outdoor pool; whirlpool. Complimentary coffee in lobby. Restaurant adj 7 am-11 pm. Ck-out 11 am. Business servs avail. Exercise equipt; weights, treadmill. Downhill/x-country ski 12 mi. Some balconies. Cr cds: A, C, D, DS, ER, JCB, MC, V.

D ⚓ ☀ ≈ ⊠ 🐾 SC

★ **PALACE.** *11383 US 20 W, 2 mi W on US 20, IL 84.* 815/777-2043; FAX 815/777-2625. 51 rms in motel, guest houses, 1-2 story. Some rm phones. S $30; D $55; suites $110-$200; rms in Ryan & Bedford houses $85-$175. Crib $4. Pet accepted, some restrictions. TV. Indoor whirlpool. Complimentary coffee in lobby. Restaurant nearby. Ck-out 11 am. Downhill ski 9 mi; x-country ski 6 mi. Complex consists of motel; Ryan House (1876), a 24-rm Italianate/Victorian mansion with antiques; and Bedford House (1850), an Italianate structure with original chandeliers, leaded glass and walnut staircase. Cr cds: A, DS, MC, V.

⚓ ☀ 🐾 SC

Hotel

★ ★ **DESOTO HOUSE.** *230 S Main St.* 815/777-0090; FAX 815/777-9529; res: 800/343-6562. 55 rms, 4 story. Apr-Oct: S, D $95-$160; each addl $10; suites $140-$175; package plans; lower rates rest of yr. Crib free. TV; cable (premium). VCR avail. Coffee in rms. Restaurant 7 am-3 pm, 5-10 pm. Bar 11-1 am. Ck-out 11 am. Meeting rms. Business servs avail. Free covered parking. Downhill ski 8 mi; x-country ski 9 mi.

Fireplace in suites. Renovated historic hotel built 1855. Cr cds: A, C, D, DS, MC, V.

⬜🏊🚭🔥SC

Inns

★ ★ **ALDRICH GUEST HOUSE.** *900 3rd St. 815/777-3323.* 5 rms, 2 story. No rm phones. S, D $75-$115; each addl $15. Children over 12 yrs only. TV in sitting rm; cable (premium), VCR. Complimentary full bkfst. Restaurant nearby. Ck-out 11 am, ck-in 4 pm. Street parking. Downhill/x-country ski 8 mi. Antiques. Library/sitting rm, fireplace. Screened porch. Built in 1845 by an Illinois state representative who later became a US senator from Minnesota. Totally nonsmoking. Cr cds: DS, MC, V.

🏊🚭🔥SC

✔★ **COLONIAL GUEST HOUSE.** *1004 Park Ave. 815/777-0336.* 6 rms, some A/C, 3 story. No rm phones. S $40; D $65-$85; each addl $15. Crib free. TV; cable. Complimentary continental bkfst. Ck-out 11 am, ck-in noon. Downhill/x-country ski 7 mi. Refrigerators. Porches. Antiques. Built 1826. No cr cds accepted.

🏊🚭🔥SC

★ ★ **HELLMAN GUEST HOUSE.** *318 Hill St. 815/777-3638.* 4 rms, 3 with shower only, 3 story. No rm phones. Apr-Oct: S $84-129; D $89-$129. Complimentary full bkfst. Ck-out 11 am, ck-in 4-6 pm. Downhill ski 10 mi; x-country ski 8 mi. Queen Anne-style house (1895). Scenic view of downtown. Totally nonsmoking. Cr cds: DS, MC, V.

🏊🚭

★ **LOGAN HOUSE.** *301 N Main St, at Franklin St. 815/777-0033; FAX 815/777-0049.* 6 rms, 2 story. No rm phones. May-Dec: S, D $75-$90; each addl $7; suites $90; lower rates rest of yr. TV; cable (premium), VCR avail (free movies). Complimentary continental bkfst. Restaurant (see CAFE ITALIA). Ck-out 11 am, ck-in 2 pm. Street parking. In 1855 building constructed as one of town's first hotel. Country decor in guest rms. Cr cds: A, C, DS, MC, V.

⬜🏊🔥SC

★ ★ **PARK AVENUE GUEST HOUSE.** *208 Park Ave. 815/777-1075; res: 800/359-0743.* 4 rms (3 with shower only), 3 story. No rm phones. S $70-$100; D $75-$105. Children over 12 yrs only. TV; cable (premium), VCR avail (movies). Complimentary continental bkfst. Restaurant nearby. Ck-out 11 am, ck-in 4 pm. Downhill/x-country ski 7 mi. Built in 1893; antiques. Totally nonsmoking. Cr cds: DS, MC, V.

🏊🚭🔥

★ ★ **PINE HOLLOW.** *4700 N Council Hill Rd, 2 mi N of downtown, N on Main. 815/777-1071.* 5 rms, 2 story. No rm phones. S, D $75-$120; each addl $15. Children over 12 yrs only. Complimentary continental bkfst. Restaurant nearby. Ck-out 11 am, ck-in 3 pm. On 120-acre evergreen tree farm. Country decor. Fireplaces. Totally nonsmoking. Cr cds: DS, MC, V.

🚭🔥

★ ★ **QUEEN ANNE GUEST HOUSE.** *200 Park St. 815/777-3849.* 4 rms, 2 story. Apr-Dec: S, D $85-$95; lower rates rest of yr. Complimentary continental bkfst. Ck-out 11 am, ck-in 3 pm. Downhill/x-country ski 8 mi. Built 1891; wraparound porch, library, many antiques. Totally nonsmoking. Cr cds: DS, MC, V.

🏊🚭🔥SC

★ ★ **STILLMAN'S MANSION.** *513 Bouthillier St, opp U.S. Grant house. 815/777-0557; FAX 815/777-8098.* 7 rms, 3 story. No elvtr. No rm phones. S, D $65-$150. TV; cable. Complimentary continental bkfst. Bar; dancing. Ck-out 11 am, ck-in 3 pm. Downhill/X-country ski 9-12 mi. In Italianate/Victorian mansion (1858). Antique Victorian furnishings; some fireplaces, in-rm whirlpools. Cr cds: A, DS, MC, V.

🔥

Resort

★ ★ ★ **EAGLE RIDGE INN & RESORT.** *Eagle Ridge Dr, 6 mi E on US 20, in Galena Territory. 815/777-2444; FAX 815/777-0445; res: 800/892-2269.* 80 rms, 2 story. Apr-Oct: S, D $109-$255; each addl $10; under 18 free; villas $228-$515; wkly rates; golf plan; lower rates rest of yr. Crib free. TV; cable (premium), VCR (movies $4). Indoor pool; whirlpool, poolside serv. Playground. Supervised child's activities; ages 2-16. Complimentary coffee in rms. Dining rm 7 am-3 pm, 5-10:30 pm; Fri-Sat to 11 pm. Rm serv. Bar 11-1 am; entertainment exc Mon. Ck-out noon, ck-in 4 pm. Meeting rms. Business servs avail. Bellhops. Sundries. Airport, bus depot transportation. Tennis. 9-hole golf course; three 18-hole golf courses; greens fee $77, pro, putting green, driving range. Canoes, pontoon-boats. Bike rental. Sand beach, private lake, marina. Downhill ski 10 mi; x-country ski on site. Trail rides. Hayrides, sleigh rides. Soc dir. Game rm. Exercise equipt; treadmill, stair machine, sauna. Massage. Minibars; some refrigerators. Private patios, balconies. Located on a bluff, overlooking a lake. Cr cds: A, C, D, DS, MC, V.

⬜🏊🏌🏃🏊🏃🔥🚭

Restaurants

★ **BUBBA'S.** *300 N Main, at Franklin. 815/777-8030.* Hrs: 4-10 pm. Closed Easter, Dec 25. Seafood menu. Bar. Semi-a la carte: dinner $12.95-$21.95. Specialties: New Orleans jambalaya, grilled swordfish with shallots, filet mignon. Former ice cream parlor (1895). Smoking in bar only. Cr cds: A, DS, MC, V.

★ ★ **CAFE ITALIA.** *(See Logan House Inn) 815/777-0033.* Hrs: 11 am-3 pm, 5-10 pm; Sat & Sun from 4:30 pm. Res accepted. Italian, Amer menu. Bar. Semi-a la carte: lunch $4.95-$8.95, dinner $8.95-$18.95. Child's meals. Specializes in pasta, barbecued ribs, steak. Built 1855. Cr cds: A, C, D, DS, MC, V.

★ ★ **FRIED GREEN TOMATOES.** *1301 Irish Hollow Rd. 815/777-3938.* Hrs: 11 am-2:30 pm, 5-9:30 pm; Fri-Sat to 10 pm. Closed Thanksgiving, Dec 25. Res accepted. Italian, Amer menu. Bar. Semi-a la carte: lunch $5.95-$9.95, dinner $9.95-$19.95. Specialties: salmon Florentine, pasta aglio, fried green tomatoes, Black Angus beef. Pianist Sat. Outdoor dining. Three dining levels in historic (1851) rural setting. Cr cds: A, MC, V.

⬜

✔★ **GRANT'S PLACE.** *515 S Main St, on 2nd floor of Galena Cellars Winery. 815/777-3331.* Hrs: 11 am-10 pm. Bar. Semi-a la carte: lunch $4-$7, dinner $9.95-$15.95. Specializes in steak, sandwiches, fish. Outdoor dining. General U.S. Grant memorabilia; woodcuts of Grant and Civil War soldiers. Cr cds: A, MC, V.

★ **LOG CABIN.** *201 N Main St. 815/777-0393.* Hrs: 11 am-10 pm; Fri, Sat to 11 pm. Closed Mon; Thanksgiving, Dec 24-25. Res accepted. Bar. Semi-a la carte: lunch $2.95-$7.95, dinner $4.75-$15. Child's meals. Specializes in steak, seafood. Pianist Fri, Sat. No cr cds accepted.

⬜

★ **SILVER ANNIE'S LTD.** *124 N. Commerce St, at Perry. 815/777-3131.* Hrs: 5-9 pm; Fri & Sat to 10 pm. Closed Thanksgiving, Dec 24, 25. Res accepted. Italian, Amer menu. Bar. Semi-a la carte: dinner $8.50-$17.95. Child's meals. Specializes in fettucine, pork chops, seafood. Own desserts. Entertainment Fri-Mon. Totally nonsmoking. Cr cds: A, C, D, DS, MC, V.

Galesburg (C-3)

(See also Bishop Hill, Moline, Monmouth)

Settled 1837 **Pop** 33,530 **Elev** 773 ft **Area code** 309 **Zip** 61401
Information Convention & Visitors Bureau, 292 E Simmons St, PO Box 749; 309/343-1194.

Eastern pioneers came to this area on the prairie to establish a community centering around a school for the training of ministers, Knox College. The town was named for their leader, G.W. Gale. Galesburg was an important station on the Underground Railroad. It is also the birth and burial place of poet Carl Sandburg.

What to See and Do

Carl Sandburg State Historic Site (1860). Restored birthplace cottage; antique furnishings, some from Sandburg family; adjoining museum contains memorabilia. Remembrance Rock, named for Sandburg's historical novel, is a granite boulder under which his ashes were placed. (Daily; closed Jan 1, Thanksgiving, Dec 25) 331 E 3rd St. Phone 309/342-2361. **Free.**

Knox College (1837). (1,000 students) Old Main (1856), original college building and site of Lincoln-Douglas debate. Fine Arts Center houses exhibits by students and faculty. Tours (when school is in session). Cherry & South Sts, 2 blks S of Public Square. Phone 309/341-7313.

Lake Storey Recreational Area. Waterpark (Memorial Day-Labor Day); boat rentals. 18-hole golf (late Mar-Nov; fee); tennis. Picnicking (Apr-Oct), playground, gardens, concessions. Camping (mid-Apr-mid-Oct; fee; hook-ups, dump station, 2-wk max). Pets on leash only. (Daily) ¼ mi N on US 150, then ½ mi W on S Lake Storey Rd. Phone 309/345-3683.

Annual Events

Railroad Days. Tour of train, yards, depot; memorabilia displays, carnival, fun runs, street fair. 4th wkend June.

Knox County Fair. 8 mi SE, off I-74 exit 51 in Knoxville. Grandstand, racetrack, carnival, exhibit halls. Phone 309/289-2714. Late July.

Stearman Fly-In. Airport. Air shows, exhibits, Stearman contests. 1st wkend after Labor Day.

Motel

✔★★ **COMFORT INN.** *907 W Carl Sandburg Dr (US 150 E).* 309/344-5445. 46 rms, 2 story. May-Sept: S $50.95-$65.95; D $55.95-$70.95; each addl $5; under 18 free; higher rates: Railroad Days, Stearman Fly-in wkend; lower rates rest of yr. Crib free. Pet accepted. TV; cable (premium), VCR avail. Complimentary continental bkfst. Complimentary coffee in lobby. Restaurant nearby. Ck-out 11 am. Meeting rm. Business servs avail. Cr cds: A, C, D, DS, ER, MC, V.

⬚ 🐾 ⌁ 🔥 SC

Motor Hotels

★★★ **JUMER'S CONTINENTAL INN.** *E Main St, at I-74.* 309/343-7151; FAX 309/343-7151, ext. 264; res: 800/285-8637. 148 rms, 2 story. S $63-$71; D $69-$77; each addl $6; suites $130; under 18 free; wkend rates. Crib free. Pet accepted. TV; cable (premium), VCR avail. Indoor pool; whirlpool, sauna. Complimentary coffee in lobby. Restaurant 6:30 am-10 pm. Rm serv. Bar 11-midnight; Sun from noon; entertainment. Ck-out noon. Coin lndry. Meeting rms. Business servs avail. Bellhops. Valet serv. Sundries. Gift shop. Free airport, RR station transportation. Golf privileges. Health club privileges. Putting green. Many private patios. In-rm whirlpool. Cr cds: A, C, D, DS, MC, V.

⬚ 🐾 🧍 ⌁ 🏌 ⌁ 🔥 SC

★ **RAMADA INN.** *29 Public Sq, just off Main St.* 309/343-9161; FAX 309/343-0157. 96 rms, 7 story. S $50-$55; D $55-$60; each addl $5. Crib free. Pet accepted. TV; cable (premium), VCR avail (movies $6). Indoor pool; whirlpool. Complimentary coffee in lobby. Restaurant. Ck-out noon. Meeting rms. Business servs avail. In-rm modem link. Health club privileges. Game rm. Balconies. Near Knox College campus. Cr cds: A, C, D, DS, JCB, MC, V.

⬚ 🐾 ⌁ ⌁ 🔥 SC

Restaurants

★ **LANDMARK CAFE AND CRÊPERIE.** *62 S Seminary St.* 309/343-5376. Hrs: 11 am-9 pm; Fri to 10 pm; Sat 9 am-10 pm; Sun 9 am-9 pm. Closed some major hols. Res accepted. French, Amer menu. A la carte entrees: bkfst $3.95-$7.50. Semi-a la carte: lunch, dinner $4.95-$12.95. Specializes in European-style crêpes, spinach bisque, health foods. Own desserts. Patio dining. Cr cds: A, C, D, DS, MC, V.

⬚ ⊐

✔★ **OOGIE'S.** *1721 N Henderson (US 150 W).* 309/344-1259. Hrs: 6 am-11 pm. Closed Dec 25. Res accepted. Serv bar. Semi-a la carte: bkfst $2.50-$6, lunch $4-$7, dinner $5-$11. Child's meals. Specializes in home-cooking, ribs, fish. Cr cds: DS, MC, V.

⬚

★ **PACKINGHOUSE.** *441 Mulberry.* 309/342-6868. Hrs: 11 am-2 pm, 5-9 pm; Fri, Sat to 10 pm; Sun noon-8 pm. Closed some major hols. Res accepted. Serv bar. Semi-a la carte: lunch $4.50-$6.95, dinner $8.95-$16.95. Child's meals. Specializes in prime rib, steak, seafood. Salad bar. Own baking. In former meat packing plant (1912). Cr cds: A, C, D, DS, MC, V.

⬚ SC ⊐

★★ **THE STEAK HOUSE.** *951 N Henderson (US 150).* 309/343-9994. Hrs: 5-11 pm. Closed Sun; major hols. Res accepted. Bar 2 pm-1 am; Fri, Sat to 2 am. Semi-a la carte: dinner $8.95-$25. Specializes in aged prime beef, cornish game hen, seafood. Cr cds: A, DS, MC, V.

⊐ ♥

Geneva (B-5)

(For accommodations see Aurora, St Charles)

Settled 1833 **Pop** 12,617 **Elev** 720 ft **Area code** 630 **Zip** 60134 **E-mail** chamber@www-geneva.com **Web** www.geneva.com
Information Chamber of Commerce, 8 S 3rd St, PO Box 481; 630/232-6060.

Lured by the stories of soldiers returning from the Black Hawk War, Easterners settled here on both sides of the Fox River. Geneva became a rallying place and supply point for pioneers continuing farther west. The first retail establishment was a hardware and general store; the second sold satin and lace, which began Geneva's unique tradition as a place hospitable to highly specialized retailing. (Today, the town has more than 100 specialty stores.) Geneva's greatest asset, however, is its historic district, which has more than 200 buildings listed on the National Register of Historic Places. Cyclists and hikers enjoy the trails that wind through the parks adjacent to the Fox River.

What to See and Do

Garfield Farm Museum. This 281-acre living history farm (currently under restoration) includes 1846 brick tavern, 1842 haybarn and 1849 horse barn, poultry, oxen, sheep, gardens and prairie. Special events throughout the yr. Grounds (June-Sept, Wed, Sun; other times by appt). 5 mi W on IL 38 to Garfield Rd, near La Fox. Phone 630/584-8485. ¢¢

Wheeler Park. This 57-acre park features flower and nature gardens, hiking; tennis, ball fields; access to riverside bicycle trail; picnicking. Miniature golf (late May-early Sept, daily; rest of May & Sept, Fri-Sun; fee). Park (daily). Off IL 31, N of IL 38. Phone 630/232-4542 (park) or 630/208-1179 (golf). **Free.** Also in park is

Geneva Historical Society Museum. Five rms of exhibits highlighting Native Americans, pioneers, Civil War and the turn of the century; local memorabilia, documents; toys and youth gallery. (Apr-Oct, Wed-Sun, afternoons) Phone 630/232-4951. **Free.**

Annual Events

Geneva on the River. 1st wkend May.

Swedish Days. Six-day festival with parade, entertainment, arts & crafts, music, food. Begins Tues after Father's Day.

Festival of the Vine. Autumn harvest celebration. Food, wine tasting. Music, craft show, antique carriage rides. 2nd wkend Sept.

Christmas Walk. 1st Fri & Sat Dec.

Restaurants

★ ★ **MILL RACE INN.** *4 E State St, jct IL 38 & IL 25. 630/232-2030.* Hrs: 11:30 am-9 pm; Fri, Sat to 10 pm; Sun bkfst 10 am-2 pm. Closed Dec 25. Res accepted. Bar. Semi-a la carte: lunch $5.25-$11.25, dinner $13.95-$23.95. Sun bkfst $6.95-$10.95. Child's meals. Specializes in seafood, prime rib, Swedish meatballs. Own pastries. Entertainment Tues-Sat. Valet parking. Gazebo dining. Country decor. 1842 blacksmith shop; fireplaces. On Fox River. Family-owned. Cr cds: A, C, D, MC, V.

 D SC

★ ★ **RIVERWALK.** *35 N River Lane. 630/232-1330.* Hrs: 11 am-4 pm, 5-10 pm; Fri, Sat to 11 pm; Sun 4-9 pm; Sun brunch 10 am-2:30 pm. Res accepted. Continental menu. Bar. Semi-a la carte: lunch $5-$8, dinner $10-$20. Sun brunch 12.95. Child's meals. Specializes in prime rib, filet mignon, stuffed brook trout. Terraced dining with view of Fox River. Cr cds: C, D, DS, MC, V.

D

Unrated Dining Spot

LITTLE TRAVELLER ATRIUM CAFE. *404 S 3rd St. 630/232-4200.* Hrs: 9:30 am-5 pm; Sat to 5:30 pm; buffet (exc Sat) 1 pm sitting. Closed Sun; also major hols. Res accepted; required buffet lunch. A la carte entrees: lunch $2-$5. Buffet: lunch $6.50. Specialties: tea sandwich plate, seafood salad, Shanghai chicken salad. English-type tea room within Victorian mansion with boutique & specialty shops. Fashion show during wkday lunch buffet. Family-owned. Cr cds: MC, V.

Glen Ellyn (D-2 see Chicago map)

(See also Wheaton)

Pop 24,944 **Elev** 750 ft **Area code** 630 **Zip** 60137 **E-mail** chamber@glen-ellyn.com **Web** www.glen-ellyn.com
Information Chamber of Commerce, 444 N Main St; 630/469-0907.

Glen Ellyn contains more than 24 houses that are more than 100 years old and are listed as historic sites. Although not open to the public, the houses are identified by plaques and make for a pleasant walking tour. Most can be found between the 300 and 800 blocks on Main St as well as on Forest and Park Sts north of the railroad. Glen Ellyn's many antique shops make the town popular with collectors and weekend browsers.

What to See and Do

Stacy's Tavern Museum (1846). Old country inn was once a popular stagecoach stop for travelers going from Chicago to the Fox River Valley. Restored with period furnishings. (Mar-Dec, Wed, Sun, afternoons; closed hols) 557 Geneva Rd, at Main St. Phone 630/858-8696. **Free.**

Annual Event

Taste of Glen Ellyn. Mid-late May.

Motor Hotel

★ ★ **HOLIDAY INN.** *1250 Roosevelt Rd (IL 38), E of I-355 exit Roosevelt Rd, E. 630/629-6000; FAX 630/629-0025.* 120 rms, 4 story. S $55-$69; D $61-$75; under 18 free. Crib free. Pet accepted, some restrictions. TV; cable (premium), VCR avail. Heated pool. Complimentary coffee in lobby. Restaurant 6:30 am-2 pm, 5-10 pm. Rm serv. Bar. Ck-out 1 pm. Coin lndry. Meeting rms. Business servs avail. In-rm modem link. Health club privileges. Cr cds: A, C, D, DS, MC, V.

Restaurant

✔★ ★ **GREEK ISLANDS WEST.** *(300 E 22nd St, Lombard 60148) E on IL 38. 630/932-4545.* Hrs: 11 am-11 pm; Fri, Sat to midnight. Res accepted. Greek menu. Bar. A la carte entrees: lunch, dinner $4.75-$21.95. Child's meals. Specializes in seafood, authentic Greek cuisine. Greek, Mediterranean decor. Cr cds: A, C, D, DS, MC, V.

 D

Glenview (C-3 see Chicago map)

(See also Northbrook, Skokie, Wheeling, Wilmette)

Pop 37,093 **Elev** 635 ft **Area code** 847 **Zip** 60025
Information Chamber of Commerce, 2320 Glenview Rd; 847/724-0900.

This northern suburb of Chicago is the home of Glenview Naval Air Station.

What to See and Do

Hartung's Automotive Museum. Display of more than 100 antique autos, trucks, tractors and motorcycles; many unrestored. License plate collection; 75 antique bicycles; promotional model cars; antique auto hub caps, radiator emblems and auto mascots. Also includes some Model T cars (1909-1926), a 1926 Hertz touring car and a 1932 Essex Terraplane. (Daily, hrs vary) 3623 W Lake St, W of Glenview Naval Air Station. Phone 847/724-4354. ¢¢

The Grove National Historic Landmark. This 82-acre nature preserve includes miles of hiking trails and 3 structures: the restored 1856 Kennicott House (tours Sun, limited hrs); the Interpretative Center, a nature center museum; and the Redfield Center, a house designed by George G. Elmslie, who studied under and worked for and with Louis Sullivan. During the 1930s, this stone house was lived in by author Donald Culross Peattie, who wrote *A Prairie Grove* about his experiences at the Grove. (See ANNUAL EVENTS) Park (daily; closed Jan 1, Dec 25). 1421 N Milwaukee Ave, just S of Lake Ave. Phone 847/299-6096. **Free.**

Annual Events

Civil War Living History Days. The Grove National Historic Landmark. Features realistic battle re-enactment with hospital tent and camps of the period; participants in authentic clothing & uniforms. Exhibits, lectures, house tours. Last wkend July.

Grovefest. The Grove National Historic Landmark. Crafts, music, activities and food; costumed volunteers gather to re-create a typical afternoon of the mid-1800s. 1st Sun Oct.

Motels

★ **BUDGETEL INN.** 1625 Milwaukee Ave (IL 21). 847/635-8300; FAX 847/635-8166. 150 rms, 3 story. S $46.95-$53.95; D $52.95-$54.95; each addl $7; under 18 free. Crib free. Pet accepted, some restrictions. TV; cable (premium); VCR avail. Complimentary continental bkfst. Coffee in rms. Restaurant opp open 24 hrs. Ck-out noon. Coin lndry. Meeting rm. Business servs avail. In-rm modem link. Valet serv. Some refrigerators, microwaves. Cr cds: A, C, D, DS, MC, V.

D ⏚ ⏚ ⏚ SC

★ ★ **COURTYARD BY MARRIOTT.** 1801 N Milwaukee Ave. 847/803-2500; FAX 847/803-2520. 149 rms, 3 story. S, D $96; suites $112-$122; wkend rates. Crib free. TV; cable (premium). Indoor pool; whirlpool. Complimentary coffee in rms. Restaurant 6:30-11 am; Sat, Sun 7 am-1 pm. Bar 4-11 pm. Ck-out 1 pm. Coin lndry. Meeting rms. Business servs avail. In-rm modem link. Valet serv. Exercise equipt; weight machine, treadmill. Microwaves avail; refrigerator in suites. Balconies. Cr cds: A, C, D, DS, MC, V.

D ⏚ ⏚ ⏚ ⏚ SC

✔ ★ **FAIRFIELD INN BY MARRIOTT.** 4514 W Lake Ave. 847/299-1600; FAX 847/803-9943. 138 rms, 3 story. Apr-Oct: S, D $56.65-$67.95; each addl $3; under 18 free; lower rates rest of yr. Crib free. TV; cable (premium). Heated pool. Complimentary continental bkfst. Restaurant opp 11-2 am. Ck-out noon. Meeting rm. Business servs avail. In-rm modem link. Health club privileges. Cr cds: A, C, D, DS, MC, V.

D ⏚ ⏚ ⏚ SC

Hotel

★ ★ **DOUBLETREE GUEST SUITES.** 1400 Milwaukee Ave. 847/803-9800; FAX 847/803-8026. 251 suites, 7 story. S $169; D $184; each addl $15; under 17 free; wkend rates. Crib free. TV. Indoor pool; whirlpool. Complimentary continental bkfst. Restaurant 11 am-11 pm. Bar to 1 am. Ck-out noon. Coin lndry. Meeting rms. Business servs avail. In-rm modem link. Gift shop. Airport transportation. Exercise equipt; weight machine, bicycles, sauna. Health club privileges. Refrigerators, microwaves. Cr cds: A, C, D, DS, JCB, MC, V.

D ⏚ ⏚ ⏚ ⏚ SC

Restaurants

★ ★ **BRASSERIE T.** (305 S Happ Rd, Northfield 60093) N on Waukegan Rd, E on Willow Rd, S on Happ Rd. 847/446-0444. Hrs: 11:30 am-9:30 pm; Fri, Sat to 10:30 pm; Sun from 4:30 pm. Closed Jan 1, July 4, Dec 25. Res accepted. Continental menu. Bar. A la carte entrees: lunch $5.95-$9.95, dinner $11.95-$17.95. Specialties: lamb shank, calf's liver, osso bucco. Cr cds: A, DS, MC, V.

D

★ **DAPPER'S NORTH.** 4520 W Lake Ave. 847/699-0020. Hrs: 5:30-1 am. Serv bar. Semi-a la carte: bkfst $2.70-$9.15, lunch $5.40-$7.95, dinner $7.40-$15.10. Complete meals: dinner $7.15-$15.35. Child's meals. Specializes in steak, Grecian chicken, fish. Own cheesecake, pastries. Cr cds: A, C, D, MC, V.

D ⏚

★ ★ **DRAGON INN NORTH.** 1650 Waukegan Rd (IL 43). 847/729-8383. Hrs: 11:30 am-9:30 pm; Fri to 10:30 pm; Sat 5-10:30 pm; Sun noon-9:30 pm. Closed July 4, Thanksgiving. Res accepted. Mandarin, Szechwan, Hunan menu. Bar. Semi-a la carte: lunch $4.95-$6.75, dinner $8.95-$16.95. Specialties: moo shu pork, orange beef, shrimp sauté Hunan. Parking. Chinese decor. Cr cds: A, MC, V.

⏚

✔ ★ **MYKONOS.** (8660 Golf Rd, Des Plaines) Just W of Greenwood. 847/296-6777. Hrs: 11 am-11 pm; Fri, Sat to midnight; Sun noon-11 pm. Res accepted. Greek menu. Bar. A la carte entrees: lunch from $4.50, dinner $7-$20. Specializes in whole sea bass, red snapper, octopus vinaigrette. Own pastries. Valet parking. Outdoor garden dining. Cr cds: A, DS, MC, V.

D ⏚

★ **PERIYAKI GREEK TAVERN.** 9860 Milwaukee Ave. 847/296-2232. Hrs: 11 am-11 pm; Fri, Sat to midnight. Closed Thanksgiving. Res accepted. Greek menu. Bar. Semi-a la carte: lunch, dinner $6.25-$18.95. Specializes in fresh fish, wood-roasted chicken, lamb dishes. Parking. Outdoor dining. Greek village atmosphere. Cr cds: A, C, D, DS, MC, V.

D ⏚

★ **WILLOW ON WAGNER.** 1519 Wagner Rd, I-94, exit Lake Ave W 1 mi. 847/724-5100. Hrs: 11:30 am-2:30 pm, 5-9 pm; Fri, Sat to 10:30 pm; Sun 4-9 pm. Closed Dec 25. Res accepted. Semi-a la carte: lunch $4.95-$8.50, dinner $7.95-$15.95. Child's meals. Specializes in prime rib, chicken, seafood. Parking. Overlooks garden. Cr cds: A, C, D, DS, MC, V.

D ⏚

Grayslake (B-2 see Chicago map)

(For accommodations see Gurnee, Libertyville, Waukegan)

Pop 7,388 **Elev** 790 ft **Area code** 847 **Zip** 60030
Information Chamber of Commerce, 164 Hawley, PO Box 167; 847/223-6888.

What to See and Do

Holiday Park. Many summer activities, including water slide (fee), sand beaches (bathhouses), bumper boats, paddle & rowboats, tennis, miniature golf. Playground, picnic areas. Baseball diamonds. Cafeteria, concession. (Memorial Day-Labor Day) 5½ mi W on IL 120 & IL 134, ½ mi E of US 12. Phone 847/546-8222. Parking ¢

Annual Event

Lake County Fair. Fairgrounds. Rodeo, exhibits, contests, midway; horse show, tractor & horse pulls. Phone 847/223-2204. Late July.

Restaurant

★ ★ ★ **COUNTRY SQUIRE.** 19133 W IL 120, just W of US 45 on IL 120. 847/223-0121. Hrs: 11 am-10 pm; Sat to 11 pm; Sun 10 am-9 pm; Sun brunch to 2 pm. Closed Mon. Res accepted. Continental menu. Bar. Semi-a la carte: lunch $7-$13, dinner $9.95-$21. Sun brunch $7.95-$14.95. Child's meals. Specialties: roast duckling, shrimp de jonghe, veal Oscar. Entertainment Fri-Sun. Parking. Restored Georgian mansion (1938), once owned by Wesley Sears; extensive gardens. Cr cds: A, C, D, DS, MC, V.

D

Great Lakes Naval Training Center

(see Waukegan)

Greenville (G-4)

(See also Vandalia)

Settled 1815 **Pop** 5,000 (est) **Elev** 619 ft **Area code** 618 **Zip** 62246
E-mail raldv@greenville.edu **Web** www.greenvilleillinois.com
Information Chamber of Commerce, 404 S Third St; 618/664-9272.

This rural community, nestled in the center of Bond County, is within easy commuting distance of downtown St Louis, Missouri. The community is host to a number of manufacturing companies and the home of Greenville College.

What to See and Do

Bock Museum. Inside the original Almira College house (1855) is a collection of works by sculptor Richard W. Bock (1865-1949), who between 1895 and 1915, executed a number of works for Frank Lloyd Wright-designed buildings. Also on display are Wright-designed prototypes of leaded-glass windows and lamps for Wright's Dana House in Springfield. (Mon-Fri; limited hrs Sat) Greenville College, College Ave. Phone 618/664-2800. **Free.**

Motel

★★ **BEST WESTERN COUNTRY VIEW INN.** *RR 4, Box 163, Jct I-70, IL 127.* 618/664-3030. 83 rms, 2 story. May-Sept: S $39-$43; D $47-$53; each addl $4; under 18 free; lower rates rest of yr. Crib $2. Pet accepted, some restrictions; $2. TV; cable. Heated pool. Complimentary continental bkfst. Restaurant adj 6 am-10 pm. Ck-out noon. Meeting rm. Microwaves avail. Cr cds: A, C, D, DS, ER, MC, V.

Gurnee (A-3 see Chicago map)

(See also Libertyville, Waukegan)

Pop 13,701 **Elev** 700 ft **Area code** 847 **Zip** 60031 **E-mail** econinfo@lakecountry-il.org **Web** www.lakecountry-il.org/
Information Lake County Chamber of Commerce, 5221 W Grand Ave, 60031-1818; 847/249-3800.

What to See and Do

Gurnee Mills Mall. More than 250 stores can be found in this indoor mall; food courts. (Daily) I-94 at I-132. Phone 847/263-7500or 800/YES-SHOP.

Six Flags Great America. This 200-acre entertainment center features rides, shows, shops and restaurants. Among the rides and attractions are The Giant Drop, a seated, vertical, high-speed drop; *Batman,* The Ride, a suspended looping thrill ride; Iron Wolf, a stand-up looping steel roller coaster; ShockWave steel roller coaster; American Eagle, a double-racing wooden roller coaster; Condor, a spinning thrill ride; water rides; and a children's area. Theaters feature live stage shows daily. (4th wk May-last wk Aug, daily; late Apr-4th wk May & Sept-mid-Oct, wkends) Admission includes all rides & shows. On Grand Ave, off I-94, exit IL 132. Phone 847/249-1776. ¢¢¢¢

Motels

★★ **BUDGETEL INN.** *5688 N Ridge Rd.* 847/662-7600; FAX 847/662-5300. 106 rms, 4 story. Memorial Day-Labor Day: S, D $99.95; suites $109.95; lower rates rest of yr. Crib free. Pet accepted. TV; cable (premium). Complimentary continental bkfst. Complimentary coffee in rms. Restaurant adj 7 am-10 pm. Ck-out noon. Business servs avail. In-rm

modem link. Coin lndry. Meeting rm. Refrigerator, microwave in suites. Cr cds: A, C, D, DS, MC, V.

★★ **COMFORT INN.** *6080 Gurnee Mills Circle E, adj to mall.* 847/855-8866. 63 rms, 3 story. June-Sept: S, D $125; each addl $5; suites $125; under 18 free; lower rates rest of yr. Crib free. TV; cable (premium). Indoor pool; whirlpool. Complimentary continental bkfst. Restaurant opp. Ck-out 11 am. Meeting rm. Refrigerator, microwave in suites. Cr cds: A, C, D, DS, MC, V.

★★ **FAIRFIELD INN BY MARRIOTT.** *6090 Gurnee Mills Circle E, adj to mall.* 847/855-8868. 63 rms, 3 story. Apr-Dec: S $98.95-$109.95; D $104.95-$119.95; suites $114.95-$139.95; under 18 free; higher rates some hols; lower rates rest of yr. Crib free. TV; cable (premium). Indoor pool; whirlpool. Complimentary continental bkfst. Restaurant nearby. Ck-out noon. Meeting rm. Business servs avail. Refrigerator, microwave in suites. Cr cds: A, C, D, DS, MC, V.

Motor Hotels

★★ **HAMPTON INN.** *5550 Grand Ave (IL 132), jct I-94 & IL 132.* 847/662-1100; FAX 847/662-2556. 134 rms, 5 story. Mid-May-mid-Sept: S, D $119; under 18 free; lower rates rest of yr. Crib free. TV; cable (premium), VCR avail. Heated pool. Complimentary continental bkfst. Restaurant adj. Business servs avail. In-rm modem link. Sundries. Game rm. Health club privileges. Some refrigerators. Balconies. Six Flags Great America 2 blks. Cr cds: A, C, D, DS, MC, V.

★★ **HOLIDAY INN.** *6161 W Grand Ave, jct IL 132W & I-94.* 847/336-6300; FAX 847/336-6303. 223 rms, 4 story. S, D $79-$139; suites $159; under 18 free. Crib free. TV; cable (premium). Heated pool; whirlpool. Restaurant 6:30 am-10 pm. Rm serv. Bar 4 pm-1 am. Ck-out noon. Coin lndry. Meeting rms. Business servs avail. In-rm modem link. Valet serv. Exercise equipt; bicycle, treadmill. Game rm. Great America 1 mi. Cr cds: A, C, D, DS, JCB, MC, V.

Inn

★★ **SWEET BASIL HILL FARM.** *15937 W Washington St (15937), I-94 exit 132E.* 847/244-3333; FAX 847/263-6693. 3 suites, 2 story, 1 cottage. S, D $85-$150; cottage $125; wkly rates. TV; VCR. Complimentary full bkfst. Business servs avail. X-country ski on site. Hiking trails. Converted farmhouse on 7 1/2 acres; sheep, llamas. Herb garden. Near Great America, Gurnee Mills Mall. Cr cds: C, D, DS, MC, V.

Havana (E-3)

(See also Petersburg)

Settled 1824 **Pop** 3,610 **Elev** 470 ft **Area code** 309 **Zip** 62644
Information Chamber of Commerce, PO Box 116; 309/543-3528.

Once a bustling steamboat and fishing port at the confluence of the Spoon and Illinois rivers, Havana is now a quiet river town, important as a grain center with a few light industries. One of the famous Lincoln-Douglas debates took place in what is now Rockwell Park.

What to See and Do

⊠ **Dickson Mounds State Museum.** Exhibits include multimedia programs relating to Native American inhabitants over 12,000-yr time span. Also agricultural plot and remains of excavated houses. Picnic area. (Daily; closed some major hols) 5 mi NW via IL 78/97, on hill above confluence of Spoon and Illinois rivers. Phone 309/547-3721. **Free.**

Illinois River National Wildlife & Fish Refuges. These 4,488 acres are used as a resting, breeding and feeding area for waterfowl. Concentrations of shorebirds (Aug-Sept). Eagles are seen here (Nov-Feb). Sport fishing (daily) and waterfowl hunting (fall) permitted in specified areas. Designated public-use areas open all yr. Interpretive nature trail; wheelchair access. 9 mi NE on Manito Rd. Contact Refuge Manager, US Fish and Wildlife Service, Illinois River National Wildlife & Fish Refuges, RR 2, PO Box 61B; 309/535-2290. **Free.**

Annual Event

Spoon River Scenic Drive. 5 mi NW on IL 78/97 to Dickson Mounds, then marked, circular route through Fulton County. Autumn drive through small towns and rolling, wooded countryside noted for fall color (complete drive 140 mi); 19th- and early 20th-century crafts, exhibits, demonstrations; antiques, collectibles; produce, food. Phone 309/547-3234. 1st & 2nd wkend Oct.

Highland Park (A-6)

(See also Chicago, Highwood, Northbrook)

Settled 1834 **Pop** 30,575 **Elev** 690 ft **Area code** 847 **Zip** 60035
Information Chamber of Commerce, 600 Central Ave, Suite 205; 847/432-0284.

What to See and Do

Francis Stupey Log Cabin (1847). Oldest structure in town; restored with period furnishings. (May-Oct, Sun; also by appt) 1750 block of St Johns Ave. Phone 847/432-7090. **Free.**

Highland Park Historical Society. Restored Victorian house (1871) has several period rms; changing exhibits of local artifacts. On grounds is the Walt Durbahn Tool Museum with household items and primitive implements used in lumbering and local trades. (Daily; closed hols) Headquarters in Jean Butz James Museum, 326 Central Ave. Phone 847/432-7090. **Free.**

Seasonal Event

Ravinia Festival. On Green Bay Rd at Lake Cook Rd. Concerts by the Chicago Symphony Orchestra, guest soloists; chamber music, pop, jazz and New Perspectives series; also dance and ballet. Pavilion and outdoor seating. For schedule, fees phone 312/728-4642. Early June-early Sept.

Motel

★ ★ ★ **COURTYARD BY MARRIOTT.** *1505 Lake Cook Rd. 847/831-3338; FAX 847/831-0782.* 149 units, 3 story. S, D $96-$109; suites $149; under 18 free. Crib free. TV; cable (premium). Indoor pool; whirlpool. Complimentary coffee in rms. Restaurant 6:30-10:30 am; Sat, Sun 7 am-noon. Bar 5-10 pm. Ck-out noon. Coin lndry. Meeting rms. Business servs avail. In-rm modem link. Valet serv. Sundries. Exercise equipt; weight machine, treadmill. Refrigerator, microwave in suites. Private patios, balconies. Cr cds: A, C, D, DS, MC, V.

D ⟋ ✕ ⟍ ⟍ SC

Restaurants

★ **CAFE CENTRAL.** *455 Central Ave. 847/266-7878.* Hrs: 11:30 am-9 pm; Fri, Sat to 10:30 pm; Sun 4-8 pm. Closed Mon; Jan 1, July 4, Dec 25. Res accepted (dinner). French menu. Bar. Semi-a la carte: lunch $6-$9, dinner $11-$17. Child's meals. Specializes in lamb shank, roasted duckling, bouillabaisse. Outdoor dining. Casual cafe dining. Totally nonsmoking. Cr cds: A, C, D, DS, MC, V.

D

★ ★ ★ **CARLOS'.** *429 Temple Ave, at Highwood, 1½ blks E of Green Bay Rd. 847/432-0770.* An outstanding selection of wines complements the vibrantly flavored cuisine in this warm and friendly restaurant, set unobtrusively in a vintage brick building off the main thoroughfare. French menu. Specializes in fresh seafood, game, fowl. Own pastries. Hrs: 5:30-9:30 pm. Closed Tues; major hols. Res accepted. Serv bar. Wine cellar. A la carte entrees: dinner $24.50-$29.50. Degustation menu: dinner $70 & $100. Valet parking. Jacket. Cr cds: A, C, D, DS, JCB, MC, V.

✔★ **LITTLE SZECHWAN.** *1900 First St. 847/433-7007.* Hrs: 5-9:30 pm; Fri, Sat to 10:30 pm; Sun to 9 pm. Closed Thanksgiving. Res accepted. Szechwan, mandarin menu. A la carte entrees: dinner $12.50-$15. Specialties: kung bau chicken, crispy duck, Taiwanese chicken rolls. Outdoor dining. Chinese decor; masks, costumes, murals. Totally nonsmoking. Cr cds: A, C, D, MC, V.

D

✔★ **PANDA PANDA.** *1825 Second St. 847/432-9470.* Hrs: 11:30 am-9:30 pm; Fri, Sat to 10:30 pm. Closed Thanksgiving. Res accepted. Chinese menu. Bar. Semi-a la carte: lunch $5.50-$6.50, dinner $7.95-$24. Specialties: orange beef, smoked tea duck, pot stickers. Chinese decor; panda murals. Cr cds: A, MC, V.

★ ★ **TIMBERS CHAR HOUSE.** *295 Skokie Valley Rd. 847/831-1400.* Hrs: 11:30 am-10 pm; Fri to 10:30 pm; Sat noon-5, 10-30 pm; Sun 4:30-8:30 pm. Closed Jan 1, July 4, Thanksgiving, Dec 25. Res accepted. Bar. Semi-a la carte: lunch $4.25-$11.95, dinner $7.95-$22.95. Child's meals. Specializes in chicken, barbecued ribs, steak. Own desserts. Parking. Cr cds: A, C, D, DS, MC, V.

D ⟍

Highwood (B-3 see Chicago map)

(See also Highland Park)

Pop 5,331 **Elev** 685 ft **Area code** 847 **Zip** 60040

Inn

★ ★ **DEER PATH INN.** *(255 E Illinois St, Lake Forest 60045)* 5 mi N on Sheridan Rd. 847/234-2280; FAX 847/234-3352. 56 rms, 3 story, 32 suites. S $120-$150; D $130-$160; each addl $10; suites $180-$190. Crib $10. TV; cable (premium), VCR avail. Complimentary full bkfst. Restaurant 6:30 am-10 am, 11:30 am-2 pm, 5-10 pm; wkends noon-10 pm. Rm serv. Ck-out noon, ck-in 3 pm. Business center. In-rm modem link. Luggage handling. Coin lndry. Health club privileges. Some refrigerators, microwaves. Built in 1929. Cr cds: A, C, D, DS, MC, V.

D ⟍ ⟍ SC ⟍

Restaurants

★ ★ **DEL RIO.** *228 Green Bay Rd. 847/432-4608.* Hrs: 5-10 pm; Fri, Sat to 11 pm. Closed some hols. Northern Italian menu. Bar. Semi-a la carte: dinner $11.75-$24.50. Specializes in homemade pasta, seafood, veal Del Rio. Parking. Italian cafe decor. Cr cds: A, C, D, DS, MC, V.

✔★ **EGG HARBOR CAFE.** (512 N Western Ave, Lake Forest 60045) 5 mi N on Sheridan Rd, E on Western Ave. 847/295-3449. Hrs: 6:30 am-2 pm. Closed Thanksgiving, Dec 25. Semi-a la carte: bkfst $3.95-$7.95, lunch $4.95-$7.95. Child's meals. Specializes in eggs Benedict, gourmet pancakes, sandwiches. Country decor; chicken & egg theme. Totally nonsmoking. Cr cds: A, DS, MC, V.

★ ★ ★ **ENGLISH ROOM.** (255 E Illinois St, Lake Forest 60045) 5 mi N on Sheridan Rd. 847/234-2280. Hrs: 6:30 am-2:30 pm, 5-9 pm; Fri, Sat to 10 pm; Sun 11 am-2:30 pm (brunch), 5-9 pm. Res accepted. Continental menu. Bar. Bkfst buffet $10.50. Semi-a la carte: lunch $7.50-$16.50. A la carte entrees: dinner $14-$29. Sun brunch $25. Child's meals. Own desserts. Parking. Outdoor dining. English manor house decor; wall prints, antiques. Jacket. Totally nonsmoking. Cr cds: A, C, D, DS, JCB, MC, V.

✔★ ★ ★ **FROGGY'S.** 306 Green Bay Rd. 847/433-7080. Hrs: 11:30 am-2 pm, 5-10 pm; Fri to 11 pm; Sat 5-11 pm. Closed Sun; major hols. French menu. Bar. Wine list. Semi-a la carte: lunch $8.95-$15.95, dinner $12.95-$17.95. Complete meals: lunch $22.95, dinner $28.95. Own pastries. Cr cds: C, D, DS, MC, V.

★ ★ ★ **GABRIEL'S.** 310 Green Bay Rd. 847/433-0031. Hrs: 5-10 pm. Closed Sun, Mon; major hols. Res accepted. French, Italian menu. Bar. Wine cellar. A la carte entrees: dinner $22-$29. Complete meals: dinner $40. Specialties: rack of lamb, papillotte (Chilean sea bass), risotto. Own desserts. Parking. Outdoor dining. European bistro atmosphere with open kitchen. Cr cds: A, C, D, DS, MC, V.

★ ★ **RIGOLETTO.** (293 E Illinois St, Lake Forest 60045) 5 mi N on Sheridan Rd. 847/234-7675. Hrs: 11:30 am-3 pm, 5-10 pm; Fri to 11 pm; Sat 5-11 pm; Sun 5-9 pm. Closed Mon; some major hols. Res accepted. Italian menu. Bar. Semi-a la carte: lunch $7-$14, dinner $10-$25. Specializes in fresh fish, pasta, veal. Contemporary decor with Italian influence. Cr cds: A, C, D, MC, V.

★ ★ **SOUTH GATE CAFE.** (665 Forest Ave, Lake Forest 60045) at Market Square, 5 mi N on Sheridan Rd. 847/234-8800. Hrs: 11 am-9 pm; Fri, Sat to 10 pm; Sun to 8 pm. Closed most major hols. Res accepted. Bar. A la carte entrees: lunch $5.50-$12.95, dinner $9.95-$22.00. Specializes in fresh seafood, pasta, pizza. Own baking. Casual dining in former fire station; overlooking town square. Cr cds: A, C, D, DS, MC, V.

Hillside (D-3 see Chicago map)

(See also Elmhurst, Hinsdale, La Grange)

Pop 7,672 **Elev** 659 ft **Area code** 708 **Zip** 60162

Motel

★ ★ **HOLIDAY INN.** 4400 Frontage Rd, at I-290W, exit Wolf Rd. 708/544-9300; FAX 708/544-9310. 248 rms, 3 story. S, D $89; wkend rates. Crib free. Pet accepted. TV; cable (premium). Heated pool. Restaurant 6 am-2 pm, 5-10 pm. Rm serv. Bar 11:30-2 am; dancing. Ck-out noon. Coin lndry. Meeting rms. Business servs avail. In-rm modem link. Valet serv. Golf privileges. Health club privileges. Exercise equipt; stair machine, weight machine. Cr cds: A, C, D, DS, JCB, MC, V.

Hinsdale (E-3 see Chicago map)

(See also Brookfield, Downers Grove, La Grange, Oak Brook)

Pop 16,029 **Elev** 725 ft **Area code** 630 **Zip** 60521
Information Chamber of Commerce, 22 E First St; 630/323-3952.

Named for a pioneer railroad director, Hinsdale includes what was once the town of Fullersburg. It is a quiet and secluded commuter community with a quaint shopping district.

What to See and Do

Robert Crown Center for Health Education. Programs to learn about the body's physical and emotional health. Displays include Valeda, a talking plexiglas model. (Sept-June, Mon-Fri; closed hols) Reservations required. 21 Salt Creek Lane. Phone 630/325-1900. ¢¢

Motels

★ ★ **FAIRFIELD INN BY MARRIOTT.** (820 79th St, Willowbrook) 3 mi S on IL 83. 630/789-6300. 129 rms, 3 story. Mid-May-mid-Oct: S $49-$54; D $56-$60; each addl $7; under 18 free; lower rates rest of yr. Crib free. TV; cable (premium). Heated pool. Complimentary continental bkfst. Restaurant nearby. Ck-out noon. Business servs avail. Health club privileges. Cr cds: A, D, DS, MC, V.

✔★ **RED ROOF INN.** (7535 IL 83, Willowbrook) S on IL 83. 630/323-8811; FAX 630/323-2714. 109 rms, 3 story. S $39.99-$46.99; D $46.99-$53.99; under 18 free. Crib free. Pet accepted, some restrictions. TV; cable (premium). Complimentary coffee in lobby. Restaurant adj 8 am-10 pm. Ck-out noon. Business servs avail. In-rm modem link. Cr cds: A, C, D, DS, MC, V.

Motor Hotels

★ ★ **BEST WESTERN INN.** (300 S Frontage Rd, Burr Ridge) S on I-294, then SW on I-55, exit 276A (County Line Rd S). 630/325-2900; FAX 630/325-8907. 124 rms, 3 story. S $56-$61; D $66-$71; each addl $5; suites $100-$150; under 18 free. Crib free. TV; cable (premium) VCR avail (movies). Pool. Restaurant 6:30 am-2 pm, 5-10 pm. Rm serv. Bar. Ck-out noon. Coin laundry. Meeting rms. Valet serv. Free airport transportation. Cr cds: A, C, D, DS, MC, V.

★ ★ **BUDGETEL INN.** (855 79th St, Willowbrook) 4 mi SW on IL 83. 630/654-0077; FAX 630/654-0181. 137 rms, 3 story. S $47-$58; D $54-$65; under 18 free. Crib free. Pet accepted, some restrictions. TV; cable (premium), VCR avail (movies). Complimentary continental bkfst. Restaurant nearby. Ck-out noon. Meeting rm. Business servs avail. Some refrigerators. Cr cds: A, C, D, DS, MC, V.

★ ★ ★ **HOLIDAY INN.** (7800 S Kingery Hwy, Willowbrook) On IL 83, just N of I-55. 630/325-6400; FAX 630/325-2362. 220 rms, 3 story. S $89; D $99; suites $95-$115; studio rms $85; under 19 free; wkend rates. Crib free. Pet accepted, some restrictions. TV; cable (premium), VCR avail (movies). Heated pool; lifeguard. Restaurant 6:30 am-2 pm, 5-10 pm. Rm serv. Bar 11-1 am; Fri, Sat to 2 am. Ck-out 1 pm. Meeting rms. Business servs avail. In-rm modem link. Valet serv. Gift shop. Free Midway Airport transportation. Exercise equipt; weight machine, stair machine, sauna. Luxury level. Cr cds: A, C, D, DS, JCB, MC, V.

Restaurant

✔★ **EGG HARBOR CAFE.** *777 N York Rd. 630/920-1344.* Hrs: 6:30 am-2 pm. Closed Thanksgiving, Dec 25. Semi-a la carte: bkfst $2.95-$6.95, lunch $4.95-$6.95. Child's meals. Specialties: frittatas, egg white omelettes, California club sandwiches. Contemporary country American decor. Totally nonsmoking. Cr cds: A, DS, MC, V.

Homewood (F-4 see Chicago map)

Pop 19,278 **Elev** 650 ft **Area code** 708 **Zip** 60430

This community, located 24 miles south of Chicago's Loop, boasts two city blocks of fascinating art; New York muralist Richard Haas refurbished older business buildings with trompe l'oeil artwork on the backs of the structures.

What to See and Do

Midwest Carvers Museum. Housed in historic farmhouses, museum features hundreds of examples of carver's art, including ornate doll carriage, realistically carved bald eagle. Woodcarving classes; gift shop. (Daily exc Sun; closed major hols) NE via Thornton/Blue Island Rd to 16236 Vincennes Ave in South Holland. Phone 708/331-6011. **Donation.**

Motel

★ **BUDGETEL INN.** *(17225 Halsted St, South Holland 60473) Just N of jct I-80, I-294, on IL 1. 708/596-8700; FAX 708/596-9978.* 102 rms, 2 story. S $46.95; D $55.95; each addl $7; under 18 free. Crib free. Pet accepted. TV, cable (premium). Complimentary continental bkfst. Restaurant adj open 24 hrs. Ck-out noon. Business servs avail. In-rm modem link. Valet serv. Cr cds: A, C, D, DS, MC, V.

[D] [picnic] [no-smoking] [fire] [SC]

Motor Hotel

★ ★ ★ **BEST WESTERN.** *17400 S Halsted St, on IL 1 (Halsted), jct I-80 & I-294, exit S. 708/957-1600; FAX 708/957-1963.* 202 rms, 5 story. S $65-$85; D $70-$90; each addl $5; suites $150-$400; under 18 free. Crib free. TV; cable (premium), VCR avail. Indoor/outdoor pool. Complimentary continental bkfst. Restaurant 6 am-9 pm. Rm serv. Bar 11-1 am, Fri & Sat to 2 am; entertainment Fri-Sun. Ck-out 11 am. Meeting rms. Business servs avail. Bellhops. Valet serv. Sundries. Gift shop. Barber, beauty shop. Refrigerator in suites. Cr cds: A, C, D, DS, MC, V.

[D] [pool] [no-smoking] [fire] [SC]

Restaurants

✔★ **AURELIO'S PIZZA.** *18162 Harwood Ave. 708/798-8050.* Hrs: 11:30 am-10:30 pm; Fri & Sat to midnight; Sun 4-10:30 pm. Closed major hols. Italian menu. Wine, beer. A la carte entrees: lunch, dinner $6-$12. Child's meals. Specializes in thin- and thick-crust pizza, pasta, calabrese. In former shipping warehouse. Outdoor patio. Family-owned. Cr cds: A, MC, V.

[D] [SC] [picnic]

★ ★ **DRAGON INN.** *(18431 S Halsted St, Glenwood 60425) In Glenwood Plaza Shopping Ctr, 1 mi S of I-294, I-80. 708/756-3344.* Hrs: 11:30 am-9:30 pm; Fri to 10:30 pm; Sat 4-10:30 pm; Sun noon-9:30 pm; lunch buffet to 2 pm. Closed Mon; Thanksgiving. Res accepted. Mandarin Chinese, Amer menu. Bar. Buffet: lunch $6.50. Semi-a la carte: lunch,

dinner $12-$16. Specializes in Szechwan and Hunan dishes. Cr cds: A, C, D, MC, V.

Illinois Beach State Park (A-3 see Chicago map)

(See also Gurnee, Waukegan)

(3 mi N of Waukegan, E of IL 131; off Sheridan Rd)

This 6.5-mile sand beach on Lake Michigan is a summer playground for more than 2.5 million visitors annually. The 4,160-acre park has facilities for beach swimming (no lifeguard) and has beach houses available. Other activities include fishing and hiking. There is a boat marina in the park and a boat launch. Cross-country skiing is popular in winter. The park has picnic shelters, a playground, a concession area and a lodge. Camping is permitted (standard fees). There is an interpretive center on the grounds. For information contact Site Superintendent, Zion 60099; 847/662-4811 or 847/662-4828. **Free.**

Motor Hotel

★ ★ **ILLNOIS BEACH RESORT & CONFERENCE CENTER.** *(1 Lake Front Dr, Zion 60099) 6 mi NE on IL 137 (Sheridan Rd) exit Wadsworth Rd. 847/625-7300; FAX 847/625-0665.* 92 rms, 5 with shower only, 3 story. June-early Sept: S, D $119-$129; suites $160-$180; under 16 free; wkend rates; package plans; lower rates rest of yr. Crib free. TV; cable (premium). Complimentary coffee in rms. Restaurant 7 am-10 pm. Rm serv. Bar. Ck-out 11 am. Meeting rms. Business servs avail. In-rm modem link. Shopping arcade. Exercise rm; instructor, weight machine, rowers, sauna. Indoor pool; whirlpool. Playground. Game rm. In-rm whirlpool in suites. Some balconies. Picnic tables, grills. On beach. Cr cds: A, C, D, DS, MC, V.

[D] [pool] [exercise] [fire] [picnic]

Itasca (D-2 see Chicago map)

(See also Chicago, Chicago O'Hare Airport Area, Elmhurst, Schaumburg)

Pop 6,947 **Elev** 686 ft **Area code** 630 **Zip** 60143

Hotel

★ ★ ★ **WYNDHAM NORTHWEST.** *400 Park Blvd. 630/773-4000; FAX 630/773-4087.* 408 rms, 12 story. S $139-$179; D $149-$189; each addl $15; suites from $175; under 18 free. Crib free. TV; cable (premium). Indoor pool; whirlpool. Complimentary coffee in rms. Restaurant 5:30-1 am. Bar 11:30-1 am; Fri, Sat to 2 am; entertainment. Ck-out noon. Convention facilities. Business center. In-rm modem link. Concierge. Shopping arcade. Barber, beauty shop. Valet parking. Airport transportation. Lighted tennis. Exercise rm; instructor, weights, bicycles, sauna, steam rms. Massage. Some microwaves; minibar, bathrm phone in suites. Cr cds: A, C, D, DS, ER, JCB, MC, V.

[D] [tennis] [pool] [exercise] [fire] [no-smoking] [SC] [tennis]

Resorts

★ ★ ★ **INDIAN LAKES.** *(250 W Schick Rd, Bloomingdale 60108) ¼ mi S of US 20, ½ mi W of Bloomingdale Rd. 630/529-0200; FAX 630/529-9271; res: 800/334-3417.* 308 rms, 6 story. S, D $99-$179; each addl $20; under 18 free; wkend rates; package plans. Crib free. TV; cable (premium). 2 pools, 1 indoor; whirlpool, poolside serv. Dining rm 6:30

am-10 pm. Rm serv. Bar. Ck-out noon, ck-in 4 pm. Convention facilities. Business servs avail. In-rm modem link. Bellhops. Shopping arcade. Beauty shop. Rec dir. Lighted tennis. 36-hole golf, greens fee $50-$54, pro, putting green. Miniature golf. Exercise rm; instructor, weights, bicycles, sauna. Massage. Game rm. Some balconies. Cr cds: A, C, D, DS, MC, V.

★ ★ **NORDIC HILLS RESORT & CONFERENCE CENTER.** 1401 Nordic Rd, ¼ mi N of US 20, off Lake St. 630/773-2750; FAX 630/773-3622. 228 rms, 9 story. S, D $119-$149; suites $275-$700; under 12 free; wkend rates. Crib free. TV; cable (premium). 2 pools, 1 indoor; whirlpools. Dining rms 6:30 am-10 pm; wkends to 11 pm. Rm serv. Bar 11:30-1 am, Sat to 2 am; entertainment. Ck-out noon, ck-in 4 pm. Meeting rms. Business servs avail. Lighted tennis. 18-hole golf, greens fee $45-$50, pro, putting green. X-country ski on site. Game rm. Bowling. Exercise equipt; weights, bicycles, sauna. Refrigerator in suites. Balconies. Spacious grounds. Cr cds: A, C, D, DS, MC, V.

Restaurant

★ ★ **PLENTYWOOD.** (130 S Church Rd, Bensenville) 4 blks E of IL 83, 2 blks S of IL 19. 630/860-4570. Hrs: 11:30 am-2:30 pm, 3 pm-closing; Mon to 1:30 pm; Sun noon-7 pm; early-bird dinner 3-5:30 pm. Closed Memorial Day, Labor Day, Dec 24, 25. Res accepted. Bar. Semi-a la carte: lunch $7.85-$12.75, dinner $8.75-$17.50. Child's meals. Specialties: Parmesan-crusted brook trout, prime rib, grilled pork chops. Own baking. Scenic grounds. Family-owned. Cr cds: A, C, D, DS, JCB, MC, V.

Jacksonville (F-3)

(See also Springfield)

Founded 1825 **Pop** 19,324 **Elev** 613 ft **Area code** 217 **Zip** 62650
Information Jacksonville Area Visitors & Conventions Bureau, 155 W Morton; 800/593-5678.

Although settled by Southerners, the town was largely developed by New Englanders and became an important station on the Underground Railroad. A center of education, culture and statesmanship, Jacksonville was named in honor of Andrew Jackson and nurtured the careers of Stephen A. Douglas and William Jennings Bryan. Lincoln often spoke here in the 1850s. Illinois College (1829), the oldest college west of the Alleghenies, and MacMurray College (1846) have played an important part in the city's history. This is also the home of the Illinois School for the Visually Impaired (1849), the Illinois School for the Deaf (1839) and Jacksonville Developmental Center (1846). Several national manufacturing companies are located here.

What to See and Do

Lake Jacksonville. Swimming (fee); fishing; boating (dock). Camping (mid-Apr-mid-Oct; fee). 4½ mi SE off US 67. Phone 217/479-4646 (seasonal) or 217/479-4600.

Motel

★ ★ **HOLIDAY INN.** 1717 W Morton Ave. 217/245-9571; FAX 217/245-0686. 114 rms, 2 story. S, D $56-$69; under 19 free. Crib free. Pet accepted. TV; cable (premium). VCR avail. Indoor pool; whirlpool. Complimentary coffee in lobby. Restaurant 6:30 am-2 pm, 5-10 pm. Rm serv. Bar 3:30 pm-1 am. Ck-out noon. Meeting rms. Business servs avail. In-rm

modem link. Valet serv. Health club privileges. Game rm. Some refrigerators, microwaves. Cr cds: A, C, D, DS, JCB, MC, V.

Restaurant

✔★ ★ **LONZEROTTIS.** 600 E State St, IL 72/IL 36 exit Morton Ave to Harbin, E to State St. 217/243-7151. Hrs: 11 am-2 pm, 5-9 pm; Fri, Sat to 10 pm. Closed Sun; most major hols. Res accepted. Italian, Amer menu. Bar. Semi-a la carte: lunch $3.25-$6.25, dinner $6.95-$15.50. Child's meals. Specializes in lasagne, prime rib, chicken piccata. Own baking. Outdoor dining. In restored Chicago & Alton Railroad depot (1909). Cr cds: A, DS, MC, V.

Joliet (B-5)

(See also Aurora, Lockport, Morris)

Settled 1831 **Pop** 76,836 **Elev** 564 ft **Area code** 815 **E-mail** enjoy.hccvb @internetMCI.com
Information Heritage Corridor Convention and Visitors Bureau, 81 N Chicago St, 60432; 815/727-2323 or 800/926-2262.

The Des Plaines River, the Chicago Sanitary and Ship Canal and railroad freight lines triggered Joliet's growth as a center of commerce and industry. The canal's Brandon Road Locks, to the south of Joliet, are among the largest in the world, and the canal continues to annually carry many millions of tons of barge traffic through the city. Joliet once supplied limestone (Joliet/Lemont) to much of the nation and was once a major center for steel production. Although Joliet was named in honor of Louis Jolliet, the French-Canadian explorer who visited the area in 1673, it was incorporated in 1837 as Juliet, companion to the nearby town of Romeo (now renamed Romeoville).

What to See and Do

Bicentennial Park Theater/Bandshell Complex. Joliet Drama Guild and other productions (fee). Also outdoor concerts in bandshell (June-Aug, Thurs evenings). River cruises (May-Oct; fee). Historic walks. (See ANNUAL EVENTS) 201 W Jefferson St. Phone 815/740-2298 or 815/740-2491. **Free.**

Empress Casino Joliet. (Daily) I-55 exit 248, left 3 mi to Empress Lane. Phone 888/436-7737. **Free.**

Harrah's Joliet Casino. (Daily) Downtown, at 150 N Joliet St. Phone 800/HARRAHS. **Free.**

Pilcher Park. Walking, driving and bicycle trails; nature center (daily), greenhouse. Picnicking, playground. Off US 30, on Gougar Rd. Phone 815/741-7277.

Rialto Square Theatre (1926). Performing arts center, designed by the Rapp brothers, is considered one of the most elaborate and beautiful of old 1920s movie palaces. The domed auditorium is decorated with gilded and polychrome ornamental plasterwork featuring bas-reliefs sculpted by artist Eugene Romeo. Between the blk-long lobby and auditorium is a neoclassical-detailed rotunda from which hangs a large hand-cut crystal chandelier—20 ft in length with 8 bronze arms embracing 250 lights. Tours (Tues & by appt). 102 N Chicago St. For information contact the Ticket Office, 102 N Chicago St, PO Box 792, 60434; 815/726-6600. Tours ¢¢

Annual Events

Waterway Daze. Bicentennial Park, along the waterway wall. Features parade of decorated, lighted watercraft; food, entertainment. Phone 815/740-2216. 3 days late July.

Festival of the Gnomes. Bicentennial Park. Celebration includes stage performances of gnome legends, gnome-related arts & crafts, refreshments. Costumed gnomes. Sat early Dec.

Motels

★ **COMFORT INN-NORTH.** 3235 Norman Ave (60435). 815/436-5141. 64 rms, 3 story. May-Sept: S $64.95; D $69.95; each addl $6; suites $69.95; under 18 free; higher rates special events; lower rates rest of yr. Crib free. Pet accepted. TV; cable (premium). Indoor pool; whirlpool. Complimentary continental bkfst. Restaurant nearby 6 am-11 pm. Ck-out 11 am. Game rm. Refrigerators avail. Health club privileges. Cr cds: A, C, D, DS, MC, V.

🅳 🐾 ≈ ⊠ 🔥 SC

★★ **COMFORT INN-SOUTH.** 135 S Larkin Ave (60436), I-80 exit 130B. 815/744-1770; FAX 815/744-1770, ext. 303. 67 rms, 2 story. S $54.95-$89.95; D $64.95-$89.95; each addl $6; under 18 free. Crib free. Pet accepted. TV; cable (premium). Indoor pool. Complimentary continental bkfst. Restaurant nearby. Ck-out 11 am. Meeting rm. Business servs avail. Sauna. Health club privileges. Some refrigerators. Cr cds: A, C, D, DS, MC, V.

🅳 🐾 ≈ ⊠ 🔥 SC

✔ **MANOR.** (23926 W Eames Rd, Channahon 60410) 6 mi W on I-55, at jct US 6, exit 248, 1 mi so on I-80. 815/467-5385; FAX 815/467-1617. 77 rms, 1-2 story. S, D $32-$42; each addl $6; under 12 free; wkly, monthly rates. Crib $6.30. Pet accepted. TV; cable (premium). Pool. Complimentary coffee in lobby. Restaurant opp. Ck-out 11 am. Business servs avail. Cr cds: A, C, D, MC, V.

🐾 ≈ ⊠ 🔥

✔ **MOTEL 6.** 1850 McDonough St (60436), off I-80 exit 130B. 815/729-2800; FAX 815/729-9528. 132 rms, 2 story. S $33.99; D $39.99; each addl $6; under 18 free. Pet accepted, some restrictions. TV; cable (premium). Complimentary coffee in lobby. Restaurant opp 6 am-10 pm. Ck-out noon. Business servs avail. Cr cds: A, C, D, DS, MC, V.

🅳 🐾 ⊠ 🔥 SC

★ **SUPER 8.** 1730 McDonough St (60436), I-80, exit 130B. 815/725-8855. 64 rms, 2 story. S $48-$60; D $53-$66; each addl $6; under 17 free. Crib free. TV; cable (premium). Coffee in rms. Complimentary continental bkfst. Restaurant nearby. Ck-out 11 am. Meeting rm. Business servs avail. Cr cds: A, C, D, DS, MC, V.

🅳 ⊠ 🔥 SC

Restaurants

★★ **SECRETS.** 2222 W Jefferson St (60435). 815/744-3745. Hrs: 3:30-11 pm; Sun 11:30 am-9 pm. Closed July 4, Dec 25. Res accepted. Bar to 2 am. Semi-a la carte: dinner $7.50-$16.95. Child's meals. Specializes in ribs, steak, fresh seafood. Entertainment Wed, Sat. Cr cds: A, C, D, DS, MC, V.

🅳 SC

✔★ **WHITE FENCE FARM.** (Joliet Rd, Romeoville 60439) 10 mi N, 1 mi S of I-55 exit 269. 815/838-1500. Hrs: 5-8:30 pm; Sun noon-7:30 pm. Closed Mon; Thanksgiving, Dec 24, 25; also Jan-Feb. Serv bar. Semi-a la carte: dinner $8.95-$14.95. Child's meals. Specializes in chicken, corn fritters. Antiques; car museum. Children's zoo adj. Family-owned. Cr cds: A, C, D, MC, V.

🅳

Kankakee (C-6)

Founded 1855 **Pop** 27,575 **Elev** 663 ft **Area code** 815 **Zip** 60901 **E-mail** kccvb@colint.com **Web** colint.com/kccvb/index.htm

Information Kankakee County Convention & Visitors Bureau, 1711 Rte 50 N, Bourbonnais 60914; 815/935-7390 or 800/747-4837.

Kankakee was originally a part of the old French town of Bourbonnais but was incorporated as a separate community around the Illinois Central rail lines and the river in the 1850s. The region retains early French characteristics in its old buildings and in its culture. Limestone quarried from the riverbed was used to erect many of the walls in the area.

What to See and Do

Antique shopping. There are over 20 antique malls and shops in the area, including the **Kankakee Antique Mall**, the largest antique mall in Illinois with over 50,000 sq ft and 225 dealers. It is located at 147 S Schuyler Ave, phone 815/937-4957. Contact the Convention & Visitors Bureau for a complete list of shops.

Gladiolus fields. More than 150,000 flowers are harvested here, from early summer to the first frost. (See ANNUAL EVENTS) E on IL 17 to Momence.

Kankakee County Historical Society Museum. George Gray Barnard sculptures; also Native American artifacts, Civil War relics, toys, costumes, dishes; historical library. Adj is the 1855 house in which Governor Len Small was born; many original furnishings. Also on property is restored, one-room Taylor School (1904-1954). Gift shop. (Mon-Thurs; Sat & Sun afternoons; closed Jan & Nov) Water St & 8th Ave, in Small Memorial Park. Phone 815/932-5279. **Donation.**

Kankakee River State Park. Approx 4,000 acres. Woodlands on both banks of the Kankakee River and canyon of Rock Creek. Fishing, hunting; boating (canoe rentals, ramp). Hiking. Cross-country skiing, snowmobiling. Picnicking, game and playground facilities, concession. Camping. Interpretive program. 8 mi NW on IL 102. Phone 815/933-1383. **Free.**

Olivet Nazarene University (1907). (1,996 students) On 160-acre campus are 29 major buildings including the Strickler Planetarium and Science Museum, Benner Library, Larsen Fine Arts Center; Snowbarger Athletic Park; Parrott Convocation Athletic Center. Tours. 3 mi N on US 45/52 at IL 102 in Bourbonnais. Phone 815/939-5011.

River excursions. Canoe trips on the Kankakee river ranging from two hrs to two days. Canoes, kayaks, paddles, life jackets and transportation provided. (Apr-mid-Oct, daily) Reservations suggested. Contact Reed's Canoe Trips, 907 N Indiana Ave; 815/932-2663. ¢¢¢¢-¢¢¢¢¢

Annual Events

Kankakee River Valley Bicycle Classic. Late June.

Kankakee River Fishing Derby. Early July.

Kankakee County Fair. Fairgrounds. 1st wk Aug.

Gladiolus Festival. Gladiolus fields in Momence. Thousands of visitors gather for celebration that includes parades, flower shows, antique car show. 2nd wkend Aug.

Kankakee River Valley Regatta. Features the National OPC championships for power boats; raft races, carnival, entertainment. Labor Day wkend.

Motor Hotel

★ **DAYS INN.** 1975 E Court St (IL 17), jct I-57, IL 17. 815/939-2400; FAX 815/939-7184. 98 rms, 4 story. S $47-$57; D $52-$67; each addl $6; under 12 free. Crib free. TV; cable, VCR avail. Pool. Restaurant 6-11 am. Ck-out noon. Meeting rms. Business serv avail. Cr cds: A, C, D, DS, MC, V.

🅳 ≈ ⊠ 🔥 SC

Restaurant

✔★ **HOMESTEAD.** *1230 South East Ave, jct Il 45, 52, at Schuyler Ave. 815/933-6214.* Hrs: 11 am-11 pm; Fri, Sat to12:30 am. Res accepted. Italian, Amer menu. Bar. Semi-a la carte: lunch $4.25-$8, dinner $7.95-$15.95. Child's meals. Specializes in steak, ribs, veal. Own breads. Historic building (1880). Family-owned. Cr cds: MC, V.

Kewanee (C-3)

(See also Bishop Hill)

Pop 12,969 **Elev** 820 ft **Area code** 309 **Zip** 61443 **E-mail** kchamber @inw.net
Information Chamber of Commerce, 113 E 2nd St; 309/852-2175.

What to See and Do

Historic Francis Park. Within this 40-acre park is Woodland Palace, a unique house built by Fred Francis, inventor, mechanical engineer, artist and poet. Francis began the house in 1889, incorporating many early forms of modern conveniences, including an air-cooling system, water-purification system, automatically opening and closing doors and circulating air. Also here is miniature log cabin built by Francis as memorial to his parents. Hiking. Picnicking, playground. Camping. (See ANNUAL EVENTS) (Mid-Apr-Oct, daily) 1 mi E on US 34. Phone 309/852-0511. Tours of Woodland Palace ¢

Johnson Sauk Trail State Park. A focal point of this 1,361-acre park is Ryan's Round Barn, a massive cattle barn that contains interpretive exhibits; also 58-acre man-made lake. Fishing; boating (rentals). Hiking. Ice-skating, snowmobiling, cross-country skiing. Picnicking. Camping (electric hookups, dump station). Standard fees. (See ANNUAL EVENTS) (Daily) 5 mi N on IL 78. Phone 309/853-5589.   **Free.**

Annual Events

Sauk Trail Heritage Days. Francis Park & Johnson Sauk Trail State Park. Four-day celebration includes pow wow, Native American crafts & story telling. Railroad display and demonstrations. Tours. Food. Children's activities. Fireworks. Wkend of July 4.

Hog Capital of the World Festival. Midway, entertainment, arts & crafts, variety of pork dishes. Labor Day wkend.

Motel

✔★ **KEWANEE MOTOR LODGE.** *400 S Main St. 309/853-4000; FAX 309/853-4000, ext. 401; res: 800/853-4007.* 28 rms, 2 story. S $38.75-$40.75; D $45; each addl $5. Crib $5. Pet accepted. TV; cable (premium). Complimentary coffee in lobby. Restaurant adj 6 am-10 pm. Ck-out noon. Business servs avail. Some refrigerators. Cr cds: A, C, D, DS, MC, V.

Restaurants

✔★ **ANDRIS WAUNEE FARM.** *S on US 34/IL 78. 309/852-2481.* Hrs: 5-11 pm; Fri & Sat to midnight. Closed Sun; some hols. Res accepted. Polynesian, Amer menu. Bar. Semi-a la carte: dinner $4.50-$13.95. Child's meals. Specializes in steak, prime rib, haddock. Salad bar. 3 dining rms, one with Polynesian theme. Family-owned. No cr cds accepted.

★★ **THE CELLAR.** *(137 S State St, Geneseo 61254-0012) 11 mi N on IL 78, then 14 mi W on I-80. 309/944-2177.* Hrs: 5-10 pm; Sun

11:30 am-9 pm. Closed Mon; Dec 24, 25. Res accepted. Bar 4 pm-midnight. Semi-a la carte: dinner $9.95-$23.95. Child's meals. Specializes in charcoal-broiled shrimp, steak, ribs, catfish. Casual dining in basement of downtown commercial building; original artwork. Cr cds: A, C, D, DS, MC, V.

La Grange (E-3 see Chicago map)

(See also Brookfield, Cicero, Elmhurst, Hinsdale, Oak Brook)

Pop 15,362 **Elev** 650 ft **Area code** 708 **Zip** 60525 **E-mail** info@westsuburbanchamber.org **Web** www.westsuburbanchamber.org
Information West Suburban Chamber of Commerce, 47 S 6th Ave; 708/352-0494.

What to See and Do

Historic District. Here are a number of historically and culturally significant homes dating from the late 19th and early 20th centuries; included are houses designed by such prominent architects as Frank Lloyd Wright, J.C. Llewelyn, E.H. Turnock and John S. Van Bergen. Bordered by 47th St on the S, Brainard Ave on the W and 8th Ave on the E, the area is split by the Burlington Northern Railroad tracks; an area N of the tracks, roughly bordered by Stone & Madison Aves, is also part of the Historic District.

Annual Event

Pet Parade. First begun in 1946, this parade attracts thousands of visitors each year. 1st Sat June.

Motels

✔★ ★ **BEST WESTERN INN.** *(5631 S La Grange Rd, Countryside) 4 mi S on US Rte 12/20. 708/352-2480; FAX 708/354-0998.* 47 rms, 1-2 story. June-Nov: S $51-$56; D $56-$61; each addl $5; under 18 free; lower rates rest of yr. Crib free. TV; cable (premium). Heated pool. Complimentary continental bkfst. Restaurant nearby. Ck-out noon. Cr cds: A, C, D, DS, MC, V.

★ ★ **HAMPTON INN.** *(6251 Joliet Rd, Countryside) ½ mi N of I-55, 1 mi E of I-294. 708/354-5200; FAX 708/354-1329.* 108 rms, 6 story. S $70; D $72; under 18 free. Crib free. TV; cable (premium), VCR avail. Pool privileges. Complimentary continental bkfst. Ck-out noon. Business servs avail. In-rm modem link. Cr cds: A, C, D, DS, MC, V.

Motor Hotel

★ ★ ★ **HOLIDAY INN.** *(6201 Joliet Rd, Countryside) at jct US 45. 708/354-4200; FAX 708/354-4241.* 305 rms, 7 story. S, D $99; suites from $129-$159; under 18 free; package plans. Crib free. TV; cable (premium), VCR avail (movies). Indoor pool; wading pool, poolside serv. Complimentary coffee. Restaurant 6 am-10 pm. Rm serv. Bar 11-1 am; dancing Tues-Sat. Ck-out noon. Meeting rm. Business servs avail. In-rm modem link. Sundries. Exercise equipt; weights, stair machine, sauna. Pool; whirlpool. Game rm. Rec rm. Cr cds: A, C, D, DS, JCB, MC, V.

Libertyville (B-3 see Chicago map)

(See also Grayslake, Gurnee)

Founded 1836 **Pop** 19,174 **Elev** 700 ft **Area code** 847 **Zip** 60048
Information Chamber of Commerce, 731 N Milwaukee Ave; 847/680-0750.

Marlon Brando, Helen Hayes and Adlai Stevenson are a few of the famous personalities who have lived in Libertyville. The St Mary of the Lake Theological Seminary (Roman Catholic) borders the town; there are four lakes near the village limits.

What to See and Do

Cuneo Museum & Gardens. Opulent Venetian-style mansion featuring great hall with arcade balconies, chapel with stained glass and fresco ceiling, ship's rm with hidden bookshelves. Collection of master paintings, 17th-century tapestries, Oriental rugs, Capo-di-monte porcelain. 75-acre grounds include fountains, gardens, conservatory. (Daily exc Mon) S on IL 21, then W on IL 60 in Vernon Hills at 1350 N Milwaukee. Phone 847/362-2025. ¢¢¢

David Adler Cultural Center. The summer residence of the distinguished neo-classical architect David Adler. Folk concerts, barn dances and children's events (fee for all). Exhibits and tours. 1700 N Milwaukee Ave. Phone 847/367-0707. **Free.**

Lambs Farm. Includes children's farmyard, small animal nursery and miniature golf (fees), thrift shop, country store, bakery, ice cream parlor, restaurant. Fire engine, pony and hay rides. Miniature train rides (fee). Gift shops. Nonprofit residential and vocational community benefitting mentally retarded adults. (Daily; closed hols) Jct I-94 & IL 176 exit. Phone 847/362-6774 (events hotline) or 847/362-4636. **Free.**

Motels

★ **BEST INNS OF AMERICA.** *1809 N Milwaukee Ave. 847/816-8006.* 90 rms, 3 story. Mid-June-mid-Sept: S $47.88-$51.88; D $53.88-$61.88; each addl $7; under 18 free; lower rates rest of yr. Crib free. Pet accepted. TV; cable (premium). Heated pool. Complimentary continental bkfst. Restaurant nearby. Ck-out 1 pm. Meeting rm. Some refrigerators. Cr cds: A, C, D, DS, MC, V.

D ⟲ ⊠ 🐾 SC

✔★ **BEST WESTERN HITCH INN POST.** *1765 N Milwaukee Ave (IL 21), at jct IL 137. 847/362-8700; FAX 847/362-8725.* 137 rms, 1-2 story. S $47-$55; D $47-$80; each addl $6; suites $86-$92; under 12 free. Crib $3. TV; cable (premium), VCR avail. Indoor pool; whirlpool. Complimentary continental bkfst. Restaurant 11 am-10 pm. Rm serv. Bar 11-1 am. Ck-out noon. Coin lndry. Business servs avail. In-rm modem link. Valet serv. Gift shop. Exercise equipt; weights, bicycles, sauna. Game rm. Some refrigerators, microwaves. Automobile museum on site. Cr cds: A, C, D, DS, MC, V.

D ⊠ 🏋 ⊠ 🐾 SC

Restaurants

★★ **GALE STREET INN.** *(906 Diamond Lake Rd, Mundelein 60060) 5 mi SW on Diamond Lake Rd. 847/566-1090.* Hrs: 11 am-10 pm; Fri, Sat to midnight. Closed Mon; Thanksgiving, Dec 25. Res accepted. Bar. Semi-a la carte: lunch $3.95-$6.95, dinner $7.95-$22.95. Specializes in barbecued baby-back ribs, prime rib, steak. Salad bar. Entertainment Tues-Sat. Patio dining. Multi-level dining overlooking Diamond Lake. Nautical decor. Cr cds: A, C, D, DS, MC, V.

★ **THE LAMBS COUNTRY INN.** *At jct I-94 & IL 176. 847/362-5050.* Hrs: 11 am-8 pm; Sun to 7 pm; Sun brunch 10:30 am-2:30 pm. Closed some major hols. Res accepted; required Fri-Sun (summer). Serv bar. Semi-a la carte: lunch $5-$8, dinner $7-$14. Sun brunch $12.95.

Child's meals. Specializes in fried chicken, prime rib, barbecued ribs. Salad bar. Own baking. Country inn atmosphere. Petting zoo adj. Cr cds: A, C, D, DS, MC, V.

D 🖾

★ **MEADOWS 21 & BUFFALO BAR AND GRILL.** *1760 N Milwaukee Ave (IL 21), just S of IL 137. 847/362-8202.* Hrs: 11 am-10 pm. Closed Sun. Res accepted. Bar. Semi-a la carte: lunch $6-$8, dinner $7.95-$13. Child's meals. Specializes in ribs, black Angus, ostrich burgers. Entertainment. Patio dining. American Southwest decor. Cr cds: A, D, DS, MC, V.

D 🖾

★★★ **TAVERN IN THE TOWN.** *519 N Milwaukee Ave (IL 21). 847/367-5755.* Hrs: 11:30 am-2 pm, 6-9 pm; Fri, Sat from 6 pm. Closed Sun; most major hols. Res accepted. Continental menu. Bar. Wine cellar. Semi-a la carte: lunch $6.95-$11.95, dinner $12.95-25. Specializes in grilled fish, seasonal game, roasted beef tenderloin. Cr cds: A, C, D, DS, MC, V.

🖾

Lincoln (E-4)

(See also Bloomington, Decatur, Springfield)

Founded 1853 **Pop** 15,418 **Elev** 591 ft **Area code** 217 **Zip** 62656 **E-mail** tourism@abelink.com
Information Abraham Lincoln Tourism Bureau of Logan County, 303 S Kickapoo St; 217/732-8687.

Of all the cities named for Abraham Lincoln, this is the only one named with his knowledge and consent and before he was elected president. Lincoln participated in the legal work involved in the organization of the townsite and its incorporation as the seat of Logan County. Later he acquired a lot here as compensation for a note he had endorsed.

What to See and Do

Mt Pulaski Court House State Historic Site (1848). This restored Greek-revival building served as county courthouse until 1855. It is one of two surviving Eighth Circuit courthouses in Illinois visited by Lincoln. Interpretive program. (Tues-Sat afternoons; closed most major hols) 12 mi SE on IL 121, in Mt Pulaski. Phone ahead for hrs, 217/792-3919. **Donation.**

Postville Court House State Historic Site. Replica on site of original courthouse that Henry Ford acquired and restored for his Greenfield Village museum (see DEARBORN, MI). Lincoln practiced law in the original courthouse twice a year while Postville was the county seat (1840-1848). Interpretive program. (See ANNUAL EVENTS) (Fri & Sat afternoons; closed most major hols) 914 5th St, I-55 Business on the W side of town. Phone 217/732-8930. **Donation.**

Annual Events

Logan County Fair. Fairgrounds. Tractor pulls, agricultural and farm machinery exhibits; horse races; livestock shows. Early Aug.

1800s Craft Fair. Postville Court House. Artisans demonstrate skills from 1800s, including blacksmithing, quilting, wood carving & broom making. Traditional music. Phone 217/732-8930. Late Aug.

Abraham Lincoln National Railsplitter Contest & Crafts Festival. Fairgrounds. Contests, entertainment, flea market. Phone 217/732-7146. Mid-Sept.

Motels

★★ **COMFORT INN.** *2811 Woodlawn Rd, I-55 exit 126. 217/735-3960; FAX 217/735-3960, ext. 304.* 52 rms, 2 story, 6 suites. S $46.95-$62.95; D $49.95-$62.95; each addl $5; suites $54.95-$64.95;

under 18 free. Crib free. Pet accepted. TV; cable (premium), VCR avail. Indoor pool; whirlpool. Complimentary continental bkfst. Restaurant adj 5:30 am-11 pm. Ck-out 11 am. Meeting rms. Business servs avail. Game rm. Refrigerators, microwaves in suites. Cr cds: A, C, D, DS, MC, V.

★ **DAYS INN.** *2011 N Kickapoo St. 217/735-1202; FAX 217/735-1202, ext. 507.* 60 rms. S, D $39-$60; each addl $5; under 12 free. Crib free. Pet accepted, some restrictions; $10/day. TV; cable (premium). Indoor pool. Complimentary continental bkfst. Restaurant nearby. Ck-out noon. Meeting rms. Business servs avail. Sundries. Cr cds: A, C, D, DS, MC, V.

Restaurant

★ **TROPICS.** *1007 Hickox Dr. 217/732-6710.* Hrs: 6:15 am-10 pm; Sun buffet 11 am-9 pm. Bar. Complete meals: bkfst $1.89-$4.39, lunch $2.99-$6.25, dinner $5.29-$22.49. Buffet (Sun): $7.99. Specializes in steak, seafood, ribs. Salad bar. Tropical decor. Cr cds: A, C, D, DS, MC, V.

D

Lincoln's New Salem State Historic Site

(see Petersburg)

Lockport (F-2 see Chicago map)

(For accommodations see Joliet)

Founded 1836 **Pop** 9,401 **Elev** 604 ft **Area code** 815 **Zip** 60441
Information Chamber of Commerce, 132 E 9th; 815/838-3357.

Lockport was founded as headquarters of the Illinois and Michigan Canal. In its heyday, the town boasted five different locks (four actually remain). Shipbuilding was once an important industry. The Old Canal Town National Historic District preserves several buildings from this bygone era.

What to See and Do

Illinois and Michigan Canal Museum (1837). Includes artifacts, pictures and documents relating to the construction and operation of the canal. Guided tours by costumed docents. (Daily, afternoons; closed hols, also wks of Thanksgiving & Dec 25) Canal Commissioner's office, 803 S State St. Phone 815/838-5080. **Free.** Also here are

Pioneer Settlement. Log cabins, village jail, root cellar, tinsmith and blacksmith shops, workshop, one-room schoolhouse, mid-19th century farmhouse, smokehouse, privy and railroad station. (Mid-Apr-Oct, afternoons) **Free.**

Old Stone Annex Building. Depicts early banking history and other exhibits. (Mid-Apr-Oct, daily) **Free.** Adj is the

Gaylord Bldg (1838). Includes the Lockport Gallery, a branch site of the Illinois State Museum, which features art of various media by the state's past and present artists (daily exc Mon). Also in the building is the I & M Canal Visitor Center with interpreters and theater productions that highlight the area (Wed-Sun), and restaurant with views of the canal (daily exc Mon). 200 W 8th St. Phone 815/838-7400 (gallery), -4830 (visitor center) or -6500 (restaurant).

Annual Events

Old Canal Days. Pioneer craft demonstrations, horse-drawn wagon tours, I & M Canal walking tours, Lockport prairie tours, museum open house, races, games, carnival, entertainment, food. Phone 815/838-4744. 3rd wkend June.

Western Open Golf Tournament. Approx 8 mi N via Archer Ave, at Cog Hill Golf Course in Lemont. Early July.

Restaurants

★ ★ **PUBLIC LANDING.** *200 W 8th St.* 815/838-6500. Hrs: 11:30 am-2 pm, 5-9 pm; Fri to 10 pm; Sat 5-10 pm; Sun 4-8 pm. Closed Mon. Bar. A la carte entrees: lunch $5.95-$8.95. Semi-a la carte: dinner $12.95-$22.95. Child's meals. Specializes in seafood, chicken, prime rib. Own pastries. Built 1838; an Illinois Historic Landmark. Overlooks Illinois and Michigan Canal. Regional museum, art gallery adj. Cr cds: MC, V.

★ ★ **TALLGRASS.** *1006 S State.* 815/838-5566. Hrs: 6-9 pm. Closed Mon, Tues; most major hols. Res required. French menu. Bar. Wine cellar. Prix fixe: dinner $45, $55. Specialties: lobster soufflé, tower of Belgian chocolate, fresh seasonal dishes. Own baking. Victorian decor; many antiques and stained glass. Jacket. Cr cds: MC, V.

Macomb (D-2)

(See also Galesburg, Monmouth)

Founded 1830 **Pop** 19,952 **Elev** 700 ft **Area code** 309 **Zip** 61455 **E-mail** chamber@macomb.com
Information Macomb Area Chamber of Commerce, 804 W Jackson, PO Box 274; 309/837-4855.

Originally known as Washington, the town was renamed to honor General Alexander Macomb, an officer in the War of 1812. Macomb is best known as the home of Western Illinois University.

What to See and Do

Argyle Lake State Park. The park has 1,700 acres with a 95-acre lake. Fishing, hunting; boating (ramp, rentals; motors, 10 hp limit). Hiking. Cross-country skiing, snowmobiling. Picnicking, playground, concession, shelter house. Camping (showers). Standard fees. (Daily) 7 mi W on US 136, then 1½ mi N. Phone 309/776-3422. **Free.**

Spring Lake Park. On 300 acres. Fishing. Picnicking. Camping (fee). 3 mi N on US 67, then 2 mi W, then 1 mi N. Phone 309/833-2052. **Free.**

Western Illinois University (1899). (12,000 students) The 1,050-acre campus includes an art gallery (Mon-Fri, free); 600,000 volume library; Illinois/National Business Hall of Fame in Stipes Hall; agricultural experiment station at N edge of campus; Geology Museum, 1st flr Tillman Hall; and a 9-hole public golf course, Tower Rd (Apr-Oct, daily; fee). 900 W Adams St, NW edge of city. Phone 309/298-1993. Also on campus are

WIU Museum. Houses antique farm equipment, early 1900s store and medical exhibits, trapping equipment; various artifacts of the region. (Mon-Fri) Sherman Hall, 3rd floor. Phone 309/298-1727 or 309/298-1808. **Free.**

Biological Sciences Greenhouse. Gardens and nature area; includes tropical and temperate plants, native aquatic, prairie and woodland plants and herbs. (Mon-Fri) S of Waggoner Hall. Phone 309/298-1004. **Free.**

Motel

★★ **DAYS INN.** *1400 N Lafayette.* 309/833-5511; FAX 309/836-2926. 144 rms, 2 story. S $48-$55; D $53-$63; each addl $6; suites $95-$125; higher rates: Labor Day, special events. Crib free. Pet accepted. TV; cable (premium); VCR avail. Pool; wading pool, poolside serv. Playground. Restaurant 6 am-2 pm, 5-10 pm. Bar 4 pm-1 am; entertainment Fri, Sat. Ck-out noon. Coin lndry. Meeting rms. Business servs avail. In-rm modem link. Some refrigerators, microwaves. Cr cds: A, C, D, DS, JCB, MC, V.

D 🐾 ≈ 🏊 🔥 SC

Marion (J-4)

(See also Benton, Carbondale)

Founded 1839 **Pop** 14,545 **Elev** 448 ft **Area code** 618 **Zip** 62959 **E-mail** marionchamber@midamer.net **Web** www.cc.marion.il.us

Information Greater Marion Area Chamber of Commerce, 2305 W Main St, PO Box 307; 618/997-6311.

A regional trade center serving 90,000 people, Marion is the seat of Williamson County, which in the 1920s and 1930s was known as "bloody Williamson County" due to both gang warfare and labor unrest among coal miners. Today, Marion is best known as the location of the maximum-security US Federal Penitentiary.

What to See and Do

⭐ **Crab Orchard National Wildlife Refuge.** Refuge for wintering Canada geese includes 7,000-acre Crab Orchard Lake, W of headquarters; Little Grassy Lake, 8 mi S; and Devil's Kitchen Lake, just E of Little Grassy. Swimming; fishing, hunting, trapping; boat ramps and rentals. Nature trails. Picnicking. Camping at Crab Orchard, Little Grassy and Devil's Kitchen (fees; rest rms, showers at all campgrounds). Pets on leash only. Headquarters (Mon-Fri; closed hols). Area (all yr, daily). Headquarters, 5 mi W on IL 13, then 2½ mi S on IL 148. Phone 618/997-3344, ext 320. ¢¢

Ferne Clyffe State Park. Caves, gorges, canyons on 1,125 acres. Fishing, hunting. Hiking, riding trails. Picnicking. Camping, equestrian camping. Nature preserve. Standard fees. (Daily) 15 mi S off IL 37, in Goreville. Phone 618/995-2411. **Free.**

Lake of Egypt. Activities on 2,300-acre stocked lake include waterskiing; fishing; boating (rentals, launching). Camping. 8 mi S via I-57, IL 37. For camping information contact Pyramid Acres Campground & Marina, 618/964-1184; or Egyptian Hills Camping & Marina, 618/996-3449.

Annual Event

Williamson County Fair. June.

Motels

★ **BEST INNS OF AMERICA.** *RR 8, Box 70, IL 13, off I-57 exit 54B.* 618/997-9421. 104 rms, 2 story. S $37-$45; D $46.88-$60.88; under 18 free. Crib free. TV; cable. Pool. Complimentary continental bkfst. Restaurant nearby. Ck-out 1 pm. Cr cds: A, C, D, DS, MC, V.

D ≈ 🏊 🔥 SC

★ **BEST WESTERN AIRPORT INN.** *RR 8, Box 348-1, IL 13, adj to Williamson County Airport.* 618/993-3222; FAX 618/993-8868. 34 rms, 2 story, 10 suites. S $39-$49; D $44-$54; each addl $5; suites $52-$72; under 12 free; higher rates SIU special events. Crib free. Pet accepted. TV. Pool. Complimentary continental bkfst. Restaurant nearby. Ck-out 11 am. Meeting rms. Business servs avail. Free airport transportation. Refrigerator, wet bar in suites. Cr cds: A, C, D, DS, MC, V.

D 🐾 ≈ ✈ 🏊 🔥 SC

★★ **COMFORT INN.** *2600 W Main St, off I-57 exit 53, near Williamson County Airport.* 618/993-6221; FAX 618/993-8964. 122 rms, 2 story, 34 suites. S $51; D $56; each addl $5; suites $59-$64; under 18 free. Crib free. TV; cable. Heated pool. Complimentary continental bkfst. Restaurant adj 6 am-10 pm. Ck-out noon. Meeting rm. Free airport transportation. Exercise equipt; weight machines, bicycles. Refrigerator, microwave, minibar in suites. Cr cds: A, C, D, DS, JCB, MC, V.

D ≈ 🏃 ✈ 🏊 🔥 SC

Restaurant

★★ **TONY'S STEAK HOUSE.** *105 S Market St.* 618/993-2220. Hrs: 4-10:30 pm. Closed Sun; major hols. Res accepted. Bar to midnight. Complete meals: dinner $6.95-$19.95. Specializes in fresh-cut steak, prime rib. Cr cds: A, C, D, DS, ER, JCB, MC, V.

🍴

Marshall (F-6)

(For accommodations see Terre Haute, IN)

Founded 1835 **Pop** 3,555 **Elev** 641 ft **Area code** 217 **Zip** 62441
Information Chamber of Commerce, PO Box 263; 217/826-2034.

The site on which Marshall is now located was purchased from the federal government in 1833 by Colonel William Archer and Joseph Duncan, sixth governor of Illinois. They named the town after John Marshall, fourth Chief Justice of the United States Supreme Court. Seat of Clark County, Marshall serves as a business center for the surrounding agricultural community.

What to See and Do

Lincoln Trail State Park. The Lincoln family passed through here en route from Indiana in 1830. This 1,022-acre park has fishing in a man-made lake; boating (ramp, rentals; motors, 10 hp limit). Hiking. Picnicking, concession. Camping. Standard fees. (Daily) 2 mi S off IL 1. Phone 217/826-2222. **Free.**

Mill Creek Park. Swimming, fishing, boating. Camping; cabins. Bridle, ATV trails. (Daily) 7 mi NW on Lincoln Heritage Trail (RR 2). Phone 217/889-3601 or 217/889-3901. **Free.**

Annual Event

Autumn Fest. Town Square. 3rd wkend Sept.

Mattoon (F-5)

(See also Arcola, Charleston, Effingham)

Founded 1854 **Pop** 18,441 **Elev** 726 ft **Area code** 217 **Zip** 61938
Information Mattoon Chamber of Commerce, 1701 Wabash Ave; 217/235-5661 or -5666.

Named for a railroad official who built the Big Four Railroad from St Louis to Indianapolis, Mattoon is an industrial town and a retail and market center for the surrounding farm area. Products vary from heavy road machinery to bagels and magazines. In 1861, General Ulysses S. Grant mustered the 25th Illinois Infantry into service in Mattoon.

What to See and Do

Lake Mattoon. Fishing; boating, launching facilities. Picnicking. Camping. 6 mi S on US 45, I-57, then 3 mi W.

Annual Event

Bagelfest. World's biggest bagel breakfast. Bagelfest Queen Pageant, Beautiful Bagel Baby Contest. Parade, talent show, music. Phone 217/235-5661. 5 days late July.

Motel

★ ★ **RAMADA INN & CONFERENCE CENTER.** *300 Broadway Ave E, just off IL 16 on access road, 1 mi E of US 45, 1 mi W of I-57 exit IL 16 (W). 217/235-0313; FAX 217/235-6005.* 124 rms, 2 story. S $51-$90; D $59-$90; each addl $5; suites $76-$95; under 20 free. Crib free. Pet accepted. TV; cable (premium). 2 pools, 1 indoor; whirlpool, sauna. Complimentary coffee. Restaurant 6 am-10 pm. Bar 11:30-1 am. Ck-out noon. Coin lndry. Meeting rms. Business servs avail. Atrium. Game rm. Rec rm. Cr cds: A, C, D, DS, ER, JCB, MC, V.

Restaurant

✔ ★ ★ **AJ'S.** *(203 E Main, Shelbyville 62565) 24 mi W on US 16. 217/774-5616.* Hrs: 10 am-10 pm; Sun from 4 pm. Closed some major hols; also Sun Labor Day-Memorial Day. Res accepted. Continental menu. Bar. Semi-a la carte: lunch $3.95-$5.95, dinner $9.95-$14.95. Child's meals. Specializes in barbecue ribs, steak, sandwiches. Brick bldg in historic area with hardwood floors, tin ceiling. Cr cds: A, DS, MC, V.

McHenry (A-5)

(See also Gurnee, Woodstock)

Pop 16,177 **Elev** 761 ft **Area code** 815 **Zip** 60050
Information Chamber of Commerce, 1257 N Green St; 815/385-4300.

What to See and Do

Moraine Hills State Park. Three small lakes on 1,690 acres. Fishing; boating (rentals). Bike, hiking trails (11 mi). Cross-country skiing (rentals). Picnicking, concession. Nature center. (Daily; closed Dec 25) Standard fees. On S River Rd. Phone 815/385-1624. **Free.**

Volo Auto Museum and Village. Display of more than 170 antique and collector cars. Gift, antique and craft shops. Autos displayed and sold. Restaurant. (Daily; closed hols) 5 mi E on IL 120 in Volo. Phone 815/385-3644. **¢¢**

Motels

★ **DAYS INN.** *(11200 US 12, Richmond 60071) 11 mi N on US 12/IL 31. 815/678-4711; FAX 815/678-4623.* 60 rms, 2 story. May-Sept: S $59-$69; D $65-$74; family, wkly, wkend, hol rates; higher rates special events; lower rates rest of yr. Crib free. Pet accepted, some restrictions. TV. Pool. Complimentary continental bkfst. Restaurant adj. Ck-out 11 am. Downhill/x-country ski 12 mi. Cr cds: A, C, D, DS, JCB, MC, V.

★ ★ **RAMADA TAMARA ROYALE CONFERENCE CENTER.** *4100 Shamrock Lane (IL 31). 815/344-5500; FAX 815/344-5527.* 58 rms, 2-3 story. S $70-$88; D $80-$98; each addl $10; suites $175-$225. Crib free. TV; cable (premium). Indoor pool; whirlpool. Complimentary coffee in lobby. Restaurant 7 am-2 pm, 5-10 pm. Rm serv. Bar; entertainment wkends. Ck-out noon. Meeting rms. Business servs avail. X-country ski 13 mi. Whirlpool in suites. Health club privileges. Picnic tables. In Chain O'Lakes region. Cr cds: A, C, D, DS, MC, V.

Motor Hotel

★ ★ ★ **HOLIDAY INN.** *(800 S IL 31, Crystal Lake 60014) 10 mi S on IL 31. 815/477-7000; FAX 815/477-7027.* 196 rms, 6 story. S $78-$99; D $78-$109; each addl $10; suites $159; under 18 free. Crib free. Pet accepted. TV; cable (premium). Indoor pool; whirlpool. Complimentary coffee in lobby. Restaurant 6:30 am-10 pm; Fri, Sat to 11 pm. Rm serv. Bar from 11 am. Ck-out noon. Meeting rms. Bellhops. Gift shop. Free RR station, bus depot transportation. Exercise equipt; weight machine, stair machine, sauna. Cr cds: A, C, D, DS, JCB, MC, V.

Restaurants

★ **JENNY'S AT CHAPEL HILL COUNTRY CLUB.** *2500 N Chapel Hill Rd. 815/385-0333.* Hrs: 4:30-9 pm; Fri, Sat to 10 pm; Sun 3-8 pm; Sun brunch 10 am-2 pm. Closed Mon, Tues; Dec 25. Res accepted. Bar. Semi-a la carte: dinner $6.95-$18.95. Sun brunch $7.95. Child's meals. Specializes in prime rib, seafood, filet mignon. Salad bar. Own pastries. Entertainment wkends. View of club grounds. Cr cds: A, C, D, DS, MC, V.

D

★ ★ **LE VICHYSSOIS.** *(220 W IL 120, Lakemoor) 2 mi W of US 12 on IL 120. 815/385-8221.* Hrs: 5:30 pm-closing; Sun from 4:30 pm. Closed Mon, Tues; major hols. Res accepted. French menu. Serv bar. Wine list. Semi-a la carte: dinner $15-$25; prix fixe $21.50. Specialties: Dover sole, salmon en croute, rack of lamb. Own pastries, ice cream. French provincial decor; country inn atmosphere. Cr cds: C, D, JCB, MC, V.

D

Moline (C-2)

(See also Rock Island)

Founded 1848 **Pop** 43,202 **Elev** 580 ft **Area code** 309 **Zip** 61265 **E-mail** cvb@quadcities.com **Web** quadcities.com/cvb
Information Cities Convention & Visitors Bureau, 2021 River Dr; 309/788-7800 or 800/747-7800.

Settled by a significant number of Belgians, Moline takes its name from the French *moulin* (mill), in reference to the many mills that were built along the Mississippi to take advantage of the limitless supply of waterpower. Today the city produces goods varying from farm implements to elevators. Moline and Rock Island, along with Bettendorf and Davenport, Iowa (across the Mississippi River), comprise the Quad Cities metropolitan area.

What to See and Do

Center for Belgian Culture. Houses Belgian memorabilia. (Wed & Sat afternoons) 712 18th Ave. Phone 309/762-0167. **Free.**

★ **Deere & Company.** World headquarters for manufacturers of farm, industrial, lawn and garden equipment. Administrative Center (1964), designed by Eero Saarinen, who also designed the arch in St Louis, is considered a masterpiece of modern architecture. On 1,000 acres overlooking Rock River Valley, the center consists of main office building with display floor; 400-seat auditorium; and the newer West Office Bldg. Main office building was constructed of corrosion-resistant unpainted steel and is set across the floor of a wooded ravine; display floor includes three-dimensional mural, designed by Alexander Girard, composed of more than 2,000 items dating from 1837 to 1918 that relate to agriculture and life in mid-America during that period. West Office Bldg (1978), designed by Roche and Dinkeloo with a skylighted interior garden court, has been cited for its harmonious relation to the original buildings. Grounds include two large pools with many fountains and an island with a Henry Moore sculpture. Tours of Administrative Center (Mon-Fri; closed hols). Factory tours (by appt; phone 309/765-4207, 309/765-4208 or 309/765-4235; children over 11 yrs only). Main building (daily), John Deere Rd. Phone 309/765-8000. **Free.**

John Deere Commons. On the banks of the Mississippi River, this complex is home to the **John Deere Pavilion**, a visitor center with interactive displays about agriculture and vintage and modern John Deere equipment. Also here are a John Deere Store; a restaurant; a hotel; **The MARK** of the Quad Cities, a 12,000-seat arena hosting high-profile events; and **Centre Station**, the transportation hub and Information Center for the Quad Cities. (Daily) 2021 River Dr. Phone 309/765-1001. **Free.**

Niabi Zoo. Miniature railroad (fee); children's zoo; picnicking, snack bar. (Daily; closed Jan 1 & Dec 25) Free admission Tues. 10 mi SE on US 6, in Coal Valley. Phone 309/799-5107. **¢¢**

Motels

★ ★ **BEST WESTERN AIRPORT INN.** *2550 52nd Ave. 309/762-9191.* 50 rms, 2 story. May-Sept: S, D $58-$85; each addl $5; under 12 free; lower rates rest of yr. Crib $3. TV; cable (premium). Indoor pool; whirlpool. Complimentary continental bkfst. Restaurant opp open 24 hrs. Ck-out 11 am. Business servs avail. Downhill/x-country ski 15 mi. Some refrigerators. Near Quad City Airport. Cr cds: A, C, D, DS, MC, V.

[D] [≈] [≋] [⊠] [✎] [SC]

★ ★ **HAMPTON INN.** *6920 27th St, near jct I-74 & I-280, adj to Quad City Airport. 309/762-1711; FAX 309/762-1788.* 138 rms, 2 story. S, D $51-$66; suites $99-$150; under 18 free. Pet accepted. TV; cable (premium). Heated pool. Complimentary continental bkfst. Restaurant adj 7 am-10:30 pm. Ck-out noon. Meeting rm. Business servs avail. Valet serv. Free airport transportation. Health club privileges. Cr cds: A, C, D, DS, MC, V.

[D] [⚲] [≈] [✈] [⊠] [✎] [SC]

★ ★ **LA QUINTA INN.** *5450 27th St, near Quad City Airport. 309/762-9008; FAX 309/762-2455.* 126 rms, 2 story. May-Sept: S $47-$54; D $52-$55; each addl $5; under 18 free; lower rates rest of yr. Crib $5. Pet accepted. TV; cable (premium). Heated pool. Complimentary continental bkfst. Restaurant nearby. Ck-out noon. Coin lndry. Meeting rm. Business servs avail. In-rm modem link. Airport transportation. Downhill ski 15 mi. Some refrigerators. Cr cds: A, C, D, DS, MC, V.

[D] [⚲] [≈] [≋] [✈] [⊠] [✎] [SC]

★ ★ **RAMADA INN.** *2620 Airport Rd, Airport Rd at jct I-74 & I-280. 309/797-1211; FAX 309/764-4313.* 92 rms, 2 story. S, D $61-$110; each addl $5; under 8 free. Crib free. TV; cable (premium). VCR avail. 2 pools, 1 indoor; whirlpool. Complimentary coffee in lobby. Restaurant 6 am-2 pm, 5-10 pm. Ck-out noon. Meeting rms. Business servs avail. In-rm modem link. Free airport transportation. Exercise equipt; weight machine, treadmill. Private patios, balconies. Cr cds: A, C, D, DS, JCB, MC, V.

[D] [≈] [✗] [✈] [⊠] [SC]

Restaurants

★ ★ **C'EST MICHELE.** *1514 5th Ave. 309/762-0585.* Hrs: 6:30 pm-midnight. Closed Sun-Tues; Thanksgiving, Dec 24, 25. Res required. French menu. Serv bar. Complete meals: dinner $30. Specialties: magret de canard, châteaubriand, veau aux moriel. Pianist. Elegant decor. Jacket. Cr cds: A, C, D, MC, V.

[D] [⛛]

✔ ★ ★ **TORTILLA FLATS.** *3939 16th St (John Deere Expy). 309/797-5296.* Hrs: 11 am-10 pm; Fri, Sat to 11 pm; Sun from 4 pm. Closed Easter, Thanksgiving, Dec 25. Res accepted. Mexican, Amer menu. Bar. Semi-a la carte: lunch $5.25-$10.75, dinner $5.95-$14.25. Child's meals. Specializes in enchiladas, steak, salads. Entertainment Tues-Sat. Outdoor dining. Cr cds: A, DS, MC, V.

[D]

Monmouth (D-2)

(See also Galesburg)

Founded 1831 **Pop** 9,489 **Elev** 770 ft **Area code** 309 **Zip** 61462
Information Monmouth Area Chamber of Commerce, 620 S Main St, PO Box 857; 309/734-3181.

Monmouth was named to commemorate the Revolutionary War battle of Monmouth, New Jersey, and was the birthplace of Wyatt Earp. There is a memorial to Earp in Monmouth Park. The town is located on the prairie in a region famous for the production of corn, soybeans, hogs and cattle.

What to See and Do

Buchanan Center for the Arts. Art and cultural exhibits in a modern gallery. (Daily exc Sun) 64 Public Square. Phone 309/734-3033. **Free.**

Pioneer Cemetery. Relatives of Wyatt Earp are buried here. E Archer Ave near 5th St.

Wyatt Earp Birthplace. The US Deputy Marshal's first family home from his birth in 1848 to 1850, when the family left for the California gold rush. (Memorial Day-Labor Day, Sun afternoons; also by appt) 406 S Third St. Phone 309/734-3181. **Donation.**

Annual Event

Warren County Prime Beef Festival. Beef and hog shows and auctions. Displays, events, entertainment, carnival, parade. 4 days beginning Wed after Labor Day.

Motel

✔ ★ ★ **MELING'S.** *1129 N Main St, at jct US 34, 67. 309/734-2196; FAX 309/734-2127.* 55 rms, 1-2 story. S $33.95; D $39.30-$43.35; each addl $5. Crib free. Pet accepted. TV; cable. Restaurant 5:30 am-9:30 pm; dining rm 11 am-1:30 pm, 5-8 pm; Sun 7 am-8 pm. Bar, closed Sun. Ck-out 11 am. Lndry facilities. Meeting rm. Business servs avail. Sundries. Free RR station, bus depot transportation. Cr cds: A, C, D, DS, MC, V.

[⚲] [⊠] [✎]

Morris (C-5)

(See also Joliet, Ottawa)

Founded 1842 **Pop** 10,270 **Elev** 519 ft **Area code** 815 **Zip** 60450
Information Grundy County Chamber of Commerce & Industry, 112 E Washington St; 815/942-0113.

What to See and Do

Gebhard Woods State Park. The I & M Canal flows along the south edge of this 30-acre park, which offers fishing and canoeing in small ponds, Nettle Creek and the canal. Hiking, biking. Snowmobiling. Picnicking. Primitive camping. Standard fees. (Daily) W edge of town. Phone 815/942-0796. **Free.**

Illinois and Michigan Canal State Trail. The I & M Canal, completed at a cost of $9.5 million in 1848, stretched 96 mi linking Lake Michigan and Chicago with the Illinois River at La Salle. Four state parks have been established on the 60-mi trail, among them Buffalo Rock (see OTTAWA). Phone 815/942-0796.

Annual Event

Grundy County Corn Festival. Music, horse show, parade. Last wk Sept.

Motel

★ ★ **HOLIDAY INN.** *200 Gore Rd (IL 47), just N of I-80. 815/942-6600; FAX 815/942-8255.* 120 rms, 2 story. S $55-62; D $61-$68; each addl $6; under 18 free. Crib free. Pet accepted, some restrictions. TV; cable. Heated pool; wading pool. Restaurant 6 am-2 pm, 5-10 pm. Rm serv. Bar 4 pm-midnight; closed Sun. Ck-out noon. Meeting rms. Business servs avail. In-rm modem link. Valet serv. Sundries. Cr cds: A, C, D, DS, JCB, MC, V.

Restaurants

★ ★ **DRAKE'S FARM.** *5595 E Pine Bluff Rd, 6 mi SE on Pine Bluff, 6 mi E of IL 47. 815/942-5580.* Hrs: 11 am-8 pm; Fri to 10 pm; Sun from 11 am; Sun brunch to 3 pm. Closed Mon-Thurs (Jan-Mar); July 4, Dec 24, 25. Res accepted. Bar. Semi-a la carte: lunch $4.95-$7.95, dinner $7.45-$15.95. Sun brunch $10.95. Specializes baby back ribs, giant shrimp, roast duck. Organist Sat evenings. View of terraced gardens, lake. Cr cds: A, C, D, MC, V.

SC

✓ ★ **R PLACE.** *21 Romines Dr, at jct of I-80 exit 112B & IL 47. 815/942-3690.* Open 24 hrs. Res accepted. Semi-a la carte: bkfst $2.95-$4.70, lunch $4.95-$9.95, dinner $5.10-$9.95. Child's meals. Specializes in hamburgers, seasonal dishes. Own baking. Salad bar. Truck stop with Victorian-era decor; chandeliers, Tiffany-style lamps; extensive collection of Americana, antique toys, mechanical puppets, gas-station memorabilia. Family-owned. No cr cds accepted.

D SC

★ **ROCKWELL INN.** *2400 US 6W, 1/2 mi S of I-80 exit IL 47 S (Morris). 815/942-6224.* Hrs: 11 am-10 pm. Closed Dec 25. Res accepted. Bar. Semi-a la carte: lunch $4.75-$11.75, dinner $8.75-$19.75. Sun brunch $12.50. Child's meals. Specializes in prime rib, chicken picatta, steak. Salad bar. Entertainment Fri & Sat evenings. Norman Rockwell prints; bar from 1893 Columbian Exposition. Cr cds: C, D, DS, MC.

D

Mt Vernon (H-4)

(See also Benton, Centralia, Du Quoin, Salem)

Pop 16,988 **Elev** 500 ft **Area code** 618 **Zip** 62864 **Web** southern illinois.com/cvb

Information Convention and Visitors Bureau, 200 Potomac Blvd; 618/242-3151 or 800/252-5464.

What to See and Do

Mitchell Museum. Changing art exhibits, including American Impressionist paintings in permanent collection. The 85-acre grounds include an art museum, outdoor sculpture park, arts & crafts instruction center and nature trails. (Tues-Sat, also Sun afternoons; closed hols) Richview Rd. Phone 618/242-1236. **Free.**

Annual Events

Sweetcorn-Watermelon Festival. Entertainment, flea market, parade. Free sweetcorn and watermelon served. 3rd wk Aug.

Cedarhurst Craft Fair. Richview Rd. Entertainment, food, juried art & craft show. Sat & Sun after Labor Day.

Motels

✓ ★ **BEST INNS OF AMERICA.** *222 S 44th St, jct I-57/64 & IL 15 (Broadway) exit 95. 618/244-4343.* 153 rms, 2 story. Mid-May-Oct: S $37.88; D $45.88; each addl $7; under 18 free; golf plan; lower rates rest of yr. Crib free. Pet accepted, some restrictions. TV; cable (premium). Pool. Complimentary continental bkfst. Restaurant adj open 24 hrs. Ck-out 1 pm. Cr cds: A, C, D, DS, MC, V.

★ ★ **DRURY INN.** *Box 805, 2 mi W, just off IL 15, 1/2 blk E of jct I-57, I-64. 618/244-4550.* 82 rms, 3 story. S $57; D $64-$70; each addl $7; under 18 free. Crib free. Pet accepted. TV; cable. Pool. Complimentary continental bkfst. Restaurant adj open 24 hrs. Ck-out noon. Meeting rms. Sundries. Some refrigerators, microwaves. Cr cds: A, C, D, DS, MC, V.

D

✓ ★ **RAMADA.** *I-57 & IL 15. 618/244-3670; FAX 618/244-6904.* 188 rms, 4 story. S $55-$61; D $61-$67; each addl $6; under 18 free; wkend rates. Crib free. Pet accepted. TV, cable (premium). Indoor pool; whirlpool. Complimentary continental bkfst. Restaurant 6 am-2 pm, 5-10 pm. Rm serv. Bar 11-1 am; Fri, Sat to 2 am; Sun to 10 pm; entertainment Tues-Sun. Ck-out noon. Meeting rms. Business center. In-rm modem link. Bellhops. Valet serv. Free airport, bus depot transportation. Exercise equipt; bicycles, rowers, sauna. Game rm. Rec rm. Cr cds: A, C, D, DS, JCB, MC, V.

Motor Hotel

★ ★ **HOLIDAY INN.** *222 Potomac, I-57/64 & IL 15 exit 95. 618/244-7100; FAX 618/242-8876.* 236 rms, 5 story. S $52-$74; D $56-$74; suites $156-$232; each addl $7; under 18 free; golf plan. Crib free. Pet accepted, some restrictions. TV; cable. Indoor pool; whirlpool. Restaurants 6 am-10 pm. Rm serv. Bar 11-2 am. Ck-out 1 pm. Meeting rms. Valet serv. Sundries. Free airport transportation. Saunas. Cr cds: A, C, D, DS, JCB, MC, V.

D

Restaurant

✓ ★ **EL RANCHERITO.** *4303 Broadway Ave. 618/244-6121.* Hrs: 11 am-10 pm; Fri, Sat to 11 pm. Closed Thanksgiving. Res accepted. Mexican menu. Bar. Semi-a la carte: lunch $2.99-$4.99, dinner $2.99-$10. Child's meals. Specializes in fajotas, chimichangas. Two-level dining with Mexican decor. Cr cds: MC, V.

D SC

Naperville (E-2 see Chicago map)

(See also Aurora, Downers Grove, Wheaton)

Settled 1831 **Pop** 85,351 **Elev** 700 ft **Area code** 630

Information Visitors Bureau, 131 W Jefferson Ave, 60540; 630/355-4141 or 800/642-STAY.

Naperville, oldest town in Du Page County, was settled by Captain Joseph Naper. Soon after, in the late 1830s, settlers of German ancestry came from Pennsylvania to transform the prairie into farmland. Although today's city is at the center of a "research and high technology corridor" and has been cited as one of the fastest growing suburbs in the nation, Naperville retains something of the atmosphere of a small town with its core of large Victorian houses and beautiful historic district. The downtown shopping district features over 100 shops and restaurants in historic buildings; it adjoins the Riverwalk, a three-and-a-half-mile winding brick pathway along the DuPage River.

What to See and Do

Naper Settlement. A 12-acre living history museum of 25 buildings in a village setting depicts a 19th-century, northern Illinois town (ca 1830-1900). Tours by costumed guides include four residences of the period; Martin-Mitchell mansion, with period furnishings; several public buildings and working businesses such as a printshop, smithy and stonecutter's shop. Also Les Schrader Art Gallery with a 42-painting exhibit depicting the growth and development of a Midwest town and museum shop. Special events throughout yr (fee). (See ANNUAL EVENT) Aurora Ave, between Webster St & Porter Ave. For hrs phone 630/420-6010. ¢¢

Annual Event

Christmas in the Village. Naper Settlement. 19th-century festivities; decorations of period. Dec.

Motels

★ ★ ★ **COURTYARD BY MARRIOTT.** *1155 E Diehl Rd (60563). 630/505-0550; FAX 630/505-8337.* 147 rms, 3 story. S, D $93; suites $119; under 12 free; wkly rates. Crib free. TV; cable (premium), VCR avail. Indoor pool; whirlpool. Restaurant 6:30-10 am, 4-9 pm; wkends 7 am-noon, 5-9 pm. Rm serv. Bar 4-11 pm. Ck-out 1 pm. Coin lndry. Meeting rms. Business servs avail. In-rm modem link. Valet serv. Exercise equipt; weight machines, treadmill. Health club privileges. Some refrigerators; microwaves avail. Private patios, balconies. Cr cds: A, C, D, DS, MC, V.

D ≃ 𝝙 ⬛ 🐾 SC

✔ ★ **EXEL INN.** *1585 N Naperville/Wheaton Rd (60563). 630/357-0022.* 123 rms, 3 story. S $47-$56; D $50-$59; each addl $5; under 18 free. Crib free. TV; cable (premium). Complimentary continental bkfst. Restaurant nearby. Ck-out noon. Coin lndry. Business servs avail. In-rm modem link. Microwaves avail. Cr cds: A, C, D, DS, MC, V.

D ⬛ 🐾 SC

★ ★ **HAMPTON INN.** *1087 Diehl Rd (60563). 630/505-1400; FAX 630/505-1416.* 128 rms, 4 story. S, D $74-$79; under 18 free; wkend rates. Crib free. TV; cable (premium). Heated pool. Complimentary continental bkfst. Meeting rms. Business servs avail. In-rm modem link. Exercise equipt; weight machine, bicycle. Game rm. Health club privileges. Cr cds: A, C, D, DS, MC, V.

D ≃ 𝝙 ⬛ 🐾 SC

✔ ★ **RED ROOF INN.** *1698 W Diehl Rd (60563). 630/369-2500; FAX 630/369-9987.* 119 rms, 3 story. May-Sept: S $54.99-$68.99; D $62.99-$76.99; under 18 free; lower rates rest of yr. Crib free. Pet accepted. TV; cable (premium). Complimentary coffee in lobby. Restaurant opp. Ck-out noon. Business servs avail. In-rm modem link. Cr cds: A, C, D, DS, MC, V.

D 🐾 ≃ 🐾

★ ★ **TRAVELODGE.** *1617 Naperville Rd (60563). 630/505-0200.* 102 rms, 3 story. Apr-Sept: S $48-$57; D $53-$62; each addl $5; under 17 free; higher rates major hols; lower rates rest of yr. Crib free. TV; cable (premium). Complimentary continental bkfst. Complimentary coffee in rms. Restaurant nearby. Ck-out noon. Coin lndry. Business servs avail. In-rm modem link. Health club privileges. Some refrigerators, microwaves. Cr cds: A, C, D, DS, JCB, MC, V.

D ⬛ SC

Motor Hotel

★ ★ ★ **WYNDHAM GARDEN.** *1837 Centre Point Circle (60563). 630/505-3353; FAX 630/505-0176.* 143 rms, 4 story, 39 suites. S, D $99; suites $119; wkend rates. Crib free. TV; cable (premium). Indoor pool; whirlpool. Complimentary coffee in rm. Restaurant 6:30 am-10 pm. Rm serv from 5 pm. Bar 4 pm-midnight. Ck-out noon. Meeting rms. Business

servs avail. In-rm modem link. Exercise equipt; treadmill, bicycles. Some refrigerators; microwaves avail. Cr cds: A, C, D, DS, ER, JCB, MC, V.

D ≃ 𝝙 ⬛ 🐾 SC

Hotels

★ ★ ★ **HILTON.** *(3003 Corporate West Dr, Lisle 60532) I-88, exit Warrenville Rd. 630/505-0900; FAX 630/505-8948.* 309 rms, 8 story. Apr-Nov: S $115-$150; D $125-$165; each addl $15; suites $295-$325; lower rates rest of yr. Crib free. TV; cable (premium), VCR avail. Indoor pool; whirlpool. Complimentary coffee in rms. Restaurant 6 am-10 pm. Ck-out noon. Meeting rms. Business servs avail. Exercise equipt; bicycles, weight machine. Health club privileges. Game rm. Some refrigerators. Cr cds: A, C, D, DS, ER, JCB, MC, V.

D ≃ 𝝙 ⬛ 🐾 SC

★ ★ **HOLIDAY INN SELECT.** *1801 N Naper Blvd (60540), S of I-88 Naperville Rd exit. 630/505-4900; FAX 630/505-8239.* E-mail mail@naperselect.com; web www.naperselect.com. 299 rms, 7 story. S $97; D $107; suites $250; under 19 free; wkend rates. Crib free. TV; cable (premium), VCR avail. Indoor pool. Restaurant 6 am-11 pm. Rm serv. Bar from 11:30 am, wkends 11-1 am. Ck-out noon. Business center. In-rm modem link. Exercise equipt; bicycles, treadmill, sauna. Health club privileges. Cr cds: A, C, D, DS, JCB, MC, V.

D ≃ 𝝙 ⬛ 🐾 SC 🏊

★ ★ ★ **HYATT.** *(1400 Corporetum Dr, Lisle 60532) E on I-88 to Naperville Rd, S to Warrenville Rd, E to IL 53. 630/852-1234; FAX 630/852-1260.* 311 rms, 13 story. S $103-$125; D $128-$140; each addl $25; wkend rates. Crib free. TV; cable (premium), VCR avail. Indoor pool; whirlpool, poolside serv. Coffee in rms. Restaurant 6 am-2 pm, 5-10 pm. Bar 11 am-midnight, Fri, Sat to 2 am. Ck-out noon. Convention facilities. Business servs avail. In-rm modem link. Concierge. Exercise equipt; weight machine, bicycles, sauna. Refrigerators avail. Cr cds: A, C, D, DS, JCB, MC, V.

D ≃ 𝝙 ⬛ 🐾 SC

★ ★ **RADISSON.** *(3000 Warrenville Rd, Lisle 60532) I-88, Naperville Rd exit. 630/505-1000; FAX 630/505-1165.* 242 rms, 8 story. S $109-$159; D $124-$174; each addl $15; suites from $119; under 18 free; wkend packages. Crib free. TV; cable (premium), VCR avail. Indoor pool; whirlpool. Complimentary coffee in lobby. Restaurant 6 am-10 pm. Bar 11-1 am, wkends to 2 am. Ck-out noon. Convention facilities. Business servs avail. In-rm modem link. Concierge. Gift shop. Exercise rm; instructor, weight machine, stair machine, sauna. Massage. Game rm. Microwaves avail. Luxury level. Cr cds: A, C, D, DS, ER, JCB, MC, V.

D ≃ 𝝙 ⬛ 🐾 SC

Restaurants

✔ ★ ★ **CASA LUPITA.** *1633 N Naper Blvd (60563). 630/505-7037.* Hrs: 11 am-11 pm; Sun brunch 10 am-2 pm. Closed Thanksgiving, Dec 25. Mexican menu. Bar. Semi-a la carte: lunch $4.99-$11.99, dinner $6.99-$11.99. Sun brunch $9.95. Child's meals. Specializes in seafood, burritos, fajitas. Outdoor dining. Mexican villa decor; piñata. Cr cds: A, C, D, DS, MC, V.

D ⬛

★ ★ ★ **EMILIO'S MESON SABIKA.** *1025 Aurora Ave (60540). 630/983-3000.* E-mail msabika@aol.com. Hrs: 11:30 am-10 pm; Fri to 11 pm; Sat 5-11 pm; Sun 4-9 pm. Closed major hols. Res accepted. Spanish menu. Bar. Wine list. Semi-a la carte: lunch $6-$12, dinner $15-$20. Specialties: scalloped shrimp & salmon, patatas con alioli, queso de cabra al horno. Own pastries. Flamenco entertainment Fri. Patio dining. In Victorian mansion (ca 1847). Cr cds: A, C, D, MC, V.

D ⬛

★ ★ **MONTPARNASSE.** *200 E 5th Ave (60563). 630/961-8203.* Hrs: 11:30 am-2:30 pm, 6-9 pm. Closed Sun; major hols. Res accepted. French menu. Setups. Semi-a la carte entrees: lunch $8-$15, dinner

$18-$29. Complete meals $45. Specialties: creme brûlée, carré d'agneau, grilled pheasant. Own baking. Entertainment Sat. In converted furniture factory. Cr cds: A, C, D, DS, MC, V.

D

Nauvoo (D-1)

(See also Macomb)

Settled 1839 **Pop** 1,108 **Elev** 659 ft **Area code** 217 **Zip** 62354
Information Tourist Center, 1295 Mulholland (IL 96), PO Box 41; 217/453-6648.

Once the largest city in Illinois, Nauvoo has a colorful history. When the Mormon prophet Joseph Smith was driven out of Missouri, he came with his Latter-day Saints to the tiny village called Commerce, on a promontory overlooking the Mississippi River, and established what was virtually an autonomous state. A city of 8,000 houses was created, and in 1841 construction began on a great temple. A schism in the church and the threat of Mormon political power led to riots and persecution of the Mormons. Joseph Smith and his brother were arrested and murdered by a mob while in the Carthage jail. Brigham Young became leader of the Nauvoo Mormons. When the city charter was repealed and armed clashes broke out anew, Young led much of the population westward in 1846 to its final settlement in Utah. Nauvoo became a ghost city, and the almost-completed temple was set on fire by an arsonist. In 1849, the Icarians, a band of French communalists, migrated to Nauvoo from Texas and established their short-lived experiment in communal living. They attempted to rebuild the temple, but a storm swept the building back into ruin. The Icarians failed to prosper and in 1856 moved on. The city was gradually resettled by a more conventional group of Germans, who developed the wine culture begun by the French group.

What to See and Do

Baxter's Vineyards. Established 1857. Tours, wine tasting. (Daily; closed Jan 1, Thanksgiving, Dec 25) 2010 E Parley St. Phone 217/453-2528. **Free.**

Joseph Smith Historic Center. A 50-min tour begins in visitors center and includes a 12-min slide presentation. (Daily; closed Jan 1, Thanksgiving, Dec 25) 149 Water St, 1 blk W of IL 96. Phone 217/453-2246. **Free.** Tour includes

Grave of Joseph Smith and burial place of Smith's wife Emma and brother Hyrum; the location of these graves, originally kept secret, was eventually lost; they were found in 1928 after an extensive search.

Joseph Smith Homestead (1803). Log cabin that the prophet occupied upon coming to Nauvoo in 1839; it is the town's oldest structure; period furnishings.

Smith's Mansion (1843). Refined, federal-style frame house occupied by Smith from 1843-1844; period furnishings.

Smith's Red Brick Store (1842). Merchandise on shelves reflects items sold in 1842-1844.

◼ **Nauvoo Restoration, Inc Visitor Center.** Center has a 20-min movie on Nauvoo history; exhibits; pamphlet with suggested tour and information on points of interest. (Daily) Young & N Main Sts. Phone 217/453-2237. **Free.** Guide service in the following buildings

Print Shop. Restored offices of Mormon newspaper and post office. Kimball & Main Sts.

Heber C. Kimball Home. Restored house of one of Joseph Smith's 12 apostles. Munson & Partridge Sts.

Brigham Young Home. Restored house of Joseph Smith's successor. Kimball & Granger Sts.

Wilford Woodruff Home. Restored house of apostle and missionary. Durphy & Hotchkiss Sts.

Also here are Seventy Hall, an 1840s meetinghouse, Lyon Drug Store, the Nauvoo Temple site, Montrose Crossing Monument, Sarah Kimball Home, William Weeks Home, Noble-Smith Home, Pendleton log house, Webb blacksmith and wagon shop, Stoddard tin shop, Riser Cobbler shop, 1840 theater, brick kiln, Clark store, Old Post Office and Merryweather Mercantile, Joseph Coolidge House with barrel, candle and pottery-making, Jonathan Browning Gunshop, Scovil Bakery and other significant structures. **Free.**

Nauvoo State Park. Restored house with wine cellar and century-old vineyard adjoining; museum (May-Sept). Fishing; boating (ramp, electric motors only). Hiking. Picnic area (shelter), playgrounds. Camping. (SEE ANNUAL EVENTS) Standard fees. (Daily) S on IL 96. On 148 acres. Phone 217/453-2512. **Free.**

Old Carthage Jail (1839-1841). Restored jail where Joseph Smith and his brother were killed; 30-min tour; visitor center has 18-min film presentation, pamphlets, exhibits. (Daily) 307 Walnut St in Carthage; 12 mi S on IL 96, then 14 mi E on US 136. Phone 217/357-2989. **Free.**

Annual Events

Musical Production, *City of Joseph.* Main & Young Sts. 2nd wk Aug.

Grape Festival. Nauvoo State Park. Includes classic French ceremony of Wedding of the Wine and Cheese. Labor Day wknd.

Motels

★ **NAUVOO.** *1610 Mulholland St (IL 96).* 217/453-2219. 11 rms, 8 with shower only. S $38; D $45; each addl $5; under 12 free. Crib avail. TV; cable (premium). Restaurant nearby. Ck-out 11 am. Picnic tables. Totally nonsmoking. Cr cds: DS, MC, V.

★ ★ **NAUVOO FAMILY.** *1875 Mulholland.* 217/453-6527; res: 800/416-4470; FAX 217/453-6601. Web www.nauvoonet.com. 71 rms, 2 story, 19 suites. Apr-Nov: S $44-$51; D $49-$56; suites $75-$90; under 12 free; lower rates rest of yr. Crib free. Pet accepted, some restrictions. TV; cable (premium). Restaurant nearby. Ck-out 11 am. Meeting rms. Indoor pool. Cr cds: A, D, MC, V.

✔★ **NAUVOO FAMILY MOTEL.** *150 N Warsaw St.* 217/453-6527. Web www.nauvoonet.com. 37 rms, 9 kit. units. May-Oct: S $38; D $49; each addl $4; kit. units $45-$67; lower rates rest of yr. Crib $3. TV; cable (premium). Ck-out 11 am. Coin lndry. Some refrigerators. Cr cds: A, DS, MC, V.

Inns

★ ★ **HOTEL NAUVOO.** *1290 Mulholland, center of town on IL 96.* 217/453-2211. 8 rms. S, D $47.50-$58; each addl $5; suites $58-$88. Closed mid-Nov-mid-Mar. TV; cable (premium). Restaurant (see HOTEL NAUVOO). Bar. Ck-out 11 am, ck-in 4 pm. Restored historic inn (1840), originally a private residence. No cr cds accepted.

★ ★ **MISSISSIPPI MEMORIES.** *1 Riverview Terr, 3 mi S on IL 96.* 217/453-2771. 4 rms, 2 story. S $59; D $89. Closed wk of Dec 25. TV avail. Complimentary full bkfst. Ck-out 10 am. In wooded area overlooking Mississippi River. Piano in sitting rm. Totally nonsmoking. Cr cds: MC, V.

Restaurant

✔★ ★ ★ **HOTEL NAUVOO.** *(See Hotel Nauvoo Inn)* 217/453-2211. Hrs: 5-8:30 pm; Fri, Sat to 9 pm; Sun brunch 11 am-3 pm. Closed Mon; also mid-Nov-mid-Mar. Res accepted. Bar. Semi-a la carte: dinner $5.50-$14.95. Buffet: dinner $10.11. Sun brunch $11.95. Serv charge 12%.

Specializes in catfish, chicken, ham. Salad bar. Restored 1840 Mormon residence. Family-owned. No cr cds accepted.

Unrated Dining Spot

GRANDPA JOHN'S. *1255 Mulholland St (IL 96). 217/453-2310.* Hrs: 7:15 am-5 pm. Closed Jan-Feb. Semi-a la carte: bkfst $1.50-$5, lunch $1.75-$6. Lunch buffet $5.95. Child's meals. Specializes in fried chicken, Swiss steak, homemade bakery goods. Original artwork; antiques. Established 1912. Totally nonsmoking. No cr cds accepted.

D

Normal
(see Bloomington)

Northbrook (C-3 see Chicago map)

(See also Glenview, Highland Park, Wheeling)

Pop 32,308 **Elev** 650 ft **Area code** 847 **Zip** 60062
Information Chamber of Commerce, 2002 Walters Ave; 847/498-5555.

The earliest European settlers in the Northbrook area were German immigrants, who arrived after the construction of the Erie Canal in 1825. In 1901 the town was incorporated as Shermerville, in honor of one of the founding families. Brickyards played a major role in the prosperity and growth of the community. After the Chicago fire of 1871, brick manufacturing surpassed farming as a leading industry; 300,000 bricks per day were produced between 1915 and 1920. In 1923, Shermerville was renamed Northbrook in reference to the middle forks of the north branches of the Chicago River, which run through the town. Today Northbrook, located in the heart of Chicago's North Shore, is the headquarters of a number of major corporations.

What to See and Do

☒ **Chicago Botanic Garden.** Managed by the Chicago Horticultural Society, this garden includes 300 acres of formal plantings, lakes, lagoons and wooded naturalistic areas. Specialty gardens include bulb, aquatic, perennial and herb landscaped demonstration gardens; Japanese garden; English walled garden; prairie and nature trail; fruit and vegetable garden; heritage garden; rose garden; waterfall garden; sensory garden for the visually impaired and learning garden for the disabled. The Education Center consists of an auditorium, floral arts museum, exhibit hall, shop, greenhouses, concession. Narrated tram ride. (Daily; closed Dec 25) 1/2 mi E of I-94 (US 41), Lake Cook Rd exit, on Lake Cook Rd in Glencoe. Phone 847/835-5440. Per vehicle ¢¢

River Trail Nature Center. A 300-acre nature preserve within the Forest Preserve District of Cook County. Nature trails; interpretive museum (daily exc Fri); special activities (see ANNUAL EVENT); naturalist. (Daily; closed Jan 1, Thanksgiving, Dec 25) 3120 N Milwaukee Ave, 1/2 mi S of Willow Rd. Phone 847/824-8360.   **Free.**

Annual Event

Maple Sugar Festival. River Trail Nature Center. Native American, pioneer and modern methods of maple sugaring demonstrated by staff naturalist. Sun late Mar.

Motel

★ ★ **COURTYARD BY MARRIOTT.** *(800 Lake Cook Rd, Deerfield 60015) approx 1 mi W of Waukegan Rd, at Pfingsten Rd. 847/940-8222; FAX 847/940-7741.* 131 rms, 2 story, 18 suites. Apr-Oct: S $106; D $116; suites $139; wkend rates; lower rates rest of yr. Crib free. TV; cable

(premium). Indoor pool; whirlpool. Complimentary coffee in rms. Restaurant 6:30-10 am; Sat, Sun 7-11 am. Bar 4:30-10:30 pm. Ck-out noon. Coin lndry. Meeting rms. Business servs avail. In-rm modem link. Valet serv. Exercise equipt; weight machine, bicycles. Refrigerators, microwaves avail. Private patios, balconies. Cr cds: A, C, D, DS, MC, V.

D ≈ ⊁ ⊠ ⊠ SC

Motor Hotel

★ ★ **RESIDENCE INN BY MARRIOTT.** *(530 Lake Cook Rd, Deerfield 60015) approx 1/2 mi W of Waukegan Rd. 847/940-4644; FAX 847/940-7639.* 128 kit. suites, 2 story. Kit. suites $129-$169; wkend rates. Crib free. Pet accepted. TV; cable (premium). Heated pool; whirlpool. Complimentary continental bkfst. Complimentary coffee in rms. Restaurant nearby. Ck-out noon. Coin lndry. Meeting rm. Business servs avail. In-rm modem link. Valet serv Mon-Fri. Sundries. Exercise equipt; bicycles, treadmill. Microwaves; many fireplaces. Balconies. Picnic tables, grills. Cr cds: A, D, DS, JCB, MC, V.

D ⊁ ≈ ⊁ ⊠ ⊠ SC

Hotels

★ ★ ★ **EMBASSY SUITES.** *(1445 Lake Cook Rd, Deerfield 60015) off I-294, E of Lake Cook Rd exit. 847/945-4500; FAX 847/945-8189.* 237 suites, 7 story. Apr-mid-Dec: S $119-$179; D $134-$194; each addl $15; under 12 free; wkend rates; lower rates rest of yr. Crib free. TV; cable (premium). Indoor pool; whirlpool. Complimentary full bkfst. Complimentary coffee in rms. Restaurant 11 am-10 pm; Fri, Sat to 11 pm. Bar 11:30 am-midnight; Sun from noon. Ck-out noon. Coin lndry. Meeting rms. Business servs avail. In-rm modem link. Gift shop. Exercise equipt; weights, bicycles, sauna. Refrigerators, wet bars, microwaves. Cr cds: A, C, D, DS, JCB, MC, V.

D ≈ ⊁ ⊠ ⊠ SC

★ ★ ★ **HILTON.** *2855 N Milwaukee Ave (IL 21). 847/480-7500; FAX 847/480-0827.* 247 rms, 10 story. S $105-$165; D $115-$180; each addl $15; suites $375-$600; under 18 free; wkend rates. Crib free. TV; cable (premium), VCR avail. Indoor pool; whirlpool. Restaurant 6 am-11 pm. Bar 11-2 am. Ck-out noon. Meeting rms. Business center. In-rm modem link. Concierge. Airport transportation $13. Exercise equipt; weights, bicycles, sauna. Gift shop. Bathrm phones, refrigerators, mini-bars; microwaves avail. Adj to forest preserve. Luxury level. Cr cds: A, C, D, DS, JCB, MC, V.

D ≈ ⊁ ⊠ ⊠ SC ⊁

★ ★ **HYATT.** *(1750 Lake Cook Rd, Deerfield 60015) Off I-294, Lake Cook Rd exit. 847/945-3400; FAX 847/945-3563.* 300 rms, 6 story. S, D $94-$169; each addl $25; under 18 free; wkend rates. Crib free. TV; cable (premium). Indoor pool; whirlpool. Complimentary coffee in lobby. Restaurant 6:30 am-10 pm. Bar 11:30 am-midnight. Ck-out noon. Convention facilities. Business servs avail. In-rm modem link. Exercise equipt; weights, treadmill, sauna. Refrigerators avail. Cr cds: A, C, D, DS, ER, JCB, MC, V.

D ≈ ⊁ ⊠ ⊠ SC

★ ★ **MARRIOTT SUITES.** *(2 Parkway N, Deerfield 60015) I-94 exit Deerfield Rd then 1/3 mi W to Parkway N. 847/405-9666; FAX 847/405-0354.* 251 suites, 7 story. S, D $109-$140; under 18 free; family, wkly, wkend rates. Crib free. Pet accepted, some restrictions. TV; cable (premium), VCR avail. 2 pools, 1 indoor; whirlpool, poolside serv. Complimentary coffee in rms. Restaurant 6:30 am-11 pm. Bar. Ck-out 1 pm. Coin lndry. Convention facilities. Business center. In-rm modem link. Gift shop. Exercise equipt; weight machine, bicycles, sauna. Health club privileges. Refrigerators, wet bars; microwaves avail. Picnic tables. Cr cds: A, C, D, DS, ER, JCB, MC, V.

D ⊁ ≈ ⊁ ⊠ ⊠ SC ⊁

★ ★ **RADISSON.** *2875 N Milwaukee.* 847/298-2525; FAX 847/298-4615. 310 rms, 4 story, 30 suites. Mar-Nov: S $89-$149; D $99-$159; each addl $10; suites $175-$195; under 18 free; lower rates rest of yr. Crib free. Pet accepted, some restrictions; deposit. TV; cable (premium), VCR avail (movies). Complimentary coffee in lobby. Restaurant 8 am-10 pm. Bar 4 pm-midnight. Ck-out noon. Convention facilities. Business center. Concierge. Gift shop. Free airport transportation. Exercise equipt; treadmill, stair machine. Heated pool; whirlpool. Many balconies. Cr cds: A, C, D, DS, MC, V.

D ✸ ≋ ✕ ⚞ SC ⚓

★ ★ **SHERATON-NORTH SHORE.** *933 Skokie Blvd. 847/498-6500; FAX 847/498-9558.* 380 rms, 10 story. S $89-$138; D $101-$148; each addl $12; suites from $225; under 18 free; wkend rates. TV; cable (premium). Indoor pool; whirlpool. Complimentary coffee in rms. Restaurant 6:30 am-11 pm. Bar 11-1 am; Sat to 2 am. Ck-out noon. Coin lndry. Convention facilities. Business center. Gift shop. Airport transportation. Exercise equipt; weight machines, treadmill, sauna. Health club privileges. Refrigerators avail. Luxury level. Cr cds: A, C, D, DS, ER, JCB, MC, V.

D ≋ ✕ ⚞ SC ⚓

Restaurants

★ ★ **CEILING ZERO.** *500 Anthony Trail. 847/272-8111.* Hrs: 11:30 am-2 pm, 5:30-9 pm; Fri to 10 pm; Sat 5:30-10 pm; Sun 5:30-9 pm. Closed major hols. Res accepted. Continental menu. Bar. Semi-a la carte: lunch $6-$12, dinner $11-$24. Specializes in fresh seafood, rack of lamb, duck. Own pastries. Parking. Cr cds: A, C, D, DS, MC, V.

⬒

★ ★ **FRANCESCA'S NORTH.** *1145 Church St. 847/559-0260.* Hrs: 11:30 am-2 pm, 5-9 pm; Fri to 10:30 pm; Sat 5-10:30 pm; Sun 5-9 pm. Res accepted (lunch). Italian menu. Bar. Semi-a la carte: lunch $5.95-$8.95, dinner $8.95-$19.95. Child's meals. Specializes in veal, chicken, fish. Contemporary Italian decor with extensive black-and-white photo collection. Cr cds: A, MC, V.

⬒

★ **FRANCESCO'S HOLE IN THE WALL.** *254 Skokie Blvd. 847/272-0155.* Hrs: 11:30 am-2:15 pm, 5-9:15 pm; Fri to 10:15 pm; Sat 5-10:15 pm; Sun 4-8:45 pm. Closed Tues; most major hols; also Jan. Italian menu. Wine, beer. A la carte entrees: lunch $3.50-$10, dinner $10-$19.95. Specializes in veal, chicken, spinach bread. Own pasta. Totally nonsmoking. No cr cds accepted.

★ ★ ★ **STEFANI'S.** *601 Skokie Blvd. 847/564-3950.* Hrs: 11:30 am-3 pm, 5-10 pm; Fri to 11 pm; Sat 5-11 pm; Sun 4-9 pm. Closed major hols. Res accepted. Northern Italian menu. Bar. Wine list. Semi-a la carte: lunch $5-$12, dinner $7.95-$25. Specializes in pasta, seafood, veal. Parking. Cr cds: A, C, D, MC, V.

D ⬒

✔★ **TONELLI'S.** *1038 Waukegan Rd (IL 43). 847/272-4730.* Hrs: 11 am-10:30 pm; Mon to 10 pm; Fri to 11:30 pm; Sat 4-11:30 pm; Sun 4-10 pm. Closed major hols. Italian, Amer menu. Bar. Semi-a la carte: lunch $4-$6.95, dinner $6.50-$13.25. Child's meals. Specialties: Lake Superior whitefish, veal piccante, mussels with linguine, pizza. Parking. Cr cds: A, MC, V.

D ⬒

Unrated Dining Spot

ED DEBEVIC'S. *(660 Lake Cook Rd, Deerfield) N on Pfingsten Rd to Lake Cook Rd, 2 blks E. 847/945-3242.* Hrs: 11:30 am-10 pm; Fri, Sat to 11 pm. Closed Thanksgiving, Dec 25. Res accepted. Bar. Semi-a la carte: lunch, dinner $3.60-$7.25. Child's meals. Specializes in chili, hamburgers, chicken. Salad bar. Parking. 1950s-style diner. Jukebox. Cr cds: A, DS, MC, V.

D

Oak Brook (E-3 see Chicago map)

(See also Brookfield, Downers Grove, Elmhurst, Hinsdale, La Grange)

Pop 9,178 **Elev** 675 ft **Area code** 630 **Zip** 60521
Information Village of Oak Brook, 1200 Oak Brook Rd; 630/990-3000.

Known as Fullersburg in the mid-1800s, Oak Brook is the home of Butler National Golf Club. Sports and recreation have long been important in this carefully planned village; it has established and maintains 12 miles of biking and hiking paths and over 450 acres of parks and recreation land. Today, Oak Brook is identified as both a mecca for international polo players and as the headquarters of many major corporations.

What to See and Do

Fullersburg Woods Environmental Center. Observation of wildlife in natural setting (all yr); environmental center and theater, native marsh ecology exhibit; two nature trails. (Daily) 3609 Spring Rd. Phone 630/850-8110. **Free.**

Graue Mill and Museum. Restored mill built in 1852; the only operating water-powered gristmill in the state. Miller demonstrates grinding of corn on buhrstones. Exhibits include farm and home implements of the period; rooms in Victorian and earlier periods; demonstrations of spinning and weaving. (Mid-Apr-mid-Nov, daily) York & Spring Rds. Phone 630/655-2090. ¢¢

Seasonal Event

Sunday Polo. Phone 630/990-2394. Mid-June-mid-Sept.

Motels

★ ★ **CLUBHOUSE INN.** *(630 Pasquinelli Dr, Westmont 60559) 3 mi W on Ogden Ave. 630/920-2200; FAX 630/920-2766.* Web www.clubhouseinn.com. 137 rms, 2 story, 19 suites. S $85; D $99; each addl $10; suites $103; under 16 free; wkend rates. Crib free. TV; cable (premium). Indoor pool; whirlpool. Complimentary full bkfst. Restaurant opp 9 am-10:30 pm. Ck-out noon. Coin lndry. Meeting rms. Business servs avail. In-rm modem link. Health club privileges. Microwaves avail. Cr cds: A, C, D, DS, MC, V.

D ≋ ⚞ ⚟ ⚞ SC

★ ★ **COMFORT SUITES.** *(17 W 445 Roosevelt Rd, Oakbrook Terrace 60181) W of IL 83, Roosevelt Rd exit. 630/916-1000; FAX 630/916-1068.* 104 suites, 3 story. S $81; D $91; each addl $10; under 18 free. Crib free. TV; cable (premium), VCR avail (movies). Indoor pool; whirlpool. Complimentary full bkfst. Complimentary coffee in rms. Restaurant nearby. Ck-out noon. Coin lndry. Meeting rms. Business servs avail. In-rm modem link. Valet serv. Exercise equipt; weight machine, treadmill, sauna. Refrigerators, microwaves. Cr cds: A, C, D, DS, MC, V.

D ≋ ✕ ⚞ ⚞ SC

★ ★ **COURTYARD BY MARRIOTT.** *(6 Trans Am Plaza Dr, Oakbrook Terrace 60181) 2 mi W off Butterfield Rd. 630/691-1500; FAX 630/691-1518.* 147 rms, 3 story. S, D $95-$99; suites $104-$112; under 18 free; wkend rates. TV; cable (premium), VCR avail. Indoor pool; whirlpool. Coffee in rms. Restaurant 6:30-10:30 am, 5-10 pm. Rm serv. Bar 4-11 pm. Ck-out 1 pm. Coin lndry. Meeting rms. Business servs avail. In-rm modem link. Valet serv. Exercise equipt; weight machine, treadmill. Refrigerator in suites. Balconies. Cr cds: A, C, D, DS, MC, V.

D ≋ ✕ ⚞ ⚞ SC

✔ ★ **HAMPTON INN.** *(222 E 22nd St, Lombard 60148) Off I-88 Highland Ave (N) exit, ½ mi to 22nd St. 630/916-9000; FAX 630/916-8016.* 130 rms, 4 story. S $75; D $80; under 18 free. Crib free. TV; cable (premium). Complimentary continental bkfst. Restaurant nearby. Ck-out noon. Meeting rms. Business servs avail. In-rm modem link. Exercise equipt; stair machine, treadmill. Cr cds: A, C, D, DS, MC, V.

[D] [symbols] [SC]

★ ★ **HAMPTON INN.** (2222 Enterprise Dr, Westchester 60154) 3 mi E on I-294, exit Cermak Rd E. 708/409-1000; FAX 708/409-1055. 112 rms, 4 story. S, D $81-$84; under 18 free; wkend rates. Crib free. TV; cable (premium), VCR avail. Complimentary continental bkfst. Restaurant opp 11 am-10 pm. Ck-out noon. Meeting rms. Business servs avail. Exercise equipt; bicycle, treadmill. Cr cds: A, C, D, DS, JCB, MC, V.

[D] [symbols] [SC]

★ ★ **LA QUINTA.** (1 S 666 Midwest Rd, Oakbrook Terrace 60181) 2 mi W on 22nd St. 630/495-4600; FAX 630/495-2558. 150 rms, 3 story. S $75-$82; D $82-$89; each addl $7; under 18 free. Crib free. Pet accepted, some restrictions. TV; cable (premium). Heated pool. Complimentary continental bkfst. Coffee in rms. Restaurant adj open 24 hrs. Ck-out noon. Meeting rms. Business servs avail. In-rm modem link. Free local transportation. Cr cds: A, C, D, DS, MC, V.

[D] [symbols] [SC]

Motor Hotels

★ ★ **DRAKE.** 2301 S York Rd, at Cermak Rd, near jct I-88 & I-294. 630/574-5700; FAX 630/574-0830. 165 rms, 4 story. S, D $89-$161; each addl $10; suites $135-$350; under 18 free; wkend packages. Crib free. TV; cable (premium), VCR avail. 2 pools, 1 indoor; whirlpool, poolside serv, lifeguard in summer. Restaurant 6:30 am-10 pm. Rm serv. Bar 11-1 am. Ck-out 1 pm. Meeting rms. Business center. In-rm modem link. Bellhops. Valet serv. Tennis. 18-hole golf course opp. Exercise rm; instructor, weights, treadmills, sauna. Lawn games. Refrigerator, minibar in some suites. Cr cds: A, C, D, DS, MC, V.

[D] [symbols] [SC]

★ ★ **RESIDENCE INN BY MARRIOTT.** (2001 S Highland Ave, Lombard 60148) 2 mi S, off I-88 Highland Ave exit. 630/629-7800; FAX 630/629-6987. 144 rms, 2 story. S $89-$129; D $109-$159; under 18 free; wkly, wkend, hol rates. Crib free. Pet accepted; $50. TV; cable, VCR avail (movies). Heated pool; whirlpool. Complimentary continental bkfst. Restaurant nearby. Ck-out noon. Coin lndry. Sundries. Exercise equipt; weight machine, treadmill. Lawn games. Microwaves. Picnic tables. Cr cds: A, C, D, DS, MC, V.

[D] [symbols] [SC]

Hotels

★ ★ ★ **HILTON SUITES.** (10 Drury Lane, Oakbrook Terrace 60181) N of I-88, off I-88. 630/941-0100; FAX 630/941-0299. 212 suites, 10 story. S, D $155; under 18 free. Crib free. Pet accepted, some restrictions. TV; cable (premium), VCR (movies). Indoor pool; whirlpool. Complimentary full bkfst. Complimentary coffee in rms. Restaurant 11:30 am-1:30 pm, 5-10 pm. Rm serv from 5 pm. Bar 4 pm- midnight. Ck-out noon. Meeting rms. Business center. In-rm modem link. Gift shop. Exercise equipt; weight machine, stair machine, sauna. Health club privileges. Microwaves. Drury Lane Theater adj. Cr cds: A, C, D, DS, MC, V.

[D] [symbols] [SC]

★ ★ **HYATT REGENCY.** 1909 Spring Rd. 630/573-1234; FAX 630/573-1909. 423 rms, 7 story. S $135-$160; D $160-$185; each addl $25; suites $350-$700; parlor $250-$350; under 18 free; wkend rates. Crib free. TV; cable (premium), VCR avail. Indoor pool; whirlpool. Restaurants 6:30 am-10:30 pm. Rm serv. Bar 11:30-1 am. Ck-out noon. Convention facilities. Business center. Sundries. Gift shop. Free local transportation. Exercise equipt; weights, bicycles. Microwaves avail. 7-story circular, tiered lobby. Shopping center adj. Luxury level. Cr cds: A, C, D, DS, ER, JCB, MC, V.

[D] [symbols] [SC]

★ ★ ★ **MARRIOTT.** 1401 W 22nd St. 630/573-8555; FAX 630/573-1026. 347 rms, 12 story. S $139; D $149; each addl $10; suites

$149-$250; under 18 free; wkend rates. Crib free. Pet accepted. TV; cable (premium), VCR avail. Heated pool; whirlpool, poolside serv. Complimentary coffee in lobby. Restaurant 6:30 am-11 pm. Rm serv. Bar 11-1 am; Sun to midnight. Ck-out 1 pm. Coin lndry. Meeting rms. Business center. In-rm modem link. Gift shop. Valet. Exercise equipt; weights, stair machine, sauna. Some bathrm phones; microwaves avail. Luxury levels. Cr cds: A, C, D, DS, JCB, MC, V.

[D] [symbols] [SC]

★ ★ ★ ★ **OAK BROOK HILLS.** 3500 Midwest Rd (60522). 630/850-5555; FAX 630/850-5569; res: 800/445-3315. This elegantly furnished hotel sits on 150 acres of manicured grounds including duck ponds and a challenging golf course. 382 rms, 11 story, 38 suites. S $167-$197; D $177-$207; each addl $15; suites $350-$650; under 16 free. Crib free. TV; cable (premium), VCR avail (movies). 2 pools, 1 indoor; whirlpools, poolside serv. Restaurants 6:30 am-10:30 pm. Rm serv 24 hrs. Bars 10-1 am; wkends to 2 am; entertainment. Ck-out 1 pm. Convention facilities. Business center. In-rm modem link. Concierge. Shopping arcade. Barber, beauty shops. Lighted tennis. 18-hole golf, greens fee $65-$75, pro, putting green. X-country ski on site. Exercise rm; instructor, weight machine, bicycles, saunas. Lawn games. Refrigerators, minibars, bathrm phones. Balconies. Luxury level. Cr cds: A, C, D, DS, JCB, MC, V.

[D] [symbols]

★ ★ ★ **RENAISSANCE.** 2100 Spring Rd, at I-88 W Cermak exit. 630/573-2800; FAX 630/573-7134. Web www.renaissance.com. 166 rms, 10 story. S $159-$189; D $174-$204; each addl $15; suites $400; under 18 free; wkend package plans. Crib free. TV; cable (premium), VCR avail (free movies). Heated rooftop pool; wading pool, poolside serv. Complimentary continental bkfst. Complimentary coffee in rms. Restaurant 6:30 am-10:30 pm. Rm serv 24 hrs. Bar 11:15-1 am. Ck-out 1 pm. Meeting rms. Business center. Concierge. Exercise equipt; weights, bicycles, sauna. Minibars. Cr cds: A, C, D, DS, ER, JCB, MC, V.

[D] [symbols] [SC]

★ ★ ★ **WYNDHAM GARDEN.** (17 W 350 22nd St, Oakbrook Terrace 60181) 630/833-3600; FAX 630/833-7037. 222 rms, 7 story. S $109; D $119; suites $206; under 12 free. Crib free. TV; cable (premium). Indoor pool; whirlpool. Complimentary coffee in rms. Restaurant 6 am-10 pm. Rm serv. Bar to midnight. Ck-out noon. Meeting rms. Business servs avail. Sundries. Golf privileges. Exercise equipt; bicycles, treadmill. Some refrigertors. Cr cds: A, C, D, DS, MC, V.

[D] [symbols] [SC]

Restaurants

★ ★ **BRAXTON SEAFOOD GRILL.** 3 Oak Brook Center Mall, just off IL 83. 630/574-2155. Hrs: 11:30 am-10 pm; Fri, Sat to 11 pm; Sun 11:30 am-9 pm. Closed some major hols. Res accepted. Bar. Semi-a la carte: lunch $6.95-$12.95, dinner $8.95-$19.95. Child's meals. Specializes in seafood, steak. Own baking. Dixieland jazz Fri, Sat. Nautical decor. Cr cds: A, C, D, DS, MC, V.

[D] [symbol]

★ ★ **FOND DE LA TOUR.** 40 N Tower Rd, 1.5 mi W of 22nd St/IL 83. 630/620-1500. Hrs: 11:30 am-2:30 pm, 5:30-10 pm; Sat from 6 pm. Closed Sun; major hols. Res accepted. French menu. Bar to 1 am. Wine list. Semi-a la carte: lunch $9.95-$15.95, dinner $20.95-$26.95. Specializes in veal, lobster, rack of lamb. Own pastries. Pianist (wkends). Valet parking. French cafe decor. Cr cds: A, C, D, DS, MC, V.

[D]

★ **MELTING POT.** (17 W 633 Roosevelt Rd, Oakbrook Terrace 60181) 2 mi NW on Roosevelt Rd. 630/495-5778. Hrs: 5-11 pm; Fri, Sat to midnight; Sun to 10 pm. Closed most major hols. Res accepted. Bar. Semi-a la carte: dinner $9.99-$15.99. Specializes in fondues, combination platters. Parking. Traditional fondue dining experience. Cr cds: A, C, D, DS, MC, V.

[D] [symbol]

★ ★ ★ **MORTON'S OF CHICAGO.** *(1 Westbrook Corp Center, Westchester 60153) 2 mi E on 22nd St at Wolf Rd. 708/562-7000.* Hrs: 11:30 am-2:30 pm, 5:30-11 pm; Sat from 5 pm; Sun 5-10 pm. Closed some hols. Res accepted. Bar. Wine list. A la carte entrees: lunch $7.95-$18.95, dinner $16.95-$29.95. Specializes in steak, lobster, prime rib. Valet parking. Cr cds: A, C, D, JCB, MC, V.

✔★ ★ **PEPPER MILL.** *(18 W 066 22nd St, Oakbrook Terrace 60181) 1 1/2 mi E on 22nd St. 630/620-5656.* Hrs: 6 am-midnight; Fri, Sat to 2 am. Closed Thanksgiving, Dec 25. Res accepted. Continental menu. Serv bar. Semi-a la carte: bkfst $3.50-$6.50, lunch $4.95-$8, dinner $7.95-$15. Child's meals. Specializes in pasta, steaks, fresh seafood. Salad bar. Patio dining. Casual atmosphere. Cr cds: A, DS, MC, V.

D

★ **ZARROSTA GRILL.** *118 Oak Brook Center Mall. 630/990-0177.* Hrs: 11:15 am-10 pm; Mon to 9:30 pm; Fri, Sat to 11 pm; Sun noon-8 pm. Closed some major hols. Res accepted. Continental menu. Wine list. Semi-a la carte: lunch $6.75-$12.95, dinner $7.25-$18.25. Complete meals: dinner $14.95-$24.95. Specializes in seafood, duck salad, mixed grill. Own pastries. Outdoor patio dining. Casual atmosphere with art-deco touch. Cr cds: A, C, D, MC, V.

D

Oak Lawn (B-6)

Pop 56,182 **Elev** 615 ft **Area code** 708
Information Chamber of Commerce, 5314 W 95th St, 60453; 708/424-8300.

In 1856, Oak Lawn was a settlement known as Black Oaks Grove. When the Wabash Railroad began to lay tracks through the community in 1879, an agreement was made with the railroad builder to create a permanent village. As a result of this agreement, the new town of Oak Lawn was officially established in 1882.

Motels

✔★ ★ **BUDGETEL INN.** *(12801 S Cicero, Alsip 60658) I-294 exit Cicero Ave. 708/597-3900; FAX 708/597-3979.* Web www.budgetel.com. 102 rms, 3 story. S, D $59.95-$105.95; suites $69.95-$109.95. Crib free. Pet accepted. TV; cable (premium), VCR avail (movies). Complimentary continental bkfst. Coffee in rms. Restaurant nearby. Ck-out noon. Meeting rm. Business servs avail. Some refrigerators. Cr cds: A, C, D, DS, MC, V.

D

★ ★ **EXEL INN.** *(9625 S 76th Ave, Bridgeview 60455) 4 mi W on 95th St (US 12/20), then N on IL 43. 708/430-1818; FAX 708/430-1894.* 113 rms, 3 story. S $46-$90; D $53-$130; under 18 free. Crib free. Pet accepted, some restrictions. TV; cable (premium). Complimentary continental bkfst. Coffee in rms. Restaurant nearby. Ck-out noon. Coin lndry. Business servs avail. Game rm. Exercise equipt; bicycle, treadmill. Microwaves avail. Cr cds: A, C, D, DS, MC, V.

D

★ ★ **HAMPTON INN.** *(13330 S Cicero Ave, Crestwood 60445) 3 mi S on Cicero Ave. 708/597-3330; FAX 708/597-3691.* Web www.hamptoninn.com. 123 rms, 4 story. S $72-$92; D $78-$92; under 18 free; higher rates New Years Eve. Crib free. Pet accepted, some restrictions. TV; cable (premium), VCR avail. Indoor pool. Complimentary continental bkfst. Restaurant nearby. Ck-out noon. Meeting rms. Business servs avail. In-rm modem link. Free airport transportation. Exercise equipt; weight machine, bicycle. Cr cds: A, C, D, DS, JCB, MC, V.

D

Motor Hotels

★ ★ ★ **HOLIDAY INN.** *4140 W 95th St (60453). 708/425-7900; FAX 708/425-7918.* 140 rms, 5 story. S $89-$109; D $99-$119; each addl $10; under 19 free. Crib free. TV; cable (premium). Heated pool. Complimentary coffee in lobby. Restaurant 6:30 am-10 pm; wkends from 7 am. Rm serv. Bar 11-2 am. Ck-out noon. Meeting rms. Business servs avail. In-rm modem link. Valet serv. Sundries. Free airport transportation. Luxury level. Cr cds: A, C, D, DS, ER, JCB, MC, V.

★ ★ **RADISSON-ALSIP.** *(5000 W 127th St, Alsip 60658) S on IL 50. 708/371-7300; FAX 708/371-9949.* 193 rms, 5 story. S, D $89-$109; each addl $10; suites $175; under 19 free; wkend rates. Crib free. TV; cable (premium). Indoor pool. Restaurant 7 am-10 pm. Rm serv. Bar 11 am-midnight; wkends to 2 am. Ck-out noon. Coin lndry. Meeting rms. Business servs avail. In-rm modem link. Bellhops. Sundries. Free Midway Airport transportation. Exercise equipt; treadmill, stair machine. Game rm. Some balconies; microwaves avail. Cr cds: A, C, D, DS, JCB, MC, V.

D

Hotel

★ ★ ★ **HILTON.** *9333 S Cicero Ave (60453), at jct US 12, 20 & IL 50. 708/425-7800; FAX 708/425-8111.* E-mail joangeary@hilton.com; web www.hilton.com. 173 rms, 12 story. S $105-$140; D $114-$150; each addl $10; suites $329-$629; family, wkend, monthly rates. Crib free. TV; cable (premium), VCR avail. Indoor pool; whirlpool. Complimentary continental bkfst. Complimentary coffee in rms. Restaurant (see WHITNEY'S). Bar 11-2 am, Sun from noon; entertainment Tues-Sat. Ck-out noon. Meeting rms. Business servs avail. In-rm modem link. Gift shop. Free Midway Airport transportation. Exercise equipt; weight machine, stair machine, sauna. Luxury level. Cr cds: A, C, D, DS, ER, MC, V.

D

Restaurants

★ ★ **OLD BARN.** *(8100 S Central Ave, Burbank 60459) 2 mi N on Cicero Ave, then 1/2 mi W on 79th St. 708/422-5400.* Hrs: 11:30 am-3 pm, 4-9 pm; Fri, Sat 5-10 pm; early-bird dinner Mon-Thur 4-6 pm. Closed some major hols. Res accepted. Bar. Semi-a la carte: lunch $5-$8, dinner $8.95-$20. Child's meals. Specializes in prime rib, roast duck, barbecued ribs. Valet parking. Original building (1933) was speak-easy during prohibition; original door buzzer. Family-owned. Cr cds: A, C, D, DS, MC, V.

D

★ ★ **WHITNEY'S.** *(See Hilton Hotel) 708/229-8888.* Hrs: 6:30 am-10:30 pm; Fri to 11:30 pm; Sat 7 am-11:30 pm; Sun 7 am-10 pm; early-bird dinner Mon-Thurs 5-6 pm; Sun brunch 8 am-1:45 pm. Res accepted. Continental menu. Bar; Fri, Sat to 2 am. Semi-a la carte: bkfst $2.75-$10.75, lunch $7.95-$9.95, dinner $12.95-$21.95. Sun brunch $8.95. Child's meals. Specializes in strip steak, halibut, grilled pork chops. Pianist Tues-Sat. Contemporary decor. Cr cds: A, C, D, DS, MC, V.

Oak Park (D-3 see Chicago map)

(See also Cicero)

Settled 1837 **Pop** 53,648 **Elev** 620 ft **Area code** 708
Information Oak Park Chamber of Commerce, 1010 Lake St, Suite 102, 60301-1106; 708/848-8151.

Oak Park, one of Chicago's oldest suburbs, is a village of well-kept houses and magnificent trees. The town is internationally famous as the birthplace of Ernest Hemingway and for its concentration of prairie-school houses by

Frank Lloyd Wright and other modern architects of the early 20th century. Wright both lived in the town and practiced architecture from his Oak Park studio between 1889 and 1909.

What to See and Do

Ernest Hemingway Museum. Exhibits include rare photos, artifacts and letters. Six-min video presentation. Walking tours of Hemingway sites, including birthplace. (Sat, also Fri & Sun afternoon; closed some major hols) 200 N Oak Park Ave, in Arts Center. Phone 708/848-2222. ¢¢

Frank Lloyd Wright Home and Studio. Wright built this house in 1889, when he was 22 yrs old. He remodeled the inside on an average of every 18 months, testing his new design ideas while creating the prairie style of architecture in the process. Guided tours (daily, inquire for schedule; closed Jan 1, Thanksgiving, Dec 25). National Trust for Historic Preservation property. 951 Chicago Ave. Phone 708/848-1976. ¢¢¢

★ **Oak Park Visitors Center.** Information, guidebooks; orientation program on Frank Lloyd Wright Prairie School of Architecture National Historic District; recorded walking tour; admission tickets for tours of Wright's home and studio; other walking tours. (Daily) 158 N Forest Ave, at Lake St. Phone 708/848-1976. Tours ¢¢¢

Pleasant Home Mansion. Opulent 30-rm mansion designed by prominent prairie-school architect George W. Maher in 1897. Second floor is home to the historical society and museum. (Thurs-Sun afternoons, guided tours on the hr) 217 S Home Ave. Phone 708/383-2654. ¢¢

Unity Temple (Unitarian Universalist Church). National landmark was designed by Frank Lloyd Wright in 1906. The church is noted as his first monolithic concrete structure and his first public building. 20-min cassette-guided tour (Mon-Fri, afternoons; wkend tours avail). 875 Lake St. Phone 708/848-6225. ¢¢

Olney (G-5)

Pop 8,664 **Elev** 482 ft **Area code** 618 **Zip** 62450
Information Chamber of Commerce, 309 E Main St, PO Box 575; 618/392-2241.

Olney is locally famous as the "home of the white squirrels." Local legend has it that the white squirrels first appeared here in 1902 when a hunter captured a male and female albino and put them on display. An outraged citizen, learning of their capture, ordered their release into the woods. Although the male was killed shortly thereafter, baby white squirrels were seen in the woods weeks later. The population has since increased to approximately 800 of these unusual albino squirrels. Olney is serious about its albino colony and has passed laws for their protection, including right-of-way for the white squirrels on any street in town.

What to See and Do

Bird Haven-Robert Ridgway Memorial. Arboretum and bird sanctuary on 18 acres. Established on land purchased in 1906 by Robert Ridgway, noted naturalist, scientist, artist and author. The sanctuary contains dozens of varieties of trees, shrubs and vines, many of which are still being identified; nature trails; replica of the original porch of the Ridgway cottage; Ridgway's grave; information center gazebo. (Daily) N on East St to Miller's Grove. **Free.**

Annual Events

Richland County Fair. Fairgrounds on IL 130. Livestock shows & exhibits, car races, horse show, entertainment, food. Phone 618/863-2606. Wk mid-July.

Fall Festival of Arts & Crafts. Juried fine arts & crafts show. Phone 618/395-4444. Last Sat Sept.

Oregon (B-4)

(For accommodations see De Kalb, Dixon, Rockford)

Settled 1833 **Pop** 3,891 **Elev** 702 ft **Area code** 815 **Zip** 61061
Information Chamber of Commerce, 201 N 3rd St, Suite 14; 815/732-2100.

Generations of artists have found inspiration in the scenic beauty of the region surrounding Oregon. In 1898, sculptor Lorado Taft and others founded a colony for artists and writers. Located on Rock River, Oregon is the home of Lorado Taft Field Campus, Northern Illinois University.

What to See and Do

Castle Rock State Park. On 2,000 acres. Fishing; boating (motors, launching ramp). Hiking & ski trails; tobogganing. Picnicking. Nature preserve. Canoe camping only (May-Oct; fee). Approx 4 mi SW on IL 2. Phone 815/732-7329. **Free.**

Ogle County Historical Society Museum (1878). Restored frame house was home of Chester Nash, inventor of the cultivator. Displays local historical exhibits. (May-Oct, Thurs & Sun, limited hrs; also by appt) 111 N 6th St. Phone 815/732-6876. **Free.**

Oregon Public Library Art Gallery. Displays work of the original Lorado Taft Eagle's Nest art group. (Daily exc Sun; closed hols) 300 Jefferson St. Phone 815/732-2724. **Free.**

Rose of Rock River. Lunch and dinner excursions aboard turn-of-the-century paddlewheeler along Rock River (2-2½ hrs). (Apr-Oct, daily) Departs from Maxson Manor, 1469 Illinois St (IL 2N). Phone 815/732-6761. ¢¢¢¢¢

Scenic drive N on IL 2, along the Rock River. Two mi N of town is

Stronghold Castle. Replica of old English castle built in 1929 by newspaper publisher Walter Strong; now owned by the Presbytery of Blackhawk, Presbyterian Church. Grounds (daily). (See ANNUAL EVENT) Phone 815/732-6111. Tours ¢ Farther N on IL 2 and on the E side of the Rock River is

Lowden Memorial State Park. Park established on 207 acres in memory of former Illinois Governor Frank O. Lowden, who lived nearby. Fishing; boating (ramp). Hiking. Picnicking, concession. Camping. Standard fees. (Mid-May-mid-Oct) Phone 815/732-6828. **Free.** On the bluffs above Rock River is

Monument to the Native American. Rising 48 ft above brush-covered bluffs, this monumental work by Lorado Taft was constructed in 1911 of poured Portland cement. The statue is usually referred to as **Blackhawk** and is regarded as a monument to him.

Soldiers Memorial. War memorial by beaux-arts sculptor Lorado Taft, completed in 1916, consists of two life-size soliders on either side of an allegorical figure symbolizing peace. On courthouse square, downtown.

White Pines Forest State Park. On 385 acres. Contains the southernmost large stand of virgin white pine in Illinois. Fishing. Hiking. Cross-country skiing. Picnicking, concession, lodge, dining facilities. Camping. Standard fees. 8 mi W on Pines Rd, near Mt Morris. Phone 815/946-3717. **Free.**

Annual Event

Autumn on Parade. Farmers' market, entertainment, parade, demonstrations; tours of Stronghold Castle. 1st wkend Oct.

Ottawa (C-4)

(See also Morris, Peru)

Founded 1829 **Pop** 17,451 **Elev** 480 ft **Area code** 815 **Zip** 61350 **E-mail** ottawa@ivnet.com **Web** ottawa.il.us

Information Ottawa Area Chamber of Commerce & Industry, 100 W Lafayette St, PO Box 888; 815/433-0084.

Founded by the commissioners of the Illinois and Michigan Canal, Ottawa took root only after the Black Hawk War. The first of the Lincoln-Douglas debates took place in the town's public square; a monument in Washington Park marks the site. Located at the confluence of the Fox and Illinois rivers, many industries are now located in this "Town of Two Rivers."

What to See and Do

Belle of the Rock. Scenic excursions on Illinois River with views of Effigy Tumuli, Eagle Cliff, Starved Rock. (May-Oct, Thurs-Sun, afternoons) Starved Rock Marina, 6 mi W on Dee Bennett Rd. Phone 815/433-4218. ¢¢¢

Buffalo Rock State Park. Part of the I & M Canal State Trail on 243 acres. Live buffalo. Hiking; picnicking (shelters), playground. 5 mi W off US 6 on Dee Bennett Rd. Phone 815/433-2220 or 815/942-0796.   **Free.**   Adj is

> **Effigy Tumuli Sculpture.** The largest earth sculptures since Mt Rushmore were formed as part of a reclamation project on the site of a former strip mine. Fashioned with the use of earthmoving equipment, the five enormous figures—a snake, turtle, catfish, frog and water strider—were deliberately designed and formed to recall similar earth sculptures done by pre-Columbian Native Americans as ceremonial or burial mounds called *tumuli.* (Daily) Phone the Canal Visitor Center, 815/942-0796 or 815/433-2220.   **Free.**

Skydive Chicago, Inc. Largest skydiving center in midwest. (Daily) Ottawa Airport, off I-80. Phone 815/433-0000.   ¢¢¢¢¢

Starved Rock State Park (see). 10 mi W on IL 71.

William Reddick Mansion (1855). Italianate, antebellum mansion has 22 rms and ornate walnut woodwork amd ornamental plasterwork; period rm contains many original furnishings. House served as public library from 1889 through early 1970s. Mansion (Mon-Fri); guided tours (by appt). 100 W Lafayette St. Contact the Chamber of Commerce office, located on the main floor of the mansion, phone 815/433-0084.

Annual Event

Ottawa's Riverfest Celebration. Parade, fireworks, carnival, family activities, Gospel concert and Polkafest. Phone 815/433-0161. 12 days Late July-early Aug.

Motor Hotel

✔★ ★ **OTTAWA INN-STARVED ROCK.** *3000 Columbus St, at jct IL 23 & I-80. 815/434-3400; FAX 815/434-3904.* 120 rms, 2 story. S, D $39.95-$44.95; each addl $6; suites $58-$76; under 13 free. Crib free. TV; cable. Indoor pool; whirlpool. Restaurant 7 am-1 pm, 5-9:15 pm; Sun 7 am-noon. Bar 11 am-midnight; Fri, Sat to 1 am. Ck-out 11 am. Meeting rms. Business servs avail. Cr cds: A, C, D, DS, MC, V.

 SC

Restaurants

✔★ **CAPTAIN'S COVE BAR AND GRILL.** *At Starved Rock Marina, 5 mi S of I-80, Utica exit (IL 178), Dee Bennett Rd. 815/434-0881.* Hrs: 11 am-10 pm. Closed Tues. Res accepted. Bar. Semi-a la carte: lunch, dinner $4.25-$13.95. Specializes in steak, seafood, pasta. Own

desserts. Entertainment wkends (in season). Outdoor dining. Screened deck overlooks Illinois River, Starved Rock Canyon Basin. Cr cds: MC, V.

★ **MONTE'S RIVERSIDE INN.** *903 E Norris Dr. 815/434-5000.* Hrs: 11 am-9 pm; Sat 4-10 pm. Closed Dec 25. Res accepted. Semi-a la carte: lunch $4.95-$7.95, dinner $7.95-$18.95. Specializes in prime rib, pasta, chicken. Adj boat docking at Fox River. Cr cds: A, MC, V.

D

Peoria (D-3)

(See also Bloomington)

Settled 1691 **Pop** 113,504 **Elev** 510 ft **Area code** 309 **Web** peoriacvb. peoria.il.us

Information Convention & Visitors Bureau, 403 NE Jefferson, 61603; 309/676-0303 or 800/747-0302.

In the heart of a rich agricultural basin on the Illinois River, Peoria is the oldest settlement in the state. Louis Jolliet and Père Marquette, along with a French party, discovered the area in 1673. La Salle established Fort Crève Coeur on the eastern shore of Peoria Lake (a wide stretch in the Illinois River) in 1680. In 1691-1692, Tonti and LaForest established Fort St Louis II on a site within the city. The settlement that grew around the fort has, except for a brief period during the Fox Wars, been continuously occupied since. The British flag flew over Peoria from 1763 to 1778; and for a short time in 1781, the Spanish held Peoria. The city is named for the Native Americans that occupied the area when the French arrived.

Peoria is the international headquarters of Caterpillar Inc, makers of earthmoving equipment used worldwide. The city is also known for steel, information-high tech firms, which are relatively new to the area, and agricultural-based companies, including stockyards and a commodity market. Peoria is the home of Bradley University (1897) and the University of Illinois-Peoria College of Medicine.

What to See and Do

Eureka College (1855). (500 students) Liberal arts and sciences. One of the first coeducational colleges in the country. The school's most famous graduate is Ronald Reagan. Cerf Center houses a collection of Reagan memorabilia from his acting and political careers; also of interest are the historic Burrus Dickinson Hall (1857) and the Chapel (1869). 18 mi E on US 24 in Eureka. Phone 309/467-6318.

Forest Park Nature Center. More than 800 acres of hardwood forest with reconstructed prairie (1½ acres); nature trails (5 mi); natural science museum. (Daily) 5809 Forest Park Dr, ½ mi off IL 29. Phone 309/686-3360.   **Free.**

Glen Oak Park & Zoo. Park on heavily wooded bluffs includes zoo with more than 250 species; amphitheater (concerts in summer); Queen Anne/Victorian pavilion, tennis courts, playground, fishing lagoon, concession. Prospect Rd & McClure Ave. Phone 309/682-1200 (park); 309/686-3365 (zoo). Zoo   ¢¢   Also here is

> **George L. Luthy Memorial Botanical Garden.** All-season gardens, rose garden, herb garden, perennial garden on 4½ acres. Conservatory includes floral display areas, tropical plants; orchid, Easter lily display; also mum display (Nov), poinsettia display (Dec). Conservatory (daily; special schedule for displays). Gardens (daily). Phone 309/686-3362. **Donation.**

Jubilee College State Historic Site. Historic site, on 90 acres, preserved Jubilee College campus, one of the first educational institutions in Illinois (1840-1852). Original Gothic-revival building and chapel are restored. Hiking. Picnicking. (Daily; closed Jan 1, Thanksgiving, Dec 25) 15 mi NW on US 150, in Brimfield. Phone 309/243-9489. 3 mi NW on US 150 is

Jubilee College State Park. More than 3,000-acre park with hiking and bridle trails. Cross-country, snowmobile trails. Picnicking. Camping. Standard fees. Phone 309/446-3758. **Free.**

Lakeview Museum of Arts and Sciences. Contains permanent and changing exhibits in the arts and sciences; 300-seat auditorium for concerts, lectures, movies; natural science history area; Children's Discovery Center; special exhibits. Gift shop. Sculpture garden and picnic area. (Daily exc Mon; closed hols) 1125 W Lake Ave, at University St N. Phone 309/686-7000. ¢¢　Also here is the

Planetarium. Multimedia shows and constellation programs (Wed, Sat, Sun; schedule varies). Largest scale model of our solar system. Phone 309/686-NOVA. ¢¢

Metamora Courthouse State Historic Site. One of the two remaining court structures on the old Eighth Judicial Circuit, the circuit on which Lincoln practiced law for 12 yrs. The building (1844), constructed of native materials, is a fine example of classical-revival architecture. On the first floor is a museum containing collection of pioneer artifacts and an exhibit pertaining to the old Eighth Judicial Circuit; on the second floor is the restored courtroom. Guide service. (Daily; closed Jan 1, Thanksgiving, Dec 25) 10 mi NE on IL 116, at 113 E Partridge in Metamora. Phone 309/367-4470. **Free.**

Peoria Historical Society maintains

Flanagan House. Oldest standing house in Peoria (ca 1837), Federal in style, contains pre-Civil War furniture, primitive kitchen, children's room with antique toys, carpenter's shop with large collection of antique tools. Location on bluffs above Illinois River affords beautiful view of entire river valley. (Mon-Fri; closed major hols) 942 NE Glen Oak Ave. Phone 309/674-1921 ¢¢　Also

Pettengill-Morron House (1868). Italianate/Second Empire mansion, built by Moses Pettengill, was purchased by Jean Morron in 1953 to replace her ancestral house, which was being destroyed to make way for a freeway. She moved a two-century accumulation of household furnishings and family heirlooms, as well as such architectural pieces as the old house's cast-iron fence, chandeliers, marble mantles and brass rails from the porch. (Tues-Sat; closed major hols) (See ANNUAL EVENTS) 1212 W Moss Ave. Phone 309/674-4745. ¢¢

Spirit of Peoria. Replica of turn-of-the-century sternwheeler, offers cruises along Illinois River. 1½-hr sightseeing cruise (Wed, Fri, Sun); Starved Rock State Park cruise, with overnight stay (Mon-Tues); Peoria to Pere Marquette State Park cruise, with two-night stay (Mon-Wed). Departs from The Landing at foot of Main St. Phone 309/699-7232 or 800/676-8988 for schedule and fees.

Theater.

Peoria Players. Dramas, comedies, musicals. (Early Sept-early May, Tues-Sun; closed hols) 4300 N University St. Phone 309/688-4473.

Corn Stock Theater. Theater-in-the-round summer stock under circus-type big top; dramas, comedies, musicals. (June-Aug) Bradley Park, near Park Rd & Nebraska Ave. Phone 309/676-2196.

Wheels O'Time Museum. Many antique autos, old tractors and farm implements, fire engines, antique clocks, musical instruments, tools, model railroads and railroad memorabilia, kitchen equipment, early radios; hands-on exhibits; outdoor display of steam-era train; changing exhibits; many items relating to Peoria history. (May-Oct, Wed-Sun, also Memorial Day, July 4, Labor Day) 8 mi N on IL 88, at 11923 N Knoxville Ave. Phone 309/243-9020. ¢¢

⊠ **Wildlife Prairie Park.** Wildlife and nature preserve with animals native to Illinois in natural habitats along wood-chipped trails: bears, cougars, bobcats, wolves, red foxes and more. Pioneer homestead has working farm from late 1800s with an authentic log cabin and one-room schoolhouse. Walking trails, playground, picnicking, food service; informational slide show (free); lectures and special events throughout summer; 24-inch scale railroad runs along park perimeter. Park (daily); buildings, train, activities (Mar-mid-Dec, daily). No pets permitted. 10 mi W via I-74, Edwards exit 82, then 3 mi S on Taylor Rd. Phone 309/676-0998. ¢¢

Annual Events

Steamboat Days. Riverboat races, boat parade; band concerts, carnival; entertainment, pageant. 4 days at Father's Day wkend.

Spoon River Valley Scenic Drive. 19 mi W on IL 116 at Farmington, then marked, circular route through Fulton County. Autumn drive through small towns and rolling, wooded countryside noted for fall color (complete drive 140 mi); 19th- and early 20th-century crafts, exhibits, demonstrations, antiques, collectibles; produce, food. Phone 309/547-3234. Usually 1st two full wkends Oct.

Candlelight Christmas. Victorian Christmas setting at Pettengill-Morron House. Carolers and costumed volunteers in Christmas setting of Victorian period. Phone 309/674-4745. Nov-mid-Dec.

Motels

★ **BEST WESTERN EASTLIGHT INN.** *(401 N Main St, East Peoria 61611) 1 blk S of I-74 exit 95A.* 309/699-7231. 199 rms, 2 story. Apr-Sept: S $56; D $64; each addl $8; under 12 free; lower rates rest of yr. Crib free. Pet accepted, some restrictions. TV; cable (premium), VCR avail. Indoor pool; whirlpool. Complimentary continental bkfst. Restaurant adj 6 am-10 pm. Bar 4 pm-1 am. Ck-out noon. Coin lndry. Meeting rms. Business servs avail. Free airport, bus depot transportation. Exercise equipt; weight machine, stair machine, sauna. Cr cds: A, C, D, DS, MC, V.

D ⊬ ≈ ✕ ⊠ 🕆 🐾 SC

★★ **COMFORT SUITES.** *4021 N War Memorial Dr (61614), I-74 exit 89.* 309/688-3800. 66 suites, 2 story. S $54.95-$64.95; D $63.45-$69.95; each addl $5; under 18 free. Crib free. Pet accepted. TV; cable (premium). Indoor pool; whirlpool. Complimentary continental bkfst. Restaurant nearby. Ck-out 11 am. Meeting rm. Business servs avail. In-rm modem link. Health club privileges. Game rm. Cr cds: A, C, D, DS, ER, JCB, MC, V.

D ⊬ ≈ ⊠ 🕆 🐾 SC

★★ **FAIRFIELD INN BY MARRIOTT.** *4203 N War Memorial Dr (61614), off I-74 exit 89 to Northwoods Mall access road.* 309/686-7600; FAX 309/686-7600, ext. 709. 135 rms, 3 story. S $45-$65; D $52-$65; each addl $7; under 18 free. Crib free. TV; cable (premium), VCR avail. Heated pool. Complimentary continental bkfst. Restaurant nearby. Ck-out noon. Meeting rm. Business servs avail. In-rm modem link. Health club privileges. Cr cds: A, C, D, DS, MC, V.

D ≈ ⊠ 🕆 🐾 SC

✔★ **RED ROOF INN.** *4031 N War Memorial Dr (61614).* 309/685-3911; FAX 309/685-3941. 108 rms, 2 story. S $35.99-$49.99; D $38.99-$59.99; under 18 free. Crib free. Pet accepted. TV; VCR avail. Complimentary coffee in lobby. Ck-out noon. Business servs avail. Cr cds: A, C, D, DS, MC, V.

D ⊬ ⊠ 🕆

★★ **SIGNATURE INN.** *4112 N Brandywine (61614), near I-74 exit 89 E & War Memorial Dr.* 309/685-2556. 124 rms, 3 story. S $60-$63; D $67-$70; each addl $7; under 17 free; wkend rates Nov-Apr. Crib free. TV; cable (premium), VCR avail (movies). Pool. Complimentary continental bkfst. Restaurant nearby. Ck-out noon. Meeting rms. Business center. In-rm modem link. Exercise equipt; bicycle, stair machine. Health club privileges. Cr cds: A, C, D, DS, ER, MC, V.

D ≈ ✕ ⊠ 🕆 SC 🏃

Motor Hotel

★★ **HAMPTON INN.** *(11 Winners Way, East Peoria 61611) IL 116, I-74 exit 95B.* 309/694-0711; FAX 309/694-0407. 154 rms, 5 story. S $69; D $79; suites $125-$150; under 18 free; higher rates Dec 31. Crib free. TV; cable (premium), VCR. Indoor pool; whirlpool. Complimentary continental bkfst. Restaurant nearby. Ck-out noon. Meeting rms. Business servs avail. In-rm modem link. Bellhops. Free airport, bus depot transportation. Exercise equipt; weights, stair machine. Refrigerator in suites. Cr cds: A, C, D, DS, MC, V.

Hotels

★ ★ HOLIDAY INN CITY CENTER. *500 Hamilton Blvd (61602).* *309/674-2500; FAX 309/674-1205.* 286 rms, 9 story. S $79-$89; D $89-$99; each addl $10; suites $105-$350; under 12 free. Crib free. Pet accepted. TV; cable. Pool. Coffee in rms. Restaurant 6 am-10 pm. Bar 11-2 am. Ck-out noon. Convention facilities. Business center. In-rm modem link. Gift shop. Barber. Free airport, bus depot transportation. Exercise equipt; weight machine, stair machine. Luxury level. Cr cds: A, C, D, DS, JCB, MC, V.

★ ★ ★ JUMER'S CASTLE LODGE. *117 N Western Ave (61604),* at Moss Ave. *309/673-8040; FAX 309/673-9782; res: 800/285-8627.* 175 rms, 4 story. S $79-$128; D $88-$135; each addl $10; studio rms $89; under 18 free. Crib free. Pet accepted. TV; cable (premium), VCR avail. Pool; whirlpool. Complimentary coffee in lobby. Restaurant (see JUMER'S). Bar 11-1 am; entertainment exc Sun. Ck-out noon. Meeting rms. Business servs avail. In-rm modem link. Valet parking. Free airport transportation. Sauna. Health club privileges. Game rm. Some fireplaces. Bavarian decor. Cr cds: A, C, D, DS, MC, V.

★ ★ PERE MARQUETTE. *501 Main St (61602).* *309/637-6500; FAX 309/637-6500; res: 800/447-1676.* 288 rms, 12 story. S $89; D $99; each addl $15; suites $175-$500; kit. units $175-$500; studio rms $175; under 18 free; wkly, wkend rates. Crib free. Pet accepted. TV; cable (premium). Restaurants 6 am-10 pm. Bar. Ck-out noon. Convention facilities. Business servs avail. In-rm modem link. Gift shop. Free covered parking. Free airport transportation. Tennis privileges. Golf privileges. Exercise equipt; weights, bicycles, treadmill, stair machine. Health club privileges. Refrigerator in suites. Restored 1920s hotel. Cr cds: A, C, D, DS, MC, V.

Restaurants

✔★ ★ ★ JUMER'S. *(See Jumer's Castle Lodge Hotel)* *309/673-8181.* Hrs: 6:30 am-10 pm; Fri to 11 pm; Sat 7 am-11 pm; Sun 7 am-10 pm; hols 7 am-8 pm; early-bird dinner 4:30-6 pm. Res accepted. German, Amer menu. Bar. Semi-a la carte: bkfst $1.95-$7.50, lunch $4.75-$6.95, dinner $7.50-$14.95. Child's meals. Specialties: Wienerschnitzel, pork roast, prime rib of beef. Own baking. Entertainment exc Sun. Bavarian decor; antiques. Family-owned. Cr cds: A, C, D, DS, MC, V.

★ ★ PAPARAZZI. *(4315 W Voss St, Peoria Heights 61614)* 5 mi NE. *309/682-5205.* Hrs: 5:30-10:30 pm. Closed Sun, Mon; some major hols; also early June. Res accepted. Continental menu. Wine, beer. A la carte entrees: dinner $5-$11. Specializes in pasta, veal. European cafe ambience. Totally nonsmoking. Cr cds: C, D, MC, V.

★ ★ ★ STEPHANIE. *1825 N Knoxville Ave (61603).* *309/682-7300.* Hrs: 11 am-2 pm, 5:30-9 pm; Sat 11 am-1:30 pm, 5:30-9:30 pm; Sun 4-9 pm. Closed major hols. Res accepted. Wine list. Semi-a la carte: lunch $3.75-$13, dinner $9.75-$19.75. Specializes in Midwestern American cooking with Mediterranean and Asian influences. Own baking. Cr cds: A, C, D, DS, MC, V.

Père Marquette State Park (G-2)

(For accommodations see Alton, also see Cahokia)

(5 mi W of Grafton on IL 100)

This is Illinois' largest state park, with 8,000 acres at the confluence of the Illinois and Mississippi rivers. It is named after Père Jacques Marquette, who passed the site with Louis Jolliet in 1673. They were the first white men to enter the present state of Illinois.

Fishing, hunting; boating (ramp, motors). Hiking, bridle paths (horses may be rented). Picnic areas, playground, concession, lodge, restaurant. Campgrounds (standard fees). Interpretive center. Schedule of free guided trips is posted in the visitor center. For information contact the Park Superintendent, PO Box 158, Grafton 62037; 618/786-3323 or 618/786-2331 (lodge).

Peru (C-4)

(See also Ottawa)

Settled 1830 **Pop** 9,302 **Elev** 500 ft **Area code** 815 **Zip** 61354

Information Illinois Valley Area Chamber of Commerce, 300 Bucklin St, PO Box 446, La Salle 61301; 815/223-0227.

What to See and Do

La Salle County Historical Museum. (1848). Exhibits include pioneer furnishings, Native American artifacts and agricultural displays; Lincoln carriage; historical library, local memorabilia. Prairie grass area; blacksmith shop, turn-of-the-century barn and one-room schoolhouse. (Fri-Sun; closed hols) 5 mi E on I-80, 1 1/2 mi S on US 178, at Canal & Mill Sts in Utica. Phone 815/667-4861. ¢

Lake de Pue. Waterskiing; fishing; boating (ramp). Picnicking. 6 mi W on IL 29.

Matthiessen State Park. This 1,938-acre park is particularly interesting for its geological formations, which can be explored via 7 mi of hiking trails. Hikers should remain on marked trails because of steep cliffs and the depth of the canyon. The upper area and bluff tops are generally dry and easily hiked, but trails into the interiors of the two dells can be difficult, especially in spring and early summer. The dells feature scenic waterfalls. Also here is a replica of a small fort stockade of the type built by the French in the Midwest during the late 1600s and early 1700s. Horseback riding (wkends). Model airplane field; archery range with a sight-in area and eight separate fields. Cross-country skiing. Bridle trails. Picnicking, playground, vending area, park office (in dells area). Observation platform. (Daily) 9 mi SE via I-80E, IL 178S in Utica. For information contact Site Superintendent, PO Box 381, Utica 61373; 815/667-4868. **Free.**

Starved Rock State Park (see). 6 mi E on I-80 to Utica exit, then S on IL 178. Near the park is

Illinois Waterway Visitor Center. Located at the Starved Rock Lock and Dam; site offers excellent view across river to Starved Rock. The history of the Illinois River from the time of the Native American, the French explorers, the construction of canals to the modern Illinois Waterway, is portrayed in a series of exhibits. The role of river transport in the nation's economy is also highlighted, with actual riverboat pilot house on display. Featured is a 3-screen, 12-min slide presentation, "The Connecting Link," tracing humans' use of the Illinois River for more than 6,000 yrs. (Daily) E on Dee Bennett Rd, S of Utica. Phone 815/667-4054. **Free.**

Annual Events

Winter Wilderness Weekend. Departs from Starved Rock Visitor Center. Guided hikes to see the spectacular ice falls of Starved Rock (see). Cross-country skiing (rentals, instruction). Phone 815/667-4906. Jan.

Cross-Country Ski Weekend. Starved Rock Visitor Center. Guided ski-hikes to Starved Rock (see) and Matthiessen State Park; ski rentals, instruction. Phone 815/667-4906. Feb.

Wildflower Pilgrimage. Starved Rock Visitor Center. Guided hikes to Starved Rock (see). Phone 815/667-4906. May.

Montreal Canoe Weekends. Begins at Point Shelter at E end of Starved Rock. Ride a replica of the 34-ft "voyageur canoe" that the French used to explore North America. Phone 815/667-4906. June.

National Championship Boat Races. Lake de Pue. 17 classes of power boats compete for national title; beer gardens and live entertainment. Phone 815/447-2848. Late July.

National Sweet Corn Festival. Approx 15 mi N via US 51 in Mendota. Music, parades, Sweet Corn Queen competition, carnival, 6-mi race. 2nd wkend Aug.

Motels

★ ★ **COMFORT INN.** 5240 Trompeter Rd. 815/223-8585; FAX 815/223-9292. 50 rms, 3 story. S $58-$63; D $62-$68; each addl $4; suite $70-$74; under 18 free. Crib free. TV; cable (premium). Pool. Complimentary continental bkfst. Restaurant nearby. Ck-out 11 am. Coin lndry. Meeting rm. Business servs avail. Some refrigerators. Cr cds: A, C, D, DS, MC, V.

D ⛱ ⊠ 🐾 SC

✔★ **LASALLE PERU INN.** (I-80 & IL 251 (May Rd), LaSalle 61301) ¼ mi N on IL 251 at I-80 exit 75. 815/224-2500; FAX 815/224-3693. 104 rms, 2 story. S $32-$59; D $39-$65; each addl $8; under 18 free. Crib free. Pet accepted. TV; VCR avail (movies). Pool. Complimentary coffee in lobby. Restaurant 11 am-8 pm. Ck-out noon. Coin lndry. Meeting rms. Business servs avail. Valet serv. Cr cds: A, C, D, DS, ER, JCB, MC, V.

D 🐾 ⛱ ⊠ 🐾 SC

★ **SUPER 8.** 1851 May Rd, I-80 & US 251. 815/223-1848. 62 rms, 3 story. June-Sept: S $36.88; D $47.88; each addl $5; under 12 free; higher rates special events; lower rates rest of yr. Crib free. Pet accepted, some restrictions. TV; cable (premium), VCR avail (movies). Complimentary coffee in lobby. Restaurant opp 11 am-9 pm. Ck-out 11 am. Cr cds: A, C, D, DS, JCB, MC, V.

D 🐾 ⊠ 🔥 SC

Inn

★ **YESTERDAYS MEMORIES.** (303 E Peru, Princeton 61356) 815/872-7753. 4 rms, 3 share bath, 2 story. S $50; D $55; each addl $10; under 3 free. Crib free. TV; VCR avail (movies). Complimentary continental bkfst. Restaurant nearby. Ck-out 11 am, ck-in 2 pm. X-country ski 5 mi. Built in 1852; antiques. Totally nonsmoking. No cr cds accepted.

🐾 ⊠ 🐾

Restaurants

✔★ **THE MAPLES.** 1401 Shooting Park Rd. 815/223-1938. Hrs: 11 am-2 pm, 5-10 pm; Sun to 8 pm (buffet only); Mon to 2 pm. Closed July 4. Res accepted. Bar. Buffet: lunch $5.95; Semi-a la carte: dinner $4.95-$11. Buffet (Sun): lunch, dinner $7.95. Child's meals. Salad bar. Family-owned. Cr cds: A, C, D, MC, V.

D ⊡

★ ★ **RED DOOR INN.** 1701 Water St. 815/223-2500. Hrs: 11 am-2 pm, 5-11 pm; Sat 4 pm-midnight; Sun 4-10 pm. Closed some hols.

Res accepted. Bar. Complete meals: lunch $4.75-$12.75, dinner $10-$25. Specialties: steak Diane, châteaubriand, fresh seafood. Salad bar. Own baking. In historic 1850 riverhouse. Cr cds: A, MC, V.

D ⊡

★ **UPTOWN BAR & GRILL.** (601 1st St, La Salle 61301) 815/224-4545. Hrs: 11 am-11 pm; Sun noon-10 pm. Closed Thanksgiving, Dec 25. Res accepted. Bar. Semi-a la carte: lunch $7-$9, dinner $15-$20. Child's meals. Specializes in steak, pasta, seafood. Casual atmosphere. Seasonal outdoor dining. Cr cds: A, DS, MC, V.

D

Petersburg (E-3)

(See also Havana, Springfield)

Founded 1833 **Pop** 2,261 **Elev** 524 ft **Area code** 217 **Zip** 62675
Information Chamber of Commerce, 125 S 7th St, PO Box 452; 217/632-7363.

Surveyed by Abraham Lincoln in 1836, Petersburg was made the seat of Menard County in 1839. Most of the residents of nearby New Salem then moved to Petersburg, and the village where Lincoln spent six years and began his political career eventually sank into ruin. Ironically, it was a later generation of Petersburg residents who were responsible for the rebirth of New Salem.

What to See and Do

Edgar Lee Masters Memorial Home. Boyhood residence of the poet. Living rm restored to 1870-1875 period. Rest of house is museum of family history. (Memorial Day-Labor Day, daily, limited hrs) Contact the Chamber of Commerce. Jackson & 8th Sts. Phone 217/632-7363. **Free.**

 Lincoln's New Salem State Historic Site. The wooded, 700-acre park incorporates a complete reconstruction, based upon original maps and family archives, of New Salem as the village appeared when Lincoln lived there (1831-1837). Authentic reconstruction began in the early 1930s, with much of the work carried out by the New Deal's Civilian Conservation Corps (CCC). Today, New Salem consists of 12 timber houses, a school and 10 shops, stores or industries, including the Denton Offutt store (where Lincoln first worked), the Lincoln-Berry store, the Rutledge tavern and the saw and gristmill. The only original building is the Onstot cooper shop, which was discovered in Petersburg and returned to its original foundation in 1922. Interior furnishings are, for the most part, authentic to the 1830s period of Lincoln's residency. A variety of programs are offered throughout the yr: self-guided tours; historical demonstrations; interpreters in period clothing; scheduled special events (see ANNUAL EVENTS); rides in horse-drawn wagon. Visitor center offers 18-min orientation film; exhibits. Picnicking, concession. Gift shop. Camping, tent & trailer sites (standard fees). (Daily; closed Jan 1, Thanksgiving, Dec 25) 2 mi S on IL 97. Phone 217/632-4000. **Free.** Also here are

Talisman **River Boat.** Replica of *Talisman,* small riverboat that went up the Sangamon River in Lincoln's day, offers hrly trips in season. (May-Labor Day, daily exc Mon; after Labor Day-Oct, Sat & Sun only) Dock near gristmill, across IL 97 from park. Phone 217/632-7681 or 217/632-2219. ¢¢

Kelso Hollow Outdoor Theatre. Performances nightly (early June-late Aug, Thurs-Sun). Phone 800/710-9290. ¢¢¢

Oakland Cemetery. Graves of Ann Rutledge, who some believe to have been Lincoln's first love, and poet Edgar Lee Masters, Petersburg native who wrote the *Spoon River Anthology.* Oakland Ave.

Annual Events

Summer Festival at New Salem. Lincoln's New Salem State Historic Site. Re-enactment of a summer day in early 1830s New Salem; crafts; interpretive activities. Wkend mid-July.

"Prairie Tales" at New Salem. Lincoln's New Salem State Historic Site. Two-day festival of nationally acclaimed storytellers. Early Aug.

Traditional Music Festival. Lincoln's New Salem State Historic Site. Mid-Sept.

Candlelight Tour of New Salem. Lincoln's New Salem State Historic Site. Early Oct.

Inn

★ ★ **THE OAKS.** *510 W Sheridan, 4 mi W on IL 97, exit Sheridan Rd. 217/632-5444; res: 888/724-6257.* 5 rms, 2 share bath, 1 with shower only, 3 story, 1 suite. No rm phones. S, D $70-$90; each addl $10; suite $125; under 12 free. TV in some rms. Complimentary full bkfst; afternoon refreshments. Ck-out 11 am, ck-in 3-6 pm. Luggage handling. Valet serv. Many fireplaces. 19th century mansion; scenic views; antiques. Cr cds: DS, MC, V.

⊠ ⊁ SC

Unrated Dining Spot

MUD PIES' TEA ROOM. *115 S 7th St. 217/632-2828.* Hrs: 11 am-3 pm. Closed Sun, Mon; most major hols. Res accepted. Semi-a la carte: bkfst, lunch $3.75-$6. Child's meals. Specializes in chicken salad sandwiches, mudslides. In 1860s bldg; gift shop adj. Totally nonsmoking. Cr cds: D, MC, V.

Quincy (E-1)

Settled 1822 **Pop** 39,681 **Elev** 601 ft **Area code** 217 **Zip** 62301 **E-mail** chamber@ltm.com **Web** quincychamber.org

Information Quincy Area Chamber of Commerce, 300 Civic Center Plaza, Ste 245, 62301-4169; 217/222-7980.

Quincy, seat of Adams County, was named for President John Quincy Adams. Located on the east bank of the Mississippi River, the town was the site of the sixth Lincoln-Douglas debate, October 13, 1858; a bronze bas-relief in Washington Park marks the spot. Quincy was, in the mid-19th century, the second-largest city in Illinois, and an industrial, agricultural and river transportation center. Today, the city, which remains a center of industry, is known for its historical business district and fine Victorian residences.

What to See and Do

John Wood Mansion (1835). This two-story, Greek-revival mansion was the residence of the founder of Quincy and a former governor of Illinois. Moved to its present location in about 1860, the house was cut in half and moved across a special bridge. Restored; original furnishings of the period including the first piano in Quincy, three-story Victorian doll house; artifacts of the area; traveling exhibits; museum. (Apr-Oct, Sat & Sun; also by appt) 425 S 12th St. Phone 217/222-1835. ¢

Quincy Museum. Located in the Newcomb-Stillwell mansion, a Richardson Romanesque-style building. Rotating exhibits and a children's discovery rm. (Tues-Sun afternoons) 1601 Maine St. Phone 217/224-7669. ¢

Motel

✔★ ★ **TRAVELODGE.** *200 S 300 St. 217/222-5620; FAX 217/224-2582.* 63 rms, 2 story. S $44; D $50-$56; each addl $5; under 12 free. Crib free. Pet accepted, some restrictions; $10. TV; cable (premium). Complimentary continental bkfst. Complimentary coffee in rms. Restaurant 11 am-11 pm. Rm serv. Bar. Ck-out noon. Business servs avail. Coin lndry. Pool. Some refrigerators, microwaves. Some balconies. Picnic table. Cr cds: A, C, D, DS, MC, V.

 D ✔ ⊁ SC

Rockford (A-4)

(See also De Kalb, Freeport, Oregon)

Founded 1834 **Pop** 139,426 **Elev** 721 ft **Area code** 815 **E-mail** rkfdcvb@wwa.com

Information Rockford Area Convention & Visitors Bureau, Memorial Hall, 211 N Main St, 61101; 815/963-8111 or 800/521-0849.

The state's second-largest city grew up on both sides of the Rock River and took its name from the ford that was used by the Galena-Chicago Stagecoach Line. The early settlers of Rockford were primarily from New England. Today, much of its population is of Swedish and Italian descent. A commercial center for a vast area, it is the largest manufacturer of screw products and fasteners in the United States and one of the most important machine-tool producers in the world.

What to See and Do

Anderson Japanese Gardens. Formal 7-acre gardens with waterfall, ponds, bridges, tea house, guest house and footpaths. (May-Oct, daily) Spring Creek & Highcrest Rds. Phone 815/877-2525. ¢¢

Burpee Museum of Natural History. Two Victorian mansions with exhibits of Illinois wildlife, birds, reptiles, mammals, fossils, minerals; Rock River Valley Native American exhibit (737 N Main). (Daily exc Mon; closed major hols) 813 N Main St. Phone 815/965-3132. ¢¢

Discovery Center Museum. Hands-on learning museum with more than 120 exhibits illustrating scientific and perceptual principles; visitors can leave their shadow hanging on a wall, create a bubble window, see a planetarium show, learn how a house is built, star in a TV show or create music in a sound studio. Adj Rock River Discovery Park features weather station, earth and water exhibits. (Daily exc Mon, also some Mon hols) 711 N Main St, in Riverfront Museum Park. Phone 815/963-6769. ¢¢

Erlander Home Museum (1871). Rockford's Swedish heritage is reflected in this two-story brick house built for John Erlander, an early Swedish settler. Restored Victorian interior; display of numerous pioneer artifacts. (Sun, limited hrs; also by appt; closed hols, 3rd Sun Mar, also Jan) 404 S 3rd St. Phone 815/963-5559. ¢

Magic Waters. This 35-acre water theme park includes 5 5-story water slides; wave pool; hot tubs; children's wading pool; island tree house; sand beach; tubing river; playground; concession, picnicking. (Memorial Day-Labor Day, daily) US 20 & US 51 in Cherry Valley. Phone 815/332-3260 or 800/373-1679. ¢¢¢

Midway Village & Museum Center. Museum contains permanent and changing exhibits of area history; aviation gallery. Village features blacksmith shop, general store, bank, schoolhouse, church, police station, town hall, law office, residences, hospital, plumbing shop and hotel. (Mar-Dec, daily) 6799 Guilford Rd. Phone 815/397-9112. ¢¢

Rock Cut State Park. On 3,092 acres on two man-made lakes. Swimming beach (Memorial Day-Labor Day); fishing; boating (ramp, rentals; motors, 10 hp limit). Horseback trail. Cross-country skiing, snowmobiling, ice-boating & -fishing. Picnicking, concession. (Daily) NE via IL 251, W on IL 173. Phone 815/885-3311. **Free.**

Rockford Art Museum. Permanent collection of 19th- and 20th-century American and European paintings. Also sculpture, graphics, photographs, decorative arts; changing exhibits. (Daily exc Mon; closed hols) (See ANNUAL EVENTS) 711 N Main St. Phone 815/968-2787. **Free.**

Sightseeing.

Rockford Trolley. Scenic ride along the Rock River and Sinnissippi Park aboard replica of a turn-of-the-century trolley car; narrated. (June-early Sept, Tues, Thurs, Sat & Sun) Phone 815/987-8893. ¢¢

Forest City Queen. Narrated tours; dinner cruises. (June-early Sept, Wed-Sun; closed July 4) Phone 815/987-8893. ¢¢

Sinnissippi Gardens. Sunken gardens, 30-ft-tall floral clock, greenhouse with aviary, lagoon; bike and exercise trail. (Daily exc Dec 25) 1300-1900 N 2nd St. Phone 815/987-8858. **Free.**

Time Museum. Historical collection of timekeeping devices from early instruments to the atomic clock; includes the most complicated astronomical clock ever constructed. Video program hrly. (Daily exc Mon) 7801 E State St, on premises of Best Western Clock Tower Resort (see MOTOR HOTELS). Phone 815/398-6000, ext 2941. ¢¢

Tinker Swiss Cottage Museum. Built 1865 by a mayor of Rockford to duplicate a Swiss chalet. The 20-rm house contains Victorian furniture, art, textiles, porcelain and handcrafted treasures from the Tinker family. The house features elaborate parquet floors, fine woodwork and intricately painted ceiling and wall murals; walnut spiral staircase. Tours. (Daily exc Mon; closed hols) 411 Kent St, at S Main St. Phone 815/964-2424. ¢¢

Trailside Centre. Pony and horse-drawn wagon rides; petting corral, riding stable, horsemanship classes; special events. (Apr-Oct, daily) Fee for activities. 5209 Safford Rd, in Lockwood Park. Phone 815/987-8809. **Free.**

Annual Events

Snow Sculpting Competition. Teams from throughout Illinois compete to represent the state at national and international competitions. Phone 815/987-8800. Early Jan.

Winnebago County Fair. W on US 20, in Pecatonica. Aug.

Greenwich Village Art Fair. Rockford Art Museum. Wkend mid-Sept.

Seasonal Events

Rockford Speedway. 5 mi N, 9500 Forest Hills Rd. Stock car racing; special auto events. Phone 815/633-1500. Apr-Sept.

New American Theater. 118 N Main St. Professional theater; six mainstage shows each season. Wed-Sun. Phone 815/964-8023. Sept-June.

Motels

★ ★ **BEST WESTERN COLONIAL INN.** 4850 E State St (US 20) (61108). 815/398-5050; FAX 815/398-5050, ext. 404. 84 rms, 2-3 story. S $60-$80; D $67-$88; suites $90-$154; under 12 free. Crib $3. Pet accepted. TV; cable, VCR avail (movies). Indoor pool; whirlpool. Complimentary coffee in lobby. Restaurant adj 11 am-11:30 pm. Bar noon-2 am. Ck-out noon. Meeting rm. Business servs avail. Exercise equipt; weight machine, bicycle. Refrigerator in suites. Rockford College adj. Cr cds: A, C, D, DS, ER, JCB, MC, V.

D ⚡ ≈ 🏋 ✕ ⊠ 🔥 SC

★ ★ **COMFORT INN.** 7392 Argus Dr (61107). 815/398-7061. 64 rms, 3 story. May-Oct: S $59.95; D $64.95; each addl $5; under 18 free; lower rates rest of yr. Crib free. Pet accepted, some restrictions. TV; cable (premium). Indoor pool. Complimentary continental bkfst. Restaurant nearby. Ck-out 11 am. Business servs avail. X-country ski 10 mi. Game rm. Some refrigerators. Cr cds: A, C, D, DS, MC, V.

D ⚡ ≈ ⚡ ⊠ ⊠ SC

★ ★ **COURTYARD BY MARRIOTT.** 7676 E State St (US 20) (61108), jct I-90. 815/397-6222; FAX 815/397-6254. 148 rms, 2-3 story. S $81; D $91; suites $105-$115; under 12 free; wkend rates. Crib free. TV; cable (premium). Indoor pool; whirlpool. Complimentary coffee in rms. Restaurant 6:30-10:30 am; Sat, Sun 7-11:30 am. Bar. Ck-out noon. Coin lndry. Meeting rms. Business servs avail. In-rm modem link. Valet serv. Exercise equipt; weights, stair machine. Balconies. Cr cds: A, C, D, DS, MC, V.

D ≈ 🏋 ✕ ⊠ 🔥 SC

✔ ★ **EXEL INN.** 220 S Lyford Rd (61108), at I-90 & US 20 Business. 815/332-4915; FAX 815/332-4843. 101 rms, 2 story. S $39.99-$47.99; D $45.99-$52.99; each addl $5; under 18 free. Crib free. Pet accepted; some restrictions. TV; cable (premium). Complimentary continental bkfst. Restaurant opp. Ck-out noon. Coin lndry. In-rm modem link. Cr cds: A, C, D, DS, MC, V.

D ⚡ ✕ 🔥 SC

★ ★ **FAIRFIELD INN BY MARRIOTT.** 7712 Potawatomi Trail (State St) (61107), jct I-90 & US 20 Business. 815/397-8000. 135 rms, 3 story. S $49.95-$69.95; D $54.95-$72.95; each addl $10; under 18 free. Crib free. TV; cable (premium). Pool. Complimentary continental bkfst. Restaurant adj 6 am-10 pm. Ck-out noon. Meeting rms. Business servs avail. In-rm modem link Cr cds: A, C, D, DS, MC, V.

D ≈ ⊠ 🔥 SC

★ ★ **HOWARD JOHNSON.** 3909 S 11th St (61109), at IL 251 Bypass 20, near Greater Rockford Airport. 815/397-9000; FAX 815/397-9000, ext. 150. 146 rms, 2 story. S $49-$70; D $59-$75; each addl $5; kit. apts $600/month; under 18 free; wknd rates. Crib free. TV; cable (premium), VCR avail (movies). Indoor pool; whirlpool. Playground. Coffee in rms. Restaurant 6 am-midnight. Bar from 11 am. Ck-out noon. Coin lndry. Meeting rms. Business servs avail. In-rm modem link. Sundries. Free airport transportation. Tennis. Exercise equipt; weight machine, stair machine, sauna. Game rm. Private patios, balconies. Cr cds: A, C, D, DS, MC, V.

D ⚡ 🏃 ≈ 🏋 ✈ ⊠ 🔥 SC

✔ ★ **RED ROOF INN.** 7434 E State St (US 20 Business) (61108). 815/398-9750; FAX 815/398-9761. 108 rms, 2 story. S $39.99-$60.99; D $44.99-$70.99; each addl $9; under 18 free. Crib free. TV; cable (premium). Complimentary coffee in lobby. Ck-out noon. Business servs avail. Cr cds: A, C, D, DS, MC, V.

D ⊠ 🔥

✔ ★ ★ **SWEDEN HOUSE LODGE.** 4605 E State St (61108). 815/398-4130; FAX 815/398-9203; res: 800/886-4138. 107 rms, 2-3 story. S $38.75-$48.75; D $40.75-$52.75; suites $49.75-$64.75; each addl $2; under 18 free. Crib free. Pet accepted, some restrictions. TV; cable (premium), VCR avail (movies). Indoor pool; whirlpool. Ck-out noon. Meeting rms. Business servs avail. Valet serv. Sundries. Exercise equipt; stair machine, rower. Game rm. Cr cds: A, C, D, DS, MC, V.

⚡ ≈ ✕ 🏋 🔥 SC

Motor Hotels

★ ★ ★ **BEST WESTERN CLOCK TOWER RESORT & CONFERENCE CENTER.** 7801 E State St (61125), at jct I-90, US 20 Business. 815/398-6000; FAX 815/398-0443. 253 rms, 2 story. S $95-$154; D $105-$164; suites $157-$250; under 18 free; wknd package plan. Crib free. TV; cable (premium), VCR (movies $6). 3 pools, 1 indoor; 2 wading pools, whirlpools, poolside serv, lifeguard. Playground. Supervised child's activities (late May-Oct). Complimentary coffee in rms. Restaurants 6 am-11 pm. Rm serv 7 am-10 pm. Bar 11-2 am, Sun 12:30-11 pm; entertainment. Ck-out noon. Coin lndry. Convention facilities. Business center. In-rm modem link. Valet serv. Shopping arcade. Airport transportation. Indoor/outdoor tennis. Exercise rm; instructor, weights, sauna, steam rm. Game rm. Some refrigerators. Many private patios, balconies. Picnic tables. Time Museum on grounds. Dinner theater. Cr cds: A, C, D, DS, MC, V.

D 🏃 ≈ 🏋 ✕ ⊠ 🔥 SC 🎿

★ ★ **HAMPTON INN.** 615 Clark Dr (61107). 815/229-0404; FAX 815/229-0175. 122 rms, 4 story. May-Oct: S, D $79-$89; under 18 free; lower rates rest of yr. Crib free. TV; cable (premium). Indoor pool; whirlpool. Complimentary continental bkfst. Restaurant adj 10 am-10 pm. Ck-out noon. Meeting rm. Business servs avail. In-rm modem link. X-country ski 15 mi. Exercise equipt: treadmill, stair machine. Cr cds: A, C, D, DS, MC, V.

D ≈ ✕ 🏋 ⊠ 🔥 SC

★ ★ **HOLIDAY INN.** 7550 E State St (61125), I-90 exit 63. 815/398-2200; FAX 815/229-3122. 202 rms, 7 story. S $75; D $82; each addl $7; suites $145; under 18 free; higher rates New Years Eve. Crib free. TV; cable (premium). Indoor pool; whirlpool. Restaurant 7 am-9 pm. Rm serv. Bar 11-2 am. Ck-out noon. Meeting rms. Business servs avail. In-rm modem link. Gift shop. Barber, beauty shop. Free airport transportation.

Exercise equipt; treadmill, stair machine. Game rm. Cr cds: A, C, D, DS, JCB, MC, V.

★ ★ **RESIDENCE INN BY MARRIOTT.** *7542 Colosseum Dr (61107), I-90 & US 20 Bus. 815/227-0013; FAX 815/227-0013, ext. 405.* 94 kit. units, 3 story. S, D $99-$144. Crib free. Pet accepted; $100 & $5/day. TV; cable (premium). Indoor pool; whirlpool. Complimentary coffee in rms. Complimentary continental bkfst. Restaurant nearby. Ck-out noon. Coin lndry. Meeting rm. Business servs avail. In-rm modem link. Exercise equipt; weight machine, stair machine. Cr cds: A, C, D, DS, JCB, MC, V.

Restaurants

★ **CAFE PATOU.** *3929 Broadway (61108), in Tiffany Court Mall. 815/227-4100.* Hrs: 11:30 am-2 pm, 5:30-10 pm; Mon from 5:30 pm. Closed Sun; some major hols. Res accepted. Continental menu. Bar. A la carte entrees: lunch $6.50-$12.50, dinner $9-$23. Child's meals. Specialties: flat breads, roasted lobster, Alaskan caribou tenderloin. Jazz quartet Thurs, Fri. Casual French country atmosphere. Own baking. Cr cds: A, C, D, DS, MC, V.

☐ D

★ ★ **GIOVANNI'S.** *610 N Bell School Rd (61107), W of jct I-90 & US 20 Business. 815/398-6411.* Hrs: 11:30 am-2 pm, 5:30-10 pm; Sat from 5:30 pm. Closed Sun; major hols. Res accepted. Bar. Extensive cognac list. A la carte entrees: lunch $5.95-$9.50, dinner $12.95-$21.95. Child's meals. Specializes in seafood, steak, veal. Own baking. Cr cds: A, C, D, DS, MC, V.

☐ D

🖝★ ★ **GREAT WALL CHINESE RESTAURANT.** *4228 E State. 815/226-0982.* Hrs: 11:30 am-2 pm, 4:30-10 pm; Fri, Sat to 11 pm; Sun to 9 pm; Sun brunch 11:30 am-2:30 pm. Closed major hols. Res accepted. Mandarin, Szechwan menu. Bar. A la carte entrees: lunch $3.95-$5.25, dinner $5.95-$12. Complete meals: dinner $9.50-$11.50. Sun brunch buffet $7.50. Specialties: moo shu pork, Great Wall steak, black bean chicken. Mandarin decor. Cr cds: A, MC, V.

★ **MICHAELS AT PERRYVILLE.** *601 N Perryville Rd (61107). 815/226-8286.* Hrs: 11:30 am-2 pm, 5-10 pm; Sat & Sun from 5 pm. Closed most major hols. Res accepted, required wknds. Bar. Semi-a la carte: lunch $5-$12, dinner $11-$20. Child's meals. Specializes in prime rib, steak, seafood. Contemporary decor. Wine selection display. Cr cds: A, C, D, DS, MC, V.

☐ D

Rock Island (C-2)

(See also Moline)

Settled 1828 **Pop** 40,552 **Elev** 560 ft **Area code** 309 **Zip** 61201 **E-mail** cvb@quadcities.com **Web** quadcities.com/cvb

Information Quad Cities Convention & Visitors Bureau, 2021 River Dr, Moline, 61265; 309/788-7800 or 800/747-7800.

One of the cities of the Quad-City metropolitan area (along with Moline, IL, and Bettendorf and Davenport, IA), Rock Island is rich in Native American, steamboat and Civil War lore. Here Lincoln was sworn into the Illinois Militia under Zachary Taylor, and here Black Hawk and his warriors were defeated. The great steamboat era brought nearly 2,000 ships annually to Rock Island, and the first railway bridge across the Mississippi was opened here in 1855. One of the most important and notorious Union military prisons of the Civil War was on the 1,000-acre island in the river. Rock Island Arsenal, one of the largest manufacturing arsenals in the world, was established in 1862. Augustana College (1860), which has an art gallery, geology museum and planetarium, is located here.

What to See and Do

Black Hawk State Historic Site. These wooded, steeply rolling hills provided the site on which the westernmost battle of the Revolutionary War was fought. The area was occupied for nearly a century by the capital villages of the Sauk and Fox nations. The Watch Tower, on a promontory 150 ft above the Rock River, provides a view of the river valley and surrounding countryside. Hauberg Indian Museum contains an outstanding collection of Native American artifacts, paintings and relics; dioramas of Sauk and Fox daily life, prehistoric display; also changing displays. Fishing. Hiking. Picnicking. (Daily) On S edge of town. Phone 309/788-0177 (park) or 309/788-9536 (museum). **Donation.**

Rock Island Arsenal and US Army Armament, Munitions and Chemical Command. On Arsenal Island, between Rock Island, IL, and Davenport, IA, are the Rock Island Arsenal Museum, which contains an extensive firearms collection and Court of Patriots memorial (daily; closed hols; free; phone 309/782-5021); a replica of Ft Armstrong blockhouse; Colonel Davenport house (Sat-Sun, fee; phone 309/786-7336); Confederate soldiers cemetery; the Rock Island National Cemetery, at the E end of the island, which has approximately 13,000 interments. Site of the first railroad bridge to span the Mississippi, lock and dam with visitor center (daily; phone 309/794-5338). Bicycle trail (7 mi) around island. Phone 309/782-6001.

Seasonal Event

Genesius Guild. Lincoln Park, 40th St & 11th Ave. Free open-air presentations of opera, Shakespeare and Greek classics. Sat & Sun evenings. Phone 309/788-7113. Mid-June-mid-Aug.

Inn

★ ★ **VICTORIAN INN.** *702 20th St. 309/788-7068; res: 800/728-7068.* 5 rms, 4 with shower only, 3 story. S, D $65-$85. Crib free. TV; cable (premium), VCR avail. Complimentary full bkfst. Restaurant nearby. Ck-out 11 am, ck-in 3 pm. Victorian house, built in 1876; furnished with antiques. Cr cds: A, MC, V.

Rosemont

(see Chicago O'Hare Airport Area)

St Charles (D-1 see Chicago map)

(See also Aurora, Elgin, Geneva)

Settled 1838 **Pop** 22,501 **Elev** 697 ft **Area code** 630 **E-mail** stc-cvb@elnet.com

Information Greater St Charles Convention & Visitors Bureau, 311 N 2nd St, PO Box 11, 60174; 630/377-6161 or 800/777-4373.

Located on the Fox River just one hour from Chicago, St Charles is a residential and light-industry town. The downtown areas on both sides of the river contain antique and specialty shops housed in historic buildings.

What to See and Do

Kane County Flea Market. One of the nation's largest flea and antique markets. (First Sun & preceding Sat of month) Kane County Fairgrounds, on Randall Rd S of IL 64. ¢¢

Outlet mall. The Piano Factory. Housed in a former piano factory built in 1901, this mall contains over two dozen outlet stores, antique stores and a restaurant. (Daily) 410 S 1st St. Phone 630/584-2099.

Pottawatomie Park. One mi of frontage on the Fox River with swimming pools (1st wkend June-Labor Day; fee), 9-hole golf (Mar-Oct; fee), tennis,

18-hole miniature golf (fee); playgrounds, ball fields. Also access to the Fox River Trail, used for biking, jogging and cross-country skiing. Outdoor concerts (summer). Picnic area, snack bars. (Daily) On 2nd Ave, ½ mi N of Main St (IL 64). Phone 630/584-1055. ¢¢ Also here are

Saint Charles Belle II and *Fox River Queen.* These 132-passenger paddle-wheel boats offer afternoon sightseeing trips (45 min) along the Fox River. Boats depart from the park and follow the river trail of the Pottawatomie. (June-Aug, daily; May & Sept-mid-Oct, Sat & Sun) For schedule and fees phone 630/584-2334.

Annual Events

Pride of the Fox RiverFest. Four-day event features river events, food, entertainment, craft show. 2nd wkend June.

Scarecrow Festival. Downtown, Lincoln Park. Display of up to 100 scarecrows; entertainment, food, crafts. 2nd full wkend Oct.

Motels

★ ★ **BEST WESTERN INN.** *1635 E Main St (IL 64, North Ave) (60174).* 630/584-4550; FAX 630/584-5221. 54 rms, 2 story. June-Sept: S $55-$65; D $59-$70; each addl $5; under 16 free; lower rates rest of yr. Crib free. TV; cable. Heated pool; whirlpool. Complimentary continental bkfst. Restaurant adj 5:30 am-11 pm. Ck-out noon. Coin lndry. Business servs avail. Sundries. Exercise equipt; weight machine, stair machine. Cr cds: A, C, D, DS, MC, V.

D ⊠ ✗ ⊠ ⊠ SC

★ **DAYS INN.** *100 S Tyler Rd (60174).* 630/513-6500; FAX 630/513-6501. 80 rms, 3 story. S $75-$90; D $77-$90; each addl $5; suites $85-$125; under 12 free. TV; cable (premium). Pool. Complimentary continental bkfst. Restaurant nearby. Ck-out 11 am. Coin lndry. Meeting rm. Business servs avail. Some refrigerators. Cr cds: A, C, D, DS, MC, V.

D ⊠ ⊠ ⊠ SC

✔ ★ **DU WAYNE.** *(27 W 641 North Ave, W Chicago 60185) 8 mi E on IL 64; E of IL 59.* 630/231-1040. 35 rms, 1-2 story. S, D $40-$51; each addl $3. TV. Heated pool. Playground. Restaurant adj 6:30 am-8 pm. Ck-out 11 am. Coin lndry. Business servs avail. Sundries. Picnic tables. Cr cds: A, C, D, MC, V.

⊠ ⊠

Restaurants

 ✔ ★ **FILLING STATION ANTIQUE EATERY.** *3 N Main St.* 630/584-4414. Hrs: 11 am-9 pm; Fri, Sat to 10 pm; Sun to 8 pm. Closed Jan 1, Easter, Memorial Day, Thanksgiving. Amer menu. Bar. Semi-a la carte: lunch $4.50-$6.95, dinner $6.95-$10.95. Child's meals. Specialties: Tex-Mex barbecued ribs, fajitas, oversized sandwiches. Entertainment Wed-Sat. Outdoor dining. Casual dining in renovated 1930s filling station; antiques. Cr cds: C, D, MC, V.

D

★ ★ **OLD CHURCH INN.** *18 N 4th St.* 630/584-7341. Hrs: 11 am-3 pm, 5:30-9 pm; Fri, Sat to 10 pm; Sun brunch 10:30 am-2:30 pm. Closed major hols. Res accepted. Continental menu. Bar. Semi-a la carte: lunch $5.25-$9.95, dinner $10.95-$18.95. Sun brunch $15.95. Child's meals. Specialties: beef Wellington, wall-eyed pike, rack of lamb. Entertainment wkends. Restored church (1851); original restored pews, stained-glass windows. Cr cds: A, C, D, DS, MC, V.

D SC

✔ ★ **SZECHWAN.** *117 W Main St (60174).* 630/513-1889. Hrs: 11:30 am-9:30 pm; Fri, Sat to 10:30 pm. Closed Thanksgiving, Dec 25. Res accepted. Chinese menu. Bar. Semi-a la carte: lunch $5.75, dinner $7.25-$16.95. Specializes in Szechwan cuisine. Oriental decor. Cr cds: A, C, D, DS, MC, V.

⊡

Salem (G-4)

(For accommodations see Centralia, Mt Vernon)

Pop 7,470 **Elev** 544 ft **Area code** 618 **Zip** 62881
Information Greater Salem Chamber of Commerce, 615 W Main St; 618/548-3010.

Salem is an important city in the oil-producing area of south-central Illinois. It is the birthplace of William Jennings Bryan, whose statue by Gutzon Borglum stands in Bryan Memorial Park.

What to See and Do

Halfway Tavern. Tavern received name for being halfway between St Louis, MO, and Vincennes, IN. Present structure is reconstructed; the original was built in 1818 and served as a stagecoach stop until 1861. Located on the trail used by George Rogers Clark when he crossed Illinois in 1799, the tavern was frequently used by Abraham Lincoln as a stopover. Interior not open to public. 7 mi E on US 50.

Ingram's Log Cabin Village. On 74 acres with 17 authentic log buildings dating from 1818-1860; 13 authentically furnished and open to the public. Picnicking. (Mid-Apr-mid-Nov, daily) 12 mi N via IL 37 in Kinmundy. Phone 618/547-7123 or 618/547-3241. ¢

One-Room Schoolhouse. Restored schoolhouse contains artifacts, old photos; traces the history of every one-room school district in Marion County. (Apr-Aug, Sat, limited hrs; other times by appt) N on IL 37, located on campus of Salem Community High School. Phone 618/548-2499 or 618/532-9026. **Free.**

Stephen A. Forbes State Park. Approx 3,100 acres. Swimming, waterskiing; fishing, hunting; boating (ramp, rentals, motors). Hiking, bridle trails. Picnicking, concession. Camping, horse campground. Standard fees. 8 mi E on US 50, then 7 mi N on Omega Rd, in Kinmundy. Phone 618/547-3381.

William Jennings Bryan Birthplace/Museum (1852). Restored house contains personal artifacts and memorabilia of the famous orator, who was born here in 1860. (Daily exc Thurs, afternoons; closed hols) 408 S Broadway. Phone 618/548-7791. **Free.**

Annual Event

Marion County Fair. Fairgrounds. Early July-Aug.

Schaumburg (C-2 see Chicago map)

(See also Arlington Heights, Chicago O'Hare Airport Area, Itasca)

Pop 68,586 **Elev** 799 ft **Area code** 847
Information Greater Woodfield Convention & Visitors Bureau, 1375 E Woodfield Rd, Suite 100, 60173; 847/605-1010 or 800/847-4849.

Motels

★ ★ **HAMPTON INN.** *1300 E Higgins Rd (60173).* 847/619-1000; FAX 847/619-1019. 127 rms, 4 story. S, D $85-$95; under 18 free; wkend rates. Crib free. TV; cable (premium). Complimentary continental bkfst. Restaurant nearby. Ck-out noon. Meeting rms. Business servs avail. Exercise equipt; treadmill, stair machine. Cr cds: A, C, D, DS, MC, V.

D ✗ ⊠ ⊠ SC

★ ★ **HOMEWOOD SUITES.** *815 E American Lane (60173).* 847/605-0400; FAX 847/619-0990. 108 kit. suites, 3 story. S, D $99-$139; extended stay rates. Crib free. Pet accepted, some restrictions; $75 refundable. TV; cable (premium), VCR (movies $4). Pool; whirlpool. Complimentary continental bkfst. Complimentary coffee in rms. Restaurant nearby. Ck-out noon. Coin lndry. Meeting rms. Business center. In-rm modem link. Valet serv. Gift shop. Exercise equipt; weight machine, stair machine. Health club privileges. Microwaves. Picnic tables, grills. Cr cds: A, C, D, DS, MC, V.

D ✦ ≋ 🏃 ⊠ 🔥 SC ⛷

★ ★ **LA QUINTA MOTOR INN.** *1730 E Higgins Rd (IL 72) (60173), I-290 exit Higgins Rd, adj to Woodfield Mall.* 847/517-8484; FAX 847/517-4477. 127 rms, 3 story. S $74-$81; D $81-$88; under 18 free; wkend rates. Crib free. Pet accepted. TV; cable (premium). Heated pool. Complimentary continental bkfst. Restaurant adj open 24 hrs. Ck-out noon. Meeting rms. Business servs avail. In-rm modem link. Valet serv. Health club privileges. Some refrigerators; microwaves avail. Cr cds: A, C, D, DS, MC, V.

D ✦ ≋ ⊠ 🔥 SC

✔★ **RED ROOF INN.** *(2500 Hassell Rd, Hoffman Estates 60195) S of I-90 Barrington Rd exit.* 847/885-7877; FAX 847/885-8616. 118 rms, 3 story. S $46-$64; D $50-$70; each addl $7. Crib avail. Pet accepted. TV; cable (premium). Complimentary coffee in lobby. Restaurant opp 6 am-11 pm. Ck-out noon. Meeting rm. Business servs avail. In-rm modem link. Cr cds: A, C, D, DS, MC, V.

D ✦ ⊠ 🔥

Motor Hotels

★ ★ **EMBASSY SUITES.** *1939 N Meacham Rd (60173).* 847/397-1313; FAX 847/397-9007. 209 suites, 7 story. S $169; D $189; each addl $15; under 18 free; wkend packages. Crib free. TV; cable (premium), VCR avail. Indoor pool; whirlpool. Complimentary full bkfst. Complimentary coffee in rms. Restaurant 11 am-10 pm. Rm serv. Bar 11:30 am-midnight. Ck-out noon. Coin lndry. Meeting rms. Business servs avail. In-rm modem link. Gift shop. Airport transportation. Exercise equipt; treadmill, stair machine, saunas. Health club privileges. Refrigerators, microwaves. Cr cds: A, C, D, DS, JCB, MC, V.

D ≋ 🏃 ⊠ 🔥 SC

★ ★ **HOLIDAY INN.** *1550 N Roselle Rd (60195).* 847/310-0500; FAX 847/312-0579. 142 rms, 6 story. S, D $99-$119; suites $145; wkend rates. Crib $10. TV; cable (premium). Complimentary coffee in lobby. Restaurant 6:30-1 am. Rm serv. Ck-out noon. Meeting rms. Business servs avail. In-rm modem link. Health club privileges. Heated pool; whirlpool. Refrigerators avail. Cr cds: A, C, D, DS, JCB, MC, V.

D ≋ ⊠ 🔥 SC

Hotels

★ ★ ★ **HYATT REGENCY WOODFIELD.** *1800 E Golf Rd (IL 58) (60173), opp Woodfield Mall.* 847/605-1234; FAX 847/605-0328. 469 rms, 5 story. S $180; D $200; each addl $25; suites $250-$515; under 18 free; wkend rates. Crib free. TV; cable (premium), VCR avail. 2 pools, 1 indoor; wading pool, whirlpool. Restaurants 6:30 am-11 pm. Bar 11:30-2 am. Ck-out noon. Convention facilities. Business servs avail. In-rm modem link. Concierge. Gift shop. Barber. Exercise equipt; bicycles, treadmill, sauna. Refrigerators avail. Some private patios, balconies. Cr cds: A, C, D, DS, ER, JCB, MC, V.

D ≋ 🏃 ⊠ 🔥 SC

★ ★ ★ **MARRIOTT.** *50 N Martingale Rd (60173).* 847/240-0100; FAX 847/240-2388. 394 rms, 14 story. S $149-$169; D $159-$179; suites $250; family, wkend rates. Crib free. Pet accepted, some restrictions. TV; cable (premium). Indoor/outdoor pool; whirlpool, poolside serv. Complimentary coffee in rms. Restaurant 6:30 am-11 pm. Bar 11-2 am. Ck-out 1 pm. Coin lndry. Convention facilities. Business center. In-rm modem link. Gift shop. Exercise equipt; weights, bicycles, sauna. Some private patios. Luxury level. Cr cds: A, C, D, DS, ER, JCB, MC, V.

D ✦ ≋ 🏃 ⊠ 🔥 SC ⛷

★ ★ **WYNDHAM GARDEN.** *800 National Pkwy (60173), 1¾ mi W of IL 53 exit Higgins Rd W.* 847/605-9222; FAX 847/605-9240. 188 rms,

6 story. S, D $190-$220; under 18 free; wkend rates. Crib free. TV; cable (premium). Indoor pool; whirlpool. Complimentary continental bkfst. Complimentary coffee in rms. Restaurant 6:30 am-1 pm. Bar to 11 pm. Ck-out noon. Meeting rms. Business servs avail. In-rm modem link. Exercise equipt; bicycles, stair machine, sauna. Health club privileges. Cr cds: A, C, D, DS, ER, JCB, MC, V.

D ≋ 🏃 ⊠ 🔥 SC

Restaurants

✔★ ★ **COUNTRY BISTRO.** *(700 W Northwest Hwy, Barrington 60010) W on I-90 to IL 59N, N at Barrington Rd exit, NW on Northwest Hwy, at The Foundry.* 847/842-1300. Hrs: 11:30 am-2 pm, 5-8:30 pm; Fri, Sat 5-9:30 pm; Sun from 5 pm. Res accepted; required Fri, Sat dinner. French menu. Bar. Semi-a la carte: lunch $6-$12, dinner $10-$16. Child's meals. Specializes in pork tenderloin, escargot, salmon. Country French decor. Totally nonsmoking. Cr cds: A, C, D, MC, V.

D

★ ★ **MILLROSE.** *(45 S Barrington Rd, South Barrington 60010) 5 mi W on I-90, exit Barrington Rd.* 847/382-7673. Hrs: 11-2 am; Sat from 10 am; Sun 10 am-10 pm; Sun brunch to 1:30 pm. Res accepted. Bar. Semi-a la carte: lunch $5.95-$9.95, dinner $9.95-$25.95. Sun brunch $10.95. Child's meals. Specializes in baby back ribs, steak, chops. Outdoor dining. Tri-level dining; brewery, gift shop; on 14 acres. Cr cds: A, C, D, DS, MC, V.

D ⊰

✔★ **RON SANTO'S AMERICAN ROTISSERIE.** *1925 N Meacham Rd (60173).* 847/397-2676. Hrs: 11:30 am-10 pm; Fri, Sat to 11 pm; Sun to 9 pm. Closed July 4, Thanksgiving, Dec 24, 25. Bar. Semi-a la carte: lunch $5.95-$8.95, dinner $6.95-$16.95. Child's meals. Specializes in wood-roasted rotisserie chicken, ribs, pasta. Sports bar atmosphere, baseball memorabilia. Cr cds: A, D, DS, MC, V.

D ⊰

Schiller Park

(see Chicago O'Hare Airport Area)

Skokie (C-4 see Chicago map)

(See also Evanston, Wilmette)

Pop 59,432 **Elev** 623 ft **Area code** 847 **E-mail** skokiechamber @internetmci.com

Information Chamber of Commerce, 8322 Lincoln Ave, PO Box 53; 847/673-0240.

Originally called Niles Center, it was not until 1940 that the village changed its name to Skokie. In its early history, the farmers of the area produced food for the growing city of Chicago; market trails carved by farm wagons later became paved roads, which accounts for the odd curves of Lincoln Avenue. Today, Skokie is the location of many major corporate headquarters.

What to See and Do

North Shore Center for the Performing Arts. Houses two individual theaters, Centre East and Northlight Theatre, that offer many types of peformances. 9501 Skokie Blvd. For ticket information phone 847/679-9501.

Motel

★ ★ **HOWARD JOHNSON.** *9333 Skokie Blvd (60077). 847/679-4200; FAX 847/679-4218.* 132 rms, 2-5 story. S $92-$102; D $107-$116; each addl $10; under 18 free. Crib free. Pet accepted. TV; cable (premium), VCR avail. Indoor pool; whirlpool. Complimentary bkfst buffet. Restaurant adj 11:30 am-11 pm. Bar 11:30 am-midnight. Ck-out 1 pm. Meeting rms. Businss servs avail. In-rm modem link. Valet serv. Exercise equipt; bicycles, stair machine, sauna. Microwave avail. Private patios, balconies. Cr cds: A, C, D, DS, JCB, MC, V.

D ⟨⟩ ≋ ⨉ ⟩⟨ ⟩ SC

Motor Hotel

★ ★ **HOLIDAY INN NORTHSHORE.** *5300 W Touhy Ave (60077). 847/679-8900; FAX 847/679-7447.* 244 rms, 2-4 story. S, D $113-$130; each addl $10; under 19 free; higher rates: Dec 31, Northwestern Univ graduation. Crib free. Pet accepted. TV; cable (premium). Indoor pool; whirlpool. Restaurant 6:30 am-2 pm, 5-10 pm; Fri, Sat to 11 pm. Rm serv. Bar 11-1 am. Ck-out noon. Coin lndry. Meeting rms. In-rm modem link. Valet serv. Gift shop. Exercise equipt; bicycle, treadmill, sauna. Game rm. Microwaves avail. Cr cds: A, C, D, DS, JCB, MC, V.

D ⟨⟩ ≋ ⨉ ⟩⟨ ⟩ SC

Hotel

★ ★ **DOUBLETREE.** *9599 Skokie Blvd (60077), at Golf Rd (IL 58). 847/679-7000; FAX 847/674-5204.* 366 rms, 11 story. S, D $124-$185; each addl $15; suites $225-$400; under 17 free; wkend rates. Crib free. Pet accepted, some restrictions; $250 deposit. TV; cable (premium). Indoor/outdoor pool; poolside serv. Restaurant 6 am-11 pm. Rm serv 24 hrs. Bar 4 pm-1 am. Ck-out noon. Convention facilities. Business center. In-rm modem link. Concierge. Gift shop. Airport transportation. Exercise equipt; weight machine, bicycles. Health club privileges. Luxury level. Cr cds: A, C, D, DS, ER, MC, V.

D ⟨⟩ ≋ ⨉ ⟩⟨ ⟩ SC ⟨⟩

Restaurants

★ ★ **DON'S FISHMARKET & TAVERN.** *9335 Skokie Blvd (60077). 847/677-3424.* Hrs: 11:30 am-2:30 pm, 5-10 pm; Fri, Sat to 11 pm; Sun 4-9 pm. Early bird dinner 5-6 pm. Closed Jan 1, Thanksgiving, Dec 25. Res accepted. Bar. Semi-a la carte: lunch $4.75-$9.95, dinner $12.95-$23.95. Specializes in fresh seafood, chicken, steak. Nautical decor. Cr cds: A, C, D, DS, MC, V.

D

★ ★ **MYRON & PHIL'S.** *(3900 W Devon Ave, Lincolnwood 60659) N on I-94, exit Peterson Ave, N on Cicero to Devon, 15 blks E. 847/677-6663.* Hrs: 11:30 am-11 pm; Sat 5 pm-midnight; Sun 3:30-10 pm. Closed Thanksgiving, Dec 25. Res accepted. Bar. Semi-a la carte: lunch $7.95-$9.95, dinner $13.95-$28.95. Specializes in seafood, steak, ribs. Piano bar Fri, Sat. Valet parking. Family-owned. Cr cds: A, C, D, DS, MC, V.

D ⟋

Springfield (E-3)

(See also Jacksonville, Lincoln, Petersburg)

Settled 1819 **Pop** 105,227 **Elev** 600 ft **Area code** 217 **E-mail** mailbox@springfield.il.us **Web** springfield.il.us/visit

Information Convention & Visitors Bureau, 109 N 7th, 62701; 217/789-2360 or 800/545-7300.

Near the geographical center of the state, Springfield, the capital of Illinois, is surrounded by rich farmland underlaid with veins of coal, which were, at one time, intensively mined. The city has the grace of a Southern capital, the economic stability of an educational, professional and service-oriented center and the fame of having been Abraham Lincoln's home for a quarter of a century.

Illinois had already become a state when Elisha Kelly came to the area from North Carolina. Impressed by fertile land and plentiful game, he later returned and settled with his father and four brothers. A small community formed around the Kelly cabin. When Sangamon County was created in 1821, Springfield was selected as the seat and named for a nearby spring located on Kelly land. On February 25, 1837, as a result of a campaign led by Lincoln, Springfield, then a town of 1,500, was proclaimed the state capital. In April of that year, Lincoln moved to Springfield from New Salem. He practiced law, married and raised his family in the new capital. On February 11, 1861, Lincoln made his famous farewell address when he left to become president. In May of 1865, Lincoln's body was returned to Springfield to be buried in the city's Oak Ridge Cemetery.

What to See and Do

Dana-Thomas House State Historic Site (1902-1904). Designed by Frank Lloyd Wright for Springfield socialite Susan Lawrence Dana, this 15-rm house is the best-preserved and most complete of the architect's Prairie period. The fully restored, highly unified interior boasts terra-cotta sculptures, more than 100 pieces of original furniture, 250 art-glass windows and 200 art-glass light fixtures and light panels. This house was one of the largest and most elaborate of Wright's career. (Wed-Sun) 301 E Lawrence Ave, at 4th, 2 blks S of Governor's Mansion. For tour schedule phone 217/782-6776. **Donation.**

Daughters of Union Veterans National Headquarters. Civil War relics, documents. (Mon-Fri; also by appt) 503 S Walnut St. Phone 217/544-0616. **Free.**

Edwards Place (1833). Built by Benjamin Edwards (brother of Ninian Edwards, early Illinois governor married to Mary Todd Lincoln's older sister), this Italianate mansion was Springfield's social and political center in yrs before Civil War; Lincoln addressed public from front gallery. Well-preserved house is furnished with original pieces and period antiques. (Wed-Sat, limited hrs) 700 N 4th St. Phone 217/523-2631.   **Free.**   Adj is

Springfield Art Association. Working studios, library, exhibition galleries. (Mon-Fri) Phone 217/523-2631.   **Free.**

Executive Mansion. Red-brick Italianate mansion has been residence of Illinois governors since 1855; Georgian detailing dates from 1970s remodeling. Half-hr tours through 14 rms. (Tues, Thurs & Sat; closed hols) On Jackson St between 4th & 5th Sts. Phone 217/782-6450.   **Free.**

Henson Robinson Zoo. A 14-acre zoo with exotic and domestic animals, reptile house, nocturnal animal house, monkey island; penguin exhibit; contact area; picnic area. (Mid-Apr-Oct, daily) 1100 E Lake Dr, 4 mi SE on Lake Springfield. Phone 217/753-6217.   ¢

Lincoln Memorial Garden & Nature Center. An 80-acre garden of trees, shrubs and flowers native to Illinois designed in naturalistic style by landscape architect Jens Jensen. Extensive display of spring wildflowers late Apr-early May; fall foliage mid-Oct. Nature trails (5 mi). Cross-country skiing in winter. Nature Center contains exhibits and shop (daily exc Mon; closed Dec 24-Jan 1). Garden (daily). (See ANNUAL EVENTS) 2301 E Lake Dr, 8 mi S, on E bank of Lake Springfield. Phone 217/529-1111.   **Free.**

⭐ **Lincoln shrines.**

Old State Capitol State Historic Site. Restored Greek-revival sandstone structure was first state house in Springfield (state's fifth). Although first occupied in 1839, it was not fully completed until 1853; it became the Sangamon County courthouse after being vacated by the state in 1876. Called the most historic structure west of the Alleghenies, it was here that Lincoln made his famous "House Divided" speech. Restored between 1966 and 1969, interior features intersecting double staircases; reconstructed house, senate and supreme court chambers; state offices. Living history program (Fri & Sat; no programs May). (Daily; closed most major hols) Downtown Mall, between Adams, Washington, 5th & 6th Sts. Phone 217/785-7960. **Donation.**

Lincoln-Herndon Law Office Building. Restored building from which Lincoln practiced law. (Daily; closed most major hols) 6th & Adams Sts, opp Old State Capitol. Phone 217/785-7289. **Donation.**

Lincoln Home National Historic Site. Site includes four city blks restored to 1860 appearance, the last year of the Lincoln's 17-yr residency. Federal-style Lincoln house was originally a single-story cottage, which Mary Todd Lincoln had remodeled to her own design. Based upon magazine drawings made while Lincoln was president-elect, the interior has been refurbished/restored with Lincoln family furnishings, period artifacts, reproduced wallpapers and window hangings. Visitor center includes exhibits, film, bookstore. Tickets required to tour house (obtain at visitor center; free). (Daily; closed Jan 1, Thanksgiving, Dec 25) Parking (fee). Visitor center at 426 S 7th St, approx 5 blks S & E of Old State Capitol. Phone 217/492-4150. **Free.**

Lincoln Depot. Restored depot where Lincoln delivered his farewell address before departing for Washington on Feb 11, 1861. Exhibits; slide show. (Apr-Aug, daily) Monroe St between 9th & 10th Sts. Phone 217/544-8695 or 217/788-1356. **Free.**

Lincoln Tomb State Historic Site. Under 117-ft granite obelisk, a belvedere, accessible via exterior staircases, offers views of 10-ft statue of Lincoln and 4 heroic groupings representing Civil War armed forces. Tomb interior follows circular route lined with statues commemorating periods of Lincoln's life. In center of domed burial chamber is monumental sarcophagus. However, Lincoln is actually buried 10 ft below (grave robbers made attempts upon the remains). Mary Todd Lincoln and three of four Lincoln sons are interred within the wall opposite. Self-guided tours; interpretive program. (Daily; closed most major hols) (See SEASONAL EVENTS) Oak Ridge Cemetery. Approx 16 blks N of Old State Capitol, via 2nd St to N Grand, then W to Monument Ave. Phone 217/782-2717. **Free.**

Oliver P. Parks Telephone Museum. Contains more than 100 antique telephones dating from 1882; film, exhibits and displays relating to the telephone. (Mon-Fri) 529 S 7th St. **Free.**

Springfield Children's Museum. Exhibits and programs featuring art, architecture, health, nature and science. Children can discover weather phenomena, dig for a fossil or put on a puppet show. (Daily exc Tues; closed major hols) 619 E Washington St. Phone 217/789-0679. ¢¢

State Capitol. One of the tallest buildings in central Illinois, the capitol dome, 405 ft high, can be seen for miles across the prairie. Built between 1868 and 1888, the state house is a Victorian combination of Renaissance revival and Second Empire. Marble, granite, bronze, black walnut, encaustic tiles, stained and etched glass and stencil work were employed throughout the structure; heroically scaled murals depict state history. Free guide service, 1st flr information desk (every 30 min, daily; closed Jan 1, Thanksgiving, Dec 25). 2nd St & Capitol Ave. Phone 217/782-2099. **Free.**

Capitol Complex Visitors Center. Displays, brochures, information. Picnic shelters. (Daily; closed Jan 1, Thanksgiving, Dec 25) Capitol Ave, between Edwards & Monroe Sts. Phone 217/524-6620.

Illinois State Museum. Contains natural history, geology, anthropology and art exhibits with life-size dioramas of wildlife and early inhabitants of Illinois; displays depict the state's botanical, zoological, ecological and Native American heritage; art galleries of photography, fine and decorative arts with works by 19th- and 20th-century Illinois artists. Special hands-on discovery rm for children. Audio tours (fee); special programs, films, lectures, tours. (Mon-Sat, also Sun afternoons; closed some major hols) Spring & Edwards Sts. Phone 217/782-7386. **Free.**

Thomas Rees Memorial Carillon. A 132-ft tower with 3 observation decks and 66-bell carillon. Bell museum. Concerts (summer, daily exc Mon; rest of yr, wkends only). 10-min film. (See ANNUAL EVENTS) Washington Park, Fayette Ave & Chatham Rd. Phone 217/753-6219. ¢

Annual Events

Maple Syrup Time. Lincoln Memorial Garden & Nature Center. Watch maple syrup being made, from tapping trees to boiling the sap. Sat & Sun afternoons, mid-Feb-early Mar.

International Carillon Festival. Thomas Rees Memorial Carillon, Washington Park. Evening concerts by visiting international carillonneurs (exc Wed). Entertainment. Phone 217/544-1751. Mid-June.

Summer Festival. New Salem Village. Phone 217/632-4000. Early July.

Springfield Air Rendezvous. Capital Airport. Phone 217/789-4400. Mid-July.

Illinois State Fair. For information contact PO Box 19427, 62794; 217/782-6661. Aug 8-17.

Ethnic Festival. State Fairgrounds. Ethnic foods, cultural exhibits; entertainment. Labor Day wkend.

LPGA State Farm Rail Classic. Rail Golf Club. Women's professional 54-hole golf tournament. Phone 217/528-5742. Labor Day wkend.

Seasonal Events

Municipal Band Concerts. Douglas Park. Fifty-piece concert band performs a wide variety of music. Tues & Thurs evenings. June & July.

114th Infantry Retreat Ceremony. Lincoln Tomb State Historic Site. Illinois Volunteer Infantry, in authentic period uniforms, demonstrates drill movements and musket firings as part of a retreat ceremony. Tues, June-Aug.

Springfield Muni Opera. 815 E Lake Dr. Broadway musicals presented in outdoor theater. Phone 217/793-6656. June-Aug.

Motels

(Rates are generally higher during state fair)

★ ★ **BEST INNS OF AMERICA.** 500 N 1st St (62702), at Carpenter Ave. 217/522-1100; FAX 217/753-8589; res: 800/237-8466. 91 rms, 2 story. S $48-$54; D $53-$61; each addl $7; under 18 free. Crib free. Pet accepted, some restrictions. TV; cable (premium), VCR avail. Pool. Complimentary continental bkfst. Restaurant adj 7 am-10 pm. Ck-out 1 pm. Coin lndry. In-rm modem link. Cr cds: A, C, D, DS, MC, V.

🆔 🐾 ≋ 🛏 🔥 SC

★ ★ **COMFORT INN.** 3442 Freedom Dr (62704), IL 36 exit 93. 217/787-2250. 67 rms, 2 story. S, D $52.95-$62.95; each addl $5; under 18 free; wkend rates. Crib free. Pet accepted. TV; cable (premium). Indoor pool; whirlpool. Complimentary continental bkfst. Restaurant adj 6 am-midnight. Ck-out 11 am. Meeting rm. In-rm modem link. Some refrigerators, microwaves. Cr cds: A, C, D, DS, MC, V.

🆔 🐾 ≋ 🛏 🔥 SC

★ ★ **COURTYARD BY MARRIOTT.** 3462 Freedom Dr (62704). 217/793-5300. 78 rms, 3 story. S, D $65-$80; suites $100-$120; under 16 free; wkly, wkend, hol rates. Crib free. TV; cable (premium). Indoor pool; whirlpool. Complimentary coffee in rms. Restaurant adj 6:30 am-9:30 pm. Bar 5-10 pm. Ck-out noon. Coin lndry. Meeting rms. Business servs avail. In-rm modem link. Sundries. Valet serv. Exercise equipt; weight machines, bicycles. Refrigerator in suites; microwaves avail. Cr cds: A, C, D, DS, MC, V.

🆔 ≋ 🏋 🛏 🔥 SC

✔★ **DAYS INN.** 3000 Stevenson Dr (62703). 217/529-0171; FAX 217/529-9431; res: 800/329-7466. 155 rms, 2 story. S $49-$56; D $56-$63; each addl $5; under 12 free; higher rates special events. Crib free. Pet accepted. TV; cable (premium). Pool. Complimentary continental bkfst. Ck-out noon. Meeting rms. Business servs avail. Free airport transportation. Microwaves avail. Picnic tables. Cr cds: A, C, D, DS, JCB, MC, V.

D ⊡ ⊡ ⊡ ⊡ SC

★ ★ **HAMPTON INN.** 3185 S Dirksen Pkwy (62703). 217/529-1100; FAX 217/529-1105. 123 rms, 4 story. S $55-$62; D $60-$67; suite $90; under 18 free. Crib free. Pet accepted, some restrictions. TV; cable (premium). Indoor pool; whirlpool. Complimentary continental bkfst. Restaurants nearby. Ck-out noon. Meeting rms. Business servs avail. Valet serv, wkdays. Exercise equipt; weight machine, bicycle. Refrigerator in suite. Cr cds: A, C, D, DS, MC, V.

D ⊡ ⊡ ⊡ ⊡ ⊡

★ ★ **RAMADA INN-SOUTH PLAZA.** 625 E St Joseph St (62703). 217/529-7131; FAX 217/529-7160. 116 rms, 2 story. S $61, D $67; each addl $6; suites $100-$150; under 18 free. Crib free. Pet accepted, some restrictions. TV; cable (premium), VCR avail. Heated pool. Complimentary coffee in lobby. Restaurant 6:30 am-2 pm, 5-9 pm. Rm serv. Ck-out noon. Coin lndry. Meeting rms. Business servs avail. In-rm modem link. Valet serv. Airport transportation. Health club privileges. Some refrigerators, microwaves. Cr cds: A, C, D, DS, MC, V.

D ⊡ ⊡ ⊡ ⊡ SC

★ ★ **RAMADA LIMITED.** 3281 Northfield Dr (62702), I-55 exit 100B, N on Dirksen Pkwy. 217/523-4000; FAX 217/523-4080. 97 rms, 2 story. S $53; D $59 each addl $6; suites $90-$125; under 18 free. Crib free. TV; cable (premium). Indoor pool. Complimentary continental bkfst. Complimentary coffee in rms. Restaurant nearby. Ck-out noon. Coin lndry. Meeting rms. Business servs avail. Valet serv. Free airport transportation. Exercise equipt; weight machine, treadmill. Refrigerator in suites; microwaves avail. Cr cds: A, C, D, DS, JCB, MC, V.

D ⊡ ⊡ ⊡ ⊡ ⊡ SC

✔★ **RED ROOF INN.** 3200 Singer Ave (62703), off I-55S exit 96B. 217/753-4302; FAX 217/753-4319. 108 rms, 2 story. S $29-$57; D $40-$55; under 18 free. Crib free. Pet accepted. TV; cable (premium). Complimentary coffee in lobby. Restaurants nearby. Ck-out noon. Business servs avail. In-rm modem link. Cr cds: A, C, D, DS, MC, V.

D ⊡ ⊡ ⊡ SC

★ ★ **SUPER 8-SOUTH.** 3675 S Sixth St (62703), off I-55 exit 92A. 217/529-8898; FAX 217/529-4354. 122 rms, 3 story. S $32.99-$60.88; D $32.99-$85.88; each addl $5; suites $45.88-$99.88; under 12 free; higher rates special events; lower rates winter months. Crib free. Pet accepted, some restrictions. TV; cable. Complimentary coffee. Restaurants nearby. Ck-out 11 am. Coin lndry. Meeting rms. Business servs avail. Some refrigerators, microwaves. Some balconies. Cr cds: A, C, D, DS, ER, MC, V.

D ⊡ ⊡ ⊡ ⊡ SC

Hotels

★ ★ ★ **HILTON.** 700 E Adams St (62701). 217/789-1530; FAX 217/789-0709. 367 rms, 30 story. S, D $99-$129; each addl $10; suites $119-$600; under 18 free; wkend rates. Crib free. Pet accepted, some restrictions. TV; cable (premium). Indoor pool. Restaurants 6:30 am-10 pm. Bar 2 pm-2 am; entertainment. Ck-out noon. Convention facilities. Business servs avail. Shopping arcade. Barber, beauty shop. Free airport, RR station transportation. Exercise rm; instructor, weight machines, bicycles, sauna. Luxury level. Cr cds: A, C, D, DS, ER, JCB, MC, V.

D ⊡ ⊡ ⊡ ⊡ ⊡ ⊡ SC

★ ★ **RENAISSANCE.** 701 E Adams St (62701). 217/544-8800; FAX 217/544-9607. 316 rms, 12 story. S $106-$148; D $114-$124; suites $180-$450; under 18 free; wkend rates. Crib free. Covered parking $5, valet $6. TV; cable (premium). Indoor pool; whirlpool. Coffee in rms. Restaurant 6:30 am-11 pm. Rm serv to 2 am. Bar. Ck-out noon. Convention facilities. Business center. In-rm modem link. Concierge. Gift shop. Free airport, RR station transportation. Exercise equipt; weight machine,

bicycles, sauna. Game rm. Bathrm phones. Luxury level. Cr cds: A, C, D, DS, ER, JCB, MC, V.

D ⊡ ⊡ ⊡ ⊡ ⊡ SC ⊡

Restaurants

★ ★ **BAUR'S.** 620 S First St (62704). 217/789-4311. Hrs: 11 am-2 pm, 5-10 pm; Sat from 5 pm; Sun brunch 10 am-2 pm. Summer hrs vary. Res accepted. Continental menu. Bar to 1 am. Semi-a la carte: lunch $4.25-$9, dinner $14.95-$24.95. Sun brunch $12.95. Child's meals. Specialties: Dover sole, tournedos Massena, German veal. Own pastries. Pianist wkends. Antiques. In restored stable building. Cr cds: A, C, D, DS, ER, MC, V.

D ⊡

★ ★ **CHESAPEAKE SEAFOOD HOUSE.** 3045 Clear Lake Ave (62702). 217/522-5220. Hrs: 4-10 pm; Fri, Sat to 11 pm. Closed Sun; Dec 25. Res accepted. Bar. Semi-a la carte: dinner $10-$20. Child's meals. Specializes in steak, seafood, barbecue ribs. In mansion (1860); nautical decor. Cr cds: A, C, D, DS, MC, V.

D ⊡

✔★ ★ **MALDANER'S.** 222 S 6th St (62701). 217/522-4313. Hrs: 11 am-2:30 pm, 5-10 pm. Closed Sun; also Jan 1, July 4, Dec 25. Res accepted. Continental menu. Bar. Semi-a la carte: lunch $2-$7, dinner $4.50-$20. Specialties: pistaccio-crusted salmon, braised pork shank, chicken with truffles. Own baking. Restored 19th-century bar. Features late 1930s art. Cr cds: A, MC, V.

D ⊡

Unrated Dining Spot

HERITAGE HOUSE. 3851 S 6th St. 217/529-5571. Hrs: 11 am-8:30 pm; Fri & Sat to 9 pm. Closed Dec 25. Res accepted. Smorgasbord: lunch $5.25, dinner $7.25. Specializes in catfish, fried shrimp, roast beef. Salad bar. Cr cds: C, D, MC, V.

D SC

Starved Rock State Park (C-4)

(See also Ottawa, Peru)

(2 mi S of La Salle on IL 351, then 4 mi E on IL 71)

Illinois' second-oldest state park (1911) occupies 2,630 acres on the Illinois River between La Salle and Ottawa. Starved Rock, a sandstone butte that rises 125 feet from the river, was the site of Fort St Louis, built by La Salle in 1682 and abandoned in 1702. The name is derived from a Native American legend that a band of Illiniwek, isolated by their enemies, starved to death on the rock.

The park has scenic trails, sandstone bluffs and canyons formed by the surging rivers of melting glaciers. In spring there are often waterfalls in the canyons. While there are no true caves, erosion has created overhangs, undercuts and cavelike depressions in the sandstone. There are 15 miles of well-marked hiking trails through a very wide variety of plant life that provides food and shelter to an abundant wildlife population. Spring wildflowers are prolific; more than 200 types can be found. Park activities include fishing, boating (ramp, rentals) as well as hiking. There are bridle trails. Picnic grounds, concessions, campgrounds and horse campgrounds are available (standard fees). The visitor center has exhibits on park history, and an interpretive program is offered. Within the park are a lodge (see RESORT) and cafe. Contact Site Superintendent, PO Box 509, Utica 61373; 815/667-4726 or 815/667-4906 (visitor center).

Resort

✔★ ★ **STARVED ROCK LODGE.** *(Box 570, Utica 61373) In state park, NW entrance on IL 178, 4 mi S of I-80 Utica exit 81. 815/667-4211; FAX 815/667-4455.* 72 lodge rms, 2-3 story, 21 units in log cabins. S, D $56-$78; each addl $9; under 12 free. Crib $3. TV; cable (premium), VCR avail (movies). Saunas. Indoor pool; wading pool, whirlpool. Dining rm 8 am-8 pm. Snack bar. Bar 11 am-11 pm. Ck-out 11 am, ck-in 3 pm. Meeting rms. Business servs avail. Gift shop. Golf privileges. Canoeing. X-country ski on site. Tobogganing. Hiking. Large lobbies, stone fireplace, Native American mementos. Rolling, wooded country. Cr cds: A, C, D, DS, MC, V.

Union (A-5)

(For accommodations see Elgin)

Pop 542 **Elev** 842 ft **Area code** 815 **Zip** 60180

What to See and Do

Antique Village Museum and Wild West Town. Large displays, including antique phonographs, movies, music boxes, toys, telephones; military collection; general store. Outdoor Western village features Wild West gunfights, pony rides, panning for gold pyrite, gift shops. (June-Aug, daily; Apr-May & Sept-Oct, wkends) US 20 & S Union Rd. Phone 815/923-2214. ¢¢¢

Illinois Railway Museum. Outdoor displays, on 56 acres, of historic and antique railroad cars, steam engines, coaches and trolleys; rides (3¹/₂-mi). Picnicking. (Memorial Day-Labor Day, daily; May & Sept, Sat & Sun; Apr & Oct, Sun only) Special events throughout the yr. Admission includes unlimited rides. Olson Rd. Phone 815/923-4000. ¢¢¢

McHenry County Historical Museum. Contains artifacts dating from first settlement in the 1830s to the present; also local history research library (by appt). On the grounds are rural schoolhouse (1895) and original log cabin (1847), authenically furnished, and used for pioneer demonstrations. (May-Oct, Tues-Fri afternoons, also Sun afternoons) 6422 Main St. Phone 815/923-2267. ¢¢

Urbana

(see Champaign/Urbana)

Vandalia (G-4)

(See also Altamont, Greenville)

Founded 1819 **Pop** 6,114 **Elev** 515 ft **Area code** 618 **Zip** 62471
Information Tourism Committee, Chamber of Commerce, 1408 N 5th St, PO Box 238; 618/283-2728.

The Illinois State Legislature chose the wilderness in the Kaskaskia River Valley as the site for the state's second capital, laid out the city and sold lots. Vandalia housed the state legislature from 1819 to 1839, when Abraham Lincoln led a successful campaign to transfer the capital to Springfield.

What to See and Do

Little Brick House Museum. Simple Italianate architecture with six restored rms furnished primarily in the 1820-1839 period; antique wallpapers, china, wooden utensils, dolls, doll carriages, pipes, parasols, powder horn, oil portraits and engravings. Berry-Hall Rm contains memorabilia of James Berry, artist, and James Hall, writer. Pays tribute to members of the Tenth General Assembly of Illinois. Outbuildings and period garden with original brick pathways around house. (days open varies; by appt) 621 St Clair St. Phone 618/283-0024. ¢¢

Ramsey Lake State Park. Approx 1,880 acres with 47-acre lake stocked with bass, bluegill and redear sunfish. Fishing, hunting; boating (ramp, rentals, electric motors only). Hiking, horseback riding. Picnicking (shelters), concession. Camping (standard fees). 13 mi N on US 51, then W on 2900N. Phone 618/423-2215. **Free.**

★ **Vandalia Statehouse State Historic Site.** Lincoln and Stephen Douglas served in the House of Representatives in this two-story, classical-revival building that townspeople built in 1836 in an effort to keep the capital in Vandalia. Many antiques and period furnishings. Guide service. (Daily; closed Dec-Feb, Mon-Tues; major hols) (See ANNUAL EVENT) 315 W Gallatin St. Phone 618/283-1161. **Free.**

Annual Event

Grande Levée. Vandalia Statehouse State Historic Site. Capital Days (1820-1839) are celebrated with period crafts, music and food. Candlelight tour of the building. Father's Day wkend.

Motels

✔★ **DAYS INN.** *1920 Kennedy Blvd. 618/283-4400; FAX 618/283-4240.* 95 rms, 2 story. Late May-early Sept: S $44; D $50; each addl $6; under 13 free; wkly rates; higher rates special events; lower rates rest of yr. Crib free. Pet accepted; $10 deposit. TV; cable (premium), VCR avail (movies). Complimentary continental bkfst. Restaurant 6 am-9 pm. Rm serv. Ck-out noon. Bellhops. Heated pool. Playground. Game rm. Cr cds: A, D, DS, MC, V.

✔★ **JAY'S.** *1 mi N on US 40 (IL 185), 1 blk SW of jct I-70 & US 51. 618/283-1200; FAX 618/283-2363.* 21 rms, 2 story. S $35; D $45-$47. Crib free. Pet accepted. TV; cable (premium). Pool privileges adj. Coffee in rms. Restaurant 6 am-10 pm. Bar 4 pm-midnight. Ck-out noon. Sundries. Cr cds: A, D, DS, MC, V.

➥ 🐾 SC

★ ★ **RAMADA LIMITED.** *US 40W, I-70 exit 61. 618/283-1400; FAX 618/283-3465.* 61 rms, 2 story. May-Oct: S, D $49-$57; each addl $8; suites $69-$77; under 12 free; lower rates rest of yr. Crib free. Pet accepted; $10 deposit. TV; cable (premium), VCR avail. Pool. Complimentary full bkfst. Restaurant adj 7 am-9 pm; Fri, Sat to 10 pm. Ck-out noon. Meeting rms. Business servs avail. Exercise equipt; weight machine, bicycle. Refrigerator, microwaves in suites. Cr cds: A, C, D, DS, MC, V.

D ➥ 🏊 🚴 🐾 SC

★ **TRAVELODGE.** *1500 N 6th St, 1 blk SW of jct I-70 & US 51, exit 63. 618/283-2363; FAX 618/283-2363, ext. 131.* 48 rms, 2 story. S $40; D $46-$48; each addl $5. Crib free. Pet accepted. TV; cable (premium). Pool. Playground. Complimentary coffee in rms. Restaurant adj 6 am-10 pm. Bar 4 pm-midnight. Ck-out noon. Sun deck. Cr cds: A, C, D, DS, ER, JCB, MC, V.

D ➥ 🏊 🚴 🐾 SC

Waukegan (A-6)

(See also Gurnee)

Settled 1835 **Pop** 69,392 **Elev** 644 ft **Area code** 847 **E-mail** econinfo@lakecounty-il.org **Web** www.lakecounty-il.org
Information Lake County Chamber of Commerce, 5221 W Grand Ave, Gurnee, 60031; 847/249-3800.

On the site of what was once a Native American village and a French trading post, Waukegan was first incorporated as Little Fort because of a French stockade there. It was barred to settlement by treaty for many years, but after the establishment of a general store by a Chicago merchant, it became a United States port of entry and thrived. On April 2, 1860, Lincoln delivered his "unfinished speech" here—he was interrupted by a fire. Waukegan is the most industrialized of all communities on the lakeshore north of Chicago. Waukegan Port, on Lake Michigan, provides dockage for lake-going vessels that serve local industry. Waukegan was the birthplace of comedian Jack Benny and author Ray Bradbury, who has used the town as a background in many of his works.

What to See and Do

Great Lakes Naval Training Center. This 1,600-acre installation on Lake Michigan, 1,000 mi from salt water, has been the training site for more than 3 million Navy recruits. The training center includes 20 technical schools, a recruit training command and a large Navy hospital. There are more than 30 separate commands, several with worldwide missions. The base is closed to the public except on special occasions. Tours. (Daily) 3 mi E off I-94. Phone 847/688-2201.   **Free.**

Illinois Beach State Park (see). 3 mi N, E of IL 131; off Sheridan Rd.

Motels

★ ★ **BEST INNS OF AMERICA.** *31 N Green Bay Rd (IL 131) (60085). 847/336-9000.* 89 rms, 2 story. Mid-June-Sept: S $55.88; D $72.88; each addl $7; under 18 free; lower rates rest of yr. Crib free. TV; cable (premium). Heated pool. Complimentary continental bkfst. Restaurant nearby. Ck-out 11 am. In-rm modem link. Six Flags Great America, Naval training center nearby. Cr cds: A, C, D, DS, MC, V.

D ≋ ⊁ 🔥 SC

✔★ **COMFORT INN.** *3031 Belvidere Rd (IL 120) (60085). 847/623-1400; FAX 847/623-0686.* 64 rms, 2 story. May-Sept: S, D $44-$90; each addl $6; under 18 free; lower rates rest of yr. Crib free. TV; cable (premium). Complimentary continental bkfst. Restaurant adj 11 am-10 pm. Ck-out 11 am. Meeting rms. Business servs avail. Sundries. Six Flags Great America, Great Lakes Naval Training Center nearby. Cr cds: A, C, D, DS, ER, MC, V.

D ⊁ 🔥 SC

★ **HOLIDAY INN EXPRESS.** *619 S Green Bay Rd (60085). 847/662-3200; FAX 847/662-7275.* 88 rms, 2 story. June-Aug: S, D $99.95; suites $109.95; each addl $17; lower rates rest of yr. Crib free. TV; cable, VCR avail (movies). Complimentary continental bkfst. Restaurant opp open 24 hrs. Ck-out noon. Meeting rm. Business servs avail. In-rm modem link. Airport transportation. Game rm. Health club privileges. Some refrigerators. Cr cds: A, C, D, DS, JCB, MC, V.

D ⊁ 🔥 SC

★ **SUPER 8.** *630 N Green Bay Rd (60085). 847/249-2388.* 61 rms, 3 story. Apr-Sept: S $51.88-$71.88; D $51.88-$78.88; each addl $5; under 12 free; lower rates rest of yr. Crib free. Pet accepted; $25. TV; cable (premium). Complimentary coffee in lobby. Restaurant nearby. Ck-out 11 am. Business servs avail. Cr cds: A, C, D, DS, JCB, MC, V.

D ✔ ⊁ 🔥 SC

Motor Hotels

★ ★ ★ **COURTYARD BY MARRIOTT.** *800 Lakehurst Rd (60085), jct IL 43 & 120. 847/689-8000; FAX 847/689-0135.* 149 rms, 3 story. June-Aug: S $99; D $109; suites $129-$149; under 17 free; wkly, wkend rates; lower rates rest of yr. Crib free. TV; cable (premium). Indoor pool; whirlpool. Complimentary coffee in rms. Restaurant 6:30-11 am. Bar 5-10 pm. Ck-out 1 pm. Coin lndry. Meeting rms. Business servs avail. In-rm modem link. Valet serv. Exercise equipt; bicycles, treadmills. Health club privileges. Some refrigerators, microwaves. Private patios, balconies. Six Flags Great America nearby. Cr cds: A, C, D, DS, MC, V.

D ≋ ⊁ ⊁ 🔥 SC

★ ★ **RAMADA INN.** *200 N Green Bay Rd (IL 131) (60085), IL 132, E to Green Bay Rd. 847/244-2400; FAX 847/249-9716.* 181 rms, 2 story. June-Aug: S $85; D $95; each addl $5; under 18 free; lower rates rest of yr. Crib free. TV; cable (premium). Indoor pool; whirlpool. Restaurant 6:30 am-10 pm. Rm serv. Bar 11-1 am. Ck-out noon. Meeting rms. Business servs avail. Bellhops. Gift shop. Exercise equipt; weight machine, bicycles, sauna. Game rm. Some refrigerators, microwaves. Cr cds: A, C, D, DS, ER, JCB, MC, V.

D ≋ ⊁ ⊁ 🔥 SC

Restaurants

★ ★ **MATHON'S.** *6 E Clayton St (60085). 847/662-3610.* Hrs: 11 am-9 pm; Fri, Sat to 10 pm; Sun 3-9 pm. Closed Mon; Jan 1, Thanksgiving, Dec 25. Res accepted. Bar. Complete meals: lunch $4.95-$9.95, dinner $7.95-$19.95. Child's meals. Specializes in fresh fish, steaks, chops. Nautical decor. Cr cds: A, C, D, DS, MC, V.

★ ★ **THE PARKWAY.** *3035 Belvidere Rd (IL 120) (60085). 847/336-0222.* Hrs: 11:30 am-9 pm; Sat from 4 pm; Sun 4-8 pm; major hols from noon. Res accepted. Bar to 11 pm; wkends to midnight. Semi-a la carte: lunch $4.95-$9.95, dinner $9.95-$16.95. Child's meals. Specializes in filet mignon, prime rib, seafood. Own cakes, pies. Three dining rms. Contemporary decor. Cr cds: A, C, D, DS, MC, V.

Wheaton (B-5)

(For accommodations see Geneva, Glen Ellyn, Naperville)

Pop 51,464 **Elev** 753 ft **Area code** 630 **Zip** 60187
Information Greater Wheaton Chamber of Commerce, 303 W Front, 61087; 630/668-6464.

Wheaton, the seat of Du Page county, is primarily a residential community with 39 churches and the headquarters of approximately two dozen religious publishers and organizations. The town's most famous citizens are football great Red Grange; Elbert Gary, who created the Indiana steel city that bears his name; and evangelist Billy Graham.

What to See and Do

Cantigny. This is the 500-acre estate of the late Robert R. McCormick, editor and publisher of the *Chicago Tribune*. Picnic area, woodland trails; 10 acres of formal gardens. (Daily) On Winfield Rd, S of IL 38. Phone 630/668-5161. Per vehicle   ¢¢   On grounds are

Robert R. McCormick Museum. Georgian residence begun by Joseph Medill (1896), enlarged by his grandson, Robert McCormick, in the 1930s. Original furnishings; unique Chinese mural in dining rm; personal artifacts, photographs, paintings. Chamber music presentation (summer, Sun, limited hrs; rest of yr, 1st Sun of month); reservation required. Guided tours (Mar-Dec, daily exc Mon; Feb, Fri-Sun; closed Thanksgiving, Dec 25, also Jan). Per vehicle   ¢¢

First Division Museum. Narrated displays dramatize story of First Infantry Division in action in World Wars I & II and Vietnam. (Mar-Dec, daily exc Mon; Feb, Fri-Sun; closed Thanksgiving, Dec 25, also Jan). Per vehicle ¢¢

Cosley Animal Farm & Museum. Children's petting zoo; antique farm equipment display; railroad caboose and equipment; aviary; herb garden; outdoor education center. (Daily; closed Jan 1, Thanksgiving, Dec 25) 1356 N Gary Ave. Phone 630/665-5534. **Free.**

Du Page County Historical Museum. Historic Romanesque limestone building (1891) houses changing exhibitions on county history; costume gallery; period rms. Extensive HO model railroad display. Research library. (Mon, Wed, Fri-Sun; closed major hols) 102 E Wesley St. Phone 630/682-7343. **Free.**

Wheaton College (1860). (2,500 students) Liberal arts, Conservatory of Music, Graduate School. 501 E College Ave. Tours, phone 630/752-5000. On campus are art exhibits, the Perry Mastodon Exhibit and

Billy Graham Center Museum. Museum features exhibits on the history of evangelism in America and the ministries of the Billy Graham Evangelistic Assn; also Rotunda of Witnesses, Gospel theme area. (Mon-Sat, also Sun afternoons; closed some hols) Phone 630/752-5909.

Marion E. Wade Center. Collection of books and papers of seven British authors: Owen Barfield, G.K. Chesterton, C.S. Lewis, George MacDonald, Dorothy L. Sayers, J.R.R. Tolkien and Charles Williams. (Daily exc Sun; closed hols) Housed in the Wheaton College Library. Phone 630/752-5908.

Annual Events

Du Page County Fair. Fairgrounds, 2015 W Manchester Rd. Phone 630/668-6636. Late July.

Autumn Fest. Memorial Park. 3rd wkend Sept.

Wheeling (C-3 see Chicago map)

(See also Arlington Heights, Glenview, Northbrook)

Pop 29,911 **Elev** 650 ft **Area code** 847 **Zip** 60090 **Web** www.wheeling.com

Information Wheeling/Prospect Heights Area Chamber of Commerce and Industry, 395 E Dundee Rd; 847/541-0170.

The Wheeling area was first occupied by the Potawatomi. Settlers arrived in 1833 and began farming the fertile prairie soil. In 1836, a stage coach route was established along Milwaukee Avenue, which was the main northbound route out of Chicago. The first commercial enterprise was a tavern-hotel (1837), followed by the establishment of a brewery (1850) on the Des Plaines River.

Motels

★ ★ **COURTYARD BY MARRIOTT.** *(505 Milwaukee Ave, Lincolnshire 60069)* I-294 to Half Day Rd exit, 3½ mi W to Milwaukee Ave, then S. 847/634-9555; FAX 847/634-8320. 146 rms, 3 story. S, D $99-$109; each addl $10; suites $108-$116; wkend rates. Crib free. TV; cable (premium). Indoor pool. Complimentary coffee in rms. Restaurant 6:30-10:30 am. Bar 5-11 pm. Ck-out 1 pm. Coin lndry. Meeting rms. Business servs avail. In-rm modem link. Airport transportation. Exercise equipt; treadmill, stair machine. Some refrigerators. Private patios, balconies. Cr cds: A, C, D, DS, MC, V.

D ≊ ᛪ ⋈ ⚲ SC

★ ★ **EXEL INN.** *(540 N Milwaukee Ave, Prospect Heights 60070)* S on Milwaukee Ave. 847/459-0545; FAX 847/459-8639. 123 rms, 3 story. S $37.99-$59.99; D $46.99-$59.99; suites $90-$130; under 18 free; wkly rates. Crib free. Pet accepted, some restrictions. TV. Compli-

mentary continental bkfst. Complimentary coffee in rms. Restaurant nearby. Ck-out noon. Coin lndry. Business servs avail. In-rm modem link. Health club privileges. Game rm. Some refrigerators; microwaves avail. Cr cds: A, C, D, DS, MC, V.

D ⛵ ⋈ ⚲ SC

Motor Hotel

★ ★ **HAWTHORN SUITES.** *(10 Westminster Way, Lincolnshire 60069)* jct I-94 & Half Day Rd (IL 22). 847/945-9300; FAX 847/945-0013. 125 kit. suites, 3 story. May-Oct: S, D $119-$170; wkend rates; lower rates rest of yr. Crib free. TV; cable (premium). Indoor pool; whirlpool. Complimentary full bkfst. Complimentary coffee in rms. Ck-out noon. Coin lndry. Meeting rms. Business servs avail. In-rm modem link. Valet serv. Sundries. Tennis privileges. Exercise equipt; treadmill, stair machine. Microwaves. Cr cds: A, C, D, DS, MC, V.

D ⛵ ᛪ ⋈ ⚲ SC

Resort

★ ★ ★ **MARRIOTT'S LINCOLNSHIRE RESORT.** *(10 Marriott Dr, Lincolnshire 60069)* off Milwaukee Ave (IL 21), ½ mi S of Half Day Rd (IL 22). 847/634-0100; FAX 847/634-1278. 390 rms, 3 story. S, D $99-$159; suites from $250-$290; under 18 free; wkend rates; theater packages; golf plans. Crib free. Pet accepted, some restrictions. TV; cable (premium), VCR avail. 2 pools, 1 indoor; wading pool, whirlpool, poolside serv, lifeguard. Playground. Supervised child's activities (May-Oct). Complimentary coffee in lobby. Restaurants 6:30 am-11 pm. Rm serv. Bars 11-1 am. Ck-out noon, ck-in 4 pm. Coin lndry. Convention facilities. Business center. Valet serv. Concierge. Gift shop. Airport transportation. Sports dir. Indoor tennis, pro. 18-hole golf, greens fee $50-$60, pro, putting green. Canoeing, paddleboating. Lawn games. Entertainment Thurs-Sat. 900-seat theater-in-the-round featuring musical comedies. Game rm. Exercise rm; instructor (by appt), weights, bicycles, sauna, steam rm. Massage. Minibars; some refrigerators. Some private patios. Picnic tables. Luxury level. Cr cds: A, C, D, DS, ER, JCB, MC, V.

D ⛵ ᛪ ᛪ ≊ ᛪ ⋈ ⚲ SC ⚶

Restaurants

★ ★ **94TH AERO SQUADRON.** *1070 S Milwaukee Ave (IL 21), adj to Palwaukee Airport.* 847/459-3700. Hrs: 11:30 am-2:30 pm, 4-11 pm; Sun from 4 pm; Sun brunch 9 am-2 pm. Res accepted. Bar Fri, Sat to 1:30 am. Semi-a la carte: lunch $5.95-$10.95, dinner $9.95-$24.95. Sun brunch $16.95. Child's meals. Specializes in prime rib, pasta, seafood. Own baking. Parking. Outdoor dining. Country French farmhouse decor, fireplace, WW I memorabilia throughout. Interior, grounds simulate farmhouse under siege; sandbags, checkpoint at bridge, airplanes, military apparatus. Cr cds: A, C, D, DS, MC, V.

D ⌣

★ ★ **ASPEN GRILLE.** *(250 Marriott Dr, Lincolnshire 60069)* NW on Milwaukee Ave, 1 blk S of IL 22. 847/634-0700. Hrs: 11 am-10 pm; Fri, Sat to 11 pm; Sun from 10 am; Sun brunch to 2 pm. Closed Thanksgiving, Dec 25. Res accepted. Bar. Semi-a la carte: lunch $8-$13, dinner $12-$18. Sun brunch $5.95-$9.95. Child's meals. Specializes in steak, seafood, pasta. Valet parking Fri, Sat (dinner). Outdoor dining. Contemporary ski-lodge atmosphere. Cr cds: A, D, DS, MC, V.

D ⌣

★ ★ **BOB CHINN'S CRAB HOUSE.** *393 S Milwaukee Ave (IL 21).* 847/520-3633. E-mail crabhse@bobchinns.com; web www.bobchinns.com. Hrs: 11 am-2:30 pm, 4:30-10:30 pm; Fri to 11:30 pm; Sat noon-11:30 pm; Sun 3-10 pm. Closed Thanksgiving, Dec 25. Bar. Semi-a la carte: lunch $4.95-$10.95, dinner $10.95-$25.95. Child's meals (dinner). Specializes in garlic Dungeness crab, soft-shell & stone crab, 12 varieties of fresh fish daily. Salad bar, raw seafood bar. Own baking. Parking. Valet serv. Cr cds: A, C, D, DS, JCB, MC, V.

D ⌣

★ **CRAWDADDY BAYOU.** *412 N Milwaukee Ave, ¼ mi S of Lake Cook Rd.* 847/520-4800. Web www.cybersystems.com/crawdaddy. Hrs: 11 am-2:30 pm, 5-10 pm; Fri to 11 pm; Sat 5-11 pm; Sun 11 am-2 pm, 4-9 pm. Cajun/Creole menu. Bar. Semi-a la carte: lunch $6.95-$13.95, dinner $8.95-$18.95. Child's meals. Specialties: boiled crawfish, chicken & smoked sausage gumbo, etoufeé. Own desserts. Zydeco music. Valet parking. Outdoor dining. Authentic Louisiana bayou decor. Cr cds: A, D, DS, MC, V.

D ⊒

★★ **DON ROTH'S.** *61 N Milwaukee Ave (IL 21).* 847/537-5800. Web www.aenglobal.com/donroths.html. Hrs: 11:30 am-2:30 pm, 5:30-9:30 pm; Fri 5:30-10 pm; Sat 5-10:30 pm; Sun 4-8:30 pm. Closed Dec 25. Res accepted. Bar. Semi-a la carte: lunch $5.95-$11.95, dinner $15.95-$26.95. Specializes in prime rib, fresh fish. Parking. Outdoor dining. In converted farmhouse. Family-owned. Cr cds: A, D, DS, MC, V.

D ⊒

★★ **GILARDI'S.** *(23397 US 45N, Vernon Hills 60061) at Milwaukee Ave (IL 21).* 847/634-1811. Hrs: 11 am-10 pm; Fri to 11 pm; Sat 4-11 pm; Sun 4-9 pm. Closed most major hols. Res accepted Sun-Thurs. Italian, Amer menu. Bar. Semi-a la carte: lunch $5.95-$8.95, dinner $10.95-$24.95. Specializes in fresh seafood, veal Vesuvio, 8-finger cavatelli. Valet parking (dinner). Entertainment Fri, Sat. In turn-of-the-century mansion; art-deco decor. Cr cds: A, DS, MC, V.

D ⊒

★★ **HANS' BAVARIAN LODGE.** *931 N Milwaukee Ave (IL 21).* 847/537-4141. Hrs: 11:30 am-10 pm; Fri to 11 pm; Sat 4-11 pm; Sun noon-9 pm. Closed Mon; Jan 1, July 4, Dec 24-26. Res accepted. German, Amer menu. Bar. Semi-a la carte: lunch $5-$9.25, dinner $9.95-$18.95. Child's meals. Specialties: Wienerschnitzel, sauerbraten, roast duck. Zither player, pianist Fri; accordionist Sat, Sun. Parking. Outdoor dining. Oktoberfest tent dining 2 wks late Sept-Oct. Beer stein collection. Cr cds: A, C, D, DS, MC, V.

D ⊒

★★ **HARRY CARAY'S.** *933 N Milwaukee Ave, 2 blks N of Lake Cook Rd.* 847/537-2827. Web www.harrycaray.com. Hrs: 11 am-10 pm; Fri to 11 pm; Sat 4-11 pm; Sun 3-9 pm. Res accepted. Bar. Semi-a la carte: lunch $7.95-$10.95, dinner $8.95-$25.95. Child's meals. Specializes in Vesuvio-style prime steaks, fresh seafood, pasta. Valet parking. Outdoor dining. Casual, sports-oriented dining area with Chicago Cubs baseball memorabilia. Cr cds: A, C, D, DS, JCB, MC, V.

D ⊒

★★★★ **LE FRANÇAIS.** *269 S Milwaukee Ave (IL 21).* 847/541-7470. Beginning with the welcome at the door, dinner at this charming French country inn re-created in the northwestern suburbs of Chicago is outstanding. The imaginative cuisine, employing sauces that are mostly lighter than they used to be; an exceptionally entensive wine list; and the superbly informative and friendly service make dinner here a reason in itself to go to the Chicago area. Contemporary French menu. Specialties: nage de homard fumé sauce aux herbe, magret de canard du jour, white chocolate Delice with fresh raspberries. Menu changes frequently. Own desserts, pastries, chocolates. Hrs: 11:30 am-2, 5:30-9 pm; Sat 2 dinner sittings, 6-6:30 pm & 9-9:30 pm; Mon from 5:30 pm; early-bird dinner 5-6 pm. Closed Sun; major hols; also 1st wk Jan. Res accepted. Serv bar. Extensive wine list. A la carte entrees: lunch $13.75-$15.50, dinner $28.50-$32.00. Prix fixe: lunch (Tues-Fri) 4-course $27, dinner (Mon-Thurs) degustation $75. Valet parking. Chef-owned. Jacket (dinner). Cr cds: A, D, DS, MC, V.

D

★★ **WEBER GRILL.** *920 N Milwaukee Ave, 3 blks N of Lake Cook Rd.* 847/215-0996. Hrs: 11:30 am-2:30 pm, 4:30-10 pm; Fri to 11 pm; Sat noon-2:30 pm, 4:30-11 pm; Sun 3-9 pm. Closed some major hols. Res accepted. Bar. Semi-a la carte: lunch $4.95-$14.75, dinner $9.99-$26.50.

Child's meals. Specializes in Weber-kettle grill cooking, steak, barbecued ribs. Own pastries. Parking. Outdoor dining. Cr cds: A, C, D, DS, MC, V.

D ⊒

Wilmette (C-4 see Chicago map)

(For accommodations see Evanston, Glenview, Skokie)

Settled 1829 **Pop** 26,690 **Elev** 610 ft **Area code** 847 **Zip** 60091
Information Chamber of Commerce, 1150 Wilmette Ave; 847/251-3800.

This community was once owned by a Native American woman, who received the land under a government treaty. The town carries the name of her French-Canadian husband, Antoine Ouilmette.

What to See and Do

Baha'i House of Worship. Spiritual center of the Baha'i faith in the US, a remarkable nine-sided structure given lightness and grace by the use of glass and tracery. It is 191 ft high and overlooks Lake Michigan. Surrounded by nine gardens and fountains. Exhibits and slide programs in visitors center on lower level. (Daily) Sheridan Rd & Linden Ave. Phone 847/853-2300. **Free.**

Gillson Park. Contains Wilmette Beach with 1,000 ft of sandy shoreline, lifeguards & beach house (June-Labor Day, daily; fee), sailing (lessons); fishing pier. Tennis. Cross-country skiing, ice-skating. Picnic facilities, playground, concession. Sunfish and Hobie 16 catamaran rentals. Park (daily). Washington & Michigan Aves. Phone 847/256-6100. ¢¢

Historical Museum. Local history; costumes; rotating exhibits; archives, reference library. (Sept-June, Tues-Thurs, Sat & Sun afternoons; closed major hols & wk of Dec 25) 609 Ridge Rd. Phone 847/853-7666. **Free.**

Kohl Children's Museum. Science and history participatory exhibits designed for children ages 1-10; miniature food store; make-up area; special activities. (Daily; closed some hols) 165 Green Bay Rd. Phone 847/251-7781 or 847/256-6056. ¢¢

Restaurants

★ **BÊTISE.** *1515 N Sheridan Rd, in Plaza del Lago Shopping Center.* 847/853-1711. Hrs: 11:30 am-2 pm, 5:30-9 pm; Fri, Sat to 10 pm; Sun 5:30-9 pm; Sun brunch 11 am-2 pm. Closed most major hols. Res accepted. French bistro menu. Serv bar. Semi-a la carte: lunch $8-$14, dinner $22-$26. Sun brunch $8-$12. Specializes in roasted chicken, fresh fish, loin of lamb. Own desserts. Art displays. Cr cds: A, C, D, DS, MC, V.

D

★★ **TANGLEWOOD.** *(566 Chestnut St, Winnetka 60093) N on Green Bay Rd, W on Spruce, 1 blk to Laundry Mall.* 847/441-4600. Hrs: 11:30 am-9 pm; Fri, Sat to 10 pm. Closed Sun; major hols. Res accepted. Continental menu. Serv bar. Semi-a la carte: lunch $5-$9, dinner $8-$18. Child's meals. Specialties: salmon with wild mushrooms, curried lamb shank, grilled shrimp fettuccine. Outdoor dining. Fireplace, skylights. Cr cds: A, MC, V.

D

Unrated Dining Spots

CONVITO ITALIANO. *1515 N Sheridan Rd, in Plaza del Lago Shopping Center.* 847/251-3654. Hrs: 11:30 am-8:30 pm; Fri, Sat to 10 pm; Sun to 8 pm. Closed hols. Italian menu. Wine, beer. Semi-a la carte: lunch $4.75-$12, dinner $7-$15. Specializes in pasta, fresh salads.

Authentic regional Italian restaurant and market. Cr cds: A, C, D, DS, MC, V.

WALKER BROS ORIGINAL PANCAKE HOUSE. *153 Green Bay Rd. 847/251-6000.* Hrs: 7 am-10:30 pm; Fri, Sat to 11 pm. Closed Thanksgiving, Dec 25. A la carte entrees: bkfst, lunch, dinner $2.50-$6.25. Child's meals. Specializes in apple pancakes, German pancakes, egg-white omelettes. Stained-glass collection, many antiques. Cr cds: DS, MC, V.

Woodstock (A-5)

(See also Gurnee, McHenry)

Pop 14,353 **Elev** 942 ft **Area code** 815 **Zip** 60098 **E-mail** wdstkcoc@il-icom.net **Web** www.woodstock-coc.org
Information Chamber of Commerce, 136 Cass St; 815/338-2436.

Orson Welles, who went to school and performed his first Shakespearean role here, once described Woodstock as the "grand capital of mid-Victorianism in the Midwest." The Victorian charm has been carefully retained, especially in the town square with its ornate gazebo, wooded park, cobblestone streets and many historic houses and buildings that now contain antique shops.

What to See and Do

Chester Gould-Dick Tracy Museum. Exhibits include permanent collection of original art of Tracy; also Gould family memorabilia, Chester Gould's original drawing board, and various changing exhibits. Gift shop. (Thurs-Sat, also Sun afternoons) In Old Courthouse Arts Center on Woodstock Sq, 101 N Johnson St. Phone 815/338-8281. **Free.**

Woodstock Opera House (1889). Restored; built in a style described as "steamboat Gothic" in reference to the exterior's resemblance to a cathedral and the interior's similarity to the salon of a Mississippi River steamboat. Especially worth noting is the stencilled auditorium ceiling. (Daily) 121 Van Buren St. For program schedule phone 815/338-5300. **Free.**

Seasonal Event

Mozart Festival. Woodstock Opera House (see). Performances by Woodstock Festival Orchestra and renowned soloists. 3 wkends Aug.

Motel

✔★ ★ **DAYS INN.** *990 Lake St. 815/338-0629; FAX 815/338-0895.* 45 rms, 3 story. S $50; D $55-$110; each addl $5; under 12 free. Crib free. TV; cable (premium), VCR avail (movies). Indoor pool. Complimentary continental bkfst. Restaurant adj open 24 hrs. Ck-out noon. Meeting rm. Business servs avail. Game rm. Some refrigerators. Cr cds: A, C, D, DS, MC, V.

Indiana

Population: 5,544,159
Land area: 35,936 square miles
Elevation: 320-1,257 feet
Highest point: Near Bethel (Wayne County)
Entered Union: December 11, 1816 (19th state)
Capital: Indianapolis
Motto: The Crossroads of America
Nickname: The Hoosier State
State flower: Peony
State bird: Cardinal
State tree: Tulip tree
State fair: Early-mid-August 1998, in Indianapolis
Time zone: Eastern and Central

At the crossroads of the nation, Indiana is one of the most typically American states in the country. Against a still visible background of Native American history and determined pioneer struggle for survival, it stands out today as a region that has come of age. It is a manufacturing state with widely distributed industrial centers surrounded by fertile farmlands and magnificent forests.

In the wooded hill country north of the Ohio River are pioneer villages where time seems to have stood still. Central Indiana is one of the richest agricultural regions in the United States. The Calumet District in the northwest has a large industrial area. Miles of sand dunes and beaches have made Lake Michigan's south shore the state's summer playground. In the northeastern section are hundreds of secluded lakes, a fisherman's paradise. Trails at state parks and recreation areas are marked for hiking and horseback riding. In the winter, skiing, ice skating and tobogganing are popular sports.

Indiana's highways and roads are lined with reminders of its colorful history. A pre-Columbian race of mound builders developed a highly ceremonial culture here. Their earth structures can still be seen in many parts of the state. In 1673 two Frenchmen, Father Marquette and Louis Jolliet, wandered across northern Indiana and preached to the Native Americans. Between 1679 and 1685 Indiana was thoroughly explored by Robert de La Salle and became a part of the French provinces of Canada and Louisiana. After the French and Indian War, most of Indiana came under British control (1763), which was violently opposed by a Native American confederation led by Chief Pontiac. In 1779, General George Rogers Clark occupied southern Indiana with French assistance and claimed it for the State of Virginia. But Virginia was unable to control the region as the British. Indiana became public domain in 1784 and remained chiefly Native American territory during the next 15 years.

Continuing pressure by the federal government in Washington and by white settlers on Native American land led the great Shawnee chief Tecumseh to form an unsuccessful confederation of Indian Nations, extending from the Great Lakes to the Gulf of Mexico. The Battle of Tippecanoe in 1811, brought about by General William Henry Harrison while Tecumseh was in the South, dealt a fatal blow to the Native American organization. In 1812, Native Americans, their towns and granaries burned by federal troops and militia, made a last furious attempt to defend their

land. But Tecumseh's death in the Battle of the Thames in 1813 marked the end of the Native American era. In 1816 Indiana became the 19th state of the Union. Abraham Lincoln was 7 years old when his family moved to southern Indiana in 1816. He lived here for 14 years.

Today, Indiana's industries manufacture transportation equipment, electrical supplies, heavy industrial machinery and food products. More than 60 percent of the building limestone used in the United States is supplied by quarries in the Hoosier State. Soft coal deposits, mainly found in southwest Indiana, are the most abundant natural resource. Indiana's principal farm products are soybeans, tomatoes, corn, spearmint, peppermint, livestock, poultry, wheat and dairy products.

Several explanations have been offered as to why Indianans are called "Hoosiers." The most logical is that in 1826, a contractor on the Ohio Falls Canal at Louisville, Samuel Hoosier, gave employment preference to men living on the Indiana side of the river. The men in his work gangs were called "Hoosier's men," then "Hoosiers."

When to Go/Climate

Hot, humid summers and cold, snowy winters are the norm in Indiana. The flat terrain provides no buffer against wind and storms, and tornadoes are not uncommon in spring and summer.

AVERAGE HIGH/LOW TEMPERATURES (°F)

INDIANAPOLIS

Jan 34/17	**May** 74/52	**Sept** 78/56
Feb 38/21	**June** 83/61	**Oct** 66/44
Mar 51/32	**July** 86/65	**Nov** 52/34
Apr 63/42	**Aug** 84/63	**Dec** 39/23

FORT WAYNE

Jan 30/15	**May** 71/49	**Sept** 76/54
Feb 34/18	**June** 81/59	**Oct** 63/43
Mar 46/29	**July** 85/63	**Nov** 49/34
Apr 60/39	**Aug** 82/61	**Dec** 36/22

Parks and Recreation Finder

Directions to and information about the parks and recreation areas below are given under their respective town/city sections. Please refer to those sections for details.

Key to abbreviations: I.P. = Interstate Park; N.B.C. = National Battlefield & Cemetery; N.B.P. = National Battlefield Park; N.F. = National Forest; N.G. = National Grassland; N.H. = National Historical Park; N.H.S. = National Historic Site; N.M. = National Monument; N.Mem. = National Memorial; N.M.P. = National Military Park; N.P. = National Park; N.Pres. = National Preserve; N.R. = National Recreational Area; N.R.R. = National Recreational River; N.S. = National Seashore; N.S.T. = National Scenic Trail; N.V.M. = National Volcanic Monument; S.B. = State Beach; S.C.P. = State Conservation Park; S.G. = State Garden; S.H.A. = State Historic Area; S.H.P. = State Historical Park; S.N.A. = State Natural Area; S.P. = State Park; S.R. = State Reserve; S.R.A. = State Recreation Area; S.Res.P. = State Resort Park; S.R.P. = State Rustic Park.

NATIONAL PARK AND RECREATION AREAS

Place Name	Listed Under
George Rogers Clark N.H.	VINCENNES
Hoosier N.F.	BEDFORD
Indiana Dunes National Lakeshore	same
Lincoln Boyhood N.Mem.	same

STATE RECREATION AREAS

Place Name	Listed Under
Brookville Lake State Reservoir	CONNERSVILLE
Brown County S.P.	same
Clifty Falls S.P.	MADISON
Harmonie S.P.	NEW HARMONY
Indiana Dunes S.P.	same
Lake Monroe (Paynetown S.R.A.)	BLOOMINGTON
Lieber S.R.A.	GREENCASTLE
Lincoln S.P.	LINCOLN BOYHOOD NATIONAL MEMORIAL & LINCOLN STATE PARK
McCormick's Creek S.P.	BLOOMINGTON
Mounds S.P.	ANDERSON
Pokagon S.P.	ANGOLA
Potato Creek S.P.	SOUTH BEND
Raccoon Lake S.R.A.	ROCKVILLE
Salamonie Reservoir, Dam & Forest	WABASH
Shades S.P.	CRAWFORDSVILLE
Shakamak S.P.	same
Spring Mill S.P.	same
Summit Lake S.P.	NEW CASTLE
Tippecanoe River S.P.	same
Turkey Run S.P.	same
Whitewater Memorial S.P.	CONNERSVILLE
Yellowwood State Forest	NASHVILLE

Water-related activities, hiking, biking, various other sports, picnicking and visitor centers, as well as camping, are available in many of these areas. Standard admission fees to state parks are: $2/carload (out-of-state, $5/carload); $18/yr permit; use of horses, fee varies. Camping, limited to 2 wks, is on a first-come basis at most parks: $5-$13/night/site/family; winter, half price. Camping permitted all yr except at Bass Lake. Campsite reservations are accepted for all parks except at Harmonie, Huntington Lake, Shades, Summit Lake and Tippecanoe. Several parks have housekeeping cabins. Six parks have inns, open all year. Pools and beaches are open from Memorial Day-late Aug (varies at each park); swimming permitted only when lifeguards are on duty. Pets on leash only. For detailed information contact the Indiana Dept of Natural Re-

sources, Div of State Parks and Reservoirs, 402 W Washington, W-298, Indianapolis 46204; 317/232-4124.

SKI AREAS

Place Name	Listed Under
Bendix Woods Ski Area	SOUTH BEND
Paoli Peaks Ski Area	FRENCH LICK
Ski World Ski Area	NASHVILLE

FISHING & HUNTING

Nonresident licenses are available for hunting, 5-day hunting, deer hunting, fishing (1-, 3- and 7-day; annual) and trapping; trout/salmon, game bird, and waterfowl stamps. Resident licenses are available for hunting, deer hunting, hunting & fishing, 1-day fishing, trapping and turkey hunting. Youth hunting license allows children under 18 to hunt all game. Residents ages 17-65 and all non-residents must obtain fishing license. For additional information, including exceptions, bag limits and license fees, contact Div of Fish and Wildlife, Dept of Natural Resources, 402 W Washington St, Rm W273, Indianapolis 46204; 317/232-4080. A free bimonthly newsletter,

Focus, is available to keep sportsmen up to date on division activities. Write to *Focus* at the same address.

Driving Information

Safety belts are mandatory for all persons in front seat of vehicle. Children under 5 years must be in an approved passenger restraint anywhere in vehicle: ages 3 and 4 may use a regulation safety belt; age 2 and under must use an approved safety seat. For further information phone 317/232-1295.

INTERSTATE HIGHWAY SYSTEM

The following alphabetical listing of Indiana towns in *Mobil Travel Guide* shows that these cities are within 10 miles of the indicated Interstate highways. A highway map, however, should be checked for the nearest exit.

Highway Number	Cities/Towns within 10 miles
INTERSTATE 64	Corydon, Jeffersonville, New Albany, Wyandotte.
INTERSTATE 65	Columbus, Indianapolis, Jeffersonville, Lafayette, New Albany, Remington.
INTERSTATE 69	Anderson, Angola, Fort Wayne, Huntington, Indianapolis, Marion, Muncie, Noblesville.
INTERSTATE 70	Brazil, Greencastle, Greenfield, Indianapolis, New Castle, Richmond, Terre Haute.
INTERSTATE 74	Batesville, Crawfordsville, Indianapolis.
INTERSTATE 94	Hammond, Michigan City.

Additional Visitor Information

Six-issue subscriptions to *Outdoor Indiana* may be obtained by contacting Dept of Natural Resources, 402 W Washington, Rm W-160, Indianapolis 46204; 317/232-4200. This official publication of the Department of Natural Resources is $10 for 1 year or $18 for 2 years.

Brochures on attractions, calendar of events, information about historic sites and other subjects are available from the Indiana Dept of Commerce, Tourism & Film Development Div, One N Capitol St, Suite 700, Indianapolis 46204; 800/289-6646.

There are Welcome Centers on highways entering southern Indiana as well as travel information centers located at highway rest areas throughout Indiana. Those who stop by will find information and brochures most helpful in planning stops at points of interest. All are open daily, 24 hours.

Anderson (E-5)

(See also Indianapolis, Muncie)

Founded 1823 **Pop** 59,459 **Elev** 883 ft **Area code** 765 **E-mail** andersonvcb@iquest.net **Web** www.madtourism.com
Information Anderson/Madison County Visitors and Convention Bureau, 6335 S Scatterfield Rd, 46013; 765/643-5633 or 800/533-6569.

Originally, this was the site of a Delaware village in the hills south of the White River. The city was named for Kikthawenund, also called Captain Anderson, a well-known chief of the Delawares. The discovery of natural gas pockets underneath the city in 1886 sparked a ten-year boom, which gave the city the title "Queen of the Gas Belt." One hundred Newport-style gaslights have been added to what is now known as Historic 8th Street. Restored Victorian homes reflect the area's fashionable past.

Anderson is the seat of grain and livestock-producing in Madison County and an important manufacturing center. Two subsidiaries of General Motors, Delco-Remy America and Delphi Interior Lighting Systems, manufacture automotive equipment. Other industrial products include castings, glass, cabinets, corrugated boxes, recreation equipment and packaging machinery. The international headquarters of the nonsectarian Church of God is in Anderson.

What to See and Do

Anderson University (1917). (2,000 students) School of Theology (Sept-June) has collection of Holy Land artifacts. Also on campus are the Jessie Wilson Art Galleries, Boehm Bird Collection and 2,250-seat Reardon Auditorium. The Indianapolis Colts hold summer training camp here (mid-July-mid-Aug). Tours (by appt). E 5th St & College Dr. Phone 765/649-9071. **Free.**

Gruenewald Historic House (1873). Twelve-rm, Second Empire town house of successful German saloonkeeper, decorated in style of 1890s. (Apr-mid-Dec) Living history tours (by appt). House tours (Tues-Fri). 626 Main St. Phone 765/646-5771. ¢¢

Historic West 8th Street. Eleven blks of restored Victorian homes lined with Newport-style gaslights, re-create the 1890s. Tours during Gaslight Festival (see ANNUAL EVENTS). Phone 765/643-5633. **Free.**

Historical Military Armor Museum. Large collection of light-weight tanks from WWI to the present; completely restored and operational. Rides given in military tank or land tract vehicle, weather permitting (addl fee). (Tues, Thurs & Sun; closed most major hols) 2330 Crystal St, I-69 exit 26. Phone 765/649-TANK or 800/875-8265. ¢

Mounds State Park. Within this 259-acre park of rolling woodlands are several well-preserved earth formations constructed many centuries ago by a prehistoric race of Adena-Hopewell mound builders. On bluffs overlooking the White River are earth structures that were once an important center of an ancient civilization of which very little is known. The largest earth structure is 9 ft high and nearly 1/4 mi in circumference. Smaller structures nearby include conical mounds and a fiddle-shaped earthwork. 2 mi E on IN 232.

Park facilities include swimming pool; fishing on White River. Hiking trails. Cross-country skiing. Picnicking, playground, concession. Camping. Nature center; naturalist service. Standard fees. (Daily) Phone 765/642-6627.

Paramount Theatre and Ballroom. Restored 1929 atmospheric theatre designed to appear as a Spanish courtyard. Tours (by appt; closed hols) 1124 Meridian Plaza. Phone 765/642-1234. Tours ¢

Annual Events

"Little 500." Anderson Speedway, 1311 Pendleton Ave. Auto races. Reservations necessary. Phone 765/642-0206. Wkend of Indianapolis "500."

Victorian Gaslight Festival. Historic West 8th St. 1890s atmosphere with home tours, events, food, arts & crafts, parade. 2nd wkend June.

Free Fair. Athletic Park Fairgrounds. Phone 765/646-5661. Late June-early July.

Motels

(Rates may be higher during Indianapolis "500")

✔★ **BEST INNS OF AMERICA.** *5706 Scatterfield Rd (46013).* 765/644-2000; res: 800/237-8466. 93 rms, 2 story. S $43.88-$50.88; D $46.88-$53.88; each addl $7; under 18 free. Crib free. Pet accepted. TV; cable. Complimentary continental bkfst. Restaurant adj 6 am-10 pm. Ck-out 1 pm. Cr cds: A, C, D, DS, MC, V.

D ✔ ⊠ ⊠ SC

★ **COMFORT INN.** *2205 E 59th St (46013).* 765/644-4422. 56 rms, 2 story, 14 suites. Mar-July: S $38-$44; D $42-$59; each addl $5; suites $45-$61; under 19 free; wkend rates; lower rates rest of yr. Crib free. Pet accepted, some restrictions. TV; cable. Indoor pool; whirlpool. Complimentary continental bkfst. Ck-out 11 am. Game rm. Refrigerator, microwave in suites. Cr cds: A, C, D, DS, ER, JCB, MC, V.

D ⚡ 🏊 🏊 🐾 SC

★ ★ **HOLIDAY INN.** *5920 Scatterfield Rd (IN 109 Bypass) (46013), at jct I-69.* 765/644-2581; FAX 765/642-8545. 158 rms, 2 story. S, D $79-$94; each addl $7; under 18 free; 2-day min: Indianapolis "500." Crib free. Pet accepted. TV; cable (premium). 2 pools, 1 indoor; whirlpool, poolside serv. Coffee in rms. Restaurants 6-10 am, 11 am-midnight. Rm serv. Bar 11-2 am, Sun noon-midnight; entertainment. Ck-out 11 am. Coin lndry. Meeting rms. Business servs avail. In-rm modem link. Bellhops. Valet serv. Gift shop. Free Anderson airport transportation. Sauna. Cr cds: A, C, D, DS, JCB, MC, V.

D ⚡ 🏊 🏊 🐾 SC

★ **LEES INN.** *2114 E 59th St (46013).* 765/649-2500; FAX 765/643-0349; res: 800/733-5337. 72 rms, 2 story. S, D $69-$145; each addl $10; under 15 free. Crib free. TV; cable. Complimentary continental bkfst. Restaurant adj 7 am-10 pm. Ck-out noon. Meeting rms. Cr cds: A, C, D, DS, MC, V.

D 🏊 🐾 SC

★ **RAMADA INN.** *5901 Scatterfield Rd (IN 109 Bypass) (46013).* 765/649-0451; FAX 765/649-5484. 115 rms, 2 story. S $65-$75; D $71-$89; each addl $10; suites $139-$145; under 12 free. Pet accepted, some restrictions; $25. TV; cable. Indoor pool; whirlpool, poolside serv. Restaurant 6:30 am-10 pm. Rm serv. Bar noon-midnight; Fri, Sat to 2 am; entertainment. Ck-out noon. Coin lndry. Meeting rms. Sundries. Tennis. Sauna. Cr cds: A, C, D, DS, MC, V.

D ⚡ 🏊 🏊 🐾 SC

Angola (A-6)

(See also Auburn)

Pop 5,824 **Elev** 1,055 ft **Area code** 219 **Zip** 46703 **E-mail** lakes101@locl.net **Web** www.lakes101.org
Information Steuben Co Tourism Bureau, 207 S Wayne St; 800/LAKE-101.

This is a tranquil town in the northeastern corner of Indiana's resort area. The wooded hills surrounding Angola provide more than 100 lakes for swimming, boating and fishing in the summer and ice-skating in the winter.

What to See and Do

Crooked Lake. Approx 800 acres. Camping, picnicking, swimming, boating and fishing. 2 mi W on US 20, then 3 mi N on I-69.

Pokagon State Park. A 1,203-acre park on the shores of Lake James and Snow Lake in the heart of the northern Indiana lake country. Swimming beach, bathhouse, lifeguard, waterskiing; fishing; boating (rentals). Hiking trails, saddle barn. Skiing, ice-skating, tobogganing, ice fishing. Picnicking, concession. Camping. Nature center; wildlife exhibit; naturalist service. Standard fees. (Daily) 6 mi N on US 27. Phone 219/833-2012.

Resort

★ ★ **POTAWATOMI INN.** *6 Lane 100 A Lake James, 6 mi N on IN 127, 1/2 mi W of I-69 in Pokagon State Park (entrance fee, Apr-Oct & wkends Nov-Mar).* 219/833-1077; FAX 219/833-4087. 126 rms in 2-story inn, 16 cabin-style rms, 3 suites. S $43-$55; D & cabin-style rms $56-$62; suites $109-$119. Crib $3. TV. Indoor pool; whirlpools. Dining rm 7 am-8 pm. Ck-out noon, ck-in 4 pm. Meeting rms. Business servs avail. Gift shop. Grocery in summer. Guest lndry. Tennis. X-country ski on site. Exercise equipt; bicycle, treadmill, sauna. Hayrides. Private beach; lifeguard in summer. Dock, boats. Tobogganing. Game rm. Lawn games. Fireplace.

On Lake James. Built in 1926 in the Pokagon State Park, land acquired from the Potawatomi Indians. Cr cds: A, DS, MC, V.

D 🏊 ⚡ 🏊 🏊 🚶 🏊 🏊

Restaurant

★ ★ ★ **THE HATCHERY.** *118 S Elizabeth St.* 219/665-9957. Hrs: 5-9 pm; Fri, Sat to 10 pm. Closed Sun; major hols. Res accepted; required in summer. Bar 4 pm-midnight. Wine cellar. Semi-a la carte: dinner $13-$19. Specializes in fresh seafood, lamb, steak. Patio dining. Entertainment Fri, Sat. Cr cds: A, C, D, DS, MC, V.

D

Auburn (B-6)

(See also Angola, Fort Wayne)

Pop 9,379 **Elev** 870 ft **Area code** 219 **Zip** 46706
Information Chamber of Commerce, 136 W 7th St; 219/925-2100.

What to See and Do

Auburn-Cord-Duesenberg Museum. More than 140 examples of these and other well-known antique, classic and special-interest cars are displayed in the original showroom of the Auburn Automobile Co; collections of automotive literature. (Daily; closed Jan 1, Thanksgiving, Dec 25) (See ANNUAL EVENT) 1600 S Wayne St. Phone 219/925-1444. ¢¢¢

Gene Stratton Porter Historic Site. Home of well-known Indiana author/naturalist/photographer. Built on Sylvan Lake in a forested area with a great variety of wildflowers and wildlife; designed by Mrs Porter and completed in 1914. Two-story log cabin furnished with many original pieces, photographs, memorabilia. Special events. Tours of cabin (Mar-Dec, daily exc Mon; closed Easter, Thanksgiving, Dec 25). 25 NW via I-69, US 6, IN 9, near Rome City. Phone 219/854-3790. **Free.**

National Automotive and Truck Museum. More than 100 cars and trucks on display with a focus on post-WWI automobiles; also auto-related exhibits. (Daily; closed Jan 1, Thanksgiving, Dec 25) 1000 Gordon M. Buerig Place. Phone 219/925-9100. ¢¢

Annual Event

Auburn-Cord-Duesenberg Festival. Auto auction, classic car show, parades, many events. Phone 219/925-3600. Early Sept.

Motels

★ ★ **AUBURN INN.** *225 Touring Dr.* 219/925-6363; res: 800/255-2541. 53 rms, 2 story. Apr-Oct: S $60-$150; D $68-$150; each addl $8; suites $125; under 16 free; wkend rates. Crib free. TV; cable. Heated pool. Complimentary bkfst buffet. Ck-out noon. Meeting rms. Business servs avail. Health club privileges. Cr cds: A, C, D, DS, MC, V.

D 🏊 🏊 🐾 SC

✔ **COUNTRY HEARTH INN.** *1115 W 7th St (IN 8).* 219/925-1316; FAX 219/927-8012; res: 800/848-5767. Web www.travelbase.com/country-hearth-auburn. 78 rms, 2 story. S $61-$67; D $63-$69; each addl $6; suites, kit. units $70-$78; under 18 free. Crib free. TV; cable (premium). Pool. Complimentary continental bkfst. Ck-out noon. Meeting rm. Business servs avail. Health club privileges. Cr cds: A, C, D, DS, MC, V.

D 🏊 🏊 🐾 SC

★ **HOLIDAY INN EXPRESS.** *404 Touring Dr.* 219/925-1900; FAX 219/927-1138. E-mail cndmgment@aol.com. 70 rms, 3 story. S $74-$80; D $80-$85; suites $90-$95; under 18 free; higher rates special events. Pet accepted. TV; cable (premium). Complimentary continental bkfst. Coffee in rms. Restaurant 6 am-10 pm. Ck-out noon. Meeting rm.

Business servs avail. In-rm modem link. Coin lndry. Health club privileges. Indoor pool; whirlpool. Some refrigerators, microwaves. Cr cds: A, C, D, DS, JCB, MC, V.

D ⚲ ⚒ 🔥 SC

Aurora (G-6)

Founded 1819 **Pop** 3,825 **Elev** 501 ft **Area code** 812 **Zip** 47001
Information Office of the Mayor, PO Box 158; 812/926-1777.

What to See and Do

Hillforest (ca 1855). Fully restored Italian Renaissance villa on 10 acres. Architecture and period furnishings incorporate characteristics of steamboat era. (Apr-mid-Dec, daily exc Mon; closed Thanksgiving) (See ANNUAL EVENTS) 213 5th St. Phone 812/926-0087. ¢¢

Annual Events

Aurora Farmers Fair. Three-day fair featuring rides, games, parade; entertainment. 1st wkend Oct.

Victorian Christmas. Hillforest. Re-creation of a Victorian Christmas. First 2 wkends Dec.

Restaurants

★ ★ **TREE HOUSE.** 10768 Gatch Hill Rd (US 50). 812/926-3737. Hrs: 11 am-9 pm; Fri, Sat to 10 pm; Sun to 8 pm. Closed Mon; Dec 25, also 2 wks Jan. Res accepted. Serv bar. Semi-a la carte: lunch $3.50-$13.95, dinner $8.95-$31.90. Sun buffet $11.95. Child's meals. Specializes in prime rib, seafood. Salad bar. Interior courtyard with live tree in center. Cr cds: A, C, D, DS, MC, V.

D

★ **WHISKY'S.** (US 50 at Front St, Lawrenceburg 47025) approx 5 mi E on US 50. 812/537-4239. Hrs: 11:30 am-10 pm; Sat 4-11 pm. Closed Sun; Easter, July 4, Dec 25. Res accepted Mon-Fri. Bar. Semi-a la carte: lunch, dinner $4.95-$16.50. Child's meals. Specializes in pork ribs. Dining in two restored bldgs (circa 1850 & 1835) joined together. Cr cds: A, DS, MC, V.

D

Batesville (G-6)

Pop 4,720 **Elev** 983 ft **Area code** 812 **Zip** 47006

What to See and Do

Whitewater Canal State Historic Site. Includes part of a restored 14-mi section of the Whitewater Canal, which provided transportation between Hagerstown and the Ohio River at Lawrenceburg from 1836-1860. *Ben Franklin III* canal boat offers horse-drawn boat cruise (25 min) through the Duck Creek aqueduct (1848) to the canal's only remaining operating lock (May-Oct, Wed-Sun; other times by appt). Working gristmill in Metamora (Wed-Sun; free). Fishing, hiking, canoeing and picnicking permitted along the canal. 14 mi N on US 52 in Metamora. Phone 317/647-6512. **Free;** Canal boat cruise ¢

Inn

✔★ ★ **SHERMAN HOUSE.** 35 S Main St (IN 229). 812/934-2407; FAX 812/934-1230. 23 rms, 2 story. S $44-$55; D $51-$55; suites $66; under 12 free. Crib free. TV; cable (premium). Restaurant (see SHERMAN

HOUSE). Bar 11 am-midnight. Ck-out 11 am, ck-in 1 pm. Meeting rms. Business servs avail. Gift shop. Exercise equipt; bicycle, treadmill. Inn since 1852. Cr cds: A, C, D, MC, V.

D 🍴 ⚒ 🔥 SC

Restaurant

★ ★ **SHERMAN HOUSE.** (See Sherman House Inn) 812/934-2407. Hrs: 6:30 am-9 pm; Fri, Sat to 10 pm; Sun to 8 pm. Closed Jan 1, Dec 25. Res accepted. German, Amer menu. Bar. Semi-a la carte: bkfst $2.50-$4, lunch $2.95-$6.25, dinner $8.95-$15.95. Child's meals. Specializes in châteaubriand, veal. Salad bar. Lobster tank. Old World atmosphere. Established in 1852. Cr cds: A, C, D, MC, V.

D

Bedford (H-4)

(See also Bloomington, French Lick)

Founded 1825 **Pop** 13,817 **Elev** 699 ft **Area code** 812 **Zip** 47421
Information Chamber of Commerce, 1116 16th St, PO Box 1193; 812/275-4493.

Bedford is the center of Indiana limestone quarrying, one of the state's foremost industries. Limestone quarried here was used in the construction of the World War Memorial in Indianapolis, the Empire State Building in New York and the Federal Triangle in Washington, DC.

This is an agricultural area producing livestock, grain and fruit. Headquarters of Hoosier National Forest and Wayne National Forest (see IRONTON, OH) are here. Williams Dam, 11 miles southwest on IN 450, offers fishing on the White River.

What to See and Do

Bluespring Caverns. One of the world's largest cavern systems; more than 20 mi of explored passageways and 15 mi of underground streams join to form the large river upon which tour boats travel. Electric lighting reveals many unusual sights, including eyeless blindfish and blind crawfish. Picnicking. Gift shop. (Apr-Oct) 6 mi SW via US 50. Phone 812/279-9471. ¢¢

Hoosier National Forest. Approx 189,000 acres spread through 9 counties. Swimming, boats; picnicking; hiking; horseback trails; fishing, hunting; nature study; historic sites. Campsites at Hardin Ridge (Monroe Co), German Ridge, Saddle Lake, Celina Lake (Perry Co) and Springs Valley (Orange County) recreation areas. Campsites on first-come basis. Both N and S of Bedford: to reach the N portion, NE on IN 58 (or E on US 50 then N on IN 446); to reach the S portion, SW on US 50 (or S on IN 37 & W on IN 60). Contact Forest Supervisor, US Forest Service, 811 Constitution Ave; 812/275-5987. Fees are charged at recreation sites for camping; entrance fee at Hardin Ridge. In portion of the forest S of Bedford is

Pioneer Mothers Memorial Forest. An 88-acre forest of virgin timber that includes white oak and black walnut trees of giant dimensions. From Paoli, S on IN 37, in Orange Co.

Lawrence County Historical Museum. Display of Indiana limestone, Native American artifacts, Civil War items, pioneer relics, World War I & II items; genealogical library. (Mon-Fri; closed hols) County Courthouse basement, Rm 12. Phone 812/275-4141. **Free.**

Osborne Spring Park. Approx 30 acres. Restored log cabin (1817). Camping (fee); picnicking. (Daily) 17 mi NW via IN 58 to Owensburg, then 3 mi NW on Osborne Spring Rd. ¢¢

Spring Mill State Park (see). On IN 60, 10 mi S in Mitchell.

Motels

✔★ **MARK III.** *1711 M Street (US 50).* 812/275-5935. 21 rms, 2 story. S $35; D $38; each addl $3; under 12 free. Crib free. Pet accepted, some restrictions. TV; cable (premium). Complimentary coffee in rms. Restaurant adj 11 am-midnight. Ck-out 11 am. Grill. Cr cds: A, C, D, DS, MC, V.

⊡ ⊡ ⊡ ⊡ SC

★ ★ **STONEHENGE.** *911 Constitution Ave.* 812/279-8111; FAX 812/279-0172; res: 800/274-2974. E-mail henge@kiva.net. 97 rms, 3 story. S $60-$125; D $66-$135; each addl $4; under 16 free. Crib $6. TV; cable (premium). Pool. Restaurant 6 am-9 pm; Fri to 10 pm; Sat 5-10 pm. Rm serv. Bar 4-10 pm; closed Sun. Ck-out noon. Meeting rms. Business servs avail. Health club privileges. Cr cds: A, C, D, DS, MC, V.

D ⊡ ⊡ ⊡ SC

Bloomington (G-4)

(See also Bedford, Nashville)

Settled 1818 **Pop** 60,633 **Elev** 745 ft **Area code** 812 **Web** www.visit bloomington.com

Information Bloomington/Monroe County Convention and Visitors Bureau, 2855 N Walnut St, 47404; 812/334-8900 or 800/800-0037.

Bloomington is an industrial and college town, the seat of Monroe County. Limestone quarries and mills in the vicinity contributed to its early industrial growth. The electronics industry and tourism play an important part in the city's economy today.

What to See and Do

Brown County State Park (see). 17 mi E on IN 46.

Butler Winery. Wines made in cellar; cheeses & preserves; tastings. (Daily; closed Jan 1, Dec 25) 1022 N College Ave. Phone 812/339-7233. **Free.**

Indiana University (1820). (34,863 students) One of the outstanding state universities in the country. Notable are the Lilly Library of Rare Books (daily exc Sun); Dailey Family Collection of Hoosier art and Thomas Hart Benton murals in auditorium (daily exc Sun; special tours, phone 812/855-9528); Art Museum (daily exc Mon); Glenn Black Laboratory of Archaeology (daily); Hoagy Carmichael Room (by appt); William H. Mathers Museum (daily exc Mon; summer hrs vary); Musical Arts Center (tours by appt, phone 812/855-9055). All buildings closed univ hols. 5 blks E of public square.

Lake Monroe. Joint project of Indiana Dept of Natural Resources and US Army Corps of Engineers. A 10,000-acre lake with approx 150-mi shoreline. Picnicking, waterskiing; swimming at Hardin Ridge, Fairfax and Paynetown areas (Memorial Day-Labor Day); fishing (all yr); boating (ramps); tent & trailer sites (standard fees; no camping at Fairfax). Paynetown State Recreation Area (standard fees). Hardin Ridge Federal Recreation Area in Hoosier National Forest (see BEDFORD). 7 mi SE via IN 46 to IN 446. Contact Monroe Reservoir, Dept of Natural Resources, 4850 South State Rd 446, 47401; 812/837-9546 or 812/837-9318. Per vehicle ¢

McCormick's Creek State Park. The creek plunges headlong through a limestone canyon in this 1,833-acre park to join the White River at its border. Trails, bridle paths and roads lead through beech and pine forests, ravines and gullies. Wolf Cave and the stone bridge over McCormick's Creek are unusual features. Swimming pool; creek fishing. Tennis. Picnicking, playground. Camping, cabins, inn. Nature center; nature trails, naturalist service. Standard fees. 12 mi NW on IN 46. Phone 812/829-2235. Per vehicle ¢

Monroe County Historical Society Museum. Displays depicting history of county and limestone industry. (Tues-Sat, also Sun afternoons; closed major hols) 6th & Washington Sts. Phone 812/332-2517. **Free.**

Oliver Winery. Tastings; preserves & gift items. Tours (wkends). (Mon-Sat, also Sun afternoons; closed Jan 1, Thanksgiving, Dec 25, election days) 7 mi N on IN 37. Phone 812/876-5800 or 800/25-TASTE. **Free.**

Annual Events

Little 500 Bicycle Race. Indiana University campus. Bicycle and tricycle races, golf jamboree, entertainment. Phone 812/855-9152. Apr.

Monroe County Fair. Monroe County Fairgrounds. Rodeo; midway; exhibits. Late July-early Aug.

Madrigal Feasts. Indiana University Campus. Phone 812/334-8900. Dec.

Motel

★ ★ **HAMPTON INN.** *2100 N Walnut (47401), IN 37 exit College to Walnut.* 812/334-2100; FAX 812/334-8433. 131 rms, 4 story. S $63; D $71; under 18 free. Crib free. Pet accepted, some restrictions. TV; cable (premium), VCR avail. Pool. Complimentary continental bkfst. Restaurant adj open 24 hrs. Ck-out noon. Meeting rms. Business servs avail. In-rm modem link. Valet serv. Downhill/x-country ski 12 mi. Some in-rm whirlpools. Cr cds: A, C, D, DS, MC, V.

D ⊡ ⊡ ⊡ ⊡ ⊡ SC

Motor Hotels

★ ★ ★ **COURTYARD BY MARRIOTT.** *310 S College Ave (47403).* 812/335-8000; FAX 812/336-9997. 117 rms, 5 story. S, D $79-$84; suites $140; under 18 free; higher rates special events. Crib free. TV; cable (premium). Complimentary coffee in rms. Restaurant nearby. Ck-out noon. Business servs avail. In-rm modem link. Coin lndry. Downhill ski 10 mi. Exercise equipt; weights, bicycle. Indoor pool; whirlpool. Refrigerator, microwave, wet bar in suites. Cr cds: A, C, D, DS, JCB, MC, V.

D ⊡ ⊡ ⊡ ⊡ ⊡ SC

★ ★ ★ **HOLIDAY INN.** *1710 Kinser Pike (47404), jct IN 37 & IN 46.* 812/334-3252; FAX 812/333-1702. 189 rms, 4 story. S $69-$83; D $78-$99; each addl $6; under 18 free. Crib free. TV; cable (premium). Indoor pool; whirlpool. Coffee in rms. Restaurant 6:30 am-10 pm. Rm serv. Bar 2 pm-3 am; Sun to midnight. Ck-out noon. Meeting rms. Business servs avail. In-rm modem link. Free airport transportation. Sundries. Downhill ski 10 mi; x-country ski 15 mi. Sauna. Game rm. Microwaves avail. Univ stadium 2 blks. Cr cds: A, C, D, DS, MC, V.

D ⊡ ⊡ ⊡ ⊡ SC

Resort

★ ★ ★ **CLARION FOURWINDS.** *Fairfax Rd (47402), 8 mi S on IN 37, then 3 mi E on Smithville Rd to Fairfax Rd; on Lake Monroe.* 812/824-9904; FAX 812/824-9816. 126 rms, 3 story. May-Oct: S, D $126-$140; suites $225-$400; lower rates rest of yr. TV; cable (premium), VCR avail. Indoor/outdoor pool; whirlpool. Playground. Supervised child's activities (Memorial Day-Labor Day). Dining rm 7 am-2 pm, 6-9 pm; Fri, Sat to 10:30 pm. Rm serv. Snack bar. Deli. Box lunches. Picnics. Bar; entertainment. Ck-in noon, ck-in 4 pm. Meeting rms. Business servs avail. Grocery. Package store. Airport transportation. Golf privileges; pro. Miniature golf. Downhill/x-country ski 20 mi. Public beach. Boat rental, marina. Lawn games. Soc dir; entertainment, movies. Shared patios, balconies. Picnic tables. Landscaped grounds. Overlooks Lake Monroe Reservoir. Cr cds: A, C, D, DS, ER, JCB, MC, V.

⊡ ⊡ ⊡ ⊡ ⊡ SC

Restaurants

★ **COLORADO STEAKHOUSE.** *1800 N College Ave (47401).* 812/339-9979. Hrs: 11 am-10 pm; Sat to 11 pm. Closed Dec 25.

Res accepted. Bar to midnight. Semi-a la carte: lunch $5-$8, dinner $9.95-$18.95. Child's meals. Specializes in smoked ribs, salmon, shrimp. Atrium dining area. Cr cds: A, C, D, DS, MC, V.

D

✔★ **GRISANTI'S.** *850 Auto Mall Rd (IN 46), adj College Mall. 812/339-9391.* Hrs: 11 am-10 pm; Fri, Sat to 11 pm; Sun to 9 pm. Closed Thanksgiving, Dec 25. Italian menu. Bar. Semi-a la carte: lunch $4.75-$7, dinner $8-$14. Specializes in chicken, seafood, lasagne. Own pasta. Italian country atmosphere. Cr cds: A, D, DS, MC, V.

D

★ **LE PETIT CAFE.** *308 W 6th St (47401). 812/334-9747.* Hrs: 11 am-2 pm, 5:30-9 pm; Sat, Sun to 10 pm. Closed Mon; most major hols. Res accepted. Continental menu. Wine, beer. Semi-a la carte: lunch $5-$10, dinner $13-$20. Specializes in steak Diane, fish, crêpes. Own pasta. Casual dining. Family-owned. Cr cds: MC, V.

Brazil (F-3)

(For accommodations see Greencastle, Terre Haute)

Pop 7,640 **Elev** 659 ft **Area code** 812 **Zip** 47834
Information Clay County Chamber of Commerce, PO Box 23; 812/448-8457.

A former mining center, Brazil was also widely known for its manufacture of building brick, tile and block coal. Bituminous coal is taken extensively from huge open strip mines. Farmers in surrounding Clay County grow corn, wheat, soybeans and raise livestock. Brazil was named for the South American country.

What to See and Do

Clay County Historical Museum. Post office has been utilized as museum offering exhibits of past and present. (Mar-Dec, Sat & Sun afternoon; closed hols) 100 E National Ave. Phone 812/446-4036. **Free.**

Forest Park. Outdoor auditorium and stadium; 18-hole golf adj (fee); swimming pool, wading pool (Memorial Day-Labor Day; fee); playground, ball fields, picnic areas (shelters); Sun evening band concerts in summer. Log cabins preserved from pioneer days, with a display of relics. The Chafariz dos Contas, a granite fountain presented to the city by the Republic of Brazil, is located here. S on IN 59. 812/442-5681 (golf) or 812/448-2752 (pool). **Free.**

Annual Event

Christmas in the Park. Forest Park. Includes parade, holiday fireworks display, musical events and decorated homes and businesses. Phone 812/448-8457. Day after Thanksgiving-Dec 26.

Brown County State Park (G-4)

(For accommodations see Columbus, Nashville)

(S and E of Nashville on IN 46)

There are 15,800 acres of hilly woodland here, with two lakes, streams, a covered bridge and miles of drives and trails. Among the wildlife commonly seen here are white-tailed deer, raccoon, gray squirrel and various birds, including the robin, white-breasted nuthatch, blue jay, cardinal and junco.

This is the largest of Indiana's parks. Swimming (Memorial Day-Labor Day); fishing. Hiking, bridle trails, saddle barn (Apr-Nov). Picnicking, concession (Apr-Nov). Camping. Nature center, naturalist service; 80-foot observation tower with view on Weed Patch Hill. (Daily) Standard fees. Contact Superintendent, PO Box 608, Nashville 47448; 812/988-6406.

Columbus (G-5)

(See also Bloomington, Nashville)

Settled 1820 **Pop** 31,802 **Elev** 656 ft **Area code** 812
Information Visitors Center, 506 5th St, 47201; 812/372-1954.

The architectural designs of many modern buildings in Columbus have attracted international attention. In the heart of the prairie, the project was launched in the late 1930s with the commissioning of Eliel Saarinen to design a church. Since then, more than 50 public and private buildings have been designed by architects such as Saarinen, John Carl Warnecke, Harry Weese, I.M. Pei, Kevin Roche, Eliot Noyes and J.M. Johansen.

What to See and Do

Indianapolis Museum of Art-Columbus. Displays changing exhibits from the Indianapolis Museum of Art (see INDIANAPOLIS) collection. Special exhibitions. (Daily exc Sun; closed major hols) 390 The Commons. Phone 812/376-2597. **Free.**

Otter Creek Golf Course. Bent grass tees; 90 sand bunkers; rolling hills; Robert Trent Jones design. Golf packages. (Mar-Nov) 4 mi E on IN 46. Phone 812/579-5227. ¢¢¢¢¢

Visitors Center. A slide presentation and gift shop are also here. Architectural tours of the town are given; reservations advised. (Apr-Oct, daily; rest of yr, daily exc Sun; closed Dec 25) 506 5th St. Phone 812/372-1954. Tours ¢¢¢

Motor Hotels

(Rates may be higher during Indianapolis "500," Kentucky Derby)

★ ★ ★ **HOLIDAY INN.** *2480 Jonathan Moore Pike (IN 46) (47201), at jct I-65 & IN 46. 812/372-1541; FAX 812/378-9049.* 253 rms, 2-7 story. S $59-$98; D $69-$108; each addl $10; suites $150-$250; under 18 free. Crib free. TV; cable (premium). Indoor pool; whirlpool. Restaurant 6 am-10 pm. Rm serv. Bars 10:30 am-midnight, 5-11 pm; entertainment. Ck-out 11 am. Convention facilities. Business servs avail. In-rm modem link. Bellhops. Sundries. Barber, beauty shop. Exercise equipt; weights, bicycles, sauna. Game rm. Atrium. Many antiques. Turn-of-the-century atmosphere. Cr cds: A, C, D, DS, JCB, MC, V.

D ≋ 🏋 🏊 🛥 🌊 **SC**

★ ★ **RAMADA INN.** *2485 Jonathan Moore Pike (IN 46) (47201), just E of jct I-65. 812/376-3051; FAX 812/376-0949.* 166 rms, 3 story. S $68-$98; D $78-$118; each addl $10; suites $85-$250; under 18 free. Crib free. TV; cable (premium). 2 pools, 1 indoor; whirlpool. Restaurant 6 am-10 pm. Rm serv. Bar. Ck-out noon. Meeting rms. Business servs avail. In-rm modem link. Valet serv. Sundries. Lighted tennis. Exercise equipt; weight machine, bicycles. Paddle boats. Refrigerators, microwaves avail. On 10 acre lake. Cr cds: A, C, D, DS, JCB, MC, V.

D 🚴 ⛵ ≋ 🏊 🏋 🌊 **SC**

Connersville (F-6)

(For accommodations see Batesville)

Founded 1813 **Pop** 15,550 **Elev** 835 ft **Area code** 765 **Zip** 47331 **E-mail** chamber@comsys.net **Web** www.connersvillein.com/chamber
Information Chamber of Commerce, 504 Central Ave; 765/825-2561.

John Connor, who established a fur-trading post here in 1808, later founded the town. Connor was kidnapped from his parents as a child and raised by Native Americans. He served as a Native American guide for General William H. Harrison in 1812, took a Native American wife and became a wealthy landowner and businessman.

The Auburn, Cord, McFarlan and Lexington automobiles were once manufactured here. Today, the most important industrial products are dishwashers, automobile components and building supplies.

What to See and Do

Brookville Lake State Reservoir. US government flood-control project, now a state recreation area. Approx 16,500 acres. Swimming, waterskiing; fishing; boating (ramps, rentals). Hiking; hunting. Picnicking. Camping. Standard fees. (Mon-Fri) 12 mi E on IN 44 to Liberty, then 5 mi S on IN 101. Phone 765/647-2657. Per vehicle ¢

Mary Gray Bird Sanctuary of the Indiana Audubon Society. Has 686 wooded acres with marked trails and picnicking facilities. Museum and library (by appt). (Daily) 3¹/₂ mi S on IN 121, then 3¹/₂ mi W on County Rd 350 S.Contact Sanctuary Manager, 3497 S Bird Sanctuary Rd; 765/827-0908. **Donation.**

Whitewater Memorial State Park. More than 1,700 acres, with lake. Swimming beach, bathhouse; fishing; boating (electric motors only; ramps, dock, rentals). Hiking, bridle trails. Picnicking (shelters), concession. Campground, family cabins. Solar-heated visitor center. Park (daily). Standard fees. 12 mi E on IN 44 to Liberty, then 1 mi S on IN 101. Phone 765/458-5565. Per vehicle ¢

Whitewater Valley Railroad. Round-trip excursions on vintage railroad cars. (May-Sept, Sat, Sun & hols; Oct, Thurs, Fri) 1 mi S on IN 121. Contact PO Box 406; 765/825-2054. ¢¢¢¢

Annual Event

Fayette County Free Fair. Park Rd. Agricultural and industrial displays; midway, entertainment, horse racing. Last wkend July-early Aug.

Corydon (J-4)

(See also New Albany, Wyandotte)

Founded 1808 **Pop** 2,661 **Elev** 549 ft **Area code** 812 **Zip** 47112 **E-mail** info@tourindiana.com **Web** www.tourindiana.com
Information Chamber of Commerce of Harrison County, 310 N Elm St; 812/738-2137.

Corydon was the scene of the only battle fought on Indiana soil during the Civil War. A Confederate raiding party under General John Hunt Morgan occupied the town briefly on July 9, 1863, holding the home guard captive.

What to See and Do

Battle of Corydon Memorial Park. Approx 5¹/₃ acres, with period cabin, authentic Civil War cannon and nature trail. Park marks the site of one of the few Civil War battles fought on Northern soil, July 9, 1863. (Daily) S on IN 135 Business. Phone 812/738-8236. **Free.**

Buffalo Trace Park. Approx 150 acres with sports facilities, camping (fee), picnicking. Thirty-acre lake with swimming, fishing, boating, petting zoo;

bumper boats. (May-Oct, daily) Some fees. Approx 10 mi N on IN 135, then ¹/₂ mi E on US 150, near Palmyra. Phone 812/364-6112. Per vehicle ¢

Corydon Capitol State Historic Site. Corydon was the seat of the Indiana Territorial government (1813-1816) when the first constitutional convention assembled here. Following Indiana's admission to the Union in 1816, this building was the state capitol, housing the first sessions of the state legislature and supreme court, until 1825. Construction of the blue limestone building started in 1814 and was completed in 1816. Nearby is Governor Hendricks' headquarters, home of Indiana's second governor; restored. (Daily exc Mon; closed some hols) Capitol Ave. Phone 812/738-4890. **Free.** Nearby is

> **Constitution Elm Monument.** Indiana's first constitution was drawn up here in June, 1816, in the shade of this large elm tree. High St.

Governor Hendricks' Home (1817). Governor's headquarters from 1822-1825. A restoration project by the State of Indiana portrays Indiana homelife in three distinct time periods between 1820 and 1880. (Daily exc Mon; closed some hols) 202 E Walnut St. Phone 812/738-4890. **Free.**

Industrial tour. Zimmerman Art Glass. Glass sculpturing, paperweights and hand-blown objects. (Tues-Sat) 395 Valley Rd. Phone 812/738-2206. **Free.**

Marengo Cave Park. Dripstone Trail tour (1 mi) of underground cave features huge corridors with colorful formations. Crystal Palace Tour (¹/₃ mi) features underground palace. (Daily; closed Thanksgiving, Dec 25) Also picnic area (shelters), swimming (fee), nature trail, camping (Apr-Oct); trail rides (summer, daily; spring & fall, wkends; fee). Approx 10 mi N of I-64 via IN 66 exit 92, on IN 64 at Marengo. Phone 812/365-2705. ¢¢¢

Squire Boone Caverns and Village. Caverns discovered in 1790 by Daniel Boone's brother, Squire, while hiding from Native Americans. Travertine formations, stalactites, stalagmites, underground streams and waterfalls. Above-ground village includes restored working gristmill, petting zoo, craft shops, demonstrations. Hayrides; 110 acres of forest with nature trails and picnic areas. One-hr cavern tours. (Memorial Day wkend-Labor Day wkend, daily) Admission includes all activities and facilities. 10 mi S on IN 135. Phone 812/732-4381. ¢¢¢

Annual Events

Popcorn Festival. Town Square. 3rd Sat May.

Harrison County Fair. Livestock, poultry, farm and 4-H Club exhibits; harness racing. Held annually since 1860. July.

Motel

✔★ **BEST WESTERN OLD CAPITOL INN.** IN 135 & I-64. 812/738-4192; FAX 812/738-4192, ext. 316. 77 rms, 2 story. S $46-$60; D $56-$68; each addl $8; higher rates Kentucky Derby. Crib free. TV; cable. Pool. Complimentary coffee in lobby. Ck-out noon. Meeting rms. Business servs avail. Sundries. Cr cds: A, C, D, DS, ER, JCB, MC, V.

≋ ⊠ 🔥 SC

Inn

★ ★ **KINTER HOUSE.** 101 S Capitol Ave. 812/738-2020; FAX 812/738-7430. 15 rms, 3 story. July-Oct: S, D $49-$99; under 12 free; higher rates wkends; lower rates rest of yr. TV; cable (premium), VCR avail. Complimentary full bkfst. Ck-out 11 am, ck-in 1 pm. Business servs avail. Lighted tennis privileges, pro. 18-hole golf privileges, greens fee $15-$20, pro. Brick Victorian house (1873); antique furnishings. Totally nonsmoking. Cr cds: A, DS, MC, V.

D 🖈 🎿 ⊠ 🔥

Restaurant

★ **MAGDALENA'S.** 104 Chestnut St. 812/738-8075. Hrs: 9 am-9:30 pm; Fri, Sat to 10:30 pm; Sun from 11 am. Closed some major hols. Res accepted. Wine. A la carte entrees: bkfst $1-$4, lunch $3-$5.99, dinner $7-$14.99. Specializes in homemade soup, steak, chicken. Ice cream parlor. Casual dining. Cr cds: A, D, DS, MC, V.

D SC 🔧

Crawfordsville (E-3)

Settled 1822 **Pop** 13,584 **Elev** 769 ft **Area code** 765 **Zip** 47933 **E-mail** mcvcb@tctc.com **Web** www.tctc.com/~mcvcb

Information Montgomery County Visitors & Convention Bureau, 412 E Main St; 765/362-5200 or 800/866-3973.

Crawfordsville, "Athens of the Hoosier State," has long been a literary center. It has been the home of nearly a dozen authors and playwrights, among them General Lew Wallace, who wrote *Ben Hur* here; Maurice Thompson, author of *Alice of Old Vincennes* and Meredith Nicholson, author of *House of a Thousand Candles*. Wabash College is located here.

Printing, steel and the production of travel trailers, fencing, nails and plastics are some of the local industries. Montgomery County, of which Crawfordsville is the seat, is a rich corn and hog region.

What to See and Do

Clements Canoes. Canoe livery with more than 500 units avail. Canoe on Sugar Creek, designated by the DNR as the state's most scenic waterway. Various length trips avail; also guided or self-guided rafting avail. (Apr-Oct, daily) 613 Old Lafayette Rd. Phone 765/362-2781. ¢¢¢¢

Ben Hur Museum. The study of General Lew Wallace, author of *Ben Hur*; he was also a soldier, diplomat and painter. Memorabilia from the movie *Ben Hur* along with war relics, art objects and personal items. (June-Aug, daily exc Mon; early Apr-May & Sept-Oct, Tues-Sun afternoons) E Pike St & Wallace Ave. Phone 765/362-5769. ¢

Lake Waveland. A 360-acre lake with canoeing, boating (rentals; fee), swimming, waterslide; fishing. Tennis courts. Also 248-acre park with camping (fee), tent and trailer sites (fee), showers, picnic area. (Apr-Oct) 13 mi S via IN 47 in Waveland. Phone 765/435-2073. Per vehicle ¢¢

Lane Place. Greek-revival residence of Henry S. Lane (1811-1881), Indiana governor and US senator. Collection of colonial, federal and Victorian furnishings, dolls and china; Civil War memorabilia; furnished log cabin (by appt). (Apr-Oct, Tues-Fri, Sun; closed most hols) (See ANNUAL EVENTS) 212 S Water St. Phone 765/362-3416. ¢

Old Jail Museum. Completed in 1882, the building's unique feature is a two-story cylindrical cellblock; the cells rotate while the bars remain stationary. Sheriff's residence has changing exhibits. (June-Aug, daily; Apr-May & Sept-Oct, Wed-Sun, afternoons) (See ANNUAL EVENTS) 225 N Washington St. Phone 765/362-5222. **Free.**

Shades State Park. Approx 3,000 acres of woods. Deep ravines, high sandstone cliffs, overlooks. Fishing in Sugar Creek. Hiking trails. Picnicking, playground. Campsites (no electric hookups). Backpack & canoe camps. Naturalist service (May-Aug). (Daily) Standard fees. 9 mi SW on IN 47, then 5 mi W on IN 234. Phone 765/435-2810. Per vehicle ¢

Turkey Run State Park (see). 23 mi SW on IN 47.

Annual Events

Sugar Creek Canoe Race. Race begins at Clements Canoes. Late Apr.

Strawberry Festival. Lane Place. Sport tournaments, parade, arts & crafts, food, entertainment. 2nd wkend in June.

Old Jail Museum Breakout. Old Jail Museum. Craft booths, refreshments; entertainment. Phone 765/362-5222. Labor Day.

Christmas Candlelight Tour. Historic homes and churches; food, entertainment. Horse-drawn sleigh rides. 2nd wkend Dec.

Motels

★ ★ **HOLIDAY INN.** *2500 N Lafayette Rd, jct US 231 & I-74.* *765/362-8700.* 150 rms, 2 story. S, D $65-$75; each addl $6; under 19 free; higher rates Indianapolis "500" (2-day min). Crib free. Pet accepted. TV; cable (premium), VCR avail. Heated pool. Restaurant 6 am-2 pm, 5-9 pm. Rm serv. Bar 11 am-midnight, Fri, Sat noon-2 am, Sun from 3 pm; entertainment. Ck-out noon. Coin lndry. Meeting rms. Business servs avail. In-rm modem link. Valet serv. Sundries. Game rm. Some microwaves. Cr cds: A, C, D, DS, JCB, MC, V.

D ⊷ ≈ ⛱ 🐾 SC

★ ★ **HOLIDAY INN.** *(I-65 & IN 39, Lebanon 46052) 765/482-0500; FAX 765/482-0311.* 209 rms, 2 story. S, D $79-$99; each addl $8; suites $154; under 19 free; higher rates special events. Crib free. TV; cable, VCR. Complimentary coffee in rms. Restaurant 7 am-10 pm; Fri, Sat to 11 pm. Rm serv. Bar from noon; Fri, Sat to midnight. Ck-out 11 am. Meeting rms. Business center. In-rm modem link. Bellhops. Valet serv. Sundries. Gift shop. Coin lndry. 18-hole golf privileges. Exercise equipt; bicycle, treadmill. Indoor pool; whirlpool. Playground. Game rm. Some refrigerators, microwaves, wet bars. Cr cds: A, C, D, DS, ER, JCB, MC, V.

D 🏃 ≈ 🏌 ⛱ 🐾 SC 🎿

Restaurant

✔ ★ **BUNGALOW.** *210 E Pike St. 765/362-2596.* Hrs: 11 am-2 pm, 4:30 pm-midnight; Tues to 2 pm; Fri to 2 am; Sat 5 pm-2 am. Closed Sun; major hols. Res accepted. Italian, Amer menu. Bar. Lunch $4.95-$7.95, dinner $8.95-$16.95. Specializes in steak, chicken Alfredo. Cr cds: D, MC, V.

Elkhart (A-4)

(See also Goshen, Mishawaka, Nappanee, South Bend)

Founded 1832 **Pop** 43,627 **Elev** 748 ft **Area code** 219 **E-mail** ecconv @amishcountry.org **Web** www.amish-country.org

Information Elkhart County Convention and Visitor Bureau, 219 Caravan Dr, 46514; 219/262-8161 or 800/262-8161.

Located at the confluence of the St Joseph and Elkhart rivers and on Christiana Creek, Elkhart is a community of bridges. Originally a crossroads of Native American trails, the town was named for a small island in the St Joseph River that Native Americans said was shaped like an elk's heart.

A 19th-century grocer (cornetist in the town band) suffered an injured upper lip in a brawl and devised a soft rubber mouthpiece for cornets. He received so many requests for mouthpieces that in 1875 he rented a one-room building and started the manufacture of brass cornets. This led to Elkhart's becoming the band instrument center of the country. Approximately 50 percent of the nation's band instruments are manufactured here by 15 firms.

Elkhart also has many industrial plants, producing diverse items such as pharmaceuticals, mobile homes, recreational vehicles, electronic components, construction machinery and plastic machinery.

What to See and Do

Elkhart County Historical Museum. Furnished cottage; Victorian home, country store, schoolroom, barn; rm depicting a 1930s house; uniforms from Civil War through Vietnam; research library; Native American artifacts; railroad rm; special programs. (Wed-Fri & Sun; closed hols; also mid-Dec-Feb) 304 W Vistula St, 8 mi E via IN 120 (Vistula St), in Bristol. Phone 219/848-4322. ¢¢

Midwest Museum of American Art. Permanent collection of 19th- and 20th-century artists, including Rockwell, Wood, Avery and Grandma

Moses; traveling exhibits; lectures; tours. (Daily exc Mon; closed major hols) 429 S Main St. Phone 219/293-6660. ¢¢

National New York Central Railroad Museum. Large collection of memorabilia from NYC railroad stations and rail cars, along with videos of NYC trains in action. Housed in a late 1880s freight house, the museum also boasts 3 restored locomotives: a 3001 L-3a "Mohawk" steam locomotive (the only one of its kind in existence), the E-8 diesel locomotive and the GG-1 electric locomotive. (Tues-Sun, limited hrs; closed major hols) 721 S Main St. Phone 219/294-3001. ¢

Ruthmere (ca 1910). Restored mansion features elaborate handcrafted ceilings, walls and woodwork; murals, silk wall coverings, period furnishings; landscaped grounds. Guided tours (Apr-mid-Dec, Tues-Sat; closed hols). 302 E Beardsley Ave. Phone 219/264-0330. ¢¢

S. Ray Miller Antique Auto Museum. More than 35 antique and classic cars on display; dozens restored to showroom quality. Includes 1930 Duesenberg "J" Murphy convertible, 1928 Rolls-Royce Phantom I Town Car, 1931 Stutz and 1954 Corvette. Also extensive collection of radiator auto emblems; artifacts of early auto industry; vintage clothing. (Daily; closed some hols) 2130 Middlebury St. Phone 219/522-0539. ¢¢

Woodlawn Nature Center. A 10-acre trail system provides a forest in its natural state for exploring and a center with displays and nature library. In the center, a working beehive, a Native American artifacts rm and a rare collection of bird eggs gathered in 1896 can be found. (Tues-Sat; closed hols) 604 Woodlawn Ave. Phone 219/264-0525. ¢

Motels

(Rates may be higher during Mobile Home Show, football wkends)

  ★ ★ **COMFORT INN.** *3321 Plaza Ct (46514), Cassopolis & IN 19.* 219/264-0404. 54 rms, 2 story. S $53; D $61; each addl $8; suites $95; under 18 free. Crib free. Pet accepted, some restrictions. TV; cable (premium). Pool. Complimentary continental bkfst. Restaurant adj 4-10 pm. Ck-out 11 am. Business servs avail. Whirlpools in suites. Cr cds: A, C, D, DS, MC, V.

  ✔★ **ECONO LODGE.** *3440 Cassopolis (IN 19) (46514).* 219/262-0540. 35 rms, 2 story. May-Oct: S $36-$50; D $44-$60; each addl $6; suites $65-$85; under 16 free; family, wkend rates; higher rates special events; lower rates rest of yr. Crib $6. Pet accepted, some restrictions. TV; cable (premium), VCR avail. Complimentary continental bkfst. Restaurant opp 6 am-midnight. Ck-out 11 am. Coin lndry. Business servs avail. Golf privileges. Cr cds: A, C, D, DS, JCB, MC, V.

  ★ ★ **KNIGHTS INN.** *3252 Cassopolis St (IN 19) (46514).* 219/264-4262; res: 800/843-5644. 118 rms, 10 kit. units. S $32.95-$70; D $35.95-$70; each addl $5; kit. units $39.95-$70; under 18 free. Crib free. Pet accepted; deposit. TV; cable (premium). Pool. Complimentary coffee in lobby. Restaurant opp open 24 hrs. Ck-out 11 am. Meeting rm. Business servs avail. In-rm modem link. Some refrigerators, microwaves. Cr cds: A, C, D, DS, MC, V.

  ★ ★ ★ **RAMADA INN.** *3011 Belvedere Rd (46514), I-80/90 exit 92, 2 blks S.* 219/262-1581; FAX 219/262-1590. 145 rms, 2 story. Apr-Sept: S $67-$79; D $75-$89; each addl $8; suites, kit. units $91-$98; under 18 free; lower rates rest of yr. Crib free. Pet accepted, some restrictions. TV; cable (premium), VCR avail. 2 pools, 1 indoor; whirlpool, poolside serv. Playground. Complimentary continental bkfst. Restaurant 6:30 am-2 pm, 5-9 pm. Rm serv. Bar 5-10 pm; Fri, Sat to 2 am; Sun 12:30-9 pm; entertainment. Ck-out noon. Meeting rms. Business center. In-rm modem link. Game rm. Putting green. Downhill ski 10 mi; x-country 5 mi. Sauna. Health club privileges. Some refrigerators. Cr cds: A, C, D, DS, MC, V.

  ✔★ **RED ROOF INN.** *2902 Cassopolis St (IN 19) (46514).* 219/262-3691; FAX 219/262-3695. 80 rms, 2 story. S $40.99-$65.99; D $40.99-$79.99; under 19 free; 2-day min football wkends; higher rates special events. Crib free. Pet accepted. TV; cable (premium). Complimen-

tary coffee in lobby. Restaurant adj open 24 hrs. Ck-out noon. Business servs avail. Downhill ski 20 mi. Cr cds: A, C, D, DS, MC, V.

  ★ ★ **SIGNATURE INN.** *3010 Brittany Ct (46514).* 219/264-7222. 125 rms, 2 story. S $64-$68; D $71-$75; under 18 free. Crib free. TV; cable (premium), VCR avail. Pool. Complimentary continental bkfst. Restaurant nearby. Ck-out noon. Meeting rms. Business center. In-rm modem link. Health club privileges Cr cds: A, C, D, DS, MC, V.

  ★ ★ **WESTON PLAZA.** *2725 Cassopolis St (IN 19) (46514).* 219/264-7502; FAX 219/264-0042; res: 800/521-8400. 202 rms, 2 story. S, D $60-$85; studio rms $60-$75; under 8 free. Crib free. TV; cable. Indoor pool; whirlpool, poolside serv. Complimentary coffee in lobby. Restaurant 6 am-2 pm, 5-9:30 pm; wkend hrs vary. Rm serv. Bar 4 pm-1 am; entertainment. Ck-out noon. Coin lndry. Meeting rms. Valet serv. Sundries. Putting green. Downhill/x-country ski 10 mi. Rec rm. Game rm. Sauna. Massage. Health club privileges. Refrigerators. Cr cds: A, D, DS, MC, V.

Restaurant

  ★ ★ **MATTERHORN.** *2041 Cassopolis St (IN 19) (46514).* 219/262-1509. Hrs: 11 am-2 pm, 5-10 pm; Sat from 5 pm; Sun brunch 10 am-2 pm. Closed Dec 25. Res accepted. Bar 10:30 am-11 pm. Semi-a la carte: lunch $3.95-$7.95, dinner $10.95-$17.95. Buffet: lunch (Mon-Fri) $5.95, dinner (Fri) $17.95. Sun brunch $8.95. Child's meals. Specializes in prime rib, steak, seafood. Cr cds: A, C, D, DS, MC, V.

Evansville (K-2)

(See also New Harmony)

Founded 1819 **Pop** 126,272 **Elev** 394 ft **Area code** 812
Information Evansville Convention & Visitors Bureau, 401 SE Riverside Dr, 47713; 812/425-5402 or 800/433-3025.

Separated from Kentucky by the Ohio River, Evansville has retained some of the atmosphere of the busy river town of the days when steamboats plied the waters of the Ohio and Mississippi rivers. The largest city in southern Indiana, Evansville combines the pleasant and leisurely ways of the South with the industrious activity of the North.

Evansville is the principal transportation, trade and industrial center of southwestern Indiana. A modern river/rail/highway terminal facilitates simultaneous exchange of cargo between trucks, freight trains and riverboats. Local industry manufactures refrigerators, agricultural equipment, aluminum ingots and sheets, furniture, textiles, nutritional and pharmaceutical products, beer and plastics.

The Ohio River offers many recreational opportunities for boating, swimming, waterskiing and fishing.

What to See and Do

 Angel Mounds State Historic Site. Largest and best preserved group of prehistoric mounds (1250-1450) in Indiana. Approx 100 acres. Interpretive center has film, exhibits, model of an excavation and artifacts; reconstructed dwellings on grounds. (Mid-Mar-Dec, daily exc Mon; closed major hols) 7 mi E on IN 662 at 8215 Pollack Ave. Phone 812/853-3956. **Free.**

Burdette Park. County park, approx 160 acres. Fishing, picnicking (shelters); cabins; pool & waterslides (summer); miniature golf (Apr-Oct); tennis courts. Some fees. 6 mi SW. Phone 812/435-5602.

Evansville Museum of Arts and Science. Permanent art, history and science exhibits; sculpture garden, Koch Planetarium (fee), steam train and station. Rivertown USA, re-creation of turn-of-the-century village.

Tours. (Daily exc Mon; closed major hols) 411 SE Riverside Dr, on Ohio River. Phone 812/425-2406.   **Free.**

Historic Reitz Home (1871). French Second Empire mansion of pioneer lumber baron John Augustus Reitz; gold leaf cornices, family furniture. (Feb-mid-Dec, Wed-Sun afternoons; closed major hols) 224 SE First St, in Historic Riverfront District. Phone 812/426-1871.   ¢¢

Mesker Park Zoo. Zoo has more than 700 animals; a bird collection; children's zoo. Also the Discovery Center Education Bldg. Tour train and paddleboats (Apr-Oct). (Daily) NW edge of town in Mesker Park, 2421 Bement Ave. Phone 812/428-0715.   ¢¢

University of Southern Indiana (1965). (7,500 students) On 300-acre campus is the Bent Twig Outdoor Education Center, 25 acres with foot trails, log lodges and a lake (daily). 5 mi W on IN 62 (Lloyd Expy). Phone 812/464-8600 or 812/464-1755.

Wesselman Park. Approx 400 acres; picnicking, tennis, handball, softball, basketball; bike trails; jogging trail; playground; 18-hole golf course (fee). Half of park is devoted to nature preserve (free, phone 812/479-0771). Swimming pool and ice rink complex (fees) adj (phone 812/479-0989). 5 mi E at N Boeke Rd & Iowa St. Phone 812/424-6921.   **Free.**   Also here is

  Roberts Municipal Stadium. Ice shows, circuses, rodeos, musicals, concerts, basketball tournaments. 2600 Division St, Lloyd Expy exit Vann St. Phone 812/476-1383.

Annual Events

Ohio River Arts Festival. Mother's Day wkend.

Freedom Festival. Citywide. More than 30 events, including parade, hot air balloon races, fireworks, food. Hydroplane racing. Phone 812/464-9576. June 14-July 4.

Germania Männerchor Volkfest. German food, beer and music. Phone 812/422-1915. Mid-Aug.

Seasonal Event

Evansville Philharmonic Orchestra. Phone 812/425-5050. Sept-May.

Motels

★ **COMFORT INN.** *5006 E Morgan Ave (47715). 812/477-2211.* 52 rms, 3 story, 11 suites. S, D $59.95-$64.95; each addl $7; suites $64.95-$71.25; under 18 free. Crib free. TV; cable. Indoor pool; whirlpool. Complimentary continental bkfst. Ck-out 11 am. Business servs avail. Game rm. Cr cds: A, C, D, DS, ER, JCB, MC, V.

D ≈ ⊁ 🔥 SC

★ **DAYS INN.** *5701 US 41N (47711), 8 mi N on US 41, near Regional Airport. 812/464-1010; FAX 812/464-2742.* 120 rms, 3 story. S $54-$59; D $59-$65; each addl $5; suites $80-$125; under 18 free. Crib free. TV; cable (premium). Indoor pool; whirlpool. Complimentary continental bkfst. Restaurant 6:30 am-1:30 pm, 5-10 pm. Rm serv. Bar 5-11 pm; Fri, Sat to 2:30 am; closed Sun. Ck-out noon. Meeting rms. Business servs avail. In-rm modem link. Valet serv. Free airport transportation. Sauna. Cr cds: A, C, D, DS, MC, V.

D ≈ ✈ 🔥 SC

★ **DRURY INN.** *3901 US 41N (47711), near airport. 812/423-5818.* 151 rms, 4 story. S $63-$79; D $73-$89; each addl $8; under 18 free. Crib free. Pet accepted. TV; cable. Indoor pool; whirlpool. Complimentary continental bkfst. Restaurant adj open 24 hrs. Ck-out noon. Coin lndry. Business servs avail. In-rm modem link. Valet serv. Exercise equipt; bicycle, treadmill. Cr cds: A, C, D, DS, MC, V.

D 🐾 ≈ ⊁ 🔥 SC

✔★ ★ **FAIRFIELD INN BY MARRIOTT.** *7879 Eagle Crest Blvd (47715). 812/471-7000.* 118 rms, 3 story. S, D $55.50-$65.50; each addl $7; under 18 free. Crib free. TV; cable (premium). Complimentary continental bkfst. Restaurant nearby. Ck-out noon. Business servs avail. In-rm

modem link. Valet serv. Exercise equipt; treadmill, stair machine. Indoor pool. Cr cds: A, C, D, DS, MC, V.

≈ ⊁ 🔥 SC

✔★ **FAIRFIELD INN BY MARRIOTT.** *5400 Weston Rd (47712). 812/429-0900.* 110 rms, 4 story. S, D $55.50-$65.50; each addl $7; under 18 free. Crib free. TV; cable (premium). Complimentary continental bkfst. Restaurant nearby. Ck-out noon. Meeting rm. Business servs avail. In-rm modem link. Coin lndry. Exercise equipt; bicycle, treadmill. Indoor pool. Cr cds: A, C, D, DS, MC, V.

D ≈ ⊁ 🔥 SC

★ ★ **HAMPTON INN.** *8000 Eagle Crest Blvd (47715), at Lloyd Expwy and I-164. 812/473-5000; FAX 812/479-1664.* 143 rms, 5 story. S, D $57-$68; under 19 free. Crib free. TV; cable (premium). VCR avail. Indoor pool. Complimentary continental bkfst. Restaurant adj 6 am-10 pm. Ck-out noon. Meeting rms. Business servs avail. Valet serv. Exercise equipt; weight machine, bicycles. Cr cds: A, C, D, DS, MC, V.

D ≈ ⊁ 🔥 SC

★ ★ **HOLIDAY INN AIRPORT.** *4101 US 41N (47711), near Evansville Regional Airport. 812/424-6400; FAX 812/424-6409.* 198 rms, 1-2 story. S, D $79; each addl $10; suites $89; under 19 free; wkend rates. Crib free. TV; cable (premium), VCR avail. Indoor pool; wading pool, whirlpool. Playground. Restaurant 6 am-10 pm; Sun 7 am-9 pm. Rm serv. Bar from noon. Ck-out 11 am. Guest lndry. Meeting rms. Business center. In-rm modem link. Sundries. Free airport transportation. Exercise equipt; weight machine, bicycles, sauna. Solardome pavilion. Game rm. Cr cds: A, C, D, DS, JCB, MC, V.

≈ ⊁ ✈ 🔥 SC 🏌

★ ★ **HOLIDAY INN-EAST.** *100 S Green River Rd (47715). 812/473-0171; FAX 812/473-5021.* 109 rms, 2 story. S $60-$72; D $67-$79; under 19 free. Crib free. TV; cable (premium). Pool. Ck-out noon. Business servs avail. In-rm modem link. Sundries. Cr cds: A, C, D, DS, ER, JCB, MC, V.

D ≈ ⊁ 🔥 SC

★ **SIGNATURE INN.** *1101 N Green River Rd (47715). 812/476-9626.* 125 rms, 2 story. S, D $67-$74; under 18 free. Crib free. TV; cable (premium). Pool. Complimentary continental bkfst. Restaurant nearby. Ck-out noon. Meeting rms. Business servs avail. In-rm modem link. Health club privileges. Cr cds: A, D, DS, MC, V.

D ≈ ⊁ SC

★ **STUDIO PLUS.** *301 Eagle Crest Dr (47715), 8 mi E on Lloyd Expy. 812/479-0103; FAX 812/469-7172.* Web www.studioplus.com. 71 kit. units, 3 story. S $59-$69; D $89; wkend, wkly, monthly rates. Crib free. Pet accepted; $200. TV; cable (premium). Complimentary coffee in rms. Restaurant nearby. Ck-out noon. Business servs avail. In-rm modem link. Valet serv. Coin lndry. Exercise equipt; bicycle, stair machine. Pool. Microwaves. Cr cds: A, C, D, DS, MC, V.

D 🐾 ≈ ⊁ 🔥 SC

Motor Hotel

★ ★ **BERNIE LITTLE'S RIVER HOUSE.** *20 Walnut St (47708). 812/425-6500; FAX 812/423-7216; res: 800/824-6710.* 91 rms, 2 & 6 story. S $95; D $105; each addl $10; suites $117-$165; under 12 free. Crib free. TV; cable, VCR avail (movies). Complimentary bkfst buffet. Restaurant 6:30 am-11 pm. Rm serv Mon-Fri. Bar 11 am-11:30 pm. Ck-out 1 pm. Meeting rms. Business servs avail. In-rm modem link. Bellhops. Valet serv. Airport, bus depot transportation. Exercise equipt; bicycles, rowing machine. Whirlpool. Some refrigerators. Private patios, balconies. View of Ohio River. Cr cds: A, C, D, DS, MC, V.

D ⊁ 🔥 SC

Hotel

★ ★ ★ **MARRIOTT-AIRPORT.** *7101 US 41N (47711), adj to Evansville Regional Airport. 812/867-7999; FAX 812/867-0241.* 201 rms, 5 story. S, D $99-$129; each addl $10; suites $250-$350; wkend rates. Crib free. TV; cable (premium). Indoor pool; whirlpool. Restaurant 6 am-2 pm, 5-11 pm. Bar 4 pm-2 am. Ck-out 11 am. Meeting rms. Business servs avail. Free airport transportation. Exercise equipt; weight machines, bicycle. Game rm. Balconies. Cr cds: A, C, D, DS, ER, JCB, MC, V.

D ⌦ 🍴 ✈ ⌦ 🏊 SC

Restaurant

★ ★ **ELLIOTT'S.** *4701 E Powell Ave (47715). 812/473-3378.* Hrs: 4-10 pm; Sun 11 am-8 pm; early-bird dinner Sun-Thurs 4-6 pm. Closed Jan 1, Dec 24, 25. Res accepted. Bar 3:30 pm-midnight; Fri, Sat to 2 am. Semi-a la carte: lunch, dinner $7.95-$19.95. Child's meals. Specializes in steak, seafood. Casual dining. Cr cds: A, DS, MC, V.

D ⌦

Fort Wayne (C-6)

(See also Auburn)

Settled ca 1690 **Pop** 173,072 **Elev** 767 ft **Area code** 219 **E-mail** fwcvb@fwai.org **Web** www.fwcvb.ortg

Information Fort Wayne/Allen County Convention & Visitors Bureau, 1021 S Calhoun St, 46802; 219/424-3700 or 800/767-7752.

The Fort Wayne area is one of the most historically significant in Indiana. The point where the St Joseph and St Mary's rivers meet to form the Maumee was, for many years before and after the first European explorers ventured into eastern Indiana, the headquarters of the Miami Native Americans. Among the first settlers were French fur traders; a French fort was established about 1690. The settlement became known as Miami Town and Frenchtown. In 1760, English troops occupied the French fort, but were driven out three years later by warriors led by Chief Pontiac. During the next 30 years Miami Town became one of the most important trading centers in the West. President Washington sent out two armies in 1790 and 1791 to establish a fort for the United States at the river junction, but both armies were defeated by the Miami under the leadership of the famous Miami chief, Little Turtle. A third American army, under General "Mad Anthony" Wayne, succeeded in defeating Little Turtle and set up a post, Fort Wayne, across the river from Miami Town. From this humble beginning Fort Wayne has grown steadily. Today it is the second-largest city in Indiana and a commercial center.

Establishment of the first railroad connections with Chicago and Pittsburgh in the 1850s laid the foundation for the city's development. Today its widely diversified companies include General Electric, Phelps Dodge, ITT, Lincoln National Corporation, North American Van Lines, Central Soya, Essex Group, General Motors, Magnavox, Uniroyal, Goodrich Tire Company and many others. Most of the world's wire die tools come from here.

Fort Wayne is home to Indiana University-Purdue University at Fort Wayne (1964), St Francis College (1890) and the Indiana Institute of Technology (1930).

What to See and Do

Allen County-Fort Wayne Historical Society Museum. Exhibits on six themes: earliest times to the Civil War; 19th-century industrialization (1860s-1894); culture and society (1894-1920); 20th-century technology & industry (1920-present); old city jail and law enforcement (1820-1970); ethnic heritage. Special temporary exhibits. (Daily exc Mon; closed major hols) 302 E Berry St, in Old City Hall. Phone 219/426-2882. ¢

Cathedral of the Immaculate Conception and Museum. Bavarian stained-glass windows. Features Gothic wood carvings at the main altar, statues and furnishings; wood-carved reredos in the sanctuary. Museum at SW corner of Cathedral Square (Wed-Fri and 2nd & 4th Sun; also by appt). Cathedral (daily; closed hols). 1100 blk of S Calhoun St. Phone 219/424-1485. Museum **Free.**

Embassy Theatre. Entertainment and cultural center hosts musicals, concerts, ballet companies; distinctive architecture; Grand Page pipe organ. Tours (Mon-Fri, by appt). 121 W Jefferson St. Phone 219/424-6287. ¢

Foellinger-Freimann Botanical Conservatory. Showcase House with seasonally changing displays of colorful flowers; Tropical House with exotic plants; Arid House with cacti and other desert flora native to Sonoran desert. Cascading waterfall. (Daily; closed Dec 25) 1100 S Calhoun St. Phone 219/427-6440. ¢¢

Fort Wayne Children's Zoo. Especially designed for children. Exotic animals, pony rides, train ride, contact area; 22-acre African Veldt area allows animals to roam free while visitors travel by miniature safari cars; tropical rain forest; also 5-acre Australian Outback area with dugout canoe ride; kangaroos, Tasmanian devils. (Late Apr-mid-Oct, daily) 3411 Sherman Blvd, in Franke Park. Phone 219/427-6800. ¢¢

Fort Wayne Museum of Art. A 1,300-piece permanent collection; changing exhibitions. Art classes, interactive programs and lectures. (Daily exc Mon; closed hols) 311 E Main St. Phone 219/422-6467. ¢¢

Lakeside Rose Garden. Approx 2,000 plants of about 225 varieties; display rose garden (June-mid-Oct). Garden (all yr, daily). 1500 Lake Ave. Phone 219/427-1267. **Free.**

The New Lincoln Museum. Extensive collection of literature about Abraham Lincoln; paintings, personal items. (Daily exc Mon) 200 E Berry St. Phone 219/455-3864. ¢¢

Annual Events

Germanfest. Celebration of city's German heritage; ethnic food, music, exhibits. Phone 800/767-7752. 4 days mid-June.

Three Rivers Festival. More than 280 events, including parades, balloon races, arts & crafts, Highland games, music, ethnic dancing, sports and fireworks at various locations in Fort Wayne. Phone 219/745-FEST. 9 days mid-July.

Johnny Appleseed Festival. Johnny Appleseed Park. Pioneer village; period crafts; contests, entertainment, Living History Hill, farmers' market. Phone 219/427-6000. 3rd wkend Sept.

Old City Hall's Gingerbread Festival. Display of more than 100 regional gingerbread creations. Thanksgiving-mid-Dec.

Seasonal Event

Foellinger Theatre. Sherman St, in Franke Park. Concerts and special attractions. Covered open-air theater. Programs vary. Phone 219/482-2785 or 219/483-0057 (off-season). June-Sept.

Motels

★ ★ **COURTYARD BY MARRIOTT.** *1619 W Washington Center Rd (46818), I-69 exit 111B. 219/489-1500; FAX 219/489-3273.* 142 rms, 2 story. S, D $69-$79; suites $89-$229; under 18 free. Crib free. TV; cable (premium). Indoor/outdoor pool; whirlpool. Ck-out noon. Meeting rms. Business servs avail. In-rm modem link. Valet serv. Sundries. Exercise equipt; weight machine, treadmill. Refrigerator in some suites. Cr cds: A, C, D, DS, JCB, MC, V.

D ⌦ 🍴 ⌦ 🏊 SC

✔★ **DAYS INN.** *3730 E Washington Blvd (46803). 219/424-1980; FAX 219/422-6525.* 120 rms, 2 story. S $28-$34; D $36-$41; each addl $4; under 12 free; wkly, monthly rates. Crib free. Pet accepted. TV; cable (premium). Pool. Restaurant 6 am-1:30 pm, 4:30-10 pm. Bar. Ck-out

11 am. Coin lndry. Meeting rms. Business servs avail. X-country ski 18 mi. Some refrigerators. Cr cds: A, C, D, DS, JCB, MC, V.

★ ★ **DON HALL'S GUESTHOUSE.** *1313 W Washington Center Rd (46825), I-69 exit 111B.* 219/489-2524; FAX 219/489-7067; res: 800/348-1999. 130 rms, 2 story. S, D $63-$69; suites $90; wkend rates. Crib free. TV; cable (premium). 2 pools, 1 indoor; whirlpool. Complimentary continental bkfst. Complimentary coffee in rms. Restaurant 6 am-11 pm; Sun to 9 pm. Rm serv. Bar 11-1 am, Sun to 10 pm; entertainment Tues-Sat. Ck-out 1 pm. Meeting rms. In-rm modem link. Sundries. Free airport transportation. Exercise equipt; stair machine, bicycles. Cr cds: A, C, D, DS, MC, V.

★ **RAMADA.** *1212 Magnavox Way (IN 14) (46804).* 219/436-8600; FAX 219/432-9764. 148 rms, 2 story. S $50-$64; D $55-$60; each addl $5; suites $59-$64; under 18 free; wkend rates. Crib free. TV; cable. Heated pool. Coffee in rms. Restaurant 7 am-2 pm, 5-9 pm. Rm serv. Bar; entertainment wkends. Ck-out noon. Coin lndry. Meeting rms. Business servs avail. Health club privileges. Microwaves avail. Cr cds: A, C, D, DS, JCB, MC, V.

✔ **RED ROOF INN.** *2920 Goshen Rd (US 33/30) (46808).* 219/484-8641; FAX 219/484-3441. 79 rms, 2 story. S, D $43.99-$71.99; under 18 free. Crib free. Pet accepted. TV. Complimentary coffee in lobby. Ck-out noon. Cr cds: A, C, D, DS, MC, V.

★ ★ **RESIDENCE INN BY MARRIOTT.** *4919 Lima Rd (46808).* 219/484-4700; FAX 219/484-9772. 80 kit. units, 2 story. S, D $109-$129; higher rates special events. Crib free. Pet accepted; $50-$100. TV; cable (premium), VCR avail (movies). Complimentary continental bkfst. Coffee in rms. Restaurant nearby. Ck-out noon. Health club privileges. Heated pool. Playground. Microwaves; many fireplaces. Cr cds: A, C, D, DS, JCB, MC, V.

★ **SIGNATURE INN.** *1734 W Washington Center Rd (46818).* 219/489-5554; FAX 219/489-5554, ext. 500. 100 rms, 2 story. S $64; D $72; under 17 free; wkend rates. Crib free. TV; cable (premium), VCR avail. Pool. Complimentary continental bkfst. Ck-out noon. Meeting rms. Business servs avail. In-rm modem link. Sundries. Cr cds: A, C, D, DS, MC, V.

Motor Hotels

★ ★ **HOLIDAY INN.** *3939 Ferguson Rd (46809), near Fort Wayne Airport.* 219/747-9171; FAX 219/747-1848. 147 rms, 2 story. S, D $78; suites $150; family, wkend rates. Crib free. TV; cable. Heated pool. Restaurant 6 am-2 pm, 5:30-10 pm. Rm serv. Bar 2 pm-midnight, Fri, Sat to 2 am. Ck-out noon. Meeting rms. Business servs avail. Bellhops. Valet serv. Free airport transportation. Golf privileges. Exercise equipt; weights, bicycles, sauna. Cr cds: A, C, D, DS, MC, V.

★ ★ **MARRIOTT.** *305 E Washington Center Rd (46825).* 219/484-0411; FAX 219/483-2892. 223 rms, 2-6 story. S $130; D $140; each addl $10; suites $235-$350; under 18 free; wkend package. Crib free. Pet accepted. TV; cable (premium). Indoor/outdoor pool; whirlpool, poolside serv. Restaurant 6 am-10 pm; Fri, Sat to 11 pm. Rm serv. Bar 11-2:30 am. Ck-out noon. Coin lndry. Meeting rms. Business servs avail. In-rm modem link. Bellhops. Valet serv. Sundries. Gift shop. Free airport transportation. Putting green. Exercise equipt; weights, bicycles. Game rm. Lawn games. Some refrigerators. Picnic tables. Cr cds: A, C, D, DS, ER, JCB, MC, V.

Hotels

★ ★ ★ **HILTON.** *1020 S Calhoun St (46862).* 219/420-1100; FAX 219/424-7775. 250 rms, 9 story. S $89-$149; D $99-$159; each addl $10; suites $190-$350; under 18 free. Crib free. TV; cable. Indoor pool; whirlpool. Restaurants 6 am-11 pm. Bar. Ck-out 11 am. Convention facilities. Business servs avail. In-rm modem link. Free airport transportation. Concierge. Gift shop. Exercise equipt; weights, bicycles. Garden lounge in lobby. Adj Grand Wayne Convention Center. Luxury level. Cr cds: A, C, D, DS, ER, MC, V.

★ ★ **HOLIDAY INN-DOWNTOWN.** *300 E Washington Blvd (US 24) (46802).* 219/422-5511; FAX 219/424-1511. 208 rms, 14 story, 28 suites. S $79-$89; D $89-$99; each addl $5; suites $119-$190; under 18 free; wkend packages. Crib free. TV; cable. Indoor pool; whirlpool. Coffee in rms. Restaurant 6 am-2 pm, 5-10 pm. Bar 5 pm-midnight; entertainment. Ck-out noon. Coin lndry. Meeting rms. Business servs avail. In-rm modem link. Free airport, bus depot transportation. Exercise equipt; weights, bicycles. Game rm. Luxury level. Cr cds: A, C, D, DS, JCB, MC, V.

Restaurants

★ ★ ★ **CAFE JOHNELL.** *2529 S Calhoun St (46856), 1 blk W of US 27.* 219/456-1939. Hrs: 11:30 am-2 pm, 6-9 pm; Sat 5-10 pm. Closed Sun; major hols. Res accepted. French, continental menu. Bar. Wine cellar. Semi-a la carte: lunch $4-$12, dinner $15-$30. Complete meals: dinner $18. Specialties: caneton à l'orange flambé, tournedos de boeuf Rossini, sole amandine de Dover. Own pastries. Victorian atmosphere. Collection of original 17th-to-20th-century art. Family-owned. Cr cds: A, C, D, MC, V.

★ ★ **DON HALL'S-THE FACTORY.** *5811 Coldwater Rd (US 27) (46825).* 219/484-8693. Hrs: 11 am-11 pm; Fri, Sat to midnight; Sun to 8 pm. Closed major hols, except Labor Day. Res accepted Sun-Thurs. Bar. Semi-a la carte: lunch $2.25-$7.50, dinner $6.50-$16. Child's meals. Specializes in Greek salad, steak, prime rib. Family-owned. Cr cds: A, C, D, DS, MC, V.

✔ ★ ★ **ELEGANT FARMER.** *1820 Coliseum Blvd N.* 219/482-1976. Hrs: 11 am-2 pm, 5-9 pm; Sat from 4:30 pm; Sun brunch 10 am-2 pm. Closed major hols. Res accepted. Bar. Semi-a la carte: lunch $3.50-$6.50, dinner $6.50-$13.50. Sun brunch $6.95. Child's meals. Specializes in prime rib, steak, seafood. Salad bar. Cr cds: A, MC, V.

✔ ★ ★ **FLANAGAN'S.** *6525 Covington Rd.* 219/432-6666. Hrs: 11-1 am; Fri, Sat to 2 am; Sun to 11 pm. Closed Thanksgiving, Dec 25. Res accepted. Bar. Semi-a la carte: lunch $4-$7, dinner $6-$11. Child's meals. Specializes in baby back ribs, pasta, seafood. Victorian decor; garden gazebo, carousel. Antiques on display. Cr cds: A, DS, MC, V.

French Lick (H-3)

(See also Bedford)

Founded 1811 **Pop** 2,087 **Elev** 511 ft **Area code** 812 **Zip** 47432

Information French Lick-West Baden Chamber of Commerce, PO Box 347; 812/936-2405.

In the early 18th century this was the site of a French trading post. The post, plus the existence of a nearby salt lick, influenced the pioneer founders of the later settlement to name it French Lick.

Today this small community is a well-known health and vacation resort centered around the French Lick springs, situated on 1,600 acres of woodland. Near it is an artesian spring, Pluto, covered by an edifice of marble and tile. The water contains a high concentration of minerals.

What to See and Do

Diesel Locomotive Excursion. French Lick, West Baden and Southern Railway operates a diesel locomotive that makes 20-mi round trip through wooded limestone country and a 2,200-ft tunnel. Train departs from the Monon Railroad station in French Lick (Apr-Nov, Sat & Sun; also Memorial Day, July 4, Labor Day). Museum (Mon-Fri, free). On IN 56. Contact Indiana Railway Museum, Inc, PO Box 150; 812/936-2405. ¢¢¢

Paoli Peaks Ski Area. Quad, 3 triple chairlifts, 4 surface tows; snowmaking, rentals, school, patrol; cafeteria. Longest run 3,300 ft; vertical drop 300 ft. (Dec-Mar, daily; open 24 hrs on wkends) N via IN 56, then E on US 150; 1½ mi W of Paoli off US 150. Phone 812/723-4696, 812/723-4698 (snow conditions). ¢¢¢-¢¢¢¢¢

Annual Event

Orange County Pumpkin Festival. Parades, arts & crafts displays, entertainment. Last wk Sept or 1st wk Oct.

Motel

★ **LANE.** *IN 56, ½ mi N on IN 56, 1½ mi S of US 150. 812/936-9919.* 43 rms. S, D $40; each addl $6. Crib $6. Pet accepted. TV; cable (premium). Pool. Restaurant nearby. Ck-out 11 am. Picnic tables. Grill. Cr cds: MC, V.

D 🐾 ➿ 🔥

Inn

★ **BRAXTON HOUSE.** *(210 N Gospel St (IN 37), Paoli 47454) N on IN 145, approx 10 mi E on US 150. 812/723-4677; res: 800/627-2982.* 6 rms, 5 with shower only, 3 story. No rm phones. S $40-$45; D $60-$65. Crib free. TV in guest area. Complimentary full bkfst. Restaurant nearby. Ck-out 11 am, ck-in 3 pm. Downhill ski 3 mi. Queen Anne Victorian built in 1893. Cr cds: A, DS, MC, V.

🐾 SC

Resort

★ ★ ★ **FRENCH LICK SPRINGS.** *8670 West IN 56, 2 mi S of US 150. 812/936-9300; FAX 812/936-2100; res: 800/457-4042.* 500 rms, 6 story. MAP: S $119; D $149; each addl $40; suites $157-$450; EP: S, D $89-$99; ski, golf, tennis plans; wkly, hol packages. TV; cable (premium). 2 pools, 1 indoor; whirlpool. Supervised child's activities (mid-Apr-mid-Nov), ages 5 and over. Dining rms 6 am-10 pm. Rm serv. Bar 11-1 am; entertainment. Ck-out noon, ck-in 4 pm. Convention facilities. Business servs avail. In-rm modem link. Sundries. Barber, beauty shop. Indoor/outdoor lighted tennis, pro. Two 18-hole golf courses, greens fee $18-$48, driving range. Downhill ski 9 mi; x-country ski on site. Stables. Indoor/outdoor games. Soc dir. Rec rm. Bowling, billiards. Exercise rm; instructor, weight machines, bicycles, sauna, steam rm. Mineral baths, massage. Country estate setting on 2,600 acres; landscaped grounds, gardens, woodland trails. Cr cds: A, D, DS, MC, V.

D 🐾 🏃 🎿 ➿ 🍴 🐾 🔥 SC

Cottage Colony

★ **PATOKA LAKE VILLAGE-THE PINES.** *Rte 2, Box 255E, 10 mi S on IN 145, at jct Lake Village Dr. 812/936-9854.* 12 log cabins. No rm phones. S, D $89; each addl (after 2nd person) $10; 6-12, $5; under 6 free; wkly rates. Crib free. Pet accepted. TV. Playground. Ck-out 11 am.

Coin lndry. Meeting rms. Microwaves. Picnic tables, grills. Surrounded by woods; near lake. Cr cds: A, DS, MC, V.

🐾 🔥

Geneva (Adams Co) (D-6)

(For accommodations see Fort Wayne)

Pop 1,280 **Elev** 846 ft **Area code** 219 **Zip** 46740

This town in eastern Indiana, near the Ohio border, is surrounded by the "Limberlost Country," which Gene Stratton Porter used as background for her romantic stories of life in the swamplands. Geneva is near the headwaters of the Wabash River and includes a large settlement of Old Order Amish families.

What to See and Do

Amishville. Amish house (tour); farm, barn, animals; working gristmill; buggy rides. Picnicking, swimming, fishing. Camping (Apr-Oct); activities; restaurant. (Apr-mid-Dec, daily; closed Thanksgiving) Some fees. 3 mi E via local road. Phone 219/589-3536. Tour ¢¢

Bearcreek Farms. Entertainment complex: restaurants, theater, shops, miniature golf course, general store. Fishing. 4 mi SE near Bryant. Phone 219/997-6822. Some fees. Lodging avail (res required), phone 800/288-7630.

Limberlost State Historic Site. A 14-rm cedar log cabin, for 18 yrs the residence of Gene Stratton Porter, author/naturalist/photographer, and her family. Furniture, books and photographs. (Mid-Mar-Dec, Wed-Sat, also Sun afternoons; closed most hols) E of US 27 at S edge of town. Phone 219/368-7428. **Free.**

George Rogers Clark National Historical Park

(see Vincennes)

Goshen (B-5)

(See also Elkhart, Mishawaka, Nappanee)

Settled 1830 **Pop** 23,797 **Elev** 799 ft **Area code** 219 **Zip** 46526 **E-mail** goshencc@tln.net **Web** www.goshen.org

Information Chamber of Commerce, 232 S Main St; 219/533-2102 or 800/307-4204.

What to See and Do

Mennonite Historical Library. Anabaptist, Mennonite and Amish research collection; genealogical resources. (Daily exc Sun; closed most hols) Goshen College campus, 1700 S Main St. Phone 219/535-7418. **Free.**

Parks. Fishing, picnicking, nature trails, winter sports. Contact the Elkhart County Park Dept, 117 N 2nd St, Rm 111; 219/535-6458.

Ox Bow. Also canoeing; sports fields, archery. (Daily) 5 mi NE off US 33. Per vehicle (Apr-Oct) ¢

Bonneyville Mill. Restored gristmill (May-Oct, daily). Park (daily). 9 mi N on IN 15 to Bristol, then 2½ mi E on IN 120, ½ mi S on County 131. **Free.**

The Old Bag Factory. Restored factory (1890) houses various types of craftsmen as well as 17 shops. (Daily exc Sun; closed some hols) 1100 Chicago Ave. Phone 219/534-2502.   **Free.**

Motels

🖊★★ **BEST WESTERN INN.** *900 Lincolnway East (US 33).* 219/533-0408. 77 rms, 2 story. S $53-$59; D $58-$61; each addl $3; under 12 free. Crib free. Pet accepted. TV; cable (premium), VCR avail. Complimentary continental bkfst. Restaurant opp 7 am-10 pm. Ck-out 11 am. Business servs avail. In-rm modem link. Valet serv Mon-Fri. Exercise equipt; weight machine, bicycle. Cr cds: A, C, D, DS, JCB, MC, V.

★★ **COURTYARD BY MARRIOTT.** *1930 Lincolnway East (US 33).* 219/534-3133; FAX 219/534-6929. 91 rms, 2 story. S, D $59-$79; suites $79-$179; under 16 free; higher rates football wknds. Crib free. TV; cable (premium). Indoor/outdoor pool. Complimentary full bkfst. Restaurant nearby. Ck-out noon. Meeting rms. Business servs avail. In-rm modem link. Exercise equipt: bicycle, stair machine. Cr cds: A, C, D, DS, MC, V.

★★ **GOSHEN INN & CONFERENCE CENTER.** *1375 Lincoln Way E.* 219/533-9551; FAX 219/533-2840; 800 888/2GOSHEN. E-mail thegosheninn@aol.com; web www.gosheninn.com. 211 rms, 2 story. Late May-Sept: S, D $69; under 18 free; higher rates football wkends; lower rates rest of yr. Crib free. TV; cable (premium). Indoor pool. Complimentary full bkfst. Restaurant 6 am-2 pm, 5-9 pm. Rm serv. Bar. Ck-out 11 am. Coin lndry. Meeting rms. Business servs avail. Putting green. Exercise equipt; weight machine, bicycle. Game rm. Cr cds: A, C, D, DS, MC, V.

Inns

★★ **CHECKERBERRY.** *62644 Country Rd 37.* 219/642-4445. 14 rms, 3 story, 3 suites. S $80-$100; D $112-$150; each addl $30; suites $160-$325; wkly, wkend rates. TV; VCR avail. Pool. Complimentary continental bkfst. Coffee in rms. Restaurant (see CHECKERBERRY). Ck-out 11 am, ck-in 1 pm. Business servs avail. In-rm modem link. Tennis. Putting green. Lawn games. Refrigerators; microwaves avail. In scenic rural Amish area; contemporary French, Amer decor. Totally nonsmoking. Cr cds: A, MC, V.

★★ **ESSENHAUS COUNTRY INN.** *(240 US 20, Middlebury 46540)* Approx 5 mi N on IN 15, then 5 mi E on US 20. 219/825-9447; res: 800/455-9471. Web www.essenhaus.com. 40 rms, 2 story. S $59-$69; D $79-$89; each addl $10; suites $99-$130; under 12 free. Crib $4. TV; cable. Complimentary coffee in lobby. Dining rm 6 am-8 pm; Fri, Sat to 9 pm. Ck-out 11 am, ck-in 3 pm. Meeting rm. Business servs avail. Whirlpool in suites. Amish country setting; handcrafted furnishings, antiques. Totally nonsmoking. Cr cds: A, DS, MC, V.

★★ **INDIAN CREEK.** *20300 CR 18 (46528).* 219/875-6606; FAX 219/875-3968. E-mail 71224.1462@compuserve.com; web www.bestinns.net/usa/in/indiancreek.html. 5 rms, 4 with shower only, 3 story, 1 suite. S $69; D $79; each addl $20; suites $99; under 4 free. Crib free. TV; VCR avail (movies). Complimentary full bkfst. Ck-out 10:30 am, ck-in 4-6 pm. Business servs avail. Luggage handling. 18-hole golf privileges, greens fee $15-$22, putting green, driving range. Picnic tables, grills. Country Victorian decor; family antiques. Totally nonsmoking. Cr cds: A, DS, MC, V.

★★ **VARNS GUEST HOUSE.** *(205 S Main St (IN 13), Middlebury 46540)* E on IN 4, 5 mi N on IN 13. 219/825-9666; res: 800/398-5424 (IN). 5 rms, 2 story. 1 rm phone. S, D $75; each addl $10. TV in sitting rm; cable. Complimentary continental bkfst. Restaurant nearby. Ck-out, ck-in 11 am. Built 1898; wrap around porch. Totally nonsmoking. Cr cds: DS, MC, V.

Restaurants

★★ **BUGGY WHEEL.** *(160 Morton St, Shipshewana 46565)* E on IN 4, N on IN 13. 219/768-4444. Hrs: 7 am-7 pm; Fri, Sat to 8 pm. Closed Sun; some major hols. Res accepted Fri, Sat. Semi-a la carte: bkfst $2-$6.99, lunch, dinner $4.99-$10.50. Child's meals. Specializes in broasted chicken, meat loaf, casseroles. Salad bar. Oak woodwork crafted by Amish carpenter. No cr cds accepted.

★★ **CHECKERBERRY.** *(See Checkerberry Inn)* 219/647-4445. Hrs: 11:30 am-1 pm, 6-9 pm. Closed Sun, Mon; Jan 1. Res required. Semi-a la carte: lunch $8-$13.50, dinner $28-$42. Specializes in seasonal wild game, crispy salmon, chicken breast. Own pasta, desserts. Country French decor on 100 acres of farmland. Cr cds: A, MC, V.

Greencastle (F-3)

(See also Brazil, Terre Haute)

Founded 1823 **Pop** 8,984 **Elev** 849 ft **Area code** 765 **Zip** 46135
Information Chamber of Commerce, 2 S Jackson St, PO Box 389; 765/653-4517.

Greencastle is within 15 miles of two man-made lakes—Racoon Lake Reservoir and Cataract Lake—with boating and camping facilities.

What to See and Do

DePauw University. (1837). (2,100 students) Liberal arts; School of Music; founded by Methodist Church. State's oldest Methodist church is on campus as well as Indiana Journalism Hall of Fame and nation's first Greek-letter sorority, Kappa Alpha Theta. Restored 19th-century classroom building. Tours (by appt). Phone 765/658-4800.

Lieber State Recreation Area. Approx 775 acres on Cataract Lake (1,500 acres). Swimming beach, lifeguard, bathhouse, waterskiing; fishing; boating (dock, rentals). Picnicking, concession. Camping. Activity center (Memorial Day-Labor Day). Adj are 342 acres of state forest and 7,300 acres of federal land, part of Cagles Mill Flood Control Reservoir Project. Standard fees. 8 mi S via US 231, then 4 mi SW on IN 42. Phone 765/795-4576. Per vehicle ¢

Inn

★★★ **WALDEN.** *2 Seminary Sq, adj to DePauw University.* 765/653-2761; FAX 765/653-4833. E-mail walden@ccrtc.com. 55 rms, 2 story. S $70; D $80; each addl $8; suites $120-$130; under 12 free; wknd rates; higher rates Indianapolis "500." Crib $8. TV. Restaurant (see DIFFERENT DRUMMER). Rm serv. Ck-out 1 pm, ck-in 4 pm. Meeting rms. Business servs avail. Tennis privileges. Amish furniture. Cr cds: A, C, D, DS, MC, V.

Restaurant

★ ★ ★ **DIFFERENT DRUMMER.** *(See Walden Inn)* 765/653-2761. E-mail walden@ccrtc.com. Hrs: 6 am-2 pm, 5-9 pm; Fri, Sat until 10 pm. Closed Dec 25. Res accepted. Bar 11-2 am; Sun noon-midnight. Wine list. A la carte entrees: bkfst $2.50-$6, lunch $4.95-$7.95, dinner $14.50-$24.50. Specialties: filet mignon, Atlantic salmon, lamb. Own breads. Classical American decor; some Amish furnishings. Cr cds: A, C, D, DS, ER, JCB, MC, V.

D

Greenfield (F-5)

(See also Indianapolis)

Pop 11,657 **Elev** 888 ft **Area code** 317 **Zip** 46140
Information Greater Greenfield Chamber of Commerce, 1 Courthouse Plaza; 317/462-4188.

This town is the birthplace of poet James Whitcomb Riley.

What to See and Do

James Whitcomb Riley Home (1850). Boyhood home of the poet from 1850-1869. Riley wrote "When the Frost Is on the Punkin" and many other verses in Hoosier dialect. Tours. Museum adj. (Apr-late Dec, Mon-Sat, also Sun afternoons) 250 W Main St. Phone 317/462-8539. ¢

Old Log Jail & Chapel-in-the-Park Museums. Historical displays include arrowheads, clothing, china; local memorabilia. (Apr-Nov, Sat & Sun) Corner of E Main & N Apple Sts. Phone 317/462-7780. ¢

Annual Event

James Whitcomb Riley Festival. Parade, carnival, entertainment, arts & crafts. Held wkend closest to Riley's birthday, Oct 7.

Motel

★ **LEE'S INN.** 2270 N State St. 317/462-7112; FAX 317/462-9801. 100 rms, 2 story. S, D $59-$67; each addl $7; suites $89-$119; under 15 free; higher rates Indianapolis 500. Crib avail. Pet accepted. TV; cable. Complimentary continental bkfst. Ck-out noon. Meeting rms. Valet serv. Cr cds: A, C, D, DS, JCB, MC, V.

D ⚡ 🏊 🐾 SC

Hammond (B-2)

(See also Chicago, IL)

Pop 84,236 **Elev** 591 ft **Area code** 219
Information Chamber of Commerce, 7034 Indianapolis Blvd, 46324; 219/931-1000.

Hammond is one of the highly industrialized cities of the Calumet area on the southwest shore of Lake Michigan. The Indiana-Illinois state line is two blocks away from Hammond's business district and separates it from its sister community, Calumet City, Illinois. Hammond is also adjacent to Chicago. Industrial products manufactured here include railway supplies and equipment, cold-drawn steel, car wheels, forgings, printing and hospital and surgical supplies.

What to See and Do

Little Red Schoolhouse (1869). Oldest one-rm schoolhouse in Lake County. Used as presidential campaign headquarters by William Jennings Bryan. Original desks, tower bell, books, desk and tools. (See ANNUAL EVENTS) (By appt) 7205 Kennedy Ave. Phone 219/844-5666. **Free.**

Wicker Memorial Park. 18-hole golf, driving range, pro shop (Apr-Oct, daily). Tennis; batting cages; miniature golf; cross-country skiing; picnicking; playground; restaurant. Park (daily). Parking fee (summer). Some fees. S on US 41 at jct US 6, in Highland. Phone 219/838-3420. **Free.**

Annual Events

Little Red Schoolhouse Festival. Corn and potato roast, parade, entertainment, arts & crafts, food booths. Last Sat & Sun June.

August Fest. Carnival, food, entertainment. Phone 219/853-6378. 7 days Aug.

International Culture Festival. Ethnic food, entertainment, arts & crafts. Phone 219/931-5100. 2nd wkend Sept.

Motor Hotels

★ ★ **HOLIDAY INN.** 3830 179th St (46323), I-80/94 exit Cline Ave S. 219/844-2140; FAX 219/845-7760. 154 rms, 4 story. S, D $76.50-$116.50; under 18 free. Crib free. Pet accepted, some restrictions. TV; cable (premium). Heated pool; poolside serv. Restaurant 6:30-9:30 am, 6-9 pm. Rm serv. Bar 4 pm-1 am; Sat to 2 am. Ck-out noon. Coin lndry. Meeting rms. Business servs avail. In-rm modem link. Bellhops. Valet serv. Sundries. Exercise equipt; weight machine, bicycle. Luxury level. Cr cds: A, C, D, DS, JCB, MC, V.

D ⚡ 🏊 ✈ 🐾 ⚒ SC

★ ★ **OLYMPIA PLAZA HOTEL.** 4125-41 Calumet Ave (46327). 219/933-0500; res: 800/562-5987; FAX 219/933-0506. 89 rms, 2 story, 9 suites. S $65; D $75; each addl $10; suites $95-$105; under 12 free. Crib free. TV; cable. Complimentary continental bkfst. Complimentary coffee in rms. Restaurant nearby. Ck-out 11 am. Meeting rms. Business servs avail. In-rm modem link. Coin lndry. Exercise equipt; bicycle, treadmill. Some in-rm whirlpools, refrigerators, microwaves, fireplaces. Cr cds: A, C, D, DS, MC, V.

D ✈ 🐾 ⚒ SC

Restaurant

★ ★ **PHIL SMIDT'S.** 1205 N Calumet Ave (US 41) (46320). 219/659-0025. Hrs: 11:15 am-9 pm; Fri, Sat to 10 pm; Sun 2:30-7:30 pm. Closed Sun Jan-Apr; hols. Res accepted. Bar. Semi-a la carte: lunch $6.95-$13, dinner $9.95-$24.50. Child's meals. Specializes in lake perch, frogs' legs, seafood. Cr cds: A, C, D, MC, V.

D ⊐

Huntington (C-5)

(See also Fort Wayne, Wabash)

Founded 1831 **Pop** 16,389 **Elev** 739 ft **Area code** 219 **Zip** 46750 **E-mail** scarende@huntington.in.us **Web** www.huntington.in.us/visitors
Information Huntington County Visitor & Convention Bureau, PO Box 212; 219/359-8687 or 800/848-4282.

Originally called Wepecheange, the town was later named for Samuel Huntington, a member of the first Continental Congress. Huntington lies in a farming and industrial area and is home to Huntington College (1897).

What to See and Do

Forks of the Wabash. Treaty grounds of Miami Native Americans. Tours of Miami Chief Richardville Home & Log House. Hiking trails. Picnic area. 2 mi W on US 24. Phone 219/356-1903 or 800/848-4282. (See ANNUAL EVENTS)

Huntington Reservoir. A 900-acre lake. Swimming at Little Turtle Area (Memorial Day-Labor Day, daily); primitive campsites (all yr; fee). Fishing, boating (launch); hunting; archery range, shooting range; picnicking; hiking trails; interpretive programs. Office (May-Labor Day, daily; rest of yr, Mon-Fri; closed major hols exc Memorial Day, July 4, Labor Day). 2 mi S on IN 5. Phone 219/468-2165. Daily fee per vehicle ¢

The Dan Quayle Center & Museum Only vice presidential museum in the country has exhibits and educational programs about our nation's past vice presidents. Special focus on the 5 Indiana natives who have held the position. (Tues-Sat, also Sun afternoons; closed major hols) 815 Warren St. Phone 219/356-6356. **Free.**

Annual Events

Huntington County Heritage Days. Parade, bed race, ducky run; arts & crafts, food, entertainment. Thurs-Sun, 3rd wk June.

Forks of the Wabash Pioneer Festival. Pioneer food, pioneer arts & crafts demonstrations, Civil War encampment, antique show, banjo and fiddle contest. Last wkend Sept.

Indiana Dunes National Lakeshore (A-3)

(For accommodations see Hammond, Michigan City)

(Along southern shore of Lake Michigan, between Gary and Michigan City)
In 1966, 8,000 acres surrounding Indiana Dunes State Park (see) were established as Indiana Dunes National Lakeshore. Another 7,139 acres have since been acquired, and development continues.

The lakeshore contains a number of distinct environments: clean, sandy beaches; huge sand dunes, many covered with trees and shrubs; several bogs and marshes; and the various plants and animals peculiar to each. To preserve these environments, dune buggies and off-road vehicles are prohibited.

The visitor center is located at the junction of Kemil Rd & US 12, 3 miles east of IN 49 (daily; closed Jan 1, Thanksgiving, Dec 25). Facilities include a hard-surfaced nature trail for the disabled. Day-use facilities include West Beach, north of US 12 between Gary and Ogden Dunes, which has swimming (lifeguard), bathhouse, visitor information center, picnic area and marked nature trails; Bailly Homestead and Chellberg Farm area, between US 12 and 20, feature restored homestead, turn-of-the-century Swedish farm, hiking trails, cultural events and a visitor information center. Other lifeguarded beaches are located on State Park/Kemil Rd, off US 12. The Horse Trail, north of US 20, has a picnic area, parking facilities and marked hiking, cross-country skiing and riding trails. On US 12, near Michigan City, is Mount Baldy, largest dune in the Lakeshore, with hiking trails and a beach. Camping is available just off the intersection of IN 12 and Broadway, near Beverly Shores (tent & trailer sites; rest rms). Contact Superintendent, 1100 N Mineral Springs Rd, Porter 46304; 219/926-7561.

Indiana Dunes State Park (A-3)

(For accommodations see Hammond, Michigan City)

(Approximately 15 mi E of Gary via US 12; 4 mi N of Chesterton on IN 49)
This beautiful and unique 2,182-acre state park extends 3 miles along Lake Michigan's south shore, with white sand dunes and beaches that can accommodate thousands of bathers. Approximately 1,800 acres are densely forested hills with a wide variety of rare flowers and ferns, creating an almost tropical appearance in summer. Many of the sand dunes continue to shift, creating hills such as 192-foot Mount Tom. There are 17 miles of marked hiking trails through forest and dune country. Swimming. Cross-country skiing in winter (rentals). Picnic facilities, snack bar, store. Campgrounds. Nature center, naturalist service. Standard fees. Phone 219/926-4520 or 219/926-1952.

Indianapolis (F-4)

(See also Anderson, Greenfield)

Founded 1820 **Pop** 731,327 **Elev** 717 ft **Area code** 317 **Web** www.indy.org
Information Convention & Visitors Association, 1 RCA Dome, Suite 100, 46225; 317/639-4282.

The present site of Indianapolis was an area of rolling woodland when it was selected by a group of 10 commissioners as the location of the new Indiana state capital on June 7, 1820. It was chosen because it was close to the geographical center of the state. Only scattered Native American villages and two white settlers and their families were located in the region at the time. The city was laid out in the wheel pattern of Washington, DC. In January, 1825, the capital of Indiana was moved here from Corydon.

In its early days the city grew mainly because of its importance as seat of the state government. By the turn of the century Indianapolis had emerged as an important manufacturing center in the Midwest and the commercial center of the rich agricultural region surrounding it.

It is the largest city in Indiana, one of the leading US distribution hubs and an important business and financial center. The annual 500-mile automobile race at the Indianapolis Motor Speedway, an outstanding race course, has brought international fame to the city. Indianapolis is also referred to as the nation's amateur sports capital. Indianapolis hosts several US Olympic trials. Among the city's industrial products are pharmaceuticals, airplane and automobile parts, television sets, electronic equipment and medical diagnostic equipment.

Transportation

Indianapolis Intl Airport: Information 317/487-9594; lost & found, 317/487-5084; weather, 317/635-5959; cash machines, adj Delta and USAir ticket offices.
Car Rental Agencies: See IMPORTANT TOLL-FREE NUMBERS.
Public Transportation: Buses (Metro Transit), phone 317/635-3344.
Rail Passenger Service: Amtrak 800/872-7245.

What to See and Do

Butler University (1855). (4,000 students) The 290-acre campus is located 7 mi N of downtown Indianapolis. 4600 Sunset Ave. Phone 317/940-8000. On campus are

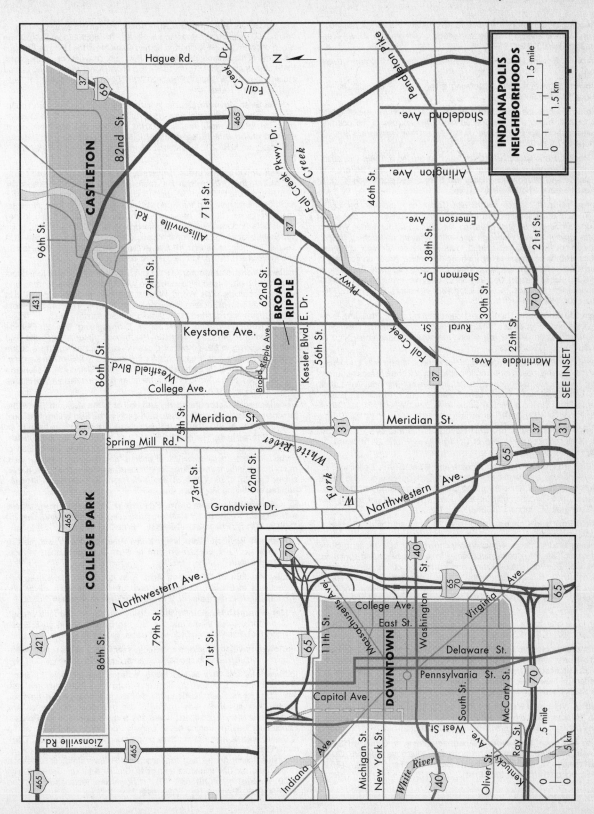

Hague Rd.

N

CASTLETON

82nd St.

Fall Creek Dr.

Fall Creek

465

37
69

Fall Creek Pkwy. Dr.

Pendleton Pike

Shadeland Ave.

INDIANAPOLIS
NEIGHBORHOODS

1.5 mile
1.5 km
0   0

96th St.

71st St.

79th St.

Allisonville Rd.

37

Arlington Ave.

46th St.

Emerson Ave.

21st St.

431

62nd St.

BROAD
RIPPLE

Keystone Ave.

Broad Ripple E. Dr.

Kessler Blvd. E. Dr.

56th St.

Fall Creek

38th St.

Rural St.

Sherman Dr.

30th St.

25th St.

70

86th St.

Westfield Blvd.

College Ave.

75th St.

Meridian St.

31

Meridian St.

Martindale Ave.

SEE INSET

37

31

Spring Mill Rd.

73rd St.

62nd St.

White River

W. Fork

Northwestern Ave.

65

37

31

COLLEGE PARK

465

Grandview Dr.

Northwestern Ave.

79th St.

71st St.

421

86th St.

Zionsville Rd.

465

70

65
40

65

DOWNTOWN

College Ave.

East St.

Massachusetts Ave.

Washington St.

Virginia Ave.

65

11th St.

65

Delaware St.

Pennsylvania St.

70

Capitol Ave.

South St.

McCarty St.

.5 mile

Michigan St.

New York St.

West St.

Indiana Ave.

White River

Kentucky Ave.

Oliver St.

Ray St.

40

.5 km

0
0

Holcomb Observatory & Planetarium. Features the largest telescope in Indiana, a 38-inch Cassegrain reflector. Planetarium shows (seasonal). Phone 317/283-9333. ¢

Hilton U. Brown Theatre. Covered outdoor theater. Programs (May-Aug).

Clowes Memorial Hall. Performing arts center. Programs (all yr). Phone 317/940-9696.

Hinkle Fieldhouse and Butler Bowl. 10,800 seats; home of Butler basketball and one of the first university fieldhouses in the country. Home football games are played in the Butler Bowl, which seats 20,000. Phone 317/940-9375.

City Market. Renovated marketplace was constructed in 1886. This building and two adj areas feature smoked meat, dairy, specialty bakery and fruit stands and ethnic foods. (Daily exc Sun; closed some hols) 222 E Market St. Phone 317/634-9266. **Free.**

Conner Prairie. A 250-acre historic site. Costumed interpreters depict life and times of early settlement in this 1836 village; contains 39 buildings, including Federal-style brick mansion (1823) built by fur trader William Conner (guided tours). Working blacksmith, weaving and pottery shops; woodworkers complex; self-guided tours. Visitor center with changing exhibits. Hands-on activities at Pioneer Adventure Area; games, toys. Picnic area, restaurant, gift shop. (May-Oct, daily exc Mon; Apr & Nov, Wed-Sun; closed Easter, Dec 25) Special events throughout yr. 13400 Allisonville Rd, approx 6 mi N of Expy 465, in Fishers. Phone 317/776-6000 or 800/966-1836. ¢¢¢

Crown Hill Cemetery. Third-largest cemetery in nation. President Benjamin Harrison, poet James Whitcomb Riley, novelist Booth Tarkington and gangster John Dillinger are among the notables buried here. 700 W 38th St. Phone 317/925-8231.

Eagle Creek Park. Approx 3,800 acres of wooded terrain with 1,300-acre reservoir. Fishing; boat ramps, rentals; shelters; golf course; cross-country skiing; hiking trails; playgrounds; swimming beach (Memorial Day-Labor Day), bathhouse, water sports center; nature center. Picnicking. (Daily; some facilities closed in winter) Some fees. 7840 W 56th St, just W of I-465. Phone 317/327-7110. Per vehicle ¢¢

Easley's Winery. Sales rm; wine tasting (21 yrs and over). Tours by appt. (Daily; closed hols) 205 N College Ave. Phone 317/636-4516. **Free.**

Eiteljorg Museum of American Indian and Western Art. Collections of Native American and American Western art. Considered one of the finest collections of its kind. (June-Aug, Mon-Sat, also Sun afternoons; rest of yr, Tues-Sat, also Sun afternoons; closed Jan 1, Thanksgiving, Dec 25) 500 W Washington St. Phone 317/636-9378. ¢¢

Garfield Park and Conservatory. This 128-acre park features restored pagoda, conservatory (daily exc Mon; closed hols; free), sunken gardens, and illuminated fountains. Conservatory shows (fee): bulb (spring); chrysanthemum (late Nov); poinsettia (Dec). Picnic area; swimming pool (late May-Labor Day, daily; fee); tennis and horseshoe courts; other sports facilities. (Daily; facilities closed hols) Musical programs in amphitheater (early June-late Aug, Thurs-Sun; free). 2450 S Shelby St at Raymond St & Garfield Dr. Phone 317/327-7184 (conservatory) or 317/327-7220 (Garfield Park).

Gray Line bus tours. Contact Indianapolis Sight-Seeing, Inc, 9075 N Meridian, 46260; 317/573-0699.

★ **Historic Lockerbie Square.** Late 19th-century private houses have been restored in this 6-blk area. Cobblestone streets, brick sidewalks and the fine architecture make this an interesting area for sightseeing. Bounded by New York, College, Michigan & East Sts. Phone 317/639-4646. Walking tour ¢¢   Here is

James Whitcomb Riley Home. Maintained in same condition as when the "Hoosier Poet" lived here (1893-1916). Tours (daily exc Mon; closed major hols). 528 Lockerbie St. Phone 317/631-5885. ¢

Hook's Historical Drug Store & Pharmacy Museum. Ornate 1852 furnishings, drugstore and medical antiques; operating soda fountain. (Daily; closed major hols; also Mon in winter) Indiana State Fairgrounds, 1180 E 38th St. Phone 317/924-1503. **Free.**

Indiana Convention Center & RCA Dome. Features 5 exhibition halls, 3 ballrms, 50 meeting rms and various offices. The 60,500-seat RCA Dome is one of only a few air-supported domed stadiums in the US. The Dome is the home of the Indianapolis Colts football team, conventions, auto shows, trade shows and more. Tours (daily exc RCA Dome event days; closed major hols). 100 S Capitol. Phone 317/237-5200 (Dome tours), 317/262-3410 (Center). Tours ¢¢

Indiana State Museum. Depicts Indiana's history, art, science and popular culture with five floors of displays. Exhibits include the Indiana Museum of Sports, Indiana radio, forests of 200 yrs ago, a small-town community at the turn of the century, paintings by Indiana artists. Changing exhibits. (Daily; closed hols) 202 N Alabama St, at Ohio St. Phone 317/232-1637. **Free.**

Indiana University—Purdue University Indianapolis (organized 1969). (28,345 students) More than 200 areas of study offered in 19 schools. Home of Indiana University Medical Center, one of the foremost research and treatment centers in the world and a primary international center for sports medicine, fitness, heart research, cancer treatment and kidney transplants. Includes five teaching hospitals and 90 clinics. IUPUI hosts many national and international athletic competitions. Home of the RCA Tennis Championships (see ANNUAL EVENTS). Main site on W Michigan St, one mi W of downtown. Phone 317/274-5555.

Indiana World War Memorial Plaza. A 5-blk area dedicated to Indiana citizens who gave their lives in the two World Wars and the Korean and Vietnam conflicts. The World War Memorial in middle of plaza is a massive edifice of Indiana limestone and granite. The Shrine Room (upper level) is dedicated to the American flag; Military Museum (lower level). (Wed-Sun; closed Jan 1, July 4, Thanksgiving, Dec 25) Outside in the center of the S stairway stands a bronze statue, *Pro Patria*. The 4-story building in NE corner of plaza is national headquarters of the American Legion. Landscaped parks are located N & S of the building; Veterans Memorial Plaza has flags of 50 states. (Daily) 431 N Meridian St, bounded by New York, St Clair, Meridian & Pennsylvania Sts. Phone 317/232-7615. **Free.**

★ **Indianapolis Motor Speedway and Hall of Fame Museum.** Site of the famous 500-mi automobile classic held each yr the Sun before Memorial Day (see ANNUAL EVENTS). Many innovations in modern cars have been tested at races here. The oval track is 2½ mi long, lined by grandstands, paddocks and bleachers accommodating 238,000 spectators. Hall of Fame Museum (fee) has exhibit of antique and classic passenger cars, many built in Indiana; more than 30 Indianapolis winning race cars. (Daily; closed Dec 25) 4790 W 16th St, 7 mi NW. Phone 317/484-6747. Grounds are free exc during May; track tour ¢

★ **Indianapolis Museum of Art.** Extensive collections with many special exhibits (fee). Tours. (Daily exc Mon; closed Jan 1, Thanksgiving, Dec 25) 1200 W 38th St. Phone 317/923-1331. **Free.**   Includes

Krannert Pavilion. Collection features American, Asian and pre-Columbian art; 20th-century art and textiles. Outdoor concert terrace, sculpture court.

Lilly Pavilion of Decorative Arts. French chateau showcases two centuries of English, Continental and American furniture, silver and ceramics. Also examples of 18th-century German porcelain. Tours.

Mary Fendrich Hulman Pavilion. Collection features Baroque through Neo-Impressionist works and the Eiteljorg Gallery of African & South Pacific Art. Allen Whitehill Clowes Special Exhibition Gallery.

Clowes Pavilion. Medieval and Renaissance art; J.M.W. Turner watercolors; lecture hall with special programs; courtyard garden.

Indianapolis Zoo. This 64-acre facility includes state's largest aquarium, enclosed whale & dolphin pavilion and more than 2,000 animals from around the world. Sea lions, penguins, sharks, polar bears; daily whale and dolphin shows; camels and reptiles of the deserts; lions, giraffes and elephants in the Plains; tigers, bears and snow monkeys in the Forests. Encounters features domesticated animals from around the world and a 600-seat outside arena offers daily programs and demonstrations. Commons Plaza includes restaurant and snack bar; additional animal exhibits; amphitheater for shows and concerts. Horse-drawn streetcar, elephant, camel, carousel and miniature train rides. Stroller & locker rentals. (Daily) 1200 W Washington St (US 40), in downtown Indianapolis. Phone 317/630-2030. Parking ¢; Zoo ¢¢¢

Madame Walker Theatre. The Walker Theatre, erected and embellished in an African and Egyptian motif, was built in 1927 as a tribute to Madame C.J. Walker, America's first self-made female millionaire. The renovated theater now has theatrical productions, concerts and other cultural events. The center serves as an educational and cultural center for the city's black community. Tours (by appt; fee). (Daily exc Sat) 617 Indiana Ave. Phone 317/236-2099.   **Free.**

Morris-Butler House (1864). A museum of Victorian lifestyles from 1850-1880. Belter & Meeks furniture, paintings, silver and other decorative arts. Special events. (Daily exc Mon; closed hols, also Jan) 1204 N Park Ave. Phone 317/636-5409.   ¢

President Benjamin Harrison Memorial Home (1874). Residence of 23rd president of the US. Sixteen rms with original furniture, paintings and family's personal effects. Herb garden. Guided tours (every 30 min). (Daily; closed some major hols, also 500 Race Day) 1230 N Delaware St. Phone 317/631-1898.   ¢

Professional sports.

   NBA (Indiana Pacers). Market Square Arena, 300 E Market Sq. Phone 317/263-2100.

   NFL (Indianapolis Colts). RCA Dome, 100 S Capitol Ave. Phone 317/297-2658.

Scottish Rite Cathedral. Structure of Tudor-Gothic design, built in 1929. The 212-ft tower has a carillon of 54 bells; auditorium has a 7,500-pipe organ. Interior is elaborately decorated. Tours. (Mon-Fri; closed wkends & hols) 650 N Meridian St. Phone 317/262-3100.   **Free.**

State Capitol (1878-1888). Structure of Indiana limestone with copper dome. (Mon-Fri; closed hols) Tours by appt. Between Washington & Ohio Sts and Capitol & Senate Aves. Phone 317/233-5293.   **Free.**

The Children's Museum. The largest of its kind; exhibits cover science, social cultures, space, history and exploration. SpaceQuest Planetarium (fee), Welcome Center, 30-ft-high Water Clock, Playscape gallery for preschoolers, Computer Discovery Center, hands-on science exhibits, simulated limestone cave, carousel rides (fee), performing arts theater, special exhibits. The largest gallery, Center for Exploration, is designed for ages 12 and up. Fee for special programs & exhibits. (Memorial Day-Labor Day, daily; rest of yr, daily exc Mon; closed Thanksgiving, Dec 25) 3000 N Meridian St. Phone 317/924-5431.   ¢¢¢

⭐ **Union Station.** Historic railway station fully restored as "festival market-place" with more than 75 stores, restaurants and entertainment establishments. (Daily) 39 W Jackson Pl. Phone 317/267-0701.   **Free.**

Annual Events

"500" Festival. Month-long celebration precedes the Indianapolis "500," held Memorial Day wkend. Numerous events include the 500 Ball, Mechanic's Recognition Party, Delco Electronics 500 Festival Parade, Mini-Marathon, Memorial Service. Phone 317/636-4556. May.

Indianapolis "500." For ticket information, contact the Indianapolis Motor Speedway. Sun before Memorial Day.

RCA Championships (tennis). Indianapolis Tennis Center, 815 W New York St. 10,000-seat stadium. World-class players compete in wk-long event. Contact 815 W New York St, 46202; 317/632-4100 or 800/622-LOVE. Mid-Aug.

Indiana State Fair. Fairgrounds. E 38th St between College Ave & Fall Creek Pkwy. Grand circuit horse racing, livestock exhibitions, entertainment and special agricultural exhibits. Phone 317/927-7500 or 317/923-3431 (evenings). Early-mid-Aug.

Village Tour of Homes. 135 S Elm, 13 mi NW in Zionsville. Several restored homes. Phone 317/873-3836. 1st wkend Oct.

Blue River Valley Pioneer Fair. Fairgrounds off I-74 in Shelbyville.Demonstrations, exhibits, entertainment. 1st wkend Oct.

Seasonal Events

Entertainment. Indianapolis Civic Theater, 1200 W 38th St, 46208, 317/923-4597; Circle Theatre (Indianapolis Symphony Orchestra and a variety of other shows), 45 Monument Circle, 46204, 317/639-4300. Dance

Kaleidoscope (Oct-Nov, Mar & June), 4600 Sunset Ave, 317/940-6555; Indiana Repertory Theater (Oct-May), 140 W Washington St, 46204, 317/635-5252; Indianapolis Ballet Theater (Sept-May), 502 N Capitol, Suite B, 46204, 317/637-8979; American Cabaret Theatre (all yr), 401 E Michigan St., 46204, 317/631-0334. Butler University, Christian Theological Seminary and Marian College offer a variety of productions throughout the academic yr; contact the individual schools for details.

Additional Visitor Information

The Indianapolis City Center, 201 S Capitol Ave, Pan Am Plaza, Suite 200, 46225, phone 317/237-5200 or 800/323-INDY, has general information brochures, maps and tourist guidebooks (daily). Information is also available through the Convention & Visitors Assoc, 1 RCA Dome, Suite 100, 46225, phone 317/639-4282.

   This is Indianapolis magazine, available locally, has up-to-date information on events and articles of interest to visitors.

City Neighborhoods

Many of the restaurants, unrated dining establishments and some lodgings listed under Indianapolis include neighborhoods as well as exact street addresses. Geographic descriptions of these areas are given, followed by a table of restaurants arranged by neighborhood.

Broad Ripple: North of Downtown; south of Broad Ripple Ave, west of Keystone Ave, north of Kessler Blvd and east of College Ave.

Castleton: Northeast area of city south of 96th St, west of IN 37, north of 82nd St and east of Keystone Ave.

College Park: South of I-465, west of Meridian St, north of 86th St and east of Zionsville Rd.

Downtown: South of 11th St, west of College Ave, north of McCarty St and east of West St and Indiana Ave. **North of Downtown:** North of I-65. **South of Downtown:** South of I-70.

INDIANAPOLIS RESTAURANTS BY NEIGHBORHOOD AREAS
(For full description, see alphabetical listings under Restaurants)

BROAD RIPPLE
Aristocrat Pub. 5212 N College Ave
Jazz Cooker. 925 E Westfield Blvd

COLLEGE PARK
Kona Jack's. 9419 N Meridian
Wildcat Brewing Company. 9111 N Michigan Rd

DOWNTOWN
Benvenuti. 1 N Pennsylvania St
The Majestic. 47 S Pennsylvania
Restaurant At The Canterbury (Canterbury Hotel). 123 S Illinois
St Elmo Steak House. 127 S Illinois

NORTH OF DOWNTOWN
Hollyhock Hill. 8110 N College Ave
Iron Skillet. 2489 W 30th St
Peter's. 8505 Keystone Crossing Blvd
Ruth's Chris Steak House. 9445 Threel Rd

   Note: When a listing is located in a town that does not have its own city heading, it will appear under the city nearest to its location. In these cases, the address and town appear in parenthesis immediately following the name of the establishment.

Motels

(Rates are usually higher during Indianapolis "500" and state fair; may be 3-day min.)

   ★ **COMFORT INN.** *5040 S East St (US 31S) (46227), south of downtown.* 317/783-6711; FAX 317/787-3065. 104 rms, 3 story. S

$49-$65; D $55-$90; each addl $5; under 18 free. Crib free. Pet accepted, some restrictions. TV; cable (premium). Pool. Complimentary continental bkfst. Restaurant nearby. Ck-out noon. Business servs avail. Refrigerator in suites. Cr cds: A, C, D, DS, JCB, MC, V.

[D] [icons] SC

★ **COUNTRY HEARTH INN.** *3851 Shore Dr (46254), I-465 exit 17, north of downtown.* 317/297-1848; FAX 317/297-1848, ext. 125; res: 800/848-5767. 83 rms, 2 story, 12 suites. S $53-$65; D $59-$71; each addl $6; suites, kits. $74-$86; under 18 free. Crib free. TV; cable (premium). Pool. Complimentary continental bkfst. Restaurant adj 6 am-10 pm. Ck-out noon. Meeting rms. Business servs avail. Health club privileges. Cr cds: A, C, D, DS, MC, V.

[D] [icons] SC

★★ **COURTYARD BY MARRIOTT.** *8670 Allisonville Rd (46250), in Castleton.* 317/576-9559; FAX 317/576-0695. 146 rms, 3 story. S, D $92; each addl $10; suites $107-$117; under 18 free; wkend rates. Crib free. TV; cable (premium). Indoor pool; whirlpool. Continental bkfst. Complimentary coffee in rms. Bar. Ck-out noon. Coin lndry. Meeting rms. Business servs avail. In-rm modem link. Valet serv. Sundries. Exercise equipt; weight machine, bicycles. Refrigerators in suites. Balconies. Cr cds: A, C, D, DS, MC, V.

[D] [icons]

★★ **COURTYARD BY MARRIOTT.** *10290 N Meridian St (46209), in College Park.* 317/571-1110; FAX 317/571-0416. 149 rms, 4 story. S, D $92-$108; each addl $10; suites $125-$145; under 18 free; higher rates special events. Crib free. TV; cable (premium). Complimentary coffee in rms. Bar 4-11 pm. Ck-out 1 pm. Meeting rms. Business servs avail. In-rm modem link. Sundries. Coin lndry. Exercise equipt; weight machine, stair machine. Indoor pool; whirlpool. Refrigerator in suites. Cr cds: A, C, D, DS, MC, V.

[D] [icons] SC

★★ **COURTYARD BY MARRIOTT-AIRPORT.** *5525 Fortune Circle E (46241), at Intl Airport, south of downtown.* 317/248-0300; FAX 317/248-1834. 151 rms, 4 story. S $89; D $99; each addl $10; suites $120; higher rates special events. Crib free. TV; cable (premium). VCR avail. Indoor pool; whirlpool. Continental bkfst. Complimentary coffee in rms. Restaurant nearby. Bar 5-11 pm; closed Sun. Ck-out noon. Meeting rms. Business servs avail. Sundries. Free airport transportation. Exercise equipt; weight machine, bicycles. Balconies. Cr cds: A, C, D, DS, MC, V.

[D] [icons] SC

★ **DRURY INN.** *9320 N Michigan Rd (46268), in College Park.* 317/876-9777; FAX 317/876-9777, ext. 473. 110 rms, 4 story. S $63-$73; D $73-$83; each addl $10; under 18 free; some wkend rates. Crib free. Pet accepted, some restrictions. TV; cable (premium). Pool. Complimentary bkfst. Restaurant nearby. Ck-out noon. Meeting rms. Business servs avail. In-rm modem link. Sundries. Cr cds: A, C, D, DS, MC, V.

[D] [icons] SC

✓★ **FAIRFIELD INN BY MARRIOTT.** *8325 Bash Rd (46250), in Castleton.* 317/577-0455. 132 rms, 3 story. S, D $56-$69; each addl $8; under 18 free. Crib free. TV; cable (premium). Heated pool. Complimentary continental bkfst. Restaurant nearby. Ck-out noon. Business servs avail. In-rm modem link. Cr cds: A, C, D, DS, MC, V.

[D] [icons] SC

★★ **HAMPTON INN.** *7220 Woodland Dr (46278), I-465 & 71st St, north of downtown.* 317/290-1212; FAX 317/291-1579. 124 rms, 4 story. S, D $69-$74; under 18 free. Crib free. Pet accepted, some restrictions. TV; cable (premium). Indoor pool; whirlpool. Complimentary continental bkfst. Restaurant adj 24 hrs. Ck-out noon. Meeting rms. Business servs avail. In-rm modem link. Valet serv. Exercise equipt; weight machine, bicycles. Cr cds: A, C, D, DS, MC, V.

[D] [icons] SC

★★ **HAMPTON INN-EAST.** *2311 N Shadeland Ave (46219), east of downtown.* 317/359-9900; FAX 317/359-1376. 125 rms, 4 story. S $64-$68; D $68-$76; under 18 free. Crib free. Pet accepted, some restrictions. TV; cable (premium). Indoor pool; whirlpool. Complimentary continental bkfst. Restaurant nearby. Ck-out noon. Meeting rm. Business servs avail. In-rm modem link. Cr cds: A, C, D, DS, MC, V.

[D] [icons] SC

★★ **HOMEWOOD SUITES.** *2501 E 86th St (46240), north of downtown.* 317/253-1919; FAX 317/255-8223. 116 suites, 3 story. No elvtr. S, D $94-$104; higher rates special events. Crib free. Pet accepted; $50. TV; cable (premium), VCR. Complimentary continental bkfst. Coffee in rms. Ck-out noon. Meeting rms. Business center. In-rm modem link. Valet serv. Coin lndry. Exercise equipt; weight machine, stair machine, sauna. Heated pool; whirlpool. Refrigerators, microwaves. Cr cds: A, C, D, DS, MC, V.

[D] [icons] SC

★ **LA QUINTA-EAST.** *7304 E 21st St (46219), north of downtown.* 317/359-1021; FAX 317/359-0578. 122 rms, 2 story. S, D $53-$62; each addl $7; under 18 free. Crib free. TV; cable (premium). Heated pool. Continental bkfst. Coffee in rms. Restaurant adj 6 am-11 pm. Ck-out noon. Coin lndry. Valet serv. Cr cds: A, C, D, DS, MC, V.

[D] [icons] SC

★ **RAMADA INN-EAST.** *7701 E 42nd St (46226), north of downtown.* 317/897-4000; FAX 317/897-8100. 192 rms, 2 story. S $64-$66; D $69-$71; each addl $5; suites $110-$160; under 18 free. Crib $10. TV; cable (premium). 2 pools, 1 indoor. Restaurant 6 am-10 pm; Sun to 2 pm. Rm serv. Bars. Ck-out noon. Meeting rms. Business servs avail. Cr cds: A, C, D, DS, MC, V.

[icons] SC

★ **RENAISSANCE TOWER.** *230 E 9th St (46204), downtown.* 317/261-1652; res: 800/676-7786; FAX 317/262-8648. 80 kit. units, 6 story. S, D $75; higher rates special events. TV; cable, VCR avail. Complimentary coffee in rms. Ck-out noon. Business servs avail. In-rm modem link. Valet serv. Coin lndry. Microwaves. Cr cds: A, DS, MC, V.

[D] [icons] SC

★★ **SIGNATURE INN.** *4402 E Creek View Dr (46237), I-65 & Southport Rd, south of downtown.* 317/784-7006. 101 rms, 2 story. S, D $65-$72; under 18 free; wkend rates Nov-Apr. Crib free. TV; cable (premium). Pool. Complimentary continental bkfst. Restaurant adj 6 am-10 pm. Ck-out noon. Meeting rms. Business servs avail. In-rm modem link. Valet serv. Sundries. Health club privileges. Microwaves avail. Cr cds: A, D, DS, MC, V.

[D] [icons] SC

Motor Hotels

★★ **AMERISUITES.** *9104 Keystone Crossing (46240), north of downtown.* 317/843-0064; FAX 317/843-1851. 126 suites, 6 story. S, D $81-$109; each addl $10. Crib free. TV; cable (premium), VCR (movies). Complimentary continental bkfst. Ck-out noon. Meeting rms. Business center. In-rm modem link. Valet serv (Mon-Fri). Coin lndry. Exercise equipt; treadmill, bicycle. Health club privileges. Heated pool. Refrigerators, microwaves, wet bars. Cr cds: A, C, D, DS, MC, V.

[D] [icons] SC

★ **COMFORT INN.** *5855 Rockville Rd (46224), near Intl Airport, west of downtown.* 317/487-9800; FAX 317/487-1125. 94 rms, 4 story, 24 suites. S $79-$180; D $84-$185; each addl $5; suites $91-$185; under 18 free. Crib free. TV; cable. Complimentary continental bkfst. Coffee in rms. Ck-out noon. Meeting rms. Business servs avail. In-rm modem link. Bellhops. Valet serv. Sundries. Coin lndry. Free airport transportation. Exercise equipt; bicycle, stair machine. Indoor pool; whirlpool.

Playground. Game rm. Some refrigerators, microwaves, wet bars; in-rm whirlpool in suites. Cr cds: A, C, D, DS, JCB, MC, V.

★★★ DOUBLETREE GUEST SUITES. *(11355 N Meridian St, Carmel 46032) Approx 15 mi N on Meridian St (US 31).* 317/844-7994; FAX 317/844-2118. 137 suites, 3 story. S, D $85-$129; each addl $15; under 18 free. Crib free. TV; cable. Indoor/outdoor pool; whirlpool, poolside serv. Complimentary coffee in rms. Restaurant 6:30 am-11 pm. Rm serv. Bar from 5 pm. Ck-out noon. Meeting rms. Business servs avail. Exercise equipt; bicycles, stair machine. Refrigerators, microwaves. Private patios. Cr cds: A, C, D, DS, MC, V.

★★ HAMPTON INN. *105 S Meridian St (46225), downtown.* 317/261-1200; FAX 317/261-1030. 180 rms, 9 story, 22 suites. S $88-$109; D $99-$109; suites $104-$159; under 18 free; higher rates special events. Crib free. Valet parking $8. TV; cable (premium). Complimentary continental bkfst. Restaurant 11 am-midnight. Rm serv. Bar. Ck-out noon. Meeting rms. Business servs avail. In-rm modem link. Bellhops. Valet serv. Exercise equipt; bicycle, treadmill. Some in-rm whirlpools, refrigerators, wet bars. Cr cds: A, C, D, DS, MC, V.

★★★ HOLIDAY INN SELECT-NORTH. *3850 De Pauw Blvd (46268), in College Park, at I-465 & US 421 exit 27.* 317/872-9790; FAX 317/871-5608. 349 rms, 5 story. S, D $99-$109; suites $170; under 18 free; wkend rates. Crib free. TV; cable (premium). Heated pool; whirlpool. Coffee in rms. Restaurant 6 am-10 pm. Rm serv. Bar 11-2 am. Ck-out 11 am. Coin lndry. Convention facilities. Business servs avail. In-rm modem link. Bellhops. Valet serv. Gift shop. Sundries. Putting green. Exercise equipt; weight machine, treadmill, sauna. Private patios; balconies. Cr cds: A, C, D, DS, JCB, MC, V.

★★ HOLIDAY INN-EAST. *6990 E 21st St (46219), east of downtown.* 317/359-5341; FAX 317/351-1666. 184 rms, 6 story. S, D $89; higher rates special events. Crib free. Pet accepted. TV; cable (premium). Complimentary full bkfst (Mon-Fri). Coffee in rms. Restaurant 6 am-11 pm; Fri-Sun to midnight. Rm serv. Bar. Ck-out noon. Meeting rms. Business center. In-rm modem link. Bellhops. Valet serv. Sundries. Coin lndry. Exercise equipt; treadmill, stair machine. Indoor pool; whirlpool. Game rm. Cr cds: A, C, D, DS, JCB, MC, V.

★★★ MARRIOTT. *7202 E 21st St (46219), I-70E & I-465, east of downtown.* 317/352-1231; FAX 317/352-9775. 252 rms, 3-5 story. S, D, studio rms $119; each addl $10; suites $300; under 18 free; wkend rates; higher rates Memorial Day wkend. Crib free. Pet accepted, some restrictions. TV; cable, VCR avail. Indoor/outdoor pool; wading pool, whirlpool, poolside serv. Complimentary coffee in lobby. Restaurant 6 am-10 pm. Rm serv. Bar 11-1 am, Sun to midnight. Ck-out noon. Coin lndry. Meeting rms. Business center. In-rm modem link. Bellhops. Valet serv. Sundries. Gift shop. Tennis privileges. Putting green. Exercise equipt; weight machine, bicycles. Rec rm. Some private patios. Luxury level. Cr cds: A, C, D, DS, JCB, MC, V.

★ RAMADA-AIRPORT. *2500 S High School Rd (46241), at Intl Airport, south of downtown.* 317/244-3361; FAX 317/241-9202. 288 rms, 6 story. S $119; D $129; each addl $10; suites $195-$275; under 18 free; higher rates special events. Crib $10. TV; cable (premium). Indoor pool. Restaurant 6-11 am, 5-10 pm. Rm serv. Bar 11-1 am. Ck-out noon. Meeting rms. Business servs avail. In-rm modem link. Bellhops. Sundries. Gift shop. Free airport transportation. Cr cds: A, C, D, DS, MC, V.

★ ST VINCENT MARTEN HOUSE. *1801 W 86th St (46260), north of downtown.* 317/872-4111; FAX 317/875-7162; res: 800/736-5634. 176 rms, 2 story. S, D $89-$99; each addl $10; suites $135-$250; under 18 free. Crib free. TV; cable. Indoor pool. Restaurant 6:30 am-2 pm, 5:30-10 pm. Rm serv. Bar 5 pm-midnight. Ck-out noon. Coin lndry. Meeting rms.

Business servs avail. In-rm modem link. Bellhops. Valet serv. Exercise equipt; weight machine, treadmill, sauna. Some refrigerators. St Vincent's Hospital adj. Cr cds: A, C, D, DS, MC, V.

★★★ WYNDHAM GARDEN. *251 E Pennsylvania Pkwy (46280), I-465 & US 31N to 103rd St, north of downtown.* 317/574-4600; FAX 317/574-4633. 171 rms, 6 story. S, D $89-$109; suites $109-$129. Crib free. TV; cable, VCR avail. Indoor pool; whirlpool. Complimentary coffee in rms. Restaurant 6:30 am-10 pm. Rm serv from 5 pm. Bar 11 am-midnight. Ck-out noon. Meeting rms. Business servs avail. Sundries. Exercise equipt; weight machine, bicycles. Cr cds: A, C, D, DS, ER, JCB, MC, V.

Hotels

★★★ CANTERBURY. *123 S Illinois (46225), downtown.* 317/634-3000; FAX 317/685-2519; res: 800/538-8186. 99 rms, 12 story. S $175-$200; D $200-$225; each addl $25; suites $400-$1,200; lower rates wkends. Crib $25. Garage $12/day. TV; cable, VCR avail. Complimentary continental bkfst. Restaurant (see RESTAURANT AT THE CANTERBURY). Afternoon tea 4-5:30 pm. Ck-out noon. Meeting rms. Business servs avail. In-rm modem link. Concierge. Bathrm phones, minibars. 2-story atrium lobby. Formal decor; 4-poster beds, Chippendale-style furniture. Historic landmark; built 1926. Cr cds: A, C, D, DS, ER, JCB, MC, V.

★★ CROWNE PLAZA-UNION STATION. *123 W Louisiana St (46225), at Union Station, downtown.* 317/631-2221; FAX 317/236-7474. 275 rms, 3 story, 33 suites. S, D $125-$155; suites $185-$250; under 18 free; wkend rates; higher rates Dec 31. Crib free. Valet parking $10. TV; cable. Indoor pool; whirlpool. Restaurant 6 am-midnight. Bar 4 pm-midnight. Ck-out noon. Convention facilities. Business servs avail. In-rm modem link. Concierge. Free airport transportation. Exercise equipt; bicycles, rowers. Rec rm. First US "union" railway depot (1853); Pullman sleeper cars from the 1920s house hotel's suites. Cr cds: A, C, D, DS, MC, V.

★★★ DOUBLETREE-UNIVERSITY PLACE. *850 W Michigan St (46206), on campus of Indiana University, downtown.* 317/269-9000; FAX 317/231-5168; res: 800/627-2700. 278 rms, 10 story. Mar-May, Sept-Nov: S, D $169; suites $250-$600; lower rates rest of yr. Crib avail. Garage parking $4.75. TV; cable (premium). Coffee in rms. Restaurant 6 am-midnight. Bar from 11 am. Ck-out noon. Convention facilities. Business center. In-rm modem link. Gift shop. Barber. Health club privileges. Refrigerators. Cr cds: A, C, D, DS, MC, V.

★★★ EMBASSY SUITES. *110 W Washington St (46204), downtown.* 317/236-1800; FAX 317/236-1816. 360 suites, 18 story. S $139-$179; D $159-$219; under 18 free. Crib free. Parking in/out $5. TV; cable, VCR avail. Indoor pool; whirlpool. Complimentary full bkfst. Complimentary coffee in rms. Restaurant 11 am-10 pm; Sat, Sun from 5 pm. Bar to 1 am. Ck-out noon. Convention facilities. Business servs avail. In-rm modem link. Shopping arcade. Exercise equipt; weights, bicycles. Refrigerators, microwaves. Cr cds: A, C, D, DS, JCB, MC, V.

★★★ EMBASSY SUITES. *3912 Vincennes Rd (46268-3024), I-465N & US 421, north of downtown.* 317/872-7700; FAX 317/872-2974. 221 suites, 8 story. S, D $109-$189; under 12 free; wkend plan. Crib avail. TV; cable (premium). Indoor pool; whirlpool. Complimentary full bkfst; afternoon refreshments. Complimentary coffee in rms. Restaurant 11 am-2 pm, 5-11 pm. Bar from 4 pm. Ck-out noon. Meeting rms. Business servs avail. In-rm modem link. Gift shop. Exercise equipt; bicycles, treadmill, sauna. Game rm. Refrigerators, microwaves. Cr cds: A, C, D, DS, MC, V.

★★★ HYATT REGENCY. *One South Capitol (46204), downtown.* 317/632-1234; FAX 317/231-7569. 500 rms, 21 story. S $175; D $200; each addl $25; suites $350-$1,000; parlor $175-$700; under 18 free;

some wkend rates. Valet, garage parking $9. Crib free. TV; VCR avail. Indoor pool. Restaurants 6 am-midnight. Bars 11-2 am. Ck-out noon. Convention facilities. Business center. In-rm modem link. Concierge. Barber, beauty shop. Exercise equipt; weight machine, bicycles. Massage. Atrium. Revolving restaurant. Cr cds: A, C, D, DS, ER, JCB, MC, V.

★ ★ ★ **OMNI-NORTH.** *8181 N Shadeland Ave (46250), I-69 N exit 82nd St, north of downtown.* 317/849-6668; FAX 317/849-4936. 215 rms, 6 story. S, D $89-$149; suites $149-$250; wkend rates. Crib free. TV; cable (premium). Indoor pool. Complimentary coffee in rms. Restaurant 7 am-10 pm; wkend hrs vary. Rm serv to midnight. Bar 11:30 am-midnight. Ck-out noon. Coin lndry. Meeting rms. In-rm modem link. Gift shop. Exercise equipt; bicycles, weight machine; sauna. Game rm. Many refrigerators. Cr cds: A, D, DS, JCB, MC, V.

★ ★ ★ **OMNI SEVERIN.** *40 W Jackson Place (46225), at Union Station, downtown.* 317/634-6664; FAX 317/767-0003. 423 rms, 13 story. S, D $119-$189; each addl $20; suites $225-$675; under 18 free. Crib free. Garage parking $5. TV; cable, VCR avail. Indoor pool; poolside serv. Coffee in rms. Restaurant 6 am-11 pm. Bar 11-1 am. Ck-out noon. Convention facilities. Business center. In-rm modem link. Concierge. Gift shop. Exercise equipt; weight machine, bicycles. Some refrigerators. Built in 1913. Across from Union Station. Cr cds: A, C, D, DS, MC, V.

★ ★ ★ **RADISSON.** *8787 Keystone Crossing (46240), at 86th St & Keystone Ave, connected to Fashion Mall, north of downtown.* 317/846-2700; FAX 317/846-2700, ext. 402. 552 units, 2-12 story. S, D $179; each addl $15; suites $199; under 17 free; wkend rates. Crib free. TV; cable (premium), VCR avail (movies). Indoor pool; whirlpool, poolside serv. Restaurants 6:30 am-11 pm. Rm serv to midnight. Bar 5 pm-2 am. Ck-out noon. Guest lndry. Convention facilities. Business center. In-rm modem link. Shopping arcade. Garage parking. Sauna. Health club privileges. Game rm. Refrigerator in suites. Cr cds: A, C, D, DS, ER, JCB, MC, V.

★ ★ ★ **RADISSON HOTEL CITY CENTER.** *31 W Ohio St (46204), downtown.* 317/635-2000; FAX 317/638-0782. 374 rms, 21 story. S $99-$169; D $99-$184; each addl $15; suites $139-$199; under 18 free. Crib free. Garage $8. TV; cable, VCR avail. Pool; poolside serv. Restaurant 6:30 am-midnight. Bars 11-1 am. Ck-out noon. Convention facilities. Business center. Health club privileges. Luxury level. Cr cds: A, C, D, DS, MC, V.

★ ★ ★ **THE WESTIN.** *50 S Capitol (46204), downtown.* 317/262-8100; FAX 317/231-3928. 573 rms, 15 story. S $194; D $224; each addl $30; suites $224-$1,000; under 18 free. Crib free. Valet, garage parking $8. TV; cable, VCR avail. Indoor pool; whirlpool. Restaurant 6:30 am-11 pm. Rm serv 24 hrs. Bar 11-2 am, Sun to midnight. Ck-out noon. Convention facilities. Business center. In-rm modem link. Concierge. Exercise equipt; bicycles, treadmill. Health club privileges. Some bathrm phones, minibars. Luxury level. Cr cds: A, C, D, DS, JCB, MC, V.

Restaurants

✔★ **ARISTOCRAT PUB.** *5212 N College Ave (46220), in Broad Ripple.* 317/283-7388. Hrs: 11 am-11 pm; Wed, Thurs to midnight; Fri, Sat to 1 am; Sun from 10 am; Sun brunch to 3 pm. Closed some major hols. Bar. Semi-a la carte: lunch, dinner $4.95-$14.95. Sun brunch $4.95-$7. Child's meals. Specializes in pasta. Parking. Outdoor dining. Casual atmosphere. Cr cds: A, C, D, DS, MC, V.

★ ★ ★ **BENVENUTI.** *1 N Pennsylvania St (46225), downtown.* 317/633-4915. Hrs: 5:30-9 pm; wkends to 9:30 pm. Closed Sun; major hols. Res accepted; required wkends. Italian menu. Bar. Wine list. A la

carte entrees: dinner $22-$32.50. Specializes in pasta, fish, veal chops. Elegant atmosphere with European flair. Jacket. Cr cds: A, D, MC, V.

★ ★ **GLASS CHIMNEY.** *(12901 Old Meridian St, Carmel 46032) I-465 NE to Meridian St, 12 mi N to 126th St, E to Old Meridian St.* 317/844-0921. Hrs: 5-10 pm; Fri, Sat to 11 pm. Closed Sun; Thanksgiving, Dec 25. Res accepted. Continental menu. Bar. Semi-a la carte: dinner $15-$38. Specializes in veal, seafood, steak. Outdoor dining. Elegant European decor. Cr cds: A, D, MC, V.

★ ★ **HOLLYHOCK HILL.** *8110 N College Ave (46240), north of downtown.* 317/251-2294. Hrs: 5-8 pm; Sun noon-7:30 pm. Closed Mon; July 4, Dec 24 & 25. Res accepted. Serv bar. Complete meals: dinner $12.95-$17.50. Child's meals. Specializes in fried chicken, seafood, steak. Tea room atmosphere. Family-owned. Cr cds: A, MC, V.

★ ★ **IRON SKILLET.** *2489 W 30th St (46222), at Cold Spring Rd, north of downtown.* 317/923-6353. Hrs: 5-8:30 pm; Sun noon-7:30 pm. Closed Mon, Tues; Dec 24, 25; also 1st wk July. Res accepted. Serv bar. Complete meals: dinner $11.95-$15.95. Child's meals. Specializes in steak, skillet-fried chicken, fresh fish. Family-style dining. Blackboard menu. Parking. Converted homestead (1870); overlooks golf course. Family-owned. Cr cds: A, C, D, DS, MC, V.

✔★ **JAZZ COOKER.** *925 E Westfield Blvd (46220), in Broad Ripple.* 317/253-2883. Hrs: 5-10 pm; Sun to 9 pm. Closed most major hols. Res accepted. Bar. A la carte entrees: dinner $9.25-$15. Specializes in Cajun, Creole dishes. Entertainment Thurs-Sun (summer). Outdoor dining. New Orleans atmosphere. Cr cds: A, C, D, DS, MC, V.

★ ★ **KONA JACK'S.** *9419 N Meridian (46260), in College Park area.* 317/843-1609. Hrs: 11 am-10 pm; Sat 5-11 pm. Closed Sun; major hols. Res accepted. Semi-a la carte: lunch $4-$8.95, dinner $10.95-$29.95. Specializes in seafood, sushi. Parking. Outdoor dining. Nautical decor. Cr cds: A, D, DS, MC, V.

★ ★ **THE MAJESTIC.** *47 S Pennsylvania (46204), downtown.* 317/636-5418. Hrs: 11 am-2 pm, 5-9 pm. Closed Sun; some major hols. Res accepted. Continental menu. Bar. Semi-a la carte: lunch $4.95-$12.95, dinner $12.95-$38.95. Child's meals. Specializes in seafood, steak, chicken. Own pasta, pastries. Old bldg with stained glass, Tiffany fixtures, handcarved bar. Cr cds: A, C, D, DS, MC, V.

★ ★ ★ **PETER'S.** *8505 Keystone Crossing Blvd (46240), north of downtown.* 317/465-1155. Hrs: 5-10 pm; Fri, Sat to 10:30 pm. Closed Sun; major hols. Res accepted. Bar. A la carte entrees: dinner $12.95-$23.95. Specializes in Indiana duckling, fresh fish, desserts. Parking. Cr cds: A, C, D, MC, V.

★ ★ ★ **RESTAURANT AT THE CANTERBURY.** *(See Canterbury Hotel)* 317/634-3000. Hrs: 7-10:30 am, 11:30 am-2 pm, 5:30-10 pm; Fri, Sat to 11 pm; Sun brunch 10:30 am-2 pm. Res accepted. Continental menu. Bar. Wine list. A la carte entrees: bkfst $4.50-$14.95, lunch $6.95-$14.95, dinner $16.50-$29.50. Sun brunch $6.95-$13.95. Specializes in seafood, veal. Own baking. Valet parking. International decor; artwork. Jacket (dinner). Cr cds: A, C, D, DS, ER, JCB, MC, V.

★ ★ ★ **RUTH'S CHRIS STEAK HOUSE.** *9445 Threel Rd (46240), at 96th & Keystone, north of downtown.* 317/844-1155. Hrs: 5-11 pm; Sun 4-10 pm. Closed some major hols. Res accepted; required hols. Bar. Extensive wine list. Semi-a la carte: dinner $16-$30. Specializes in steak, pork chop, seafood. Own baking. Parking. English country atmosphere. Cr cds: A, MC, V.

D

★ ★ **ST ELMO STEAK HOUSE.** *127 S Illinois (46204), downtown.* 317/637-1811. Hrs: 4-10:30 pm; Sun 5-9:30 pm. Closed major hols. Res accepted. Bar. Semi-a la carte: dinner $16.95-$34.95. Specializes in steak, fresh seafood. Turn-of-the-century decor, historic photographs. Cr cds: A, C, D, DS, MC, V.

D

★ **WILDCAT BREWING COMPANY.** *9111 N Michigan Rd (46268), in College Park.* 317/872-3446. Hrs: 11 am-11 pm; Sun to 10 pm. Closed Thanksgiving, Dec 25. Res accepted. Bar to 2 am. Semi-a la carte: lunch $5-$11, dinner $7-$19. Specializes in prime rib, Italian dishes, Mexican dishes. Microbrewery can be viewed from two dining areas. Cr cds: A, DS, MC, V.

Jasper (J-3)

Pop 10,030 **Elev** 472 ft **Area code** 812 **Zip** 47546

Monastery Immaculate Conception (1867). Historic monastery, home to the Sisters of St Benedict, is located on 190 acres. The church, one of the most famous examples of Romanesque architecture in the country, features brilliant stained-glass windows, handsome wood panels and pews hand-carved in Oberammergau, and an interior dome rising 87 ft from the marble floor. An information office at the main entrance has historical display, a scale model of the entire complex and a video about the monastery. Guided tours (by appt). Monastery (daily). S on IN 162, in Ferdinand at 802 E 10th St. Phone 812/367-1411.

Motels

★ ★ **BEST WESTERN DUTCHMAN INN.** *(406 E 22nd St, Huntingburg 47542)* Approx 4 mi S on US 231. 812/683-2334. 94 rms, 2 story. S, D $49-$89; under 18 free. Crib free. TV; cable (premium), VCR avail. Pool; wading pool. Restaurant 6 am-2 pm, 4:30-9 pm. Bar 4-11 pm. Ck-out 11 am. Meeting rms. Business servs avail. Valet serv. Some in-rm steam baths; microwaves avail. Cr cds: A, C, D, DS, MC, V.

D

✔★ **DAYS INN.** *Jct IN 162 & IN 164.* 812/482-6000; FAX 812/482-7207. 84 rms, 2 story. S $52-$60; D $66-$72; each addl $6; under 18 free. Crib free. Pet accepted, some restrictions; $5. TV; cable (premium), VCR avail. Pool. Complimentary continental bkfst. Restaurant adj. Ck-out noon. Meeting rms. Business servs avail. Valet serv. Sundries. Some refrigerators. Cr cds: A, C, D, DS, MC, V.

D

Motor Hotel

★ ★ **HOLIDAY INN.** *US 231, 1¹/₂ mi S.* 812/482-5555; FAX 812/482-7908. 200 rms, 2 story. May-Aug: S, D $99-$125; under 19 free; lower rates rest of yr. Crib free. TV; cable (premium). Indoor pool; wading pool, whirlpool. Restaurant 6 am-2 pm, 5-9 pm. Rm serv. Bar 3 pm-1:30 am, closed Sun. Ck-out noon. Coin lndry. Convention facilities. Business servs avail. In-rm modem link. Game rm. Rec rm. Exercise equipt; bicycle, rower, sauna. Cr cds: A, C, D, DS, JCB, MC, V.

D

Restaurant

★ ★ **SCHNITZELBANK.** *393 Third Ave.* 812/482-2640. Hrs: 8 am-10 pm. Closed Sun; major hols. German, Amer menu. Bar to 11 pm.

Semi-a la carte: bkfst, lunch $3-$6.95, dinner $5.50-$19.95. Specializes in steak, seafood. Salad bar. Bavarian decor. Cr cds: DS, MC, V.

D SC

Jeffersonville (J-5)

(See also New Albany)

Founded 1802 **Pop** 21,841 **Elev** 448 ft **Area code** 812 **Zip** 47130 **E-mail** jkeith@sunnyside.win.net **Web** www.sunnysideoflouisville.org

Information Southern Indiana Convention and Tourism Bureau, 315 Southern Indiana Ave; 812/282-6654 or 800/552-3842.

Jeffersonville, on the north bank of the Ohio River, opposite Louisville, Kentucky, has a proud history as a shipbuilding center. One of the oldest towns in Indiana, it was built according to plans by Thomas Jefferson. The city is an industrial manufacturing center and a terminal for the American Commercial Line, Inc, a large river transportation company. Grain, tobacco, strawberries and dairy goods are the main farm products in surrounding Clark County.

What to See and Do

Colgate Clock. Said to be the second-largest clock in the world (40 ft in diameter). Atop the Clarksville Colgate-Palmolive plant.

Howard Steamboat Museum. Housed in 22-rm mansion featuring stained- and leaded-glass windows, hand-carved panels, brass chandeliers, a grand stairway, Victorian furniture (1893); steamboat models, shipyard artifacts & tools, pictures and other memorabilia (1834-1941). Tours (daily exc Mon; closed major hols). 1101 E Market St. Phone 812/283-3728. ¢¢

Annual Events

Victorian Chautauqua. Howard Steamboat Museum. Victorian-style cafe, speakers, children's activities. Phone 812/283-3728. Mid-May.

Steamboat Days Festival. On the riverfront, downtown. Parade, entertainment, 5K run. Phone 812/284-BOAT. Early or mid-Sept.

Motel

(Rates are generally much higher during Kentucky Derby)

✔★ **BEST WESTERN GREENTREE INN.** *(1425 Broadway St, Clarksville 47129)* N of Louisville, KY on I-65 at IN 131 exit. 812/288-9281. 107 rms. S $49; D $60-$65; each addl $5. Crib free. Pet accepted, some restrictions. TV; cable (premium). Pool. Restaurant adj open 24 hrs. Ck-out noon. Business servs avail. In-rm modem link. Health club privileges. Bathrm phones. Cr cds: A, C, D, DS, ER, JCB, MC, V.

D SC

Hotels

★ ★ ★ **HOLIDAY INN LAKEVIEW.** *(505 Marriott Dr, Clarksville 47129)* 2 mi N on I-65 at Stansifer exit. 812/283-4411; FAX 812/288-8976. 356 rms, 3-10 story. S $72; D $78; each addl $6; suites $90-$200; under 18 free; wknd rates. Crib free. TV; cable. 2 pools; 1 indoor; poolside serv. Playground. Coffee in rms. Restaurant 6:30 am-2 pm, 5-10 pm. Bar 11-1 am; entertainment. Ck-out noon. Coin lndry. Convention facilities. Business servs avail. Gift shop. Barber, beauty shop. Free airport transportation. Tennis. Miniature golf. Exercise equipt; bicycles, treadmill. Refrigerators in suites. Private patios, balconies. Picnic tables. Heliport. Scenic grounds with lake view. Cr cds: A, C, D, DS, MC, V.

D SC

★ **RAMADA.** *700 W Riverside Dr.* 812/284-6711; FAX 812/283-3686. 186 units, 10 story, 20 suites. S $72; D $82; each addl $10;

suites $95-$145; under 18 free. Crib free. Pet accepted, some restrictions. TV; cable (premium). Pool. Restaurant 6:30 am-2 pm, 5-10 pm. Bar 5 pm-2 am. Ck-out noon. Meeting rms. Business servs avail. Free airport transportation. Game rm. On Ohio River. Cr cds: A, C, D, DS, MC, V.

D ⮐ ⌕ ⌕ ⌕ SC

Kokomo (D-4)

(See also Logansport, Peru)

Founded 1842 **Pop** 44,962 **Elev** 810 ft **Area code** 765 **E-mail** kokomoin @holli.com **Web** www.holli.com/kokomoin

Information Kokomo Indiana Visitors Bureau, 112 N Washington St, 46901; 765/457-6802 or 800/837-0971.

This is a lively manufacturing center, where the first clutch-driven automobile with electric ignition was invented by Elwood Haynes. Since then Kokomo manufacturers have invented several more useful items, from the first pneumatic rubber tire to canned tomato juice. The automobile industry is represented by Delco Electronics and Chrysler plants, which manufacture automotive entertainment systems, semiconductor devices, transmissions and aluminum die castings. Indiana University has a branch here, and Grissom Air Force Base is located 14 miles north of town.

What to See and Do

Elwood Haynes Museum. Home of Elwood Haynes; memorabilia, items relating to early development of the automobile; 1905 and 1924 Haynes cars on display; industrial exhibits; also Haynes Stellite (alloy used in space ships). (Daily exc Mon; closed hols) 1915 S Webster St. Phone 765/456-7500. **Free.**

Haynes Memorial. Pumpkinvine Pike is site of the first successful road test of Haynes' car. 3 mi E, off US 31 Bypass.

Highland Park. County's last covered bridge was moved here from Vermont. Recreational facilities. (Daily) 1402 W Defenbaugh St. Phone 765/452-0063. **Free.** Also in park are

"Old Ben." An enormous, stuffed Hereford steer that weighed 4,720 pounds, was 16 ft, 8 inches long and 6 ft, 4 inches high. His life ended in 1910, at the height of his fame, when he slipped and fell on ice.

Sycamore stump. The original tree died in the early 1900s, leaving a stump that measures 51 ft in circumference. The interior of the stump has held 24 people and once served as a telephone booth.

Seiberling Mansion (1891). This late-Victorian-style mansion houses exhibits of historical and educational interest; county history; manufacturing artifacts. (Tues-Sun, afternoons; closed some hols; also Jan) 1200 W Sycamore St. Phone 765/452-4314. ¢

Annual Events

Greentown Glass Festival. E on I-35, in downtown Greentown. Commemorates the production of Greentown Glass. Carnival, beauty pageant, antique show, many events. 2nd wkend June.

Howard County Fair. Greentown fairgrounds. Last wk July.

Motels

✔★★ **FAIRFIELD INN BY MARRIOTT.** *1717 E Lincoln Rd (46902), 3¹/₂ mi S on US 31 exit Lincoln Rd.* 765/453-8822. 61 rms, 3 story, 20 suites. S $58-$72; D $62-$72; each addl $5; suites $79; under 18 free; higher rates special events. TV; cable (premium). Complimentary continental bkfst. Ck-out noon. Meeting rm. Business servs avail. In-rm modem link. Indoor pool; whirlpool. Game rm. Some refrigerators, microwaves. Cr cds: A, D, DS, MC, V.

D ⌕ ⌕ ⌕ SC

★★ **HOLIDAY INN EXPRESS.** *511 Albany Dr (47902), 3¹/₂ mi S on US 31.* 765/453-2222. 79 rms, 3 story. S, D $73-$84; suites $99-$154; under 19 free; higher rates special events. Crib avail. TV; cable (premium). Complimentary continental bkfst. Coffee in rms. Restaurant opp 11 am-11 pm. Ck-out 11 am. Meeting rms. Business servs avail. In-rm modem link. Coin lndry. Exercise equipt; treadmill, rowers. Indoor pool. Bathrm phones, refrigerators, microwaves, wet bars; some in-rm whirlpools, fireplaces. Cr cds: A, C, D, DS, JCB, MC, V.

D ⌕ ⌕ ⌕ ⌕ SC

✔★ **MOTEL 6.** *2808 S Reed Rd (46902).* 765/457-8211. 93 rms, 2 story. S $39-$45; D $45-$51; each addl $3; under 18 free; higher rates Indianapolis "500" wkend (2-day min). Crib free. TV; cable. Complimentary coffee. Restaurant adj 6 am-11 pm. Ck-out noon. Cr cds: A, D, DS, MC, V.

⌕ ⌕ SC

★★ **RAMADA INN.** *1709 E Lincoln Rd (46902).* 765/459-8001. 132 rms, 3 story. No elvtr. S $55-$89; D $60-$95; each addl $10; under 18 free; wkend rates; higher rates Indianapolis "500" wkend (2-day min). Crib free. TV; cable. Indoor pool. Restaurant 6 am-2 pm, 5-10 pm; Sat, Sun from 7 am. Rm serv. Bar 4 pm-1 am, Thurs-Sat to 2 am, Sun to midnight; entertainment. Ck-out noon. Meeting rms. Business servs avail. Free airport transportation. Exercise equipt; weight machine, rowers, sauna. Health club privileges. Picnic tables. Cr cds: A, C, D, DS, ER, MC, V.

D ⌕ ⌕ ⌕ ⌕ SC

★ **SIGNATURE INN.** *4021 S LaFountain (46902).* 765/455-1000. 101 rms, 2 story. S $48-$57; D $55-$58; under 17 free; wkend plans; higher rates: Indy "500." Crib free. Indoor pool; whirlpool. Complimentary continental bkfst. Ck-out noon. Meeting rms. Exercise equipt; weight machine, stair machine. Cr cds: A, C, D, DS, ER, MC, V.

D ⌕ ⌕ ⌕ ⌕ SC

Restaurants

✔★★ **COLORADO STEAK HOUSE.** *3201 S LaFountain (46902).* 765/455-1280. Hrs: 11 am-10 pm; Fri, Sat to 11 pm; Sun to 9 pm; Sun brunch to 2 pm. Res accepted. Bar. Semi-a la carte: lunch $5-$8, dinner $9-$15. Sun brunch $8.95. Child's meals. Specializes in Black Angus beef, seafood, steak. Cr cds: A, C, D, DS, MC, V.

D

★ **WHEATFIELD.** *2900 S Washington St (46902).* 765/453-1200. Hrs: 6:30 am-10:30 pm. Res accepted. Serv bar. Semi-a la carte: bkfst $1.95-$7.40, lunch $2.95-$8, dinner $5.95-$18.95. Child's meals. Specializes in seafood, ribs, steak, salads. Cr cds: A, MC, V.

D SC

Lafayette (D-3)

Founded 1825 **Pop** 43,764 **Elev** 560 ft **Area code** 765

Information Convention and Visitors Bureau, 301 Frontage Rd, PO Box 5547, 47903; 765/447-9999 or 800/872-6648.

Lafayette, on the east bank of the Wabash River, was named for the Marquis de Lafayette, who served as a general under George Washington in the Revolutionary War.

The city is surrounded by an extensive farm area, including cattle and dairy farms. A large number of diversified industries in the area manufacture automotive gears and supplies, electrical equipment and pharmaceuticals.

On the west bank of the river in West Lafayette is Purdue University. Established as an agricultural college in 1869, Purdue is also noted for many other programs, especially engineering.

What to See and Do

Clegg Botanical Garden. Approx 15 acres of rugged terrain with glacier-made ridges, native trees and wildflowers, ravines; nature trails, lookout point. (Daily) E on IN 25 to County Rd 300N, then 1 mi E to County Rd 400E, then 1¼ mi S. Phone 765/423-1325.   **Free.**

Columbian Park. Indoor zoo with petting zoo (daily; closed Thanksgiving, Dec 25). Amusement park; outdoor theater; water slide, swimming pool; tennis courts; concession, picnicking. Facilities (Memorial Day-Labor Day, daily exc Mon). Park (daily). Some fees. 5 mi SW via I-65, to IN 26 Lafayette exit. Phone 765/447-9351.   **Free.**

Fort Ouiatenon (1717). A 30-acre park; replica blockhouse with 18th-century French trading post. Museum depicts history of French, Native American, British and American struggles to control Wabash Valley. (Memorial Day-Labor Day, daily exc Mon; early Apr-Memorial Day & Labor Day-late Oct, wkends) (See ANNUAL EVENTS) Picnicking, boating. Park (daily). 4 mi SW of West Lafayette on S River Rd. Phone 765/743-3921 or 765/742-8411.   **Free.**

Greater Lafayette Museum of Art. Maintains permanent collection of 19th- and 20th-century American art; East and Weil Galleries present contemporary and historical exhibits. Rental gallery, library, gift shop. Art classes, lectures and workshops. (Tues-Sun afternoons; closed major hols & Aug) 101 S 9th St. Phone 765/742-1128.   **Free.**

Purdue University (1869). (36,163 students) More than 140 major buildings on 1,579 acres with private airport. In West Lafayette via I-65, IN 26. Contact Visitor Information Center; 765/494-INFO.

Tippecanoe Battlefield Museum and Park. Site of 1811 battle in which soldiers of the Fourth Regiment and local militia led by Gen William H. Harrison, territorial governor of Indiana, defeated a confederation of Native Americans headed by The Prophet, brother of Tecumseh. Wabash Heritage Trail begins here. (See ANNUAL EVENTS) (Daily) I-65 at IN 43 exit, in Battle Ground. Phone 765/567-2147.   ¢

Tippecanoe County Historical Museum. Collection of Americana, including artifacts from the Tippecanoe Battlefield and Fort Ouiatenon, exhibited in an English Gothic-style mansion (1852). (Daily exc Mon; closed hols & Jan) 909 South St. Phone 765/742-8411.   ¢¢

Wolf Park. Education/research facility, home to several packs of wolves, a small herd of bison, some coyotes and foxes. See wolves close at hand as they eat and socialize. (May-Nov, Mon-Sun afternoons; closed hols) Also "wolf howl" (all yr, Fri evenings; inquire for hrs). 10 mi NE via I-65, exit 178 or IN 43. Phone 765/567-2265.   ¢¢

Annual Events

Fiddlers' Gathering. Tippecanoe Battlefield. Old-time folk and country musicians from across the country. Late June.

Feast of the Hunters' Moon. Fort Ouiatenon. Re-enactment of life 250 yrs ago, when the fort soldiers, Canadian traders, Native Americans and backwoodsmen gathered to trade and celebrate the fall season. Phone 765/742-8411. Mid-Oct.

Motels

✔★ **FAIRFIELD INN BY MARRIOTT.** 4000 State Rd 26 E (47905). 765/449-0083. 79 rms, 3 story, 11 suites. S $59-$69; D $59-$79; each addl $10; suites $59-$79; under 18 free; higher rates special events. Crib free. TV; cable (premium). Complimentary continental bkfst. Restaurant adj 6 am-11 pm. Ck-out noon. Meeting rms. Business servs avail. In-rm modem link. Health club privileges. Indoor pool; whirlpool. Game rm. Refrigerator, microwave in suites. Cr cds: A, C, D, DS, MC, V.

D 🛏 🖬 🐾 SC

★★ **HOMEWOOD SUITES.** 3939 IN 26E (47905). 765/448-9700; FAX 765/449-1297. 84 kit. suites, 3 story. S, D $89-$152; under 18 free; higher rates: university events, Indy "500". Crib free. Pet accepted, some restrictions. TV; cable, VCR (movies). Heated pool; whirlpool. Complimentary continental bkfst. Complimentary coffee in rms. Restaurant nearby. Ck-out noon. Coin lndry. Meeting rms. Business center. In-rm modem link. Sundries. Gift shop. Free airport, RR station, bus depot transportation. Exercise equipt; weight machine, treadmill, sauna. Lawn games. Microwaves. Cr cds: A, C, D, DS, JCB, MC, V.

D 🐾 🛏 🏋 🖬 🐾 🖬

★★ **LEES INN.** 4701 Meijer Ct (47905). 765/447-3434; FAX 765/448-6105. 81 rms, 3 story. S $79-$119; D $89-$129; each addl $10; suites $99-$250; under 18 free; higher rates Indy "500." Crib free. TV; cable (premium). Complimentary continental bkfst. Restaurant opp 6 am-10 pm. Ck-out noon. Meeting rms. Business servs avail. In-rm modem link. Indoor pool; whirlpool. Refrigerators, minibars, wet bars. Cr cds: A, D, DS, MC, V.

D 🛏 🖬 🐾 SC

★★ **SIGNATURE INN.** 4320 IN 26 E (47905). 765/447-4142. 121 rms, 2 story. S $62; D $72; under 18 free; higher rates: Indy "500," football wkends. Crib free. TV; cable. Pool. Complimentary continental bkfst. Restaurant nearby. Ck-out noon. Meeting rms. Business servs avail. Cr cds: A, C, D, DS, MC, V.

D 🛏 🖬 🐾 SC

Motor Hotels

★★★ **HOLIDAY INN.** 5600 IN 43N (47906), at jct I-65 & IN 43 exit 178. 765/567-2131; FAX 765/567-2511. Web www.nlci.com/holiday. 150 rms, 4 story. S $55-$74; D $60-$76; each addl $6; under 18 free; higher rates: football games, Indianapolis "500," other special events. Crib free. Pet accepted. TV. Indoor pool. Restaurant 6 am-10 pm. Bar 4 pm-1 am. Ck-out 11 am. Free guest lndry. Meeting rms. Valet serv. Golf privileges. Sauna. Game rm. Cr cds: A, C, D, DS, JCB, MC, V.

D 🐾 🏋 🛏 🖬 🐾 SC

★★★ **RADISSON INN.** 4343 IN 26E (47905). 765/447-0575; FAX 765/447-0901. 124 rms, 6 story. S, D $89-$99; each addl $10; suites $145; under 18 free; higher rates: Indianapolis "500," university events (2-day min). Crib free. Pet accepted, some restrictions. TV; cable (premium). Indoor pool; whirlpool. Complimentary coffee in rm. Restaurant 6:30 am-2 pm, 5-10 pm. Rm serv. Bar 4 pm-midnight; pianist exc Mon, Thurs. Ck-out noon. Coin lndry. Meeting rms. In-rm modem link. Valet serv. Sauna. Refrigerators. Cr cds: A, C, D, DS, JCB, MC, V.

D 🐾 🛏 🖬 🐾 SC

★★ **UNIVERSITY INN.** (3001 Northwestern Ave, West Lafayette 47906) 4 mi W on US 52, at Cumberland Ave. 765/463-5511; FAX 765/497-3850; res: 800/777-9808. E-mail uicc@nlci.com; web www.nlci.com/inn. 149 rms, 3 story. S, D $66-$68; each addl $5; suites $100-$200; under 18 free; higher rates: motor races, football wkends (2-night min), university events. Crib free. TV; cable. Indoor pool; whirlpool. Restaurant 5:30-9:30 pm; Fri, Sat to 11 pm. Rm serv. Bar 4-11 pm. Ck-out 11 am. Meeting rms. Business servs avail. Free airport transportation. Exercise equipt; weight machine, rower. Microwave in suites. Garden atrium. Cr cds: A, D, DS, JCB, MC, V.

D 🛏 🏋 🖬 🐾 SC

Restaurant

★★★ **SORRENTO.** (601 Sagamore Pkwy W, West Lafayette 47906) 2 mi W on US 52 Bypass. 765/463-5537. Hrs: 11 am-midnight; Sun 4-10:30 pm; brunch 11 am-4 pm (exc Sun). Closed Jan 1 (until 4 pm), Dec 25. Res accepted. French, Italian menu. Bar. Wine list. Semi-a la carte: lunch $4-$10, dinner $9-$20. Brunch $2.95-$4.95. Child's meals. Specializes in veal, steak. Waterfalls. Stained glass, crystal chandeliers. Cr cds: A, C, D, DS, MC, V.

La Porte (A-3)

(See also Michigan City, South Bend)

Founded 1832 **Pop** 21,507 **Elev** 807 ft **Area code** 219 **Zip** 46350
Information Chamber of Commerce, 414 Lincolnway, PO Box 486; 219/362-3178.

This is a busy manufacturing center and a popular resort area in both winter and summer. City lakes offer fishing, ice fishing, snowmobiling and other recreational activities. Seven lakes with fishing and boating facilities border the town on the north and west. Chief industrial products are industrial fans, coil coating, corrugated and plastic containers, rubber products, iron and metal castings.

What to See and Do

Door Prairie Museum. Collection covers over 100 yrs of automobiles, including models by Citroen, Ford, Mercedes Benz, Rolls Royce, Tucker. (May-Nov, Tues-Sun) 2405 Indiana Ave, 1 mi S on US 35. Phone 219/326-1337. ¢¢

Kingsbury Fish & Wildlife Area. Approx 5,000 acres of state hunting and fishing areas with access to Kankakee River and Tamarack Lake. Area includes nature trails, target shooting, hunting; boating/canoeing; picnicking; birdwatching. Mixsawbah State Fish Hatchery adj. (Daily) 5 mi SE via US 35, exit County 500 S. Phone 219/393-3612.

La Porte County Historical Society Museum. Period rms, archives, antique gun collection. (Mon-Fri & 1st Sun of month; closed hols) County Complex. 813 Lincolnway. Phone 219/326-6808, ext 276. **Free.**

Annual Event

La Porte County Fair. Fairgrounds. Exhibits, livestock judging, harness races, shows, food, rides. Phone 219/362-2647. July.

Motor Hotel

★ ★ **PINE LAKE HOTEL & CONFERENCE CENTER.** *444 Pine Lake Ave (IN 35).* 219/362-4585; FAX 219/324-6993; res: 800/374-6338. 146 rms, 2-4 story. S $69-$99; D $79-$99; each addl $10; under 18 free; higher rates special events. Crib free. Pet accepted. TV; cable (premium). Indoor/outdoor pool; whirlpool, poolside serv. Restaurant 6 am-2 pm, 5-10 pm. Rm serv. Bar 11 am-midnight, wkend hrs vary. Ck-out 11 am. Meeting rms. Business servs avail. Shopping arcade. Barber, beauty shop. Downhill ski 12 mi; x-country ski 10 mi. Exercise equipt; weights, weight machine, sauna. Rec rm. Game rm. Cr cds: A, C, D, DS, JCB, MC, V.

D ⟨icons⟩ SC

Inn

★ ★ **ARBOR HILL INN.** *263 W Johnson Rd, 2 mi NW on US 35N.* 219/362-9200. 7 rms, 3 with shower only, 3 story, 4 suites. S, D $71-$99; suites $103-$189; higher rates special events. Crib free. TV; cable (premium). Complimentary continental bkfst. Ck-out 11 am, ck-in 4 pm. Business servs avail. In-rm modem link. Luggage handling. Downhill ski 10 mi; x-country ski 1 mi. Refrigerators. In-rm whirlpool, fireplace in suites. Some balconies. Built in 1910; Greek Revival, turn-of-the-century design. Totally nonsmoking. Cr cds: A, DS, MC, V.

D ⟨icons⟩

Restaurants

★ **REED'S STATE STREET PUB.** *502 State St.* 219/326-8339. Hrs: 11 am-2 pm, 5-9 pm; Fri, Sat to 10 pm. Closed Sun; Jan 1, Dec 25. Res accepted. Bar. Semi-a la carte: lunch $4.95-$10, dinner $6.95-

$18.95. Child's meals. Specializes in prime rib, steak, pasta, seafood. Historic art prints, stained-glass church windows. Cr cds: A, MC, V.

★ ★ **TANGERINE.** *601 Michigan Ave.* 219/326-8000. Hrs: 11 am-2 pm, 5-9:30 pm; Fri to 10 pm; Sat 5-10 pm. Closed Sun; major hols. Res accepted. Bar. Semi-a la carte: lunch $3.95-$7.95, dinner $10.95-$17.95. Specializes in beef Wellington, prime rib, duck. Former hotel, built in mid-1800s. Cr cds: A, MC, V.

⟨icon⟩

Lincoln Boyhood National Memorial & Lincoln State Park (J-3)

(See also Santa Claus)

(4 mi W of Santa Claus on IN 162)

Lincoln spent his boyhood years (1816-1830) in this area, reading books, clerking at James Gentry's store and helping his father with farm work. When Lincoln was 21, his family moved to Illinois, where his political career began. The 200-acre wooded and landscaped park includes the grave of Nancy Hanks Lincoln, mother of Abraham Lincoln. She was 35 years old, and Abraham was 9, when she died on October 5, 1818.

The Memorial Visitor Center has information available on the park, including the Cabin Site Memorial, the park's two miles of walking trails and the gravesite. A film is shown at the visitor center every hour depicting Lincoln's Indiana years. Nearby, on the original Thomas Lincoln tract, is the Lincoln Living Historical Farm, with a furnished log cabin similar to the one the Lincolns lived in, log buildings, animals and crops of a pioneer farm. Costumed pioneers carry out family living and farming activities typical of an early 19th-century farm. Farm (mid-Apr-Sept). (Daily; closed Jan 1, Thanksgiving, Dec 25) Phone 812/937-4541. Per person ¢; Per family ¢¢

Approx 1,700 acres with a 58-acre lake. Swimming, bathhouse; fishing; boating (no motors; rentals). Hiking trails. Picnic areas, concessions. Primitive and improved camping, cabins, group camp. Naturalist service (June-Aug). Standard fees. Phone 812/937-4710 or 812/937-4541.

The Lincoln Amphitheatre has an outdoor musical/theatrical production about the life of Lincoln when he lived in Indiana between the ages of 7 and 21. Drama is in a covered amphitheater near the site of Lincoln's home. (June-Aug, nightly exc Mon) Phone 800/264-4-ABE.

Logansport (C-4)

(See also Kokomo, Peru)

Founded 1828 **Pop** 16,812 **Elev** 620 ft **Area code** 219 **Zip** 46947
Information Logansport/Cass County Chamber of Commerce, 300 E Broadway, Suite 103; 219/753-6388.

Located at the confluence of the Wabash and Eel rivers, Logansport is situated in the agricultural heartland. An active trading center for more than a century, batteries, auto-related components and cement are among the commodities produced here. The rivers and many nearby lakes offer fishing and hunting.

The town was named in honor of James Logan, nephew of the famous Shawnee chief, Tecumseh. Captain Logan was fatally wounded by British-led Native Americans after having served with distinction as leader of a company of Native American scouts fighting for the United States in the War of 1812.

What to See and Do

Cass County Historical Museum (Jerolaman-Long House). Antique china collection; Native American artifacts; paintings, local memorabilia. (Tues-Sat & 1st Sun of month; closed hols) 1004 E Market St. Phone 219/753-3866. **Free.**

France Park. A 500-acre park with waterfall; 100-yr-old log cabin at entrance. Swimming beach (Memorial Day-Labor Day), water slide (fee), scuba diving; fishing. Nature trail; miniature golf (fee), shuffleboard; rock-hounding. Cross-country skiing (fee), snowmobiling, ice fishing, ice-skating. Picnicking (shelters). Primitive & improved camping, camp store. (Daily) 4 mi W via US 24. Phone 219/753-2928. ¢

Indiana Beach. Rides, games, arcades; beach, swimming; shops. Cottages and camping. Amusement area (mid-May-Labor Day, daily; early May & early Sept, wkends only). 306 Indiana Beach Dr, approx 20 mi W via US 24, in Monticello. Phone 219/583-4141. ¢

Riverside Park. Includes historic Dentzel carousel (1902); model train. Park includes playground, tennis courts, basketball court, ball fields, miniature golf, picnic area. Park (daily). Fee for some activities. Riverside Dr, between 11th & 15th Sts. Phone 219/753-6969.

Annual Event

Iron Horse Festival. Iron Horse Museum, One Iron Horse Sq (4th & Melbourne). Railroad festival; restored Vandalia railroad station with train & artifacts. Phone 219/722-IRON or 219/753-6388. Mid-July.

Motel

✔★★ **HOLIDAY INN.** 3550 Market St. 219/753-6351; FAX 219/722-1568. 95 rms, 2 story. S $60-$86; D $66-$92; each addl $6; suites $125; under 19 free; higher rates Indianapolis "500." Crib free. Pet accepted. TV; cable. Heated pool. Restaurant 6 am-10 pm. Rm serv. Bar 4 pm-midnight. Ck-out noon. Meeting rms. Sundries. Free local airport transportation. Cr cds: A, C, D, DS, JCB, MC, V.

D ✦ ≈ ⊠ 🔥 SC

Madison (H-5)

Settled 1809 **Pop** 12,006 **Elev** 497 ft **Area code** 812 **Zip** 47250 **Web** www.seidata.com/~dhodges/madnet/madison.html

Information Madison Area Convention and Visitors Bureau, 301 E Main St; 812/265-2956 or 800/559-2956.

Between the Ohio River and Crooked Creek, the settlement of Madison grew rapidly during the river transport days of the 1850s and was briefly the largest city in Indiana, with a population of 5,000. Many of the fine homes reflect the architecture of pre-Civil War days in the South. The 555-acre campus of Hanover College (1827) overlooks the river.

What to See and Do

Clifty Falls State Park. From a high, wooded plateau, this 1,360-acre park offers a view of the Ohio River and its traffic, as well as hills on the Kentucky shore. It also contains waterfalls of Clifty Creek and Little Clifty Creek, bedrock exposures, numerous fossil beds and a deep boulder-strewn canyon reached by the sun at high noon only; variety of wildlife, regional winter vulture roost. Swimming pool (Memorial Day-Labor Day; fee). Tennis. Picnicking (shelters, fireplaces), playground, concession. Inn in park has lodgings all yr (for reservations contact PO Box 387; 812/265-4135). Primitive and developed camping (fee). Naturalist service; nature center. 1 mi W on IN 56. Phone 812/265-1331. Per vehicle ¢

Dr. William Hutchings Hospital Museum. A 19th-century Greek-revival building, which served as office and hospital of a "horse-and-buggy" doctor in the late 1800s. Furnishings, surgical tools and medical library. (Mid-Apr-Oct, daily) 120 W 3rd St. Phone 812/265-2967. ¢¢

Judge Jeremiah Sullivan House (1818). Federal-style furnished home; pioneer kitchen, smokehouse, bake oven. (Mid-Apr-Oct, daily) 304 W 2nd St.Phone 812/265-2967. ¢¢ Nearby is

Talbot-Hyatt Pioneer Garden. Frontier garden including many regional plants and flowers. Some plants brought from Virginia. (Daily) **Free.**

Lanier State Historic Site. Greek-revival mansion completed in 1844 for James F.D. Lanier, a financier who loaned the state of Indiana a total of $1,040,000 when its treasury was in need during the Civil War. Some original possessions. (Daily exc Mon; closed some hols) 511 W 1st St, between Elm & Vine. Phone 812/265-3526. **Free.**

Schofield House (1809-1814). Two-story, handmade, sun-dried brick tavern-house; early Federal style. (Apr-Nov, daily exc Tues; candlelight tours by appt) 217 W 2nd St. Phone 812/265-4759 or 812/867-3434. ¢

Shrewsbury House (1846-1849). Example of Greek-revival architecture, with a free-standing spiral staircase. Period furnishings. (Apr-Dec, daily; rest of yr, by appt) 301 W 1st St. Phone 812/265-4481. ¢¢

Annual Event

Regatta and Governor's Cup Race. Hydroplanes compete on the Ohio River. Phone 812/265-5000. Late June-early July.

Motel

★★★ **OGLE HAUS INN.** (1013 W Main St, Vevay 47043) 20 mi E on IN 56. 812/427-2020; FAX 812/427-3397; res: 800/545-9360. 54 rms, 2 story, 6 suites. Apr-Oct: S $70; D $75; each addl $5; suites $135-$160; under 16 free; lower rates rest of yr. Crib free. TV; cable (premium). Heated pool. Restaurant 7 am-8 pm, wkends to 9 pm. Rm serv. Bar 11 am-10 pm, wkends to midnight; entertainment. Ck-out noon. Guest lndry. Meeting rms. Business servs avail. Free airport transportation. Downhill ski 20 mi. Refrigerator in suites. Balconies. Whirlpool, fireplace in suites. On Ohio River. Cr cds: A, C, D, DS, MC, V.

D ≈ ⊠ 🔥 SC

Restaurant

★★ **KEY WEST SHRIMP HOUSE.** 117 Ferry St (IN 56), at end of Ohio River Bridge. 812/265-2831. Hrs: 11 am-2 pm, 5-9 pm; Sun noon-8 pm. Closed Mon. Semi-a la carte: lunch $4.25-$7.25, dinner $10.45-$20.95. Child's meals. Specializes in seafood, steak. Salad bar. Own desserts. Century-old building; fireplace. Cr cds: A, D, DS, MC, V.

Marion (D-5)

(See also Peru, Wabash)

Settled 1826 **Pop** 32,618 **Elev** 815 ft **Area code** 765 **E-mail** marionin@comteck.com **Web** www.comteck.com~marionin

Information Marion/Grant County Convention & Visitors Bureau, 217 S Adams St, 46952; 765/668-5435 or 800/662-9474.

An industrial center and farm trading town, Marion lies on the Mississinewa River. Its principal industrial products are automotive parts, video display and components, plastics, glass, paper and wire products. Indiana Wesleyan University (1920) is located here.

What to See and Do

Fairmount, Hometown of James Dean (1950s screen idol). S via I-69, exit 55 then W on IN 26. In Fairmount is

James Dean/Fairmount Historical Museum. Contains the most complete collection of articles of James Dean. Also here are exhibits by Jim Davis, creator of the cartoon cat Garfield. (Mar-Nov, Mon-Sat, also Sun afternoons; rest of yr, by appt) 203 E Washington St. Phone 765/948-4555. ¢

The James Dean Gallery. Extensive collection of memorabilia and archives dealing with the career of James Dean. Exhibit includes clothing from his films, high school yearbooks, original movie posters from around the world. (Daily; closed Jan 1, Thanksgiving, Dec 25) 425 N Main St. Phone 765/948-3326. ¢¢

Matthews Covered Bridge. Cumberland Covered Bridge (1876-1877), 175-ft long, spans the Mississinewa River. 5 mi E via IN 18, S via I-69 then E on IN 26, in Matthews.

Miami Indian Historical Site. Large Native American cemetery with memorials; hiking trails, fishing, hunting. (Daily) 7 mi NW via IN 15, then W on 600 N St. Phone 765/668-5435. **Free.**

Mississinewa Lake. 15 mi NW, off IN 15 (see PERU).

Annual Events

Marion Easter Pageant. Marion Coliseum between Washington & Branson Sts. 2,000 in cast. Evening of Good Friday and Easter Sunday morning.

Fairmount Museum Days/Remembering James Dean. James Dean/Fairmount Historical Museum. Large car show, James Dean look-alike contest, parade, downtown street fair. Last full wkend Sept.

Mississinewa 1812. Battle re-enactment with period food, crafts and storytelling. Phone 765/662-0096. Early Oct.

Motel

★ ★ **COMFORT SUITES.** *1345 N Baldwin Ave (46952).* 765/651-1006; FAX 765/651-0145. 62 suites, 2 rms. S $74-$99; D $79-$99; each addl $5; under 18 free; higher rates special events. Crib avail. TV; cable (premium). Complimentary continental bkfst. Coffee in rms. Ck-out noon. Meeting rms. Business servs avail. In-rm modem link. Valet serv. Coin lndry. Exercise equipt; rowers, stair machine, sauna. Indoor pool; whirlpool. Refrigerators, microwaves; some bathrm phones, in-rm whirlpools. Cr cds: A, C, D, DS, JCB, MC, V.

D ⊠ 🏃 ⊠ 🔥 SC

Motor Hotel

★ ★ **HOLIDAY INN.** *501 E Fourth St (46952).* 765/668-8801; FAX 765/662-6827. 120 rms, 5 story. S, D $65-$89; under 19 free. Crib free. TV; cable (premium). Pool. Coffee in rms. Restaurant 6 am-3 pm, 5-10 pm; Sat from 7 am; Sun 7 am-3 pm, 5-9 pm. Rm serv. Bar 4 pm-midnight, closed Sun. Ck-out noon. Meeting rms. Sundries. Cr cds: A, C, D, DS, MC, V.

D ⊠ ⊠ 🔥 SC

Merrillville (B-2)

Pop 27,257 **Elev** 661 ft **Area code** 219 **Zip** 46410
Information Chamber of Commerce, 255 W 80th Pl; 219/769-8180 or 800/252-3948.

Once a thriving stop-off point for the many wagon trains headed west, Merrillville has left its rural beginnings to become a regional center of commerce; it has also established its identity as a leader in commercial-industrial development. Area parks and nearby agricultural lands provide pleasant surroundings.

What to See and Do

Lemon Lake County Park. Approx 290 acres of recreation facilities adj to Cedar Lake. Park offers fishing, paddleboats; basketball & tennis courts, volleyball, softball fields; hiking/fitness/jogging trails; picnicking (shelters). Arboretum. (Daily) 1 mi E via US 30, then S on IN 55, SW of Crown Point. Phone 219/769-7275 or 219/755-3685. ¢

Star Plaza Theatre. 3,400-seat theater hosts top-name performers. Bill changes weekly and offers a variety of entertainers from comedians to rock & roll, jazz, country and pop artists. (See HOTEL) I-65 & US 30. Phone 219/769-6600. ¢¢¢¢

Motels

✔ ★ ★ **FAIRFIELD INN BY MARRIOTT.** *8275 Georgia St.* 219/736-0500; FAX 219/736-0500, ext. 709. 132 rms, 3 story. S $64; D $69; each addl $3; under 18 free; higher rates wkends. Crib free. TV; cable (premium). VCR avail. Heated pool. Complimentary continental bkfst. Restaurant nearby. Ck-out noon. Business servs avail. In-rm modem link. Health club privileges. Cr cds: A, C, D, DS, MC, V.

D ⊠ ⊠ 🔥 SC

★ **RED ROOF INN.** *8290 Georgia St, 1/2 mi SW of jct I-65 & US 30 exit 253B.* 219/738-2430; FAX 219/738-2436. 108 rms, 2 story. S $39-$45; D $45-$51; each addl $6; under 18 free. Crib free. TV; cable (premium). Complimentary coffee. Ck-out noon. Business servs avail. In-rm modem link. Cr cds: A, C, D, DS, MC, V.

D ⊠ 🔥 SC

Hotel

★ ★ ★ **RADISSON HOTEL AT STAR PLAZA.** *800 E 81st Ave, I-65 & US 30, at Star Plaza Theater Complex.* 219/769-6311; FAX 219/769-1462. 347 rms, 4 story. S $89-$135; D $99-$145; each addl $10; suites $225-$800; under 18 free; wkday, wkend packages. Crib free. Pet accepted. TV; cable (premium), VCR avail (movies). 2 pools, 1 indoor; poolside serv. Playground. Complimentary coffee in rms. Restaurant 6:30 am-10 pm. Bar 11:30-2 am, Sun 5 pm-midnight; entertainment. Ck-out 11 am. Coin lndry. Convention facilities. Business servs avail. In-rm modem link. Shopping arcade. Barber, beauty shop. Valet parking. Exercise equipt; weights, bicycles. Game rm. Bathrm phones; some refrigerators, in-rm whirlpools, saunas; microwaves avail. Health club privileges. Private patios, balconies. Cr cds: A, C, D, DS, ER, MC, V.

D ⊠ ⊠ 🏃 ⊠ 🔥 SC

Restaurant

★ ★ ★ **LOUIS' BON APPETIT.** *(302 S Main St, Crown Point) S on IN 55.* 219/663-6363. Hrs: 5:30-9:30 pm; Sun 11 am-2 pm. Closed Mon; Dec 24, 25. Res accepted. French menu. Serv bar. Wine list. Semi-a la carte: dinner $12-$26. Sun brunch $9.75. Specializes in confit of duck, loin of lamb, pork tenderloin, fish. Own baking. Outdoor dining. In 19th-century mansion; antiques. Cr cds: A, C, D, DS, JCB, MC, V.

D

Michigan City (A-3)

(See also La Porte)

Founded 1833 **Pop** 33,822 **Elev** 600 ft **Area code** 219 **Zip** 46360 **E-mail** lpccvb@netnitco.net **Web** www.harborcountry-in.org
Information La Porte County Convention & Visitors Bureau, 1503 S Meer Rd; 800/634-2650. There is a visitor center directly off I-94, exit 40B.

This is Indiana's summer playground on the southeast shore of Lake Michigan. In the center of the famous Indiana sand dunes region, Michigan City offers miles of fine beaches. For fishermen, the lake offers coho salmon (late Mar-Nov), chinook salmon, lake trout and perch.

What to See and Do

Barker Mansion (1900). A 38-rm mansion modeled after an English manor house; marble fireplaces; Tiffany glass; Italian sunken garden.

Tours (June-Oct, daily; rest of yr, Mon-Fri). 631 Washington St. Phone 219/873-1520. ¢

John G. Blank Center for the Arts. Painting, sculpture, graphic art exhibits of regional, national and international origin. Performing arts events. (Daily exc Sun; closed hols) 312 E 8th St. Phone 219/874-4900. ¢

Indiana Dunes State Park (see). 11 mi W on US 12, IN 49. Also here is Indiana Dunes National Lakeshore (see).

Lighthouse Place Outlet Center. More than 135 outlet stores. (Daily) Sixth & Wabash Sts. Phone 219/879-6506.

Washington Park. Swimming beach; yacht basin, marina; picnic facilities, concession; fishing; tennis courts; observation tower. Zoo (daily). Recreational facilities (daily). Amphitheater (Thurs evening & wkend band concerts in summer). Sr citizens center (Mon-Fri). N end of Franklin St. Phone 219/873-1506 (park), 219/873-1510 (zoo). Some fees (Mar-Dec).Per vehicle parking ¢¢; Zoo ¢¢ Also here is

> **Old Lighthouse Museum** (1858). Marine exhibits, Fresnel lens, shipbuilding tools, local history displays. Site of launching of first submarine on Great Lakes in 1845. (Mar-Dec, daily exc Mon; closed hols) Phone 219/872-6133. ¢

Annual Events

Michigan City Summer Festival. City-wide. Parades, concerts, fireworks. Early July.

Lakefront Music Fest. Washington Park. Mid-July.

Motels

✔★ **AL & SALLY'S.** *3221 W Dunes Hwy (US 12). 219/872-9131.* 16 rms. May-late Sept: S $30-$40; D $40-$50; each addl $5; lower rates rest of yr. Crib $5. TV; cable (premium). Heated pool. Playground. Complimentary coffee in rms. Restaurant nearby. Ck-out 11 am. Lighted tennis. Downhill ski 15 mi; x-country ski 3 mi. Lawn games. Refrigerators. Picnic tables. Located in Indiana Dunes National Lakeshore. Cr cds: A, DS, MC, V.

★ **BLACKHAWK.** *3651 W Dunes Hwy (US 12). 219/872-8656; FAX 219/872-5427.* 20 rms, showers only. May-Sept: S, D $35-$55; family, wkly, wkend rates; ski plans; lower rates rest of yr. Pet accepted; $20 deposit. TV; cable (premium). Heated pool. Complimentary coffee in lobby. Ck-out 11 am. Downhill/x-country ski 8 mi. Refrigerators. Picnic tables. Cr cds: A, MC, V.

★★ **HOLIDAY INN.** *5820 S Franklin St (US 421). 219/879-0311; FAX 219/879-2536.* 165 rms, 2-3 story. S, D $76-$89; suites $150; under 18 free. Crib free. TV; cable (premium). Indoor pool. Complimentary coffee in lobby. Restaurant 6:30 am-10 pm. Rm serv. Bar 3 pm-1 am; Sun to midnight. Ck-out 11 am. Meeting rms. Business servs avail. Exercise equipt; bicycles, treadmill. X-country ski 5 mi. Health club privileges. Some refrigerators. Balconies. Cr cds: A, C, D, DS, JCB, MC, V.

★ **KNIGHTS INN.** *201 W Kieffer Rd, US 421 exit 34B. 219/874-9500; FAX 219/874-5122; res: 800/219-9555.* 103 rms. Mid-June-mid-Sept: S, kit. units $58-$99; D $68-$99; under 16 free; higher rates special events; lower rates rest of yr. Crib free. Pet accepted, some restrictions. TV; cable (premium). Pool. Complimentary coffee in lobby. Ck-out 11 am. Meeting rm. Some refrigerators. Cr cds: A, C, D, DS, ER, MC, V.

★ **RED ROOF INN.** *110 W Kieffer Rd. 219/874-5251; FAX 219/874-5287.* 79 rms, 2 story. S $35-$42; D $41-$48; under 18 free. Crib free. Pet accepted. TV; cable (premium). Complimentary coffee in lobby.

Restaurant opp 6 am-10 pm. Ck-out noon. Business servs avail. In-rm modem link. Sundries. Cr cds: A, C, D, DS, MC, V.

Inns

★★★ **CREEKWOOD.** *US 20/35, at I-94 exit 40B. 219/872-8357.* 13 rms, 2 story. S $108-$153; D $118-$163; each addl $16; suite $200. Crib $8. Closed early Jan. TV; VCR avail (movies). Whirlpool. Complimentary continental bkfst. Ck-out noon, ck-in 4 pm. Business servs avail. Downhill ski 20 mi; x-country ski on site. Lawn games. Exercise equipt; treadmill, rower. Refrigerators; some fireplaces. Some private patios. Reconstructed from remains of early 1800s trading post-way station. On 33 wooded acres; hiking trails; near Lake Michigan. Cr cds: A, D, MC, V.

★★ **DUNELAND BEACH INN.** *3311 Pottawattamie Trail. 219/874-7729; res: 800/423-7729; FAX 219/874-0053.* 10 rms, 5 with shower only, 2 story. May-Oct: S, D $69-$89; lower rates rest of yr. TV. Complimentary full bkfst. Complimentary coffee in rms. Restaurant (see HUNTER). Ck-out 11 am, ck-in 3 pm. Business servs avail. Luggage handling. Valet serv. Lighted tennis. X-country ski 5 mi. Many in-rm whirlpools. Some balconies. On beach. Turn-of-the-century inn built in 1892; country atmosphere. Totally nonsmoking. Cr cds: A, C, D, DS, MC.

Restaurants

★★ **BASIL'S.** *521 Franklin Square. 219/872-4500.* Hrs: 4:30-10 pm; Sat 5:30-10:30 pm. Closed Sun; Thanksgiving, Dec 25. Bar. Semi-a la carte: dinner $12-$19. Specializes in chops, seafood, steak. Entertainment wkends. Paintings by local artists. Family-owned. Cr cds: A, C, D, MC, V.

★★ **HUNTER.** *(See Duneland Beach Inn) 219/874-7729.* Hrs: 5-9 pm. Closed Sun-Tues. Res accepted; required Fri, Sat. Continental menu. Bar. Semi-a la carte: dinner $10-$25. Specializes in venison steak, Dover sole, roast duckling. Own baking. Intimate dining in country French atmosphere with white brick fireplace and oil paintings. Cr cds: A, D, DS, MC, V.

Mishawaka (A-4)

(See also Elkhart, Goshen, South Bend)

Founded 1832 **Pop** 42,608 **Elev** 720 ft **Area code** 219 **E-mail** cvbsjco@aol.com

Information South Bend-Mishawaka Convention & Visitors Bureau, 401 E Colfax Ave, Suite 310, PO Box 1677, South Bend 46634-1677; 219/234-0051 or 800/828-7881.

Directly east of South Bend, Mishawaka is mainly an industrial city. Divided by the St Joseph River, it was named for a beautiful daughter of Chief Elkhart of the Shawnee, who lived in this region before 1800.

In the southwestern part of the city is a Belgian quarter populated by some 6,000 Flemish-Dutch speaking citizens, most of whom came to Mishawaka following World War I.

What to See and Do

100 Center Complex. 35 retail shops; also restaurants, movie theater; lodging, entertainment; arts & crafts festival 2nd wk July. (Daily) 700 Lincoln Way W. Phone 219/259-7861. **Free.**

Hannah Lindahl Children's Museum. Hands-on exhibits with scientific and historical items. Also re-created here is a brick street of stores from the 1800s, a traditional Japanese house and a Survive Alive House that teaches fire prevention. (Sept-May, Tues-Fri, 1st & 2nd Sat of each month; June, Tues-Thurs) 1402 S Main St. Phone 219/258-3056. ¢

Merrifield Park. This 31-acre park features a 1.3-acre Japanese garden. Also swimming, water slide, fishing, boating (launch), ice-skating, playground; picnic area. (Daily) 1000 E Mishawaka Ave. Phone 219/258-1664. ¢

Restaurants

✔★★ **DOC PIERCE'S.** *120 N Main St (46544). 219/255-7737.* Hrs: 11 am-2 pm, 5-10 pm; Fri, Sat to 11 pm. Closed Sun; major hols. Res accepted. Bar. Semi-a la carte: lunch $3.95-$6.25, dinner $6.25-$14.95. Specializes in aged steak, shrimp. 1920s decor. Cr cds: A, C, D, DS, MC, V.

★ **PAT'S COLONIAL PUB.** *901 W Fourth St (46544), US 33 (Lincoln Hwy) E to Logan St S. 219/259-8282.* Hrs: 11 am-11 pm; Mon to 9 pm; Sat from 4 pm. Closed Sun; major hols. Res accepted. Bar. A la carte entrees: lunch $3.25-$6.50. Complete meals: lunch $5.95-$7.95, dinner $7.95-$19.95. Specializes in steak, lake perch, seafood. Casual dining. Cr cds: A, MC, V.

Muncie (E-5)

(See also Anderson, New Castle)

Founded 1818 **Pop** 71,035 **Elev** 950 ft **Area code** 765 **E-mail** mvb @ecicnet.org

Information Muncie-Delaware County Convention & Visitors Bureau, 425 N High St, 47305; 765/284-2700 or 800/568-6862.

This area was once the home of the Munsee tribe of the Delaware. The town became an agricultural trading center during the first half of the 19th century; with the construction of railroads and the discovery of natural gas it developed into an industrial city. Many industrial plants are located here.

Ball Corporation, which for years produced the famous Ball jars, maintains its international headquarters in Muncie. The five Ball brothers took an active part in the city's life and in many philanthropic undertakings. They also supported a number of other industrial enterprises and contributed substantially to Ball State University.

Muncie became nationally famous in the 1930s as the subject of sociological studies of a "typical" small city by Robert and Helen Lynd, *Middletown* and *Middletown in Transition.*

What to See and Do

Appeal to the Great Spirit. Copy of Cyrus Dallin's famous statue, which stands in front of Boston Museum of Fine Arts. N bank of White River at Walnut St & Granville Ave.

Ball Corporation Museum. Extensive collection of rare Ball glass food preserving jars and current company products. (Mon-Fri; closed hols) 345 S High St. Phone 765/747-6100. **Free.**

Ball State University (1918). (20,300 students) Purchased by the Ball family and presented to the state of Indiana. Campus has a state-of-the-art telecommunication production facility (phone 765/285-1481); planetarium and observatory (phone 765/285-8871 or 765/285-8862; free). Tours. (Mon-Fri) 2000 University Ave. Phone 765/285-5683. Also on campus are

Museum of Art. Collections of 18th- and 19th-century paintings, prints and drawings; contemporary works; changing exhibits. (Daily exc Mon) Fine Arts Bldg. Phone 765/285-5242. **Free.**

Christy Woods. A 17-acre biology department laboratory with arboretum, gardens and greenhouses. Extensive assemblage including the Wheeler Orchid Collection. Tours (by appt). Phone 765/285-8839 or 765/285-8820. **Free.**

Minnetrista Cultural Center. A 70,000-sq-ft facility exhibiting the history, art and industry of east central Indiana. Changing exhibits feature Native American history, the family, technology and the art of east central Indiana. Nationally touring science exhibits offered each spring and fall. Floral gardens, landscaped lawns and an historic apple orchard surround the center. (Daily exc Mon; closed Dec 25) 1200 N Minnetrista Pkwy. Phone 765/282-4848. ¢¢

Muncie Children's Museum. Exhibits allow visitors to explore the world around them in this completely hands-on museum. Outdoor learning center. Changing exhibits. Gift shop. (Daily exc Mon; closed major hols) 515 S High St. Phone 765/286-1660. ¢¢

Oakhurst Gardens. Six-acre gardens house many naturalized plants. Renovated home (1895) of George, Frances and Elizabeth Ball has exhibits on gardens and natural history. One-hr guided tours. (Daily exc Mon) 1200 N Minnetrista Pkwy. Phone 765/282-4848 or 800/4-CULTURE. ¢¢

Prairie Creek Reservoir. A 2,333-acre park with 1,252-acre lake. Picnicking, concession. Boating (10 mph limit); fishing; swimming (Memorial Day-Labor Day); playground. Camping. Some fees. 6 mi SE on Burlington Dr. Phone 765/747-4776.

Annual Events

Glass Days. Late May.

Delaware County Fair. Fairgrounds, Wheeling Ave. 2 wks mid-late July.

Seasonal Event

International Dragway. 5 mi NE on IN 67 near Albany. Drag racing Sat. Phone 765/789-8470. Apr-Oct.

Motels

✔★ **DAYS INN.** *3509 Everbrook Lane (47304). 765/288-2311.* 62 rms, 2 story. S $45-$50; D $50-$65; each addl $5; under 12 free; higher rates: Indianapolis "500", university events. Crib free. Pet accepted. $20 deposit. TV. Complimentary continental bkfst. Restaurant nearby. Ck-out 11 am. Health club privileges. Cr cds: A, C, D, DS, MC, V.

D ✔ 🏊 ➘ 🐾 SC

★ **LEE'S INN.** *3302 N Everbrook Lane (47304). 765/282-7557; FAX 765/282-0345; res: 800/733-5337.* 92 rms, 2 story. S $64; D $74; each addl $7; suites $81-$157; under 15 free; higher rates Indianapolis "500". Crib avail. Pet accepted. Complimentary continental bkfst. Restaurant nearby. Ck-out noon. Meeting rms. Valet serv. Health club privileges. Minibars. Cr cds: A, DS, MC, V.

D ✔ 🏊 ➘ 🐾 SC

★ **RAMADA INN.** *3400 S Madison St (47302). 765/288-1911; FAX 765/282-9458.* 148 rms, 2 story. S, D $52-$109; under 18 free. Crib avail. Pet accepted, some restrictions. TV; cable (premium), VCR avail. Pool. Complimentary continental bkfst. Restaurant 6:30 am-2 pm, 5-10 pm; Sun 7 am-2 pm. Rm serv. Bar 2 pm-1 am; entertainment. Ck-out noon. Coin lndry. Meeting rms. Business servs avail. Valet serv. Cr cds: A, C, D, DS, JCB, MC, V.

D ✔ 🏊 ➘ 🐾 SC

★ **SIGNATURE INN.** *3400 N Chadam Lane (47304). 765/284-4200.* 101 rms, 2 story. S, D $71-$78; under 17 free; higher rates: James Dean wkend, Indianapolis "500". Crib free. TV; cable. Pool. Complimentary continental bkfst. Restaurant nearby. Ck-out noon. Meeting rms. Sundries. Health club privileges. Cr cds: A, D, DS, MC, V.

D 🏊 ➘ 🐾 SC

Hotel

★ ★ ★ **RADISSON.** 420 S High St (47305). 765/741-7777; FAX 765/747-0067. 130 rms, 7 story, 28 suites. S, D $75-$86; suites $86-$225; under 17 free; wkend rates. Crib free. Pet accepted. TV; cable (premium). Indoor pool; whirlpool. Restaurant 6:30 am-10 pm. Rm serv 24 hrs. Bar noon-midnight; wkends to 1 am; entertainment. Ck-out noon. Meeting rms. Business servs avail. Free airport transportation. Health club privileges. Microwaves avail. Cr cds: A, C, D, DS, MC, V.

⬛ 🛎 ≋ ⬛ 🔥 SC

Restaurant

★ ★ ★ **FOXFIRES.** 3300 Chadam Ln (47304). 765/284-5235. Hrs: 5-11 pm. Closed Sun; some major hols. Res accepted; required hols. Continental menu. Bar. Wine cellar. Semi-a la carte: dinner $7-$32. Complete meal: dinner $23-$48. Specializes in broiled bone-on beef tenderloin, wild game, fresh seafood. Two distinct dining areas—one casual and one formal—offer different menus; contemporary decor. Cr cds: A, D, DS, MC, V.

⬛ 🔲

Nappanee (B-4)

(See also Elkhart, Goshen, Warsaw)

Founded 1874 **Pop** 5,510 **Elev** 878 ft **Area code** 219 **Zip** 46550 **E-mail** acre@npcc.net **Web** www.amish-country.com

Information Amish Acres Visitor Center, 1600 W Market; 219/773-4188 or 800/800-4942.

Many Amish-run farms dot the countryside surrounding Nappanee. Rich, productive soil makes agricultural crops a major part of the economy; local industry manufactures kitchen cabinets, mobile homes, recreational vehicles, vitreous steel products and furniture.

What to See and Do

✪ **Amish Acres.** Restored Amish homestead and farm. Guided tours, horse-drawn rides, music theater (fees); bakery, restaurant (see), inns, shops. (Daily) 1 mi W on US 6. Phone 219/773-4188. **Free.**

Annual Event

Amish Acres Arts & Crafts Festival. Amish Acres (see). Entries from many states; paintings, ceramics, jewelry; entertainment, dancing, feasts. Mid-Aug.

Motels

★ ★ **NAPPANEE INN.** 2004 W Market St. 219/773-5999; FAX 219/773-5988; res: 800/800-4942. E-mail acre@npcc.nft; web www.amish acres.com. 66 rms, 2 story. June-Oct: S $59-$79; D $64-$89; each addl $10; under 18 free; higher rates special events; lower rates rest of yr. Crib free. TV; cable (premium), VCR avail. Heated pool. Complimentary continental bkfst. Restaurant nearby. Ck-out noon. Business servs avail. The inn takes its name from the Nappanee House, the town's first hotel, which opened in 1875. Part of a restored 80-acre farm. Cr cds: A, D, DS, MC, V.

⬛ ≋ ⬛ SC

★ ★ **OAKWOOD INN.** (849 E Lake View Rd, Syracuse 46567) 9 mi E on US 6, 2 mi S on IN 13. 219/457-5600; FAX 219/457-3104. 78 rms, 3 story, 10 suites. June-Aug: S, D $85-$110; suites $105-$160; lower rates rest of yr. Crib free. TV; cable (premium), VCR (movies). Complimentary continental bkfst. Complimentary coffee in rms. Restaurant 11 am-2 pm, 5:30-7 pm. Ck-out 11 am. Business servs avail. In-rm modem link. Bellhops. Gift shop. Coin lndry. 18-hole golf privileges, putting green, driving range. Exercise equipt; weight machine, stair machine. Playground. Some in-rm whirlpools; refrigerators, microwaves avail. Picnic tables. On lake. Totally nonsmoking. Cr cds: A, DS, MC, V.

⬛ 🛎 🏊 ≋ 🔥 SC

Motor Hotel

★ ★ **THE INN AT AMISH ACRES.** 1234 W Market (US 6). 219/773-2011; FAX 219/773-2078. 64 rms, 2 story, 16 suites. June-Labor Day: S $92; D $97; each addl $10; suites $113-$118; under 18 free; higher rates Village Art Festival, university football wkends; lower rates rest of yr. Crib free. TV; cable (premium). Pool. Complimentary continental bkfst. Restaurant nearby. Ck-out noon. Meeting rms. Business servs avail. Free airport transportation. Some refrigerators, microwaves. Cr cds: D, DS, MC, V.

⬛ ≋ ⬛ 🔥 SC

Restaurant

✔ ★ ★ ★ **AMISH ACRES.** 1600 W Market St. 219/773-4188. Hrs: 11 am-7 pm; Sun, hols to 6 pm. Closed Jan-Feb. Complete meals: lunch $5.95-$8.95, dinner $8.95-$13.95. Child's meals. Specializes in Amish cooking (family style), cider-baked ham, roast turkey. Own baking. Early Amer decor. Located in historic farm; combination tour tickets including dinner $23. Theater May-late Dec. Family-owned. Cr cds: C, D, DS, MC, V.

⬛

Nashville (G-4)

(See also Bloomington, Columbus)

Pop 873 **Elev** 629 ft **Area code** 812 **Zip** 47448 **E-mail** tour@brown county.com **Web** www.browncounty.com

Information Brown County Convention & Visitors Bureau, Main & Van Buren Sts, PO Box 840; 812/988-7303 or 800/753-3255.

The heart of Brown County, Nashville has been called "log cabin country" because of its many log cabins. This area is also known for art, antiques and collectibles.

What to See and Do

Bill Monroe Bluegrass Hall of Fame. Museum of memorabilia from bluegrass and country western performers; log cabin. Special events throughout the summer. (June-Oct, daily exc Mon) 5 mi N via IN 135, in Bean Blossom. Phone 812/988-6422. ¢¢¢

Brown County Art Gallery. Permanent and changing exhibits of Indiana art. (Daily; closed Jan 1, Dec 25) 1 Artist Dr. Phone 812/988-4609. **Free.**

Brown County Art Guild. Changing exhibits; Goth estate collection. (Mar-Dec, daily; rest of yr, by appt only) Van Buren St. Phone 812/988-6185. **Donation.**

Brown County State Park (see). 2 mi SE of town on IN 46.

Country Museum. Weaving and spinning rm; antiques; log cabin (ca 1845); county doctor's office and furnishings; blacksmith shop, Old Log Jail (fee). (May-Oct, Tues-Sat) 1 blk E of courthouse. Phone 812/988-6422. ¢¢

Hoosier National Forest. S of town (see BEDFORD).

Ski World. Two chairlifts, 4 rope tows; patrol, school, rentals; snowmaking; cafeteria & lounge. Longest run 3,400 ft; vertical drop 325 ft. Dry toboggan slide; summer amusement area. (Apr-Oct, mid-Dec-early Mar, daily) 4 mi W via IN 46. Phone 812/988-6638. Summer ¢¢; Winter ¢¢¢-¢¢¢¢¢

T.C. Steele State Historic Site. Home and studio of Impressionistic artist Theodore C. Steele (1847-1926). Site includes 15 acres of gardens, 4 hiking trails, and exhibits of more than 60 Steele canvases. (Mid-Mar-Dec, daily exc Mon; closed most hols) 8 mi W on IN 46 to Belmont, then 1½ mi S on T.C. Steele Rd. Phone 812/988-2785. **Free.**

Yellowwood State Forest. A 23,326-acre forest with three lakes. Fishing; boating (ramp, rentals). Hiking trails. Picnicking (shelter), playground. Primitive camping; horseback riders' camp. Standard fees. 7 mi W on IN 46. Phone 812/988-7945. **Free.**

Annual Event

Log Cabin Tour. Unescorted tours of five log homes in Brown County. Contact the Convention & Visitors Bureau. Early June.

Seasonal Event

Brown County Playhouse. Presents four theater productions. Phone 812/855-1103 or 812/988-2123. June-Aug, Wed-Sun; Sept-Oct, Fri-Sun.

Motels

★ ★ ★ **BROWN COUNTY INN.** *Box 128, 2 blks S on IN 135, at IN 46. 812/988-2291; FAX 812/988-8312; res: 800/772-5249.* 99 rms, 2 story. Apr-Oct: S, D $65-$106; each addl $6; under 18 free; lower rates rest of yr. Crib free. TV; cable. Indoor/outdoor pool. Playground. Restaurant (see THE HARVEST). Bar 11:30 am-11 pm, Sat to 1 am; entertainment Fri, Sat. Ck-out noon. Meeting rms. Tennis. Downhill ski 5 mi; x-country ski 2 mi. Miniature golf. Game rm. Lawn games. Rustic; many antiques. Cr cds: A, C, D, DS, MC, V.

🅳 🏊 ⛷ 🏔 🎿 🔥 SC

★ ★ **SALT CREEK INN.** *551 E State Rd 46, ½ mi E on IN 46, at Salt Creek Rd. 812/988-1149.* 66 rms, 2 story, 20 kit. units (no equipt). S $40-$75; D $48-$83; each addl $5; suites $85-$110; kit. units $53-$85; under 16 free. Pet accepted, some restrictions; $5. TV; cable. Complimentary coffee in lobby. Restaurant nearby. Ck-out 11 am. Downhill ski 5 mi. Cr cds: A, DS, MC, V.

🅳 🐾 🏊 🔥 SC

★ ★ **SEASONS LODGE.** *560 IN 46 East, approx ⅓ mi E of jct IN 135 & 46. 812/988-2284; res: 800/365-7327 (IN).* 80 rms, 2 story. S, D $60-$115; each addl $5; under 18 free. TV; cable, VCR avail (movies). Indoor/outdoor pool. Playground. Restaurant 7 am-9 pm. Rm serv. Bar noon-10 pm; Sat, Sun to 1 am; entertainment Fri, Sat. Ck-out noon. Meeting rms. Business servs avail. Sundries. Golf 2 mi. Downhill ski 4 mi; x-country ski 1 mi. Game rm. Lawn games. Some fireplaces. Private patios, balconies. Adj to Brown County State Park. Cr cds: A, C, D, DS, MC, V.

🅳 🏊 🏃 🛥 🔥 SC

Inns

★ **ALLISON HOUSE.** *90 S Jefferson St, downtown. 812/988-0814.* 5 rms, 2 story. No rm phones. S, D $95; 2-day min. Complimentary full bkfst. Restaurant nearby. Ck-out 11 am, ck-in 2 pm. Downhill ski 5 mi, x-country ski 3 mi. Built in 1883; within walking distance to Arts & Crafts colony. Totally nonsmoking. No cr cds accepted.

🏊 🛥 🔥

★ ★ **CORNERSTONE INN.** *54 E Franklin St. 812/988-0300; FAX 812/988-0200.* E-mail tiltonteam@aol.coom; web www.cornerstone .inn.com. 16 rms, 3 story, 2 suites. June-Dec: S, D $90-$105; suites $145; under 12 free; special package plans; lower rates rest of yr. TV; VCR avail. Complimentary full bkfst. Restaurant nearby. Ck-out 11 am, ck-in 3 pm. Luggage handling. Bathrm phones. In-rm whirlpool in suites. Totally nonsmoking. Cr cds: A, DS, MC, V.

🅳 🛥 🔥 SC

Restaurants

★ ★ **THE HARVEST.** *(See Brown County Inn Motel)* 812/988-2291, ext. 301. Hrs: 7 am-2 pm, 4:30-8:30 pm; Fri, Sat to 9 pm; Sun 7 am-8:30 pm, brunch to 11:30 am. Res accepted. Bar 11:30-1 am. Semi-a la carte: bkfst $4.25-$6.95, lunch $4.95-$6.95, dinner $8.95-$16.95. Sun brunch $6.95. Child's meals. Specializes in prime rib, chicken. Salad bar. Entertainment Fri, Sat. Outdoor dining. Cr cds: A, D, DS, MC, V.

🅳 SC

★ **NASHVILLE HOUSE.** *Main St at Van Buren. 812/988-4554.* Hrs: 11:30 am-8 pm; Fri, Sat to 9 pm. Closed Tues exc in Oct; also late Dec-early Jan. Res accepted. Semi-a la carte: lunch $6.95-$11.95, dinner $10.45-$18.95. Child's meals. Specializes in baked ham, fried chicken, fried biscuits and apple butter. Limited menu. Bake shop. Rustic country atmosphere; fireplace. Family-owned. Cr cds: DS, MC, V.

🅳

✔★ **THE ORDINARY.** *Van Buren St. 812/988-6166.* Hrs: 11:30 am-8 pm; Fri, Sat to 10 pm. Closed Mon (exc Oct), Jan 1, Thanksgiving, Dec 24, 25, 31. Res accepted. Bar. Semi-a la carte: lunch $3.75-$8.50, dinner $11.50-$18.95. Child's meals. Specializes in sandwiches, wild game, barbequed ribs. Entertainment Fri, Sat. Rustic country tavern. Cr cds: DS, MC, V.

🅳

New Albany (J-5)

(See also Corydon, Jeffersonville)

Founded 1813 **Pop** 36,322 **Elev** 450 ft **Area code** 812 **Zip** 47150 **E-mail** jkeith@sunnyside.win.net **Web** www.sunnysideoflouisville.org

Information Southern Indiana Convention and Tourism Bureau, 315 Southern Indiana Ave, Jeffersonville 47130; 812/282-6654 or 800/552-3842.

Opposite Louisville, Kentucky, on the Ohio River, New Albany has the first public high school in Indiana, established 1853. In the last century this city was famous for its shipyards. Two of the best-known Mississippi and Ohio River steamers, the *Robert E. Lee* and the *Eclipse,* were built here. Today it is a plywood center; other principal products are furniture, machine tools, electronic equipment, frozen food and fertilizer.

What to See and Do

Blue River Canoe Trips. Canoe trips (7-58 mi), some including camping (2-4 days). (Apr-Oct) Contact Cave Country Canoes, PO Box 145, Milltown 47145. Approx 20 mi W via IN 64 in Milltown, at bridge and dam. Phone 812/633-4993. ¢¢¢¢- ¢¢¢¢¢

Culbertson Mansion State Historic Site. A 25-rm, Second Empire/Victorian residence built in 1869. Period furnishings; cantilevered three-story staircase, hand-painted frescoed ceilings. Serpentine stone walks. Guided tours. (Mar-Dec, daily exc Mon; closed major hols) 914 E Main St. Phone 812/944-9600. **Free.**

Floyd County Museum. History and heritage of the area; changing exhibits depict early settlers, steamboat building era, Civil War and industrial period. Hand-carved animated diorama. Art gallery has works by local and regional artists; lectures; demonstrations; workshops. Gift shop. (Tues-Sat; closed major hols) 201 E Spring St. Phone 812/944-7336. **Free.**

Scribner House (1814). Oldest house in New Albany, built by one of the city's founders. Collection of antiques, paintings, toys and textiles; period furnishings. Tours (by appt). State & Main Sts, SE corner. Phone 812/944-7330 or 812/949-1776. ¢

Annual Event

Harvest Homecoming. Wk-long festivities include open house on Mansion Row, parade, hot air balloon race, music. Early Oct.

Inn

★ ★ **HONEYMOON MANSION.** 1014 E Main St. 812/945-0312; res: 800/759-7270. 6 rms, 3 story. No rm phones. S, D $69.95-$139.95; wkend, hol plans. Children over 12 yrs only. TV; cable (premium), VCR. Complimentary full bkfst. Ck-out noon, ck-in 2 pm. Concierge serv. Luggage handling. Business servs avail. Free airport transportation. Some in-rm whirlpools. Restored 1850 mansion; Victorian chapel. Totally nonsmoking. Cr cds: MC, V.

D ⊠ 🐾 SC

New Castle (E-5)

(For accommodations see Muncie, Richmond)

Founded 1819 **Pop** 17,753 **Elev** 1,055 ft **Area code** 765 **Zip** 47362
Information Chamber of Commerce, 100 S Main St, Suite 108, PO Box 485; 765/529-5210.

New Castle is a productive city; numerous plants manufacture hundreds of diversified products.

What to See and Do

Henry County Historical Society Museum (1870). Residence of Civil War general William Grose; houses pioneer and war relics, Wilbur Wright memorabilia, collection of World War I items; genealogical records. (Daily exc Sun, limited hrs; closed hols) 606 S 14th St. Phone 765/529-4028. **Free.**

Henry County Memorial Park. More than 300 acres; lake; picnic facilities, playground, 18-hole golf (fee), ball fields, concession; open-air theater; boats (fee); fishing; ice-skating; auditorium. (Daily) 1½ mi N on IN 3. Phone 765/529-1004. **Free.**

Summit Lake State Park. Approx 2,550 acres, including 800-acre lake. Swimming, boating. Hiking. Camping. Naturalist service (summer). (All yr) Standard fees. 9 mi NE on IN 3 to IN 36. Phone 765/766-5873. Per vehicle ¢

The Indiana Basketball Hall of Fame. "The home of Hoosier hysteria," a 14,000-sq-ft brick and glass museum, honors the spirit of basketball as well as the game's historical significance and outstanding individuals. An auditorium, library, interactive exhibits and video inventory of game films and interviews all help explore what basketball means to Indiana's culture, history and personality. (Daily exc Mon; closed Jan 1, Thanksgiving, Dec 25) 1 Hall of Fame Ct. Phone 765/529-1891. ¢¢

New Harmony (J-1)

(See also Evansville)

Founded 1814 **Pop** 846 **Elev** 384 ft **Area code** 812 **Zip** 47631

During the first half of the 19th century, this was the site of two social experiments in communal living. New Harmony was founded by members of the Harmony Society, under the leadership of George Rapp, who had come with many of his followers from Württemberg, Germany and settled at Harmony, Pennsylvania. In 1814 the society came to Indiana. The deeply religious members believed in equality, mutual protection and common ownership of property, practiced celibacy and prepared for the imminent return of Christ. In a 10-year period they succeeded in transforming 30,000 acres of dense forest and swampland into farms and a town that

was the envy of the surrounding region. In 1825 it was sold to Robert Owen, a Scottish industrialist, social reformer and communal idealist. Rapp and his followers returned to Pennsylvania.

Owen, supported by his four sons and William Maclure, attempted to organize a new social order, eliminating financial exploitation, poverty and competition. He tried to establish a model society in New Harmony, with equal opportunities for all, full cooperative effort and advanced educational facilities to develop the highest type of human beings. Within a short time, many of the world's most distinguished scientists, educators, scholars and writers came to New Harmony, which became one of the scientific centers of America. Owen's original experiment was doomed to early failure, mainly because of his absence from the community and rivalry among his followers. But the scientists and educators stayed on. The first US Geological Survey was done here, and the Smithsonian Institution has its origins in this community.

The town is in a rural area surrounded by rich farmland. Historic New Harmony and the New Harmony State Historic Sites are dedicated to the efforts and contributions made to Indiana's development by the founders and settlers of this community. Many of the buildings and old homes still dominate New Harmony today.

What to See and Do

★ **Tour tickets** at The Atheneum Visitors' Center, North & Arthur Sts. (Daily) Phone 812/682-4488. ¢¢-¢¢¢

1830 Owen House. Example of English architectural style.

1850 Doctor's Office. Collection of medical equipment and apothecary workshop from mid- to late 1800s.

David Lenz House (1820). Harmonist frame residence furnished with Harmonist artifacts. 324 North St.

Dormitory Number 2 (1822). An example of Harmonist brick institutional architecture. Houses exhibits on education and printing in old New Harmony.

Early West Street Log Structures. Reconstructed buildings establish the character of early Harmonist streetscape (1814-1819).

George Keppler House (1820). Harmonist frame residence contains David Dale Owen geological collection.

Harmonie State Park. Approx 3,500 acres of open fields & woods on banks of Wabash River. Swimming pool; boating (launch, ramp), fishing. Nature & hiking trails, bicycling (rentals). Picnicking (shelters), playground. Camping (tent & trailer sites, electrical hookups; cabins). Interpretive, cultural arts programs. (Daily) Standard fees. 4 mi S on IN 69, then 1 mi W on Harmonie Pkwy. Phone 812/682-4821. Per vehicle ¢

Harmonist Cemetery. 230 members of the Harmony Society are buried here in unmarked graves dating from 1814-1824. Site includes several prehistoric Woodland mounds and an apple orchard.

Lichtenberger Building/Maximilian-Bodmer Exhibit. Exhibit of Maximilian-Bodmer expedition (1832-1834) of upper Missouri region includes original lithographs of field sketches and original prints of life among the Mandan.

Macluria Double-Log Cabin (1775). Oldest structure in New Harmony.

Murphy Auditorium (1913). Facility is used for performing arts, lectures, theater and local events. Professional summer theatre under direction of University of Southern Indiana. Phone 812/465-1635 (June-Sept).

Robert Henry Fauntleroy House (1822-1840). Harmonist family residence. Enlarged and restyled by Robert and Jane Owen Fauntleroy. House museum contains period furniture.

Roofless Church (1959). Interdenominational church, designed by Philip Johnson, commemorates New Harmony's religious heritage. Jacques Lipchitz's sculpture, Descent of the Holy Spirit, is in center. Phone 812/682-4431. **Free.**

Salomon Wolf House (1823). Building houses electronic scale model of New Harmony in 1824. Audiovisual program.

Scholle House. Former Harmonist residence now houses changing exhibits.

The Atheneum Visitors' Center. Documentary film. Orientation area in building designed by Richard Meier. All tours begin here; tickets must be purchased here to view sites. North & Arthur Sts.

The Labyrinth. Circular maze of shrubbery created to symbolize the twists and choices along life's pathway.

Thrall's Opera House. Originally Harmonist Dormitory Number 4 and later converted to a concert hall by Owen descendants.

Tillich Park (1963). Burial place of German theologian Paul Johannes Tillich. Engraved stones contain selections of Dr. Tillich's writing.

Workingmen's Institute (1894). One of America's first free public libraries, begun in 1838. Archives of early New Harmony manuscript collections, art gallery, museum, public library. (Tues-Sat; closed hols) 407 W Tavern St. Phone 812/682-4806. ¢

Motel

★ ★ ★ **NEW HARMONY INN.** *North & Brewery Sts, off I-64. 812/682-4491; FAX 812/682-4491, ext. 329; res: 800/782-8605.* 90 rms, 3 story. Apr-Oct: S $65; D $75; each addl $10; under 12 free; lower rates rest of yr. Crib free. TV; cable, VCR avail. Indoor pool. Restaurant (see RED GERANIUM). Bar. Ck-out noon. Meeting rms. Business servs avail. Tennis. Exercise equipt; weights, bicycles, whirlpool, sauna. Rec rm. Some refrigerators, fireplaces. Balconies. Pastoral landscape. Chapel. Cr cds: A, DS, MC, V.

D ⚓ ≋ ⚼ ⋉ 🐾 SC

Restaurant

★ ★ **RED GERANIUM.** *(See New Harmony Inn Motel) 812/682-4431.* Hrs: 11 am-10 pm; Fri, Sat to 11 pm; Sun to 8 pm. Closed Mon; Jan 1, Dec 25. Bar to 11 pm. Semi-a la carte: lunch $4.95-$10.75, dinner $14.95-$23.95. Specialties: charcoal-broiled prime rib, old-fashioned Shaker lemon pie. Garden rm with painted orchard ceiling. Cr cds: A, DS, MC, V.

D ⋉

Peru (C-4)

(For accommodations see Kokomo, Logansport, Marion; also see Wabash)

Founded 1826 **Pop** 12,843 **Elev** 650 ft **Area code** 765 **Zip** 46970 **Web** www.miamicochamber.com

Information Peru/Miami County Chamber of Commerce, 2 N Broadway, Suite 202; 765/472-1923.

Peru is an industrial and agricultural trading community on the banks of the Wabash, near the confluence of the Mississinewa and Wabash rivers. The surroundings are filled with historic landmarks and memories of the times when the Miami made their home here, and the great Tecumseh tried to unite the various Native American tribes into one nation. Peru was once the largest circus winter quarters in the world, home of the famous Hagenbeck-Wallace circus. Peru was also the home town of composer Cole Porter; his birthplace was a large frame house that is now a duplex apartment at the northeast corner of Huntington & E 3rd St.

What to See and Do

Circus Museum. Vast collection of circus memorabilia and relics, historical items from professional circuses and the Peru Amateur Circus. (Daily; closed hols) (See ANNUAL EVENTS) 154 N Broadway. Phone 765/472-3918. **Donation.**

Miami County Museum. Exhibits on the circus, pioneers, Miami tribe, Victorian rms and stores, Cole Porter; Art Room. (Tues-Sat; closed Jan 1, July 4, Thanksgiving, Dec 25) 51 N Broadway. Phone 765/473-9183. ¢

Mississinewa Lake. A 3,200-acre lake. Boating (fee); waterskiing, swimming (Memorial Day-Labor Day, daily). Picnicking; hiking trails. Camping (fee). Fishing, hunting in season. (Mid-May-mid-Sept, daily) 7 mi SE via IN 19, E on County Rd 500S. Phone 765/473-6528. Per vehicle ¢-¢¢

Annual Events

Circus City Festival. Circus Museum. Amateur circus, museum, displays, performances, rides, booths; parade (last Sat). Phone 765/472-3918. Mid-July.

Heritage Days. Miami County Courthouse Sq. Celebrates the county's pioneer heritage. Phone 765/473-9183. 2nd wkend Sept.

Plymouth (B-4)

(See also South Bend)

Founded 1834 **Pop** 8,303 **Elev** 799 ft **Area code** 219 **Zip** 46563 **E-mail** mccvb@skyenet.net

Information Marshall County Convention and Visitors Bureau, 220 N Center St; 219/936-9000 or 800/626-5353.

Plymouth is a farming and industrial center. Southwest of the town was the site of the last Potawatomi village in this area. In 1838 their chief, Menominee, refused to turn his village over to white squatters and made a last unsuccessful stand against soldiers secretly sent by the governor of Indiana. The surviving 859 men, women and children were dispossessed and evacuated by the government to Kansas. So many members of the tribe died of malaria that fresh graves were left at every campsite during their long and tragic journey.

What to See and Do

Chief Menominee Monument. A granite memorial with a statue of Menominee at the site of his original village. SW of town at Twin Lakes.

Marshall County Historical Museum. Relics pertaining to local history; Native American artifacts; genealogical materials. (Daily exc Mon; closed hols) 123 N Michigan St. Phone 219/936-2306. **Free.**

Annual Event

Marshall County Blueberry Festival. Centennial Park. Parade, exhibits, tractor pull, "Blueberry Stomp" road race, canoe & bike races, balloon race, circus, fireworks. Labor Day wkend.

Motels

★ ★ **CULVER COVE.** *(319 E Jefferson St, Culver 46511) 219/842-2683; FAX 219/842-2821.* 80 kit. units, 2 story. May-Aug: S, D $105-$152; suites $152-$184; wkly, wkend rates; higher rates special events; lower rates rest of yr. Crib free. TV; cable (premium), VCR avail. Complimentary continental bkfst. Complimentary coffee in rms. Restaurant 11 am-2 pm, 5-8 pm; Fri, Sat to 9 pm. Rm serv. Bar 4 pm-midnight. Ck-out 11 am, ck-in 3 pm. Meeting rms. Business servs avail. In-rm modem link. Valet serv. Barber, beauty shop. Coin lndry. Tennis. Exercise equipt; weights, weight machine, sauna. Massage. Rec rm. Indoor pool; whirlpool. On beach. Microwaves, fireplaces; many in-rm whirlpools. Balconies. Picnic tables. On lake. Cr cds: A, C, D, DS, MC, V.

D ⚓ ≋ ⚼ ⋉ 🐾 SC

★ ★ **HOLIDAY INN.** *2550 N Michigan St. 219/936-4013; FAX 219/936-4553.* 108 rms, 2 story. S, D $59-$64; each addl $5; under 19 free; higher rates special events. Crib free. Pet accepted. TV; cable (premium). Pool. Restaurant 6:30 am-9 pm; Fri, Sat to 10 pm; Sun 7 am-9 pm. Rm serv. Bar 11-1 am; wkend hrs vary. Ck-out noon. Coin lndry. Meeting rms. Business servs avail. In-rm modem link. Sundries. 18-hole golf course adj. Health club privileges. Cr cds: A, C, D, DS, JCB, MC, V.

D ⚓ ≋ ⋉ 🐾 SC

Richmond (E-6)

(See also New Castle)

Settled 1806 **Pop** 38,705 **Elev** 980 ft **Area code** 765 **Zip** 47374

Information Richmond/Wayne County Tourism Bureau, 5701 National Rd E; 765/935-8687 or 800/828-8414.

Established by Quakers, this city on the Whitewater River, is one of Indiana's leading industrial communities; it is the trade and distribution center for agriculturally rich Wayne County.

What to See and Do

Antique Alley. Over 900 dealers display their treasures within a 33-mi stretch through and around Richmond. Contact Tourism Bureau for complete listing.

Earlham College (1847). (1,200 students) Liberal arts. Owns and operates Conner Prairie. W of Whitewater River on US 40. Phone 765/983-1200. On campus are Lilly Library, Stout Memorial Meetinghouse, Runyan Student Center and

Joseph Moore Museum of Natural Science. Birds and mammals in natural settings, fossils, mastodon and allosaurus skeletons. (Academic yr, Mon, Wed, Fri & Sun; rest of yr, Sun only) Phone 765/983-1303. **Free.**

Glen Miller Park. A 194-acre park; E.G. Hill Memorial Rose Garden, 9-hole golf (fee), natural springs, picnic shelters, concessions, fishing, paddleboats, playground, tennis courts and outdoor amphitheatre (summer concerts). 2514 E Main St (US 40). Phone 765/983-7285. **Free.** Also in the park is

The German Friendship Garden. Features 200 German hybridized roses sent by the German city of Zweibrücken, from its own rose garden. In bloom May-Oct. 2500 National Rd E.

Hayes Regional Arboretum. A 355-acre site with trees, shrubs and vines native to this region; 40-acre beech-maple forest; auto tour (3.5 mi) of site. Fern garden; spring house. Hiking trails; solar greenhouse; bird sanctuary; nature center with exhibits; gift shop. (Daily exc Mon; closed major hols) 801 Elks Rd, 2 mi W of jct US 40 & I-70. Phone 765/962-3745. **Free.**

Huddleston Farmhouse Inn Museum. Restored 1840s farmhouse/inn complex with outbuildings once served National Road travelers. (May-Aug, Tues-Sat, also Sun afternoons; rest of yr, Tues-Sat only; closed some hols; also Jan) 1 mi W on US 40, at W edge of town, in Cambridge City. Phone 765/478-3172. ¢

Indiana Football Hall of Fame. History of football in Indiana; photos, plaques, memorabilia of more than 300 inductees. High schools, colleges and universities are represented. (Mon-Fri, also by appt; closed hols) N 9th & A Sts. Phone 765/966-2235. ¢

Levi Coffin House State Historic Site (1839). Federal-style brick home of Quaker abolitionist who helped 2,000 fugitive slaves escape to Canada; period furnishings. Tours (Tues-Sat, afternoons; closed July 4). 113 US 27N, in Fountain City. Phone 765/847-2432. ¢

Madonna of the Trails. One of 12 monuments erected along Old National Rd (US 40) in honor of pioneer women. US 40.

Middlefork Reservoir. A 405-acre park with 175-acre stream and spring-fed lake. Fishing; boating (dock rental); bait & tackle supplies. Hiking trails. Picnicking, playground. Sylvan Nook Dr, 2 mi N on IN 27, just S of I-70. Phone 765/983-7293. **Free.**

Wayne County Historical Museum. Pioneer rms include general store; bakery, cobbler, print, bicycle, blacksmith and apothecary shops; log cabin (1823), loom house; agricultural hall; decorative arts gallery; antique cars and old carriages; Egyptian mummy; collections of the Mediterranean world. (Feb-Dec, daily exc Mon; closed Jan 1, Easter, Thanksgiving, Dec 25) (See ANNUAL EVENTS) 1150 N A St, at 12th St. Phone 765/962-5756. ¢¢

Annual Events

Rose Festival. Moonlight parade, entertainment, arts & crafts and concerts under the stars. Phone 765/935-7673. June.

Pioneer Day Festival. Wayne Country Historical Museum. Pioneer crafts, food. Sun after Labor Day.

Motels

(Rates may be higher during the Indianapolis "500")

✔★ **BEST WESTERN IMPERIAL.** *3020 E Main St. 765/966-1505.* 44 rms, 2 story. S, D $29-$52; each addl $5; kit. units $10 addl; under 12 free; higher rates rest for special events. Crib $2. TV; cable. Heated pool. Complimentary continental bkfst. Restaurant nearby. Ck-out noon. Some microwaves, refrigerators. Cr cds: A, C, D, DS, MC, V.

≈ ⊠ 🔥 SC

★ **COMFORT INN.** *912 Mendelson Dr, I-70 exit 151.* 765/935-4766. 52 rms, 2 story. S, D $54.95-$59.95; each addl $5; suites $61.95-$69.95; under 18 free. Crib free. Pet accepted. Indoor pool; whirlpool. Restaurant adj 6 am-8 pm. Ck-out 11 am. Game rm. Refrigerators, microwaves in suites. Cr cds: A, C, D, DS, MC, V.

D 🐾 ≈ ⊠ 🔥 SC

✔★ **KNIGHTS INN.** *419 Commerce Dr, I-70 at US 40 exit 156 A.* 765/966-6682. 103 rms, 10 kits. S, D $37.95-$49.95; each addl $5; kit. units $41.95-$49.95; under 18 free; higher rates special events. Crib free. Pet accepted. TV; cable (premium), VCR avail. Pool. Complimentary coffee in lobby. Restaurant adj 6 am-10 pm; Fri, Sat open 24 hrs. Ck-out noon. Meeting rm. Some refrigerators. Cr cds: A, C, D, DS, MC, V.

🐾 ≈ ⊠ 🔥 SC

★★ **LEE'S INN.** *6030 National Rd E, I-70 exit 156A.* 765/966-6559; FAX 765/966-7732; res: 800/733-5337. 91 rms, 2 story, 12 suites. S $65-$85; D $75-$95; each addl $10; suites $73-$162; under 16 free. Crib free. Pet accepted. TV; cable (premium), VCR avail. Complimentary continental bkfst. Restaurant adj 6 am-10 pm. Ck-out noon. Meeting rms. Business servs avail. Health club privileges. Some in-rm whirlpools, microwaves. Cr cds: A, C, D, DS, MC, V.

D 🐾 ⊠ 🔥 SC

★ **RAMADA INN.** *4700 National Rd E (Main St), 1 mi W of I-70 exit 156 A.* 765/962-5551; FAX 765/966-6250. 158 rms, 2 story. S, D $68-$98; each addl $10; under 18 free. Crib free. Pet accepted, some restrictions. TV; cable. Heated pool. Restaurant 11 am-11 pm. Rm serv. Bar. Ck-out noon. Meeting rms. Business servs avail. Valet serv. Sundries. Game rm. Health club privileges. Cr cds: A, C, D, DS, MC, V.

D 🐾 ≈ ⊠ 🔥 SC

Hotel

★★ **CLARION LELAND.** *900 South A St, I-70 exit 151.* 765/966-5000; FAX 765/962-0887; res: 800/535-2630. 112 rms, 7 story. S, D $70-$110; each addl $10; under 18 free; wknd rates. Crib free. Pet accepted, some restrictions. TV; cable (premium), VCR avail. Indoor pool. Restaurant 6 am-10 pm. Bar; entertainment Sat. Ck-out noon. Meeting rms. Business servs avail. Concierge. Health club privileges. In-rm whirlpools, microwaves avail. Restored hotel (1928); Queen Anne furnishings. Cr cds: A, C, D, DS, ER, JCB, MC, V.

D 🐾 ≈ ⊠ 🔥 SC

Restaurants

★★ **OLDE RICHMOND INN.** *138 S Fifth St. 765/962-2247.* Hrs: 11 am-9 pm; Fri, Sat to 10 pm; Sun to 8 pm. Closed Jan 1, Labor Day, Dec 25. Res accepted. Continental menu. Bar. Semi-a la carte: lunch $5-$11, dinner $9-$27. Child's meals. Specializes in fresh seafood, steak. Outdoor dining. Restored mansion built 1892. Cr cds: MC, V.

★ **TASTE OF THE TOWN.** *1616 E Main St. 765/935-5464.* Hrs: 11 am-10 pm; Fri to midnight; Sat 4 pm-midnight; Closed Sun; some major hols. Res accepted. Italian, Amer menu. Bar. Complete meals: lunch $4.50-$5.95, dinner $6.95-$14.95. Child's meals. Specializes in home-made soup, steak, seafood. Entertainment Fri, Sat 8:30 pm-midnight. Casual dining. Cr cds: A, DS, MC, V.

Rockville (F-2)

(For accommodations see Terre Haute)

Pop 2,706 **Elev** 711 ft **Area code** 765 **Zip** 47872 **E-mail** alynk@ticz.com **Web** www.coveredbridges.com
Information Convention & Visitors Bureau, PO Box 165; 765/569-5226.

What to See and Do

⭐ **Historic Billie Creek Village.** Re-created turn-of-the-century village and working farmstead with 3 covered bridges; more than 30 buildings, including one-rm schoolhouse, country store, blacksmith shop, burr mill, livery; governor's house, log cabin; nature preserve; special events (see ANNUAL EVENTS). Weaving, candle dipping and many other old-time craft demonstrations (Memorial Day wkend-Halloween wkend, wkends). Self-guided tours (Jan-late Dec, Mon-Fri; free admission). 1 mi E on US 36. For further information contact RR 2, Box 27; 765/569-3430. Wkend admission ¢¢

Raccoon Lake State Recreation Area. Approx 4,000 acres on reservoir. Swimming, waterskiing; fishing; boating (rentals). Campground. Standard fees. 9 mi E on US 36. Phone 765/344-1412. Per vehicle (Mar-Oct) ¢¢

Shades State Park. Approx 25 mi NE via US 41, IN 47, 234 (see CRAWFORDSVILLE).

Turkey Run State Park (see). 10 mi NE via US 41, IN 47.

Annual Events

Parke County Maple Fair. 4-H Fairground. Celebration of maple sugar harvest. Bus & self-guided tours to 6 maple camps. Arts & crafts. Last wkend Feb & 1st wkend Mar.

Civil War Days. Historic Billie Creek Village. State's largest re-enactment of Civil War battle; costumes, battlefield; ladies tea; dance. Mid-June.

Sorghum & Cider Fair. Historic Billie Creek Village. Cider made in copper kettles; sorghum cane squeezed by horse-powered press. Mid-Sept.

Parke County Covered Bridge Festival. Arts & crafts, craft demonstrations; food; animals and rides at living museum. Activities county-wide. Mid-Oct.

Old Fashioned Arts and Crafts Christmas. Historic Billie Creek Village. Christmas celebration at village. Early Dec.

Santa Claus (J-3)

Founded 1846 **Pop** 927 **Elev** 519 ft **Area code** 812 **Zip** 47579

This is a small, one-street town with a first-class post office. Its name has made it particularly significant to millions of Americans at Christmas time. At the start of the season several hundred thousand parcels and a million other pieces of mail arrive at the post office from all over the country, to be remailed with the Santa Claus postmark.

What to See and Do

Holiday World & Splashin' Safari. Holiday World theme park includes more than 60 rides, games, shows, exhibits and attractions themed around Christmas, July 4th and Halloween. Live music; high-dive shows; Lincoln-era exhibit; wax museum; antique toy and doll museums; craftspersons at work; petting zoo; and Santa himself! Sidewalk and indoor restaurants. (Mid-May-Aug, daily; early May & Sept-early Oct, wkends) Jct IN 162, 245. Phone 800-GO-SANTA. ¢¢¢¢¢ Admission includes rides, shows, exhibits and

Splashin' Safari Water Park. Offers adult and children's water slides, an action river, children's activity pool, and a sandy beach area. (Memorial Day wkend-Labor Day)

Shakamak State Park (G-2)

(For accommodations see Terre Haute)

(2 mi W of Jasonville on IN 48)

More than 1,766 acres with 3 artificial lakes stocked with game fish. Swimming pool, lifeguard, bathhouse; boating (rentals, no gasoline motors). Picnicking, playground. Hiking. Camping, trailer facilities; cabins. Naturalist service (May-Aug); nature center. Standard fees. Phone 812/665-2158. Per vehicle ¢¢

South Bend (A-4)

(See also Elkhart, La Porte, Mishawaka)

Founded 1823 **Pop** 105,511 **Elev** 710 ft **Area code** 219 **E-mail** cvbsjco@aol.com
Information South Bend-Mishawaka Convention and Visitors Bureau, 401 E Colfax Ave, Suite 310, PO Box 1677, 46634; 219/234-0051 or 800/828-7881.

South Bend is probably most famous, at least in the eyes of football fans, as the home of the "fighting Irish" of Notre Dame. A visit to the campus, distinguished by the massive golden dome of the Administration Building, is worth the trip. Indiana University also has a branch here.

Two Frenchmen, Father Marquette and Louis Jolliet, who traveled through northern Indiana between 1673-1675, were the first Europeans to enter the South Bend area. In December, 1679, the famous French writer and explorer René Robert Cavelier, Sieur de la Salle, proceeded from here with 32 men to the Mississippi River. During a second trip in 1681, La Salle negotiated a peace treaty between the Miami and Illinois Confederations under an oak tree known as the Council Oak. The first permanent settlers arrived in 1820, when Pierre Freischuetz Navarre set up a trading post for the American Fur Company.

South Bend was founded in 1823 by Alexis Coquillard, who, with his partner Francis Comparet, bought the fur trading agency from John Jacob Astor. Joined by Lathrop Taylor, another trading post agent, Coquillard was instrumental in promoting European settlement of the area and in the construction of ferries, dams and mills, which began the industrial development of the town.

Industries formerly based in South Bend and contributing to its growth were the Studebaker auto plant and the Oliver Corporation. The St Joseph River runs at its southernmost bend through the center of the city, which was officially named South Bend by the US Post Office Department in 1830.

What to See and Do

Century Center. Multipurpose facility, designed by Philip Johnson and John Burgee, housing a convention center, performing arts and art centers, museum and park area. General building (daily; closed most major hols). 120 S St Joseph St. Phone 219/235-9711. Parking ¢ Within the center is

South Bend Regional Museum of Art. Permanent collection, changing exhibitions. Classes, lecture series. Museum shop. (Tues-Fri, also Sat & Sun afternoons) Phone 219/235-9102. **Free.**

College Football Hall of Fame. Sports shrine and museum dedicated to the preservation of college football. The educational and interpretive exhibits bring to life the history, color and pageantry of the game. (Daily; closed Jan 1, Thanksgiving and Dec 25). 111 South St Joseph St. Phone 219/235-9999. **¢¢¢**

East Race Waterway. Only man-made whitewater raceway in North America. Recreational, instructional & competitive canoeing, kayaking, rafting. Lighted sidewalks, foot bridges, seating areas. (June-Aug, Wed, Thurs, Sat & Sun; closed for races) E side of St Joseph River at South Bend Dam, downtown. Phone 219/233-6121. **¢¢**

Northern Indiana Center for History. Includes permanent, temporary and interactive exhibition galleries; research library. Permanent exhibits depict history of the St Joseph River Valley Region of Northern Indiana and Southern Michigan. 808 W Washington, located in the West Washington National Historic District. For information on hours, admission fees and special exhibitions, phone 219/235-9664. On the grounds is the

Copshaholm, Historic Oliver Mansion. Built in 1895-1896 by the Oliver family, this 38-rm mansion is complete with original furnishings. **Copshaholm Carriage House** serves as the visitor center for the historical complex; also houses a gift shop. The grounds include 3 acres of historic gardens, tennis court, tea house, sunken Italian gardens, fountain and more. The mansion, gardens and carriage house are on the National Register of Historic Places. Guided tours. (Daily exc Mon) Phone 219/235-9664. **¢¢**

Parks.

Leeper. Tennis (daily, fee); fragrance garden for the visually impaired; Pierre Navarre Cabin (1820), was the home and fur-trading post of South Bend's first settler. Michigan St, on US 31. Phone 219/235-9405. **¢¢**

Pinhook. Historical park has lagoon, picnic area; fishing and small boating. 2901 N Riverside Dr, 1 mi W. Phone 219/235-9417. **Free.**

Potawatomi Park. Lighted tennis courts & softball diamond; zoo (Mar-Dec; fee); conservatories; tropical gardens; concerts; picnic area (fee). Swimming (mid-June-late Aug, daily; fee). 500 Greenlawn. Phone 219/235-9800. **¢¢**

City Greenhouses and Conservatory. Spring, mum and Christmas flower shows. (Daily; closed major hols) 2105 Mishawaka Ave. Phone 219/235-9442. **¢**

Rum Village. Nature center, picnic area, hiking & nature trails on 160 acres of woodland. Also contains Safetyville, miniature village teaching youngsters pedestrian, bike and auto safety. W Ewing St, 1½ mi W of US 33. Phone 219/235-9455. **Free.**

St Patrick's Park. Swimming, canoeing, boat launch; hiking; picnicking; cross-country skiing. (Daily) (See SEASONAL EVENTS) 7 mi N near US 31, on the St Joseph River. Phone 219/277-4828. Wkend admission, per vehicle ¢

Bendix Woods. Picnicking, nature center. Hiking; exercise trail; cross-country skiing. (Daily) 12 mi W on IN 2. Phone 219/654-3155. Wkend admission, per vehicle (May-Oct) **¢¢**

Potato Creek State Park. Approx 3,800 acres. Swimming beach (lifeguard); fishing on Lake Worster; boating, canoeing, paddleboats (rentals). Hiking, paved bike trails (rentals). Cross-country skiing (rentals). Picnicking (shelter rentals). Camping, horse camping (tie-rail at site), cabins. Nature center, naturalist service (all yr). Standard fees. (Daily) 7 mi S on US 31, then 4 mi W on IN 4. Phone 219/656-8186. Per vehicle ¢

Saint Mary's College (1844). (1,600 women) Music, theatrical and art events throughout the yr. Campus tours (by appt). 2 mi N on US 33 at IN Toll Rd exit 77. Phone 219/284-4626 for ticket and event information.

The Studebaker National Museum. Houses and displays the Studebaker vehicle collection and artifacts. Exhibits depict evolution of the industry in the US from 1852-1966, the 114-yr span of the company. Shows more than 80 Studebaker wagons, carriages and motorized vehicles, including carriages of four US presidents. Also features a hands-on science and technology center. (Daily; closed some hols). 525 S Main St. Phone 219/235-9714. **¢¢**

★ **University of Notre Dame** (1842). (10,126 students) One of leading universities in the US; noted for its biotechnology and vector biology research, and studies focusing on radiation, aerodynamics and social ministry. The school is a major center for constitutional law studies. N on US 31, 33 & I-80, 90. Phone 219/631-5726. On campus are

Snite Museum of Art. Contains more than 19,000 works of art representing ancient to contemporary periods. Included are works of Chagall, Picasso, Rodin and Boucher as well as 18th- and 19th-century European art. (Daily exc Mon; closed hols) Phone 219/631-7960. **Free.**

The Basilica of the Sacred Heart (1871). Contains French stained-glass windows and a baroque altar in Our Lady Chapel. Its spire houses the oldest carillon in North America. Contains works by famed Croatian sculptor Ivan Mestrovic. Phone 219/631-7091. A short distance from the church is

Grotto of Our Lady of Lourdes. Replica of original in the French Pyrenees.

Administrative Building (1879). The "Golden Dome" houses Columbus murals by Luigi Gregori, a former director of the university's art department and portrait painter at the Vatican Museum in the late 1860s. Phone 219/631-5726.

Notre Dame Hesburgh Library (1963). South wall of 2-million volume library has ten-storied granite mural, "The Word of Life." Phone 219/631-5252.

Joyce Center (1968). A 10½-acre complex under twin domes for athletic, cultural and civic events. Includes Sports Heritage Hall, with memorabilia from Notre Dame sports history. Phone 219/631-5030.

Guided tours of the 1,250-acre campus can be arranged at the Dept of Public Relations and Information. (Summer, Mon-Fri; academic yr, by appt; closed hols) Phone 219/631-5726. For a list of daily events phone 219/631-5110. **Free.**

Annual Event

Ethnic Festival. Parade, performances. Arts and crafts. 4th of July wkend.

Seasonal Events

Minor League Baseball. Stanley Coveleski Regional Baseball Stadium. 501 W South St. 5,000 seat baseball stadium. Home of the South Bend Silver Hawks. Apr-Aug.

Firefly Festival of the Performing Arts. St Patrick's Park. Plays, music, concerts in outdoor amphitheater. Mid-June-early Aug, wkends.

Motels

(Rates may be higher football wkends)

★★ **BEST INNS OF AMERICA.** *425 Dixie Hwy (46637).* 219/277-7700; FAX 219/277-7700, ext. 113; res: 800/237-8466. 93 rms, 2 story. May-Nov: S, D $45.88-$56.88; each addl $6; under 18 free; lower rates rest of yr. Crib free. Pet accepted, some restrictions. TV; cable. Complimentary continental bkfst. Restaurant nearby. Ck-out 1 pm. Meeting rm. Cr cds: A, C, D, DS, MC, V.

D 🐾 ⊠ 🏂 **SC**

★ **DAYS INN.** *52757 US 31N (46637).* 219/277-0510; FAX 219/277-9316. 180 rms, 3 story. S $39-$60; D $49-$70; each addl $5; under 8 free; higher rates special events. Crib free. Pet accepted. TV; cable (premium). Pool. Playground. Complimentary continental bkfst. Ck-out noon. Meeting rm. Business servs avail. In-rm modem link. Cr cds: A, C, D, DS, ER, JCB, MC, V.

[D] [icons] SC

★★ **HOLIDAY INN-UNIVERSITY AREA.** *515 Dixie Hwy (46637). 219/272-6600; FAX 219/272-5553.* 220 rms, 2 story. S $89-$99; D $99-$110; each addl $10; under 18 free; wknd, hol rates. Crib free. Pet accepted, some restrictions. TV; cable (premium). 2 pools, 1 indoor; wading pool, whirlpool. Complimentary continental bkfst. Coffee in rms. Restaurant 7-10 am, 11 am-1 pm, 5:30-9:30 pm. Rm serv. Bar 11 am-midnight; Fri, Sat to 1 am. Ck-out noon. Coin lndry. Meeting rms. Business servs avail. Bellhops. Free airport transportation. Exercise equipt; weight machine, bicycle, sauna. Game rm. Rec rm. Balconies. Picnic tables. Cr cds: A, C, D, DS, JCB, MC, V.

[D] [icons] SC

★ **KNIGHTS INN.** *236 Dixie Way N (US 31) (46637). 219/277-2960; FAX 219/277-0203; res: 800/843-5644.* 108 rms. S $34.95-$49.95; D $38.95-$54.95; each addl $6; kit. units $42.95-$64.95; under 18 free; higher rates special events. Crib free. TV; cable (premium). Complimentary continental bkfst. Restaurant nearby. Ck-out noon. Business servs avail. X-country ski 15 mi. Cr cds: A, C, D, DS, JCB, MC, V.

[D] [icons] SC

★★ **MORRIS INN OF NOTRE DAME.** *Notre Dame Ave (46556), on campus. 219/631-2000; FAX 219/631-2017.* 92 rms, 3 story. S $72-$86; D $80-$94; under 12 free. Crib free. TV, cable. Complimentary coffee in lobby. Restaurant (see MORRIS INN). Rm serv. Bar. Ck-out noon. Meeting rms. Business servs avail. Bellhops. Sundries. Gift shop. Tennis. 9-hole golf course, greens fee $10. Downhill ski 1 mi, x-country ski 20 mi. Exercise equipt; weight machine, bicycles. Some refrigerators. Picnic tables. Cr cds: A, C, D, DS, MC, V.

[D] [icons]

★★ **SIGNATURE INN.** *215 Dixie Way S (46637). 219/277-3211.* 123 rms, 2 story. S $70-$72; D $77-$79; each addl $7; under 17 free; higher rates special events. Crib free. TV; cable (premium). Pool, whirlpool. Complimentary continental bkfst. Restaurant opp open 24 hrs. Ck-out noon. Meeting rms. Business servs avail. In-rm modem link. Exercise equipt; weight machine, bicycles. Cr cds: A, C, D, DS, MC, V.

[D] [icons] SC

✔★ **SUPER 8.** *52825 US 33N (46637). 219/272-9000; FAX 219/273-0035.* 111 rms, 2 story. S $42.95; D $52.85; each addl $4; under 17 free; higher rates special events. TV; cable (premium). Complimentary continental bkfst. Ck-out 11 am. X-country ski 10 mi. Some refrigerators, microwaves, in-rm whirlpools. Cr cds: A, C, D, DS, MC, V.

[icons] SC

Motor Hotels

★★ **INN AT SAINT MARY'S.** *53993 US 31/33N (46637). 219/232-4000; FAX 219/289-0986; res: 800/947-8627.* 150 rms, 3 story, 80 suites. S $84; D $94; suites $99-$159; under 18 free; higher rates special events. Crib free. TV; cable (premium), VCR. Complimentary continental bkfst. Restaurant nearby. Bar. Ck-out noon. Coin lndry. Meeting rms. Business center. In-rm modem link. Gift shop. Free airport, RR station, bus depot transportation. Exercise equipt; bicycle, treadmill. Refrigerator, microwave in suites. Cr cds: A, C, D, DS, MC, V.

[D] [icons]

★★ **RESIDENCE INN BY MARRIOTT.** *716 N Niles Ave (46617). 219/289-5555.* 80 kit. suites, 2 story. July-Nov: S, D $99-$129; higher rates graduation; lower rates rest of yr. Crib free. Pet accepted; $100. TV; cable (premium), VCR avail (movies). Heated pool; whirlpool. Playground. Complimentary continental bkfst. Complimentary coffee in rms. Restaurant nearby. Ck-out noon. Coin lndry. Meeting rms. Business servs avail. Exercise equipt; weights, bicycle. Microwaves. Balconies. Cr cds: A, C, D, DS, JCB, MC, V.

[D] [icons]

Hotels

★★ **HOLIDAY INN-DOWNTOWN.** *213 W Washington St (46601), in Valley American Bank Bldg, 8th-16th floors. 219/232-3941; FAX 219/284-3715.* 177 rms. S, D $69-$125; each addl $10; suites $105-$150; under 19 free; higher rates special events. Crib free. TV; cable (premium). Indoor pool. Complimentary coffee in lobby. Restaurant 6:30 am-2 pm, 5-10 pm. Rm serv 6:30 am-9:30 pm. Bar 11:30-1 am; Sun noon-midnight. Ck-out noon. Meeting rms. Business servs avail. Free airport transportation. Exercise equipt; bicycles, treadmills. X-country ski 9 mi. Massage. Health club privileges. Cr cds: A, C, D, DS, JCB, MC, V.

[D] [icons] SC

★★★ **MARRIOTT.** *123 N St Joseph St (46601). 219/234-2000; FAX 219/234-2252.* Web www.marriott.com/marriott/sbnin. 300 rms, 9 story. S $89-$150; D $99-$170; suites $295-$425; under 18 free; wknd packages; higher rates special events. Crib free. Garage. TV; cable (premium), VCR avail (movies). Indoor pool; whirlpool, poolside serv. Restaurant 6:30 am-10 pm; Sun from 7 am; wknd hrs vary. Bar 3 pm-1:30 am. Ck-out noon. Convention facilities. Business center. In-rm modem link. Gift shop. Garage. X-country ski 9 mi. Exercise equipt; bicycles, treadmill, sauna. Game rm. Atrium. Connected to Century Center. Cr cds: A, C, D, DS, ER, JCB, MC, V.

[D] [icons] SC

Inns

★★ **THE BOOK INN.** *508 W Washington (46601). 219/288-1990.* E-mail bookinn@aol.com; web members.aol.com/bookinn/. 5 rms, 1 with shower only, 2 story, 2 suites. S, D, suites $75-$120; higher rates special events. TV; VCR avail (movies). Complimentary full bkfst. Restaurant adj 11:30 am-10 pm. Business servs avail. Luggage handling. X-country ski 4 mi. Built in 1872; contains used bookstore. Totally nonsmoking. Cr cds: A, MC, V.

[icons]

★★ **OLIVER INN.** *630 W Washington St (46601). 219/232-4545; res: 888/697-4466; FAX 219/288-9788.* E-mail oliver@michiana.org; web michiana.org/users/oliver. 9 rms, 2 share bath, 3 story. S, D $75-$125; higher rates special events. Pet accepted, some restrictions. TV; cable (premium). Complimentary continental bkfst; afternoon refreshments. Restaurant adj 11:30 am-2 pm, 5-10 pm; Fri to 11 pm; Sat 4:30-11 pm; Sun 4-9 pm; Sun brunch 9 am-2 pm. Ck-out 11 am, ck-in 4-6 pm. Business servs avail. Luggage handling. 18-hole golf privileges, pro, putting green. Downhill/x-country ski 20 mi. Lawn games. Some fireplaces. Picnic tables. Built in 1886; Victorian decor. Totally nonsmoking. Cr cds: A, DS, MC, V.

[icons] SC

★★ **QUEEN ANNE INN.** *420 W Washington St (46601). 219/234-5959; res: 800/582-2379; FAX 219/234-4324.* 6 rms, 3 story, 1 suite. S $65-$200; D $70-$185; each addl $15; suite $105; special package plans. TV; VCR avail (movies). Complimentary full bkfst. Restaurant nearby. Ck-out 11 am, ck-in 4 pm. Business servs avail. Street parking. Free airport transportation. X-country ski 4 mi. Some fireplaces. Built in 1893; Victorian decor. Totally nonsmoking. Cr cds: A, MC, V.

[icons]

Restaurants

★★★ **CARRIAGE HOUSE.** *24460 Adams Rd (46628), I-80/90 exit 72. 219/272-9220.* Hrs: 5-9:30 pm. Closed Sun, Mon; most major hols; also early Jan. Res accepted. Continental menu. Bar. Complete meals: dinner $16-$28. Specialties: chicken Chardonnay, beef Wellington, roast rack of lamb. Own baking. Outdoor dining. Restored church (ca 1850); European-style dining. Cr cds: A, C, D, MC, V.

[D]

★★ **DAMON'S.** *52885 US 31N (46637). 219/272-5478.* Hrs: 11 am-11 pm; Fri, Sat to midnight; Sun to 10 pm. Closed Thanksgiving, Dec

25. Res accepted. Bar. Semi-a la carte: lunch $4.95-$15.95, dinner $5.95-$15.95. Child's meals. Specializes in onion loaf, barbecued ribs, barbecued chicken. Cr cds: A, C, D, DS, MC, V.

D SC

★ ★ LASALLE GRILL. 115 W Colfax (46601). 219/288-1155. E-mail lasalle@tcpbbs.net; web www.lasallegrill.com. Hrs: 5-10 pm; Fri, Sat to 11 pm. Closed Sun; most major hols. Res accepted. Bar. Semi-a la carte: dinner $14.25-$28.95. Specializes in prime steak, grilled salmon, seasonal game. Own baking. Mix of contemporary and traditional decor. Cr cds: A, C, D, DS, MC, V.

D

★ ★ MORRIS INN. (See Morris Inn of Notre Dame Motel) 219/631-2020. Hrs: 7-10:30 am, 11:30 am-2 pm, 5:30-8:30 pm; Sun brunch 11:30 am-2 pm. Closed mid-Dec-early Jan. Res accepted; required lunch. Bar. Semi-a la carte: bkfst $3-$6, lunch $4.75-$5.50, dinner $9.95-$24.95. Sun brunch $7.95-$14.95. Child's meals. Specializes in fresh fish, chicken dishes, prime rib. Own ice cream. Traditional American fine dining; contemporary decor with some original art. Totally nonsmoking. Cr cds: A, C, D, DS, MC, V.

D

★ ★ TIPPECANOE PLACE. 620 W Washington (46601). 219/234-9077. Hrs: 11:30 am-2 pm, 5-10 pm; Fri to 10:30 pm; Sat 4:30-10:30 pm; Sun 4-9 pm; Sun brunch 9 am-2 pm. Res accepted. Bar to 11:30 pm, wkends to midnight. Wine list. Semi-a la carte: lunch $6-$10, dinner $14-$19. Sun brunch $10.95. Specializes in seafood, prime rib, steaks. Own pastries. Parking. Former Studebaker mansion (1886-1889); many antiques. Cr cds: A, C, D, MC, V.

D

Spring Mill State Park (H-4)

(For accommodations see Bedford, Bloomington)

(3 mi E of Mitchell on IN 60)

In this 1,319-acre park an abandoned pioneer village has been restored in a small valley among wooded hills. Built around a gristmill, which dates to 1817, are the log shops and homes of a pioneer trading post. The village's main street is flanked by a tavern, distillery, post office and an apothecary shop. A small stream flowing through the valley turns an overshot waterwheel at the gristmill and furnishes power for a sawmill. The homes of the pioneers have been furnished with household articles from a century ago.

The Virgil I. Grissom Memorial, dedicated to the Indiana astronaut who was the second American in space, is located here. In the building are space exhibits, a slide show and a visitor center.

In the surrounding forest, which includes 60 acres of woods, are some of the largest oak and tulip trees in Indiana. Some of the many caverns in the park have underground streams with blind fish. In Twin Caves, boat trips may be taken on underground stream (Apr-Oct). Park facilities include swimming pool, lifeguard; fishing; boating (rentals, no motors) on a 30-acre artificial lake. Hiking trails, tennis. Picnicking. Camping. Inn has accommodations (phone 812/849-4081). Standard fees. Phone 812/849-4129. Per vehicle (Apr-Oct) ¢¢

Terre Haute (F-2)

(See also Brazil, Greencastle, Rockville)

Founded 1816 **Pop** 57,483 **Elev** 507 ft **Area code** 812 **E-mail** thcvb @holli.com **Web** www.terrehaute.com

Information Terre Haute Convention & Visitors Bureau, 643 Wabash Ave, 47807; 812/234-5555 or 800/366-3043.

Terre Haute was founded as a river town on the lower Wabash River and has become an important industrial, financial, agricultural, educational and cultural center.

The plateau on which the city is built (27 square miles) was named *Terre Haute* (high land) by the French, who governed this area until 1763. The dividing line that separated the French provinces of Canada and Louisiana runs through this section. American settlers arrived with the establishment of Fort Harrison in 1811. In later years, it became a terminal for river trade on the Wabash, Ohio and Mississippi rivers to New Orleans. Many wagon trains with westbound settlers passed through here. The advance of the railroads made large-scale coal operations possible; Terre Haute became a railroad and coal mining center and developed a highly diversified industrial and manufacturing complex.

Novelist Theodore Dreiser, author of *Sister Carrie* and *An American Tragedy*, and his brother, Paul Dresser, composer of Indiana's state song, "On the Banks of the Wabash," lived here. Eugene V. Debs founded the American Railway Union, first industrial union in America, in Terre Haute. The city is also the home of Rose-Hulman Institute of Technology (1874).

What to See and Do

Children's Science & Technology Museum. Hands-on museum exhibits allow visitors, both young and old, to experience science, to explore the world around them and to understand today's ever changing technology. (Tues-Sat; closed Jan 1, Thanksgiving, Dec 25) 523 Wabash Ave. Phone 812/235-5548. ¢¢

Deming Park. 177 acres of wooded hills; swimming pool (June-Labor Day, fee), fishing; cross-country skiing (rentals), tennis, picnicking, concession; miniature train rides (wkends & hols, fee); water slide (fee), 18-hole Frisbee disc course. E end of Ohio Blvd at Fruitridge Ave. Phone 812/232-2727. **Free.**

Dobbs Park & Nature Center. Approx 100 acres. A 25-acre state nature preserve; 2½-acre lake, fishing; 4-acre wetlands area; 4 mi of nature trails; interpretive nature center; butterfly & hummingbird garden (June-Sept). Tree nursery. Picnicking (shelters). (Daily) 4 mi E via IN 42 at jct IN 46. Phone 812/877-1095. **Free.** Also here is

Native American Museum. Exhibits include dwellings, clothing, weapons and music of Eastern Woodland Native American cultures. Hands-on activities. Phone 812/877-6007. **Free.**

Eugene V. Debs Home. Restored home of the labor and Socialist leader; memorabilia. (Wed-Sun afternoons; slso by appt; closed hols) 451 N 8th St. Phone 812/232-2163 or 812/237-3443. **Free.**

Farrington's Grove Historical District. More than 800 residential dwellings in a 70-sq-blk area; homes dating from 1849.

Fowler Park Pioneer Village. An 1840s pioneer village with 12 log cabins, a general store, schoolhouse and gristmill. (Daily) 10654 Bono Rd. Phone 812/462-3391. **Free.**

Historical Museum of the Wabash Valley. Local exhibits in 15 rms of 1868 house; one-rm school, country store, military rm, dressmaker's shop. (Daily exc Mon; closed hols) 1411 S 6th St, at Washington Ave. Phone 812/235-9717. **Free.**

Indiana State University (1865). (11,500 students) Turman Gallery in the Center for Performing and Fine Arts has paintings, sculpture, ceramics, jewelry (Tues-Fri, Sun; free). Cunningham Memorial Library houses the Cordell Collection of rare and early English language dictionaries. Historic Condit House (1860), office of the university president, is an example of

Italianate architecture. Campus tours. Bounded by 3rd (US 41), 9th, Cherry & Tippecanoe Sts. For university events phone 812/237-3773.

Paul Dresser Birthplace State Shrine & Memorial. Restoration of mid-19th-century workingman's home; birthplace of Dresser, composer of popular songs. (May-Sept, Sun; also by appt) 1st & Farrington Sts in Fairbanks Park. Phone 812/235-9717.   **Free.**

Saint Mary-of-the-Woods College (1840). (1,245 students) On beautiful 67-acre campus. Nation's oldest Catholic liberal arts college for women. Tours by appt. 4¹/₂ mi NW on US 150. Phone 812/535-5212.

Sheldon Swope Art Museum. The museum's permanent collections range from ancient to contemporary art with a collection of 19th- and 20th-century American paintings and master prints. Special exhibits, films, lectures, classes and performing arts events. (Daily; closed hols) 25 S 7th St. Phone 812/238-1676.   **Free.**

Annual Events

Maple Sugarin' Days. Prairie Creek Park.Demonstrations of syrup-making process at syrup camp. Actual syrup-making takes place in hand-hewn log house (1852). Phone 812/462-3391 or 812/898-2279 (wkends). Early Feb-early Mar.

Wabash Valley Festival. Fairbanks Park. Flea market, carnival, entertainment. Last wk May. Phone 812/232-2727.

Frontier Day. Wabash Valley Fairgrounds, 2 mi S on US 41. Horse show, events. July 4.

Little Italy Festival. 12 mi N via IN 63, in Clinton. Italian food, carnival, music. Labor Day wkend.

Pioneer Days. 6 mi S via US 41. Old fashioned crafts demonstrated; pioneer exhibits. Phone 812/462-3391. 1st wkend Oct.

Motels

✔★ ★ **FAIRFIELD INN BY MARRIOTT.** *475 E Margaret Ave (47802), 5 mi S on US 41 at I-70. 812/235-2444.* 62 rms, 3 story. S, D $53.99-$59.99; each addl $6; suites $85.95-$95.95; under 18 free; higher rates Indy 500. Crib free. TV; cable (premium). Complimentary continental bkfst. Restaurant opp 6 am-10 pm. Ck-out noon. Business servs avail. In-rm modem link. Indoor pool; whirlpool. Some refrigerators, microwaves. Cr cds: A, C, D, DS, MC, V.

D ≋ ⊠ 🔥 SC

★ ★ **SIGNATURE INN.** *3033 Dixie Bee Rd (US 41S) (47802), I-70 & US 41. 812/238-1461; FAX 812/238-1461, ext. 500.* 157 rms, 3 story. S, D $62-$72; each addl $7; under 18 free; wkend rates; higher rates special events. Crib free. TV; cable (premium). Pool. Continental bkfst. Ck-out noon. Meeting rms. Business servs avail. In-rm modem link. Exercise equipt; weight machine, stair machine. Cr cds: A, C, D, DS, MC, V.

D ≋ ⊼ ⊠ 🔥 SC

Motor Hotels

★ ★ **DRURY INN.** *3040 S US 41 (47802), at I-70. 812/238-1206.* 153 rms, 7 story. S $58.95; D $68.95; each addl $10; suites $125; under 18 free; higher rates special events. Crib free. TV; cable. Indoor pool. Continental bkfst. Complimentary coffee in rms. Restaurant adj 6 am-10 pm. Ck-out noon. Meeting rms. Business servs avail. Bellhops. Sundries. Cr cds: A, C, D, DS, MC, V.

≋

★ ★ **HOLIDAY INN.** *3300 US 41 S (47802), at I-70. 812/232-6081; FAX 812/238-9934.* 230 rms, 2-5 story. S, D $84-$97; suites $115-$175; under 20 free; higher rates special events. Crib free. Pet accepted. TV; cable (premium). Indoor pool; whirlpool. Complimentary coffee in rms. Restaurant 6:30 am-2 pm, 5-10:30 pm. Rm serv. Bar 11-1 am. Ck-out noon. Guest lndry. Meeting rms. Business servs avail. In-rm modem link. Bellhops. Valet serv. Exercise equipt; weights, bicycle. Cr cds: A, C, D, DS, ER, JCB, MC, V.

D ✔ ≋ ⊼ ⊠ 🔥 SC

★ ★ **LARRY BIRD'S BOSTON CONNECTION.** *555 S 3rd St (US 41) (47807), downtown. 812/235-3333; FAX 812/232-9563; res: 800/255-3399 (IN), 800/262-0033 (exc IN).* 95 rms, 4 story. S $65; D $72; suites $107; under 18 free; higher rates special events. Crib free. TV; cable (premium). Heated pool. Restaurants 6:30 am-9 pm. Rm serv. Bar 11-2 am; entertainment Fri, Sat. Ck-out noon. Meeting rms. Business servs avail. Bellhops. Sundries. Gift shop. Free airport transportation. Health club privileges. Refrigerator avail. Cr cds: A, D, DS, MC, V.

≋

★ **PEAR TREE INN.** *3050 US 41S (S Third St) (47802), I-70 & US 41S. 812/234-4268; res: 800/282-8733.* 64 rms, 4 story. S $50.95; D $60.95; each addl $10; under 18 free. Crib free. TV; cable (premium). Ck-out noon. Business serv avail. Valet serv. Sundries. Health club privileges. Cr cds: A, C, D, DS, MC, V.

D ≋ 🔥 SC

Restaurant

★ **GERHARDT'S BIERSTUBE.** *1724 Lafayette (47804). 812/466-9249.* Hrs: 11 am-2 pm, 4-9 pm; Fri to 10 pm; Sat, Sun 4-10 pm. Closed Mon; major hols. Res accepted. German menu. Bar. Semi-a la carte: lunch $2-$5.75, dinner $6.50-$14. Specializes in sauerbraten, Wienerschnitzel. German country inn atmosphere. Cr cds: A, DS, MC, V.

Tippecanoe River State Park (B-3)

(For accommodations see Plymouth)

(5 mi N of Winamac on US 35)

One of Indiana's larger state parks, its 2,761 acres stretch for more than 7 miles along the Tippecanoe River, on the east side of US 35. (The area west of the highway is operated by the Division of Fish and Wildlife as Winamac State Fish and Wildlife Area.)

Tippecanoe is ideal for outdoor enthusiasts, with its oak forests, pine plantations, fields, winding roads, marshes and an occasional sand dune. Fishing; boating (launch). Hiking, bridle trails. Cross-country skiing. Picnicking (shelter), playground. Camping (electrical hookups) & horseback camping. Group camping. Naturalist service (May-Aug). View from fire tower. Standard fees. (Daily) Phone 219/946-3213. Per vehicle   ¢¢

Turkey Run State Park (E-2)

(2 mi N of Marshall on IN 47)

This is a 2,382-acre wooded area. Within the park are deep, rock-walled prehistoric canyons and winding streams that twist through solid rock. Canoeing and fishing in Sugar Creek for bluegill, crappie and rock bass. Hiking trails (13.5 mi) lead through canyons, along cliffs and into forests. An historic house, built by one of the area's first settlers, is open for tours (seasonal).

Facilities include swimming pool. Hiking, saddle barn. Tennis. Picnicking, concession (summer). Trailer camping. Nature Center (daily; winter, wkends only); bird observation room. Planetarium. Naturalist service. Standard fees. (Daily) Phone 317/597-2635. Per vehicle   ¢¢

Motel

★ **TURKEY RUN INN.** *(RR 1, Marshall 47859) 2 mi E of jct IN 47 & US 41, in Turkey Run State Park.* 765/597-2211; FAX 765/597-2660. 82 rms, 3 story. S $47.30; D $51.70; suites $62.70; higher rates wknds. TV; VCR avail. Indoor pool. Playground. Supervised child's activities. Restaurant 7 am-8 pm. Ck-out noon. Meeting rms. Business servs avail. Gift shop. Lighted tennis. Game rm. Picnic tables, grills in park. Hiking trails; nature center. 9 & 18-hole golf courses nearby, pro. 2 lakes & Sugar Creek nearby. Cr cds: A, DS, MC, V.

[D] [symbols]

Valparaiso (B-3)

(See also Hammond, La Porte, Portage)

Founded 1865 **Pop** 24,414 **Elev** 738 ft **Area code** 219 **Zip** 46383 **E-mail** gvcc@netnitco.net
Information Chamber of Commerce, 150 Centier Square, Suite 1005, PO Box 330, 46384; 219/462-1105.

Annual Events

Porter County Fair. Porter County Expo Center. Late July.

Popcorn Festival. Downtown. Parade, 5-mi Fun Run; arts & crafts, entertainment, hot air balloon show. Phone 219/464-8332. 1st Sat after Labor Day.

Motels

★★ **COURTYARD BY MARRIOTT.** *2301 E US 30 (Morthland Ave).* 219/465-1700; FAX 219/477-2430. 111 rms, 2 story. S, D $72-$99; suites $79-$129. Crib free. TV; cable (premium). Indoor/outdoor pool. Ck-out noon. Meeting rm. Business servs avail. In-rm modem link. Valet serv. Sundries. Exercise equipt; bicycle, stair machine. Cr cds: A, C, D, DS, JCB, MC, V.

[D] [symbols] SC

✔★★ **HOLIDAY INN EXPRESS.** *760 Morthland Dr (US 30).* 219/464-8555. 54 rms, 4 story. S, D $59-$89; higher rates university related events. Crib free. TV; cable (premium). Complimentary continental bkfst. Restaurant nearby. Ck-out noon. Business servs avail. Exercise equipt; weight machine, treadmill. Cr cds: A, C, D, DS, MC, V.

[D] [symbols] SC

Vincennes (H-2)

Founded 1732 **Pop** 19,859 **Elev** 429 ft **Area code** 812 **Zip** 47591
Information Vincennes Area Chamber of Commerce, 27 N 3rd St, PO Box 553; 812/882-6440 or 800/886-6443.

This city on the banks of the Wabash River is the oldest town in Indiana. French fur traders roamed through the region as early as 1683, established a trading post and were soon followed by settlers. Fort Vincennes was built by French troops under Francis Morgamme de Vincennes in 1732. It was turned over to British control in 1763, but many of the French settlers (who frequently intermarried with Native Americans) remained in the area. In 1778, the State of Virginia furnished $12,000 and 7 companies of militia to 25-year-old George Rogers Clark and directed him to secure all land northwest of the Ohio River for Virginia. Clark's troops seized Fort Sackville in the summer of 1778, but it fell back into British hands several months later. The second and final capture of Vincennes by Clark the following year opened up the entire Northwest Territory. In 1784 the territory was ceded by Virginia to the United States and became a public domain. Vincennes was, from 1800-1813, the capital of the Indiana Territory; between 1808 and 1811 several meetings and negotiations took place here between Governor William H. Harrison and the famous Shawnee Chief Tecumseh and his brother, The Prophet. During the 18th century the town was almost entirely populated by descendants of the French founders. After 1800 a large number of Easterners and German families settled in Vincennes and advanced farming, local business and industry. The first newspaper in the Indiana Territory, the *Indiana Gazette,* was published here in 1804.

Today Vincennes is a Midwest shipping and trading center and the seat of Knox County—notable for its melons and livestock raising. For recreation, the Wabash River offers fishing and boating.

What to See and Do

Fort Knox II. Military post built and garrisoned by new American nation during early 1800s to protect western frontier prior to Battle of Tippecanoe. As tensions on the frontier increased, additional troops were gathered here, the fort having been hurriedly enlarged and strengthened by Captain Zachary Taylor in 1810. The outline of the fort is marked for self-guided tours. (Daily) 3 mi N via Fort Knox Rd.   **Free.**

George Rogers Clark National Historical Park. Memorial building (daily) commemorates the George Rogers Clark campaign during the American Revolution. Includes the site of Fort Sackville, captured from the British by Clark's force in 1779. Visitor center with museum exhibits (daily; closed Jan 1, Thanksgiving, Dec 25); film shown every half-hr. Downtown off US 50 & US 41. For information phone 812/882-1776.   ¢

Indiana Military Museum. Extensive and varied collection of military memorabilia. Military vehicles, artillery, uniforms, insignia, equipment and related artifacts spanning the Civil War to Desert Storm. Museum (May-Sept, Mon-Fri, afternoons; winter and wkends by appt; closed Jan 1, Thanksgiving, Dec 25; outdoor display (summer, daily). 4305 Bruceville Rd. Phone 812/882-8668.   ¢

Indiana Territory Site. From this 2-story capitol building, an area consisting of the present states of Indiana, Illinois, Michigan, Wisconsin and a part of Minnesota was governed in 1811. A replica of the first newspaper printing shop in Indiana is also here, where Elihu Stout first issued the *Indiana Gazette* in 1804. Nearby is the **Maurice Thompson Birthplace,** restored 1842 home of author of *Alice of Old Vincennes.* Tours (Mid-Mar-mid-Dec, Wed-Sun). First & Harrison Sts. Phone 812/882-7422.   ¢

Kimmell Park. Camping (hookups; fee); boating (ramp); fishing; picnicking. (May-Oct) Oliphant Dr. Phone 812/882-1140.

Log Cabin Visitors Center. (Mid-Mar-mid-Dec, Wed-Sun) Phone 812/882-7422.   **Free.**

Michel Brouillet Old French House (ca 1806). French Creole house; period furniture. (May-Sept, Thurs-Sun) 509 First St. Phone 812/882-7886. ¢

Old State Bank, Indiana State Memorial (1839). Operated as a bank until 1877; the oldest bank building in Indiana. Guided tours (Mid-Mar-mid-Dec, Wed-Sun; closed hols) Busseron & 2nd Sts. Phone 812/882-7422.   ¢

Ouabache Trails Park. Two picnicking areas (6 shelters); camping (tent & trailer sites, hookups, dump station); interpretive center. Nature & hiking trails. Sand volleyball court, horseshoe pits. Approx 250 acres of wooded area bordered on west by Wabash River. Contact Knox County Parks & Recreation Dept, RR 6, Box 227H; 812/882-4316. Camping (mid-Apr-late Oct)   ¢¢¢

The Old Cathedral Minor Basilica (1826). (Daily) 2nd & Church Sts. Phone 812/882-5638. **Donation.** Behind the cathedral is St Rose Chapel and

The Old French Cemetery. William Clark, Judge of the Indiana Territory, was buried here in 1802; also local Frenchmen who served in George Rogers Clark's army (1778-1779). Adj to the cathedral is

Old Cathedral Library and Museum (1794). Indiana's oldest library; more than 12,000 documents, books, artworks—some dating from 1400s. (By appt) **Donation.**

Vincennes University (1801). (7,000 students) A junior college established as Jefferson Academy; first land-grant college in the Indiana Territory. Tours. 1st & College Sts. Phone 812/888-8888.

William Henry Harrison Mansion (Grouseland) (1803-1804). Residence of the 9th President of the US while he was governor of the Indiana Territory; first brick building constructed in Indiana; 1803-1812 period furnishings. (Daily; closed Jan 1, Thanksgiving, Dec 25) 3 W Scott St, opp Indiana Territorial Capitol. Phone 812/882-2096. ¢¢

Annual Events

Spirit of Vincennes Rendezvous. Old French Commons, at Willow St & River Rd. 1700-1840 era encampment and battle re-enactment. Phone 812/882-7079. Memorial Day wkend.

Indiana State Chili Cook-off. Patrick Henry Dr, downtown. Chili cooking contest, sanctioned by Intl Chili Society. Winner advances to national cook-off. Phone 812/882-6440. 1-day event. Early or mid-Sept.

Wabash (C-5)

(For accommodations see Huntington, Marion; also see Peru)

Founded 1834 **Pop** 12,127 **Elev** 700 ft **Area code** 219 **Zip** 46992 **E-mail** wabcocvb@ctlnet.com **Web** www.communinet.org/cvb

Information Wabash County Convention & Visitors Bureau, 111 S Wabash, PO Box 746; 800/563-1169.

On March 31, 1880, the Wabash Courthouse was illuminated by four electric carbon lamps. Wabash thus became the first electrically illuminated city in the world. This is the hometown of Mark C. Honeywell, founder of the Honeywell Corporation, and country singer Crystal Gayle.

The hill from which the town overlooks the Wabash River was, in 1826, the site of the signing of the Paradise Spring Treaty, by which Chief Pierish of the Potawatomi ceded the land between the Wabash and Eel Rivers to the US government for cultivation by white settlers.

In 1835, a section of the Wabash and Erie Canal was dug through this area. Much of the work was done by immigrant Irish laborers who brought with them long-smoldering differences from the old country. On July 12, about 300 men from County Cork and a roughly equal number from the north of Ireland decided to settle old scores by fighting a battle near the present site of Wabash. The first shots had been fired when the state militia arrived and separated the two groups by force.

What to See and Do

Honeywell Center. Historic art deco building is a community center with cultural and recreational facilities; gallery; special events, concerts. Fee for some activities. (Daily; closed hols) 275 W Market St. Phone 800/626-6345. **Free.**

Salamonie Reservoir, Dam & Forest. Observation mound & nature center at Army Corps of Engineers project (daily; phone 219/782-2181). Several state recreation areas provide camping on 2,860-acre lake; also picnicking, fishing, waterskiing, hunting, swimming, hiking trails, boating, launching sites (fee) and ramps (Memorial Day-Labor Day). 7 mi NE on US 24 to Lagro, then 5 mi SE on IN 524. Contact office at Lost Bridge West State Recreation Area, 10 mi NE via US 24, then 8 mi S on IN 105 (daily); phone 219/468-2125. The state forest offers picnicking, camping and fishing in Hominy Ridge, 11-acre lake; phone 219/782-2349. Fishing below the Salamonie Reservoir Dam; phone 219/782-2181 or 219/468-2125. Standard fees at all ramps. Entrance fee at Lost Bridge West only.

Wabash County Historical Museum. Items include records and artifacts from the periods of Native American occupation, pioneer settlement and the Civil War; research materials include local newspapers dating from 1846. (Tues-Sat; closed hols) Memorial Hall, W Hill & Miami Sts, W of courthouse. Phone 219/563-0661. **Free.**

Warsaw (B-5)

(For accommodations see Nappanee)

Pop 10,968 **Elev** 828 ft **Area code** 219 **Zip** 46580 **E-mail** kccvb@kconline.com

Information Kosciusko County Convention & Visitors Bureau, 313 S Buffalo St; 219/269-6090 or 800/800-6090.

Warsaw is in the heart of the Indiana lake region and primarily a vacation resort. Many fine lakes in surrounding Kosciusko County have excellent swimming and boating facilities; fish are plentiful.

Local industry manufactures surgical supplies and movie projection screens; located here is one of the largest rotogravure printing plants in the US. Kosciusko County is also home to the world's largest duck producer, Maple Leaf Farms. One mile southeast, in Winona Lake, is Grace College (1948) and Seminary (1937).

What to See and Do

Tippecanoe Lake. Secluded 4-mi-long lake with recreational facilities. This is Indiana's deepest natural lake. 6 mi N on IN 15, then 4 mi E.

Annual Event

Back to the Days of Kosciuszko. Re-enactment of the Revolutionary War era. Food of the period, crafts, demonstrations. Participants in period clothing. Phone 219/269-6090. Mid-Oct.

Motel

★ ★ **COMFORT INN.** 2605 E Center St. 219/267-7337. 60 rms, 2 story, 8 suites. S, D $65-$79; suites $79-$129; higher rates special events. Crib free. Pet accepted; $50 deposit. TV; cable (premium). Complimentary continental bkfst. Restaurant nearby. Ck-out noon. Business servs avail. In-rm modem link. Valet serv. Health club privileges. Heated pool. In-rm whirlpool, refrigerator, microwave in suites. Picnic tables, grills. Cr cds: A, C, D, DS, MC, V.

D ⟨⟩ ≈ ⟨⟩ SC

Motor Hotel

★ ★ **RAMADA INN.** 2519 E Center St. 219/269-2323; FAX 219/269-2432. 156 rms, 4 story. S, D $76-$88; each addl $10; suites $95-$115; under 12 free; higher rates summer wknds. Crib free. Pet accepted. TV; cable, VCR avail. Complimentary coffee in rms. Restaurant 7-10:30 am, 11 am-2 pm, 5-10 pm. Rm serv. Bar. Ck-out noon. Meeting rms. Business servs avail. In-rm modem link. Valet serv. Sundries. Coin lndry. 18-hole golf privileges, pro. Exercise equipt; weights, stair machine, sauna. Indoor/outdoor pool; whirlpool, poolside serv. Game rm. Rec rm. Microwaves avail. Cr cds: A, C, D, DS, MC, V.

D ⟨⟩ ⟨⟩ ≈ ⟨⟩

Inn

★ ★ **WHITE HILL MANOR.** 2513 E Center St. 219/269-6933; FAX 219/268-1936. 8 rms, 2 with shower only, 2 story. S $70-$99; D $80-$120; each addl $15. Children over 12 yrs only. Pet accepted. TV; VCR avail (movies). Complimentary full bkfst. Complimentary coffee in rms. Restaurant nearby. Ck-out 11 am, ck-in 3 pm. Business servs avail. In-rm modem link. X-country ski 5 mi. Lawn games. Microwaves avail. Picnic tables, grills. Built in 1934; restored English Tudor manor. Totally nonsmoking. Cr cds: A, C, D, DS, MC, V.

D ⟨⟩ ≈ ⟨⟩

Wyandotte (J-4)

(For accommodations see Corydon, New Albany)

Pop 50 (est) **Elev** 760 ft **Area code** 812 **Zip** 47179

What to See and Do

Little Wyandotte Cave. Large variety of cave life and formations. Impressively illuminated. Guided tours (30-45-min). (Memorial Day-Labor Day, daily; rest of yr, daily exc Mon; closed Jan 1, Easter, Thanksgiving, Dec 25) On IN 62, 2 mi S of I-64 via IN 66 or IN 135. Phone 812/738-2782. ¢¢

⍟ **Wyandotte Caves.** Approx 7 mi of mapped passages. Features include Garden of Helictites, a large collection of gravity-defying formations; Rothrock's Cathedral, an underground mountain 105 ft high, 140 ft wide, 360 ft long; and Pillar of the Constitution, a stalagmite approx 35 ft high and 71 ft in circumference. The cave was used by prehistoric Native Americans for mining aragonite and is known to have been the source of saltpeter and Epsom salts around 1812. Jacket recommended, cave temperature 52°F. One-hr guided tours (Memorial Day-Labor Day, daily). Two-hr guided tours (Memorial Day-Labor Day, daily; rest of yr, daily exc Mon; closed Jan 1, Easter, Thanksgiving, Dec 25). Three-, five- and eight-hr tours (Sat & Sun, by res only). On IN 62, 2 mi S of I-64 via either IN 66 or IN 135. Phone 812/738-2782. ¢¢¢

Michigan

Population: 9,295,297
Land area: 56,954 square miles
Elevation: 570-1,980 feet
Highest point: Mt Arvon (Baraga County)
Entered Union: January 26, 1837 (26th state)
Capital: Lansing
Motto: If you seek a pleasant peninsula, look around you
Nickname: Wolverine State
State flower: Apple blossom
State bird: Robin
State tree: White pine
State fair: August 18-31, 1998, in Detroit
Time zone: Eastern and Central (Menominee, Dickinson, Iron and Gogebic counties)
Web: www.travel-michigan.state.mi.us

Michigan has a mighty industrial heritage and is well-known as the birthplace of the automobile industry, but rivaling the machines, mines and mills is the more than $8 billion-a-year tourist industry. The two great Michigan peninsulas, surrounded by four of the five Great Lakes, unfold a tapestry of lakeshore beaches, trout-filled streams, more than 11,000 inland lakes, nearly 7 million acres of public hunting grounds—and the cultural attractions of Dearborn, Detroit, Ann Arbor, Grand Rapids and other cities.

Michigan has a geographically split personality linked by a single—but magnificent—bridge. The Upper Peninsula faces Lake Superior on one side and Lake Michigan on the other. It revels in its north-country beauty and ruggedness. The Lower Peninsula has shores on lakes Michigan, Huron and Erie. Its highly productive Midwestern-style farmland is dotted with diversified cities.

Michigan is a four-season vacationland, with the tempering winds off the Great Lakes taming what might otherwise be a climate of extremes. In a land of cherry blossoms, tulips, ski slopes and sugar-sand beaches, you can fish through the ice, hunt deer with a bow and arrow, follow a pack of dogs on the trail of a bobcat, rough it on an uncluttered island, trace Native American paths or hunt for copper, iron ore and Lake Superior agates or Petoskey stones. One of the country's finest art museums is in Detroit, and Dearborn's Henry Ford Museum and historic Greenfield Village attract visitors from all over the world. Michigan has an increasing array of challenging resort golf courses as well as more than 700 public courses. Ann Arbor, Detroit and East Lansing offer outstanding universities.

A world center for automobile manufacture, Michigan leads in the production of automobiles and light trucks. More than two-thirds of the nation's tart red cherries are harvested here; so are more than 90 percent of the dry edible beans. This state is also one of the nation's leading producers of blueberries. Wheat, hay, corn, oats, turkeys, cattle and hogs are produced in vast quantities. The Soo Locks at Sault Ste Marie boast the two longest locks in the world that can accommodate superfreighters 1,000 feet long.

French explorers were the first known Europeans to penetrate the lakes, rivers and streams of Michigan. In their wake came armies of trappers eager to barter with the natives and platoons of soldiers to guard the newly acquired territory. Frenchmen and Native Americans teamed to unsuccessfully fight the British, who in turn were forced to retreat into Canada after the American colonies successfully revolted. The British briefly forged into Michigan again during the War of 1812, retreating finally to become Michigan's good neighbors in Canada.

There has been a wavelike pattern to Michigan's economic development. First there were the trees that created a great lumber industry. These were rapidly depleted. The copper and iron-ore mines followed. They also are now mostly inactive, although the discovery of new copper deposits is leading to renewed activity. Finally, the automobile industry, diversified industries and tourism have become successful. Today, the St Lawrence Seaway makes the cities of Michigan international ports and the state's future a prosperous one.

When to Go/Climate

Long, hard winters and hot, humid summers are common on Michigan's Upper Peninsula. The Lower Peninsula benefits from the moderating influence of the Great Lakes. Summers are warm; and brilliant fall foliage spreads southward from the Upper Peninsula beginning in September.

AVERAGE HIGH/LOW TEMPERATURES (°F)

DETROIT

Jan 30/16	May 70/47	Sept 74/53
Feb 33/18	June 79/56	Oct 62/41
Mar 44/27	July 83/61	Nov 48/32
Apr 58/37	Aug 81/60	Dec 35/21

GRAND RAPIDS

Jan 29/15	May 69/46	Sept 72/50
Feb 32/16	June 79/55	Oct 60/39
Mar 43/25	July 83/60	Nov 46/30
Apr 57/35	Aug 81/58	Dec 34/21

SAULT STE MARIE

Jan 21/5	May 63/38	Sept 66/44
Feb 23/5	June 71/46	Oct 54/36
Mar 33/15	July 76/51	Nov 40/26
Apr 48/28	Aug 74/51	Dec 26/12

Parks and Recreation Finder

Directions to and information about the parks and recreation areas below are given under their respective town/city sections. Please refer to those sections for details.

Key to abbreviations: I.P. = Interstate Park; N.B.C. = National Battlefield & Cemetery; N.B.P. = National Battlefield Park; N.F. = National Forest; N.G. = National Grassland; N.H. = National Historical Park; N.H.S. = National Historic Site; N.M. = National Monument; N.Mem. = National Memorial; N.M.P. = National Military Park; N.P. = National Park; N.Pres. = National Preserve; N.R. = National Recreational Area; N.R.R. = National Recreational River; N.S. = National Seashore; N.S.T. = National Scenic Trail; N.V.M. = National Volcanic Monument; S.B. = State Beach; S.C.P. = State Conservation Park; S.G. = State Garden; S.H.A. = State Historic Area; S.H.P. = State Historic Park; S.N.A. = State Natural Area; S.P. = State Park; S.R. = State Reserve; S.R.A. = State Recreation Area; S.Res.P. = State Resort Park; S.R.P. = State Rustic Park.

NATIONAL PARK AND RECREATION AREAS

Place Name	Listed Under
Hiawatha N.F.	ESCANABA
Huron-Manistee N.F.	MANISTEE, OSCODA
Isle Royale N.P.	same
Ottawa N.F.	IRONWOOD
Pictured Rocks National Lakeshore	MUNISING
Sleeping Bear Dunes National Lakeshore	same

STATE RECREATION AREAS

Place Name	Listed Under
Albert E. Sleeper S.P.	PORT AUSTIN
Aloha S.P.	CHEBOYGAN
Bay City S.R.A.	BAY CITY
Burt Lake S.P.	INDIAN RIVER
Cheboygan S.P.	CHEBOYGAN
Fayette S.P.	MANISTIQUE
Fort Custer S.R.A.	BATTLE CREEK
Fort Wilkins S.P.	COPPER HARBOR
Grand Haven S.P.	GRAND HAVEN
Hartwick Pines S.P.	GRAYLING
Highland S.R.A.	PONTIAC
Holland S.P.	HOLLAND
Indian Lake S.P.	MANISTIQUE
Interlochen S.P.	TRAVERSE CITY
J.W. Wells S.P.	MENOMINEE
Lakeport S.P.	PORT HURON
Ludington S.P.	LUDINGTON
Muskegon S.P.	MUSKEGON
Orchard Beach S.P.	MANISTEE
Otsego Lake S.P.	GAYLORD
Palms Book S.P.	MANISTIQUE
Petoskey S.P.	PETOSKEY
P.J. Hoffmaster S.P.	MUSKEGON
Pontiac Lake S.R.A.	PONTIAC
Porcupine Mountains Wilderness S.P.	ONTONAGON
Sterling S.P.	MONROE
Tahquamenon Falls S.P.	NEWBERRY
Van Buren S.P.	SOUTH HAVEN
Van Riper S.P.	ISHPEMING
Warren Dunes S.P.	ST JOSEPH
Waterloo S.R.A.	JACKSON
Wilderness S.P.	MACKINAW CITY
William Mitchell S.P.	CADILLAC
Wilson S.P.	HARRISON

Water-related activities, hiking, riding, various other sports, picnicking and visitor centers, as well as camping, are available in many of these areas. Motor vehicle permits are required to enter parks: $4/day (exc Warren Dunes, $5/day for nonresidents); annual sticker: $20. From May through September, about 80% of the campsites in each park are available by reservation for stays of 1-15 nights. The fee is $6-$14/night. Pets on leash only. For reservations phone 800/44-PARKS. For reservation applications and further information about state parks, contact Dept of Natural Resources, Parks and Recreation Division, PO Box 30257, Lansing 48909-7757; 517/373-9900. For information on state forests, contact Dept of Natural Resources, Forest Management Division, PO Box 30452, Lansing 48909; 517/373-1275.

SKI AREAS

Place Name	Listed Under
Alpine Valley Ski Resort	PONTIAC
Big Powderhorn Mt Ski Area	IRONWOOD
Binder Park	BATTLE CREEK
Bittersweet Ski Area	KALAMAZOO
Blackjack Ski Area	IRONWOOD
Boyne Highlands Ski Area	HARBOR SPRINGS
Boyne Mountain Ski Area	BOYNE CITY
Caberfae Peaks Ski Resort	CADILLAC
Cannonsburg Ski Area	GRAND RAPIDS
Chalet Cross-Country Ski Area	CLARE
Crystal Mountain Resort	BEULAH
Hickory Hills Ski Area	TRAVERSE CITY
Indianhead Mountain-Bear Creek Ski Resort	WAKEFIELD
Jasper Mountain	HARRISON
Maasto Hiihto Ski Trail	HANCOCK
Marquette Mt Ski Area	MARQUETTE
Mont Ripley Ski Area	HOUGHTON
Mt Holly Ski Area	HOLLY
Mt Zion Ski Area	IRONWOOD
Nub's Nob Ski Area	HARBOR SPRINGS
Pando Ski Area	GRAND RAPIDS
Pine Mt Lodge	IRON MOUNTAIN
Porcupine Mts Wilderness State Park	ONTONAGON
Shanty Creek Resort	BELLAIRE
Ski Brule	IRON RIVER
Skyline Ski Area	GRAYLING
Snowsnake Mountain	HARRISON
Sugar Loaf Resort	TRAVERSE CITY
Swiss Valley Ski Area	THREE RIVERS
Timber Ridge Ski Area	KALAMAZOO
Treetops Sylvan Resort	GAYLORD

FISHING & HUNTING

In the 1960s coho and chinook salmon were transplanted from the Pacific Northwest into the streams feeding into Lake Michigan and subsequently into lakes Huron and Superior. The success of the program was immediate and today salmon fishing, especially for chinook, is a major sport. Chinook fishing is good throughout the summer in the Great Lakes and through the early fall during the spawning season in the rivers; the fish may weigh as much as 45 pounds. Information on charter boat fishing can be obtained from Travel Michigan, Michigan Jobs Commission, PO Box 3393, Livonia 48151; 800/543-2YES.

Nonresident restricted fishing licenses: annual $26; all-species fishing including spike, salmon and brook, brown, rainbow and lake trout: $39. A fishing license for all waters is required for everyone 17 years of age and older. Resident and nonresident 24-hour fishing license $6.

Nonresident hunting licenses: small game $60; deer $120; bear $150; archery (deer only) $120. For further information on hunting and fishing, write Dept of Natural Resources, Retail Sections, PO Box 30181, Lansing 48909; phone 517/373-1204.

Driving Information

Safety belts are mandatory for all persons in front seat of vehicle. Children ages 4-16 must be in an approved passenger restraint anywhere in vehicle. Children ages 1-4 may use a regulation safety belt in back seat, but must use an approved safety seat in front seat of vehicle. Children under age 1 must use an approved safety seat anywhere in vehicle. For further information phone Office of Highway Safety Planning, 517/336-6477.

INTERSTATE HIGHWAY SYSTEM

The following alphabetical listing of Michigan towns in *Mobil Travel Guide* shows that these cities are within 10 miles of the indicated Interstate highways. A highway map, however, should be checked for the nearest exit.

Highway Number	Cities/Towns within 10 miles
INTERSTATE 69	Coldwater, Flint, Lansing, Marshall, Owosso, Port Huron.
INTERSTATE 75	Bay City, Birmingham, Bloomfield Hills, Cheboygan, Dearborn, Detroit, Flint, Frankenmuth, Gaylord, Grayling, Holly, Mackinaw City, Monroe, Pontiac, Saginaw, St Ignace, Sault Ste Marie, Warren.
INTERSTATE 94	Ann Arbor, Battle Creek, Dearborn, Detroit, Jackson, Kalamazoo, Marshall, Mount Clemens, Port Huron, St Clair, St Joseph, Warren, Ypsilanti.
INTERSTATE 96	Detroit, Grand Haven, Grand Rapids, Lansing, Muskegon.

Additional Visitor Information

Travel Michigan, Michigan Jobs Commission, PO Box 30226, Lansing 48909; phone 800/543-2YES, distributes publications including an annual travel planner, seasonal travel guides and calendars of events, and directories of lodgings, campgrounds, golf courses and charter boat and canoe companies. Travel counselors are available to assist in planning a Michigan getaway.

There are 13 Welcome Centers in Michigan, open daily; visitors who stop will find information, brochures and an extensive database of lodging facilities and attractions most helpful in planning stops at points of interest. Their locations are as follows: Clare, off US 27; Coldwater, off I-69; Dundee, off US 23; Iron Mountain, off US 2; Ironwood, off US 2; Mackinaw City, off I-75; Marquette, off US 41; Menominee, off US 41/MI 35; Monroe, off I-75; New Buffalo, off I-94; Port Huron, off I-94; St Ignace, off I-75; and Sault Ste Marie, off I-75.

Alma (H-4)

(See also Mount Pleasant)

Pop 9,034 **Elev** 736 ft **Area code** 517 **Zip** 48801

Information Chamber of Commerce, 110 W Superior St, PO Box 516; 517/463-5525.

What to See and Do

Alma College (1886). (1,250 students) An 87-acre campus. Campus tours. 190,000-volume library. Frank Knox Memorial Room in Reid-Knox building has mementos of former secretary of the Navy (by appt). 614 W Superior St. Phone 517/463-7111.

Annual Event

Highland Festival & Games. Bahlke Field at Alma College. Piping, drumming, fiddling, Ceilidh, dancing; caber toss, sheaf toss, hammer throw competitions; art fair, parade. Memorial Day wkend.

Motels

★ ★ **COMFORT INN.** 3110 W Monroe Rd. 517/463-4400; FAX 517/463-2970. 87 rms, 2 story. S, D $49-$89; each addl $5; under 18 free. Crib free. TV; cable (premium), VCR avail (movies). Indoor pool; whirlpool. Complimentary continental bkfst. Restaurant 4:30-10 pm; closed Sun, Mon. Rm serv. Bar. Ck-out 11 am. Meeting rms. Business servs avail. Valet serv. Some bathrm phones. Cr cds: A, C, D, DS, ER, MC, V.

★ **PETTICOAT INN.** 2454 W Monroe Rd. 517/681-5728. 11 rms. S $32-$36; D $36-$40; each addl $3; higher rates special events. Pet accepted. TV; cable (premium). Restaurant adj open 24 hrs. Ck-out 11 am. Country setting. Cr cds: A, DS, MC, V.

Alpena (E-5)

Pop 11,354 **Elev** 593 ft **Area code** 517 **Zip** 49707 **E-mail** alpenacv @northland.lib.mi.us **Web** www.oweb.com/upnorth/cvb

Information Convention and Visitors Bureau, 235 W Chisholm St, PO Box 65; 517/354-4181 or 800/4-ALPENA.

Located at the head of Thunder Bay, Alpena is a center for industry as well as recreation. Approximately 80 shipwrecks have occurred in this area, making it an excellent diving location.

What to See and Do

Dinosaur Gardens Prehistorical Zoo. One man's authentic reproductions of prehistoric birds and animals. (Mid-May-mid-Oct, daily) 11168 US 23, 10 mi S in Ossineke. Phone 517/471-5477. ¢¢

Island Park and Alpena Wildfowl Sanctuary. Intown wildfowl sanctuary and self-guided nature trails, fishing platforms and picnic area. US 23 N.

Jesse Besser Museum. Historical exhibits feature agricultural, lumber and early industrial era; reconstructed avenue of 1890 shops and businesses; restored cabins, Maltz Exchange Bank (1872), Green School (1895). Jesse Besser exhibit. Science exhibits include geology, natural history and archaeological displays. Also planetarium, shows (Sun; fee). Museum (daily; closed major hols). 491 Johnson St, 2 blks E off US 23. Phone 517/356-2202. ¢

Old Presque Isle Lighthouse and Museum. Nautical instruments, marine artifacts and other antiques housed in lighthouse and keeper's cottage (1840). Antiques from mid-1800s. (May-mid-Oct, daily) 23 mi N via US 23 on Presque Isle. Phone 517/595-2787. ¢

Annual Events

"Art on the Bay"—Thunder Bay Art Show. Bay View Park. 3rd wkend July.

Brown Trout Festival. Phone 517/354-4181. 3rd full wk July.

Alpena County Fair. Alpena County Fairgrounds. 1st wk Aug.

Motels

✔★ ★ **BEST WESTERN.** 1286 M-32 West (MI 32W). 517/356-9087. 36 rms, 1-2 story. Late May-Oct: S $40; D $46-$52; each addl $6; under 12 free; lower rates rest of yr. Crib $4. TV; cable (premium). Indoor

pool; whirlpool. Restaurant adj 7 am-9 pm. Bar. Ck-out 11 am. Sundries. Game rm. Cr cds: A, C, D, DS, MC, V.

★ **FLETCHER'S.** 1001 US 23N. 517/354-4191; FAX 517/354-4056; res: 800/334-5920. 96 rms, 2 story. June-Oct: S $55; D $61; each addl $6; suites $100; kit. units $75; under 16 free; wkly rates; lower rates rest of yr. Crib $6. Pet accepted. TV; cable, VCR avail. Indoor pool; whirlpool, sauna. Restaurant 7 am-10 pm. Rm serv. Bar 11-2 am; Sun from noon. Ck-out 11 am. Meeting rms. Bellhops. Free airport, bus depot transportation. Tennis. Nature trail. Refrigerators; some in-rm whirlpools. Some balconies. Grills. Overlooks wooded acres. Cr cds: A, C, D, DS, ER, MC, V.

Motor Hotel

★ ★ **HOLIDAY INN.** 1000 Chisholm (US 23N). 517/356-2151. 148 rms, 2 story. S $65-$95; D $75-$105; each addl $10; studio rms $95; under 19 free. Crib free. Pet accepted. TV; cable. Indoor pool; whirlpool, poolside serv. Restaurant 6:30 am-2 pm, 5-10 pm. Rm serv. Bar 4 pm-2 am; entertainment. Ck-out noon. Coin lndry. Meeting rms. Business servs avail. Bellhops. Valet serv. Sundries. Gift shop. Free airport, bus depot transportation. Putting green. X-country ski 8 mi. Exercise equipt; bicycle, stair machine, sauna. Game rm. Cr cds: A, C, D, DS, ER, JCB, MC, V.

Restaurant

★ ★ **THUNDERBIRD INN.** 1100 State St (US 23). 517/354-8900. Hrs: 11 am-9 pm. Closed Sun; major hols. Bar. Semi-a la carte: lunch $1.95-$6.45, dinner $6-$20. Specializes in seafood, steak, prime rib. Cr cds: MC, V.

Ann Arbor (J-5)

(See also Dearborn, Detroit, Jackson, Ypsilanti)

Settled 1823 **Pop** 109,592 **Elev** 840 ft **Area code** 734 **E-mail** a2info @annarbor.org **Web** www.annarbor.org

Information Convention & Visitors Bureau, 120 W Huron, 48104; 734/995-7281 or 800/888-9487.

Most famous as the home of the University of Michigan, Ann Arbor has a college-town atmosphere enjoyed by both students and residents. The community's economy is diversified, with more than 100 research and high-technology firms.

There are two interesting theories about the origin of the town's unusual name. One explanation is that two of the pioneer settlers had wives named Ann who liked to sit together under a wild grape arbor—hence, "Ann Arbor." The other theory, recognized by many historians, claims that the latter part of the name came from the many openings, or, in those days, "arbors," which appeared in the thick forests covering the nearby hills. The "arbors" were said to have resulted from agricultural methods of the Native Americans.

What to See and Do

Huron-Clinton Metroparks. A regional park system with 13 recreation areas located along the Huron and Clinton rivers in southeast Michigan. A motor vehicle entry permit, which is good at all metroparks, is required (free on Tues). (Also see FARMINGTON, MOUNT CLEMENS, TROY) Entry permit ¢-¢¢

Delhi. On this 50-acre site are the Delhi Rapids. Fishing; canoeing, rentals (May-Sept). Hiking trails. Cross-country skiing. Picnicking, playground. 5¹/₂ mi NW on Delhi Rd, near Huron River Dr. Phone 734/227-2757.

Dexter-Huron. Fishing; canoeing. Hiking trails. Cross-country skiing. Picnicking, playground. 7¹/₂ mi NW along Huron River Dr. Phone 734/227-2757.

Hudson Mills. More than 1,600-acre recreation area; fishing; boating, canoe rentals, camp; hiking, bicycle trail, rentals; 18-hole golf; cross-country skiing (winter); picnicking, playground; camping; activity center. 12 mi NW on N Territorial Rd. Phone 734/227-2757 or 734/426-8211.

Kempf House (1853). Unusual example of Greek-revival architecture, restored structure owned and maintained by the city of Ann Arbor. Antique Victorian furnishings; displays of local historical artifacts. Tours (Mon, Wed & Fri mornings, Sat & Sun afternoons; closed Jan & Aug). 312 S Division. Phone 734/994-4898. ¢

✪ **University of Michigan** (1817). (36,000 students) Established here in 1837, after having moved from Detroit where it was founded. One of the largest universities in the country, it makes significant contributions in teaching and research. Phone 734/764-1817. Points of particular interest are

Law Quadrangle. Quadrangle includes four beautiful Gothic-style buildings. The law library, with an underground addition, has one of the nation's most extensive collections. S State St & S University Ave. Phone 734/764-9322.

Power Center for the Performing Arts. A 1,414-seat theater houses performances of drama, opera, music and dance. 121 S Fletcher. Phone 734/763-3333.

Natural Science Museums. Anthropology, Michigan wildlife, geology and prehistoric life exhibits. (Daily; closed hols) Planetarium shows (Sat & Sun; fee). 1109 Geddes Ave. Phone 734/764-0478. **Free.**

Museum of Art. (Daily exc Mon) S State St & S University Ave. Phone 734/764-0395. **Free.**

Kelsey Museum of Ancient and Medieval Archaeology. (Sept-Apr, daily; rest of yr, daily exc Mon) 434 S State St. Phone 734/764-9304. **Free.**

Nichols Arboretum. Approx 125 acres. (Daily) Geddes Ave. **Free.**

Matthaei Botanical Gardens. Approx 250 acres including greenhouses (daily; closed hols). Seasonal exhibits. Grounds (daily). 1800 Dixboro Rd, 3 mi NE of campus. Phone 734/998-7060 or 734/998-7061. ¢

North Campus. Contains research areas; School of Music designed by Eero Saarinen; School of Art and Architecture with public art gallery (daily exc Sun); School of Engineering. 2 mi NE of central campus.

Gerald R. Ford Presidential Library. Research library that houses Ford's presidential, vice-presidential and congressional documents. (Mon-Fri; closed hols) North campus, 1000 Beal Ave. Phone 734/741-2218. **Free.**

Annual Events

Ann Arbor Summer Festival. Power Center, University of Michigan. A performing arts festival of mime, dance, theater and music; also lectures, films, and exhibits. Phone 734/995-7281. June-early July.

Street Art Fair. S University Ave, Main St, State St, Liberty St. Nearly 1,000 artists and craftspeople display and sell works. 4 days mid-July.

Motels

★★ **FAIRFIELD INN BY MARRIOTT.** *3285 Boardwalk (48108). 734/995-5200; FAX 734/995-5394.* 110 rms, 4 story. S $54.95-$69.95; D $59.95-$69.95; each addl $6; under 18 free; higher rates: football wkends, some univ events. Crib free. TV; cable (premium). Indoor pool; whirlpool. Complimentary continental bkfst. Restaurant adj 6:30 am-1 pm. Ck-out noon. Valet serv. X-country ski 3 mi. Refrigerators. Cr cds: A, C, D, DS, MC, V.

[D] [symbols] SC

★★ **HAMPTON INN-NORTH.** *2300 Green Rd (48105). 734/996-4444; FAX 734/996-0196.* 130 rms, 4 story. S $59-$85; D $66-$95; under 18 free. Crib free. Pet accepted, some restrictions. TV; cable (premium). Indoor pool; whirlpool. Complimentary continental bkfst. Restaurant nearby. Ck-out noon. Meeting rms. Business servs avail. Valet serv. X-country ski 3 mi. Cr cds: A, C, D, DS, JCB, MC, V.

[D] [symbols] SC

★★ **HAMPTON INN-SOUTH.** *925 Victors Way (48108). 734/665-5000; FAX 734/665-8452.* 150 rms, 4 story. June-Nov: S $65-$70; D $75-$80; under 18 free; 2-day min special events; higher rates special events; lower rates rest of yr. Crib free. TV; cable (premium). Indoor pool; whirlpool. Complimentary coffee in lobby. Ck-out noon. Coin lndry. Meeting rms. Business servs avail. Valet serv Mon-Fri. Exercise equipt; bicycle, stair machine. Cr cds: A, C, D, DS, JCB, MC, V.

[D] [symbols] SC

★ **LAMP POST INN.** *2424 E Stadium Blvd (48104). 734/971-8000; FAX 734/971-7483.* 54 rms, 27 with shower only, 2 story. S, D $39-$64; family, wkly rates; higher rates special events. Pet accepted, some restrictions. TV; cable, VCR avail. Pool. Complimentary continental bkfst. Ck-out 11 am. Downhill ski 20 mi; x-country ski 1¹/₂ mi. Health club privileges. Cr cds: A, D, DS, MC, V.

[D] [symbols] SC

✔ **RED ROOF INN.** *3621 Plymouth Rd (48105). 734/996-5800; FAX 734/996-5707.* 108 rms, 2 story. S $39.99-$54.99; D $48.99-$61.99; 3 or more persons $51.99-$64.99; under 18 free; higher rates special events. Crib free. Pet accepted. TV; cable (premium). Restaurant adj 6 am-midnight. Ck-out noon. X-country ski 2¹/₂ mi. Cr cds: A, C, D, DS, MC, V.

[D] [symbols]

★★ **RESIDENCE INN BY MARRIOTT.** *800 Victors Way (48108). 734/996-5666.* 112 kit. suites, 2-3 story. S, D $110-$160. Crib free. Pet accepted; fee. TV; cable (premium). Heated pool; whirlpool. Complimentary continental bkfst. Restaurant opp 6 am-11 pm. Ck-out noon. Coin lndry. Meeting rm. Valet serv. Balconies. Picnic tables, grills. Cr cds: A, C, D, DS, JCB, MC, V.

[D] [symbols] SC

Motor Hotels

★★ **COURTYARD BY MARRIOTT.** *3205 Boardwalk (48108). 734/995-5900; FAX 734/995-2937.* 160 rms, 4 story, 40 suites. S $79-$89; D $89-$99; each addl $10; suites $99-$109; under 18 free. Crib free. TV; cable (premium). Indoor pool; whirlpool. Restaurant 6:30 am-1 pm. Bar 4:30-midnight. Ck-out noon. Meeting rms. Valet serv. X-country ski 3 mi. Exercise equipt; weight machine, bicycles. Many refrigerators. Cr cds: A, C, D, DS, ER, JCB, MC, V.

[D] [symbols] SC

★★★ **CROWNE PLAZA.** *610 Hilton Blvd (48108), at State St & I-94. 734/761-7800; FAX 734/761-1040.* 200 rms, 3 story. S, D $74-$119; suites $175-$225; family, wkend rates. Crib free. TV; cable (premium). Indoor pool; whirlpool. Restaurant 6:30 am-10 pm; Sun from 7 am. Rm serv. Bar 11-1 am. Ck-out 11 am. Meeting rms. Bellhops. Valet serv. Sundries. Gift shops. X-country ski 10 mi. Exercise equipt; weight machine, treadmill, sauna. Cr cds: A, C, D, DS, JCB, MC, V.

[D] [symbols] SC

★★★ **HOLIDAY INN-NORTH CAMPUS.** *3600 Plymouth Rd (48105). 734/769-9800; FAX 734/761-1290.* 222 rms, 2-5 story. S $85; D $95; under 18 free; wkend rates. Crib free. Pet accepted, some restrictions; $50 refundable. TV; cable. Indoor/outdoor pool. Restaurant 6:30 am-10 pm; Fri, Sat to 11 pm; Sun 7:30 am-9 pm. Rm serv. Bar. Ck-out 11 am. Meeting rms. Business servs avail. Valet serv. Tennis. X-country ski 2¹/₂ mi. Exercise equipt; weight machine, bicycles. Game rm. Picnic tables. Cr cds: A, C, D, DS, ER, JCB, MC, V.

[D] [symbols] SC

★ ★ ★ **SHERATON INN.** *3200 Boardwalk (48108). 734/996-0600;* FAX 734/996-8136. 197 rms, 6 story. S, D, studio rms $79-$125; each addl $10; suites $109-$169; under 18 free; wkend rates. Crib free. TV; cable (premium). Indoor/outdoor pool; whirlpool, poolside serv. Restaurant 6:30 am-10:30 pm; Fri, Sat to 11:30 pm. Rm serv. Bar noon-1 am. Ck-out noon. Meeting rms. Business center. In-rm modem link. Bellhops. Sundries. X-country ski 10 mi. Exercise equipt; bicycle, stair machine, sauna. Health club privileges. Some refrigerators, microwaves. Cr cds: A, C, D, DS, ER, JCB, MC, V.

★ ★ ★ **WEBER'S INN.** *3050 Jackson Rd (48103). 734/769-2500;* FAX 734/769-4743; res: 800/443-3050. 160 rms, 4 story. S, D $85-$125; each addl $10; suites $199-$250; under 18 free. Crib free. TV; cable (premium), VCR avail (movies). Indoor pool; whirlpool, poolside serv. Restaurant 6:30 am-10:30 pm; Mon to 9:30 pm; Fri to midnight; Sat 8 am-midnight; Sun 8 am-9:30 pm. Rm serv. Bar 11-1:30 am; entertainment. Ck-out noon. Meeting rms. Business servs avail. In-rm modem link. Valet serv. Sundries. Tennis privileges. X-country ski 5 mi. Exercise equipt; weights, bicycles, sauna. Some refrigerators. Some rms with spiral stair-case to pool. Cr cds: A, C, D, DS, JCB, MC, V.

Hotels

★ ★ **BELL TOWER.** *300 S Thayer St (48104). 734/769-3010;* FAX 734/769-4339; res: 800/999-8693. 66 rms, 3-4 story, 10 suites. S $104; D $119; each addl $15; suites $133-$202; under 6 free. Crib free. TV; cable, VCR avail. Complimentary continental bkfst. Restaurant 6-10 pm; closed Sun. Ck-out noon. Meeting rms. Business servs avail. In-rm modem link. Free valet parking. X-country ski 2 mi. Refrigerator, minibar in suites. European-style decor, ambience. Cr cds: A, C, D, ER, MC, V.

★ ★ ★ **CAMPUS INN.** *615 E Huron St (48104). on Univ of Michi-gan campus. 734/769-2200; FAX 734/769-6222; res: 800/666-8693.* 208 rms, 15 story. S $108-$119; D $123-$134; each addl $15; suites $147-$270; under 2 free; higher rates special events (2-day min). Crib avail. TV; cable, VCR avail. Pool. Restaurant 7 am-9 pm; Fri, Sat to 10 pm. Bar from noon. Ck-out noon. Meeting rms. Business servs avail. In-rm modem link. Gift shop. X-country ski 3 mi. Exercise equipt; weight machine, treadmill, sauna. Cr cds: A, C, D, DS, MC, V.

Restaurants

✔★ **BELLA CIAO.** *118 W Liberty St. 734/995-2107.* Hrs: 5:30-10 pm. Closed major hols. Res accepted. Italian menu. Serv bar. A la carte entrees: dinner $10-$17. Specializes in veal, pasta, seafood. Outdoor dining. Cr cds: A, C, D, DS, MC, V.

★ ★ **EARLE.** *121 W Washington St. 734/994-0211.* Hrs: 5:30-10 pm; Fri to midnight; Sat 6 pm-midnight; Sun 5-9 pm. Closed hols; also Sun June-Aug. Res accepted. French, Italian provincial menu. Bar. Semi-a la carte: dinner $10-$20. Own sorbet. Pianist wkdays, jazz trio wkends. Outdoor dining. In historic brick building (1885). Cr cds: A, C, D, DS, JCB, MC, V.

★ ★ ★ **ESCOFFIER.** *300 S Thayer St. 734/995-3800.* Hrs: 6-10 pm. Closed Sun; major hols. Res accepted. French menu. Bar. Wine list. A la carte entrees: dinner $16-$21. Complete meals: dinner $23. Own pastries. Pianist. Valet parking. Outdoor dining. Cr cds: A, C, D, MC, V.

★ ★ **GANDY DANCER.** *401 Depot St. 734/769-0592.* Hrs: 11:30 am-4 pm, 5-10 pm; Fri & Sat to 11 pm; Sun 3:30-9 pm; early-bird dinner Mon-Sat 4:30-5:30 pm; Sun brunch 10 am-2 pm. Closed Jan 1, Dec 25. Res accepted. Bar. Semi-a la carte: lunch $5.50-$14, dinner $13-$30. Sun brunch $14.95. Child's meals. Specializes in fresh seafood, rack of

lamb, pasta. Own pasta. Entertainment. Valet parking. Converted railroad station. Family-owned. Cr cds: A, C, D, DS, JCB, MC, V.

★ ★ **KERRYTOWN BISTRO.** *415 N Fifth Ave. 734/994-6424.* Hrs: 11:30 am-2 pm, 5-10 pm; Sun 10:30 am-2 pm; Mon 5-9 pm; Sat, Sun brunch 10:30 am-2 pm. Closed major hols. Res accepted. French menu. Bar. A la carte entrees: lunch $5-$9, dinner $11-$19. Sat, Sun brunch $5-$7. Specialty: cassoulet à la carcassonne. French country atmosphere. Cr cds: A, MC, V.

✔★ **METZGER'S.** *203 E Washington St. 734/668-8987.* Hrs: 11 am-10 pm; Sun 11:30 am-8 pm. Closed Jan 1, Thanksgiving; also July 4-6 & Dec 24-26. German, Amer menu. Bar to midnight, Sun to 8 pm. Semi-a la carte: lunch $3-$7, dinner $6-$14. Child's meals. Specializes in sauerbraten, Wienerschnitzel, seafood. Bavarian decor; extensive stein collection. Cr cds: A, DS, MC, V.

★ ★ **MOVEABLE FEAST.** *326 W Liberty. 734/663-3278.* Hrs: 11:30 am-2 pm, 6-9 pm; Mon, Sat from 6 pm. Closed Sun; major hols. Res accepted. Serv bar. A la carte entrees: lunch $6-$8.50, dinner $14.50-$24.75. Complete meals: dinner $20-$33.25. Specializes in duck, seafood, veal. Parking. Outdoor dining. Historic Victorian house (1870). Totally nonsmoking. Cr cds: A, C, D, DS, MC, V.

★ **PAESANO'S.** *3411 Washtenaw Ave. 734/971-0484.* Hrs: 11 am-11 pm; Fri to midnight; Sat noon-midnight; Sun 10 am-10 pm; Sun brunch 10 am-2 pm; hols 3-9 pm. Closed Jan 1, Thanksgiving, Dec 25. Res accepted. Italian, Amer menu. Bar. Semi-a la carte: lunch $5.50-$9, dinner $7.50-$17.95. Sun brunch $10.95. Child's meals. Specializes in pasta, fresh seafood. Strolling mandolinists Fri. Parking. Outdoor dining. Cr cds: A, D, DS, MC, V.

★ ★ **SWEET LORRAINE'S CAFE.** *303 Detroit St (48104). 734/665-0700.* Hrs: 11 am-11 pm; Fri, Sat to midnight; Sun to 9:30 pm. Closed Mon; Jan 1, July 4, Dec 25. Bar. A la carte entrees: lunch $5-$14, dinner $5-$18. Child's meals. Specializes in vegetarian dishes, desserts. Outdoor dining. Contemporary decor. Cr cds: A, C, D, DS, MC, V.

Battle Creek (J-4)

(See also Kalamazoo, Marshall)

Settled 1831 **Pop** 53,540 **Elev** 830 ft **Area code** 616 **E-mail** bcvcb @mcimail.com

Information Greater Battle Creek/Calhoun County Visitor and Convention Bureau, 34 W Jackson St, Suite 5A, 49017; 616/962-2240 or 800/397-2240.

Battle Creek's fame was built by two cereal tycoons, W.K. Kellogg and C.W. Post. The Kellogg and Post cereal plants are the largest of their type anywhere. The city has a variety of other food-packing industries plus many heavy industries. Post and Kellogg have influenced not only the economy; signs, streets, parks and many public institutions also bear their names. The city takes its name from a "battle" that took place on the banks of the creek in 1825 between a native and a land surveyor.

What to See and Do

Binder Park Zoo. Natural exotic and domestic animal exhibits; "Z. O. & O." miniature train ride, nature trails, restaurant, gift shop. (Mid-Apr-mid-Oct, daily) Special events during Halloween & Christmas. 7400 Division Dr. Phone 616/979-1351. ¢¢

Fort Custer State Recreation Area. Swimming beach; fishing; boating (launch). Nature, bridle, and bicycle trails. Picnic areas. Hunting. Improved campgrounds (res required). Cross-country skiing, snowmobiling. (Daily) Standard fees. 8 mi W via MI 96, 5163 W Fort Custer Dr in Augusta. Phone 616/731-4200. Per car ¢¢

Kimball House Museum (1886). Restored and refurnished Victorian home; displays trace development of use of appliances, tools, medical instruments; herb garden; country store. (Fri afternoons & 2nd and 4th Sun of month; closed hols) 196 Capital Ave NE. Phone 616/966-2496. ¢

Leila Arboretum. A 72-acre park containing native trees and shrubs. W Michigan Ave at 20th St. On grounds is

Kingman Museum of Natural History. Exhibits include Journey Through the Crust of the Earth, Walk in the Footsteps of the Dinosaurs, Mammals of the Ice Age, Window to the Universe, Planetarium, Wonder of Life, Discovery Room and others. (July-Aug, daily; rest of yr, daily exc Mon; closed major hols) Phone 616/965-5117. ¢

Skiing. Binder Park. Offers trails with varying degrees of difficulty for the Nordic skier. Also golf course. (Daily; weather permitting) 6723 B Drive S. Phone 616/966-3431. ¢¢

Sojourner Truth Grave. On the cemetery's Fifth St is the plain square monument marking the resting place of this remarkable fighter for freedom. Born a slave in the 1790s, Truth gained her freedom in the 1820s and crusaded against slavery until her death in 1883. Although uneducated, she had a brilliant mind as well as unquenchable devotion to her cause. Oak Hill Cemetery, South Ave & Oak Hill Dr.

W.K. Kellogg Bird Sanctuary of Michigan State University. Experimental farm and forest nearby. Seven kinds of swans and more than 20 species of ducks and geese inhabit the ponds and Wintergreen Lake. One of the finest birds of prey collections in the Midwest, along with free roaming upland game birds. Colorful viewing all seasons of the year. Observation deck and educational displays. Grounds and reception center (daily). 13 mi NW off MI 89, 12685 E C Ave. Phone 616/671-2510. ¢

Willard Beach. Lavishly landscaped; has a wide bathing beach; pavilion; picnicking; supervised swimming. (Memorial Day-Labor Day, daily) 2 mi S, on shores of Goguac Lake. ¢

Annual Event

Cereal City Festival. On Michigan Ave. Children's Parade, Queen's Pageant, arts & crafts exhibits; also the world's longest breakfast table. 2nd Sat June.

Motels

✔★ **APPLETREE INN.** 4786 Beckley Rd (49017). 616/979-3561; FAX 616/979-1400; res: 800/388-7829. 86 rms, 9 kit. units. S $40.75-$44.75; D $42.75-$54.75; each addl $4; kit. units $51.25-$63.75; under 18 free; wkly rates; golf plans; higher rates Balloon Festival. Crib free. Pet accepted. TV; cable (premium). Coffee in rms. Complimentary continental bkfst. Restaurant opp open 24 hrs. Ck-out noon. Meeting rm. Business servs avail. Tennis privileges. X-country ski 4 mi. Health club privileges. Some in-rm whirlpools. Cr cds: A, C, D, DS, ER, MC, V.

⍟ 🐾 🏊 ⛷ 🎿 🔥 SC

★★ **BATTLE CREEK INN.** 5050 Beckley Rd (49015), I-94 at Capital Ave (exit 97). 616/979-1100; FAX 616/979-1899; res: 800/232-3405. 211 rms, 2 story. S $60-$70; D $73-$77; each addl $8; family rates, golf plans. Crib free. Pet accepted. TV; cable (premium). Indoor heated pool; poolside serv. Coffee in rms. Complimentary continental bkfst. Restaurant 6:30 am-2 pm, 5-10 pm. Rm serv. Bar 4 pm-midnight. Ck-out noon. Coin lndry. Meeting rms. Business servs avail. Valet serv. Putting green. Exercise equipt; stair machine, bicycle. Health club privileges. Game rm. Refrigerators avail. Cr cds: A, C, D, DS, JCB, MC, V.

⍟ 🐾 🏊 🎿 🎿 🔥 SC

★ **SUPER 8.** 5395 Beckley Rd (49017). 616/979-1828; FAX 616/919-1828, ext. 404. 62 rms, 3 story. No elvtr. S $35.88-$38.88; D $41.88-$48.88; each addl $5; suites $49.88-$58.88; under 12 free; higher rates special events. Crib free. TV; cable (premium). Complimentary cof-

fee. Restaurant adj 6 am-midnight. Ck-out 11 am. X-country ski 4 mi. Cr cds: A, D, DS, MC, V.

⍟ 🏊 🎿 🔥 SC

Hotel

★★★ **McCAMAMLY PLAZA.** 50 Capital Ave SW (49017). 616/963-7050; FAX 616/963-4335. 245 rms, 16 story. S $123-$153; D $133-$163; each addl $20; suites $200-$300; under 17 free; wkly, wkend rates. Crib free. TV; cable, VCR avail (movies). Indoor pool; whirlpool, poolside serv. Coffee in rms. Restaurant 6:30 am-1:30 pm, 5:30-10 pm. Bar 4 pm-1 am; entertainment exc Sun. Ck-out 1 pm. Meeting rms. Business servs avail. Shopping arcade. Free RR station, bus depot transportation. 18-hole golf privileges. X-country ski 3 mi. Exercise equipt; weights, bicycles, sauna. Refrigerators, minibars. Cr cds: A, C, D, DS, ER, JCB, MC, V.

⍟ 🏊 🏋 🏊 ⛷ 🎿 🔥 SC

Inn

★★ **GREENCREST MANOR.** 6174 Halbert Rd (49017). 616/962-8633; FAX 616/962-7254. 8 rms, 2 share bath, 3 story. S, D $75-$170. TV; cable (premium). Complimentary continental bkfst. Restaurant nearby. Ck-out 11 am, ck-in 4:30 pm. Business servs avail. 18-hole golf privileges. X-country ski 5 mi. Some in-rm whirlpools. Marble fireplaces, expansive lawns. Totally nonsmoking. Cr cds: A, D, MC, V.

🏊 🏋 🎿 🔥

Restaurant

✔★ **SAM'S JOINT.** (1600 MI 66, Athens 49051) 12 mi S on MI 66. 616/729-5010. Hrs: 5-10 pm; Sat from 4; Sun noon-8 pm. Closed Mon; Easter, Thanksgiving, Dec 25. Res accepted. Bar. Semi-a la carte: lunch, dinner $5.95-$14.95. Child's meals. Specializes in barbecued pork back ribs, open-flame prime rib. Cr cds: MC, V.

Bay City (G-5)

(See also Midland, Saginaw)

Settled 1831 **Pop** 38,936 **Elev** 595 ft **Area code** 517
Information Bay Area Convention & Visitors Bureau, 901 Saginaw St, 48708; 517/893-1222 or 888/BAY-TOWN.

Bay City is a historic port community located on Saginaw Bay, which services Great Lakes freighters as well as seagoing vessels in the handling of millions of tons of products annually. The city, which is the county seat, is noted for tree-shaded streets and residential areas with new homes and Victorian and Georgian mansions built by the 19th-century lumber barons. Industries include shipbuilding, automobile parts, petrochemicals and electronics. Sugar beet production and potato and melon crops are important to its economy.

Retail, service, specialty dining and entertainment businesses can be found in the Historic Midland Street area on the west side of Bay City.

What to See and Do

Bay City State Recreation Area. Approx 200 acres. Swimming, bathhouse; fishing; boating; hiking; picnicking; concession; camping. Standard fees. 5 mi N on MI 247, along Saginaw Bay. Phone 517/684-3020. Also here are

Jennison Nature Center. Displays on the history, geology, wildlife and general ecology of the area. Hiking trails. (Daily exc Mon; closed hols) Phone 517/667-0717. **Free.**

Tobico Marsh. 1,700 acres of wetland, the largest remaining wildlife refuge on Saginaw Bay's western shore. Two 32-ft towers allow panoramic viewing of deer, beaver, mink and hundreds of species of waterfowl and song, shore and marsh birds. Visitors Center (daily exc Mon). Killarney Beach Rd. Phone 517/684-3020. **Free.**

Bay County Historical Museum. Preserving and displaying the heritage of Bay County. Exhibits interpret life of Native Americans; depict fur trading, lumbering, shipbuilding, industrial development; life of pioneering women; changing exhibits. (Daily exc Sat; closed major hols) 321 Washington Ave. Phone 517/893-5733. **Donation.**

City Hall & Bell Tower (ca 1895). Meticulously restored Romanesque structure; council chamber has 31-ft-long woven tapestry depicting history of Bay City. View of city and its waterway from bell tower. (Mon-Fri; closed hols) 301 Washington Ave. Phone 517/893-1222. **Free.**

Deer Acres. Storybook theme park with petting zoo. Train rides (fee), antique cars, more. (Mid-May-Labor Day, daily; after Labor Day-mid-Oct, Sat & Sun) 17 mi N on MI 13, in Pinconning. Phone 517/879-2849. ¢¢¢

Scottish Rite Cathedral. The only Scottish Rite Cathedral in the state; contains Lord Cornwallis' surrender chair. (Mon-Fri) 614 Center Ave. Phone 517/893-3700. **Free.**

Annual Events

Liberty Classic & Antique Wooden Boat Show. Veterans' Memorial Park. Mid-June.

St Stanislaus Polish Festival. Lincoln Ave, S end of Bay City. Late June.

Munger Potato Festival. SE on MI 15, then E on MI 138 in Munger. 4 days late July.

Motels

★ ★ **BEST WESTERN CREEKSIDE INN.** 6285 Westside Saginaw Rd (48706), jct MI 84, I-75 exit 160. 517/686-0840; FAX 517/686-0840, ext. 397. 71 rms, 2 story. S $55-$60; D $55-$65; each addl $5; under 12 free. Crib free. TV; cable (premium). Heated pool; whirlpool, sauna. Restaurant adj 6 am-9 pm. Ck-out 11 am. Meeting rms. Business servs avail. Game rm. Some refrigerators. Private patios, balconies. Cr cds: A, C, D, DS, MC, V.

↙★ **EUCLID.** 809 N Euclid Ave (MI 13) (48706). 517/684-9455. 36 rms. S $36; D $46; 3rd addl, $4. Crib $5. TV; cable (premium). Heated pool. Playground. Restaurant nearby. Ck-out 11 am. Some refrigerators. Picnic tables, grill. Cr cds: A, C, D, DS, MC, V.

Motor Hotels

★ ★ ★ **BAY VALLEY HOTEL AND RESORT.** 2470 Old Bridge Rd (48706). 517/686-3500; FAX 517/686-6931; res: 800/292-5028. 150 rms, 3 story. Mid-Apr-Oct: S $69-$109; D $75-$115; each addl $10; suites $150; under 12 free; package plans; lower rates rest of yr. Crib free. TV; cable (premium), VCR avail. Indoor/outdoor pool; whirlpool, poolside serv. Playground. Restaurant 7 am-10 pm; Fri, Sat to 11 pm. Rm serv. Bar 11-1:30 am; Sun from noon; entertainment. Ck-out noon. Meeting rms. Business servs avail. Free airport transportation. Bellhops. Valet serv. Sundries. Indoor & outdoor tennis, pro. 18-hole golf, greens fee $46-$54, pro, putting green, driving range. X-country ski on site, instruction. Exercise rm; instructor, weights, bicycles, sauna. Game rm. Lawn games. Private patios, balconies. Picnic tables, grills. Cr cds: A, C, D, DS, MC, V.

★ ★ **HOLIDAY INN.** 501 Saginaw St (48708). 517/892-3501; FAX 517/892-9342. 100 rms, 4 story. S $70-$89; D $75-$96; each addl $7; under 18 free. Crib free. Pet accepted. TV; cable. Indoor pool; whirlpool, sauna. Restaurant 6:30 am-10 pm; Sat, Sun from 7 am. Rm serv. Bar from noon. Ck-out noon. Coin lndry. Meeting rms. Business servs avail. Valet serv. Sundries. Cr cds: A, C, D, DS, ER, JCB, MC, V.

Restaurants

★ ★ **LINDEN HOF.** 201 N Euclid Ave (MI 13). 517/686-2209. Hrs: 11 am-11 pm; Sun 11:30 am-10 pm. Closed Dec 25. Res accepted. Bar to 1 am. Semi-a la carte: lunch $3.50-$6, dinner $7.95-$16. Buffet: lunch, dinner (Fri-Sun) $7.95-$14.95. Child's meals. Salad bar. Gift shop. Family-owned. Cr cds: DS, MC, V.

★ ★ **TERRY AND JERRY'S O SOLE MIO.** 1005 Saginaw St. 517/893-3496. Hrs: 5-10 pm; Fri, Sat to 10:30 pm. Closed Mon; major hols. Res accepted. Italian, Amer menu. Bar. Semi-a la carte: dinner $8-$25. Child's meals. Specializes in veal, pasta, fresh seafood. Salad bar. Pianist, vocalist Sat. Family-owned. Cr cds: A, C, D, MC, V.

Bellaire (E-4)

Pop 1,104 **Elev** 616 ft **Area code** 616 **Zip** 49615

What to See and Do

Skiing. Shanty Creek Resort. Two separate mountains: triple, 5 double chairlifts, 2 rope tows; patrol, school, rentals; snowmaking; nursery; night skiing; lodge (see RESORT), restaurant, snack bar, entertainment; indoor/outdoor pool, 2 whirlpools; health club. 29 trails on 2 mountains; longest run approx 1 mi; vertical drop 425 ft. Cross-country trails (25 mi). (Thanksgiving-Mar, daily) Shanty Creek Rd, 2 mi SE off MI 88. Phone 616/533-8621 or 800/678-4111. ¢¢¢¢¢

Resort

★ ★ ★ **SHANTY CREEK.** 1 Shanty Rd, 2 mi SE, 1 mi E of MI 88. 616/533-8621; FAX 616/533-7001; res: 800/678-4111. 560 rms, 1-3 story. 259 kit. units (some equipt). June-Aug, winter wkends, Christmas wk: S, D $119-$129; each addl $10; kit. units $165-$330; chalets $290-$420; under 18 free; package plans; lower rates rest of yr. Crib $5. TV; cable (premium), VCR avail. 5 pools, 2 indoor; whirlpool, poolside serv. Playground. Supervised child's activities (seasonal). Dining rm 7 am-9 pm. Rm serv. Box lunches. Bars 11-2 am; Sun from noon. Ck-out noon, ck-in 6 pm. Grocery. Package store. Meeting rms. Business center. Gift shop. Free airport transportation. Sports dir. Tennis, pro. Three 18-hole golf courses, pro, putting greens, driving ranges. Downhill/x-country ski on site. Ice skating. Sleighing. Lawn games. Exercise course, hiking trails. Dancing, entertainment, movies. Rec rm. Game rm. Exercise rm; instructor, weights, bicycles, sauna, steam rm. Fireplaces. Private patios, balconies. Picnic tables, grills. Extensive grounds. Mountain bike trails (rentals). Private sand beach nearby. Cr cds: A, C, D, DS, MC, V.

Benton Harbor

(see St Joseph)

Beulah (F-3)

(For accommodations see Frankfort, Traverse City)

Pop 421 **Elev** 595 ft **Area code** 616 **Zip** 49617 **Web** www.benzie.org
Information Benzie County Chamber of Commerce, PO Box 204, Benzonia 49616; 616/882-5801.

This resort town is at the east end of Crystal Lake, which offers excellent fishing for salmon, trout, perch, bass and smelt. Skiing, ice fishing, golf and boating are also popular in the area.

What to See and Do

Benzie Area Historical Museum. Exhibits and artifacts depict area's lumbering, shipping, farming, transportation, homelife; display on Civil War author Bruce Catton. (June-Sept, Tues-Sat; Apr-May & Oct-Nov, Fri & Sat only; special tours by appt) 3 mi S on US 31 in Benzonia, 6941 Traverse Ave. Phone 616/882-5539. ¢

Gwen Frostic Prints. Original block prints designed by artist and poet Gwen Frostic are featured at this wildlife sanctuary and printing shop. Display room lets visitors observe the printing presses in operation. (Mon-Fri). (Early May-early Nov, daily; rest of yr, daily exc Sun; closed major hols) 3 mi S on US 31, 2 mi W, in Benzonia at 5140 River Rd. Phone 616/882-5505. **Free.**

Platte River State Anadromous Fish Hatchery. Michigan's largest hatchery annually produces about 9 million anadromous salmon (salmon that live in oceans or lakes and return to the rivers to spawn). This is the birthplace of the coho salmon in the Great Lakes; also produces chinook salmon. Self-guided tours (daily). 15120 US 31, 10 mi E via US 31. Phone 616/325-4611. **Free.**

Skiing. Crystal Mountain Resort. Five chairlifts, 2 rope tows; night skiing; patrol, rentals; snowmaking; nursery; lodge, condominiums, restaurant, cafeteria, bar. 25 trails; longest run 1/2 mi; vertical drop 375 ft. (Thanksgiving-early Apr, daily) Groomed, track-set cross-country trails (14 mi), lighted night trail; rentals, instruction (Dec-Mar, daily). Snowboard half-pipe. Also 2 golf courses; indoor pool, fitness center; hiking, mountain bike trails; tennis courts. 3 mi S on US 31, then 7 mi SE on MI 115 near Thompsonville. Phone 616/378-2000. ¢¢¢¢

Restaurants

★ ★ **BROOKSIDE INN.** *N on US 31.* 616/882-9688. Hrs: 8 am-9:30 pm; Fri, Sat to 11 pm; summer to midnight. Res accepted. Serv bar. Semi-a la carte: bkfst $2.75-$6.95, lunch $2.55-$6, dinner $6.75-$30. Child's meals. Specializes in steak, seafood, desserts. Tableside stone cooking. Outdoor dining. Began as an ice cream shop; country decor, antiques. Guest rms avail. Cr cds: A, D, DS, MC, V.

✔★ **CHERRY HUT.** *246 US 31.* 616/882-4431. Hrs: 11 am-9 pm; mid-June-Labor Day 10 am-10 pm. Closed Late Oct-Memorial Day. Semi-a la carte: lunch $3.65-$7.95, dinner $9.50-$11.95. Child's meals. Specialties: cherry chicken salad, cherry pie. Outdoor dining. Cr cds: DS, MC, V.

★ **SAIL INN.** *(US 31, Benzonia 49616)* 1 mi S on US 31 & MI 115. 616/882-4971. Hrs: 8 am-10 pm; Fri, Sat to 11 pm; Sun brunch 11 am-2 pm. Closed Thanksgiving, Dec 25. Bar. Semi-a la carte: bkfst, lunch $2.95-$7, dinner $6.95-$15.95. Sun brunch $7.95. Child's meals. Specializes in seafood, steak. Salad bar. Family-owned. Cr cds: A, DS, MC, V.

[D]

Big Rapids (G-4)

Settled 1854 **Pop** 12,603 **Elev** 920 ft **Area code** 616 **Zip** 49307 **Web** multimag.com/mccvb/
Information Mecosta County Convention & Visitors Bureau, 246 N State St; 616/796-7640 or 800/833-6697.

What to See and Do

Mecosta County Parks. Parks open May-Sept. No pets permitted in Brower & School Section Lake parks. Permit for all county parks ¢¢¢¢; Camping ¢¢¢; Parks include

Brower. Swimming, fishing, boating (launch). Playgrounds; tennis courts, softball diamond. Camping. 8 mi S on US 131 to Stanwood, then 1 mi W to Old State Rd, then 3 mi S. Phone 616/823-2561.

Paris. Fishing, canoeing (ramp); wildlife area. Picnicking (shelter). Camping. 6 mi N on MI 131, in Paris. Phone 616/796-3420.

Merrill Lake. Swimming (2 beaches), fishing, boating (launch, ramps). Picnicking (shelters); playgrounds. Camping. E on MI 20 to MI 66, then N, 4 mi N of Barryton. Phone 517/382-7158.

School Section Lake. Swimming beach. Picnicking (shelters), concessions, playgrounds. Camping. No motorcycles. Approx 23 mi E via MI 20. Phone 616/972-7450.

Annual Events

Springtime in Paris Festival. 5 mi N on US 131 in Paris. Street performers, musicians, art shows, exhibits, stage performances, concessions. Phone 616/796-2420. 3rd wkend June.

Labor Day Arts Fair. Hemlock Park on Muskegon River. More than 100 exhibitors of various arts & crafts; concessions. Phone 616/796-7649. Labor Day.

Motor Hotel

★ ★ ★ **HOLIDAY INN & CONFERENCE CENTER.** *1005 Perry St, at Ferris State Univ.* 616/796-4400; FAX 616/796-0220. 118 rms, 4 story. S $68-$77; D $78-$87; each addl $10; suites $150; under 18 free; golf plans. Crib free. TV; cable (premium). Indoor pool; whirlpool, sauna. Restaurant 6:30 am-10 pm; Fri, Sat 7 am-11 pm; Sun 7 am-8 pm. Rm serv. Bar 11 am-11 pm; Fri, Sat to midnight; Sun noon-9 pm. Ck-out noon. Meeting rms. Business servs avail. In-rm modem link. Valet serv. Gift shop. Tennis privileges, pro. 18-hole golf, greens fee, pro, putting green, driving range. Cr cds: A, C, D, DS, ER, JCB, MC, V.

Birmingham (J-6)

(See also Bloomfield Hills, Detroit, Southfield)

Pop 19,997 **Elev** 781 ft **Area code** 248
Information Birmingham-Bloomfield Chamber of Commerce, 124 W Maple, 48009; 248/644-1700.

Motel

★ ★ **HOLIDAY INN EXPRESS.** *145 S Hunter Blvd (MI 1) (48009).* 248/646-7300; FAX 248/646-4501. 126 rms, 2-5 story. S, D $109.95-$119.95; suites $125-$250; under 19 free; wkend rates. Crib free. TV; cable (premium). Coffee in rms. Complimentary continental bkfst. Restaurant nearby. Business servs avail. In-rm modem link. Ck-out noon. Valet serv. Refrigerators. Cr cds: A, C, D, DS, ER, JCB, MC, V.

Hotel

★ ★ ★ ★ **TOWNSEND.** *100 Townsend St (48009), downtown. 248/642-7900; FAX 248/645-9061; res: 800/548-4172.* French furniture, a wood-burning fireplace and a mahogany bookshelf full of antique books lend intimacy to the lobby here. 87 rms, 4 story, 51 suites. S from $199; D from $209; each addl $20; suites $225-$600; under 12 free. Crib free. TV; cable (premium), VCR (movies). Restaurant (see RUGBY GRILLE). Afternoon tea Tues-Sat by res; pianist. Rm serv 24 hrs. Bar to 2 am. Ck-out 1 pm. Meeting rms. Business servs avail. In-rm modem link. Concierge. Gift shop. Covered parking. Tennis privileges. Downhill ski 20 mi; x-country ski 5 mi. Exercise bicycle brought to rm on request. Health club privileges. Bathrm phones; many minibars. Balconies. Located opp park. Cr cds: A, C, D, MC, V.

Restaurants

★ ★ ★ **RUGBY GRILLE.** *(See Townsend Hotel) 248/642-7900.* Hrs: 6:30 am-midnight; Fri, Sat 7-1 am. Res accepted. Bar. Wine cellar. Prix fixe: bkfst $7.95-$19.95. A la carte entrees: lunch $9.95-$18.95, dinner $20-$40. Specialties: steak tartare, Caesar salad, black Angus beef. Own baking. Valet parking. Intimate dining rm with cherry woodwork, marble-top tables, French doors. Cr cds: A, C, D, MC, V.

Bloomfield Hills (J-6)

(See also Birmingham, Detroit, Pontiac, Southfield, Troy, Warren)

Settled 1819 **Pop** 4,288 **Elev** 830 ft **Area code** 248
Information Birmingham-Bloomfield Chamber of Commerce, 124 W Maple, Birmingham 48009; 248/644-1700.

Amasa Bagley followed a Native American trail and cleared land on what is today the business section of this small residential city. It was known as Bagley's Corners, later as Bloomfield Center and then as Bloomfield Hills. In 1904, Ellen Scripps Booth and George G. Booth, president of the Detroit *News,* bought 300 acres of farmland here, naming it Cranbrook after the English village in which Mr. Booth's father was born. Since then, they have turned the estate into a vast cultural and educational complex.

What to See and Do

Cranbrook Educational Community. This famous campus is the site of the renowned center for the arts, education, science and culture. Located on more than 300 acres, Cranbrook is noted for its exceptional architecture, gardens and sculpture. 1221 N Woodward Ave. Phone 248/645-3000. Cranbrook is composed of

Cranbrook Academy of Art and Museum. (150 students) Graduate school for the fine arts, architecture and design. Museum has international arts exhibits and collections. (Wed-Sun afternoons; closed major hols) Phone 248/645-3312. ¢¢

Cranbrook Institute of Science. Natural history and science museum with exhibits, observatory, nature center; planetarium and laser demonstrations. (Mon-Sat, also Sun afternoons; closed major hols) Phone 248/645-3200. ¢¢

Cranbrook House (1908). Tudor-style structure designed by Albert Kahn. Contains exceptional examples of decorative and fine art from the late 19th and early 20th centuries. 380 Lone Pine Rd. Phone 248/645-3149. Tours ¢¢ Surrounding Cranbrook House are

Cranbrook Gardens. Forty acres of formal and informal gardens; trails, fountains, outdoor Greek theater. (May-Aug, daily; Sept, afternoons only; Oct, Sat & Sun afternoons) Phone 248/645-3149. ¢¢

Motor Hotel

★ ★ ★ **KINGSLEY HOTEL AND SUITES.** *1475 N Woodward Ave (MI 1) (48304). 810/644-1400; FAX 810/644-5449; res: 800/544-6835.* 160 rms, 3 story. S, D $104-$114; each addl $10; suites $125-$398; under 18 free; wkend rates. Crib free. TV; cable. Indoor pool; whirlpool. Restaurant 6-1 am. Rm serv 4-11 pm; Sun to 10 pm. Bar from 11 am; Sun noon-midnight; entertainment Tues-Sat. Ck-out noon. Meeting rms. Business servs avail. Bellhops. Barber, beauty shop. Downhill ski 20 mi. Exercise equipt; weights, bicycles. Some refrigerators. Some balconies. Cr cds: A, C, D, DS, MC, V.

Restaurant

★ ★ ★ ★ **THE LARK.** *(6430 Farmington Rd, West Bloomfield 48322) N of Maple Rd (15 Mile Rd). 248/661-4466.* E-mail larkrest@aol.com; web www.thelark.com. This restaurant overlooks a walled garden filled with potted flowers and herbs, a grape arbor and a stone fountain decorated with a spouting lion's head and tile frogs. French menu. Specializes in rack of lamb, monthly theme dinners. Hrs: 6-10:30 pm (last sitting 8:30 pm); Fri, Sat to 9 pm (last sitting). Closed Sun, Mon; major hols; also 1st wk Jan & 1st wk Aug. Res required. Bar. Wine cellar. Complete meals: dinner $50-$65. Outdoor dining. Own herb garden. Cr cds: A, C, D, MC, V.

Boyne City (E-4)

(See also Charlevoix, Petoskey)

Pop 3,400 **Elev** 600 ft **Area code** 616 **Zip** 49712
Information Chamber of Commerce, 28 S Lake St; 616/582-6222.

What to See and Do

Skiing. Boyne Mountain. Triple, 6-passenger, 3 quad, 3 double chairlifts; rope tow; patrol, school, rentals; snow making; lodge (see RESORT), cafeteria, restaurant, bar; nursery. Longest run 1 mi; vertical drop 500 ft. Cross-country trails (35 mi), rentals. (Trail ticket; fee) (Late Nov-mid-Apr, daily) SE via MI 75 to Boyne Falls, off US 131. Phone 616/549-2441 or 800/462-6963. ¢¢¢¢¢

Motel

★ ★ **WATER STREET INN.** *200 Front St. 616/582-3000; FAX 616/582-3001; res: 800/456-4313.* 27 kit. units, 3 story. Late June-early Sept: S, D $145-$165; each addl $10; under 13 free; higher rates hol wks; wkly rates; ski plans; lower rates rest of yr. Crib $10. TV; cable (premium). Restaurant adj 4-10 pm; Fri, Sat to 11 pm; Sun noon-9 pm; hrs vary late June-early Sept. Ck-out 11 am. Business servs avail. Downhill ski 6 mi; x-country ski 1½ mi. In-rm whirlpools. Private patios, balconies. On Lake Charlevoix. Private swimming beach. Cr cds: MC, V.

Resort

★ ★ **BOYNE MOUNTAIN.** *(Boyne Mtn Rd, Boyne Falls 49713) SE via MI 75 to Boyne Falls exit 282, off US 131. 616/549-6000; FAX 616/549-6093; res: 800/462-6963.* 265 units in lodges, villas, condos, 1-3 story, 109 kits. Dec-mid-Mar, mid-June-Aug: S, D $72-$105; 1-3 bedrm kit. apts $135-$325; AP; package plans; lower rates rest of yr. Crib free. TV; cable, VCR avail (movies). 2 pools, heated; whirlpool. Dining rm 7 am-10 pm. Box lunches. Bar noon-2 am. Ck-out 1 pm, ck-in 5 pm. Meeting rms. Business servs avail. 9-hole & two 18-hole golf courses, greens fee $70-$80, pro. Tennis, pro. Private beach. Paddle boats. Downhill/x-country ski on site. Ice rink; rentals. Lawn games. Bicycles. Entertainment. Exercise equipt; weights, bicycles, sauna. 5,000-ft paved, lighted airstrip. Many minibars. Some balconies. Alpine-style decor; fireplace in lobby. Cr cds: A, C, D, DS, MC, V.

Restaurants

✔★ **PIPPINS.** 5 W Main, in Water Street Mall shopping center. 616/582-3311. Hrs: 8 am-9 pm; Sun to 2 pm. Closed Nov-Apr. Bar. Semi-a la carte: bkfst $2.25-$5.50, lunch $2.95-$5.50, dinner $7.95-$12.95. Child's meals. Specializes in homemade soups and desserts, broiled fresh whitefish. Cr cds: MC, V.

★★ **STAFFORD'S ONE WATER STREET.** 1 Water St. 616/582-3434. Hrs: 11:30 am-11 pm; mid-Sept-mid-June: from 4 pm; Sun noon-9 pm; early-bird dinner 4-6 pm. Closed Dec 25. Res accepted. Bar. Semi-a la carte: lunch $4.75-$9.95, dinner $16.50-$25.95. Child's meals. Specializes in regional cuisine, fresh whitefish. Entertainment Tues-Sat. Overlooks Lake Charlevoix. Cr cds: A, MC, V.

Cadillac (F-4)

Settled 1871 **Pop** 10,104 **Elev** 1,328 ft **Area code** 616 **Zip** 49601 **E-mail** cavb@netonecom.net **Web** www.michiweb.com/cadillac

Information Cadillac Area Visitor Bureau, 222 Lake St; 616/775-0657 or 800/22-LAKES.

On the shores of lakes Cadillac and Mitchell, Cadillac was founded as a lumber camp and was once the major lumber center of the area. The city today prospers on diversified industry and tourism. Named for Antoine de la Mothe Cadillac, founder of Detroit, it is also headquarters for the Huron-Manistee National Forest (see MANISTEE and OSCODA). A Ranger District office of the forests is also located here.

What to See and Do

Caberfae Peaks Ski Resort. Quad, triple, 2 double chairlifts, 2 T-bars, 2 rope tows; patrol, school, rentals; snowmaking; bar, cafeteria, lodge, motel, restaurant. (Late Nov-Apr, daily) Snowboard, cross-country and snowmobile trails. 12 mi W on MI 55. Phone 616/862-3300. ¢¢¢¢

Johnny's Game and Fish Park. Wild and tame animals; 75-ft-long elevated goat walk; fishing for rainbow trout (no license, no limit; fee). (Mid-May-Labor Day, daily) 5 mi SW on MI 115, follow signs. Phone 616/775-3700. ¢¢

William Mitchell State Park. Approx 260 acres between Cadillac and Mitchell lakes. Swimming beach, bathhouse; fishing, hunting; boating (launching, rentals). Interpretive hiking trail. Picnicking, playground. Camping (tent & trailer facilities). Visitor center. Nature study area. Standard fees. 2 1/2 mi W via MI 55 & 115. Phone 616/775-7911.

Motels

★★ **BEST WESTERN BILL OLIVER'S.** 5676 E MI 55, 4 mi W of Cadillac on MI 55. 616/775-2458; FAX 616/775-8383. 66 rms. May-mid-Oct, Dec 26-mid-Mar: D $72-$87; each addl $5; lower rates rest of yr. Crib $3. TV; cable (premium). Indoor pool; whirlpool, sauna. Playground. Restaurant 7 am-10 pm. Rm serv. Ck-out 11 am. Business servs avail. Tennis. Golf privileges. Downhill ski 12 mi; x-country ski 1/2 mi. Bowling. Game rm. Lawn games. Cr cds: A, C, D, DS, MC, V.

★★ **CADILLAC SANDS RESORT.** 6319 E MI 115. 616/775-2407; FAX 616/775-6422; res: 800/647-2637. 55 rms, 2 story. June-Sept: S, D $69.95-$125; each addl $5; under 12 free. Crib $2. Pet accepted. TV;

cable (premium). Indoor pool. Complimentary continental bkfst. Restaurant 5-10:30 pm; also Sat, Sun 8-11 am (in season). Bar 4 pm-2:30 am; entertainment. Ck-out 11 am. Meeting rm. Business servs avail. Free airport transportation. Golf privileges, putting green. Downhill ski 13 mi; x-country ski 3 1/2 mi. Lawn games. Some private patios, balconies. Boat rentals, paddleboats. Private beach; dockage. Cr cds: A, C, D, DS, MC, V.

★★ **DAYS INN.** 6001 E MI 115, 1/4 mi N of jct MI 55. 616/775-4414; FAX 616/779-0370. 60 rms, 2 story. June-Sept & Dec-Feb: S $63-$111; D $68-$121; family, mid-wk rates; lower rates rest of yr. Crib free. Pet accepted. TV; cable (premium), VCR avail (movies). Indoor pool; whirlpool. Complimentary continental bkfst. Restaurant nearby. Ck-out 11 am. Meeting rm. Business servs avail. Valet serv. Downhill ski 12 mi; x-country ski 1 mi. Volleyball. Some refrigerators. Lake 1/4 mi; swimming beach. Cr cds: A, C, D, DS, JCB, MC, V.

★★ **HAMPTON INN.** 1650 S Mitchell St. 616/779-2900; FAX 616/779-0846. 120 rms, 4 story. Memorial Day-Labor Day: S $79; D $84; family rates; lower rates rest of yr. Crib free. TV; cable (premium), VCR avail (movies). Indoor pool; whirlpool. Complimentary continental bkfst. Restaurant nearby. Ck-out 11 am. Meeting rms. Business servs avail. Valet serv. Golf privileges. Downhill ski 20 mi; x-country ski 1 mi. Cr cds: A, C, D, DS, MC, V.

★★★ **McGUIRE'S RESORT.** 7880 Mackinaw Trail. 616/775-9947; FAX 616/775-9621; res: 800/632-7302. 123 rms, 1-3 story. S $65-$79; D $69-$99; each addl $10; suites $90-$180; studio rms $90-$129; under 18 free; ski, golf plans; higher rates Dec 26-Jan 1. TV; cable. Indoor pool; whirlpool, sauna. Restaurant 7 am-10 pm; off-season to 9 pm. Rm serv. Bar 11:30-1:30 am; entertainment. Ck-out 11 am. Meeting rm. Business servs avail. Valet serv. Gift shop. Free airport, bus depot transportation. Tennis. 27-hole golf, greens fee $49-$55, putting green, driving range. Downhill ski 15 mi; x-country ski on site. Game rm. Lawn games. Private patios. Panoramic view of countryside. Cr cds: A, D, DS, MC, V.

✔★ **SOUTH SHORE RESORT.** 1246 Sunnyside Dr (MI 55). 616/775-7641; FAX 616/775-1185; res: 800/569-8651. 16 rms, 6 kits. May-mid-Sept, Oct, hunting season, Christmas wk: S $49; D $59; each addl $5; kit. units $64-$99; lower rates rest of yr. Crib free. Pet accepted. TV; cable. Complimentary coffee. Restaurant nearby. Ck-out 11 am. Business servs avail. Downhill ski 15 mi; x-country ski 3 mi. Lawn games. Private beach. Boats; launch, dock. Refrigerators. Picnic tables. Cr cds: DS, MC, V.

✔★ **SUN 'N SNOW.** 301 S Lake Mitchell, at jct MI 55 & MI 115. 616/775-9961; res: 616/477-9961; FAX 616/775-3846. 29 rms. June-Labor Day, winter wkends, Christmas wk: S $45-$54; D $59-$69; suites $90-$115; lower rates rest of yr. Crib free. Pet accepted. TV; cable. Restaurant nearby. Ck-out 11 am. Business servs avail. Downhill ski 15 mi; x-country ski 1/4 mi. Golf privileges. Lawn games. Private beach. On Lake Mitchell. Park opp. Cr cds: DS, MC, V.

✔★ **SUPER 8.** 211 MI 55W. 616/775-8561; FAX 616/775-9392. 27 rms, 2 story. Jan-Feb, June-Aug: S $46; D $65; each addl $5; under 12 free; lower rates rest of yr. Crib free. TV; VCR avail (movies). Indoor pool; whirlpool. Complimentary continental bkfst. Restaurant opp 8 am-3 pm. Ck-out 11 am. Downhill ski 15 mi; x-country ski 1/4 mi. Some refrigerators. Cr cds: A, C, D, DS, MC, V.

Restaurants

★★ **HERMANN'S EUROPEAN CAFE.** 214 N Mitchell. 616/775-9563. Hrs: 11 am-9:30 pm; Fri, Sat to 10 pm. Closed Sun; major hols. Bar. Wine list. Continental menu. Semi-a la carte: lunch $5.50-$12, dinner $8-$22. Child's meals. Specialties: Austrian apple strudel, Wienerschnitzel, fresh seafood. Own baking. Guest rms avail. Cr cds: DS, MC, V.

★ ★ **LAKESIDE CHARLIE'S.** *301 S Lake Mitchell.* 616/775-5332. Hrs: 11:30 am-10 pm; Fri, Sat to 11 pm; Sun 11 am-8 pm; early-bird dinner 4-6 pm. Closed Mon. Res accepted. Bar to midnight; Fri, Sat to 1:30 am. Semi-a la carte: lunch $5-$7, dinner $6.95-$16.95. Child's meals. Specializes in fresh seafood, prime beef. Entertainment Fri, Sat. Patio overlooking lake. Cr cds: A, DS, MC, V.

Calumet (B-1)

(For accommodations see Copper Harbor, Hancock, Houghton)

Pop 818 **Elev** 1,208 ft **Area code** 906 **Zip** 49913 **E-mail** keweenaw @portup.com **Web** www.portup.com/snow

Information Keweenaw Peninsula Chamber of Commerce, 1197 Calumet Ave; 906/337-4579 or 800/338-7982.

What to See and Do

✪ **Calumet Theatre** (1899). Built with boom town wealth and continually being restored, this ornate theater was host to such great stars as Lillian Russell, Sarah Bernhardt, Lon Chaney, Otis Skinner, James O'Neil, Douglas Fairbanks and John Philip Sousa. Guided tours (mid-June-Sept, daily). Live performances throughout the yr. 340 6th St. Phone 906/337-2610. Tours ¢¢

Restaurant

★ **OLD COUNTRY HAUS.** *2 mi N on US 41.* 906/337-4626. Hrs: 11:30 am-9 pm; Sun brunch to 2 pm. German, Amer menu. Bar. Semi-a la carte: lunch $4-$7, dinner $7-$19. Sun brunch $7.95. Specialties: Wienerschnitzel, beef rouladen, steak. Soup & salad bar. Rustic decor. Cr cds: A, DS, MC, V.

Charlevoix (E-4)

Pop 3,116 **Elev** 599 ft **Area code** 616 **Zip** 49720 **E-mail** coc@freeway.net
Information Charlevoix Area Chamber of Commerce, 408 Bridge St; 616/547-2101.

What to See and Do

Beaver Island Boat Co. A 2¼-hr trip to Beaver Island, the largest island of the Beaver Archipelago. (June-Sept, daily; mid-Apr-May & Oct-mid-Dec, limited schedule) Advance car reservations necessary. City Dock, 103 Bridge Park Dr. Phone 616/547-2311. ¢¢¢¢

Swimming, picnicking. Depot & Ferry Ave beaches; launching ramp; tennis courts; municipal 9-hole golf course (June-Labor Day); charter fishing, boat rentals (power and sail). Lake Michigan & Lake Charlevoix beaches.

Annual Events

Venetian Festival. Midway, street and boat parades, fireworks. 4th full wkend July.

Waterfront Art Fair. East Park. 2nd Sat Aug.

Apple Festival. 2nd wkend Oct.

Motels

★ **ARCHWAY.** *1440 S Bridge St (US 31), at MI 66.* 616/547-2096; FAX 616/547-9693. 14 rms. Mid-June-mid-Aug: S, D $48-$99; lower rates rest of yr. TV; cable (premium). Pool. Restaurant adj 5:30 am-3 pm. Ck-out 10 am. Free airport transportation. Downhill/x-country ski 2 mi. Picnic tables. Cr cds: DS, MC, V.

★ ★ ★ **EDGEWATER INN.** *100 Michigan Ave.* 616/547-6044; FAX 616/547-0038; res: 800/748-0424. 60 kit. suites, 3 story. July-late Aug: 1-bedrm (up to 4) $160-$205; 2-bedrm (up to 6) $225-$275; each addl adult (after 4) $5; wkly rates; higher rates: Christmas hols, special events; lower rates rest of yr. Crib free. TV; cable (premium). Indoor/outdoor pool; whirlpool. Restaurant 7 am-10 pm. Serv bar. Ck-out 11 am. Coin lndry. Meeting rm. Business servs avail. Beauty shop. Downhill/x-country ski 1 mi. Exercise equipt; bicycles, treadmill, sauna. Some in-rm whirlpools. Private patios, balconies. Picnic tables. On lake; boat slips. Cr cds: A, MC, V.

★ **LODGE OF CHARLEVOIX.** *Box 337, US 31 North.* 616/547-6565; FAX 616/547-0741. 40 rms, 2 story. July-mid-Aug, hol wkends, Christmas hols: S, D $80-$115; each addl $5; suites $155-$165; lower rates rest of yr. Crib free. TV; cable (premium). Indoor pool. Complimentary coffee. Restaurant nearby. Ck-out 11 am. Business servs avail. Downhill/x-country ski 1 mi. Some private patios, balconies. Picnic table, grill. Overlooks harbor. Cr cds: A, D, MC, V.

★ ★ **POINTS NORTH INN.** *101 Michigan Ave.* 616/547-0055; FAX 616/547-2283; res: 800/968-5433. 23 suites, 1-2 story. Mid-June-early Sept: suites $147-$252; under 12 free; wkly rates; higher rates: Venetian Festival, art festivals, hols, Octoberfest; lower rates rest of yr. Crib free. TV; cable (premium), VCR avail. Indoor/outdoor pool. Complimentary continental bkfst. Restaurant nearby. Ck-out 11 am. Coin lndry. Business servs avail. In-rm whirlpools, refrigerators. Balconies. Cr cds: A, DS, MC, V.

★ ★ **WEATHERVANE TERRACE.** *111 Pine River Lane, just N of bridge.* 616/547-9955; FAX 616/547-0070; res: 800/552-0025 (MI). 68 rms, 2-3 story. Late June-early Sept: S, D $90-$115; suites $150-$180; under 12 free; wkly rates; ski plans; higher rates: Venetian Festival, Art Fair, Dec 29-31; lower rates rest of yr. TV; cable (premium), VCR avail (movies). Heated pool; whirlpool. Complimentary continental bkfst. Restaurant adj 11 am-11 pm in season. Ck-out 11 am. Meeting rms. Business servs avail. Downhill/x-country ski 1 mi. Refrigerators, wet bars; some fireplaces, in-rm whirlpools. Many balconies. Sun deck overlooks 2 lakes, river. Cr cds: A, D, DS, MC, V.

Restaurants

★ ★ **MAHOGANY'S.** *9600 Clubhouse Dr.* 616/547-3555. Hrs: noon-2:30 pm, 6-10 pm. Closed Dec 24, 25. Res accepted. Continental menu. Bar to midnight. Wine list. Semi-a la carte: lunch $5.50-$9, dinner $15-$26. Child's meals. Specializes in veal, seafood. Entertainment Fri, Sat. Victorian country cottage. Totally nonsmoking. Cr cds: A, MC, V.

★ ★ ★ **ROWE INN.** *(6303 County 48, Ellsworth 49729) 12 mi S via County 65 to County 48, 6 mi E of US 31.* 616/588-7351. Hrs: 6-10 pm. Closed Thanksgiving, Dec 25. Res required. Serv bar. Wine cellar. Complete meals: dinner $19.50-$29.50. Specializes in seasonal cuisine. Own baking. Family-owned. Cr cds: A, DS, MC, V.

★ ★ **STAFFORD'S WEATHERVANE.** *Pine River Channel, at drawbridge. 616/547-4311.* Hrs: 11:30 am-11 pm; Sun to 10 pm; early-bird dinner 5-6 pm. Res accepted. Bar. Semi-a la carte: lunch $4.75-$9.75, dinner $9.95-$20. Child's meals. Specializes in fresh whitefish. Overlooks Pine River Channel to Lake Michigan. Cr cds: A, MC, V.

D 🍴

★ ★ **TAPAWINGO.** *(9502 Lake St, Ellsworth) 12 mi S via County 65, 6 mi E of US 31. 616/588-7971.* Hrs: 6-9:30 pm; days vary Sept-mid-Nov, mid-Dec-June. Closed some major hols; also mid-Nov-mid-Dec. Res required. Bar. Wine cellar. Prix fixe: dinner $28-$38. Specializes in regional dishes. Menu changes seasonally. Own baking. Country atmosphere. Landscaped setting on small lake. Fieldstone fireplace. Totally nonsmoking. Cr cds: MC, V.

D

Cheboygan (E-4)

(See also Indian River, Mackinaw City)

Founded 1871 **Pop** 4,999 **Elev** 600 ft **Area code** 616 **Zip** 49721 **E-mail** info@cheboygan.com **Web** www.cheboygan.com
Information Cheboygan Area Chamber of Commerce, 124 N Main St, PO Box 69; 616/627-7183 or 800/968-3302.

Surrounded by two Great Lakes and large inland lakes, the city has long been famous as a premier boating area. Cheboygan was once a busy lumber port, but now has a wide variety of industry.

What to See and Do

Cheboygan Opera House (1877). Renovated 580-seat auditorium featuring events ranging from bluegrass to ballet. Contact Chamber of Commerce for show schedule. Huron & Backus Sts.

Fishing. Locks here lift boats to Cheboygan River leading to inland waterway which includes Mullett and Burt lakes, famous for muskie, walleye, salmon and bass. Cheboygan County is the only place in the state where sturgeon spearing is legal each winter (Feb). Along the route, marinas supply cruise needs; swimming, boating. Contact the Chamber of Commerce.

State parks.

Aloha. Approx 95 acres with swimming, sand beach; fishing; boating (launch). Picnicking. Camping (dump station). Standard fees. (Daily) 9 mi S on MI 33, then W on MI 212, on Mullett Lake. Phone 616/625-2522. Per car ¢¢

Cheboygan. More than 1,200 acres with swimming; fishing, hunting; boating. Hiking. Cross-country skiing. Picnicking. Camping. Nature study. Standard fees. (Daily) 3 mi NE off US 23, on Lake Huron. Phone 616/627-2811. Per car ¢¢

The US Coast Guard Cutter *Mackinaw.* One of the world's largest icebreakers, with a complement of 80 officers and men. When in port, the *Mackinaw* is moored at the turning basin on the E side of the Cheboygan River.

Annual Event

Cheboygan County Fair. Fairgrounds. Late July-early Aug.

Motels

★ ★ **BEST WESTERN RIVER TERRACE.** *847 S Main St (US 27). 616/627-5688; FAX 616/627-2472.* 53 rms, 2 story. Late June-early Sept: S $58-$78; D $67-$107; each addl $5; lower rates rest of yr. Crib $5. TV; cable (premium), VCR avail. Indoor pool; whirlpool. Restaurant adj 6 am-midnight (winter to 11 pm). Ck-out 11 am. Business servs avail. X-country ski 5 mi. Exercise equipt; weight machine, treadmill. Some in-rm

whirlpools. Spacious grounds, excellent view of river. Cr cds: A, C, D, DS, JCB, MC, V.

D 📶 🏊 🧗 🎿 🏊

★ ★ **DAYS INN.** *889 S Main St (US 27). 616/627-3126; FAX 616/627-2889.* 28 rms, 2 story. Mid-June-mid-Sept: S $58-$98; D $62-$110; suites $75-$150; under 16 free; higher rates Labor Day wkend; lower rates rest of yr. Crib $5. Pet accepted. TV; cable (premium). Complimentary continental bkfst. Restaurant adj 6 am-11 pm. Ck-out 11 am. Free airport, bus depot transportation. X-country ski 3 mi. Refrigerators. Balconies. On river; dockage. Cr cds: A, C, D, DS, MC, V.

D 🐾 🐾 🏊 🎿 🏊 SC

Restaurant

★ ★ **HACK-MA-TACK INN.** *8131 Beebe Rd. 616/625-2919.* Hrs: 5 pm-closing. Closed mid-Oct-mid-Apr. No A/C. Bar. Semi-a la carte: dinner $12.95-$28.95. Specializes in whitefish, prime rib. Early Amer decor; fireplace. Set in wooded area. Overlooks Cheboygan River, 400-ft dock. Guest rms avail. Cr cds: C, D, DS, MC, V.

Clare (G-4)

(See also Harrison, Midland, Mount Pleasant)

Pop 3,021 **Elev** 841 ft **Area code** 517 **Zip** 48617
Information Chamber of Commerce, 609 McEwan St; 517/386-2442.

What to See and Do

Chalet Cross-Country. Groomed cross-country trails (approx 8.5 mi) graded to skier's experience; patrol, school, rentals; store. (Dec-Mar, daily; closed Dec 25) 5931 Clare Ave, 6 mi N via Old US 27. Phone 517/386-9697. ¢¢

Annual Event

Irish Festival. Mar 10-16.

Motor Hotel

★ **DOHERTY.** *604 McEwan St (Old US 27 Business). 517/386-3441; FAX 517/386-4231; res: 800/525-4115.* 92 rms, 3 story. S $36-$65; D $46-$70; each addl $5; suites $102-$115; wkly rates; golf plans. Crib $5. Pet accepted. Indoor pool; whirlpool, poolside serv. Complimentary full bkfst Mon-Fri. Restaurant (see DOHERTY). Bar 11-2 am; entertainment Wed-Sat. Ck-out noon. Meeting rms. Business servs avail. Bellhops. Valet serv. Free airport transportation. Golf privileges. Downhill ski 5 mi; x-country ski 7 mi. Game rm. Balconies. Cr cds: A, D, DS, MC, V.

D 🐾 🏊 🧗 🎿 🏊 🏊

Restaurant

★ **DOHERTY.** *(See Doherty Motor Hotel) 517/386-3441.* Hrs: 6 am-2 pm, 5-10 pm; Fri, Sat to 11 pm; Sun to 9 pm. Res accepted. Bar 11-2 am. Semi-a la carte: bkfst $4.75-$9.25, lunch $4.95-$10.25, dinner $10-$27. Child's meals. Specializes in prime rib, fresh whitefish, homemade desserts. Salad bar. Entertainment Wed, Fri, Sat. Established 1924. Family-owned. Cr cds: A, D, DS, MC, V.

D 🍴

Coldwater (J-4)

(See also Marshall)

Pop 9,607 **Elev** 969 ft **Area code** 517 **Zip** 49036
Information Coldwater/Branch County Chamber of Commerce, 20 Division St; 517/278-5985 or 800/968-9333.

What to See and Do

Tibbits Opera House (1882). Renovated 19th-century Victorian opera house. Presently home to professional summer theater series (see SEASONAL EVENT), art exhibits, a winter concert series, children's programs and community events. Originally owned and operated by businessman Barton S. Tibbits, the house attracted such performers as John Phillip Sousa, Ethel Barrymore, P.T. Barnum, John Sullivan and William Gillette. Tours (Mon-Fri). 14 S Hanchett St. Phone 517/278-6029. Tours **Free.**

Wing House Museum (1875). Historical house museum exhibiting Second Empire architectural style. Includes original kitchen and dining room in basement; collection of Oriental rugs; oil paintings; three generations of glassware; Regina music box; furniture from Empire to Eastlake styles. (Wed-Sun, afternoons; also by appt) 27 S Jefferson St. Phone 517/278-2871. ¢

Annual Events

Quincy Chain of Lakes Tip-Up Festival. 5 mi E via US 12 on Tip-Up Island in Quincy. Parade, fishing and woodcutting contests; torchlight snowmobile ride; dancing, polar bear splash, pancake breakfast, fish fry. 2nd wkend Feb.

Bronson Polish Festival Days. SW on US 12 in Bronson. Heritage fest; games, vendors, concessions, dancing. 3rd wk July.

Branch County 4-H Fair. 4-H Fairgrounds. Exhibits, animal showing, carnival booths, rides, horse show, tractor pulling. Phone 517/279-8411. 2nd wk Aug.

Seasonal Event

Tibbits Professional Summer Theatre Series. Tibbits Opera House. Resident professional company produces comedies, musicals. Phone 517/278-6029. Late June-Aug.

Motel

★ ★ **QUALITY INN.** *1000 Orleans Blvd. 517/278-2017; FAX 517/279-7214.* 122 rms, 2 story, 24 kits. May-Oct: S $60-$65; D $67-$72; each addl $7; suites, kit. units $72-$77; under 18 free; higher rates race wkends; lower rates rest of yr. Crib free. Pet accepted. TV; cable (premium). Indoor pool; whirlpool. Complimentary continental bkfst. Restaurant 11 am-2 pm, 5-8 pm; wkend hrs vary. Rm serv. Bar 5 pm-midnight; Fri, Sat to 2 am; closed Sun; entertainment Thurs-Sat. Ck-out 11 am. Meeting rms. Business servs avail. Valet serv. X-country ski 2 mi. Game rm. Cr cds: A, C, D, DS, ER, JCB, MC, V.

⠀D ⠀⠀⠀⠀⠀ SC

Inn

★ ★ **CHICAGO PIKE.** *215 E Chicago St (US 12). 517/279-8744; FAX 517/278-8597.* 8 rms, 2 story. 2 A/C. D $80-$165; each addl $20; suite $140. Closed Thanksgiving, Dec 24, 25. Children over 12 yrs only. TV; cable (premium), VCR avail (free movies). Complimentary full bkfst; afternoon refreshments. Restaurant nearby. Ck-out noon, ck-in 3 pm. Free airport transportation. Golf privileges. X-country ski 20 mi. Bicycles avail. Horse & carriage rental. Picnic tables, grills. Victorian residence (1903); antiques; period furnishings; fireplace in sitting rm. Cr cds: A, MC, V.

Copper Harbor (B-2)

(See also Calumet)

Pop 55 (est) **Elev** 621 ft **Area code** 906 **Zip** 49918 **E-mail** keweenaw @portup.com **Web** www.portup.com/snow
Information Keweenaw Peninsula Chamber of Commerce, 1197 Calumet Ave, Calumet 49913; 906/337-4579 or 800/338-7982.

Lumps of pure copper studded the lakeshore and attracted the first explorers to this area, but deposits proved thin and unfruitful. A later lumbering boom also ended. Today this northernmost village in the state is a small but beautiful resort. Streams and inland lakes provide excellent trout, walleye, bass and northern pike angling. Lake Superior yields trout, salmon and other species.

What to See and Do

Brockway Mountain Drive. 10 mi; begins ¼ mi W of jct US 41 & MI 26; lookouts; views of Lake Superior and forests.

Delaware Mine Tour. Underground guided tour of copper mine dating back to 1850s. (Mid-May-mid-Oct, daily) 11 mi W on US 41. Phone 906/289-4688. ¢¢¢

Ferry service to Isle Royale National Park (see). Four ferries and a float plane provide transportation (June-Sept, daily; some trips in May). For fees and schedule contact Park Superintendent, 906/482-0984.

Fort Wilkins State Park. Approx 200 acres. An historic army post (1844) on Lake Fanny Hooe. The stockade has been restored and the buildings have been preserved to maintain the frontier post atmosphere. Costumed guides demonstrate old army lifestyle. Fishing; boating (launch); cross-country ski trails; picnicking, playground, concession; camping. Museum with relics of early mining days and various exhibits depicting army life in the 1870s. Standard fees. (Daily) 1 mi E on US 41. Phone 906/289-4215. Per vehicle ¢¢-¢¢¢¢

Isle Royale Queen III Evening Cruises. Narrated 1½-hr cruise on Lake Superior. Reservations advised. (July 4-Labor Day, evenings) Phone 906/289-4437. ¢¢¢-¢¢¢¢

Snowmobiling. There is a series of interconnecting trails totalling several hundred miles; some overlook Lake Superior from high bluffs. Also 17 mi of cross-country trails. (Dec-Mar)

Annual Event

Brockway Mt Challenge. 15 km cross-country ski race. Phone 906/337-4579. Jan.

Motels

★ **BELLA VISTA.** *160 Sixth St, just off jct US 41 & MI 26. 906/289-4213.* 22 rms, 1-2 story, 8 kit. cottages. No A/C. Late June-mid-Oct: D $39-$52; each addl $4; cottages for 2-5, $39-$60; lower rates May-mid-June. Closed rest of yr. TV; cable (premium). Restaurant nearby. Ck-out 10 am. Some balconies. Picnic tables. Most rms overlook harbor. On Lake Superior; dock. Cr cds: MC, V.

⠀⠀⠀⠀

★ ★ **KEWEENAW MOUNTAIN LODGE.** *US 41, 1½ mi S on US 41. 906/289-4403.* 42 units, 34 cottages. No A/C. Mid-May-mid-Oct: D $60; cabins (1-2-bedrm) $65-$76. Closed rest of yr. TV; cable (premium). Restaurant 7:30 am-9 pm. Bar from noon. Ck-out 10 am. Meeting rms. Tennis. 9-hole golf, greens fee $10-$15. Lawn games. Some fireplaces. Rustic decor. On Keweenaw Peninsula near Lake Superior. Cr cds: MC, V.

⠀D ⠀⠀⠀⠀

✔★ **MINNETONKA RESORT.** *560 Gratiot St, jct US 41 & MI 26. 906/289-4449; res: 800/433-2770.* 13 motel rms, 12 cottages, 8 kits.

No A/C. Early May-late Oct: S $46; D $46-$58; cottages for 2-10, $46-$95; $285-$500/wk. Closed rest of yr. Crib $5. Pet accepted; $5. TV; cable (premium). Restaurant opp 8 am-10 pm. Ck-out 10:30 am. Gift shop. Saunas. Picnic tables, grill. Pine-paneled cottages, many overlooking harbor, lake. Astor House Museum on premises. 8 rms across street. Cr cds: DS, MC, V.

★ **NORLAND.** *2 mi E on US 41, just past Ft Wilkins State park entrance.* 906/289-4815. 8 rms, 6 kits. No A/C. Apr-Jan: S $28-$36; D $32-$44; each addl $4. Closed rest of yr. TV; cable (premium). Restaurant nearby. Ck-out 11 am. Refrigerators. Screened picnic shelter, grill. Rustic; on lake in forested area. No cr cds accepted.

Restaurant

★ **TAMARACK INN.** *512 Gratiot St.* 906/289-4522. Hrs: 8 am-9 pm. Closed 1st wk June, 2nd wk Oct. Res accepted. Semi-a la carte: bkfst $2-$6, lunch $3.75-$6, dinner $6.95-$16. Salad bar. Overlooking lake. Cr cds: MC, V.

Dearborn (J-6)

(See also Detroit, Ypsilanti)

Settled 1763 **Pop** 89,286 **Elev** 605 ft **Area code** 313
Information Chamber of Commerce, 15544 Michigan Ave, 48126; 313/584-6100.

Dearborn is the home of the Ford Motor Company Rouge Assembly Plant, Ford World Headquarters, the Henry Ford Museum and Greenfield Village. Although Dearborn has a long and colorful history, its modern eminence is due to Henry Ford, who was born here in 1863.

What to See and Do

Henry Ford Estate-Fair Lane (1913-1915). Built by automotive pioneer Henry Ford in 1915, the mansion cost in excess of $2 million and stands on 72 acres of property. The mansion, designed by William Van Tine, reflects Ford's penchant for simplicity and functionalism; its systems for heating, water, electricity and refrigeration were entirely self-sufficient at that time. The powerhouse, boathouse and gardens have been restored, and some original furniture and children's playhouse have been returned to the premises. (Apr-Dec, daily; rest of yr, daily exc Sat, one tour per day; closed Jan 1, Dec 25) 4901 Evergreen Rd (follow signs), on the University of Michigan-Dearborn Campus. Phone 313/593-5590. ¢¢¢

Henry Ford Museum and Greenfield Village. On a 254-acre setting, this is an indoor-outdoor complex that preserves a panorama of American life of the past—an unequaled collection of American historical artifacts. Built by Henry Ford as a tribute to the culture, resourcefulness and technology of the United States, the museum and village stand as monuments to America's achievements. Dedicated in 1929 to Thomas Edison, they attract visitors each year from around the world. (Daily; closed Thanksgiving, Dec 25) 20900 Oakwood Blvd, 1/2 mi S of US 12, 1 1/2 mi W of Southfield Rd. Phone 313/271-1620 or 800/343-1929.

Henry Ford Museum, occupying 12 acres, includes major collections in transportation, power and machinery, agriculture, lighting, communications, household furnishings and appliances, ceramics, glass, silver and pewter. Special exhibits, demonstrations and hands-on activities. (Daily; closed Thanksgiving, Dec 25) Phone 313/271-1620. ¢¢¢¢

Greenfield Village is comprised of more than 80 18th-19th-century buildings moved here from all over the country. Historic homes, shops, schools, mills, stores and laboratories that figured in the lives of such historic figures as Lincoln, Webster, Burbank, McGuffey, Carver, the Wright brothers, Firestone, Edison and Ford. Among the most interest-

ing are the courthouse where Abraham Lincoln practiced law, the Wright brothers' cycle shop, Henry Ford's birthplace, Edison's Menlo Park laboratory, homes of Noah Webster and Luther Burbank, 19th-century farmstead of Harvey Firestone; steam-operated industries, crafts workers, demonstrations, home activites. (Daily; closed Thanksgiving, Dec 25; interiors also closed Jan-mid-Mar) Also winter sleigh tours. Phone 313/271-1620. ¢¢¢¢   Also here is

Suwanee Park. Turn-of-the-century amusement center with antique merry-go-round, steamboat, train ride; restaurant, soda fountain. (Mid-May-Sept) Some fees.

In addition, visitors can take narrated rides in a horse-drawn carriage (fee), on a steam train (fee), or on a riverboat; 1931 Ford bus rides are also avail (mid-May-Sept). Varied activities are scheduled throughout the yr (see ANNUAL EVENTS). Meals and refreshments are available. Combination ticket for Henry Ford Museum & Greenfield Village ¢¢¢¢

Annual Events

Colonial Life Festival. Greenfield Village. Early July.

Homecoming. Ford Field. 1st wkend Aug.

Old Car Festival. Greenfield Village. 2 days mid-Sept.

Fall Harvest Days. Greenfield Village. Celebrates turn-of-the-century farm chores, rural home life and entertainment. 3 days early Oct.

Motels

★ ★ ★ **BEST WESTERN GREENFIELD INN.** *(3000 Enterprise Dr, Allen Park 48101) SE on Oakwood Blvd, at I-94 exit 206A.* 313/271-1600; FAX 313/271-1600, ext. 7189. 210 rms, 3 story. S $75-$95; D $85-$105; each addl $10; suites $99-$129; under 20 free. Crib $10. TV; cable (premium), VCR (movies). Indoor pool; whirlpool, poolside serv. Restaurant 6 am-10 pm. Rm serv. Bar 11 am-midnight. Ck-out noon. Coin lndry. Meeting rms. Business servs avail. In-rm modem link. Bellhops. Valet serv. Sundries. Free airport, RR station, bus depot transportation. Downhill ski 14 mi; x-country ski 4 mi. Exercise equipt; weights, bicycles, sauna. Bathrm phones, refrigerators; some in-rm whirlpools. Cr cds: A, C, D, DS, ER, JCB, MC, V.

★ ★ **COURTYARD BY MARRIOTT.** *5200 Mercury Dr (48126).* 313/271-1400; FAX 313/271-1184. 147 rms, 2-3 story. S, D $89-$105; suites $105-$114; under 12 free; wknd rates. Crib free. TV; cable (premium). Indoor pool; whirlpool. Coffee in rms. Bkfst avail. Bar Sun-Thurs 5:30-9:30 pm. Ck-out noon. Coin lndry. Meeting rms. Business servs avail. In-rm modem link. Valet serv (Mon-Fri). Exercise equipt; weights, bicycles. Some refrigerators. Private patios, balconies. Cr cds: A, D, DS, MC, V.

★ ★ **HAMPTON INN.** *20061 Michigan Ave (US 12) (48124).* 313/436-9600; FAX 313/436-8345. 119 rms, 4 story. S, D $77-$87; suites $122-$132; under 18 free. Crib free. TV; cable (premium). Indoor pool. Complimentary continental bkfst. Complimentary coffee in rms. Restaurant nearby. Ck-out noon. Coin lndry. Meeting rm. Business servs avail. In-rm modem link. Valet serv. Refrigerator, wet bar in suites. Overlooks Henry Ford Museum & Greenfield Village. Cr cds: A, C, D, DS, MC, V.

★ ★ **QUALITY INN FAIRLANE.** *21430 Michigan Ave (US 12) (48124).* 313/565-0800; FAX 313/565-2813. 100 rms, 2 story. S, D $89-$119; each addl $5; family, wknd rates. Crib free. TV; cable (premium), VCR avail (movies $5). Heated pool. Complimentary continental bkfst. Ck-out noon. Meeting rms. Business servs avail. In-rm modem link. Refrigerators. Near Henry Ford Museum & Greenfield Village. Cr cds: A, C, D, DS, ER, JCB, MC, V.

✔★ **RED ROOF INN.** *24130 Michigan Ave (US 12) (48124).* 313/278-9732; FAX 313/278-9741. 112 rms, 2 story. June-Aug: S $39.99-

$59.99; D $49.99-$69.99; 1-2 addl, $59.99-$69.99; under 18 free; lower rates rest of yr. Crib free. Pet accepted, some restrictions. TV; cable (premium). Complimentary coffee in lobby. Restaurant adj 6:30 am-5:30 pm; cafe opp to 11 pm. Ck-out noon. Business servs avail. Cr cds: A, C, D, DS, MC, V.

Hotels

★ ★ ★ **DEARBORN INN, A MARRIOTT HOTEL.** 20301 Oakwood Blvd (48124). 313/271-2700; FAX 313/271-7464. 222 rms, 2-4 story. 22 suites. S $119-$139; D $129-$149; suites $200-$275; under 18 free; wknd rates; package plans. Crib free. Pet accepted, some restrictions. TV; cable (premium), VCR avail. Heated pool; wading pool; poolside serv. Coffee in rms. Restaurant 6:30 am-11 pm. Bar 11-1 am; entertainment. Ck-out noon. Meeting rms. Business servs avail. In-rm modem link. Concierge. Gift shop. Tennis. Exercise equipt; treadmill, stair machine. Lawn games. Some refrigerators. Consists of Georgian-style inn built by Henry Ford (1931), two Colonial-style lodges and five Colonial-style houses; early Amer decor and furnishings. On 23 acres; gardens. Luxury level. Cr cds: A, C, D, DS, ER, JCB, MC, V.

★ ★ ★ **HYATT REGENCY.** 18600 Michigan Ave (48126), at Fairlane Town Center. 313/593-1234; FAX 313/593-3366. 771 rms, 16 story. S, D $160-$185; each addl $25; suites $350-$720; under 18 free; wknd rates. Crib free. Valet parking $9. TV; cable (premium). Indoor pool; whirlpool. Restaurants 6:30 am-midnight. Bars, 1 revolving. Ck-out noon. Convention facilities. Business center. In-rm modem link. Exercise equipt; weights, bicycles, sauna. Health club privileges. 16-story atrium, glass elevators. Near Henry Ford Museum and Greenfield Village. Cr cds: A, C, D, DS, ER, JCB, MC, V.

★ ★ ★ **THE RITZ-CARLTON, DEARBORN.** 300 Town Center Dr (48126), in Fairlane Town Center. 313/441-2000; FAX 313/441-2051. At this hotel, the service is polished and the public rooms sumptuously decorated with chandeliers, marble, art and antiques. Guest rooms are spacious and have marble bathrooms. 308 rms, 11 story. S, D $135-$195; suites $375-$900; under 12 free; wknd rates. Valet/garage parking $12. TV; cable (premium), VCR avail. Indoor pool; whirlpool; poolside serv. Restaurant (see THE GRILLE). Rm serv 24 hrs. Bar 11-1 am; entertainment. Ck-out noon. Convention facilities. Business center. In-rm modem link. Concierge. Gift shop. Tennis privileges. Golf privileges. Exercise equipt; weight machine, bicycles, sauna. Massage. Health club privileges. Bathrm phones, minibars; some wet bars; microwaves avail. Ballroom. Luxury level. Cr cds: A, C, D, DS, ER, JCB, MC, V.

Restaurants

★ ★ ★ **THE GRILLE.** (See The Ritz-Carlton, Dearborn Hotel) 313/441-2000. Hrs: 6:30 am-2:30 pm, 6-10 pm; Fri, Sat 6-11 pm; Sun brunch 10:30 am-2 pm. Res accepted. Continental menu. Bar 11-1 am; Sun to midnight. Wine cellar. A la carte entrees: bkfst $8-$13, lunch $8-$20, dinner $18-$35. Buffet: lunch $22.50. Sun brunch $35. Own baking, desserts. Pianist, harpist. Valet parking. Club-like setting; brass chandeliers, 18th- and 19th-century oil paintings. Cr cds: A, C, D, DS, ER, JCB, MC, V.

★ ★ **KIERNAN'S STEAK HOUSE.** 21931 Michigan Ave (US 12) (48124). 313/565-4260. Hrs: 11 am-11 pm; Sat from 5 pm; Sun 4-9 pm. Closed most major hols. Res accepted. Bar to midnight. Semi-a la carte: lunch $7-$17.95, dinner $9.95-$17.95. Specializes in steak, seafood, veal. Valet parking. Intimate atmosphere. Cr cds: A, MC, V.

★ ★ **MORO'S.** (6535 Allen Rd, Allen Park 48101) 313/382-7152. Hrs: 11 am-10 pm; Sat 4-10 pm; Sun 2-8 pm. Closed most major hols; also Sun June-Aug. Italian menu. Wine list. Semi-a la carte: lunch $5-$15, dinner $10-$25. Specializes in veal, steak. Casual, Italian decor. Totally nonsmoking. Cr cds: A, MC, V.

Detroit (J-6)

Founded 1701 **Pop** 1,027,974 **Elev** 600 ft **Area code** 313 **Web** www.visitdetroit.com

Information Metropolitan Detroit Convention and Visitors Bureau, 100 Renaissance Center, 19th floor, 48243; 800/DETROIT.

Suburbs Ann Arbor, Birmingham, Bloomfield Hills, Dearborn, Farmington, Mount Clemens, Plymouth, Pontiac, St Clair, Southfield, Troy, Warren, Ypsilanti. (See individual alphabetical listings.)

Detroit, a high-speed city geared to the tempo of the production line, is the symbol throughout the world of America's productive might. Its name is almost synonymous with the word "automobile." The city that put the world on wheels, Detroit is the birthplace of mass production and the producer of nearly 25 percent of the nation's automobiles, trucks and tractors. Every year a new generation of vehicles is hammered out in its factories. This is the city of Ford, Chrysler, the Fishers, Dodge and the UAW. Detroit is a major producer of space propulsion units, automation equipment, plane parts, hardware, rubber tires, office equipment, machine tools, fabricated metal, iron and steel forging, auto stampings and accessories. Being a port and border city, Detroit puts the Michigan Customs District among the nation's top five customs districts.

Founded by Antoine de la Mothe Cadillac in the name of Louis XIV of France at le place du détroit—"the place of the strait"—this strategic frontier trading post was 75 years old when the Revolution began. During the War of Independence, Detroit was ruled by Henry Hamilton, the British governor hated throughout the colonies as "the hair buyer of Detroit." He encouraged his Native Americans to take rebel scalps rather than prisoners. At the end of the war, the British ignored treaty obligations and refused to abandon Detroit. As long as Detroit remained in British hands, it was both a strategic threat and a barrier to westward expansion; however, the settlement was finally wrested away by Major General Anthony Wayne at the Battle of Fallen Timbers. On July 11, 1796, the Stars and Stripes flew over Detroit for the first time.

During the War of 1812, the fortress at Detroit fell mysteriously into British hands again, without a shot fired. It was recaptured by the Americans the following year. In 1815, when the city was incorporated, Detroit was still just a trading post; by 1837, it was a city of 10,000 people. Then, the development of more efficient transportation opened the floodgates of immigration, and the city was on its way as an industrial and shipping hub. Between 1830 and 1860, population doubled with every decade. At the turn of the century, the auto industry took hold. Today, Detroit is a leader in the fields of automation and space exploration equipment. Yet it is a city that acknowledges its traditions as a French fort and frontier trading post. It looks to the future as well as the past.

Detroit was a quiet city before the automobile—brewing beer and hammering together carriages and stoves. Most people owned their own homes—they called it "the most beautiful city in America." All this swiftly changed when the automobile age burst upon it. Growth became the important concern; production stood as the summit of achievement. The automobile lines produced a new civic personality—there was little time for culture at the end of a day on the line. The city rocketed out beyond its river-hugging confines, developing nearly 100 suburbs. Today growing pains have eased, the automobile worker has more leisure time and a new Detroit personality is emerging. Civic planning is remodeling the face of the community, particularly downtown and along the riverfront. Five minutes from downtown, twenty separate institutions form Detroit's Cultural Center—all within easy walking distance of one another.

Detroit is one of the few cities in the US where you can look due south into Canada. The city stretches out along the Detroit River between lakes Erie and St Clair, opposite the Canadian city of Windsor, Ontario (see). Detroit is 143 square miles in size and almost completely flat. The buildings

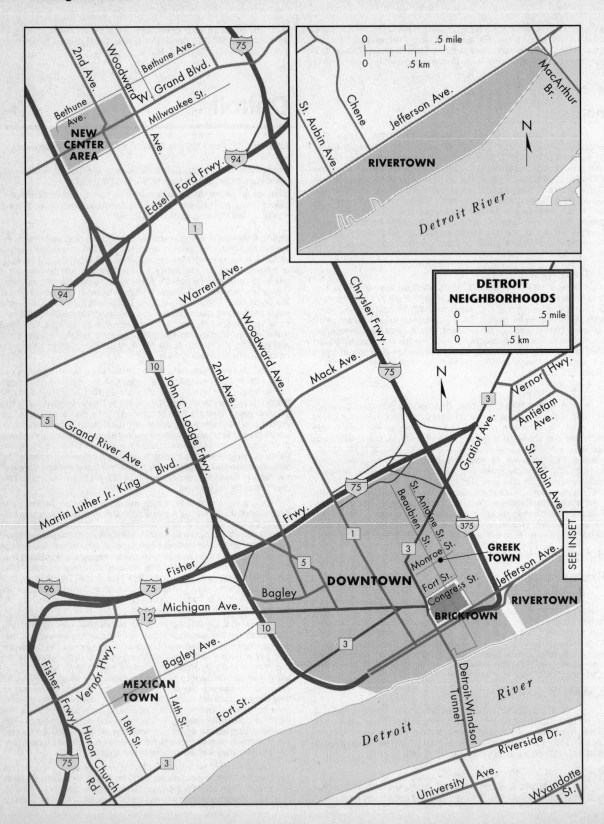

NEW CENTER AREA

2nd Ave.

Woodward

Bethune Ave.

W. Grand Blvd.

Bethune Ave.

Milwaukee St.

Ave.

75

94

Edsel Ford Frwy.

1

94

Warren Ave.

Woodward Ave.

10

Mack Ave.

Chrysler Frwy.

75

John C. Lodge Frwy.

2nd Ave.

5

Grand River Ave.

Blvd.

Martin Luther Jr. King

Frwy.

1

5

Fisher

96

75

Bagley

DOWNTOWN

Michigan Ave.

12

Bagley Ave.

10

Fisher Frwy.

Vernor Hwy.

MEXICAN TOWN

14th St.

18th St.

Fort St.

3

Huron Church Rd.

75

3

Detroit

River

University Ave.

Riverside Dr.

Wyandotte St.

Vernor Hwy.

Gratiot Ave.

3

Antietam Ave.

St. Aubin Ave.

St. Antoine St.

Beaubien St.

375

3

Monroe St.

GREEK TOWN

Fort St.

Congress St.

Jefferson Ave.

BRICKTOWN

RIVERTOWN

Detroit-Windsor Tunnel

SEE INSET

Inset (top right):

0 — .5 mile

0 — .5 km

St. Aubin Ave.

Chene

Jefferson Ave.

MacArthur Br.

RIVERTOWN

N

Detroit River

DETROIT NEIGHBORHOODS

0 — .5 mile

0 — .5 km

N

of the Renaissance Center and Civic Center are grouped about the shoreline, and a network of major highways and expressways radiate from this point, like the spokes of a fan. The original city was laid out on the lines of the L'Enfant plan for Washington, DC, with a few major streets radiating from a series of circles. As the city grew, a gridiron pattern was superimposed to handle the maze of subdivisions that had developed into Detroit's 200 neighborhoods.

These main thoroughfares all originate near the Civic Center: Fort St (MI 3); Michigan Ave (US 12); Grand River Ave (I-96); John Lodge Freeway (US 10); Woodward Ave (MI 1); Gratiot Ave (MI 3); and Fisher and Chrysler Freeways (I-75). Intersecting these and almost parallel with the shoreline are the Edsel Ford Freeway (I-94) and Jefferson Ave (US 25).

Transportation

Airport: See DETROIT WAYNE COUNTY AIRPORT AREA.

Car Rental Agencies: See IMPORTANT TOLL-FREE NUMBERS.

Public Transportation: Buses (Suburban Mobility Authority for Regional Transportation), phone 313/962-5515 or 313/935-4910 (Detroit Department of Transportation). Elevated train downtown (the People Mover), phone 800/541-RAIL.

Rail Passenger Service: Amtrak 800/872-7245.

What to See and Do

✪ **Belle Isle.** Between US and Canada, in sight of downtown Detroit, this 1,000-acre island park offers 9-hole golf, a nature center, guided nature walks, swimming, fishing (piers, docks). Picnicking, ball fields, tennis and lighted handball courts. An island park in middle of Detroit River, reached by MacArthur Bridge. Phone 313/267-7115. **Free.** Also here are

Whitcomb Conservatory. Exhibits of ferns, cacti, palms, orchids; special exhibits. (Wed-Sun) Phone 313/267-7134. ¢

Belle Isle Zoo. Animals in natural habitat. (Apr-Oct, daily) Phone 313/852-4083. ¢¢¢

Aquarium. One of the largest and oldest freshwater collections in the country. (Daily) Phone 313/267-7159. ¢

Dossin Great Lakes Museum. Scale models of Great Lakes ships; restored "Gothic salon" from Great Lakes liner; marine paintings, reconstructed ship's bridge and full-scale racing boat, *Miss Pepsi*. (Wed-Sun) Phone 313/267-6440. **Donation.**

Canada. Windsor, Ontario (see), is only a 5-min drive through the Detroit-Windsor tunnel or via the Ambassador Bridge. Tunnel & bridge tolls. Buses run every 12 min (fee). For Border Crossing Regulations, see MAKING THE MOST OF YOUR TRIP.

Children's Museum. Exhibits include "America Discovered," Inuit culture, children's art, folk crafts, birds and mammals of Michigan, holiday themes. Participatory activities relate to exhibits. Special workshops and programs and planetarium demonstrations on Sat and during vacations. (Oct-May, daily exc Sun; rest of yr, Mon-Fri; closed hols) 67 E Kirby Ave. Phone 313/494-1210. **Free.**

Civic Center. Dramatic group of buildings in a 95-acre downtown riverfront setting. Woodward & Jefferson Aves. Included in this group are

City-County Building. A $27 million, 13-story white marble office building and 19-story tower housing more than 36 government departments and courtrooms. At front entrance is massive bronze sculpture, *Spirit of Detroit*. Building (Mon-Fri; closed hols). 2 Woodward Ave. Phone 313/224-5585. **Free.**

Cobo Hall-Cobo Arena. Designed to be the world's finest convention-exposition-recreation building; features a 11,561-seat arena and 720,000 sq ft of exhibit area and related facilities. (Daily) W Jefferson Ave & Washington Blvd. For information on Cobo Conference/Exhibition Center events phone 313/887-8111.

Veterans' Memorial Building. Rises on site where Cadillac and first French settlers landed in 1701. This $5.75 million monument to the Detroit area war dead was the first unit of the $180 million Civic Center to be completed. The massive sculptured-marble eagle on the front of

the building is by Marshall Fredericks, who also sculpted *Spirit of Detroit* at City-County Building. 151 W Jefferson Ave. Phone 313/877-8111.

Mariners' Church. Oldest stone church in the city, completed in 1849, was moved 800 ft to present site as part of Civic Center plan. Since that time it has been extensively restored and a belltower with carillon has been added. Tours (by appt). 170 E Jefferson Ave. Phone 313/259-2206. **Free.**

Hart Plaza & Dodge Fountain. A $2-million water display designed by sculptor Isamu Noguchi. Jefferson Ave.

Michigan Consolidated Gas Company Building. Glass-walled skyscraper designed by Minoru Yamasaki. 1 Woodward Ave.

Detroit Historical Museum. Presents a walk through history along reconstructed streets of Old Detroit, period alcoves, costumes; changing exhibits portray city life. The museum now showcases a new automotive exhibition, celebrating the 100th anniversary of the automotive industry. (Wed-Sun; closed hols) 5401 Woodward Ave. Phone 313/833-1805. ¢

Detroit Institute of Arts (1885). One of the great art museums of the world, tells history of man through his artistic creations. Every significant art-producing culture is represented. Exhibits include *The Detroit Industry* murals by Diego Rivera, Van Eyck's *St Jerome*, Bruegel's *Wedding Dance* and Van Gogh's *Self-Portrait*; African, American, Indian, Dutch, French, Flemish and Italian collections; medieval arms and armor; an 18th-century American country house reconstructed with period furnishings. Frequent special exhibitions (fee); lectures, films. (Wed-Sun; closed Jan 1, Dec 25) 5200 Woodward Ave, between Farnsworth Ave & Kirby St. Phone 313/833-7900. ¢¢

Detroit Public Library. Murals by Coppin, Sheets, Melchers and Blashfield; special collections include National Automotive History, Burton Historical (Old Northwest Territory), Hackley (African-Americans in performing arts), Labor, Maps, Rare Books, US Patents Collection from 1790 to present. (Tues-Sat; closed hols) 5201 Woodward Ave. Phone 313/833-1000. **Free.**

Detroit Symphony Orchestra Hall (1919). Restored public concert hall features classical programs. The Detroit Symphony Orchestra performs here (Sept-May). 3711 Woodward Ave, at Parsons. Phone 313/833-3700.

Detroit Zoo. One of the world's outstanding zoos, with 40 exhibits of more than 1,200 animals in natural habitats. Outstanding chimpanzee, reptile, bear, penguin and bird exhibits. (May-Oct, daily; rest of yr, Wed-Sun; closed Jan 1, Thanksgiving, Dec 25) 10 mi N via Woodward Ave, at I-696 in Royal Oak. Phone 313/398-0903. ¢¢¢

Eastern Market (1892). Built originally on the site of an early hay and wood market, this and the Chene-Ferry Market are the two remaining produce/wholesale markets. Today the Eastern Market encompasses produce and meat-packing houses, fish markets and storefronts offering items ranging from spices to paper. It is also recognized as the world's largest bedding flower market. (Daily exc Sun; closed hols) 2934 Russell, via I-75 at Gratiot. Phone 313/833-1560. **Free.**

Fisher Building (1928). Designed by architect Albert Kahn, this building was recognized in 1928 as the most beautiful commercial building erected and given a silver medal by the Architectural League of New York. The building consists of a 28-story central tower and two 11-story wings. Housed here are the Fisher Theater, shops, restaurants, art galleries and offices. Underground pedestrian walkways and skywalk bridges connect to parking deck and eleven separate structures, including General Motors World Headquarters and New Center One. W Grand & Second Blvds. Phone 313/874-4444.

Gray Line bus tours. Contact 1301 E Warren Ave, 48207; 313/935-3808.

Historic Trinity Lutheran Church (1931). Third church of congregation founded in 1850; 16th-century-style pier-and-clerestory, neo-Gothic small cathedral. Luther tower is a copy of the tower at a monastery in Erfurt, Germany. Much statuary and stained glass. Bell tower. (Daily; no tours during services) 1345 Gratiot Ave. Phone 313/567-3100. **Donation.**

Huron-Clinton Metroparks. A system of 13 recreation areas in the surrounding suburbs of Detroit (see ANN ARBOR, FARMINGTON, MOUNT CLEMENS and TROY).

International Institute of Metropolitan Detroit. Hall of Nations has cultural exhibits from five continents (Mon-Fri; closed hols). Cultural programs and ethnic festivals throughout the yr. 111 E Kirby Ave. Phone 313/871-8600. **Free.**

Motown Museum. "Hitsville USA," the house where legends like Diana Ross and the Supremes, Stevie Wonder, Marvin Gaye, the Jackson Five and the Temptations recorded their first hits. Motown's original recording Studio A; artifacts, photographs, gold and platinum records, memorabilia. Guided tours. (Tues-Sat, also Sun & Mon afternoons) 2648 W Grand Blvd. Phone 313/875-2264. ¢¢

Museum of African-American History. Exhibitions trace the history and achievements of black people in the Americas. (Wed-Sun; closed hols) 315 E Warren Ave. In the University Cultural Center. Phone 313/833-9800. **Free.**

Professional sports.

American League baseball (Detroit Tigers). Tiger Stadium, Michigan Ave at Trumbull. Phone 313/962-4000.

NBA (Detroit Pistons). The Palace of Auburn Hills, 3777 Lapeer Rd (MI 24), Auburn Hills (see PONTIAC). Phone 248/377-0100.

NFL (Detroit Lions), Pontiac Silverdome, 1200 Featherstone Rd, Pontiac (see). Phone 248/355-4131.

NHL (Detroit Red Wings). Joe Louis Arena, 600 Civic Center Dr. Phone 313/396-7544.

Renaissance Center. Seven-tower complex on the riverfront; includes 73-story hotel (see HOTELS), offices, restaurants, bars, movie theaters, retail shops and business services. Jefferson Ave at Beaubien. Phone 313/568-5600.

Trappers Alley. Historic furrier and tannery buildings renovated as a 5-floor marketplace featuring art gallery, restaurants and shopping. (Daily; closed some major hols) 508 Monroe Ave at Beaubien, in Greektown. Phone 313/963-5445.

★ **Washington Boulevard Trolley Car.** Antique electric trolley cars provide a unique transit service to downtown hotels, the Civic Center and the Renaissance Center. From late May-Labor Day Detroit operates the only open-top double-decker trolley car in the world. (Daily) Phone 313/933-1300 for schedule. ¢

Wayne State University (1868). (34,950 students) Has 13 professional schools and colleges. The campus has almost 100 buildings, some of the most notable being the award-winning McGregor Memorial Conference Center designed by Minoru Yamasaki and its sculpture court; the Walter P. Reuther Library of Labor and Urban Affairs; and the Yamasaki-designed College of Education. Wayne has a medical campus of 16 acres adj in the Detroit Medical Center. Three theaters present performances (Oct-May & July-mid-Aug, Tues-Sat; fee); for schedule phone 313/577-2972. 656 W Kirby. For university information phone 313/577-2424.

Annual Events

International Auto Show. Cobo Hall. Jan.

Detroit Grand Prix. Belle Isle. Indy car race. Fri is Free Prix Day. Phone 313/259-7749. Early June.

International Freedom Festival. Joint celebration with Detroit and Windsor; nearly 100 events, including fireworks. Phone 313/887-8200. Late June-early July.

Michigan State Fair. Michigan Exposition & Fairgrounds. Phone 313/369-8250. Aug 18-31.

Montreux Detroit Jazz Festival. Hart Plaza, downtown. 5 days of free jazz concerts. Early Sept-Labor Day wkend.

Christmas Carnival. Cobo Conference/Exhibition Center. Displays, attractions for young and old. Phone 313/887-8200. Dec.

Seasonal Events

Horse racing.

Northville Downs. 301 S Center St in Northville. Harness racing. Over 12 yrs only. Phone 810/349-1000. Daily exc Wed. Jan-Apr & Oct-Dec.

Ladbroke-DRC. W via I-96, at 28001 Schoolcraft Rd in Livonia. Phone 313/525-7300. Thoroughbred racing. Wed-Sun. Mid-Mar-late Dec.

Hazel Park. 1650 E Ten Mile Rd. Phone 313/398-1000. Harness racing nightly exc Sun. Apr-mid-Oct.

Riverfront Festivals. Hart Plaza, downtown riverfront. Wkend festivals featuring entertainment, costumes, history, artifacts and handicrafts of Detroit's diverse ethnic populations. Different country featured most wkends. Phone 313/224-1184. May-Sept.

The Theatre Company-University of Detroit Mercy. 4001 W McNichols Rd. Dramas, comedies in university theater. Phone 313/993-1130. Sept-May.

Meadow Brook Theatre. Oakland University in Rochester (see PONTIAC).

Meadow Brook Music Festival (see PONTIAC).

Additional Visitor Information

The Metropolitan Detroit Convention and Visitors Bureau, 100 Renaissance Center, 19th Floor, 48243, phone 800/DETROIT, publishes the *Visitor's Guide to Greater Detroit*, a helpful booklet describing the area. Information is also available from the City of Detroit, Department of Public Information, 608 City-County Bldg, 48226; phone 313/224-3755. In addition, there are Detroit Visitor and Information Centers located at 100 Renaissance Center, 1st floor and at Henry Ford Museum and Greenfield Village in Dearborn (see) that provide booklets and brochures on the city. To receive an information packet on Detroit or to inquire about lodgings phone the "Whats Line," 800/DETROIT.

Detroit Metro Airport Area

For additional accommodations, see DETROIT WAYNE COUNTY AIRPORT AREA, which follows DETROIT.

City Neighborhoods

Many of the restaurants, unrated dining establishments and some lodgings listed under Detroit include neighborhoods as well as exact street addresses. Geographic descriptions of these areas are given, followed by a table of restaurants arranged by neighborhood.

Bricktown: Area of Downtown south of Fort St, west of St Antoine St, north of the Renaissance Center (Jefferson St) and east of MI3.

Downtown: South of Fisher Frwy (I-75), west of Walter P Chrysler Frwy (I-375), north of the Detroit River and east of John C Lodge Expy (MI 10).

East of Downtown: East of I-375.

Greektown: Area of Downtown on Monroe St between Beaubien St on the west and St Antoine St on the east.

Mexican Town: West of Downtown; along Bagley Ave between 14th and 18th Sts.

New Center Area: North of Downtown; south of Bethune Ave, west of Woodward, north of Milwaukee and east of MI 10.

Rivertown: East of Downtown; south of Jefferson Ave, west of MacArthur Bridge and north of the Detroit River.

DETROIT RESTAURANTS BY NEIGHBORHOOD AREAS
(For full description, see alphabetical listings under Restaurants)

DOWNTOWN
Caucus Club. 150 W Congress St
Intermezzo. 1435 Randolph St
Opus One. 565 E Larned
Traffic Jam & Snug. 511 W Canfield St
Tres Vite. 2203 Woodward Ave
The Whitney. 4421 Woodward Ave

EAST OF DOWNTOWN
Joe Muer's. 2000 Gratiot Ave
Van Dyke Place. 649 Van Dyke Ave

GREEKTOWN
Fishbone's Rhythm Kitchen Cafe. 400 Monroe St
Pegasus Taverna. 558 Monroe St

MEXICAN TOWN
El Zocalo. 3400 Bagley

NEW CENTER AREA
Pegasus In The Fisher. 3011 W Grand Blvd

RIVERTOWN
Baron's Steakhouse (The River Place Hotel). 1000 River Place
Rattlesnake Club. 300 Stroh River Place

Note: When a listing is located in a town that does not have its own city heading, it will appear under the city nearest to its location. In these cases, the address and town appear in parenthesis immediately following the name of the establishment.

Motels

★ ★ **BEST WESTERN LIVONIA PARK SUITES.** *(16999 S Laurel Park Dr, Livonia 48154) 30 mi W on I-96 to I-275, N on I-275 to jct Six Mile Rd.* 313/464-0050; FAX 313/464-5869. 123 rms, 2 story. S $59-$79; D $59-$129; each addl $8. Crib free. TV; cable (premium). Heated pool. Complimentary continental bkfst. Ck-out noon. Meeting rms. Business servs avail. In-rm modem link. X-country ski 5 mi. Exercise equipt; weight machine, rower. Refrigerators; some in-rm whirlpools, minibars. Cr cds: A, C, D, DS, ER, JCB, MC, V.

D ⊠ ≈ ✕ ⊠ ⚒ SC

★ ★ **COURTYARD BY MARRIOTT.** *(17200 N Laurel Park Dr, Livonia 48152) W via I-96 to I-275, N to Six Mile Rd.* 313/462-2000; FAX 313/462-5907. 149 rms, 3 story. S, D $96-$106; suites $125-$135; wkend rates. Crib free. TV; cable (premium). Indoor pool; whirlpool. Restaurant 6:30-10 am; Sat 7-11 am; Sun 7 am-1 pm. Bar 4-11 pm; closed Sat, Sun. Ck-out noon. Coin Indry. Meeting rms. Business servs avail. In-rm modem link. Valet serv. Downhill/x-country ski 20 mi. Exercise equipt; weights, bicycles. Refrigerator in suites. Private patios, balconies. Cr cds: A, D, DS, MC, V.

D ⊠ ≈ ✕ ⊠ ⚒ SC

★ ★ **PARKCREST INN.** *(20000 Harper Ave, Harper Woods 48225) NE on I-94, exit 224B.* 313/884-8800; FAX 313/884-7087. 49 rms, 2 story. S $59; D $67-$72; kit. units $84; family rates. Crib free. Pet accepted. TV; cable (premium). Heated pool. Restaurant 6:30-2:30 am; Sun 7:30 am-10 pm. Rm serv. Bar to 2 am. Ck-out 11 am. Valet serv. X-country ski 15 mi. Cr cds: A, C, D, DS, MC, V.

❤ ⊠ ≈ ⊠ ⚒ SC

🚶★ **SHORECREST MOTOR INN.** *1316 E Jefferson Ave (48207), downtown.* 313/568-3000; FAX 313/568-3002; res: 800/992-9616. 54 rms, 2 story. S $49-$63; D $55-$79; family, wkly, wkend rates. Crib free. Pet accepted, some restrictions. TV; cable (premium). Restaurant 6 am-10 pm; wkends from 7 am. Rm serv. Ck-out noon. Business servs avail. Valet serv. Refrigerators. Cr cds: A, C, D, DS, MC, V.

D ❤ ⚒ SC

Motor Hotel

★ ★ ★ **HOLIDAY INN.** *5801 Southfield Service Dr (48228), west of downtown.* 313/336-3340; FAX 313/336-7037. 347 rms, 6 story. S, D $99; suites $250; under 18 free; wkend rates. Crib free. TV; cable (premium). 2 pools, 1 indoor; whirlpool. Coffee in rms. Restaurant 6 am-2 pm, 5-10 pm; Sat, Sun from 7 am. Rm serv. Bar 11 am-midnight. Ck-out noon. Convention facilities. Business center. Bellhops. Gift shop. Exercise equipt; bicycles, stair machine, sauna. Game rm. Cr cds: A, C, D, DS, JCB, MC, V.

D ≈ ✕ ⊠ ⚒ SC ⚒

Hotels

★ ★ ★ **ATHENEUM.** *1000 Brush Ave (48226), in Greektown.* 313/962-2323; FAX 313/962-2424; res: 800/772-2323. 174 suites, 10 story. Suites $125-$600; each addl $20; family, wkly rates. Crib free. Valet parking $8. TV; cable (premium), VCR avail. Restaurant adj 8 am-midnight. Rm serv 24 hrs. Bar. Ck-out noon. Meeting rms. Business servs avail. In-rm modem link. Concierge. Gift shop. Exercise equipt; bicycle, stair machine. Minibars; some bathrm phones. Neoclassical structure adj International Center. Cr cds: A, C, D, DS, ER, JCB, MC, V.

D ✕ ⊠ ⚒ SC

★ ★ ★ **DOUBLETREE-DOWNTOWN.** *333 E Jefferson Ave (48226), downtown.* 313/222-7700; FAX 313/222-6509. 255 rms, 21 story. S $180-$250; D $190-$250; each addl $20; suites $250-$1,000; under 18 free; wkend rates. Valet parking $9. Crib free. TV; cable. Indoor pool; whirlpool, poolside serv. Coffee in rms. Restaurant 6:30 am-10 pm; Fri, Sat to 11 pm. Bar 11-2 am. Meeting rms. Business servs avail. In-rm modem link. Shopping arcade. Barber, beauty shop. Tennis. Racquetball. Exercise rm; instructor, weights, bicycles, sauna. Bathrm phone & TV, refrigerator in suites. Opp river. Cr cds: A, C, D, DS, MC, V.

D 🏋 ≈ ✕ ⊠ ⚒ SC 🚶

★ ★ **EMBASSY SUITES.** *(19525 Victor Pkwy, Livonia 48152) W on I-96 to I-275N, exit Seven Mile Rd E.* 313/462-6000; FAX 313/462-6003. 239 suites, 5 story. S $129-$149; D $139-$159; each addl $10; under 12 free (max 2); wkend rates; higher rates special events. Crib free. TV; cable (premium), VCR avail. Indoor pool; whirlpool. Complimentary full bkfst. Complimentary coffee in rms. Restaurant 6-9 am, 11 am-4 pm, 5-10 pm; hrs vary Fri-Sun. Bar 5 pm-midnight; closed Sun. Ck-out noon. Coin Indry. Meeting rms. Business servs avail. In-rm modem link. Gift shop. Exercise equipt; weight machine, rowers, sauna. Refrigerators. Balconies. Five-story atrium. Cr cds: A, C, D, DS, JCB, MC, V.

D ≈ ✕ ⊠ ⚒ SC

★ ★ ★ **MARRIOTT.** *(17100 Laurel Park Dr N, Livonia 48152) 30 mi W on I-96 to I-275, N on I-275 to Six Mile Rd.* 313/462-3100; FAX 313/462-2815. 224 rms, 6 story. S, D $124-$139; suites $225; family, wkend rates. Crib free. TV; cable (premium), VCR avail. Indoor pool; whirlpool, poolside serv. Restaurant 6:30 am-10 pm. Bar noon-midnight. Ck-out noon. Meeting rms. Business center. In-rm modem link. Gift shop. Free garage parking. Downhill/x-country ski 20 mi. Exercise equipt; weights, bicycles, sauna. Health club privileges. Connected to Laurel Park Mall. Luxury level. Cr cds: A, C, D, DS, ER, JCB, MC, V.

D ⊠ ≈ ✕ ⊠ ⚒ SC 🚶

★ ★ **THE RIVER PLACE.** *1000 River Place (48207), in Rivertown.* 313/259-9500; FAX 313/259-3744; res: 800/890-9505. 108 rms, 5 story, 18 suites. S $115-$185; D $135-$205; each addl $20; suites $165-$500; under 12 free; hol rates; higher rates some special events. Crib free. Valet parking $6. Pet accepted. TV; cable (premium), VCR avail. Indoor pool; whirlpool. Restaurant (see BARON'S STEAKHOUSE). Bar 11 am-11 pm; Fri, Sat to 1 am. Ck-out noon. Meeting rms. Business servs avail. In-rm modem link. Tennis privileges. Exercise rm; instructor, weight machine, treadmill, sauna. Massage. Croquet court. On Detroit River. Cr cds: A, C, D, DS, JCB, MC, V.

D ❤ 🏋 ≈ ✕ ⊠ ⚒ SC

★ ★ ★ **WESTIN-RENAISSANCE CENTER.** *Renaissance Center (48243), Jefferson Ave at Brush, downtown.* 313/568-8000; FAX 313/568-8146. 1,400 rms, 73 story. S $105-$165; D $130-$180; each addl $20; suites $330-$1,200; under 18 free; wkend rates. Crib free. Pet accepted. TV; cable, VCR avail (movies). Indoor pool. Restaurants 6 am-11 pm. Rm serv 24 hrs. Bar 11:30-1:30 am. Ck-out 1 pm. Convention facilities. Business center. In-rm modem link. Shopping arcade. Barber, beauty shop. Exercise rm; instructor, weights, bicycles, sauna. Many minibars. Luxury level. Cr cds: A, C, D, DS, ER, JCB, MC, V.

D ❤ ≈ ✕ 🏃 ⊠ ⚒ SC ⚒

Restaurants

★ ★ ★ **BARON'S STEAKHOUSE.** *(See The River Place Hotel)* 313/259-4855. Hrs: 7 am-10 pm; Fri, Sat to 11 pm; Sun 7 am-2 pm. Closed Dec 25. Res accepted. Bar to 11 pm. Semi-a la carte: bkfst

$4.95-$11.95, lunch $4.95-$16.95, dinner $13.95-$28.95. Sun brunch $12.95. Child's meals. Specializes in beef, chicken, seafood. Entertainment Fri, Sat. Outdoor dining. Overlooks Detroit River. Cr cds: A, C, D, DS, JCB, MC, V.

D

★ ★ ★ **CAUCUS CLUB.** *150 W Congress St (48226), in Penobscot Bldg, downtown.* 313/965-4970. Hrs: 11:30 am-8:30 pm; Fri to 10 pm; summer hrs vary. Closed Sat, Sun; major hols. Res accepted. Continental menu. Semi-a la carte: lunch $7.75-$17.25; dinner $15-$24. Child's meals. Specializes in fresh Dover sole, steak tartare, baby back ribs. Entertainment Mon-Fri. Cr cds: A, C, D, DS, MC, V.

✔★ **EL ZOCALO.** *3400 Bagley (48216), in Mexican Town.* 313/841-3700. Hrs: 11-1 am; Fri, Sat to 2:30 am. Closed some major hols. Res accepted Sun-Thurs. Mexican menu. Bar. Semi-a la carte: lunch $5.95-$8.95, dinner $6.35-$9.95. Specialties: chiles rellenos, queso flameado, chimichangas. Parking. Mayan and Aztec art. Cr cds: A, C, D, DS, MC, V.

★ ★ **FISHBONE'S RHYTHM KITCHEN CAFE.** *400 Monroe St (48226), at Brush Ave, in Greektown.* 313/965-4600. Hrs: 6:30 am-midnight; Fri, Sat to 1:45 am; Sun brunch 10:30 am-2:30 pm; dinner 2 pm-midnight. Closed Dec 25. Southern Louisiana, Creole, Cajun menu. Bar. Semi-a la carte: lunch $5.95-$12.95, dinner $5.95-$19.95. Sun brunch $13.95. Specialties: smoked whiskey ribs, jambalaya, crawfish etoufee. Valet parking. Bourbon Street bistro atmosphere; tin ceilings, antique lamps. Cr cds: A, C, D, DS, MC, V.

★ ★ ★ **INTERMEZZO.** *1435 Randolph St (48226), downtown.* 313/961-0707. Hrs: 11 am-10 pm; Fri, Sat to 11 pm. Closed Sun, Mon; major hols. Res accepted. Italian menu. Bar. Semi-a la carte: lunch $6-$12, dinner $12-$24. Specializes in veal, pasta. Entertainment Fri, Sat. Outdoor dining. Contemporary decor. Cr cds: A, D, DS, MC, V.

★ ★ ★ **JOE MUER'S.** *2000 Gratiot Ave (48207), east of downtown.* 313/567-1088. Hrs: 11:15 am-2:30 pm, 4:30-10 pm; Sat 5-11 pm. Closed Sun; major hols. Bar. Semi-a la carte: lunch $9-$16, dinner $19.25-$26. Child's meals. Specializes in seafood. Tudor-style with beamed ceilings. Jacket. Cr cds: A, C, D, DS, MC, V.

★ ★ ★ **OPUS ONE.** *565 E Larned (48226), downtown.* 313/961-7766. Hrs: 11:30 am-10 pm; Fri to 11 pm; Sat 5-11 pm. Closed Sun; major hols. Res accepted. Bar. Wine cellar. French, Amer menu. Semi-a la carte: lunch $8.95-$16.95, dinner $19.50-$34.50. Child's meals. Specializes in seafood, aged beef. Own baking, ice cream. Pianist Tues-Sat (dinner). Valet parking. In building designed by Albert Kahn; etched glass, original artwork. Jacket. Cr cds: A, C, D, DS, MC, V.

✔★ **PEGASUS IN THE FISHER.** *3011 W Grand Blvd (48202), in New Center Area.* 313/875-7400. Hrs: 11 am-11 pm; Mon to 9 pm; Fri to midnight; Sat 4 pm-midnight. Closed Sun; most major hols. Res accepted. Continental menu. Bar. Semi-a la carte: lunch $5-$7, dinner $7-$16. Specializes in steak, pasta, fresh seafood. Entertainment Fri & Sat evenings. Valet parking. Art-deco decor; hand-painted ceilings. Cr cds: A, C, D, DS, MC, V.

★ ★ **PEGASUS TAVERNA.** *558 Monroe St (48226), in Greektown.* 313/964-6800. Hrs: 11-1 am; Fri, Sat to 2 am; Sun to midnight. Greek, Amer menu. Bar. A la carte entrees: lunch $4.95-$7.95, dinner $5.95-$17.95. Child's meals. Specializes in lamb chops, seafood, spinach

cheese pie. Parking. Lattice-worked ceiling; hanging grape vines. Cr cds: A, D, DS, MC, V.

★ ★ ★ **RATTLESNAKE CLUB.** *300 Stroh River Place (48207), in Rivertown.* 313/567-4400. Hrs: 11:30 am-10 pm; Fri to midnight; Sat 5:30-midnight. Closed Sun; most major hols. Res accepted. Bar. Semi-a la carte: lunch $7-$18, dinner $14.95-$29.95. Specializes in seasonal dishes. Entertainment Fri, Sat. Valet parking. Outdoor dining. Modern decor; two dining areas overlook Detroit River. Cr cds: A, C, D, DS, MC, V.

✔★ ★ **TRES VITE.** *2203 Woodward Ave (48201), downtown.* 313/964-4144. Hrs: 11:30 am-8 pm; Fri to 11 pm; Sat 5-11 pm. Closed Sun (exc special events) & Mon; major hols. Res accepted. Mediterranean menu. Bar. A la carte entrees: lunch $5.95-$12.95, dinner $6.95-$17.95. Specializes in pizza, pasta, steak. Valet parking. In historic Fox Theatre building. Cr cds: A, DS, MC, V.

★ ★ ★ **VAN DYKE PLACE.** *649 Van Dyke Ave (48214), east of downtown.* 313/821-2620. Hrs: 6-9:30 pm; Fri, Sat from 5 pm. Closed Sun, Mon; major hols. Res accepted. Serv bar. Wine list. A la carte entrees: dinner $23-$28. Specializes in contemporary American fare with French accents. Own baking. Valet parking. Turn-of-the-century Louis XVI town house. Cr cds: A, D, MC, V.

★ ★ ★ **THE WHITNEY.** *4421 Woodward Ave (48201), downtown.* 313/832-5700. Hrs: 11 am-2 pm, 6-9:30 pm; Wed, Thurs 5-10 pm; Fri, Sat 5-11 pm; Sun 5-8 pm; Sun brunch 11 am-2:30 pm. Closed major hols. Res recommended. Bar 5 pm-2 am; closed Sun. Wine cellar. A la carte entrees: lunch $6.95-$16.95, dinner $16-$30. Prix fixe: dinner $44-$55. Sun brunch $21.95. Specializes in veal, beef, seafood. Own baking. Entertainment. Valet parking. Cr cds: A, D, MC, V.

Unrated Dining Spot

TRAFFIC JAM & SNUG. *511 W Canfield St (48201), at Second St, downtown.* 313/831-9470. Hrs: 11 am-9 pm; Mon to 3 pm; Thurs to 10:30 pm; Fri to midnight; Sat 5 pm-midnight. Closed Sun; most major hols. Serv bar. Semi-a la carte: lunch $6-$10, dinner $9-$13. Child's meals. Own pastries, desserts, ice cream, cheese. Micro brewery and dairy on premises. Parking. Rustic decor, many antiques. Cr cds: DS, MC, V.

Detroit Wayne County Airport Area (J-6)

(See also Dearborn, Detroit, Ypsilanti)

Services and Information

Information: 313/942-3550.

Airlines: Air Canada, America West, American, Asiana, British Airways, Continental, Delta, Great Lakes, KLM, Midwest Express, Northwest, Southwest, Spirit, TWA, United, USAir.

Motels

★ ★ **COURTYARD BY MARRIOTT.** *(30653 Flynn Dr, Romulus 48174) N on Merriman Rd to Flynn Dr.* 313/721-3200; FAX 313/721-1304. 146 rms, 3 story. S, D $93; each addl $10; suites $110; under 16 free;

wkend rates. Crib free. TV; cable (premium). Indoor pool; whirlpool. Complimentary coffee in rms. Restaurant 6:30 am-2 pm, 5-10 pm; Sat 7 am-1 pm, 5-10 pm; Sun 7 am-1 pm. Bar. Ck-out noon. Coin lndry. Meeting rms. Business servs avail. In-rm modem link. Valet serv. Free airport transportation. Exercise equipt; weight machine, treadmill. Refrigerator in suites. Balconies. Cr cds: A, C, D, DS, MC, V.

★ ★ **HAMPTON INN.** *(30847 Flynn Dr, Romulus 48174) N on Merriman Rd to Flynn Dr. 313/721-1100; FAX 313/721-9915.* 136 rms, 3 story. S, D $69.95-$89.95; under 17 free. Crib $5. TV; cable (premium). Pool. Complimentary continental bkfst. Restaurant adj 6 am-10 pm; Fri, Sat to 11:30 pm. Ck-out noon. Meeting rms. Business center. In-rm modem link. Valet serv. Free airport transportation. Cr cds: A, C, D, DS, MC, V.

★ ★ **QUALITY INN.** *(7600 Merriman Rd, Romulus 48174)* 1/2 mi N on Merriman Rd. 313/728-2430; FAX 313/728-3756. 140 rms. S, D $54-$89; each addl $5; under 12 free; wkly rates. Crib free. TV; cable (premium). Complimentary continental bkfst. Restaurant adj 11-1 am. Bar. Ck-out noon. Coin lndry. Meeting rms. Business servs avail. In-rm modem link. Free airport transportation. Cr cds: A, D, DS, MC, V.

Motor Hotels

★ ★ ★ **HILTON SUITES.** *(8600 Wickham Rd, Romulus 48174) N on Merriman Rd to Wickham Rd. 313/728-9200; FAX 313/728-9278.* 151 suites, 3 story. S $129; D $139; each addl $10; family rates. Crib free. TV; cable (premium), VCR (movies $6). Indoor/outdoor pool; whirlpool, poolside serv. Complimentary full bkfst. Complimentary coffee in rms. Restaurant 6 am-11 pm. Bar. Ck-out noon. Coin lndry. Meeting rms. Business center. In-rm modem link. Bellhops. Valet serv. Sundries. Free airport transportation. Downhill ski 10 mi. Exercise equipt; weight machine, bicycles. Game rm. Refrigerators. Some balconies. Cr cds: A, C, D, DS, MC, V.

★ ★ **RAMADA INN.** *(8270 Wickham Rd, Romulus 48174) N on Merriman Rd to Wickham Rd. 313/729-6300; FAX 313/722-8740.* 243 rms, 4 story. S, D $79-$89; each addl $10; suites from $150; family, wkend rates; package plans. Crib free. TV; cable (premium). Indoor pool. Playground. Restaurant 6 am-10 pm. Rm serv. Bar 11-2 am, Sun from noon; entertainment. Ck-out noon. Meeting rms. Business servs avail. Bellhops. Valet serv. Sundries. Free airport transportation. X-country ski 4 mi. Exercise equipt; weight machine, bicycle, sauna. Cr cds: A, C, D, DS, ER, JCB, MC, V.

Hotels

★ ★ ★ **CROWNE PLAZA.** *(8000 Merriman Rd, Romulus 48174)* 1 mi N on Merriman Rd. 313/729-2600; FAX 313/729-9414. 365 rms, 11 story. S, D $104-$132; each addl $10; suites $179-$229; family, wkend rates. Crib free. Pet accepted, some restrictions. TV; cable (premium), VCR avail. Indoor pool; whirlpool. Coffee in rms. Restaurant 6 am-10 pm. Bar noon-1 am. Ck-out noon. Convention facilities. Business center. In-rm modem link. Gift shop. Free airport transportation. Exercise equipt; weights, bicycles. Game rm. Some balconies. Luxury level. Cr cds: A, C, D, DS, JCB, MC, V.

★ ★ **MARRIOTT.** *(30559 Flynn Dr, Romulus 48174) N on Merriman Rd to Flynn Dr. 313/729-7555; FAX 313/729-8634.* 245 rms, 4 story. S, D $119; suites $350; family, wkend rates. Crib free. TV; cable (premium). Indoor pool; whirlpool. Restaurant 6:30 am-10 pm. Bar from 11 am. Ck-out noon. Meeting rms. Business servs avail. In-rm modem link. Gift shop. Free airport transportation. Downhill ski 15 mi. Exercise equipt;

weight machine, bicycles. Some bathrm phones. Refrigerator, minibar in suites. Luxury level. Cr cds: A, C, D, DS, ER, JCB, MC, V.

East Lansing

(see Lansing)

Escanaba (D-2)

Settled 1830 **Pop** 13,659 **Elev** 598 ft **Area code** 906 **Zip** 49829 **E-mail** deltacc@up.net **Web** www.DeltaMi.org

Information Delta County Area Chamber of Commerce, 230 Ludington St; 906/786-2192 or 888/335-8264.

The first European settlers in this area were lured by the pine timber, which they were quick to log; however, a second growth provides solid forest cover once again. Escanaba is the only ore-shipping port on Lake Michigan. Manufacture of paper is another important industry. Sports enthusiasts are attracted by the open water and huge tracts of undeveloped countryside. Fishing is excellent. Escanaba is the headquarters for the Hiawatha National Forest.

What to See and Do

Hiawatha National Forest. This 893,000-acre forest offers scenic drives, lake and stream fishing, hunting, swimming, sailing, motorboating, canoeing, camping, picnicking, hiking, horseback riding, cross-country skiing, snowmobiling and winter sports. It has shoreline on three Great Lakes—Huron, Michigan and Superior. The eastern section of the forest is close to Sault Ste Marie, St Ignace and the northern foot of the Mackinac Bridge. Fees charged at developed campground sites. Some fees. (Daily) For further information contact the Supervisor, 2727 N Lincoln Rd; 906/786-4062. **Free.**

Ludington Park. Fishing, boating (launch, marina; fee); swimming, bath house; tennis courts, playground, ball fields. Picnic area, tables, stoves. Scenic bike path. Pavilion, bandshell. (Apr-Nov, daily) On MI 35, overlooks Little Bay de Noc. Phone 906/786-4141. **Free.** In the park is

Delta County Historical Museum and Sand Point Lighthouse. Local historical artifacts; lumber, railroad and maritime industry exhibits; 1867 restored lighthouse (fee). (June-Labor Day, afternoons) Phone 906/786-3763. ¢

Pioneer Trail Park and Campground. A 74-acre park on the Escanaba River. Shoreline fishing, picnicking, nature trails, playground, camping (fee). (May-Sept, daily) 3 mi N on US 2/41, MI 35. Phone 906/786-1020. ¢

Annual Event

Upper Peninsula State Fair. Agricultural and 4-H exhibits, midway, entertainment. 6 days mid-Aug.

Motels

✓★ **BAY VIEW.** *(7110 US 2/41/MI 35, Gladstone 49837) 4 mi N on US 2/41 (MI 35). 906/786-2843; FAX 906/786-6218; res: 800/547-1201.* 23 rms, 1-2 story. Mid-June-mid-Sept: S $40-$55; D $45-$60; family rates; some lower rates rest of yr. Crib free. Pet accepted. TV; cable (premium). Sauna. Indoor pool. Playground. Complimentary coffee in rms. Restaurant adj 7 am-8 pm. Ck-out 11 am. Business servs avail. Some refrigerators. Picnic tables, barbecue area. Cr cds: A, DS, MC, V.

★ ★ **BEST WESTERN PIONEER INN.** *2635 Ludington St. 906/786-0602; FAX 906/786-3938.* 72 rms, 2 story. S $45-$70; D $55-$99;

each addl $5. Crib $5. TV; cable (premium). Indoor pool. Restaurant 7 am-2 pm, 5-10 pm. Bar 5 pm-2 am. Ck-out 11 am. Meeting rms. Business servs avail. Sundries. Downhill/x-country ski 7 mi. Many balconies. Cr cds: A, C, D, DS, MC, V.

★★ **DAYS INN.** *2603 N Lincoln Rd. 906/789-1200; FAX 906/789-0128.* 124 rms, 4 story. Mid-Jun-mid Sept: S, D $65-$83; each addl $6; under 12 free; lower rates rest of yr. Crib free. TV; cable. Indoor pool; whirlpool. Restaurant adj 6 am-10 pm. Bar 11:30 am-midnight; Fri, Sat to 2 am. Ck-out noon. Meeting rms. Free airport transportation. Downhill/x-country ski 7 mi. Cr cds: A, C, D, DS, JCB, MC, V.

★★ **TERRACE BAY INN.** *Box 453, 4 1/2 mi N, 1/2 blk E of US 2/41 (MI 35).* 906/786-7554. 71 rms, 1-2 story. Mid-June-Aug: S $42-$49; D $64-$74 each addl $5; under 16 free; package plans; lower rates rest of yr. Crib $2. TV; cable, VCR avail. Indoor pool; whirlpool. Restaurant 5-9 pm; June-Aug 7-11 am, 5-10 pm. Bar 5 pm-11 pm. Ck-out 11 am. Meeting rms. Business servs avail. Sundries. Tennis. Golf, driving range. Downhill ski 5 mi; x-country ski 7 mi. Exercise equipt; bicycles, treadmill, sauna. Game rm. Lawn games. Private patios, balconies. Overlooks Little Bay de Noc. Cr cds: A, C, D, DS, MC, V.

✓★ **VALU HOST.** *921 N Lincoln Rd. 906/789-1066; FAX 906/789-9202; res: 800/929-5997.* 50 rms, 2 story. June-Sept: S $34.95; D $42.95; each addl $4; under 12 free; higher rates Upper Peninsula State Fair; lower rates rest of yr. TV; cable (premium). Complimentary continental bkfst. Restaurant nearby. Ck-out 11 am. Meeting rm. Downhill/x-country ski 7 mi. Cr cds: DS, MC, V.

Restaurants

✓★★ **LOG CABIN SUPPER CLUB.** *(7531 US 2, Gladstone 49837)* 10 mi N. 906/786-5621. Hrs: 11 am-10 pm; Sun from 4 pm. Closed most major hols. Bar to midnight. Semi-a la carte: lunch $4-$6, dinner $7.95-$11.95. Complete meals: dinner $8.95-$19.95. Child's meals. Specializes in steak, fresh fish. Salad bar. Rustic decor. Overlooks Little Bay de Noc. Cr cds: MC, V.

★★ **STONEHOUSE.** *2223 Ludington St.* 906/786-5003. Hrs: 11 am-2 pm, 5-10 pm; Sat, Sun from 5 pm. Closed some major hols; also Sun Sept-Apr. Res accepted Sat-Sun. Bar to midnight. Semi-a la carte: lunch $3-$6.95, dinner $3.95-$22. Child's meals. Specializes in prime rib, seafood, veal. Collection of antique cars. Cr cds: A, C, D, DS, MC, V.

Farmington (J-5)

(See also Birmingham, Detroit, Southfield)

Pop 10,132 **Elev** 750 ft **Area code** 248
Information Chamber of Commerce, 33000 Thomas St, Suite 101, 48336; 248/474-3440.

What to See and Do

Kensington Metropark. More than 4,000 acres on Kent Lake. Two swimming beaches (Memorial Day-Labor Day, daily); boating (rentals). Biking/hiking trail. Tobogganing, skating, ice-fishing. Picnicking, concessions; 18-hole golf (fee). 45-min boat cruises on the *Island Queen* (summer, daily; fee). Nature trails; farm center, nature center. Park (daily). Free admission

Tues. 14 mi NW on I-96, Kent Lake Rd or Kensington Rd exits. Phone 248/685-1561 or 248/227-2757. Motor vehicle entry permit ¢-¢¢

Annual Event

Farmington Founders Festival. Ethnic food, arts & crafts, sidewalk sales, carnival, rides, concert, fireworks. Mid-July.

Motels

★★ **COMFORT INN.** *(30715 Twelve Mile Rd, Farmington Hills 48334)* I-696 exit 5, N on Orchard Lake Rd, then E on Twelve Mile Rd. 810/471-9220; FAX 810/471-2053. 135 rms, 4 story. S $49-$59; D $55-$65; each addl $6; suites $83; under 18 free; wkend rates. Crib free. TV; cable (premium). Continental bkfst. Restaurant nearby. Ck-out noon. Meeting rms. Valet serv. Refrigerator in suites. Balconies. Cr cds: A, C, D, DS, ER, JCB, MC, V.

★★ **HAMPTON INN.** *(20600 Haggerty Rd, Northville 48167)* S on I-275 exit 167 (Eight Mile Rd). 313/462-1119; FAX 313/462-6270. 125 rms, 4 story. S $59-$75; D $66-$85; under 18 free; wkend rates. Crib free. TV; cable (premium). Heated pool. Complimentary continental bkfst. Ck-out noon. Meeting rms. Business servs avail. In-rm modem link. Valet serv. Downhill ski 20 mi. Exercise equipt; weight machine, bicycles, sauna. Cr cds: A, C, D, DS, MC, V.

✓★ **RED ROOF INN.** *(24300 Sinacola Court, Farmington Hills 48335)* 3 mi W. 810/478-8640; FAX 810/478-4842. 108 rms. S $31.99-$33.99; D $37.99-$39.99; 3 or more $47.99; under 18 free. Crib free. Pet accepted. TV; cable. Restaurant adj open 24 hrs. Ck-out noon. Cr cds: A, C, D, DS, MC, V.

★ **TRAVELODGE.** *(21100 Haggerty Rd, Northville 48167)* S on I-275, exit Eight Mile Rd. 810/349-7400; FAX 810/349-7454. 125 rms, 2 story. S, D $48-$55; each addl $6; under 18 free; wkly rates; higher rates Dec 31. Crib free. TV; cable (premium). Complimentary continental bkfst. Complimentary coffee in rms. Restaurant adj 7 am-3 pm. Ck-out noon. Meeting rms. Business servs avail. Valet serv. Some refrigerators. Cr cds: A, C, D, DS, MC, V.

Motor Hotels

★★ **BEST WESTERN EXECUTIVE HOTEL & SUITES.** *(31525 W Twelve Mile Rd, Farmington Hills 48334)* W on I-696, Orchard Lake Rd exit. 810/553-0000; FAX 810/553-7630. 204 rms, 3 story, 44 suites. S, D $79; suites $99-$129; under 19 free; wkend rates. Crib free. TV; cable. Indoor pool; whirlpool. Restaurant 6:30 am-11 pm. Rm serv. Bar 11 am-midnight. Ck-out noon. Meeting rms. Business center. In-rm modem link. Bellhops. Valet serv. Downhill ski 20 mi. Exercise equipt; weight machine, bicycles, sauna. Some in-rm whirlpools; bathrm phone in suites. Cr cds: A, C, D, DS, ER, JCB, MC, V.

★★ **DOUBLETREE.** *(27000 Sheraton Dr, Novi 48377)* At I-96 Walled Lake/Novi Rd exit 162. 810/348-5000; FAX 810/348-2315. 217 rms, 3 story. S $88-$100; D $93-$110; each addl $10; suites $175-$275; under 12 free; wkend rates. Crib free. TV; cable (premium). 2 pools, 1 indoor; whirlpool. Restaurant 6:30 am-10:30 pm. Rm serv. Bar 11-1 am; entertainment. Ck-out noon. Meeting rms. Business servs avail. Bellhops. Valet serv. Exercise equipt; bicycle, treadmill, sauna. Cr cds: A, D, DS, JCB, MC, V.

★★ **HOTEL BARONETTE.** *(27790 Novi Rd, Novi 48377)* At I-96 Walled Lake/Novi exit 162, at Twelve Oaks Mall. 810/349-7800; FAX 810/349-7467; res: 800/395-9009. 148 rms, 3 story. S $69; D $79; each addl $10; suites $100-$275; under 12 free; wkend rates. Crib free. TV; cable, VCR (movies). Indoor pool; whirlpool. Complimentary coffee in rms. Complimentary full bkfst. Restaurant 6:30 am-10:30 pm; wkends from 7:30 am. Bar 11 am-11 pm. Ck-out noon. Meeting rms. Valet serv. Bakery. Putting green. Exercise equipt; weight machine, treadmill, sauna. Bathrm phones, minibars; some wet bars. Some balconies. Cr cds: A, C, D, DS, ER, JCB, MC, V.

★ ★ **RADISSON SUITE.** *(37529 Grand River Ave, Farmington Hills 48335) NW on Grand River Ave, at Halstead Service Dr S. 810/477-7800; FAX 810/477-6512.* 137 suites, 4 story. S, D $99; wkend rates. Crib free. TV; cable (premium), VCR avail. Indoor pool; whirlpool. Complimentary continental bkfst. Coffee in rms. Restaurant 6:30 am-2 pm, 5-10 pm. Rm serv. Bar 5 pm-midnight. Ck-out noon. Meeting rms. Business servs avail. Valet serv. Downhill ski 20 mi. Exercise equipt; weight machine, bicycles, sauna. Refrigerators. Cr cds: A, C, D, DS, ER, JCB, MC, V.

★ ★ **WYNDHAM GARDEN.** *(42100 Crescent Blvd, Novi 48375) At jct I-96 & Novi Rd, behind Novi Town Center. 810/344-8800; FAX 810/344-8535.* 148 rms, 2 story, 22 suites. S $84; D $94; each addl $10; suites $94-$104; under 18 free; wkend rates. Crib free. TV; cable. Indoor pool; whirlpool, sauna. Complimentary coffee in rms. Restaurant 6:30 am-2 pm, 5-10 pm; Sat, Sun from 7 am. Rm serv (dinner). Bar. Ck-out noon. Meeting rms. Valet serv. Health club privileges. Refrigerators avail. Cr cds: A, C, D, DS, ER, JCB, MC, V.

Hotel

★ ★ ★ **HILTON.** *(21111 Haggerty Rd, Novi 48375) NW on Grand River Ave, then S on Haggerty Rd to jct Eight Mile Rd. 810/349-4000; FAX 810/349-4066.* 239 rms, 7 story. S $105-$145; D $110-$160; each addl $15; suites $275-$525; family, wkend rates. Crib free. Pet accepted, some restrictions. TV; cable (premium). Pool; whirlpool. Restaurant 6:30 am-11 pm. Rm serv 24 hrs. Bar 11-2 am. Ck-out noon. Meeting rms. Business servs avail. In-rm modem link. Downhill ski 10 mi; x-country ski 2 mi. Exercise equipt; weights, bicycles, sauna. Refrigerator in suites. Cr cds: A, C, D, DS, ER, JCB, MC, V.

Inn

★ **BOTSFORD.** *(28000 Grand River Ave/I-96 Business, Farmington Hills 48336) NW on Grand River Rd, at jct Eight Mile Rd. 810/474-4800; FAX 810/474-7669.* 65 rms. S $65-$75; D $70-$85; each addl $5; suites $75-$95; under 12 free; monthly rates. Crib $5. TV; cable (premium). Complimentary full bkfst. Coffee in rms. Dining rm 7 am-10 pm. Bar 11 am-midnight. Ck-out 1 pm, ck-in 3 pm. Guest lndry. Meeting rms. Tennis. Early Amer, Victorian furnishings; many antiques. Built in 1836; restored by Henry Ford. Cr cds: A, C, D, DS, MC, V.

Restaurants

★ ★ **AH WOK.** *(41563 W Ten Mile Rd, Novi) NW on Grand River Ave, then W on Ten Mile Rd, just past Meadowbrook Rd. 810/349-9260.* Hrs: 11 am-9:30 pm; Fri to 11:30 pm; Sat 4 pm-11:30 pm; Sun noon-9:30 pm. Closed major hols. Res accepted wkends. Chinese menu. Serv bar. Semi-a la carte: lunch $5.50-$9.95, dinner $7.50-$18. Specialties: Peking duck, Szechwan dumplings, hot & sour soup. Parking. Cr cds: A, C, D, MC, V.

✔★ ★ ★ **FIVE LAKES GRILL.** *(424 N Main St, Milford 48381) 10 mi W on I-96, 6 mi N on MI 59. 810/684-7455.* Hrs: 4-10 pm; Fri, Sat to 11 pm. Closed Sun; most major hols. Res accepted. Bar. Semi-a la carte: dinner $11.50-$20. Child's meals. Specializes in fusion cooking. Modern bistro decor. Cr cds: A, MC, V.

★ ★ **LITTLE ITALY.** *(227 Hutton St, Northville 48167) S on I-275, exit Eight Mile Rd, then 3 mi W. 810/348-0575.* Hrs: 11:30 am-2:30 pm, 5-10 pm; Fri to 11 pm; Sat 5-11 pm; Sun 4-9 pm; closed some major hols. Res accepted. Italian menu. Bar. Semi-a la carte: lunch $6.95-$9.50, dinner $10.95-$21.95. Specializes in veal, seafood. Parking. Converted residence; small, intimate dining areas; antiques, original art. Cr cds: A, MC, V.

★ ★ **MacKINNON'S.** *(126 E Main St, Northville 48167) S on I-275, exit Eight Mile Rd, then 3 mi W. 810/348-1991.* Hrs: 11 am-10 pm; Fri, Sat to 11 pm. Closed Sun. Res accepted. Continental menu. Bar to 11 pm. Semi-a la carte: lunch $4.95-$10.95, dinner $13.95-$25.95. Specialties: charcoal duck, rack of lamb. Outdoor dining. Victorian atmosphere; stained-glass windows. Cr cds: A, C, D, DS, MC, V.

★ **ROCKY'S OF NORTHVILLE.** *(41122 W Seven Mile Rd, Northville) S on I-275, exit Seven Mile Rd, then 1½ mi W. 810/349-4434.* Hrs: 11:30 am-10 pm; Fri, Sat to 11 pm; Sun 1-9 pm. Closed Jan 1, Dec 25. Bar. Semi-a la carte: lunch $4.95-$10.95, dinner $8.95-$15.50. Child's meals. Specializes in seafood, pasta, steak. Parking. Outdoor dining. Cr cds: A, C, D, DS, MC, V.

★ ★ **TOO CHEZ.** *(27155 Sheraton Dr, Novi) NW via I-96, Walled Lake/Novi exit 162. 810/348-5555.* Hrs: 11:30 am-2:30 pm, 5:30-10 pm; Fri, Sat to 11 pm. Closed Sun; Dec 25. Continental menu. Res accepted. Bar. Wine list. A la carte entrees: lunch $5-$9, dinner $8-$30. Child's meals. Own baking. Parking. Outdoor dining. Cr cds: A, C, D, DS, MC, V.

Flint (H-5)

(See also Holly, Owosso, Saginaw)

Settled 1819 **Pop** 140,761 **Elev** 750 ft **Area code** 810 **E-mail** /staff @Flint.org **Web** flint.org

Information Flint Area Convention and Visitors Bureau, 519 S Saginaw St, 48502; 810/232-8900 or 800/25-FLINT.

Once a small, wagon-producing town, Flint is now an important automobile manufacturer. The fur trade brought Flint its first prestige; lumbering opened the way to carriage manufacturing, which prepared the city for the advent of the automobile. General Motors, the city's major employer, has Buick plants here. One of the largest cities in the state, it also has many other industrial firms.

What to See and Do

County recreation areas. For additional information phone 810/736-7100.

Genesee-C.S. Mott Lake. Approx 650 acres. Swimming; fishing; boating (launches, fee). Snowmobiling. Picnicking with view of Stepping Stone Falls. Riverboat cruises (fee). (Memorial Day-Labor Day) **Free.**

Holloway Reservoir. Approx 2,000 acres. Swimming; water sports; fishing; boating (launches, fee). Snowmobiling. Picnicking. Camping (fee). (Daily) 12 mi E on MI 21, then 8 mi NE via MI 15, Stanley Rd. **Free.**

Crossroads Village/Huckleberry Railroad. Restored living community of the 1860-1880 period; 28 buildings and sites including a railroad depot, carousel, Ferris wheel, general store, schoolhouse and several homes; working sawmill, gristmill, cidermill, blacksmith shop; 8-mi steam train ride; entertainment. Paddlewheel riverboat cruises (fee). Special events most wkends. (Memorial Day-Labor Day, daily; Sept, wkends; also special Halloween programs, Dec holiday lighting spectacular) G-6140 Bray Rd, 6 mi NE via I-475, at exit 13. Phone 810/736-7100. General admission ¢¢¢

Flint College and Cultural Corporation. A complex that includes the University of Michigan-Flint (5,700 students), Mott Community College, Whiting Auditorium, Flint Institute of Music, Bower Theater. 1241 Kearsley St. Phone 810/760-1087 (Cultural Center). Also here are

Flint Institute of Arts. Permanent collections include Renaissance decorative arts, Oriental Gallery, 19th- and 20th-century paintings and sculpture, paperweights; changing exhibits. (Daily exc Mon; closed hols) In the Cultural Center, 1120 E Kearsley St. Phone 810/234-1695. **Free.**

Robert T. Longway Planetarium. Ultraviolet, fluorescent murals; Spitz projector. Exhibits (Mon-Fri). Programs (phone for schedule). 1310 E Kearsley St. Phone 810/760-1181. ¢¢

Sloan Museum. Collection of antique autos and carriages, most manufactured in Flint; exhibitions of Michigan history; health and science exhibits. (Daily exc Mon; closed hols) 1221 E Kearsley St. Phone 810/760-1169. ¢¢

For-Mar Nature Preserve and Arboretum. Approx 380 acres. Nature trails, indoor and outdoor exhibits, two interpretive buildings. Guided hikes (fee). 2142 N Genesee Rd. Phone 810/789-8567. Naturalist programs ¢

Motels

★ ★ **HOLIDAY INN EXPRESS.** *1150 Robert T. Longway Blvd (48503). 810/238-7744; FAX 810/233-7444.* 124 rms, 5 story. S $51-$59; D $56-$64; under 18 free. Crib free. TV; cable (premium). Complimentary continental bkfst. Ck-out noon. Meeting rm. Business center. In-rm modem link. Valet serv. Free airport transportation. Downhill ski 20 mi. Health club privileges. Cr cds: A, C, D, DS, MC, V.

D ⊠ ⊠ ⊠ SC ⊼

✓ ★ **RED ROOF INN.** *G-3219 Miller Rd (48507). 810/733-1660; FAX 810/733-6310.* 107 rms, 2 story. June-mid-Sept: S $34.99-$42; D $42-$49; 3 or more $52-$56; under 18 free; lower rates rest of yr. Crib free. TV; cable (premium). Restaurant adj 6:30 am-11 pm. Business servs avail. Ck-out noon. Cr cds: A, C, D, DS, MC, V.

D ⊠ ⊠

✓ ★ **SUPER 8.** *3033 Claude Ave (48507), at I-75 exit 117. 810/230-7888.* 62 rms, 3 story. No elvtr. S $38.98; D $44.98; each addl $6; under 12 free; higher rates Buick Open. Pet accepted. TV; cable. Complimentary coffee in lobby. Restaurant nearby. Ck-out 11 am. Cr cds: A, C, D, DS, JCB, MC, V.

D ⊠ ⊠ ⊠ SC

Motor Hotel

★ ★ ★ **HOLIDAY INN GATEWAY CENTRE.** *5353 Gateway Centre (48507), at US 23 exit 90 (Hill Rd E), near Bishop Intl Airport. 810/232-5300; FAX 810/232-9806.* 171 rms, 4 story. S $99-$129; D $99-$149; each addl $10; suites $114-$229; family, wkly rates. Crib free. TV; cable. Indoor pool; whirlpool, sauna. Restaurant 6:30 am-10 pm; Fri, Sat 7 am-11 pm. Rm serv. Bar 11:30 am-midnight; Fri, Sat to 2 am. Ck-out noon. Coin lndry. Meeting rms. Business servs avail. In-rm modem link. Bellhops. Valet serv. Concierge. Free airport, RR station, bus depot transportation. Game rm. Some refrigerators, wet bars. Picnic tables. Cr cds: A, C, D, DS, ER, JCB, MC, V.

D ⊠ ✈ ⊠ ⊠ SC

Hotel

★ ★ **RIVERFRONT.** *One Riverfront Center West (48502), at Saginaw St. 810/239-1234; FAX 810/239-5843.* 369 rms, 16 story. S, D $89; suites $99-$295; under 18 free. Crib free. TV; cable. Indoor pool; whirlpool. Restaurant 6:30 am-11 pm; Fri, Sat to 1 am. Bar. Ck-out noon. Meeting rms. Business center. Free garage parking. Free airport transportation. Concierge. Exercise equipt; stair machine, bicycle. Game rm. Some refrigerators. On river. Cr cds: A, C, D, DS, ER, JCB, MC, V.

D ⊠ ✈ ⊠ ⊠ SC ⊼

Inn

★ ★ **BONNYMILL.** *(710 Broad St, Chesaning 48616) N via I-75 to MI 57, then 18 mi W. 517/845-7780; FAX 517/845-5165.* 29 rms, 3 story, 11 suites. S, D $65-$95; each addl $10; suites $135-$145; under 11 free; winter rates. Crib free. TV; cable (premium), VCR avail (movies). Complimentary full bkfst; afternoon refreshments. Complimentary coffee in rms. Dining rm 7:30-9 am; Sat, Sun 8-9:30 am. Rm serv. Ck-out 11 am, ck-in 3 pm. Business servs avail. Valet serv. Airport transportation. Golf privileges. X-country ski 7 mi. Balconies. Picnic tables. Rebuilt from 1920 farmer's grain mill. Antique winding oak staircase. Cr cds: A, DS, MC, V.

D ⊠ ⊼ ⊠ ⊠

Restaurants

★ ★ ★ **CHESANING HERITAGE HOUSE.** *(605 Broad St, Chesaning 48616) N via I-75 to MI 57, then 18 mi W. 517/845-7700.* Hrs: 11 am-9:30 pm; Sat to 10 pm; Sun noon-9 pm. Closed Dec 24, 25. Res accepted. Bar to midnight; Fri, Sat to 1 am. Semi-a la carte: lunch $3.75-$11.95, dinner $9.95-$19.95. Child's meals. Specializes in stuffed pork tenderloin, prime rib, seafood. Outdoor dining. Victorian decor; crystal chandelier, fireplace. Georgian-revival mansion (1908) converted into nine dining areas. Cr cds: A, DS, MC, V.

D ♥

★ ★ ★ **MAKUCH'S RED ROOSTER.** *3302 Davison Rd. 810/742-9310.* Hrs: 11 am-9 pm; Fri to 10 pm; Sat 5-10 pm. Closed Sun; major hols. Res accepted. Bar. Semi-a la carte: lunch $4.50-$11.95; dinner $18.95-$29.95. Child's meals. Specializes in Caesar salad, fresh seafood, steak. Own baking. Tableside preparation. Family-owned. Cr cds: MC, V.

Frankenmuth (H-5)

(See also Bay City, Flint, Saginaw)

Settled 1845 **Pop** 4,408 **Elev** 645 ft **Area code** 517 **Zip** 48734 **E-mail** chamber@frankenmuth.org **Web** www.frankenmuth.org

Information Convention & Visitors Bureau, 635 S Main St; 517/652-6106 or 800/FUN-TOWN.

This city was settled by 15 immigrants from Franconia, Germany, who came here as Lutheran missionaries to spread the faith to the Chippewas. Today, Frankenmuth boasts authentic Bavarian architecture, flower beds and warm German hospitality.

What to See and Do

⊠ **Bronner's Christmas Wonderland.** Thought to be the world's largest Christmas store: more than 50,000 trims and gifts from around the world. Multi-image presentation "World of Bronner's" (18 min); outdoor Christmas lighting display along Christmas Lane (dusk-midnight). (Daily; closed most hols). 25 Christmas Lane. Phone 517/652-9931 or 800/ALL-YEAR (recording).

Factory Outlet Stores. More than 100 outlet stores can be found at Manufactures Marketplace and The Village Shops at Birch Run. (Daily) Approx 5 mi S on I-75, exit 136. Phone 517/624-9348.

Frankenmuth Historical Museum. Local historical exhibits, hands-on displays, audio recordings and cast-form life figures. Gift shop features folk art. (Mon-Sat, also Sun afternoons; closed most hols) 613 S Main St. Phone 517/652-9701. **¢**

Frankenmuth Riverboat Tours. Narrated tours (45 min) along Cass River. (May-Oct, daily, weather permitting) Board at dock behind Riverview Cafe, 445 S Main St. Phone 517/652-8844. **¢¢**

Glockenspiel. Tops the Bavarian Inn (see RESTAURANTS); 35-bell carillon with carved wooden figures moving on a track acting out the story of the Pied Piper of Hameln. 713 S Main St.

Michigan's Own Military & Space Museum. Features uniforms, decorations and photos of men and women from Michigan who served the nation in war and peace; also displays on Medal of Honor recipients, astronauts, former governors. (Mar-Dec, daily; closed Easter, Dec 25) 1250 S Weiss St. Phone 517/652-8005. **¢¢**

Annual Event

Bavarian Festival. Heritage Park. Celebration of German heritage. Music, dancing, parades & other entertainment; food; art demonstrations and agricultural displays. Phone 517/652-8155. 9 days mid-June.

Motels

★ ★ ★ **BAVARIAN INN LODGE.** *1 Covered Bridge Lane. 517/652-7200; FAX 517/652-6711.* 354 units, 4 story. June-Oct: S $95; D $99-$125; suites $125-$195; lower rates rest of yr. Crib $5. TV; cable, VCR avail. 3 indoor pools; whirlpools. Restaurant 7 am-9 pm. Rm serv. Bar to 12:30 am; entertainment. Ck-out 11 am. Meeting rms. Business servs avail. Airport transportation. Gift shops. Tennis. Exercise equipt; weight machine, treadmill. 2 game rms. Lawn games. Balconies. View of Cass River. Cr cds: DS, MC, V.

★ ★ ★ **ZEHNDERS BAVARIAN HAUS.** *1365 S Main. 517/652-6144; FAX 517/652-9777; res: 800/863-7999.* 137 rms, 2 story. Early June-late Oct: D $85-$125; suites $165-$200; lower rates rest of yr. Crib free. TV; cable (premium). Indoor/outdoor pool; whirlpool. Restaurant 7:30-10:30 am. Ck-out 11 am. Business servs avail. 18-hole golf privileges. Exercise equipt; treadmill, bicycles, sauna. Game rm. Private balconies. Cr cds: DS, MC, V.

Restaurants

★ ★ **BAVARIAN INN.** *713 S Main St (MI 83). 517/652-9941.* Hrs: 11 am-9:30 pm. Closed Dec 24 evening; also 1st wk Jan. Res accepted. German, Amer menu. Bar; imported wine, beer. Semi-a la carte: lunch $4-$7.50, dinner $9.75-$15.75. Child's meals. Specializes in Bavarian dinner, family-style chicken dinner. Bavarian atmosphere; 35-bell carillon with moving figurines. Bakery. Established 1888. Family-owned. Cr cds: A, DS, MC, V.

D

★ ★ **ZEHNDER'S.** *730 S Main St (MI 83). 800/863-7999.* Hrs: 8 am-9:30 pm. Closed Dec 24. Bar. Semi-a la carte: bkfst $4.95-$7.95, lunch $5.95-$8.95, dinner $11.50-$16.50. Child's meals. Specializes in all-you-can-eat family-style chicken dinner, steak, seafood. Early Amer decor. Bakery. Gift shop. Family-owned. Cr cds: DS, MC, V.

D

Frankfort (F-3)

(See also Beulah)

Pop 1,546 **Elev** 585 ft **Area code** 616 **Zip** 49635 **Web** www.benzie.org
Information Benzie County Chamber of Commerce, PO Box 204, Benzonia 49616; 616/882-5801 or 800/882-5801.

An important harbor on Lake Michigan, Frankfort is a popular resort area. Fishing for coho and chinook salmon is excellent here. Frankfort is the burial site of Father Marquette. Nearby is Sleeping Bear Dunes National Lakeshore (see). Development of the lakeshore is complete with 40-slip marina, gas, sewage pumpout, electricity and bathing facilities.

Motels

★ **BAY VALLEY INN.** *1561 Scenic Hwy (MI 22), 1 1/2 mi S. 616/352-7113; FAX 616/352-7114; res: 800/352-7113.* 20 rms. Memorial Day-Labor Day: S $45-$55; D $65-$75; suite $90; family, wkly rates; lower rates rest of yr. Crib free. Pet accepted. TV; cable, VCR avail (free movies). Playground. Complimentary continental bkfst. Ck-out 11 am. Free lndry. Meeting rms. Business servs avail. Downhill/x-country ski 18 mi. Rec rm. Refrigerators. Picnic tables, grills. Cr cds: A, DS, MC, V.

★ ★ **HARBOR LIGHTS.** *15 Second St, W end of Main St on Lake Michigan, 7 blks W of MI 22. 616/352-9614; FAX 616/352-6580; res: 800/346-9614.* 57 rms, 33 A/C, 2 story, 45 condominiums. July, Aug: D $85-$95; kit. units $80-$120; condo units $110-$225; wkly rates; ski, golf plans; lower rates May-mid-June, after Labor Day-Oct. Crib free. TV; cable. Indoor pool; whirlpool. Ck-out 11 am. Meeting rm. Business servs avail. Downhill ski 18 mi; x-country ski 3 mi. Lawn games. Some in-rm whirlpools. Some balconies. Park, beach opp. Some rms with lake view. Cr cds: DS, MC, V.

Resort

★ ★ **CHIMNEY CORNERS.** *1602 Crystal Dr (MI 22). 616/352-7522.* 8 rms in lodge, all share bath, 1-2 story, 7 kit. apts (1-2 bedrm), 13 kit. cottages for 1-20. No A/C. Mid-June-Labor Day: lodge rms for 2, $40-$45 (maid serv avail); kit. apts for 2-6, $760-$795/wk; kit. cottages $1,100-$1,300/wk; lower rates May-mid-June, after Labor Day-Oct. Closed rest of yr. Crib free. Pet accepted, some restrictions. TV in lobby; cable. Playground. Dining rm in season 8-10:30 am, noon-2 pm. Ck-out 10 am, ck-in 3 pm. Grocery, coin lndry, package store 7 mi. Tennis. Private beach; rowboats, hoists; paddle boats. Sailboats. Fireplaces. Many private patios. Picnic tables, grills. 1,000-ft beach on Crystal Lake, 300 acres of wooded hills. Cr cds: V.

Restaurants

★ **HOTEL FRANKFORT.** *231 Main St. 616/352-4303.* Hrs: 8 am-9 pm; Fri, Sat to 10 pm; June-Aug to 10 pm. Res accepted. Bar. Semi-a la carte: bkfst $2.05-$6.95, lunch $2.95-$7, dinner $7.95-$19.95. Child's meals. Specializes in prime rib, Icelandic scrod, desserts. Pianist. Victorian decor; gingerbread woodwork on exterior. Guest rms avail. Cr cds: A, DS, MC, V.

D

★ **MANITOU.** *4349 Scenic Hwy (MI 22), 9 mi N. 616/882-4761.* Hrs: 4:30-10 pm; early-bird dinner to 6 pm Thurs-Sun. Closed Dec-Apr. Res accepted. Wine, beer. Semi-a la carte: dinner $8.95-$29.95. Specialties: fresh broiled whitefish, sautéed perch, rack of lamb. Outdoor dining. Wildlife theme. Cr cds: MC, V.

✔★ ★ **WHARFSIDE.** *300 Main St. 616/352-5300.* Hrs: 11 am-9 pm. Closed Sun, Mon; Thanksgiving, Dec 25. Amer, Italian menu. Serv bar. Semi-a la carte: lunch $4.50-$8.95, dinner $9.95-$15.95. Child's meals. Specializes in steak, pasta. Overlooks Lake Michigan. Totally nonsmoking. Cr cds: A, D, DS, MC, V.

D

Gaylord (E-4)

(See also Boyne City, Grayling)

Settled 1873 **Pop** 3,256 **Elev** 1,349 ft **Area code** 517 **Zip** 49735
Information Gaylord Area Convention & Tourism Bureau, 101 W Main, PO Box 3069; 517/732-4000 or 800/345-8621.

What to See and Do

Otsego Lake State Park. Approx 60 acres. Swimming beach, bathhouse, waterskiing; fishing for pike, bass, perch; boating (rentals, launch); picnicking, playground, concession; camping. (Mid-Apr-mid-Oct) Standard fees. 7 mi S off I-75 on Old US 27. Phone 517/732-5485. Per car ¢¢

Skiing. Treetops Sylvan Resort. Double, 2 triple chairlifts, 4 rope tows; patrol, school, rentals; cafeteria, bar. 18 runs; longest run 1/2 mi; vertical drop 225 ft. (Dec-mid-Mar, daily) 10 mi of cross-country trails; 31/2 mi of lighted trails. 5 mi E via MI 32 to Wilkinson Rd. Phone 517/732-6711 or 800/444-6711. ¢¢¢¢¢

Annual Events

Winterfest. Ski racing and slalom, cross-country events, snowmobile events, activities for children, snow sculpting, downhill tubing. Fees for some events. Late Jan-early Feb.

Alpenfest. Participants dressed in costumes of Switzerland, carnival, pageant, grand parade; "world's largest coffee break." 3rd wkend July.

Otsego County Fair. 1st full wk Aug.

Motels

✔★ **BEST WESTERN ROYAL CREST.** *803 S Otsego Ave (Old US 27).* 517/732-6451; FAX 517/732-7634; res: 800/876-9252. 44 rms, 1-2 story. Mid-May-Oct, Christmas wk, ski wkends: S $59-$79; D $69-$89; each addl $6; under 16 free; lower rates rest of yr. Crib free. Pet accepted. TV; cable. Complimentary continental bkfst. Complimentary coffee in rms. Ck-out 11 am. Exercise equipt; treadmill, stair machine, sauna. Whirlpool. Downhill/x-country ski 3 mi. Cr cds: A, C, D, DS, ER, MC, V.

D ✔ ≋ ⅄ 🚶 ♨ SC

★ ★ **COMFORT INN.** *137 West St.* 517/732-7541; FAX 517/732-0930. 117 rms, 2 story. Memorial Day-Labor Day, ski wkends, Christmas wk: S, D $85-$120; each addl $5; golf packages; lower rates rest of yr. Crib free. TV; cable (premium). Indoor pool; whirlpool. Restaurant 7 am-10 pm; Sun to noon. Ck-out 11 am. Business servs avail. Downhill/x-country ski 1/2 mi. Exercise equipt; treadmill, stair machine. Cr cds: A, C, D, DS, JCB, MC, V.

D ≋ ≋ ⅄ 🚶 ♨ SC

★ ★ **DAYS INN.** *1201 W Main St (MI 32).* 517/732-2200; FAX 517/732-0300. 95 rms, 2 story. Mid-June-early Sept: S $79-$115; D $89-$115; each addl $5; family rates; ski, golf plans; higher rates late Dec-Jan 1; lower rates rest of yr. Crib free. TV; cable (premium). Indoor pool; whirlpool. Complimentary continental bkfst. Restaurant adj 6 am-10 pm. Ck-out 11 am. Coin Indry. Meeting rm. Business servs avail. Downhill ski 4 mi; x-country ski 11/2 mi. Exercise equipt; weight machine, stair machine, sauna. Game rm. Refrigerators. Cr cds: A, C, D, DS, JCB, MC, V.

D ≋ ≋ ⅄ 🚶 ♨ SC

★ ★ ★ **HOLIDAY INN.** *833 W Main St (MI 32).* 517/732-2431; FAX 517/732-9640. 140 rms, 2 story. Mid-June-Sept, ski wkends, Christmas wk: S, D $85-$91; each addl $6; under 19 free; golf plans; lower rates rest of yr. Crib free. Pet accepted. TV; cable, VCR avail (movies). Indoor pool; whirlpool. Restaurant 6 am-10 pm. Rm serv. Bar 3 pm-midnight. Ck-out 11 am. Coin Indry. Meeting rms. Business servs avail. Valet serv. Sundries. Downhill/x-country ski 4 mi. Exercise equipt; bicycle, stair machine, sauna. Game rm. Cr cds: A, C, D, DS, JCB, MC, V.

D ✔ ≋ ≋ ⅄ 🚶 ♨ ≋ ⅄ ♨ SC

Resorts

★ **EL RANCHO STEVENS.** *2332 E Dixon Lake Rd, Exit I-75 exit #279, 1 mi N on Old US 27 to McCoy Rd, 3 mi E to E. Dixon Lake Rd.* 517/732-5090. 32 rms in 2 lodges, 2-3 story. No A/C. Memorial Day-Sept (2-night min), MAP: S $110-$128; D $83-$99/person. Closed rest of yr. Crib free. Heated pool. Free supervised child's activities. Teen club. Dining rm 6-9 pm. Snacks; barbecues. Bar noon-midnight. Ck-out 11 am, ck-in 3 pm. Grocery, coin Indry, package store 3 mi. Meeting rms. Free airport transportation. Sports dir; instructors. Tennis. Sand beach; water sports, paddle boats, boats. Waterskiing avail. Hayrides. Nature hike. Lawn games. Soc dir; entertainment, dancing. Game rm. Rec rm. Picnic tables. 1,000 acres on Lake Dixon. Cr cds: DS, MC, V.

✔ ⅄ 🚶 ≋ ≋ ♨

★ ★ ★ **GARLAND.** *(County Rd 489, Lewiston 49756)* 30 mi SE on Country Rd 489. 517/786-2211; FAX 517/786-2254; res: 800/968-0042. 58 rms in main bldg, 60 cottages. May-Oct, MAP: S $60; D $199-$209; cottages $159; family, wkly, wkend, hol rates; golf, ski plans; lower rates rest of yr. Closed wk of Thanksgiving, mid-Mar-Apr. Crib free. TV; cable, VCR avail. 2 pools, 1 indoor; whirlpool, poolside serv. Restaurant 6 am-11 pm; winter hrs vary. Rm serv. Box lunches. Bar 6-2 am; entertainment. Ck-out 11 am, ck-in 4 pm. Grocery, coin Indry 5 mi. Bellhops. Valet serv. Concierge. Meeting rms. Business servs avail. Airport transportation. Sports dir. Lighted tennis. 72-hole golf course, pro, greens fee $75, putting green, driving range. Downhill ski 12 mi; x-country ski on site. Sleighing. Hiking. Bicycles. Lawn games. Soc dir. Exercise equipt; bicycles, weight machine, sauna, steam rm. Massage. Refrigerators. Balconies. Picnic tables. Cr cds: A, C, D, DS, MC, V.

D ✔ ⅄ 🚶 ≋ ≋ ⅄ ♨ ≋

★ ★ **MARSH RIDGE.** *4815 Old 27 South.* 517/732-6794; FAX 517/732-0467; res: 800/743-7529 (MI). 59 rms, 1-2 story, 5 kit. units. Mid-May-late Oct, late Dec-late Mar: S, D $95-$160; each addl $10; kit. units up to 4, $250; under 16 free; ski, golf plans; lower rates rest of yr. TV; cable (premium). Heated pool; whirlpool, sauna. Restaurant 7 am-10 pm; 5-9 pm off season. Ck-out 11 am. Meeting rms. Business servs avail. 18-hole golf, greens fee (incl cart) $48-$54, putting green, lighted driving range. Downhill ski 5 mi; lighted x-country ski on site. Rec rm. Lawn games. Refrigerators; some fireplaces. Private patios, balconies. Picnic tables. Cr cds: A, D, MC, V.

D ≋ ⅄ 🚶 ≋ ≋ ♨ SC

★ ★ ★ **TREETOPS SYLVAN RESORT.** *3962 Wilkinson Rd.* 517/732-6711; FAX 517/732-6595; res: 800/444-6711. 228 rms in main buildings, 2-3 story, 30 rms in chalets, 2 story, 12 kits. May-Sept, Dec 25-Feb: S $79-$134; D $99-$144; each addl $6; chalet rms $160-$294; kit. units $104-$114; under 18 free; MAP avail; ski, golf plans; lower rates rest of yr. Crib $5. TV; cable, VCR avail. 4 pools, 2 indoor; whirlpools, poolside serv. Playground. Supervised child's activities, ages 1-12 yrs. Coffee in rms. Dining rm (public by res) 8 am-10 pm; Fri, Sat to 10:30 pm. Snack bar; box lunches; picnics. Rm serv. Bar to 2 am. Ck-out noon, ck-in 4 pm. Meeting rms. Business servs avail. Airport transportation. Lighted tennis. 81-hole golf, greens fee $60-$68, pro, putting green, driving range. Downhill/x-country ski on site; rentals. Exercise equipt; stair machine, weight machines, sauna. Lawn games. Hiking trails. Soc dir. Game rm. Many refrigerators. Many private patios, balconies. Picnic tables, grills. 4,000-acre hilltop complex on the crest of Pigeon River Valley. Cr cds: A, C, D, MC, V.

D ✔ ⅄ ⅄ 🚶 ≋ ≋ ⅄ ♨

Restaurants

★ **SCHLANG'S BAVARIAN INN.** *Old US 27S. 517/732-9288.* Hrs: 5-10 pm; Closed Sun; most major holidays. German, Amer menu. Bar. Semi-a la carte: dinner $10.95-$23. Specializes in pork chops, baked whitefish, ribeye steak. Authentic Bavarian atmosphere; fireplace. Family-owned. Cr cds: MC, V.

★ ★ **SUGAR BOWL.** *216 W Main St (MI 32). 517/732-5524.* Hrs: 7 am-11 pm; Sun to 10 pm. Closed Easter, Thanksgiving, Dec 25; also last wk Mar & 1st wk Apr. Res accepted. Greek, Amer menu. Bar. Semi-a la carte: bkfst $2.50-$6.25, lunch $3.75-$6.95, dinner $4.50-$25. Child's meals. Specializes in fresh Lake Superior whitefish, charcoal-broiled steak. Greek gourmet table. Salad bar. Fireplace. Family-owned. Cr cds: A, DS, MC, V.

Glen Arbor (F-3)

(See also Leland, Traverse City)

Settled 1848 **Pop** 250 (est) **Elev** 591 ft **Area code** 616 **Zip** 49636

This community, situated on Lake Michigan, lies just north of Sleeping Bear Dunes National Lakeshore (see).

Annual Event

Glen Arbor Antique Show and Festival. Antique show and sale. Phone 616/334-3238. Last wkend June.

Resort

★ ★ ★ **THE HOMESTEAD.** *Woodridge Rd (MI 22). 616/334-5000; res: 616/334-5100; FAX 616/334-5120.* 210 condos, 2-3 story, 77 lodge rms. No A/C in condos. July-Labor Day: condos $167-$419; lodge rms $133-$175; MAP avail; lower rates May-June, early Sept-Oct. Closed Apr, Nov; wkdays mid-Dec-early Mar. TV; cable. 3 heated pools, sauna, poolside serv in season. Playground. Supervised child's activities (July-Sept). Restaurant 8 am-10 pm. Bar noon-1 am in season. Ck-out 11 am, ck-in 5 pm. Grocery, package store on site. Meeting rms. Business servs avail. Sports dir. Tennis, pro (July-Sept). 9-hole par-3 golf, pro. Private beach; swimming. Sailboats, canoes. Charter fishing. Downhill/x-country ski on site. Skating. Bicycles. Exercise course. Entertainment. Many fireplaces. Patios, balconies. On Lake Michigan shoreline. Cr cds: DS, MC, V.

Restaurants

★ ★ **JACK'S GLEN LAKE INN.** *(4566 MacFarland Rd, Maple City 49664) 6 mi SE on County 675, 4¹/₂ mi SE of MI 22 in Burdickville. 616/334-3900.* Hrs: 8 am-2 pm, 5-9 pm. Closed Mon. Res accepted. Continental menu. Serv bar. Semi-a la carte: bkfst $3-$6, lunch $4-$6, dinner $8-$14. Specializes in chicken, pasta. Family-owned. Totally nonsmoking. Cr cds: DS, MC, V.

★ ★ **LA BÉCASSE.** *(9001 S Dunn's Farm Rd, Maple City 49664) 5 mi S on County Hwy 675 to jct County Hwy 616, in Burdickville. 616/334-3944.* Hrs: 5:45-9:15 pm. Closed Mon; Tue May-mid-June; most major hols; also mid-Oct-late Dec & mid-Mar-early May. Res accepted. French menu. Serv bar. Semi-a la carte: dinner $16-$25. Specializes in profiteroles, veal, wild game dishes. Outdoor dining. European-style cafe. Cr cds: A, DS, MC, V.

✔★ **WESTERN AVENUE GRILL.** *6410 Western Ave. 616/334-3362.* Hrs: 11 am-9 pm. Closed Mon-Wed; Thanksgiving, Dec 25. Serv bar. Semi-a la carte: lunch $3.95-$6.95, dinner $7.95-$13.95. Specializes in seafood, pasta, ribs. Modern rustic decor. Cr cds: A, DS, MC, V.

Grand Haven (H-3)

(See also Grand Rapids, Holland, Muskegon)

Settled 1834 **Pop** 11,951 **Elev** 590 ft **Area code** 616 **Zip** 49417 **E-mail** 2042712@mcimail.com

Information Grand Haven/Spring Lake Area Visitors Bureau, One S Harbor Dr; 616/842-4499 or 800/303-4096.

Through this port city at the mouth of the Grand River flows a stream of produce for all the Midwest. The port has the largest charter fishing fleet on Lake Michigan and is also used for sport fishing, recreational boating and as a Coast Guard base. Connecting the pier to downtown shops is a boardwalk and park.

What to See and Do

Grand Haven State Park. Almost 50 acres on Lake Michigan beach. Swimming, bathhouse; fishing. Picnicking (shelter), playground, concession. Camping. Standard fees. (Daily) 1 mi SW. Phone 616/798-3711. Per car ¢¢

Harbor Trolleys. Two different routes: Grand Haven trolley operates between downtown and state park; second trolley goes to Spring Lake. (Memorial Day-Labor Day, daily) Transfer point at Chinook Pier. Phone 616/842-3200. ¢

Municipal Marina. 57 transient slips; fish cleaning station; stores and restaurants; trolley stop. At foot of Washington St, downtown.Phone 616/847-3478. Also docked here is the

Harbor Steamer. Stern-wheel paddle boat cruises to Spring Lake; scenic views, narrated by captain. (Mid-May-Sept, daily) 301 N Harbor. For reservations, schedule phone 616/842-8950. ¢¢¢

Musical Fountain. Said to be the world's largest electronically controlled musical fountain; water, lights and music are synchronized. Programs (Memorial Day-Labor Day, nightly; May & rest of Sept, Fri & Sat only). Special Christmas nativity scene in Dec covering all of Dewey Hill. Dewey Hill. Phone 616/842-2550.

Annual Events

Winterfest. Music, dance, parade, children's activities. Early Feb.

Polar Ice Cap Golf Tournament. Spring Lake. 18-hole, par-3 golf game on ice. Feb.

Great Lakes Stunt Kite Festival. Grand Haven State Park. Phone 616/846-7501. May.

National Coast Guard Festival. Includes a parade, carnival, craft exhibit, ship tours, pageant and variety shows, fireworks. Late July-early Aug.

Seasonal Event

On the Waterfront Big Band Concert Series. Wed evenings. July-Aug.

Motels

(Rates may be higher during Tulip Time and Coast Guard festivals)

★ ★ **BEST WESTERN BEACON.** *1525 S Beacon Blvd (US 31). 616/842-4720.* 101 rms. May-Sept: S $46-$60; D $58-$120; each addl $4; under 12 free; higher rates special events; lower rates rest of yr. Crib $2. TV; cable (premium). Heated pool. Restaurant adj 6 am-11 pm. Ck-out 11 am. Free airport, bus depot transportation. X-country ski 8 mi. Some in-rm whirlpools, refrigerators. Picnic tables. Cr cds: A, C, D, DS, MC, V.

★ ★ **DAYS INN.** *1500 S Beacon Blvd (US 31). 616/842-1999; FAX 616/842-3892.* 100 rms, 2 story. May-early Sept: S, D $69-$110; each addl $6; lower rates rest of yr. Crib free. TV; cable. Indoor pool; whirlpool. Complimentary continental bkfst. Restaurant 11:30 am-10 pm; Sun 10:30 am-2 pm. Rm serv. Bar noon-midnight. Ck-out noon. Coin lndry. Meeting rms. Business servs avail. Downhill ski 2 mi; x-country ski 6 mi. Game rm. Cr cds: A, C, D, DS, JCB, MC, V.

D ⚡ ≈ ⬛ 🔥 SC

✔★ **FOUNTAIN INN.** *1010 S Beacon Blvd (US 31). 616/846-1800; FAX 616/847-9287; res: 800/745-8660.* 47 rms, 2 story. Mid-May-Labor Day: S, D $49.95-$89.95; each addl $5; higher rates special events; lower rates rest of yr. TV; cable. Complimentary continental bkfst. Restaurant nearby. Ck-out 11 am. Meeting rms. X-country ski 3 mi. Cr cds: A, DS, MC, V.

D ⚡ ⬛ 🔥 🖊

Inns

★ ★ **HARBOR HOUSE.** *114 South Harbor Dr. 616/846-0610; FAX 616/846-0530; res: 800/841-0610.* 17 rms, 3 story, 1 suite. Memorial Day-Labor Day: S, D $120-$140; each addl $25; suite $140-$180; higher rates wkends (2-day min); lower rates rest of yr. Closed Dec 24, 25. TV in sitting rm; cable. Complimentary continental bkfst. Restaurant nearby. Ck-out 11 am, ck-in 2 pm. Business servs avail. Downhill ski 2 blks; x-country ski 15 mi. Game rm. Some balconies. Early American decor. Totally nonsmoking. Cr cds: MC, V.

D ⚡ ⬛ 🖊

★ ★ **ROYAL PONTALUNA.** *(1870 Pontaluna Rd, Spring Lake 48456) 616/798-7271; FAX 616/798-7271; res: 800/856-3545.* 5 rms, 2 story. No rm phones. May-Sept: S, D $85-$135; each addl $25; lower rates rest of yr. TV; cable (premium), VCR (movies). Indoor pool; whirlpool, sauna. Complimentary continental bkfst. Restaurant nearby. Ck-out 11 am, ck-in 4 pm. Lighted tennis. X-country ski on site. Rec rm. Totally nonsmoking. Cr cds: A, D, MC, V.

⚡ 🛷 ⬛ 🖊 SC

Restaurant

★ **ARBOREAL INN.** *(18191 174th Ave, Spring Lake 49456) 3 mi N on US 31 to Van Wagoner Rd, then left to 174th Ave, then right 1/4 mi. 616/842-3800.* Hrs: 11 am-2 pm, 5-10 pm; Sat from 5 pm. Closed Sun; some major hols. Res accepted. Bar. A la carte entrees: lunch $5-$11, dinner $12.95-$26.95. Specialties: tournedos Oscar, whitefish jardiniere. Early American decor. Cr cds: A, DS, MC, V.

D 🍴

Grand Marais (C-3)

Pop 350 (est) **Elev** 640 ft **Area code** 906 **Zip** 49839
Information Chamber of Commerce, PO Box 139; 906/494-2447.

On the shore of Lake Superior, Grand Marais has a harbor with marina and is surrounded by cool, clear lakes, trout streams and agate beaches. In the winter, there is snowmobiling and cross-country skiing.

What to See and Do

Pictured Rocks National Lakeshore. This scenic stretch of shoreline begins at the western edge of Grand Marais and continues west to Munising (see). Hiking, swimming, hunting, fishing, rock climbing, cross-country skiing and snowmobiling.

Annual Events

500-Mile Snowmobile Endurance Run. Mid-Jan.

Music and Arts Festival. 2nd wkend Aug.

Motel

★ ★ **BUDGET HOST-WELKER'S RESORT.** *Box 277, on Canal St, 1 mi E of MI 77. 906/494-2361; FAX 906/494-2371.* 41 rms, 1-2 story, 9 kit. cottages. Some A/C. Some rm phones. S $34-$47; D $40-$52; each addl $5; kit. cottages $227-$297/wk. Crib $5. Pet accepted. TV; cable (premium), VCR avail (movies $5). Indoor pool; whirlpool, sauna. Playground. Restaurant 7:30 am-8:30 pm. Bar. Ck-out 11 am, cottages 10 am. Coin lndry. Meeting rm. Business servs avail. Tennis. Lawn games. On Lake Superior; private beach. Cr cds: A, DS, MC, V.

D 🐾 🎣 🛷 ≈ ⬛ 🔥

Grand Rapids (H-3)

(See also Grand Haven, Holland, Muskegon)

Settled 1826 **Pop** 189,126 **Elev** 657 ft **Area code** 616 **E-mail** grcvb @mcimail.com **Web** www.grcvb.org

Information Grand Rapids/Kent County Convention & Visitors Bureau, 140 Monroe Center NW, 49503; 616/459-8287 or 800/678-9859.

Grand Rapids, a widely known furniture center and convention city, is located on the site where Louis Campau established a Native American trading post in 1826. The city derives its name from the rapids in the Grand River, which flows through the heart of the city. There are 50 parks here, totalling 1,270 acres. Calvin College and Calvin Seminary (1876) are located here; several other colleges are in the area.

Thirty-eighth president Gerald R. Ford was raised in Grand Rapids and represented the Fifth Congressional District in Michigan from 1948 to 1973, when he became the nation's vice president.

What to See and Do

Blandford Nature Center. More than 140 acres of woods, fields and ponds with self-guiding trails; guided tours (fee); interpretive center has exhibits, live animals; furnished pioneer garden; one-room schoolhouse. (Mon-Fri, also Sat & Sun afternoons; closed hols) 1715 Hillburn Ave NW. Phone 616/453-6192. **Free.**

Fish Ladder. A unique fish ladder for watching salmon leap the rapids of the Grand River during spawning season. Sixth St dam.

⭐ **Frederik Meijer Gardens.** Botanic garden and sculpture park includes 15,000-sq-ft glass conservatory, desert garden, exotic indoor and outdoor gardens, more than 50 bronze works in sculpture park. Also outdoor nature trails and tram tour. Gift shop, restaurant. (Daily; closed Jan 1, Dec 25) 3411 Bradford NE. Phone 616/957-1580. ¢¢

⭐ **Gerald R. Ford Museum.** Exhibits tracing the life and public service of the 38th president of the US. A 28-min introductory film on Ford; reproduction of the White House Oval Office; educational exhibits on the US House of Representatives and the presidency; American Bicentennial Exhibit. (Daily; closed Jan 1, Thanksgiving, Dec 25) 303 Pearl St NW. Phone 616/451-9263. ¢

Grand Rapids Art Museum. Collections include Renaissance, German Expressionist, French and American paintings; graphics and a children's gallery augmented by special traveling exhibitions. (Daily exc Mon; closed hols) 155 Division St N. Phone 616/459-4677. ¢¢

John Ball Zoo. Includes zoological gardens, aquarium and conservatory; Adventureland with children's zoo featuring a 60-ft waterfall and petting zoo; African Forest Edge exhibit, penguin exhibit, herpetarium/nocturnal animal exhibits; picnic area. (Daily) 1300 W Fulton St. Phone 616/336-4300. ¢¢

La Grande Vitesse. This 42-ton stabile was created by Alexander Calder. County Building, downtown.

Meyer May House (1908). Frank Lloyd Wright house from the late prairie period. Authentically restored with all architect-designed furniture, leaded-glass windows, lighting fixtures, rugs and textiles. Tours begin at visitor center, 442 Madison St SE. (Tues, Thurs & Sun; schedule varies) 450 Madison St SE. Phone 616/246-4821.   **Free.**

Skiing.

Cannonsburg. Quad, triple and double chairlifts, 2 T-bars, 8 rope tows. Longest run approx ⅓ mi; vertical drop 250 ft. Patrol, school, equipment rentals; snowmaking; nursery; cafeteria, bar. (Thanksgiving-mid-Mar, daily) 6800 Cannonsburg Rd, 10 mi NE via US 131, W River Dr. Phone 616/874-6711 or 800/253-8748(IL, IN, OH) for snow conditions.   ¢¢¢¢

Pando. 6 rope tows, 7 lighted runs; patrol, school, rentals; grooming equipment, snowmaking; cafeteria. (Dec-Mar, Thurs-Sun) 7 mi of cross-country trails; 3 mi of lighted trails, track-setting equipment; rentals. 8076 Belding Rd NE, 12 mi NE on MI 44, in Rockford. Phone 616/874-8343. ¢¢¢;   Wkends ¢¢¢¢

Van Andel Museum Center of Grand Rapids. Exhibits of regional cultural and natural history, including mammals, birds, furniture, Woodland artifacts, re-creation of 1890s Grand Rapids street scene and 1928 carousel. Chaffee Planetarium offers laser light shows (fee); phone 616/456-DOME. (Daily; closed hols) 272 Pearl St NW. Phone 616/456-3977.   ¢¢

Annual Event

Festival '97. Calder Plaza. Arts & crafts shows, entertainment, international foods. 1st full wkend June.

Seasonal Event

Community Circle Theater. Phone 616/456-6656. John Ball Park Pavilion; mid-May-Sept, Wed-Sun. Magic Circle Children's Theater; June-Aug, Tues-Sat.

Motels

(Rates may be higher during Tulip Time Festival, mid-May)

★ ★ **AMERIHOST INN.** *2171 Holton Court NW (49544).* *616/791-8500; FAX 616/791-8630.* 60 rms, 2 story. June-Aug: S $58-$73; D $63-$78; each addl $8; suites $99-$129; under 17 free; lower rates rest of yr. Crib free. TV; cable (premium). Indoor pool; whirlpool, sauna. Complimentary continental bkfst. Restaurant adj 5:30 am-11 pm. Ck-out noon. Meeting rm. Business servs avail. Valet serv. Downhill/x-country ski 15 mi. Exercise equipt; bicycles, weight machines. Some refrigerators. Cr cds: A, C, D, DS, JCB, MC, V.

[D] [icons] SC

★ ★ **BEST WESTERN GRANDVILLE INN.** *(3425 Fairlanes Ave, Grandville 49418)* I-196 W exit 69A E (Chicago Dr) to Fairlanes Ave. *616/532-3222; FAX 616/532-4959.* 82 units, 2 story. S $62-$120; D $69-$120; each addl $5; suites $94-$120; under 12 free. Crib $5. TV; cable (premium). Indoor pool. Complimentary continental bkfst. Ck-out 11 am. Coin lndry. Meeting rm. Business servs avail. Downhill ski 20 mi; x-country ski 10 mi. Game rm. Adj to Grand Village Mall. Cr cds: A, C, D, DS, MC, V.

[D] [icons]

★ ★ **COMFORT INN.** *4155 28th St SE (49512),* S on US 131, then E on MI 11. *616/957-2080; FAX 616/957-9712.* 109 rms, 3 story. S $57; D $63; suites $73; under 18 free; wkend rates. Crib free. TV; cable (premium). Complimentary continental bkfst. Restaurant adj 6 am-10 pm. Ck-out noon. Meeting rm. Business servs avail. Valet serv. Downhill ski 15 mi; x-country ski 4 mi. Some balconies. Cr cds: A, C, D, DS, ER, JCB, MC, V.

[D] [icons] SC

✔ ★ **EXEL INN.** *(4855 28th St SE, Kentwood 49512)* 11 mi SE, ½ mi W of I-96 exit 43A. *616/957-3000; FAX 616/957-0194.* 110 rms, 2

story. S $36.99-$38.99; D $41.99-$47.99; each addl $4; under 18 free. Crib free. Pet accepted. TV. Complimentary continental bkfst. Ck-out noon. Downhill ski 15 mi; x-country ski 4 mi. Cr cds: A, C, D, DS, MC, V.

[D] [icons] SC

★ ★ **HAMPTON INN.** *4981 28th St SE (49512).* *616/956-9304; FAX 616/956-6617.* 120 rms, 2 story. S $57-$61; D $64-$68; each addl $7; under 18 free. Crib free. TV; cable (premium). Heated pool. Complimentary continental bkfst. Restaurant adj 11 am-10 pm. Ck-out noon. Meeting rm. Business servs avail. Valet serv. Downhill ski 15 mi; x-country ski 4 mi. Exercise equipt; weight machines, bicycles. Cr cds: A, C, D, DS, MC, V.

[D] [icons] SC

✔ ★ **RED ROOF INN.** *5131 28th St SE (49512), just W of I-96 exit 43A.* *616/942-0800; FAX 616/942-8341.* 107 rms, 2 story. S $40.99-$47.99; D $46.99-$54.99; 1st addl $6; under 18 free. Crib free. Pet accepted. TV; cable (premium). Complimentary coffee in lobby. Restaurant adj 6 am-11 pm; Fri, Sat 24 hrs; Sun to 10 pm. Ck-out noon. Business servs avail. Downhill ski 15 mi; x-country ski 5 mi. Cr cds: A, C, D, DS, MC, V.

[D] [icons]

★ ★ **RESIDENCE INN BY MARRIOTT.** *2701 E Beltline SE (49546).* *616/957-8111; FAX 616/957-3699.* 96 kit. suites, 2 story. Suites $102-$135; under 12 free. Crib free. Pet accepted, some restrictions; $60 & $6/day. TV; cable (premium), VCR avail. Heated pool; whirlpool. Complimentary continental bkfst. Restaurant adj 11-2 am. Ck-out noon. Coin lndry. Meeting rm. Business servs avail. Valet serv. Free airport transportation. Downhill ski 15 mi; x-country ski 5 mi. Exercise equipt; stair machine, bicycle. Health club privileges. Private patios; some balconies. Picnic tables, grills. Cr cds: A, C, D, DS, JCB, MC, V.

[D] [icons] SC

★ **SWAN INN.** *(5182 Alpine Ave NW, Comstock Park 49321)* 7 mi NW on MI 37. *616/784-1224; FAX 616/784-6565; res: 800/875-7926.* 40 rms, 1-2 story, 4 kits. S $35-$39; D, kit. units $46-$56; each addl $2; under 12 free; wkly rates. Crib free. TV; cable (premium). Heated pool. Restaurant 6 am-10 pm; Sun to 4 pm. Rm serv. Ck-out 11:30 am. Coin lndry. Meeting rms. Business servs avail. Downhill/x-country ski 12 mi. Cr cds: A, C, D, DS, MC, V.

[D] [icons] SC

Motor Hotels

★ ★ **BEST WESTERN MIDWAY.** *4101 28th St SE (49512).* *616/942-2550; FAX 616/942-2446.* 146 rms, 3 story. S $82-$92; D $92-$102; each addl $10; under 18 free; wkend, hol rates. Crib free. TV; cable (premium). Indoor pool; whirlpool, poolside serv. Complimentary full bkfst. Complimentary coffee in rms. Restaurant 7 am-2 pm, 5-10 pm; Sun 6:30 am-2 pm, 5-9 pm. Rm serv. Bar noon-midnight; Fri, Sat to 2 am. Ck-out noon. Meeting rms. Business servs avail. Bellhops. Valet serv. Free airport transportation. Downhill ski 14 mi; x-country ski 4 mi. Exercise equipt; bicycles, weight machine, sauna. Health club privileges. Game rm. Rec rm. Some refrigerators, balconies. Picnic tables. Cr cds: A, C, D, DS, MC, V.

[D] [icons] SC

★ ★ ★ **CROWNE PLAZA.** *5700 28th St SE (MI 11) (49546).* *616/957-1770; FAX 616/957-0629.* 318 rms, 3-5 story. S, D $90-$126; suites $255; under 18 free; wkend packages. Crib free. TV; cable (premium), VCR avail (movies). Indoor/outdoor pool; whirlpool, poolside serv. Restaurant 6:30 am-10 pm. Rm serv. Bar 11-2 am; Sun noon-midnight. Ck-out noon. Coin lndry. Meeting rms. Business servs avail. Bellhops. Valet serv. Gift shop. Free airport transportation. Tennis privileges. 18-hole golf privileges, greens fee $30, pro, putting green. Downhill ski 14 mi; x-country ski 5 mi. Exercise equipt; weights, bicycles, sauna. Private patios, balconies. Cr cds: A, C, D, DS, JCB, MC, V.

[D] [icons] SC

★ ★ **DAYS INN.** *310 Pearl St (49504).* *616/235-7611; FAX 616/235-1995.* 175 units, 8 story. S, D $49-$96; each addl $7; suites

$74-$96; under 16 free; ski plans; higher rates special events. Crib free. TV; cable (premium), VCR avail. Indoor pool; whirlpool. Restaurant 6 am-10 pm; wknd hrs vary. Rm serv. Bar 11-1 am; Sun to 10 pm. Ck-out 11 am. Meeting rms. Business servs avail. Bellhops. Valet serv. Downhill/x-country ski 12 mi. Exercise equipt; bicycles, stair machine. Refrigerator in suites. Cr cds: A, C, D, DS, MC, V.

D ⚡ ≈ ✕ 🔆 🐾 SC

★ ★ **HARLEY HOTEL.** 4041 Cascade Rd SE (49546). 616/949-8800; FAX 616/949-4303. 149 rms, 2 story. S $75-$95; D $85-$105; each addl $10; suites $180; family, wknd rates. Crib free. TV; cable (premium). Indoor/outdoor pool; sauna. Restaurant 6:30 am-10 pm; Fri, Sat to 11 pm. Rm serv. Bar 4 pm-midnight; Fri, Sat to 1 am; entertainment Fri, Sat. Ck-out 11 am. Meeting rms. Business servs avail. Bellhops. Valet serv. Sundries. Free airport transportation. Lighted tennis. Downhill/x-country ski 4 mi. Lawn games. Private patios, balconies. Cr cds: A, C, D, DS, MC, V.

D ⚡ 🏌 ≈ 🔆 🐾 SC

★ ★ ★ **HILTON.** 4747 28th St SE (49512), near Kent County Airport. 616/957-0100; FAX 616/957-2977. 226 rms, 4 story. S $81-$87; D $90-$96; each addl $9; suites $150-$325; studio rms $79-$152; family, ski, wkend rates. Crib free. TV; cable (premium). Indoor pool; whirlpool. Restaurant 6:30 am-11 pm; Sat, Sun from 7 am. Rm serv. Bar 11-2 am. Ck-out noon. Meeting rms. Business servs avail. In-rm modem link. Bellhops. Valet serv Mon-Fri. Free airport transportation. Downhill ski 14 mi; x-country ski 4 mi. Exercise equipt; weights, bicycles, sauna. Some refrigerators. Cr cds: A, C, D, DS, ER, MC, V.

D ⚡ ≈ ✕ 🔆 🐾 SC

★ ★ ★ **HOLIDAY INN AIRPORT EAST.** 3333 28th St SE (49512). 616/949-9222; FAX 616/949-3841. 200 rms, 5 story. S, D $85; family, wkend rates. Crib free. TV; cable (premium). Indoor pool; whirlpool, sauna, poolside serv. Restaurant 6:30 am-10 pm; Fri to 11 pm; Sat 7 am-11 pm; Sun 7 am-10 pm. Rm serv. Bar 4 pm-midnight. Ck-out noon. Meeting rms. Business servs avail. Bellhops. Valet serv. Free airport transportation. Downhill ski 15 mi; x-country ski 3 mi. Rec rm. Putting green. Cr cds: A, C, D, DS, ER, JCB, MC, V.

D ⚡ ≈ 🔆 🐾 SC

★ ★ **HOLIDAY INN SOUTH.** 255 28th St SW (49548), US 131 28th St exit 81. 616/241-6444; FAX 616/241-1807. 156 rms, 5 story. S $65-$80; under 19 free. Crib free. TV; cable (premium), VCR avail. 2 pools, 1 indoor; whirlpool, poolside serv. Restaurant 6:30 am-11 pm. Rm serv. Bar 11-1 am. Ck-out noon. Meeting rms. Business servs avail. In-rm modem link. Bellhops. Valet serv. Downhill ski 12 mi; x-country ski 3 mi. Exercise equipt; bicycles, stair machine, sauna. Holidome. Health club privileges. Game rm. Rec rm. Cr cds: A, C, D, DS, ER, JCB, MC, V.

D ⚡ ≈ ✕ 🐾 SC

★ ★ **LEXINGTON HOTEL SUITES.** 5401 28th St Court SE (49546). 616/940-8100; FAX 616/940-0914; res: 800/441-9628. 121 suites, 3 story. S $79-$99; D $87-$107; each addl $8; under 18 free; higher rates special events. Crib free. TV; cable (premium). Indoor pool; whirlpool. Complimentary continental bkfst; afternoon refreshments. Complimentary coffee in rms. Restaurant nearby. Ck-out noon. Coin lndry. Meeting rms. Business servs avail. Valet serv. Free airport transportation. Downhill ski 15 mi; x-country ski 5 mi. Exercise equipt; weight machine, bicycles. Refrigerators. Cr cds: A, C, D, DS, JCB, MC, V.

D ⚡ ≈ ✕ 🐾 SC

★ ★ **NEW ENGLAND SUITES HOTEL.** 2985 Kraft Ave SE (49512). 616/940-1777; FAX 616/940-9809; res: 800/784-8371. 40 suites, 2 story. S $75, D $80. Crib free. Pet accepted. TV; cable (premium), VCR avail (movies free). Complimentary continental bkfst. Complimentary coffee in rms. Restaurant nearby. Ck-out noon. Business servs avail. Valet serv. Refrigerators. Cr cds: A, C, D, DS, MC, V.

D 🐾 🔆 🐾 SC

★ ★ **QUALITY INN TERRACE CLUB.** 4495 28th St SE (49512). 616/956-8080; FAX 616/956-0619. 126 rms, 3 story. S $69-$99; D $79-$109; each addl $10; suites $109-$139; under 18 free; wkly, wkend

rates; ski, golf plans. Crib free. TV; cable (premium). Indoor pool; whirlpool. Complimentary full bkfst. Complimentary coffee in rms. Restaurant nearby. Ck-out noon. Coin lndry. Meeting rms. Business servs avail. In-rm modem link. Free airport transportation. Downhill ski 15 mi; x-country ski 3 mi. Exercise equipt; weights, bicycles. Refrigerator, minibar in suites. Cr cds: A, C, D, DS, ER, JCB, MC, V.

D ⚡ ≈ ✕ 🔆 🐾 SC

Hotels

★ ★ ★ ★ **AMWAY GRAND PLAZA.** Pearl St (49503), at Monroe Ave. 616/774-2000; FAX 616/776-6496; res: 800/253-3590. In this renovated 1913 hotel, chandeliers, period furnishings and many antiques set a grandiose mood. 682 rms, 29 story. S $91-$155; D $107-$185; each addl $15; suites $215-$1,100; under 12 free; wknd rates. Crib free. TV; cable (premium), VCR avail. Indoor pool; whirlpool, poolside serv. 7 restaurants. Rm serv 24 hrs. Bars 11:30-2 am; Sun from noon; entertainment exc Sun. Ck-out noon. Meeting rms. Business center. Concierge. Shopping arcade. Barber, beauty shop. Airport transportation. Lighted tennis. Downhill ski 15 mi; x-country ski 10 mi. Exercise rm; instructor, weights, bicycles, sauna. Massage. Bathrm phone, refrigerator in suites. Some balconies. On the Grand River. Luxury level. Cr cds: A, C, D, DS, JCB, MC, V.

D ⚡ 🏌 ≈ ✕ 🔆 🐾 SC 🚶

★ ★ **HOLIDAY INN NORTH.** 270 Ann St NW (49504), US 131 exit 88. 616/363-9001; FAX 616/363-0670. 164 rms, 7 story. S $74, D $82; each addl $8; under 20 free; ski plan; wknd, hol rates. Crib free. Pet accepted, some restrictions. TV; cable (premium), VCR avail. Indoor pool; whirlpool, sauna, poolside serv. Restaurant 6:30 am-10 pm; Fri, Sat 7 am-11 pm. Bar 11-1 am; entertainment. Ck-out noon. Coin lndry. Meeting rms. Business servs avail. Downhill/x-country ski 14 mi. Game rm. Picnic tables. On Grand River. Cr cds: A, C, D, DS, JCB, MC, V.

D 🐾 ≈ ≈ 🔆 🐾 SC

Restaurants

✔★ ★ **ARNIE'S BAKERY.** 3561 28th St SE (49512), in Eastbrook Mall. 616/956-7901. Hrs: 7 am-10:30 pm; Sat from 8 am; Sun 9 am-3 pm. Closed some major hols. Semi-a la carte: bkfst $3-$6, lunch $5-$7, dinner $6-$10.50. Child's meals. Specializes in desserts, sandwiches. Pianist. Retail bakery. Cr cds: A, MC, V.

D ⬛ ♥

★ ★ **DUBA'S.** 420 E Beltline NE (49506). 616/949-1011. Hrs: 11 am-10 pm; Fri, Sat to 11 pm. Closed Sun; hols. Res accepted. Bar. Semi-a la carte: lunch $5.95-$10, dinner $13.95-$22. Child's meals. Specializes in prime rib, fish. Parking. Family-owned. Cr cds: A, MC, V.

D

★ ★ **GIBSON'S.** 1033 Lake Dr (49506). 616/774-8535. Hrs: 11:30 am-11 pm; Sat from 5 pm. Closed July 4, Thanksgiving, Dec 25; also Sun from June-Aug. Res accepted. Continental menu. Bar 11:30-1 am. Wine list. Semi-a la carte: lunch $5-$11.50, dinner $11.75-$25. Specializes in aged beef, lamb, fowl. Own baking, ice cream. Parking. Patio dining. In former Franciscan friary (1860s). Cr cds: A, D, DS, MC, V.

D

★ ★ **GRAND RIVER SALOON.** 151 Ottawa St NW (49503). 616/458-2229. Hrs: 11-1 am; Sat from noon. Closed Sun; most major hols. Res accepted. Continental menu. Bar to 2 am. A la carte entrees: lunch $5-$8, dinner $7-$14. Specializes in steak. Outdoor dining. English pub atmosphere. Cr cds: A, DS, MC, V.

D ⬛

★ **JOHN BRANN'S STEAKHOUSE CASCADE.** 5510 28th St SE (49512). 616/285-7800. Hrs: 11 am-10:30 pm; Fri, Sat to 11 pm; Sun 10 am-9 pm; early-bird dinner Sun-Thurs 4-8 pm; Sun brunch to 2:30 pm. Closed Thanksgiving, Dec 25. Res accepted. Bar to 2 am. Semi-a la carte: lunch $5.99-$8.99, dinner $7.99-$15.99. Sun brunch $8.99. Child's meals.

Specialties: steak, prime rib. Salad bar. Family-owned. Cr cds: A, C, D, DS, MC, V.

 (icon: D, icon)

★★ **KENTWOOD STATION.** (1665 Viewpond Dr, Kentwood 49508) S on US 131, exit 44th St, then S on Kalamazoo Ave. 616/455-4150. Hrs: 11:30 am-2 pm, 5-9 pm; Fri to 10 pm; Sat 5-10 pm. Closed Sun; hols. Res accepted. Bar to 11 pm, Fri, Sat to midnight. Semi-a la carte: lunch $4.95-$8.50, dinner $10.25-$16.75. Child's meals. Specializes in prime rib, seafood, homemade soup. Salad bar. Parking. Railroad decor. Cr cds: A, MC, V.

✓★★ **PIETRO'S.** 2780 Birchcrest St SE (49506). 616/452-3228. Hrs: 11:30 am-10 pm; Fri to 11 pm; Sat 3-11 pm; Sun noon-10 pm. Closed Thanksgiving, Dec 25. Northern Italian, Amer menu. Bar. Semi-a la carte: lunch $6-$7, dinner $7-$11. Child's meals. Specializes in fresh pasta, chicken, veal dishes. Parking. Outdoor dining. Cr cds: A, DS, MC, V.

★★ **REMBRANDT'S.** 333 Bridge St NW (49503), in Bridgewater Place Bldg. 616/459-8900. Hrs: 11:30 am-11 pm; Mon to 2 pm; Sat from 5 pm. Closed Sun; most major hols. Res accepted. Bar. Semi-a la carte: lunch $5.50-$12, dinner $13.50-$29.95. Child's meals. Specializes in seafood, steak. Overlooks Grand River. Cr cds: A, DS, MC, V.

★★ **SAYFEE'S.** 3555 Lake Eastbrook Blvd SE (49546). 616/949-5750. Hrs: 11 am-11 pm. Closed Sun exc Mother's Day & Easter; some major hols. Continental menu. Bar. Semi-a la carte: lunch $4.95-$11.50, dinner $6.95-$18.95. Child's meals. Specializes in steak, seafood. Band Tues-Sat. Valet parking wkends. Cr cds: A, C, D, DS, MC, V.

★★ **SCHNITZELBANK.** 342 Jefferson Ave SE (49503). 616/459-9527. Hrs: 11 am-8 pm; Fri to 9 pm; Sat 4:30-9 pm. Closed Sun; hols. Res accepted. German, Amer menu. Bar. Semi-a la carte: lunch $4.50-$7.95, dinner $8.95-$18.50. Specialties: sauerbraten, roast chicken, Wienerschnitzel. Parking. Bavarian atmosphere. Family-owned. Cr cds: A, MC, V.

★★ **SHANGHAI GARDEN.** 5595 28th St SE (49512). 616/942-5120. Hrs: Chinese restaurant: 11:30 am-10 pm; Sat noon-11 pm; Sun noon-9 pm. Lunch buffet $6.25. Sun brunch $9.65. Japanese restaurant: 4:30-10 pm only. Res accepted. Oriental menu. Bar. Chinese (semi-a la carte): lunch $4.75-$6.25, dinner $5.45-$16.95. Japanese (semi-a la carte): dinner $10.25-$25.95. Specializes in mandarin, Szechwan & Hunan dishes; Japanese steak house hibachi-style cooking. Parking. Two distinct dining areas separated by bridge over pond, garden. Cr cds: A, C, D, DS, MC, V.

✓★★ **WYOMING CATTLE CO.** (1820 44th St SW, Wyoming 49509) 616/534-0704. Hrs: 11 am-10 pm; Fri, Sat to 11 pm. Closed Thanksgiving, Dec 24, 25. Bar to 11 pm. Semi-a la carte: lunch $4.50-$7.95, dinner $6.75-$18.95. Specializes in steak. Outdoor dining. Western decor. Cr cds: A, DS, MC, V.

Grayling (F-4)

(See also Gaylord, Houghton Lake)

Pop 1,944 **Elev** 1,137 ft **Area code** 517 **Zip** 49738 **E-mail** visitor @grayling-mi.com **Web** www.grayling-mi.com
Information Grayling Area Visitors Council, PO Box 217; 800/937-8837.

What to See and Do

Canoe trips. There are many canoe liveries in the area, with trip itineraries for the Manistee and Au Sable rivers. Contact Grayling Area Visitors Council for details.

Hartwick Pines State Park. Approx 9,700 acres. Fishing for trout, perch and largemouth bass; hunting; marked cross-country ski trails; picnicking, playground, concession; camping. Three-dimensional exhibits in interpretive center tell the story of the white pine. Log memorial building, lumberman's museum near virgin pine forest; "Chapel in the Pines." Naturalist. Standard fees. (Daily) 7 mi NE on MI 93. Phone 517/348-7068. Per car ¢¢

Skyline Ski Area. Chairlift, 9 rope tows; patrol, school, rentals; cafeteria; ski shop. Longest run approx 1/2 mi; vertical drop 210 ft. (Mid-Dec-Mar, daily) 2 mi S off I-75, exit 251. Phone 517/275-5445. ¢¢¢¢¢

Annual Events

Winter Wolf Festival. Early Feb.

World's Championship Au Sable River Festival & Marathon. This canoe marathon starts at Grayling and ends in Oscoda (see) on Lake Huron. Arts & crafts, parade, car show. Last full wkend July.

Motels

★★★ **HOLIDAY INN.** 2650 I-75 S Business, at exit 254. 517/348-7611; FAX 517/348-7984. 151 rms, 2 story. July-Aug: S, D $89-$109; each addl $6; suites $150-$175; under 19 free; lower rates rest of yr. Pet accepted. TV; cable (premium), VCR avail. Indoor pool; wading pool, whirlpool, poolside serv. Playground. Restaurant 6 am-2 pm, 5-10 pm; Sun 6 am-9 pm. Rm serv. Bar 11-2 am; entertainment. Ck-out 11 am. Meeting rms. Business servs avail. Bellhops. Valet serv. Sundries. Airport, bus depot transportation. Downhill ski 5 mi; x-country ski on site. Game rm. Lawn games. Exercise equipt; weight machine, bicycle, sauna. Picnic tables. On wooded property. Some refrigerators. Cr cds: A, C, D, DS, ER, JCB, MC, V.

★ **HOSPITALITY HOUSE.** 1232 I-75 Business Loop. 517/348-8900; FAX 517/348-6509; res: 800/722-4151. 80 rms, 1-2 story. Memorial Day-Labor Day, wkends: S, D $60-$80; each addl $5; suites $110-$165; under 16 free; lower rates rest of yr. Crib free. TV; cable (premium), VCR avail (movies $4). Indoor pool; whirlpool. Restaurant 6:30 am-2 pm, 5-9 pm. Rm serv. Business servs avail. Valet serv. Free airport, bus depot transportation. Downhill/x-country ski 3 mi. Game rm. Refrigerators. Cr cds: A, C, D, DS, MC, V.

✓★ **NORTH COUNTRY LODGE.** Box 290, 3/4 mi N on Old US 27, I-75 Business. 517/348-8471; FAX 517/348-6114; res: 800/475-6300. 24 rms, 8 kits. Mid-June-Labor Day, winter wkends, Christmas wk: S, D $40-$90; each addl $2; kit. units $45-$65; suite $125-$150; family, wkly rates; lower rates rest of yr. Crib free. Pet accepted. TV; cable. Restaurant nearby. Ck-out 11 am. Free airport, bus depot transportation. Downhill/x-country ski 3 mi. Cr cds: A, C, D, DS, MC, V.

✓★ **POINTE NORTH OF GRAYLING.** 1/2 mi N on Old US 27, I-75 Business. 517/348-5950. 21 rms. Mid-June-Labor Day, Christmas wk, winter wkends: S $35-$50; D $50-$65; each addl $5; kit. unit $65-$75;

lower rates rest of yr. TV; cable (premium). Ck-out 10 am. Downhill ski 3 mi; x-country ski 2 mi. Refrigerators. Picnic table, grill. Cr cds: A, D, DS, MC, V.

✔★ **SUPER 8.** 5828 Nelson A Miles Pkwy. 517/348-8888; FAX 517/348-2030. 61 rms, 2 story. Apr-Sept: S $46.69; D $55.88-$67.88; each addl $4; under 12 free; lower rates rest of yr. TV; cable (premuim). Pet accepted. Complimentary continental bkfst. Restaurant adj open 24 hrs. Ck-out 11 am. Meeting rm. Coin lndry. Downhill ski 1 mi; x-country ski 6 mi. Lawn games. Cr cds: A, C, D, DS, MC, V.

Cottage Colony

★ **PENROD'S.** 100 Maple St, 100 Maple St. 517/348-2910; 800 888/467-4837. 11 cabins, 7 kits. Cabins for 2-3, $45-$60; kit. cabins for 2-3, $55-$60; kit. cabins for 4-6, $80-$90; wkly rates. TV. Playground. Restaurant nearby. Ck-out 11 am, ck-in 2 pm. Grocery, package store 3 blks. Bi-wkly maid serv. Free airport, bus depot transportation. Canoe trips, rentals. Inner tubes. Lawn games. Picnic tables, grills. Rustic log cabins; some with screened porches. 6¹/₂ acres on Au Sable River. Cr cds: DS, MC, V.

Hancock (C-1)

(See also Copper Harbor, Houghton)

Pop 4,547 **Elev** 686 ft **Area code** 906 **Zip** 49930 **E-mail** keweenaw @portup.com **Web** www.portup.com/snow
Information Keweenaw Peninsula Chamber of Commerce, 326 Shelden Ave, PO Box 336, Houghton 49931; 906/482-5240 or 800/338-7982.

Named for John Hancock, the town is the home of Suomi College (1896), the only Finnish college in the United States.

What to See and Do

Maasto Hiihto Ski Trail. A 9¹/₂-mi public cross-country ski trail with beginner-to-expert trails groomed daily. (Dec-Apr, daily, 24 hrs) ¹/₂ mi N via US 41, then 2 mi N on side road. Phone 906/482-2388. **Free.**

Quincy Mine Steam Hoist. This 790-ton hoist was used at the Quincy Copper Mine between 1920 and 1931; it could raise 10 tons of ore at a speed of 3,200 ft per minute from an inclined depth of more than 9,000 ft. Also guided tour of mine shafts (45 min). (Mid-May-mid-Oct, daily) 1 mi N on US 41. Phone 906/482-3101. Mine and hoist tour with tram ride ¢¢¢¢; surface tour with tram ride ¢¢¢; tram ride ¢¢

Motel

✔★★ **BEST WESTERN COPPER CROWN.** 235 Hancock Ave (US 41S). 906/482-6111; FAX 906/482-0185. 47 rms, 2 story. S $45-$55; D $50-$60; each addl $3; under 12 free; higher rates special events. TV; cable (premium). Indoor pool; whirlpool, saunas. Restaurant adj 6 am-6 pm. Ck-out 11 am. Meeting rm. Business servs avail. Sundries. Downhill/x-country ski 1 mi. Some carports. Cr cds: A, C, D, DS, MC, V.

Harbor Springs (E-4)

(See also Petoskey)

Settled 1827 **Pop** 1,540 **Elev** 600 ft **Area code** 616 **Zip** 49740 **E-mail** harbor@freeway.net **Web** www.harborsprings-mi.com
Information Harbor Springs Chamber of Commerce, 205 State St; 616/526-7999.

Known as a year-round vacation spot, Harbor Springs is a picturesque town on Little Traverse Bay.

What to See and Do

Andrew J. Blackbird Museum. Museum of the Ottawa; artifacts. (Memorial Day-Labor Day, daily; Sept-Oct, wkends) Fee for special exhibits. 368 E Main St. Phone 616/526-7731. ¢

Shore Drive. Along MI 119, one of the most scenic drives in the state. Passes, through Devil's Elbow and Springs area, said to be haunted by an evil spirit.

Skiing.

Nub's Nob. Two double, 3 quad, 3 triple chairlifts; patrol, school, rentals; snowmaking; cafeteria, bar. Longest run approx 1 mi; vertical drop 427 ft. (Thanksgiving-Easter, daily) Half-day rates. Cross-country trails (same seasons, hrs as downhill skiing); night skiing (5 nights/wk). 500 Nub's Nob Rd, 5 mi NE. Phone 616/526-2131. ¢¢¢¢¢

Boyne Highlands. Four triple, 4 quad chairlifts, rope tow; patrol, school, rentals; snowmaking; cafeteria, restaurant, bar, nursery; lodge (see RESORT). (Thanksgiving Day wkend-mid-Apr, daily) Wkend plan. Cross-country trails (4 mi); rentals. 4¹/₂ mi NE off MI 119. Phone 616/526-2171 or 800/GO-BOYNE. ¢¢¢¢

Motels

★ **BIRCHWOOD INN.** 7077 Lake Shore Dr (MI 119). 616/526-2151; res: 800/530-9955. 48 rms, 1-2 story, 2 suites in lodge. Mid-June-mid-Oct: S, D, suites $55-$99; each addl $10; kit. suites $105-$215; lower rates rest of yr. Crib $10. TV; cable. Heated pool. Playground. Complimentary continental bkfst. Restaurant adj 5:30-10 pm. Ck-out 11 am. Meeting rms. Business servs avail. Tennis. Downhill ski 8 mi; x-country ski 1 mi. Refrigerators avail. Private patios, balconies. Cr cds: MC, V.

★★ **COLONIAL INN.** 210 Artesian Ave. 616/526-2111. 45 rms, 2 story, 8 kits. Late June-early Sept: S, D $108-$158; kit. units $138-$188; lower rates May-late June & early Sept-Oct; also some wkends. Closed rest of yr. TV; cable. Heated pool; whirlpool. Complimentary continental bkfst (July-Aug). Restaurant nearby 11 am-10 pm. Bar 5-11 pm. Ck-out 11 am. Meeting rm. Refrigerators avail; some fireplaces. Porches, balconies. Built 1894; landscaped grounds. Lake 1 blk. Cr cds: MC, V.

★ **HARBOR SPRINGS COTTAGE INN.** 145 Zoll St. 616/526-5431. 21 rms, 2 A/C, 4 kits. Mid-June-Labor Day: S, D $82-$92; kit. units $98; under 14 free; lower rates rest of yr. Crib $5. TV; cable. Complimentary continental bkfst. Ck-out 11 am. Downhill/x-country ski 5 mi. Guest bicycles, sailboats. Little Traverse Bay opp. Cr cds: A, DS, MC, V.

Inn

★★★ **KIMBERLY COUNTRY ESTATE.** 2287 Bester Rd. 616/526-7646; FAX 616/526-8054. 9 rms, 3 with shower only, 2 story. S, D $135-$250; suites $250. Children over 12 yrs only. Some TVs. Heated pool. Complimentary continental bkfst. Restaurant nearby. Ck-out 11 am, ck-in 2-6 pm. Luggage handling. Downhill/x-country ski 5 mi. Rec rm. Lawn games. Totally nonsmoking. Cr cds: A, MC, V.

Resort

★ ★ ★ **BOYNE HIGHLANDS.** *600 Highlands Dr, 4 mi N of MI 119.* 616/526-3000; FAX 616/526-3095; res: 800/GO-BOYNE. 234 rms, 3 story, 128 condo units. June-Aug, mid-Dec-Mar: D $90-$150; condo units $150-$300; ski, golf plans; lower rates rest of yr. TV; cable. Heated pools; whirlpool. Dining rm 7 am-10:30 pm. Bar 4 pm-2 am. Ck-out 1 pm, ck-in 5 pm. Coin lndry. Meeting rms. Business servs avail. Grocery 2 mi; package store 1 mi. Tennis. 72-hole golf, greens fee $70-$99, 2 driving ranges, 2 putting greens. Downhill/x-country ski on site. Ice skating. Lawn games. Hiking. Game rm. Entertainment, dancing. Exercise equipt; weights, bicycles, sauna. Some private patios, balconies. European atmosphere. On 6,000 acres. Cr cds: A, D, DS, MC, V.

Restaurants

★ ★ **ARBORETUM.** *Lake Shore Dr, 3 mi N on MI 119.* 616/526-6291. Hrs: 5:30-10 pm. Closed Nov & Apr; also Sun-Tues Dec-Mar. Res accepted. Bar. Semi-a la carte: dinner $8.95-$23.95. Child's meals. Specializes in lamb, veal, whitefish. Pianist May-Oct; Fri, Sat winter. Valet parking. Cr cds: C, D, DS, MC, V.

✔★ ★ **LEGS INN.** *(6425 Lake Shore Dr, Cross Village) 21 mi N on MI 119 (Lake Shore Dr).* 616/526-2281. Hrs: noon-9 pm; July-Labor Day noon-10 pm. Closed late-Oct-late-May. No A/C. Polish, Amer menu. Bar. Semi-a la carte: lunch $5-$7, dinner $9-$15. Child's meals. Specialties: pierogi, stuffed cabbage, goulash. Entertainment Fri-Sun. Fieldstone exterior with roofline railing composed of inverted stove legs; collection of wooden sculptures & curios; warm, cheerful atmosphere. Cr cds: MC, V.

★ **THE NEW YORK.** *101 State St.* 616/526-1904. Hrs: 11 am-10 pm; Fri to 11 pm; Sat 10 am-11 pm; Sun from 10 am. Closed Thanksgiving, Dec 25; also Apr. Res accepted. Continental menu. A la carte entrees: bkfst $3.95-$7.95, lunch $4.95-$8.95, dinner $9-$20. Specializes in veal, pasta, fresh fish. Victorian-style former hotel building. Cr cds: A, MC, V.

★ ★ **STAFFORD'S PIER.** *102 Bay St.* 616/526-6201. Hrs: 11:30 am-11 pm; Sun to 10 pm. Res accepted. Bar. Semi-a la carte: lunch $5.50-$10.75, dinner $9.50-$28. Child's meals. Specializes in whitefish. Outdoor dining. Overlooks harbor. Family-owned. Cr cds: A, MC, V.

Harrison (G-4)

(For accommodations see Clare, Houghton Lake)

Pop 1,835 **Elev** 1,186 ft **Area code** 517 **Zip** 48625
Information Chamber of Commerce, 809 N 1st St, PO Box 682; 517/539-6011.

What to See and Do

Skiing.

Jasper Mountain. Chairlift, 4 rope tows; patrol, school, rentals, snowmaking; cafeteria; bar. Longest run 1,800 ft; vertical drop 200 ft. (Mid-Dec-mid-Mar, daily; also Wed-Sat evenings) 5 mi W of US 27 on US 10,

then 1½ mi S of Farwell on unnumbered road. Phone 517/588-2945 or 800/9JASPER. ¢¢¢¢

Snowsnake Mountain. Triple chairlift, 5 rope tows; patrol, school, rentals; snowmaking; snack bar. Longest run approx ½ mi; vertical drop 210 ft. Night skiing. (Mid-Dec-mid-Mar, daily) Cross-country trails. 3407 Mannsiding Rd, 5 mi S on US 27. Phone 517/539-6583. ¢¢¢¢

Wilson State Park. Approx 35 acres on the shore of Budd Lake. Swimming; fishing for largemouth bass, bluegill, perch. Picnicking, playground. Camping. Standard fees. 1 mi N on Old US 27. Phone 517/539-3021. Per vehicle ¢¢

Annual Events

Frostbite Open. Winter golf tournament. Feb.

Clare County Fair. Clare County Fairgrounds. Late July-early Aug.

Holland (H-3)

(See also Grand Haven, Saugatuck)

Founded 1847 **Pop** 30,745 **Elev** 610 ft **Area code** 616 **E-mail** louii @macatawa.org **Web** www.holland-chamber.org
Information Holland Area Chamber of Commerce, 272 E 8th St, PO Box 1888, 49422-1888; 616/392-2389.

In 1847, a group of Dutch seeking religious freedom left the Netherlands and settled in this area because its sand dunes and fertile land reminded them of their homeland. Today much of the population is of Dutch descent. The town prides itself on being the center of Dutch culture in the United States. The city is located at the mouth of the Black River, on the shores of Lake Macatawa, and has developed a resort colony along the shores of lakes Macatawa and Michigan.

What to See and Do

Cappon House (1874). Italianate house of first mayor of Holland. Original furnishings, millwork. (May-Sept, Fri & Sat afternoons or by appt) Washington Blvd & W 9th St. Phone 616/392-6740 or 616/392-9084. ¢¢

Dutch Village. Buildings of Dutch architecture; canals, windmills, tulips, street organs, Dutch dancing; animals, movies, rides; wooden shoe carving & other crafts; museum, tours; restaurant. (Mid-Apr-late Oct, daily) 1 mi NE on US 31. Phone 616/396-1475. ¢¢

Holland Museum. Features decorative arts from the Netherlands Collection, the Volendam Room. Permanent and changing exhibits pertaining to local history. Gift shop. (Daily exc Tues; closed major hols) 31 W 10th St. Phone 616/392-9084 or 616/392-1362. ¢¢

Holland State Park. This 143-acre park includes a ¼-mi beach on Lake Michigan. Swimming, bathhouse; boating (launch), fishing. Picnicking, playground, concessions. Camping. Standard fees. 7 mi W off US 31. Phone 616/399-9390. Per car ¢¢

Hope College (1866). (2,550 students) Liberal arts. Tours of campus. Theater series (July-Aug, fee; phone 616/394-7890). Between College & Columbia Aves. Phone 616/392-5111.

⭐ **Windmill Island.** The 225-yr-old windmill, "De Zwaan" (the swan), is the only operating imported Dutch windmill in the US. It was relocated here by special permission of the Dutch government, as the remaining windmills in the Netherlands are considered historic monuments. It is still used today to grind flour. The imported carousel, "Draaimolen," offers free rides. (May-Aug, daily; Labor Day-Oct, limited hrs) 7th St & Lincoln. Phone 616/396-5433. ¢¢ Includes

Little Netherlands. A miniature reproduction of old Holland; 20-min film on Dutch windmills in the posthouse; klompen dancing in summer; exhibits, tulips.

Wooden Shoe Factory. Factory operations can be viewed by public (daily exc Sun). Also gift shop (daily; hrs may be limited off-season). 447 US 31 at 16th St. Phone 616/396-6513. ¢

Annual Event

Tulip Time Festival. A celebration of Dutch heritage: 1,800 klompen dancers, 3 parades, street scrubbing, Dutch markets, musical and professional entertainment and millions of tulips. Phone 616/396-4221 or 800/822-2770. 10 days mid-May.

Motels

(Rates are generally higher during Tulip Time Festival)

★ ★ **COUNTRY INN BY CARLSON.** *12260 James St (49424), adj Manufacturers Marketplace.* 616/396-6677; FAX 616/396-1197; res: 800/456-4000. 116 rms, 2 story. July-Aug: S $74-$88; D $89-$99; each addl $5; under 18 free; lower rates rest of yr. Crib free. TV; cable, VCR avail. Complimentary continental bkfst. Coffee in rms. Restaurant nearby. Ck-out noon. Meeting rms. Business servs avail. Valet serv. X-country ski 5 mi. Bathrm phones. Country-style decor. Cr cds: A, C, D, DS, MC, V.

✔★ **SUPER 8.** *680 E 24th St (49423).* 616/396-8822; FAX 616/396-2050. 68 rms, 3 story, 6 suites. May-Labor Day: S $52.88; D $57.88; each addl $6; suites $85; under 12 free; wkend rates; lower rates rest of yr. Crib free. TV; cable (premium). Complimentary coffee in lobby. Restaurant nearby. Ck-out 11 am. Coin lndry. Business servs avail. In-rm modem link. Valet serv. X-country ski 3 mi. Cr cds: A, C, D, DS, MC, V.

Motor Hotel

★ ★ ★ **HOLIDAY INN.** *650 E 24th St (49423).* 616/394-0111; FAX 616/394-4832. 168 units, 4 story. May-Nov: S $80-$105; D $87-$113; under 17 free; lower rates rest of yr. TV; cable (premium). Indoor pool. Restaurant 6 am-10 pm. Rm serv. Bar 4 pm-2 am; entertainment exc Sun. Ck-out noon. Meeting rms. Business servs avail. Bellhops. Free airport, RR station, bus depot transportation. X-country ski 3 mi. Exercise equipt; weights, bicycles, sauna. Game rm. Rec rm. Refrigerator in suites. Patios, balconies. Cr cds: A, C, D, DS, JCB, MC, V.

Inn

★ ★ **DUTCH COLONIAL.** *560 Central Ave (49423).* 616/396-3664; FAX 616/396-0461. 5 rms, 1 with shower only, 1-3 story. D $75-$150; each addl $20; 3-day min hols. Complimentary full bkfst. Ck-out 11 am, ck-in 3 pm. In-rm modem link. X-country ski 3 mi. Picnic tables. Built 1928; many antiques. Totally nonsmoking. Cr cds: A, DS, MC, V.

Restaurants

✔★ **84 EAST PASTA ETC.** *84 E 8th St (49423).* 616/396-8484. Hrs: 11 am-11 pm. Closed Sun; major hols. Italian, Amer menu. Bar. A la carte entrees: lunch $5-$7, dinner $6-$9. Child's meals. Specializes in pasta. Casual decor. Cr cds: A, MC, V.

✔★ **8TH STREET GRILLE.** *20 W 8th St (49424).* 616/392-5888. Hrs: 11 am-11 pm. Closed Sun; major hols. Wine, beer. Semi-a la carte: lunch, dinner $3.95-$12. Specializes in soup, sandwiches. Early 1920s-style cafe. Cr cds: A, MC, V.

★ ★ ★ **ALPENROSE.** *4 E 8th St (49423).* 616/393-2111. Hrs: 11 am-9 pm; summer to 10 pm, Fri & Sat to 10:30 pm; Sun brunch 10:30 am-2 pm. Closed Dec 25; also Mon evenings Jan-Apr. Res accepted. Austrian, continental menu. Serv bar. Extensive wine list. Semi-a la carte: lunch $5.95-$8.95, dinner $8.95-$17.95. Sun brunch $13.95. Child's meals. Specialties: chicken shortcake, Wienerschnitzel. Outdoor dining. Authentic Austrian-style dining. Totally nonsmoking. Cr cds: A, DS, MC, V.

★ ★ **THE HATCH.** *1870 Ottawa Beach Rd.* 616/399-9120. Hrs: 5:30-10 pm; Fri, Sat to 10:30 pm; Sun 5-9 pm; Sun brunch 10:30 am-2:30 pm. Closed Jan 1, Dec 25. Res accepted. Bar to midnight. Semi-a la carte: dinner $10-$20. Sun brunch $10. Child's meals. Specializes in steak. Entertainment Thurs-Sat 9 pm-1 am. Parking. Nautical decor. Cr cds: A, MC, V.

✔★ ★ **KUIPERS' SANDY POINT.** *(7175 Lake Shore Dr, West Olive 49460)* 616/399-6161. Hrs: 11 am-3 pm, 5-9 pm; Fri, Sat to 10 pm. Closed Sun, Mon. Res accepted. Bar. Semi-a la carte: lunch $3.75-$6.95, dinner $8.95-$15.95. Child's meals. Specializes in barbecued ribs, fresh seafood. Entertainment Fri, Sat. Parking. Cr cds: A, DS, MC, V.

★ **PEREDDIES.** *447 Washington Square (49423).* 616/394-3061. Hrs: 10 am-9:30 pm; Fri, Sat to 10:30 pm. Closed Sun; major hols. Res accepted; required Fri, Sat. Italian menu. Serv bar. Semi-a la carte: lunch $5-$10, dinner $15-$20. Specializes in pasta. European-style cafe with deli and Italian galleria. Cr cds: A, D, MC, V.

★ ★ ★ **SANDPIPER.** *(2225 South Shore Dr, Macatawa 49434) 4 mi W on 16th St to S Shore Dr.* 616/335-5866. Hrs: 5-9:30 pm; Sun to 8:30 pm. Winter 5-8:30 pm; Fri, Sat to 9 pm. Closed Jan 1, Dec 25; also Sun in winter. Res accepted; required Fri & Sat. Bar. Wine list. A la carte entrees: dinner $14.25-$22. Child's meals. Specializes in seafood. Parking. Overlooks Lake Macatawa. Cr cds: A, DS, MC, V.

★ ★ **TILL MIDNIGHT.** *208 College Ave (49423).* 616/392-6883. Hrs: 11 am-2:30 pm, 5 pm-midnight. Closed Sun; most major hols. Res accepted. Eclectic menu. Bar. A la carte entrees: lunch $6-$8, dinner $15-$22. Child's meals. Specializes in breads, desserts. Modern art by local artist adorn the walls. Totally nonsmoking. Cr cds: A, DS, MC, V.

Holly (H-5)

(For accommodations see Detroit, Flint, Pontiac)

Pop 5,595 **Elev** 937 ft **Area code** 810 **Zip** 48442

Information Chamber of Commerce, 115 S Saginaw St, PO Box 214; 810/634-1900.

What to See and Do

Davisburg Candle Factory. Located in 125-yr-old building; produces unique and beautiful handcrafted candles. Unusual taper production line. Showroom and gift shop. Demonstrations by appt (wkdays). (Daily) 634 Broadway; 2 mi S, then 3 mi E on Davisburg Rd. Phone 810/634-4214. **Free.**

⊠ **Historic Battle Alley.** Once known for its taverns and brawls, Battle Alley is now a restored 19th-century street featuring antiques, boutiques, specialty shops, craftsmen; dining at the Historic Holly Hotel (see RESTAURANT). On the Alley is a mosaic of the bicentennial logo made from 1,000 red, white and blue bricks. (Daily; closed major hols) Downtown, State and National Historic District. **Free.**

Mt Holly Ski Area. Quad, 3 triple, 3 double chairlifts, 5 rope tows; patrol, school, rentals; snowmaking; 2 cafeterias, 2 bars. (Dec-Mar, daily; closed Dec 24 eve) 13536 S Dixie Hwy, 7 mi NE off I-75. Phone 810/634-8269. ¢¢¢¢¢

Annual Events

Michigan Renaissance Festival. 1 mi N of Mt Holly on Dixie Hwy. Festivities include jousting tournaments, entertainment, food and crafts in Renaissance-style village. Phone 810/634-5552. 8 wkends Aug-Sept.

Carry Nation Festival. Re-creation of Carry Nation's 1908 visit to Holly. The "temperance crusader" charged down Battle Alley with her famed umbrella, smashing bottles and a few heads along the way. Pageant, parade, antique car show, race, games, arts & crafts show, model railroad. Wkend after Labor Day.

Dickens Christmas. Re-creates the Dickensian period with carolers, town crier, strolling characters, skits, bell choirs, street hawkers, carriage rides. Thanksgiving wkend-wkend before Dec 25.

Restaurant

★ ★ **HISTORIC HOLLY HOTEL.** 110 Battle Alley. 810/634-5208. Hrs: 11 am-3 pm, 5-10 pm; Fri, Sat to 11 pm; Sun noon-8 pm; Sun brunch 11 am-3 pm. Closed major hols. Res accepted. Bar. Semi-a la carte: lunch $3.50-$8.95, dinner $14.95-$27.95. Sun brunch $14.95. Specialties: beef Wellington, medallions of beef. Own baking. Comedy theater Thurs-Sat; pianist Sat. In restored hotel (1891); Victorian decor. Cr cds: A, C, D, MC, V.

SC

Houghton (C-1)

(See also Calumet, Hancock)

Settled 1843 **Pop** 7,498 **Elev** 607 ft **Area code** 906 **Zip** 49931 **E-mail** keweenaw@portup.com **Web** www.portup.com/snow

Information Keweenaw Peninsula Chamber of Commerce, 326 Shelden Ave, PO Box 336; 906/482-5240 or 800/338-7982.

Houghton and its sister city, Hancock (see), face each other across the narrowest part of Portage Lake. This is the area of America's first mining capital, the scene of the first great mineral strike in the Western Hemisphere. The copper-bearing geological formations are believed to be the oldest rock formations in the world. The great mining rush of 1843 and the years following brought people from all over Europe. Two main ethnic groups are identifiable today: Cornishmen, who came from England; and Finns, who have made this their cultural center in the US.

What to See and Do

Ferry service to Isle Royale National Park (see). Four ferries and a float plane provide transportation (June-Sept, daily; some trips in May). For fees and schedule contact Park Superintendent, 906/482-0984.

Michigan Technological University (1885). (6,200 students) Campus tours leave from University Career Center in Administration Bldg. (See ANNUAL EVENT) 1400 Townsend Dr. Phone 906/487-1885. On campus is

A.E. Seaman Mineralogical Museum. Exhibits one of the nation's best mineral collections. (May-Oct, daily exc Sun; rest of yr, Mon-Fri; closed hols) In Electrical Energy Resources Center. Phone 906/487-2572. ¢¢

Skiing. Mont Ripley Ski Area. Double chairlift, T-bar; patrol, school, rentals; cafeteria. (Early Dec-late Mar, daily; closed Dec 25) ½ mi E on MI 26. Phone 906/487-2340. ¢¢¢¢¢

Annual Event

Winter Carnival. Michigan Technological University. Snow sculptures and statues; dogsled and snowshoe racing, broomball, skiing, skating; skit contests; Queen Coronation and Snoball Dance. Phone 906/487-2818. Late Jan-early Feb.

Motels

★ ★ **BEST WESTERN FRANKLIN SQUARE INN.** 820 Shelden Ave. 906/487-1700; FAX 906/487-9432. 105 rms, 7 story. June-Oct: S $65-$75; D $72-$82; each addl $6; suites $95-$110; under 12 free; higher rates special events; lower rates rest of yr. Crib $4. TV; cable (premium). Indoor pool; whirlpool, sauna. Restaurant 6:30 am-10 pm. Rm serv. Bar 2 pm-2 am. Ck-out 11 am. Meeting rms. Business servs avail. Downhill ski 3 mi; x-country ski 5 mi. Refrigerator avail. Cr cds: A, C, D, DS, JCB, MC, V.

★ **CHIPPEWA.** (PO Box 470, Chassell 49916) 7 mi SE on US 41. 906/523-4611. 15 rms, 7 kit. units. June-mid-Oct: S $36; D $44-$46; kit. units for 2-6, $50-$70; lower rates rest of yr. Crib $2. TV; cable. Restaurant adj 7 am-8 pm; Sun from 8 am-7 pm. Ck-out 10 am. Meeting rms. Downhill ski 9 mi; x-country ski 1 blk. Picnic tables. Some rms overlook bay of Portage Lake. City park with beach, playground, picnic area & boat launch adj. Cr cds: C, D, DS, MC, V.

✓ ★ **L'ANSE.** (Rt 2 Box 506, L'Anse 49946) 33 mi SW on US 41. 906/524-7820; FAX 906/524-7247; res: 800/800-6198. 21 rms, 2 with shower only, 1 story. S $26-$34; D $36; each addl $2; higher rates special events. Crib $2. Pet accepted, some restrictions. TV; cable (premium). Complimentary coffee in lobby. Ck-out 11 am. X-country ski 2 mi. Cr cds: C, D, DS, MC, V.

★ **SUPER 8.** (790 Michigan Ave, Baraga 49908) 30 mi SW on MI 38, 1 mi W of US 41. 906/353-6680; FAX 906/353-7246. 40 rms, 2 story. S $41.88; D $49.88; each addl $6; under 12 free. Crib $2. Pet accepted. TV; cable. Complimentary continental bkfst. Restaurant opp. Ck-out 11 am. Meeting rm. Business servs avail. X-country ski 8 mi. Cr cds: A, C, D, DS, MC, V.

✓ ★ **SUPER 8.** 1200 E Lakeshore Dr. 906/482-2240; FAX 906/482-0686. 86 rms, 2 story. S $48-$53; D $53-$58; each addl $3; suites $75; under 12 free. Crib $3. TV; cable (premium). Indoor pool; whirlpool, sauna. Complimentary continental bkfst. Restaurant nearby. Ck-out 11 am. Meeting rm. Downhill ski 1 mi; x-country ski ½ mi. Cr cds: A, C, D, DS, MC, V.

★ **VACATIONLAND.** US 41 SE, 2 mi SE on US 41. 906/482-5351; res: 800/822-3279. 24 rms, 1-2 story. July-Labor Day: S $38-$58; D $42-$58; family rates; lower rates rest of yr. Crib $2. TV; cable (premium). Heated pool; sauna. Continental bkfst. Complimentary coffee in lobby. Restaurant nearby. Ck-out 11 am. Sundries. Downhill ski 5 mi; x-country ski 3 mi. Picnic tables. 18-hole golf adj. Cr cds: A, C, D, DS, MC, V.

Motor Hotel

★ **BEST WESTERN KING'S INN.** 215 Sheldon Ave. 906/482-5000; FAX 906/482-9795. 68 rms, 4 story. July-Sept: S $61-$82; D $67-$88; each addl $6; under 17 free; lower rates rest of yr. Crib free. Pet accepted. TV; cable (premium), VCR avail (movies). Indoor pool; whirlpool, sauna. Complimentary continental bkfst. Restaurant adj 11 am-midnight. Ck-out 11 am. Meeting rm. Valet serv. Downhill ski 2 mi; x-country ski 3 mi. Cr cds: A, C, D, DS, MC, V.

Restaurants

★ ★ **ONIGAMING SUPPER CLUB.** *3 mi S on US 41. 906/482-2714.* Hrs: 5-10 pm. Closed Nov-Apr. Res accepted. Bar. Semi-a la carte: dinner $9.25-$16.50. Child's meals. Specializes in planked Lake Superior trout, barbecued ribs, steak. On land of former yacht club (1894); dining in rebuilt clubhouse. Deep-water docking. Cr cds: MC, V.

★ ★ **THE SUMMER PLACE.** *(Box 356, Chassell 49916) 4¹/2 mi S on US 41. 906/523-4848.* Hrs: 5-9 pm; Fri, Sat to 10 pm. Closed Mon; also Jan-Apr. Res accepted. Bar. Semi-a la carte: dinner $8.95-$15.95. Specializes in marinated steak, fresh Lake Superior trout. Porch dining. Overlooks Portage Lake. Cr cds: A, C, D, DS, MC, V.

Houghton Lake (F-4)

(See also Grayling, Harrison)

Pop 3,353 **Elev** 1,162 ft **Area code** 517 **Zip** 48629 **Web** www.go vacation.com

Information Chamber of Commerce, 1625 W Houghton Lake Dr; 517/366-5644 or 800/248-LAKE.

This little village is the gateway to a popular north country resort area including 3 of the largest inland lakes in the state and 200,000 acres of state forests.

What to See and Do

Higgins Lake. One of the most beautiful in America, Higgins Lake covers 9,600 acres and has 20 mi of sandy shoreline. N on US 27.

Houghton Lake. Largest inland lake in Michigan. The source of the Muskegon River. This lake has a 32-mi shoreline and 22,000 acres of water. Also 200 mi of groomed and marked snowmobile trails. A variety of resorts are in the area. At N end of village.

St Helen Lake. This pine-bordered lake has 12 mi of shoreline. E on MI 55, then N on MI 76.

Annual Events

Tip-Up-Town USA Ice Festival. Ice fishing contests, games, food, parade, carnival. 3rd & 4th wkend Jan.

Historical Roundup. Contests, demonstrations; antique cars; displays of logging era; flea market; museum, restored village. Early Aug.

Motels

(Rates may be higher during Tip-Up-Town USA Ice Festival)

★ ★ **VAL HALLA.** *9869 Old US 27. 517/422-5137.* 12 rms, 2 kits. Memorial Day wkend-Labor Day: S, D $45-$62; each addl $5; 2-bedrm kit. apts $525/wk; some lower rates rest of yr. Crib $1. Pet accepted. TV. Heated pool. Restaurant nearby. Ck-out 11 am. Free airport transportation. Putting green. Downhill ski 17 mi; x-country ski 2 mi. Lawn games. Private patios. Picnic table, grills. Cr cds: MC, V.

★ **VENTURE INN.** *8939 Old US 27, at jct MI 55. 517/422-5591.* 12 rms. Mid-June-Labor Day: S $40-$45; D $50; each addl $5; higher rates hols; lower rates rest of yr. Crib $2. TV. Heated pool. Complimentary coffee in rms. Restaurant opp open 24 hrs. Ck-out 11 am. Downhill ski 20 mi; x-country ski 10 mi. Cr cds: MC, V.

[D] [≋] [🏊] [🐾] [SC]

Cottage Colony

★ **MORRIS'S NORTHERNAIRE.** *11544 W Shore Dr. 517/422-6644.* 6 cottages for 3-8, 5 with shower only. May-Labor Day: S, D $75; lower rates rest of yr. Crib free. TV; cable. Playground. Restaurant nearby. Ck-out 10 am. Grocery 3 mi. Coin lndry 1 mi. Lawn games. Picnic tables. On beach. Cr cds: MC, V.

★ ★ **WOODBINE VILLA.** *12122 W Shore Dr. 517/422-5349.* 9 kit. cottages. No A/C. Wkly: 2-4, $525; 4-6, $575-$625; daily rates Apr-mid-June & Labor Day-late Nov; higher rates special events. Crib free. TV; cable. Playground. Restaurant nearby. Ck-out 10 am, ck-in 4 pm. Grocery, package store 2 mi, coin lndry 3 blks. Sand beach, dock; motors, rowboats. Downhill ski 15 mi; x-country ski 5 mi. Sauna. Lawn games. Picnic table, grill. Fish-cleaning house. Screened porches. Rustic setting with private beach on Houghton Lake. Cr cds: MC, V.

Restaurants

✔★ **COYLES.** *9074 Old US 27. 517/422-3812.* Hrs: 8 am-10 pm; Fri, Sat to 11 pm; winter hrs vary. Closed Dec 25. Res accepted. Serv bar. Semi-a la carte: bkfst 99¢-$5, lunch $2.39-$6, dinner $4.29-$11.99. Child's meals. Specializes in chicken, seafood, smorgasbord. Salad bar. Cr cds: DS, MC, V.

★ ★ **HOLIDAY ON THE LAKE.** *100 Clearview (Old US 27), ¹/2 mi N of MI 55. 517/422-5195.* Hrs: 11:30 am-10 pm; hrs vary off season. Closed Dec 25. Res accepted. Bar to 2:30 am. Semi-a la carte: lunch $2.99-$5.99, dinner $5.95-$29.95. Child's meals. Specializes in prime rib. Salad bar. Entertainment. Cr cds: A, DS, MC, V.

[D] [SC] [≋]

Hulbert (D-4)

(For accommodations see Newberry; also see Soo Junction)

Pop 250 (est) **Elev** 750 ft **Area code** 906 **Zip** 49748

North of Hulbert is a particularly wild portion of the Upper Peninsula with much wildlife. Popular activities are fishing for northern pike, bass, perch and trout on Hulbert Lake, canoeing and other outdoor sports.

What to See and Do

Tahquamenon Falls State Park. E on MI 28, then approx 15 mi N on MI 123 (see NEWBERRY).

Tom Sawyer Riverboat. A 17-mi cruise down Tahquamenon River with nature and folklore talks; 1¹/2-mi train ride through virgin hardwood forest to state park; short walk to Upper Tahquamenon Falls. (Mid-June-early Oct, daily; Memorial Day-mid-June, wkends) 10 mi N off MI 28 at Slater's Landing. Phone 906/876-2331 or 906/632-3727 (winter). ¢¢¢¢

Indian River (E-4)

(See also Cheboygan, Petoskey)

Pop 2,500 **Elev** 616 ft **Area code** 616 **Zip** 49749
Information Chamber of Commerce, 3435 S Streets Hwy, PO Box 57; 616/238-9325.

What to See and Do

Burt Lake State Park. Approx 400 acres. Beach, beachhouse, waterskiing; fishing for walleyed pike, perch; boating (ramp, rentals); picnicking, playground, concession; camping. Standard fees. (May-Oct, daily) 1/2 mi S off I-75, exit 310. Phone 616/238-9392. Per car ¢¢

Canoeing. Trips on Sturgeon and/or Pigeon rivers; difficulty varies with streams. Various trips offered. Reservations advised.

   Tomahawk Trails Canoe Livery. (May-Oct, daily) Contact PO Box 814; 616/238-8703.

   Sturgeon & Pigeon River Outfitters. Canoeing, tubing, kayaking. (May-mid-Sept) Contact 4271 S Straits Hwy; 616/238-8181.

Cross in the Woods. Wooden crucifix 55 ft tall. Outdoor shrines. (Mar-Nov, daily) 1 mi W of I-75 exit 310, on MI 68. Phone 616/238-8973. **Free.**

Motel

   ✔★ **NOR-GATE.** *4846 S Straits Hwy (Old US 27). 616/238-7788.* 12 rms, 3 kits. S $28-$35; D $36-$40; each addl $3; kit. units $36-$67; wkly rates. Crib $5. TV; cable (premium). Complimentary coffee in lobby. Restaurant nearby. Ck-out 11 am. Picnic tables. State park 1/2 mi. Cr cds: DS, MC, V.

[symbols]

Iron Mountain (D-1)

(See also Iron River, Ishpeming)

Settled 1878 **Pop** 8,525 **Elev** 1,138 ft **Area code** 906 **Zip** 49801
Information Tourism Assn of the Dickinson County Area, 333 S Stephenson Ave, PO Box 672; 906/774-2945 or 800/236-2447.

After more than a half-century of production, the underground shaft mines of high-grade ore deposits here have closed. Logging, tourism and wood products are the main economic factors now, and Iron Mountain is the distribution point for the entire Menominee Range area. A nearby bluff heavily striped with iron ore gave the city its name. Abandoned mines, cave-ins and a huge Cornish mine pump, preserved as tourist attractions, are reminders of mining days.

What to See and Do

Iron Mountain Iron Mine. Mine train tours 2,600 ft of underground drifts, tunnels, 400 ft below surface. Working machinery, museum. Tours (June-mid-Oct, daily). 8 mi E on US 2 in Vulcan. Phone 906/563-8077. ¢¢¢

Lake Antoine Park. Improved county campgrounds (fee); swimming, boating, waterskiing, nature trail, picnicking, concession; band concerts. (Memorial Day-Labor Day, daily) 2 mi NE. Phone 906/774-8875. Camping ¢¢¢

Menominee Range Historical Museum. More than 100 exhibits depict life on the Menominee Iron Range in the 1880s and early 1900s; one-room school, Victorian parlor, trapper's cabin, country store. (Mid-May-Nov, daily; rest of yr, by appt) 300 E Ludington St, in Carnegie Public Library. Phone 906/774-4276. ¢¢; Combination ticket ¢¢¢ includes

Cornish Pumping Engine & Mining Museum. Features largest steam-driven pumping engine built in US, with 40'-diameter flywheel in engine and weighing 160 tons; also display of underground mining equipment used in Michigan; World War II glider display. (Mid-May-Nov, daily; rest of yr by appt) Kent St. Phone 906/774-1086. ¢¢

Skiing. Pine Mt Lodge. Three double chairlifts, rope tow; snow making, patrol, school, rentals; 9-hole golf; 2 tennis courts; indoor/outdoor pools; restaurant, cafeteria, bar; lodge, condos. Longest run approx 3/4 mi; vertical drop 400 ft. (Late Nov-early Apr, daily) Cross-country trails. N332 Pine Mountain Rd, 2 1/2 mi N off US 2/141. Phone 906/774-2747 or 800/321-6298 (Nov-Apr). ¢¢¢¢

Annual Event

Pine Mt Ski Jumping Tournament. Pine Mt Lodge. Feb.

Seasonal Event

Festival of the Arts. Crafts demonstrations, antique car show, concerts, square and folk dancing, community theater, international foods. Mid-June-mid-Aug.

Motels

   ★★ **BEST WESTERN EXECUTIVE INN.** *1518 S Stephenson Ave (US 2). 906/774-2040; FAX 906/774-0238.* 57 rms, 2 story. June-Sept: S $56; D $63; each addl $6; lower rates rest of yr. Crib free. Pet accepted. TV; cable (premium), VCR avail (movies $2.50). Indoor pool. Complimentary continental bkfst. Ck-out 11 am. Downhill/x-country ski 3 mi. Cr cds: A, C, D, DS, MC, V.

[symbols]

   ★★ **COMFORT INN.** *1555 N Stephenson Ave. 906/774-5505; FAX 906/774-2631.* 48 rms, 2 story. S $49-$69; D $55-$75; each addl $6; under 18 free. Crib free. TV; cable (premium), VCR avail. Complimentary continental bkfst. Restaurant nearby. Ck-out 11 am. Meeting rm. Business servs avail. Valet serv. Coin lndry. Downhill/x-country ski 2 mi. Exercise equipt; bicycles, weight machine. Some refrigerators. Cr cds: A, C, D, DS, ER, JCB, MC, V.

[symbols]

   ★ **SUPER 8.** *2702 N Stephenson Ave (US 2). 906/774-3400; FAX 906/774-9903.* 90 rms, 2 story. S $40.88; D $52.88; each addl $6; suites $60.88-$66.88; under 12 free. Crib free. TV; cable (premium), VCR avail (movies). Pool; whirlpool, sauna. Complimentary continental bkfst. Restaurant nearby. Ck-out 11 am. Coin lndry. Meeting rm. Business servs avail. Downhill/x-country ski 4 mi. Some refrigerators. Picnic tables. Cr cds: A, D, DS, MC, V.

[symbols]

   ✔★ **TIMBERS MOTOR LODGE.** *200 S Stephenson Ave (US 2). 906/774-7600; FAX 906/774-6222; res: 800/433-8533.* 53 rms, 2 story. S $34-$38; D $44; each addl $5; suites $54. Crib $4. TV; cable (premium). Indoor pool; whirlpool. Restaurant nearby. Ck-out noon. Meeting rms. Business servs avail. In-rm modem link. Downhill/x-country ski 1 1/2 mi. Exercise equipt; treadmill, stair machine, sauna. Cr cds: A, D, DS, MC, V.

[symbols]

Iron River (D-1)

(For accommodations see Iron Mountain)

Pop 2,095 **Elev** 1,510 ft **Area code** 906 **Zip** 49935 **E-mail** iccoc@up.net **Web** www.iron.org/

Information Iron County Chamber of Commerce, 50 E Genesee St; 906/265-3822 or 888/TRY-IRON.

Just north of the Wisconsin-Michigan state line, Iron River was one of the last of the large mining towns to spring up on the Menominee Range. Lumbering has also played a prominent part in the town's past. Ottawa National Forest (see IRONWOOD) lies a few miles to the west, and a Ranger District office is located here.

What to See and Do

Iron County Museum. Indoor/outdoor museum of 19 buildings. Miniature logging exhibit with more than 2,000 pieces; iron mining dioramas; more than 100 major exhibits; log homestead; 1896 one-room schoolhouse; logging camp, home of composer Carrie Jacobs-Bond; Lee LeBlanc Wildlife Art Gallery. Annual ethnic festivals (Scandinavian, Polish, Italian, Yugoslavian-inquire for schedule). (Mid-May-Oct, daily; rest of yr, by appt) 2 mi S on County 424 in Caspian. Phone 906/265-2617. ¢¢

Ski Brule. Four chairlifts, 2 T-bars, pony lift, rope tow; patrol, school, rentals, snow making; chalet and condo lodging; restaurant, cafeteria, bar. 14 runs, longest run 1 mi; vertical drop 500 ft. (Nov-Apr, daily) Cross-country trails. 119 Big Bear Rd, 3 mi SW off MI 189. Phone 906/265-4957 or 800/362-7853. ¢¢¢¢

Annual Events

Bass Festival. Canoe races on the Paint River, softball game, barbecue, music and events at Runkle Park and Runkle Lake. 1st wkend July.

Ferrous Frolics. Iron County Museum. Arts, crafts, demonstrations, band concert, flea market. 3rd wkend July.

Upper Peninsula Championship Rodeo. Fairgrounds. Late July.

Iron County Fair. Fairgrounds. 4 days late Aug.

Ironwood (B-3)

(See also Wakefield; also see Hurley, WI)

Settled 1885 **Pop** 6,849 **Elev** 1,503 ft **Area code** 906 **Zip** 49938

Information Ironwood Area Chamber of Commerce, 213 S Marquette St; 906/932-1122.

Ironwood is a center for summer and winter recreation. The first part of Gogebic County to be settled, the town was linked at first with fur trading. It quickly blossomed into a mining town when a deposit of iron was found in what is now the eastern section of the city. John R. Wood, one of the first mining captains, was known as "Iron" because of his interest in ore—thus, the name Ironwood.

What to See and Do

Black River Harbor. Picnicking, playground; camping; deep-sea fishing boats for rent; boat rides, Lake Superior cruises. 4 mi E, then 15 mi N on County 513.

Copper Peak Ski Flying. The only ski flying facility in North America, and one of six in the world, where athletes test their skill in an event that requires more athletic ability than ski jumping; skiiers reach speeds of more than 60 mi per hour and fly farther than 500 ft. International tournament held every winter. In summer, chairlift and elevator rides take visitors 240 ft above the crest of Copper Peak for view of three states, Lake

Superior and Canada. (Mid-June-Labor Day, daily; Sept-Oct, wkends) 12 mi N on County 513. Phone 906/932-3500. Chairlift ¢¢

Hiawatha—World's Tallest Indian. Statue of famous Iroquois stands 52 ft high and looks N to the legendary "shining big-sea-water"—Gitchee Gumee, also known as Lake Superior. Houk St.

Little Girl's Point Park. Notable for the agate pebbles on the beaches. Picnic tables (fee), campsites (fee); Native American burial grounds. (May-Sept) County 505N, 18 mi N, off US 2; on Lake Superior. Phone 906/932-1420.

Ottawa National Forest. Wooded hills, picturesque lakes and streams, waterfalls, J.W. Toumey Nursery, Black River Harbor, North Country National Scenic Trail, Watersmeet Visitor Center and Sylvania, Sturgeon River Gorge and McCormick Wildernesses are all part of this 953,600-acre forest. Fishing for trout, muskie, northern pike, walleyed pike, bass and panfish; hunting for big and small game; swimming; canoeing, boat landing, Hiking; cross-country & downhill skiing. Picnicking. Camping. Some fees. (Daily) E via US 2, MI 28.Contact Supervisor, 2100 E Cloverland Dr; 906/932-1330. **Free.**

Skiing.

Mt Zion. One of the highest points on the Gogebic Range, with 1,750-ft altitude, 1,150 ft above Lake Superior. Double chairlift, 2 rope tows; patrol, school, rentals; snack bar. Longest run 3/4 mi; vertical drop 300 ft. (Mid-Dec-Mar, daily exc Mon; closed Dec 25) 2 mi of cross-country trails, rentals. 3/4 mi N of US 2. Phone 906/932-3718. ¢¢¢

Big Powderhorn Mt. Eight double chairlifts; patrol, school, rentals; 3 restaurants, cafeteria, 3 bars. 24 runs; longest run 1 mi; vertical drop 600 ft. (Thanksgiving-early Apr, daily) 2 mi NE off US 2 on Powderhorn Rd. Phone 906/932-4838 or 906/932-3100 (reservations only). ¢¢¢¢¢

Blackjack. Four chairlifts, 2 rope tows; patrol, school, rentals; cafeteria, restaurant, bar; nursery, lodging. Longest run 5,300 ft; vertical drop 465 ft. (Nov-Mar, daily) 12 mi E of MI 51 via US 2, Blackjack exit. Phone 906/229-5115 or 906/229-5157 (reservations only). ¢¢¢¢

Annual Event

Gogebic County Fair. Fairgrounds. Phone 906/932-1420. 2nd wkend Aug.

Motels

 BLACK RIVER LODGE. N 12390 Black River Rd, 2 mi E on US 2 then 4 mi N on Powderhorn Rd. 906/932-3857; res: 800/666-9916. 25 rms, 12 A/C, 2 story, 4 townhouses (no A/C), some kits. Dec-Mar: S $25-$50; D, suites $35-$98; kit. units $45-$100; townhouses $80-$180; wkly rates; ski plans; AP, MAP avail; lower rates rest of yr. Crib free. TV; cable (premium), VCR avail. Indoor pool; whirlpool. Playground. Restaurant (hrs vary). Bar 6 pm-2 am. Ck-out 11 am. Meeting rms. Downhill ski 1½ mi; x-country ski on site. Lawn games. Game rm. Hiking. Fish/hunt guides. Some refrigerators. Picnic tables, grill. Cr cds: DS, MC, V.

★ ★ **COMFORT INN.** 210 E Cloverland Dr (US 2). 906/932-2224; FAX 906/932-9929. 63 rms, 2 story. Late Dec-early Jan: S $71.88-$85; D $87-$92; each addl $6; under 18 free; lower rates rest of yr. Crib free. TV; cable (premium), VCR avail (movies). Indoor pool; whirlpool. Complimentary continental bkfst. Restaurant opp open 24 hrs. Ck-out 11 am. Meeting rm. Business servs avail. Downhill/x-country ski 6 mi. Some refrigerators, wet bars. Cr cds: A, C, D, DS, ER, JCB, MC, V.

Restaurant

★ **MAMA GET'S.** E5964 US 2. 906/932-1322. Hrs: 4-10 pm. Closed July 4, Thanksgiving, Dec 25. Bar. Semi-a la carte: dinner $5-$16. Child's meals. Specializes in Mexican dishes, steaks, ribs. Live music Wed. Log cabin with floor to ceiling fieldstone fireplace. Cr cds: MC, V.

Ishpeming (D-2)

(See also Iron Mountain, Marquette)

Founded 1844 **Pop** 7,200 **Elev** 1,411 ft **Area code** 906 **Zip** 49849
E-mail ishnegcc@vp.net **Web** www.upsell.com/ish-neg/chamber.html
Information Ishpeming-Negaunee Area Chamber of Commerce, 661 Palms Ave; 906/486-4841.

Iron mines gave birth to this city and still sustain it. Skiing is the basis of its recreation and tourism business. In 1887, three Norwegians formed a ski club in Ishpeming, which is a Native American word for "high grounds." That ski club eventually became a national ski association.

What to See and Do

★ **National Ski Hall of Fame and Ski Museum.** Affiliated with the US Ski Association. Houses national trophies and displays of old skis and ski equipment, including a replica of the oldest-known ski and ski pole in the world. Roland Palmedo National Ski Library, collection of ski publications for researchers in house only. (Daily; closed Jan 1, Easter, Thanksgiving, Dec 25) Between 2nd & 3rd Sts, on US 41. Phone 906/485-6323 or 906/485-6324. ¢¢

Suicide Bowl. Includes five ski-jumping hills from mini-hill to 70-m hill. There are also four cross-country trails; one is lighted for evening use. On Cliffs Dr at E end of city. Phone 906/485-4242. ¢¢

Van Riper State Park. Approx 1,000 acres on Lake Michigamme. Swimming, waterskiing, bathhouse; fishing; boating (ramp, rentals); hunting; hiking; picnic grounds, concession, playground, camping. Standard fees. (Daily) 17 mi W on US 41. Phone 906/339-4461. Per car ¢¢

Annual Event

Annual Ski Jumping Championships. Paul Bietila Memorial. Also cross-country ski race. Feb.

Motel

★★ **BEST WESTERN COUNTRY INN.** *850 US 41W. 906/485-6345; FAX 906/485-6348.* 60 rms, 2 story. Mid-June-Oct: S $65; D $70; each addl $5; family rates; ski plans; lower rates rest of yr. Crib free. TV; cable (premium). Indoor pool; whirlpool. Complimentary coffee in lobby. Restaurant adj 6 am-10 pm; Fri, Sat to 11 pm. Ck-out noon. Business servs avail. Downhill ski 15 mi; x-country ski 2 mi. Game rm. Cr cds: A, C, D, DS, MC, V.

D ⛷ 🏊 ⚒ 🐾 SC

Isle Royale National Park (B-1)

(N of Upper Peninsula, on island in Lake Superior)

This unique wilderness area, covering 571,790 acres, is the largest island in Lake Superior, 15 miles from Canada (the nearest mainland), 18 miles from Minnesota and 45 miles from Michigan. There are no roads, and no automobiles are allowed. The main island, 45 miles long and 8½ miles across at its widest point, is surrounded by more than 400 smaller islands. Isle Royale may be reached by boat from Houghton or Copper Harbor (see) in Michigan or from Grand Portage in Minnesota; or by seaplane from Houghton. Schedules vary; inquire each year around January 1. Contact, Isle Royale National Park, 800 E Lakeshore Dr Houghton, MI 49931; 906/482-0984 or -0986.

The only wildlife here are those animals able to fly, swim, drift across the water or travel on ice. Moose, wolf, fox and beaver are the dominant mammals; however, before 1900 no moose existed on the island. The current population of 500 evolved from a few moose that either swam or crossed the ice to reach the island in 1912. In the winter of 1949 wolves came across on the ice and stayed. More than 200 species of birds have been observed, including loons, bald eagles and ospreys.

Prehistoric peoples discovered copper on the island 4,000 years ago. Later, white men tried to mine in a number of places. The remains of these mining operations may still be seen; some of the ancient mining pits date back 3,800 years.

There are more than 165 miles of foot trails leading to beautiful inland lakes, more than 20 of which have game fish, including pike, perch, walleye and, in a few, whitefish cisco. There are trout in many streams and lakes. Fishing is under National Park Service and Michigan regulations (see FISHING & HUNTING in state text). Boat rental and charter fishing is available at Rock Harbor Lodge (see). Basic supplies are available on the island in limited quantities. Nights are usually cold; bring warm clothing and be prepared to rough it. Group camping may not exceed 10 persons; inquire for group information; group campsites must be reserved. The park is open from approximately May to October.

Rock Harbor Lodge is at the east end of the island, about 3½ mi E of Mott Island, which is the Park Service headquarters during the summer. The lodge offers rooms, cabins, restaurant and a camp store. Room reservations should be made at least three weeks in advance; lodge open June through Labor Day. For lodge information write National Park Concessions, PO Box 405, Houghton, MI 49931 (summer); or Mammoth Cave National Park, Mammoth Cave, KY 42259 (winter).

Jackson (J-4)

(See also Ann Arbor, Battle Creek, Lansing)

Founded 1829 **Pop** 37,446 **Elev** 960 ft **Area code** 517
Information Convention & Tourist Bureau, 6007 Ann Arbor Rd, 49201; 517/764-4440.

Four major highways and heavy rail traffic make this a transportation center. Industries are the foundation of the city's economy. In Jackson on July 6, 1854, the Republican Party was officially born at a convention held "under the green spreading oaks," as there was no hall large enough to accommodate the delegates. Each year the city attracts thousands of tourists, who use it as a base to explore more than 200 natural lakes in Jackson County.

What to See and Do

Cascades Falls Park. Approx 465 acres. Picnicking, playground; 18-hole miniature golf, driving range; fitness and jogging trail; basketball, horseshoe courts; fishing ponds and pier; paddle-boating (rentals); pier; tennis courts; restaurant. Some fees. Brown St, via I-94 to exit 138. Phone 517/788-4320. Also here are

Sparks Illuminated Cascades Waterfalls. Approx 500 ft of water cascading over 16 waterfalls and 6 fountains in continually changing patterns of light, color and music. (Memorial Day-Labor Day, nightly) Phone 517/788-4320 or 517/788-4277. ¢¢ Fee includes

Cascades-Sparks Museum. Depicts early history of falls and its builder, Captain William Sparks; original drawings, models, audiovisual displays. (Memorial Day-Labor Day, nightly) Phone 517/788-4320.

Clark Lake. Approx 550 acres of woodland, lake and sandy beaches. Includes golf, sailing, riding, fishing and shuffleboard facilities. For a complete guide to lakes and streams, contact the Convention & Tourist Bureau. 10 mi S on US 127, then E on unnumbered road.

Dahlem Environmental Education Center. Nature center with 5 mi of trails through forests, fields, marshes; ½-mi "special needs" trail for the disabled; visitors center with exhibits, gift shop. (Daily exc Mon) 7117 S Jackson Rd. Phone 517/782-3453. **Free.**

Ella Sharp Park. Approx 530 acres with 18-hole golf course, tennis courts, ballfields, swimming pool, miniature golf, picnic facilities, formal gardens. (Daily) 3225 4th St, at S edge of city. Phone 517/788-4040. **Free.** In park is

Ella Sharp Museum. Complex includes Victorian farmhouse, historic farm lane, one-room schoolhouse, log cabin, galleries with rotating art and historic exhibits; studios; planetarium; visitors center. (Daily exc Mon; closed major hols) Phone 517/787-2320. ¢¢

⚡ **Michigan Space Center.** US space artifacts and memorabilia displayed in geodesic dome, including Gemini trainer, Apollo 9 Command Module, replica of space shuttle, *Challenger* memorial, space food, space suits, lunar rover, moon rock, satellites, orbiters, landers, giant rocket engines; films and special presentations. Picnicking and children's play areas. Gift shop. (May-Labor Day, daily; Jan-Apr, daily exc Mon; rest of yr, phone for schedule; closed Jan 1, Easter, Thanksgiving, Dec 25) 2111 Emmons Rd, adj to Jackson Community College. Phone 517/787-4425. ¢¢

Republican Party founding site. Marked with a tablet dedicated by President William Howard Taft. W Franklin & 2nd Sts.

Waterloo Farm Museum. Tours of furnished pioneer farmhouse (1855-1885), bakehouse, windmill, farm workshop, barn, milk cellar, log house, granary. (June-Aug, Tues-Sun afternoons; Sept, Sat & Sun; Pioneer Festival 2nd Sun Oct) 10 mi E via I-94 to exit 150, N on Mt Hope Rd, E on Waterloo-Munith Rd, at 9998 Waterloo-Munith Rd, near Waterloo. Phone 517/596-2254. ¢¢

Waterloo State Recreation Area. This is the state's largest recreation area, with 20,072 acres. Swimming, beach, bathhouse, waterskiing; fishing; boating (ramp, rentals) on numerous lakes; horseback riding; nature trails; hunting; picnicking, concession; cabins, tent & trailer sites; geology center. Standard fees. 15 mi E on I-94, then N on unnumbered road. Phone 313/475-8307.

Annual Events

Rose Festival. Ella Sharp Park. Parade, pageant, garden tours, entertainment. Phone 517/787-2065. Mid-May-mid-June.

Hot-Air Balloon Jubilee. Jackson County Airport. Competitive balloon events; skydivers; arts & crafts. Phone 517/782-1515. Mid-July.

Jackson County Fair. Stage shows; displays of produce, handicrafts, farm animals; midway shows; rides. Phone 517/788-4405. Aug 4-10.

Civil War Muster & Battle Re-enactment. Cascade Falls Park. Thousands of participants re-create a different Civil War battle each year; living history demonstrations, parades, food, entertainment. 3rd wkend Aug.

Seasonal Events

Harness racing. Jackson Harness Raceway, Jackson County Fairgrounds. Parimutuel betting. Phone 517/788-4500. Spring and fall meets.

Michigan Speedway. SE on MI 50 to US 12, then 1 mi W.NASCAR, ARCA, IROC and Indy Car races on a 2-mi oval track. Contact 12626 US 12, Brooklyn 49230; 517/592-6671 or 800/354-1010. Mid-June-mid-Aug.

Motels

🚶★ **BUDGETEL INN.** 2035 Service Dr (49201). 517/789-6000; FAX 517/782-6836. 67 rms, 2 story. S $39.95-$52.95; D $46.95-$59.95; family rates. Crib free. Pet accepted. TV, cable (premium). Complimentary continental bkfst. Complimentary coffee in rms. Restaurant adj 6:30 am-10 pm. Ck-out noon. Meeting rm. Business servs avail. Valet serv. Some refrigerators. Cr cds: A, C, D, DS, MC, V.

D 🐾 🏊 🐾 SC

★★ **COUNTRY HEARTH INN.** 1111 Boardman Rd (49202). 517/783-6404; res: 800/848-5767. 73 rms, 2 story. S $53-$67; D $59-$73; each addl $6; kit. units $67-$73; under 18 free; higher rates auto races. Crib free. TV; cable. Complimentary continental bkfst. Restaurant nearby.

Ck-out noon. Business servs avail. Health club privileges. Country-inn decor. Cr cds: A, C, D, DS, MC, V.

D 🏊 🐾 SC

★★ **HOLIDAY INN.** 2000 Holiday Inn Dr (49202), jct US 127 & I-94 exit 138. 517/783-2681; FAX 517/783-5744. 184 rms, 2 story. S, D $65-$85; under 19 free; wknd, special events rates. Crib free. Pet accepted. TV; cable (premium), VCR avail. Heated pool; whirlpool, sauna. Restaurant 6:30 am-2 pm, 5-10 pm. Rm serv. Bar 4 pm-midnight, Sun 5-10 pm. Ck-out 11 am. Coin lndry. Meeting rms. Business servs avail. Bellhops. Putting green; miniature golf. X-country ski 10 mi. Game rm. Cr cds: A, C, D, DS, JCB, MC, V.

D 🐾 🏌 🏊 🐾 SC

Restaurants

★★ **BRANDYWINE PUB & FOOD.** 2125 Horton Rd (49203). 517/783-2777. Hrs: 4-10 pm; Fri, Sat to 11 pm; early-bird dinner Mon-Fri 4-6 pm. Closed Sun; most major hols. Res accepted. Bar. Semi-a la carte: dinner $8.95-$18.95. Child's meals. Specializes in fresh fish, steak, vegetables. Early 1920s atmosphere; Tiffany-style lighting. Cr cds: A, MC, V.

D 🐾

★★ **GILBERT'S STEAK HOUSE.** 2323 Shirley Dr (49202), jct I-94 & US 127N. 517/782-7135. Hrs: 11 am-10 pm; Fri, Sat to 11 pm; Sun noon-7 pm. Closed some major hols. Res accepted. Bar. Semi-a la carte: lunch $4.95-$8.50, dinner $9.95-$19.95. Child's meals. Specializes in steak, prime rib, seafood. Victorian atmosphere. Cr cds: A, C, D, DS, MC, V.

D 🐾

Kalamazoo (J-3)

(See also Battle Creek, Paw Paw, Three Rivers)

Settled 1829 **Pop** 80,277 **Elev** 780 ft **Area code** 616 **E-mail** cvb @sapien.net

Information Kalamazoo County Convention and Visitors Bureau, 128 N Kalamazoo Mall, 49007; 616/381-4003 or 800/222-6363.

Yes, there really is a Kalamazoo—a unique name, immortalized in song and verse. The name is derived from the Native American name for the Kalamazoo River, which means "where the water boils in the pot." The concept is noted not only in the community's name but also in its cultural, industrial and recreational makeup. Diversified industry from bedding plants to pharmaceuticals thrive here. Many recreational activities complete the picture.

What to See and Do

Bronson Park. A bronze tablet marks the spot where Abraham Lincoln made an antislavery speech in 1856. Extending for 2 blks on South St.

Crane Park. Formal floral gardens, tennis courts. Park St, at the crest of Westnedge Hill overlooking city.

Echo Valley. 60 mph tobogganing (toboggans furnished), ice-skating (rentals). (Dec-Mar, Fri-Sun; closed Dec 25) 8495 East H Ave. Phone 616/349-3291 or 616/345-5892. ¢¢¢

Gilmore-CCCA Museum. More than 120 antique autos tracing the significant technical developments in automotive transportation; on 90 acres of landscaped grounds. (Mid-May-mid-Oct, daily) 6865 Hickory Rd, 15 mi NE via MI 43 in Hickory Corners. Phone 616/671-5089. ¢¢¢

⚡ **Kalamazoo Air Zoo** (Kalamazoo Aviation History Museum). Restored aircraft of World War II period, many in flying condition; exhibits, video theater, flight simulator, observation deck. Tours of Restoration Center (May-Sept). Flight of the Day (May-Sept, afternoons). (Daily) 3101 E

Milham Rd, on the grounds of Kalamazoo/Battle Creek Airport. Phone 616/382-6555. ¢¢¢

Kalamazoo College (1833). (1,300 students) Private, liberal arts college. Red brick streets and Georgian architecture characterize this school, one of the 100 oldest colleges in the nation. A 3,023-pipe organ is in Stetson Chapel; Bach Festival (Mar); Festival Playhouse (June-July). 1200 Academy St. Phone 616/337-7000.

Kalamazoo Institute of Arts. Galleries, school, shop, library and auditorium. Collection of 20th-century American art; circulating exhibits. (Daily exc Mon; closed hols; also Aug) 314 S Park St. Phone 616/349-7775 or 616/349-3959. **Donation.**

Kalamazoo Nature Center. Interpretive Center; restored 1860s pioneer homestead; nature trails (tours by appt); barnyard (May-Labor Day); Public Orientation Room programs, slides, movies, live animals. (Daily; closed most major hols) 7000 N Westnedge Ave, 5 mi N. Phone 616/381-1574. ¢¢

Kalamazoo Valley Museum. Includes Mary Jane Stryker Interactive Learning Hall with an interactive theater, science gallery, Challenger Learning Center, Egyptian artifacts and Universe Theater and Planetarium. (Mon-Sat, Sun afternoons) 230 N Rose St. Phone 616/373-7990. Interactive Learning Hall ¢; Planetarium-Theater ¢

Skiing.

Timber Ridge Ski Area. Four chairlifts, Pomalift, 3 rope tows; patrol, school; snow making; snack bar, cafeteria, 2 bars. Store, repairs, rentals. 15 trails; longest run 2/3 mi; vertical drop 250 ft. (Late Nov-mid-Mar, daily) 5 mi N on US 131, then W at D Ave exit. Phone 616/694-9449 or 800/253-2928 (snow conditions). ¢¢¢¢¢

Bittersweet Ski Area. Four triple chairlifts, double chairlift, 5 rope tows; school; lodge, cafeteria, bar. 16 trails; longest run 2,300 ft; vertical drop 300 ft. (Dec-Mar, daily) 18 mi N via US 131, MI 89 W to Jefferson Rd exit. Phone 616/694-2820. ¢¢¢¢¢

Western Michigan University (1903). (28,000 students) Contemporary plays, musical comedies, operas and melodramas offered in Shaw and York theaters. Touring professional shows, dance programs and entertainers in Miller Auditorium; dance and music performances are featured in the Irving S. Gilmore University Theatre Complex. Art exhibits in Sangren Hall and East Hall. Inquire for schedules. W Michigan Ave. Phone 616/387-1000.

Annual Events

Maple Sugaring Festival. Kalamazoo Nature Center. Mar.

Kalamazoo County Flowerfest. July.

Kalamazoo County Fair. Aug.

Wine and Harvest Festival. Kalamazoo-Paw Paw. 1st wkend Sept.

Motels

★ ★ **BEST WESTERN KELLY INN.** 3640 E Cork St (49001). 616/381-1900; FAX 616/373-6136. 124 rms, 3 story. S, D $67-$74; each addl $8; under 14 free. Crib free. TV; cable (premium), VCR avail (movies $5). Indoor pool; whirlpool, sauna. Complimentary continental bkfst. Restaurant nearby. Ck-out noon. Meeting rms. Business servs avail. Valet serv. Downhill/x-country ski 15 mi. Cr cds: A, C, D, DS, ER, MC, V.

D ✔ ≈ ⊠ 🐾 SC

✔★ ★ **FAIRFIELD INN BY MARRIOTT.** 3800 E Cork St (49001), near Municipal Airport. 616/344-8300; FAX 616/344-8300, ext. 709. 133 rms, 3 story. Late May-mid-Sept: S $39.95; D $55.95; each addl $3; under 18 free; lower rates rest of yr. Crib free. TV; cable. Heated pool. Complimentary continental bkfst. Restaurant adj 6 am-midnight. Ck-out noon. Meeting rm. Business servs avail. Valet serv. Downhill/x-country ski 15 mi. Cr cds: A, D, DS, MC, V.

D ✔ ≈ ⊠ 🐾 SC

★ ★ **HOLIDAY INN-AIRPORT.** 3522 Sprinkle Rd (49002). 616/381-7070; FAX 616/381-4341. 146 rms, 2 story. S, studio rms $75; D $83; under 18 free. Crib free. Pet accepted. TV; cable (premium), VCR

avail. 2 pools, 1 indoor; whirlpool, sauna, poolside serv. Restaurant 6:30 am-10 pm; Fri, Sat to 11 pm. Rm serv. Bar 11:30 am-midnight; closed Sun. Ck-out noon. Coin lndry. Meeting rms. Business servs avail. Bellhops. Valet serv. Sundries. Free airport transportation. Downhill/x-country ski 15 mi. Adj to stadium. Cr cds: A, C, D, DS, ER, JCB, MC, V.

D ✔ ≈ ⊠ 🐾 SC

★ ★ **LA QUINTA.** 3750 Easy St (49002), near Municipal Airport. 616/388-3551; FAX 616/342-9132. 122 rms, 2 story. S $48; D $54; each addl $6; under 18 free. Crib free. Pet accepted. TV; cable (premium). Heated pool. Complimentary continental bkfst. Restaurant adj 6 am-11 pm. Ck-out noon. Meeting rms. Business servs avail. Valet serv. Free airport, RR station, bus depot transportation. Downhill/x-country ski 15 mi. Cr cds: A, C, D, DS, MC, V.

D ✔ ≈ ≈ ✈ ⊠ 🐾 SC

✔★ **RED ROOF INN-WEST.** 5425 W Michigan Ave (49009). 616/375-7400; FAX 616/375-7533. 108 rms, 2 story. S $36-$45; D $40-$52; 3 or more $50; under 18 free; higher rates special events. Crib free. Pet accepted. TV. Complimentary bkfst. Restaurant nearby. Ck-out noon. Business servs avail. Downhill ski 8 mi; x-country ski 3 mi. Picnic tables, grill. Cr cds: A, C, D, DS, MC, V.

D ✔ ≈ ⊠ 🐾

★ ★ **RESIDENCE INN BY MARRIOTT.** 1500 E Kilgore Rd (49001), near Municipal Airport. 616/349-0855; FAX 616/349-0855, ext. 211. 83 kit. suites, 2 story. S, D $105-$130; under 12 free; wkly rates; ski, golf plans. Crib free. Pet accepted. TV; cable, VCR avail (movies). Heated pool; whirlpool. Complimentary full bkfst. Complimentary coffee in rms. Restaurant nearby. Ck-out noon. Coin lndry. Meeting rms. Business servs avail. In-rm modem link. Bellhops. Valet serv. Free airport, RR station, bus depot transportation. 9-hole golf privileges. Downhill/x-country ski 20 mi. Health club privileges. Some fireplaces. Picnic tables, grills. Cr cds: A, C, D, DS, JCB, MC, V.

D ✔ ≈ 🧍 ≈ ✈ ⊠ 🐾 SC

✔★ **SUPER 8.** 618 Maple Hill Dr (49009). 616/345-0146. 62 rms, 3 story. No elvtr. Apr-Oct: S $41.88; D $48.88-$52.88; under 12 free; lower rates rest of yr. Crib free. Pet accepted. TV; cable (premium). Complimentary coffee in lobby. Restaurant adj 7 am-10 pm. Ck-out 11 am. Downhill ski 11 mi. Some refrigerators. Cr cds: A, C, D, DS, MC, V.

D ✔ ≈ ⊠ 🐾

Motor Hotel

★ ★ **HOLIDAY INN-WEST.** 2747 S 11th St (49009). 616/375-6000; FAX 616/375-1220. 186 rms, 4 story. S, D $79-$89; studio rms $79; under 19 free. Crib free. Pet accepted. TV. Indoor pool; whirlpool, poolside serv. Restaurant 6:30 am-10:30 pm; Fri, Sat to 11 pm. Rm serv. Bar 11:30 am-midnight; Fri, Sat to 1 am. Ck-out 11 am. Coin lndry. Meeting rm. Business servs avail. Bellhops. Valet serv. Putting green. Downhill ski 8 mi; x-country ski 3 mi. Exercise rm; stair machine, bicycles, sauna. Game rm. Cr cds: A, C, D, DS, ER, JCB, MC, V.

D ✔ ≈ ≈ 🧍 ⊠ 🐾 SC

Hotel

★ ★ ★ **RADISSON PLAZA-KALAMAZOO CENTER.** 100 W Michigan Ave (49007). 616/343-3333; FAX 616/381-1560. 281 rms, 9 story. S $99-$125; D $109-$134; each addl $10; suites $150-$275; family rates; ski, golf plans. Crib free. Garage $4; valet $6. TV; cable. Indoor pool; whirlpool. Restaurant (see WEBSTER'S). Bar 11-1:30 am. Ck-out noon. Convention facilities. Business servs avail. In-rm modem link. Concierge. Shopping arcade. Free airport, RR station, bus depot transportation. Downhill/x-country ski 16 mi. Exercise rm; instructor, weights, treadmill, sauna. Bathrm phone, refrigerator, wet bar in some suites. Cr cds: A, C, D, DS, ER, JCB, MC, V.

D ✔ ≈ 🧍 ⊠ 🐾 SC

Inns

★ ★ **HALL HOUSE.** *106 Thompson St (49006). 616/343-2500; res: 800/421-4414.* 4 rms, 3 story. S, D $75-$109; 2-night min some special events; wkly rates. TV; cable. Complimentary bkfst. Georgian Colonial-revival building (1923). Original artwork. Some antiques. Cr cds: A, DS, MC, V.

★ ★ **STUART AVENUE.** *229 Stuart Ave (49007). 616/342-0230; FAX 616/385-3442.* 17 rms in 4 buildings, 2-3 story, 6 suites, 12 kit. units. S $49-$69; D $59-$79; each addl $10; suites $80-$130; kit. units $150-$250/wk (2 wk min); wkly rates. Crib $10. TV; cable. Complimentary continental bkfst; afternoon refreshments. Restaurant nearby. Ck-out noon, ck-in 4 pm. Meeting rms. Downhill/x-country ski 15 mi. Some fireplaces. Consists of three Victorian houses. Parlors, sitting rms; gold gaslight chandeliers, antiques. Landscaped garden with gazebo, lily pond. Totally nonsmoking. Cr cds: A, C, D, DS, MC, V.

Restaurants

★ ★ ★ **BLACK SWAN.** *3501 Greenleaf Blvd (49008), in Parkview Hills Development. 616/375-2105.* Hrs: 11:30 am-2 pm, 5-10 pm; Sun 5-8 pm; Sun brunch 11 am-2 pm. Closed major hols. Res accepted. Continental menu. Bar to midnight. Semi-a la carte: lunch $5.95-$9.95, dinner $14.95-$19.95. Sun brunch $11.95. Child's meals. Specializes in fish, beef Wellington. Valet parking. Overlooks lake. Cr cds: A, C, D, DS, MC, V.

★ ★ **BRAVO.** *5402 Portage Rd (49002). 616/344-7700.* Hrs: 11:30 am-10 pm; Fri to 11 pm; Sat 5 pm-11 pm; Sun 4-9 pm; Sun brunch 11 am-2 pm. Closed some major hols. Res accepted. Italian, Amer menu. Bar. Semi-a la carte: lunch $5-$10, dinner $8.95-$16.95. Sun brunch $12.95. Child's meals. Specialties: scampi with linguine, veal with morels, minestrone. Wood-burning pizza oven. Contemporary Italian decor. Cr cds: A, DS, MC, V.

★ ★ ★ **WEBSTER'S.** *(See Radisson Plaza-Kalamazoo Center Hotel)* 616/343-4444. Hrs: 11:30 am-2 pm, 5:30-10 pm; Fri, Sat to 11 pm. Closed Sun; most major hols. Res accepted. Continental menu. Bar. Semi-a la carte: lunch $9.95, dinner $12.95-$21.95. Specialties: beef Wellington, seafood. Entertainment. Club atmosphere. Jacket. Totally nonsmoking. Cr cds: A, C, D, DS, ER, JCB, MC, V.

Lansing & East Lansing (H-4)

Settled 1847 **Pop** Lansing, 127,321; East Lansing, 50,677 **Elev** 860 ft
Area code 517 **E-mail** glcvb-info@lansing.org **Web** www.lansing.org

Information Greater Lansing Convention & Visitors Bureau, 119 Pere Marquette, PO Box 15066, 48901; 517/487-6800 or 800/968-8474.

When the capital of Michigan moved here in 1847 for lack of agreement on a better place, the "city" consisted of one log house and a sawmill. Today, in addition to state government, Lansing is the headquarters for many trade and professional associations and has much heavy industry. R.E. Olds, who built and marketed one of America's earliest automobiles, started the city's industrial growth. Lansing is the home of the BOC Lansing Product Team of General Motors, and many allied industries. East Lansing, a neighboring community, is the home of the Michigan State University Spartans and is part of the capital city in all respects except government.

What to See and Do

BoarsHead Theater. A regional center with a professional resident theater company. Center for the Arts, 425 S Grand Ave. For schedule phone 517/484-7805.

Brenke River Sculpture and Fish Ladder. Located at North Lansing Dam on the Riverfront Park scenic walk, sculpture encompasses the ladder designed by artist/sculptor Joseph E. Kinnebrew and landscape architect Robert O'Boyle. 2 mi N via Washington Ave.

Fenner Nature Center. Park features a bald eagle, two waterfowl ponds, replica of a pioneer cabin and garden, five miles of nature trails through a variety of habitats; picnicking. Nature center with small animal exhibits (daily exc Mon). Trails (daily). 2020 E Mt Hope Ave, at Aurelius Rd. Phone 517/483-4224. **Free.**

Impression 5 Science Center. Center has more than 200 interactive, hands-on exhibits, including computer lab, chemistry experiments; restaurant. (Mon-Sat, also Sun afternoons) 200 Museum Dr. Phone 517/485-8116. ¢¢

Michigan Historical Museum (Michigan Library & Historical Center). Exhibits include a copper mine, sawmill and 54-ft-high relief map of Michigan; audiovisual programs, hands-on exhibits. (Daily; closed state hols) 717 W Allegan St. Phone 517/373-3559. **Free.**

Michigan State University (1855). (42,000 students) Founded as the country's first agricultural college and forerunner of the nationwide land-grant university system, MSU, located on a 5,300-acre landscaped campus with 7,800 different species and varieties of trees, shrubs and vines, is known for its research, Honors College and many innovations in education. Among the interesting features of the campus are Abrams Planetarium (shows: Fri-Sun; fee; phone 517/355-4672); Horticultural Gardens; W.J. Beal Botanical Garden; Breslin Student Events Center (box office phone 517/432-5000); Wharton Center for Performing Arts (box office, phone 517/432-2000); Michigan State University Museum (Mon-Sat, also Sun afternoons, closed hols); and Kresge Art Museum (Mon-Wed & Fri, also Thurs, Sat & Sun afternoons; closed hols). In East Lansing. Phone 517/353-7631.

Potter Park Zoo. Zoo on the Red Cedar River; has more than 400 animals. Educational programs, camel and pony rides, playground, concession and picnic facilities. (Daily) 1301 S Pennsylvania Ave. Phone 517/483-4222. ¢; Parking ¢

★ **R.E. Olds Transportation Museum.** Named after Ransom Eli Olds, the museum houses Lansing-built vehicles including Oldsmobile, REO, Star and Durant autos; REO and Duplex trucks, bicycles, airplanes; period clothing, photographic display of Olds' Victorian home and a "Wall of Wheels" from the Motor Wheel Corp. (Daily; closed Jan 1, Dec 25) 240 Museum Dr. Phone 517/372-0422. ¢¢

State Capitol Building. Dedicated 1879, this was one of the first state capitols to emulate the dome and wings of the US Capitol in Washington, DC. Interior walls and ceilings reflect the work of many skilled artisans, muralists and portrait painters. Tours (daily). Capitol & Michigan Aves. Phone 517/373-2353. **Free.**

The Ledges. Edging the Grand River, the Ledges are quartz sandstone 300 million yrs old. They are considered a good rock climbing area for the experienced. (Daily) 10 mi W via MI 43 in Grand Ledge. Phone 517/627-7351. Per car ¢

Woldumar Nature Center. A 188-acre wildlife preserve; nature walks, interpretive center (Mon-Fri; closed hols). Trails open for hiking and skiing (daily, dawn-dusk). 5539 Lansing Rd. Phone 517/322-0030. ¢

Annual Events

East Lansing Art Festival. Artists' work for sale, continuous performances, ethnic foods, children's activities. Phone 517/337-1731. 3rd wkend May.

Mint Festival. 18 mi N via US 27 in St Johns. Queen contest, parade, mint farm tours, antiques, arts & crafts, flea market, entertainment. Phone 517/224-7248. 2nd wkend Aug.

Riverfest. Riverfront Park. Competitive water activities, ethnic foods, arts & crafts, lighted float parade. Labor Day wkend.

Motels

★ ★ ★ **BEST WESTERN MIDWAY.** *(7711 W Saginaw Hwy, Lansing 48917)* 517/627-8471; FAX 517/627-8597. 149 rms, 2-3 story. Sept-May: S $65-$82; D $70-$87; each addl $5; under 12 free; lower rates rest of yr. Crib free. Pet accepted. TV; cable (premium). Indoor pool; whirlpool. Coffee in rms. Restaurant 6:30 am-10 pm; wkend hrs vary. Rm serv. Bar 11-2 am. Ck-out noon. Meeting rms. Business servs avail. Bellhops. Valet serv. Sundries. Free airport transportation. Exercise equipt; rower, stair machine, sauna. Game rm. Refrigerators avail. Cr cds: A, C, D, DS, JCB, MC, V.

D ★ ≈ ✗ ≊ ▨ SC

★ ★ **CLUBHOUSE INN.** *(2710 Lake Lansing Rd, Lansing 48912)* 517/482-0500; FAX 517/482-0557. 129 rms, 2 story, 17 suites. S $56; D $64; suites $70-$105; under 16 free. Crib free. TV; cable (premium), VCR avail. Indoor pool; whirlpool. Complimentary full bkfst. Ck-out noon. Coin lndry. Meeting rms. Business center. Valet serv. X-country ski 5 mi. Private patios, balconies. Picnic tables, grills. Cr cds: A, C, D, DS, MC, V.

D ★ ≈ ≊ ▨ ♣

★ ★ **COMFORT INN.** *(2209 University Park Dr, Okemos 48864)* E via I-96, exit 110. 517/349-8700; FAX 517/349-5638. 160 rms, 2 story. S, D $59-$95; each addl $6; suites $85-$115; under 18 free; higher rates special events. Crib free. TV; cable, VCR avail. Heated pool; whirlpool. Complimentary continental bkfst. Restaurant adj 6 am-midnight. Ck-out 11 am. Meeting rm. Business servs avail. X-country ski 5 mi. Exercise equipt; treadmill, bicycles, sauna, steam rm. Wet bar, whirlpool in suites. Cr cds: A, D, DS, MC, V.

D ★ ≈ ✗ ≊ ▨ SC

★ ★ **FAIRFIELD INN BY MARRIOTT.** *(2335 Wood Lake Dr, Okemos 48864)* 517/347-1000; FAX 517/347-5092. 79 rms, 2 story. S $59; D $64; each addl $5; suites $125; under 18 free. Crib free. TV; cable (premium). Indoor pool; whirlpool. Complimentary continental bkfst. Restaurant nearby. Ck-out noon. Valet serv. Game rm. Some refrigerators. Cr cds: A, C, D, DS, MC, V.

D ≈ ▨ ▨ SC

★ ★ **HAMPTON INN.** *(525 N Canal Rd, Lansing 48917)* 517/627-8381; FAX 517/627-5502. 109 rms, 3 story. S, D $53-$66; suites $84; under 18 free. Crib free. TV; cable (premium). Complimentary continental bkfst. Restaurant adj 6 am-10 pm. Ck-out noon. Meeting rms. Business servs avail. Valet serv. Refrigerator in suites. Some balconies. Cr cds: A, C, D, DS, ER, MC, V.

D ▨ ▨ SC

✔★ **RED ROOF INN-EAST.** *(3615 Dunckel Rd, Lansing 48910)* 517/332-2575; FAX 517/332-1459. 80 rms, 2 story. S $41-$51; D $42-$54; each addl $6; under 18 free. Crib free. Pet accepted. TV. Restaurant opp 7 am-11 pm. Ck-out noon. Business servs avail. X-country ski 7 mi. Cr cds: A, C, D, DS, MC, V.

D ★ ≈ ▨

Motor Hotels

★ ★ ★ **HARLEY.** *(3600 Dunckel Dr, Lansing 48910)* 517/351-7600; FAX 517/351-4640. 150 rms, 2 story. S $71-$110; D $81-$112; each addl $10; suites $175; under 18 free; wkly rates. Crib free. TV; cable (premium). 2 pools, 1 indoor; whirlpool. Restaurant 6:30 am-11 pm; Sat, Sun from 7 am. Rm serv. Bar 11-1 am; entertainment exc Sun. Ck-out 11 am. Meeting rm. Business servs avail. Bellhops. Valet serv. Sundries. Free airport, RR station, bus depot transportation. Lighted tennis. Putting green. X-country ski 7 mi. Exercise equipt; bicycle, rower, sauna. Lawn games. Game rm. Private patios, balconies. Cr cds: A, C, D, DS, MC, V.

D ★ ♣ ≈ ✗ ≊ ▨ SC

★ ★ ★ **MARRIOTT UNIVERSITY PLACE.** *(300 MAC Ave, East Lansing 48823)* Adj to Michigan State Univ. 517/337-4440; FAX 517/337-

5001. 180 rms, 7 story. S, D $99; each addl $10; under 19 free; wkend rates; higher rates: univ football wkends, graduation. Crib free. TV; cable (premium). Indoor pool; whirlpool. Complimentary coffee in lobby. Restaurant 6:30 am-midnight; Sat from 7 am; Sun 7 am-10 pm. Rm serv. Bar 11 am-midnight; Sun to 10 pm. Ck-out noon. Coin lndry. Meeting rms. Business servs avail. Bellhops. Valet serv. Sundries. Free garage parking. Free airport transportation. Exercise equipt; weight machine, bicycles, sauna. Balconies. Cr cds: A, C, D, DS, JCB, MC, V.

D ≈ ✗ ≊ ▨ SC

★ ★ **QUALITY SUITES.** *(901 Delta Commerce Dr, Lansing 48917)* 517/886-0600; FAX 517/886-0103. 117 suites, 4 story. S $89; D $99; each addl $10; under 18 free; wkend rates. Crib free. TV; cable (premium), VCR avail (movies). Complimentary full bkfst. Restaurant nearby. Ck-out 11 am. Meeting rms. Business servs avail. Valet serv. Sundries. Free airport transportation. Exercise equipt; bicycles, treadmill, whirlpool, sauna. Refrigerators. Some balconies. Cr cds: A, C, D, DS, MC, V.

D ✗ ≊ ▨ SC

★ ★ **RESIDENCE INN BY MARRIOTT.** *(1600 E Grand River Ave, East Lansing 48823)* 517/332-7711; FAX 517/332-7711, ext. 6005. 60 kit. suites, 2 story. S $115; D $165; each addl $10; family rates. Crib free. TV; cable (premium), VCR avail (movies). Heated pool; whirlpool. Complimentary continental bkfst. Complimentary coffee in rms. Restaurants nearby. Ck-out noon. Coin lndry. Business servs avail. Valet serv. Health club privileges. Balconies. Picnic table, grill. Cr cds: A, D, DS, JCB, MC, V.

D ≈ ▨ ▨

★ ★ ★ **SHERATON.** *925 S Creyts Rd (48917).* 517/323-7100; FAX 517/323-2180. 219 rms, 5 story. S $105; D $115; each addl $12; suites $225; under 18 free; wkend rates. Crib free. TV; cable (premium). Indoor pool; whirlpool. Coffee in rms. Restaurant 6:30 am-midnight. Rm serv. Bar 11-2 am. Ck-out noon. Meeting rms. Business servs avail. Bellhops. Gift shop. Free airport transportation. X-country ski 5 mi. Exercise equipt; treadmills, bicycles, whirlpool, sauna. Some refrigerators. Cr cds: A, C, D, DS, ER, JCB, MC, V.

D ≈ ≈ ✗ ≊ ▨ SC

Hotels

★ ★ ★ **HOLIDAY INN-SOUTH.** *(6820 S Cedar St, Lansing 48911)* 517/694-8123; FAX 517/699-3753. 300 rms, 5 story. S $97-$113; D $107-$123; each addl $10; suites $160-$350; under 18 free; wkend rates. Crib free. TV; cable. Indoor pool; whirlpool. Coffee in rms. Restaurant 6:30 am-10 pm. Bar 4 pm-1 am. Ck-out noon. Convention facilities. Business servs avail. Airport, RR station, bus depot transportation. X-country ski 3 mi. Exercise equipt; weights, bicycles, sauna. Sun deck. Game rm. Refrigerators. Cr cds: A, C, D, DS, ER, JCB, MC, V.

D ★ ≈ ✗ ≊ ▨ SC

★ ★ ★ **RADISSON.** *(111 N Grand Ave, Lansing 48933)* 517/482-0188; FAX 517/487-6646. 260 rms, 11 story. S, D $115; suites $185-$199; under 19 free. Crib free. TV; cable (premium). Indoor pool; whirlpool. Coffee in rms. Restaurant 6 am-11 pm. Bar 11-1 am. Ck-out noon. Convention facilities. Business servs avail. Concierge. Gift shop. Free valet parking. Free airport, RR station, bus depot transportation. X-country ski 6 mi. Exercise equipt; bicycles, stair machine, sauna. Bathrm phone; refrigerator in suites. Cr cds: A, C, D, DS, ER, JCB, MC, V.

D ★ ≈ ✗ ≊ ▨ SC

Inn

★ ★ **DUSTY'S ENGLISH INN.** *(728 S Michigan Rd, Eaton Rapids 48827)* 517/663-2500; FAX 517/663-2643; res: 800/858-0598. 10 rms, 3 story. S $75-$145; D $85-$155; each addl $15; suites $135-$155. Children over 12 yrs only. TV; cable (premium), VCR avail. Pool. Complimentary continental bkfst. Restaurant 11:30 am-1:30 pm, 5:30-8:30 pm. Ck-out 11 am, ck-in 3 pm. Business servs avail. 18-hole golf privileges.

X-country ski on site. Built in 1927; furnished with antiques. Totally non-smoking. Cr cds: DS, MC, V.

Restaurant

★ **PARTHENON.** *(227 S Washington Square, Lansing 48933)* 517/484-0573. Hrs: 7 am-8 pm. Closed Sun; major hols. Res accepted. Greek, Amer menu. Bar. Complete meals: bkfst $2.35-$5.75. Semi-a la carte: lunch $5.25-$7.95, dinner $8.95-$16.95. Specialties: souvlakia, moussaka, scorpios. Cr cds: A, C, D, DS, MC, V.

Leland (E-3)

(See also Glen Arbor)

Pop 400 (est) **Elev** 602 ft **Area code** 616 **Zip** 49654

What to See and Do

⭐ **Boat trips to Manitou Islands.**The *Mishe-mokwa* makes daily trips in summer, including overnight camping excursions, to North and South Manitou Islands (see SLEEPING BEAR DUNES NATIONAL LAKESHORE); also evening cocktail cruise (by res only). (June-Aug, daily; May & Sept-Oct, Fri-Mon & Wed) Leland Harbor. Phone 616/256-9061. ¢¢¢¢-¢¢¢¢¢

Motel

★ ★ **LELAND LODGE.** *565 E Pearl St.* 616/256-9848; FAX 616/256-8812. 18 rms, 2 story, 4 kits. Mid-June-Labor Day: S, D $89-$149; each addl $10; kit. units $805-$995/wk; lower rates rest of yr. Crib free. TV; cable. Complimentary continental bkfst wkends (in season). Restaurant 11 am-10 pm; off-season to 9 pm. Rm serv. Bar 11 am-11 pm. Ck-out 11 am. Business servs avail. 18-hole golf privileges. Cr cds: A, DS, MC, V.

Inn

★ ★ **MANITOU MANOR.** *147 N Manitou Trail W, Lake Leelanau, 3 mi S on MI 22.* 616/256-7712. 6 rms. No A/C. Memorial Day-mid-Oct: S $85-$95; D $110-$159; each addl $15; family, wkly rates; lower rates rest of yr. TV in sitting rm; VCR. Complimentary full bkfst. Ck-out 11 am, ck-in 3 pm. Downhill ski 5 mi; x-country ski on site. Library. Totally nonsmoking. Historic (1878) farmhouse with 6 acres of cherry trees. Cr cds: DS, MC, V.

Restaurants

★ ★ **BLUE BIRD.** *102 River St.* 616/256-9081. Hrs: 11:30 am-3 pm, 5-9 pm; Sun 4-9 pm; Late-Nov-Mar: Sun brunch 10 am-2 pm; Fri, Sat 5-9 pm. Closed first 3 wks Nov; also Mon Apr-mid-June, after Labor Day-Oct. Res accepted. Bar 11:30 am-midnight. Semi-a la carte: lunch $3-$8.50, dinner $8.95-$16.95. Child's meals. Specializes in prime rib, seafood, Great Lakes fish. Salad bar. Overlooks channel. Family-owned. Cr cds: MC, V.

★ ★ **THE COVE.** *111 River St.* 616/256-9834. Hrs: 11 am-10 pm. Closed mid-Oct-mid-May. Res accepted. Bar. Semi-a la carte: lunch $3.95-$7.95, dinner $9.95-$19.95. Child's meals. Specializes in seafood. Outdoor dining. On channel overlooking Lake Michigan. Cr cds: A, MC, V.

★ ★ **LEELANAU COUNTRY INN.** *(149 E Harbor Hwy, Maple City 49664) 8 mi S on MI 22.* 616/228-5060. Hrs: 5-9 pm; early-bird dinner 5-6 pm; hrs vary Nov-May. Closed Dec 24, 25, 26. Res accepted. Semi-a la carte: dinner $9.95-$18.95. Child's meals. Specializes in fresh seafood, prime rib, pasta. Own desserts. Converted house (1891); guest rms avail. Cr cds: A, MC, V.

Ludington (G-3)

(See also Manistee)

Settled 1880 **Pop** 8,507 **Elev** 610 ft **Area code** 616 **Zip** 49431 **E-mail** suelacvb.com **Web** www.ludingtoncvb.com

Information Ludington Area Convention & Visitor Bureau, 5827 W US 10; 616/845-0324 or 800/542-4600.

A large passenger car ferry and freighters keep this important Lake Michigan port busy. First named Père Marquette, in honor of the missionary-explorer who died here in 1675, the community later adopted the name of its more recent founder, James Ludington, a lumber baron. Ludington draws vacationers because of its long stretch of beach on Lake Michigan and miles of forests, lakes, streams and dunes surrounding the town. The Père Marquette River has been stocked with chinook salmon; fishing boats may be chartered.

What to See and Do

Auto ferry service (to Manitowoc, WI). Amenities include museum, game room, theater, staterooms, food service. (May-Oct, daily) End of US 10. Phone 616/845-5555 or 800/841-4243. ¢¢¢¢¢

Ludington Pumped Storage Hydroelectric Plant. Scenic overlooks beside Lake Michigan and the plant's 840-acre reservoir. One of the world's largest facilities of this type. (Apr-Nov, daily) 6 mi S on S Lakeshore Dr. **Free.** Footpaths connect to

Mason County Campground and Picnic Area. Picnicking, playground. Camping (hookups). (Memorial Day-Labor Day, daily) S Old US 31 to Chauvez Rd, then 1 1/2 mi S. Phone 616/845-7609. Camping per site ¢¢¢

Ludington State Park. Approx 4,500 acres on lakes Michigan and Hamlin and the Sable River. Swimming, bathhouse, waterskiing; fishing; boating (ramp, rentals); hunting. Cross-country skiing. Picnicking, playground, concession. Camping. Visitor center (May-Sept). Standard fees. 8 1/2 mi N on MI 116. Phone 616/843-8671. Per vehicle ¢¢

Père Marquette Memorial Cross. Towers high into the skyline, overlooks the harbor and Lake Michigan. Near the harbor.

Stearns and Waterworks parks. These two parks join together to form the city's western boundary; 1/2-mi swimming beach (lifeguard, June-Labor Day); fishing; boating, ramps, launch, 150-slip marina. Picnicking, playground, miniature golf, shuffleboard. Fee for some activities.

White Pine Village. Historical buildings re-create small-town Michigan life in the late 1800s; general store, trapper's cabin, courthouse/jail, town hall, one-room school and others. (June-early Sept, daily exc Mon) 3 mi S via US 31 to Iris Rd, follow signs. Phone 616/843-4808. ¢¢

Motels

★ **FOUR SEASONS.** *717 E Ludington Ave (US 10).* 616/843-3448; res: 800/968-0180. 33 rms. Mid-June-mid-Oct: S, D $45-$99; higher rates: hols, festivals; lower rates rest of yr. Crib free. TV; cable (premium), VCR avail. Complimentary continental bkfst. Coffee in rms. Restaurant nearby. Ck-out 11 am. Free airport transportation. Golf privileges. X-country ski 6 mi. Cr cds: DS, MC, V.

★ **LANDS INN.** *4079 W US 10. 616/845-7311; FAX 616/843-8551.* 116 rms, 4 story. Mid-May-early Sept: S $89; D $99; each addl $10; suites $125; under 16 free; wkly rates; golf plans; lower rates rest of yr. Crib free. TV; cable (premium). Indoor pool; whirlpool, sauna. Restaurant 6:30 am-10 pm. Rm serv. Bar 5 pm-midnight; entertainment Thurs-Sat. Ck-out 10 am. Coin lndry. Meeting rms. Business servs avail. Game rm. Cr cds: A, C, D, DS, MC, V.

D ≈ ⌧ 🐾 SC

★ **MARINA BAY.** *604 W Ludington Ave (US 10). 616/845-5124; FAX 616/843-7929; res: 800/968-1440.* 24 rms, 1-2 story. Late June-early Sept: S, D $60-$135; each addl $5; higher rates special events; lower rates rest of yr. Crib free. TV; cable (premium), VCR avail (movies $2). Complimentary coffee in lobby. Restaurant nearby. Ck-out 11 am. Business servs avail. Free airport transportation. X-country ski 4 mi. Some in-rm whirlpools. Cr cds: DS, MC, V.

≈ 🐾

★ **MILLER'S LAKESIDE.** *808 W Ludington Ave (US 10). 616/843-3458; FAX 616/843-3450; res: 800/843-2177.* 52 rms. Mid-May-mid-Sept: S, D $65-$80; each addl $5; suites $95; higher rates: hols, special events; wkly rates off-season; lower rates rest of yr. Crib free. TV; cable (premium), VCR avail. Heated pool. Restaurant nearby. Ck-out 11 am. Business servs avail. Free airport transportation. X-country ski 5 mi. Public beach, launching ramp, park, miniature golf opp. Cr cds: A, DS, MC, V.

D ≈ ≈ ⌧ 🐾 SC

★ **NADER'S LAKE SHORE MOTOR LODGE.** *612 N Lakeshore Dr. 616/843-8757; res: 800/968-0109.* 26 rms, 2 kits. Mid-June-early Sept: S, D $64; kit. units $50-$58; lower rates May-mid-June, early Sept-Oct. Closed rest of yr. Crib free. TV; cable. Heated pool. Restaurant nearby. Ck-out 11 am. Lawn games. Refrigerators. Private patios. Picnic tables. Beach 1 blk. Cr cds: A, D, DS, MC, V.

🐾 ≈ 🐾 SC

★★ **SNYDER'S SHORELINE INN.** *903 W Ludington Ave (US 10). 616/845-1261; FAX 616/843-4441.* 44 rms, 2 story, 8 suites. Mid-June-Oct: S $69-$199; D $89-$249; each addl $20; suites $159-$249; higher rates special events; lower rates May-mid-June. Closed rest of yr. TV; cable (premium), VCR avail (free movies). Heated pool; whirlpool. Complimentary continental bkfst. Ck-out 11 am. Business servs avail. Free airport transportation. Many refrigerators; some wet bars. Balconies. On lake; swimming beach. Cr cds: A, D, DS, MC, V.

D ≈ ⌧ 🐾

✔★★ **VIKING ARMS.** *930 E Ludington Ave (US 10). 616/843-3441; FAX 616/845-7703.* 45 rms. Mid-May-mid-Oct: S $40-$150; D $49-$150; each addl $5; family rates; higher rates: hols, special events; lower rates rest of yr. Crib $2. TV; cable, VCR (movies $3). Heated pool; whirlpool. Complimentary continental bkfst. Coffee in rms. Restaurant nearby. Ck-out 11 am. Meeting rm. Business servs avail. Free airport transportation. X-country ski 7 mi. Some in-rm whirlpools, fireplaces. Cr cds: A, C, D, DS, MC, V.

D ≈ ≈ ⌧ 🐾

Inn

★★ **HISTORIC NICKERSON INN.** *(262 W Lowell St, Pentwater 49449) approx 15 mi S on US 31. 616/869-6731; FAX 616/869-6151; res: 800/742-1288.* 12 rms, 4 with shower only, 3 story. No rm phones. June-Oct: S, D $100-$185; each addl $25; lower rates rest of yr. Children over 11 yrs only. Complimentary full bkfst. Restaurant (see HISTORIC NICKERSON INN). Ck-out 11 am, ck-in 2 pm. Luggage handling. X-country ski 2 mi. Built in 1914; furnished with antiques. Cr cds: MC, V.

≈ ⌧ 🐾

Restaurants

★★ **GIBBS.** *3951 W US 10/31. 616/845-0311.* Hrs: 11:30 am-9 pm; summer to 10 pm; Sat, Sun 8 am-10 pm. Closed Jan-mid-Feb. Res accepted. Bar. Semi-a la carte: bkfst $1.95-$5.95, lunch $2.95-$9.95, dinner $5.50-$24.95. Child's meals. Salad bar. Own ice cream. Family-owned. Cr cds: A, DS, MC, V.

★★ **HISTORIC NICKERSON INN.** *(See Historic Nickerson Inn) 616/869-6731.* Hrs: 6-9:30 pm; Sun 8 am-1 pm, 6-9:30 pm. Closed Dec 25. Res accepted. Eclectic menu. Serv bar. Semi-a la carte: bkfst $3.95-$8.95, lunch $6.95-$13.95, dinner $10.95-$27.95. Specializes rack of lamb, seafood. Outdoor dining. Overlooks Lake Michigan. Totally nonsmoking. Cr cds: MC, V.

D

★★ **SCOTTY'S.** *5910 E Ludington Ave (US 10). 616/843-4033.* Hrs: 11:30 am-2 pm, 5-10 pm; Sat from 5 pm; Sun 9 am-1 pm. Closed Thanksgiving, Dec 25. Res accepted. Bar. Semi-a la carte: lunch $3.50-$7.95, dinner $8.50-$18.95. Child's meals. Specializes in prime rib, steak, seafood. Family-owned. Cr cds: A, MC, V.

D ⌧

Mackinac Island (D-4)

(See also Mackinaw City, St Ignace)

Pop 469 **Elev** 600-925 ft **Area code** 906 **Zip** 49757 **Web** www.mackinac.com
Information Chamber of Commerce, PO Box 451; 906/847-3783 or 800/4-LILACS.

(By ferry from St Ignace and Mackinaw City. By air from Pellston, Detroit and St Ignace.)

Labeled the "Bermuda of the North," Mackinac (MAK-i-naw) Island retains the atmosphere of the 19th century and the imprint of history. In view of the Mackinac Bridge, it has been a famous resort for the last century. The island was called "great turtle" by Native Americans who believed that its towering heights and rock formations were shaped by supernatural forces. Later, because of its strategic position, the island became the key to the struggle between England and France for control of the rich fur trade of the great Northwest. Held by the French until 1760, it became English after Wolfe's victory at Québec, was turned over to the United States at the close of the American Revolution, reverted to the British during the War of 1812 and finally was restored to the US.

With the decline of the fur trade in the 1830s, Mackinac Island began to develop its potential as a resort area. Southern planters and their families summered here prior to the Civil War; wealthy Chicagoans took their place in the years following. No automobiles are allowed on the island; transportation is by horse and carriage or bicycle. Horse and carriages and bicycles can be rented. Passenger ferries make regularly scheduled trips to the island from Mackinaw City and St Ignace, or visitors can reach the island by air from St Ignace, Pellston or Detroit.

What to See and Do

Ferry services.

Shepler's Mackinac Island Ferry. Departs 556 E Central Ave, Mackinaw City or from downtown, St Ignace. (Early May-early Nov) Phone 616/436-5023. Round trip ¢¢¢¢

Arnold Transit Co. Fifteen-min trip from St Ignace or Mackinaw City. (May-Dec, daily) Phone 906/847-3351. ¢¢¢¢¢

Star Line Ferry. "Hydro Jet" service from Mackinaw City and St Ignace. (May-Oct) Phone 800/638-9892. ¢¢¢¢

Mackinac Island Carriage Tours, Inc. Narrated, historic and scenic horse-drawn carriage tour (1³⁄₄ hrs) covering 20 sights. (Mid-May-mid-Oct, daily; some tours avail rest of yr) Main St. Phone 906/847-3307. ¢¢¢¢

✪ **Mackinac Island State Park.** Comprises approx 80 percent of the island. Michigan's first state park has views of the Straits of Mackinac, prehistoric geological formations, including Arch Rock, shoreline and in-land trails. Visitor center at Huron St has informative exhibits, slide presentation and guidebooks (mid-May-mid-Oct, daily). British Landing Nature Center (May-Labor Day). (Daily) Phone 906/847-3328.   **Free.**   Here is

Fort Mackinac (1780-1895). High on a bluff overlooking the Straits of Mackinac, this 18th-19th-century British and American military outpost is complete with massive limestone ramparts, cannon, guardhouse, blockhouses, barracks; 14 buildings restored; costumed interpreters, re-enactments, children's discovery room, crafts demonstrations; rifle and cannon firings; audiovisual presentation. (Mid-May-mid-Oct, daily) ¢¢¢   Included in admission are

Indian Dormitory (1838). Built as a place for Native Americans to live during annual visits to the Mackinac Island office of the US Indian Agency; interpretive displays, craft demonstrations; murals depicting scenes from Longfellow's "Hiawatha." (Mid-June-Labor Day, daily)

Benjamin Blacksmith Shop. A working forge in replica of blacksmith shop dating from 1880s. (Mid-June-Labor Day, daily) Market St.

Beaumont Memorial. Monument to Dr. William Beaumont, who charted observations of the human digestive system by viewing this action through an opening in the abdomen of a wounded French-Canadian. (Mid-June-Labor Day, daily)

Other places of interest included in the admission price are Mission Church (1830), Biddle House (1780) and McGulpin House.

Marquette Park. Statue of Father Marquette, historic marker and 66 varieties of lilacs dominate this park. Main St.

Annual Events

Lilac Festival. 2nd wk June.

Sailing races. Port Huron-to-Mackinac and Chicago-to-Mackinac. Mid- & late July.

Hotels

★ ★ ★ **ISLAND HOUSE.** *Main St.* 906/847-3347; FAX 906/847-3819; res: 800/626-6304. 97 rms, 42 A/C, 4 story. Mid-June-Labor Day: S, D $117-$160; each addl $20; suites $400; under 13 free; MAP avail; lower rates after Labor Day-mid-Oct, mid-May-mid-June. Closed rest of yr. Crib free. Indoor pool; whirlpool, steam rm. Restaurant (see GOVNOR'S DINING ROOM). No rm serv. Bar noon-2 am; entertainment exc Mon. Ck-out 11 am. Meeting rms. Business servs avail. Airport transportation. Tennis privileges. Golf privileges. One of first summer hotels on island (1852); Victorian architecture. Lake opp. Cr cds: MC, V.

⛷🏌🏊🎿🔥

★ ★ ★ **LAKE VIEW.** *Huron St, opp ferry docks.* 906/847-3384; FAX 906/847-6283. 85 rms, some A/C, 4 story. May-Oct: S $129-$255; D $159-$275; each addl $15; under 16 free. Closed rest of yr. Crib free. Indoor pool; whirlpool, sauna. Restaurant 7:30 am-10 pm, off season to 8 pm. Ck-out 11 am. Meeting rms. Business servs avail. Lake opp. Cr cds: DS, MC, V.

D 🏊🎿🐾

★ ★ ★ **LILAC TREE.** *Main St.* 906/847-6575; FAX 906/847-3501. 39 suites, 3 story. July-Aug: S, D $175-$250; family, hol rates; lower rates May-June, Sept-Oct. Closed rest of yr. Crib free. TV; cable (premium). Complimentary coffee in rms. Restaurant 11 am-2 pm. No rm serv. Ck-out 11 am. In-rm modem link. Shopping arcade. Refrigerators. Balconies. Each suite uniquely decorated; antique and reproduction furnishings. Cr cds: A, DS, MC, V.

D 🐾

Inns

★ ★ **BAY VIEW AT MACKINAC.** *100 Huron St, 100 Huron St.* 906/847-3295; FAX 906/847-6219. 20 air-cooled rms, 10 with shower only, 3 story. No rm phones. Mid-June-mid-Sept: S, D $95-$285; wkly rates; wkends (2-day min); lower rates May-mid-June, mid-Sept-Oct. Closed rest of yr. Adults only. TV; VCR in suites. Complimentary continental bkfst. Restaurant opp 7 am-10 pm. Ck-out 11 am, ck-in 3 pm. Some balconies. Built 1891 in Grand Victorian style; on bay. Totally nonsmoking. Cr cds: MC, V.

D 🐾🎿🐾

★ ★ ★ **IROQUOIS ON THE BEACH.** *Main St, downtown.* 906/847-3321. 47 rms, 3 story. No A/C. Mid-June-mid-Sept: S, D $115-$268; each addl $15; suites $345; spring, fall packages; lower rates mid-May-mid-June, mid-Sept-late Oct. Closed rest of yr. TV in some rms, sitting rm. Continental bkfst 7-11:30 am. Restaurant (see CARRIAGE HOUSE). Rm serv. Ck-out noon, ck-in 3 pm. Business servs avail. Luggage handling. Valet serv. 18-hole golf privileges. Overlooks water, private beach. Cr cds: DS, MC, V.

🏌🐾

Resorts

★ ★ ★ **GRAND HOTEL.** *6 blks from dock.* 906/847-3331. 286 rms, 6 story. Mid-May-Oct, MAP: S $275; D $240-$500; each addl $75. Serv charge 18%. Closed rest of yr. Crib avail. Heated pool; whirlpool, sauna, lifeguard. Restaurant 8 am-8:45 pm. Afternoon tea. Rm serv. Box lunches. Bar to 2 am. Ck-out noon, ck-in 3 pm. Convention facilities. Valet serv. Tennis, pro. 18-hole golf, greens fee $25, putting green. Bicycles. Exercise trail. Lawn games. Rec rm. Entertainment. Some balconies. Large veranda overlooks Straits of Mackinac, formal gardens. On 500 acres; 2,000-acre state park adj. Cr cds: A, DS, MC, V.

D 🐾🏌🏊🎿🐾

★ ★ ★ **MISSION POINT.** *¹⁄₂ mi E.* 906/847-3312; FAX 906/847-3833; res: 800/833-7711. 236 air-cooled rms, 2-3 story, 90 suites. Late June-early Sept: S, D $160-$300; each addl $20; suites $210-$695; under 18 free; MAP avail; higher rates: July 4, yacht races (3-day min); lower rates mid-May-late June, early Sept-mid-Oct. Closed rest of yr. Crib free. TV; cable (premium), VCR avail. Heated pool; whirlpool, poolside serv. Supervised child's activities; ages 4-12. Dining rm 7 am-11 pm. Rm serv. Snack bar. Box lunches. Picnics. Bar 11-2 am. Ck-out 11 am, ck-in 3 pm. Grocery, coin lndry, package store ¹⁄₂ mi. Meeting rms. Business center. Concierge. Gift shop. Tennis. Golf privileges. Sunset cruises Sat evenings (in season). Bicycle rentals. Lawn games. Soc dir. Movies nightly. Game rm. Exercise equipt; weight machines, bicycles, sauna. 18 acres on lakefront. Cr cds: A, DS, MC, V.

D 🏌🏊🎿🐾🐾 SC 🐾

Restaurants

★ ★ **CARRIAGE HOUSE.** *(See Iroquois On The Beach Inn)* 906/847-3321. Hrs: 11:30 am-10 pm; in season from 8 am. Closed mid-Oct-Memorial Day. Res accepted. No A/C. Bar. A la carte entrees: bkfst from $6.95. Semi-a la carte: lunch $7.50-$13.75, dinner $17.75-$28.25. Child's meals. Specializes in whitefish, prime rib, veal. Outdoor dining. Overlooks water. Family-owned. Cr cds: DS, MC, V.

★ ★ **GOVNOR'S DINING ROOM.** *(See Island House Hotel)* 906/847-3347. Hrs: 7:30-10:30 am, 5:30-10 pm. Closed mid-Oct-mid-May. Bar noon-2 am. Buffet: bkfst $12.95. Semi-a la carte: dinner $12.95-$26.95. Specializes in prime rib, pasta. Entertainment exc Mon. In Mackinac Island's oldest hotel (1852). Cr cds: MC, V.

D ♥

Mackinaw City (D-4)

(See also Cheboygan, Mackinac Island, St Ignace)

Settled 1681 **Pop** 875 **Elev** 590 ft **Area code** 616 **Zip** 49701 **E-mail** BJones@freeway.net **Web** www.mackinawcity.com

Information Greater Mackinaw Area Chamber of Commerce, 706 S Huron, PO Box 856, phone 616/436-5574; or the Mackinaw Area Tourist Bureau, phone 800/666-0160.

The only place in America where one can see the sun rise on one Great Lake (Huron) and set on another (Michigan), Mackinaw City sits in the shadow of the Mackinac Bridge. The French trading post built here became Fort Michilimackinac about 1715. It was taken over by the British in 1761 and two years later was captured by Native Americans. The British reoccupied the fort in 1764. The fort was rebuilt on Mackinac Island (see) during 1780-1781.

What to See and Do

⭐ **Colonial Michilimackinac.** Reconstructed French and British outpost and fur-trading village of 1715-1781; costumed interpreters provide music and military demonstrations, pioneer cooking and crafts, children's program and re-enactments of French colonial wedding and arrival of the Voyageurs. Working artisans, musket and cannon firing (mid-June-Labor Day, daily). Murals, dioramas in restored barracks (mid-May-mid-Oct, daily). Re-created Native American encampment (mid-June-Labor Day). Archaeoligical tunnel "Treasures from the Sand"; Visitors can view the longest ongoing archaeological dig in US (mid-June-Labor Day, daily). Visitor Center, audiovisual presentation. At S end of Mackinac Bridge. Phone 616/436-5563. ¢¢¢

Mill Creek. Scenic 625-acre park features working water-powered sawmill (1790); nature trails, forest demonstration areas, maple sugar shack, active beaver colony, picnicking. Sawmill demonstrations; archaeological excavations (mid-June-Labor Day, Mon-Fri). Visitor Center, audiovisual presentation. (Mid-May-mid-Oct, daily) 3 mi SE via US 23. Phone 616/436-7301. ¢¢

Mackinac Bridge. This imposing structure has reduced crossing time to the Upper Peninsula over the Straits of Mackinac to 10 min. Connecting Michigan's upper and lower peninsulas between St Ignace (see) and Mackinaw City, the 8,344-ft distance between cable anchorages makes it one of the world's longest suspension bridges. (Total length of steel superstructure: 19,243 ft; height above water at midspan: 199 ft; clearance for ships: 155 ft) Fine view from the bridge. Auto toll ¢

Mackinac Island ferries.

Shepler's Mackinac Island Ferry. (Early May-early Nov) Phone 616/436-5023. ¢¢¢¢

Arnold Transit Company. (May-Dec, daily) Phone 906/847-3351. ¢¢¢¢

Star Line Ferry. "Hydro-Jet" (May-Oct) Phone 616/436-5045. ¢¢¢¢

Wilderness State Park. Approx 8,200 acres. Beaches, waterskiing; fishing; boating (launch); hunting in season; snowmobiling, cross-country skiing; picnic areas, playgrounds. Trailside cabins, camping. Standard fees. 11 mi W of I-75, on Lake Michigan and Straits of Mackinac. Phone 616/436-5381. Per car ¢¢

Annual Events

Colonial Michilimackinac Pageant. Pageant and re-enactment of Chief Pontiac's capture of the frontier fort in 1763; parade, muzzle-loading contests. 3 days Memorial Day wkend.

Women's Club Antique Show. 1st Tues Aug.

Mackinac Bridge Walk. Recreational walk for all across Mackinac Bridge (some lanes open to motor vehicles). Labor Day morning.

Seasonal Event

Vesper Cruises. Arnold's Line Dock. Phone 616/436-5622. Sun evening. July-Sept.

Motels

⭐ **BEACHCOMBER.** *1011 S Huron Ave (US 23).* 616/436-8451. 22 rms. July-early Aug: S, D $65-$115; each addl $3; cottage $550/wk; higher rates: July 4, antique car show, Labor Day wkend (2-day min); lower rates mid-Apr-June, early Sept-Oct. Closed rest of yr. Crib free. Pet accepted, some restrictions. TV; cable (premium). Restaurant nearby. Ck-out 10 am. Refrigerators avail. Picnic tables. On lake; private beach. Cr cds: A, DS, MC, V.

D ⮐ ⮐ 🏊 🐾 SC

⭐⭐ **BEST WESTERN.** *112 Old US 31.* 616/436-5544; FAX 616/436-7180. 73 rms, 2 story. Late June-early Sept: S $46-$89; D $52-$95; each addl $5; higher rates: Labor Day wkend (2-day min), special events; lower rates mid-Apr-late June, early Sept-Oct. Closed rest of yr. Crib $4. TV; cable (premium), VCR avail. Indoor pool; whirlpool. Complimentary contintental bkfst. Restaurant nearby. Ck-out 11 am. Coin lndry. In-rm modem link. Refrigerators; some in-rm whirlpools. Cr cds: A, C, D, DS, MC, V.

🏊 🏊 🐾 SC

⭐ **CHEROKEE SHORES.** *925 S Huron Ave.* 616/436-8621; res: 800/748-0124. 24 rms, 1-2 story, 9 cottages. July-late Aug: S $38-$60; D $40-$79; each addl $3-$5; higher rates: auto shows, hol wkends, Labor Day wkend (3-day min), special events; lower rates May-June, late Aug-Oct. Closed rest of yr. Crib $3. TV; cable (premium). Indoor pool privileges. Playground. Complimentary coffee in lobby. Restaurant opp 7 am-11 pm. Ck-out 10:30 am. Business servs avail. Lawn games. Some refrigerators. Picnic area, grill. Beach. Cr cds: DS, MC, V.

⮐

⭐⭐ **CHIPPEWA MOTOR LODGE.** *929 S Huron Ave (US 23).* 616/436-8661; res: 800/748-0124. 39 rms, 1-3 story. July-late Aug: S, D $49-$85; each addl $3-$5; under 12 free; higher rates: wkends, auto shows, Labor Day wkend (3-day min), special events; lower rates May-June, late Aug-Oct. Closed rest of yr. Crib $4. TV; cable (premium). Indoor pool; whirlpool. Playground. Complimentary coffee. Restaurant opp 7 am-10 pm. Ck-out 10:30 am. Business servs avail. Lawn games. Game rm. Picnic tables, grill. Patio; sun deck. Landscaped grounds. Private beach on Lake Huron. Cr cds: DS, MC, V.

D ⮐ 🏊 🏊 🐾

⭐⭐ **COMFORT INN.** *611 S Huron Ave (US 23).* 616/436-5057. 60 rms, 3 story. No elvtr. Late June-early Sept: S, D $88-$130; each addl $6; under 18 free; higher rates: Labor Day wkend, antique auto show (3-day min); lower rates May-late June, early Sept-Oct. Closed rest of yr. Crib $6. TV; cable (premium). Indoor pool; whirlpool. Restaurant nearby. Ck-out 10 am. Refrigerators. Balconies. On lake, beach. Cr cds: A, C, D, DS, ER, JCB, MC, V.

D 🏊 🏊 🐾 SC

⭐⭐ **DAYS INN.** *825 S Huron Ave (US 23).* 616/436-5557; FAX 616/436-5703. 84 rms, 2 story. Late June-early Sept: S $64-$144; D $68-$148; each addl $6; under 12 free; higher rates: summer hols, antique car show, special events; 2-day min Labor Day, antique car show; lower rates Apr-late June & early Sept-Oct. Closed rest of yr. TV; cable, VCR avail. Indoor pool; whirlpool, sauna. Playground. Complimentary coffee. Restaurant 7 am-9 pm. Rm serv. Ck-out 11 am. Coin lndry. Meeting rm. Putting green. Game rm. Lawn games. Refrigerators avail. Balconies. Picnic table. On lake; ferry terminal adj. Cr cds: A, C, D, DS, JCB, MC, V.

D 🏊 🏊 🐾 SC

⭐ **HOLIDAY INN EXPRESS.** *364 Louvingney St.* 616/436-7100; FAX 616/436-7070. 71 rms, 3 story. Mid-June-early Sept: S $75-$145; D $81-$145; each addl $6; family rates; higher rates special events; lower rates rest of yr. Crib free. TV; cable (premium), VCR (movies). Indoor pool; whirlpool. Complimentary continental bkfst. Restaurant opp 8 am-10 pm. Ck-out 11 am. Coin lndry. Business servs avail. X-country ski 7 mi. Exercise equipt; weight machine, bicycles, sauna. Game rm. Some refrigerators. Balconies. Lake, swimming beach 3 blks. Cr cds: A, C, D, DS, JCB, MC, V.

[D] [≈] [≋] [🏃] [⛷] [🔥] [SC]

★ **HOWARD JOHNSON.** *150 Old US 31.* 616/436-5733. 46 rms, 1-2 story. Late June-Aug: S $75; D $98; each addl $5; family rates; higher rates July 4; higher rates and 2-day min Labor Day, Antique Car Show; lower rates Sept-Oct & May-late June. Closed rest of yr. Crib free. TV; cable (premium). 2 pools, 1 indoor; whirlpool. Playground. Complimentary coffee in lobby. Restaurant nearby. Ck-out 11 am. Cr cds: A, C, D, DS, JCB, MC, V.

[D] [≈] [≋] [🔥] [SC]

★ **KEWADIN.** *619 S Nicolet St (MI 108).* 616/436-5332. 76 rms, 2 story. Mid-June-early Sept: S $64.50-$84.50; D $69.50-$84.50; each addl $5; family rates; higher rates special events; lower rates May-mid-June, early Sept-mid-Oct. Closed rest of yr. Crib free. Pet accepted. TV; cable. Heated pool. Playground. Restaurant nearby. Ck-out 11 am. Refrigerators. Cr cds: A, C, D, DS, MC, V.

[⛷] [≈] [≋] [🔥] [SC]

★ ★ **LA MIRAGÉ.** *699 N Huron Ave.* 616/436-5304. 25 rms, 2 story. July-early Sept: S, D $45-$95; each addl $5; family, wkly rates; higher rates: antique auto show, hol wkends, special events (2-day min); lower rates May-June, early Sept-Oct. Closed rest of yr. Crib $4. Pet accepted, some restrictions. TV; cable. Indoor pool; whirlpool, sauna. Restaurant nearby. Ck-out 11 am. Some in-rm whirlpools, saunas, refrigerators. Beach opp. Cr cds: A, D, DS, MC, V.

[D] [⛷] [≈] [≋] [🔥]

✔★ ★ **MOTEL 6.** *206 Nicolet St.* 616/436-8961; FAX 616/436-7317; res: 800/388-9508. 53 rms, 2 story. Mid-June-Labor Day: S, D $38.95-$88.95; each addl $6; higher rates: hol wkends, special events; Labor Day wkend (2-day min); lower rates rest of yr. Crib free. Pet accepted; $3. TV; cable (premium). Indoor pool; whirlpool. Restaurant adj 7 am-10 pm. Ck-out 11 am. X-country ski on site. Some refrigerators. Cr cds: A, C, D, DS, MC, V.

[D] [⛷] [≈] [≋] [🔥]

★ ★ **PARKSIDE INN-BRIDGESIDE.** *102 Nicolet St.* 616/436-8301; res: 800/827-8301. 44 rms, 1-2 story. Late June-early Sept: S, D $48-$88; family rates; higher rates: antique auto show, hol wkends; lower rates May-late June, early Sept-late Oct. Closed rest of yr. Crib $3. Pet accepted, some restrictions. TV; cable (premium). Indoor pool; whirlpool. Restaurant adj 6 am-10 pm. Ck-out 10 am. Game rm. Refrigerators avail. Picnic tables, sun deck. Some rms overlook lake, bridge. Colonial Michilimackinac State Park opp. Cr cds: A, DS, MC, V.

[D] [⛷] [≈] [≋] [🔥] [SC]

★ ★ **QUALITY INN.** *917 S Huron Ave (US 23).* 616/436-5051; FAX 616/436-7221. 60 rms, 1-2 story. Late June-early Sept: S $65.50; D $85-$109.50; each addl $5; family rates; higher rates: hol wkends, antique auto show, Labor Day wkend (2-day min); lower rates mid-Apr-late June, early Sept-Oct. Closed rest of yr. Pet accepted, some restrictions. TV; cable (premium), VCR avail. Indoor pool; whirlpool, sauna. Playground. Restaurant nearby. Ck-out 10 am. Business servs avail. Lawn games. Many refrigerators. Many balconies. Picnic area, grills. Private beach on Lake Huron. Near ferry dock. Cr cds: A, C, D, DS, ER, JCB, MC, V.

[D] [⛷] [▱] [≈] [≋] [🔥] [SC]

★ ★ **RAMADA LIMITED-WATERFRONT.** *723 S Huron Ave (US 23).* 616/436-5055; FAX 616/436-5921. 42 rms, 3 story. Late June-early Sept: S, D $79-$129; each addl $5; suites $150; Labor Day wkend (3-day min), special events (2-day min); lower rates mid-Apr-late June, early Sept-Oct. Closed rest of yr. Crib free. TV; cable (premium), VCR avail. Indoor pool; whirlpools. Complimentary continental bkfst. Restaurant

opp 7 am-10:30 pm. Ck-out 11 am. Business servs avail. Refrigerators. Balconies. On beach. Cr cds: A, C, D, DS, JCB, MC, V.

[D] [▱] [≈] [≋] [🔥]

★ **STARLITE BUDGET INNS.** *116 Old US 31.* 616/436-5959; FAX 616/436-5101; res: 800/288-8190. 33 rms. Mid-July-late Aug: S $49-$59; D $52-$60; family, wkly rates; higher rates: July 4, Labor Day, auto show; lower rates May-mid-July & late Aug-Oct. Closed rest of yr. Crib free. Pet accepted, some restrictions; $5. TV; cable (premium). Heated pool. Playground. Complimentary coffee in rms. Restaurant nearby. Ck-out 10 am. Refrigerators. Cr cds: A, D, DS, MC, V.

[D] [⛷] [≈] [≋] [🔥] [SC]

★ **SUPER 8.** *601 N Huron Ave.* 616/436-5252; FAX 616/436-7004. 50 rms, 2 story. July-mid-Oct: S $74-$135; D $79-$145; each addl $6; higher rates special events (2-day min); lower rates rest of yr. Crib $6. Pet accepted, some restrictions. TV; cable, VCR avail. Indoor pool; whirlpool, sauna. Complimentary coffee in lobby. Restaurant nearby. Ck-out 11 am. Coin lndry. Game rm. Refrigerators avail. Some balconies. Cr cds: A, C, D, DS, MC, V.

[D] [⛷] [≈] [≋] [🔥] [SC]

★ ★ **SURF.** *907 S Huron Ave (US 23).* 616/436-8831; res: 800/822-8314. 40 rms, 1-2 story. Late June-early Sept: S, D $65-$95; each addl $5; family, wkly rates off-season; lower rates May-late June, early Sept-Oct. Closed rest of yr. Crib $5. Pet accepted, some restrictions; $5-$10. TV; cable (premium). Indoor pool; whirlpool. Playground. Complimentary coffee. Restaurant nearby. Ck-out 11 am. Business servs avail. Lawn games. Refrigerators. Balconies, patios. Grills. Private sand beach; overlooks Lake Huron. Cr cds: A, DS, MC, V.

[D] [⛷] [▱] [≈] [≋] [🔥] [SC]

✔★ ★ **WATERFRONT INN.** *1009 S Huron Ave (US 23).* 616/436-5527; res: 800/962-9832. 69 rms. July-early Sept: S $63-$71.95; D $49-$96.95; each addl $5; kit. units (up to 6) $435/wk; higher rates: Labor Day wkend, antique auto show (3-day min); lower rates rest of yr. Pet accepted, some restrictions. TV; cable (premium). Pool; whirlpool. Playground. Coffee in rms. Restaurant nearby. Ck-out 11 am. Picnic table. Private beach on Lake Huron. Cr cds: A, DS, MC, V.

[D] [⛷] [▱] [≈] [≋] [🔥] [SC]

Motor Hotel

★ ★ **RAMADA.** *450 S Nicolet (MI 108).* 616/436-5535; FAX 616/436-5489. 162 rms, 3 story. Mid-June-early Sept: S $60.50-$92.50; D $66.50-$92.50; each addl $8; under 18 free; lower rates rest of yr. Crib free. TV; cable (premium), VCR avail. Indoor pool; whirlpool, sauna. Complimentary coffee. Restaurant 6:30 am-11 pm; off season to 9 pm. Rm serv. Bar 3 pm-2 am. Ck-out 11 am. Coin lndry. Meeting rms. X-country ski 5 mi. Game rm. Refrigerators; some in-rm whirlpools. Cr cds: A, C, D, DS, MC, V.

[D] [≈] [≈] [≋] [🔥] [SC]

Restaurants

★ ★ **'NEATH THE BIRCHES.** *Old US 31, 1 mi S on Old US 31.* 616/436-5401. Hrs: 4-10 pm; early-bird dinner 4-6 pm. Closed late Oct-mid-May. Res accepted. Bar. Semi-a la carte: dinner $8.95-$32.95. Child's meals. Specializes in prime rib, whitefish. Salad bar. Family-owned. Cr cds: A, C, D, DS, MC, V.

★ ★ **DAM SITE INN.** *(Pellston 49769) 18 mi S via US 31, then 1 blk E.* 616/539-8851. Hrs: 5-10 pm; Sun 3-9 pm; late Apr-May, Sept-late Oct to 9 pm; Sun to 8 pm. Closed late Oct-late Apr; also Mon Sept-June. No A/C. Bar. Semi-a la carte: dinner $9.50-$24.75. Specializes in own noodles, buttermilk biscuits, whitefish. Family-style chicken dinner. Open kitchen. Fireplace. Overlooks dam. Cr cds: MC, V.

[D]

✔★ **EMBERS.** *810 S Huron Ave (US 23), opp Arnold Dock. 616/436-5773.* Hrs: 7 am-10 pm. Closed mid-Nov-early Apr. Bar 8-1 am. Semi-a la carte: bkfst $1.95-$6.50, lunch $3.95-$6.95, dinner $6.95-$16.99. Buffet: bkfst $4.49, lunch $4.99, dinner $8.99. Specializes in fresh whitefish, soups, bread pudding. Cr cds: DS, MC, V.

SC

★ **PANCAKE CHEF.** *325 Central Ave. 616/436-5578.* Hrs: 7 am-10 pm; off-season to 9 pm. Semi-a la carte: bkfst $2.95-$6.25, lunch $3.50-$6.50, dinner $7.95-$12.95. Buffet: bkfst $5.95, dinner $8.95. Specializes in variety of pancakes, steak, fish. Salad bar. Cr cds: D, DS, MC, V.

D

Unrated Dining Spot

THE FORT. *400 N Louvingny, opp Colonial Michilimackinac. 616/436-5453.* Hrs: 7:30 am-10 pm; Apr-May & Sept-Oct from 8 am. Closed Nov-Mar. Bar. Buffet: bkfst $3.99, lunch $5.49, dinner $7.99. Child's meals. Specializes in fish, baked chicken & ham, smorgasbord meals. Salad bar. Cr cds: DS, MC, V.

Mancelona

(see Bellaire)

Manistee (F-3)

(See also Ludington)

Pop 6,734 **Elev** 600 ft **Area code** 616 **Zip** 49660 **Web** www.manistee.com:80/~edo/chamber/

Information Manistee Area Chamber of Commerce, 11 Cypress St; 616/723-2575 or 800/288-2286.

With Lake Michigan on the west and the Manistee National Forest on the east, this site was once the home of 1,000 Native Americans who called it Manistee—"spirit of the woods." In the mid-1800s this was a thriving lumber town, serving as headquarters for more than 100 companies. When the timber supply was exhausted, the early settlers found other sources of revenue. Manistee is rich in natural resources including salt, oil and natural gas. A Ranger District office of the Huron-Manistee National Forest is located in Manistee.

What to See and Do

Huron-Manistee National Forest. This 520,968-acre forest is the Manistee section of the Huron-Manistee National Forest (for Huron section see OSCODA). The forest includes the Lake Michigan Recreation Area, which contains trails and panoramic views of the sand dunes and offers beaches; fishing in lakes and in the Pine, Manistee, Little Manistee, White, Little Muskegon and Père Marquette rivers; hiking, bicycle and vehicle trails; hunting for deer and small game; camping, picnicking, boating; winter sports include downhill & cross-country skiing, snowmobiling, ice fishing & ice sailing. Fees charged at recreation sites. (Daily) E and S of town, via US 31 & MI 55. For further information contact Forest Supervisor, 412 Red Apple Rd; 800/821-6263. **Free.**

Manistee County Historical Museum. Fixtures and fittings of 1880 drugstore and early general store; Victorian period rms, historical photographs; Civil War, marine collections; antique dolls, costumes, housewares. (June-Sept, daily exc Sun; rest of yr, Tues-Sat; closed most hols) Russell Memorial Bldg, 425 River St. Phone 616/723-5531. ¢

Old Waterworks Building. Logging wheels, early lumbering, shipping and railroad exhibits; Victorian parlor, barbershop, shoe shop, kitchen. (Late June-Aug, Tues-Sat) W 1st St. Phone 616/723-5531. **Donation.**

Orchard Beach State Park. High on a bluff overlooking Lake Michigan; 201 acres. Swimming beach. Hiking. Picnicking, playground, stone pavilion. Camping. 2 mi N on MI 110. Contact Park Manager, 2064 Lakeshore Rd; 616/723-7422. Entrance/vehicle ¢¢

Ramsdell Theatre & Hall (1903). Constructed by T.J. Ramsdell, pioneer attorney, this opulant building is home to the Manistee Civic Players, who present professional and community productions throughout the yr; also art and museum exhibits. Tours (June-Aug, Wed & Sat; rest of yr, by appt). 101 Maple St at 1st. Phone 616/723-9948 or 616/723-7188. **Donation.**

Annual Events

Muzzle-loaders Shoot Time at Manistee. Old Fort Rendezvous. Traditional shooting events, costumed participants. Phone 616/723-9016. Late June.

National Forest Festival. Boat show; car show; US Forestry Service forest tours; parades, athletic events, raft and canoe races, Venetian boat parade, fireworks. Sponsored by the Chamber of Commerce; phone 616/723-2575. Wk of July 4.

Motels

✔★ ★ **BEST WESTERN.** *200 Arthur St (US 31), near Manistee-Blacker Airport. 616/723-9949; FAX 616/723-8807.* 72 rms, 2 story. Late May-Oct: S $48-$90; D $54-$100; each addl $6; lower rates rest of yr. Crib $6. TV; cable (premium). Indoor pool. Restaurant 6 am-10 pm. Bar 2 pm-2 am. Ck-out 11 am. Meeting rms. Business servs avail. Free airport transportation. X-country ski 3 mi. Exercise equipt; weight machine, bicycle. Game rm. Sun deck. Manistee Lake opp. Cr cds: A, C, D, DS, MC, V.

D ⊠ ≋ ✕ ✕ ⋈ ⋒ SC

★ ★ **DAYS INN.** *1462 S US 31. 616/723-8385; FAX 616/723-8385, ext. 112.* 90 rms, 2 story. July-Sept: S, D $75-$99; each addl $6; under 12 free; lower rates rest of yr. Crib free. TV; cable, VCR avail (movies). Indoor pool; whirlpool. Continental bkfst. Restaurant opp 5 am-midnight. Ck-out 11 am. Coin lndry. Meeting rms. Business servs avail. Sundries. Free airport transportation. X-country ski 3 mi. Game rm. Cr cds: A, D, DS, MC, V.

D ⊠ ≋ ⋈ ⋒ SC

★ **MANISTEE INN & MARINA.** *378 River St. 616/723-4000; FAX 616/723-0007; res: 800/968-6277.* 25 rms, 2 story. Mid-May-mid-Sept: S $47-$68; D $58-$73; each addl $8; whirlpool rms $72-$91; family, wkly rates; lower rates rest of yr. Crib free. TV; cable, VCR (movies $2). Complimentary continental bkfst. Restaurant nearby. Ck-out 11 am. Coin lndry. Meeting rm. Business servs avail. X-country ski 10 mi. Refrigerators avail; some wet bars. Cr cds: A, C, D, DS, MC, V.

D ⋐ ⊠ ⋈ ⋒ SC

Manistique (D-3)

Pop 3,456 **Elev** 600 ft **Area code** 906 **Zip** 49854
Information Schoolcraft County Chamber of Commerce, US 2, PO Box 72; 906/341-5010.

Manistique, the county seat of Schoolcraft County, has a bridge in town named "The Siphon Bridge" that is partially supported by the water that flows underneath it. The roadway is approximately four feet below the water level. Fishing for salmon is good in the area. A Ranger District office of the Hiawatha National Forest (see ESCANABA) is located here.

What to See and Do

State parks.

Indian Lake. Approx 550 acres. Swimming, sand beach, bathhouse, waterskiing; fishing for pike, perch, walleye, bass and bluegill; boating (rentals, launch); hiking. Picnicking. Camping. (Daily) 6 mi W on US 2, then 3 mi N on MI 149, 1/2 mi E on County Rd 442. Phone 906/341-2355. Entrance/vehicle ¢¢

Palms Book. Approx 300 acres. Here is Kitch-iti-ki-pi, the state's largest spring, 200 ft wide, 40 ft deep; 16,000 gallons of water per minute form a stream to Indian Lake. Observation raft for viewing the spring. Picnicking, concession. No camping allowed. Standard fees. Closed in winter. S on US 2 to Thompson, then 12 mi NW on MI 149. Phone 906/341-2355. Entrance/vehicle ¢¢

Fayette. Approx 700 acres. Fayette, formerly an industrial town producing charcoal iron (1867-1891), is now a ghost town; self-guided tour of restored remains; interpretive center (May-Oct). Swimming; fishing. Picnicking, playground. Camping. 15 mi W on US 2, then 17 mi S on MI 183 to Fayette on Big Bay de Noc. Phone 906/644-2603. Entrance/vehicle ¢¢

Thompson State Fish Hatchery. 7 mi SW via US 2, MI 149. For days open phone 906/341-5587. **Free.**

Motels

★ ★ **BEST WESTERN BREAKERS.** *East US 2 (Lake Shore), 2 mi E of Manistique on US 2. 906/341-2410; FAX 906/341-2207.* 40 rms. Mid-June-early Sept: S $65; D $70; each addl $5; studio rms $75-$85; under 13 free; lower rates rest of yr. Crib free. TV; cable (premium), VCR avail (movies). Indoor/outdoor pool; whirlpool. Restaurant 7 am-9 pm. Ck-out 11 am. Overlooks Lake Michigan. Private beach opp. Cr cds: A, C, D, DS, MC, V.

★ **BUDGET HOST.** *Rte 1 Box 1505, 3 1/2 mi E on US 2. 906/341-2552.* 26 rms, 13 A/C ($5 addl for A/C). Mid-June-Labor Day: S, D $40-$55; each addl $5; suites $65-$100; lower rates rest of yr. Crib $3. TV; cable (premium). Heated pool. Restaurant adj 5 am-11 pm; bar. Ck-out 11 am. Business servs avail. Free airport, bus depot transportation. X-country ski 5 mi. Lawn games. Cr cds: A, C, D, DS, ER, MC, V.

★ **ECONO LODGE.** *Box 184, 1 1/4 mi E on US 2. 906/341-6014.* 31 rms. July-Labor Day: S, D $58-$66; each addl $5; under 18 free; lower rates rest of yr. Pet accepted; $5. TV; cable (premium). Complimentary continental bkfst. Restaurant nearby. Ck-out 11 am. X-country ski 10 mi. Lake Michigan boardwalk opp. Cr cds: A, C, D, DS, JCB, MC, V.

✔★ **HOLIDAY.** *Rte 1, 4 mi E on US 2. 906/341-2710.* 20 rms. No A/C. June-Labor Day: D $46; lower rates rest of yr. Crib $5. Pet accepted. TV; cable (premium). Heated pool. Playground. Complimentary continental bkfst. Restaurant nearby. Ck-out 11 am. Lawn games. Picnic tables. Cr cds: A, DS, MC, V.

★ **NORTHSHORE MOTOR INN.** *1967 E Lakeshore Dr. 906/341-2420; res: 800/297-7107.* 12 rms. July-Aug: S, D $42-$60; each addl $4; under 12 free; lower rates rest of yr. Crib free. TV; cable (premium). Restaurant nearby. Ck-out 11 am. Downhill ski 1 1/2 mi; x-country ski 6 mi. Picnic tables. Opp lake, beach. Cr cds: A, C, D, DS, MC, V.

Inn

★ **CELIBETH HOUSE.** *(Blaney Park Rd (M-77), Blaney Park 49836) 22 mi E on US 2, then 1 mi N on MI 77. 906/283-3409.* 7 air-cooled rms, 3 story. No rm phones. S $45-$48; D $48-$53; each addl $10; suite $78; under 7 free. Closed Dec-Apr. Complimentary continental bkfst.

Restaurant nearby. Ck-out 11 am, ck-in 3 pm. X-country ski 11 mi. Picnic tables. Renovated house (1895) used as logging company's headquarters and then as part of resort. Antiques, sitting rm with fireplace. On 85 acres overlooking private lake. Totally nonsmoking. Cr cds: MC, V.

Marquette (C-2)

(See also Ishpeming)

Settled 1849 **Pop** 21,977 **Elev** 628 ft **Area code** 906 **Zip** 49855 **E-mail** mqtinfo@up.net **Web** www.marquette.org

Information Marquette Area Chamber of Commerce, 501 S Front St; 906/226-6591.

The largest city in the Upper Peninsula, Marquette is the regional center for retailing, government, medicine and iron ore shipping. Miles of public beaches and picnic areas flank the dock areas on Lake Superior. Rocks rise by the water and bedrock runs just a few feet below the surface. The city is named for the missionary-explorer Father Jacques Marquette, who made canoe trips along the shore here in 1669-71. At the rear flank of the city is sand-plain-blueberry country, as well as forests and mountains of granite and iron.

What to See and Do

Marquette County Historical Museum. Exhibits of regional historical interest; J.M. Longyear Research Library. (Mon-Fri; closed hols) 213 N Front St. Phone 906/226-3571. ¢

Marquette Mt Ski Area. Three double chairlifts, rope tow; patrol, school, rentals; snowmaking, night skiing, wkly NASTAR; cafeteria, bar; nursery. Longest run 1 1/4 mi; vertical drop 600 ft. (Late Nov-Mar, daily) Cross-country trails (3 mi) nearby. 3 mi SW on County 553. Phone 906/225-1155. ¢¢¢¢

Mt Marquette Scenic Outlook Area. Provides lovely view. (May-mid-Oct, daily) 1 mi S via US 41. **Free.**

Northern Michigan University (1899). (8,900 students) The 300-acre campus includes the Superior Dome, the world's largest wooden dome (spans 5.1 acres); Lee Hall Gallery; and a five-acre technology and applied sciences center. Olson Library has Tyler Collection on early-American literature. The school has been designated an Olympic Education Center. Tours avail. Presque Isle Ave. Phone 906/227-1700. For information on Olympic Education Center, phone 906/227-2888.

Presque Isle Park. Picnic facilities (4 picnic sites for the disabled), swimming, water slide (fees), boating (launch, fee), nature trails, cross-country skiing, tennis courts and playground. (May-Oct, daily; rest of yr, open only for winter sports) On the lake in NE part of city. Phone 906/228-0460. **Free.** Near the park is

Upper Harbor ore dock. Several million tons of ore are shipped annually from this site; the loading of ore freighters is a fascinating sight to watch. Adj parking lot for viewing and photography.

Statue of Father Marquette. On top of a bluff overlooking the site of the first settlement. Marquette Park.

Sugar Loaf Mt. A 3,200-ft trail leads to summit for panoramic view of Lake Superior coastline and forestland. 7 mi N on County 550.

Tourist Park. Swimming, fishing, playground; tent & trailer sites (mid-May-mid-Oct, daily; fee). Entrance fee charged during Hiawatha Music Festival (see ANNUAL EVENTS). On County 550. Phone 906/225-1555 (summer); 906/228-0460 (winter). **Free.**

Annual Events

Red Earth Loppet. 22- and 42-km cross-country ski race. Late Feb or early Mar.

International Food Festival. Ellwood Mattson Lower Harbor Park. Ethnic foods, crafts, music. July 4 wkend.

Hiawatha Music Festival. Tourist Park. Bluegrass, traditional music festival. 3rd wkend July.

Art on the Rocks. Presque Isle Park. Nationwide art display & sale. Last full wkend July.

Seafood Festival. Ellwood Mattson Lower Harbor Park. Wkend before Labor Day.

Motels

★ **CEDAR MOTOR INN.** 2523 US 41W. 906/228-2280. 44 rms, 1-2 story. Mid-June-mid-Oct: S, D $44-$56; each addl $3; lower rates rest of yr. Crib $5. TV; cable (premium). Indoor pool; whirlpool, sauna. Coffee in rms. Restaurant nearby. Ck-out 11 am. Meeting rm. Business servs avail. In-rm modem link. Downhill ski 5 mi; x-country ski 3 mi. Sun deck. Cr cds: A, D, DS, MC, V.

★ **DAYS INN.** 2403 US 41W. 906/225-1393; FAX 906/225-1393, ext. 177. 65 rms. July-Sept: S, D $55-$85; each addl $6; family rates; lower rates rest of yr. Crib free. TV; cable (premium). Indoor pool; whirlpool, sauna. Complimentary continental bkfst. Restaurant nearby. Ck-out 11 am. Downhill ski 5 mi; x-country ski 3 mi. Some refrigerators. Cr cds: A, C, D, DS, MC, V.

✔★ **IMPERIAL.** 2493 US 41W. 906/228-7430; FAX 906/228-3883; res: 800/424-9514. 43 rms, 2 story. June-Oct: S $38; D $44; each addl $3; lower rates rest of yr. Crib $5. TV; cable (premium). Indoor pool; sauna. Coffee in lobby. Restaurants nearby. Ck-out 11 am. Business servs avail. Downhill ski 5 mi; x-country ski 3 mi. Game rm. Cr cds: A, C, D, DS, MC, V.

★ ★ **TIROLER HOF.** 150 Carp River Hills (US 41S), MI 28. 906/226-7516; res: 800/892-9376. 44 rms, 36 A/C, 2 story. Mid-May-mid-Oct: S $42; D $50-$52; each addl $5; suites $68; studio rms $50-$52; lower rates rest of yr. Crib avail. TV; cable (premium). Playground. Restaurant (in season) 7:30-10 am, 5:30-9 pm. Ck-out 11 am. Coin lndry. Meeting rm. Downhill/x-country ski 1½ mi. Rec rm. Sauna. Private patios, balconies. Picnic tables, grills. On 13 acres; pond. Overlooks Lake Superior. Cr cds: A, DS, MC, V.

✔★ **VALUE HOST.** 1101 US 41W. 906/225-5000; FAX 906/225-5096. 52 rms, 2 story. May-Oct: S $34.45-$37.45; D $38.45-$48.50; each addl $5; family rates; lower rates rest of yr. Crib free. TV; cable (premium). Complimentary continental bkfst. Ck-out 11 am. Meeting rm. Business servs avail. Downhill/x-country ski 4 mi. Sauna. Whirlpool. Some refrigerators. Picnic tables. Cr cds: DS, MC, V.

Motor Hotels

★ ★ **HOLIDAY INN.** 1951 US 41W. 906/225-1351; FAX 906/228-4329. 203 rms, 5 story. S, D $75-$79; each addl $4; family; ski plans. Crib free. Pet accepted. TV; cable (premium). Indoor pool; whirlpool, sauna. Restaurant 6 am-2 pm, 5-10 pm. Rm serv. Bar 3 pm-2 am; Sun to midnight. Ck-out noon. Meeting rm. Business servs avail. Bellhops. Valet serv. Sundries. Free airport transportation. Downhill ski 7 mi; x-country ski 3 mi. Health club privileges. Nature trails. Picnic tables. Cr cds: A, C, D, DS, ER, JCB, MC, V.

★ ★ **RAMADA INN.** 412 W Washington St (US 41 Business). 906/228-6000; FAX 906/228-2963. 113 rms, 2-7 story. S $70-$120; D $80-$150; each addl $5; under 18 free. Crib free. Pet accepted. TV; cable (premium). Indoor pool; whirlpool, sauna. Restaurant 6 am-10 pm; Fri, Sat to 11 pm. Rm serv. Bar 11-2 am. Ck-out noon. Coin lndry. Meeting rms.

Business servs avail. Airport transportation. Downhill ski 5 mi; x-country ski ½ mi. Many poolside rms. Cr cds: A, C, D, DS, MC, V.

Restaurants

✔★ **ENTRE AMIGOS.** 142 W Washington, at town center. 906/228-4531. Hrs: 11 am-10:30 pm; in season to 11:30 pm; Sun brunch 10 am-2 pm. Res accepted. Mexican, Amer menu. Bar 4 pm-2 am; Sun to midnight. Semi-a la carte: lunch, dinner $3-$14. Sun brunch $7.95. Child's meals. Specializes in wet burrito, fajitas, grilled steaks. Cr cds: A, DS, MC, V.

★ ★ **NORTHWOODS SUPPER CLUB.** 260 Northwoods Rd. 906/228-4343. Hrs: 11 am-11 pm; Sun 10 am-10 pm; Sun brunch 10 am-2 pm. Closed Dec 24-26. Res accepted. Bar. Semi-a la carte: lunch $3.95-$7, dinner $9-$21. Buffet (dinner): Tues $10.95, Fri $14.95. Sun brunch $8.95. Child's meals. Specializes in steak, seafood, fresh Lake Superior fish. Salad bar. Own baking. Entertainment Fri-Sun; summer Wed-Sun. Rustic atmosphere; 5 fireplaces. Family-owned. Cr cds: A, DS, MC, V.

Marshall (J-4)

Founded 1830 **Pop** 6,891 **Elev** 916 ft **Area code** 616 **Zip** 49068
Information Chamber of Commerce, 109 E Michigan; 616/781-5163 or 800/877-5163.

Marshall was, at one time, slated to be Michigan's capital—a grand governor's mansion was built, land was set aside for the capitol and wealthy and influential people swarmed into the town. In 1847, Marshall lost its capital bid to Lansing. Today, many of the elaborate houses and buildings of the period remain, and more than 30 historical markers dot the city's streets.

What to See and Do

American Museum of Magic. Display of vintage magical equipment, rare posters, photographs and personal effects of some of the well-known magicians of history. (By appt) 107 E Michigan Ave. Phone 616/781-7674. ¢¢

Honolulu House Museum (1860). This exotic structure, blending traditional Italianate architecture with tropical motifs of island plantation houses, was built by first US Consul to the Sandwich Islands (now Hawaii); period furnishings, artifacts. Also headquarters of Marshall Historical Society, which provides free self-guided walking tour brochures listing town's many interesting 19th-century buildings and more than 30 historical markers. (May-Oct, daily; rest of yr, wkends) 107 N Kalamazoo Ave. Phone 616/781-8544 or 800/877-5163. ¢¢

Annual Events

Welcome to My Garden Tour. Tour of Marshall's most distinctive gardens. Phone 616/781-8547. 2nd wkend July.

Historic Home Tour. Informal tours of nine 19th-century homes, including Honolulu House (see), Governor's Mansion and Capitol Hill School. 1st wkend after Labor Day.

Inns

★ ★ **McCARTHY'S BEAR CREEK.** 15230 C Drive N. 616/781-8383. 14 rms, 2-3 story. No rm phones. S, D $65-$98; each addl $10. Crib free. Complimentary continental bkfst. Ck-out noon, ck-in 3 pm. X-country ski 12 mi. Some balconies. Picnic tables. Rms in renovated house and dairy barn (1948); country decor, antiques. On wooded knoll overlooking Bear Creek; handbuilt fieldstone fencing. Cr cds: A, MC, V.

★ ★ NATIONAL HOUSE. 102 S Parkview. 616/781-7374; FAX 616/781-4510. 16 rms, 2 story. S, D $69-$130; each addl $10; under 6 free. Closed Dec 24-25. Crib free. TV; cable (premium); VCR avail. Complimentary bkfst. Restaurant nearby. Ck-out noon, ck-in after 3 pm. Business servs avail. Airport transportation. X-country ski 10 mi. Oldest operating inn in state; authentically restored, antique furnishings. Established in 1835. Cr cds: A, MC, V.

Restaurant

★ ★ SCHULER'S OF MARSHALL. 115 S Eagle St. 616/781-0600. Hrs: 11 am-10 pm; Sat to 11 pm; Sun to 9 pm; Sun brunch 10 am-2 pm; hols to 9 pm. Closed Dec 25. Res accepted. Bar; wknds to midnight. Semi-a la carte: lunch $5.75-$8.95, dinner $12.95-$19.95. Sun brunch $11.95. Child's meals. Specializes in prime rib, rotisserie chicken, fresh fish. Own desserts. Menu changes seasonally. Patio dining. 3 dining rms with fireplaces. Bakery on premises. Family-owned. Cr cds: A, C, D, DS, MC, V.

Unrated Dining Spot

CORNWELL'S TURKEYVILLE. 18935 15½ Mile Rd, 4 mi N of I-94 on I-69N to exit 42, then ½ mi W. 616/781-4293. Hrs: 11 am-8 pm; Sun to 6 pm. Closed late Dec-mid-Jan. Avg ck: lunch, dinner $4-$9. Child's meals. Specializes in various turkey meals. Dinner theater. Outdoor dining. Family-owned. Cr cds: MC, V.

Menominee (E-2)

(For accommodations see Marinette, WI)

Settled 1796 **Pop** 9,398 **Elev** 600 ft **Area code** 906 **Zip** 49858
Information Menominee Area Chamber of Commerce, 1005 10th Ave, PO Box 427; 906/863-2679.

Because of water transportation and water power, many manufacturing industries have located in Menominee. Green Bay and the Menominee river form two sides of the triangle-shaped city. Across the river is the sister city of Marinette, Wisconsin (see). Established as a fur-trading post, later a lumbering center, Menominee County is the largest dairy producer in the state of Michigan. Menominee is a Native American word for "wild rice," which once grew profusely on the riverbanks.

What to See and Do

First St Historic District. Variety of specialty shops located in a setting of restored 19th-century buildings. Marina, parks, restaurants, galleries. From 10th Ave to 4th Ave.

Henes Park. Small zoo with deer yards, nature trails, bathing beach and picnic area. (Memorial Day-mid Oct, daily) Henes Park Dr, NE of city off MI 35. Phone 906/863-2656.   **Free.**

J.W. Wells State Park. Approx 700 acres, including 2 mi along Green Bay and 1,400 ft along Big Cedar River. Swimming, bathhouse, waterskiing; fishing; boating (ramp); hunting; snowmobiling, cross-country skiing; picnicking, playground; camping, cabins & shelters. Standard fees. 23 mi NE on MI 35, Cedar River. Phone 906/863-9747. Per vehicle   ¢¢

Menominee Marina. One of the best small-craft anchorages on the Great Lakes. Swimming beach; lifeguard. (May-Oct, daily) 1st St between 8th & 10th Aves. Phone 906/863-8498 or 906/863-5101.

Stephenson Island. Reached by bridge that also carries traffic between the sister cities on US 41 (see MARINETTE, WI). On island are picnic areas and an historical museum. In middle of Menominee River.

Annual Event

Waterfront Festival. Entertainment, music & dancing, footraces, fireworks, food, parade. 4 days, 1st wkend Aug.

Midland (G-5)

(See also Bay City, Mount Pleasant, Saginaw)

Pop 38,053 **Elev** 629 ft **Area code** 517 **E-mail** tourism@macc.org **Web** www.macc.org
Information Midland County Convention & Visitors Bureau, 300 Rodd St, Ste 101, 48640; 517/839-9901or 888/4-MIDLAND.

Midland owed its prosperity to the lumber industry until Herbert Henry Dow founded The Dow Chemical Company in 1897.

What to See and Do

Architectural Tour. Self-guided driving tour of buildings designed by Alden B. Dow, son of Herbert H. Dow. The younger Dow studied under Frank Lloyd Wright at Taliesin. He designed more than 45 buildings in Midland, including the architect's house and studio, churches, Stein House (his Taliesin apprentice project) and the Whitman House, for which he won the 1937 Grand Prix for residential architecture. Many buildings are privately owned and not open to the public. Maps and audio cassettes are available at the Midland Center for the Arts. Audio cassettes   ¢¢

Chippewa Nature Center. On 900 acres; 12 mi of marked and mowed trails; wildflower walkway and pond boardwalk; Homestead Farm; reconstructed 1870s log cabin, barn, sugarhouse, one-room schoolhouse; visitor center; museum depicting evolutionary natural history of the Saginaw Valley; auditorium; library; seasonal programs. (Daily; closed Thanksgiving, Dec 25) 400 S Badour Rd. Phone 517/631-0830.   **Free.**

★ **Dow Gardens.** Gardens, originally grounds of the residence of Herbert H. Dow, founder of The Dow Chemical Co, include 96 acres of trees, flowers, streams, waterfalls. (Daily; closed Jan 1, Thanksgiving, Dec 24 afternoon, Dec 25 & Dec 31 afternoon) Tours by appt. Entrance at Eastman Rd & W St Andrews. Phone 517/631-2677.   ¢¢

Herbert H. Dow Historical Museum. Composed of replicated Evans Flour Mill and adjacent buildings that housed Dow's Midland Chemical Company, predecessor to The Dow Chemical Company. Interpretive galleries include Joseph Dow's workshop, Herbert Dow's office, drillhouse with steam-powered brine pump, laboratory; audiovisual theater. (Wed-Sat, also Sun afternoons; closed hols) 3200 Cook Rd, 2 mi NW via W Main St. Phone 517/832-5319.   ¢¢

Midland Center for the Arts. Designed by Alden B. Dow. Houses Hall of Ideas, a museum of science, technology, health, history and art exhibits. Also concerts, plays. Architectural tour begins here. (Daily; closed major hols) 1801 W St Andrews. Phone 517/631-5930. Hall of Ideas   ¢¢

Annual Events

Maple Syrup Festival. Chippewa Nature Center. Mid-Mar.

Matrix: Midland Festival. Midland Center for the Arts. Celebration of the arts, sciences, humanities; classical & popular music, theater, dance; lectures by noted professionals. Phone 517/631-7557. Late May-mid-June.

Fall Festival. Chippewa Nature Center. 1st wkend Oct.

Motels

★ ★ ★ BEST WESTERN VALLEY PLAZA. 5221 Bay City Rd (48642). 517/496-2700; FAX 517/496-9233. 161 rms, 2 story. S $59-$69;

D $69-$79; suites $110-$155; under 18 free; higher rates wkends. Crib free. Pet accepted, some restrictions. TV; cable. Indoor pool; wading pool. Restaurant 6 am-10 pm; Sat from 7 am; Sun to noon. Rm serv. Bar noon-1 am. Ck-out noon. Meeting rms. In-rm modem link. Bellhops. Valet serv. Gift shop. Free airport transportation. Health club privileges. Game rm. Lawn games. Small lake with beach. Cr cds: A, C, D, DS, MC, V.

★★ **HOLIDAY INN.** *1500 W Wackerly St (48640). 517/631-4220; FAX 517/631-3776.* 236 rms, 2 story. S $74-$139; D $84-$147; each addl $10; under 18 free; wkend rates. Crib free. Pet accepted, some restrictions. TV; cable (premium). Indoor pool; whirlpool, poolside serv. Restaurant 6 am-3 pm, 5:30-10 pm. Rm serv. Bar 11:30-2 am; entertainment. Ck-out noon. Meeting rms. Business center. In-rm modem link. Bellhops. Valet serv. Sundries. Gift shop. Free airport transportation. Tennis privileges. X-country ski 2 mi. Exercise equipt; weights, bicycles, sauna. Game rm. Minibars. Cr cds: A, C, D, DS, JCB, MC, V.

★ **REST ALL INN.** *(4955 S Garfield Rd, Auburn 48611) E on US 10, at Garfield Rd. 517/662-7888; FAX 517/662-7607; res: 800/866-4322.* 61 rms, 3 story. S $39; D $47-$53; each addl $3; suite $68-$71; under 12 free; wkly rates. Crib free. TV; cable (premium). Complimentary coffee in lobby. Restaurant adj open 24 hrs. Ck-out 11 am. Coin lndry. Free airport transportation. Downhill ski 15 mi. Game rm. Some refrigerators. Cr cds: DS, MC, V.

Restaurant

★★★ **CAFE EDWARD.** *5010 Bay City Rd (48642). 517/496-3351.* Hrs: 5-9 pm. Closed Sun exc Mother's & Father's Day; Thanksgiving, Dec 25. Res accepted. Serv bar. Wine cellar. Complete meals: dinner $9-$20. Own baking, ice creams, sauces. Cr cds: A, MC, V.

Monroe (K-5)

(See also Detroit; also see Toledo, OH)

Settled 1780 **Pop** 22,902 **Elev** 599 ft **Area code** 734 **Zip** 48161
Information Monroe County Chamber of Commerce, PO Box 1094; 734/457-1030.

Originally called Frenchtown because of the many French families that settled here, this city on Lake Erie was renamed in 1817 in honor of President James Monroe. The river that flows through the center of the city was named the River Aux Raisin because of the many grapes growing in the area. At one time, Monroe was briefly the home of General George Armstrong Custer of "Little Bighorn" fame.

What to See and Do

Monroe County Historical Museum. Exhibits of General George Custer, Woodland Native Americans, pioneers, War of 1812; trading post, country store museum. (Summer, daily; rest of yr, Wed-Sun; closed Jan 1, Easter, Thanksgiving, Dec 25) 126 S Monroe St. Phone 734/243-7137. ¢
River Raisin Battlefield Visitor Center. Interprets fierce War of 1812 battle of River Raisin (Jan 1813). Nearly 1,000 US soldiers from Kentucky clashed with British, Native American and Canadian forces on this site; only 33 Americans escaped death or capture. Exhibits of weapons and uniforms, dioramas; fiber optic audiovisual map program. (Memorial Day-Labor Day, daily; rest of yr, wkends; closed some major hols) 1402 Elm Ave, just off I-75 at Elm Ave exit. Phone 734/243-7136 or 734/243-7137. **Free.**

Sterling State Park. 1,001 acres. Swimming, waterskiing; fishing, boating (ramp); hiking; picnicking, playground, concession; camping. Standard fees. N of city, off I-75. Phone 734/289-2715. Per car ¢¢

Annual Events

Monroe County Fair. Monroe County Fairgrounds, jct MI 50 & Raisinville Rd. Rides, concessions, merchant buildings. Phone 734/241-5775. Late July-early Aug.
Old French Town Days. An 18th-century festival; revolutionary battles, military and militia encampments, period music, Children's Corner, period crafts; also voyageurs and their canoes. Phone 734/243-7137. Last full wkend Aug.

Motel

★ **ECONO LODGE.** *1440 N Dixie Hwy (MI 50). 734/289-4000; FAX 734/289-4262.* 115 rms, 2 story. S $40-$51; D $54-$72; each addl $6; under 12 free. Crib free. Pet accepted. TV; cable (premium), VCR avail. Indoor pool; whirlpool, sauna. Restaurant 5 am-10 pm. Rm serv. Bar 11-2 am. Ck-out noon. Meeting rms. Business servs avail. In-rm modem link. Game rm. Private patios, balconies. Cr cds: A, D, DS, MC, V.

Motor Hotel

★ **HOLIDAY INN.** *1225 N Dixie Hwy (MI 50). 734/242-6000; FAX 734/242-0555.* 127 rms, 4 story. S $60; D $68; each addl $8; under 18 free; wkend rates off-season; golf plans. Crib free. Pet accepted. TV; cable (premium), VCR avail. Indoor pool; whirlpool, sauna, poolside serv. Restaurant 6 am-10 pm. Rm serv. Bar 11-2 am; Sun noon-midnight; entertainment exc Sun. Ck-out noon. Meeting rms. In-rm modem link. Bellhops. Valet serv. Sundries. Golf privileges. Game rm. Cr cds: A, C, D, DS, JCB, MC, V.

Mount Clemens (J-6)

Pop 18,405 **Elev** 614 ft **Area code** 810
Information Central Macomb County Chamber of Commerce, 58 S Gratiot, 48043; 810/463-1528.

What to See and Do

Art Center. Exhibits and classes, sponsors tours. Sales gallery, gift shop. Holiday Fair (Dec). (Mon-Fri, limited hrs Sat; closed July & Aug) 125 Macomb Place. Phone 810/469-8666. **Free.**
Crocker House (1869). This Italianate-style building, home of the Macomb County Historical Society, was originally owned by the first two mayors of Mount Clemens; period rooms, changing exhibits. (Mar-Dec, Tues-Thurs; also first Sun each month) 15 Union St. Phone 810/465-2488. ¢
Metro Beach Metropark. Park features 3/4-mi beach (late May-Sept, daily), pool (Memorial Day-Labor Day, daily; fee), bathhouse; boating, marinas, ramps, launch, dock (fee). 18-hole, par-3 golf course, miniature golf, shuffleboard, tennis, group rental activity center, playgrounds. Picnicking, concessions. Nature center. (Daily, hrs vary) No pets. Free admission Tues. 4 mi SE off I-94 on Lake St Clair, exit 236. Phone 810/463-4581. Motor vehicle entry permit ¢

Annual Events

Parade of Lights Water Fantasy. On Clinton River. Parade of decorated and lighted boats. 1st Sat Aug.
Farm City Festival. Late Aug.

Motel

★ ★ **COMFORT INN.** (11401 Hall Rd, Utica 48317) E on MI 59, at jct MI 59 & MI 53. 810/739-7111; FAX 810/739-1041. 104 rms, 3 story. S $59-$70; D $59-$80; each addl $5; under 16 free. Crib free. TV; cable (premium), VCR avail (movies). Complimentary continental bkfst. Restaurant nearby. Ck-out noon. Coin lndry. Business servs avail. In-rm modem link. Valet serv. Airport transportation. Downhill ski 10 mi; x-country ski 6 mi. Cr cds: A, C, D, DS, ER, JCB, MC, V.

D ⚡ ⛼ 🔥 SC

Mount Pleasant (G-4)

(See also Alma, Clare, Midland)

Pop 23,285 **Elev** 770 ft **Area code** 517 **Zip** 48858 **E-mail** visitor @mtpleasant.com **Web** www.mtpleasant.com
Information Convention & Visitors Bureau, 114 E Broadway; 800/772-4433.

What to See and Do

Central Michigan University (1892). (16,300 students) Phone 517/774-4000. Here are

Clarke Historical Library. Rare books, manuscripts; historical documents of Northwest Territory; children's library; changing exhibits. (School year, Mon-Fri, phone for hrs; closed hols) 4th floor of Park Library. Phone 517/774-3352. **Free.**

Center for Cultural & Natural History. Includes 45 exhibits and dioramas on anthropology, history and natural science. (Daily; closed hols) Rowe Hall. **Free.**

Soaring Eagle Casino. Includes 2,500-seat Bingo Hall, slot machines, blackjack, craps and roulette. Saginaw Chippewa Campground is nearby. (Daily) 2395 S Leaton Rd. Phone 888/7-EAGLE-7. **Free.**

Annual Events

Maple Syrup Festival. Approx 5 mi S via US 27, in Shepherd. Last wkend Apr.

Apple Fest. 1st wkend Oct.

Motels

★ ★ **COMFORT INN UNIVERSITY PARK.** 2424 S Mission St, adj to Central Michigan Univ. 517/772-4000; FAX 517/773-6052. 138 rms, 2 story, 12 suites. S, D $48.50-$119.50; each addl $5; suites $135; under 18 free; wkly, wkday rates; golf plans; higher rates: CMU football wkends, festivals. Crib free. Pet accepted. TV; cable (premium), VCR (movies). Indoor pool. Complimentary continental bkfst. Restaurant nearby. Ck-out noon. Coin lndry. Meeting rms. Business servs avail. In-rm modem link. Game rm. Cr cds: A, D, DS, ER, JCB, MC, V.

D ⚡ ⛼ 🔥 SC

★ ★ **HOLIDAY INN.** 5665 E Pickard Rd. 517/772-2905; FAX 517/772-4952. 184 rms, 2-3 story. S, D $58-$145; each addl $10; under 12 free; golf plan. Crib free. Pet accepted. TV; cable (premium). 2 pools, 1 indoor; whirlpool. Playground. Coffee in rms. Restaurants 6:30 am-10 pm; Sun to 8 pm. Rm serv. Bar noon-2 am; Sun to 8 pm; entertainment exc Sun. Ck-out 11 am. Coin lndry. Meeting rms. Business servs avail. In-rm modem link. Bellhops. Valet serv. Sundries. Free airport, bus depot transportation. Lighted tennis. 36-hole golf, greens fee $35-$65, putting green, driving range. Exercise equipt; weights, stair machine, sauna. Rec rm. Lawn games. In-rm whirlpools, refrigerators; some minibars. Balconies. Cr cds: A, C, D, DS, JCB, MC, V.

D ⚡ 🏃 ⛳ ⛼ 🎾 🔥 SC

★ **SUPER 8.** 2323 S Mission. 517/773-8888; FAX 517/772-5371. 143 rms, 3 story. Apr-Sept: S $54.88-$84.88; D $59.88-$89.88; each addl $5; under 16 free; lower rates rest of yr. Crib free. Pet accepted. TV; cable (premium), VCR avail (movies). Complimentary continental bkfst. Restaurant nearby. Ck-out noon. Meeting rm. Business servs avail. Valet serv. Tennis privileges. X-country ski 3 mi. Some refrigerators. Cr cds: A, C, D, DS, JCB, MC, V.

D ⚡ 🏃 ⛼ 🔥 SC

Restaurant

★ ★ ★ **EMBERS.** 1217 S Mission St (US 27 Business). 517/773-5007. Hrs: 5 pm-9 pm; Fri, Sat to 10 pm; Sun 10 am-7 pm; Sun brunch to 2 pm. Closed most major hols. Res accepted. Serv bar. Semi-a la carte: dinner $15.95-$25.95. Sun brunch $10.95. Child's meals. Specializes in pork chops, charcoal-broiled lobster tail, steak. Smorgasbord 1st & 3rd Thurs. Own baking. Open charcoal grill. Family-owned. Cr cds: A, C, D, DS, MC, V.

D ⛽

Munising (D-3)

Pop 2,783 **Elev** 620 ft **Area code** 906 **Zip** 49862
Information Alger Chamber of Commerce, 422 E Munising Ave, PO Box 405; 906/387-2138.

Colorful sandstone formations, waterfalls, sand dunes, agate beaches, hiking trails and outdoor recreational facilities are part of the Hiawatha National Forest and the Pictured Rocks National Lakeshore, which stretches eastward from Munising along 42 miles of the south shore of Lake Superior. Camping areas are plentiful in the Lakeshore, Hiawatha National Forest and on Lake Superior. A Ranger District office of the Hiawatha National Forest (see ESCANABA) is located in Munising.

What to See and Do

Pictured Rocks Boat Cruise. A 37-mi cruise on the *Miners Castle, Pictured Rocks, Grand Island* or *Miss Superior.* (June-early Oct, daily) City Pier, Elm Ave. Phone 906/387-2379. ¢¢¢¢¢

★ **Pictured Rocks National Lakeshore.** Along a 15-mi section of the Lake Superior shoreline are multicolored sandstone cliffs rising to heights of 200 ft. Here the erosive action of the waves, rain and ice has carved the cliffs to create caves, arches, columns and promontories. Although many consider views from a boat superior, most sections are accessible by trails and roads that provide spectacular views of the cliffs and the lake (most roads closed in winter). The cliffs give way to 12 mi of sand beach followed by the Grand Sable Banks; 5 sq mi (3,200 acres) of sand dunes are perched atop the banks. Also here are waterfalls, inland lakes, ponds, streams, hardwood and coniferous forests and numerous birds and animals.

Visitor activities include sightseeing, hiking, swimming, scuba diving, fishing, boating, hunting, photography and picnicking. Offered in summer are guided historical walks and campfire programs; in winter there is snowmobiling, cross-country skiing on groomed and tracked ski trails and snowshoeing. Also here are the Grand Marais Maritime Museum (summer) and Munising Falls Interpretive Center (summer, daily). There are three drive-in campgrounds (fee) and numerous hike-in backcountry campsites (permit required, free, obtain from any visitor station). Pets are not permitted in the backcountry; must be on leash in other areas. Visitors can obtain information at Pictured Rocks National Lakeshore-Hiawatha National Forest Visitor Information Station (daily); Munising Headquarters (Mon-Fri); or Grand Sable Visitor Center (summer). For further information contact the Superintendent, PO Box 40; 906/387-3700. **Free.**

Annual Event

Pictured Rocks Road Race. Course runs over wooded, hilly trails, roads passing waterfalls, streams and Lake Superior. Late June.

Motels

 ALGER FALLS. *Rte 1, Box 967, 2 mi E on MI 28/94. 906/387-3536.* 17 rms. July-Labor Day: S $39-$45; D $45-$50; kit. cottages $55-$65; lower rates rest of yr. Crib $4. Pet accepted. TV; cable. Restaurant nearby. Ck-out 11 am. X-country ski 3 mi. Rec rm. Picnic tables. Wooded area with trails. Cr cds: DS, MC, V.

★ **BEST WESTERN.** *Box 310, 3 mi E on MI 28. 906/387-4864; FAX 906/387-2038.* 80 rms, 2 story. Late June-Aug: S, D $59-$64; each addl $5; suites $80-$95; lower rates rest of yr. Crib $5. Pet accepted. TV. Indoor pool; whirlpool, sauna. Restaurant 7 am-10 pm. Bar 11-1 am; Sun from noon. Ck-out 11 am. Meeting rm. Business servs avail. Picnic tables. Some refrigerators. Cr cds: A, D, DS, MC, V.

★ ★ **COMFORT INN.** *PO Box 276, on MI 28E. 906/387-5292; FAX 906/387-3753.* 61 rms, 2 story. S, D $63-$95. Crib free. Pet accepted. TV; cable (premium), VCR (movies). Indoor pool; whirlpool. Complimentary continental bkfst. Ck-out 11 am. Coin lndry. Meeting rms. Business servs avail. X-country ski 6 mi. Exercise equipt; bicycle, stair machine. Game rm. Cr cds: A, C, D, DS, ER, JCB, MC, V.

★ ★ **DAYS INN.** *M-28 E, 5 blks SE on MI 28. 906/387-2493; FAX 906/387-5214.* 66 rms. July-Sept & late Dec: S, D $65-$85; kit. units $125; lower rates rest of yr. Crib free. TV; cable (premium), VCR (movies). Indoor pool; whirlpool, sauna. Restaurant adj 6 am-11 pm. Ck-out 11 am. Business servs avail. X-country ski 1 mi. Cr cds: A, C, D, DS, JCB, MC, V.

 SUNSET RESORT. *1315 Bay St, 1315 Bay St. 906/387-4574.* 16 units (1-3-rm), 6 kits. No A/C. June-Labor Day: S, D $49-$55; kit. units $54-$60; lower rates rest of yr. Closed 3rd wk Oct-Apr 30. Crib $1. Pet accepted. TV; cable. Playground. Complimentary coffee. Restaurant nearby. Ck-out 11 am. Lawn games. Picnic tables, grills. On Lake Superior; dockage. Cr cds: MC, V.

 SUPER 8. *MI 28 & Fed Hwy 13. 906/387-2466; FAX 906/387-2355.* 29 rms, 2 story. Mid-June-Labor Day, Dec-Mar: S $45.88; D $55.88-$65.88; each addl $5; suite $73.88; under 12 free; lower rates rest of yr. Crib free. TV; cable (premium). Complimentary continental bkfst. Restaurant nearby. Ck-out 11 am. X-country ski 3 mi. Whirlpool, sauna. Some refrigerator. Cr cds: A, C, D, DS, JCB, MC, V.

Restaurant

 SYDNEY'S. *4 blks SE on MI 28. 906/387-4067.* Hrs: 6 am-10 pm; Sun brunch 8 am-1 pm. Bar 3 pm-2 am. Semi-a la carte: bkfst $1.50-$4.50, lunch, dinner $5-$13.50. Sun brunch $6. Specializes in fresh lake trout, whitefish, steak. Salad bar. Cr cds: A, C, D, MC, V.

Muskegon (H-3)

(See also Grand Haven, Whitehall)

Settled 1810 **Pop** 40,283 **Elev** 625 ft **Area code** 616
Information Muskegon County Convention & Visitors Bureau, 610 W Western Ave, 49440; 800/235-3866 or 800/250-WAVE.

Muskegon County is located in the western part of the lower peninsula, along 26 miles of Lake Michigan shoreline. Muskegon Channel, which runs from Lake Michigan through the sand dunes to Muskegon Lake, opens the harbor to world trade. It has 80 miles of waterfront, including 10 miles of public waterfront, and 3,000 acres of public parks—an acre for every 50 persons in the county. The downtown has been enclosed as a climate-controlled shopping and business mall.

Muskegon Lake, largest of 40 lakes in Muskegon County, is the focal point of the area comprised of Muskegon, Muskegon Heights, North Muskegon, Norton Shores, Roosevelt Park and surrounding townships. Fishing for coho, chinook salmon, lake trout, perch, walleye and other fish is good here; ice fishing is popular in the winter months. The first freshwater reef in North America, a natural fish attractant, is located in Lake Michigan, off Pere Marquette Park.

What to See and Do

Hackley & Hume Historic Site. Restored Queen Anne/Victorian mansions (1888-1889) built by two wealthy lumbermen; elaborately carved woodwork, stenciled walls, 15 Renaissance-style stained-glass windows, tiled fireplaces with carved mantels, period furniture. Tours (mid-May-Sept, Wed, Sat & Sun; also some wkends in Dec). 472 and 484 W Webster. Phone 616/722-7578. ¢

Michigan's Adventure Amusement Park. More than 20 amusement rides, including Wolverine Wildcat, largest wooden roller coaster in the state; Corkscrew roller coaster, Mammoth River water slide, log flume; games, arcade. Also water park with wave pool, lazy river, body flumes, tube slides. (Mid-May-early Sept, daily) 4750 Whitehall Rd, 8 mi N on US 31 via Russell Rd exit. Phone 616/766-3377.   ¢¢¢¢

Muskegon Museum of Art. Permanent collection includes American and European paintings, an extensive print collection, Tiffany and contemporary glass, paintings by Hopper, Inness, Whistler, Homer, Wyeth and others. (Daily exc Mon; closed major hols) 296 W Webster Ave. Phone 616/722-2600. **Donation.**

Muskegon State Park. A 1,165-acre area with replica of frontier blockhouse on one of the park's highest sand dunes, observation point. Swimming, beaches, bathhouse, waterskiing; fishing, boating (ramp, launch). Twelve miles of hiking trails; cross-country skiing; skating rink. Picnicking, concession, playground. Camping (electrical hookups). Standard fees. On MI 213. Phone 616/744-3480. Per vehicle   ¢¢

Muskegon Trolley Company. Two routes cover north side, south side and downtown; each trolley stops at 11 locations, including Hackley & Hume Historic Site, USS *Silversides,* Muskegon State Park and Pleasure Island Water Fun Park. (Memorial Day-Labor Day, daily; no trips during special events) Phone 616/724-6420. ¢

P.J. Hoffmaster State Park. More than 1,000 acres include forest-covered dunes along 2½ mi of Lake Michigan shoreline. Swimming, sandy beach. Ten mi of trails, Dune Climb Stairway to top of one of highest dunes, observation deck. Cross-country ski trails (3 mi). Picnicking, concession. Camping (electric hookups, dump station). Visitors center has displays, exhibits on dune formation (daily). Standard fees. S on Henry St to Pontaluna Rd, then W on Lake Harbor Rd. Phone 616/798-3711. Per car ¢¢   Also here is

Gillette Visitor Center. Sand dune interpretive center. Multi-image slide presentations on the Great Lakes & dune habitats; dune ecology exhibit, hands-on classroom; seasonal animal exhibits. (Daily) 6585 Lake Harbor Rd. Phone 616/798-3573.

Pleasure Island Water Fun Park. River country area featuring Black Hole slide, Runaway River inner-tube slide, Lazy River tube ride, swimming area, beach; bumper and pedal boats, water cannons; miniature golf, volleyball, arcade, children's area; picnicking, concessions. (Memorial Day-Labor Day, daily) S on Henry St to Pontaluna Rd, 1½ mi W of US 31. Phone 616/798-7857. All-inclusive pass ¢¢¢¢-¢¢¢¢¢

USS Silversides. Famous World War II submarine that served with Pacific Fleet along Japan's coasts. The *Silverside's* outstanding aggressive war record included sinking 23 enemy ships, embarking on special minelaying and reconnaisance missions and rescuing two American aviators downed in air strikes over Japan. Guided tours. (June-Aug, daily; Apr-May & Sept-Oct, Sat & Sun) No high heels, skirts. Bluff St at Muskegon Channel. Phone 616/755-1230. ¢¢

Annual Events

Muskegon Summer Celebration. Family music & entertainment parade, midway, food & beer tents, Venetian boat parade. Phone 616/722-6520. June & July.

Muskegon Air Fair. More than 100 military and civilian aircraft; displays. Phone 616/798-4596. Mid-July.

Muskegon Shoreline Spectacular. Pere Marquette Park. Concerts, sporting events, arts & crafts, hot-air balloon rides. Phone 616/737-5791. Labor Day wkend.

Seasonal Event

Muskegon Race Course. S on US 31, at jct I-96. Harness racing, parimutuel betting; 2,122-seat grandstand, 468-seat clubhouse, concessions. Phone 616/798-7123. Wed & Fri-Sun evenings. Apr-mid-Oct.

Motels

★ **BEL-AIRE.** *4240 Airline Rd (49444), near county airport.* 616/733-2196. 16 rms. June-Aug: S $48; D $58; each addl $5; higher rates special events; lower rates rest of yr. Crib $3. TV; cable (premium). Restaurant nearby. Ck-out 11 am. X-country ski 5 mi. Cr cds: A, DS, MC, V.

★ ★ **BEST WESTERN PARK PLAZA.** *2967 Henry St (49441).* 616/733-2651; FAX 616/733-5202. 108 rms, 4 story. June-Aug: S, D $64-$80; each addl $6; suites $90-$160; under 11 free; wkly rates; golf plan; lower rates rest of yr. Crib free. TV; cable, VCR avail (movies). Sauna. Indoor pool. Restaurant 7 am-11 pm. Rm serv. Bar noon-2 am; entertainment Wed-Sat. Ck-out noon. Meeting rms. Business servs avail. Valet serv. Free airport, RR station, bus depot transportation. Game rm. Rec rm. Cr cds: A, C, D, DS, ER, JCB, MC, V.

✔ ★ **DAYS INN.** *3450 Hoyt St (49444), off Seaway Dr.* 616/733-2601; res: 800/368-4571. 107 rms, 2 story. S $70.95; D $79.95; each addl $5. Crib free. TV; cable (premium), VCR avail (movies). Heated pool; whirlpool. Complimentary continental bkfst. Restaurant nearby. Ck-out 11 am. Coin lndry. Meeting rms. Business servs avail. X-country ski 5 mi. Cr cds: A, C, D, DS, MC, V.

★ **SUPER 8.** *3380 Hoyt St (49444).* 616/733-0088. 62 rms, 2 story. Apr-Sept: S $39.88; D $50.88; each addl $5; under 12 free; lower rates rest of yr. TV; cable (premium), VCR avail (movies). Restaurant nearby. Ck-out 11 am. Business servs avail. Cr cds: A, C, D, DS, MC, V.

Motor Hotel

★ ★ ★ **HOLIDAY INN-MUSKEGON HARBOR.** *939 3rd St (49440).* 616/722-0100; FAX 616/722-5118. 201 rms, 8 story. S, D $80-$100; each addl $10; suites $195-$275; studio rms $80-$100; family rates. Crib free. TV; cable, VCR avail (movies). Indoor pool; whirlpool. Restaurant 6:30 am-10 pm; wkends 7 am-11 pm. Rm serv. Bar 2 pm-midnight; Fri,

Sat to 1 am. Ck-out 11 am. Meeting rms. Business servs avail. Bellhops. Valet serv. Gift shop. Free airport, bus depot transportation. Exercise equipt; treadmill, bicycles, steam rm, sauna. Cr cds: A, C, D, DS, JCB, MC, V.

Restaurants

✔ ★ **HOUSE OF CHAN.** *375 Gin Chan Ave (49444).* 616/733-9624. Hrs: 11:30 am-10 pm; Fri to 11 pm; Sat 4-11 pm; Sun 11 am-9 pm. Closed Mon; Dec 25. Res accepted. Wine. Chinese, Amer menu. Semi-a la carte: lunch $5-$7, dinner $8-$12. Buffet: lunch $5.25, dinner $8.98-$9.95. Sun brunch $7.95. Child's meals. Specialties: Beijing shrimp, crispy chicken, crispy fish. Pagoda in center of large dining rm. Cr cds: A, MC, V.

★ ★ **RAFFERTY'S DOCKSIDE.** *601 Terrace Point Blvd (49441).* 616/722-4461. Hrs: 11:30 am-11 pm; Sun to 4 pm. Closed some major hols. Res accepted. Bar. Semi-a la carte: lunch $4.95-$9.95, dinner $8.95-$18.95. Child's meals. Specializes in salads, steak, fresh fish. Outdoor dining. Overlooks marina. Cr cds: A, DS, MC, V.

★ ★ **TONY'S CLUB.** *785 W Broadway (49441).* 616/739-7196. Hrs: 11:30 am-10 pm; Fri to 11 pm; Sat 5-11 pm; early-bird dinner Mon-Sat 4:30-6:30 pm. Closed Sun; most major hols. Res accepted. Bar. Semi-a la carte: lunch $4.25-$7.95, dinner $9.50-$14.95. Child's meals. Specializes in steak, pasta, chicken. Valet parking. Stained-glass windows depicting Mediterranean scenes. Family-owned since 1969. Cr cds: A, C, D, DS, MC, V.

Newberry (D-4)

(See also Hulbert, Soo Junction)

Pop 1,873 **Elev** 788 ft **Area code** 906 **Zip** 49868
Information Newberry Area Chamber of Commerce, PO Box 308; 906/293-5562 or 800/831-7292.

What to See and Do

Luce County Historical Museum (1894). Restored Queen Anne structure; the stone on the lower portion is Marquette or Jacobsville sandstone, some of the oldest rock in the country. Originally a sheriff's residence and jail, it was saved from razing and is now a museum. The stateroom fireplace is original; many of the rooms have been refurbished to hold records, books and other artifacts; jail cells are still intact. (Tues-Thurs) 411 W Harrie St. Phone 906/293-5753 or 906/293-5946. **Free.**

Seney National Wildlife Refuge. 95,455 acres; Canada geese, bald eagles, sandhill cranes, loons, deer, beaver, otter; several species of ducks. Visitor center has exhibits, films and information on wildlife observation (mid-May-Sept, daily). Headquarters (Mon-Fri). Self-guided auto tour (mid-May-mid-Oct). Half-mi nature trail (daylight hrs). Fishing, picnicking. Limited hunting. Pets on leash only. 3 mi S on MI 123, then 23 mi W on MI 28 to Seney, then 5 mi S on MI 77. Phone 906/586-9851. **Free.**

Tahquamenon Falls State Park. Approx 35,000 acres of scenic wilderness; includes Upper (40 ft) and Lower Falls (a series of several scenic falls of lesser height). Swimming, fishing, boating (rentals, launch); snowmobiling, cross-country skiing, hunting in season; playground, picnicking, concession; camping near rapids and near shore of Whitefish Bay, Lake Superior. Standard fees. 30 mi NE on MI 123. Phone 906/492-3415. Per car ¢¢

Annual Event

Lumberjack Days. 1 mi N on MI 123, at Tahquamenon Logging Museum. Wood carvings, traditional music, logging contests, lumberjack breakfast. Wkend late Aug.

Motels

★ ★ **COMFORT INN.** *Jct MI 28 & MI 123. 906/293-3218; FAX 906/293-3435.* 54 rms, 2 story. Early June-Oct & Dec-Mar: S, D $50-$84; each addl $6; under 18 free; lower rates rest of yr. Crib free. TV; cable. Restaurant opp 6 am-midnight. Ck-out 10 am. Coin lndry. Meeting rm. Business servs avail. Valet serv. X-country ski ¾ mi. Game rm. Some in-rm whirlpools. Cr cds: A, C, D, DS, ER, JCB, MC, V.

D 🏊 🎿 ✗ 🐾 SC

★ ★ **DAYS INN.** *MI 28 & Co Rd 403. 906/293-4000; FAX 906/293-4005.* 66 rms, 2 story. June-Aug, mid-Dec-Feb: S $60-$90; D $66-$105; each addl $6; under 12 free; lower rates rest of yr. Crib free. TV; cable (premium). Indoor pool; whirlpool, sauna. Complimentary continental bkfst. Coin lndry. X-country ski 2 mi. Game rm. Some refrigerators. Cr cds: A, C, D, DS, ER, JCB, MC, V.

D 🏊 🎿 ✗ 🐾 SC

★ **GATEWAY.** *MI 123. 906/293-5651; res: 800/791-9485.* 11 rms, 1 story. No rm phones. July-Sept, late Dec-Apr: S $40; D $44-$49; each addl $4; suite $52-$64; lower rates rest of yr. Crib free. TV; cable (premium). Restaurant nearby. Ck-out 10 pm. X-country ski 4 mi. Cr cds: DS, MC, V.

🎿 ✗ 🐾

★ **MANOR.** *Rte 04, Box 979, S Newberry Ave (MI 123), 3 mi N of jct MI 28. 906/293-5000.* 12 rms. Mid-June-mid-Oct, Christmas wk: S, D $38-$58; each addl $4; suites $54-$72; family rates; lower rates rest of yr. Crib free. Pet accepted. TV; cable (premium). Restaurant nearby. Ck-out 10 am. Lawn games. Cr cds: DS, MC, V.

🐾 ✗ 🐾 SC

🗸★ **ZELLAR'S VILLAGE INN.** *S Newberry Ave (MI 123), 2½ mi N of jct MI 28. 906/293-5114; FAX 906/293-5116.* 20 rms. S $40; D $50-$60; each addl $4. Crib $5. Pet accepted. TV; cable (premium). Restaurant 6 am-10 pm. Rm serv. Bar. Ck-out 11 am. Meeting rms. Business servs avail. In-rm modem link. Sundries. Game rm. Cr cds: A, C, D, DS, MC, V.

D 🐾 ✗ 🐾 SC

New Buffalo

(For accommodations see St Joseph; also see Niles)

Pop 2,317 **Elev** 630 ft **Area code** 616 **Zip** 49117 **E-mail** hccc@hc.cns.net **Web** www.harborcountryguide.com
Information Harbor County Chamber of Commerce, 530 S Whittaker, Ste #5; 616/469-5409.

Because of its proximity to large midwestern cities, Lake Michigan and beaches, New Buffalo and the Harbor County area have become a popular resort community for year-round vacationers.

What to See and Do

Red Arrow Highway. Many antique stores, inns, galleries, shops and restaurants can be found along this road that travels from Union Pier to Sawyer, between Lake Michigan and the Interstate. I-94, exits 4B, 6 or 12.

Niles (K-3)

(For accommodations see St Joseph; also see New Buffalo, Mishawaka, IN, South Bend, IN)

Pop 12,458 **Elev** 658 ft **Area code** 616 **Zip** 49120
Information Four Flags Council on Tourism, 321 E Main, PO Box 10; 616/683-3720.

Niles calls itself the "city of four flags" because the banners of France, England, Spain and the United States each have flown over the area. Montgomery Ward and the Dodge brothers are native sons of the town.

What to See and Do

Fernwood Botanic Gardens. The scenic grounds comprise 100 acres of woodland trails, spring-fed ponds, a tall grass prairie & nearly 20 gardens, including rock and fern gardens and Japanese garden. Nature center features hands-on educational exhibits and panoramic bird observation windows. (Daily exc Mon; closed Thanksgiving, Dec 25) 13988 Range Line Rd, 5 mi NW via US 31/33, Walton Rd exit. Phone 616/695-6491. ¢¢

Fort St Joseph Museum. Contains one of the top five Sioux art collections in the nation. Includes autobiographical pictographs by Sitting Bull and Rain-In-The-Face. Other collections are Fort St Joseph (1691-1781) and Potawatomi artifacts, local history memorabilia. (Wed-Sat; closed hols) 508 E Main St. Phone 616/683-4702. **Donation.**

Annual Event

Four Flags Area Apple Festival. Phone 616/683-8870. 4th wk Sept.

Ontonagon (A-4)

Pop 2,040 **Elev** 620 ft **Area code** 906 **Zip** 49953
Information Ontonagon County Chamber of Commerce, PO Box 266; 906/884-4735.

A Ranger District office of the Ottawa National Forest (see IRONWOOD) is located here.

What to See and Do

Porcupine Mountains Wilderness State Park. This 63,000-acre forested, mountainous semiwilderness area harbors otters, bears, coyotes, bald eagles and many other species. There are many streams and lakes with fishing for bass, perch, trout; boating (launch). Hunting in season for grouse, deer and bear. Downhill & cross-country skiing; snowmobiling. Hiking trails with overnight rustic cabins (reservations avail) and shelters; scenic overlooks, waterfalls, abandoned mine sites. Visitor center. Picnicking, playground. Camping. Standard fees. (Daily) 20 mi W on MI 107, on shore of Lake Superior. Phone 906/885-5275. Per car ¢¢ In the park is

Ski area. Triple, double chairlifts, T-bar, rope tow; patrol, school, rentals; snack bar. Longest run 6,000 ft; vertical drop 600 ft. 25 mi of cross-country trails. (Mid-Dec-Mar, daily; closed Dec 25) Phone 906/885-5275. ¢¢¢¢¢

Motels

★ ★ **BEST WESTERN PORCUPINE MOUNTAIN LODGE.** *120 Lincoln Ave. 906/885-5311; FAX 906/885-5847.* 71 rms, 3 story. June-mid-Oct & late Dec-late Mar: S, D $75-$100; each addl $5; family rates; ski plan; lower rates rest of yr. Crib free. TV; cable (premium), VCR avail. Sauna. Indoor pool; whirlpool. Complimentary continental bkfst. Restaurant 7 am-9:30 pm; off season from 4:30 pm. Bar 1 pm-2 am. Ck-out 11 am. Meeting rms. Business servs avail. Gift shop. Airport transportation.

Downhill/x-country ski 3 mi. Game rm. Rec rm. Picnic tables. On lake; swimming beach. Cr cds: A, C, D, DS, MC, V.

D ⌖ ⌖ ⌖ ⌖ ⌖ SC

★ **LAMBERT'S CHALET COTTAGES.** *287 Lakeshore Rd. 906/884-4230.* 13 kit. cottages for 2-8 (1-2-bedrm), 2 vacation homes for 2-12 (3-bedrm). No A/C. S, D $52-$82; each addl $10; vacation homes $215; under 18, $5. Crib avail. TV; cable (premium). Restaurant nearby. Ck-out 11 am. Gift shop. Free airport transportation. Downhill/x-country ski 15 mi. Many fireplaces. Picnic tables, grills. Private beach on Lake Superior. Cr cds: A, DS, MC, V.

⌖ ⌖ ⌖ ⌖ ⌖

★ ★ **MOUNTAIN VIEW.** *(237 MI 107, Silver City) Approx 15 mi W on MI 64. 906/885-5256; FAX 906/885-5205; res: 800/435-5256.* 11 cottages. No A/C. Late June-Aug: S, D $99-$119; each addl $10; lower rates rest of yr. Crib free. TV; cable, VCR (movies). Complimentary coffee in rms. Restaurant nearby. Ck-out 11 am. Downhill/x-country ski 1 mi. Refrigerators avail. Cr cds: A, DS, MC, V.

D ⌖ ⌖ ⌖

Oscoda (F-5)

(See also Tawas City)

Pop 1,061 **Elev** 590 ft **Area code** 517 **Zip** 48750 **Web** www.oscoda.com
Information Oscoda-Au Sable Chamber of Commerce, 4440 N US 23; 517/739-7322 or 800/235-4625.

This is a resort community where the Au Sable River, a famous trout stream, empties into Lake Huron. In 1890, when it was a logging town, Oscoda reached a population of 23,600.

What to See and Do

Huron-Manistee National Forest. This 427,000-acre forest is the Huron section of the Huron-Manistee National Forest (for Manistee section see MANISTEE). A major attraction of the forest is the Lumberman's Monument overlooking the Au Sable River. A three-figure bronze memorial, depicting a timber cruiser, sawyer and river driver, commemorates the loggers who cut the virgin timber in Michigan in the latter part of the 19th century. The visitor center at the monument offers interpretations of this colorful era (Memorial Day-Labor Day). Scenic drives; beaches, swimming, streams and lakes; trout fishing and canoe trips down the Au Sable River; hunting for deer and small game; camping; picnicking; winter sports areas. (Daily) W of town on River Rd. Contact Huron Shores Ranger Station, US Forest Service, 5761 Skeel Ave; 517/739-0728. Fees charged at recreation sites. **Free.**

Paddle-wheeler boat trips. Boat makes 19-mi (2-hr) round trips on Au Sable River. (Memorial Day-mid-Oct, daily; schedule may vary, reservations advised) *Au Sable River Queen,* Foote Dam, 6 mi W on River Rd. Phone 517/739-7351. ¢¢¢

Annual Event

Au Sable River International Canoe Marathon. This 120-mi marathon begins in Grayling (see) and ends in Oscoda. Held in conjunction with Au Sable River Days festival. Last wkend July.

Motels

★ **LAKE TRAIL.** *5400 N US 23. 517/739-2096; FAX 517/739-2565; res: 800/843-6007.* 42 rms, 1-2 story, 20 suites, 2 kit. cottages. S $49; D $49-$125; each addl $6; suites $72-$125; kit. cottages $85 ($525/wk in season); under 12 free. Crib free. TV; cable, VCR avail (movies $4). Complimentary continental bkfst. Ck-out 11 am. Airport transportation. Lighted tennis. Lawn games. Some refrigerators. Balconies.

Picnic tables, grills. On lake; paddle boats, wave runners avail; swimming beach. Cr cds: DS, MC, V.

D ⌖ ⌖ ⌖ ⌖ ⌖

★ ★ **REDWOOD MOTOR LODGE.** *3111 N US 23. 517/739-2021; FAX 517/739-1121.* 37 rms, 1-2 story, 9 kit. cottages. S, D $47-$125; each addl $5; under 5 free. Crib free. TV; cable (premium). Sauna. Indoor pool; whirlpool. Playground. Bar 4 pm-midnight. Ck-out 11 am. Meeting rm. Game rm. Lawn games. Picnic tables, grill. Private beach on Lake Huron opp. Cr cds: A, C, D, DS, MC, V.

D ⌖ ⌖ SC

Owosso (H-5)

(For accommodations see Flint, Lansing)

Settled 1836 **Pop** 16,322 **Elev** 730 ft **Area code** 517 **Zip** 48867
Information Owosso-Corunna Area Chamber of Commerce, 215 N Water St; 517/723-5149.

Owosso's most famous sons were James Oliver Curwood, author of many wildlife novels about the Canadian wilderness, and Thomas E. Dewey, governor of New York and twice Republican presidential nominee. The city, rising on the banks of the Shiawassee River, has five parks and many industries.

What to See and Do

Curwood Castle. This replica of a Norman castle, thought to be architecturally unique in the state, was used as a studio by James Oliver Curwood, author and conservationist. It is maintained as a museum with Curwood memorabilia and local artifacts displayed. (Tues-Sun afternoons; closed hols) 224 Curwood Castle Dr. Phone 517/723-8844, ext 554. **Donation.**

Annual Events

Curwood Festival. River raft, bed and canoe races, juried art show, pioneer displays and demonstrations, fun run, parade, entertainment. 1st full wkend June.

Shiawassee County Fair. County Fairgrounds, 2900 E Hibbard in Corunna. Agricultural and home economics exhibits, rides. Phone 517/743-2223. 1st wk Aug.

Paw Paw (J-3)

(See also Kalamazoo)

Pop 3,169 **Elev** 740 ft **Area code** 616 **Zip** 49079
Information Chamber of Commerce, PO Box 105; 616/657-5395.

The center of an important grape-growing area, this town takes its name from the Paw Paw River, so designated by Native Americans for the papaw trees that grew along its banks.

What to See and Do

Maple Lake. Created in 1908 when river waters were dammed for electric power. Picnicking, boating and swimming on Maple Island.

Winery tours.

Warner Vineyards. Produce wine, champagne and juices. Tours and tasting. (Daily; closed some major hols) 706 S Kalamazoo St, 3 blks N of I-94. Phone 616/657-3165. **Free.**

St Julian Wine Co. The oldest and largest winery in the state; wine tasting. Tours every ½-hour. (Mon-Sat, also Sun afternoons; closed some major hols) 716 S Kalamazoo St, 2 blks N of I-94 exit 60. Phone 616/657-5568. **Free.**

Motel

✔★ **MROCZEK INN.** *139 Ampey Rd. 616/657-2578.* 43 rms, 2 story. S $35.95; D $39.95-$42.95; 3-4 persons $44.95. Crib free. TV. Complimentary coffee in lobby. Restaurant nearby. Ck-out 11 am. Downhill ski 20 mi. Cr cds: A, D, DS, MC, V.

Petoskey (E-4)

(See also Boyne City, Charlevoix, Harbor Springs)

Settled 1852 **Pop** 6,056 **Elev** 786 ft **Area code** 616 **Zip** 49770 **E-mail** chamber@petoskey.com **Web** www.petoskey.com

Information Petoskey Regional Chamber of Commerce, 401 E Mitchell St; 616/347-4150.

A popular resort stretching along Little Traverse Bay, Petoskey is known for its historic Gaslight Shopping District. A diverse industrial base provides a viable year-round economy.

What to See and Do

Little Traverse Historical Museum. Housed in a former railroad depot, visitors can see historical exhibits from the area's Native American, pioneer and Victorian past. (May-Nov, daily). Waterfront Park. Phone 616/347-2620.

Petoskey State Park. A 305-acre park with swimming beach, beach house; fishing. Hiking. Cross-country skiing. Picnicking, playground. Camping (electrical hookups, dump station). Standard fees. 4 mi NE, on MI 119. Phone 616/347-2311.

St Francis Solanus Indian Mission (1859). Built of square hand-cut timbers, held together by dovetailed corners. Native American burial grounds (not open to public) adj the church. W Lake St.

Annual Event

Art in the Park. Phone 616/347-4150. 3rd Sat July.

Motels

★★ **BAYWINDS INN.** *909 Spring St (US 131). 616/347-4193; FAX 616/347-5927; res: 800/204-1748.* 48 rms, 2 story. Mid-June-Labor Day, late Dec-Mar: S, D $89-$97; each addl $5; lower rates rest of yr. Crib $5. TV; cable (premium). Indoor pool; whirlpool. Complimentary continental bkfst. Ck-out 11 am. Downhill/x-country ski 10 mi. Exercise equipt; weight machine, treadmill. Game rm. Refrigerators, some balconies. Some in-rm whirlpools. Cr cds: A, D, DS, MC, V.

✔★ **ECONO LODGE.** *1858 US 131S. 616/348-3324; FAX 616/348-3521.* 60 rms, 2 story. Mid-June-early Sept: S $46-$85; D $51-$95; family rates; ski, package plans; lower rates rest of yr. Crib avail. Pet accepted. TV; cable. Indoor pool; whirlpool. Complimentary continental bkfst. Restaurant nearby. Ck-out 11 am. Business servs avail. Downhill ski 15 mi; x-country ski 10 mi. Cr cds: A, D, DS, MC, V.

Motor Hotel

★★ **HOLIDAY INN.** *1444 US 131 S. 616/347-6041.* 144 rms, 5 story. July-Aug: S, D $85; under 19 free; hol rates; ski, golf plans; higher rates wkends, Dec 20-Jan 2; lower rates rest of yr. Crib free. TV; cable

(premium). Indoor pool; whirlpool. Playground. Complimentary coffee in rms. Restaurant 7 am-2 pm, 5-10 pm. Rm serv. Bar 4 pm-midnight; Fri, Sat to 2 am; entertainment Fri, Sat. Ck-out noon. Coin lndry. Meeting rms. Business servs avail. Bellhops. Valet serv. Gift shop. Downhill/x-country ski 15 mi. Exercise equipt; weight machine, bicycles. Game rm. Balconies. Cr cds: A, C, D, DS, ER, JCB, MC, V.

Hotel

★★ **STAFFORD'S PERRY.** *Bay & Lewis Sts. 616/347-4000; FAX 616/347-0636; res: 800/456-1917.* 81 rms, 3 story. Late June-early Sept, wkends Sept-Feb & Christmas wk: S, D $75-$175; suites $185; ski packages; lower rates rest of yr. Crib $5. TV; cable, VCR avail. Restaurant 7-10:30 am, 11:30 am-2:30 pm, 5:30-10 pm. Bar noon-11 pm. Ck-out 11 am. Meeting rms. Business servs avail. Downhill/x-country ski 8 mi. Exercise equipt; bicycle, rower. Whirlpool. Some private patios, balconies. Cr cds: A, MC, V.

Inn

★★★ **STAFFORD'S BAY VIEW.** *613 Woodland Ave, 1 mi N on US 31. 616/347-2771; FAX 616/347-3413; res: 800/456-1917.* 31 rms, 3 story, 11 suites. July-Aug, late-Dec: S, D $118-$168; each addl $18; suites $195; under 3 free; ski plan; lower rates rest of yr. Crib $5. Complimentary full bkfst. Restaurant (see STAFFORD'S BAY VIEW INN). Ck-out 11 am, ck-in after 3 pm. Business servs avail. Valet serv. Tennis privileges. Downhill ski 6 mi; x-country ski on site. Sleigh rides. Bicycles. Lawn games. Picnic tables. Victorian-style inn with green, mansard roof (1886); antiques, reproductions. Overlooks Little Traverse Bay. Cr cds: A, MC, V.

Restaurants

★★ **ANDANTE.** *321 Bay St. 616/348-3321.* Hrs: 5:30-9 pm. Closed Sun, Mon (Oct-May); most major hols. Res accepted. Eclectic menu. Serv bar. Semi-a la carte: dinner $26-$39. Overlooks Little Traverse Bay. Totally nonsmoking. Cr cds: A, MC, V.

★★ **STAFFORD'S BAY VIEW INN.** *(See Stafford's Bay View Inn) 616/347-2771.* Hrs: 8-10:30 am, noon-2:30 pm, 5:30-9 pm; Fri, Sat to 10 pm; Sun brunch 10 am-2 pm. Res accepted. Semi-a la carte: bkfst $5.50-$10.50, lunch $6-$9.50, dinner $15.50-$24. Sun brunch $16.95. Specializes in fresh lake fish. Own pasta. Family-owned. Views of bay. Cr cds: A, MC, V.

★ **VILLA.** *887 Spring St (US 131). 616/347-1440.* Hrs: 4:30-11 pm. Closed Easter, Thanksgiving, Dec 24, 25. Italian menu. Serv bar. Semi-a la carte: dinner $15.95-$25.95. Child's meals. Specialties: veal scaloppine, seafood fettucine Alfredo. Salad bar. Cr cds: A, MC, V.

Plymouth (J-5)

Pop 9,560 **Elev** 730 ft **Area code** 313 **Zip** 48170
Information Chamber of Commerce, 386 S Main St; 313/453-1540.

Plymouth is a quaint town with historical attractions and unique shopping areas.

Annual Events

Ice Sculpture Spectacular. Hundreds of ice sculptures line the streets and fill Kellogg Park, as professional and student chefs compete with each other carving huge blocks of ice; the sculptures are lighted at night. Mid-Jan.

Fall Festival. Antique mart, music, ethnic food. 1st wkend after Labor Day.

Thanksgiving in Plymouth. Festivities include re-enactment of the first Thanksgiving. Nov.

Motels

★ ★ **FAIRFIELD INN BY MARRIOTT.** *(5700 Haggerty Rd, Canton 48187)* S on I-275 exit 25, W on Ford Rd to Haggerty. *313/981-2440; FAX 313/981-2440, ext. 709.* 133 rms, 3 story. S, D $55-$75; each addl $7; under 18 free. Crib free. TV; cable (premium). Heated pool. Complimentary continental bkfst. Restaurant 6 am-10 pm. Ck-out noon. Business servs avail. Valet serv. Cr cds: A, D, DS, MC, V.

D ≈ ⊠ ⊼ SC

★ ★ **QUALITY INN.** 40455 Ann Arbor Rd. *313/455-8100; FAX 313/455-5711.* 123 rms, 2 story. S, D $69-$86; family, wkend rates. Crib free. TV; cable (premium). Pool. Coffee in rms. Complimentary continental bkfst. Restaurant adj 11-2 am. Ck-out noon. Meeting rms. Business servs avail. In-rm modem link. Valet serv. Health club privileges. Cr cds: A, C, D, DS, JCB, MC, V.

D ≈ ⊠ ⊼ SC

✔ ★ **RED ROOF INN.** 39700 Ann Arbor Rd, at I-275 exit 28. *313/459-3300; FAX 313/459-3072.* 109 rms, 2 story. S $33.99-$48.99; D $41.99-$50.99; under 18 free. Crib free. Pet accepted. TV; cable (premium). Restaurant opp open 24 hrs. Ck-out noon. In-rm modem link. Cr cds: A, C, D, DS, MC, V.

D ✔ ⊠ ⊼

Restaurants

★ ★ ★ **CAFE BON HOMME.** 844 Penniman. *313/453-6260.* Hrs: 11:30 am-9 pm; Sat noon-10 pm. Closed Sun; major hols. Res accepted. Contemporary European menu. Bar. Semi-a la carte: lunch $6.95-$12.95, dinner $19.95-$26.95. Specialties: beef Wellington, rack of lamb, whitefish. Cr cds: A, C, D, MC, V.

D

★ ★ **ERNESTO'S.** 41661 Plymouth Rd. *313/453-2002.* Hrs: 11 am-3 pm, 5-10 pm; Fri & Sat 11 am-11 pm; Sun noon-9 pm. Jan 1, Dec 25. Res accepted. Italian menu. Bar. Semi-a la carte: lunch $7.25-$12.95, dinner $13.95-$24.95. Specializes in lamb chops, veal, pasta. Pianist Tues-Sat, strolling minstrels Mon-Thurs. Outdoor dining. Cr cds: A, D, DS, MC, V.

D

Pontiac (J-6)

(See also Bloomfield Hills, Detroit, Southfield)

Founded 1818 **Pop** 71,166 **Elev** 943 ft **Area code** 248

Information Oakland County Division, Greater Detroit Chamber of Commerce, 1760 S Telegraph Rd, Suite 207, Bloomfield Hills 48302, phone 248/456-8600 or 248/644-1229; or the Metropolitan Detroit Convention & Visitors Bureau, 100 Renaissance Center, 19th floor, Detroit 48243, phone 800/DETROIT.

What was once the summer home of Chief Pontiac of the Ottawas is now the home of the Pontiac Division of General Motors. A group of Detroit businessmen established a village here that became a way station on the

wagon trail to the west. The Pontiac Spring Wagon Works, in production by the middle 1880s, is the lineal ancestor of the present industry. Pontiac is surrounded by 11 state parks, and 400 lakes are within a short distance.

What to See and Do

Alpine Valley Ski Resort. 10 chairlifts, 14 rope tows; patrol, school, rentals, snowmaking; bar, cafeteria. Longest run approx 1/3 mi; vertical drop 320 ft. (Nov-Mar, daily; closed Dec 24 afternoon & Dec 25 morning) 12 mi W of Telegraph Rd on MI 59 (Highland Rd), at 6775 E Highland, near Milford. Phone 248/887-2180 or 248/887-4183 (snow conditions). ¢¢¢¢¢

Oakland University (1959). (12,500 students) On the grounds of the former Meadow Brook Farms estate of Mr. and Mrs. Alfred G. Wilson. The Eye Research Institute is internationally recognized; Center for Robotics and Advanced Automation promotes education, research and development in high technology and manufacturing methods. (See SEASONAL EVENTS) 3 mi NE off I-75, in Rochester. Phone 248/370-2100. Also on campus are

Meadow Brook Hall (1926-1929). English Tudor mansion (100 rms) with nearly all original furnishings and art objects; antique needlepoint draperies, 24 fireplaces; library has hand-carved paneling; dining room has sculptured ceiling; ballroom has elaborate stone- and woodwork. Serves as cultural and conference center of the university. (July-Aug, afternoons; rest of yr, Sun afternoons) Phone 248/370-3140. ¢¢¢

Meadow Brook Art Gallery. Series of contemporary, primitive and Oriental art exhibitions, including permanent collection of African art; outdoor sculpture garden adj to music festival grounds. (Oct-May, daily exc Mon) Phone 248/370-3005. **Free.**

Meadow Brook Theatre. Professional company. (Early Oct-mid-May, daily exc Mon; matinees Wed, Sat & Sun) Phone 248/377-3300.

Professional sports.

NBA (Detroit Pistons). The Palace of Auburn Hills, 3777 Lapeer Rd (MI 24), Auburn Hills. Phone 248/377-0100.

NFL (Detroit Lions). Pontiac Silverdome, 1200 Featherstone Rd. Phone 248/355-4131.

State recreation areas.

Pontiac Lake. Approx 3,700 acres. Swimming, bathhouse, waterskiing; fishing; boating (launch); horseback riding, riding stable; hunting in season, archery and rifle ranges; winter sports; picnicking, playground, concession; camping. Standard fees. 7 mi W on MI 59. Contact Park Manager, 7800 Gale Rd, Rte 2, 48327; 248/666-1020. Per car ¢¢

Highland. On 5,524 wooded acres. Swimming, bathhouse; fishing; boating (launch); hiking; horseback riding, hunting in season; cross-country skiing; picnicking, playground, concession; camping. Standard fees. 17 mi W on MI 59. Phone 248/685-2433.

Seasonal Event

Meadow Brook Music Festival. Oakland University. Concerts featuring popular and classical artists. Dining and picnicking facilities. Phone 248/567-6000. Mid-June-Aug.

Motels

★ ★ ★ **COURTYARD BY MARRIOTT.** *(1296 Opdyke Rd, Auburn Hills 48326)* just N of I-75 & MI 59. *248/373-4100; FAX 248/373-1885.* 148 rms, 2-3 story, 10 suites. Apr-July: S $92; D $102; each addl $10; suites $110-$120; under 14 free; wkly, wkend, hol rates; ski plans; higher rates sports wkends; lower rates rest of yr. Crib free. TV; cable (premium). VCR avail. Indoor pool; whirlpool. Complimentary coffee in rms. Bkfst and evening refreshments avail. Bar 4-11 pm. Ck-out noon. Coin lndry. Meeting rms. Business center. In-rm modem link. Valet serv. Downhill ski 10 mi; x-country ski 2 mi. Exercise equipt; weights, bicycle. Some refrigerators, minibars. Balconies. Cr cds: A, C, D, DS, ER, MC, V.

D ✔ ≈ ⊼ ⊠ ⊼ SC

✔ ★ ★ **FAIRFIELD INN BY MARRIOTT.** *(1294 Opdyke Rd, Auburn Hills 48326)* I-75 exit 79 (University Dr). *248/373-2228.* 134 rms, 3 story. S $36.95-$49.95; D $48.95-$59.95; under 18 free; higher rates: special events, wkends. Crib free. TV; cable (premium). Heated pool. Complimentary continental bkfst. Restaurant adj 6 am-11 pm. Ck-out noon. Valet serv (Mon-Fri). In-rm modem link. Downhill/x-country ski 10 mi. Near Palace, Silverdome, Pine Knob Music Theatre. Cr cds: A, C, D, DS, MC, V.

★ ★ HAMPTON INN. (1461 N Opdyke Rd, Auburn Hills 48326) I-75 exit 79 (University Dr). 248/370-0044; FAX 248/370-9590. 124 rms, 3 story. S $58-$65; D $65-$72; under 17 free. Crib free. TV; cable (premium), VCR avail (movies). Pool. Complimentary continental bkfst. Ck-out noon. Meeting rms. In-rm modem link. Valet serv. Downhill/x-country ski 10 mi. Exercise equipt; bicycle, stair machine. Cr cds: A, C, D, DS, MC, V.

Motor Hotel

★ ★ ★ HILTON SUITES. (2300 Featherstone Rd, Auburn Hills 48326) Just W of I-75, opp Silverdome. 248/334-2222; FAX 248/334-2922. 224 suites, 5 story. S, D $89-$149; each addl $15; family, wkend rates; package plans. Crib free. Pet accepted, some restrictions. TV; cable (premium), VCR (movies $3). Indoor pool; whirlpool. Complimentary full bkfst. Complimentary coffee in rms. Restaurant 6-9:30 am, 11:30 am-1:30 pm, 5:30-10 pm; wkend hrs vary. Rm serv. Bar. Ck-out noon. Coin lndry. Meeting rms. Business center. In-rm modem link. Bellhops. Sundries. Valet serv. Gift shop. Golf privileges. Downhill/x-country ski 12 mi. Exercise equipt; weights, treadmill, sauna. Game rm. Refrigerators. Some balconies. Cr cds: A, C, D, DS, ER, JCB, MC, V.

Restaurants

★ ★ MUSKIES IRVIN PIER. (3880 Lapeer Rd, Auburn Hills 48326) Off I-75 exit 81, opp Palace of Auburn Hills. 248/373-7330. Hrs: 11:30 am-10 pm; Fri to 11 pm; Sat 5-11 pm. Closed Sun, major hols. Res accepted. Bar. Semi-a la carte: lunch $3.50-$8.95, dinner $3.50-$19. Child's meals. Specializes in fresh seafood, pizza baked in wood-burning oven. Cr cds: A, C, D, DS, MC, V.

[D]

★ ★ PIKE STREET. 18 W Pike St (48432). 248/334-7878. Hrs: 11 am-3 pm, 5-10 pm; Fri, Sat to 11 pm. Closed major hols. Res accepted. Bar. Semi-a la carte: lunch $5.75-$11, dinner $13-$26. Specializes in innovative American cuisine. Entertainment Thurs-Sat. Valet parking. Cr cds: A, C, D, DS, MC, V.

[D]

Port Austin (G-6)

Pop 815 Elev 600 ft Area code 517 Zip 48467

What to See and Do

Albert E. Sleeper State Park. 1,003 acres. Sand beach, bathhouse; hunting; fishing; hiking; cross-country skiing; picnicking, playground; camping. Standard fees. (Daily) 13 mi S on MI 25, on Saginaw Bay, Lake Huron. Phone 517/856-4411. Per car ¢¢

Huron City Museum. Nine preserved buildings from the 1850-90 Victorian era, including the LaGasse Log Cabin, Phelps Memorial Church, Point Aux Barques US Life Saving Station, Hubbard's General Store, Community House/Inn, Brick Museum, Carriage Shed and Barn; and House of Seven Gables, former residence of Langdon Hubbard and later Dr. William Lyon Phelps (addl fee). Buildings house period furnishing and memorabilia. Tours (July-Labor Day, daily exc Tues). (Daily) 7930 Huron City Rd, 8 mi E on MI 25. Phone 517/428-4123. ¢¢¢

Port Huron (H-6)

(See also St Clair)

Pop 33,694 Elev 600 ft Area code 810 Zip 48060

Information Greater Port Huron Area Chamber of Commerce, 920 Pine Grove Ave; 810/985-7101.

Fort Gratiot Lighthouse, oldest on the Great Lakes, marks the St Clair Straits. The famous International Blue Water Bridge (toll), south of the lighthouse, crosses to Sarnia, ON (see). (For Border Crossing Regulations see MAKING THE MOST OF YOUR TRIP.)

What to See and Do

Lakeport State Park. 565 acres on Lake Huron. Beach, bathhouse, waterskiing; fishing for perch; boating (ramp); hiking; picnicking, concession, playground; camping (fee). (Daily) 10 mi N on MI 25. Phone 810/327-6765. Per car ¢¢

Museum of Arts and History. Historical and fine arts exhibits; pioneer log home, Native American collections, Thomas Edison's boyhood home archaeological exhibit, marine lore, natural history exhibits, period furniture; also lectures. (Wed-Sun; closed hols) (See ANNUAL EVENTS) 1115 6th St. Phone 810/982-0891. Donation. Also here is

Huron Lightship Museum. Lightships were constructed as floating lighthouses, anchored in areas where lighthouse construction was not possible, using their powerful lights and fog horns to guide ships safely past points of danger. Built in 1920, the Huron was stationed at various shoals in Lake Michigan and Lake Huron until her retirement in 1971. (June-Sept, Wed-Sun afternoons or by appt) ¢

Annual Events

Feast of the Ste Claire. Pine Grove Park. Re-enactment of 18th-century crafts, lifestyles, battles; also foods, fife & drum corps. Memorial Day wkend.

Blue Water Festival/Mackinac Race. Mid-July.

Pioneer Day. On Museum of Arts and History grounds. Festival of folklife. Traditional food, crafts and music. 3rd Sun Sept.

Motels

★ ★ COMFORT INN. 1700 Yeager St. 810/982-5500; FAX 810/982-7199. 80 rms, 2 story, 16 suites. June-Aug: S $54-$59; D $59-$64; each addl $5; suites $89-$99; under 18 free; higher rates special events; lower rates rest of yr. Crib free. TV; cable (premium), VCR avail. Indoor pool; whirlpool. Complimentary continental bkfst, coffee in lobby. Restaurant opp 6 am-10 pm. Ck-out 11 am. Coin lndry. Meeting rms. In-rm modem link. Valet serv. Exercise equipt; weight machine, bicycles. Game rm. Refrigerator in suites. Cr cds: A, C, D, DS, ER, JCB, MC, V.

[D]

★ KNIGHTS INN. 2160 Water St. 810/982-1022; FAX 810/982-0927; res: 800/843-5644. 104 units. Apr-Oct: S $51.95-$62.95; D $57.99-$67.95; each addl $5; kit. units $61.95-$77.95; under 18 free; lower rates rest of yr. Crib free. Pet accepted. TV; cable (premium), VCR avail. Pool. Coffee in rms. Restaurant nearby. Ck-out noon. Cr cds: A, C, D, DS, MC, V.

[D]

★ ★ ★ THOMAS EDISON INN. 500 Thomas Edison Pkwy. 810/984-8000; FAX 810/984-3230; res: 800/451-7991. 149 rms, 3 story, 12 suites. S, D $85-$120, each addl $10; suites $150-$345. Crib free. TV; cable (premium), VCR avail. Indoor pool; whirlpool. Restaurant 7 am-11 pm; Sun 8 am-9 pm. Rm serv. Bar 11-2 am; entertainment (days vary). Ck-out noon. Meeting rms. Business center. Bellhops. Sundries. Gift shop. Tennis privileges. Golf privileges. Exercise rm; instructor, weight machine, bicycles, sauna. Bathrm phones. Balconies. Opp river. Cr cds: A, C, D, DS, MC, V.

Restaurant

★ ★ **FOGCUTTER.** *511 Fort St, atop Port Huron Ofc Ctr. 810/987-3300.* Hrs: 11 am-10 pm; Sat from noon; Sun noon-7 pm. Closed Jan 1, Memorial Day, Labor Day, Dec 25. Res accepted. Bar. Lunch $4.95-$8.95, dinner $9.85-$19.95. Child's meals. Specializes in Swiss onion soup, almond-fried jumbo shrimp, prime rib. Panoramic view. Cr cds: A, C, D, DS, MC, V.

Romulus

(see Detroit Wayne County Airport Area)

Saginaw (H-5)

(See also Bay City, Midland)

Settled 1816 **Pop** 69,512 **Elev** 595 ft **Area code** 517
Information Saginaw County Convention and Visitors Bureau, 901 S Washington Ave, 48601; 517/752-7164 or 800/444-9979.

When this was the land of the Sauk, the trees grew so thick that it was always night in the swamps on both sides of the Saginaw River. When the loggers "brought daylight to the swamp," the city became the timber capital of the world. When the trees were depleted, Saginaw turned its attention to industry and agriculture. Today, it is the home of numerous General Motors plants and is a leading manufacturer of malleable castings, as well as marketer of sugar beets, beans, bran and wheat.

What to See and Do

Andersen Water Park & Wave Pool. Park features pool with 3-ft waves, wading pool, 350-ft double water slide and other water activities. (Memorial Day wkend-Labor Day wkend, daily) Under 10 with adult only; children must be 4 ft in height to ride water slide. Rust Ave (MI 46) & Fordney St. Phone 517/759-1386. ¢¢

Castle Museum of Saginaw County History. Housed in a replica of a French chateau; collections pertaining to the history of the Saginaw Valley and central Michigan. (Daily; closed major hols) 500 Federal. Phone 517/752-2861. ¢

Children's Zoo. Small animals, including llamas, macaws, swans, snakes and porcupines. Contact yard featuring goats; train & pony rides (fees); lectures; educational programs. (Mid-May-Labor Day, daily) S Washington Ave & Ezra Rust Dr, in Celebration Square. Phone 517/759-1657. ¢

Japanese Cultural Center & Tea House. Unique showplace on Lake Linton, designed by Yataro Suzue; gift from sister city of Tokushima, Japan. Tea service (fee); garden. (Daily exc Mon) 527 Ezra Rust Dr. Phone 517/759-1648.

Marshall M. Fredericks Sculpture Gallery. Houses an extraordinary collection of more than 200 works by the world renowned sculptor. (Daily exc Mon) 2250 Pierce Rd, at Saginaw Valley State University. Phone 517/790-5667. **Donation.**

Saginaw Art Museum. Permanent and changing exhibits of paintings, sculpture, fine art; children's gallery; historic formal garden. (Daily exc Mon; closed hols) 1126 N Michigan Ave. Phone 517/754-2491. **Donation.**

Annual Events

Greek Festival. 4th wkend June.

Rendezvous Pageant. 3rd wkend Aug.

Saginaw County Fair. 1st wk after Labor Day.

Seasonal Event

Saginaw Harness Raceway. 2701 E Genesee Ave, N via I-75, Bridgeport exit. Over 12 yrs only. For schedule phone 517/755-3451. Racing season May-late Aug.

Motels

★ ★ **HAMPTON INN.** *2222 Tittabawassee Rd (48604). 517/792-7666; FAX 517/792-3213.* 120 rms, 2 story. S $56-$60; D $63-$67; under 18 free. Crib free. TV; cable (premium), VCR avail. Heated pool. Complimentary continental bkfst, coffee in lobby. Restaurant nearby. Ck-out noon. Meeting rms. Valet serv. Downhill ski 10 mi. Game rm. Cr cds: A, D, DS, MC, V.

✓★ **SUPER 8.** *4848 Town Centre Rd (48603). 517/791-3003.* 62 rms, 3 story. Apr-Sept: S $37.88; D $43.84-$47.88; each addl $5; suite $53.88; under 12 free; lower rates rest of yr. Crib free. Pet accepted, some restrictions. TV; cable (premium). Restaurant nearby. Ck-out 11 am. Cr cds: A, C, D, DS, MC, V.

Motor Hotel

★ ★ **FOUR POINTS BY SHERATON.** *4960 Towne Centre Rd (48604). 517/790-5050; FAX 517/790-1466.* 156 rms, 6 story. S $68-$98; D $78-$108; each addl $10; under 18 free; wkend plan. Crib free. Pet accepted, some restrictions; $20 refundable. TV; cable (premium), VCR avail. Indoor/outdoor pool; whirlpool. Restaurant 6:30 am-10 pm. Rm serv. Bar 11-2 am; entertainment. Ck-out noon. Meeting rms. Business servs avail. Bellhops. Valet serv. Free airport transportation. Sauna. Health club privileges. Game rm. Country French decor. Cr cds: A, C, D, DS, ER, JCB, MC, V.

Inn

★ ★ **MONTAGUE.** *1581 S Washington Ave (48601). 517/752-3939; FAX 517/752-3159.* 18 rms, 16 with bath, 2-3 story. S $55-$140; D $65-$150; each addl $10. Crib free. TV; cable. Complimentary continental bkfst. Dining rm (public by res) 11:30 am-2 pm, 6-10 pm; closed Sun, Mon. Ck-out noon, ck-in 3 pm. Health club privileges. Lawn games. On lake. Restored Georgian mansion (1929); antiques. Cr cds: A, MC, V.

Restaurants

★ ★ **HOLLY'S LANDING.** *1134 N Niagara St (48602). 517/754-4461.* Hrs: 11 am-10 pm; Fri to 11 pm; Sat 11:30 am-11 pm; Sun noon-9 pm. Res accepted. Bar 11 am-11 pm; Fri, Sat to 2 am. Semi-a la carte: lunch $5.50-$7.95, dinner $9.75-$17.95. Child's meals. Specializes in steak, seafood, prime rib. Nautical decor. Overlooks river. Cr cds: A, D, DS, MC, V.

★ ★ **TREASURE ISLAND.** *924 N Niagara St (48602). 517/755-6577.* Hrs: 11 am-11 pm; Fri, Sat to midnight. Closed Sun. Res accepted. Bar to midnight. Complete meals: lunch $4.95-$9.95, dinner $12.95-$18.95. Child's meals. Specializes in prime rib, lobster, fresh fish. Entertainment Thurs-Sat. Outdoor dining. Overlooks river. Cr cds: A, DS, MC, V.

St Clair (H-6)

(See also Detroit, Mount Clemens, Port Huron, Warren)

Pop 5,116 **Elev** 600 ft **Area code** 810 **Zip** 48079

Motels

★ ★ ★ **RIVER CRAB BLUE WATER INN.** *1337 N River Rd (MI 29).* 810/329-2236; FAX 810/329-6056; res: 800/468-3727. 21 rms. May-Labor Day: S, D $92.50; each addl $5; under 16 free; lower rates rest of yr. Crib free. TV; cable (premium). Heated pool. Complimentary continental bkfst. Restaurant (see RIVER CRAB). Bar 4:30-11 pm; off-season hrs vary. Ck-out 11 am. Business servs avail. Refrigerators. All rms overlook river. Cr cds: A, C, D, DS, MC, V.

★ ★ **ST CLAIR INN.** *500 N Riverside (MI 29).* 810/329-2222; FAX 810/329-2348; res: 800/482-8327. 96 rms, 3 story. S, D $80-$145; each addl $10; suites $100-$300; family rates. Crib free. TV; cable, VCR avail. Indoor pool; whirlpool. Restaurant (see ST CLAIR INN). Rm serv. Bar 11-2 am; entertainment Tues-Sat. Ck-out noon, ck-in 3 pm. Business servs avail. Bellhops. Valet serv. Tennis privileges. 18-hole golf privileges. Health club privileges. Game rm. Some bathrm phones. Private patios, balconies. Overlooks St Clair River. Cr cds: A, C, D, DS, MC, V.

Restaurants

★ ★ **RACHELLE'S ON THE RIVER.** *119 Clinton St.* 810/329-7159. Hrs: 11:30 am-10 pm; Fri, Sat to 11 pm; Sun to 9 pm; winter hrs vary. Closed Dec 25. Res accepted. Bar. A la carte: lunch $5-$13; dinner $5-$18. Child's meals. Specializes in fresh seafood, pasta. Entertainment Thurs-Sat. Outdoor dining. Scenic setting on Pine River. Cr cds: A, D, DS, MC, V.

★ ★ **RIVER CRAB.** *(See River Crab Blue Water Inn Motel)* 810/329-2261. Hrs: 11:30 am-10:30 pm; early-bird dinner Mon-Fri 4-6 pm. Closed Jan 1, Dec 24, 25. Res accepted. Bar. A la carte entrees: lunch $6-$15, dinner $9-$30. Sun brunch $15.95. Child's meals. Specializes in clam bakes, Maine lobster, Charley's chowder. Entertainment. Valet parking. Outdoor dining. Cr cds: A, C, D, DS, MC, V.

★ ★ **ST CLAIR INN.** *(See St Clair Inn Motel)* 810/329-2222. Hrs: 7-10:30 am, 11:30 am-4 pm, 5-10 pm; Fri, Sat to midnight; Sun 8 am-noon, 1-9 pm. Res accepted. Bar. Semi-a la carte: bkfst $4-$11, lunch $8-$14, dinner $15-$40. Child's meals. Specializes in prime rib, seafood, steak. Entertainment Tues-Sat. Valet parking Fri, Sat. Outdoor dining. River view. Cr cds: A, C, D, DS, MC, V.

St Ignace (D-4)

(See also Mackinac Island, Mackinaw City)

Pop 2,568 **Elev** 600 ft **Area code** 906 **Zip** 49781 **E-mail** StIgnaceTA@northernway.net **Web** visit-USA.com/Mackinac

Information St Ignace Area Chamber of Commerce, 560 N State St; 906/643-8717 or 800/338-6660.

Located at the north end of the Mackinac Bridge, across the Straits of Mackinac from Mackinaw City (see), St Ignace was founded more than 300 years ago by the famous missionary/explorer, Père Marquette. St Ignace is the gateway to Michigan's Upper Peninsula, which offers beautiful scenery and vast opportunities for outdoor recreation. A Ranger District office of the Hiawatha National Forest (see ESCANABA) is located in St Ignace.

What to See and Do

Father Marquette National Memorial. This 52-acre memorial pays tribute to the life and work of the famed Jesuit explorer who came to area in the 1600s. Adj Mackinac Bridge Authority Plaza.

Mackinac Island ferries. Fifteen-min trips to the island.

Arnold Transit Co. (May-Dec, daily) Phone 906/847-3351. ¢¢¢¢

Shepler's. (Early May-early Nov, daily) Phone 616/436-5023. ¢¢¢¢

Star Line Ferry. "Hydro Jet" service (May-Oct). Contact 590 N State St; for fee information phone 906/643-7635.

Marquette Mission Park and Museum of Ojibwa Culture. Gravesite of Father Marquette. Museum interprets 17th-century Native American life and the coming of the French. (Memorial Day-Labor Day, daily; after Labor Day-rest of Sept, Tues-Sat) Phone 906/643-9161. ¢

Annual Events

Down Memory Lane Parade and Straits Area Antique Auto Show. Last Sat June.

Mackinac Bridge Walk. The only day each year when walking across the bridge is permitted (some lanes open to motor vehicles). Labor Day.

Arts & Crafts Dockside & St Ignace Powwow. Juried show held in conjunction with the Bridge Walk; traditional Native American powwow. Labor Day wkend.

Motels

★ ★ **AURORA BOREALIS.** *635 W US 2.* 906/643-7488; res: 800/462-6783. 56 rms, 2 story. Late June-mid-Aug: S $74; D $79; each addl $5; higher rates: Labor Day (2-day min), Auto Show (3-day min); lower rates May-late June & mid-Aug-Oct. Closed rest of yr. Crib $5. TV; cable (premium). Restaurant adj 7 am-10 pm. Ck-out 10 am. Cr cds: DS, MC, V.

 ★ **BAY VIEW BEACHFRONT RESORT.** *1133 N State St (I-75 Business).* 906/643-9444. 19 rms. Late June-Labor Day: S, D $42-$54; each addl $4; under 12, $2; lower rates mid-May-late June, after Labor Day-late Oct. Closed rest of yr. Crib free. TV; cable. Restaurant nearby. Ck-out 10 am. Free airport transportation. Picnic tables, grill. On Lake Huron, private beach. Cr cds: DS, MC, V.

★ ★ ★ **BEST WESTERN GEORGIAN HOUSE LAKEFRONT INN.** *1131 N State St (I-75 Business).* 906/643-8411; FAX 906/643-8924. 85 rms, 2-3 story. June-Labor Day: S, D $89-$128; each addl $5; under 12 free (max 2); wkday rates; higher rates & 3-day min Labor Day, Auto Show; lower rates rest of yr. Crib $5. TV; cable (premium). Indoor pool; whirlpool. Playground. Restaurant (May-Oct) 7 am-10 pm. Ck-out 11 am. Coin lndry. Business servs avail. In-rm modem link. Free airport transportation. Downhill ski 5 mi; x-country ski 2 mi. Miniature golf. Lawn games. Picnic tables, grill. On Lake Huron; sun deck. Cr cds: A, C, D, DS, MC, V.

★ ★ **BUDGET HOST GOLDEN ANCHOR.** *700 N State St (I-75 Business).* 906/643-9666; FAX 906/643-9126. 56 rms, 2 story. Mid-June-Labor Day: S, D $54-$92; each addl $4; higher rates special events, holidays, Auto Show (3-day min); Labor day (2-day min); lower rates rest of yr. Crib free. Pet accepted; $20 refundable. TV; cable (premium). Indoor pool; whirlpool. Guest lndry. Playground. Ck-out 11 am. Business servs avail. In-rm modem link. Downhill/x-country ski 5 mi. Some refrigerators, in-rm whirlpools. Sun deck. Overlooks Moran Bay. Ferry 1 blk. Cr cds: A, C, D, DS, MC, V.

★ ★ **COMFORT INN.** *927 N State St. 906/643-7733; FAX 906/643-6420.* 100 rms, 4 story. July-late Aug: S, D $68-$130; each addl $5; under 18 free; higher rates (2-day min): car show, Labor Day; lower rates late Aug-Dec, Apr-June. Closed rest of yr. Crib $5. TV; cable (premium). Indoor pool; whirlpool. Playground. Complimentary continental bkfst. Ck-out 11 am. Coin lndry. Meeting rm. Business servs avail. Exercise equipt; weight machine, bicycle. Game rm. Lawn games. Refrigerators. Balconies. Picnic tables. On beach. Cr cds: A, C, D, DS, JCB, MC, V.

D ≈ ⚽ ⊠ 🔥 SC

★ ★ **DAYS INN.** *1074 N State St (I-75 Business). 906/643-8008; FAX 906/643-9400.* 120 rms, 2-3 story. Late June-early Sept: S $59-$99; D $64-$104; each addl $6; suites $96-$156; under 13 free; higher rates & 3-day min: Labor Day, Auto Show; lower rates rest of yr. Crib free. TV; cable (premium). Sauna. 2 indoor pools; whirlpools. Complimentary continental bkfst. Restaurant opp 7 am-10 pm. Ck-out 10 am. Coin lndry. Free local airport, bus depot transportation. Game rm. Refrigerators avail. Some balconies. Cr cds: A, C, D, DS, JCB, MC, V.

D ≈ ⊠ 🔥

★ ★ **ECONO LODGE.** *1030 N State St (I-75 Business). 906/643-8060; res: 800/752-3454.* 47 rms, 2 story. Late June-late Aug: S, D $62-$92; each addl $6; higher rates and 2-day min Labor Day, Car Show; lower rates May-late June & late Aug-mid-Oct. Closed rest of yr. Crib free. TV; cable (premium). Indoor pool; whirlpool. Playground. Restaurant adj 7:30 am-9 pm. Ck-out 10 am. In-rm modem link. Some refrigerators. Cr cds: A, D, DS, MC, V.

D ≈ ⊠ 🔥

★ ★ **HARBOUR POINTE.** *797 N State St (I-75 Business). 906/643-9882; FAX 906/643-6946; res: 800/642-3318.* 123 rms, 1-3 story. No elvtr. July-late Aug: S, D $69-$135; higher rates: hols, auto show, boat show; Labor Day (2-day min); lower rates May-June, late Aug-Oct. Closed rest of yr. Crib $5. TV; cable (premium), VCR avail. 2 pools, 1 indoor; 3 whirlpools. Playground. Complimentary continental bkfst. Restaurant nearby. Ck-out 11 am. Coin lndry. Meeting rms. Business servs avail. Free airport, bus depot transportation. Game rm. Lawn games. Some refrigerators. Balconies. Picnic tables. On lake. Cr cds: A, DS, MC, V.

D ≈ ⊠ 🔥 SC

★ ★ **HOWARD JOHNSON-LODGE DUPONT.** *913 Boulevard Dr. 906/643-9700; FAX 906/643-6762.* 57 rms, 2 story. Mid-June-mid-Sept: S $68-$76; D $73-$87; each addl $6; under 18 free; higher rates: Labor Day (2-day min), auto show (3-day min); lower rates rest of yr. Crib free. Pet accepted; $6. Indoor pool; whirlpool. TV; cable, VCR avail. Complimentary coffee in lobby. Restaurant nearby. Ck-out noon. Coin lndry. Meeting rms. Sundries. X-country ski 7 mi. Game rm. Cr cds: A, C, D, DS, ER, JCB, MC, V.

D ♨ ≋ ≈ ⊠ 🔥 SC

✔ ★ ★ **K ROYALE MOTOR INN.** *1037 N State St (I-75 Business). 906/643-7737; res: 800/882-7122.* 95 rms, 3 story. S, D $38-$92; each addl $5; higher rates: Labor Day (2-day min), Auto Show (3-day min), special events. Closed Nov-Mar. Crib avail. TV; cable (premium). Indoor pool; whirlpool. Playground. Complimentary continental bkfst. Restaurant opp 7:30 am-10 pm in season. Coin lndry. Ck-out 10 am. Free airport, bus depot transportation. Game rm. Refrigerators. Balconies. Picnic tables. Sun deck. Overlooks Lake Huron; private beach. Cr cds: DS, MC, V.

D ≈ ⊠ 🔥 SC

★ ★ **KEWADIN SHORES INN.** *1140 N State St (I-75 Business). 906/643-9141; res: 800/KEWADIN.* 71 rms, 3 story. S, D $59-$79; package plans; higher rates: antique auto show, hols. Crib free. TV; cable (premium). Heated pool. Playground. Restaurant nearby. Ck-out 11 am. Free airport transportation. Game rm. Lawn games. Picnic tables, grills. Nature trail. Cr cds: A, C, D, DS, MC, V.

D ≈ ⊠ 🔥 SC

★ **THUNDERBIRD MOTOR INN.** *10 S State St. 906/643-8900.* 34 rms, 2 story. Mid-June-Labor Day: S, D $70-$125; each addl $5; higher rates (3-day min): Labor Day, Car Show; lower rates Labor Day-Oct,

mid-May-mid-June. Closed rest of yr. Crib $4. TV; cable (premium). Restaurant nearby. Ck-out 11 am. Cr cds: D, MC, V.

D ⊠ 🔥 SC

★ **TRADEWINDS.** *1190 N State St. 906/643-9388; FAX 906/643-7253; res: 800/677-8162.* 25 rms. No rm phones. Late June-Labor Day: S, D $55; each addl $4; higher rates (3-day min) Labor Day, Car Show; lower rates Labor Day-mid-Oct, late May-late June. Closed rest of yr. TV; cable (premium). Pool. Playground. Complimentary coffee in rms. Restaurant adj 7 am-11 pm. Ck-out 11 am. Picnic tables. Overlooks Lake Huron. Cr cds: MC, V.

≈ 🔥

St Joseph (J-3)

(See also New Buffalo, Niles)

Pop 9,214 **Elev** 630 ft **Area code** 616 **Zip** 49085
Information Cornerstone Alliance, 185 E Main St, PO Box 428, Benton Harbor 49023; 616/925-6100.

This town is opposite Benton Harbor on the St Joseph River.

What to See and Do

Deer Forest. Approx 30 acres; more than 500 animals and birds; Story Book Lane, "Santa's Summer Home," train, children's rides, stage events, picnicking. (Memorial Day-Labor Day, daily) Approx 12 mi NE via I-94, in Coloma. Phone 616/468-4961 or 800/752-DEER. ¢¢

Krasl Art Center. Three galleries house contemporary and traditional works, fine and folk arts, local and major museum collections; art reference library; lectures, tours, films; gift shop. (Daily; closed hols) 707 Lake Blvd. Phone 616/983-0271. **Free.**

Warren Dunes State Park. 1,499 acres on Lake Michigan. Swimming, beach house. Hiking. Picnicking, playground, concession. Camping, cabins. 200 acres of virgin forest in Warren Woods. Standard fees. (Daily) 14 mi S via MI 63 & I-94, in Sawyer. Phone 616/426-4013. Per car ¢¢

Annual Events

Blossomtime Festival. A spring salute to agriculture, industry and recreation in southwestern Michigan; Blessing of the Blossoms; Blossomtime Ball, Grand Floral Parade. Late Apr-early May.

Lake Bluff Art Fair. Lake Bluff Park. One of the major art shows in the state. 2nd wkend July.

Venetian Festival. Boat parades, fireworks, concerts, land & water contests, races, sand-castle sculptures, food booths, photography competition. Phone 616/983-7917. Late July.

Tri-State Regatta. Labor Day wkend.

Motels

✔ ★ ★ **BEST WESTERN GOLDEN LINK LODGE.** *2723 Niles Ave (MI 63). 616/983-6321; FAX 616/983-7630.* 36 rms, 2 story, 2 kits. May-Sept: S $31-$38; D $49-$55; each addl $4; suite $52-$55; kit. units $38-$52; under 12 free; wkly rates off-season; lower rates rest of yr. Crib $4. TV; cable (premium). Heated pool. Complimentary continental bkfst. Restaurant adj open 24 hrs. Ck-out noon. X-country ski 5 mi. Many refrigerators. Cr cds: A, C, D, DS, MC, V.

≋ ≈ ⊠ 🔥 SC

★ ★ **COMFORT INN.** *(1598 Mall Dr, Benton Harbor 49022) I-94 exit 29. 616/925-1880.* 52 rms, 2 story. Mid-May-mid-Sept: S $59.95; D $64.95; family rates; lower rates rest of yr. Crib free. Pet accepted. TV; cable (premium). Indoor pool; whirlpool. Complimentary continental bkfst.

Restaurant nearby. Ck-out 11 am. Business servs avail. Game rm. Some refrigerators. Cr cds: A, D, DS, MC, V.

★ ★ **COURTYARD BY MARRIOTT.** (1592 Mall Dr, Benton Harbor 49022) I-94 exit 29. 616/925-3000; FAX 616/925-8796. 98 rms, 2 story. May-Sept: S, D $77-$96; suites $129-$299; lower rates rest of yr. Crib free. TV; cable. Indoor/outdoor pool. Complimentary coffee. Restaurant nearby. Ck-out noon. Meeting rms. Business servs avail. In-rm modem link. Valet serv. X-country ski 5 mi. Exercise equipt; treadmill, stair machine. Picnic tables. Cr cds: A, C, D, DS, MC, V.

★ ★ **DAYS INN.** (2699 MI 139S, Benton Harbor 49022) 5 mi SE on MI 139, at I-94 exit 28. 616/925-7021; FAX 616/925-7115. 122 rms, 2 story. May-Labor Day: S $47-$58; D $59-$70; each addl $5; under 16 free; higher rates festivals; lower rates rest of yr. Crib free. TV, VCR avail (movies). Indoor pool; whirlpool. Restaurant open 24 hrs. Rm serv 8 am-9 pm. Ck-out noon. Coin lndry. Meeting rm. Business servs avail. Valet serv. Sundries. X-country ski 20 mi. Exercise equipt; weights, bicycles, sauna. Game rm. Some refrigerators. Private patios, balconies. Cr cds: A, C, D, DS, MC, V.

✔ ★ **SUPER 8.** (1950 E Napier Ave, Benton Harbor 49022) I-94 exit 30. 616/926-1371; FAX 616/926-1371, ext. 169. 62 rms, 3 story. S $35.88-$47.88; D $46.88-$60.88; under 12 free; higher rates wkends, special events. Crib free. Pet accepted. TV; cable (premium). Complimentary coffee in lobby. Restaurant nearby. Ck-out 11 am. Business servs avail. Cr cds: A, C, D, DS, MC, V.

Motor Hotel

★ ★ **QUALITY INN.** (2860 MI 139 S, Benton Harbor 49022) 5 mi NE on I-94, exit 28. 616/925-3234; FAX 616/925-6131. 150 rms, 2 story. June-Sept: S $63-$75; D $68-$75; each addl $5; under 18 free; golf plan; lower rates rest of yr. Crib free. TV; cable (premium). Indoor/outdoor pool; whirlpool. Restaurant 6:30 am-10 pm; Sat 7 am-11 pm; Sun 7 am-9 pm. Rm serv 4 pm-midnight. Ck-out 11 am. Meeting rms. Business servs avail. Bellhops. Gift shop. Free RR station, bus depot transportation. Exercise equipt; weight machine, bicycles, sauna. Game rm. Rec rm. Cr cds: A, C, D, DS, ER, JCB, MC, V.

Hotel

★ ★ **BOULEVARD ALL SUITE.** 521 Lake Blvd. 616/983-6600; FAX 616/983-0520; res: 800/875-6600. 85 suites, 7 story. Suites $97-$128; each addl $10; under 12 free; golf plans; higher rates Memorial Day wkend, Venetian Festival (2-day min); lower rates rest of yr. Crib free. TV; cable (premium), VCR avail. Complimentary continental bkfst. Coffee in rms. Restaurant 7 am-2 pm, 5:30-10 pm. Bar from 5 pm. Ck-out noon. Meeting rms. Business center. Health club privileges. Refrigerators, wet bars. Cr cds: A, DS, MC, V.

Restaurants

★ ★ **PIER III.** 105 Main St (I-94 Business). 616/983-2334. Hrs: 7 am-10 pm; Fri, Sat to 11 pm; early-bird dinner Mon-Fri 4:30-6:30 pm; Sat 4-5:30 pm, Sun. Closed Dec 25. Res accepted. Bar. Semi-a la carte: bkfst from $2.99, lunch $6-$12, dinner $8-$26. Child's meals. Specializes in perch, steak, house salad. Open-hearth grill. Nautical decor. Cr cds: A, DS, MC, V.

★ ★ **SCHULER'S OF STEVENSVILLE.** (5000 Red Arrow Hwy, Stevensville) 5 mi S on Red Arrow Hwy (I-94) at exit 23. 616/429-3273.

Hrs: 11 am-10 pm; Fri, Sat to 11 pm; Sun 11 am-10 pm; hols noon-8 pm. Closed Dec 25. Res accepted. Semi-a la carte: lunch $5.95-$9.50, dinner $6.95-$18.50. Sun brunch $9.95. Child's meals. Specializes in prime rib, pork chop, fresh seafood. Old English theme; stone fireplace. Family-owned. Cr cds: A, C, D, DS, MC, V.

Saugatuck (H-3)

(See also Holland, South Haven)

Pop 954 **Elev** 600 ft **Area code** 616 **Zip** 49453

Information Saugatuck-Douglas Visitors & Convention Bureau, PO Box 28; 616/857-1701.

Long one of the major art colonies in the Midwest, Saugatuck/Douglas is growing as a year-round resort area. It offers beautiful beaches for swimming and surfing on Lake Michigan, hiking and cross-country skiing in the dunes, canoeing and boating on the Kalamazoo River, yachting from marinas and a charming shopping area. The northern end of the village covers an ancient Native American burial ground. During the summer months, arts & crafts shows are abundant.

What to See and Do

Fenn Valley Vineyards and Wine Cellar. Self-guided tour overlooking wine cellar; audiovisual program, wine tasting. (Daily; closed Jan 1, Easter, Thanksgiving, Dec 25) 5 mi SE via I-196 exit 34, at 6130 122nd Ave in Fennville. Phone 616/561-2396. **Free.**

Keewatin Marine Museum. Tours of restored, turn-of-the-century, passenger steamship of the Canadian Pacific railroad; maintained as "in-service" ship; features original, elegant furnishings, carved paneling, brass fixtures. Quadruple-expansion engine rm also open to tours. (Memorial Day-Labor Day, daily) Harbour Village, just S of the Saugatuck-Douglas Bridge. Phone 616/857-2107 or 616/857-2151, ext 415. ¢¢

Saugatuck Dune Rides. Buggy rides over the sand dunes near Lake Michigan. (May-Sept, daily; Oct, wkends only) 1/2 mi W of I-196, exit 41. Phone 616/857-2253. ¢¢¢

Sightseeing cruises.

Star of Saugatuck. Stern-wheel paddleboat with narrated tours on the Kalamazoo River and Lake Michigan (weather permitting). (Early May-Sept, daily; Oct, wkends only) At the Fish Dock, 716 Water St. Phone 616/857-4261. ¢¢¢

City of Douglas. Scenic afternoon, buffet brunch luncheon & dinner cruises to Lake Michigan via Kalamazoo River. (Memorial Day wkend-Labor Day, daily) Docked just S of the Douglas-Saugatuck Bridge. Phone 616/857-2107 or 616/857-2151, ext 415. ¢¢¢-¢¢¢¢

Annual Event

Harbor Days. Venetian boat parade, family activities. Last wkend July.

Motels

(Rates may be higher during Tulip Time Festival, mid-May)

★ ★ **LAKE SHORE RESORT.** 2885 Lake Shore Dr. 616/857-7121. 30 rms. June-mid-Sept, hols: S, D $95-$130; each addl $30; lower rates May, mid-Sept-Oct. Closed rest of yr. TV; cable. Heated pool. Continental bkfst. Restaurant nearby. Ck-out 11 am. Viewing decks overlook lake. Wooded area; nature trails, bicycling, private beach on Lake Michigan. Cr cds: MC, V.

★ ★ **SHANGRAI-LA.** 6190 Blue Star Hwy (County A2). 616/857-1453; FAX 616/857-5905; res: 800/877-1453. 20 rms. May-Labor Day: S $40-$85; D $45-$95; each addl $5; lower rates rest of yr. Closed

Jan. Crib $5. TV; VCR (movies $3). Heated pool. Restaurant nearby. Ck-out 11 am. X-country ski 4 mi. Lawn games. Refrigerators avail. Picnic tables, grill. Cr cds: A, DS, MC, V.

★ ★ **TIMBERLINE.** *Blue Star Hwy (County A2), 1 mi N of Saugatuck-Douglas Bridge.* 616/857-2147; res: 800/257-2147. 28 rms. May-early Sept: S $55-$85; D $60-$95; each addl $5; lower rates rest of yr. Crib free. TV; cable (premium). Heated pool. Playground. Complimentary coffee. Restaurant nearby. Ck-out 11 am. Free airport, bus depot transportation. X-country ski 2½ mi. Game rm. Lawn games. Cr cds: A, DS, MC, V.

Inns

★ ★ **KINGSLEY HOUSE.** *(626 W Main St, Fennville 49408) 8 mi SE on MI 89.* 616/561-6425. 8 rms, 4 with shower only, 3 story, 3 suites. No rm phones. Apr-Oct: S $80; D $80-$90; suites $95-$145; 2-day min wkends, 3-day min hols; lower rates rest of yr. Children over 12 years only. TV in suites; VCR avail. Complimentary full bkfst wkends. Restaurant nearby. Ck-out 11 am, ck-in 4 pm. Luggage handling. X-country ski 5 mi. Bicycles avail. Victorian house built 1886; antiques. Totally nonsmoking. Cr cds: A, DS, MC, V.

★ ★ **MAPLEWOOD.** *428 Butler St.* 616/857-1771; FAX 616/857-1773; res: 800/650-9790. 15 rms, 11 with shower only, 2 story. May-Oct: S, D $110-$155; each addl $15; under 5 free; lower rates rest of yr. Crib free. TV; cable. Heated pool. Complimentary full bkfst. Restaurant nearby. Ck-out noon, ck-in 3-6 pm. 18-hole golf privileges. X-country ski 3 mi. Built in 1860; antiques. Totally nonsmoking. Cr cds: A, MC, V.

★ ★ **PARK HOUSE.** *888 Holland St.* 616/857-4535; FAX 616/857-1065; res: 800/321-4535. 9 rms, 2 story, 3 suites, 6 cottages. Some rm phones. S, D $85-$150; suites $150; cottage $115-$225; wkly rates; 2-day min wkends Sept-June, 3-day min wkends July-Aug. TV in parlor, suites, cottages; VCR avail (movies). Complimentary full bkfst. Restaurant adj (in season) 7 am-3 pm. Ck-out 11 am, ck-in 3 pm. Business servs avail. X-country ski 2 mi. Many fireplaces. Some balconies. Picnic tables, grill. White, clapboard house built for lumberman (1857); oldest house in Saugatuck, once visited by Susan B. Anthony. Sitting rm; wide-planked pine floors, antiques. Cr cds: A, DS, MC, V.

★ ★ **ROSEMONT INN BED & BREAKFAST.** *83 Lake Shore Dr.* 616/857-2637; res: 800/721-2637. Web www.saugatuck.com. 14 rms, 2 story. Mid-June-mid-Sept: S, D $130-$235; each addl $35; 3-day min hols; lower rates rest of yr. Adults only. TV; cable. Sauna. Heated pool; whirlpool. Complimentary full bkfst; afternoon refreshments. Restaurant nearby. Ck-out noon, ck-in 3 pm. Business servs avail. In-rm modem link. Golf privileges. X-country ski on site. Rec rm. On Lake Michigan; swimming beach. Built 1901. Totally nonsmoking. Cr cds: A, DS, MC, V.

★ ★ **SHERWOOD FOREST.** *938 Center St, S on Blue Star Hwy (County A2), right on Center St.* 616/857-1246; FAX 616/857-1996; res: 800/838-1246. 5 rms, shower only, 2 story, 1 kit. cottage. No rm phones. Memorial Day-Labor Day: S, D $70-$140; cottage $750/wk; higher rates wkends (also 2-day min); lower rates rest of yr. TV in sitting rm; VCR (free movies). Heated pool, whirlpool. Complimentary continental bkfst. Ck-out noon, ck-in 3 pm. X-country ski. Bicycles avail. Picnic tables. Near Lake Michigan, beach. Victorian-style house built 1890s; many antiques. Totally nonsmoking. Cr cds: DS, MC, V.

★ **TWIN GABLES COUNTRY INN.** *900 Lake St.* 616/857-4346; FAX 616/857-1092; res: 800/231-2185. 14 rms, 2 story, 3 cottages (1-2 bedrm). No rm phones. May-Oct: S, D $68-$98; each addl $10-$15; cottages $495-$720/wk; under 3 free; wkly rates; lower rates rest of yr. TV

in sitting rm. Heated pool; whirlpool. Complimentary continental bkfst. Ck-out 11 am, ck-in 3 pm. Free airport, RR station, bus depot transportation. X-country ski 3 mi. Picnic tables, grills. Fireplace in sitting rm, embossed tin ceilings and walls; antiques. Near lake. Cr cds: A, DS, MC, V.

★ ★ ★ **WICKWOOD.** *510 Butler St.* 616/857-1465; FAX 616/857-1552. 11 rms, 2 story, 2 suites. No rm phones. May-Nov: S, D $165-$175; suites $185-$195; lower rates rest of yr. Closed Dec 24, 25. Complimentary continental bkfst. Restaurant nearby. Setups. Ck-out noon, ck-in 3 pm. Business servs avail. X-country ski 5 mi. Inn (1940) designed after English country house; library, sitting rm, antiques. Screened gazebo. Cr cds: MC, V.

Restaurants

★ **CHEQUERS.** *220 Culver St.* 616/857-1868. Hrs: 11:30 am-10 pm; Sat to 11 pm; Sun noon-10 pm; winter hrs vary. Closed Jan 1, Dec 25. English pub menu. Bar. Semi-a la carte: lunch $4-$8, dinner $9-$14.50. Specialties: shepherd's pie, fish & chips. English-style pub. Cr cds: A, D, MC, V.

✔★ **LOAF & MUG.** *236 Culver St.* 616/857-2974. Hrs: 8 am-3 pm; Fri & Sat to 8 pm. Closed some major hols; also wk of Christmas. No A/C. Semi-a la carte: bkfst $2.75-$9.50, lunch, dinner $5.95-$10. Specializes in deli-style sandwiches & soups. Entertainment June-Aug. Outdoor garden dining. Cr cds: A, DS, MC, V.

★ ★ **TOULOUSE.** *248 Culver St.* 616/857-1561. Hrs: 5-10 pm; Fri, Sat to 11 pm; Sun from noon; winter hrs may vary. Closed Jan 1, Dec 25; also Mon-Wed winter months. Res accepted. French menu. Bar. Semi-a la carte: dinner $14.95-$27.95. Specializes in cassoulet, seafood, french country cuisine. Patio dining. French country atmosphere. Cr cds: A, D, DS, MC, V.

Sault Ste Marie (D-5)

(See also Sault Ste Marie, ON, Canada)

Settled 1668 **Pop** 14,689 **Elev** 613 ft **Area code** 906 **Zip** 49783
Information Chamber of Commerce, 2581 I-75 Business Spur; 906/632-3301 or 800/MI-SAULT.

Sault Ste Marie (SOO-Saint-Marie) is the home of one of the nation's great engineering marvels—the locks of St Mary's River. Along the river the locks lower or raise lake and ocean vessels 21 feet between Lake Superior and Lake Huron in 6 to 15 minutes. From April to December, about 100 vessels a day pass through with no toll charge. The cascades of the river, which made the locks necessary, give the city its name: the French word for a cascade is *sault* and the name of the patron saint was Mary; combined, the two made Sault de Sainte Marie or "Leap of the Saint Mary's."

The only entrance into Canada for almost 300 miles, the Sault Ste Marie community began in 1668 when Father Jacques Marquette built the first mission church here. An international bridge spans the St Mary's River to Sault Ste Marie, Ontario (toll). (For Border Crossing Regulations see MAKING THE MOST OF YOUR TRIP.) A Ranger District office of the Hiawatha National Forest (see ESCANABA) is located in Sault Ste Marie.

What to See and Do

Federal Building. Grounds occupy what was the site of Jesuit Fathers' mission, and later the original site of Fort Brady (1822) before it was moved. Ground floor houses **River of History Museum,** an interpretive center depicting the history of the St Mary's River. E Portage Ave.

Lake Superior State University (1946). (3,000 students) This hillside campus was the second site of historic Fort Brady after it was moved from its original location; many old buildings, including some that were part of the fort, still stand. Library's Marine Collection on Great Lakes Shipping open on request. Carillon concerts (June-Sept, twice daily; free). Headquarters of the famous Unicorn Hunters, official keepers of the Queen's English. Tours. Phone 906/635-2315.

Museum Ship Valley Camp and Great Lakes Maritime Museum. Great Lakes Marine Hall of Fame. Ship's store, picnic area & park. (Mid-May-mid-Oct, daily) 5 blks E of locks. Phone 906/632-3658. ¢¢

★ **"Soo" Locks.** The famous locks can be seen from both the upper and lower parks paralleling the locks. The upper park has three observation towers. There is a scale model of the locks at the east end of the MacArthur Lock and a working lock model, photos and a movie in visitor building in upper park. (Mar-Feb, daily) Phone 906/632-3311. **Free.**

Soo Locks Boat Tours. Two-hr narrated excursions travel through the Soo Locks, focusing on their history. Sunset dinner cruises (approx 2³/₄ hrs; res suggested). (Mid-May-mid-Oct, daily) Docks located at 515 & 1157 E Portage Ave. Phone 906/632-6301 or 906/632-2512. ¢¢¢¢-¢¢¢¢¢

Tower of History. A 21-story observation tower with 20-mi view of Canadian and American cities; show in lobby, displays. (Mid-May-mid-Oct, daily) 501 E Waterstreet. Phone 906/632-3658. ¢¢

Twin Soo Tour. Guided tour (2-4 hrs) of both Canadian & American cities of Sault Ste Marie; provides view of Soo Locks; passengers may disembark in Canada. (June-Oct, daily) 315-317 W Portage Ave. Phone 906/635-5241. ¢¢ Also here is

The Haunted Depot. Guided tours through depot's many unusual chambers; visitors can "fall uphill" in the mystery bedroom, walk through a "storm" in the cemetery, "lose their heads" at the guillotine. (June-Oct, daily) Phone 906/635-5912. ¢¢

Motels

✔★★ **BEST WESTERN COLONIAL INNS.** 4281 I-75 Business, ¹/₄ mi E of I-75 on I-75 Business, exit 392. 906/632-2170; FAX 906/632-7877. 110 rms, 2 story. S, D $45-$120; family rates; package plans. Crib free. TV; cable (premium), VCR avail. Sauna. Indoor pool. Complimentary continental bkfst. Restaurant nearby. Ck-out 11 am. Coin lndry. In-rm modem link. Game rm. Refrigerators. Cr cds: A, C, D, DS, ER, MC, V.

🅳 ≋ ⊠ 🔥 SC

★★ **COMFORT INN.** 4404 I-75 Business, exit 392, at Cascade Crossings Mall. 906/635-1118; FAX 906/635-1119. 66 rms, 2 story. May-Oct: S $84; D $94; each addl $8; under 18 free; lower rates rest of yr. Crib free. TV; cable (premium). Heated pool. Complimentary continental bkfst. Restaurant adj. Ck-out 11 am. Cr cds: A, C, D, DS, ER, JCB, MC, V.

🅳 ≋ ⊠ 🔥 SC

★ **CRESTVIEW THRIFTY INNS.** 1200 Ashmun St (I-75 Business). 906/635-5213; FAX 906/635-9672; res: 800/955-5213. 44 rms. July-mid-Oct: S $54; D $64-$74; package plans; lower rates rest of yr. Crib free. Pet accepted. TV; cable (premium). Complimentary coffee in lobby. Restaurant nearby. Ck-out 11 am. In-rm modem link. Some refrigerators. Locks 1 mi. Cr cds: A, D, DS, MC, V.

✔ ⊠ 🔥 SC

★★ **DAYS INN.** 3651 I-75 Business Spur. 906/635-5200; FAX 906/635-9750. 85 rms, 2 story. June-Oct: S, D $90-$145; each addl $6; under 12 free; higher rates special events, hols; lower rates rest of yr. Crib free. TV; cable (premium), VCR avail (movies). Indoor pool; whirlpool. Complimentary coffee in lobby. Restaurant adj 7 am-10 pm. Ck-out 11 am.

Coin lndry. In-rm modem link. Valet serv. X-country ski 5 mi. Game rm. Refrigerator avail. Cr cds: A, C, D, DS, MC, V.

🅳 ≋ ⊠ 🔥 SC

★ **DORAL.** 518 E Portage Ave. 906/632-6621; res: 800/998-6720. 20 rms, 2 story. Mid-June-Oct: S $56; D $66; each addl $6; under 12 free; lower rates mid-Apr-mid-June. Closed rest of yr. TV; cable. Sauna. Heated pool; whirlpool. Restaurant nearby. Ck-out 10 am. Game rm. Lawn games. Picnic tables. Cr cds: DS, MC, V.

≋ ⊠ 🔥

★ **LAWSON.** 2049 Ashmun St (I-75 Business). 906/632-3322; res: 800/457-8536. 16 rms, 3 story. July-Oct: S $48; D $62; each addl $4; lower rates rest of yr. Crib $2. TV; cable (premium), VCR avail. Complimentary coffee in lobby. Restaurant nearby. Ck-out 11 am. Airport transportation. X-country ski ¹/₄ mi. Some refrigerators. Cr cds: A, DS, MC, V.

≋ ⊠ 🔥 SC

★★ **RAMADA INN.** 3290 Ashmun St, 1³/₄ mi S on I-75 Business. 906/635-1523; FAX 906/635-2941. 130 rms, 2 story. Mid-June-mid-Oct: S, D $70-$95; each addl $10; suites from $110; under 18 free; lower rates rest of yr. Crib free. TV; cable. Indoor pool; whirlpool. Playground. Restaurant 6 am-10 pm. Rm serv. Bar noon-2 am; entertainment Wed-Sun. Ck-out noon. Meeting rms. Business servs avail. Valet serv. Sundries. X-country ski on site. Exercise equipt; weights, bicycles, sauna. Game rm. Cr cds: A, C, D, DS, MC, V.

🅳 ≋ 🎿 ⊠ 🔥 SC

★ **SEAWAY.** 1800 Ashmun St (I-75 Business). 906/632-8201; FAX 906/632-8210; res: 800/782-0466. 18 rms. June-mid-Sept: S $63.70; D $68.25; each addl $5; lower rates rest of yr. Crib free. Pet accepted, some restrictions. TV; cable. Complimentary coffee in lobby. Restaurant opp 5 am-midnight. Ck-out 10 am. Free airport transportation. Downhill ski 18 mi; x-country ski ¹/₄ mi. Cr cds: A, C, D, DS, MC, V.

✔ ⊠ 🔥 SC

★ **SUPER 8.** 3826 I-75 Business Spur. 906/632-8882; FAX 906/632-3766. 61 rms, 2 story. July-Aug: S $54.88-$70.88; D $60.88-$72.88; under 12 free; lower rates rest of yr. Crib free. Pet accepted, some restrictions; $50 deposit. TV; cable (premium). Complimentary continental bkfst. Restaurant nearby. Ck-out 11 am. Coin lndry. Cr cds: A, C, D, DS, MC, V.

🅳 ✔ ⊠ 🔥 SC

Hotel

★★★ **OJIBWAY.** 240 W Portage St. 906/632-4100; FAX 906/632-6050; res: 800/654-2929 (MI). 71 rms, 6 story. June-mid-Oct: S $128; D $132; each addl $5; suites $240; under 18 free; package plans; lower rates rest of yr. Crib free. TV; cable (premium). Sauna. Indoor pool; whirlpool. Restaurant (see FREIGHTERS). No rm serv. Bar noon-2 am; entertainment Fri, Sat. Ck-out 11 am. Meeting rms. Business servs avail. In-rm modem link. Some in-rm whirlpools. Overlooking Soo Locks. Cr cds: A, C, D, DS, MC, V.

🅳 ≋ ⊠ 🔥 SC

Restaurants

★ **ANTLER'S.** 804 E Portage Ave. 906/632-3571. Hrs: 11 am-10 pm; Fri, Sat to 11 pm. Closed some major hols. Bar. Semi-a la carte: lunch, dinner $4.95-$22.95. Child's meals. Specializes in steak, seafood, barbecued ribs. Rustic atmosphere. Historic building (1800s). Same owner since 1947. Cr cds: A, D, DS, MC, V.

★★ **FREIGHTERS.** (See Ojibway Hotel) 906/632-4211. Hrs: 6 am-10 pm; Sun brunch 11 am-2:30 pm. Closed Dec 25. Bar noon-2 am. Semi-a la carte: bkfst $4-$5, lunch $5-$7, dinner $14-$25. Sun brunch $10.95. Child's meals. Specializes in seafood, prime rib. Extensive beer selection. Bi-level dining on river, overlooking Soo Locks. Cr cds: A, D, DS, MC, V.

D SC

Sleeping Bear Dunes National Lakeshore (E-3)

(For accommodations see Glen Arbor, Leland, Traverse City)

(On Lake Michigan shoreline between Frankfort and Leland)

In 1970, Congress designated the Manitou Islands and 35 miles of mainland Lake Michigan shoreline in the vicinity of Empire as Sleeping Bear Dunes National Lakeshore. An Ojibway legend tells of a mother bear, who with her two cubs tried to swim across Lake Michigan from Wisconsin to escape from a forest fire. Nearing the Michigan shore, the exhausted cubs fell behind. Mother bear climbed to the top of a bluff to watch and wait for her offspring. They never reached her. Today she can still be seen as the Sleeping Bear, a solitary dune higher than its surroundings. Her cubs are the Manitou Islands, which lie a few miles offshore.

The lakeshore's variety of landforms support a diversity of interrelated plant habitats. Sand dune deserts contrast sharply with hardwood forests. There are stands of pine, dense cedar swamps and a few secluded bogs of sphagnum moss. Against this green background are stands of white birch. In addition, the park supports many kinds of animal life, including porcupine, deer, rabbit, squirrel, coyote and raccoon. More than 200 species of birds may be seen. Fishing and hunting are state-regulated; a Michigan license is required. Bass, bluegill, perch and pike are plentiful; salmon are numerous in the fall.

Dune Climb takes visitors up 150 feet on foot through the dunes for a panoramic view of Glen Lake and the surrounding countryside. Pierce Stocking Scenic Drive, a 7-mile loop, is a road with self-guiding brochure available that offers visitors an opportunity to view the high dunes and overlooks from their cars (May-Oct; free).

Sleeping Bear Point Maritime Museum, 1 mi W of Glen Haven on MI 209, located in the restored US Coast Guard Station, contains exhibits on the activities of the US Life-Saving Service and the US Coast Guard and the general maritime activities these organizations have aided on the Great Lakes. A restored boat house contains original and replica surf boats and other related rescue equipment. (Memorial Day-Labor Day, daily).

South Manitou Island, an 8-square-mile, 5,260-acre island with 12 miles of shoreline has a fascinating history. Formed from glacial moraines more than 10,000 years ago, the island slowly grew a covering of forest. European settlers and the US Lighthouse Service, attracted by the forest and the natural harbor, established permanent sites here as early as the 1830s. On the southwest corner is the Valley of the Giants, a grove of white cedar trees more than 500 years old. There are three developed campgrounds on the island; ranger-guided tours of 1873 lighthouse.

North Manitou Island, nearby, is a 28-square-mile wilderness with 20 miles of shoreline. There are no facilities for visitors. All travel is by foot and is dependent on weather. Camping is allowed under wilderness regulations; no ground fires are permitted. There is no safe harbor or anchorage on either of the Manitou islands; however, from May-Oct, the islands are accessible by commercial ferry service from Leland (see).

Camping is available at D.H. Day and Platte River campgrounds (May-Nov; dump station; fee); camping is limited to 14 days. Pets on leash only. Information may be obtained from Headquarters in Empire (daily; closed hols). The visitor center there has information on self-guided trails, hiking, cross-country skiing, evening campfire programs, maritime & natural history exhibits and other park activities (daily; closed major hols). For further information and fees contact Chief of Interpretation, 9922 Front St, Empire 49630; 616/326-5134.

Soo Junction (D-4)

(For accommodations see Newberry; also see Hulbert)

Pop 100 (est) **Elev** 840 ft **Area code** 906 **Zip** 49868

What to See and Do

Toonerville Trolley and Riverboat Trip to Tahquamenon Falls. Narrated 6½-hr, 53-mi round trip through Tahquamenon region via narrow-gauge railroad and riverboat, with 1¼-hr stop at Upper Tahquamenon Falls. Trolley leaves Soo Junction (mid-June-early Oct, daily). For further details contact Tahquamenon Boat Service, Inc, RR 2, Box 938, Newberry 49868; 906/876-2311. ¢¢¢¢

Southfield (J-6)

(See also Birmingham, Bloomfield Hills, Detroit, Farmington, Pontiac)

Pop 75,728 **Elev** 684 ft **Area code** 248
Information Chamber of Commerce, 4000 Town Center, Suite 53, 48075; 248/353-6444.

Southfield, a northwestern suburb of Detroit, is the largest office center in the Detroit metro area. It is also home to the Lawrence Institute of Technology and has branch campuses of Wayne State University, Central Michigan University and the University of Phoenix.

Motels

★ ★ ★ **COURTYARD BY MARRIOTT.** 27027 Northwestern Hwy (MI 10) (48034). 810/358-1222; FAX 810/354-3820. 147 rms, 2-3 story. S $89; D $99; suites $99-$109; wknd rates; higher rates special events. Crib free. TV; cable (premium). Indoor pool; whirlpool. Restaurant 6:30-10 am. Serv bar. Ck-out noon. Coin lndry. Meeting rms. Business servs avail. In-rm modem link. Valet serv. Exercise equipt; weights, bicycles. Balconies. Cr cds: A, C, D, DS, MC, V.

D ≈ ✗ ⚓ 🐾 SC

★ ★ **HAMPTON INN.** 27500 Northwestern Hwy (MI 10) (48034). 810/356-5500; FAX 810/356-2083. 153 rms, 2 story. S $65-$75; D $75-$85; under 18 free; some wkly, wknd rates. Crib free. TV; cable. Indoor pool; whirlpool. Complimentary continental bkfst. Restaurant nearby. Ck-out noon. Coin lndry. Meeting rms. Business servs avail. In-rm modem link. Valet serv. Downhill/x-country ski 20 mi. Exercise equipt; weights, bicycles. Picnic tables. Cr cds: A, C, D, DS, MC, V.

D ≈ ≈ ✗ ⚓ 🐾 SC

✓★ **MARVINS GARDEN INN.** 27650 Northwestern Hwy (48034). 810/353-6777; FAX 810/353-2944. 110 rms, 2 story. S, D $40-$45; family rates. Crib $6. TV; cable (premium). Complimentary continental bkfst. Complimentary coffee in rms. Restaurant nearby. Ck-out noon. Meeting rms. Some refrigerators. Cr cds: A, C, D, DS, MC, V.

D ⚓ 🐾 SC

Motor Hotel

★ ★ ★ **HOLIDAY INN.** 26555 Telegraph Rd (48034). 810/353-7700; FAX 810/353-8377. 417 rms, 2-16 story. S, D $75-$81; each addl $8; suites $175-$249; under 19 free; wknd rates. Crib free. Pet accepted, some restrictions. TV; cable (premium). Indoor pool; whirlpool. Restaurant 6:30 am-2 pm, 5-10 pm; Sat, Sun from 7 am. Rm serv. Bar 11-1 am. Ck-out noon. Coin lndry. Convention facilities. Bellhops. Sundries. Gift shop.

Barber, beauty shop. Downhill/x-country ski 20 mi. Game rm. Rec rm. Many rms in circular tower. Cr cds: A, C, D, DS, JCB, MC, V.

Hotels

★ ★ **HILTON GARDEN INN.** *26000 American Dr (48034).* *810/357-1100; FAX 810/799-7030.* 195 rms, 7 story. S, D $89; each addl $10; suites $175; under 12 free; wkend rates. Crib free. Pet accepted, some restrictions. TV; cable (premium). Indoor pool; whirlpool. Restaurant 6-10 am, 11 am-2 pm, 5-10 pm; wkend hrs vary. Bar 5 pm-midnight. Ck-out 1 pm. Meeting rms. Business center. In-rm modem link. Exercise equipt; weight machine, stair machine, sauna. Cr cds: A, C, D, DS, ER, JCB, MC, V.

★ ★ ★ **MARRIOTT.** *27033 Northwestern Hwy (MI 10) (48034).* *810/356-7400; FAX 810/356-5501.* 222 rms, 6 story. S, D $109-$129; suites $250; under 16 free; wkend rates. Crib free. TV; cable, VCR avail. Indoor pool; whirlpool. Restaurant 6:30 am-11 pm. Bar 11-1 am. Ck-out noon. Meeting rms. In-rm modem link. Concierge. Gift shop. Exercise equipt; weights, bicycles, sauna. Health club privileges. Refrigerator. Luxury level. Cr cds: A, C, D, DS, ER, JCB, MC, V.

★ ★ **RADISSON PLAZA AT TOWN CENTER.** *1500 Town Center (48075).* *810/827-4000; FAX 810/827-1364.* 385 rms, 12 story. S $123-$163; D $135-$175; each addl $15; suites $180-$425; under 17 free. Crib free. Valet parking $6. TV; cable (premium), VCR avail. Indoor pool; whirlpool, poolside serv. Restaurant 6:30 am-10:30 pm. Rm serv 24 hrs. Bar 11-2 am; Sun noon-midnight; entertainment Tues-Sat. Ck-out noon. Convention facilities. Business servs avail. In-rm modem link. Concierge. Downhill/x-country ski 20 mi. Exercise equipt; weights, bicycles, sauna. Refrigerators avail. Luxury level. Cr cds: A, C, D, DS, JCB, MC, V.

Restaurants

✔ ★ ★ ★ **CHIANTI VILLA ITALIA.** *28565 Northwestern Hwy (48034).* *810/350-0055.* Hrs: 11:30 am-10 pm; Fri to 11 pm; Sat 4-11 pm; Sun 4-8:30 pm. Closed Memorial Day, Dec 25. Res accepted. Italian menu. Bar. A la carte entrees: lunch $5.95-$9.95, dinner $8.95-$15.95. Child's meals. Specializes in pasta. Italian villa decor. Cr cds: A, D, DS, MC, V.

★ ★ ★ **GOLDEN MUSHROOM.** *18100 W Ten Mile Rd (48075).* *810/559-4230.* Hrs: 11:30 am-4 pm, 5-11 pm; Fri to midnight; Sat 5:30 pm-midnight. Closed Sun; major hols. Res accepted. Continental menu. Bar 11:30 am-midnight. A la carte entrees: lunch $9-$15, dinner $20.50-$32.50. Specializes in wild game dishes. Own baking. Valet parking. Cr cds: A, C, D, DS, JCB, MC, V.

★ ★ **LE METRO.** *29855 Northwestern Hwy (MI 10) (48034), in Applegate Square.* *810/353-2757.* Hrs: 11:30 am-10 pm; Fri, Sat to 11 pm; early-bird dinner Mon-Fri 4:30-6:30 pm; Sun 4:30-5:30. Closed major hols. Res accepted. Bar. Semi-a la carte: lunch $5.95-$12.95, dinner $7.25-$18. Specialties: Norwegian salmon, stuffed medallions of provimi veal, pasta. Entertainment Wed, Thurs. Parking. Lively atmosphere. Cr cds: A, C, D, DS, MC, V.

★ ★ **MORTON'S OF CHICAGO.** *One Town Square (48076), between Civic Center Dr & Lahser.* *810/354-6006.* Hrs: 5:30-11 pm; Sun 5-10 pm. Closed major hols. Res accepted. Bar. A la carte entrees: dinner $16.95-$59.90. Specializes in fresh seafood, beef. Valet parking (dinner).

Menu recited. Semi-formal steak house atmosphere. Cr cds: A, C, D, MC, V.

★ ★ **SWEET LORRAINE'S CAFE.** *29101 Greenfield Rd (48076).* *810/559-5985.* Hrs: 11 am-10:30 pm; Fri, Sat to midnight; Sun to 9 pm. Closed some hols. Bar. A la carte entrees: lunch $4.95-$9.95, dinner $9.45-$16.95. Specialties: pecan chicken, Jamaican "Jerk" chicken & shrimp Creole, vegetarian entrees. Modern-style bistro. Cr cds: A, C, D, DS, MC, V.

✔ ★ ★ ★ **TOM'S OYSTER BAR.** *29106 Franklin Rd (48034).* *810/356-8881.* Hrs: 11 am-midnight. Closed Jan 1, Dec 25. Res accepted. Bar. Semi-a la carte: lunch $5-$10, dinner $10-$18. Child's meals. Specializes in seafood. Entertainment. Outdoor dining. Contemporary decor. Cr cds: A, C, D, DS, MC, V.

South Haven (J-3)

(See also Saugatuck)

Pop 5,563 **Elev** 618 ft **Area code** 616 **Zip** 49090 **E-mail** lakemicvb @cybersol.com

Information Lakeshore Convention & Visitors Bureau, 415 Phoenix St; 616/637-5252.

A five-mile beach on Lake Michigan and surrounding lakes make sport fishing a popular summer pastime in South Haven; numerous marinas and charter boat services are available in the area.

What to See and Do

Liberty Hyde Bailey Birthsite Museum. The 19th-century house of the famous botanist and horticulturist; family memorabilia, period furnishings, Native American artifacts. (Tues & Fri afternoons; closed major hols) 903 S Bailey Ave. Phone 616/637-3251. **Donation.**

Michigan Maritime Museum. Exhibits of Great Lakes maps, photographs, maritime artifacts, historic boats; public boardwalk and park. (All yr; phone for schedule) 260 Dyckman Ave, at the bridge. Phone 616/637-8078. ¢¢

Van Buren State Park. 326 acres include scenic wooded sand dunes. Swimming, bathhouse; hunting; picnicking, playground, concession; camping. 4 mi S off I-196. Phone 616/637-2788. Per car ¢¢

Annual Events

Harborfest. Dragon boat races, arts & crafts, musical entertainment, children's activities. 3rd wkend June.

National Blueberry Festival. Arts & crafts, entertainment, children's parade, 5K run. 2nd wkend Aug.

Motels

✔ ★ ★ **ECONO LODGE.** *09817 MI 140, I-196 exit 18.* *616/637-5141; FAX 616/637-1109.* 60 rms. May-Sept: S $70-$82; D $80-$90; each addl $5; suites $100-$120; under 18 free; higher rates: Tulip Festival, some hols; lower rates rest of yr. Crib $5. Pet accepted. TV; cable (premium), VCR avail (movies). Playground. Indoor pool. Complimentary coffee in rms. Restaurant adj 6:30 am-8 pm; Fri, Sat to 10 pm. Bar. Ck-out 11 am. Coin lndry. Valet serv. Downhill ski 20 mi; x-country ski 5 mi. Exercise rm; instructor, weights, bicycles, sauna. Cr cds: A, C, D, DS, JCB, MC, V.

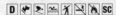

★ **LAKE BLUFF.** 76648 11th Ave. 616/637-8531; FAX 616/637-8532; res: 800/686-1305 (Great Lakes states & PA). 49 rms, 17 kits. May-Sept: S, D $62-$195; kit. units $69-$135; wkly rates; lower rates rest of yr. Crib free. TV. Sauna. Heated pool; wading pool, whirlpool. Coffee in rms. Restaurant nearby. Ck-out 11 am. Business servs avail. Free bus depot transportation. X-country ski 2 mi. Lawn games. Rec rm. Picnic tables, grills. On Lake Michigan. Cr cds: A, C, D, DS, MC, V.

Inn

★★ **YELTON MANOR.** 140 N Shore Dr. 616/637-5220; FAX 616/637-4957. 17 rms, 3 story. No rm phones. July-Labor Day: S, D $90-$205; lower rates rest of yr. TV; cable, VCR avail (movies). Complimentary full bkfst. Restaurant nearby. Ck-out 11 am, ck-in 3 pm. Concierge. Luggage handling. Business servs avail. 18-hole golf privileges. X-country ski 1 mi. Built in 1890; antiques. Totally nonsmoking. Cr cds: A, MC, V.

Restaurants

✔★ **CLEMENTINE'S.** 500 Phoenix St. 616/637-4755. Hrs: 11 am-11 pm; Sun noon-10 pm. Closed some major hols. Bar. Semi-a la carte: lunch $4-$7, dinner $4-$12. Child's meals. Specializes in pan-fried perch, sandwiches, onion rings. Built 1903; original tin ceiling. Brass chandeliers, old photographs. Cr cds: A, DS, MC, V.

★ **MAGNOLIA GRILLE/IDLER RIVERBOAT.** 515 Williams St, #10. 616/637-8435. Hrs: 11 am-midnight. Closed Nov-mid-Apr. Res accepted. Continental menu. Bar. Semi-a la carte: lunch $3.50-$6.50, dinner $12.50-$18.95. Child's meals. Specializes in prime rib, seafood, Cajun dishes. Outdoor dining. On historic riverboat (1897), overlooking Black River. Cr cds: A, C, D, DS, MC, V.

Tawas City (F-5)

Pop 2,009 **Elev** 587 ft **Area code** 517 **Zip** 48763 **E-mail** jgackstetter @voyager.net **Web** www.tawas.com

Information Tawas Area Chamber of Commerce, 402 Lake St, PO Box 608, 48764; 517/362-8643 or 800/55-TAWAS.

A Ranger District office of the Huron-Manitee National Forest (see MANITEE and OSCODA) is located in East Tawas.

Annual Events

Perchville USA. Perch fishing festival featuring parade, fishing contests, softball, go-cart races. 1st wkend Feb.

MarinerFest. Festival with Beach Bash, carnival, lighted boat parade, fish boil, antique car show. 3rd wkend July.

Tawas Bay Waterfront Art Show. Tawas City Park. More than 200 professional and amateur artists display art and craftwork; juried show. 1st wkend Aug.

Motels

★ **DALE.** 1086 US 23. 517/362-6153. 16 rms. June-Nov: S $40-$60; D $50-$65; each addl $4; lower rates rest of yr. TV; cable (premium). Complimentary coffee in rms. Restaurant nearby. Ck-out 11

am. Bus depot transportation. X-country ski 7 mi. Refrigerators avail. Cr cds: A, C, D, DS, MC, V.

★★★ **HOLIDAY INN.** (300 E Bay St, East Tawas 48730) SW on US 23. 517/362-8601; FAX 517/362-5111. 103 rms, 2 story. July-Aug: S, D $99-$140; each addl $8; suites $146; under 18 free; ski, golf plans; higher rates: major hols, Perchville USA; lower rates rest of yr. Crib free. TV; cable (premium). Sauna. Indoor pool; whirlpool, poolside serv. Playground. Free supervised child's activities (July-Aug). Restaurant 6:30 am-10 pm. Rm serv. Bar 11 am-midnight; Fri, Sat 10-2 am; entertainment exc Sun. Ck-out noon. Coin lndry. Meeting rms. Business servs avail. In-rm modem link. Valet serv. Sundries. Gift shop. Golf privileges. X-country ski 5 mi. Beach; jet ski, paddle boats, rafts. Game rm. Lawn games. Cr cds: A, C, D, DS, DS, JCB, MC, V.

★ **TAWAS.** 1124 US 23. 517/362-3822. 21 rms. June-Aug: S, D $53-$99; each addl $5; lower rates rest of yr. Crib $5. TV; cable (premium). Sauna. Pool; whirlpool. Playground. Complimentary coffee. Ck-out 11 am. X-country ski 15 mi. Game rm. Lawn games. Refrigerators; some in-rm whirlpools. Cr cds: A, D, DS, MC, V.

Restaurant

✔★ **GENII'S FINE FOODS.** (601 W Bay St, East Tawas) SW on US 23. 517/362-5913. Hrs: 7 am-9 pm; wkends to 10 pm in season. Closed Dec 25. Res accepted. Semi-a la carte: bkfst $1.35-$5.25, lunch $3.75-$4.75, dinner $4.95-$11. Child's meals. Specializes in fish, steak, spaghetti. Salad bar. Own pies. Rustic decor; overlooks lake. Cr cds: DS, MC, V.

Three Rivers (J-3)

(See also Kalamazoo)

Pop 7,413 **Elev** 810 ft **Area code** 616 **Zip** 49093
Information Chamber of Commerce, 103 S Douglas Ave; 616/278-8193.

What to See and Do

Swiss Valley Ski Area. Three chairlifts, 4 rope tows; patrol, school, rentals, ski shop; snowmaking; NASTAR; restaurant, cafeteria, bar. Vertical drop, 225 ft. Night skiing. (Dec-Mar, daily) 10 mi W on MI 60, then N on Patterson Hill Rd, in Jones. Phone 616/244-5635 or 616/244-8016 (snow conditions). ¢¢¢¢

Inns

★★ **MENDON COUNTRY INN.** (440 W Main St, Mendon 49072) Approx 12 mi E on MI 60. 616/496-8132; FAX 616/496-8403; res: 800/304-3366. 18 rms, 2 story. No rm phones. S, D $69-$159; each addl $10. Children over 12 yrs only. TV in sitting rm. Complimentary continental bkfst. Restaurant nearby. Ck-out 11 am, ck-in 3 pm. Concierge. Luggage handling. Business servs avail. 18-hole golf privileges. X-country ski 15 mi. Some refrigerators. Built in 1843; antiques. Totally nonsmoking. Cr cds: A, DS, MC, V.

★★ **SANCTUARY AT WILDWOOD.** (58138 MI 40, Jones 49061) Approx 10 mi W on US 60. 616/244-5910; res: 800/249-5910. 11 rms, 2 story. No rm phones. Mid-May-Oct: S, D $99-$179; each addl $10; lower rates rest of yr. TV. Pool. Complimentary continental bkfst. Restaurant nearby. Ck-out 11 am, ck-in 3 pm. X-country ski on site. Totally nonsmoking. Cr cds: A, DS, MC, V.

Traverse City (F-3)

Settled 1847 **Pop** 15,155 **Elev** 600 ft **Area code** 616 **Zip** 49684
Information Traverse City Convention and Visitors Bureau, 101 W Grandview Pkwy; 616/947-1120.

A one-acre cherry orchard, planted here in the 1880s, has multiplied to such an extent that today the entire region produces more than 75 million pounds of cherries a year. Traverse City is now one of the largest cherry marketing cities in the country, as well as a year-round resort. There are 6 ski areas within 35 miles of town. More than 30 public and private golf courses are also found in the area.

What to See and Do

Clinch Park. Zoo and aquarium featuring animals native to Michigan (mid-Apr-Nov, daily). Con Foster Museum has exhibits on local history, Native American and pioneer life & folklore (Memorial Day-Labor Day, daily). Steam train rides; marina (May-Oct). Grandview Pkwy & Cass St. Phone 616/922-4904 (zoo) or 616/922-4905 (museum). Some fees. Docked in marina is

Schooner *Madeline.* Full-scale replica of 1850s Great Lakes vessel. Original *Madeline* served as first school in Grand Traverse region. Tours (early May-late Sept, Wed-Sun afternoons). Phone 616/946-2647. **Donation.**

Interlochen Center for the Arts. The Interlochen Arts Academy, a fine arts boarding high school, is located here (Sept-May). Concerts by students, faculty and internationally known guests; art exhibits, drama and dance productions (all yr). Approx 2,500 students assemble here every summer to study music, art, drama and dance (see SEASONAL EVENT). 13 mi SW via US 31, then 2 mi S on MI 137, in Interlochen. Phone 616/276-6230.

Interlochen State Park. A 187-acre park with sand beach on Green and Duck lakes. Swimming, bathhouse; fishing; boating (rentals, launch); picnicking, playground, concession; camping; pavilion. Standard fees. 15 mi SW via US 31, then S on MI 137, in Interlochen, adj to National Music Camp. Phone 616/276-9511. Per car ¢¢

L. Mawby Vineyards/Winery. Wine tasting. Guided tours (May-Oct, Thurs-Sat; by appt only). 7 mi N via MI 22 toward Suttons Bay, then 1 mi W on Hilltop Rd, ¼ mi N on Elm Valley Rd. Phone 616/271-3522. **Free.**

Scenic drive. Extends length of Old Mission Peninsula. At tip is the midway point between the North Pole and the Equator (the 45th parallel). On it stands the Old Mission Lighthouse, one of the first built on the Great Lakes. N on MI 37.

Skiing.

Hickory Hills. Five rope tows; snowmaking; patrol, snack bar. (Mid-Dec-mid-Mar, daily; closed Jan 1, Dec 25) Lighted cross-country trails (fee). 2 mi W of Division St (US 31) on Randolph Rd. Phone 616/947-8566. ¢¢¢

Sugar Loaf Resort. Six chairlifts, beginners' lift; night skiing; rentals, school; snowmaking; 20 slopes; 17 mi of groomed and tracked cross-country trails. 3 restaurants, 2 bars, entertainment. Vertical drop 500 ft. Kids Klub for children, nursery. 18-hole golf; mountain biking (rentals). 7 mi W on MI 72, then 11 mi NW on County 651, follow signs. Phone 616/228-5461 or 800/968-0576. ¢¢¢¢

Annual Event

National Cherry Festival. More than 130 activities, including pageants, water sports, queen's coronation, Junior Royale, Heritage and Cherry Royale parades, band competitions and regattas. Early July.

Seasonal Event

Interlochen Arts Camp. Interlochen Center for the Arts. A variety of performing arts events by students and visiting professionals. Mid-June-early Sept.

Motels

★ ★ **BAYSHORE.** *833 E Front St (49686).* 616/935-4400; *FAX 616/935-0262; res:* 800/634-4401. 120 rms, 4 story. Late June-late Aug: S, D $125-$170; each addl $10; suites $280; under 12 free; lower rates rest of yr. Crib free. TV; cable (premium). Indoor pool; whirlpool. Complimentary continental bkfst. Restaurant opp 7 am-11 pm. Ck-out 11 am. Meeting rm. Business servs avail. Sundries. Coin lndry. Free airport transportation. Downhill/x-country ski 5 mi. Exercise equipt; bicycle, treadmill. Game rm. Cr cds: A, C, D, DS, MC, V.

★ ★ **BEACH CONDOMINIUMS.** *1995 US 31N (49686).* 616/938-2228; *FAX 616/938-9774.* 30 kit. units, 3 story. Late June-early Sept: S, D $119-$239; ski, 5-day package plans; lower rates rest of yr. Crib $10. TV; cable (premium). Heated pool; whirlpool. Ck-out 11 am. Business servs avail. Downhill ski 1½ mi; x-country ski 4½ mi. In-rm whirlpools. Private patios, balconies. On bay; sand beach, lake swimming. Cr cds: A, DS, MC, V.

★ ★ **BEACH HAUS RESORT.** *1489 US 31N (49686).* 616/947-3560; *FAX 616/947-0199.* 29 rms, 2 story. Mid-June-Labor Day: S, D $106-$150; each addl $5; lower rates mid-May-mid-June, after Labor Day-Oct. Closed rest of yr. Crib free. TV; cable. Complimentary continental bkfst. Restaurant opp open 24 hrs. Ck-out 11 am. Coin lndry. Business servs avail. Free airport, bus depot transportation. Refrigerators. Many private patios, balconies. Picnic tables, grills. On Miracle Mile. Private beach; dockage. Cr cds: MC, V.

★ ★ **BEST WESTERN FOUR SEASONS.** *305 Munson Ave (US 31) (49686).* 616/946-8424; *FAX 616/946-1971.* 111 rms. June-Oct: S, D $101-$139; each addl $7; under 18 free; wknd rates; lower rates rest of yr. Crib $7. TV; cable (premium), VCR avail. 2 pools, 1 indoor; whirlpool. Restaurant nearby. Ck-out 11 am. Business servs avail. Downhill ski 3 mi; x-country ski 6 mi. Game rm. Some refrigerators, in-rm whirlpools. Cr cds: A, C, D, DS, MC, V.

★ ★ **DAYS INN.** *420 Munson Ave (US 31) (49686), near Cherry Capital Airport.* 616/941-0208; *FAX 616/941-7521.* 183 rms, 2 story. Mid-June-Labor Day: S, D $110-$125; each addl $2-$5; suites $127-$140; under 12 free; lower rates rest of yr. Crib free. TV; cable (premium), VCR avail (movies $5). Indoor pool; whirlpool. Playground. Complimentary continental bkfst. Restaurant adj 7 am-10 pm. Ck-out 11 am. Coin lndry. Meeting rms. Business servs avail. Free airport transportation. Downhill ski 3 mi; x-country ski 6 mi. Some in-rm whirlpools. Cr cds: A, C, D, DS, ER, JCB, MC, V.

★ ★ **ELK RAPIDS BEACH RESORT.** *(8975 N Bayshore Dr, Elk Rapids 49629) 17 mi N on US 31.* 616/264-6400; *res:* 800/748-0049. 25 kit. condos, 3 story. No elvtr. Memorial Day wkend-Labor Day: $110-$155; each addl $10; wkly rates; lower rates rest of yr. TV; cable. Heated pool. Complimentary coffee in rms. Ck-out 10:30 am. Coin lndry. Downhill/x-country ski 17 mi. Grills. Opp lake, beach. Cr cds: A, DS, MC, V.

★ ★ **GRAND BEACH RESORT HOTEL.** *1683 US 31N (49686).* 616/938-4455; *FAX 616/938-4435; res:* 800/968-1992. 95 rms, 3 story. Mid-June-Labor Day: S, D $112-$142; each addl $10; suites $188-$228; family rates; ski, golf plans; lower rates rest of yr. Crib $5. TV; cable (premium), VCR (movies $3). Indoor pool; whirlpool. Complimentary continental bkfst. Restaurant nearby. Ck-out 11 am. Coin lndry. Meeting rm.

Business servs avail. Downhill/x-country ski 2 mi. Exercise equipt; weight machine, stair machine. Game rm. Refrigerators, wet bars. Balconies. On lake; swimming beach. Cr cds: A, C, D, DS, MC, V.

★ ★ **HAMPTON INN.** *1000 US 31N (49686).* 616/946-8900; FAX 616/946-2817. 127 rms, 4 story. June-Sept: S, D $105-$120; under 19 free; lower rates rest of yr. Crib free. TV; cable (premium). Indoor pool; whirlpool. Complimentary continental bkfst. Ck-out noon. Meeting rm. Business servs avail. In-rm modem link. Valet serv Mon-Fri. Golf privileges 2 mi. Downhill/x-country ski 5 mi. Exercise equipt; bicycles, stair machine. Some refrigerators. Opp beach. Cr cds: A, C, D, DS, MC, V.

★ ★ **HERITAGE INN.** *417 Munson Ave (US 31) (49686).* 616/947-9520; FAX 616/947-9523; res: 800/968-0105. 39 rms, 2 story. Mid-June-early Sept: S, D $90-$140; each addl $4-$6; lower rates rest of yr. Crib $5. TV; cable (premium), VCR (movies $2). Heated pool. Continental bkfst. Restaurant opp 7 am-10 pm. Ck-out 11 am. Downhill ski 3 mi; x-country ski 6 mi. Exercise equipt; weight machines, bicycles. Game rm. Some in-rm whirlpools. Picnic tables. Cr cds: A, C, D, DS, MC, V.

★ **MAIN STREET INN.** *618 E Front St (49686).* 616/929-0410; FAX 616/929-0489; res: 800/255-7180. 95 rms, 21 kit. units. June-Aug: S, D $89.95-$125; each addl $6; kit. units $99.95; under 18 free; lower rates rest of yr. Crib free. Pet accepted. TV; cable (premium), VCR avail (movies). Heated pool. Ck-out 11 am. Coin lndry. Meeting rm. Business servs avail. Downhill ski 5 mi; x-country ski 8 mi. Putting green. Opp beach. Cr cds: A, C, D, DS, ER, MC, V.

★ ★ **NORTH SHORE INN.** *2305 US 31N (49686).* 616/938-2365; FAX 616/938-2368; res: 800/938-2365. 26 rms, 9 with shower only, 3 story. June-Labor Day: S, D $69-$195; under 18 free; lower rates rest of yr. Crib free. TV; cable (premium), VCR avail. Heated pool. Restaurant nearby. Ck-out 11 am. Coin lndry. Downhill/x-country ski 1 mi. Some refrigerators. Totally nonsmoking. Cr cds: A, DS, MC, V.

★ ★ **PINECREST.** *360 Munson Ave (49686).* 616/947-8900; res: 800/223-4433. 35 rms, 2 story. July-Aug: S $90-$110; D $95-$110; lower rates rest of yr. Crib free. TV; cable (premium), VCR (movies). Heated pool; whirlpool. Complimentary continental bkfst. Restaurant adj 6 am-11 pm. Ck-out 11 am. X-country ski 6 mi. Refrigerators avail. Cr cds: A, C, D, DS, MC, V.

★ ★ **POINTES NORTH INN.** *2211 US 31N (49686).* 616/938-9191; FAX 616/938-0070; res: 800/968-3422. 52 rms, 3 story. Mid-June-Aug: S, D $135-$145; under 12 free; wkly rates; lower rates rest of yr. Crib free. TV; cable, VCR avail (movies $3). Heated pool. Complimentary continental bkfst. Restaurant adj 8 am-11 pm. Ck-out 11 am. Downhill/x-country ski 1½ mi. Refrigerators. Private patios, balconies. Private beach. Cr cds: A, MC, V.

★ ★ **SUGAR BEACH.** *1773 US 31N (49686).* 616/938-0100; FAX 616/938-0200; res: 800/509-1995. 95 rms, 3 story. Mid-June-Labor Day: S, D $122-$238; each addl $5-$10; suites $238-$264; lower rates rest of yr. Crib $5. TV; cable (premuim), VCR avail (movies). Indoor pool; whirlpool. Complimentary continental bkfst. Restaurant opp 10 am-midnight. Ck-out 11 am. Coin lndry. Meeting rm. Business servs avail. Downhill ski 3 mi; x-country ski 5 mi. Game rm. Exercise equipt; bicycles, weight machine. Some refrigerators. Cr cds: A, C, D, DS, MC, V.

★ ★ **TRAVERSE BAY INN.** *2300 US 31N (49686).* 616/938-2646; FAX 616/938-5845; res: 800/968-2646. 24 rms, 2 story. July-late Aug: S $55; D $65; suites $95-$165; under 12 free; lower rates rest of yr. Crib free. Pet accepted. TV; cable (premium), VCR avail (movies). Pool;

whirlpool. Playground. Restaurant nearby. Ck-out 11 am. Business servs avail. Gift shop. Valet serv. Coin lndry. Downhill/x-country ski 1 mi. Game rm. Some refrigerators. Cr cds: A, DS, MC, V.

Motor Hotel

★ ★ ★ **HOLIDAY INN.** *615 E Front St (49686).* 616/947-3700; FAX 616/947-0361. 179 rms, 4 story. June-Labor Day: S, D $140-$170; each addl $8; under 19 free; lower rates rest of yr. Crib free. Pet accepted. TV; cable (premium). Indoor pool; whirlpool. Restaurant 7-1 am. Rm serv. Ck-out 11 am. Meeting rm. Business servs avail. Bellhops. Sundries. Gift shop. Valet serv. Free airport, bus depot transportation. Downhill ski 5 mi; x-country ski 8 mi. Exercise equipt; bicycle, weight machine, sauna. Game rm. Lawn games. Some refrigerators. Cr cds: A, C, D, DS, JCB, MC, V.

Hotel

★ ★ ★ **PARK PLACE.** *300 E State St, near Cherry Capital Airport.* 616/946-5000; FAX 616/748-0133. 140 rms, 10 story. June-Oct: S, D $125-$150; each addl $15; suites $175-$250; ski, golf plans; lower rates rest of yr. Crib free. TV; cable (premium). Indoor pool; whirlpool, poolside serv. Restaurant 6:30 am-11 pm. Bar 11 am-midnight, Fri & Sat to 2 am; entertainment Fri, Sat. Ck-out 11 am. Meeting rms. Business servs avail. Free airport, bus depot transportation. Downhill ski 5 mi; x-country ski 1 mi. Exercise equipt; weights, treadmill, sauna. Bathrm phones, refrigerators. Some balconies. Restored to 1930s appearance; Victorian decor. Cr cds: A, C, D, DS, ER, JCB, MC, V.

Resorts

★ ★ ★ **CRYSTAL MOUNTAIN.** *(12500 Crystal Mountain Dr, Thompsonville 49683)* 30 mi SW on US 31 to MI 115. 616/378-2000; FAX 616/378-4594; res: 800/968-7686. 81 motel rms, 2-3 story, 98 kits. (some equipt), 68 condos (1-3 bedrm) & 22 houses (2-3 bedrm). A/C in motel, most condos/houses. Jan-Feb & mid-June-Aug: S, D $79-$135; each addl $15; condos $139-$347; houses $237-$376; family, wkly rates; ski, golf plans; MAP avail; higher rates hols; lower rates rest of yr. Crib free. TV; cable. 2 pools, 1 indoor; whirlpool, poolside serv. Playground. Supervised child's activities (seasonal). Dining rm 7 am-9 pm. Snack bar. Bar; hrs vary. Ck-out noon, ck-in 5 pm (6 pm in winter). Coin lndry. Grocery, package store 2 mi. Meeting rms. Gift shop. Sports dir. Tennis. 27-hole golf, greens fee $40, 10-acre golf practice center, driving range. Downhill/x-country ski on site; rentals. Sleighing. Hiking. Bicycles (rentals). Lawn games. Chairlift rides (summer). Soc dir. Game rm. Exercise equipt; weight machine, treadmill. Many refrigerators, wet bars. Balconies. Picnic tables, grills. Cr cds: A, D, DS, MC, V.

★ ★ ★ **GRAND TRAVERSE.** *(6300 US 31N, Grand Traverse Village 49610)* 6 mi NE on US 31. 616/938-2100; FAX 616/938-5494; res: 800/748-0303. 426 rms, 6-15 story; 200 kit. condos (1-3 bedrm), 50 studio condos, 2-5 story. May-Oct: S, D $150-$210; each addl $15; condos $130-$275; suites $420-$590; wkly, ski, golf plans; lower rates rest of yr. Crib free. TV; cable (premium), VCR. 4 pools, 2 indoor; whirlpool, poolside serv, lifeguard. Supervised child's activities; to age 15. Dining rm 6:30 am-11 pm. Box lunches. Deli. Picnics. Rm serv 7 am-11 pm; Fri, Sat to midnight; off-season to 10 pm. Bar noon-2 am; entertainment, dancing. Ck-out 11 am, ck-in 4 pm. Business center. Valet serv. Grocery 1 blk. Coin lndry, package store 1 mi. Convention facilities. Free airport, bus depot transportation on property shuttle. Sports dir. Indoor, outdoor tennis, pro. 36-hole golf, greens fee $25-$45 for 9 holes, $35-$100 for 18 holes, pro, putting green, driving range. Swimming beach, snack bar, paddleboats, jet skis. Downhill ski 3 mi; x-country ski on site. Ski rentals; sleighing; tobogganing; ice rink, rentals. Horse-drawn carriage rides (summer), horse-drawn sleigh rides (winter). Soc dir; entertainment, dancing. Game rm. Exercise rm; instructor, weights, bicycles, sauna. Fish store. Many refrigerators; some fireplaces. Many private patios, balconies. Cr cds: A, C, D, DS, JCB, MC, V.

★ ★ **SUGAR LOAF.** (4500 Sugar Loaf Mt Rd, Cedar 49621) 7 mi W on MI 72, then 11 mi NW on County 651, follow signs. 616/228-5461; FAX 616/228-6545; res: 800/968-0576. 150 rms in 2-4 story lodge, 53 town houses (2-4 bedrm), 2 story, 16 condo units. July-Aug: S, D $99-$109; each addl $10; studio rms $120-$130; kit. units $145-$320; under 18 free; MAP avail; ski, golf plans; higher rates Christmas hols. Closed Apr & Nov. Crib free. TV; cable. 3 pools, 1 indoor; whirlpool. Supervised child's activities (Dec-Mar, July-Aug). Dining rm (public by res) 7 am-2 pm, 5:30-10 pm; hrs vary off-season. Bar 4 pm-midnight. Ck-out 11 am, ck-in 5 pm. Meeting rms. Business servs avail. Gift shop. Tennis. 36-hole championship golf, greens fee $39-$60, pro, putting green, driving range. Lawn games. Downhill/x-country ski on site; instructor, rentals, ski shop. Soccer field. Entertainment. Game rm. Exercise equipt; weight machine, bicycles. Bike rentals. Some refrigerators. 3,500-ft paved airstrip. Cr cds: A, C, D, DS, MC, V.

Restaurants

✔★ **AUNTIE PASTA'S.** 2030 S Airport Rd. 616/941-8147. Hrs: 11 am-10 pm; Sun from noon. Closed Thanksgiving, Dec 24-25. Italian menu. Bar to 11 pm. Semi-a la carte: lunch $3.95-$7.95, dinner $7.25-$14.95. Child's meals. Specializes in fresh pasta. Own bread, sauces. Parking. Cr cds: A, DS, MC, V.

★ ★ **BAY WINDS.** 1265 US 31N (49686). 616/929-1044. Hrs: 11 am-10 pm; Fri & Sat to 11 pm; Sun bkfst buffet 9 am-1 pm. Closed Dec 24, 25. Res accepted. Bar 11:30 am-midnight; Fri & Sat to 1 am. Semi-a la carte: lunch $4-$6.95, dinner $4.25-$16.95. Buffet bkfst $5.95. Child's meals. Specializes in prime rib, New York strip, seafood. Own desserts. Entertainment. Parking. Outdoor dining. Cr cds: A, C, D, DS, MC, V.

★ ★ ★ **BOWERS HARBOR INN.** 13512 Peninsula Dr (49686). 616/223-4222. Hrs: 5-10 pm; Fri & Sat to 11 pm; Nov-Apr to 9 pm; Fri, Sat to 10 pm. Closed Thanksgiving, Dec 24-25. Res required. Bar. Semi-a la carte: dinner $18-$28. Child's meals. Specialty: fish in a bag. Parking. In historic mansion (1880); early Amer decor. Overlooks bay. Cr cds: A, DS, MC, V.

✔★ **LA SEÑORITA.** 1245 S Garfield St. 616/947-8820. Hrs: 11 am-10 pm; Fri & Sat to 11 pm; Sun noon-10 pm; summer to 11 pm, Fri, Sat to midnight. Closed Easter, Thanksgiving, Dec 25. Mexican, Amer menu. Bar 4 pm-midnight. Semi-a la carte: lunch $4-$6, dinner $5-$10. Child's meals. Specializes in fajitas. Parking. Mexican decor, artifacts. Cr cds: A, C, D, MC, V.

✔★ ★ **REFLECTIONS.** 2061 US 31N (49686). 616/938-2321. Hrs: 7 am-3 pm, 5-10 pm; Sun brunch 11 am-2 pm. Closed Dec 24, 25. Res accepted. Bar to midnight. Semi-a la carte: bkfst $4.95-$7.95, lunch 6.95-$8.95, dinner $6.25-$17.95. Sun brunch $7.95-$12.95. Specializes in seafood. Entertainment Fri, Sat. Overlooks Little Traverse Bay. Cr cds: A, C, D, MC, V.

★ **SCHELDE'S.** 714 Munson Ave (49686). 616/946-0981. Hrs: 11 am-10 pm; Fri & Sat to 11 pm. Closed Thanksgiving, Dec 24, 25. Bar 11 am-midnight. Semi-a la carte: lunch $4.95-$7.25 dinner $6-$15. Child's meals. Specializes in prime rib. Salad bar. Parking. Cr cds: A, DS, MC, V.

✔★ **SWEITZER'S.** 13890 W Bay Shore Dr. 616/947-0493. Hrs: 7 am-9 pm; Sun 8 am-8 pm; Sun brunch 8 am-2 pm. Closed Dec 25. Res

accepted. Serv bar. Semi-a la carte: bkfst $2-$5.50, lunch $4-$6.50, dinner $7.95-$14.95. Sun brunch $5.95. Child's meals. Specializes in seafood, steak. Salad bar. Parking. Cr cds: A, DS, MC, V.

★ ★ ★ **WINDOWS.** 7677 W Bay Shore Dr. 616/941-0100. Hrs: 5-10 pm. Closed Dec 25; also Mon Sept-May & Sun Nov-May. Res accepted. Bar. Semi-a la carte: dinner $16.95-$26.50. Child's meals. Specializes in fresh seafood, beef. Own chocolates, ice cream. Parking. Outdoor dining. View of bay. Totally nonsmoking. Cr cds: C, D, MC, V.

Troy (J-6)

(See also Detroit, Pontiac, Warren)

Settled 1820 **Pop** 72,884 **Elev** 670 ft **Area code** 248
Information Chamber of Commerce, 4555 Corporate Dr, Suite 300, 48098; 248/641-8151.

The year 1819 saw the first land grants in the area that was eventually to become Troy. By 1837 the city was becoming a center for trade between Detroit and Pontiac, and today is the home of many large corporations.

What to See and Do

Stony Creek Metropark. More than 4,000 acres. Swimming beaches with bathhouse, lifeguard (Memorial Day-Labor Day, daily). Fishing; boating (ramp, rentals). Bicycling (rentals, trails). Winter sports. Picnicking, playground; golf (fee). Nature center with trails, exhibits. (Summer, daily) Pets on leash only. Approx 6 mi N on MI 150 (Rochester Rd) to 26 Mile Rd. Phone 248/781-4242. (Also see ANN ARBOR, FARMINGTON and MOUNT CLEMENS) Motor vehicle entry permit (free on Tues): wkdays ¢; wkends & hols ¢¢

Troy Museum and Historical Village. Village museum including 1820 log cabin, 1832 Caswell House, 1877 Poppleton School, 1880 general store, 1890 blacksmith shop and 1900 print shop; exhibits, displays. (Daily exc Mon; closed some major hols; also Dec 24, 31) 60 W Wattles Rd, 1 mi NE of I-75, Big Beaver Rd exit. Phone 248/524-3570. **Free.**

Motels

★ ★ ★ **COURTYARD BY MARRIOTT.** 1525 E Maple Rd (48083). 810/528-2800; FAX 810/528-0963. 147 rms, 3 story, 14 suites. S $89; D $99; suites $109; under 16 free; wkly, wkend rates; higher rates special events. Crib free. TV; cable (premium), VCR avail. Indoor pool; whirlpool. Complimentary coffee in rms. Bkfst avail. Restaurant adj 11-1 am. Ck-out 1 pm. Coin lndry. Meeting rms. Business center. In-rm modem link. Valet serv. Downhill ski 15 mi. Exercise equipt; weight machine, bicycle. Refrigerator in suites. Balconies. Cr cds: A, C, D, DS, MC, V.

★ ★ **FAIRFIELD INN BY MARRIOTT.** (32800 Stephenson Hwy, Madison Heights 48071) Approx 2 mi S via I-75 exit 65B. 810/588-3388. 134 rms, 3 story. S, D $55-$69; each addl $7; under 18 free; wkend rates. Crib free. TV; cable (premium). Pool. Complimentary continental bkfst in lobby. Restaurant adj 11-2 am. Ck-out noon. Valet serv. Cr cds: A, D, DS, MC, V.

★ ★ **HAMPTON INN.** (32420 Stephenson Hwy, Madison Heights 48071) Approx 2 mi S via I-75 exit 65B. 810/585-8881; FAX 810/585-9446. 124 rms, 4 story. S $53-$65; D $57-$70; under 18 free. Crib free. Pet accepted, some restrictions. TV; cable (premium). Complimentary continental bkfst, coffee. Restaurant nearby. Ck-out noon. Meeting rm.

In-rm modem link. Valet serv. Exercise equipt; weights, bicycles, sauna. Cr cds: A, C, D, DS, MC, V.

[D] [🛉] [✗] [⅀] [🔥] [SC]

✔★ **RED ROOF INN.** 2350 Rochester Court (48083). 810/689-4391; FAX 810/689-4397. 109 rms, 2 story. S $36.99-$44.99; D $42.99-$50.99; 3 or more $58.99; under 18 free. Crib free. Pet accepted. TV; cable (premium). Restaurant nearby. Ck-out noon. In-rm modem link. X-country ski 10 mi. Cr cds: A, C, D, DS, MC, V.

[D] [🛉] [⅀] [🔥]

★★ **RESIDENCE INN BY MARRIOTT.** 2600 Livernois Rd (48083). 810/689-6856; FAX 810/689-3788. 152 kit. suites, 2 story. May-Sept: S $109-$129; D $119-$179; family, wkly, wkend, hol rates; 2-day min hols; lower rates rest of yr. Crib free. Pet accepted, some restrictions; $6/day. TV; cable (premium), VCR avail. Heated pool; whirlpool. Complimentary coffee in rms. Complimentary continental bkfst. Restaurant opp 7 am-8 pm. Ck-out noon. Coin lndry. In-rm modem link. Valet serv. Downhill/x-country ski 20 mi. Health club privileges. Balconies. Picnic tables. Cr cds: A, C, D, DS, MC, V.

[D] [🛉] [≈] [⅀] [🔥] [SC]

Motor Hotels

★★ **DRURY INN.** 575 W Big Beaver Rd (48084). 810/528-3330. 153 rms, 4 story. S, D $66-$76; each addl $6; under 18 free; wkend rates. Crib free. Pet accepted, some restrictions. TV; cable (premium), VCR avail. Pool. Complimentary continental bkfst. Restaurant adj 6 am-midnight; Thurs-Sat open 24 hrs. Ck-out noon. Meeting rms. In-rm modem link. Valet serv. X-country ski 4 mi. Health club privileges. Cr cds: A, C, D, DS, MC, V.

[D] [🛉] [≈] [⅀] [🔥] [SC]

★★★ **HILTON INN NORTHFIELD.** 5500 Crooks Rd (48098), at I-75. 810/879-2100; FAX 810/879-6054. 191 rms, 3 story. S $114-$134; D $124-$144; each addl $10; suites $250-$350; family, wkend rates; package plans. Crib free. Pet accepted, some restrictions. TV; cable (premium). Sauna. Indoor pool. Coffee in rms. Restaurant 6:30 am-11 pm; Sat, Sun from 7 am. Rm serv. Bar 10:30-2 am; entertainment. Ck-out noon. Meeting rms. Business center. In-rm modem link. Bellhops. Valet serv. Sundries. X-country ski 3 mi. Game rm. Some refrigerators. Private patios, balconies. Cr cds: A, C, D, DS, ER, MC, V.

[🛉] [≈] [⅀] [🔥] [SC] [🏃]

★★ **HOLIDAY INN.** 2537 Rochester Ct (48083). 810/689-7500; FAX 810/689-9015. 153 rms, 4 story. S $78-$88; D $85-$95; suites $92-$109; under 18 free; wkend rates. Crib free. Pet accepted, some restrictions. TV; cable, VCR avail. Heated pool; poolside serv. Restaurant 6:30 am-1 pm, 5:30-10 pm; Sat & Sun from 7 am. Rm serv. Bar. Ck-out noon. Coin lndry. Meeting rms. In-rm modem link. Bellhops. Valet serv. X-country ski 5 mi. Exercise equipt; weights, bicycles, sauna. Cr cds: A, C, D, DS, JCB, MC, V.

[D] [🛉] [≈] [✗] [⅀] [🔥] [SC]

★★ **SOMERSET INN.** 2601 W Big Beaver Rd (48084). 810/643-7800; FAX 810/643-2296; res: 800/228-8769. 250 rms, 13 story. S $110-$130; D $125-$145; each addl $15; suites $225-$325; family, wkend rates. Crib free. TV; cable. Heated pool. Restaurant 6 am-11 pm; Sat, Sun from 7 am. Rm serv. Bar 11-1 am. Ck-out noon. Meeting rms. Business center. In-rm modem link. Bellhops. Valet serv. Shopping arcade. Health club privileges. Cr cds: A, C, D, DS, MC, V.

[D] [≈] [⅀] [🔥]

Hotels

✔★★★ **DOUBLETREE GUEST SUITES.** 850 Tower Dr (48098). 810/879-7500; FAX 810/879-9139. 251 suites, 8 story. S, D $85-$175; each addl $20; under 18 free; wkend rates. Crib free. TV; cable. Indoor pool; whirlpool, poolside serv. Coffee in rms. Restaurant 6:30 am-10 pm. Bar 11:30 am-midnight. Ck-out 11 am. Convention facilities. In-rm modem link. Gift shop. X-country ski 4 mi. Exercise equipt; weights, bicycles, sauna. Bathrm phones, refrigerators, minibars. Cr cds: A, C, D, DS, ER, JCB, MC, V.

[D] [≈] [✗] [⅀] [🔥] [SC]

★★★ **MARRIOTT.** 200 W Big Beaver Rd (48084). 810/680-9797; FAX 810/680-9774. 350 rms, 17 story. S $139-$144; D $169-$174; each addl $30; suites $600; under 18 free; wkend rates. Crib free. Pet accepted. Valet parking $4/day, $8/overnight; free garage. TV; cable (premium), VCR avail. Indoor pool; whirlpool, poolside serv. Restaurant 7 am-11 pm. Bar 4 pm-1 am; entertainment Tues-Sat. Ck-out noon. Convention facilities. Business servs avail. In-rm modem link. Concierge. Gift shop. X-country ski 5 mi. Exercise equipt; stair machine, treadmill, sauna. Refrigerators avail. Luxury level. Cr cds: A, C, D, DS, ER, MC, V.

[D] [🛉] [≈] [✗] [⅀] [🔥] [SC]

Restaurants

✔★★ **MON JIN LAU.** 1515 E Maple Rd (48083). 810/689-2332. Hrs: 11-1 am; Fri to 2 am; Sat 4 pm-2 am; Sun 3 pm-midnight; hols 4 pm-2 am. Closed Thanksgiving, Dec 25. Res accepted. Asian, Amer menu. Bar. Semi-a la carte: lunch $5.95-$8.95, dinner $8.50-$12.95. Child's meals. Specialties: Mongolian rack of lamb, chili pepper squid, Chinese angel hair pasta. Asian atmosphere. Family-owned. Cr cds: A, C, D, MC, V.

★★ **PICANO'S.** 3775 Rochester Rd (48083). 810/689-8050. Hrs: 11 am-10:30 pm; Fri, Sat to 11 pm; Sun noon-9:30 pm. Closed some major hols. Italian menu. Bar. Semi-a la carte: lunch $7-$10, dinner $8-$16. Specializes in veal, chicken, pasta. Own pasta. Valet parking. Modern Italian decor; mural. Cr cds: A, D, DS, MC, V.

[D]

★★ **STELLINE.** 2801 W Big Beaver Rd (48084). 810/649-0102. Hrs: 11 am-10 pm, 5-10 pm; Sun noon-4 pm. Closed some major hols. Northern Italian menu. Bar. Semi-a la carte: lunch $5.95-$11.95, dinner $6.95-$19.95. Specializes in pasta dishes. Valet parking. Cr cds: A, D, DS, MC, V.

[D] [🔲]

Wakefield (B-3)

(See also Ironwood)

Pop 2,318 **Elev** 1,550 ft **Area code** 906 **Zip** 49968

What to See and Do

Indianhead Mountain-Bear Creek Ski Resort. Quad, triple, 3 double chairlifts; Pomalift, 2 T-bars; beginner's lift; patrol, school, rentals; NASTAR (daily); snowmaking; lodge (see RESORT), restaurants, cafeterias, bars; nursery. Longest run 1 mi; vertical drop 638 ft. (Nov-mid-Apr, daily) 500 Indianhead Rd, 1 mi W on US 2, then 1 mi N. Phone 906/229-5181 or 800/3-INDIAN. ¢¢¢¢

Motel

✔★ **REGAL COUNTRY INN.** 1602 E US 2, 1 mi E on US 2. 906/229-5122. 18 rms, 2 story. July-Aug, mid-Nov-Easter: S $28-$48; D $38-$58; each addl $10; higher rates Christmas hols; lower rates rest of yr. Crib free. TV; cable. Complimentary continental bkfst. Restaurant nearby. Ck-out 11 am. Downhill/x-country ski 2 mi. Sauna. 1950s ice cream parlor on premises. Cr cds: A, DS, MC, V.

[≈] [⅀] [🔥] [SC]

Resort

★ ★ **INDIANHEAD MOUNTAIN.** *500 Indianhead Rd, 1 mi W on US 2, then 1 mi N. 906/229-5181; FAX 906/229-5920; res: 800/346-3426.* 62 rms, 2-3 story, 51 chalets, 32 condo units. S, D $58-$160; mid-wk rates; ski plan. Closed mid-Apr-June & Oct-mid-Nov. Pet accepted. TV; cable, VCR avail (movies). Indoor pool; whirlpool. Playground. Supervised child's activities (Nov-mid-Apr). Dining rm 7:30 am-9 pm. Bar 8-2 am, Sun from noon, summer from 4 pm. Ck-out 11 am, ck-in 4 pm. Meeting rms. Business servs avail. Free bus depot transportation. Tennis. 9-hole, par 3 golf, greens fee $6-$10. Downhill ski on site. Hiking, mountain biking, nature trails. Game rm. Exercise rm; instructor, weights, bicycles, sauna. Cr cds: A, DS, MC, V.

Warren (J-6)

(See also Detroit, St Clair, Troy)

Pop 144,864 **Elev** 615 ft **Area code** 810
Information Chamber of Commerce, 30500 Van Dyke Ave, Suite 118, 48093; 810/751-3939.

Warren, a northern suburb of Detroit, is the third largest city in Michigan. It is home of the General Motors Technical Center, designed by Eero Saarinen, as well as other offices of many large automotive manufacturers. A small, farmland community until the 1930s, Warren erupted almost overnight when General Electric's Carboloy Division established a factory in the area. Soon other major manufacturers set up plants in Warren and the city boomed.

Motels

★ ★ ★ **BEST WESTERN STERLING INN.** *(34911 Van Dyke Ave, Sterling Heights 48312) N on MI 53 (Van Dyke Ave), at 15 Mile Rd. 810/979-1400; FAX 810/979-0430.* 160 rms, 2-3 story. S $69-$85; D $69-$90; each addl $5; suites $135-$275; under 12 free; wkend rates. Crib free. TV; cable. Indoor pool; whirlpool. Restaurant 6-11 pm; Fri to midnight; Sat 7 am-midnight; Sun 7 am-10 pm. Rm serv. Bar from 11 am; Sat to midnight; Sun noon-10 pm. Ck-out noon. Meeting rms. Business servs avail. In-rm modem link. Valet serv. Downhill/x-country ski 18 mi. Exercise equipt; weight machine, bicycles, sauna. Refrigerators; some in-rm whirl-pools, bathrm phones. Cr cds: A, C, D, DS, MC, V.

★ ★ ★ **COURTYARD BY MARRIOTT.** *30190 Van Dyke Ave (48093). 810/751-5777; FAX 810/751-4463.* 147 rms, 3 story, 14 suites, 113 kit. units. S $85; D $95; each addl $10; suites $95-$105; under 5 free; wkend rates. Crib free. TV; cable (premium), VCR avail. Indoor pool; whirlpool. Complimentary coffee in rms. Bkfst avail. Restaurant adj open 24 hrs. Ck-out 1 pm. Coin lndry. Meeting rms. In-rm modem link. Valet serv. Exercise equipt; weights, bicycle. Refrigerators in suites. Balconies. Cr cds: A, C, D, DS, MC, V.

✔ ★ ★ **FAIRFIELD INN BY MARRIOTT.** *7454 Convention Blvd (48092). 810/939-1700; FAX 810/939-1700, ext. 709.* 132 rms, 3 story. S, D $45-$59; each addl $7; under 18 free. Crib free. TV; cable (premium). Heated pool. Complimentary continental bkfst. Restaurant nearby. Ck-out noon. In-rm modem link. Valet serv. Cr cds: A, C, D, DS, MC, V.

★ ★ **GEORGIAN INN.** *(31327 Gratiot Ave, Roseville 48066) 13 Mile Rd at I-94. 810/294-0400; FAX 810/294-1020; res: 800/477-1466.* 111 rms, 2 story. Mid-May-mid-Sept: S, D $60-$73; each addl $5; suites $135; kit. units $81; under 12 free; lower rates rest of yr. Crib free. Pet accepted, some restrictions. TV; cable. Heated pool; poolside serv. Restaurant 6 am-11 pm. Rm serv. Bar. Ck-out noon. Coin lndry. Meeting rms. Business

servs avail. In-rm modem link. Valet serv. Exercise equipt; weights, bicy-cle. Game rm. Cr cds: A, C, D, DS, MC, V.

★ ★ **HAMPTON INN.** *7447 Convention Blvd (48092). 810/977-7270; FAX 810/977-3889.* 124 rms, 3 story. S $52-$57; D $58-$63; suites $75-$81; under 18 free; wkend rates. Crib $6. TV; cable (premium). Complimentary continental bkfst. Restaurant nearby. Ck-out noon. Meeting rms. In-rm modem link. Valet serv. X-country ski 20 mi. Refrigerator, wet bar in suites. Cr cds: A, D, DS, MC, V.

★ ★ **HOLIDAY INN EXPRESS.** *11500 Eleven Mile Rd (48089), I-696 exit Hoover Rd. 810/754-9700; FAX 810/754-0376.* 125 rms, 2 story. S, D $62; under 17 free; wkend rates. Crib free. TV; cable (premium). Pool. Complimentary continental bkfst. Restaurant adj 11 am-midnight. Ck-out noon. Meeting rms. In-rm modem link. Valet serv. Cr cds: A, C, D, DS, ER, JCB, MC, V.

★ ★ **HOMEWOOD SUITES.** *30180 N Civic Center Dr (48093). 810/558-7870; FAX 810/558-8072; res: 800/225-5466.* 76 kit. suites, 3 story. Suites $64-$139. Crib avail. Pet accepted, some restrictions; $100 refundable. TV; cable (premium), VCR. Pool; whirlpool. Complimentary continental bkfst. Complimentary coffee in rms. Restaurant nearby. Ck-out noon. Coin lndry. Meeting rms. Business center. In-rm modem link. Valet serv. Sundries. Gift shop. Downhill/x-country ski 20 mi. Exercise equipt; weight machine, bicycles. Grills. Cr cds: A, C, D, DS, MC, V.

✔ ★ **RED ROOF INN.** *26300 Dequindre Rd (48091). 810/573-4300; FAX 810/573-6157.* 136 rms, 2 story. S $32.99-$42.99; D $46.99-$53.99; 3 or more $44.99-$60.99; under 18 free; higher rates special events. Crib free. Pet accepted, some restrictions. TV; cable (premium). Complimentary coffee. Restaurant nearby. Ck-out noon. Business servs avail. In-rm modem link. Cr cds: A, C, D, DS, MC, V.

★ ★ **RESIDENCE INN BY MARRIOTT.** *30120 Civic Center Dr (48093). 810/558-8050; FAX 810/558-8214.* 133 kit. suites, 3 story. Mid-May-mid-Sept: S, D $104; under 18 free; wkly, wkend rates; lower rates rest of yr. Crib free. Pet accepted; $50 deposit & $8/day. TV; cable (premium), VCR. Pool; whirlpool. Complimentary coffee in rms. Complimentary continental bkfst. Restaurant nearby. Ck-out noon. Coin lndry. In-rm modem link. Valet serv. Exercise equipt; weight machine, bicycle. Health club privileges. Some balconies. Picnic tables. Cr cds: A, C, D, DS, ER, JCB, MC, V.

Restaurant

★ ★ **ANDIAMO ITALIA.** *7096 Fourteen Mile Rd (48092). 810/268-3200.* Hrs: 11 am-11 pm; Fri to midnight; Sat 4 pm-midnight; Sun 4-9 pm. Closed some major hols. Italian menu. Bar. Semi-a la carte: lunch $8-$14, dinner $9-$22. Specializes in pasta, gnocchi, bocconcini di vitello. Valet parking. Player piano. Cr cds: A, MC, V.

Whitehall (H-3)

(For accommodations see Muskegon)

Pop 3,027 **Elev** 593 ft **Area code** 616 **Zip** 49461
Information White Lake Area Chamber of Commerce, 124 W Hanson St; 616/893-4585 or 800/879-9702.

What to See and Do

Montague City Museum. History of lumbering era, artifacts; displays on Montague resident Nancy Ann Fleming, who was Miss America 1961. (June-Aug, Sat & Sun) N on US 31 Business, at Church & Meade Sts in Montague. Phone 616/894-6813. **Donation.**

White River Light Station Museum. In 1875 lighthouse made of Michigan limestone and brick; ship relics and artifacts including binnacle, ships helm, chronograph, compasses, sextant, charts; models, photographs, paintings. View of Lake Michigan's sand dunes along coastline. (Memorial Day-Labor Day, daily exc Mon; Sept, wkends) 6199 Murray Rd, S of the channel on White Lake. Phone 616/894-8265. ¢

World's Largest Weather Vane. This 48-ft-tall structure weighs 4,300 pounds and is topped with a model of the lumber schooner *Ella Ellenwood* that once traversed the Great Lakes. Trademark of Whitehall Products Ltd, the company that created it, the vane is mentioned in the *Guinness Book of Records.* Just S of town on US 31 Business, at edge of White Lake in Montague.

Seasonal Event

Summer concerts. White Lake Music Shell, Launch Ramp Rd, in Montague. Phone 616/893-4585. Mid-June-late Aug.

Ypsilanti (J-5)

(See also Ann Arbor)

Settled 1823 **Pop** 24,846 **Elev** 720 ft **Area code** 313 **Zip** 48197
Information Ypsilanti Area Visitors and Convention Bureau, 301 W Michigan Ave, Suite 101; 313/483-4444.

Established as a Native American trading post, this city was later named for a young Greek patriot, Demetrius Ypsilanti. The city had stations on the Underground Railroad before the Civil War. There are many fine examples of Greek-revival architecture. A two-block area, known as Depot Town, has renovated houses and storefronts, most of which are at least 150 years old, as well as antique shops and restaurants.

What to See and Do

Eastern Michigan University (1849). (25,000 students) The university is home to Quirk/Sponberg Dramatic Arts Theaters, Pease Auditorium, Bowen Field House, Rynearson Stadium, Olds Student Rec Center; Ford Art Gallery with changing exhibits (Mon-Fri; phone 313/487-1268; free); Intermedia Art Gallery (free). Tours (by appt) depart from historic Starkweather Hall. (Daily) Phone 313/487-1849 or 313/487-INFO.

Ford Lake Park. This park offers fishing, boating (launch; fee); volleyball, tennis and handball courts; horseshoes; softball field; 4 picnic shelters. (Daily; some fees May-Sept) 9075 S Huron River Dr. Phone 313/485-6880 or 313/483-0774. Per vehicle ¢¢

Ypsilanti Historical Museum. Victorian house with 11 rms, including a special children's rm and craft rm; exhibits. (Thurs, Sat & Sun) Ypsilanti Historical Archives are located here and are open for research pertaining to local history and genealogy (Mon-Fri mornings). 220 N Huron St. Phone 313/482-4990. **Donation.**

Ypsilanti Monument and Water Tower. Marble column with a bust of Demetrius Ypsilanti, Greek patriot. Century-old water tower. Cross & Washtenaw Sts.

Annual Events

Frog Island Festival. Showcase for diverse jazz styles and talents. Phone 313/761-1800. Late June.

Ypsilanti Summer Music Games. Drum and bugle corps from across Canada and the US. Phone 313/483-4444. Late July.

Ypsilanti Heritage Festival. Riverside Park. Classic cars, arts & crafts, 18th-century encampment, jazz competition and continuous entertainment. Phone 313/483-4444. 3rd full wkend Aug.

Festival of Lights. Riverside Park. Thousands of lights create a winter fantasy land. Late Nov-Dec.

Hotel

★ ★ ★ **MARRIOTT.** *1275 S Huron St, I-94 exit 183.* 313/487-2000; FAX 313/481-0700. 236 rms, 8 story. May-Oct: S, D $95-$135; under 12 free; golf plan; wkend rates; lower rates rest of yr. Crib free. TV; cable (premium), VCR avail. Indoor pool; whirlpool. Restaurant 6:30 am-10 pm. Bar 11-2 am, Sun noon-midnight. Ck-out noon. Convention facilities. Business servs avail. In-rm modem link. Concierge. Gift shop. 18-hole golf, pro, putting green, driving range. Exercise equipt; weight machine, bicycles, sauna. Health club privileges. Game rm. Bathrm phones. Luxury level. Cr cds: A, C, D, DS, ER, MC, V.

Restaurant

★ ★ **HAAB'S.** *18 W Michigan Ave.* 313/483-8200. Hrs: 11 am-9 pm; Fri, Sat to 10 pm. Closed Dec 25. Res accepted. Bar. Semi-a la carte: lunch $4-$8, dinner $6-$16. Child's meals. Specializes in steak. Early Amer decor. Building dates from 19th century. Family-owned. Cr cds: A, C, D, DS, JCB, MC, V.

SC ➔

Ohio

Population: 10,847,115
Land area: 41,004 square miles
Elevation: 433-1,550 feet
Highest point: Campbell Hill (Logan County)
Entered Union: March 1, 1803 (17th state)
Capital: Columbus
Motto: With God, all things are possible
Nickname: Buckeye State
State flower: Scarlet carnation
State bird: Cardinal
State tree: Ohio buckeye
State fair: Early-mid-August 1998, in Columbus
Time zone: Eastern
Web: www.travel.state.oh.us

Ohio is a combination of rich agricultural farmland and forests, as well as a center for technology, education, industry and recreation. Its farmland is dotted with major industrial cities and crisscrossed by roads and railways that carry most of the traffic between the East and Middle West. Taking its name from the Iroquois word for "something great," the state has produced its share of great men, including Thomas Edison, astronauts John Glenn and Neil Armstrong and eight of the nation's presidents—William Harrison, Grant, Hayes, Garfield, Benjamin Harrison, McKinley, Taft and Harding.

The earliest inhabitants of the area were prehistoric people who built more than 10,000 mounds, many of them effigy mounds of great beauty. The first European to explore the Ohio area was probably the French explorer La Salle, in about 1669. Conflicting French and British claims of the area led to the French and Indian War, which ended in a treaty giving most of France's lands east of the Mississippi to Great Britain.

The Northwest Ordinance of 1787 set up the Northwest Territory, of which the future state of Ohio was a division. New Englanders of the Ohio Company bought land in the Muskingum River Valley and founded Marietta, the first permanent settlement. Other settlements soon sprang up along the Ohio River. The area grew as Revolutionary War veterans received land in payment for their services. Ohio became a state in 1803.

Though Ohioans had mixed feelings about the issue of slavery and the Civil War, about 345,000 men responded to Union calls for volunteers—more than twice the state's quota. Ohio also provided several Union commanders, including Ulysses S. Grant and William T. Sherman.

After the Civil War ended, Ohio's abundant natural resources and its strategic position between two of the country's principal waterways—Lake Erie on the north and the Ohio River on the south—paved the way for rapid industrialization and growth. Today, Ohio has many major metropolitan areas, but its citizens are equally proud of Ohio's excellent park system, its wealth of small, tree-shaded towns and its "queen city," Cincinnati.

When to Go/Climate

Ohio summers can be hot and humid, especially in the south. The Lake Erie shore areas often experience cooler summer temperatures than elsewhere in the state, but can be subject to harsh winter winds and sudden snowstorms.

AVERAGE HIGH/LOW TEMPERATURES (°F)

CLEVELAND

Jan 32/18	**May** 69/47	**Sept** 74/54
Feb 35/19	**June** 78/57	**Oct** 62/44
Mar 46/28	**July** 82/61	**Nov** 50/35
Apr 58/37	**Aug** 81/60	**Dec** 37/25

COLUMBUS

Jan 34/19	**May** 72/50	**Sept** 76/55
Feb 38/21	**June** 80/58	**Oct** 65/43
Mar 51/31	**July** 84/63	**Nov** 51/34
Apr 62/40	**Aug** 82/61	**Dec** 39/25

Parks and Recreation Finder

Directions to and information about the parks and recreation areas below are given under their respective town/city sections. Please refer to those sections for details.

Key to abbreviations: I.P. = Interstate Park; N.B.C. = National Battlefield & Cemetery; N.B.P. = National Battlefield Park; N.F. = National Forest; N.G. = National Grassland; N.H. = National Historical Park; H.N.S. = National Historic Site; N.M. = National Monument; N.Mem. = National Memorial; N.M.P. = National Military Park; N.P. = National Park; N.Pres. = National Preserve; N.R. = National Recreational Area; N.R.R. = National Recreational River; N.S. = National Seashore; N.S.T. = National Scenic Trail; N.V.M. = National Volcanic Monument; S.B. = State Beach; S.C.P. = State Conservation Park; S.G. = State Garden; S.H.A. = State Historic

Area; S.H.P. = State Historic Park; S.N.A. = State Natural Area; S.P. = State Park; S.R. = State Reserve; S.R.A. = State Recreation Area; S.Res.P. = State Resort Park; S.R.P. = State Rustic Park.

NATIONAL PARK AND RECREATION AREAS

Place Name	Listed Under
Hopewell Culture N.H.	CHILLICOTHE
Lawnfield (James A. Garfield N.H.S.)	MENTOR
Perry's Victory and International Peace Memorial	PUT-IN-BAY
Wayne N.F.	IRONTON
William Howard Taft N.H.S.	CINCINNATI

STATE RECREATION AREAS

Place Name	Listed Under
Alum Creek S.P.	DELAWARE
Beaver Creek S.P.	EAST LIVERPOOL
Blue Rock S.P.	ZANESVILLE
Buck Creek S.P.	SPRINGFIELD
Buckeye Lake S.P.	NEWARK
Burr Oak S.P.	ATHENS
Caesar Creek S.P.	WILMINGTON
Catawba Island S.P.	PORT CLINTON
Cowan Lake S.P.	WILMINGTON
Crane Creek S.P.	TOLEDO
Delaware S.P.	DELAWARE
Dillon S.P.	ZANESVILLE
East Fork S.P.	CINCINNATI
East Harbor S.P.	PORT CLINTON
Geneva S.P.	GENEVA-ON-THE-LAKE
Grand Lake-St Marys S.P.	CELINA
Headlands Beach S.P.	MENTOR
Hocking Hills S.P.	same
Hueston Woods S.P.	OXFORD
Independence Dam S.P.	DEFIANCE
Indian Lake S.P.	BELLEFONTAINE
John Bryan S.P.	SPRINGFIELD
Kelleys Island S.P.	KELLEYS ISLAND
Lake Erie Island S.P.	PUT-IN-BAY
Lake Hope S.P.	ATHENS
Little Miami Scenic S.P.	WILMINGTON
Mary Jane Thurston S.P.	BOWLING GREEN
Malabar Farm S.P.	MANSFIELD
Maumee Bay S.P.	TOLEDO
Mosquito Lake S.P.	WARREN
Mount Gilead S.P.	same
Paint Creek S.P.	CHILLICOTHE
Portage Lakes S.P.	AKRON
Punderson S.P.	CHARDON
Salt Fork S.P.	CAMBRIDGE
Shawnee S.P.	PORTSMOUTH
Strouds Run S.P.	ATHENS
West Branch S.P.	KENT

Water-related activities, hiking, riding, various other sports, picnicking, camping and visitor centers are available in many of these areas. Camping is permitted all year in 57 parks: $8-$19/site/night, no reservations. Reservations taken by application beginning Mar 1 for Rent-A-Camp program (May-Sept) at many parks: $20-$30/site/night, includes all equipment. Reservations taken up to 1 year in advance for housekeeping cabins at 16 parks (all yr-round): $64-$140/night; June-Aug, by the week only, $285-$725/week. Resort lodges are also available. Pets allowed in designated campsites only. For details contact Information Center, Ohio Dept of Natural Resources, Division of Parks & Recreation, 1952 Belcher Dr, Bldg C-3, Columbus 43224-1386; 614/265-6561.

CALENDAR HIGHLIGHTS

JULY

Antique Car Parade (Hamilton). Courthouse Square. 300 cars in one of the nation's oldest antique car parades. Phone 513/863-2334.

Football's Greatest Weekend (Canton). Pro Football Hall of Fame. Events include parade, induction ceremony, AFC-NFC Hall of Fame Pro Game. Phone 330/456-7253 or 800/533-4302.

AUGUST

Boat Regatta (Put-in-Bay and Vermilion). More than 200 sailboats race to Vermilion. Phone 216/967-6634.

All-American Soap Box Derby (Akron). Derby Downs, Municipal Airport. More than 200 boys and girls (9-16 yrs) from US and abroad compete with homemade, gravity-powered cars for scholarships, prizes. Phone 330/733-8723.

Ohio State Fair (Columbus). Expositions Center. Agricultural and industrial exposition plus grandstand entertainment, pageants and horse show. Phone 614/644-3247 or 800/BUCKEYE.

NEC "World Series of Golf" (Akron). Firestone Country Club. International competition. Phone 330/644-2299.

SEPTEMBER

Riverfest (Cincinnati). Celebration of Cincinnati's river heritage held along the city's waterfront parks. Entertainment includes sky diving and waterskiing performances, amusement rides, riverboat cruises and fireworks. Phone Convention and Visitors Bureau, 800/CINCY-USA.

OCTOBER

Bob Evans Farm Festival (Gallipolis). Bob Evans Farm. Bluegrass and country entertainment; food, 150 heritage craftspeople and demonstrations; Appalachian clogging, square dancing. Camping. Phone 614/245-5305 or 800/994-FARM.

DECEMBER

Christmas Candle Lightings (Coshocton). Roscoe Village. Tree and candle lighting ceremonies; hot-mulled cider and ginger cookies. Phone 800/877-1830.

Christmas in Zoar (New Philadelphia). Tours of private houses, craft show, German food, strolling carolers and tree lighting ceremony. Phone 330/874-3011.

SKI AREAS

Place Name	Listed Under
Alpine Valley Ski Area	CLEVELAND
Boston Mills Ski Area	AKRON
Brandywine Ski Area	AKRON
Clear Fork Ski Area	MANSFIELD
Mad River Mt Ski Resort	BELLEFONTAINE
Snow Trails Ski Area	MANSFIELD

FISHING & HUNTING

Annual fishing license $15, nonresident $24; 3-day permit $15. Hunting license $15 (resident youth $8), nonresident $91. Special deer and wild turkey permits $20. Fur-taker permit $11. Wetlands habitat stamp $11. Tourist small game permit $25. Hunting forbidden on Sunday except for coyote, fox, woodchuck and waterfowl in season. For latest game and fishing regulations contact the Department of Natural Resources, Division of Wildlife, 1840 Belcher Dr, Columbus 43224-1329; 614/265-6300 or 800/WILDLIF.

Driving Information

Safety belts are mandatory for all persons in front seat of vehicle. Children under 4 years or under 40 pounds in weight must be in an approved safety seat anywhere in vehicle. For further information phone 614/466-2550.

INTERSTATE HIGHWAY SYSTEM

The following alphabetical listing of Ohio towns in *Mobil Travel Guide* shows that these cities are within 10 miles of the indicated Interstate highways. A highway map should, however, be checked for the nearest exit.

Highway Number	Cities/Towns within 10 miles
INTERSTATE 70	Cambridge, Columbus, Dayton, Newark, St Clairsville, Springfield, Vandalia, Zanesville.
INTERSTATE 71	Akron, Cincinnati, Cleveland, Columbus, Delaware, Lebanon, Mansfield, Mason, Mount Gilead, Strongsville, Wilmington.
INTERSTATE 75	Bowling Green, Cincinnati, Dayton, Findlay, Lebanon, Lima, Mason, Miamisburg, Middletown, Piqua, Sidney, Toledo, Vandalia, Wapakoneta.
INTERSTATE 76	Akron, Kent, Youngstown.
INTERSTATE 77	Akron, Brecksville, Cambridge, Canton, Cleveland, Gnadenhutten, Marietta, Massillon, New Philadelphia.
INTERSTATE 90	Ashtabula, Chardon, Cleveland, Geneva-on-the-Lake, Mentor, Painesville.

Additional Visitor Information

For free travel information contact Ohio Division of Travel and Tourism, PO Box 1001, Columbus 43216, 800/BUCKEYE (Mon-Fri, 9 am-8 pm; Sat, Sun 9 am-6 pm). The Ohio Historical Society is a good source for historical information; contact Director, 1982 Velma Ave, Columbus 43211, phone 614/297-2300.

Travel information centers are located on interstate highways at eleven key roadside rest areas. These centers offer free brochures containing information on Ohio's attractions and events; staff are also on hand to answer any questions.

Akron (C-5)

(See also Aurora, Canton, Cleveland, Kent, Massillon)

Founded 1825 **Pop** 223,019 **Elev** 1,027 ft **Area code** 330 **E-mail** jsksales@aol.com

Information Akron/Summit Convention & Visitors Bureau, 77 E Mill St, 44308-1401; 330/374-7560 or 800/245-4254.

The "rubber capital of the world" is 35 miles south of the St Lawrence Seaway, on the highest point on the Ohio and Erie Canal, covering an area of approximately 54 square miles. Metropolitan Akron has many manufacturing plants as well as strong service, trade and government sectors. Although best known for its rubber factories, housing corporate headquarters of four major rubber companies, Akron is also a center for polymer research.

Akron owes its start to the Ohio and Erie Canal, which was opened to traffic in 1827. General Simon Perkins, commissioner of the Ohio Canal Fund, seeing the trade possibilities, laid out the town two years earlier. The seat of Summit County was already thriving when Dr. Benjamin Franklin

Goodrich organized the first rubber plant in 1870. This event aroused little interest and it took the "horseless carriage" to spark the future of Akron. By 1915 it was a boom town. The major rubber companies maintain large research laboratories and developmental departments. Other products range from fishing tackle to plastics and industrial machine products.

What to See and Do

Akron Art Museum. Regional, national and international art, 1850 to present; also changing exhibits; sculpture garden. (Daily exc Mon; closed hols) 70 E Market St. Phone 330/376-9185.   **Free.**

Akron Civic Theatre (1929). Lavishly designed by Viennese architect John Eberson to resemble a night in a Moorish garden, complete with blinking stars and floating clouds. The theater is one of four atmospheric-type facilities of its size remaining in the country. (Daily) 2 182 S Main St. Phone 330/535-3179 or 330/535-3178 (recording).

Akron Zoological Park. This 26-acre zoo features more than 300 birds, mammals, and reptiles from around the world. Exhibits include the Ohio Farmyard where children can pet and feed the animals, walk-through aviary, and underwater viewing window for observing the river otters. (Mid-Apr-mid-Oct, daily; also for special events during Halloween wk and Dec 25 wk). 500 Edgewood Ave. Phone 330/375-2525 or 330/375-2555. ¢¢

Cuyahoga River Gorge Reservation. Part of park system. On N bank is the cave where Mary Campbell, first white child in the Western Reserve, was held prisoner by Native Americans. 3 mi N of Main & Market Sts.

Cuyahoga Valley National Recreation Area. 32,000 acres. Beautiful and varied area with extensive recreational facilities, many historic sites and entertainment facilities; 20-mi long, fully accessible Ohio & Erie Canal Towpath Trail. Artistic events, performances, campfire programs, nature walks. Two visitor centers (daily; closed some hols). Park (daily). Fee for some activities. Located along 22 mi of the Cuyahoga River just N of Akron. Phone 800/445-9667. Also here is

> **Dover Lake Park.** Swimming, beach, wave pool, water slides, tube slides; concessions, pavilions; chairlift ride, camping, picnic grounds. (Memorial Day-Labor Day, daily) Approx 13 mi N on OH 8, then 1 mi W on OH 82, then S on Brandywine Rd, then W on Highland (Vaughn) Rd. Phone 330/467-7946.   ¢¢¢¢

Goodyear World of Rubber. Historic and product displays. A 1-hr tour includes movies on tire production. (Mon-Fri; closed hols) 4th floor Goodyear Hall; 1201 E Market St, 1½ mi E of OH 8, on I-76, at jct Goodyear Blvd. Phone 330/796-6546.   **Free.**

Hale Farm and Village. Authentic Western Reserve house (ca 1825), other authentic buildings in a village setting depict northeastern Ohio's rural life in the mid-1800s; pioneer implements; craft demonstrations, special events; farming; costumed guides. (May-Oct, Wed-Sun) Approx 10 mi N on unnumbered road at 2686 Oak Hill Rd in Bath (10 mi S of I-80 exit 11); in Cuyahoga Valley National Recreation Area. Phone 330/666-3711 or 800/589-9703.   ¢¢ Also here is

> **Cuyahoga Valley Scenic Railroad.** Scenic railroad trips through the Cuyahoga Valley National Recreation Area between Cleveland and Akron aboard vintage railroad cars pulled by first generation ALCO diesels. Stations include Independence (S of Cleveland), Hale Farm, Akron Valley Business District, NPS Canal Visitor Center, Howard St & Quaker Square in Akron. Reservations required. For schedule phone 330/657-2000 or 800/468-4070.   ¢¢¢¢

Inventure Place. Dedicated to the creative process; houses interactive exhibit area, national inventors hall of fame. (Daily exc Mon) 221 S Broadway St. Phone 800/968-IDEA.   ¢¢¢

Naturealm Visitors Center. A 4,000-sq-ft "Gateway to Nature" underground exhibit area surrounded by many sights and sounds of nature. (Daily; closed hols) 1828 Smith Rd. Phone 330/865-8065.   **Free.**

Portage Lakes State Park. Several reservoir lakes totaling 2,520 acres. Swimming; fishing, hunting; boating (dock, launch). Hiking; snowmobiling. Picnicking (shelter). Camping (campground located 5 mi from park headquarters), pet camping. Standard fees. 4 mi S off OH 93, 619. Phone 330/644-2220.   **Free.**

Portage Princess Cruise. Cruise the glacier-made lakes on enclosed riverboat (May-Oct 13, daily). On OH 619, 4 mi W of I-77. Phone 330/499-6891. ¢¢¢

Quaker Square. Shopping, hotel, restaurants and entertainment center in the original mills and silos of the Quaker Oats Company. Historical displays including famous Quaker Oats advertising memorabilia and Railways of America model train collection. (Daily; closed major hols) 135 S Broadway, in downtown area. Phone 330/253-5970. **Free.**

Skiing.

Boston Mills. 4 triple, 2 double chairlifts, 2 handle tows; patrol, school, rentals; snowmaking; cafeteria; bar. Longest run 1,800 ft; vertical drop 250 ft. (Dec-mid-Mar, daily) 9 mi N on OH 8 to exit 12, then W on OH 303 to Riverview Rd in Peninsula, then N to Boston Mills Rd. Phone 216/657-2334 or 216/467-2242 (Cleveland); 216/655-6703 (snow conditions), 216/656-4489 (Cleveland). ¢¢¢¢¢

Brandywine. Triple, 4 quad chairlifts, 3 handle tows; patrol, school, rentals, 27 snowmaking systems; cafeteria; bars. Longest run 1,800 ft; vertical drop 250 ft. (Early Dec-late Feb, daily) Approx 13 mi N on OH 8, then 4 mi W on Highland Rd. Phone 216/657-2334 or 216/467-2242 (Cleveland); 216/655-6703 (snow conditions) or 216/656-4489 (Cleveland). ¢¢¢¢

Stan Hywet Hall and Gardens. Tudor-revival-style manor house built by F.A. Seiberling, co-founder of Goodyear Tire & Rubber; contains 65 rms with antiques and art treasures dating from the 14th century. More than 70 acres of grounds and gardens. (Daily exc Mon; closed major hols, also 2 wks Jan) 714 N Portage Path, 1½ mi N of jct OH 18. Phone 330/836-5533. ¢¢¢

Summit County Historical Society. 550 Copley Rd. Phone 330/535-1120. Museums include

Perkins Mansion (1837). Greek-revival home built of Ohio sandstone by Simon Perkins, Jr, on 10 landscaped acres. (Daily exc Mon; closed hols; also Jan) 550 Copley Rd at S Portage Path. ¢¢

John Brown Home. Remodeled residence where the abolitionist lived 1844-1846. (Daily exc Mon; closed hols; also Jan) 514 Diagonal Rd at Copley Rd. ¢¢

The University of Akron (1870). (27,000 students) Third-largest four-yr university in Ohio; known for its Colleges of Polymer Science, Polymer Engineering and Fine and Applied Arts. The E.J. Thomas Performing Arts Hall is home to the Ohio Ballet and Akron Symphony. Bierce Library houses many collections including the Archives of the History of American Psychology. Campus tours arranged through Admissions. Just E of downtown. Office phone 330/972-7100; 330/972-7111 (for general information). Also here is

Hower House (1871). A 28-rm Victorian mansion, second empire Italianate-style architecture, built by John Henry Hower; lavish furnishing from around the world. (Feb-Dec, Wed-Fri & Sun afternoons; closed most major hols) 60 Fir Hill. Phone 330/972-6909. ¢¢

The Winery at Wolf Creek. Tasting rm overlooks vineyard & lake. (Tues-Sat; closed hols) Approx 1½ mi N of I-76, at exit 14, 2637 S Cleveland-Massillon Rd in Norton. For details phone 330/666-9285. **Free.**

Annual Events

All-American Soap Box Derby. Derby Downs, Municipal Airport. More than 200 boys and girls (9-16 yrs) from US and abroad compete with homemade, gravity-powered cars for scholarships, prizes. Phone 330/733-8723. 1st or 2nd wk Aug.

NEC "World Series of Golf." Firestone Country Club. International competition. Phone 330/644-2299. Late Aug.

Yankee Peddler Festival. 10 mi S on OH 21S, in Canal Fulton, at Clay's Park Resort. Arts, crafts, entertainment, costumes, food of pioneer period 1776-1825. Phone 800/535-5634. Last 3 wkends Sept.

Harvest Festival. Hale Farm and Western Reserve Village. Celebrates end of the harvest season. Hands-on 19th-century rural activities include cider pressing, hayrides, crafts; musical entertainment, food. Phone 330/666-3711 or 800/589-9703. Early Oct.

Wonderful World of Ohio Mart. Stan Hywet Hall. Renaissance Fair with handicrafts, food, entertainment. Phone 330/836-5533. Early Oct.

Seasonal Events

Ohio Ballet. E.J. Thomas Hall, University of Akron. For schedule, reservations phone 330/972-7900. Performances in Feb, Apr, July, Aug & Nov.

Blossom Music Center. 1145 W Steels Corners Rd, in Cuyahoga Falls, approx 8 mi N on OH 8, then W; Ohio Tpke exits 11, 12; in Cuyahoga National Recreation Area. Summer home of Cleveland Orchestra; symphony, jazz, pop, rock, country music concerts. For schedule phone 330/920-8040. Late May-mid-Sept.

Akron Symphony Orchestra. E.J. Thomas Hall, University of Akron. Phone 330/535-8131. Sept-May.

Motels

★ ★ **BEST WESTERN EXECUTIVE INN.** 2677 Gilchrist Rd (44305), I-76 exit 27. 330/794-1050; FAX 330/794-8495. 120 rms, 3 story. May-Sept: S $57-$63; D $63-$70; each addl $6; under 17 free; lower rates rest of yr. Crib free. TV; cable (premium), VCR avail. Heated pool. Restaurant 6 am-10 pm; Sat from 7 am; Sun 7 am-8 pm. Rm serv. Bar 11-2 am exc Sun. Ck-out noon. Meeting rms. Business servs avail. Valet serv. Exercise equipt; bicycles, stair machine. Cr cds: A, C, D, DS, ER, MC, V.

D ≈ ⚹ ⊠ ⚹ SC

✔ ★ ★ **COMFORT INN WEST.** 130 Montrose West Ave (44321), I-77, exit 137B. 330/666-5050; FAX 330/668-2550. 132 rms, 2 story. S $55-$85; D $55-$95; each addl $8; under 19 free; wkend rates. Crib free. TV; cable (premium), VCR avail (movies). Indoor pool, whirlpool. Complimentary continental bkfst. Restaurant nearby. Ck-out 11 am. Coin lndry. Meeting rm. Business servs avail. In-rm modem link. Valet serv. Health club privileges. Some refrigerators, wet bars. Cr cds: A, C, D, DS, JCB, MC, V.

D ≈ ⊠ ⚹ SC

★ ★ **HOLIDAY INN-SOUTH.** I-77 & Arlington Rd (44312), exit 120. 330/644-7126; FAX 330/644-1776. 131 rms, 2 story. S $59-$65; D $60-$65; each addl $6; suites $130-$185; under 18 free. Crib free. Pet accepted. TV; cable. Pool; poolside serv. Restaurant 6 am-10 pm; Sat, Sun from 7 am. Rm serv. Bar 11-2:30 am; entertainment Tues-Sat. Ck-out noon. Meeting rms. Business servs avail. Bellhops. Valet serv. Sundries. Airport transportation. Cr cds: A, C, D, DS, JCB, MC, V.

D ✔ ≈ ⊠ ⚹ SC

✔ ★ **RED ROOF INN.** 99 Rothrock Rd (44321), OH 18 & I-77. 330/666-0566; FAX 330/666-6874. 108 rms, 2 story. S $35.99-$41.99; D $39.99-$49.99; each addl $7; under 18 free. Crib free. Pet accepted. TV; cable (premium). Complimentary coffee. Restaurant adj 6 am-10 pm. Ck-out noon Business servs avail. Cr cds: A, C, D, DS, MC, V.

D ✔ ⊠ ⚹ SC

Motor Hotels

★ ★ **HOLIDAY INN AKRON/FAIRLAWN.** 4073 Medina Rd (44333), I-77 exit 137A. 330/666-4131; FAX 330/666-7190. 165 rms, 4 story. S, D $65-$90; each addl $8; under 19 free. Crib free. TV; cable (premium). Heated pool. Restaurant 6:30 am-10 pm; Fri, Sat to midnight. Rm serv. Ck-out noon. Coin lndry. Meeting rms. Business servs avail. In-rm modem link. Valet serv. Sundries. Exercise equipt; weight machine, bicycles. Health club privileges. Cr cds: A, C, D, DS, JCB, MC, V.

D ≈ ⚹ ⊠ ⚹ SC

★ ★ ★ **RADISSON INN.** 200 Montrose West Ave (44321). 330/666-9300; FAX 330/668-2270. 130 rms, 4 story. S, D $100-$130; each addl $10; suites $150; under 18 free; wkend rates; higher rates NEC World Series of Golf. Crib free. TV; cable. Indoor pool. Coffee in rms. Restaurant 6 am-2 pm, 5-10 pm. Rm serv. Bar to 10 pm. Ck-out noon. Meeting rms. Business servs avail. In-rm modem link. Valet serv. Sundries. Airport transportation. Exercise equipt; weights, bicycles, whirlpool, sauna. Mini-bars; some refrigerators. Some balconies. Cr cds: A, C, D, DS, ER, JCB, MC, V.

[D] [symbols] [SC]

Hotels

★ ★ ★ HILTON INN-WEST. *3180 W Market St (44333). 330/867-5000; FAX 330/867-1648.* 204 rms, 4 story. S $79-$115; D $89-$125; each addl $10; suites $110-$140; studio rms $75; family rates. Crib free. Pet accepted. TV; cable. 2 pools, 1 indoor; poolside serv. Restaurant 6:30 am-10 pm; Fri, Sat from 7:30 am. Rm serv. Bar 11:30-2 am, Sun 4 pm-midnight; entertainment Fri, Sat. Ck-out noon. Coin lndry. Meeting rms. Business center. In-rm modem link. Bellhops. Valet serv. Sundries. Gift shop. Airport transportation. Exercise equipt; weights, bicycles, sauna, whirlpool. Some refrigerators. Cr cds: A, C, D, DS, MC, V.

[D] [symbols] [SC]

★ ★ ★ HILTON QUAKER SQUARE. *135 S Broadway (44308). 330/253-5970; FAX 330/253-2574.* 196 rms, 8 story. S, D $89-$135; each addl $15; suites $220-$295; studio rms $110-$150; family rates, wknd packages. Crib free. TV; cable. Indoor pool. Restaurant 6:30 am-11 pm; Sun 7 am-10 pm. Bar 11-2:30 am; entertainment wkends. Ck-out noon. Meeting rms. Business center. Airport transportation. Exercise equipt; bicycle, stair machine. Balconies. Historic building; all rms are in grain silos, built in 1932 for Quaker Oats Co. Cr cds: A, C, D, DS, MC, V.

[D] [symbols] [SC]

Restaurants

✔★ ART'S PLACE. *(2225 State Rd, Cuyahoga Falls) N on I-77. 330/928-2188.* Hrs: 11 am-10 pm; Fri to 11 pm; Sat 4-11 pm; Sun noon-7 pm. Res accepted. Bar to 1 am. Semi-a la carte: lunch $4.15-$6.75, dinner $5.50-$12.95. Child's meals. Specializes in prime rib, chicken, barbecued ribs. Parking. Cr cds: A, DS, MC, V.

[D] [symbol]

✔★ HOUSE OF HUNAN. *(2717 W Market St, Fairlawn) 3 mi NW. 330/864-8215.* Hrs: 11:30 am-10 pm; Fri to 11 pm; Sat noon-11 pm; Sun noon-10 pm; early-bird dinner Mon-Sat 4-6 pm; Sun noon-4 pm. Res accepted. Chinese menu. Bar. A la carte entrees: lunch $4.50-$7.50, dinner $5.25-$12.95. Specializes in Hunan and Szechwan dishes. Parking. Oriental decor. Cr cds: A, D, DS, MC, V.

[SC] [symbol]

★ ★ ★ LANNING'S. *826 N Cleveland-Massillon Rd. 330/666-1159.* Hrs: 5:30-11 pm; Sat 5 pm-midnight. Closed Sun; major hols. Res accepted. Bar from 4 pm. Semi-a la carte: dinner $14-$27.50. Specializes in steak, fresh seafood. Pianist Sat. Valet parking. Mediterranean decor. View of stream. Family-owned. Jacket. Cr cds: A, C, D, DS, MC, V.

[symbol]

★ ★ ★ TANGIER. *532 W Market St. 330/376-7171.* Hrs: 11:30 am-11 pm; Sun to 3 pm. Closed most major hols. Res accepted. Continental menu. Bar to 2:30 am. Semi-a la carte: lunch $5.95-$8.95, dinner $8.95-$23. Child's meals. Specialties: rack of lamb Phoenicia, authentic Mediterranean feast. Own baking. Entertainment. Parking. Floor shows. Mediterranean-Middle Eastern decor. Cr cds: A, C, D, DS, MC, V.

[D] [SC] [symbol]

✔★ ★ TRIPLE CROWN. *(335 S Main, Munroe Falls) 2 mi E of Rte 8. 330/633-5325.* Hrs: 11 am-10 pm; Sun 3-8 pm; early-bird dinner Tues-Fri 4-6 pm; Sun brunch 10 am-2:30 pm. Closed major hols. Res accepted. Bar. Semi-a la carte: lunch $4.85-$10.95, dinner from $7.95. Sun brunch $8.95. Child's meals. Specializes in fish, steak. Pianist. Parking. Horseracing memorabilia. Cr cds: A, DS, MC, V.

[D] [SC] [symbol]

Alliance (C-6)

(See also Akron, Canton, Kent, Massillon, Youngstown)

Settled 1805 **Pop** 23,376 **Elev** 1,174 ft **Area code** 330 **Zip** 44601 **E-mail** allcham@alliancelink.com **Web** www.rodman.lib.oh.us/chamber
Information Chamber of Commerce, 210 E Main St; 330/823-6260.

What to See and Do

Glamorgan Castle. Historic complex (1904) built by Colonel William H. Morgan. (Mon-Fri, afternoon tours; also by appt) 200 Glamorgan Ave. Phone 330/821-2100. **Donation.**

Mabel Hartzell Museum. Furniture, clothes of 18th and 19th centuries, local historical items, early pewter, glass, china in century-old house. (June-Aug, Sun exc hols; wkdays & rest of yr, by appt) 840 N Park Ave. Phone 330/823-4115 or 330/821-4256. **Donation.**

Mount Union College (1846). (1,375 students) Liberal arts college. On campus is Crandall Art Gallery (Sept-Apr, Mon-Fri; closed hols; free). Guided tours. 1972 Clark Ave. Phone 330/821-5320.

Annual Event

Carnation Festival. Honoring state flower. 2nd wk Aug.

Motor Hotel

★ ★ COMFORT INN. *2500 W State St. 330/821-5555; FAX 330/821-4919.* 113 rms, 5 story. S $50; D $54; each addl $5; suites $80-$115; under 18 free. Crib free. Pet accepted, some restrictions; $10. TV; cable (premium), VCR avail (movies). Indoor pool; whirlpool. Complimentary continental bkfst. Ck-out noon. Coin lndry. Meeting rms. Business servs avail. Bellhops. Exercise equipt; weight machine, bicycles. Cr cds: A, C, D, DS, JCB, MC, V.

[D] [symbols] [SC]

Ashtabula (A-6)

(See also Geneva-on-the-Lake, Painesville)

Settled 1796 **Pop** 21,633 **Elev** 695 ft **Area code** 440 **Zip** 44004
Information Ashtabula Area Chamber of Commerce, 4536 Main Ave, PO Box 96; 440/998-6998.

This modern harbor at the mouth of the Ashtabula River is an important shipping center for coal and iron ore. Swimming, fishing and boating are possible in Lake Erie.

What to See and Do

Conneaut Historical Railroad Museum. Museum in former New York Central depot; memorabilia of early railroading, model engines. Adj on siding are the *Old Iron Horse 755* (retired Nickel Plate RR locomotive) and a caboose, which may be boarded. (Memorial Day-Labor Day, daily) Children 11 yrs & under only with adult. 12 mi NE on US 20 to Conneaut, at 342 Depot St, just off Broad St. Phone 440/599-7878. **Free.**

Great Lakes Marine & US Coast Guard Memorial Museum. In former lighthouse keeper's home built 1898. Includes working scale model of Hulett ore unloading machine, ship's pilot house, marine artifacts, paintings, photos, models, handmade miniature tools. Guides; tours (by appt, all yr). View of river, harbor, docks; picnicking. (Memorial Day-Oct, Fri-Sun & hols, afternoons) 1071-73 Walnut Blvd. Phone 440/964-6847. **Donation.**

Annual Events

Blessing of the Fleet. Boat parades on lake; tours, art shows, fireworks. 1st wkend June.

Ashtabula County Dog Days. Downtown. Rides, entertainment, food. Late July.

Ashtabula County Fair. In Jefferson. Mid-Aug.

Covered Bridge Festival. Fairgrounds. 2nd wkend Oct.

Motels

✔★ **CEDARS.** 2015 W Prospect Rd (US 20). 440/992-5406; FAX 440/992-5943; res: 800/458-2015. 15 rms. S $40; D $50-$65; each addl $5. TV; cable (premium). Restaurant nearby. Ck-out 11 am. Business servs avail. Cr cds: A, C, D, DS, MC, V.

★★ **HOLIDAY INN.** (Austinburg 44010) 8 mi SW, at jct OH 45, I-90 Warren-Ashtabula exit 223. 440/275-2711; FAX 440/275-7314. 119 rms, 2 story. S $70-$80; D $75-$95; under 18 free. Crib free. TV; cable (premium). VCR avail. Heated pool. Coffee in rms. Restaurant 6 am-2 pm, 5-10 pm. Rm serv. Bar 5 pm-midnight. Ck-out noon. Coin lndry. Meeting rms. Business servs avail. In-rm modem link. Bellhops. Sundries. Cr cds: A, C, D, DS, ER, JCB, MC, V.

★ **TRAVELODGE.** (2352 OH 45, Austinburg 44010) 8 mi SW, at jct OH 45, I-90 Warren-Ashtabula exit 223. 440/275-2011; FAX 440/275-1253. 48 rms, 2 story. S $50-$60; D $58-$74; each addl $5; under 18 free. Crib free. TV; cable. Pool. Coffee in rm. Complimentary continental bkfst in lobby. Ck-out noon. Business servs avail. Cr cds: A, C, D, DS, ER, MC, V.

Restaurant

★★ **EL GRANDE.** 2145 W Prospect St. 440/998-2228. Hrs: 11 am-9 pm; Fri to 10 pm; Sat 4-11 pm. Closed Sun, Mon; major hols. Italian, Amer menu. Semi-a la carte: lunch $3.95-$9.95, dinner $5.45-$13.45. Specializes in steak, pasta, seafood. Western decor. Cr cds: MC, V.

Athens (F-4)

Founded 1800 **Pop** 21,265 **Elev** 723 ft **Area code** 614 **Zip** 45701
Information Athens County Convention & Visitors Bureau, PO Box 1019; 614/592-1819 or 800/878-9767.

The establishment of Ohio University, oldest college in what was the Northwest Territory, created the town of Athens. It is also the seat of Athens County. A Ranger District office of the Wayne National Forest (see IRONTON) is located here.

What to See and Do

Ohio University (1804). (18,000 students) First university in Northwest Territory. Information and self-guided tours of historic campus available at Visitors Center, Richland Ave. Athens Campus. Phone 614/593-2097.

State parks.

Lake Hope. Over 3,220 acres. Swimming, lifeguard, bathhouse May-Labor Day); fishing, boating (rentals); concession; picnicking, hiking; 69 cabins, lodge; camping, pet camping; nature center with naturalist (May-Labor Day). Standard fees. 14 mi NW on OH 56, then 6 mi S on OH 278 in Zaleski State Forest. Phone 614/596-5253. **Free.**

Strouds Run. On 161-acre Dow Lake. Swimming, lifeguard (Memorial Day-Labor Day); fishing, boating (rentals); picnicking, hiking; concession; camping, pet camping. Standard fees. (Daily) 5 mi E off US 50. Phone 614/592-2302. **Free.**

Burr Oak. More than 2,500 acres. Swimming, lifeguard, bathhouse (Memorial Day-Labor Day); fishing, boating (rentals, ramp) picnicking, hiking; nearby golf course; cabins, lodge (614/767-2112); camping. Standard fees. 3 mi N on US 33, then 14 mi N on OH 13, borders on Wayne National Forest (see IRONTON). Phone 614/767-3570 (park office). **Free.**

Wayne National Forest. Sections W, N & E (see IRONTON).

Seasonal Event

Ohio Valley Summer Theater. Elizabeth Baker Theater & Forum Theater, Ohio University. For schedule phone 614/593-4800. June-July.

Motels

★★ **AMERIHOST INN.** 20 Home St, US 33 State St Exit. 614/594-3000; FAX 614/594-5546. 102 rms, 2 story. S, D $69-$79; each addl $6; under 12 free; higher rates special events. Crib free. TV. Indoor pool; whirlpool. Complimentary continental bkfst. Restaurant adj 6 am-10 pm. Ck-out noon. Meeting rm. Exercise equipt; stair machine, bicycle, sauna. Cr cds: A, C, D, DS, MC, V.

✔★ **DAYS INN.** 330 Columbus Rd, at US 33, from E Columbus Rd exit. 614/592-4000; FAX 614/593-7687. 60 rms, 2 story. S, D $50-64; each addl $6; under 14 free; higher rates special events. Crib free. TV; cable (premium). Complimentary continental bkfst. Restaurant nearby. Ck-out noon. Business servs avail. Miniature golf, driving range adj. Cr cds: A, C, D, DS, MC, V.

Motor Hotel

★★★ **OHIO UNIVERSITY INN.** 331 Richland Ave. 614/593-6661; FAX 614/592-5139. 143 rms, 2-3 story. S, D $79-$89; under 12 free; higher rates special events. Crib free. TV; cable. Pool. Restaurant 6:30 am-2 pm, 5-10 pm; Sun, hols 7 am-9 pm. Rm serv. Bar. Ck-out noon. Meeting rms. Business servs avail. Sundries. Some private patios, balconies. Cr cds: A, C, D, DS, MC, V.

Resort

✔★ **BURR OAK.** (Glouster 45732) 29 mi N, off OH 78, 4 mi NE of Glouster. 614/767-2112. 60 rms in 3-story lodge; 30 kit. cottages, 2-bedrm. Apr-Oct: S, D $65-$99; each addl $5; kit. cottages $95 ($495/wk); under 12 free; some lower rates rest of yr. Crib free. TV; VCR avail (movies). Indoor pool. Playground. Dining rm 7 am-9 pm. Bar. Ck-out noon. Meeting rms. Business servs avail. Sundries. Gift shop. Lighted tennis. Game rm. Overlooks Burr Oak Lake; all state park facilities avail. Cr cds: A, D, MC, V.

Restaurants

★★ **SEVEN SAUCES.** 66 N Court. 614/592-5555. Hrs: 5-9 pm; Fri, Sat to 10 pm; Sun to 8:30 pm. Closed major hols. Res accepted. Continental menu. Bar (Fri & Sat only). A la carte entrees: dinner $7.95-$15.95. Specializes in seafood, steak, international dishes. Cr cds: A, DS, MC, V.

★★ **SYLVIA'S.** 4 Depot St. 614/594-3484. Hrs: 11 am-2 pm, 5-9 pm; Fri, Sat to 10 pm; Sun from 5 pm. Closed major hols; also 1 wk

Aug. Italian menu. Bar. Semi-a la carte: lunch $5-$9, dinner $8-$18. Child's meals. Specializes in pasta, seafood, chicken. Patio dining. Contemporary decor. Cr cds: A, MC, V.

Aurora (B-5)

(See also Akron, Cleveland, Kent, Warren)

Pop 9,192 **Elev** 1,130 ft **Area code** 330 **Zip** 44202

What to See and Do

Geauga Lake. A 120-acre lake with boardwalk; wave pool, water slides, swimming. Amusement park with rides including 4 roller coasters and historic carousel; Turtle Beach; live musical shows; Cinema 180. (Memorial Day-Labor Day, daily; May & Sept, wkends only) 5 mi N on OH 43. Phone 330/562-7131, 330/562-8303 or 800/THE-WAVE. ¢¢¢¢¢

⭐ **Sea World.** An 80-acre marine-life park; live shows including the killer whale Shamu, dolphins, seals and otters; also water-ski and boat show. Major exhibits are the Penguin Encounter, Shamu's Happy Harbor (adults & kids play area) and World of the Sea aquarium. Also featured is Shark Encounter; five species inhabit this unique underwater experience that actually brings visitors into the world of the shark; a moving walkway partially surrounded by huge, curved acrylic panels immerses guests 7 ft into the exhibit and 6 ft under the surface of the water. (Mid-May-early Sept, daily) 1100 Sea World Dr, 2 mi NW. Phone 330/562-8101. General admission ¢¢¢¢¢

Motel

⭐⭐⭐ **BEST WESTERN AURORA WOODLANDS RESORT.** *800 N Aurora Rd (OH 43). 330/562-9151; FAX 330/562-5701.* 144 rms, 2 story. May 16-Sept 13: S, D $148-$168; each addl $10; suites $275; under 18 free; lower rates rest of yr. Crib free. TV; cable (premium). Indoor heated pool; whirlpool, lifeguard. Restaurant 6:30 am-2 pm, 5-10 pm. Rm serv. Bar 11-2 am. Ck-out 11 am. Coin lndry. Meeting rms. Business servs avail. Valet serv. Sundries. Exercise equipt; weights, treadmill, sauna. Game rm. Cr cds: A, C, D, DS, ER, MC, V.

Restaurant

⭐⭐ **WELSHFIELD INN.** *(14001 Main Market, Burton) 15 mi NE via OH 43, OH 44 & US 422. 330/834-4164.* Hrs: 11:30 am-2:30 pm, 4:30-9 pm; Fri to 10 pm; Sat to 2:30 pm, 4:30-10 pm; Sun noon-8 pm. Closed Mon. Res accepted; required some hols. Serv bar. Semi-a la carte: lunch $2.50-$10.95, dinner $9.50-$21.95. Child's meals. Specializes in fresh salmon, baked chicken, prime rib. Cr cds: A, DS, MC, V.

Beachwood (B-5)

(See also Brecksville, Cleveland)

Pop 10,677 **Area code** 216 **Zip** 44122

The suburb of Beachwood is located east of Cleveland.

What to See and Do

Shaker Lakes Regional Nature Center. This 300-acre tract has nature and hiking trails, bird observation area, 2 man-made lakes. (Mon-Sat, also Sun afternoons) 6N to OH 87, at 2600 S Park Blvd in Shaker Heights. Phone 216/321-5935. **Free.**

Thistledown Racing Club. Thoroughbred horse racing; parimutuel betting. (Mar-late May, Sat-Sun; late May-Dec, daily) At Northfield and Emery Rd, in North Randall. Phone 216/662-8600. ¢¢

Motel

⭐ **TRAVELODGE.** *3795 Orange Place. 216/831-7200; FAX 216/831-0616.* 128 rms, 2 story. May-Sept: S $60-$71; D $66-$78; each addl $6; under 18 free; summer packages; lower rates rest of yr. Crib free. TV; cable. Complimentary continental bkfst. Coffee in rms. Ck-out 11 am. Meeting rms. Business servs avail. Sundries. Airport transportation. Some refrigerators. Cr cds: A, C, D, DS, ER, JCB, MC, V.

Motor Hotels

⭐⭐⭐ **COURTYARD BY MARRIOTT.** *3695 Orange Place, at I-271 & Chagrin Blvd. 216/765-1900; FAX 216/765-1841.* 113 rms, 4 story. S, D $95-$109; each addl $10; suites $150; under 18 free; wkend rates. Crib free. TV; cable (premium). Heated pool. Complimentary coffee in rms. Restaurant. Rm serv. Bar. Ck-out noon. Meeting rms. Business servs avail. Valet serv. Some refrigerators. Some balconies. Cr cds: A, D, DS, MC, V.

⭐ **HOLIDAY INN.** *3750 Orange Place. 216/831-3300; FAX 216/831-0486.* 169 rms, 4 story. S, D $115; under 19 free. Crib free. TV; cable (premium). Indoor/outdoor pool; sauna, lifeguard. Restaurant 6:30 am-10 pm. Rm serv. Bar 11-1 am, Sun 1-10 pm. Ck-out 11 am. Coin lndry. Meeting rms. Business servs avail. In-rm modem link. Valet serv. Sundries. Downhill/x-country ski 7 mi. Cr cds: A, C, D, DS, ER, JCB, MC, V.

⭐⭐⭐ **MARRIOTT-EAST.** *3663 Park East Dr. 216/464-5950; FAX 216/464-6539.* 403 rms, 4-7 story. S, D $79-$165; suites $225-$500; under 18 free. Crib free. Pet accepted; fee. TV; cable (premium), VCR avail. Indoor/outdoor pool; whirlpool, lifeguard, poolside serv. Restaurant 6:30 am-11 pm; Sat, Sun from 7 am. Rm serv. Bar 11:30-2 am. Ck-out noon. Coin lndry. Convention facilities. Business center. Bellhops. Concierge. Gift shop. Downhill ski 15 mi; x-country ski 10 mi. Exercise equipt; weights, bicycles, sauna. Game rm. Rec rm. Some refrigerators. Luxury level. Cr cds: A, C, D, DS, ER, JCB, MC, V.

⭐⭐⭐ **RADISSON INN.** *26300 Chagrin Blvd. 216/831-5150; FAX 216/765-1156.* 196 rms, 2-4 story. May-Sept: S, D $105; each addl $10; suites $150-$185; under 18 free; lower rates rest of yr. Crib free. TV; cable (premium). Heated pool. Restaurants 6:30 am-10 pm. Rm serv 7 am-10 pm. Bar 11 am-midnight. Ck-out noon. Coin lndry. Meeting rms. Business servs avail. Gift shop. Valet serv. Barber. Downhill ski 12 mi; x-country ski 1 1/2 mi. Exercise equipt; weight machine, bicycles. Some refrigerators. Cr cds: A, C, D, DS, ER, JCB, MC, V.

Hotel

⭐⭐⭐ **EMBASSY SUITES.** *3775 Park East Dr. 216/765-8066; FAX 216/765-0930.* 216 suites, 4 story. S $155; D $170; each addl $15; under 16 free; higher rates New Year's Eve. Crib free. TV; cable (premium), VCR avail. Indoor pool; whirlpool, lifeguard. Complimentary full bkfst; evening refreshments. Complimentary coffee in rms. Restaurant 11:30 am-10 pm; Fri, Sat to 11 pm. Bar. Ck-out 1 pm. Coin lndry. Meeting rms. Business servs avail. In-rm modem link. Gift shop. Downhill/x-country ski 12 mi. Exercise equipt; weights, bicycles, sauna. Game rm. Refrigerators. Cr cds: A, C, D, DS, MC, V.

Restaurants

★ ★ **CHARLEY'S CRAB.** *25765 Chagrin Blvd.* 216/831-8222. Hrs: 11:30 am-10 pm; Sat to 11 pm; Sun 4-10 pm; early-bird dinner Mon-Sat 5-6 pm; Sun 4-10 pm. Closed major hols. Res accepted. Bar. Semi-a la carte: lunch $6.75-$18, dinner $11.50-$30. Child's meals. Specializes in fresh fish, pasta. Valet parking. Cr cds: A, C, D, DS, MC, V.

★ ★ **INN AT HUNTERS HOLLOW.** *(100 N Main St, Chagrin Falls 44022) E on US 422, off Chagrin Blvd.* 216/656-2949. Hrs: 11:30 am-10 pm; Fri & Sat to 11 pm. Closed Sun; major hols. Res accepted. American menu. Bar to 1:30 am. Lunch $6-$10, dinner $15-$25. Specializes in fresh fish, homemade pasta, lamb. Entertainment. Valet parking. Cr cds: A, C, D, DS, MC, V.

★ ★ **LION & LAMB.** *(30519 Pine Tree Rd, Pepper Pike) S on I-271, exit Chagrin Blvd, at Landers Circle & Chagrin Blvd.* 216/831-1213. Hrs: 11:30 am-3 pm, 5-10 pm; Fri, Sat to 11 pm. Closed Sun; major hols. Res accepted. Italian, Amer menu. Bar 11-2:30 am. Semi-a la carte: lunch $4.95-$6.75, dinner $12.50-$26.95. Entertainment exc Sun. Family-owned. Cr cds: A, D, DS, MC, V.

★ ★ ★ **RISTORANTE GIOVANNI.** *25550 Chagrin Blvd.* 216/831-8625. Hrs: 11:30 am-2:30 pm, 5:30-9:30 pm; Sat 5:30-10:30 pm. Closed Sun; major hols. Res required. Northern Italian menu. Bar. Wine list. Semi-a la carte: lunch $6.50-$14.95, dinner $18.50-$34. Specializes in fresh seafood, homemade pasta. Own baking, desserts. Valet parking. Jacket. Cr cds: A, C, D, DS, MC, V.

★ ★ **SAMURAI JAPANESE STEAK HOUSE.** *23611 Chagrin Blvd.* 216/464-7575. Hrs: 11:30 am-2 pm, 5:30-10 pm; Fri to 11 pm; Sat 5-11 pm; Sun 4:30-9 pm. Closed July 4, Thanksgiving, Dec 25. Res accepted. Japanese menu. Bar. Semi-a la carte: lunch $5.95-$9.50, dinner $12.50-$25.95. Child's meals. Specialties: teppanyaki filet mignon and sirloin steak, shrimp flambé. Table-side cooking. Valet parking. Cr cds: A, D, DS, MC, V.

★ ★ **SHUHEI.** *23360 Chagrin Blvd (44022).* 216/464-1720. Hrs: 11:30 am-2:30 pm, 5:30-10 pm; Fri, Sat to 11 pm; Sun 5-9 pm. Closed most major hols. Res accepted. Japanese menu. Bar. Semi-a la carte: lunch $8.50-$14.50, dinner $15.95-$23.50. Specializes in seafood, poultry. Japanese decor. Jacket. Cr cds: A, C, D, DS, MC, V.

Bellefontaine (D-2)

(See also Lima, Sidney)

Settled 1806 **Pop** 12,142 **Elev** 1,251 ft **Area code** 937 **Zip** 43311 **E-mail** jwagner@logancountyohio.com **Web** www.logancountyohio.com

Information Greater Logan County Convention and Tourist Bureau, 100 S Main St; 937/599-2016.

The French name, which means "beautiful fountain," resulted from the natural springs at the site. An industrial town, this area was once a Shawnee village called Blue Jacket's Town, for a white man who was captured by the Shawnee, married the chief's daughter and became chief of the tribe. The area is rich in Native American lore, Revolutionary history and scenic and recreational attractions. At Campbell Hill, the elevation is 1,550 feet, the highest point in Ohio.

What to See and Do

Indian Lake State Park. Recreational area and summer resort. Land once belonged to Wyandot, Shawnee and other tribes. More than 640 acres of land with a 5,800-acre water area. Swimming; fishing for bass, crappie, channel catfish and bluegill; boating (dock, launch, rentals). Hiking trails. Snowmobiling on frozen lake. Picnicking, concession. Camping. Standard fees. (Daily) 12 mi NW off US 33. Phone 937/843-2717. **Free.**

Mad River Mt Ski Resort. Triple, 2 double chairlifts, T-bar, 3 rope tows; patrol, school, rentals; snowmaking; lodge, cafeteria, bar. Slopes (1,000-3,000 ft). (Dec-Mar, daily) 5 mi SE on US 33. Phone 937/599-1015. ¢¢¢¢

Ohio Caverns. Noted for the coloring and white crystal formations; illuminated. Picnicking. One-hr guided tours covering one mi. (Daily; closed Thanksgiving, Dec 25) 8 mi S on US 68 to West Liberty, then 3 mi SE on OH 245. Phone 937/465-4017. ¢¢¢

Piatt Castles. Castle Mac-A-Cheek (1868) is the Norman-style home of Civil War General Abram Sanders Piatt; original furnishings, firearms, Native American artifacts, patent models, extensive library. **Mac-O-Chee** (1881) is the Flemish-style home of social critic, writer, editor and Civil War Colonel Donn Piatt; European and Asian furnishings and objects. Both Castles (Apr-Oct, daily; Mar, wkends). Guided tours. 7 mi S on US 68 to West Liberty, then 1 mi E on OH 245. Phone 937/465-2821. Each castle ¢¢

Zane Caverns. Illuminated stalactites, stalagmites; display of cave pearls; guided tour. Gift shop. (May-Sept, daily; rest of yr, Wed-Sun) 7092 OH 540. Phone 937/592-9592. ¢¢¢   Also here is

Southwind Park. Picnicking, playground; cabins & camping (fee); swimming pond; hiking trails. Pets (on leash). For further information contact Zane Caverns. ¢

Annual Event

Logan County Fair. Harness racing. Mid-late July.

Motels

★ ★ **COMFORT INN.** *260 Northview Dr, 3 mi N of OH 68 at US 33.* 513/599-6666; FAX 513/599-2300. 73 rms, 2 story. S $58-$77; D $47.70-$82; each addl $5; suites $82-$96; under 18 free. Crib free. Pet accepted; $10. TV; cable (premium), VCR avail (movies). Heated pool. Complimentary continental bkfst. Restaurant nearby. Bar; entertainment. Ck-out noon. Coin lndry. Meeting rms. In-rm modem link. Sundries. Downhill ski 8 mi. Exercise equipt; stair machine, treadmill. Some refrigerators, microwaves. Cr cds: A, C, D, DS, JCB, MC, V.

★ ★ **HOLIDAY INN.** *1134 N Main St, 2 mi N on OH 68 at US 33.* 513/593-8515; FAX 513/593-4802. 103 rms, 2 story. S, D $69; each addl $5; under 18 free. Crib free. Pet accepted, some restrictions. TV; cable (premium), VCR avail. Indoor pool. Restaurant 6 am-2 pm, 5-10 pm; Sun to 8 pm. Rm serv. Bar 4 pm-1 am; entertainment Tues-Sat. Ck-out noon. Coin lndry. Meeting rms. In-rm modem link. Downhill ski 5 mi. Exercise equipt; weights, stair machine. Cr cds: A, C, D, DS, JCB, MC, V.

Bellevue (B-3)

(See also Fremont, Milan, Norwalk, Sandusky)

Settled 1815 **Pop** 8,146 **Elev** 751 ft **Area code** 419 **Zip** 44811
Information Chamber of Commerce, 110 W Main St; 419/483-2182.

What to See and Do

Historic Lyme Village. The John Wright Victorian mansion is featured with several other buildings that have been moved here and restored to create village depicting 19th-century life. (June-Aug, daily exc Mon; May & Sept, Sun only) Several events throughout the yr. 2 mi E on OH 113. Phone 419/483-4949 or 419/483-6052. ¢¢

Mad River and NKP Railroad Society Museum. Display of various old railroad cars, artifacts; gift shop. (Memorial Day-Labor Day, daily; May & Sept-Oct, wkends only) 253 S West St. Phone 419/483-2222. **Donation.**

Seneca Caverns. One of Ohio's largest natural caverns, it is actually a unique "earth crack," created by undetermined geologic forces. Eight rooms on 7 levels; Old Mist'ry River flows at lowest level (110 ft); lighted. One-hr guided tours; constant temperature of 54°F. (Memorial Day-Labor Day, daily; May & Sept-mid-Oct, wkends only). 3 mi S on OH 269, then 2 mi W on Thompson Township Road 178. Phone 419/483-6711. ¢¢¢

Motel

★ ★ **BEST WESTERN RESORT INN.** *1120 E Main St. 419/483-5740.* 89 rms, 1-2 story. Late June-early Sept: S, D $59-$79; each addl $4; suites $135-$250; higher rates wkends; lower rates rest of yr. Crib $10. TV; cable (premium). 2 pools, 1 indoor; whirlpool. Restaurant 6 am-9 pm. Bar. Ck-out 11 am. Coin lndry. Meeting rms. Sundries. Exercise equipt; weights, bicycles, sauna. Refrigerators; microwaves avail. Cr cds: A, C, D, DS, ER, MC, V.

D ⚓ ≋ 𝔛 ⊠ 🐾 SC

Restaurant

✔★ ★ **McCLAIN'S.** *137-139 Main St, jct US 20 & OH 269. 419/483-2727.* E-mail wwemclains@onebellevue. Hrs: 11 am-10 pm. Closed Sun; some major hols. Bar. Semi-a la carte: lunch, dinner $3.25-$13. Child's meals. Specializes in barbecued ribs, steak, prime rib, seafood. Old-time decor. Family-owned since 1880. Cr cds: MC, V.

D

Bowling Green (B-2)

(See also Findlay, Fremont, Toledo)

Founded 1834 **Pop** 28,176 **Elev** 705 ft **Area code** 419 **Zip** 43402
Information Chamber of Commerce, 163 N Main St, PO Box 31; 419/353-7945 or 800/866-0046.

Surrounded by rich farmland, Bowling Green is an educational center with diversified industries. It is also the seat of Wood County.

What to See and Do

Bowling Green State University (1910). (18,000 students) Attractive 1,300-acre campus. Undergraduate colleges of arts and sciences, education, health and human services, music, business administration and technology; graduate college. A golf course and an all-yr ice-skating arena are open to the public (fees). E Wooster St, just W of I-75. Phone 419/372-2531. Located on campus is

The Educational Memorabilia Center (1875). Restored one-room schoolhouse and memorabilia collection; more than 1,500 items reminiscent of education's past, such as desks, slates, inkwells, McGuffey's Readers, maps, globes; potbellied stove and 100-yr-old pump organ. (Sat & Sun afternoons; wkdays, by appt; closed hols & school breaks). 900 blk of E Wooster. Phone 419/372-7405. **Free.**

Mary Jane Thurston State Park. A 555-acre park. Fishing; boating (unlimited horsepower, dock, launch); hunting; hiking; sledding. Picnicking (shelter). Tent camping. Standard fees. 4 mi NW on OH 64, then 8 mi W on OH 65, near Napoleon. Phone 419/832-7662.

Annual Events

Wood County Fair. County Fairgrounds. Agricultural & livestock shows, displays, rides & concessions. Early Aug.

National Tractor Pulling Championship. World's largest outdoor pull held at Wood Co Fairgrounds. Phone 419/354-1434. Mid-Aug.

Motor Hotel

(Rates may be higher special university wkends)

★ ★ **DAYS INN.** *1550 E Wooster St, I-75 exit 181, opp Bowling Green Univ. 419/352-5211; FAX 419/354-8030.* 100 rms, 2 story. S $45-$53; D $54-$58; each addl $6; higher rates special events. Crib $6. TV; cable (premium). Complimentary continental bkfst. Complimentary coffee in rms. Ck-out 11 am. Microwaves avail. Cr cds: A, C, DS, MC, V.

D ⊠ 🐾 SC

Restaurants

✔★ **JUNCTION BAR & GRILL.** *110 N Main St. 419/352-9222.* Hrs: 11 am-10 pm; Fri, Sat to 11 pm; Sun to 9 pm. Closed Easter, Thanksgiving, Dec 25. Res accepted. Mexican, Amer menu. Bar. Semi-a la carte: lunch $1.99-$6.45, dinner $1.99-$12.95. Child's meals. Specializes in appetizers, steak. Cr cds: A, DS, MC, V.

★ ★ **KAUFMAN'S.** *163 S Main St, I-75 Bowling Green Univ exit. 419/352-2595.* Hrs: 11-12:30 am. Closed Sun; major hols. Res accepted. Bar to 1 am. Semi-a la carte: lunch $3-$7.50, dinner $5-$26.45. Buffet: dinner (Fri, Sat) $14.95. Child's meals. Specializes in steak, seafood, prime rib. Salad bar. Family-owned. Cr cds: A, C, D, DS, MC, V.

Brecksville (B-5)

(See also Beachwood, Cleveland)

Pop 11,818 **Elev** 900 ft **Area code** 440 **Zip** 44141
Information Chamber of Commerce, 10107 Brecksville Rd; 440/526-7350.

The suburb Brecksville is located approximately nine miles south of Cleveland and is adjacent to the Cuyahoga Valley National Recreation Area.

Motel

★ ★ **COMFORT INN.** *(6191 Quarry Ln, Independence 44131)* N via I-77, Rockside Rd exit. 440/328-7777. 90 rms, 3 story. June-Aug: S $60-$72; D $68-$80; under 18 free; lower prices rest of yr. TV; cable; VCR (movies $4). Pool. Complimentary continental bkfst. Restaurant adj 6 am-10 pm. Ck-out noon. Meeting rms. Business servs avail. Sundries. Cr cds: A, C, D, DS, MC, V.

D ≋ ⊠ 🐾 SC

Motor Hotels

★ ★ ★ **HILTON-SOUTH.** *(6200 Quarry Ln, Independence 44131)* N on I-77, at Rockside Rd. 440/447-1300; FAX 440/642-9334. 195 rms, 5 story. S $105-$115; D $110-$140; each addl $12; wkend, family rates. Crib free. Pet accepted; some restrictions. TV; cable. Indoor/outdoor pool; poolside serv (summer), lifeguard. Playground. Coffee in rms. Restaurant 6 am-10 pm; Fri, Sat to 11 pm. Rm serv. Entertainment. Ck-out noon. Meeting rms. Business servs avail. In-rm modem link. Bellhops. Gift shop. Free airport transportation. Tennis. Exercise equipt; weights, bicycle, whirlpool, sauna. Cr cds: A, C, D, DS, ER, JCB, MC, V.

D ⚓ 🐎 ≋ 𝔛 ⊠ 🐾 SC

★ ★ **HOLIDAY INN.** *(6001 Rockside Rd, Independence 44131)* N on I-77, just E of Rockside Rd exit. 440/524-8050; FAX 440/524-9280. 363 rms, 5 story. S $89-119; D $99-$119; under 19 free. Crib free. TV; cable (premium), VCR avail. Indoor pool; sauna. Coffee in rms. Restaurant 6:30 am-10 pm. Rm serv. Bar 11-2 am; entertainment exc Sun. Ck-out noon. Coin lndry. Convention facilities. Business servs avail. Bellhops.

Valet serv. Gift shop. Free airport transportation. Cr cds: A, C, D, DS, JCB, MC, V.

D ≈ ⇘ 🔥 SC

Hotel

★ ★ ★ HARLEY HOTEL-SOUTH. *(5300 Rockside Rd, Independence 44131) At I-77 Rockside Rd exit. 440/524-0700; FAX 440/524-6477.* 184 rms, 5 story. S $115; D $125; each addl $10; under 18 free. Crib free. TV; cable (premium), VCR avail. Indoor/outdoor pool; whirlpool, sauna. Restaurant 6:30 am-10 pm; Fri, Sat to 11 pm. Bar 11:30-1 am, Fri, Sat to 2 am, Sun 1-11 pm, entertainment Sat. Ck-out 11 am. Meeting rms. Business servs avail. In-rm modem link. Lighted tennis. Free airport transportation. Luxury level. Cr cds: A, C, D, DS, MC, V.

D 🏃 ≈ ⇘ 🔥 SC

Restaurant

★ ★ MARCO POLO'S. *8188 Brecksville Rd. 440/526-6130.* Hrs: 11:30 am-10 pm; Fri to midnight; Sat 4 pm-midnight; Sun 9:30 am-9 pm. Closed Dec 25. Res accepted. Italian menu. Bar to 2:30 am; Sun 1 pm-midnight. Semi-a la carte: lunch $5.99-$8.95, dinner $7.95-$19.95. Specializes in pasta. Entertainment Fri, Sat. Former stagecoach stop, built 1800s. Beamed ceilings with large iron chandeliers. Cr cds: A, C, D, DS, MC, V.

D SC

Cambridge (E-5)

(See also Gnadenhutten, Zanesville)

Founded 1806 **Pop** 11,748 **Elev** 886 ft **Area code** 614 **Zip** 43725 **E-mail** 102062.2555@compuserve.com

Information Visitors & Convention Bureau, 2250 Southgate Pkwy, PO Box 427; 614/432-2022 or 800/933-5480.

Cambridge, an important center for the glassmaking industry, was named by early settlers who came from the English Isle of Guernsey. At one time a center of mining and oil, it is located at the crossroads of three major federal highways.

What to See and Do

Degenhart Paperweight and Glass Museum. Large collection of Midwestern pattern glass, Cambridge glass and Degenhart paperweights. Gift shop. (Mar-Dec, daily; rest of yr, Mon-Fri; closed major hols) 65323 Highland Hills Rd; E on US 22, to Highland Hills Rd at intersection of US 22 & I-77. Phone 614/432-2626. ¢

Industrial tours.

Boyd's Crystal Art Glass. Glass factory and showroom; glass from molten form to finished product. Tours of factory (Mon-Fri; closed hols) and showroom (June-Aug, daily exc Sun; rest of yr, Mon-Fri; closed hols). 1203 Morton Ave. Phone 614/439-2077. **Free.**

Mosser Glass. Glass-making tours; gift shop. (Mon-Fri; closed major hols; also 1st 2 wks July, last wk Dec) US 22 E, 1/2 mi W via I-77 exit 47. Phone 614/439-1827. **Free.**

Muskingum Watershed Conservancy District. Seneca Lake Park. A 3,550-acre lake offers swimming; fishing; boating (180-hp limit), marina. Playground. Class A tent & trailer sites at marina and park (daily; hookups). Pets on leash. 9 mi S on I-77, then 7 mi E on OH 313, then 2 mi S on OH 574 to park entrance. Phone 614/685-6013. Park (Memorial Day-Labor Day, daily). Per vehicle ¢¢

Salt Fork State Park. A 20,181-acre park with swimming; fishing; boating (rentals, docks, marina). Hiking trails; golf. Picnicking (shelter), concession, lodge. Tent & trailer sites, cabins (reservations accepted). Standard fees. 9 mi NE off US 22. Phone 614/439-2751 (park) or 800/282-7275 (reservations).

The Cambridge Glass Museum. More than 5,000 pieces of Cambridge glass and pottery made between 1902-1954. (June-Oct, daily exc Sun; closed hols) 812 Jefferson Ave. Phone 614/432-3045. ¢

Annual Event

Salt Fork Arts and Crafts Festival. City Park. Early Aug.

Seasonal Event

The Living Word Outdoor Drama. On S OH 209W, at 6010 College Hill Rd. Ohio's Passion Play in outdoor amphitheater retells the life of Jesus Christ. For reservations phone 614/439-2761. Thurs-Sat. Late June-early Sept.

Motels

(Rates may be higher during Jamboree in the Hills Festival)

✔ ★ BEST WESTERN. *1945 Southgate Pkwy, I-70 exit 178. 614/439-3581; FAX 614/439-1824.* 95 rms, 2 story. S, D $79-$110; each addl $10; under 18 free; higher rates special events. Crib $1. Pet accepted. TV; cable, VCR avail (movies). Pool. Restaurant adj. Bar 11-2 am. Ck-out 11 am. Business servs avail. Cr cds: A, C, D, DS, MC, V.

D 🐾 ≈ ⇘ 🔥 SC

✔ ★ HOLIDAY INN. *Southgate Pkwy, 1 mi SW on OH 209, 1/4 mi N of jct I-70 exit 178. 614/432-7313; FAX 614/432-2337.* 109 rms, 2 story. May-Nov: S $49-$139; D $57-$147; each addl $8; under 18 free; lower rates rest of yr. Crib free. Pet accepted. TV; cable. Pool. Restaurant 6 am-10 pm; Sat, Sun 7 am-11 pm. Rm serv. Bar 4 pm-midnight, Sun 5-10 pm. Ck-out noon. Coin lndry. Meeting rms. Business servs avail. Health club privileges. Cr cds: A, C, D, DS, JCB, MC, V.

D 🐾 ≈ ⇘ 🔥 SC

★ ★ SALT FORK RESORT & CONFERENCE CENTER. *N on I-77 exit 47, 6 mi NE on US 22, in Salt Fork State Park. 614/439-2751; FAX 614/432-6615; res: 800/282-7275 (OH).* 148 rms in lodge, 3 story, 54 2-bedrm kit. cottages (no A/C, no rm phones in cottages). S, D $99-$144; each addl $5; cottages $120-$135 ($600-$700/wk); under 18 free; wkly rates; golf plans. Crib free. TV; cable; VCR avail (movies). 2 pools, 1 indoor; wading pool, poolside serv. Playground. Dining rm 7-11 am, noon-2 pm, 5-8 pm. Snack bar. Bar 5-9 pm. Ck-out noon (lodge), 10 am (cottages). Coin lndry. Meeting rooms. Business servs avail. Gift shop. Lighted tennis. 18-hole golf, greens fee $14-$15.50, pro. Exercise equipt; stair machine, bicycles, sauna. Marina; canoes, motorboats, rowboats, sailboats. Fish/hunt guides. Hiking trails. Game rm. Rec rm. Lawn games. Some refrigerators. Private patios, balconies. Picnic tables. Cr cds: A, C, D, DS, MC, V.

D ➹ 🏃 🎿 🏃 ≈ 🍴 ⇘ SC

★ TRAVELODGE. *at jct OH 209, I-70 exit 178. 614/432-7375; FAX 614/432-5808.* 48 rms, 2 story. May-Oct: S, D $59-$70; each addl $5; under 18 free; lower rates rest of yr. Crib free. TV; cable. Heated pool; whirlpool, sauna. Complimentary coffee in-rms. Restaurant adj 6 am-10 pm. Ck-out noon. Business servs avail. Valet serv. Health club privileges. Some balconies. Cr cds: A, C, D, DS, MC, V.

D ➹ ≈ ⇘ 🔥 SC

Restaurant

★ HOUSE OF HUNAN. *2400 E Wheeling Ave, I-77 N, exit 146. 614/439-5252.* Hrs: 11 am-9:30 pm; Fri, Sat to 10 pm; Sun from 11:30 am. Closed Thanksgiving, Dec 25. Res accepted. Chinese menu. Bar. Semi-a la carte: lunch $4.50-$4.95, dinner $6.50-$13.95. Cr cds: MC, V.

Canton (C-5)

(See also Akron, Alliance, Massillon, New Philadelphia, Wooster)

Settled 1805 **Pop** 84,161 **Elev** 1,060 ft **Area code** 330 **Web** www.visitcantonohio.com

Information Canton/Stark County Convention & Visitors Bureau, 229 Wells Ave NW, 44703-2642; 800/533-4302.

John Saxton, grandfather of Mrs. William McKinley, first published the still-circulating *Ohio Repository* (*The Repository* today) in 1815. In 1867 William McKinley opened a law office in the town, and in 1896 conducted his "front porch campaign" for the presidency. After his assassination his body was brought back to Canton for burial. Because of his love for the red carnation, it was made the state flower.

This large steel-processing city, important a century ago for farm machinery, is in the middle of rich farmland, on the edge of "steel valley" where the three branches of Nimishillen Creek come together. It is one of the largest producers of specialty steels in the world.

What to See and Do

Canton Classic Car Museum. Collection of antique, classic cars; fire pumper; police bandit car; cars of '50s and '60s; restoration shop; memorabilia, period fashions, advertising, nostalgia and popular culture. (Daily; closed Easter, Thanksgiving, Dec 25) 555 Market Ave S. Phone 330/455-3603. ¢¢

Canton Garden Center. Tulips, daffodils, peonies, chrysanthemums; five senses garden; JFK memorial fountain with continuous flame (daily). Garden Center (Tues-Fri). 1615 Stadium Park NW, in Stadium Park. Phone 330/455-6172; 330/489-3015. **Free.**

Harry London Chocolate Factory. Tours (daily). (Daily, closed major hols) 5353 Lauby Rd. Phone 330/494-0833 or 800/321-0444. ¢

Hoover Historical Center. Hoover farmhouse restored to Victorian era; boyhood home of W.H. Hoover, founder of the Hoover Company. One of the most extensive antique vacuum cleaner collections in the world; memorabilia reflecting the growth and development of the company and the industry; changing exhibits; herb gardens. Tours (July). (Daily exc Mon; closed hols) 2225 Easton St NW, in North Canton. Phone 330/499-0287. **Free.**

McKinley National Memorial. Tomb, statue of McKinley; panoramic view of city. McKinley Monument Dr NW. (Daily) Adj is

McKinley Museum of History, Science and Industry (1963). McKinley memorabilia; **Discover World,** an interactive science center; Historical Hall; Street of Shops. (Daily; planetarium shows Sat & Sun; closed most hols) 800 McKinley Monument Dr NW. Phone 330/455-7043. ¢¢¢

★ **Pro Football Hall of Fame** (1963). Museum, a 5-building complex, dedicated to the game and its players; memorabilia; research library; movie theater; museum store. (Daily; closed Dec 25) (See ANNUAL EVENT). 2121 George Halas Dr NW, N of Fawcett Stadium, adj to I-77. Phone 330/456-8207. ¢¢¢

Waterworks Park. Picnic facilities (tables, cooking stoves, shelter), playground. Between Tuscarawas St W & 7th St NW. Phone 330/489-3015.

Annual Event

Football's Greatest Weekend. Pro Football Hall of Fame. Events include parade, induction ceremony, AFC-NFC Hall of Fame Pro Game. Late July-early Aug.

Motels

✔★ **COMFORT INN.** *5345 Broadmoor Cr NW (44709).* 330/492-1331; FAX 330/492-9093. 124 rms, 3 story. S $55-$61; D $65-$91; each addl $6; under 18 free; wkend rates; golf plans; higher rates Hall of Fame wk. Crib free. TV; cable (premium). Pool. Complimentary conti-

nental bkfst. Restaurant nearby. Ck-out noon. Meeting rms. Business servs avail. In-rm modem link. Valet serv. Health club privileges. Cr cds: A, C, D, DS, ER, JCB, MC, V.

D ≈ 🐾 ➤ 🐾 SC

★ ★ **HAMPTON INN.** *5335 Broadmoor Circle (44709), I-77 exit 109.* 330/492-0151; FAX 330/492-7523. 108 rms, 4 story. S $53-$69; D $57-$69; under 18 free; higher rates special events. Crib free. TV; cable. Complimentary continental bkfst. Restaurant nearby. Ck-out noon. Meeting rms. In-rm modem link. Valet serv. Health club privileges. Game rm. Cr cds: A, C, D, DS, MC, V.

D ➤ 🐾 SC

★ ★ **HOLIDAY INN-BELDON VILLAGE.** *4520 Everhard Rd NW (44718), I-77 exit 109.* 330/494-2770; FAX 330/494-6473. 196 rms, 2-3 story. S $79-$86; D $87-$94; each addl $8; suites $150; under 19 free; higher rates Hall of Fame wkend. Crib free. Pet accepted. TV. Pool; poolside serv. Restaurant 6:30 am-10 pm; Sun from 7 am. Rm serv. Bar 2 pm-2:30 am; entertainment. Ck-out noon. Meeting rms. Business servs avail. In-rm modem link. Free airport transportation. Health club privileges. Cr cds: A, C, D, DS, JCB, MC, V.

D 🐾 ≈ ➤ 🐾 SC

✔★ **RED ROOF INN.** *5353 Inn Circle Ct NW (44720), I-77 exit 109.* 330/499-1970; FAX 330/499-1975. 108 rms, 2 story. S $37.99-$40.99; D $44.95-$51.99; each addl $7; under 18 free. Crib free. Pet accepted. TV. Restaurant adj 6 am-10 pm. Ck-out noon. Business servs avail. Cr cds: A, C, D, DS, MC, V.

D 🐾 ➤ 🐾 SC

Motor Hotel

★ ★ **SHERATON INN.** *4375 Metro Circle NW (44720), I-77 exit 109.* 330/494-6494; FAX 330/494-7129. 152 rms, 6 story. S $75-$109; D $85-$119; each addl $10; suites $125-$250; under 18 free; higher rates Hall of Fame wkend. Crib free. TV; cable (premium). Indoor/outdoor pool; poolside serv. Restaurant 6:30 am-10 pm. Rm serv. Bar 1 pm-2 am, Sun noon-midnight. Ck-out noon. Meeting rms. Business center. Bellhops. Valet serv. Free airport transportation. Exercise equipt; weights, bicycles, whirlpool, sauna. Game rm. Some refrigerators. Cr cds: A, C, D, DS, ER, MC, V.

D ≈ 🏃 ➤ 🐾 SC 🚶

Hotel

★ ★ ★ **HILTON.** *320 Market Ave S (44702).* 330/454-5000; FAX 330/454-5494. 170 rms, 8 story. S $70-$95; D $80-$105; suites $195-$295; under 18 free. Crib free. TV; cable. VCR avail (movies). Indoor pool. Restaurant 6:30 am-10:30 pm; Sat, Sun from 7 am. Rm serv. Bar 11-2 am. Ck-out noon. Meeting rms. Business servs avail. Gift shop. Free airport transportation. Exercise equipt; weight machine, bicycle, whirlpool, sauna. Game rm. Cr cds: A, C, D, DS, JCB, MC, V.

D ≈ 🏃 ➤ 🐾 SC

Restaurants

✔★ **JOHN'S GRILLE.** *2749 Cleveland Ave (44709).* 330/454-1259. Hrs: 7 am-11 pm; Fri, Sat to midnight. Closed Sun; major hols. Bar. Semi-a la carte: bkfst $3.50-$5.50, lunch $5.50-$14.50, dinner $8.95-$14.95. Specializes in steak, seafood. Casual decor. Cr cds: A, D, DS, MC, V.

D

★ ★ ★ **LOLLI'S.** *4801 Dressler Rd NW, I-77 exit 109.* 330/492-6846. Hrs: 11:30 am-2:30 pm, 5-10 pm; Sat from 5 pm. Closed Sun; major hols. Res accepted. Italian menu. Bar. Wine list. Semi-a la carte: dinner

$7.95-$16.95. Specializes in fresh pasta, fish, veal medallions. Own baking. Family-owned. Cr cds: A, D, DS, MC, V.

Celina (D-1)

(See also Van Wert, Wapakoneta)

Settled 1834 **Pop** 9,650 **Elev** 876 ft **Area code** 419 **Zip** 45822
Information Celina-Mercer County Chamber of Commerce, 226 N Main St; 419/586-2219.

Celina is on Grand Lake, a 17,500-acre man-made lake lined with houses and resorts. The town is a home for metal products, dairying and wood fabricating industries and it also attracts anglers and vacationers.

What to See and Do

Grand Lake-St Marys State Park. Offers swimming; fishing (panfish, bass); boating, (marina, rentals, ramps). Snowmobiling. Picnicking (shelters), concession. Camping. Standard fees. The lake is Ohio's largest inland lake (15,000 acres). The park is 7 mi E on OH 703, then follow park signs. Phone 419/394-2774.

Mercer County Courthouse. Greek architecture with great bronze doors opening on halls of marble; dome of colored glass has near-perfect acoustics. (Mon-Fri) Main & Market Sts. **Free.**

Mercer County Historical Museum, the Riley Home. History of area depicted by 18th- and 19th-century artifacts including Native American, medical and farm; also pioneer home furniture displays. (Wed-Fri & Sun) 130 E Market St. Phone 419/586-6065. **Free.**

Annual Event

Celina Lake Festival. At jct US 127 & OH 29. Antique car show, parade, triathlon, arts & crafts show, fireworks. Usually late July.

Motel

✔★★ **COMFORT INN.** *1421 OH 703E. 419/586-4656; FAX 419/586-4152.* 40 rms, 1-2 story. S $53-$56; D $57-$60; each addl $6; suite $85-$95; kit. units $57-$59; under 18 free; higher rates special events. Crib $5. TV; cable (premium). Complimentary continental bkfst. Restaurant adj 11 am-10 pm. Ck-out 11 am. Sundries. Microwaves avail. Cr cds: A, C, D, DS, ER, JCB, MC, V.

D ⩥ ⩥ SC

Chardon (B-5)

(For accommodations see Aurora, Cleveland, Mentor, Painesville)

Pop 4,446 **Elev** 1,225 ft **Area code** 216 **Zip** 44024
Information Chardon Area Chamber of Commerce, 112 E Park St; 216/285-9050.

What to See and Do

Geauga County Historical Society-Century Village. Restored 19th-century Western Reserve village with homes, shops, school, country store. All original with period furnishings (1798-1875). (May-Oct, daily exc Mon; Mar-Apr & Nov-Dec 24, Sat & Sun; closed Easter, Thanksgiving) Museum and country store (Mar-Dec 24). 8 mi S on OH 44 then 3 mi E on OH 87, at 14653 E Park St in Burton. Phone 216/834-4012. ¢¢

Materials Park Geodesic Dome. An 11-story latticework of aluminum tubing designed by R. Buckminster Fuller; world headquarters of ASM

International; mineral garden with more than 75 ore specimens. (Daily) 10 mi S on OH 44, then 6 mi W on OH 87. Phone 216/338-5151. **Free.**

Punderson State Park. A 990-acre park with a 90-acre lake. Swimming; fishing; boating (rentals). Hiking; golf. Winter sports area, snowmobiling. Snack bar, lodge (pool, summer). Camping, cabins. Standard fees. (Daily) 10 mi S via OH 44, then W 1 mi on OH 87. Phone 216/564-2279. **Free.**

Annual Event

Geauga County Maple Festival. Demonstrations of making syrup, candy, cream and other maple products; beard and ax-throwing contests; entertainment. Phone 216/286-3007. Wkend after Easter.

Restaurants

★★ **BASS LAKE TAVERN.** *426 South St. 216/285-3100.* Hrs: 11:30 am-2:30 pm, 5-10 pm; Sun 5-9 pm; early-bird dinner Mon-Fri 5-6:30 pm. Closed major hols. Res accepted. Bar. Semi-a la carte: lunch $8-$15, dinner $15-$24. Specializes in chops & steaks, game, seafood. Entertainment Fri, Sat. Outdoor dining. Casual country atmosphere. Cr cds: A, D, DS, MC, V.

★★ **THE INN AT FOWLER'S MILL.** *10700 Mayfield Rd. 216/286-3111.* Hrs: 11:30 am-2:30 pm, 5:30-9:30 pm; Fri, Sat 5:30-10:30 pm; Sun 10 am-2:30 pm. Closed Mon. Res accepted; required hols. Closed major hols. Continental menu. Bar to 4:30-11 pm; Fri, Sat to midnight. Semi-a la carte: lunch $4.95-15.95. Child's meals. Specializes in fresh seafood, steaks. Outdoor dining. Cr cds: A, D, DS, MC, V.

D ⩥

Chillicothe (F-3)

Settled 1796 **Pop** 21,923 **Elev** 620 ft **Area code** 614 **Zip** 45601
Information Chamber of Commerce, 165 S Paint St, phone 614/772-4530; or the Ross-Chillicothe Convention & Visitors Bureau, PO Box 353, phone 614/775-0900 or 800/413-4118.

Chillicothe, first capital of the Northwest Territory, became the first capital of Ohio in 1803. Among the early settlers from Virginia who were active in achieving statehood for Ohio were Edward Tiffin, first state governor and Thomas Worthington, governor and US senator. The Greek-revival mansions, which give Paint St its character today, were built for the pioneer statesmen.

On the west side of Scioto River Valley, 45 miles south of the present capital, Chillicothe is quite industrialized, though still fringed by wheat fields. Papermaking, begun in the early 1800s, is still an essential industry here. Just east of town is Mount Logan, which is pictured on the State Seal.

What to See and Do

Adena State Memorial (1807). Restored 1807 mansion of Ohio's 6th governor, Thomas Worthington; period furnishings. (Memorial Day wkend-Labor Day, Wed-Sat, also Sun afternoons; after Labor Day-Oct, wkends only) At S end of Adena Rd, off Pleasant Valley Rd. ¢¢

Franklin House. This 1907 prairie-style home houses museum devoted primarily to the women of Ross County; rotating exhibits of period costumes and accessories, coverlets, quilts and linens, decorative arts. (Apr-Nov, Tues-Sun afternoons; rest of yr, Sat & Sun afternoons) 80 S Paint St. Phone 614/772-1936. ¢

Hopewell Culture National Historical Park. At this site are 23 prehistoric Hopewell burial mounds (200 B.C. to A.D. 500), concentrated within a 13-acre area surrounded by an earthwall. Self-guided trails; wayside exhibits. Visitor center with museum exhibits (daily; closed Jan 1, Thanksgiving, Dec 25). W bank of Scioto River, 4 mi N on OH 104. Phone 614/774-1125. ¢

James M. Thomas Telecommunication Museum. Collection of documents and equipment depicting evolution of modern phone service. (Mon-Fri; closed hols) 68 E Main St, in Chillicothe Telephone Co. Phone 614/772-8200. **Free.**

Knoles Log Home. This simple 2-story log home (1800-1825) features open hearth cooking, kitchen garden, early household utensils and tools; also on-site demonstrations (seasonal). (Apr-Nov, Tues-Sun afternoons; rest of yr, Sat & Sun afternoons) 39 W 5th St. Phone 614/772-1936. ¢

Paint Creek State Park. Large lake offers swimming; fishing; boating (ramp, rentals). Hiking, bridle trails. Cross-country skiing, snowmobiling. Camping (tent rentals). Paint Creek Pioneer Farm; living history program, summer programs. Standard fees. 25 mi W off US 50 in Bainbridge. Phone 513/365-1401 (park office).

Ross County Historical Society Museum. Housed in an 1838 Federal-style home, museum features 3 floors of exhibits, antiques, furnishings, pioneer crafts and toys. Includes Constitution Room, Civil War Room, Indian Room and Camp Sherman Room. Tours; inquire for schedule. (Apr-Nov, Tues-Sun afternoons; rest of yr, Sat & Sun afternoons) 45 W 5th St. Phone 614/772-1936. ¢

Seip Mound State Memorial. Prehistoric burial mound, 250 ft long and 30 ft high, surrounded by smaller mounds and earthworks. Exhibit pavilion; picnicking. (Daily) 14 mi SW on S side of US 50. This archaeological site is operated by the Ohio Historical Society, phone 614/297-2630. **Free.**

Seven Caves. A natural attraction of 7 caves centered on self-guided walk along trails winding up and down the sides of cliffs, into canyons and gorges; rock formations; wooded park. Picnic area, snack bar. (Daily) 15 mi E of Hillsboro on US 50. Phone 513/365-1283. ¢¢¢

Yoctangee Park. Swimming pool (fee), 12-acre lake. Six tennis courts, basketball and volleyball courts, softball diamonds. Picnicking facilities, playground. Yoctangee Blvd & Riverside St. **Free.**

Annual Events

Feast of the Flowering Moon. Downtown. Native American, frontier and early American feast featuring Native American demonstrations and encampment, crafts and parade. Phone 614/775-0900. Memorial Day wkend.

Fall Festival of Leaves. 19 mi W on US 50, in Bainbridge. Arts & crafts demonstrations, entertainment; scenic self-guided tours. Phone 614/634-2085. 3rd wkend Oct.

Seasonal Event

Tecumseh! Sugarloaf Mountain Amphitheater, 5 mi NE off US 23, OH 159 N exit. Epic outdoor drama depicts the struggle of Tecumseh, the legendary Shawnee warrior who nearly united all the Native American nations. Museum, open-air restaurant, backstage tours. Phone 614/775-0700 (after Mar 1). Nightly exc Sun. Mid-June-early Sept.

Motels

★ **COMFORT INN.** 20 North Plaza Blvd. 614/775-3500; FAX 614/775-3588. 109 rms, 2 story. S, D $65-$75; each addl $5; under 17 free. Crib free. Pet accepted. TV; cable. Heated pool. Coffee in rms. Complimentary continental bkfst. Restaurant nearby. Bar; entertainment Fri, Sat. Ck-out noon. Meeting rms. Business servs avail. Valet serv. Complimentary health club privileges. Cr cds: A, C, D, DS, ER, JCB, MC, V.

★★ **DAYS INN.** 1250 N Bridge St. 614/775-7000; FAX 614/773-1622. 155 rms, 2 story. S, D $62-$75; each addl $6; under 19 free. Crib free. Pet accepted. TV; cable (premium). Heated pool; poolside serv. Complimentary coffee in rms. Restaurant 6 am-2 pm, 4-9 pm; Sun 7 am-2 pm, brunch 10 am-2 pm. Rm serv. Bar 4 pm-2 am; closed Sun; entertainment Fri, Sat. Ck-out noon. Coin lndry. Meeting rms. Business servs avail. Valet serv. Cr cds: A, C, D, DS, JCB, MC, V.

✔★ **TRAVELODGE.** 1135 E Main St, at jct US 50, 23, 35. 614/775-2500; FAX 614/775-2500, ext. 166. 59 rms. S, D $45-$69; each addl $5; under 18 free. Crib free. TV. Pool. Coffee in rms. Restaurant opp 6 am-11 pm. Ck-out noon. Meeting rm. Business servs avail. Cr cds: A, C, D, DS, MC, V.

Restaurant

★ **DAMON'S.** 10 N Plaza Blvd, OH 159 at OH 35 on US 23. 614/775-8383. Hrs: 11 am-10 pm; Fri, Sat to 11 pm; Sun to 9 pm. Closed major hols. Res accepted Sun-Thurs. Bar. Semi-a la carte: lunch $4.45-$7.95, dinner $6.95-$15.95. Child's meals. Specializes in ribs, onion rings. Casual atmosphere. Cr cds: A, MC, V.

Cincinnati (F-1)

(See also Hamilton, Mason)

Settled 1788 **Pop** 364,040 **Elev** 683 ft **Area code** 513 **E-mail** info@cincyusa.com **Web** www.cincyusa.com

Information Greater Cincinnati Convention & Visitors Bureau, 300 W 6th St, 45202; 800/CINCY-USA.

Cincinnati was a bustling frontier riverboat town and one of the largest cities in the nation when poet Henry Wadsworth Longfellow immortalized it as the "queen city of the West." Although other cities farther west have since outstripped it in size, Cincinnati is still the Queen City to its inhabitants and to the many visitors who are rediscovering it. With a wealth of fine restaurants, a redeveloped downtown with Skywalk, its own *Montmartre* (Mt Adams) and the "beautiful Ohio" flowing alongside, Cincinnati has a cosmopolitan flavor uniquely its own.

Early settlers chose the site because it was an important river crossroads used by Native Americans. During 1788 and 1789, three small settlements—Columbia, North Bend and Losantiville—were founded. In 1790, Arthur St Clair, governor of the Northwest Territory, changed the name of Losantiville to Cincinnati, in honor of the revolutionary officers' Society of the Cincinnati, and made it the seat of Hamilton County. Despite smallpox, insects, floods and crop failures, approximately 15,000 settlers came in the next 5 years. They had the protection of General Anthony Wayne, who broke the resistance of the Ohio Native Americans. In the early 1800s a large influx of immigrants, mostly German, settled in the area.

In the 1840s and 1850s Cincinnati boomed as a supplier of produce and goods to the cotton-growing South and great fortunes were accumulated. During the Civil War the city was generally loyal to the Union, although its location on the Mason-Dixon line and the interruption of its trade from the South caused mixed emotions. After the Civil War, prosperity brought art, music, a new library and a professional baseball team. A period of municipal corruption in the late 19th century was ended by a victory for reform elements and the establishment of a city-manager form of government, which has earned Cincinnati the title of America's best-governed city.

Today, the city is the home of two universities, several other institutions of higher education and has its own symphony orchestra, opera and ballet. Cincinnati has also nearly completed a glittering multimillion dollar redevelopment of its downtown area and renovation of its riverfront into an entertainment and recreation center. Major hotels, stores, office complexes, restaurants, entertainment centers and the Cincinnati Convention Center are now connected by a skywalk system, making the city easily accessible to pedestrians. One can still echo the words of Charles Dickens, who described the city in 1842 as "a place that commends itself . . . favorably and pleasantly to a stranger."

Transportation

Car Rental Agencies: See IMPORTANT TOLL-FREE NUMBERS.

Public Transportation: Bus (Queen City Metro), 513/621-4455.

Rail Passenger Service: Amtrak 800/872-7245.

Airport Information

Cincinnati/Northern Kentucky Intl Airport: Information 606/283-3151; 606/283-3123 (lost and found); 513/241-1010 (weather); cash machines, Terminal D.

What to See and Do

Airport Playfield. Baseball fields; 18- and 9-hole golf courses, driving range, miniature golf; tennis courts. Paved bike & hike trail; bike rentals. Skateboard facility. Land of Make Believe playground with wheelchair accessible play equipment; jet plane, stagecoach; "Spirit of '76" picnic area. Summer concerts. (May-Sept, daily) Some fees. Beechmont Levee & Wilmer Ave, 8 mi E. Phone 513/321-6500.

Bicentennial Commons at Sawyer Point. Overlooks with different views of the Ohio River; 4-mi Riverwalk has geologic timeline of the river. Performance pavilion and amphitheater. Tennis pavilion with eight courts; skating pavilion; three sand volleyball courts; fitness area with exercise stations. Picnicking, playground. Dining area with umbrella tables. Some fees. On Pete Rose Way, E of Riverfront Coliseum, along Ohio River. Phone 513/352-4000 or 513/352-4026.

Carew Tower. Cincinnati's tallest building—48 stories. Observation tower (Tues-Sat; closed hols). 5th & Vine Sts. Phone 513/241-3888 or 513/579-9735. ¢

Children's Museum of Cincinnati. More than 200 hands-on displays for preschoolers to preteens. Special performances, interactive & educational programs. (Wed-Sun) 700 W Pete Rose Way, Longworth Hall. Phone 513/421-5437. ¢¢¢

Cincinnati Fire Museum. Restored firehouse (1907) exhibits firefighting artifacts preserved since 1808; hands-on displays; emphasis on fire prevention. (Daily exc Mon; closed hols) 315 W Court St. Phone 513/621-5553. ¢¢

Cincinnati Zoo and Botanical Garden. Features more than 750 species in a variety of naturalistic habitats, including its world-famous gorillas and white Bengal tigers. The Cat House features 16 species of cats; Insect World is a one-of-a-kind exhibit. Jungle Trails exhibit is an indoor/outdoor rainforest. Rare okapi, walrus, Komodo Dragons and giant eland are also on display. Participatory children's zoo. Animal shows (summer). Elephant and camel rides. Picnic areas, restaurant. (Daily) 3400 Vine St. Phone 513/281-4701 (recording) or 513/281-4700. ¢¢¢

City Hall (1888). Houses many departments of city government. The interior includes a grand marble stairway with historical stained-art glass windows at the landings and murals on the ceiling. (Mon-Fri) 801 Plum St, at 8th St. Phone 513/352-3000.

Civic Garden Center of Greater Cincinnati. Specimen trees; perennials, dwarf evergreens, herbs, raised vegetable gardens; greenhouse; gift shop; library. (Tues-Sat; closed hols) 2715 Reading Rd. Phone 513/221-0981. **Free.**

Contemporary Arts Center. Changing exhibits and performances of recent art. (Daily; closed hols) 115 E 5th St. Phone 513/721-0390. ¢

East Fork State Park. This 10,580-acre park includes rugged hills, open meadows and reservoir. Swimming beach, lifeguard; fishing; boating. Hiking (overnight hiking areas with permit from park office), bridle trails. Picnicking. Camping. Standard fees. Off OH 125, 4 mi SE of Amelia. Phone 513/734-4323.

Eden Park. More than 185 acres initially called "the Garden of Eden." Ice-skating on Mirror Lake. The Murray Seasongood Pavilion features spring & summer band concerts and other events. Picnicking. Four overlooks with scenic views of Ohio River, city and Kentucky hillsides. At Gilbert Ave between Elsinore & Morris. Cultural institutions within park include

Cincinnati Art Museum. Houses paintings, sculpture, prints, photographs, costumes, decorative and tribal arts and musical instruments, representing most major civilizations for the past 5,000 yrs. Also examples of Cincinnati decorative arts, such as art furniture and Rookwood pottery. Continuous schedule of temporary exhibits. Restaurant, gift shop. (Daily exc Mon; closed major hols) Tours for the visually impaired (call Education Department for appt). Phone 513/721-5204. ¢¢

Krohn Conservatory. Floral conservatory of more than 5,000 species of exotic plants, including a 5-story tall indoor rain forest complete with 20-ft waterfall; major collection of unusual epiphytic plants. Individual horticultural houses contain palm, desert, orchid and tropical collections. Themed flower and garden shows 6 times annually. Guided tours avail. Gift shop. (Daily; extended hrs for hol shows) Eden Park Dr, 1 mi E via Fort Washington Way and Martin St, or Gilbert Ave. Phone 513/352-4086. **Free.**

Cincinnati Playhouse in the Park. Professional regional theater, located in Eden Park, presenting classic and contemporary plays and musicals on two stages: the Robert S. Marx Theater and the Thompson Shelterhouse. (Mid-Sept-late July, daily exc Mon; Wed matinee) Dinner avail before each performance. 962 Mt Adams Circle. For schedule and reservations phone 513/421-3888 or 800/582-3208 (in OH).

Fountain Square Plaza. Center of downtown activity whose focal point is the Tyler Davidson Fountain, cast in Munich, Germany and erected in Cincinnati in 1871. The sculpture, whose highest point is the open-armed Genius of Water, symbolizes the many values of water. A bandstand pavilion enables lunch hour audiences to enjoy outdoor performances. Horsedrawn carriage tours of downtown also begin at the square.

Hamilton County Courthouse. Good example of adapted Greek Ionic architecture; contains one of America's most complete law libraries. (Mon-Fri; closed hols) 1000 Main St, between Court St & Central Pkwy. Phone 513/632-8250.

Harriet Beecher Stowe Memorial. Famous author of *Uncle Tom's Cabin* lived here from 1832-1836. Completely restored with some original furnishings. (Tues-Thurs) 2950 Gilbert Ave. Phone 513/632-5120. **Donation.**

Hebrew Union College—Jewish Institute of Religion (1875). (120 students) First institution of Jewish higher learning in the United States. Graduate school offers a variety of programs. Klau Library includes Dalsheimer Rare Book Bldg with rare remnants of Chinese Jewry and collections of Spinoza and Americana. American Jewish Archives Building is dedicated to study and preservation of American Jewish historical records. Archaeological exhibits and Jewish ceremonial objects are in the Skirball Museum Cincinnati Branch. Guided tours (by appt). 3101 Clifton Ave, I-75 Hopple St exit. Phone 513/221-1875.

Historic Loveland Castle. A one-fifth scale, medieval stone castle built by one man over a period of 50 yrs. (Apr-Sept, daily; rest of yr, Sat & Sun; closed Dec 25) 12025 Shore Dr. Phone 513/683-4686. ¢

John Hauck House Museum. Ornate 19th-century stonefront town house in historic district. Restored home contains period furnishings, memorabilia, antique children's toys, special displays. (Thurs & Sun; also special Christmas hrs; closed hols) 812 Dayton St. Phone 513/721-3570. ¢

Meier's Wine Cellars. Country wine store, tasting room. 45-min tours (June-Oct, daily exc Sun). 6955 Plainfield Pike, in Silverton; NE on US 22 or N on I-71 exit 10 (Stewart Rd), right on Stewart Rd and follow signs. Phone 513/891-2900 or 800/346-2942. **Free.**

Mount Airy Forest and Arboretum. First municipal reforestation project in the US. More than 1,450 acres include 800 acres of conifers and hardwoods, 300 acres of native hardwoods and 241 acres of grasslands. The 120-acre arboretum (guided tours by appt, phone 513/541-8176) includes specialty gardens, floral displays, and extensive plant collections. Area is used by students and amateur and professional gardeners as a testing area for observation of growth, habits and tolerance of plants. Nature trails. Picnic areas, lodges. (Daily) 5080 Colerain Ave, 8 mi NW on US 27, off I-75. Phone 513/352-4080. **Free.**

Mt Adams. Mt Adams is the *Montmartre* of Cincinnati; its narrow streets, intimate restaurants, boutiques and art stores give the area a European flavor. Area directly SW of Eden Park, on hill overlooking Cincinnati and the Ohio River.

Paramount's Kings Island. 20 mi N on I-71 (see MASON).

Professional sports.

National League baseball (Cincinnati Reds). Cinergy Field. Phone 513/421-4510.

NFL (Cincinnati Bengals). Cinergy Field. Phone 513/621-3550.

Public Landing. Where first settlers touched the shore and first log cabin was built. Center of river trade; look for paddlewheelers. Cinergy Field and six Ohio River bridges to northern Kentucky. Foot of Broadway.

River cruises.

Delta Queen, Mississippi Queen, and *American Queen* all paddlewheelers, make 3-12-night cruises on the Ohio, Mississippi, Cumberland and Tennessee rivers. Phone 800/543-1949. ¢¢¢¢

BB Riverboats. Variety of cruises including sightseeing, lunch and dinner cruises (res required), all-day, half-day and moonlight trips. 1 mi SE via I-75 exit 192, foot of Madison, located at Covington (KY) Landing. For schedule phone 606/261-8500. Fees vary. Sightseeing ¢¢¢

Scenic drives. On Columbia Pkwy to Ault Park, with views of Ohio River; and on Central Pkwy (US 27), along old Miami-Erie Canal to Mt Airy Forest.

Sharon Woods Village. A 30-acre historic village recaptures life in southwestern Ohio prior to 1880. Nine buildings (1804-1880), reconstructed and authentically restored and refurnished. Special exhibits and events; period craft demonstrations; guided tours. (May-Oct, Wed-Sun) N on I-75, E on I-275, exit at US 42 S, then 1 mi S; entrance to Sharon Woods Park on left. Phone 513/563-9484. ¢¢

Taft Museum. Federal-period mansion, built 1820, houses world-renowned art collection of Charles and Anna Taft. A museum since 1932, it was restored to its original appearance and decorated in the style of that period. European and American paintings include Rembrandt, Turner, Whistler and Sargent; European decorative arts; French enamels; Chinese porcelains. Formal gardens. (Mon-Sat; also Sun & hol afternoons; closed major hols) 316 Pike St, at 4th St. Phone 513/241-0343. ¢¢

Trailside Nature Center. Discovery center has displays on local birds, mammals, insects and geology. Wkend nature walks and program (all yr). (Tues-Sat; also Sun afternoons) In Burnet Woods. Phone 513/751-3679. **Free.**

★ **Union Terminal.** (1933) Famous Art Deco landmark, noted for its mosaic murals, Verona marble walls, terrazzo floors and large domed rotunda. Cafe and museum shops. 1301 Western Ave. Also in terminal are

Cincinnati History Museum. Permanent exhibit on the Public Landing of Cincinnati; also temporary exhibits. Library (daily exc Sun; free). (Daily; closed Thanksgiving, Dec 25) 1301 Western Ave. Phone 513/287-7030. ¢¢

Museum of Natural History & Science. Natural history of Ohio Valley. Wilderness Trail with Ohio flora and fauna and full scale walk-through replica of a cavern with 32-ft waterfall; Children's Discovery Center. (Daily; closed Thanksgiving, Dec 25) 1301 Western Ave. Phone 513/287-7020. ¢¢

Omnimax Theater. A 260-degree domed screen 5 stories high and 72 ft wide. Films change every six months. (Daily; closed Thanksgiving, Dec 25) Phone 513/287-7000. ¢¢¢

University of Cincinnati (1819). (37,000 students) Includes 18 colleges and divisions, of which Music, Law, Medicine and Pharmacy are among the oldest west of the Alleghenies. Founded as Cincinnati College; chartered 1870 as municipal university; became a full state university July 1, 1977. The College-Conservatory of Music has an extensive schedule of performances, phone 513/556-4183. On campus is Tangeman University Center (daily exc Sun; closed most hols). Bounded by Clifton & Jefferson Aves, Calhoun St & Martin Luther King Dr. Phone 513/556-6000.

William Howard Taft National Historic Site. Birthplace and boyhood home of the 27th president and Chief Justice of the US Supreme Court. Four rms with period furnishings; other rooms contain exhibits on Taft's life and careers. (Daily; closed Jan 1, Thanksgiving, Dec 25) 2038 Auburn Ave. Phone 513/684-3262. **Free.**

Xavier University (1831). (6,800 students) Campus tours. 3800 Victory Pkwy. Phone 513/745-3000.

Annual Events

May Festival. Cincinnati Music Hall, 1241 Elm St. Oldest continuous choral festival in the nation; choral and operatic masterworks. Phone 513/381-3300 for schedule and information. Last 2 wkends May.

Coors Light Festival. Cinergy Field features top name performers in soul, rhythm & blues. For details phone 513/871-3900. Late July.

Riverfest. Celebration in honor of Cincinnati's river heritage held along the city's waterfront parks. Entertainment includes sky diving and waterskiing performances, amusement rides, riverboat cruises and fireworks. For details contact the Convention & Visitors Bureau. Labor Day wkend.

Oktoberfest-Zinzinnati. Downtown Cincinnati becomes a German biergarten for this festive wkend. Nonstop German music, singing, dancing, food, and thousands of gallons of beer. Mid-Sept.

Seasonal Events

River Downs Race Track. 6301 Kellogg Ave, 10 mi E on US 52. Thoroughbred racing. Phone 513/232-8000. Daily exc Thurs. Mid-Apr-Labor Day & mid-Oct-mid-Nov.

Turfway Park Race Course. 10 mi SW off I-75 via exit 184, on Turfway Pike in Florence, KY. Phone 606/371-0200 or 800/733-0200. Thoroughbred racing Wed-Sun. Early Sept-early Oct & late Nov-Mar.

Cincinnati Opera. Music Hall. Nation's second-oldest opera company offers a summer season plus special performances throughout year. Capsulized English translations projected above the stage complement all productions. Phone 513/241-ARIA. Mid-June-mid-July.

Cincinnati Ballet. 1216 Central Pkwy. Performs five-series program at the Aronoff Center, both contemporary and classical works. For schedule, tickets phone 513/621-5219. Oct-May; also *Nutcracker* staged at Music Hall during Dec.

Cincinnati Symphony Orchestra. 1241 Elm St, in Music Hall. Nation's fifth oldest orchestra presents symphony and pops programs. For schedule phone 513/381-3300. Sept-May.

Additional Visitor Information

The Greater Cincinnati Convention and Visitors Bureau, 300 W 6th St, 45202, phone 800/CINCY-USA, has interesting tourist guides and maps. Visitor information centers are located at 5th & Vine Sts at Fountain Square, and two others are located off southbound I-71 & I-75.

City Neighborhoods

Many of the restaurants, unrated dining establishments and some lodgings listed under Cincinnati include neighborhoods as well as exact street addresses. Geographic descriptions of Downtown and Mt Adams are given, followed by a table of restaurants arranged by neighborhood.

Downtown: South of Central Pkwy, west of I-71, north of the Ohio River and east of I-75. **North of Downtown:** North of Central Pkwy. **East of Downtown:** East of I-71. **West of Downtown:** West of I-71/I-75.

Mt Adams: South of Eden Park, west of Columbia Pkwy, north of I-471 and east of I-71.

CINCINNATI RESTAURANTS BY NEIGHBORHOOD AREAS
(For full description, see alphabetical listings under Restaurants)

DOWNTOWN
La Normandie Tavern and Chophouse. 118 E Sixth St
Leboxx Cafe. 819 Vine St
Maisonette. 114 E 6th St
Mecklenburg Gardens. 302 E University
Nicola's. 1420 Sycamore St
Orchid's (Omni Netherland Plaza Hotel). 35 W 5th St
The Palace (Cincinnatian Hotel). 601 Vine St
The Phoenix. 812 Race St
Pigalls Cafe. 127 W 4th St

Primavista. 810 Matson Place
Seafood 32 (Regal Cincinnati Hotel). 150 W Fifth St

NORTH OF DOWNTOWN
Aglamesis Bros. 3046 Madison Rd
Chateau Pomije. 2019 Madison Rd
Cheng-1 Cuisine. 203 W McMillan St
Chester's Road House. 9678 Montgomery Rd
China Gourmet. 3340 Erie Ave
Darci's. 7328 Kenwood Rd
DeSha's. 11320 Montgomery Rd
The Diner on Sycamore. 1203 Sycamore St
Forest View Gardens. 4508 North Bend Rd
Germano's. 9415 Montgomery Rd
Grand Finale. 3 East Sharon Ave
House of Tam. 889 W Galbraith Rd
Lenhardt's. 151 W McMillan St
Montgomery Inn. 9440 Montgomery Rd
Pacific Moon. 8300 Market Place Ln
Tandoor. 8702 Market Place Ln
Window Garden. 3077 Harrison Ave

EAST OF DOWNTOWN
The Blackstone. 455 Delta Ave
Heritage. 7664 Wooster Pike (OH 50)
National Exemplar (Best Western Mariemont Inn Motel). 6880 Wooster Pike
The Precinct. 311 Delta Ave

WEST OF DOWNTOWN
Fore & Aft. 7449 Forbes Rd

MT ADAMS
Adrica's. 934 Hatch St
Celestial. 1071 Celestial St
Cherrington's. 950 Pavilion St
Montgomery Inn Boathouse. 925 Eastern Ave
Petersen's. 1111 St Gregory
Rookwood Pottery. 1077 Celestial St
Teak. 1049 St Gregory

Note: When a listing is located in a town that does not have its own city heading, it will appear under the city nearest to its location. In these cases, the address and town appear in parenthesis immediately following the name of the establishment.

Motels

(Rates may be higher during Kool Jazz Festival)

★ ★ **AMERISUITES.** 11435 Reed Hartman Hwy (45241). 513/489-3666; FAX 513/489-4187. 127 suites, 6 story. May-Sept: S, D $99-$149; each addl $10; under 18 free; lower rates rest of yr. Crib avail. Pet accepted. TV; cable (premium), VCR (movies). Heated pool. Complimentary continental bkfst. Restaurant nearby. Ck-out noon. Meeting rms. Business center. Valet serv. Coin lndry. Exercise equipt; treadmill, stair machine. Health club privileges. Microwaves. Cr cds: A, C, D, DS, MC, V.

🅳 ⛵ ≋ 🏋 ≋ 🐾 SC 🏊

★ ★ ★ **BEST WESTERN MARIEMONT INN.** 6880 Wooster Pike (45227), east of downtown. 513/271-2100; FAX 513/271-1057. 60 rms, 3 story. S $59-$62; D $64-$71; each addl $5; suites $79-$89; under 12 free. Crib free. TV; cable (premium). Complimentary coffee in lobby. Restaurant (see NATIONAL EXEMPLAR). Rm serv. Bar 11 am-midnight. Ck-out noon. Coin lndry. Business servs avail. In-rm modem link. Valet serv. Cr cds: A, C, D, DS, JCB, MC, V.

🐾 SC

★ ★ **COMFORT INN.** 9011 Fields Ertel Rd (45249), I-71 exit 19, north of downtown. 513/683-9700; FAX 513/683-1284. 115 rms, 3 story. May-Sept: S, D $89-$115; each addl $10; under 18 free; lower rates rest of yr. Crib free. TV; cable (premium). Pool. Complimentary continental bkfst. Restaurant adj open 24 hrs. Ck-out 11 am. Meeting rms. Business servs avail. Valet serv. Health club privileges. Cr cds: A, C, D, DS, MC, V.

🅳 ≋ ≋ 🐾 SC

★ ★ **COMFORT SUITES.** (11349 Hartman Hwy, Blue Ash 45241) N on I-71, W on OH 126 to Reed Hartman Hwy. 513/530-5999; FAX 513/530-0179. 50 suites, 3 story. Mid-June-late Aug: S, D $150; each addl $6; under 17 free; lower rates rest of yr. Crib free. TV; cable (premium), VCR avail (movies). Pool. Complimentary continental bkfst. Coffee in rms. Bar 4:30-11 pm; closed Sat, Sun. Ck-out 11 am. Meeting rms. Business servs avail. Valet serv. Sundries. Exercise equipt; weight machine, bicycles, sauna. Health club privileges. Refrigerators. Cr cds: A, C, D, DS, MC, V.

🅳 ≋ 🏋 ≋ 🐾 SC

★ ★ **COURTYARD BY MARRIOTT.** (4625 Lake Forest Dr, Blue Ash 45242) I-275 exit 47. 513/733-4334; FAX 513/733-5711. Web www.courtyard.com. 149 rms, 2-3 story. May-Aug: S, D $94-$109; under 12 free; suites $109-$119; wkend rates; lower rates rest of yr. Crib free. TV; cable (premium). Indoor pool; whirlpool. Complimentary coffee in lobby. Restaurant 6:30-10:30 am; wkends 7-11:30 am. Bar 5-11 pm. Ck-out 1 pm. Coin lndry. Meeting rms. Business servs avail. Exercise equipt; weight machines, stair machine. Health club privileges. Microwaves in suites. Sun deck. Cr cds: A, C, D, DS, MC, V.

🅳 ≋ 🏋 ≋ 🐾 SC

✔ ★ ★ **CROSS COUNTRY INN.** (330 Glensprings Dr, Springdale 45246) N on I-75 to I-275W, exit at OH 4 (exit 41). 513/671-0556; FAX 513/671-4953; res: 800/621-1429. 120 rms, 2 story. S $37.99-$44.99; D $49.99-$56.99; each addl $8; under 18 free. Crib free. TV; cable (premium). Heated pool. Complimentary coffee in lobby. Restaurant adj 11 am-midnight. Ck-out noon. Meeting rm. Business servs avail. Cr cds: A, C, D, DS, MC, V.

🅳 ≋ ≋ 🐾 SC

✔ ★ ★ **CROSS COUNTRY INN.** 4004 Williams Dr (45255), off I-275 exit 65 at OH 125, south of downtown. 513/528-7702; FAX 513/528-1246. 128 rms, 2 story. S, D $35.99-$54.99; under 18 free. Crib free. TV; cable (premium). Pool. Complimentary coffee in lobby. Restaurant adj 6 am-11 pm. Ck-out noon. Business servs avail. Health club privileges. Cr cds: A, DS, MC, V.

🅳 ≋ ≋ 🐾 SC

★ ★ **FAIRFIELD INN BY MARRIOTT.** (11171 Dowlin Rd, Sharonville 45241) I-75 exit 15, then 1 blk E. 513/772-4114. 135 rms, 3 story. Mat-Oct: S, D $45-$83; each addl $7; under 18 free; higher rates special events; lower rates rest of yr. Crib free. TV; cable (premium). Pool. Complimentary continental bkfst. Restaurant adj 6 am-midnight. Ck-out noon. Meeting rms. Business servs avail. In-rm modem link. Valet serv. Health club privileges. Cr cds: A, C, D, DS, MC, V.

🅳 ≋ ≋ 🐾 SC

★ ★ **HAMPTON INN.** 10900 Crowne Point Dr (45241), off I-75 exit 15, north of downtown. 513/771-6888; FAX 513/771-5768. Web www.hampton-inn.com. 130 rms, 4 story. June-Aug: S, D $79-$89; under 18 free; higher rates special events; lower rates rest of yr. Crib free. TV; cable (premium). Pool. Complimentary continental bkfst. Restaurant nearby. Ck-out noon. Meeting rm. Business servs avail. Health club privileges. Cr cds: A, C, D, DS, MC, V.

🅳 ≋ ≋ 🐾 SC

✔ ★ **RED ROOF INN.** 11345 Chester Rd (45246), I-75 Sharon Rd exit 15, north of downtown. 513/771-5141; FAX 513/771-0812. 108 rms, 2 story. S $45.99-$55.99; D $50.99-$69.99; each addl $7; under 18 free; higher rates special events. Crib $5. Pet accepted. TV; cable (premium). Restaurant adj 11-2 am. Ck-out noon. Business servs avail. Valet serv. Health club privileges. Cr cds: A, C, D, DS, MC, V.

🐾 ≋ 🐾

★ ★ **RESIDENCE INN BY MARRIOTT.** 11689 Chester Rd (45246), north of downtown. 513/771-2525; FAX 513/771-3444. 144 kit.

suites, 1-2 story. 1 bedrm $89-$129; 2 bedrm $109-$159; higher rates July. Pet accepted; $75-$95. TV; cable (premium). Pool; whirlpool. Complimentary continental bkfst. Ck-out noon. Coin lndry. Business servs avail. Valet serv. Health club privileges. Microwaves. Picnic tables, grills. Cr cds: A, C, D, DS, JCB, MC, V.

★ ★ **SIGNATURE INN.** 8870 Governor's Hill Dr (45249), off I-71 & Mason-Montgomery Rd, exit 19, north of downtown. 513/683-3086; FAX 513/683-3086, ext. 500. 99 rms, 2 story. Memorial Day-Labor Day: S, D $99-$115; under 17 free; lower rates rest of yr. Crib free. TV; cable (premium), VCR avail. Pool. Complimentary continental bkfst. Ck-out noon. Meeting rms. Business center. In-rm modem link. Health club privileges. Game rm. Cr cds: A, C, D, DS, MC, V.

★ **SUPER 8.** 11335 Chester Rd (45246), I-75 Sharon Rd exit 15, north of downtown. 513/772-3140; FAX 513/772-1931. 144 rms, 2 story. S $46-$73; D $53-$80; each addl $7; under 18 free; higher rates: wkends, special events. Crib free. Pet accepted, some restrictions. TV; cable (premium). Pool. Complimentary continental bkfst. Restaurant adj 11 am-11 pm. Ck-out noon. Coin lndry. Meeting rms. Business servs avail. Valet serv. Cr cds: A, C, D, DS, MC, V.

Motor Hotels

★ ★ **HARLEY.** 8020 Montgomery Rd (45236), I-71 exit 12, north of downtown. 513/793-4300; FAX 513/793-1413. Web www.harleyhotels.com. 152 rms, 2 story. S, D $110-$120; each addl $10; under 18 free. Crib free. TV; cable (premium). 2 pools, 1 indoor; whirlpool. Restaurant 6:30 am-10 pm; Fri, Sat to 11 pm; Sun 7 am-9 pm. Rm serv. Bar; entertainment Fri, Sat. Ck-out 11 am. Meeting rms. Business center. Bellhops. Lighted tennis. Putting green. Exercise equipt; bicycles, stair machine, sauna. Rec rm. Private patios, balconies. Cr cds: A, C, D, DS, JCB, MC, V.

★ ★ **IMPERIAL HOUSE.** 5510 Rybolt Rd (45248), I-74 exit 11, north of downtown. 513/574-6000; FAX 513/574-6566; res: 800/543-3018. 196 rms, 2-5 story, 27 kits. S $49-$76; D $58-$76; each addl $5; suites $130-$150; family rates. Crib free. TV; cable (premium). Pool. Restaurant 6:30 am-10 pm. Bar 11-2:30 am; Sun 1 pm-1 am; entertainment Thur-Sat. Ck-out noon. Coin lndry. Meeting rms. Business servs avail. In-rm modem link. Sundries. Sauna, steam rm. Cr cds: A, C, D, DS, MC, V.

★ ★ **QUALITY HOTEL & SUITES CENTRAL.** 4747 Montgomery Rd (45212), north of downtown, OH 42 at Norwood Lateral. 513/351-6000; FAX 513/351-0215. 146 rms, 8 story. S, D $76-$99; each addl $5; under 18 free; wkend rates. Pet accepted. TV; cable (premium), VCR avail. Pool; poolside serv. Complimentary continental bkfst. Restaurant 11 am-2:30 pm, 5-10:30 pm; Sat 7-10 am, 5-11:30 pm; Sun 7-10 am, 4-9 pm. Rm serv. Bar 11-2 am, Sat from 1 pm, Sun 4-11 pm. Ck-out noon. Meeting rms. Business center. In-rm modem link. Bellhops. Free airport transportation. Health club privileges. Some bathrm phones; refrigerators, microwaves in suites. Some private patios, balconies. Picnic tables, grills. Cr cds: A, C, D, DS, ER, JCB, MC, V.

★ ★ **WOODFIELD SUITES.** (11029 Dowlin Dr, Sharonville 45241) 12 mi N on I-75 exit 15. 513/771-0300; res: 800/338-0008; FAX 513/771-6411. 151 suites, 7 story. May-Oct: S, D $89-$189; each addl $10; under 17 free; lower rates rest of yr. Crib free. Pet accepted, some restrictions; $10. TV; cable (premium), VCR avail. Complimentary continental bkfst. Coffee in rms. Restaurant nearby. Ck-out noon. Meeting rms. Business servs avail. In-rm modem link. Bellhops. Valet serv (Mon-Fri). Coin lndry. Exercise equipt; treadmills, stair machines. Indoor pool; whirl-

pool. Rec rm. Refrigerators, microwaves; some wet bars, in-rm whirlpools. Cr cds: A, C, D, DS, MC, V.

Hotels

★ ★ ★ **CINCINNATIAN.** 601 Vine St (45202), downtown. 513/381-3000; FAX 513/651-0256; res: 800/942-9000. E-mail info @cincinnatianhotel.com; web www.cincinnatianhotel.com. 147 rms, 8 story. S, D $205-$270; suites $450-$1,500; under 12 free; wkend rates. Crib free. Covered parking $14. TV; cable (premium), VCR avail. Restaurant 6:30 am-11 pm (also see THE PALACE). Rm serv 24 hrs. Bar 11:30 am-11 pm; entertainment. Ck-out noon. Meeting rms. Business servs avail. Concierge. Exercise equipt; weight machine, bicycles, sauna. Bathrm phones, minibars; microwave avail. Landmark hotel (1882); restored. Cr cds: A, C, D, DS, JCB, MC, V.

★ ★ **CROWNE PLAZA.** 15 W Sixth St (45202), at Vine St, downtown. 513/381-4000; FAX 513/381-5158. Web www.crowneplaza.com. 326 rms, 11 story. S, D $139-$159; suites $200-$350; family rates. Crib free. Valet parking (fee). TV; cable (premium). Coffee in rms. Restaurant 6 am-11 pm; Sun to 10 pm. Bar 11-2 am. Ck-out 1 pm. Convention facilities. Business center. Concierge. Barber, beauty shop. Exercise equipt; weights, bicycles, sauna. Whirlpool. Refrigerators, minibars. Cr cds: A, C, D, DS, ER, JCB, MC, V.

★ ★ ★ **EMBASSY SUITES BLUE ASH.** 4554 Lake Forest Dr (45242), north of downtown at Reed Hartman Hwy. 513/733-8900; FAX 513/733-3720. E-mail cybga@aol.com. 235 suites, 5 story. S, D $89-$179; each addl $10; under 12 free; higher rates special events. Crib free. TV; cable (premium). Indoor pool; whirlpool. Complimentary full bkfst. Complimentary coffee in rms. Restaurant 11:30 am-10 pm. Bar 5 pm-1 am; closed Sun. Ck-out noon. Coin lndry. Meeting rms. Business servs avail. Gift shop. 18-hole golf privileges. Exercise equipt; weight machine, bicycles, sauna. Health club privileges. Refrigerators, microwaves, wet bars. Balconies. Cr cds: A, C, D, DS, JCB, MC, V.

★ ★ **GARFIELD HOUSE.** 2 Garfield Place (45202), 2 blks W of Fountain Square, downtown. 513/421-3355; FAX 513/421-3729; res: 800/367-2155. 133 kit. suites, 16 story. 1-bedrm $165-$185; 2-bedrm $175-$200; penthouse suites $425-$1,200; monthly rates. Crib free. Pet accepted; $75. Garage parking $4-$8. TV; cable (premium), VCR avail. Complimentary continental bkfst. Complimentary coffee in rms. Restaurant 11 am-9 pm; wkends from 5 pm. Rm serv 5-10 pm. Bar. Ck-out noon. Coin lndry. Meeting rms. Business servs avail. Exercise equipt; weight machine, stair machine. Health club privileges. Microwaves. Some balconies. Cr cds: A, C, D, DS, MC, V.

★ ★ ★ **HOLIDAY INN.** 4501 Eastgate Blvd (45245), east of downtown. 513/752-4400; FAX 513/753-3178. 247 rms, 6 story. S, D $94-$99; each addl $10; suites $200-$275; under 18 free; wkend rates; higher rates special events. Crib free. TV; cable (premium). Complimentary coffee in rms. Restaurant 6:30 am-11 pm; Sun to 10 pm. Bar 11 am-midnight; Sun to 10 pm. Ck-out 11 am. Meeting rms. Business center. Gift shop. Exercise equipt; bicycle, treadmill. Health club privileges. Indoor pool; whirlpool. Bathrm phone, in-rm whirlpool, refrigerator, microwave, wet bar in suites. Cr cds: A, C, D, DS, JCB, MC, V.

★ ★ **HOLIDAY INN-QUEENSGATE.** 800 W Eighth St (45203), I-75 at Linn, west of downtown. 513/241-8660; FAX 513/241-9057. 246 rms, 11 story. S, D $99-$119; suites $189-$210; under 18 free. Crib free. Pet accepted. TV; cable (premium). Pool. Coffee in rms. Restaurant 6:30 am-2 pm, 5-9 pm. Bar 4 pm-2 am; closed Sun. Ck-out noon. Coin lndry. Meeting rms. Business servs avail. In-rm modem link. Exercise equipt;

stair machine, bicycle. Health club privileges. Refrigerators avail. Cr cds: A, C, D, DS, ER, JCB, MC, V.

D [symbols] SC

★ ★ **HYATT REGENCY.** *151 W Fifth St (45202), downtown.* *513/579-1234; FAX 513/579-0107.* Web www.hyatt.com. 485 rms, 22 story. S, D $187-$214; each addl $25; suites $400-$750; under 18 free; wkend rates; higher rates special events. Crib free. TV; cable (premium). Indoor pool; whirlpool, poolside serv. Restaurant 6:30 am-midnight. Bar 11-2:30 am. Ck-out noon. Convention facilities. Business center. Concierge. Shopping arcade. Barber. Exercise equipt; weight machines, bicycles, sauna. Some bathrm phones; refrigerator in suites. Luxury level. Cr cds: A, C, D, DS, JCB, MC, V.

D [symbols] SC

★ ★ ★ **MARRIOTT-NORTHEAST.** *9664 Mason-Montgomery Rd (45040), NE on I-71 exit 19, north of downtown.* *513/459-9800; FAX 513/459-9808.* 303 rms, 6 story. S, D $119-$139; each addl $10; suites $225; under 12 free; higher rates special events. Crib avail. TV; cable (premium). Complimentary coffee in rms. Restaurant 6:30 am-2 pm, 5-10:30 pm. Bar 11:30-1 am. Ck-out noon. Convention facilities. Business center. In-rm modem link. Gift shop. Exercise equipt; bicycle, weight machine. 2 pools, 1 indoor; poolside serv. Bathrm phone, refrigerator in suites. Luxury level. Cr cds: A, C, D, DS, JCB, MC, V.

D [symbols] SC

★ ★ ★ **OMNI NETHERLAND PLAZA.** *35 W Fifth St (45202), off I-75, downtown.* *513/421-9100; FAX 513/421-4291.* 607 rms, 29 story. S $175-$210; D $205-$235; each addl $30; suites $250-$1,680; under 18 free; wkly, wkend rates. Crib free. Valet parking. TV; cable (premium), VCR avail. Indoor pool. Restaurant (see ORCHID'S). Bar 11-2 am; entertainment. Ck-out noon. Business center. Concierge. Shopping arcade. Health club privileges. Some private patios. Cr cds: A, C, D, DS, ER, JCB, MC, V.

D [symbols] SC

★ ★ **REGAL CINCINNATI.** *150 W Fifth St (45202), I-75 exit 5th St, downtown.* *513/352-2100; FAX 513/352-2148.* 882 rms, 21-32 story. S, D $94-$179; each addl $10; suites $250-$1,100; under 18 free. Crib free. Garage $13. TV; cable (premium). Heated pool. Restaurants 6:30 am-11 pm; Sun to 10 pm (also see SEAFOOD 32). Bars 11-2:30 am; Sun from 1 pm. Ck-out 11 am. Convention facilities. Business center. In-rm modem link. Concierge. Shopping arcade. Barber. Health club privileges. Luxury level. Cr cds: A, C, D, DS, JCB, MC, V.

D [symbols] SC

★ ★ **SHERATON-SPRINGDALE.** *(11911 Sheraton Lane, Springdale 45246) N on OH 4, at I-275 exit 41.* *513/671-6600; FAX 513/671-0507.* 267 rms, 10 story. May-Aug: S $99-$109; D $109-$119; each addl $10; suites $130-$150; under 18 free; package plans; lower rates rest of yr. Crib free. TV; cable (premium), VCR avail. Indoor pool; whirlpool. Coffee in rms. Restaurant 6:30 am-10 pm; Fri, Sat to 11 pm. Bar 11-2 am; entertainment. Ck-out noon. Coin lndry. Meeting rms. Business servs avail. In-rm modem link. Gift shop. Exercise equipt; weight machine, bicycle. Game rm. Some bathrm phones. Cr cds: A, C, D, DS, MC, V.

D [symbols] SC

★ ★ **VERNON MANOR.** *400 Oak St (45219), north of downtown.* *513/281-3300; FAX 513/281-8933; res: 800/543-3999.* Web vernon/manor.com. 173 rms, 7 story. S, D $150-$165; each addl $15; suites $235-$450; studio rms $175-$195; under 16 free. Crib free. TV; cable (premium). Complimentary coffee in lobby. Restaurant 6:30 am-10 pm; Sun brunch 10:30 am-2:30 pm. Bar 11-2 am; Sun 1 pm-midnight. Ck-out noon. Coin lndry. Meeting rms. Business center. In-rm modem link. Barber. Valet parking. Exercise equipt; weights, treadmill. Some refrigerators. Cr cds: A, C, D, DS, MC, V.

D [symbols] SC

★ ★ ★ **WESTIN.** *Fountain Sq (45202), 5th & Vine Sts, downtown.* *513/621-7700; FAX 513/852-5670.* 448 rms, 17 story. S $195-$205; D $215-$235; each addl $20; suites $300-$1,200; under 18 free; wkend packages. Crib free. Garage $13.95. TV; cable (premium), VCR avail. Indoor pool; whirlpool, poolside serv. Complimentary coffee in rms. Res-

taurant 6:30 am-10 pm; Fri, Sat to midnight. Rm serv 24 hrs. Bar 11:30-2:30 am; Sun from 1 pm. Ck-out 1 pm. Convention facilities. Business center. In-rm modem link. Shopping arcade. Valet parking. Exercise equipt; weights, bicycles, sauna, steam rm. Massage. Some bathrm phones, refrigerators. Sun deck. Luxury level. Cr cds: A, C, D, DS, ER, JCB, MC, V.

D [symbols] SC

Restaurants

✔ ★ **ADRICA'S.** *934 Hatch St (45202), in Mt Adams.* *513/721-5329.* Hrs: 5-11 pm; Fri, Sat to midnight. Closed Jan 1, Dec 25. Res accepted. Italian menu. Bar. A la carte entrees: dinner $7.95-$12.95. Specialties: hand-tossed fresh pizza, lasagne, eggplant Parmesan. Outdoor patio dining. Cr cds: A, C, D, DS, MC, V.

[symbol]

★ ★ **BLACK FOREST.** *(8675 Cincinnati-Columbus Rd, Pisgah 45069) 3¹/₂ mi N of I-275, exit 46, on OH 42.* *513/777-7600.* Hrs: 11:30 am-2 pm, 4:30-10 pm; Fri to 11 pm; Sat 4:30-11 pm; Sun 4:30-10 pm. Closed some major hols. Res accepted. German menu. Bar. Semi-a la carte: lunch $4.25-$9, dinner $6.95-$17. Buffet: lunch $5.95. Child's meals. Specialties: Wienerschnitzel, Oktoberfest chicken, sauerbraten. German band Fri, Sat. Parking. Old World German decor. Family-owned. Cr cds: A, C, D, DS, MC, V.

D [symbol]

★ ★ **THE BLACKSTONE.** *455 Delta Ave, east of downtown.* *513/321-0010.* Hrs: 5-11 pm; Fri, Sat to midnight; Sun 11 am-3 pm, 4:30-8:30 pm. Closed major hols. Res accepted. Bar. Semi-a la carte: dinner $11.95-$22.95. Child's meals. Specializes in fresh fish, pasta. Parking. Patio dining. Cr cds: A, C, D, DS, MC, V.

D [symbol]

★ ★ ★ **CELESTIAL.** *1071 Celestial St (45202), in Highland Tower Apts, in Mt Adams.* *513/241-4455.* Hrs: 11:30 am-2:30 pm, 5:30-10 pm; Fri, Sat to 11 pm. Closed Sun; some major hols. Res accepted. Continental menu. Bar. Wine list. Semi-a la carte: lunch $6.50-$13.50, dinner $18.95-$24.50. Specializes in game, fresh seafood. Own baking. Jazz Tues-Sat. Free valet parking. Panoramic view of city. Jacket. Cr cds: A, C, D, MC, V.

D [symbol]

✔ ★ ★ **CHATEAU POMIJE.** *2019 Madison Rd (45208), north of downtown.* *513/871-8788.* Hrs: 11 am-2:30 pm, 5:30-9:30 pm; Fri to 10:30 pm; Sat 5:30-10:30 pm. Closed Sun; major hols. Continental menu. Wine, beer. Semi-a la carte: lunch $6-$10, dinner $10-$18. Specialties: cioppino, Chateau chicken, fresh salmon. Own desserts. Street parking. Outdoor dining. Casual, cafe dining; adj wine shop. Cr cds: DS, MC, V.

D

★ **CHENG-1 CUISINE.** *203 W McMillan St (45219), north of downtown.* *513/723-1999.* Hrs: 11 am-10 pm; Fri to 10:30 pm; Sat noon-10:30 pm; Sun 4:30-10 pm. Closed Thanksgiving, Dec 25. Chinese menu. Serv bar. Semi-a la carte: lunch $4.25-$5.75, dinner $5.50-$12.95. Specialties: cashew chicken, pan-fried moo-shu, sizzling shrimp & scallops. Cr cds: A, DS, MC, V.

D [symbol]

★ ★ **CHERRINGTON'S.** *950 Pavilion St (45202), in Mt Adams.* *513/579-0131.* Hrs: 7-10 am, 11 am-3 pm, 5-9 pm; Fri, Sat to 11 pm; Sat 8-11:30 am, 5-11 pm; Sun 11 am-3 pm, 4-9 pm. Closed Mon; some major hols. Res accepted. Bar. Semi-a la carte: bkfst $2.95-$6.95, lunch $4.95-$8.95, dinner $8.95-$22.95. Specializes in fresh seafood. Outdoor dining. Blackboard menu. Guitarist Fri, Sat. Renovated residence (1880). Cr cds: A, C, D, MC, V.

[symbol]

★ ★ **CHESTER'S ROAD HOUSE.** *9678 Montgomery Rd (45242), north of downtown.* *513/793-8700.* Hrs: 11:30 am-2:30 pm, 5-10 pm; Fri to 10:30 pm; Sat to 11 pm; Sun 5-9 pm. Closed Jan 1, July 4, Dec 25; also Super Bowl Sun. Res accepted. Bar. Semi-a la carte: lunch

$6.50-$9.50, dinner $9.50-$22.95. Specializes in fresh seafood, rack of baby lamb, steak. Salad bar. Parking. Garden atmosphere; in converted brick farmhouse (1900). Family-owned. Cr cds: A, C, D, DS, MC, V.

[D] [⌴]

★ ★ CHINA GOURMET. 3340 Erie Ave (45208), Hyde Park East, north of downtown. 513/871-6612. Hrs: 11:30 am-10:30 pm; Fri to 11 pm; Sat noon-11 pm. Closed Sun; major hols. Res accepted. Chinese menu. Bar. A la carte entrees: lunch $6-$9.95, dinner $9.95-$27.50. Specializes in fresh seafood. Parking. Cr cds: C, D, MC, V.

[D] [⌴]

★ ★ DeSHA'S. 11320 Montgomery Rd (45249), north of downtown, 1 mi N of I-275. 513/247-9933. Hrs: 11 am-2:30 pm, 5-10 pm; Fri to 11 pm; Sat 5-11 pm; Sun brunch 10 am-2 pm. Closed Jan 1, Dec 25. Res accepted. Bar. Semi-a la carte: lunch $8-$10, dinner $12-$20. Sun brunch $11.95. Child's meals. Specializes in steak, prime rib, seafood. Parking. Outdoor dining on patio. Casually elegant dining. Cr cds: A, C, D, DS, MC, V.

[D] [⌴]

✔ ★ THE DINER ON SYCAMORE. 1203 Sycamore St, north of downtown. 513/721-1212. Hrs: 11 am-midnight; Fri, Sat to 1 am; Sun brunch 11 am-2:30 pm. Closed Dec 25. Bar. Semi-a la carte: lunch, dinner $4.95-$15.95. Sun brunch $4.95-$7.25. Child's meals. Specialties: Caribbean white crab chili, seafood Diablo, crab cakes. Parking. Outdoor dining. Nostalgic diner atmosphere. Cr cds: A, C, D, DS, MC, V.

[D] [⌴]

★ FORE & AFT. 7449 Forbes Rd, off US 50 (River Rd), 12 mi west of downtown,. 513/941-8400. Hrs: 11 am-10 pm; Fri to 11 pm; Sat 4 pm-11 pm. Closed Jan 1, Dec 24, 25. Res accepted. Bar. Semi-a la carte: lunch $5.75-$14.95, dinner $8.75-$17.95. Child's meals. Specializes in hand-cut steak, prime rib, seafood. Parking. Outdoor dining. Floating barge on Ohio River; nautical memorabilia. Cr cds: A, MC, V.

[SC] [⌴]

★ FOREST VIEW GARDENS. 4508 North Bend Rd (45211), S of I-74 exit 14, north of downtown. 513/661-6434. Hrs: Edelweiss Rm: 11 am-2 pm, 5-7:30 pm; Sat from 5 pm; Show Rm: Broadway music shows (sittings): Thurs 6 pm, Fri 7 pm, Sat 5 & 8 pm, Sun 5 pm. Closed Mon; Dec 24, 25; also 1st wk Jan. Res accepted; required for shows. German, Amer menu. Bar. Semi-a la carte: lunch $3.95-$7.50, dinner $11.95-$18.95. Child's meals. Specializes in Wienerschnitzel, sauerbraten, prime rib. Parking. Outdoor dining in beer garden. Bavarian Fest atmosphere. Banquet-style seating. Family-owned. Cr cds: A, C, D, DS, MC, V.

[D] [⌴]

★ ★ GERMANO'S. 9415 Montgomery Rd (45242), north of downtown. 513/794-1155. Web www.cincy.com/dining/germano. Hrs: 11:30 am-2:30 pm, 5:30-10 pm; Fri to 11 pm; Sat 5-11 pm. Closed Sun; Easter, Thanksgiving, Dec 25. Res accepted (dinner). Italian menu. Serv bar. Semi-a la carte: lunch $5.95-$8.95, dinner $10.95-$21.95. Specializes in pasta, seafood, veal. Own desserts. Tuscan decor with framed art, tapestries. Totally nonsmoking. Cr cds: A, DS, MC, V.

[D]

★ ★ GRAND FINALE. 3 East Sharon Ave, north of downtown. 513/771-5925. Hrs: 11:30 am-10:30 pm; Fri, Sat to 11 pm; Sun 5-10 pm; Sun brunch 10:30 am-3 pm. Closed Mon; Dec 25. Continental menu. Bar. Semi-a la carte: lunch $4.95-$11.95, dinner $14.95-$19.95. Sun brunch $10.95. Child's meals. Specialties: steak salad Annie, chicken Ginger, rack of lamb. Own baking. Parking. Outdoor dining. Remodeled turn-of-the-century saloon. Cr cds: A, C, D, DS, MC, V.

[D] [⌴]

★ ★ HERITAGE. 7664 Wooster Pike (OH 50) (45227), east of downtown. 513/561-9300. Web theheritage.com. Hrs: 11:30 am-2:30 pm, 5-9 pm; Sat 5-10 pm; Sun 10:30 am-2 pm, 5-9 pm. Closed some major hols. Res accepted. Bar. Wine list. Semi-a la carte: lunch $5.95-$8.95, dinner $13.95-$20.95. Sun brunch $12.95. Child's meals. Specializes in

regional American cuisine. Own baking. Valet parking. Outdoor dining. Restored 1827 farmhouse. Own herb garden. Family-owned. Cr cds: A, C, D, DS, MC, V.

[⌴]

✔ ★ ★ HOUSE OF TAM. 889 W Galbraith Rd, Finneytown at Winton, north of downtown. 513/729-5566. Hrs: 11 am-9:30 pm; Fri to 10 pm; Sat 5-10:30 pm. Closed Sun; some major hols. Res accepted. Chinese menu. Bar. Semi-a la carte: lunch $4.50-$6.50, dinner $5.95-$15.95. Specialties: pine nuts chicken, sea emperor's feast, strawberry chicken. Parking. Totally nonsmoking. Cr cds: A, DS, MC, V.

[D]

★ ★ LA NORMANDIE TAVERN AND CHOPHOUSE. 118 E Sixth St, downtown. 513/721-2761. Web www.maisonette.com. Hrs: 11:30 am-2:30 pm, 5-11 pm; Sat from 5 pm. Closed Sun; major hols. Res accepted. Bar. Semi-a la carte: lunch $6.99-$12.50, dinner $15.50-$24.50. Specializes in aged beef, fresh fish. Valet parking. Four-sided fireplace. Family-owned. Cr cds: A, C, D, DS, MC, V.

[⌴]

✔ ★ LEBOXX CAFE. 819 Vine St (45202), downtown. 513/721-5638. Hrs: 11:30 am-8 pm. Closed Sat, Sun; major hols. Contemporary Amer menu. Semi-a la carte: lunch $2-$5, dinner $4-$6. Child's meals. Specializes in meatloaf, ribs, burgers. Casual decor. Cr cds: A, DS, MC, V.

[D] [⌴]

★ LENHARDT'S. 151 W McMillan St (45219), I-71 exit 4, north of downtown. 513/281-3600. Hrs: 11 am-9:30 pm; Sat from 4 pm. Closed Sun, Mon; July 4; also 1st 2 wks Aug, 2 wks at Christmas. Res accepted. German, Hungarian menu. Bar 7 pm-2 am; closed Sun. Semi-a la carte: lunch $3.75-$9.50, dinner $7.95-$15.95. Specialties: Wienerschnitzel, sauerbraten, Hungarian goulash. Free parking. Former Moerlin brewery mansion. Cr cds: A, DS, MC, V.

[⌴]

★ ★ ★ ★ MAISONETTE. 114 E 6th St, downtown. 513/721-2260. Web www.maisonette.com. Exceptionally attentive service puts guests at ease to enjoy Chef Jean-Robert de Cavel's blend of classical and modern cuisine. The three salmon-colored dining rooms are adorned with paintings by famous Cincinnati artists, including Frank Duvanek, whose self-portrait hangs over the bar. French cuisine. Specialties: escalopes de foie gras, fresh, imported French fish dishes, seasonal offerings. Own pastries. Hrs: 11:30 am-2:30 pm, 6-10:30 pm; Mon from 6 pm; Sat 5:30-11 pm. Closed Sun; major hols. Res accepted. Bar. Wine cellar. A la carte entrees: lunch $13.75-$17.75, dinner $25-$36. Valet parking (dinner). Jacket. Cr cds: A, C, D, DS, MC, V.

[D]

✔ ★ ★ MECKLENBURG GARDENS. 302 E University (45219), downtown. 513/221-5353. Hrs: 11 am-10 pm; Fri to 11 pm; Sat, Sun 5-10 pm. Closed major hols. Res accepted. German menu. Bar to 1 am. Semi-a la carte: lunch $5-$9, dinner $7-$17. Specialties: sauerbraten, potato pancakes, Mecklenburg pies. Own desserts. Entertainment Wed, Fri, Sat. Valet parking Fri, Sat. Outdoor dining. Casual dining; grapevine motif. Cr cds: A, C, D, DS, MC, V.

[D] [⌴]

★ ★ MONTGOMERY INN. 9440 Montgomery Rd, north of downtown. 513/791-3482. Web www.montgomeryinn.com. Hrs: 11 am-10:30 pm; Fri to midnight; Sat 3 pm-midnight; Sun 3-9:30 pm. Closed major hols. Res accepted. Bar. A la carte entrees: lunch $4.50-$8.50, dinner $12.50-$20.95. Child's meals. Specializes in barbecued ribs, chicken. Parking. Family-owned. Cr cds: A, C, D, DS, MC, V.

[D] [⌴]

★ ★ MONTGOMERY INN BOATHOUSE. 925 Eastern Ave, 1 mi E of Riverfront Stadium, on OH 50/52, Mt Adams. 513/721-7427. Web www.montgomeryinn.com. Hrs: 11 am-10:30 pm; Fri to 11 pm; Sat 3-11 pm; Sun 3-10 pm. Closed major hols. Res accepted Sun-Fri. Bar. A la carte entrees: lunch $4.95-$17.95, dinner $9.95-$22.95. Child's meals. Specializes in barbecued ribs, seafood, chicken. Valet parking. Outdoor dining (in season). Unique circular building, located at the river; scenic view. Cr cds: A, DS, MC, V.

D ⊒

✔★ **NATIONAL EXEMPLAR.** *(See Best Western Mariemont Inn Motel)* 513/271-2103. Hrs: 7 am-2 pm, 5:30-10 pm; Fri, Sat to 10:30 pm; Sun 5-9 pm. Closed Dec 25. Res accepted. Bar. Semi-a la carte: bkfst $3.25-$6.95, lunch $4.50-$6.95, dinner $9.95-$16.95. Child's meals. Specializes in omelettes, steak, seafood. Casual early American decor. Cr cds: A, DS, MC, V.

D

★★ **NICOLA'S.** *1420 Sycamore St (45210), downtown.* 513/721-6200. Hrs: 11:30 am-2 pm, 5:30-10 pm; Fri to 11 pm; Sat 5:30-11 pm. Closed Sun; major hols. Res accepted. Northern Italian menu. Bar. Semi-a la carte: lunch $5.50-$9.95, dinner $9.95-$28. Specializes in regional Italian dishes, fresh fish. Own pasta, desserts. Valet parking. Outdoor dining. Contemporary decor; casual dining. Cr cds: A, C, D, DS, MC, V.

D ⊒

★★★★ **ORCHID'S.** *(See Omni Netherland Plaza Hotel)* 513/421-1772. Located in the Carew Tower's grand Omni Netherland Plaza, this restaurant in the Palm Court echoes the elegant, art-deco atmosphere of the hotel. The menu features creative American cuisine. Specializes in fresh seafood, veal, beef. Hrs: 11 am-2 pm, 6-10 pm; Sat 6-11 pm; Sun from 6 pm; Sun brunch 10 am-2 pm. Res accepted. Bar to 2 am; Sun 1 pm-midnight. Wine list. Semi-a la carte: lunch $13.25-$18.95. A la carte entrees: dinner $24.95-$54. Sun brunch $21.95. Pianist; jazz Fri, Sat evenings. Valet parking. Cr cds: A, C, D, DS, ER, JCB, MC, V.

D ⊒

★ **PACIFIC MOON.** *8300 Market Place Ln (45242), north of downtown.* 513/891-0091. Hrs: 11 am-10 pm; Fri, Sat to 11 pm. Closed Thanksgiving. Res accepted. Asian menu. Bar. Semi a-la carte: lunch $5.50-$9.50, dinner $12-$22. Specializes in pork, seafood, chicken. Entertainment Sat. Outdoor dining. Contemporary decor. Cr cds: A, C, D, DS, JCB, MC, V.

D ⊒

★★★ **THE PALACE.** *(See Cincinnatian Hotel)* 513/381-6006. E-mail info@concinnatianhotel.com; web www.cincinnatianhotel.com. Hrs: 6:30 am-2:30 pm, 6-10:30 pm; Sun to 9:30 pm; Sun brunch (Labor Day-Mother's Day) 10:30 am-2 pm. Res accepted. Bar 11-1 am; Fri, Sat to 2 am. Wine list. A la carte entrees: bkfst $5.75-$14.95, lunch $6.50-$17, dinner $22-$32. Specializes in seafood, rack of lamb, steak. Own baking. Pianist, jazz trio, harpist (dinner). Valet parking. Jacket. Cherry-wood paneling, decorative columns, and tables with silver table lamps create an elegant neoclassical setting. Cr cds: A, C, D, DS, JCB, MC, V.

D ♥

★ **PETERSEN'S.** *1111 St Gregory, in Mt Adams.* 513/651-4777. Hrs: 11:30 am-10 pm; Fri, Sat to 11 pm. Closed Sun; major hols. Wine. A la carte entrees: lunch $4.75-$9.75, dinner $6.75-$13.75. Specializes in black bean burrito, pasta, desserts. Jazz Mon-Sat. Cr cds: A, C, D, DS, MC, V.

D ⊒

★★★ **THE PHOENIX.** *812 Race St (45202), downtown.* 513/721-2255. Hrs: 5-9 pm; Sat 5:30-10 pm. Closed Sun, Mon; major hols. Res accepted. Wine cellar. A la carte entrees: dinner $11.95-$24.95. Specializes in seafood, pasta, lamb chops. Pianist Sat. Valet parking. Formal dining. Built in 1893; white marble staircase, 12 German stained-glass windows from the 1880s, hand-carved library breakfront built on site in 1905. Totally nonsmoking. Cr cds: A, C, D, DS, MC, V.

D

★★ **PIGALLS CAFE.** *127 W 4th St, downtown.* 513/651-2233. Hrs: 11 am-2:30 pm, 5-10 pm; Fri to 11 pm; Sat 5-11 pm. Closed Sun; major hols. Italian, Amer menu. Bar. Semi-a la carte: lunch $6.99-$9.99,

dinner $8.99-$18.99. Specialties: calypso coconut shrimp, Pigalls cafe salad, fresh seafood. Valet parking Fri, Sat. Bistro-style cafe with murals of Paris. Cr cds: A, C, D, DS, MC, V.

D ⊒

★★★ **THE PRECINCT.** *311 Delta Ave (45226), east of downtown.* 513/321-5454. Hrs: 5-10 pm; Fri, Sat to 11:30 pm. Closed some major hols. Res accepted. Bar 5 pm-2:30 am. Wine list. Semi-a la carte: dinner $16.95-$28.50. Specializes in steak, veal, fresh seafood. Own pastries. Entertainment. Valet parking. In 1890s police station. Cr cds: A, C, D, DS, MC, V.

D

★★ **PRIMAVISTA.** *810 Matson Place (45204), Price Hill, downtown.* 513/251-6467. Hrs: 5:30-10 pm; Fri from 5 pm; Sat 5-11 pm; Sun 5-9 pm. Closed major hols. Res accepted. Italian menu. Bar. Semi-a la carte: dinner $13.95-$28.95. Specialties: Branzino con Aragosta, Costolette di Vitello. Contemporary Italian decor, view of river. Cr cds: A, D, DS, MC, V.

D ⊒

★ **ROOKWOOD POTTERY.** *1077 Celestial St (45202), in Mt Adams.* 513/721-5456. Hrs: 11 am-10 pm; Fri, Sat to 11:30 pm. Closed Memorial Day, Thanksgiving, Dec 25. Bar. Semi-a la carte: lunch $5-$10, dinner $9-$17. Child's meals. Specializes in gourmet burgers, seafood, salads. Free parking. Originally housed production of Rookwood Pottery; some seating in former pottery kilns. Collection of Rookwood Pottery. Cr cds: A, C, D, MC, V.

SC ⊒

★★ **SEAFOOD 32.** *(See Regal Cincinnati Hotel)* 513/352-2160. Hrs: 5-10 pm; Fri, Sat to 11 pm. Closed Sun; Thanksgiving, Dec 25. Res accepted. Bar. Semi-a la carte: dinner $17.50-$24.95. Specialties: wild mushroom-crusted salmon, cioppino Thirty-2. Entertainment. Revolving restaurant overlooks the city. Cr cds: A, D, DS, MC, V.

D ⊒

✔★ **TANDOOR.** *8702 Market Place Ln (45242), north of downtown.* 513/793-7484. Hrs: 11:30 am-2 pm, 5:30-9:30 pm; Fri, Sat to 10:30 pm. Closed Sun; Dec 25. Res accepted. Northern India menu. Bar. Buffet: lunch $6.50. Complete meal: lunch, dinner $4.95-$18.95. Specializes in tandoori cooking. Outdoor dining. Indian decor. Cr cds: A, C, D, MC, V.

D ⊒

✔★ **TEAK.** *1049 St Gregory (45202), in Mt Adams.* 513/665-9800. Hrs: noon-3 pm, 5-9 pm; Fri to 10 pm; Sat 3-11 pm; Sun 5-9 pm. Closed major hols. Res accepted. Thai menu. Bar. Complete meals: lunch, dinner $6.50-$14.95. Specializes in noodle dishes, curry dishes. Outdoor dining. Contemporary decor with Thai art. Cr cds: A, C, D, DS, MC, V.

⊒

★ **WINDOW GARDEN.** *3077 Harrison Ave, I-75 Harrison Ave exit, north of downtown.* 513/481-2743. Hrs: 11 am-8 pm; Sun brunch to 2 pm. Closed Dec 25. Res accepted; required hols. Bar. Semi-a la carte: lunch $5-$7.75, dinner $7.95-$14.95. Sun brunch buffet $9.50. Child's meals. Parking. Cr cds: A, C, D, DS, MC, V.

SC ⊒

Unrated Dining Spots

AGLAMESIS BROS. *3046 Madison Rd, north of downtown.* 513/531-5196. Hrs: 10 am-10 pm; Fri, Sat to 11 pm; Sun noon-10 pm. Closed Jan 1, Easter, Dec 25. Avg ck: $5.50. Specializes in homemade ice cream & candy. Old-time ice cream parlor; established 1908. Family-owned. Cr cds: MC, V.

DARCI'S. *7328 Kenwood Rd, north of downtown.* 513/793-2020. Hrs: 7 am-10 pm; Fri, Sat to 11 pm. Closed Thanksgiving, Dec 25. French menu. Wine, beer. A la carte entrees: bkfst 89¢-$6.89, lunch, dinner $1.49-$12.99. Specializes in croissants, French delicatessen foods. Own baking. Cr cds: A, MC, V.

D

Cleveland (B-5)

Founded 1796 **Pop** 505,616 **Elev** 680 ft **Area code** 216
Information Convention & Visitors Bureau of Greater Cleveland, 3100 Terminal Tower, 50 Public Square, 44113; 216/621-4110 or 800/321-1001.
Suburbs Beachwood, Brecksville, Mentor, Strongsville. (See individual alphabetical listings.)

Ohio's second-largest city extends 50 miles east and north along the shore of Lake Erie and 25 miles south inland. It is a combination of industrial flats, spacious suburbs, wide principal streets and an informality due partially to its diverse population. Many nationalities have contributed to its growth—Poles, Italians, Croats, Slovenes, Serbs, Lithuanians, Germans, Irish, Romanians, Russians and Greeks. Formerly the various national groups divided regionally, but this is less true today. Cleveland has more than 600 churches, 11 colleges, one metropolitan newspaper and several suburban weeklies, as well as a progressive independent mayor-council form of government. A transportation crossroads and a big steel, electrical and machine-tool center, the city also serves as home to the famed Cleveland Clinic.

Cleveland's history has been peppered with industrial giants—John D. Rockefeller, Mathers of iron and shipping, Mark Hanna of steel and political fame, the Van Sweringens and others. The village, founded by Moses Cleaveland, profited by the combination of Great Lakes transportation and fertile country. At the time, northern Ohio was still almost entirely unoccupied; growth was slow. Not until 1827, when the Ohio Canal was opened to join Lake Erie with the Ohio River, did the town start to expand. Incoming supplies of coal and iron ore led to the manufacture of locomotives and iron castings. Before the Civil War the city had surpassed Columbus in population to become the second largest in the state and was changing from a commercial to an industrial center. The boom era after World War I saw the birth of Shaker Heights, one of the more affluent suburbs, the Terminal Tower Group of buildings downtown and the Group Plan, with civic buildings all surrounding the central mall.

The layout of the city is systematic. All the main avenues lead to the Public Square (Tower City Center), where the Terminal Tower is located. The east-west dividing line is Ontario St, which runs north and south through the square. The north and south streets are numbered; the east and west thoroughfares are avenues, with a few roads and boulevards. Euclid Ave is the main business street running through Cleveland and many of its suburbs. Many of the early buildings have been razed and replaced by planned urban architecture, while other buildings are being restored. "Millionaire's row" and the magnificent mansions on Euclid Ave are all but gone. The Cuyahoga River Valley, where refineries, oil tanks and steel mills once made many fortunes, now is known for its entertainment and dining area along the river called the Flats. The 39 city parks and 17,500 acres of metropolitan parks are still a tribute to what was once called "forest city." Cleveland is also home to many universities including Case Western Reserve, John Carroll and Cleveland State.

Transportation

Car Rental Agencies: See IMPORTANT TOLL-FREE NUMBERS.
Public Transportation: Buses & trains (RTA), phone 216/621-9500.
Rail Passenger Service: Amtrak 800/872-7245.

Airport Information

Cleveland Hopkins Intl Airport: Information 216/265-6000; 216/265-6030 (lost and found); 216/931-1212 (weather).

What to See and Do

Alpine Valley Ski Area. Area has quad, double chairlifts, J-bar, 2 rope tows; patrol, school, rentals; snowmaking; cafeteria, lounge. Longest run 1/3-mi; vertical drop 240 ft. (Early Dec-early Mar) 10620 Mayfield Rd, 30 mi E on US 322, in Chesterland. Phone 216/285-2211 or 216/729-9775 (snow conditions). ¢¢¢¢

Beck Center for the Cultural Arts/Lakewood Little Theater. (Sept-June; reduced schedule July-Aug) 17801 Detroit Ave, in Lakewood. Phone 216/521-2540.

Brookside Park. A 157-acre park with tennis courts; athletic fields. Picnic areas. Denison Ave and Fulton Pkwy, 4 mi SW of Public Square (downtown) on I-71. Also here is

Cleveland Metroparks Zoo. Seventh oldest zoo in the country, with more than 3,300 animals occupying 165 acres. Includes mammals, land and water birds; animals displayed in naturalized settings. More than 600 animals and 7,000 plants are featured in the 2-acre Rain Forest exhibit. (Daily; closed Jan 1, Dec 25) 3900 Brookside Park Dr. Phone 216/661-6500. ¢¢¢

Cleveland Health Education Museum. More than 200 participatory exhibits and displays on the human body including Juno, the transparent talking woman; Wonder of New Life; giant tooth; and Family Discovery Center. (Daily; closed hols) 8911 Euclid Ave, East Side. Phone 216/231-5010. ¢¢

Cleveland Hopkins International Airport. Municipally owned; 1,800 acres. Observation deck (May-Nov, weather permitting; free). 5300 Riverside Dr, 12 mi SW of Public Square (downtown). Adj is

NASA Lewis Visitor Center. The display and exhibit area features the Space Shuttle, space station, aeronautics and propulsion, planets and space exploration; also Skylab 3, an Apollo capsule and communications satellites. (Daily; closed major hols) 21000 Brookpark Rd. Phone 216/433-2001. **Free.**

Cleveland Institute of Art (1882). (460 students) Professional education in the visual arts. Professional and student exhibition gallery (Sept-May, daily; rest of yr, Mon-Fri; closed most hols). 11141 East Blvd & 11610 Euclid Ave in University Circle. Phone 216/421-7000.

Cleveland Institute of Music (1920). (Students: conservatory, 300; preparatory, 3,500) This internationally recognized school provides preparatory study and professional training as well as free public concerts and recitals. Tours. 11021 East Blvd. Phone 216/791-5000.

Cleveland Metroparks System. Established in 1917, the system today consists of more than 19,000 acres of land in 12 reservations, their connecting parkways and Cleveland Metroparks Zoo. More than 100 mi of parkways provide scenic drives, picnic areas and play fields; wildlife management areas and waterfowl sanctuaries; hiking and bridle trails, stables; golf courses; swimming, boating and fishing; tobogganing, sledding, skating and cross-country skiing areas; and 4 nature centers offering nature exhibits and programs. Phone 216/351-6300.

Cleveland Museum of Natural History. Dinosaurs, mammals, birds, geological specimens, gems; exhibits on prehistoric Ohio, North American native cultures, ecology; Woods Garden, live animals; library. (Daily; closed major hols). Wade Oval at University Circle. Phone 216/231-4600. ¢¢ Also here is

Ralph Mueller Planetarium. Shows (Mid-June-Aug, daily; rest of yr, Sat & Sun). Observatory (Sept-May, Wed on cloudless nights; planetarium program on cloudy nights). Children's programs. ¢

Cleveland Play House. America's oldest regional, professional, Equity theater presents traditional American classics and premiere productions of new works in three theaters; organized in 1915. (Sept-June, daily exc Mon, also wkend matinees) 8500 Euclid Ave. Phone 216/795-7000.

Cleveland State University (1964). (18,200 students) James J. Nance College of Business Administration, Fenn College of Engineering, Cleveland-Marshall College of Law, College of Urban Affairs, Graduate Studies, Education, Arts and Sciences. Campus tours. Euclid Ave & E 24th St. Phone 216/687-2000.

Dittrick Museum of Medical History. Collection of objects relating to history of medicine, dentistry, pharmacy, nursing; doctor's offices of 1880

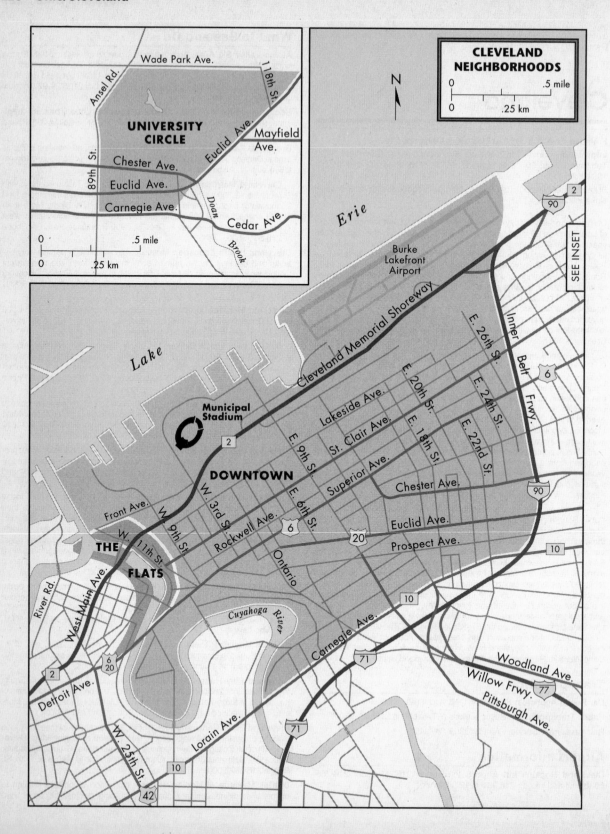

CLEVELAND NEIGHBORHOODS

0 .5 mile
0 .25 km

UNIVERSITY CIRCLE

Wade Park Ave.

Ansel Rd.

118th St.

89th St.

Euclid Ave.

Mayfield Ave.

Chester Ave.

Euclid Ave.

Carnegie Ave.

Doan Brook

Cedar Ave.

0 .5 mile
0 .25 km

N

Erie

Lake

Burke Lakefront Airport

SEE INSET

90

2

6

Cleveland Memorial Shoreway

E. 26th St.

E. 24th St.

E. 22nd St.

E. 20th St.

E. 18th St.

Inner Belt Frwy.

Municipal Stadium

2

DOWNTOWN

Lakeside Ave.

St. Clair Ave.

Superior Ave.

Chester Ave.

Euclid Ave.

Prospect Ave.

90

E. 9th St.

E. 6th St.

Front Ave.

W. 3rd St.

Rockwell Ave.

6

20

10

10

THE FLATS

W. 11th St.

W. 9th St.

River Rd.

West Main Ave.

Ontario

Cuyahoga River

Carnegie Ave.

71

Woodland Ave.

Willow Frwy.

77

Pittsburgh Ave.

2

6

20

Detroit Ave.

Lorain Ave.

W. 25th St.

71

10

42

and 1930; exhibits on development of medical concepts in the Western Reserve to the present. Also history of the X-ray and microscopes. (Daily exc Sun; closed hols & day after Thanksgiving) 11000 Euclid Ave, 3rd floor of Allen Memorial Medical Library, University Circle area. Phone 216/368-3648. **Free.**

Dunham Tavern Museum. Restoration of early stagecoach stop (1824) between Buffalo and Detroit; historic museum with changing exhibits; period furnishings. (Wed & Sun afternoons; closed major hols) 6709 Euclid Ave, East Side. Phone 216/431-1060. ¢

Edgewater Park. A 119-acre park with swimming beach; fishing; boating (ramps, marina). Biking; fitness course. Picnic grounds (pavilions), playground, concessions. Scenic overlook. (Daily) West Blvd & Cleveland Memorial Shoreway; unit of Cleveland Lakefront State Park on Lake Erie. Phone 216/881-8141. **Free.**

Euclid Beach Park. A 51-acre park with swimming beach; fishing access. Picnic grounds, concession. 16300 Lakeshore Blvd; unit of Cleveland Lakefront State Park on Lake Erie. Phone 216/881-8141. **Free.**

Gordon Park. A 117-acre park with fishing piers; boat ramp. Picnic area, playground. (Daily) E 72nd St and Cleveland Memorial Shoreway; unit of Cleveland Lakefront State Park on Lake Erie. Phone 216/881-8141. **Free.**

Great Lakes Science Center. More than 350 hands-on exhibits explain scientific principles and topics specifically relating to the Great Lakes region. Also features an OmniMax domed theater. (Daily; closed some hols) 601 Erieside Ave. Phone 216/694-2000. ¢¢¢

Hanna Fountain Mall. Rectangular section in downtown heart of city, with plaza, fountains and memorial to World War II veterans. Surrounding the mall are the following governmental and municipal buildings

City Hall. Lakeside Ave & E 6th St, overlooking Lake Erie.

County Court House and Administration Building. Justice Center. Ontario & Lakeside Ave.

Federal Buildings. Courts, customs, passport bureau. (Old) at Superior Ave and Public Square and (new) at E 6th St & Lakeside Ave.

Public Library. Business and Science Building adjoining, separated by a reading garden; special exhibits. (Daily; closed hols) 325 Superior Ave, near Public Square. Phone 216/623-2800.

Public Auditorium and Convention Center. Seats 10,000; includes ballroom, music hall, little theater and 375,000 sq ft of usable space. Space for 28 events at one time. St Clair Ave, E 6th St & Lakeside Ave.

High-level bridges. Main Avenue Bridge, Lorain Carnegie Bridge, Innerbelt Freeway Bridge, all spanning Cuyahoga River Valley.

John Carroll University (1886). (4,500 students) Arts and sciences, business and graduate schools in 21 Gothic-style buildings on 60-acre campus. Large collection of G. K. Chesterton works. Warrensville Center & Fairmount Blvd, in University Heights. Phone 216/397-1886.

Karamu House and Theater. Multicultural center for the arts. Classes/workshops in music, creative writing, dance, drama and visual arts; dance, music and theatrical performances (Sept-June); two theaters, art galleries. Fee for some activities. 2355 E 89th St at Quincy Ave. Phone 216/795-7070.

Lake Erie Nature and Science Center. Features animals, marine tanks, petting pen, nature displays, wildlife/teaching garden; planetarium show (fee). Science Center (daily; closed some major hols). 28728 Wolf Rd, 14 mi W on US 6 or I-90 to Bay Village, in Metropark Huntington, West Side. Phone 216/871-2900.

Lake View Cemetery. Graves of President James A. Garfield, Mark Hanna, John Hay, John D. Rockefeller. Garfield Monument (Apr-mid-Nov, daily). Cemetery (daily). 12316 Euclid Ave, at E 123rd St, East Side. Phone 216/421-2665.

Oldest Stone House Museum (1838). Authentically restored and furnished with early 19th-century artifacts; herb garden. Guided tour by costumed hostess. (Feb-Nov, Wed & Sun afternoons; closed hols) 5 mi W, 1 blk N of US 6 in Lakewood, at 14710 Lake Ave, West Side. Phone 216/221-7343. **Donation.**

Playhouse Square Center. Three restored theaters form one of the nation's largest performing and entertainment centers. Performances include legitimate theater, Broadway productions, popular and classical music, ballet, opera and children's theater. 1501 Euclid Ave. Phone 216/241-6000.

Professional sports.

American League baseball (Cleveland Indians). Jacobs Field, Ontario & Carnegie. Phone 216/420-4200.

NBA (Cleveland Cavaliers). Gund Arena, Ontario & Huron. Phone 216/420-2000.

⭐ **Rock and Roll Hall of Fame and Museum.** A striking composition of geometric shapes, this building is now the permanent home of the Hall of Fame. More than 50,000 sq ft of exhibition areas explore rock's ongoing evolution and its impact on culture. Interactive database of rock and roll songs; videos; working studio with DJs conducting live broadcasts; exhibits on R & B, soul, country, folk and blues music. (Memorial Day-Labor Day, daily; rest of yr, daily exc Mon; closed Jan 1, Thanksgiving, Dec 25) North Coast Harbor, E 9th St Pier. Phone 216/781-ROCK. ¢¢¢¢

Rockefeller Park. Connects Wade Park and Gordon Park. A 296-acre park with lagoon area, playground, tennis courts, picnic facilities. Also here are

Cultural Gardens. Chain of gardens combining landscape architecture and sculpture of 24 nationalities. Along East & Martin Luther King, Jr Blvds. (Daily) **Free.**

Rockefeller Greenhouse. Japanese, Latin American and peace gardens; garden for the visually impaired; seasonal displays. (Daily) 750 E 88th St. Phone 216/664-3103. **Free.**

Sightseeing tours.

***Goodtime III* boat cruise.** Two-hr sightseeing and dance cruises on Cuyahoga River, lake and harbor. Leaves pier at E 9th St. (Mid-June-Sept, daily; limited schedule rest of yr) Phone 216/861-5110. Sightseeing cruise ¢¢; Dance cruise ¢¢¢¢; Dinner cruise ¢¢¢¢¢

***Nautical Queen* boat cruise.** Lunch, brunch and dinner cruises. For details, contact E 9th St Pier, North Coast Harbor, 44113 or phone 216/696-8888.

Cuyahoga Valley Line Steam Railroad. Scenic railroad trips between Independence (S of Cleveland) and Akron aboard vintage train. (See AKRON)

Lolly the Trolley Tours of Cleveland. One- and two-hr tours leave from Burke Lakefront Airport. Advance reservations requested. Phone 216/771-4484 or 800/848-0173. ¢¢¢

Steamship *William G. Mather* Museum. Former flagship of the Cleveland Cliffs Iron Company, this 618-ft steamship is now a floating discovery center. Built in 1925 to carry iron ore, coal, grain and stone throughout the Great Lakes, she now houses exhibits and displays focusing on the heritage of the "Iron Boats." Her forward cargo hold is an exhibit hall and also houses a theater and gift shop. Guided and self-guided tours of the vessels are available (depending upon the time of yr); visitors will see the pilot house, crew and guest quarters, galley, guest and officers' dining room and the 4-story engine rm. (June-Aug, daily; May & Sept-Oct, Sat-Sun) 1001 E 9th St Pier. Phone 216/574-6262. ¢¢

Temple Museum of Religious Art. Jewish ceremonial objects; antiquities of the Holy Land region. (Daily, by appt; closed Jewish and natl hols) 1855 Ansel Rd, University Circle area. Phone 216/831-3233. **Free.**

The Cleveland Arcade (1890). This 5-story, enclosed shopping mall, one of the world's first, features more than 80 shops and restaurants. (Daily exc Sun) 401 Euclid Ave, between Superior & Euclid at E 4th St, downtown. Phone 216/621-8500.

⭐ **The Cleveland Museum of Art.** Extensive collections of approx 30,000 works of art represent a wide range of history and culture; included are arts of the Islamic Near East, the pre-Columbian Americas and European and Asian art; also African, Indian, American, ancient Roman and Egyptian art. Concerts, lectures, special exhibitions, films; cafe. Museum entrance from East Blvd. (Daily exc Mon; closed some major hols) Parking (fee). 11150 East Blvd at University Circle. Phone 216/421-7340. **Free.**

The Cleveland Orchestra. One of the world's finest orchestras. Outstanding soloists and guest conductors. (Mid-Sept-mid-May, Tues & Thurs-Sun) Severance Hall, 11001 Euclid Ave at East Blvd. Phone 216/231-1111.

During summer months orchestra performs at Blossom Music Center, approx 28 mi S via US 422, OH 8 (see AKRON).

Tower City Center. A former railroad station and terminal, built in the 1920s. "The Avenue," a 3-level marble, glass and brass complex of dining, entertainment and retail establishments, has an 80-ft high skylight, a 55-ft glass dome, 26 escalators and elevators and a 40-ft-long fountain. An underground walkway connects Tower City to the Gateway Complex containing Jacobs Field and Gund Arena. Terminal Tower (ca 1930) was reborn again in the 1990s as the nucleus of Tower City Center. On the 42nd floor of this 52-story building is an observation deck (Sat & Sun). Public Square, downtown. For further information check Terminal Tower Lobby; phone 216/621-7981. Observation deck ¢

USS COD. World War II Submarine credited with 7 successful war patrols that sank more than 27,000 tons of Imperial Japanese shipping. Tours include all major compartments of this completely restored *Gato* class submarine. (May-Sept, daily) Docked at N Marginal Rd, between E 9th St & Burke Lakefront Airport. Phone 216/566-8770. ¢¢

Wade Park. More than 80 acres; lake; rose and herb gardens. Euclid Ave near 107th St at University Circle. **Free.** Also here is

Garden Center of Greater Cleveland. Changing displays of indoor plants; horticultural library (Mon-Fri; also Sat & Sun afternoons; closed hols). Herb, rose, perennial, wildflower, Japanese and reading gardens surround the building (grounds all yr, daily). 11030 East Blvd. Phone 216/721-1600. **Free.**

Western Reserve Historical Society Museum and Library. Changing exhibits; special programs; genealogy department; costume collection; American decorative arts. (Daily exc Mon; closed hols) 10825 East Blvd in University Circle. Phone 216/721-5722. ¢¢ Also here and included in admission is

Frederick C. Crawford Auto-Aviation Collection. Antique cars and planes; motorcycles and bicycles; National Air Racing exhibit; Main Street, Ohio, 1890. (Daily exc Mon; closed hols)

Wildwood Park. An 80-acre park with fishing; boating (ramps). Picnic grounds, playground, concession. Lakeshore Blvd and Neff Rd; unit of Cleveland Lakefront State Park on Lake Erie. Phone 216/881-8141. **Free.**

Annual Events

Tri-City JazzFest. Phone 216/987-4444. Mar.

Slavic Village Harvest Festival. Slavic Village (Fleet Ave at 55th St). Phone 216/271-5591. Mid-Aug.

Cuyahoga County Fair. Fairgrounds, in Berea. One of largest in the state. Phone 216/243-0090. Early or mid-Aug.

Cleveland National Air Show. Burke Lakefront Airport. Phone 216/781-0747. Labor Day wkend.

Additional Visitor Information

Tourist information may be obtained from the Convention & Visitors Bureau of Greater Cleveland, 3100 Terminal Tower, 50 Public Square, 44113, phone 216/621-4110 or 800/321-1001. An information booth is located in the Terminal Tower Building on Public Square, Hopkins International Airport and Powerhouse & Nautica Boardwalk in The Flats.

Cleveland Magazine and *Northern Ohio Live,* at newsstands, have up-to-date information on cultural events and articles of interest to visitors.

City Neighborhoods

Many of the restaurants, unrated dining establishments and some lodgings listed under Cleveland include neighborhoods as well as exact street addresses. Geographic descriptions of these areas are given, followed by a table of restaurants arranged by neighborhood.

Downtown: South of Lake Erie, west of I-90, north of Carnegie Ave and east of the Cuyahoga River. **South of Downtown:** South of OH 10. **West of Downtown:** West of Cuyahoga River.

The Flats: Area along both sides of the Cuyahoga River south of Front Ave and north of Superior Ave.

University Circle: East of Downtown; south of Wade Park Ave, west of Euclid Ave, north of Cedar Ave and east of E 89th St.

CLEVELAND RESTAURANTS BY NEIGHBORHOOD AREAS
(For full description, see alphabetical listings under Restaurants)

DOWNTOWN
Alvie's. 2033 Ontario St
Diamondback Brewing Company. 724 Prospect Ave
John Q's Steakhouse. 55 Public Sq
Marlin. 1952 E 6th St
Morton's of Chicago. 1600 W Second St
New York Spaghetti House. 2173 E 9th St
Piccolo Mondo. 1352 W 6th St
Riverview Room (The Ritz-Carlton, Cleveland). 1515 W Third St
Sammy's. 1400 W 10th St
Sans Souci (Renaissance Hotel). 24 Public Square
Sweetwater's Cafe Sausalito. 1301 E 9th St

SOUTH OF DOWNTOWN
Johnny's Bar. 3164 Fulton Rd

WEST OF DOWNTOWN
Don's Lighthouse Grille. 8905 Lake Ave
Great Lakes Brewing Co. 2516 Market St
Heck's Cafe. 2927 Bridge Ave
Keka. 2523 Market Ave
Miracles'. 2391 W 11th St
Parker's. 2801 Bridge Ave

THE FLATS
Watermark. 1250 Old River Rd

UNIVERSITY CIRCLE
Baricelli Inn (Baricelli Inn). 2203 Cornell Rd
Classics (Omni International Hotel). 2065 E 96th St
Club Isabella. 2025 University Hospital Dr
Guarino's. 12309 Mayfield Rd
That Place on Bellflower. 11401 Bellflower Rd

Note: When a listing is located in a town that does not have its own city heading, it will appear under the city nearest to its location. In these cases, the address and town appear in parenthesis immediately following the name of the establishment.

Motels

★ ★ **COMFORT INN.** (17550 Rosbough Dr, Middleburg Heights 44130) approx 13 mi S on I-71 exit 235. 216/234-3131; FAX 216/234-6111. 136 rms, 3 story. S, D $79-$99; each addl $5; under 18 free; wkend rates. Crib free. Pet accepted, some restrictions. TV; cable (premium). Pool. Complimentary continental bkfst. Coffee in rms. Restaurant nearby. Ck-out noon. Meeting rms. Business center. Valet serv. Sundries. Free airport transportation. Microwaves avail. Cr cds: A, C, D, DS, ER, JCB, MC, V.

D 🐾 ≈ ⊠ 🏊 SC 🏃

✓★ **CROSS COUNTRY INN.** (7233 Engle Rd, Middleburg Heights 44130) 13 mi S on I-71 exit 235. 216/243-2277; FAX 216/243-9852. 112 rms, 2 story. S $44.99-$51.99; D $47.99-$54.99; each addl $7; under 18 free. Crib free. TV; cable (premium). Heated pool. Complimentary coffee in lobby. Restaurant adj open 24 hrs. Ck-out noon. Meeting rm. Downhill ski 18 mi; x-country ski 5 mi. Cr cds: A, D, DS, MC, V.

D 🏊 ≈ ⊠ 🔥 SC

★ ★ **FAIRFIELD INN BY MARRIOTT.** (16644 Snow Rd, Brook Park 44142) S on I-90, W then S on I-71, near Intl Airport. 216/676-5200; FAX 216/676-5200, ext. 709. 135 rms, 3 story. May-Aug: S, D $67.95; each addl $7; under 18 free; lower rates rest of yr. Crib free. TV; cable (premium). Pool. Complimentary continental bkfst. Ck-out noon. Business servs avail. Cr cds: A, D, DS, MC, V.

D ≋ ⋈ 🔥 SC

✔★ **RED ROOF INN.** *(17555 Bagley Rd, Middleburg Heights 44130) 13 mi SW via I-71 exit 235.* 216/243-2441; FAX 216/243-2474. 117 rms, 3 story. S $42.99-$54.99; D $47.99-$56.99; each addl $10; under 18 free. Crib free. Pet accepted. TV; cable (premium). Complimentary coffee. Restaurant nearby. Ck-out noon. Cr cds: A, C, D, DS, MC, V.

D 🐾 ⋈ 🔥

★★★ **RESIDENCE INN BY MARRIOTT.** *(17525 Rosbough Dr, Middleburg Heights 44130) 16 mi S on I-71 exit 235.* 216/234-6688; FAX 216/234-3459. 158 kit. suites, 2 story. S, D $109-$169; wkend, wkly, monthly rates. Crib free. Pet accepted, some restrictions. TV; cable (premium), VCR avail (movies). Heated pool; whirlpool. Complimentary continental bkfst. Complimentary coffee in rms. Restaurant adj 6 am-midnight. Ck-out noon. Coin lndry. Business servs avail. Valet serv. Sundries. Airport transportation. Downhill ski 15 mi; x-country ski 5 mi. Lawn games. Exercise equipt; bicycles, treadmill. Microwaves; many fireplaces. Picnic tables, grills. Cr cds: A, C, D, DS, JCB, MC, V.

D 🐾 ≋ ≋ 🏃 ⋈ 🔥 SC

Motor Hotel

★★ **HARLEY HOTEL-WEST.** *(17000 Bagley Rd, Middleburg Heights 44130) I-71 Bagley Rd exit.* 216/243-5200; FAX 216/243-5240. Web www.harleyhotels.com. 253 rms, 2 story. S $86-$96; D $96-$112; each addl $10; suites $125-$195; under 18 free; wkend rates. Crib free. TV; cable (premium). 2 pools, 1 indoor; wading pool, lifeguard. Restaurant 6:30 am-10 pm; Fri, Sat to 11 pm. Rm serv. Bar; entertainment Fri, Sat. Ck-out 11 am. Coin lndry. Meeting rms. In-rm modem link. Bellhops. Valet serv. Sundries. Free airport transportation. Sauna. Cr cds: A, C, D, DS, MC, V.

D ≋ ⋈ 🔥 SC

Hotels

★★★ **EMBASSY SUITES.** *1701 E 12th St (44114), downtown.* 216/523-8000; FAX 216/523-1698. Web www.embassy-suites.com. 268 suites, 10 story. S, D $119-$169; under 18 free; kit. units $119-$169; wkend rates. Crib free. Pet accepted. Valet parking $12. TV; cable. Indoor pool. Complimentary coffee in rms. Restaurant 6:30 am-10:30 pm. Bar 11-1 am. Ck-out noon. Coin lndry. Meeting rms. In-rm modem link. Concierge. Lighted tennis. Exercise equipt; weights, bicycles, sauna. Minibars, microwaves. Balconies. Cr cds: A, C, D, DS, ER, JCB, MC, V.

D 🐾 ⛷ ≋ 🏃 ⋈ 🔥 SC

★★★ **MARRIOTT AIRPORT.** *4277 W 150th St (44135), west of downtown.* 216/252-5333; FAX 216/251-1508. Web www.marriott.com. 371 rms, 4-9 story. S $139; D $159; suites $175-$350; under 18 free; wkend package. Crib free. Pet accepted; $50. TV; cable (premium), VCR avail. Indoor pool; whirlpool, poolside serv. Restaurant 6 am-11 pm. Bar 11:30-2 am. Ck-out noon. Coin lndry. Convention facilities. Business servs avail. In-rm modem link. Gift shop. Free airport transportation. Exercise equipt; weights, bicycles, sauna. Cr cds: A, C, D, DS, ER, JCB, MC, V.

D 🐾 ≋ 🏃 ✈ ⋈ 🔥 SC

★★★ **MARRIOTT DOWNTOWN AT KEY CENTER.** *127 Public Sq (44114), downtown.* 216/696-9200; FAX 216/696-0966. 400 rms, 25 story. S, D $159-$169; suites $250-$750; under 18 free. Crib free. Garage $13. TV; cable (premium), VCR avail. Indoor pool; whirlpool. Restaurant 6 am-11 pm. Bar 11-2 am. Ck-out noon. Coin lndry. Convention facilities. Business center. In-rm modem link. Concierge. Gift shop. Exercise equipt; weight machine, treadmill, sauna. Minibars. Luxury level. Cr cds: A, C, D, DS, ER, JCB, MC, V.

D ≋ 🏃 ⋈ 🔥 SC 🏋

★★★ **OMNI INTERNATIONAL.** *2065 E 96th St (44106), at Carnegie, in University Circle area.* 216/791-1900; FAX 216/231-3329. 302

rms, 17 story. S, D $209; each addl $10; suites $225-$1,300; under 18 free. Crib free. Garage parking $8. TV; cable (premium), VCR avail. Restaurant (see CLASSICS). Bar 11-1 am; Sat, Sun from noon. Ck-out noon. Convention facilities. Business servs avail. In-rm modem link. Gift shop. Entertainment in lobby. Exercise equipt; weights, bicycle. Minibars. Luxury level. Cr cds: A, C, D, DS, MC, V.

D 🏃 ≋ 🔥 SC

★★★ **RADISSON INN-CLEVELAND AIRPORT.** *(25070 Country Club Blvd, North Olmsted 44070) 12 mi W on I-480, exit 6B, then N adj Great Northern Mall.* 216/734-5060; FAX 216/734-5471. 140 rms, 6 story. May-Oct: S, D $139-$149; each addl $10; suites $160; under 18 free; wkend, hol rates; higher rates conventions; lower rates rest of yr. Crib free. TV; cable (premium), VCR avail. Indoor pool; whirlpool. Complimentary coffee in rms. Restaurant 6:30 am-2 pm, 5-10 pm; Sat, Sun from 7 am. Bar 11 am-11 pm. Ck-out noon. Meeting rms. Business servs avail. In-rm modem link. Free airport transportation. Downhill ski 15 mi; x-country ski 10 mi. Exercise equipt; stair machine, bicycle, sauna. Some refrigerators; microwaves avail. Some balconies. Cr cds: A, C, D, DS, ER, JCB, MC, V.

D ⛷ ≋ 🏃 ✈ ⋈ 🔥 SC

★★★ **RENAISSANCE.** *24 Public Square (44113), downtown.* 216/696-5600; FAX 216/696-0432. 491 rms, 14 story. S $125-$204; D $125-$224; each addl $20; suites $250-$1,500; under 18 free; wkend rates. Crib free. TV; cable (premium), VCR avail (movies). Indoor pool. Complimentary coffee. Restaurant (see SANS SOUCI). Bar 11-2 am; entertainment. Ck-out noon. Convention facilities. Business center. In-rm modem link. Concierge. Gift shop. Garage parking. Exercise rm; instructor, weights, bicycles, sauna. Health club privileges. Bathrm phones, refrigerators, minibars. 10-story indoor atrium. Luxury level. Cr cds: A, C, D, DS, ER, JCB, MC, V.

D ≋ 🏃 ⋈ 🔥 SC ✈

★★★★ **THE RITZ-CARLTON, CLEVELAND.** *1515 W Third St (44113), at Tower City Center, downtown.* 216/623-1300; FAX 216/623-0515. Web www.ritzcarlton.com. China cabinets in the halls and guest rooms with easy chairs add Victorian flourish to the modern elegance of this hotel. 208 rms, 7 story, 21 suites. S, D $149-$209; suites $259-$359; under 12 free; wkend rates. Pet accepted. Valet parking (fee). TV; cable, VCR avail (movies). Indoor pool; whirlpool, poolside serv. Restaurant (see RIVERVIEW ROOM). Afternoon tea. Rm serv 24 hrs. Bar 11:30-1 am; pianist. Ck-out noon. Meeting rms. Business center. In-rm modem link. Concierge. Exercise equipt; weight machine, bicycles, sauna. Massage. Health club privileges. Bathrm phones, minibars. Luxury level. Cr cds: A, C, D, DS, ER, JCB, MC, V.

D 🐾 ≋ 🏃 ⋈ 🔥 ✈

★★★ **SHERATON-CITY CENTER.** *777 St Clair Ave (44114), downtown.* 216/771-7600; FAX 216/566-0736. 470 rms, 22 story. S, D $154; each addl $15; suites $179-$850; under 18 free. Crib free. Garage $13. TV; cable (premium). Restaurant 6:30 am-11 pm. Bar from 11 am, Sun from 1 pm. Ck-out noon. Convention facilities. Business center. In-rm modem link. Gift shop. Airport transportation. Exercise equipt; weight machine, bicycle. Health club privileges. Many rms with view of lake. Luxury level. Cr cds: A, C, D, DS, MC, V.

D 🏃 ⋈ 🔥 SC ✈

★★★ **WYNDHAM.** *1260 Euclid Ave (44115).* 216/615-7500; FAX 216/615-3355. 205 rms, 14 story. S $149-$189; D $169-$209; each addl $20; suites $249; under 16 free. Crib avail. Valet parking $15. TV; cable. Indoor pool; whirlpool. Complimentary coffee in rms. Restaurant 6 am-10:30 pm. Bar to 2 am. Ck-out noon. Meeting rms. Business servs avail. Sundries. Valet serv. Exercise equipt; bicycle, treadmill, sauna. Health club privileges. Cr cds: A, C, D, DS, MC, V.

D ≋ 🏃 🔥 SC

Inn

★★★ **BARICELLI.** *2203 Cornell Rd (44106), at Cornell & Murray Hill, in University Circle area.* 216/791-6500; FAX 216/791-9131. 7 rms, 3 story. S, D $125-150. TV; cable. Complimentary continental bkfst. Dining rm (see BARICELLI INN). Ck-out 11 am, ck-in 2 pm. Business servs avail. Antiques, stained glass. Brownstone (1896) with individually decorated rms. Cr cds: A, C, D, MC, V.

Restaurants

★ ★ ★ **BARICELLI INN.** (See Baricelli Inn) 216/791-6500. Hrs: 5:30-11 pm. Closed Sun; most major hols. Res accepted. Continental menu. Wine, beer. Semi-a la carte: dinner $19.50-$39. Specialties: lobster & crab ravioli, beef tenderloin. Outdoor dining. Fireplaces, stained glass and paintings throughout room. Cr cds: A, C, D, MC, V.

★ **CABIN CLUB.** (30651 Detroit Rd, Westlake 44145) 216/899-7111. Hrs: 11 am-10:30 pm; Fri, Sat to 11:30 pm; Sun 4-10:30 pm. Closed most major hols. Res accepted. Bar to 1 am. Semi-a la carte: lunch $8-$16, dinner $15-$30. Child's meals. Specializes in steak, seafood, chicken. Log cabin decor. Cr cds: A, D, MC, V.

★ ★ **CENA COPA.** (2206 Lee Rd, Cleveland Heights 44118) 8 mi E on US 322. 216/932-6995. Hrs: 5:30-10 pm; Fri, Sat to 11 pm. Closed Sun; major hols. Res accepted; required Fri, Sat. Continental menu. Bar to 11 pm; Fri, Sat to midnight. Semi-a la carte: dinner $15.95-$24.95. Specializes in seafood. Own baking. Jazz Thurs. Valet parking. Outdoor dining. Contemporary, black-and-white decor. Cr cds: A, MC, V.

★ ★ ★ **CLASSICS.** (See Omni International Hotel) 216/791-1300. Hrs: 11:30 am-2:30 pm, 5:30-9:30 pm; Sat 5-10 pm. Closed Sun; major hols. Res accepted. Continental menu. Bar to 11 pm. Wine list. Semi-a la carte: lunch $15-$20, dinner $19-$29. Specialties: rack of lamb, steak Diane. Entertainment. Elegant decor. Jacket. Cr cds: A, C, D, DS, MC, V.

★ **CLUB ISABELLA.** 2025 University Hospital Dr (44106), in University Circle area. 216/229-1177. Hrs: 11:30 am-11 pm; Fri to 1 am; Sat 5:30 pm-1 am. Res accepted; required wkends. Bar. Semi-a la carte: lunch $4.95-$7.95, dinner $8.95-$17.95. Live jazz nightly. Valet parking (dinner). Outdoor dining. Former stagecoach house. Cr cds: A, C, D, MC, V.

★ ★ **DIAMONDBACK BREWING COMPANY.** 724 Prospect Ave (44103), downtown. 216/771-1988. Hrs: 11:30 am-10 pm; Fri to midnight; Sat 5 pm-midnight; Sun hrs vary. Closed most major hols. Res accepted. Continental menu. Bar. Semi-a la carte: lunch $6-$12, dinner $12-$24. Specializes in tapas. Own baking. Latino music Fri, Sat. Valet parking. Multi-level restaurant with brewery and champagne bar. Cr cds: A, C, D, DS, MC, V.

★ ★ **DON'S LIGHTHOUSE GRILLE.** 8905 Lake Ave (44102), west of downtown. 216/961-6700. Hrs: 11:30 am-10 pm; Fri to 11 pm; Sat 5 pm-11 pm; Sun 4:30-9 pm. Closed some major hols. Res accepted. Continental menu. Bar. Semi-a la carte: lunch $6.95-$9.95, dinner $10-$20. Specializes in fresh seafood, steaks. Valet parking. Contemporary decor. Cr cds: A, C, D, DS, MC, V.

★ ★ **GREAT LAKES BREWING CO.** 2516 Market St (44113), opp West Side Market, west of downtown. 216/771-4404. Hrs: 11:30 am-midnight; Fri, Sat to 1 am; Sun 3-10 pm. Closed major hols. Res accepted. Bar. Semi-a la carte: lunch, dinner $6-$16. Child's meals. Specializes in crab cakes, fresh pasta, seafood, brew master's pie. Own baking. Outdoor dining. Microbrewery. Located in historic 1860s brewery; turn-of-the-century pub atmosphere. Cr cds: A, C, D, MC, V.

✔★ ★ **GUARINO'S.** 12309 Mayfield Rd (44106), in University Circle area. 216/231-3100. Hrs: 11:30 am-10:30 pm; Thurs to 11 pm; Fri, Sat to 11:30 pm; Sun 1-8 pm. Closed major hols. Res accepted; required Fri, Sat. Italian, Amer menu. Bar. A la carte entrees: lunch $7-$9.25, dinner $12-$16.75. Child's meals. Specializes in Southern Italian cuisine. Valet parking. Outdoor dining. Oldest restaurant in Cleveland. In heart of Little Italy; antiques. Cr cds: A, C, D, DS, MC, V.

★ ★ **HECK'S CAFE.** 2927 Bridge Ave (44113), west of downtown. 216/861-5464. Hrs: 11:30 am-9:30 pm; Tues, Wed to 10:30 pm; Thurs to 11:30 pm; Fri, Sat to midnight; Sun brunch 11 am-3 pm. Closed major hols. Res accepted. Semi-a la carte: lunch $4.15-$8.95, dinner $4.15-$18.95. Sun brunch $6.95-$9.95. Specializes in bouillabaisse, hamburgers. Outdoor dining. In historic 19th-century building. Cr cds: A, MC, V.

★ ★ **JOHN Q'S STEAKHOUSE.** 55 Public Sq (44113), downtown. 216/861-0900. Hrs: 11:30 am-10 pm; Fri to 11 pm; Sat 4-11 pm; Sun from 4 pm. Closed major hols. Res accepted. Bar. Semi-a la carte: lunch $7.95-$18.95, dinner $15.95-$24.95. Child's meals. Specialty: 16-oz pepper steak. Vocalist Fri. Valet parking Sat. Outdoor dining. Traditional decor with dark wood floors and walls. Cr cds: A, C, D, DS, MC, V.

★ ★ **JOHNNY'S BAR.** 3164 Fulton Rd (44109), south of downtown. 216/281-0055. Hrs: 11:30 am-3 pm, 5-10 pm; Fri to 11 pm; Sat 5-11 pm. Closed Sun; most major hols. Res accepted; required Fri, Sat. Italian menu. Bar. Semi-a la carte: lunch $6-$13.95, dinner $14.50-$29.95. Specialties: "Italian Feast," veal chops. Former neighborhood grocery. Family-owned. Cr cds: A, D, MC, V.

★ ★ **KEKA.** 2523 Market Ave (44113), west of downtown. 216/241-5352. Hrs: 11:30 am-11 pm; Fri to 1 am; Sat 4 pm-1 am; Sun 5-10 pm. Closed Mon; major hols. Res accepted. Spanish menu. Bar. Semi-a la carte: lunch $4-$10, dinner $14-$20. Specializes in tapas, paella, seafood. Own baking. Jazz Wed-Fri. Valet parking. Outdoor dining. Spanish decor; high ceilings, artwork. Cr cds: A, MC, V.

✔★ ★ **LEMON GRASS.** (2179 Lee Rd, Cleveland Heights 44118) 8 mi E on US 322. 216/321-0210. Hrs: 11:30 am-2:30 pm, 5-10 pm; Fri to 11 pm; Sat 5-11 pm. Closed Sun; some major hols. Res accepted (dinner). Thai menu. Bar. Semi-a la carte: lunch $7-$10, dinner $11-$21. Specializes in seafood, curry dishes. Blues, jazz Fri. Outdoor dining. Thai decor with two distinct dining areas—one formal, one informal. Cr cds: A, MC, V.

★ ★ **MARLIN.** 1952 E 6th St (44114), downtown. 216/589-0051. Hrs: 11:30 am-10 pm; Sat from 5:30 pm. Closed Sun; most major hols. Res accepted. Contemporary Amer menu. Bar. Semi-a la carte: lunch $8.25-$14, dinner $17-$29. Specializes in seafood. Bistro decor. Cr cds: A, D, DS, MC, V.

✔★ ★ **MIRACLES'.** 2391 W 11th St (44113), 2 mi W on I-90, west of downtown. 216/623-1800. Hrs: 11:30 am-9 pm; Mon to 2:30 pm; Fri, Sat to 10 pm; Sun 10:30 am-2:30 pm (brunch). Closed most major hols. Res accepted Fri-Sun. Bar. Semi-a la carte: lunch $5-$10, dinner $8-$17. Sun brunch $4.50-$6.95. Specializes in potato pancakes, homemade soups, fresh fish. Own baking. Outdoor dining. Casual dining in 1860 bldg. Cr cds: C, D, DS, MC, V.

★ ★ ★ **MORTON'S OF CHICAGO.** 1600 W Second St (44113), downtown. 216/621-6200. Hrs: 11:30 am-2:30 pm, 5-11 pm; Sat from 5 pm; Sun 5-10 pm. Closed most major hols. Res accepted. Bar. Wine list. A la carte entrees: lunch $14-$23, dinner $21-$36. Specializes in steak, prime beef. Club atmosphere. Cr cds: A, C, D, JCB, MC, V.

★ **NEW YORK SPAGHETTI HOUSE.** *2173 E 9th St (44115), downtown.* 216/696-6624. Hrs: 11 am-9:30 pm; Fri, Sat to 10:30 pm; Sun 3-7 pm. Closed major hols. Res accepted. Italian, Amer menu. Bar. Semi-a la carte: lunch $6-$7, dinner $8-$24. Specializes in veal. Mural scenes of Italy. In former parsonage. Family-owned. Cr cds: A, DS, MC, V.

★ ★ ★ **PARKER'S.** *2801 Bridge Ave (44113), west of downtown.* 216/771-7130. French, Amer menu. Hrs: 11:30 am-2:30 pm; 5:30-9:15 pm. Closed Sun; major hols. Res accepted. Bar. Wine cellar. A la carte entrees: lunch $8-$14. Complete meals: dinner $41. Valet parking. Country French atmosphere. Jacket. Totally nonsmoking. Cr cds: A, DS, MC, V.

★ ★ **PICCOLO MONDO.** *1352 W 6th St (44113), downtown.* 216/241-1300. Hrs: 11:30 am-11 pm; Fri, Sat to midnight. Closed Sun; most major hols. Res accepted. Italian menu. Bar. Semi-a la carte: lunch $9-$20, dinner $11-$32. Specialties: veal scallopine, brick oven pizza. Italian villa decor. Cr cds: A, C, D, DS, MC, V.

★ ★ **PIER W.** *(12700 Lake Ave, Lakewood 44107) Shoreway via Rte 2 to Lake Ave.* 216/228-2250. Hrs: 11:30 am-3 pm, 5:30-10 pm; Fri, Sat 5 pm-midnight; Sun 9:30 am-2:30 pm, 4:30-10 pm; Sun brunch to 2:30 pm. Closed Dec 25. Res accepted. Bar. Semi-a la carte: lunch $5.95-$12.95, dinner $14.95-$47.95. Sun brunch $17.95. Specializes in seafood. Own pastries. Entertainment Fri, Sat. Valet parking. Nautical decor. On water with view of Lake Erie, Cleveland skyline. Cr cds: A, C, D, DS, MC, V.

✔★ **PLAYERS ON MADISON.** *(14523 Madison Ave, Lakewood 44107)* 216/521-2600. Hrs: 5-10 pm; Fri, Sat to 11 pm. Closed major hols. Italian menu. Bar. Semi-a la carte: dinner $14-$20. Specializes in pizza, pasta. Italian bistro decor. Cr cds: A, D, DS, MC, V.

★ ★ **RIVERVIEW ROOM.** *(See The Ritz-Carlton, Cleveland Hotel)* 216/623-1300. Hrs: 6:30 am-10 pm; Fri, Sat to 11 pm; Sun brunch 10:30 am-2:30 pm. Res accepted; required brunch. Contemporary Amer menu. Bar. Wine cellar. Complete meal: bkfst $10.50-$15, lunch $15-$25, dinner $30-$40. Semi-a la carte: bkfst $8.50-$12, lunch $12.50-$17.50, dinner $24-$35. Bkfst buffet $8.50-$10.50. Sun brunch $32. Child's meals. Specialty: mushroom mystic. Own baking, pasta. Valet parking. Elegant restaurant with antiques and artwork throughout; large windows offer view of river and downtown. Cr cds: A, C, D, DS, ER, JCB, MC, V.

★ ★ **SAMMY'S.** *1400 W 10th St (44113), downtown.* 216/523-5560. Web www.dinersource.com/sammys/sammmain.html. Hrs: 5:30-10 pm; Fri, Sat to midnight. Closed Sun; major hols. Res accepted. Bar. Wine list. Semi-a la carte: dinner $19.95-$28.95. Specialties: boule de neige, fresh fish. Raw bar. Own baking. Entertainment. Valet parking. In restored 1850 warehouse; view of Cuyahoga River and bridges. Cr cds: A, C, D, DS, JCB, MC, V.

★ ★ **SANS SOUCI.** *(See Renaissance Hotel)* 216/696-5600. Hrs: 11:30 am-2:30 pm, 5:30-10 pm; Fri, Sat to 11 pm; Sun from 5:30 pm. Closed most major hols. Res accepted. Mediterranean menu. Bar to 2 am. Wine list. Semi-a la carte: lunch $5.75-$15, dinner $11.95-$19.50. Specializes in seafood. Mediterranean decor. Cr cds: A, C, D, DS, JCB, MC, V.

★ ★ **SWEETWATER'S CAFE SAUSALITO.** *1301 E 9th St (44114), in the Galleria at Erieview, downtown.* 216/696-2233. Hrs: 11:30 am-9 pm; Fri, Sat to 10 pm. Closed Sun; Thanksgiving, Dec 25. Res accepted. Bar to midnight. Semi-a la carte: lunch $5.50-$10.95, dinner $6.95-$16.95. Specialties: seafood, pasta, black bean soup. Pianist Fri, Sat (dinner). Valet parking. Dinner theater package. Cr cds: A, D, DS, MC, V.

★ ★ **THAT PLACE ON BELLFLOWER.** *11401 Bellflower Rd (44106), in University Circle area.* 216/231-4469. Hrs: 11:30 am-3 pm, 5:30-10 pm; Fri, Sat to 11 pm; Sun 5-8:30 pm; Mon to 3 pm. Closed major hols. Res accepted. Varied menu. Bar. Semi-a la carte: lunch $4.95-$6.95, dinner $9.95-$16.95. Child's meals. Specializes in beef Wellington, fresh salmon. Valet parking. Outdoor dining. Converted turn-of-the-century carriage house. Cr cds: A, D, MC, V.

✔★ ★ **WATERMARK.** *1250 Old River Rd (44113), in The Flats.* 216/241-1600. Hrs: 11:30 am-10 pm; Fri, Sat to 11 pm; Sun brunch 11 am-2:30 pm. Res accepted. Bar. Semi-a la carte: lunch, dinner $7.95-$17.95. Sun brunch $15.95. Child's meals. Specializes in marinated and grilled seafood. Free valet parking. Outdoor dining. Former ship provision warehouse on Cuyahoga River. Cr cds: A, C, D, DS, JCB, MC, V.

Unrated Dining Spot

ALVIE'S. *2033 Ontario St, downtown.* 216/771-5322. Hrs: 6:30 am-7 pm; Sat 9 am-3 pm. Closed Sun; major hols. Beer. Semi-a la carte: bkfst $2-$4, lunch $2-$5. Specializes in deli foods, salads. Own soups. Family-owned. No cr cds accepted.

Columbus (E-3)

(See also Delaware, Lancaster, Newark)

Founded 1812 **Pop** 632,910 **Elev** 780 ft **Area code** 614 **Web** www.columbuscvb.org

Information Greater Columbus Convention & Visitors Bureau, 90 N High St, 43215-3014; 614/221-6623 or 800/354-2657.

Columbus was created and laid out to be the capital of Ohio; it is most attractive, with broad, tree-lined streets, parks, Ohio State University and a handsome Greek-revival capitol. Both Chillicothe and Zanesville had previously been capitals, but in 1812 two tracts were selected on the banks of the Scioto River, one for the capitol, the other for a state penitentiary, and construction began immediately. The legislature first met here in 1816.

By 1833, the new National Road reached Columbus, and stagecoach travel stimulated its growth. The first railroad reached Columbus in 1850 and from then on the city grew rapidly. Floods in 1913 made it necessary to widen the channel of the Scioto River. Levees, fine arched bridges and the Civic Center were built.

Transportation equipment, machinery, fabricated and primary metals, food, printing and publishing are among the principal industries, but education and government are Columbus's most important functions. Its people are civic-minded, sports-minded and cultured. The city has more than 900 churches and 13 colleges and universities.

What to See and Do

Camp Chase Confederate Cemetery. Burial ground for Confederate soldiers who were prisoners in the camp. Sullivant Ave between Powell Ave & Binns Blvd.

City Hall. Occupies an entire block in the Civic Center. Greco-Roman style. Municipal departments and city council chamber. N Front, W Gay, W Broad Sts & Marconi Blvd.

Columbus Museum of Art. Collections focus on 19th- and 20th-century European and American paintings, sculpture, works on paper and decorative arts; contemporary sculpture; also includes 16th- and 17th-century Dutch and Flemish Masters. Galleries arranged chronologically. Museum shop; indoor atrium; Sculpture Garden; cafe. (Daily exc Mon; closed most hols) 480 E Broad St at Washington Ave. Phone 614/221-6801. **Free.** Special exhibitions ¢¢

COSI, Ohio's Center of Science & Industry. Hands-on museum includes exhibits, programs and demonstrations. Battelle Planetarium shows (daily). Coal Mine, Hi-Tech Showcase, Free Enterprise Area, Foucault pendulum, Solar Front Exhibit Area, Computer Experience, Street of Yesteryear, Weather Station, KIDSPACE and FAMILIESPACE. (Daily) 280 E Broad St. Phone 614/228-2674. ¢¢

Federal Building. Federal offices. 200 N High St.

German Village. Historic district restored as old-world village with shops, old homes, gardens; authentic foods. Bus tour avail; inquire. (Daily) S of downtown, bounded by Livingston Ave, Blackberry Alley, Nursery Lane, Pearl Alley. Phone 614/221-8888. **Free.**

Hoover Reservoir Area. Fishing; boating. Nature trails. Picnicking. (Daily) 12 mi NE on Sunbury Rd. Phone 614/645-3350. **Free.**

Martha Kinney Cooper Ohioana Library. Reference library of books on Ohio and by Ohioans. (Mon-Fri & 1st Sat of each month; closed hols) Rm 1105, Ohio Departments Bldg, 65 S Front St, at foot of State St. Phone 614/466-3831. **Free.**

McKinley Memorial. Statue of President McKinley delivering his last address. W entrance to capitol grounds.

O'Shaughnessy Reservoir. Waterskiing; fishing; boating. Picnicking. 16 mi N on Riverside Dr, OH 257. **Free.** At reservoir dam is

Columbus Zoo. More than 11,000 birds, mammals, fish and reptiles; children's zoo. Picnic areas. (Daily) 9990 Riverside Dr. Phone 614/645-3550. ¢¢

★ **Ohio Historical Center** (1970). Modern architectural design contrasts with the age-old themes of Ohio's prehistoric culture, natural history and history. Exhibits include an archaeology mall with computer interactive displays and life-sized dioramas; a natural history mall with a mastodon skeleton and a demonstration laboratory; and a history mall with transportation, communication and lifestyle exhibits. Ohio archives and historical library (Tues-Sat). Museum (daily; closed Jan 1, Thanksgiving, Dec 25). 17th Ave at I-71. Phone 614/297-2300. ¢¢   Also here, and included in admission, is

Ohio Village (1974). Reconstruction of a rural, 1860s Ohio community with one-room schoolhouse, town hall, general store, hotel, farmhouse, barn, doctor's house and office. Costumed craftspeople operate printing, tinsmith, blacksmith, weaver's and other shops. (Apr-Dec, Wed-Sun; rest of yr, wkends only; closed Thanksgiving, Dec 24-25 & Wed following Mon hol) Phone 614/297-2680.

★ **Ohio's Prehistoric Native American Mounds.** Driving tour of approx 244 mi for a visit to several of these areas. There are more than 10,000 Native American mounds in Ohio, many of which, like the famous Serpent Mound, were built in complex and fascinating forms, such as birds, animals and snakes. Ohio State University has been responsible for the excavation and exploration of Ohio's earliest history. The Ohio Historical Center, 17th Ave at I-71 is a good place to start; here the entire prehistory is made clear in exhibits. After taking in these exhibits, take US 23 approx 46 mi S to jct US 35, then head 1 mi W to OH 104/207, then turn right (N) and go 2 mi to

Hopewell Culture National Historical Park (see CHILLICOTHE). Thirteen acres of Hopewell mounds; pottery and relics in museum. Return S on OH 104, 4 mi to Chillicothe. Here drop in at the

Ross County Historical Society Museum, 45 W 5th St (see CHILLICOTHE) and see more exhibits on the lives of the earliest dwellers in Ohio. Take US 50 approx 17 mi SW to

Seip Mound State Memorial (see CHILLICOTHE). Continue W approx 3 mi through Bainbridge and turn S on OH 41 approx 12 mi to

Fort Hill State Memorial (see). This ancient fortification, probably built by the Hopewell, is of great interest. Continue S on OH 41 approx 9 mi to Locust Grove, turn W on OH 73 approx 4 mi to the famous

Serpent Mound State Memorial (see). This is the largest (1,335 ft long) and most remarkable effigy mound in the country. Continue NW on OH 73 approx 30 mi to OH 350, turn left (W) approx 23 mi to

Fort Ancient State Memorial (see). This is one of the biggest and most impressive prehistoric earthworks in the country, built by the Hopewell between 100 B.C. and A.D. 500. Best return route to Columbus is via OH 350 W to I-71, then 76 mi NE to Columbus.

Ohio State Capitol. Fine building that has at its northwest corner a group of bronze statues by Levi T. Scofield. The sculpture depicts Ohio soldiers and statesmen under Roman matron Cornelia. Her words, "These are my jewels," refer to Grant, Sherman, Sheridan, Stanton, Garfield, Hayes and Chase, who stand below her. Rotunda. Observation window on 40th floor of State Office Tower Bldg, across from rotunda. (Daily) In a 10-acre park bounded by High, Broad, State & 3rd Sts, on US 23, 40. Phone 614/466-2125 or 800/BUCKEYE **Free.**

Ohio State University (1870). (58,000 students) One of largest universities in the country with 19 colleges, a graduate school and more than 100 departments; medical center. Libraries have more than four million volumes. Tours. N High St & 15th Ave. Visitor information center, phone 614/292-4070. Also on campus are

Wexner Center for the Arts. Contemporary art. Film, video, performing arts and education programs and exhibits. Gallery tours during exhibitions (free). (Daily exc Mon; closed hols) 15th Ave at High St. Phone 614/292-0330.

Chadwick Arboretum. 2120 Fyffe Rd. (Apr-Oct) **Free.**

Park of Roses. Contains over 10,000 rose bushes representing 350 varieties. Picnic facilities. Rose festival (early June). Musical programs Sun evenings in summer. (Daily) Acton & High Sts, 5½ mi N, in Whetstone Park. **Free.**

Santa Maria **Replica.** A full-scale, museum-quality replica of Christopher Columbus's flagship, the *Santa Maria.* Costumed guides offer guided tour of the upper and lower decks. Visitors learn of life as a sailor on voyages in the late 1400s. (Apr-Jan daily exc Mon; closed some hols) Battelle Riverfront Park, Marconi Blvd & Broad St. Phone 614/645-8760. ¢¢

The Columbus Symphony Orchestra. Performances at Ohio Theatre. 55 E State St. Box office, phone 614/228-8600.

Annual Events

Greater Columbus Arts Festival. Downtown riverfront area. Exhibits, music, dancing. Early June.

Ohio State Fair. Expositions Center, I-71 and E 17th Ave. Agricultural and industrial exposition plus grandstand entertainment, pageants and horse show. Phone 800/BUCKEYE. Early-mid-Aug.

Columbus Day Celebration. Parade, fireworks, entertainment. Early Oct.

Seasonal Events

Harness racing. Scioto Downs. 9 mi S on US 23 (S High St), 3 mi S of I-270. Restaurants. Phone 614/491-2515. Nightly exc Sun. Early May-mid-Sept.

Actors Theater. Schiller Park in German Village. Two Shakespearean productions, one American musical. Phone 614/444-6888. June-Aug.

BalletMet. Ohio Theatre, 55 E State St. For schedule phone 614/229-4848. Sept-mid-Apr.

Thoroughbred racing. Beulah Park Jockey Club. Southwest Blvd, in Grove City. Phone 614/871-9600. Daily exc Thurs. Mid-Sept-mid-May.

Opera/Columbus. English translation projected onto screen above stage. Palace Theatre, 34 W Broad St. For schedule, phone 614/461-0022. Oct-Apr.

Additional Visitor Information

Tourist brochures and a quarterly calendar of events may be obtained at the Visitor Center/gift shop in the Convention & Visitors Bureau, 90 N High St or on the 2nd level of Columbus City Center Shopping Mall, South High St & South Third St at Rich St, phone 800/345-4FUN. A third visitor information center is located at the Columbus International Airport, I-670E, I-270.

Motels

★ ★ **AMERISUITES.** 7490 Vantage Dr (43235). 614/846-4355; FAX 614/846-4493. 126 suites, 6 story. S, D $98-$118; under 12 free. Crib free. TV; cable (premium), VCR avail (movies). Heated pool. Complimentary continental bkfst. Restaurant adj 6 am-11 pm. Ck-out noon. Meeting rms. Business center. Valet serv. Coin lndry. Free airport transportation. Exercise equipt; weight machine, bicycle. Microwaves. Cr cds: A, C, D, DS, MC, V.

⊡ ≋ ✕ ⊻ 🔥 SC 🏃

★ **BEST WESTERN-EAST.** *(2100 Brice Rd, Reynoldsburg 43068)* E on I-70, exit 110. 614/864-1280; FAX 614/864-1280, ext. 388. 143 rms, 2 story. S $60-$72; D $69-$79; under 18 free; higher rates special events. Crib free. Pet accepted. TV; cable (premium). Pool; poolside serv. Restaurant 6 am-11 pm. Rm serv. Bar 11 am-midnight. Ck-out noon. Meeting rms. Businesss servs avail. Free airport transportation. Cr cds: A, C, D, DS, MC, V.

⊡ 🐾 ≋ ⊻ 🔥 SC

★★ **COURTYARD BY MARRIOTT.** *7411 Vantage Dr (43085).* 614/436-7070; FAX 614/436-4970. 145 rms, 4 story. S, D $95-$99; each addl $10; suites $105-$125; under 18 free; wkend rates. Crib free. TV; cable (premium). Indoor pool; whirlpool. Complimentary coffee in rms. Restaurant 6:30-10 am. Bar 4:30-11 pm. Ck-out 1 pm. Coin lndry. Meeting rms. Business servs avail. In-rm modem link. Valet serv (Mon-Fri). Exercise equipt; weights, bicycles. Game rm. Refrigerator in suites. Balconies. Cr cds: A, C, D, DS, MC, V.

⊡ ≋ ✕ ⊻ 🔥 SC

✔★★ **CROSS COUNTRY INN-NORTH.** *4875 Sinclair Rd (43229).* 614/431-3670; FAX 614/431-7261. 136 rms, 2 story. S $39.99-$41.99; D $46.99-$49.99; family rates. Crib free. TV; cable (premium). Heated pool. Restaurant adj 6 am-11 pm. Ck-out noon. Business servs avail. Cr cds: A, DS, MC, V.

⊡ ≋ ⊻ 🔥 SC

★★ **FAIRFIELD INN BY MARRIOTT.** *887 Morse Rd (43229).* 614/262-4000. 135 rms, 3 story. Apr-Oct: S, D $49-$66; each addl $6; under 18 free; lower rates rest of yr. Crib free. TV; cable (premium). Pool. Complimentary continental bkfst. Restaurant nearby. Ck-out noon. Meeting rm. Business servs avail. In-rm modem link. Cr cds: A, C, D, DS, MC, V.

⊡ ≋ ⊻ 🔥 SC

★★ **HAMPTON INN.** *4280 International Gateway (43219), near Port Columbus Airport.* 614/235-0717; FAX 614/231-0886. 129 rms, 4 story. S, D $65-$70; each addl $5; suites $90; under 18 free. Crib free. TV; cable (premium). Complimentary continental bkfst. Restaurant adj 6 am-midnight. Ck-out noon. Meeting rms. Business servs avail. In-rm modem link. Bellhops. Valet serv (Mon-Fri). Free airport transportation. Health club privileges. Heated pool. In-rm whirlpool in suites. Cr cds: A, C, D, DS, MC, V.

⊡ ≋ ✕ ⊻ 🔥

★★ **HOMEWOOD SUITES.** *115 Hutchinson Ave (43235), jct I-270 & US 23N.* 614/785-0001; FAX 614/785-0143; res: 800/225-5466. 99 kit. units, 3 story, 99 suites. S, D $99-$115; wkend rates. Crib free. Pet accepted; from $10/day. TV; cable (premium), VCR (movies $5). Heated pool; whirlpool. Complimentary bkfst. Complimentary coffee in rms. Restaurant adj 6 am-midnight. Ck-out noon. Coin lndry. Meeting rms. Business center. In-rm modem link. Sundries. Tennis privileges. Exercise equipt; weight machine, stair machine. Lawn games. Microwaves. Grills. Cr cds: A, C, D, DS, JCB, MC, V.

⊡ 🐾 🏃 ≋ ✕ ⊻ 🔥 SC 🏃

✔★ **RED ROOF INN-MORSE ROAD.** *750 Morse Rd (43229), I-71 Morse-Sinclair exit 16.* 614/846-8520; FAX 614/846-8526. 107 rms, 2 story. S $42.99-$52.99; D $49.99-$59.99; under 18 free. Crib free. Pet accepted. TV. Complimentary coffee in lobby. Restaurant adj 7 am-11 pm. Ck-out noon. Business servs avail. Cr cds: A, C, D, DS, MC, V.

⊡ 🐾 ⊻ 🔥 SC

★★ **SIGNATURE INN.** *6767 Schrock Hill Ct (43229), N of I-270, Cleveland Ave exit.* 614/890-8111. 125 rms, 2 story. S, D $67-$77;

under 17 free. Crib free. TV; cable (premium), VCR avail (movies). Pool. Complimentary continental bkfst. Restaurant adj 8 am-midnight. Ck-out noon. Meeting rms. Business center. Health club privileges. Cr cds: A, C, D, DS, MC, V.

⊡ ≋ ⊻ 🔥 SC 🏃

★★ **TRUEMAN CLUB HOTEL.** *900 E Dublin-Granville Rd (43229), just W of I-71 exit 117 (OH 161).* 614/888-7440; FAX 614/888-7879; res: 800/477-7888. 182 rms, 5 story, 22 suites. S, D $124-$134; each addl $10; suites $145-$155. Crib free. TV; cable (premium). Indoor pool; whirlpool. Complimentary continental bkfst. Restaurant adj 6 am-11 pm. Bar 4 pm-1 am. Ck-out noon. Coin lndry. Meeting rms. Business servs avail. Free airport transportation. Exercise equipt; bicycles, stair machines. Health club privileges. Some refrigerators, wet bars. Cr cds: A, C, D, DS, MC, V.

⊡ ≋ ✕ ⊻ 🔥 SC

Motor Hotels

✔★ **BEST WESTERN-NORTH.** *888 E Dublin-Granville Rd (43229).* 614/888-8230; FAX 614/888-8223. 180 rms, 2 story. S, D $69-$74; each addl $5; suites $95; under 18 free; wkend rates. Crib free. TV; cable (premium). 2 pools, 1 indoor. Restaurant 6:30 am-10 pm. Rm serv. Bar 5 pm-2 am. Ck-out noon. Coin lndry. Business servs avail. Valet serv. Health club privileges. Cr cds: A, C, D, DS, MC, V.

≋ ⊻ 🔥 SC

★★ **COURTYARD BY MARRIOTT.** *35 W Spring St (43215).* 614/228-3200; FAX 614/228-6752. 149 rms, 5 story. S, D $100-$107; each addl $10; suites $130-$140; under 18 free. Crib free. Valet parking $12.50. TV; cable, VCR avail. Indoor pool; whirlpool. Complimentary coffee in rms. Restaurant 6:30-10 am, 5-10 pm; Sat, Sun 7 am-noon. Bar 5-11 pm. Ck-out noon. Meeting rms. Business servs avail. In-rm modem link. Bellhops. Sundries. Valet serv. Coin lndry. Exercise equipt; bicycles, weight machine. Health club privileges. Some refrigerators. Cr cds: A, C, D, DS, MC, V.

⊡ ≋ ✕ ⊻ 🔥 SC

★★ **HARLEY.** *1000 E Dublin-Granville Rd (43229), at I-71 exit 117.* 614/888-4300; FAX 614/888-3477. Web www.harleyhotels.com. 150 rms, 2 story. S, D $102-$112; each addl $10; suites $130; under 18 free. Crib free. TV; cable (premium). Sauna. 2 pools, 1 indoor; whirlpool. Restaurant 6:30 am-10 pm. Rm serv. Bar 4:30 pm-1 am, Sun to 10 pm; entertainment wkends. Ck-out 11 am. Meeting rms. Business servs avail. Parking. Free airport transportation. Lighted tennis. Putting green. Health club privileges. Game rm. Lawn games. Private patios, balconies. Cr cds: A, C, D, DS, MC, V.

⊡ 🏃 ≋ ⊻ 🔥 SC

★★★ **HOLIDAY INN.** *175 Hutchinson Ave (43235), I-270 exit 23.* 614/885-3334; FAX 614/846-4353. 316 rms, 6 story. S, D $99-$115; suites $205-$220; under 17 free. Crib free. Pet accepted. TV; cable (premium), VCR avail. Indoor pool. Complimentary coffee in rms. Restaurant 6 am-11 pm. Rm serv. Bar. Ck-out noon. Coin lndry. Convention facilities. Business servs avail. In-rm modem link. Bellhops. Gift shop. Free airport transportation. Exercise equipt; weight machine, stair machine. Refrigerator in suites. Cr cds: A, C, D, DS, MC, V.

⊡ 🐾 ≋ ✕ ⊻ 🔥 SC

★ **HOLIDAY INN-AIRPORT.** *750 Stelzer Rd (43219), near Port Columbus Airport.* 614/237-6360; FAX 614/237-2978. 236 rms, 3 story. S $89.95-$109.95; D $108.95-$119.95; each addl $10; suites $135-$175; under 18 free; wkend rates. Crib free. Pet accepted. TV; cable. Indoor pool; whirlpool. Complimentary coffee in rms. Restaurant 6:30 am-2 pm, 5:30-10 pm. Rm serv. Bar 1 pm-midnight. Ck-out noon. Coin lndry. Meeting rms. Business servs avail. In-rm modem link. Sundries. Gift shop. Airport transportation. Exercise equipt; weights, bicycles, sauna. Cr cds: A, C, D, DS, JCB, MC, V.

⊡ 🐾 ≋ ✕ ✈ ⊻ 🔥 SC

✔★ ★ **LENOX INN.** (I-70E at OH 256, Reynoldsburg 43086) exit 112B. 614/861-7800; FAX 614/759-9059; res: 800/821-0007. 151 rms, 2 story. S, D $49-$77; each addl $6; suites $109-$134; under 18 free. Crib free. Pet accepted; $10. TV; cable (premium). Pool. Restaurant 6:30 am-10 pm. Rm serv. Bar. Ck-out 11 am. Meeting rms. Business servs avail. In-rm modem link. Valet serv. Sundries. Free airport transportation. Health club privileges. Cr cds: A, C, D, DS, MC, V.

D ⚹ ⚊ ⚹ ⚹ SC

★ ★ ★ **WOODFIN SUITES.** (4130 Tuller Rd, Dublin 43017) N on OH 315, W on I-270 to exit 20, S to Dublin Center Dr, right 1 blk to Tuller Rd. 614/766-7762; FAX 614/761-1906; res: 800/237-8811. 88 kit. suites, 2 story. 1 bedrm $140-$150; 2 bedrm $189; each addl $10; under 12 free; wkend rates. Crib free. TV; cable (premium), VCR (free movies). Heated pool; whirlpool. Complimentary bkfst buffet. Complimentary coffee in rms. Restaurant nearby. Ck-out noon. Coin lndry. Meeting rms. Business center. In-rm modem link. Valet serv. Microwaves. Cr cds: A, D, DS, MC, V.

D ⚊ ⚹ ⚹ SC 🚶

Hotels

★ ★ ★ **ADAM'S MARK.** 50 N Third St (43215), downtown. 614/228-5050; FAX 614/228-2525. 415 rms, 21 story. S, D $175-$195; each addl $20; suites $700; under 18 free; higher rates special events. Crib free. Valet parking $13; garage parking $10. TV; cable (premium), VCR avail. Restaurant 6:30 am-11 pm. Rm serv 24 hrs. Bar 11-2 am; Sun to 11 pm. Ck-out noon. Convention facilities. Business servs avail. In-rm modem link. Gift shop. Coin lndry. Exercise equipt; treadmill, stair machine, sauna. Heated pool; whirlpool. Cr cds: A, C, D, DS, JCB, MC, V.

D ⚊ ⚹ ⚹ ⚹ SC

★ ★ ★ **CONCOURSE.** 4300 International Gateway (43219), at Port Columbus Airport. 614/237-2515; FAX 614/237-6134. 147 rms, 2 story. S, D $113-$125; each addl $10. Crib free. TV; cable (premium), VCR avail (movies). 2 pools, 1 indoor; whirlpool, poolside serv. Restaurants 6 am-11 pm. Bar 11-1 am. Ck-out noon. Meeting rms. Business servs avail. In-rm modem link. Free airport transportation. Valet serv. Exercise equipt; weights, treadmills, sauna, steam rm. Cr cds: A, C, D, DS, MC, V.

⚊ ⚹ ⚹ ⚹ SC

★ ★ ★ **CROWNE PLAZA.** 33 Nationwide Blvd (43215), downtown. 614/461-4100; FAX 614/461-5828. Web www.crowneplaza.com. 384 rms, 12 story. S, D $150-$190; suites $350-$500; under 12 free; wkend rates. Crib free. Garage $13. TV; cable. Indoor pool. Coffee in rms. Restaurant 6:30 am-11 pm. Bar from 11 am. Ck-out noon. Coin lndry. Convention facilities. Business servs avail. In-rm modem link. Gift shop. Exercise equipt; weight machines, bicycles, sauna. Connected to Convention Center. Luxury level. Cr cds: A, C, D, DS, JCB, MC, V.

D ⚊ ⚹ ⚹ SC

★ ★ ★ **DOUBLETREE GUEST SUITES.** 50 S Front St (43215). 614/228-4600; FAX 614/228-0297. 194 suites, 16 story. S, D $179-$219; each addl $20; under 18 free; wkend rates; higher rates special events. Crib free. TV; cable (premium). Coffee in rms. Restaurant 6:30 am-10 pm; Sat from 7 am-11 pm; Sun 7 am-10 pm. Bar 11 am-midnight, Sun from 1 pm. Ck-out noon. Business center. In-rm modem link. Covered parking. Health club privileges. Refrigerators; microwaves avail. Opp river. Cr cds: A, C, D, DS, MC, V.

D ⚹ ⚹ SC 🚶

★ ★ ★ **EMBASSY SUITES.** 2700 Corporate Exchange Dr (43231), off I-270 exit 27. 614/890-8600; FAX 614/890-8626. 217 kit. suites, 8 story. S $109-$139; D $119-$149; each addl $10; suites $200-$300; under 18 free; wkend rates. Crib free. TV; cable (premium), VCR avail. Indoor/outdoor pool; whirlpool, poolside serv. Complimentary full bkfst. Restaurant 11 am-10 pm; wkends to 11 pm. Bar 11-1 am. Ck-out noon. Meeting rms. Business servs avail. Concierge. Gift shop. Free airport transportation. Exercise equipt; stair machine, treadmill, sauna. Game rm. Refrigerators, microwaves. Cr cds: A, C, D, DS, MC, V.

D ⚊ ⚹ 🚶 ⚹ SC

★ ★ **HOLIDAY INN-CITY CENTER.** 175 E Town St (43215). 614/221-3281; FAX 614/221-2667. 240 rms, 12 story. S, D $119-$150; under 18 free. Crib free. Pet accepted. TV; cable (premium). Pool. Complimentary coffee in rms. Restaurant 6:30 am-2 pm, 5-10 pm; Sat, Sun from 7 am. Bar 4 pm-midnight. Ck-out noon. Meeting rms. Business servs avail. Free airport transportation. Health club privileges. Cr cds: A, C, D, DS, ER, JCB, MC, V.

D ⚹ ⚊ ⚹ ⚹ SC

★ ★ **HOLIDAY INN-EAST.** 4560 Hilton Corporate Dr (43232), I-70 Hamilton Rd exit 107. 614/868-1380; FAX 614/863-3210. E-mail 102175,426@compuserve.com. 278 rms, 21 story. S, D $109-$130; each addl $10; wkend plan. Crib free. TV; cable (premium). Indoor pool; wading pool, poolside serv. Playground. Coffee in rms. Restaurant 6 am-midnight. Bar 11-2 am. Ck-out noon. Convention facilities. Business center. In-rm modem link. Free airport transportation. Exercise equipt; bicycle, stair machine, sauna. Health club privileges. Cr cds: A, C, D, DS, JCB, MC, V.

D ⚊ ⚹ 🚶 ⚹ ⚹ SC 🚶

★ ★ ★ **HYATT ON CAPITOL SQUARE.** 75 E State St (43215), at Columbus City Center. 614/228-1234; FAX 614/469-9664. Web www.hyatt.com. 400 rms, 21 story. S, D $203-$228; each addl $25; suites $250-$400; under 18 free; wkend packages. TV; cable (premium). Restaurant 6:30 am-10 pm; wkends to 11 pm. Bar 11 am-midnight; wkends to 1 am; entertainment. Ck-out noon. Meeting rms. Business center. In-rm modem link. Concierge. Shopping arcade. Exercise equipt; weights, bicycles, sauna. Massage. Some private patios, balconies. Luxury level. Cr cds: A, C, D, DS, JCB, MC, V.

D 🚶 ⚹ ⚹ SC 🚶

★ ★ ★ **HYATT REGENCY.** 350 N High St (43215), at Greater Columbus Convention Ctr. 614/463-1234; FAX 614/280-3046. Web www.hyatt.com. 631 rms, 20 story. S, D $180-$205; each addl $25; suites $625-$1,000; under 18 free. Crib free. Valet parking $14.50. TV; cable (premium). Indoor pool. Restaurant 6:30 am-2:30 pm, 5-11 pm; Thurs-Sat 5 pm-midnight; Sun 6:30 am-11 pm. Bar 11-1:30 am; entertainment. Ck-out noon. Business center. In-rm modem link. Concierge. Shopping arcade. Exercise equipt; stair machine, treadmill. Luxury level. Cr cds: A, C, D, DS, JCB, MC, V.

D ⚊ 🚶 ⚹ ⚹ SC 🚶

★ ★ ★ **MARRIOTT-NORTH.** 6500 Doubletree Ave (43229), I-71 exit 117. 614/885-1885; FAX 614/885-7222. 300 rms, 9 story. S, D $175-$190; suites $395-$450; wkend rates. Crib free. TV; cable (premium). Indoor/outdoor pool; whirlpool, poolside serv. Restaurant 6:30 am-10 pm. Bar 11:30 am-midnight. Ck-out noon. Coin lndry. Convention facilities. Business center. In-rm modem link. Gift shop. Free airport transportation. Tennis privileges. Exercise equipt; weight machine, stair machine, sauna. Health club privileges. Game rm. Refrigerator avail. Microwaves in suites. Cr cds: A, C, D, DS, MC, V.

D 🚶 ⚊ 🚶 ⚹ ⚹ SC 🚶

★ ★ **RADISSON-AIRPORT.** 1375 N Cassady Ave (43219), I-670 exit 9. 614/475-7551; FAX 614/476-1476. Web www.radisson.com. 247 units, 6 story. S, D $109-$129; each addl $10; suites $175-$250; under 18 free; wkend, hol rates. TV; cable, VCR avail. Indoor pool; whirlpool. Coffee in rms. Restaurant 6 am-midnight. Bar 10-1 am, Sun noon-midnight. Ck-out noon. Coin lndry. Meeting rms. Business servs avail. In-rm modem link. Gift shop. Free airport transportation. Exercise equipt; weights, bicycles, sauna. Some bathrm phones, refrigerators, in-rm whirlpools. Cr cds: A, C, D, DS, JCB, MC, V.

D ⚊ 🚶 ⚹ ⚹ SC

★ ★ **RADISSON-NORTH.** 4900 Sinclair Rd (43229), near jct I-71 & Morse Rd. 614/846-0300; FAX 614/847-1022. 268 rms, 5-6 story. S, D $138; each addl $10; suites $125-$175; under 18 free; wkend rates. Pet accepted, some restrictions. TV; cable (premium), VCR avail. 2 pools, 1 indoor; wading pool, whirlpool, poolside serv. Restaurant 6:30 am-2 pm, 5-11 pm. Bar 11-2 am; entertainment Thurs-Sat. Ck-out noon. Convention facilities. Business center. In-rm modem link. Gift shop. Free airport transportation. Exercise equipt; weight machines, bicycles. Game rm. Cr cds: A, C, D, DS, JCB, MC, V.

✔★★ **RAMADA UNIVERSITY.** *3110 Olentangy River Rd (43202).* 614/267-7461; FAX 614/263-5299. 239 rms, 5 story. S, D $89-$99; each addl $10; suites $175-$195; under 18 free. Crib free. TV; cable (premium), VCR avail. Pool; poolside serv. Complimentary coffee in rms. Restaurant 6 am-10 pm. Ck-out noon. Meeting rms. Business servs avail. Free airport transportation. Health club privileges. Refrigerator, minibar in suites. Cr cds: A, C, D, DS, JCB, MC, V.

★★★ **SHERATON SUITES.** *201 Hutchinson Ave (43235), just NE of jct I-270 & OH 23N.* 614/436-0004; FAX 614/436-0926. 261 suites, 9 story. S, D $140-$150; each addl $10; under 18 free; wkend, extended rates. Crib avail. TV; cable (premium), VCR avail. 2 pools, 1 indoor; whirlpool, poolside serv. Complimentary coffee in rms. Restaurant 6 am-10:30 pm; Sat from 7 am. Bar. Ck-out 1 pm. Coin lndry. Meeting rms. Business servs avail. In-rm modem link. Gift shop. Free airport transportation. Exercise equipt; stair machine, treadmill. Health club privileges. Refrigerators; microwaves avail. Cr cds: A, C, D, DS, ER, JCB, MC, V.

★★★ **WESTIN.** *310 S High St (43215).* 614/228-3800; FAX 614/228-7666. 196 rms, 6 story. S, D $155-$195; each addl $15; suites $175-$500; family rates; wkend rates; higher rates special events. TV; cable (premium). Coffee in rms. Restaurant 6 am-11 pm. Rm serv 24 hrs. Bar 3 pm-2 am. Ck-out noon. Meeting rms. Business servs avail. Health club privileges. Luxury level. Cr cds: A, C, D, DS, JCB, MC, V.

★★★ **WYNDHAM DUBLIN.** *(600 Metro Place North, Dublin 43017)* I-270 exit 17A. 614/764-2200; FAX 614/764-1213. 217 rms, 3 story. S, D $140-$160; suites $280-$400; under 18 free; wkend rates. Crib free. TV; cable (premium), VCR avail. Indoor pool. Coffee in rms. Restaurant 6:30 am-10 pm. Rm serv 24 hrs. Bar 11-1 am; Sat to 2 am; closed Sun. Ck-out 1 pm. Meeting rms. Business servs avail. In-rm modem link. Gift shop. Sauna. Health club privileges. Balconies. Cr cds: A, C, D, DS, ER, JCB, MC, V.

Inn

★★★ **WORTHINGTON.** *(649 High St, Worthington 43085) 8 mi N on High St (US 23).* 614/885-2600; FAX 614/885-1283. 26 rms, 3 story. S, D $140-$175; suites $175-$275. TV; cable. Complimentary full bkfst. Dining rm (see SEVEN STARS DINING ROOM). Rm serv. Bar 5 pm-midnight. Ck-out noon, ck-in 3 pm. Business servs avail. Concierge. Bellhops. Tennis privileges. Renovated Victorian inn. Cr cds: A, C, D, DS, MC, V.

Restaurants

✔★ **A LA CARTE.** *2333 N High St.* 614/294-6783. Hrs: 5-9:30 pm; Fri, Sat to 10:30 pm. Closed Sun, most major hols. Res accepted. Mediterranean menu. Serv bar. Wine cellar. A la carte entrees: dinner $6.95-$10.95. Specializes in fresh seafood, lamb, veal. Parking. Outdoor dining. Menu changes wkly. Cr cds: A, C, D, DS, MC, V.

★★★ **ALEX'S BISTRO.** *4681 Reed Rd, in Arlington Square Center.* 614/457-8887. Hrs: 11:30 am-2 pm, 5:30-10 pm. Closed Sun; major hols. Res accepted. French, Italian menu. Bar. Wine list. A la carte entrees: lunch $5.50-$8.95, dinner $9.50-18.50. Specializes in fresh seafood, wild game, pastas. Parking. Menu changes seasonally. French brasserie atmosphere. Cr cds: A, D, MC, V.

★★ **BEXLEY'S MONK.** *2232 East Main St (43209).* 614/239-6665. Hrs: 11:30 am-2:30 pm, 5-10 pm; Fri, Sat to 11 pm; Sun from 5 pm. Closed major hols. Res accepted. Eclectic menu. Bar. A la carte entrees: lunch $6-$11, dinner $10-$20. Specializes in seafood, pasta. Entertainment. Contemporary decor. Cr cds: A, C, D, DS, MC, V.

✔★ **BISTRO ROTI.** *1693 W Lane Ave (43221).* 614/481-7684; FAX 614/481-7814. Hrs: 11:30 am-2 pm, 5:30-10 pm; Fri, Sat to 11 pm. Closed Sun; major hols. Res accepted. Eclectic menu. Bar. Semi-a la carte: lunch $5-$10, dinner $11-$17. Specializes in seafood, pastas, chicken. Contemporary decor. Cr cds: A, C, D, DS, MC, V.

★★ **BRAVO! ITALIAN KITCHEN.** *3000 Hayden Rd (43235).* 614/791-1245. Hrs: 11 am-10 pm; Fri to midnight; Sat 5 pm-midnight; Sun 5-9:30 pm. Closed major hols. Res accepted. Italian menu. Bar. A la carte entrees: lunch $8-$10, dinner $8-$17. Specializes in northern Italian cuisine. Valet parking. Outdoor dining. Upscale bistro atmosphere. Cr cds: A, C, D, DS, MC, V.

✔★★ **CAMERON'S.** *(2894 E Main St, Bexley 43209)* E on OH 40. 614/235-3662. Hrs: 5-10 pm; Fri, Sat to 11 pm; Sun to 9 pm. Closed most major hols. Res accepted. Contemporary Amer menu. Bar to 11 pm; Fri, Sat to midnight; Sun to 10 pm. Semi-a la carte: dinner $7.50-$17.95. Child's meals. Specializes in walleye, crab cakes, rack of lamb. Jazz Mon. Valet parking. Bright, contemporary decor. Cr cds: A, C, D, DS, MC, V.

✔★ **CAP CITY DINER.** *1299 Olentangy River Rd (43212).* 614/291-3663. Hrs: 11 am-10 pm; Fri, Sat to midnight; Sun from 4 pm. Closed major hols. Contemporary Amer menu. Bar. Semi-a la carte: lunch $4.95-$8.95, dinner $5.95-$16.95. Child's meals. Specializes in veal & mushroom meatloaf, desserts. Entertainment Sun, Tues. Outdoor dining. Upscale diner. Cr cds: A, C, D, DS, MC, V.

✔★ **CHINA DYNASTY.** *1677 W Lane Ave (43221).* 614/486-7126. Hrs: 11 am-10 pm; Fri, Sat to 11 pm; Sun 11 am-9 pm. Closed July 4, Thanksgiving. Res accepted. Chinese menu. Bar. Semi-a la carte: lunch $4.50-$7.25, dinner $6.50-$12.95. Specializes in Hunan, Szechwan, Mandarin dishes. Casual Chinese decor. Cr cds: A, DS, MC, V.

★ **CLARMONT.** *684 S High St, in German Village.* 614/443-1125. Hrs: 7 am-2:30 pm, 5-10 pm; Fri, Sat 7-11 pm; Sun 4-9 pm. Closed some major hols. Res accepted. Bar to 10 pm; Fri, Sat to midnight. Semi-a la carte: bkfst $2.95-$7.50, lunch $5.95-$7.25, dinner $12.95-$21.95. Specializes in steak, fresh seafood, jumbo shrimp cocktail. Parking. Cr cds: A, C, D, MC, V.

✔★ **COOKER BAR & GRILLE.** *6193 Cleveland Ave (43229).* 614/899-7000. Hrs: 11 am-10:30 pm; Fri, Sat to 11:30 pm; Sun to 10 pm; Sun brunch 11 am-3 pm. Closed Thanksgiving, Dec 25. Bar. Semi-a la carte: lunch, dinner $6-$14.95. Sun brunch $6-$9.75. Child's meals. Specializes in prime rib, fresh fish, meatloaf. Own biscuits. Parking. Patio dining. Casual family-style dining. Cr cds: A, C, D, DS, MC, V.

★★ **ENGINE HOUSE NO. 5.** *121 Thurman Ave.* 614/443-4877. Hrs: 11:30 am-10 pm; Fri, Sat 4-11 pm; Sun 4-9 pm; early-bird dinner Mon-Sat 4-6 pm. Closed some major hols. Res accepted. Bar. Semi-a la carte: lunch $5-$16, dinner $14-$30. Child's meals. Specializes in fresh seafood, homemade pastas. Pianist Fri, Sat. Old firehouse; firefighting equipment displayed. Parking. Cr cds: A, C, D, DS, MC, V.

★★ **FIFTY-FIVE AT CROSSWOODS.** *55 Hutchinson Ave (43235).* 614/846-5555. Hrs: 11 am-2:30 pm, 5-10 pm; Fri to 11 pm; Sat

5-11 pm; Sun 5-9 pm; Sun brunch 10 am-2:30 pm. Closed major hols. Res accepted. Bar 11-1 am; Sat from 5 pm; Sun 5-10 pm. A la carte entrees: lunch $5.95-$8.95, dinner $12.95-$19.95. Sun brunch $15.95. Child's meals. Specialties: hand-cut steak, linguine fruit de mer, Maryland crab cakes. Own pasta. Parking. Cr cds: A, C, D, DS, MC, V.

D 🖃

★ ★ **FIFTY-FIVE ON THE BOULEVARD.** *55 Nationwide Blvd, opp Convention Center.* 614/228-5555. Hrs: 11 am-2:30 pm, 5-10 pm; Fri to 11 pm; Sat 5-11 pm; Sun 5-9 pm. Closed some major hols. Res accepted. Bar to 1 am. Semi-a la carte: lunch $5.95-$9.95, dinner $12.95-$19.95. Child's meals. Specializes in fresh fish, pasta, Norwegian salmon. Valet parking. Cr cds: A, C, D, DS, MC, V.

D 🖃

✔★ **GALAXY CAFE.** *(33 Beech Ridge Dr, Powell 43065)* 614/846-7776. Hrs: 11 am-3 pm, 5-9 pm; Fri to 10 pm; Sat 8 am-3 pm, 5-10 pm; Sun 8 am-2 pm. Closed Mon; major hols. Eclectic menu. Semi-a la carte: bkfst $2.50-$5, lunch $3-$8, dinner $3.50-$9.50. Child's meals. Specializes in salads, pasta, chicken. Casual decor. Totally nonsmoking. Cr cds: MC, V.

D

★ ★ **HANDKE'S CUISINE.** *520 S Front St, downtown, near German Village in Brewery district.* 614/621-2500. Hrs: 5:30-10 pm. Closed Sun; Dec 25. Res accepted. International menu. Bar. Extensive wine list. A la carte entrees: dinner $9.75-$23.75. Specializes in veal chop, duck, fresh seafood. Valet parking. Located in historic brewery building, the former Schlee Brewery; main dining rm on lower level. Cr cds: A, DS, MC, V.

★ ★ **HUNAN HOUSE.** *2350 E Dublin-Granville Rd (43229).* 614/895-3330. Hrs: 11:30 am-10 pm; Fri, Sat to 10:30 pm. Closed Thanksgiving. Res accepted. Chinese menu. Bar. A la carte entrees: lunch $5-$8, dinner $8-$18. Specialties: Szechwan, Hunan and Mandarin delicacies. Parking. Cr cds: A, C, D, MC, V.

🖃

★ ★ **HUNAN LION.** *2000 Bethel Rd (43220), in Crown Point.* 614/459-3933. Hrs: 11:30 am-10 pm; Fri, Sat to 10:30 pm. Res accepted. Chinese, Thai menu. Bar. Semi-a la carte: lunch $5.95-$8.95, dinner $8.95-$18. Specializes in Szechwan dishes, basil seafood, black pepper steak. Parking. Modern decor with Oriental touches. Cr cds: A, C, D, MC, V.

D 🖃

✔★ **K2U.** *641 N High St (43215).* 614/461-4766. Hrs: 11 am-midnight; Sat from 5 pm. Closed Sun; Memorial Day, Thanksgiving, Dec 25. Res accepted. Eclectic menu. Bar. Semi-a la carte: lunch $3-$11, dinner $3-$16. Specializes in soups, pasta, sandwiches. Entertainment Mon, Thur, Fri. Outdoor dining. Casual European-style bistro. Cr cds: A, C, D, DS, MC, V.

D

★ **KAHIKI.** *3583 E Broad St.* 614/237-5425. Hrs: 11:30 am-10:15 pm; Fri to 11:15 pm; Sat 4:30-11:15 pm; Sun brunch 11:30 am-3 pm. Closed major hols. Res accepted. Chinese, Polynesian menu. Serv bar. Semi-a la carte: lunch $5.95-$9.95, dinner $13.95-$24.95. Child's meals. Parking. Sea village decor; thatched-roof huts. Tropical rain forest, birds; aquariums; display of native objets d'art. Cr cds: A, C, D, DS, MC, V.

🖃

★ ★ **L'ANTIBES.** *772 N High St #106 (43215).* 614/291-1666. E-mail lantibe@aol.com; web users.aol.com/lantibes. Hrs: 5-9 pm; Fri, Sat to 11 pm. Closed Sun, Mon; Thanksgiving, Dec 25. Res accepted. French menu. A la carte entrees: dinner $14-$24. Specializes in fresh fish, veal, lamb. Parking. Modern decor. Art collection of owners displayed. Cr cds: A, MC, V.

D 🖃

★ ★ **LINDEY'S.** *169 E Beck St (43206).* 614/228-4343. Hrs: 11:30 am-2:30 pm, 5:30-10 pm; Thurs-Sat to midnight. Closed most major

hols. Res accepted. Bar. Semi-a la carte: lunch $5.95-$8.95, dinner $7.95-$19.95. Sun jazz brunch 11:30 am-2:30 pm. Specialties: angel hair pasta, grilled tournedos with Bearnaise sauce, gourmet pizza. Entertainment Thurs, Sun. Valet parking. Outdoor dining. Restored building (1888) in German Village. Cr cds: A, C, D, MC, V.

🖃

✔★ **MARBLE GANG.** *1052 Mt Vernon Ave, Mt Vernon Plaza shopping ctr.* 614/253-7396. Hrs: 10 am-midnight; Fri, Sat to 3:30 am. Closed Sun. Res accepted. Bar. Semi-a la carte: lunch, dinner $5.50-$12.95. Child's meals. Specialties: barbecued ribs, chicken. Jazz Thurs evenings. Cr cds: A, C, D, MC, V.

D 🖃

★ ★ ★ **MERLOT.** *(5252 Norwich St, Hilliard 43026)* 614/529-1995. Hrs: 5-10 pm. Closed Sun; major hols. Res accepted. Wine list. A la carte entrees: dinner $15-$32. Specialties: cedar-roasted salmon, honey curry roasted duckling, lobster bisque. Outdoor dining. Elegant decor. Cr cds: A, C, D, DS, MC, V.

D

★ ★ ★ **MORTON'S OF CHICAGO.** *2 Nationwide Plaza.* 614/464-4442; FAX 614/464-2940. Hrs: 5-11 pm; Sun to 10 pm. Closed major hols. Res accepted. Bar. A la carte entrees: dinner $18.95-$29.95. Specializes in prime aged beef, fresh seafood, dessert soufflés. Valet parking. Contemporary decor; in downtown office complex. Cr cds: A, C, D, DS, MC, V.

D 🖃

✔★ **OLD MOHAWK.** *821 Mohawk St (43206), in German Village.* 614/444-7204. Hrs: 11 am-midnight; Tues, Wed to 1 am; Thur, Fri to 2:30 am; Sat 9-2:30 am; Sun from 9 am. Closed some major hols. Bar. Semi-a la carte: lunch, dinner $4.95-$9.95. Specialties: turtle soup, quesadillas. Building from 1800s was once a grocery and tavern; exposed brick walls. Cr cds: A, D, MC, V.

D 🖃

★ ★ ★ **REFECTORY.** *1092 Bethel Rd.* 614/451-9774. Web www.columbuspages.com/restaurants/refectory. Hrs: 5-10:30 pm. Closed Sun; major hols. French menu. Bar 4:30 pm-midnight; Fri, Sat to 1 am. Res accepted. Wine cellar. A la carte entrees: dinner $19.95-$26.95. Specialties: cotelette de salmon, rosage d'agneau aux olives, filet de beouf à l'estragon. Own pastries. Parking. Outdoor dining. Former schoolhouse and sanctuary. Cr cds: A, C, D, DS, MC, V.

🖃

★ ★ **RIGSBY'S CUISINE VOLATILE.** *698 N High St (43215).* 614/461-7888. Hrs: 11 am-11 pm. Closed Sun. Res accepted. Mediterranean menu. Bar. A la carte entrees: lunch $8-$14, dinner $12-$24. Specializes in pasta, rack of lamb, seafood. Entertainment Wed, Thurs. Valet parking. Outdoor dining. Ultramodern decor. Cr cds: A, D, DS, MC, V.

D

✔★ **SCHMIDT'S SAUSAGE HAUS.** *240 Kossuth St.* 614/444-6808. Hrs: 11 am-10 pm; Fri to 11 pm; Sat to midnight. Closed Easter, Thanksgiving, Dec 25. German, Amer menu. Bar. Semi-a la carte: lunch $5.15-$6.95, dinner $7.15-$18.95. Child's meals. Specializes in homemade sausage, desserts. German music Thurs-Sat. Parking. Family-owned. Cr cds: A, C, D, DS, MC, V.

D 🖃

★ ★ ★ **SEVEN STARS DINING ROOM.** *(See Worthington Inn)* 614/885-2600. Hrs: 7-10 am, 11 am-3 pm, 5:30-10 pm; Fri, Sat to 11 pm; Sun 5-9 pm; Sat brunch 11 am-3 pm. Closed some major hols. Res accepted. Regional Amer menu. Bar. Wine list. Semi-a la carte: bkfst $5-$10, lunch $6.50-$12, dinner $14.95-$29.95. Sat brunch $6.50-$12, Sun buffet 11 am-2:30 pm, $14.95. Specializes in rack of lamb, fresh seafood, beef. Own baking. Entertainment Fri, Sat. Parking. Outdoor dining. Cr cds: A, C, D, DS, MC, V.

🖃

★ ★ **TAPATIO.** *491 N Park St (43215).* *614/221-1085.* Hrs: 11:30 am-3:30 pm, 5-10 pm; Fri, Sat to 11 pm; Sun 5-10 pm. Closed Thanksgiving, Dec 25. Res accepted. Eclectic menu. Bar. Semi-a la carte: lunch $4-$9, dinner $6-$22. Specializes in seafood, beef tenderloin. Outdoor dining. Modern contemporary bistro. Cr cds: A, C, D, DS, MC, V.

★ **TONY'S.** *16 W Beck St, at High St.* *614/224-8669.* Hrs: 11:30 am-10 pm; Fri to 11 pm; Sat 5:30-11 pm. Closed Sun; major hols. Res accepted. Italian menu. Bar. A la carte entrees: lunch $4-$8, dinner $8-$17. Specialties: linguine, spinach & cheese canneloni, classic Italian dishes. Pianist Sat evenings. Parking. Outdoor dining. Cr cds: A, D, MC, V.

★ **THE TOP.** *2891 E Main St.* *614/231-8238.* Hrs: 4 pm-midnight. Closed Jan 1, Dec 24, 25. Bar. Semi-a la carte: dinner $14.95-$24.95. Specializes in steak, seafood, barbecued ribs. Parking. Family-owned. Cr cds: A, C, D, DS, MC, V.

Unrated Dining Spots

KATZINGER'S. *475 S 3rd St.* *614/228-3354.* Hrs: 8:30 am-8:30 pm; Sat, Sun from 9 am. Closed Easter, Thanksgiving, Dec 25. Continental menu. Beer. A la carte entrees: lunch, dinner $2.35-$9. Child's meals. Specializes in deli, ethnic foods. Outdoor dining. Delicatessen in German Village. Totally nonsmoking. Cr cds: MC, V.

UMBERTO'S CAFFÈ DOLCE CAFE. *3145 Kingsdale Center.* *614/451-2722.* Hrs: 9 am-10 pm; Fri, Sat to 11:30 pm; Sun 11:30 am-5 pm. Closed major hols. Italian, Amer menu. Bar. Avg ck: lunch $5.45, dinner $6.95. Specializes in soup, salad, pasta. Cr cds: A, C, D, DS, MC, V.

Conneaut

(see Ashtabula)

Coshocton (D-5)

(See also Cambridge, Newark, Zanesville)

Founded 1802 **Pop** 12,193 **Elev** 775 ft **Area code** 614 **Zip** 43812
Information Coshocton County Convention & Visitors Bureau, PO Box 905; 614/622-4877 or 800/338-4724.

This unusual name was derived from travelers' spellings of Native American words meaning either "river crossing" or "place of the black bear." The settlement was first known as Tuscarawa. Coshocton is on the banks of the Muskingum River at the junction of the Tuscarawas and Walhonding rivers; Johnny Appleseed planted some of his orchards here. Specialty advertising originated in Coshocton, which has a variety of other industries including leather goods, iron pipe, plastics, pottery, appliances, rubber products, stainless steel and baskets.

What to See and Do

Roscoe Village. Visitor Center has information on canal era and historic attractions in the area; displays and continuous slide presentations. Roscoe Village creates a quaint living museum as an 1830s Ohio-Erie Canal town with pocket gardens, old-time shops, antiques, exhibits and crafts; also lodging and dining avail. Many special events throughout the yr. (Daily; closed Jan 1, Thanksgiving, Dec 25) NW edge of town on OH 16. Phone 800/877-1830. **Free.** Also in the village is

Johnson-Humrickhouse Museum. Houses four permanent galleries: Native American and Eskimo collection ranging from Stone Age to the present; Oriental Room with Chinese and Japanese collections; Early American gallery also has a pioneer room display; Decorative Arts has some European pieces. Museum also has traveling exhibits. (May-Oct, every afternoon; rest of yr, afternoons exc Mon; closed some major hols) Phone 614/622-8710. ¢

Boat trips. One-mi horse-drawn boat trips (35 min) on the Ohio-Erie Canal aboard *Monticello III.* (Memorial Day-Labor Day, daily; rest of May & after Labor Day-late Oct, wkends) Phone 614/622-7528. ¢¢

Village Exhibit Tour. Exhibit bldgs include Township Hall (1880) with one-room school exhibit; blacksmith's shop; 19th-century print shop; Craft and Learning Center with 1800s craft demonstrations; the Dr Maro Johnson Home (1833), furnished with antiques (1690-1840); the Toll House, with model locks and canal artifacts; and the Craftsman's House, an 1825 workingman's house where the art of broom making is revived. Self-guided tour of exhibit buildings (daily; closed Jan 1, Thanksgiving, Dec 25); guided tours (Jan-Mar). Phone 381 Hill St. Phone 614/622-9310 or 800/877-1830. ¢¢¢

Annual Events

Dulcimer Days. Roscoe Village. Displays, jam sessions, workshops. 3rd wkend May.

Hot Air Balloon Festival. June 6-8.

Coshocton Canal Festival. Roscoe Village. Celebrates arrival of first boat from Cleveland in 1830. Art exhibits, parades, old-time crafts, costume promenade, musical events, food. 3rd wkend Aug.

Old Time Music Fest. Roscoe Village. Banjo and barbershop music. 3rd wkend Sept.

Apple Butter Stirrin'. Roscoe Village. 3rd wkend Oct.

Christmas Candle Lightings. Roscoe Village. Tree and candle lighting ceremonies; hot-mulled cider & ginger cookies. 1st 3 Sats in Dec.

Motel

★ ★ ★ **ROSCOE VILLAGE INN.** *200 N Whitewoman St.* *614/622-2222;* res: *800/237-7397.* 51 rms, 4 story. S, D $75-$85; family rates. Crib free. TV; cable. Restaurant 7 am-2 pm, 5-9 pm; wkend hrs vary. Bar noon-11 pm; entertainment Fri. Ck-out noon. Meeting rms. Business servs avail. 18-hole golf privileges. Cr cds: A, D, DS, MC, V.

Restaurant

✔ ★ ★ **THE WAREHOUSE.** *400 N Whitewoman St.* *614/622-4001.* Hrs: 11 am-9 pm. Closed Jan 1, Dec 25. Semi-a la carte: lunch, dinner $3.50-$12.95. Child's meals. Specializing in bean soup, bran muffins. Own ice cream. In converted warehouse (1831) in Roscoe Village. Cr cds: A, DS, MC, V.

Dayton (E-2)

(See also Miamisburg, Middletown, Springfield, Vandalia)

Founded 1796 **Pop** 182,044 **Elev** 757 ft **Area code** 937
Information Dayton/Montgomery County Convention & Visitors Bureau, Chamber Plaza, One Chamber Plaza, Suite A, 45402-2400; 937/226-8211.

Dayton is situated at the fork of the Great Miami River. The river curves through the city from the northeast, uniting with the Stillwater River half-a-mile above Main Street Bridge. Mad River from the east and Wolf Creek from the west join the others four blocks from there. Dayton has 28 bridges crossing these rivers.

The first flood, in 1805, started a progression of higher levees. In 1913, the most disastrous flood took 361 lives and property worth $100 million and inspired a flood-control plan effective to date.

Here, between 1870 and 1910, James Ritty invented a "mechanical money drawer" (which only amused people at first); John Patterson, promoting this cash register, opened the first daylight factory with 80 percent glass walls; Barney Oldfield, in his "Old 999" pioneer racing car, won a local exhibition match; the Wright brothers experimented with kites, gliders, built a wind tunnel and developed the aileron; and Charles Kettering sold a big order of automobile self-starters to the Cadillac Motor Company. During and after World War I the city added Frigidaire and Wright-Patterson Air Force Base to its economic base. Today Dayton is a well-planned, well-run industrial city with a council-manager form of government.

What to See and Do

Aullwood Audubon Center and Farm. A 200-acre environmental education center and working educational farm. Interpretive museum, nature trails, exhibits. Working farm has seasonal programs. (Daily; closed some hols & hol wkends) 1000 Aullwood Rd, 10 mi NW on OH 48 to jct OH 40, at Englewood Dam. Phone 937/890-7360. ¢¢

Benjamin Wegerzyn Horticultural Center. Stillwater Gardens and wetland woods; horticultural library; Gift Gallery. Grounds (daily). 1301 E Siebenthaler. Phone 937/277-6545. **Free.**

Carillon Park. Collections depict history of transportation and early pioneer life in the area; includes original early railroad depot, section of the Miami and Erie canal fitted with an original lock; Dayton-built motor vehicles; Wright brothers' 1905 plane; 1912 steam locomotive and tender. In 18 buildings on 65 acres. (May-Oct, Tues-Sun, also Mon hols) Concerts (May-Oct, Sun; June-Aug, Sat). 2001 S Patterson Blvd, 2 mi S via I-75 to exit 51. Phone 937/293-2841. ¢¢; Also in park is

Newcom Tavern. Oldest preserved house in the city; miraculously withstood the 1913 Dayton flood. Collection of pioneer, early Dayton relics.

Dayton Museum of Discovery. Houses natural history exhibits including live animals common to Ohio; Philips Space Theater shows (daily). Bieser Discovery Center & the Dayton Science Center feature hands-on interactive exhibits and activities. (Daily exc Mon) 2600 DeWeese Pkwy. Phone 937/275-7431. ¢¢

Eastwood Lake. A 185-acre lake designed for most water sports including motor boating, fishing boats and water-skiing (even calendar days), sailboards, personal water craft, sailing, fishing boats at idle speed (odd calendar days). 35 mph speed limit and 40 power boat capacity. (Daily) OH 4 and Harshman Rd. Phone 937/275-PARK. **Free.**

Masonic Temple. Modern adaptation of Greek Ionic architecture; considered one of the most beautiful Masonic buildings in the country. (Daily) 525 W Riverview Ave at Belmonte Park N. Phone 937/224-9795. **Free.**

Paul Laurence Dunbar House State Memorial. The Dayton-born black poet and novelist lived here from 1903 until his untimely death at age 34 in 1906. (Memorial Day-Labor Day, Wed-Sun; Sept-Oct, wkends; Nov-May, Mon-Fri) 219 Paul Laurence Dunbar St. Phone 937/224-7061. ¢¢

SunWatch Prehistoric Indian Village. Reconstructed village. Planting and harvesting of Native American gardens, house construction, demonstrations and hands-on activities avail throughout the yr. Visitors information center houses audiovisual program, exhibits and life-size dioramas. Tours. (Daily; closed Thanksgiving, Dec 25) S off I-75, 2301 W River Rd. Phone 937/268-8199. ¢¢

The Dayton Art Institute. European and American paintings and sculpture; Asian Gallery; pre-Columbian arts, prints and decorative arts; changing exhibits; Experiencenter participatory gallery; reference library. Concerts. (Tues-Sun, also Mon hols; closed Dec 25) Riverview & Forest Aves. Phone 937/223-5277. ¢¢

The Old Courthouse. Classic Grecian architecture. Home of the Montgomery County Historical Society. Permanent Wright brothers display. (Tues-Sat) 3rd & Main Sts. Phone 937/228-6271. **Free.**

University of Dayton (1850). (6,700 students) Engineering, liberal arts, arts and science, law, business and education. On campus is Kennedy Union Art Gallery (academic yr; daily; free). Campus tours. 300 College Park Ave, SE part of city. Phone 937/229-4114.

Woodland Cemetery and Arboretum. Graves of Orville and Wilbur Wright, Charles F. Kettering, Deeds, Cox and Patterson. (Daily) 118 Woodland Ave. Maps avail, phone 937/222-1431.

Wright Brothers Memorial. A monolith dedicated to the "fathers" of aviation; overlooks Huffman Prairie where the Wrights practiced flying. E on OH 444 at jct old OH 4.

Wright Cycle Shop. Replica of the shop where Wright brothers performed some of their experiments, turn-of-the-century bicycles. (Sat & Sun; also by appt) 22 S Williams St. Phone 937/443-0793. **Free.**

Wright State University (1967). (17,000 students) Library contains one of the largest collections of Wright brothers memorabilia. Biological preserve with walking trails. The Creative Art Center is home to the Dayton Art Institute Museum of Contemporary Art. 8 mi E on Colonel Glenn Hwy (E 3rd St). Phone 937/873-2310.

Wright-Patterson Air Force Base. Center of research and aerospace logistics for US Air Force; also site of Air Force Institute of Technology. 10 mi NE on OH 444. On grounds is

United States Air Force Museum. One of the world's most comprehensive military aviation museums; more than 200 major historic aircraft and missiles; exhibits span period from Wright brothers to space age. IMAX theater (fee). (Daily; closed major hols) Area B, Springfield and Harshman Rds. Phone 937/255-3284. **Free.**

Annual Events

National Folk Festival. Phone 937/223-3655. 3rd wkend June.

US Air & Trade Show. Dayton International Airport. Features approx 100 outdoor exhibits; flight teams. Phone 937/898-5901. Late July.

Montgomery County Fair. Fairgrounds, 1043 S Main St. Phone 937/224-1619. Labor Day wkend.

Seasonal Event

The Dayton Art Institute Concert Series. Summer concerts in cloistered garden. Phone 937/223-5277. Feb-Mar & Oct-Nov, Sun afternoons; mid-June-early Aug, Tues evenings.

Motels

✔★ ★ **COMFORT INN.** (7907 Brandt Pike, Huber Heights 45424) 1 mi S on I-70 exit 38, off OH 201. 937/237-7477; FAX 937/237-5187. 53 rms, 2 story, 6 suites. Apr-Oct: S $61.99-$64.99; D $66.95-$69.95; suites $95-$98; under 18 free; higher rates special events; lower rates rest of yr. Crib free. TV; cable (premium). Complimentary continental bkfst. Restaurant adj open 24 hrs. Ck-out 11 am. In-rm modem link. Valet serv (Mon-Fri). Exercise equipt; bicycle, treadmill. Whirlpool. In-rm whirlpool, refrigerator, microwave, minibar in suites. Cr cds: A, C, D, DS, MC, V.

D ⟮×⟯ ⟮⟯ ⟮⟯ SC

✔★ ★ **CROSS COUNTRY INN.** 9325 N Main St (45415), at I-70 & OH 48, exit 29. 937/836-8339; FAX 937/836-1772; res: 800/621-1429. 120 rms, 2 story. S $34-$41; D $45-$47; each addl $7; under 18 free. Crib free. TV; cable (premium). Pool. Complimentary coffee in lobby. Restaurant adj 6:30 am-midnight. Ck-out noon. Business servs avail. Cr cds: A, D, DS, MC, V.

D ⟮≈⟯ ⟮⟯ ⟮⟯ SC

★ ★ **FAIRFIELD INN BY MARRIOTT.** 6960 Miller Lane (45414), I-75 exit 60. 937/898-1120. 135 rms, 3 story. S, D $57.95-$65.95; under 18 free. Crib free. TV; cable. Pool. Complimentary continental bkfst. Restaurant nearby. Ck-out noon. Meeting rm. Business servs avail. In-rm modem link. Cr cds: A, C, D, DS, MC, V.

D ⟮≈⟯ ⟮⟯ ⟮⟯ SC

★ ★ **HAMPTON INN.** 8099 Old Yankee St (45458), jct I-675 & OH 725. 937/436-3700; FAX 937/436-2995. 130 rms, 4 story. S $55-$60;

D $60-$65; under 18 free. Crib free. TV; cable (premium). Pool. Complimentary continental bkfst. Restaurant nearby. Ck-out noon. Meeting rm. Business servs avail. Exercise equipt; weight machine, stair machine. Health club privileges. Cr cds: A, C, D, DS, MC, V.

⬜⬜⬜⬜⬜⬜

★ ★ **HAMPTON INN.** *(2550 Paramount Place, Fairborn 45324) N on I-675, exit 17 to Fairfield Rd to Colonel Glen Hwy.* 937/429-5505; FAX 937/429-6828. 63 rms, 3 story, 8 suites. S, D $70-$79; suites $75-$85; under 18 free; higher rates special events; lower rates winter. Crib free. Pet accepted, some restrictions. TV; cable (premium), VCR avail. Indoor pool; whirlpool. Complimentary continental bkfst. Restaurant adj 5 am-11 pm. Ck-out noon. Business servs avail. In-rm modem link. Valet serv. Health club privileges. Refrigerator, microwave in suites. Cr cds: A, C, D, DS, MC, V.

⬜⬜⬜⬜⬜

★ ★ **HOMEWOOD SUITES.** *(2750 Presidential Dr, Fairborn 45324) 8 mi NE on I-675 exit 17.* 937/429-0600; FAX 937/429-6311; res: 800/225-5466. Web www.homewood.suites.com. 128 suites, 3 story. S, D $109-$119; family, wkly, monthly rates. Crib free. Pet accepted. TV; cable (premium), VCR (movies $6). Heated pool; whirlpool, poolside serv. Complimentary continental bkfst. Complimentary coffee in rms. Restaurant adj 6 am-11 pm. Ck-out noon. Coin lndry. Meeting rms. Business center. In-rm modem link. Bellhops. Valet serv. Sundries. Gift shop. Grocery store. Exercise equipt; weight machine, stair machine. Lawn games. Refrigerators, microwaves. Picnic tables, grills. Cr cds: A, C, D, DS, JCB, MC, V.

⬜⬜⬜⬜⬜⬜⬜⬜

★ **HOWARD JOHNSON.** *7575 Poe Ave (45414).* 937/454-0550; FAX 937/454-5566. 121 rms, 2 story. S $52-$59; D $59-$66; each addl $7; under 18 free. Crib free. Pet accepted, some restrictions; $50 deposit. TV; cable (premium), VCR avail (movies). Pool. Complimentary continental bkfst. Bar 5 pm-midnight. Ck-out noon. Guest lndry. Meeting rms. Business servs avail. Valet serv. Free airport transportation. Health club privileges. Cr cds: A, C, D, DS, MC, V.

⬜⬜⬜⬜⬜⬜

★ **QUALITY INN-SOUTH.** *1944 Miamisburg-Centerville Rd (45459), at I-675 & OH 725 W, exit 2.* 937/435-1550; FAX 937/438-1878. 72 rms, 2 story, 12 kit. units. S, D $55-$75; each addl $7; suites $65-$80; kit. units $55-$75; wkend rates; 2-day min special events. Crib free. TV; cable (premium), VCR avail. Pool. Complimentary continental bkfst. Restaurant adj 11-1 am. Ck-out noon. Business servs avail. Valet serv. Health club privileges. Some refrigerators. Cr cds: A, C, D, DS, MC, V.

⬜⬜⬜⬜⬜

✔★ **RED ROOF INN-NORTH.** *7370 Miller Ln (45414), I-75 exit 60.* 937/898-1054; FAX 937/898-1059. 109 rms, 2 story. S $37.95-$45.99; D $42.99-$58.99; each addl $5; under 18 free. Crib free. Pet accepted. TV; cable (premium). Complimentary coffee in lobby. Restaurant nearby. Ck-out noon. Business servs avail. Cr cds: A, C, D, DS, MC, V.

⬜⬜⬜⬜

Motor Hotels

★ ★ **DOUBLETREE GUEST SUITES.** *300 Prestige Place (45342).* 937/436-2400; FAX 937/436-2886. 138 suites, 3 story. S, D $145-$200; each addl $20; under 18 free; wkend rates. Crib free. TV; cable (premium), VCR avail. Indoor/outdoor pool; wading pool, whirlpool, poolside serv. Complimentary coffee in rms. Restaurant 6:30 am-2 pm, 5-10 pm. Bar 11:30 am-11 pm. Ck-out noon. Coin lndry. Meeting rms. Business servs avail. Valet serv. Exercise equipt; weights, bicycles, stair machine. Health club privileges. Game rm. Refrigerators; microwaves avail. Some private patios, balconies. Cr cds: A, C, D, DS, MC, V.

⬜⬜⬜⬜⬜⬜

★ ★ **HOLIDAY INN I-675 CONFERENCE CENTER.** *(2800 Presidential Dr, Fairborn 45324) I-675 exit 17, adj Nutter Center, opp Wright State University.* 937/426-7800; FAX 937/426-1284. 202 rms, 6 story. S, D $96-$125; each addl $10; wkend rates. Crib free. TV; cable

(premium), VCR avail. Indoor pool; whirlpool. Coffee in rms. Restaurant 6 am-10 pm. Rm serv. Bar 11-2 am; Sun to midnight; entertainment. Ck-out noon. Meeting rms. Business servs avail. Bellhops. Valet serv. Gift shop. Free airport transportation. Exercise equipt; weights, stair machine, sauna. Sun deck. Many bathrm phones. Luxury level. Cr cds: A, C, D, DS, JCB, MC, V.

⬜⬜⬜⬜⬜⬜⬜

Hotels

★ ★ ★ **CROWNE PLAZA DAYTON.** *Fifth & Jefferson Sts (45402), opp Convention Ctr.* 937/224-0800; FAX 937/224-3913. 284 rms, 14 story. S $142-$162; D $157-$177; each addl $15; suites $249-$394; under 12 free. Crib free. Pet accepted, some restrictions. TV; cable (premium). Heated pool; poolside serv. Complimentary coffee in rms. Restaurant 6:30 am-11 pm. Rm serv 24 hrs. Bar; entertainment. Ck-out noon. Meeting rms. Business servs avail. Gift shop. Exercise equipt; weight machines, stair machine. Some refrigerators. Luxury level. Cr cds: A, C, D, DS, ER, JCB, MC, V.

⬜⬜⬜⬜⬜⬜⬜⬜

★ ★ ★ **MARRIOTT.** *1414 S Patterson Blvd (45409).* 937/223-1000; FAX 937/223-7853. 399 rms, 6 story. S, D $120-$140; suites $200-$400; under 18 free; wkend rates. Crib free. Pet accepted, some restrictions. TV; cable (premium), VCR avail. Indoor/outdoor pool; whirlpool, poolside serv. Restaurant 7 am-10 pm. Bar 11-2 am; entertainment. Ck-out noon. Coin lndry. Convention facilities. Business center. In-rm modem link. Gift shop. Exercise equipt; weights, treadmill, sauna. Balconies. Luxury level. Cr cds: A, C, D, DS, ER, JCB, MC, V.

⬜⬜⬜⬜⬜⬜⬜⬜⬜

Inn

★ ★ ★ **LAKEWOOD FARM.** *(8495 OH 48, Waynesville 45068) S on OH 48, between OH 725 & OH 73.* 937/885-9850; FAX 937/885-9874. 4 rms, 2 story. S, D $65-$75; each addl $25; under 2 free. Crib free. TV in some rms; cable, VCR avail (movies). Complimentary full bkfst; afternoon refreshments. Ck-out 11 am, ck-in 3-6 pm. Business servs avail. Lawn games. Built as a gristmill in 1834; country atmosphere. On 25 acres. Totally nonsmoking. Cr cds: MC, V.

⬜⬜⬜⬜

Restaurants

★ **AMAR INDIA.** *(2759 Miamisburg-Centerville Rd, Centerville 45459) approx 2 mi S on OH 48 to OH 725, opp Dayton Mall.* 937/439-9005. Hrs: 11:30 am-2 pm, 5-10 pm; Sun noon-3 pm, 4:30-9 pm. Closed major hols. Northern Indian menu. Semi-a la carte: lunch $5-$8, dinner $8-$16. Specializes in vegetarian dishes, clay-oven breads dishes. Parking. Casual contemporary atmosphere. Cr cds: A, C, D, DS, MC, V.

⬜

✔★ **AMBER ROSE.** *1400 Valley St (45404).* 937/228-2511. Hrs: 11 am-9 pm; Mon to 2 pm; Fri, Sat to 10 pm. Closed Sun; major hols. European, Amer menu. Bar. Semi-a la carte: lunch $4.95-$8.50, dinner $10.95-$14.50. Specialties: turtle soup, Lithuanian cabbage rolls. Parking. Victorian-style residence (1906); pressed tin ceilings, original wood flooring; stained-glass windows with rose motif. Cr cds: MC, V.

⬜⬜⬜⬜

★ ★ **ANTICOLI'S.** *3045 Salem Ave (OH 49).* 937/277-2264. Hrs: 11:30 am-2:30 pm, 4:30-10 pm; Fri, Sat from 5 pm; Sun 11:30 am-8 pm; Sun brunch to 2:30 pm. Closed Mon; Jan 1, July 4, Dec 25. Res accepted. Italian menu. Bar. Semi-a la carte: lunch $3.95-$7.95, dinner $8.95-$16.95. Sun brunch $5.95-$8.95. Child's meals. Specializes in traditional and Northern Italian pasta & veal dishes, fresh fish, steak. Own baking. Parking. Italian decor. Family-owned. Cr cds: A, C, D, DS, MC, V.

⬜

★ **BARNSIDER.** *5202 N Main St (45415), on OH 48.* *937/277-1332.* Hrs: 5-10 pm; Fri, Sat 4-11 pm; Sun from noon. Closed some major hols. Bar. Semi-a la carte: dinner $10-$20. Child's meals. Specializes in steak, chops, shrimp. Parking. Family-owned. Cr cds: A, MC, V.

[D] [≈]

✔★ **BRAVO ITALIAN KITCHEN.** *2418 Centerville Rd (45459).* *937/439-1294.* Hrs: 11 am-10 pm; Fri, Sat to 11 pm. Closed Thanksgiving, Dec 25. Italian menu. Bar. Semi-a la carte: lunch $7.50-$9.50, dinner $12.50-$14.50. Child's meals. Specializes in pizza, lasagna. Upscale family dining. Cr cds: A, C, D, DS, MC, V.

[D]

✔★ **CHINA COTTAGE.** *6290 Far Hills Ave (OH 48).* *937/434-2622.* Hrs: 11 am-11 pm; Fri, Sat to midnight; Sun to 9 pm. Closed some major hols. Bar. Semi-a la carte: lunch $4-$6, dinner $6-$13. Specialties: orange chicken, Szechwan dishes, fresh fish. Parking. Cr cds: A, C, D, MC, V.

[D] [≈]

★★ **J ALEXANDER'S.** *(7970 Washington Village Dr, Centerville 45459) S on I-75, exit 44, near Dayton Mall.* *937/435-4441.* Hrs: 11 am-11 pm; Fri, Sat to midnight; Sun to 10 pm. Closed Thanksgiving, Dec 25. Bar. Semi-a la carte: lunch $5.95-$8.95, dinner $6.50-$18.95. Child's meals. Specializes in prime rib, seafood, homemade desserts. Parking. Casual dining. Cr cds: A, C, D, DS, MC, V.

[D] [≈]

★★★ **JAY'S.** *225 E 6th St.* *937/222-2892.* Hrs: 5-10:30 pm; Fri, Sat to 11 pm; Sun to 9 pm. Closed major hols. Res accepted Sun-Fri. Bar. Wine cellar. Semi-a la carte: dinner $12.50-$26.95. Child's meals. Specializes in fresh seafood, prime beef. Parking. Remodeled 1850s gristmill in Oregon Village. Cr cds: A, C, D, DS, JCB, MC, V.

[≈]

★★★ **KING COLE.** *40 N Main St, at 2nd St, in Kettering Tower, downtown.* *937/222-6771.* Hrs: 11:30 am-2 pm, 5-10 pm; Sat 5-10:30 pm. Closed Sun; major hols. Res accepted. Continental menu. Bar. Wine list. A la carte entrees: lunch $7.95-$10.95, dinner $16.50-$24.50. Specialties: sautéed veal loin, baby rack of lamb, sautéed Carolina bass. Own baking. Located on the 1st floor of a bank building. Gainsborough, Reynolds, other Old Masters originals. Cr cds: A, C, D, DS, MC, V.

[D] [≈]

★★ **KITTY'S.** *110 N Main St (45402), main floor of One Citizens Federal Centre.* *937/228-3333.* Hrs: 11 am-2 pm, 5-9 pm; Fri, Sat 5-11 pm. Closed Sun; major hols. Res accepted. Bar 11 am-9 pm. Semi-a la carte: lunch $6.50-$9.50, dinner $13.95-$21.95. Specializes in pasta, salads, California-style pizza. Bistro decor; work of regional artists displayed. Cr cds: A, C, D, DS, MC, V.

[D] [≈]

★★★ **L'AUBERGE.** *(4120 Far Hills Ave, Kettering 45419) approx 2 mi S on OH 48.* *937/299-5536.* The walls of this elegant French restaurant are hung with murals as well as contemporary paintings. Tables are set with Villeroy & Boch china. French nouvelle menu. Specializes in pâté, imported fresh seafood and game. Own baking. Hrs: 11:30 am-2:30 pm, 5-10 pm. Closed Sun; major hols. Res accepted. Bar. Wine cellar. Semi-a la carte: lunch $8.95-$12.50, dinner $21.50-$27.50. Pianist. Outdoor dining. Chef-owned. Jacket. Cr cds: A, C, D, MC, V.

[D]

★★ **LINCOLN PARK GRILLE.** *580 Lincoln Park Blvd, 1st floor of office building, 1/2 mi E of Far Hills Ave (OH 48).* *937/293-6293.* Hrs: 11 am-10 pm; Fri to 11 pm; Sat 5-11 pm; Sun (June-Aug) 5-11 pm. Closed Jan 1, Thanksgiving, Dec 25. Res accepted. Bar. Semi-a la carte: lunch $4.95-$7.95, dinner $8.95-$18.95. Pianist. Parking. Patio dining. View of Lincoln Park Commons fountain and amphitheater. Cr cds: A, C, D, MC, V.

[D] [≈]

★★ **OAKWOOD CLUB.** *2414 Far Hills Ave (45419).* *937/293-6973.* Hrs: 4:30 pm-midnight; Fri, Sat to 1 am. Closed Sun; major hols. Res accepted. Bar to 2:30 am. Semi-a la carte: dinner $13.95-$21.95. Specializes in steak, prime rib, fresh seafood. Own baking. Parking. Club atmosphere. Neiman originals on walls. Cr cds: A, C, D, MC, V.

[D] [≈]

★★★ **PEASANT STOCK.** *424 E Stroop Rd, E end of Town & Country Shopping Center.* *937/293-3900.* Hrs: 11 am-10 pm; Fri, Sat to 11 pm; Sun brunch 10:30 am-2:30 pm. Closed major hols. Bar to midnight. Semi-a la carte: lunch $5-$9, dinner $11-$19. Sun brunch $11.95. Child's meals. Specializes in fresh fish, prime rib, salads. Pianist Sun 10:30 am-2:30 pm, Mon-Wed 6-10 pm, classical guitarist Thurs-Sat 8-11 pm. Country French decor; collection of china plates displayed. Cr cds: A, C, D, DS, MC, V.

[D] [≈] [♥]

★★ **PINE CLUB.** *1926 Brown St.* *937/228-7463.* Hrs: 5 pm-1 midnight. Fri, Sat to 1 am. Closed Sun; Jan 1, Thanksgiving, Dec 25. Bar 4 pm-2 am. Wine list. Semi-a la carte: dinner $9.95-$20.95. Child's meals. Specializes in steak, veal, pork. Parking. Casual atmosphere; collection of Toby mugs & beer steins. Braille menu. No cr cds accepted.

[D] [≈]

★★ **STEVE KAO'S.** *8270 Springboro Pike, I-75 exit 44.* *937/433-2556.* Hrs: 11:30 am-9:30 pm; Fri, Sat to 11 pm; Sun noon-10 pm. Closed major hols. Res accepted. Chinese menu. Bar; entertainment. A la carte entrees: lunch $5.95-$7.25, dinner $7.95-$14.95. Specializes in Peking duck, salmon, Szechwan dishes. Parking. Cr cds: A, C, D, DS, MC, V.

[D] [≈]

✔★★ **WELTON'S.** *4614 Wilmington Pike, I-675 exit 7, then N; in Wilmington Heights Shopping Mall.* *937/293-2233.* Hrs: 5-10 pm; Fri, Sat to 11 pm. Closed Sun; some major hols. Bar. Semi-a la carte: dinner $5.95-$17.95. Specializes in fresh fish, pizza, hand-cut steak. Cr cds: A, DS, MC, V.

[D] [≈]

Defiance (B-1)

Pop 16,768 **Elev** 691 ft **Area code** 419 **Zip** 43512

Information Defiance Area Chamber of Commerce, PO Box 130; 419/782-7946.

Defiance was named for Fort Defiance (1794), which was constructed during Major General "Mad Anthony" Wayne's vigorous campaign against the Native Americans. The fort was so named after Wayne said "I defy the English, the Native Americans and all the devils in hell to take it." Defiance was also the site of a major Native American council in 1793 and is the birthplace of Chief Pontiac. Johnny Appleseed lived in Defiance during 1811-1828 while growing his pioneer apple orchards.

What to See and Do

Au Glaize Village. Over 110 acres. Replicas and restored late 19th-century buildings including Kieffer log cabin, Kinner log house; cider, sorghum and saw mills; blacksmith shop; railroad station and rolling stock; church, school, post office, gas station, dental and doctor offices; four museum buildings, black powder range. (June-Sept, wkends) Special events throughout the season. 3 mi SW off US 24 on Krouse Rd. Phone 419/784-0107 or 419/782-7255. ¢¢

Independence Dam State Park. A 604-acre park on the Maumee River. Fishing; boating (marina). Hiking. Picnicking (shelter). Camping. Standard fees. 3 mi E on OH 424. Phone 419/784-3263.

Annual Event

Flowing Rivers Festival. Site of the original Fort Defiance. Barefoot and regular waterskiing competitions, parade, art festival; fireworks. Phone 419/782-7946. Late June-early July.

Motels

★ **COMFORT INN.** *1900 N Clinton St. 419/784-4900; FAX 419/784-5555.* 62 rms, 2 story, 10 suites. S $55-$80; D $65-$90; each addl $5; suites $75-$90; under 18 free. TV; cable (premium). Indoor pool; whirlpool. Complimentary continental bkfst. Restaurant opp 11-2 am. Ck-out 11 am. Coin lndry. Meeting rms. In-rm modem link. Sundries. Refrigerator in suites. Cr cds: A, C, D, DS, JCB, MC, V.

✔★ **DAYS INN.** *1835 N Clinton St, jct US 24 & OH 66. 419/782-5555; FAX 419/782-8085.* 121 rms, 2 story. S $45; D $54; each addl $6; under 18 free. Crib free. TV; cable (premium), VCR avail. Indoor pool. Restaurant 6 am-2 pm; closed Sat, Sun. Rm serv. Bar. Ck-out noon. Meeting rms. Sundries. Cr cds: A, C, D, DS, ER, JCB, MC, V.

★ **PARAMOUNT HOTEL.** *(2395 N Scott St, Napoleon 43545)* 18 mi W on US 24 & OH 6, exit 108. 419/592-5010; res: 800/827-8641; FAX 419/592-6618. 79 rms, 2 story. S, D $53-$57; each addl $6; suites $75-$80; under 18 free; wkend rates. Crib free. Pet accepted, some restrictions. TV; cable (premium). Complimentary coffee in lobby. Restaurant 6:30 am-10 pm. Rm serv. Bar 11-1:30 am. Ck-out noon. Meeting rms. Business servs avail. Sundries. Coin lndry. Pool. Microwaves avail. Cr cds: A, C, D, DS, MC, V.

Delaware (D-3)

(See also Columbus, Marion, Mount Gilead, Mount Vernon)

Founded 1808 **Pop** 20,030 **Elev** 880 ft **Area code** 614 **Zip** 43015 **E-mail** delcocvb@midohio.net **Web** delaware.org

Information Delaware County Convention & Visitors Bureau, 44 E Winter St; 614/368-4748 or 888-335-6446.

Delaware, on the Olentangy River, derives its name and heritage from New England. Now a college town, trading center for farmers and site of diversified industry, the area was chosen by Native Americans as a campsite because of its mineral springs. The Mansion House (famous sulphur-spring resort built in 1833) is now Elliot Hall, the first building of Ohio Wesleyan University. There is a legend that President Rutherford B. Hayes (a native of Delaware) proposed to his bride-to-be, Lucy Webb (one of the school's first coeds), at the sulphur spring.

What to See and Do

Alum Creek State Park. 8,600 acres. Versatile topography and character of lake provides for abundance of activities. Swimming, waterskiing; fishing, hunting; boating. Hiking, bridle trails. Snowmobiling. Camping (rentals, fee). Nature programs. Standard fees. Daily. 6 mi E on OH 36, 37. For further information phone 614/548-4631. **Free.**

Delaware County Historical Society Museum. Relics tracing area's history from 1800. Genealogy library. (Mar-mid-Nov, Sun & Wed afternoons; also by appt; closed some major hols) 157 E William St. Phone 614/369-3831. **Free.**

Delaware State Park. 1,815-acre park with 1,330-acre lake. Swimming, bathhouse; fishing; boating (rentals, ramp). Hiking. Picnicking, concession. Camping. Standard fees. Daily. Phone 614/369-2761. **Free.**

Ohio Wesleyan University (1842). (2,000 students) Sandusky St passes thru historic 200-acre campus. Liberal arts educational institution. Mayhew

Gallery, Humphreys Art Hall (Sept-May, daily exc Sun). Gray Chapel houses one of three Klais organs in the US. Campus tours. Phone 614/369-4431 or 614/368-2000.

Olentangy Indian Caverns and Ohio Frontierland. Natural limestone cave; 55-105 ft below ground on 3 levels are various rock strata and fossils; once refuge for the Wyandot. Tours (35 min) guided and self-guided (Apr-Oct). Also re-creation of Ohio frontierland and Native American village (Memorial Day-Labor Day). 1779 Home Rd, 7 mi S, off US 23. Phone 614/548-7917. Combination ticket ¢¢¢

Perkins Observatory. Operated by Ohio Wesleyan and Ohio State universities; 32-inch reflecting telescope. (Mon-Fri; closed hols) Afternoon tour avail (limited hrs). 4 mi S on US 23. Phone 614/363-1257. **Free.**

Annual Event

Delaware County Fair. Fairgrounds, 236 Pennsylvania Ave. Grand Circuit harness racing; Little Brown Jug harness race for pacers. Usually 3rd wk Sept.

Motels

★★ **HOLIDAY INN EXPRESS.** *(16510 Square Dr, Marysville 43040)* 16 mi W on US 36. 513/644-8821. 74 rms, 2 story, 12 kit. units. S, D $65; each addl $5; suites $94; kit. units $65; under 19 free. Crib free. Pet accepted, some restrictions. TV; cable (premium), VCR avail. Complimentary bkfst. Restaurant adj 6 am-10 pm. Ck-out noon. Business center. In-rm modem link. Whirlpool in some suites. Cr cds: A, C, D, DS, MC, V.

✔★ **TRAVELODGE.** *1001 US 23N. 614/369-4421.* 32 rms, 1-2 story. S $42-$48; D $47-$59; each addl $6; under 18 free; higher rates: Little Brown Jug harness race, wkends during peak season. Crib $6. Pet accepted. TV; cable. Complimentary coffee in rms. Restaurant open 24 hrs. Ck-out noon. Meeting rms. Business servs avail. Sundries. Cr cds: A, C, D, DS, MC, V.

Restaurants

★ **BRANDING IRON.** *1400 Stratford Rd. 614/363-1846.* Hrs: 5-9:30 pm; Fri, Sat to 10:30 pm; Sun noon-8 pm. Closed Mon; Jan 1, Dec 24, 25; also first 2 wks Aug. Res accepted. Bar. Semi-a la carte: dinner $6.95-$14.95. Child's meals. Specializes in steak, barbecued ribs. Parking. Western decor. Family-owned. Cr cds: MC, V.

★ **BUN'S OF DELAWARE.** *6 W Winter St. 614/363-3731.* Hrs: 7:30 am-8 pm; Sun 11 am-7 pm. Closed Mon; major hols. Bar. Semi-a la carte: bkfst $2-$4.75, lunch $3.75-$6.75, dinner $5.35-$14.95. Child's meals. Cr cds: A, C, D, DS, MC, V.

★★ **MICHAEL OLIVERS.** *351 S Sandusky St. 614/363-1262.* Hrs: 6:30 am-10 pm; Sun 6:30 am-2 pm. Res accepted. Italian menu. Bar to 2:30 am. Semi-a la carte: bkfst $1.25-$8.95, lunch $6.45-$14.40, dinner $13.75-$22.75. Specialties: jambalaya, cordon bleu. Entertainment Thurs-Sat. Casual decor. Cr cds: A, DS, JCB, MC, V.

East Liverpool (D-6)

(For accommodations see Salem, Steubenville)

Settled 1798 **Pop** 13,654 **Elev** 689 ft **Area code** 330 **Zip** 43920

Located where Ohio, Pennsylvania and West Virginia meet on the Ohio River, East Liverpool was called Fawcett's Town (after its first settler) until

1860. Its clay deposits determined its destiny as a pottery center; everything from dinnerware to brick is produced here.

What to See and Do

Beaver Creek State Park. There are many streams in this 3,038-acre forested area that contains the ruins of the Sandy and Beaver Canal and one well-preserved lock. Gaston's Mill (ca 1837) has been restored. Fishing, hunting; canoeing. Hiking, bridle trails. Picnicking. Primitive camping. Standard fees. (Daily) 8 mi NW off OH 7. Phone 330/385-3091. **Free.**

Museum of Ceramics. History museum contains collection of regional pottery and porcelain; bone china; life size dioramas; multimedia presentation. (Mar-Nov, Wed-Sun; closed Thanksgiving) 400 E 5th St. Phone 330/386-6001. ¢¢

Pottery tours. Hall China Co. (Daily exc Sun) Anna St. Phone 330/385-2900. **Homer Laughlin China Co.** (Mon-Fri) Phone 330/387-1300, ext 667. **Pioneer Pottery.** Tours by appt. 761 Dresden Ave. Phone 330/385-4293.

Annual Event

Tri-State Pottery Festival. Pottery industry displays, plant tours, pottery olympics; art & antique show, rose show, rides. 3rd wkend June.

Elyria (B-4)

(See also Cleveland, Lorain, Oberlin, Sandusky)

Settled 1817 **Pop** 56,746 **Elev** 730 ft **Area code** 440 **Zip** 44035 **E-mail** visitors@lcvb.org **Web** www.lcvb.org

Information Lorain County Visitors Bureau, 611 Broadway, Lorain 44052; 440/245-5282 or 800/334-1673.

This retailing and industrial city, at the junction of the east and west branches of the Black River, is the seat of Lorain County. The novelist Sherwood Anderson managed a paint factory here before his literary career began. Now the city has more than 130 industries manufacturing automotive parts, golf balls, air-conditioning and home-heating units, aircraft parts and pumps and metal castings. Surrounding greenhouses and farms contribute poultry, fruits, vegetables and dairy products to the city's economy.

What to See and Do

Cascade & Elywood parks. Picnic areas, playground; trails, sledding hill; waterfalls, views of rock cliffs. Washington Ave or Furnace St off W River St.

The Hickories Museum (1894). Shingle-style mansion of industrialist Arthur Lovett Garford. Changing exhibits on Lorain County. Hicks Memorial Research Library. 509 Washington Ave. Phone 440/322-3341. Tours (Tues-Sat afternoons) ¢¢

Annual Event

Apple Festival. 3rd wkend Sept.

Motels

★ **COMFORT INN.** *739 Leona St, off OH Tpke exit 8. 440/324-7676; FAX 440/324-4046.* 66 rms, 2 story, 9 suites. June-Aug: S, D $48-$96; each addl $6; suites $70-$125; under 18 free; lower rates rest of yr. Crib $6. TV; cable (premium). Complimentary continental bkfst. Restaurant nearby. Ck-out 11 am. Coin lndry. Meeting rm. Sundries. Health club privileges. Refrigerator, microwave, in-rm whirlpool in suites. Cr cds: A, C, D, DS, ER, JCB, MC, V.

D ⚡ 🐾 SC

✔★ ★ **DAYS INN.** *621 Midway Blvd, off OH Tpke exit 8. 440/324-4444; FAX 440/324-2065.* 101 rms, 3 story, 30 suites. May-Sept: S $45-$96.95; D $45-$104.95; each addl $8; suites $69.95-$124.95; under 13 free; lower rates rest of yr. Crib free. TV; cable (premium). Indoor pool. Complimentary continental bkfst. Restaurant nearby. Ck-out noon. Coin lndry. Business servs avail. In-rm modem link. Game rm. Cr cds: A, C, D, DS, MC, V.

D ⚡ 🐾 SC

★ ★ **RAMADA INN.** *910 Lorain Blvd, off OH Tpke exit 8. 440/323-7488.* 64 rms, 2 story. May-Sept: S, D $50.95-$109.95; each addl $8; under 18 free; lower rates rest of yr. Crib $8. TV; cable (premium). Pool. Restaurant 6-10 am, 6-9 pm; wkend hrs vary. Bar from 6 pm. Ck-out noon. Meeting rms. In-rm modem link. Game rm. Cr cds: A, C, D, DS, MC, V.

D ⚡ 🐾 SC

Motor Hotel

★ ★ **HOLIDAY INN.** *1825 Lorain Blvd, off OH Tpke exit 8. 440/324-5411; FAX 440/324-2785.* 250 rms, 2-6 story. June-Aug: S, D $119-$129; each addl $10; suites $150-$175; under 18 free. Crib free. TV; cable (premium). Heated pool; poolside serv. Restaurant 6 am-10 pm. Rm serv. Bar 11:30-2 am. Ck-out noon. Coin lndry. Meeting rms. Business servs avail. In-rm modem link. Valet serv. Sundries. Free airport transportation. Health club privileges. Cr cds: A, C, D, DS, JCB, MC, V.

D ⚡ 🐾 SC

Restaurant

★ **GRASSIE'S WAYSIDE INN.** *447 Oberlin Rd. 440/322-0690.* Hrs: 10 am-10 pm. Closed Sun; major hols. Continental menu. Bar. Semi-a la carte: lunch $5-$8, dinner $8-$15. Child's meals. Specializes in skillet prime rib, fresh seafood, pasta. Family-owned. Cr cds: A, DS, MC, V.

D ⤴

Findlay (C-2)

(See also Bowling Green, Lima, Tiffin)

Founded 1821 **Pop** 35,703 **Elev** 780 ft **Area code** 419 **Zip** 45840 **E-mail** chamber@bright.net **Web** rri.bright.net/hancock/chamber

Information Hancock County Convention and Visitors Bureau, 123 East Main Cross St; 419/422-3315 or 800/424-3315.

In 1860 the editor of the Findlay *Jeffersonian,* in letters signed "Petroleum V. Nasby," attacked slavery. In the previous decade the "grapevine telegraph" and Underground Railroad, piloting runaway slaves to safety, were active in Findlay. Named for Fort Findlay, one of the outposts of the War of 1812, it is the seat of Hancock County, 45 miles south of Toledo in the state's rich farm area. Congress designated Findlay as Flag City, USA in 1974.

Tell Taylor, educated in Findlay, was inspired to write "Down by the Old Mill Stream" while fishing along the Blanchard River. Marilyn Miller, Russell Crouse, Dr. Howard T. Ricketts and Dr. Norman Vincent Peale also came from Findlay.

What to See and Do

Hancock Historical Museum. Exhibits of glass, including examples produced in Findlay during the great gas boom of the 1880s; Pendleton art glass collection. (Mon-Fri; tours, Thurs, Fri & Sun afternoons) 422 W Sandusky St. Phone 419/423-4433. **Donation.**

Mazza Gallery. Exhibited here is the Mazza Centennial Collection; original art created by illustrators of childrens' books. More than 500 works of distinguished illustrators are displayed, including those of Ezra Jack Keats,

Maurice Sendak and other Caldecott Medal winners. (Wed-Fri, also Sun afternoons; closed major hols) 1000 N Main St, lower level of Shafer Library. Phone 419/424-4777.   **Free.**

Motels

★ ★ **COUNTRY HEARTH INN.** *1020 Interstate Court.* 419/423-4303; FAX 419/423-3459; res: 800/672-7935. 72 rms, 8 suites, 10 kit. units. S $58-$73; D $64-$81; each addl $6; suites, kit. units $64-$84; under 18 free. Crib free. TV; cable (premium). Pool. Complimentary bkfst. Coffee in rms. Restaurant adj 6 am-10 pm. Ck-out noon. Meeting rms. Business servs avail. In-rm modem link. Valet serv. Microwaves avail. Cr cds: A, C, D, DS, MC, V.

D ☲ ➤ ⩘ SC

✔★ ★ **CROSS COUNTRY INN.** *1951 Broad Ave, I-75 exit 159.* 419/424-0466; FAX 419/424-1043. 120 rms. S $35.99-$42.99; D $39.99-$50.99; each addl $7; under 18 free. Crib free. TV. Heated pool. Complimentary coffee in lobby. Restaurant adj 7 am-11 pm. Ck-out noon. Cr cds: A, C, D, DS, MC, V.

D ☲ ➤ ⩘ SC

★ ★ **FAIRFIELD INN BY MARRIOTT.** *2000 Tiffin Ave.* 419/424-9940. 57 rms, 3 story, 13 suites. S $55.95-$61.95; D $55.95-$65.95; each addl $6; suites $65.95-$71.95; under 18 free. Crib $6. TV; cable (premium). Indoor pool; whirlpool. Complimentary continental bkfst. Ck-out noon. Meeting rm. Business servs avail. Valet serv. Sundries. Refrigerator in suites. Cr cds: A, D, DS, MC, V.

D ☲ ➤ ⩘ SC

★ ★ **FINDLAY INN & CONFERENCE CENTER.** *200 E Main Cross St.* 419/422-5682; FAX 419/422-5581; res: 800/825-1455. 80 rms, 3 story, 12 suites. S $58-$95; D $65-$130; suites $95-$130; wkend rates. Crib $6. TV; cable. Indoor pool; whirlpool. Complimentary continental bkfst (Mon-Fri). Restaurant 6:30 am-10 pm; Sat, Sun from 7:30 am. Rm serv. Bar. Ck-out noon. Meeting rms. Business servs avail. Bellhops. Exercise equipt; bicycles, rowers, sauna. Health club privileges. Some refrigerators; microwaves avail. Cr cds: A, C, D, DS, MC, V.

D ☲ 🏋 ➤ ⩘ SC

Fort Ancient State Memorial (F-2)

(For accommodations see Cincinnati, Dayton, Lebanon, Middletown)

(7 mi SE of Lebanon on OH 350)

Fort Ancient is one of the largest and most impressive prehistoric earthworks of its kind in the United States. The Fort Ancient earthworks were built by the Hopewell people between 100 B.C. and A.D. 500. This site occupies an elevated plateau overlooking the Little Miami River Valley. Its massive earthen walls, more than 23 feet high in places, enclose an area of 100 acres; within this area are earth mounds once used as a calendar of event markers and other archaeological features. Relics from the site and the nearby prehistoric Native American village are displayed in Fort Ancient Museum. Hiking trails. Picnic facilities. (Memorial Day-Labor Day, Wed-Sun; Apr-Memorial Day & Labor Day-Oct, wkends) Phone 513/932-4421. Per vehicle ¢¢

Fort Hill State Memorial (F-3)

(For accommodations see Chillicothe)

(5 mi N of Sinking Spring off OH 41; SW of Chillicothe via US 50, OH 41)

This is the site of a prehistoric Native American hilltop earth and stone enclosure. The identity of its builders has not been determined, but implements found in the vicinity point to the Hopewell people. There is a 2,000-foot trail that leads to the ancient earthworks. Picnic area and shelterhouse. (Daily) Phone 513/588-3221.   **Free.**

Fremont (B-3)

Founded 1820 **Pop** 17,648 **Elev** 601 ft **Area code** 419 **Zip** 43420 **E-mail** sccvb@nwohio.com **Web** www.nwohio.com/visithere/

Information Sandusky County Convention & Visitors Bureau, PO Box 643; 419/332-4470 or 800/255-8070.

Wyandot settled here as early as 1650; scouts and settlers came in the late 1700s. Fort Stephenson was built and defended in the War of 1812. Earlier known as Lower Sandusky, the town became Fremont in 1849. Rutherford B. Hayes, 19th US president, lived in Fremont and is buried here. Seat of Sandusky County, 20 miles from Lake Erie on the Sandusky River, Fremont is an industrial town known for cutlery, food processing and tools and dies. It is also an agricultural area.

What to See and Do

Hayes Presidential Center, Spiegel Grove. Rutherford B. Hayes Library, Museum and home; period and community exhibits; Hayes memorabilia. Graves of the President and Mrs. Hayes. (Daily; closed Jan 1, Thanksgiving, Dec 25) Library (daily exc Sun & hols). Tours of the residence and museum (daily). 1337 Hayes Ave at Buckland Ave. Phone 419/332-2081 or 800/998-7737. Museum ¢¢; Home ¢¢; Combination ticket ¢¢¢

Library Park. Scene of 1813 Fort Stephenson battle; "Old Betsy," only cannon used to defend the fort; Soldiers Monument. (Daily exc Sun) 423 Croghan St between Arch & High Sts. Phone 419/334-7101.   **Free.**

Annual Events

Civil War Encampment & President Hayes Birthday Reunion. Phone 800/998-7737. 1st full wkend Oct.

Haunted Hydro. Phone 419/334-2451. Oct 3-Nov 2.

Motel

★ **DAYS INN.** *3701 N OH 53, OH Tpke exit 6.* 419/334-9551. 105 rms, 2 story, 2 suites. June-Aug: S, D $38-$115; each addl $8; suites $95-$150; under 12 free; higher rates special events; lower rates rest of yr. TV; cable (premium). Pool. Playground. Restaurant 6-11 am, 5-10 pm; Sun to 11 am. Rm serv. Bar. Ck-out noon. Coin lndry. Meeting rms. Valet serv. Game rm. Cr cds: A, C, D, DS, MC, V.

D ☲ ➤ ⩘ SC

Gallipolis (G-4)

Settled 1790 **Pop** 4,831 **Elev** 576 ft **Area code** 614 **Zip** 45631 **E-mail** 102033.1264@compuserve.com **Web** www.gallipolis.org

Information Ohio Valley Visitors Center, 45 State St; 800/765-6482.

Gallipolis, "the old French city" along the Ohio River, was the second permanent settlement in Ohio. The columnist O.O. McIntyre lived in Gallipolis, often wrote about it and is buried here. The district library has an extensive collection of his work.

What to See and Do

Bob Evans Farm. A 1,100-acre farm. Hiking, horseback riding (fee); canoeing (fee); special wkend events (fee); Craftbarn and Farm Museum; craft demonstrations; domestic animals, farm crops. (Memorial Day wkend-Labor Day wkend, daily; Sept, wkends; call for schedule) 12 mi W; just off US 35, on OH 588 in Rio Grande. Phone 614/245-5305 or 800/994-FARM. **Free.**

French Art Colony. Monthly exhibits. (Daily exc Mon; closed hols) 530 1st Ave. Phone 614/446-3834. **Free.**

Our House State Memorial. Built as a tavern in 1819; restored. Lafayette stayed here. (Memorial Day-Labor Day, daily exc Mon) 434 1st St. Phone 614/446-0586 (museum). ¢¢

Annual Event

Bob Evans Farm Festival. Bob Evans Farm. Bluegrass and country entertainment; food, 150 heritage craftspeople and demonstrations; Appalachian clogging, square dancing. Camping. Phone 614/245-5305 or 800/994-FARM. Mid-Oct.

Motels

✔★ **BEST WESTERN WILLIAM ANN.** *918 Second Ave.* *614/446-3373; FAX 614/446-1337.* 56 rms, 1-2 story. S $35-$40; D $40-$45; each addl $5; suites $50-$65; under 12 free. Crib $5. Pet accepted. TV; cable. Restaurant nearby. Ck-out 11 am. Business servs avail. Cr cds: A, C, D, DS, MC, V.

⬛ ⬛ ⬛ SC

★★ **HOLIDAY INN.** *577 OH State Rt 7. 614/446-0090.* 100 rms, 2 story. S, D $59; suites $59; under 20 free. Crib free. Pet accepted. TV; cable. Pool; wading pool. Restaurant 6 am-10 pm. Rm serv. Bar 4 pm-midnight. Ck-out noon. Coin lndry. Meeting rms. Business servs avail. Sundries. Cr cds: A, C, D, DS, JCB, MC, V.

D ⬛ ⬛ ⬛ ⬛ SC

Geneva-on-the-Lake (A-6)

(For accommodations see Ashtabula, Painesville)

Founded 1869 **Pop** 1,626 **Elev** 605 ft **Area code** 216 **Zip** 44041 **Web** www.ncweb.com/gol

Information Convention and Visitors Bureau, 5536 Lake Rd; 216/466-8600 or 800/862-9948.

Geneva-on-the-Lake was Ohio's first summer resort. Its 129-year-old entertainment "strip" has a wide variety of nightlife, while Lake Erie offers boating, fishing and beaches.

What to See and Do

Ashtabula County History Museum, Jennie Munger Gregory Memorial (1823-1826). One of first frame houses built on Lake Erie's southern shore. Victorian furnishings, clothing, quilts and artifacts. (June-Sept, Wed & Sun afternoons). Lake Rd (OH 534) between Putnam Dr and Grandview Dr. Phone 216/466-7337. **Donation.**

Erieview Park. Amusement park with major & kiddie rides, water slides; train ride; arcade. Nightclub; lodging; restaurant, picnicking. (May-Sept, daily; early and late season hrs vary) 5483 Lake Rd. Phone 216/466-8650. **Free.** Rides/water slides pass ¢¢¢

Geneva State Park. This 698-acre park offers swimming; fishing, hunting; boating, 383-slip marina with 6-lane ramp. Hiking. Snowmobile & cross-country trails. Picnicking (shelter), concession. Camping, pet camping, cabins. Standard fees. (Apr-Nov; daily) Off OH 534. Phone 216/466-8400. **Free.**

Shandy Hall (1815). Western Reserve home; original furnishings; tours. (May-Oct, Tues-Sat, also Sun afternoons) 6333 S Ridge West Rd; S on OH 534, then 2 mi W on OH 84, near Unionville. Phone 216/466-3680. ¢¢

Annual Event

Geneva Grape Jamboree. Downtown. Festival marks the grape harvesting season. Grape products, grape stomping; parades, entertainment, exhibits, contests, winery tours. Phone 216/466-5262. Last full wkend Sept.

Gnadenhutten (D-5)

(For accommodations see Cambridge, Coshocton, New Philadelphia)

Settled 1772 **Pop** 1,226 **Elev** 835 ft **Area code** 614 **Zip** 44629

Gnadenhutten (ja-NA-den-hutten) is a rural center in Tuscarawas County in the Muskingum Conservancy District.

What to See and Do

Gnadenhutten Historical Park and Museum. Monument to 90 Christian Native Americans who were massacred here in 1782. Native American burial mound. Reconstructed log church and cooper's cabin. Museum. Oldest tombstone in Ohio. (Memorial Day-early Sept, daily; early Sept-Oct, wkends; rest of yr, by appt) 1 mi S. Phone 614/254-4756. **Donation.**

Tappan Lake Park. Swimming; fishing; boating (ramp), marina. Playground. Tent & trailer sites (showers, flush toilets), cabins. Standard fees. Pets on leash. (Daily) 7 mi E on US 36, 15 mi SE on US 250, W on County 55, 3 mi to park entrance. Phone 614/922-3649. Per vehicle ¢¢

Clendening Lake Marina. Fishing; boating (ramp). Motel. Tent & trailer sites. Pets on leash. (May-Oct; daily) 7 mi E on US 36 to Dennison, then 12 mi S, off OH 800. Phone 614/658-3691.

Hamilton (F-1)

(See also Cincinnati, Mason, Middletown, Oxford)

Founded 1791 **Pop** 61,368 **Elev** 580 ft **Area code** 513 **E-mail** Hamilton@ctd.com **Web** www.hamilton-ohio.com

Information Greater Hamilton Convention & Visitors Bureau, 201 Dayton St, 45011; 513/844-8080 or 800/311-5353.

Originally Fort Hamilton, an outpost of the Northwest Territory, the city became an industrial center in the 1850s with the completion of the Miami-Erie Canal. It continues as such today. Much of the rich 19th-century heritage is preserved in the large number and variety of restored homes in several historic districts.

What to See and Do

Dayton Lane Historic Area Walking Tour. Many examples of restored Victorian and turn-of-the-century architecture, mostly homes. Allow an hour. From the railroad tracks on the W to OH 4 on the E; from Buckeye St on the N to High St on the S.

German Village Walking Tour. Nine-blk area just N of the business district. German Village was part of the original city plan of 1796, with the first courts, school, newspaper and many early businesses. Allow at least 1 hr; 2 mi. Within the district are

> **Butler County Historical Museum (Benninghofen House)** (1861). Historical museum housed in Victorian Italianate mansion. Period furnishings; antique clothing, toys; doll collection; 19th-century dentist's office; local memorabilia. (Daily exc Mon; closed hols) 327 N 2nd St. Phone 513/896-9930. ¢

> **Lane-Hooven House** (1863). Unusual octagonal home in the Gothic-revival style; octagonal turret, Tudor front door, cast iron balconies, jigsaw bargeboard-decorated eaves. Exterior and interior fully restored. Home of Hamilton Community Foundation. (Daily exc wkends; closed hols) 319 N 3rd St. Phone 513/863-1389. **Free.**

Rossville Walking Tour. Ten-and-one-half-block area on the W side of the Great Miami River. Until 1855 this was the separate town of Rossville, which was laid out in 1804 as a mercantile community. More buildings survived here, because it was less susceptible to flooding than the east bank. Wide range of styles from 1830-1920. Allow 1 hr; over 2 mi; level ground except for Millikin St. Before crossing to Rossville, visit Monument Park with the 1804 Log Cabin and

> **Soldiers, Sailors and Pioneers Monument** (1902). Permanent memorial to the pioneer settlers and those of the area who fought in conflicts from the Indian Wars to Vietnam. Displays inside building. (Daily exc Sun) High & Monument Sts. Phone 513/867-5823. **Free.**

Annual Events

Ft Hamilton Days Festival. Courthouse Square. Concerts, fireworks, arts & crafts, kart races. Phone 513/524-3211. Late June.

Antique Car Parade. Courthouse Square. 300 cars in one of nation's oldest antique car parades. 4th Sat July.

Butler County Fair. Buter County Fairgrounds. Phone 513/892-1423. Last full wk July.

Ohio Honey Festival. Courthouse Square. Aug.

Dam Fest. Two-day festival centered on the Great Miami River and Miami Campus; features world champion water skiers in doubles and free-style competition; booths, games, entertainment. Phone 513/867-2281. Wkend after Labor Day.

Hotel

★ ★ **HAMILTONIAN.** *1 Riverfront Plaza (45011). 513/896-6200; FAX 513/896-9463; res: 800/522-5570.* 120 rms, 6 story. S, D $77-$84; each addl $8; suites $130-$135; wkend rates. Crib free. Pet accepted. TV; cable (premium); VCR avail. Pool. Coffee in rms. Restaurant 6:30 am-10 pm. Bar 11-1 am; Fri, Sat to 2 am. Ck-out noon. Meeting rms. Business servs avail. In-rm modem link. Indoor tennis privileges. Health club privileges. Refrigerator avail. On river. Luxury level. Cr cds: A, C, D, DS, MC, V.

Restaurant

★ ★ **ACADEMY.** *343 N Third St. 513/868-7171.* Hrs: 11 am-2 pm, 5-10 pm; Sat from 5 pm. Closed Sun; major hols. Res accepted. Bar to 2:30 am. Semi-a la carte: lunch $5.50-$8.50, dinner $13.95-$19.95. Specializes in veal, seafood, steak. Pianist Wed-Sat. Two 1850s buildings joined by garden/atrium. Cr cds: A, MC, V.

Hocking Hills State Park (F-4)

(For accommodations see Athens, Chillicothe, Lancaster)

(12 mi SW of Logan via OH 374, 664; or SE of Lancaster via US 33, SW on OH 664)

More than 2,000 acres divided into six scenic areas:

> **Ash Cave.** Natural rock shelter with 90-ft waterfall in spring and winter. Ashes from Native American campfires were found here. Picnicking, shelter, hiking; a 1/4-mile wheelchair-accessible trail to Ash Cave. (Daily) Phone 614/385-6841. **Free.**

> **Old Man's Cave.** The most popular and highly developed area. Waterfalls, gorges and caves. A hermit who lived in the main cave after the Civil War gave the cave its name. Fishing, hiking, park naturalist in summer. Picnicking, shelter, concession, restaurant. Cabins, camping. Standard fees. (Daily) Phone 614/385-6841. **Free.**

> **Rock House.** Unusual "house" formation in the sandstone cliff. Picnicking, hiking. **Free.**

> **Cantwell Cliffs, Cedar Falls, Conkie's Hollow.** Feature cliffs, good trails, rare plants and picnicking. (Daily) Phone 614/385-6341. **Free.**

Ironton (G-3)

(For accommodations see Gallipolis, Portsmouth)

Founded 1848 **Pop** 12,751 **Elev** 558 ft **Area code** 614 **Zip** 45638
Information Greater Lawrence County Convention and Visitors Bureau, PO Box 488, South Point 45680; 614/894-3838 or 614/532-9991.

Extensive ore pockets in the district once gave Ironton a thriving iron industry; the first charcoal furnace north of the Ohio River started producing pig iron here in 1826. The town was founded by one of the first ironmasters. Ironton was the southern terminus for the Detroit, Toledo and Ironton. The Chesapeake and Ohio and the Norfolk and Southern railroads still serve the area.

Ironton is now an important industrial city; many companies have large plants here.

What to See and Do

Lawrence County Museum. Changing exhibits in Italian-style villa (1870). (Early Apr-mid-Dec, Fri-Sun afternoons) 506 S 6th St. Phone 614/532-1222. **Donation.**

Wayne National Forest. Three sections make up this 202,967-acre area of SE Ohio. Private lands are interspersed within the federal land. One section is the E side of Ohio, NE of Marietta (see); the second is NE of Athens (see); and the third section is in the S tip of the state, SW of Gallipolis. The forest lies in the foothills of the Appalachian Mountains. It is characterized by rugged hills covered with diverse stands of hardwoods, pine, and cedar; lakes, rivers, and streams; springs, rock shelters, covered bridges, several trails and campgrounds are located in the forest. A Ranger District office of the forest is also located here. (Daily) For information contact the Supervisor, 219 Columbus Rd, Athens 45701; 614/592-6644. **Free.** In the forest is

> **Lake Vesuvius.** The stack of Vesuvius (1833), one of the earliest iron blast furnaces, still remains. Swimming; fishing; boating (dock; May-Sept). Hiking. Picnicking. Camping. (Daily) 10 mi N off OH 93. Phone 614/532-3223. Camping ¢¢¢

Annual Events

Tri-State Fair and Regatta. Various events held in tri-state area of Kentucky, Ohio and West Virginia. Highlights include jet-ski and powerboat races; concerts; carnival; fireworks. Phone 304/525-8141. June-Aug.

Lawrence County Fair. E on US 52, at fairgrounds in Proctorville. Mid-July.

Kelleys Island (B-3)

(For accommodations see Port Clinton, Sandusky; also see Put-in-Bay)

Founded 1833 **Pop** 172 **Elev** 598 ft **Area code** 419 **Zip** 43438
Information Chamber of Commerce, PO Box 783; 419/746-2360.

Kelleys Island, one of the largest of 20 islands in Lake Erie, is 5 miles across at the widest point. This is a vacation spot with auto and passenger service available from Marblehead on Neuman Boat Line or Kelleys Island Ferry Boat Line. Island hopping cruises are available from Port Clinton and Sandusky (see).

What to See and Do

Glacial Grooves State Memorial. Limestone with unusually long, smooth grooves made by glacial action. The largest easily accessible such grooves in North America, they were scoured into solid limestone bedrock approx 30,000 yrs ago by glacier of the great ice sheet that covered part of North America. Outdoor exhibits. (Daily) Located on the N side of Kelleys Island, W of dock, on W shore. Phone 419/797-4530.   **Free.**

Inscription Rock State Memorial. Inscription Rock is marked with prehistoric Native American pictographs. The flat-topped limestone slab displays carvings of human figures smoking pipes and wearing headdresses and various animal forms. (Daily) Located on the S shore, E of dock. Phone 419/797-4530.   **Free.**

Kelleys Island State Park. This 661-acre park offers swimming; fishing; hunting; boating (launch). Hiking. Picnicking (shelter). Camping. Standard fees. N shore. Phone 419/797-4530.

Kent (C-5)

(See also Akron, Alliance, Aurora, Canton, Cleveland)

Pop 28,835 **Elev** 1,097 ft **Area code** 330 **Zip** 44240
Information Kent Area Chamber of Commerce, 155 E Main St; 330/673-9855.

What to See and Do

Kent State University (1910). (33,000 students) Twenty schools and colleges. Non-academic campus tours arranged by University News and Information Office. On campus are the Kent State University Museum, with more than 10,000 costumes and treasures (Wed-Sat, also Sun afternoons, donation); Gallery of the School of Art in the Art Bldg and the Student Center Gallery (academic yr, Mon-Fri); Planetarium (by appt); and the May 4th Memorial, next to Taylor Hall. E Main St, 8 mi S of OH Tpke on OH 43. Phone 330/672-2727.

West Branch State Park. A 8,002-acre park with swimming; fishing; boating (launch, rentals). Hiking, bridle, snowmobiling trails. Picnicking (shelter), concession. Camping. Standard fees. (Daily) 12 mi E on OH 5. Phone 330/296-3239.   **Free.**

Motels

(Rates may be higher for special university wkends)

★ **DAYS INN.** 4422 Edson Rd, at jct I-76, OH 43. 330/677-9400; FAX 330/677-9456. 67 rms, 2 story. June-early Sept: S $53-$70; D $59-$85; each addl $6; under 12 free; lower rates rest of yr. Crib free. TV; cable. Heated pool. Complimentary continental bkfst. Restaurant nearby. Ck-out 11 am. Meeting rms. Business servs avail. Sundries. Cr cds: A, C, D, DS, JCB, MC, V.

D ⊠ ☇ ≡ 🛇 SC

★ ★ **HOLIDAY INN.** 4363 OH 43, 3 mi S on OH 43 at jct I-76. 330/678-0101; FAX 330/677-5001. 152 rms, 2 story. May-Sept: S, D $99; under 19 free; lower rates rest of yr. Crib free. Pet accepted. TV; cable (premium). Heated pool. Restaurant 6:30 am-2 pm, 5-10 pm. Rm serv. Bar. Ck-out noon. Coin lndry. Meeting rms. Business servs avail. Exercise equipt; weight machine, bicycles. Cr cds: A, C, D, DS, JCB, MC, V.

D ✔ ⊠ 🏋 ☇ 🛇 SC

★ ★ **INN OF KENT.** 303 E Main St, OH Tpke exit 13. 330/673-3411; FAX 330/673-9878. 57 rms, 2 story, some kits. June-Labor Day: S, D $55-$70; each addl $3; under 12 free; lower rates rest of yr. Crib free. Pet accepted, some restrictions. TV; cable. Indoor pool. Restaurant 7 am-2:30 pm; Fri, Sat to 9 pm. Rm serv. Ck-out noon. Coin lndry. Meeting rm. Business servs avail. Cr cds: A, C, D, DS, MC, V.

D ✔ ⊠ ☇ 🛇

✔★ **KNIGHTS INN.** 4423 OH 43, at jct I-76. 330/678-5250; FAX 330/678-7014. 99 rms, 30 kit. units. May-Sept: S, D $44.95-$49.95; each addl $6; kit. units $49.95-$54.95; under 18 free; some lower rates rest of yr. Crib free. Pet accepted. TV; cable. Pool. Restaurant adj open 24 hrs. Ck-out noon. Meeting rm. Business servs avail. Some refrigerators. Cr cds: A, DS, MC, V.

✔ ⊠ ☇ 🛇 SC

✔★ ★ **UNIVERSITY INN.** 540 S Water St (OH 43). 330/678-0123; FAX 330/678-7356. 107 rms, 7 story. June-Sept: S $55; D $55-$75; each addl $4; lower rates rest of yr. Crib free. TV; cable (premium). Heated pool. Restaurant 6:30 am-2 pm. Ck-out 11 am. Coin lndry. Meeting rms. Business servs avail. Many refrigerators. Private patios, balconies. Cr cds: A, C, D, DS, MC, V.

⊠ ☇ 🛇

Restaurant

✔★ ★ **PUFFERBELLY LTD.** 152 Franklin Ave. 330/673-1771. Hrs: 11:30 am-10 pm; Fri, Sat to 11 pm; Sun to 9 pm; Sun brunch 11 am-2:30 pm. Closed major hols. Continental menu. Bar to 1 am. Semi-a la carte: lunch $3.95-$7.95, dinner $3.95-$15.95. Sun brunch $8.95. Child's meals. Specializes in fresh seafood, steak. Historic railroad depot (1875); museum. Cr cds: A, DS, MC, V.

D ⊡

Lancaster (E-4)

(See also Columbus, Newark)

Founded 1800 **Pop** 34,507 **Elev** 860 ft **Area code** 614 **Zip** 43130 **E-mail** lancasteroh_visitorsbureau@compuserve.com
Information Fairfield County Visitors & Convention Bureau, One N Broad, PO Box 2450; 614/653-8251 or 800/626-1296.

What to See and Do

Mount Pleasant. A 250-ft rock outcropping overlooking city; was a favorite Native American lookout. Trails wind to top. In Rising Park, N High St & Fair Ave.

Square 13. Here are 19 historic buildings; a free pamphlet describing these buildings may be obtained from the Fairfield County Visitors & Convention Bureau or from the Fairfield Heritage Assn, 105 E Wheeling St; also inquire about walking tour tape rentals (free with refundable deposit). N High, Broad, Main & Wheeling Sts.

Sherman House Museum (1811). Birthplace of General William Tecumseh Sherman and Senator John Sherman (Sherman Anti-Trust Act). Civil War Museum. (Apr-mid-Dec, Tues-Sun afternoons; closed most hols) 137 E Main St. Phone 614/687-5891 or 614/654-9923. ¢¢

Mumaugh Memorial (1805-1824). 1st & 2nd floor have restored rms. (By appt only) 162 E Main St. Phone 614/687-6619. **Free.**

Stanbery-Rising (1834). Educational building for First United Methodist Church. (Not open to the public) 131 N High St.

The Georgian. (1833). Two-story brick house reflects Federal and Regency styles. Headquarters of the Fairfield Heritage Assn. (Apr-mid-Dec, Tues-Sun afternoons; closed major hols) 105 E Wheeling St. Phone 614/654-9923. ¢¢

Annual Events

Pilgrimage. Tours of mid-19th-century through modern houses and museums. Phone 614/654-9923. First wkend May.

Spring Old Car Festival. Fairfield County Fairgrounds. Antique automobiles, steam engines, old farm equipment, car parts and swap meet. Phone 800/626-1296. 1st wkend June.

Lancaster Festival. Throughout town. Features dance, musical and theatrical performances; special art and museum exhibits; children's events. Phone 614/687-4808 or 800/626-1296. 12 days mid-late July.

Zane Square Arts & Crafts Festival. Corner of Broad & Main Sts. More than 125 craftsmen display and sell handcrafted items; entertainment; street dancing. Phone 614/687-6651. Wkend mid-Aug.

Fairfield County Fair. Harness racing, exhibits, amusements. Phone 800/626-1296. Mid-Oct.

Christmas Candlelight Tour. Tour of downtown area churches; musical presentations. Tickets at The Georgian. Phone 614/654-9923 or 800/626-1296. 2nd Sat Dec.

Motels

★ ★ **AMERIHOST INN.** *1721 River Valley Circle North, at River Valley Mall (OH 33).* 614/654-5111; FAX 614/654-5108. 60 rms, 2 story. S, D $65-$95; each addl $6; under 12 free; wkly rates. Crib free. TV; cable. Indoor pool; whirlpool. Coffee in rms. Complimentary continental bkfst. Restaurant adj 7 am-midnight. Ck-out noon. Meeting rms. Business servs avail. Valet serv. Exercise equipt; bicycles, stair machine, sauna. Shopping center adj. Cr cds: A, D, DS, MC, V.

D ⌧ ⌧ ⌧ SC

★ ★ **BEST WESTERN.** *1858 N Memorial Dr.* 614/653-3040; FAX 614/653-1172. 168 rms, 2 story. S, D $52-$80; each addl $7; under 19 free. Crib free. Pet accepted. TV; cable. Pool. Complimentary coffee in rms. Restaurant 6 am-10 pm. Rm serv. Bar to 1 am. Ck-out noon. Meeting rms. Business servs avail. Valet serv. Coin lndry. Health club privileges. Some refrigerators. Cr cds: A, C, D, DS, JCB, MC, V.

D ⌧ ⌧ ⌧ SC

✔★ **KNIGHTS INN.** *1327 River Valley Blvd, at OH 33.* 614/687-4823; FAX 614/687-6276; res: 800/843-5644. 60 units, 7 kits. S, D $39-$49; each addl $6; under 18 free. Crib free. Pet accepted. TV; VCR avail (movies). Complimentary coffee in lobby. Restaurant adj 7 am-10 pm. Ck-out noon. Business servs avail. Cr cds: A, C, D, DS, ER, MC, V.

D ⌧ ⌧ ⌧ SC

Restaurant

★ ★ ★ **SHAW'S INN.** *123 N Broad St, downtown, ½ block N of Main St.* 614/654-1842. Hrs: 7-10:30 am, 11:30 am-2:30 pm, 5-10 pm; Sun 7 am-9 pm. Closed Jan 1, 2; Dec 24, 25. Res accepted. Bar. Wine list. Semi-a la carte: bkfst $3.25-$7.95, lunch $5.75-$12.95, dinner $8.95-$25. Specializes in stuffed chicken breast, prime rib, fresh seafood. Own baking. Outdoor dining. Cr cds: MC, V.

Lebanon (F-2)

(See also Cincinnati, Dayton, Mason, Middletown, Wilmington)

Settled 1796 **Pop** 10,453 **Elev** 769 ft **Area code** 513 **Zip** 45036

Information Chamber of Commerce, 120 E South St, Ste 201, phone 513/932-1100; or the Warren County Convention & Visitors Bureau, 1073 Oregonia Rd, phone 800/433-1072.

Some of the early settlers around Lebanon were Shakers who contributed much to the town's culture and economy. Though their community, Union Village, was sold over 50 years ago and is now a retirement home, local interest in the Shakers still thrives.

What to See and Do

Fort Ancient State Memorial (see). 7 mi SE on OH 350.

Glendower State Memorial (1836). Period furnishings, relics of area in Greek-revival mansion. (June-Aug, Wed-Sun; Sept-Oct, Sat & Sun) 105 Cincinnati Ave, US 42. Phone 513/932-1817 or 513/932-5366. ¢¢

Indiana & Ohio Old Time Passenger Train. Scenic train excursion. (May-Dec, Sat & Sun) For rates and schedule information, phone 513/631-INFO (recording); for reservation information, phone 513/398-8584 or 800/48-TRAIN. ¢¢¢

Valley Vineyards Winery. Tours of winery; wine tastings. (Daily; closed most major hols) 4 mi S on US 48 from I-71 then 3 mi NE on US 22. Phone 513/899-2485. **Free.**

Warren County Historical Society Museum. Historical museum portrays Warren County history from prehistoric times to present; includes exhibits of fossils and Native American artifacts; pioneer and period rooms; large indoor village green depicting 19th-century shops; extensive Shaker collection; library of historical, genealogical and Shaker material. (Daily exc Mon; closed hols) 105 S Broadway. Phone 513/932-1817. ¢¢

Annual Events

Warren County Fair. Mid-July.

Applefest. Farmers' market; crafts; entertainment; food. 4th Sat Sept.

Seasonal Event

Lebanon Raceway. Warren County Fairgrounds, OH 48N. Night harness racing. For details phone 513/932-4936. Mon, Tues, Fri & Sat. Sept-May.

Motels

★ **COUNTRYSIDE INN.** *(3802 Dry Run Rd, South Lebanon 45065)* off OH 48, E on Mason to Lebanon Rd. 513/494-1001; res: 800/905-8576. 24 rms, 1 story. June-Labor Day: S $60-$65; D $70-$85; lower rates rest of yr. Crib free. TV; cable. Pool. Complimentary coffee in lobby. Ck-out 11 am. Some refrigerators. Cr cds: DS, MC, V.

⌧ ⌧ SC

★ **KNIGHTS INN.** *725 E Main St, OH 123 at OH 48 Bypass.* 513/932-3034; res: 800/843-5644. 58 rms. May-Aug: S $55-$65; D $65-$75; each addl $5; kits. $70-$80; under 18 free; lower rates rest of yr. Crib free. TV; cable (premium). Pool. Complimentary coffee in lobby. Restaurant adj 6 am-11 pm. Ck-out 11 am. Meeting rms. Business servs avail. Microwaves in kits. Cr cds: A, C, D, DS, MC, V.

★★ **SHAKER INN.** *600 Cincinnati Ave (US 42 S). 513/932-7575; res: 800/752-6151.* Web www.lebanon-ohio.com/shaker-inn.html. 20 rms, 4 suites. Late May-early Sept: S $56-$58; D $62-$65; each addl $6; suites $75-$90; under 12 free; higher rates special events; lower rates rest of yr. Crib $4. TV; cable. Pool. Complimentary coffee in lobby. Ck-out 11 am. Refrigerators; microwaves avail. Cr cds: A, DS, MC, V.

Inn

✔★★★ **GOLDEN LAMB.** *27 S Broadway, at OH 63 & OH 123. 513/932-5065.* 18 rms, 4 story. S $65-$85; D $75-$100; each addl $10; suite $120. TV; cable. Complimentary continental bkfst. Restaurant (see GOLDEN LAMB INN). Bar. Ck-out 11 am. Business servs avail. Built 1803; rms furnished with antiques. Cr cds: A, C, D, DS, MC, V.

Restaurant

★★ **GOLDEN LAMB INN.** *(See Golden Lamb Inn) 513/932-5065.* Hrs: 11 am-3 pm, 5-9 pm; Sun noon-8 pm; early-bird dinner Mon-Fri 5-6:30 pm. Closed Dec 25. Res accepted. Bar. Semi-a la carte: lunch $8-$12, dinner $10-$20. Child's meals. Specialties: roast leg of spring lamb, roast turkey, roast duck. Antique furnishings. Cr cds: A, C, D, DS, MC, V.

Lima (C-2)

(See also Findlay, Van Wert, Wapakoneta)

Founded 1831 **Pop** 45,549 **Elev** 880 ft **Area code** 419 **Web** www.allencvb.lima.oh.us

Information Lima/Allen County Convention and Visitors Bureau, 147 N Main St, 45801; 419/222-6075 or 888/222-6075.

Lima is an industrial, agri-business and retail center.

What to See and Do

Allen County Museum. Pioneer and Native American relics; displays of fossils and minerals; railroad and street railway history; separate children's museum. Scale model of George Washington's home, Mount Vernon, in separate room. (Daily exc Mon; closed major hols) 620 W Market St. Phone 419/222-9426. **Free.**

Lincoln Park Railway Exhibit. DT & I Railroad depot, last steam locomotive built by the Lima works of Baldwin-Lima Hamilton; 1883 private car and 1882 caboose. (All yr, lighted at night) Lincoln Park, E Elm & Shawnee Sts. Free.

MacDonell House. Restored Victorian mansion, completely furnished in the style of the 1890s; listed in the National Register of Historical Places. (Daily exc Mon; closed major hols) 632 W Market St. Phone 419/224-1113. ¢

Annual Events

Square Fair/Summer Community Arts Festival. Town Square, downtown.Artists, craftsmen, ethnic food, entertainment. Phone 419/222-1096. 1st full wkend Aug.

Allen County Fair. Rides, games, livestock shows, entertainment, grandstand shows, night harness racing, displays and exhibits. Phone 419/228-7141. Late Aug.

Transportation Heritage Festival. Phone 419/222-6045. Sept.

Motor Hotel

★★★ **HOLIDAY INN.** *1920 Roschman Ave (45804). 419/222-0004; FAX 419/222-2176.* 150 rms, 4 story. S, D $86-$100; under 18 free. Crib free. Pet accepted. TV. Indoor pool; whirlpool. Playground. Restaurant 6:30 am-10 pm; Sat to 11 pm. Rm serv. Bar; entertainment Fri, Sat. Ck-out noon. Meeting rms. In-rm modem link. Sundries. Exercise equipt; weight machine, bicycles, sauna. Game rm. Rec rm. Microwaves avail. Balconies. Cr cds: A, C, D, DS, ER, JCB, MC, V.

Restaurant

✔★★ **TUDOR'S.** *2383 Elida Rd (45805). 419/331-2220.* Hrs: 11 am-10:30 pm; wkends to 11:30 pm. Closed Memorial Day, Labor Day, Dec 25. Res accepted. Bar. Semi-a la carte: lunch $3.99-$7.50, dinner $5.29-$12.99. Child's meals. Specializes in seafood, steak, barbecued ribs. Salad bar. English pub atmosphere. Family-owned. Cr cds: A, C, D, MC, V.

Lorain (B-4)

(For accommodations see Cleveland, Elyria, Oberlin, Sandusky; also see Vermilion)

Settled 1807 **Pop** 71,245 **Elev** 608 ft **Area code** 440 **E-mail** visitors@lcvb.org **Web** www.lcvb.org

Information Lorain County Visitors Bureau, 611 Broadway, 44052; 440/245-5282 or 800/334-1673.

This industrial city, on Lake Erie's south shore at the mouth of the Black River, has a fine harbor and nine major public parks. Struck by a devastating tornado in 1924, the city was rebuilt. Lorain is the birthplace of Admiral Ernest J. King, of World War II fame.

What to See and Do

Lakeview Park. A 50-acre park along lake shore. Large beach, bathhouse; boardwalk. Colored-light fountain; garden with 3,000 roses of 40 varieties; tennis, baseball, basketball, volleyball, lawn bowling. Ice-skating. Picnicking, playground, concessions. (Daily) W Erie Ave at Lakeview Dr. Phone 440/244-9000. **Free.**

Lorain Harbor. Innovative ore transfer facility regularly brings giant ore vessels to port. Several excellent vantage points for viewing (Lake Erie shipping season only).

Municipal Pier. Pier fishing; boat (launch); supplies (fuel, bait); concession. Phone 440/204-2269. **Small Boat Harbor,** Alabama Ave. (Daily) Foot of Oberlin Ave. Phone 440/244-9000. **Free.**

Annual Event

International Festival Week. Sheffield Shopping Ctr. Ten-day celebration of Lorain's ethnic diversity. Song, dance, crafts and foods of many nations; entertainers in ethnic costumes. Last wk June.

Mansfield (C-4)

(See also Mount Gilead, Mount Vernon)

Founded 1808 **Pop** 50,627 **Elev** 1,230 ft **Area code** 419 **E-mail** 76716.2602@compuserve.com

Information Mansfield/Richland County Convention & Visitors Bureau, 52 Park Ave W, 44902; 419/525-1300 or 800/642-8282.

The best view of Mansfield is from Ashland Hill across the Rocky Fork Valley. A pioneer log blockhouse, built as protection against the Native Americans in the War of 1812, still stands in South Park in the city's western section. Named for Jared Mansfield, United States Surveyor General, it is a diversified industrial center, 75 miles southwest of Cleveland. Pulitzer Prize-winning novelist Louis Bromfield was born here and later returned to conduct agricultural research at his 1,000-acre Malabar Farm.

What to See and Do

Clear Fork Reservoir. Fishing; boating (docks). Picnicking. Camping (Mar-Nov, fee). (Daily) 7 mi S on US 42, then W on OH 97. Phone 419/884-0166 (marina & camping information).   **Free.**

Kingwood Center and Gardens. Center has 47 acres of landscaped gardens, greenhouses and wooded property. French provincial mansion with horticultural library (Easter-Nov 1, Tues-Sat; also Sun afternoon; rest of yr, Tues-Sat; closed hols). Greenhouses and gardens (daily). Flower and art shows, special lectures, workshops throughout the yr. 900 Park Ave W. Phone 419/522-0211.   **Free.**

Malabar Farm State Park. Louis Bromfield's farm and house are within this 917-acre park. Fishing. Hiking, bridle trails, equestrian camp. Picnicking. Tractor-drawn wagon tour of farm; house tour. (Memorial Day-Labor Day, daily; Nov-Mar, daily exc Mon; closed some hols) (See ANNUAL EVENTS) 10 mi SE on OH 39, then S on OH 603 to Pleasant Valley Rd. Phone 419/892-2784. Tour   ¢¢

Muskingum Watershed Conservancy District. Charles Mill Lake Park. On 1,350-acre lake. Boating (10 hp limit). 9 mi E on OH 430. Phone 419/368-6885. **Pleasant Hill Lake Park.** 14 mi SE on OH 95, via OH 39 & 603. 850-acre lake. Boating (unlimited hp). Cabins. Activity center. Phone 419/938-7884. Both offer swimming; fishing; boating (ramp), marina. Playgrounds; picnicking. Camping (showers, flush toilets). (Daily) Pets on leash only. Per vehicle   ¢¢

Oak Hill Cottage (1847). With 7 gables, 5 double chimneys and 7 marble fireplaces, as well as all period furnishings of the 1800s, this restored house is considered one of the most perfect Gothic houses in the nation. (Apr-Dec, Sun afternoons; closed major hols) 310 Springmill St. Phone 419/524-1765.   ¢

Richland Carrousel Park. Features a wooden, hand-carved, hand-painted, turn-of-the-century-style carousel with 52 animals and 2 chariots. (Daily; closed major hols; may be closed for private functions, phone ahead to confirm availability) Corner 4th & Main Sts. Phone 419/522-4223. Carousel rides   ¢

Richland County Museum. Remodeled schoolhouse (ca 1847), two period rooms; local memorabilia, artifacts. (May-Oct, Sat & Sun) 7 mi SW on US 42, at 51 W Church St, in Lexington. Phone 419/884-2230. **Donation.**

Skiing.

Snow Trails. Six chairlifts; patrol, school, rentals; snowmaking; cafeteria, bar. (Dec-mid-Mar, daily) Cross-country and night skiing. Possum Run Rd, 5 mi S near jct OH 13, I-71. Phone 419/774-9818.   ¢¢¢¢¢

Clear Fork Ski Area. Area has quad, triple, double chairlifts, J-bar, 2 handle bars; patrol, school, rentals; snowmaking; cafeteria, bar. Longest run 2,000 ft; vertical drop 300 ft. (Nov-Mar, daily) 12 mi S on OH 13, then 7 mi SE on OH 97, then N on OH 95, in Butler. Phone 419/883-2000 or 800/237-5673 (snow conditions).   ¢¢¢¢¢

Annual Events

Ohio Winter Ski Carnival. Snow Trails Ski Resort. Costumes, queen contest, races, dance. Late Feb.

Richland County Fair. Fairgrounds, 750 N Home Rd. Flea market, circus; hardware and auto shows. Phone 419/747-3717. Mid-Aug.

Ohio Heritage Days. At Malabar Farm State Park. Celebration of the pioneer era with participants dressed in period clothing; apple butter-making, horse-drawn wagon rides, crafts displays, demonstrations; tour Bromfield house & farm. Phone 419/892-2784. Sept.

Seasonal Event

Auto racing. Mid-Ohio Sports Car Course. 6 mi S on US 42, then W on OH 97 to Steam Corners Rd. A 2.25-mi track. Phone 800/MID-OHIO or 419/884-4000. Usually May-Oct.

Motels

★ **BEST WESTERN INN.** *880 Laver Rd (44905), I-71 exit 176.* 419/589-2200; FAX 419/589-5624. 105 rms, 2 story. S $47-$65; D $47-$77; each addl $6; under 18 free; higher rates: special events, summer wkends. Crib free. Pet accepted. TV; cable (premium). Pool. Restaurant 6-11 am, 5-9 pm. Rm serv. Bar 5 pm-2 am. Ck-out noon. Meeting rms. Business servs avail. Cr cds: A, C, D, DS, MC, V.

D ✔ ≈ ≈ ⅍ **SC**

★★ **COMFORT INN NORTH.** *500 N Trimble Rd (44906).* 419/529-1000; FAX 419/529-2953. 114 rms, 2 story, 22 suites. S $58-$63; D $63-$68; each addl $5; suites $72-$88; under 18 free; higher rates auto racing wkends. Crib free. Pet accepted, some restrictions. TV; cable. Indoor pool. Complimentary continental bkfst. Restaurant adj 11 am-10 pm; Fri, Sat to 11 pm. Rm serv. Bar. Ck-out noon. Coin lndry. Meeting rms. Business servs avail. In-rm modem link. Sundries. Downhill/x-country ski 20 mi. Refrigerators in suites. Cr cds: A, C, D, DS, ER, JCB, MC, V.

D ✔ ≈ ≈ ⅍ **SC**

✔★ **KNIGHTS INN.** *555 N Trimble Rd (44906), just off US 30.* 419/529-2100; FAX 419/529-6679; res: 800/843-5644. 110 rms. S $35-$45; D $47-$55; each addl $5; kit. units $57-$65; under 16 free; higher rates auto races. Crib free. Pet accepted. TV; cable (premium); VCR (movies). Pool. Complimentary continental bkfst. Restaurant adj 6 am-midnight. Ck-out noon. Business servs avail. Valet serv. Sundries. Cr cds: A, C, D, DS, MC, V.

D ✔ ≈ ≈ ⅍ **SC**

✔★ **TRAVELODGE.** *90 Hanley Rd (OH 13) (44904).* 419/756-7600. 93 rms, 2 story. S $40-$47; D $42-$59; each addl $5; kit. units $52-$62; higher rates auto racing wkends; under 18 free. Crib free. Pet accepted. TV; cable. Pool. Coffee in rms. Restaurant open 24 hrs. Ck-out noon. Meeting rms. Business servs avail. Downhill/x-country ski 2 mi. Cr cds: A, C, D, DS, ER, JCB, MC, V.

✔ ≈ ≈ ⅍ **SC**

Hotel

★ **HOLIDAY INN.** *116 Park Ave W (44902).* 419/525-6000; FAX 419/525-0197. 158 rms, 7 story. S $64-$110; D $70-$110; each addl $6; suites $125-$225; under 18 free; ski plan; higher rates special events. Crib free. TV; cable (premium). Indoor pool; whirlpool. Coffee in rms. Restaurant 6:30 am-2 pm, 5-10 pm. Bar 11 am-midnight. Ck-out noon. Meeting rms. Business servs avail. In-rm modem link. Downhill ski 7 mi. Exercise equipt; weights, treadmill, sauna. Some refrigerators. Minibars. Cr cds: A, C, D, DS, ER, JCB, MC, V.

D ≈ ≈ ⚞ ⅍ **SC**

Marietta (F-5)

Founded 1788 **Pop** 15,026 **Elev** 616 ft **Area code** 614 **Zip** 45750

Information Tourist and Convention Bureau, 316 3rd St; 614/373-5178 or 800/288-2577.

General Rufus Putnam's New England flotilla, arriving at the junction of the Muskingum and Ohio rivers for western land-buying purposes, founded Marietta, the oldest settlement in Ohio. Its name is a tribute to Queen Marie Antoinette for French assistance to the American Revolution. Most of the landmarks are along the east side of the Muskingum River. Front St is approximately the eastern boundary of the first stockade, which was called Picketed Point. Later the fortification called Campus Martius was erected and housed General Putnam, Governor St Clair and other public officials.

One of the most important Ohio River ports in steamboat days, Marietta today is a beautiful tree-filled town and the home of Marietta College and manufacturers producing oil, plastics, rubber, paints, glass, dolls, safes and concrete. Information for Wayne National Forest (see IRONTON) may be obtained from the National Forest Service office in Marietta.

What to See and Do

Campus Martius, Museum of the Northwest Territory. Rufus Putnam home, which was part of the original Campus Martius Fort (1788); furnished with pioneer articles. On grounds is the Ohio Company Land Office (1788); restored and furnished. (Mar-Apr & Oct-Nov, Wed-Sun; May-Sept, daily; closed Thanksgiving) 601 2nd St & Washington St. Phone 614/373-3750. ¢¢

Industrial tours.

Rossi Pasta. Pasta makers for many fine stores offer opportunity (limited) to watch the process in factory. (Mon-Sat, also Sun afternoon; closed major hols) Also retail outlet. 114 Greene St, at Front St. For tour schedule phone 614/373-5155 or 800/227-6774. **Free.**

Fenton Art Glass Co. Handmade pressed and blown glassware. Free 45-min guided tours (Mon-Fri; closed hols, also 1st 2 wks July). Must wear shoes; no children under two. Gift shop & outlet on premises; also museum with film of tour (daily; closed major hols). 420 Caroline Ave in Williamstown, WV, across Ohio River, off I-77 exit 185. Phone 304/375-7772. Museum ¢

Mound Cemetery. A 30-ft-high conical mound stands in the cemetery where 24 Revolutionary War officers are buried. 5th & Scammel Sts.

Sacra Via St. Built originally by Mound Builders as "sacred way" to Muskingum River. Extends from Muskingum River to Elevated Square.

Muskingum Park. Riverfront common where Arthur St Clair was inaugurated first governor of the Northwest Territory in 1788; monument to westward migration sculpted by Gutzon Borglum. Between Front St & the Muskingum River, N of Putnam St.

Ohio River Museum State Memorial. Exhibits on history and development of inland waterways (May-Sept, daily; Mar-Apr & Oct-Nov, Wed-Sun; closed Thanksgiving). Steamboat *W.P. Snyder, Jr* (1918) is moored on Muskingum River; guided tours (Apr-Oct). Front & St Clair Sts. Phone 614/373-3717. ¢¢

Trolley tours. One-hr narrated tours of Marietta aboard turn-of-the-century style trolley. (July-Aug, daily exc Mon; mid-late June, Thurs-Sun; May-mid June & Sept-Oct, wkends) 127 Ohio St. For schedule, reservations phone 614/374-2233. ¢¢¢

Valley Gem **Sternwheeler.** Excursions on the Ohio and Muskingum rivers aboard sternwheeler *Valley Gem*. (June-Aug, daily exc Mon; May & Sept-Oct, wkends only) Phone 614/373-7862. Regular rides ¢¢

Annual Events

Ohio River Sternwheel Festival. Ohio Riverfront Park. Sternwheel races, fireworks, entertainment on riverfront; several sternwheel boats from across the nation. Phone Tourist and Convention Bureau for details. Wkend after Labor Day.

Indian Summer Arts and Crafts Festival. Washington County Fairgrounds, 901 Front St. Displays and demonstrations of new and traditional crafts and artwork; musicians; food; children's activities. Phone 614/373-8027. Late Sept.

Seasonal Event

Showboat *Becky Thatcher.* Rear of 237 Front St. Permanently docked sternwheeler presents showboat melodrama on its first deck. Restaurant and lounge occupy the second and third decks. Theater season may vary; phone 614/373-6033 for schedule. Late June-late Aug.

Motels

✔★ **BEST WESTERN.** *279 Muskingum Dr, I-77 exit 6.* 614/374-7211. 47 rms, 1-2 story. S $40-$50; D $50-$60; each addl $5; under 12 free. Crib free. TV; cable. Complimentary continental bkfst. Restaurant nearby. Ck-out noon. Business servs avail. Sundries. Health club privileges. Refrigerators. Picnic tables, grill. On Muskingum River; free dockage. Cr cds: A, C, D, DS, MC, V.

🏊 ⌦ 🐾 SC

★ **ECONO LODGE.** *702 Pike St, I-77 exit 1.* 614/374-8481. 48 rms, 2 story. S, D $50-$60; each addl $5. Crib free. TV; cable (premium). Pool. Complimentary continental bkfst. Restaurant nearby. Ck-out noon. Business servs avail. Cr cds: A, C, D, DS, JCB, MC, V.

D ⌦ ⌦ 🐾 SC

★ ★ **HOLIDAY INN.** *701 Pike St, I-77 exit 1.* 614/374-9660; FAX 614/373-1762. 109 rms, 2 story. S, D $49-$80; under 19 free. Crib free. TV; cable (premium). VCR avail. Pool; wading pool. Restaurant 6:30 am-2 pm, 5-10 pm; Sat, Sun from 7 am. Rm serv. Bar 4 pm-2 am; entertainment exc Sun. Ck-out noon. Meeting rms. Business servs avail. In-rm modem link. Valet serv. Sundries. Airport transportation. Cr cds: A, C, D, DS, JCB, MC, V.

D ⌦ ⌦ 🐾 SC

✔★ **KNIGHTS INN.** *506 Pike St, I-77 exit 1.* 614/373-7373; FAX 614/373-9466; res: 800/526-5947. 111 rms, 15 kit. units. S $37.95-$46.95; D $43.95-$58.95; first addl $5; kit. units $43.95-$62.95; under 18 free. Crib free. TV; cable (premium), VCR avail (movies $6). Pool. Complimentary coffee. Restaurant adj 6 am-10 pm. Business servs avail. In-rm modem link. Cr cds: A, C, D, DS, ER, MC, V.

D ⌦ ⌦ 🐾 SC

Hotel

★ ★ **LAFAYETTE.** *101 Front St, I-77 exit 1.* 614/373-5522; FAX 614/373-4684; res: 800/331-9336 (exc OH), 800/331-9337 (OH). 79 rms, 5 story. S, D $65; each addl $5; suites $70-$250; under 14 free. Crib free. TV; cable. Restaurant 6:30 am-10 pm. Bar 11-2 am. Ck-out noon. Meeting rms. Business servs avail. Gift shop. Free airport transportation. Health club privileges. Some balconies. On Ohio River. Cr cds: A, C, D, DS, MC, V.

D ⌦ 🐾 SC

Marion (D-3)

(See also Delaware, Mount Gilead)

Settled 1820 **Pop** 34,075 **Elev** 956 ft **Area code** 614 **Zip** 43302 **E-mail** evers@on-ramp.net **Web** marion.net

Information Marion Area Convention & Visitors Bureau, 1952 Marion-Mt. Gilead Rd, Suite 121; 614/389-9770 or 800/371-6688.

Marion's beginnings are due to Jake Foos, a chainman on a party surveying the territory for a proposed road in 1808. Thirsty after a meal of salt bacon, he discovered a spring. From then on the area became a stopping place for travelers. Originally named Jacob's Well for this reason, it was renamed for General Francis Marion, the "Swamp Fox" of the Revolutionary War.

Both agricultural and industrial, Marion's growth was largely influenced by the Huber Manufacturing Company, which introduced the steam shovel (1874), and Marion Power Shovels, now known as Dresser Industries. Marion is also the center of a major popcorn-producing area in the US. Its best-known citizen was Warren G. Harding, owner and publisher of the *Star*. Later he became a state senator, lieutenant governor and 29th President of the United States.

What to See and Do

Carousel Concepts. Working museum; view woodworkers carving carousel horses. (Daily) 2209 Marion-Waldo Rd. Phone 614/389-9755 or 800/279-8868. ¢¢

Harding Memorial. A ten-acre area with rows of maple trees that create the shape of a Latin cross. The circular monument is made of white Georgia marble and contains the stone coffins of Harding and his wife. Grounds (daily). Delaware Ave & Vernon Heights Blvd. **Free.**

President Harding's Home and Museum. Built during Harding's courtship with Florence Mabel Kling and where they were married in 1891. Harding administered much of his 1920 "front porch campaign" for presidency from the front of the house; the museum, at the rear of the house, was once used as the campaign's press headquarters. (Memorial Day wkend-Labor Day wkend, Wed-Sun; Apr-May, by appt; after Labor Day-Oct, Sat & Sun) 380 Mt Vernon Ave. Phone 614/387-9630. ¢¢

Stengel True Museum. Displays include Native American artifacts; china and glassware; firearms; antique watches, clocks; toys; utensils. Under age 12 with adult only. (Sat & Sun afternoons; other times by appt; closed Easter, Dec 25) 504 S State St. Phone 614/387-6140 or 614/382-2826. **Free.**

Annual Events

Marion County Fair. Late June-early July.

US Open Drum and Bugle Corps Competition. Harding High School Stadium. Phone 614/387-6736. Aug.

Popcorn Festival. Tours, food, entertainment. 1st wkend after Labor Day.

Motels

★ **COMFORT INN.** *256 Jamesway, 3 mi E on OH 95 exit 95.* 614/389-5552. 56 rms, 2 story. May-Oct: S $54-$80; D $54-$90; each addl $6; suites $65-$95; under 18 free; higher rates special events; lower rates rest of yr. Crib $6. Pet accepted, some restrictions; $6. TV; cable (premium). Complimentary continental bkfst. Restaurant opp 5 am-11 pm. Ck-out 11 am. Business servs avail. Indoor pool; whirlpool. Game rm. Refrigerator, microwave in suites. Cr cds: A, D, DS, MC, V.

[symbols] SC

★ **HARDING MOTOR LODGE.** *1065 Delaware Ave.* 614/383-6771; FAX 614/383-6733; res: 800/563-4399. 99 rms, 2 story. S, D $45; each addl $6; suites $71.25; under 18 free. Crib free. Pet accepted; $5. TV; cable (premium). Complimentary coffee in lobby. Ck-out noon.

In-rm modem link. Coin lndry. Valet serv. Microwaves avail. Cr cds: A, C, D, DS, MC, V.

[symbols] SC

✔★ **TRAVELODGE.** *1952 Marion-Mt Gilead Rd.* 614/389-4671; FAX 614/389-4671, ext. 101. 90 rms, 2 story. S $45-$60; D $47-$65; each addl $6; suites $60-$79; under 18 free. Crib free. Pet accepted; $3-$6. TV; cable (premium), VCR avail. Pool. Complimentary coffee in rms. Restaurant nearby. Ck-out noon. Meeting rms. Business servs avail. In-rm modem link. Valet serv. Health club privileges. Microwaves avail. Picnic tables. Cr cds: A, C, D, DS, ER, JCB, MC, V.

[symbols] SC

Mason (F-1)

(See also Cincinnati, Dayton, Hamilton, Lebanon, Middletown)

Pop 11,452 **Elev** 800 ft **Area code** 513 **Zip** 45040 **E-mail** mlkcoc@eos.net

Information Mason Area Chamber of Commerce, 316 W Main St; 513/398-2188.

What to See and Do

Golf Center at Kings Island. Two golf courses designed by Jack Nicklaus and architect Desmond Muirhead (fee). Grizzly Course, home of the Senior PGA Classic, features the famed 546-yard 18th hole. The 18-hole Bruin, a mid-length version of the Grizzly, features 7 par-4 holes. Also includes a tennis stadium that seats 10,500 for the ATP Championship. Restaurant, lounge, pro shop, driving range (fee) and tennis courts (fee). (Mar-Dec, daily) 6042 Fairway Dr. Phone 513/398-7700 (tee reservations) or 513/398-5200 (office).

⊞ **Paramount's Kings Island.** Premier seasonal family theme park. 350-acre facility with more than 100 rides and attractions. Includes "The Outer Limits" thrill ride and "Flight of Fear," an indoor roller coaster. (Late May-early Sept, daily; mid-Apr-late May, wkends; also selected wkends early Sept-Oct) I-71 to Kings Mills Rd exit. Phone 513/573-5700 or 800/288-0808. Two-day ticket avail. ¢¢¢¢

The Beach Waterpark. Offers 30 water slides and attractions on 35 acres, including The Aztec Adventure watercoaster and Thunder Beach, a 750,000-gallon wave pool and Lazy Miami, a meandering river slowly winding through the park. Two sand volleyball courts. A children's activity area with pools, slides and mini-waterfall. Picnic area; restaurants. (Memorial Day wkend-Labor Day, daily) 2590 Waterpark Dr, W of I-71 at Kings Mills Rd exit 25, opp Paramount's Kings Island. Phone 513/398-7946 or 800/886-7946. ¢¢¢¢

Motels

★ **BEST WESTERN KINGS ISLAND.** *9847 Escort Dr, I-71 exit 19.* 513/398-3633; FAX 513/398-3633, ext. 301. 124 rms, 2 story. S, D $49-$150; under 12 free; higher rates special events. Crib free. TV; cable (premium). Pool. Playground. Complimentary coffee. Restaurant nearby. Ck-out 11 am. Business servs avail. Game rm. Cr cds: A, C, D, DS, MC, V.

[symbols] SC

✔★ **DAYS INN KINGS ISLAND.** *9735 Mason-Montgomery Rd, at I-71 exit 19.* 513/398-3297; FAX 513/398-3297, ext. 302. 124 rms, 2 story. S, D $39-$129; higher rates for special events. Crib free. Pet accepted, some restrictions. TV; cable (premium). Pool. Playground. Complimentary continental bkfst. Restaurant adj. Ck-out 11 am. Meeting rms. Business servs avail. Game rm. Cr cds: A, C, D, DS, MC, V.

[symbols] SC

★★ **HOLIDAY INN-NORTHEAST.** *9845 Escort Dr, at I-71 exit 19.* 513/398-8015; FAX 513/398-0822. 104 rms, 2 story. S, D $79-$110;

under 19 free. Crib free. Pet accepted. TV; cable (premium). Pool. Playground. Restaurant 6:30 am-2 pm, 5-10 pm. Rm serv. Bar 6-11 pm; closed Sun. Ck-out noon. Meeting rms. Business servs avail. In-rm modem link. Cr cds: A, C, D, DS, JCB, MC, V.

★ HOUSTON. *4026 OH 42. 513/398-7277; res: 800/732-4741.* 42 rms, 6 suites. June-Labor Day: S $64.95-$67.95; D $66.95-$69.95; each addl $6; under 12 free; lower rates rest of yr. Crib free. TV; cable (premium). Pool. Restaurant adj 3:30-10 pm; Fri, Sat to 10:30 pm. Ck-out 11 am. Refrigerators avail. Cr cds: A, C, D, DS, MC, V.

Motor Hotel

★ ★ ★ KINGS ISLAND INN. *(5691 Kings Island Dr, Kings Island 45034)* I-71 Kings Mills Rd exit. *513/398-0115; FAX 513/398-1095; res: 800/727-3050.* 288 rms, 2 story. Memorial Day-Labor Day: S, D $99-$145; under 18 free; lower rates rest of yr. Crib free. TV; cable (premium). 2 pools, 1 indoor; whirlpool. Playground. Coffee in rms. Restaurant 7 am-2 pm, 5-10 pm. Rm serv. Bar 11:30-1 am, Sun 1pm-midnight; entertainment. Ck-out 11 am. Meeting rms. Business servs avail. In-rm modem link. Bellhops. Valet serv. Sundries. Gift shop. Tennis. Putting green. Game rm. Many private patios, balconies. Cr cds: A, C, D, DS, MC, V.

Restaurant

✔★ ★ HOUSTON INN. *4026 US 42. 513/398-7377.* Hrs: 3:30-10 pm; Fri, Sat to 10:30 pm; Sun 11 am-8 pm. Closed Mon; some major hols. Bar. Semi-a la carte: dinner $9-$16 Specializes in frogs' legs, seafood, steak. Salad bar. Antiques. Family-owned. Cr cds: A, C, D, DS, MC, V.

Massillon (C-5)

(For accommodations see Akron, Canton, New Philadelphia, Wooster)

Founded 1826 **Pop** 31,007 **Elev** 1,015 ft **Area code** 330 **Zip** 44646
Information Chamber of Commerce, 137 Lincoln Way E; 330/833-3146.

Massillon is an industrial center on the Tuscarawas River in northeastern Ohio.

What to See and Do

Canal Fulton and Museum. *St Helena III,* a replica of mule-drawn canal boat of the mid-19th century, takes 45-min trip on the Ohio-Erie Canal. Leaves Canal Fulton Park (June-Aug, daily; mid-May-late May & early Sept-mid-Sept, wkends only). 6 mi NW on OH 21, then 1 mi NE on OH 93. Phone 330/854-3808 or 800/HELENA-3. ¢¢¢

Massillon Museum. Historical and art exhibits. (Tues-Sat; also Sun afternoons; closed major hols) 121 Lincoln Way E. Phone 330/833-4061. **Free.**

Spring Hill (1821). Historic 19th-century home includes basement kitchen and dining rm, secret stairway, original furnishings; on grounds are springhouse, smokehouse, woolhouse and milkhouse; picnicking. (June-Aug, Wed-Sun; Apr-May & Sept-Oct, by appt) 1401 Spring Hill Lane NE, OH 241. Phone 330/833-6749. ¢¢

The Wilderness Center. Nature center on 573 acres includes 6 nature trails, 7½-acre lake, 23-ft observation platform; picnicking. Interpretive building (daily exc Mon; closed major hols). Grounds (daily). 5 mi S on US 21, then 8 mi SW on US 62 to Wilmot, then 1 mi NW on US 250. Phone 330/359-5235. **Donation.**

Mentor (B-5)

(See also Chardon, Cleveland, Geneva-on-the-Lake, Painesville)

Founded 1799 **Pop** 47,358 **Elev** 690 ft **Area code** 440 **Zip** 44060
Information Mentor Area Chamber of Commerce, 7547 Mentor Ave, Rm 302; 440/946-2625.

Site of the first Lake County settlement, Mentor was once an agricultural center. James A. Garfield resided here before his election as US president. Mentor serves as a retail trade center.

What to See and Do

Headlands Beach State Park. A 125-acre park with 1-mi-long beach on shore of Lake Erie. Swimming, lifeguard (Memorial Day-Labor Day, Fri-Sun); fishing. Picnicking, concessions. OH 44 N, to Lake Erie. Phone 440/257-1330. Per vehicle ¢¢

🟦 **Lawnfield (James A. Garfield National Historic Site).** Garfield's last house before the White House. Two floors of original furnishings; memorial library contains Garfield's books, desk. On grounds are campaign office, carriage house (both closed to the public) and picnic area. (Sat, Sun; closed some major hols) 8095 Mentor Ave, US 20. Phone 440/255-8722. ¢¢

The Holden Arboretum. Approx 7,000 varieties of plants on 3,100 acres; forests, lakes; hiking trails, picnic facilities; wildlife sanctuary; reception center. (Daily exc Mon; closed Jan 1, Dec 25) 9500 Sperry Rd, 5 mi SE; S of jct OH 306, I-90; 1 mi S to Kirtland-Chardon Rd, E 4 mi to Sperry Rd. Phone 440/946-4400. ¢¢

Wildwood Cultural Center. English Tudor Revival manor house listed on National Register of Historic Places. (Mon-Fri; closed hols) 7645 Little Mountain Rd. Phone 440/974-5735. **Free.**

Motel

★ ★ FAIRFIELD INN BY MARRIOTT-WILLOUGHBY. *(35110 Maple Grove Rd, Willoughby 44094)* E of Cleveland on I-90, exit 189 (OH 91), N on OH 91 to Maple Grove Rd. *440/975-9922.* 134 rms, 3 story. June-Aug: S, D $55-$70; lower rates rest of yr. Crib free. TV; cable (premium), VCR avail (movies). Heated pool. Complimentary continental bkfst. Restaurant opp 6 am-11 pm. Ck-out noon. Business servs avail. In-rm modem link. Health club privileges. Cr cds: A, C, D, DS, MC, V.

Motor Hotels

★ ★ CLARION-EAST. *(35000 Curtis Blvd, Eastlake 44095)* approx 5 mi W on OH 2, at SOM Center Rd (OH 91). *440/953-8000; FAX 440/953-1706.* 115 rms, 5 story. Apr-Oct: S, D $115-$125; each addl $10; suites $95-$150; under 18 free; higher rates Dec 31; lower rates rest of yr. Crib free. TV; cable (premium). Indoor pool; poolside serv. Restaurant 7 am-10 pm. Rm serv. Bar 2 pm-midnight; entertainment. Ck-out noon. Meeting rms. Business center. Valet serv. Sundries. Exercise equipt; weights, treadmill, sauna. Some bathrm phones; refrigerator, minibar in suites. Cr cds: A, C, D, DS, ER, JCB, MC, V.

★ ★ ★ HARLEY HOTEL-EAST. *(6051 SOM Center Rd, Willoughby 44094)* at jct I-90 & OH 91. *440/944-4300; FAX 440/944-5344.* 146 rms, 2 story. S, D $112-$129; under 18 free; wkend plans. Crib free. TV; cable (premium). 2 pools, 1 indoor; wading pool. Complimentary coffee. Restaurant 6:30 am-2:30 pm, 5-10 pm; Fri-Sun 7 am-11 pm. Bar 11:30-midnight; Fri, Sat to 1 am; Sun 1-9 pm. Ck-out 11 am. Coin lndry. Meeting rms. Business servs avail. In-rm modem link. Lighted tennis. Golf privileges ¼ mi. Downhill ski 18 mi; x-country ski 1 mi. Sauna. Health club privileges. Lawn games. Some refrigerators. Cr cds: A, D, DS, MC, V.

Restaurant

★ ★ **MOLINARI'S.** *8900 Mentor Ave (US 20).* 440/974-2750. Hrs: 11:30 am-2 pm, 5:30-10 pm; Mon to 2 pm; Fri, Sat to 11 pm. Closed Sun; some major hols. Res accepted. Northern Italian, California menu. Bar. Semi-a la carte: lunch $6.95-$8.95, dinner $11.95-$19.95. Specializes in pasta, rack of lamb, veal chops. Jazz Fri-Sat. Open kitchen. Contemporary decor. Cr cds: A, C, D, DS, MC, V.

Miamisburg (E-1)

(See also Dayton)

Pop 17,834 **Elev** 690 ft **Area code** 937 **Zip** 45342
Information South Metro Chamber of Commerce, 1410 B Miamisburg Centerville Rd, Centerville, 45459; 937/433-2032.

Motels

★ ★ **COURTYARD BY MARRIOTT.** *100 Prestige Place, E of I-75 exit 44.* 937/433-3131; FAX 937/433-0285. 146 rms, 3 story, 12 suites. S, D $87-$97; suites $109-$129; under 18 free; wkend rates. Crib free. TV; cable (premium). Indoor pool; whirlpool. Complimentary coffee in rms. Restaurant 6:30-10:30 am; Sat, Sun 7-11 am. Bar Mon-Thurs 5-10 pm. Ck-out 1 pm. Coin lndry. Meeting rms. Business servs avail. Valet serv. Sundries. Exercise equipt; weight machine, bicycles. Health club privileges. Refrigerator in suites. Cr cds: A, C, D, DS, MC, V.

★ **KNIGHTS INN.** *185 Byers Rd, just W of I-75 exit 44.* 937/859-8797; FAX 937/746-9109; res: 800/843-5644. 161 rms, 22 kit. units. S $37.95-$41.95; D $42.95-$46.95; kit. units $46.95-$48.95; under 18 free. Crib free. Pet accepted, some restrictions. TV; cable (premium). Pool. Complimentary continental bkfst. Restaurant adj open 24 hrs. Ck-out noon. Meeting rms. Some refrigerators. Cr cds: A, C, D, DS, MC, V.

✔★ **RED ROOF INN-DAYTON SOUTH.** *222 Byers Rd, just off I-75 exit 44.* 937/866-0705; FAX 937/866-0700. 107 rms, 2 story. S $35.99-$55.99; D $48.99-$56.99; each addl $7; under 18 free. Crib free. Pet accepted, some restrictions. TV; cable (premium). Ck-out noon. Business servs avail. In-rm modem link. Cr cds: A, C, D, DS, MC, V.

★ ★ **RESIDENCE INN BY MARRIOTT.** *155 Prestige Place, E of I-75 exit 44.* 937/434-7881; FAX 937/434-9308. 96 suites, 2 story. 1-bedrm suites $97-$125; 2-bedrm suites $120-$150. Crib free. Pet accepted; $10. TV; cable (premium). VCR avail (movies). Heated pool; whirlpool. Complimentary continental bkfst. Restaurant nearby. Ck-out noon. Coin lndry. Business servs avail. Valet serv. Health club privileges. Fireplaces. Balconies. Picnic tables, grills. Cr cds: A, C, D, DS, JCB, MC, V.

Motor Hotel

★ ★ **HOLIDAY INN-DAYTON MALL.** *31 Prestige Plaza Dr, off I-75 exit 44.* 937/434-8030; FAX 937/434-6452. 197 rms, 3 story. S, D $85-$95; under 18 free; wkend plans; higher rates special events. Crib free. TV; cable (premium). VCR avail. 2 pools, 1 indoor; wading pool. Coffee in rms. Restaurant 6:30 am-2 pm, 5-10 pm; Fri, Sat to 11 pm. Rm serv 2 pm-11 pm. Bar 11-1 am, wkend hrs vary; entertainment. Ck-out 11 am. Coin lndry. Meeting rms. Business servs avail. In-rm modem link.

Bellhops. Sundries. Putting green. Exercise equipt; treadmill, stair machine. Health club privileges. Game rm. Cr cds: A, C, D, DS, JCB, MC, V.

Inn

★ ★ ★ **ENGLISH MANOR.** *505 E Linden Ave.* 937/866-2288; res: 800/676-9456. 5 rms, 2 share bath, 3 story. No rm phones. S, D $65-$95. TV in sitting rm; cable. Complimentary full bkfst. Restaurant nearby. Ck-out 11 am, ck-in 3 pm. Restored Tudor-style mansion (1924); antiques. Totally nonsmoking. Cr cds: A, D, DS, MC, V.

Restaurants

✔★ **ALEX'S.** *125 Monarch Lane, I-75 exit 44, 2 mi W.* 937/866-2266. Hrs: 5-10 pm; Fri, Sat to 11 pm; early-bird dinner Mon-Fri 5-7 pm. Closed Sun; major hols. Res accepted. Bar to midnight; wknds to 1 am. Semi-a la carte: dinner from $7.95. Child's meals. Specializes in prime rib, steak, fresh seafood. Piano bar wkends. Cr cds: A, C, D, MC, V.

★ **BULLWINKLE'S TOP HAT BISTRO.** *19 N Main St.* 937/859-7677. Hrs: 11 am-11 pm; Fri to midnight; Sat noon-midnight. Closed Sun; major hols. Res accepted. Bar. Semi-a la carte: lunch $5.49-$6.95, dinner $8.25-$14.59. Child's meals. Specializes in baby back ribs, chicken, fish. Patrons may grill own entree. Cr cds: A, C, D, DS, MC, V.

★ ★ **PEERLESS MILL INN.** *319 S 2nd St.* 937/866-5968. Hrs: 5-9 pm; Fri, Sat to 10 pm; Sun 1-7 pm; Sun brunch 10 am-2 pm. Closed Mon; Jan 1, July 4, Dec 25. Res accepted. Bar. Semi-a la carte: dinner $12.95-$18.95. Sun brunch $10.95. Child's meals. Specializes in fresh seafood, roast duckling, prime rib. Own baking. Pianist wkends. Converted flour mill (1828). Cr cds: A, C, D, ER, MC, V.

Middletown (Butler Co) (F-1)

(For accommodations see Cincinnati, Dayton, Lebanon, Mason, Oxford)

Pop 46,022 **Elev** 650 ft **Area code** 513 **Zip** 45042 **E-mail** 6middle @infinet.com **Web** www.middletown.com/mcvb
Information Middletown Convention & Visitors Bureau, 30 City Centre Plaza; 513/422-3030 or 888/6-MIDDLE.

What to See and Do

Americana Amusement Park. Over 100 rides, shows and attractions, including 2 roller coasters and log flume; also pony rides, petting zoo; swimming. (June-Aug, daily; Apr-May & Sept, wkends only) 5757 Middletown-Hamilton Rd. Phone 800/486-3070 ¢¢¢¢ All-day ride pass ¢¢¢¢

Sorg Opera Company. Annually produces 3 major operas, fully staged with orchestra. 63 S Main St. Phone 513/425-0180. ¢¢¢¢

Annual Event

MiddFest. Celebrates international arts, history, culture, sports, and food. Phone 513/425-7707. 1st wkend Oct.

Motel

★ ★ **FAIRFIELD INN BY MARRIOTT.** 6750 Roosevelt Pkwy (45044), 1/4 mi W of I-75 exit 32 (OH 122). 513/424-5444. 57 rms, 3 story, 8 suites. S $62.95-$72.95; D $67.95-$77.95; each addl $5; suites $72.95-$82.95; under 18 free; higher rates special events. Crib free. TV; cable (premium), VCR avail. Complimentary continental bkfst. Restaurant adj 6 am-10 pm. Ck-out noon. Business servs avail. Valet serv (Mon-Fri). Indoor pool; whirlpool. Game rm. Refrigerator, microwave in suites. Cr cds: A, C, D, DS, MC, V.

D ➟ ⊱ 🔥 SC

Motor Hotel

★ ★ **MANCHESTER INN AND CONFERENCE CENTER.** 1027 Manchester Ave, downtown. 513/422-5481; res: 800/523-9126; FAX 513/422-4615. Web www.middletown.com/maninn. 79 rms, some with shower only, 5 story, 16 suites. S, D $64-$98; each addl $8; suites $84-$149; under 18 free; hol rates. Crib free. Pet accepted; $8/day. TV; cable, VCR avail. Complimentary coffee in rms. Restaurant 6:30 am-10 pm; Sat 8 am-11 pm; Sun 8 am-9 pm. Rm serv. Bar; entertainment Fri. Ck-out noon. Meeting rms. Business servs avail. In-rm modem link. Bellhops. Valet serv (Mon-Fri). Gift shop. Health club privileges. Refrigerator, microwave in suites. Microwaves avail. Cr cds: A, C, D, DS, MC, V.

D ➥ ⊱ 🔥 SC

Restaurant

✔ ★ **DAMON'S.** 4750 Roosevelt Blvd (45044), 1 1/2 mi W on OH 122. 513/423-8805. Hrs: 11 am-11 pm; Fri, Sat to midnight; Sun to 10 pm. Closed major hols. Res accepted Sun-Thurs. Bar. Semi-a la carte: lunch $4.50-$6.50, dinner $8-$15. Child's meals. Specializes in ribs, seafood. Club decor with sports memorabilia. Cr cds: A, C, D, DS, MC, V.

D ⊱

Milan (B-4)

(See also Bellevue, Oberlin, Sandusky)

Founded 1817 **Pop** 1,464 **Elev** 602 ft **Area code** 419 **Zip** 44846
Information Chamber of Commerce, PO Box 544, 419/499-2001.

Milan was founded by settlers from Connecticut, and many homes here bear the mark of New England architecture. A canal connecting the town with Lake Erie was built in 1839, making Milan one of the largest shipping centers in the Midwest at that time.

What to See and Do

Galpin Wildlife and Bird Sanctuary. Woodland with many varieties of trees, wildflowers and birds; nature trail. (Daily) 1/2 mi SE on Edison Dr. **Free.**

Milan Historical Museum. House of Dr. Lehman Galpin, Edison family doctor. Contains nationally known glass collection; doll collection; Native American artifacts; gun room, blacksmith shop, general store. (Apr-Oct, daily exc Mon) 10 Edison Dr. Phone 419/499-2968. **Donation.** Nearby are

Newton Memorial Arts Building. Displays include collections of antiques, fine arts, needlepoint & laces, netsukes (ornamental buttons or figures of ivory or wood, used to attach a purse or other article to a sash). (Apr-Oct) 10 Edison Dr. Phone 419/499-2968. **Donation.**

Sayles House. Restoration of mid-19th century home. (Apr-Oct) 10 Edison Dr at Front St. Phone 419/499-2968. **Donation.**

Thomas A. Edison Birthplace Museum. Two-story red brick house where the inventor spent his first seven years; contains some original furnishings, inventions and memorabilia. Guided tours. (June 2-Labor Day,

Tues-Sat, also Sun afternoons; Feb-June 1, & after Labor Day-Nov, Tues-Sat afternoons; closed Thanksgiving) 9 Edison Dr, 3 mi S of OH Tpke exit 7. Phone 419/499-2135. ¢¢

Motels

★ ★ **COMFORT INN.** 11020 Milan Rd (US 250), N of Tpke exit 7. 419/499-4681; FAX 419/499-3159. 102 rms, 2 story. May-Sept: S, D $58-$180; under 18 free; lower rates rest of yr. Crib $10. Pet accepted, some restrictions. TV; cable. 2 pools, 1 indoor; whirlpools. Continental bkfst. Complimentary coffee. Restaurant nearby. Ck-out noon. Coin lndry. Business servs avail. Sundries. Sauna. Cr cds: A, C, D, DS, JCB, MC, V.

D ➥ ➟ ⊱ 🔥 SC

★ ★ **RAMADA LIMITED.** 11303 Milan Rd, 3 mi N on OH 250. 419/499-4347. 56 rms, 2 story. Late-May-Aug: S $44-$154; D $47-$174; each addl $10; under 18 free; lower rates rest of yr. Crib avail. TV; cable (premium). Complimentary continental bkfst. Restaurant adj 5-9:30 pm. Ck-out noon. Business servs avail. Sundries. Coin lndry. Sauna. Indoor pool; whirlpool. Cr cds: A, C, D, DS, MC, V.

D ➟ ⊱ SC

✔ ★ **SUPER 8.** 11313 Milan Rd (US 250N). 419/499-4671. 69 rms, 2 story, 9 suites. Late May-Aug, wkends: S $53.88-$102.88; D $58.88-$123; each addl $6; suites $98.88-$174; under 12 free; lower rates rest of yr. Restaurant 5-9:30 pm; Fri, Sat to 10 pm; closed Sun night. TV; cable (premium). Pool. Complimentary continental bkfst. Ck-out noon. Coin lndry. Meeting rm. Sundries. Game rm. Some refrigerators; microwaves avail. Cr cds: A, C, D, DS, MC, V.

D ➟ ⊱ 🔥 SC

Restaurant

★ ★ **HOMESTEAD INN.** 12018 US 250. 419/499-4271. Hrs: 7 am-9 pm; Fri, Sat to 10 pm; Sun to 8 pm. Closed some major hols. Res accepted Sun-Thurs. Bar; closed Sun. Semi-a la carte: bkfst $2.85-$4.50, lunch $5.75-$7.95, dinner $12.50-$16.50. Child's meals. Specializes in beef, salads, desserts. Salad bar. Victorian house (1883). Cr cds: A, C, D, DS, MC, V.

⊱

Mound City Group National Monument

(see Chillicothe)

Mount Gilead (D-3)

(For accommodations see Delaware, Mansfield, Marion, Mount Vernon)

Pop 2,846 **Elev** 1,130 ft **Area code** 419 **Zip** 43338

What to See and Do

Mt Gilead State Park. More than 170 acres. Fishing; boating (electric motors only). Hiking. Picnicking (shelter). Camping. Standard fees. (Daily) 1 mi E on OH 95. Phone 419/946-1961. **Free.**

Mount Vernon (D-4)

(See also Mansfield, Mount Gilead, Newark)

Founded 1805 **Pop** 14,550 **Elev** 990 ft **Area code** 614 **Zip** 43050 **E-mail** knoxcvb@knox.net **Web** www.knox.net/visitor

Information Knox County Convention & Visitors Bureau, 236 S Main St; 800/837-5282.

Descendants of the first settlers from Virginia, Maryland, New Jersey and Pennsylvania still live in this manufacturing and trading center. Seat of Knox County, it is in a rich agricultural, sandstone, oil and gas producing area. It is in the largest sheep-raising county east of the Mississippi.

Johnny Appleseed owned two lots in the original village plot at the south end of Main St. Daniel Decatur Emmett, author and composer of "Dixie," was born here. The offices of the State Headquarters of the Ohio Conference of Seventh-Day Adventists are here. Colonial-style architecture has been used for many public buildings and residences.

Motel

✔★ ★ **CURTIS.** *12 Public Sq. 614/397-4334; res: 800/934-6835.* 72 rms, 2 story. S, D $46-$52; each addl $5; under 13 free. Crib free. Pet accepted. TV; cable, VCR avail (movies). Complimentary coffee in rms. Restaurant 6:30 am-2 pm, 5-9 pm. Rm serv. Bar 11-1 am. Ck-out noon. Coin lndry. Business servs avail. Valet serv. Refrigerators. Some minibars. Cr cds: A, C, D, DS, MC, V.

Inn

★ ★ ★ **WHITE OAK.** *(29683 Walhonding Rd, Danville 43014) E on US 36 to jct US 62, then 4 mi E on OH 715.* 614/599-6107. 10 rms, 1-2 story. Phones avail. S, D $75-$135; each addl $25. Children over 12 yrs only. Complimentary full bkfst. Ck-out 11 am, ck-in 3 pm. Business servs avail. Lawn games. Turn-of-the-century farmhouse with original white oak woodwork. Totally nonsmoking. Cr cds: A, DS, MC, V.

Newark (E-4)

(See also Columbus, Lancaster, Zanesville)

Founded 1802 **Pop** 44,389 **Elev** 829 ft **Area code** 614 **Zip** 43055
Information Licking County Convention & Visitors Bureau, 50 W Locust St, PO Box 702; 614/345-8224 or 800/589-8224.

This industrial city on the Licking River attracts many visitors because of its large group of prehistoric mounds. Construction of the Ohio-Erie Canal was begun here on July 4, 1825, with Governor DeWitt Clinton of New York as the official groundbreaker and speaker. The Ohio Canal was then built north to Lake Erie and south to the Ohio River.

What to See and Do

Buckeye Central Scenic Railroad. A 1¹/₂-hr scenic rail trip through Licking County. (Memorial Day wkend-Oct, wkends & hols) Also special holiday-theme trains avail (Oct & Dec). US 40. Phone 614/366-2029. ¢¢¢

Buckeye Lake State Park. Swimming, waterskiing; fishing; boating (ramp). Picnicking (shelter). Standard fees. (Daily) 11 mi S on OH 79, on Buckeye Lake (3,300 acres water and 200 acres land). Phone 614/467-2690.

Dawes Arboretum. Over 2,000 species of woody plants on 355 acres; 3-acre Japanese Garden; Cypress Swamp; All Seasons Garden; nature

trails; picnic areas and shelter; special programs. (Daily; closed Jan 1, Thanksgiving, Dec 25) 7770 Jacksontown Rd SE. Phone 614/323-2355. **Free.**

Flint Ridge State Memorial. Prehistoric Native American flint quarry; trails for the disabled and the visually impaired; picnic area. Museum (Memorial Day-Labor Day, Wed-Sun; after Labor Day-Oct, wkends only). Park (Apr-Oct). 5 mi E on OH 16, then 5 mi S on County 668. Phone 614/787-2476. ¢¢

Licking County Historical Society Museum. Restored Sherwood-Davidson House (ca 1815) with period furnishings. Adj is restored Buckingham Meeting House (ca 1835). Guided tours (Apr-Dec, daily exc Mon). 6th St at W Main, Veterans Park. Phone 614/345-4898. ¢ The Society also maintains

Webb House Museum. Home (1908) of lumber executive includes family heirloom furnishings and wooden interior features. Guided tours. (Apr-Dec, Thurs, Fri & Sun afternoons; also by appt) 303 Granville St. Phone 614/345-8540. **Free.**

Robbins-Hunter Museum in the Avery Downer House. Outstanding Greek-revival house (1842). Period furnishings; decorative and fine arts. Guided tours. (June-Dec, Tues-Sun afternoons) 221 E Broadway. Phone 614/587-0430. **Donation.**

National Heisey Glass Museum. Displays of Heiseyware manufactured in the area from 1896-1957. (Tues-Sun afternoons; closed hols) 169 W Church St, at 6th St. Phone 614/345-2932. ¢

⭐ **Newark Earthworks.** The group of earthworks here was originally one of the most extensive of its kind in the country, covering an area of more than 4 sq mi. The Hopewell (100 B.C.- A.D. 500) used their geometric enclosures for social, religious and ceremonial purposes. Remaining portions of the Newark group are Octagon Earthworks and Wright Earthworks, with many artifacts of pottery, beadwork, copper, bone and shell exhibited at the nearby Moundbuilders Museum.

Moundbuilders State Memorial. The Great Circle, 66 acres, has walls from 8 to 14 ft high with burial mounds in the center; picnic facilities. Museum containing Hopewell artifacts (Memorial Day-Labor Day, Wed-Sun; after Labor Day-Oct, wkends only). Park (Apr-Oct). SW on OH 79, at S 21st St & Cooper. Phone 614/344-1920. Museum ¢¢

Wright Earthworks. One-acre area has a 100-ft wall remnant, an important part of original Newark group. ¹/₄ mi NE of Great Circle at James & Waldo Sts. **Free.**

Octagon Earthworks. The octagon-shaped enclosure encircles 50 acres that includes small mounds, and is joined by parallel walls to a circular embankment enclosing 20 acres. N 30th St & Parkview. **Free.**

Motel

★ ★ **HOWARD JOHNSON.** *775 Hebron Rd, I-70 exit 129B.* 614/522-3191; FAX 614/522-4396. 72 rms, 2 story. S $55-$65; D $70-$80; each addl $8; suites $100-$125; under 18 free; higher rates special events. Crib free. Pet accepted. TV; cable (premium), VCR avail (movies). Indoor pool. Complimentary continental bkfst Mon-Fri. Bar 6 pm-1 am; closed Sun. Ck-out noon. Meeting rms. Business servs avail. In-rm modem link. Exercise equipt; treadmill, stair machine. Private patios, balconies. Cr cds: A, C, D, DS, JCB, MC, V.

Motor Hotel

★ ★ ★ **CHERRY VALLEY LODGE.** *2299 Cherry Valley Rd, off OH 16 between Newark & Granville.* 614/788-1200; FAX 614/788-8800; res: 800/788-8008. 120 rms, 2 story. S, D $119-$134; each addl $10; suites $165-$180; under 18 free; wkend rates; golf plan. Crib free. TV; cable (premium), VCR (movies free). 2 pools, 1 indoor; whirlpool, poolside serv. Playground. Complimentary coffee in rms. Restaurant 6:30 am-10:30 pm. Rm serv. Bar 11-1 am. Ck-out noon. Meeting rms. Business servs avail. In-rm modem link. Bellhops. Gift shop. Valet serv. Exercise equipt;

weight machine, stair machine. Landscaped grounds with lake. Cr cds: A, C, D, DS, MC, V.

⊡ ⊠ 🏃 ⊠ ⬢

Inn

★ ★ ★ **BUXTON.** *(313 E Broadway, Granville 43023) 5 mi W on OH 16, 8 mi N of I-70 at OH 37. 614/587-0001; FAX 614/587-1460.* 25 rms, 2 story. S $60-$75; D $70-$90; each addl $10; under 5 free. TV; cable. Coffee in rms. Complimentary continental bkfst. Restaurant (see BUXTON INN DINING ROOM). Ck-out noon, ck-in 2 pm. Business servs avail. 18-hole golf privileges. Refrigerators. Antiques, prints. Private patios. Rms in two houses (1812). Cr cds: A, DS, MC, V.

🏃1 ⬢ ⬛

Restaurants

★ ★ **BUXTON INN DINING ROOM.** *(See Buxton Inn) 614/587-0001.* Hrs: 6:45-10 am, 11:30 am-2 pm, 5:30-9 pm; Fri to 10 pm; Sat 8-11 am, 11:30 am-2 pm, 5:30-10 pm; Sun 9 am-8 pm; Sun brunch 11 am-2 pm. Closed Jan 1, Dec 25. Res accepted. French, Amer menu. Bar 5 pm-midnight, closed Sun. Semi-a la carte: bkfst $3.95-$6.25, lunch $4.95-$9.95, dinner $11.50-$23.95. Sun brunch $4.95-$7.95. Specialties: Louisiana chicken, coquille of seafood, triple chocolate mousse cake. Greenhouse dining. New England-style inn (1812). Cr cds: A, D, DS, MC, V.

⊡ ♥

✔★ **DAMON'S.** *1486 Granville Rd. 614/349-7427.* Hrs: 11 am-11 pm; Fri & Sat to midnight; Sun to 10 pm. Closed Dec 25. Res accepted. Bar. Semi-a la carte: lunch $3.95-$7.95, dinner $6.95-$15.95. Child's meals. Specializes in ribs, onion rings. Casual atmosphere. Cr cds: A, C, D, DS, MC, V.

⊡ ⬛

★ **NATOMA.** *10 N Park, opp courthouse. 614/345-7260.* Hrs: 11 am-10 pm; Sat from 5 pm. Closed Sun; major hols. Res accepted Mon-Fri. Bar. A la carte entrees: lunch $4.50-$9.25, dinner $7.95-$17.95. Specializes in char-broiled chicken and ribs, baby beef filet mignon. Family-owned since 1922. Cr cds: A, C, D, DS, MC, V.

⊡ ⬛

New Philadelphia (D-5)

(See also Canton, Coshocton, Gnadenhutten, Massillon)

Founded 1804 **Pop** 15,698 **Elev** 910 ft **Area code** 330 **Zip** 44663 **E-mail** Tourism@Tusco.net **Web** web/tusco.net/tourism

Information Tuscarawas County Convention & Visitors Bureau, 125 McDonald's Dr, SW; 330/339-5453 or 800/527-3387.

New Philadelphia, seat of Tuscarawas County, and its neighbor Dover still reflect the early influence of the German-Swiss who came from Pennsylvania. Some of the earliest town lots in New Philadelphia were set aside for German schools.

What to See and Do

Fort Laurens State Memorial. An 82-acre site of only American fort in Ohio during Revolutionary War. Named in honor of Henry Laurens, Continental Congress president. Built in 1778 as a defense against the British and Native Americans. Picnicking; museum has artifacts and multimedia program on American Revolution. (Memorial Day-Labor Day, Wed-Sun; after Labor Day-Oct, wkends only) 14 mi N via OH 39, I-77, OH 212 to Bolivar, then 1/2 mi S. Phone 330/874-2059. ¢¢

Muskingum Watershed Conservancy District. A Muskingum River flood control and recreation project. The district maintains a total of 10 lakes, 5 lake parks, 10 marinas and 10 campgrounds. (Daily) Main office, 1319 Third St NW. Phone 330/343-6647. Per vehicle ¢¢

Atwood Lake Park. A 1,540-acre lake with swimming; fishing; boating (25 hp limit), marinas. Golf. Restaurant. Cottages, resort. Tent & trailer sites (showers, flush toilets). Standard fees. Pets on leash only. (Daily). 12 mi E on OH 39, then N off OH 212. For park information phone 330/343-6780. Per vehicle ¢¢

Leesville Lake. Fishing and boating on 1,000-acre lake (10 hp limit). Tent & trailer sites (Apr-Oct). 12 mi E on OH 39, then S off OH 212. **Southfork Marina,** on SW shore, off OH 212; (Apr-Nov, daily) phone 614/269-5371. **Petersburg Marina,** on N shore, off OH 332; phone 330/627-4270. Pets on leash only. Fee for camping.

Schoenbrunn Village State Memorial. Partial reconstruction of the first Ohio town built by Christian Native Americans under the leadership of Moravian missionaries; one of 6 villages constructed between 1772 and 1798. Picnicking; museum. (Memorial Day-Labor Day, daily; after Labor Day-Oct, wkends only) 3 mi SE off US 250 on OH 259. Phone 330/339-3636 or 800/752-2711. ¢¢

Tuscora Park. Swimming (fee); tennis; shuffleboard; amusement rides (fee per ride), including 100-yr-old carousel; swimming (fee); picnicking; concession. (Late May-Labor Day, daily) Tuscora Ave, 1/2 mi N on OH 416. Phone 330/343-4644. **Free.**

Warther Museum. Collection of miniature locomotives by master carver Ernest Warther, carved of ebony, pearl, ivory and walnut; largest model has 10,000 parts; collection of buttons in quilt patterns and arrow points. On landscaped grounds are telegraph station, operating hand car and caboose. Tour of cutlery shop. (Daily; closed major hols) 331 Karl Ave, 1/2 mi E of I-77, in Dover. Phone 330/343-7513. ¢¢¢

Zoar State Memorial. A quaint village where the German religious Separatists found refuge from persecution (1817); an experiment in communal living that lasted for 80 yrs. Number One House on Main St houses the historical museum and has Zoar Society records, pottery and furniture. Zoar Garden, in the center of the village, follows the description of New Jerusalem in the Bible. Restoration includes the garden house, blacksmith shop, bakery, tinshop, carpenter shop. (Memorial Day-Labor Day, Wed-Sat, also Sun & hol afternoons; Apr-May & after Labor Day-Oct, wkends) I-77 exit 93; 2 1/2 mi SE on OH 212. Phone 330/874-3011. ¢¢

Annual Events

Zoar Harvest Festival. In Zoar. Antique show; 1850s craft demonstrations; music in 1853 church; museum tours, horse drawn wagon rides. Phone 330/874-2100. Early Aug.

Swiss Festival. 8 mi W on OH 39, in Sugarcreek. Swiss cheese from more than 13 factories in the area. Swiss musicians, costumes, polka bands. Steinstossen (stone-throwing), Schwingfest (Swiss wrestling); parade each afternoon. Phone 330/852-4113. 4th Fri & Sat after Labor Day.

Christmas in Zoar. Tours of private houses, craft show, German food, strolling carolers and tree lighting ceremony. Phone 330/874-3011. Early Dec.

Seasonal Event

Trumpet in the Land. Schoenbrunn Amphitheatre, off US 250 on University Dr. Outdoor musical drama by Paul Green takes you back to a time when Ohio was the western frontier of America, to witness the founding of Ohio's first settlement, Schoenbrunn, in 1772. Daily exc Mon. For reservations, information phone 330/339-1132. Mid-June-late Aug.

Motels

★ ★ **HOLIDAY INN.** *131 Bluebell Dr, I-77 exit 81. 330/339-7731; FAX 330/339-1565.* 150 rms, 2 story. S, D $79 wkdays, $89 wkends; higher rates: Hall of Fame Week, Ohio Swiss Festival. Crib free. Pet accepted. TV; cable, VCR avail. 2 pools, 1 indoor; whirlpool. Restaurant 6:30 am-10 pm. Bar 4 pm-1 am. Ck-out 11 am. Meeting rms. Business servs avail. Valet serv. Sundries. Exercise equipt; weights, bicycles, sauna. Cr cds: A, C, D, DS, MC, V.

D 🛌 ≋ 🏋 ⚓ 🔥 SC

★ **TRAVELODGE.** *1256 W. High Ave, at jct I-77 exit 81. 330/339-6671.* 62 rms, 2 story. S $53; D $70; kit. units $55-$75; each addl $5; under 18 free. Crib free. TV; cable. Pool. Coffee in rms. Restaurant adj. Ck-out noon. Business servs avail. Cr cds: A, C, D, DS, MC, V.

D ≋ ⚓ 🔥 SC

Resort

★ ★ ★ **ATWOOD LAKE.** *(2650 Lodge Road, Dellroy 44620) E on OH 39, N on OH 212, E on OH 542, on E side of Atwood Lake. 330/735-2211; FAX 330/735-2562; res: 800/362-6406.* 104 rms, 2 story, 17 kit. cottages (4-bedrm). Mid-June-Sept: S $98-$115; D $110-$125; each addl $10; cottages for 8-10, $790/wk; family rates; golf plans; lower rates rest of yr. TV; cable. 2 pools, 1 indoor; whirlpool. Playground. Free supervised child's activities (mid-June-Sept). Dining rm 7-11 am, noon-4 pm, 5-9 pm; Fri, Sat to 10 pm. Box lunches. Snack bar. Rm serv. Bar noon-2 am. Ck-out 1 pm, ck-in 4 pm. Meeting rms. Business servs avail. In-rm modem link. Gift shop. Airport, bus depot transportation. Lighted tennis, pro. 9-hole par-3 golf, 18-hole par-70 golf, pro, driving range, putting green. X-country ski on site; sledding. Exercise equipt; weights, bicycles, sauna. Motorboats, sailboats, canoes, rowboats. Bicycle rentals. Game rm. Lawn games. Picnic tables, grills at cottages. Glass walls open to patios in lodge. On hill overlooking lake; 1,540 acres. Private airstrip, heliport. A Muskingum Watershed Conservancy District facility. Cr cds: A, C, D, DS, MC, V.

D 🛌 ⚓ 🎿 🏋 ⛷ ≋ 🏋 ⚓ 🔥 SC

Oberlin (B-4)

(See also Cleveland, Elyria, Lorain, Milan, Strongsville)

Founded 1833 **Pop** 8,191 **Elev** 800 ft **Area code** 216 **Zip** 44074 **E-mail** visitors@lcvb.org **Web** www.lcvb.org

Information Lorain County Visitors Bureau, 611 Broadway, Lorain 44052; 216/245-5282 or 800/334-1673.

Oberlin College and the town were founded together. Oberlin was the first college to offer equal degrees to men and women and the first in the United States to adopt a policy against discrimination because of race. The central portion of the campus forms a six-acre public square, called Tappan Square, in the center of the town.

Charles Martin Hall, a young Oberlin graduate, discovered the electrolytic process of making aluminum in Oberlin. The Federal Aviation Agency maintains an Air Traffic Control Center here.

What to See and Do

Oberlin College (1833). (2,750 students) College of Arts and Sciences and Conservatory of Music (1867). Campus tours from admissions office, Carnegie Building. At jct OH 511, 58. Phone 440/775-8121. On campus are

Allen Memorial Art Museum. Major collection of more than 14,000 works includes 17th-century Dutch paintings, 19th- and 20th-century European works, Japanese woodcuts and contemporary works. (Daily exc Mon; closed major hols) 87 N Main. Phone 440/775-8665. **Free.**

Hall Auditorium. Dramatic arts center.

Kettering Hall of Science. Named for inventor Charles F. Kettering, the building houses departments of biology and chemistry, a biology museum, greenhouse and science library.

Conservatory of Music. Complex of buildings (1964) by architect Minoru Yamasaki; includes 667-seat Warner Concert Hall, a teaching and classroom building, rehearsal and library unit and Robertson Hall, which houses practice facilities.

Seeley G. Mudd Center. Library with more than one million volumes; also houses archives, audiovisual center.

Tours. Oberlin Historic Sites tour includes James Monroe House (1866), Little Red School House (1836) and Jewett House (1884). Phone 440/774-1700. ¢

Motel

★ ★ **OBERLIN INN.** *7 N Main, on Oberlin College campus. 216/775-1111; FAX 216/775-0676.* 76 rms, 2-3 story. S, D $78-$129; each addl $10; suites $175; under 12 free. Crib free. TV; cable (premium). Restaurant 7 am-9 pm. Rm serv. Ck-out noon. Meeting rms. Business servs avail. Valet serv. Sundries. Airport transportation. Health club privileges. Cr cds: A, C, D, DS, MC, V.

D ⚓ 🔥 SC

Oxford (F-1)

(See also Cincinnati, Hamilton, Mason, Middletown)

Founded 1810 **Pop** 18,937 **Elev** 972 ft **Area code** 513 **Zip** 45056
Information Visitors & Convention Bureau, 118 W High St, 513/523-8687; Chamber of Commerce, 513/523-5200.

Situated in the rolling hills of southwestern Ohio, this small town has many brick streets and unique shops and is home to Miami University.

What to See and Do

Hueston Woods State Park. A 3,596-acre park with swimming, bathhouse; boating (launch, rentals). Nature, hiking and bridle trails; 18-hole golf. Picnicking, concession, lodge. Camping, cabins. Nature center; naturalist. Standard fees. (Daily) 5 mi N on OH 732. Phone 513/523-6347 (park office) or 513/523-6381 (lodge & cabins). **Free.** At S entrance is

Pioneer Farm & House Museum. Farmhouse (1835) has period furniture, clothing, toys. Barn (ca 1850) has early farm implements, tools. Arts & crafts fair (1st wkend June). Apple butter-making demonstrations (2nd wkend Oct). (Memorial Day-Oct, call for hrs) Doty & Brown Rds. Phone 513/523-8005. ¢

Miami University (1809). (16,000 students) On campus are the Miami University Art Museum (daily exc Mon) and two other art galleries; zoology, geology, and anthropology museums; entomological collections; Turrell Herbarium. Campus tours. 500 E High St. Phone 513/529-1809. Also on campus is

McGuffey Museum. Restored home of William Holmes McGuffey, who compiled the *McGuffey Eclectic Readers* while a member of the faculty here; memorabilia, collection of his books. (Call for schedule) Spring & Oak Sts. Phone 513/529-2232. **Free.**

Annual Events

Outdoor Summer Music Festival. Uptown Oxford at Martin Luther King Park. Every Thurs, June & July.

Red Brick Rally Car Show. Uptown. 2nd Sun Oct.

Motels

★ ★ **AMERIHOST INN.** *6 E Sycamore St, at Main St. 513/523-0000; FAX 513/523-2093.* 61 rms, 2 story. S $54-$100; D $64-$100; each addl $5; under 12 free; higher rates Miami Univ events. Crib avail. TV; cable (premium), VCR avail. Indoor pool; whirlpool. Complimentary continental bkfst. Complimentary coffee in rms. Ck-out noon. Meeting rm. Business servs avail. Exercise equipt; bicycles, stair machine, sauna. Cr cds: A, C, D, DS, JCB, MC, V.

D ≋ 🏋 ⚓ 🔥 SC

★ ★ **HAMPTON INN.** *5056 College Corner Pike. 513/524-0114; FAX 513/524-1147.* 66 rms, 3 story. S $52-$89; D $58-$95; each addl $6; suites $89-$95; under 18 free; higher rates special events. Crib free. TV; cable (premium), VCR avail. Complimentary continental bkfst. Restaurant adj 6 am-10 pm. Ck-out 11 am. Meeting rms. Business servs avail. In-rm modem link. Valet serv. Exercise equipt; bicycle, treadmill. Indoor pool; whirlpool. Some in-rm whirlpools, refrigerators. Cr cds: A, C, D, DS, MC, V.

D ⊛ 🏊 ✕ 🐾 ⊠ 🔥 SC

★ ★ **HUESTON WOODS RESORT.** *(RR 1, College Corner 45003) 5 mi N on OH 732 in Hueston Woods State Park. 513/523-6381; FAX 513/523-1522; res: 800/282-7275.* 94 rms, 3 story, 53 kit. units. No elvtr. S, D $99-$109; each addl $5; cottages $65-$97; under 16 free. Crib free. TV; cable (premium), VCR avail (movies). 2 pools, 1 indoor; wading pool. Playground. Free supervised child's activities (June-Aug). Complimentary coffee in cabins. Restaurant. Bar evenings. Ck-out noon. Meeting rms. Business servs avail. Sundries. Lighted tennis. 18-hole golf. X-country ski on site. Exercise equipt; weight machine, stair machine, sauna. Game rm. Rec rm. Lawn games. Microwaves in cabins. Private patios, balconies. Large fireplace in lobby. Indian motif. On bluff above lake; beach. All facilities of state park avail. Cr cds: A, C, D, DS, MC, V.

D ⊷ ⛵ 🏊 🎿 ♨ ≈ ✕ ⛷ 🐾 ⊠ 🔥 SC

Painesville (B-5)

(See also Ashtabula, Cleveland, Geneva-on-the-Lake, Mentor)

Pop 15,699 **Elev** 677 ft **Area code** 216 **Zip** 44077 **E-mail** info@lakevisit.com **Web** www.lakevisit.com

Information Lake County Visitors Bureau, 1610 Mentor Ave; 216/354-2424 or 800/368-LAKE.

What to See and Do

Fairport Harbor Lighthouse and Marine Museum. Lighthouse, lightkeeper's dwelling (museum) with attached ship's pilothouse. (Memorial Day wkend-Oct 1, Wed, Sat & Sun, also major hols) 2 mi N off OH 2 at 129 2nd St, in Fairport Harbor. Phone 216/354-4825. ¢

Annual Event

Lake County Fair. Lake County Fairgrounds. Late Aug.

Inn

★ ★ **RIDER'S 1812 INN.** *792 Mentor Ave. 216/354-8200.* 10 rms, 2 story. S, D $75-$99; each addl $10. Crib free. Pet accepted. TV; cable, VCR avail (movies $2). Complimentary full bkfst in rm. Restaurant (see RIDER'S INN). Rm serv. Ck-out, ck-in flexible. Business servs avail. Bellhops. Concierge. Airport transportation. 18-hole golf privileges. Health club privileges. Original stagecoach stop (1812); historic stop on the underground railroad, some original antiques. Cr cds: A, DS, MC, V.

⊷ ✕ 🐾 ⊠ 🔥

Resort

★ ★ ★ **QUAIL HOLLOW RESORT & COUNTRY CLUB.** *(11080 Concord-Hambden Rd, Concord) S on OH 44, at I-90 exit 200. 216/352-6201; FAX 216/350-3504; res: 800/792-0258.* 169 rms, 2-4 story. Apr-Oct: S $116-$136; D $136-$156; each addl $15; under 18 free; wkend rates; ski, golf plans; lower rates rest of yr. Crib free. TV; cable, VCR avail. 2 pools, 1 indoor; whirlpool, poolside serv, lifeguard. Playground. Dining rm 6:30 am-10 pm; Fri, Sat 7 am-10 pm; Sun brunch 10:30 am-2:30 pm. Snack bar. Rm serv. Bar 11:30-2 am; entertainment Fri-Sat. Ck-out 11 am. Meeting rms. Business center. Valet serv. Gift shop. Tennis. Golf, greens fee $55-$75, pro, putting green, driving range. Downhill ski 12 mi; x-country

ski nearby. Exercise equipt; weights, bicycles, sauna. Lawn games. Private patios, balconies. Cr cds: A, C, D, DS, JCB, MC, V.

D ⊷ 🎿 ✕ ♨ ≈ ✕ ⛷ 🐾 ⊠ 🔥 SC ⊛

Restaurants

✔ ★ **DINNER BELL DINER.** *1155 Bank St. 216/354-3708.* Hrs: 8 am-9 pm; Sun to 8 pm. Closed July 4, Thanksgiving, Dec 25. Res accepted. Semi-a la carte: bkfst $2-$8.25, lunch $4-$9.95, dinner $5.75-$12.95. Specializes in prime rib, meat loaf, Greek steak tips over noodles. Eclectic decor. Photographs of celebrity guests. Cr cds: A, DS, MC, V.

D SC

★ ★ **RIDER'S INN.** *(See Rider's 1812 Inn) 216/942-2742.* Hrs: 11:30 am-9 pm; Fri, Sat to 10 pm; Sun 10 am-9pm. Closed Dec 25. Res accepted. Bar. Semi-a la carte: lunch $3.95-$8.95, dinner $8.95-$23. Sun brunch $10.95. Child's meals. Specializes in venison, duck, potato leek soup. Entertainment Fri, Sat. Outdoor dining. Features fare from original 19th century recipes. Cr cds: A, DS, MC, V.

D ♥

Piqua (D-1)

(See also Dayton, Sidney, Vandalia)

Pop 20,612 **Elev** 869 ft **Area code** 937 **Zip** 45356

Information Piqua Area Chamber of Commerce, 400 N Wayne St, PO Box 1142; 937/773-2765.

What to See and Do

✪ **Piqua Historical Area.** More than 170 acres in Great Miami River valley, near crossroads used by prehistoric people, by French and English fur traders and by soldiers of General "Mad Anthony" Wayne. (Memorial Day-Labor Day, Wed-Sun; after Labor Day-Oct, wkends only) 3½ mi NW on OH 66. Phone 937/773-2522. ¢¢ Area and fee includes

John Johnston Home (1810). Restored Dutch colonial-style farmhouse built by Ohio Indian agent and businessman. Other buildings include double pen log barn, springhouse, fruit kiln and ciderhouse; craft demonstrations.

Historic Indian Museum has artifacts from the 17th-19th centuries.

Miami and Erie Canal (1825-1845). Rides on *Gen'l Harrison,* replica of a mid-19th-century canalboat.

Annual Event

Heritage Festival. Piqua heritage re-created. Native American and square dancing; demonstrations including long rifle, blacksmith, wood carving, dulcimer, soap making, weaving; contests; food; canalboat ride. Phone 937/773-2765. Labor Day wkend.

Motor Hotel

★ ★ **COMFORT INN.** *987 E Ash St, I-75 exit 82, at Miami Valley Centre Mall. 937/778-8100; FAX 937/778-9573.* 124 rms, 5 story. S, D $68-$120; each addl $6; under 18 free. Crib free. TV; cable (premium). Indoor pool; whirlpool. Complimentary continental bkfst. Restaurant nearby. Ck-out noon. Meeting rms. Business servs avail. Valet serv. Exercise equipt; weights, stair machine. Cr cds: A, C, D, DS, ER, JCB, MC, V.

D 🏊 ✕ 🐾 ⊠ SC

Port Clinton (B-3)

(See also Fremont, Kelleys Island, Put-in-Bay, Sandusky, Toledo)

Founded 1828 **Pop** 7,106 **Elev** 592 ft **Area code** 419 **Zip** 43452
Information Chamber of Commerce, 130 Jefferson St, Suite 1B, phone, 419/734-5503; or the Ottawa County Visitors Bureau, 109 Madison St, Suite E, phone, 419/734-4386.

What to See and Do

African Safari Wildlife Park. Visitors may drive their own cars through game preserve to see lions, ostriches, giraffes, zebras, other animals roaming free in natural setting. Camel rides avail. (Mid-May-Labor Day, daily; Sept, wkends if weather permits) 4 mi E to Lightner Rd, off US 2 Bypass. Phone 419/732-3606. ¢¢¢

Camp Perry Military Reservation. Largest military camp on the Great Lakes. (Daily) 5 mi W on OH 2. Phone 419/635-4114. **Free.**

Catawba Island State Park. Fishing (perch, catfish, bluegill, bass, crappie); boating on Lake Erie (ramps). Picnicking. (Daily) 4 mi E on OH 163, then N on OH 53. Phone 419/797-4530. **Free.**

East Harbor State Park. Swimming beach, lifeguard, bathhouse (Memorial Day-Labor Day); fishing; boating, marina, docks. Hiking. Snowmobiling. Concession. Camping. Standard fees. (Daily) 7 mi E on OH 163, then N on OH 269. Phone 419/734-4424 (park), 419/734-5857 (camp) or 419/734-2289 (marina). **Free.**

Ottawa County Historical Museum. Guns, dolls, Native American and county relics; 1813 Battle of Lake Erie exhibit. (June-Aug, daily exc Sun; rest of yr, Tues-Thurs afternoons, also by appt; closed hols) W 3rd & Monroe Sts. Phone 419/732-2237. **Free.**

Perry's Victory and International Peace Memorial. 12 mi by ferry to Put-in-Bay (see).

Annual Event

National Matches. Camp Perry. Held since 1907. Hundreds of competitors each in outdoor pistol, small-bore and highpower rifle championships. Small Arms Firing Schools. Early July-mid-Aug.

Motels

✔★ **DAYS INN.** *2149 E Gill Rd. 419/734-4945; FAX 419/734-5877.* 37 rms. May-Oct: S, D $88-$138; under 12 free; lower rates rest of yr. Closed Nov-March. Crib free. TV; cable. Complimentary continental bkfst. Ck-out noon. Coin lndry. Cr cds: A, C, D, DS, MC, V.

D ⊠ 🛇 SC

★ **FAIRFIELD INN BY MARRIOTT.** *3760 E State Rd. 419/732-2434.* 64 rms, 2 story. Apr-Aug: S $68.95-$148; D $68.95-$180; under 18 free; lower rates rest of yr. Crib $10. TV; cable (premium). Complimentary continental bkfst. Ck-out noon. Business servs avail. Sundries. Coin lndry. Indoor pool. Game rm. Some in-rm whirlpools. Cr cds: A, C, D, DS, MC, V.

D ≈ 🛇 🐾 SC

★★ **PHIL'S INN.** *1704 E Perry St (OH 163). 419/734-4446; FAX 419/732-3370; res: 800/354-7445.* E-mail goodfood@philsinn.com; web www.philsinn.com. 38 rms, 2 story. Late May-Labor Day: S, D $70-$90; suites $110-$135; kit. unit $85-$115; under 12 free; lower rates rest of yr. Crib $5. TV; cable (premium). Restaurant 8 am-midnight. Bar. Ck-out noon. Valet serv. Sundries. Free airport transportation. Some refrigerators; microwaves avail. Cr cds: A, DS, MC, V.

D 🐾 SC

Restaurant

★★ **GARDEN AT THE LIGHTHOUSE.** *226 E Perry St (OH 163).* 419/732-2151. Hrs: 11 am-2 pm, 4-10 pm; early-bird dinner 4-6 pm. Closed some major hols; also Sun Sept-May. Res accepted. Continental menu. Bar. Semi-a la carte: lunch $4.50-$8.95, dinner $8.95-$21.95. Child's meals. Specializes in seafood. Patio dining. In former lighthouse keeper's building; glassed-in porch overlooking gardens. Cr cds: A, C, D, DS, MC, V.

Portsmouth (G-3)

(See also Ironton)

Founded 1803 **Pop** 22,676 **Elev** 533 ft **Area code** 614 **Zip** 45662
Information Convention & Visitors Bureau, 1020 7th St, PO Box 509; 614/353-7647.

Portsmouth is the leading firebrick and shoelace center of southern Ohio. At the confluence of the Ohio and Scioto rivers, 100 miles east of Cincinnati, it is connected to South Portsmouth, Kentucky, by bridge. The Boneyfiddle historic district in downtown Portsmouth includes many antique and specialty shops.

Portsmouth was the childhood home of cowboy movie star Roy Rogers and baseball's Branch Rickey.

What to See and Do

Brewery Arcade (1842). A former brewery, restored; now a complex of shops. 224 Second St, in the historic Boneyfiddle district.

Floodwall Murals Project. 14 murals depicting area history completed by Robert Dafford. (Daily) Along Front St at Ohio River. **Free.**

Shawnee State Forest. A 60,000-acre forest with 6 lakes. Ruffed grouse, squirrel and deer hunting in season. Bridle trail. (Daily) (See ANNUAL EVENTS) 7 mi SW on US 52, then W on OH 125. Phone 614/858-6685. **Free.** In forest is

Shawnee State Park. Swimming; fishing; boating (ramps, dock) on 68-acre lake. 18-hole golf. Picnicking (shelter), lodge. Camping, cabins. Nature Center. (Daily) Phone 614/858-4561 or 614/858-6652. **Free.**

Southern Ohio Museum and Cultural Center. Changing exhibits in visual arts; performing arts; workshops; guided tours. (Daily exc Mon; closed major hols, also Jan & Aug) Free admission Fri. 825 Gallia St. Phone 614/354-5629. ¢

The 1810 House. Original homestead built by hand. Nine rms with period furniture; handling of objects permitted. Guided tours. (May-Dec, Sat & Sun afternoons; wkdays by appt) 1926 Waller St. Phone 614/353-6344. **Free.**

Annual Events

Trout Derby. In Shawnee State Park. Phone 614/858-6652. Last wkend Apr.

Roy Rogers Festival. Downtown. Old-time Western stars, memorabilia, staged gunfights. 1st wkend June.

Charity Horse Show. Scioto County Fairgrounds. June.

Scioto County Fair. Fairgrounds. 2nd wk Aug.

River Days Festival. Downtown. Labor Day wkend.

Fall foliage hikes and tours. Shawnee State Park and Forest. Guided hikes, hoedowns, camp-outs, auto tours. 3rd wkend Oct.

Motel

★ ★ **HOLIDAY INN.** *Box 1190, 4 mi N on US 23. 614/354-2851; FAX 614/353-2084.* 100 rms, 2 story. S, D $59; under 18 free; higher rates special events. Crib free. Pet accepted, some restrictions. TV; cable. Pool. Restaurant. Rm serv. Bar 5 pm-2 am. Ck-out noon. Meeting rms. Business servs avail. In-rm modem link. Valet serv. Cr cds: A, C, D, DS, MC, V.

D ⟨symbols⟩ SC

Motor Hotel

✔★ ★ **RAMADA INN.** *711 2nd St, at jct US 23, 52. 614/354-7711; FAX 614/353-1539.* 119 rms, 5 story. S $49-$59; D $53-$69; each addl $7; under 18 free. Crib free. Pet accepted, some restrictions. TV; cable (premium). Indoor pool; wading pool, whirlpool, poolside serv. Complimentary continental bkfst. Restaurant 11 am-11 pm; Fri, Sat to midnight. Rm serv. Ck-out noon. Meeting rms. Business servs avail. Valet serv. Sundries. Health club privileges. Dockage. Some refrigerators. Cr cds: A, C, D, DS, MC, V.

D ⟨symbols⟩ SC

Restaurant

✔★ **SARAH'S.** *3732 Scioto Trail. 614/354-1299.* Hrs: 11 am-10 pm; Fri to 11 pm; Sat 5-11 pm. Closed Sun, Mon; Dec 25. Bar. Semi-a la carte: lunch $4.95-$7, dinner $7-$19.95. Child's meals. Specialties: prime rib, "oversized" salads. Decorated with antiques, artifacts; Victorian chandeliers. Cr cds: A, MC, V.

D

Put-in-Bay (B-3)

(For accommodations see Port Clinton, Sandusky; also see Kelleys Island)

Settled 1811 **Pop** 141 **Elev** 570 ft **Area code** 419 **Zip** 43456

On South Bass Island in Lake Erie, this village is an all-year resort, which can be reached by ferry (inquire as to time and seasons) from Port Clinton (phone 800/245-1538) and Catawba Point (phone 419/285-2421) or by plane from Sandusky (phone 800/368-3743). The area claims the best smallmouth black bass fishing in America in spring; good walleye fishing in June, July and August; and ice fishing for perch and walleye in winter. Boating, swimming, bicycling, picnic grounds, yachting facilities, golf and waterskiing are available. Wine is produced in the area.

What to See and Do

Crystal Cave. Unusual deposit of strontium sulphate crystals; the largest 18 inches long. Heineman Winery is located on the grounds; winery tour and tasting is included in cave tour. (Mid-May-mid-Sept, daily) 798 Catawba Ave. Phone 419/285-2811. ¢¢

Lake Erie Island State Park. Includes South Bass Island, Kelleys Island, and Catawba parks. Waterskiing; fishing; boating. Picnicking (shelter). Camping (fee); cabins (fee). Standard fees. S shore. Phone 419/797-4530.

Perry's Cave. Commodore Perry is said to have stored supplies here before the Battle of Lake Erie in 1813; later prisoners were kept here for a short time. The cave is 52 ft below the surface and is 208 ft by 165 ft; the temperature is 50°F. It has an underground stream that rises and falls with the level of Lake Erie. Picnic area avail (no water). 20-min guided tour. (June-Labor Day, daily; spring & fall, wkends; rest of yr, by appt) Catawba Ave. Phone 419/285-2405. ¢¢

Perry's Victory and International Peace Memorial. Greek Doric granite column (352 ft high) commemorates Commodore Oliver Hazard Perry's victory over the British Naval Squadron at the Battle of Lake Erie, near Put-in-Bay, in 1813. The US gained control of the lake, preventing a British invasion. Observation platform in monument (317 ft above lake) provides view of the battle site and neighboring islands on a clear day. The 3,986-mi US-Canadian boundary is the longest unfortified border in the world. Children under 16 only with adult. (May-late Oct, daily). 2 Bay View Ave. Phone 419/285-2184 or 419/285-3512. ¢

Put-in-Bay Tour Train. Departs from downtown depot and Jet Express dock. A 1-hr tour of the island (May-mid-Sept, daily). Phone 419/285-4855. ¢¢¢

Annual Event

Boat Regatta. More than 200 sailboats race to Vermilion (see). Early Aug.

St Clairsville (E-6)

(See also Steubenville)

Pop 5,162 **Elev** 1,284 ft **Area code** 614 **Zip** 43950

This charming tree-shaded town has been the seat of Belmont County since 1804.

Annual Event

Jamboree in the Hills. 4 mi W off I-70 exit 208 or 213. A 4-day country music festival featuring more than 30 hrs of music; top country stars. Camping avail. Phone 800/624-5456. 3rd wkend July.

Motels

★ ★ **DAYS INN-WEST.** *52601 Holiday Dr, off I-70 exit 220. 614/695-0100; FAX 614/695-4135.* 138 rms, 2 story. S $40-$49; D $45-$54; each addl $5. Crib free. TV. Pool; poolside serv. Complimentary continental bkfst. Restaurant 11 am-10 pm; Fri, Sat to 11 pm. Rm serv. Bar. Ck-out noon. Meeting rms. Business servs avail. Microwaves avail. Cr cds: A, D, DS, MC, V.

D ⟨symbols⟩ SC

✔★ **KNIGHTS INN.** *51260 National Rd, I-70 exit 218. 614/695-5038; FAX 614/695-3014; res: 800/835-9628.* 104 rms, 16 kits. S $36.95-$44.95; D $38.95-$54.95; each addl $7; kit. units $44.95-$69.95; under 18 free. Crib free. Pet accepted, some restrictions. TV; cable (premium), VCR avail (movies). Pool. Complimentary coffee. Restaurant nearby. Ck-out noon. Business servs avail. In-rm modem link. Some in-rm whirlpools; microwaves avail. Cr cds: A, D, DS, ER, MC, V.

D ⟨symbols⟩ SC

Sandusky (B-4)

(See also Bellevue, Milan, Port Clinton, Vermilion)

Settled 1816 **Pop** 29,764 **Elev** 600 ft **Area code** 419 **Zip** 44870 **E-mail** vcbstaff@buckeyenorth.com **Web** buckeyenorth.com

Information Visitor & Convention Bureau, 231 W Washington Row; 419/625-2984 or 800/255-3743.

On a flat slope facing 18-mile-long Sandusky Bay, this town stretches for more than 6 miles along the waterfront. Originally explored by the French, named by the Wyandot "Sandouske," meaning "at the cold water," it is the second largest coal-shipping port on the Great Lakes. It became a tourist center in 1882; automotive parts industry and manufacturing are also important to the economy.

What to See and Do

Battery Park. Piers; marina, sailing club. Lighted tennis. Picnicking (shelter), playground. Restaurant. At E end of Water St, overlooks Sandusky Bay. Phone 419/625-6142.   **Free.**

Boat trips.

    MV *Pelee Islander.* (Reservation necessary for autos.) Ferry transportation in summer to Leamington and Kingsville, Ontario (for Border Crossing Regulations see MAKING THE MOST OF YOUR TRIP). (Mid-June-Labor Day) Foot of Jackson St. Phone 519/724-2115. ¢¢¢¢-¢¢¢¢¢

    The Neuman Boat Line. Auto and passenger service to Kelleys Island (see). From Marblehead, foot of Frances St (first Sat Apr-Sun before Thanksgiving, daily). Also lunch and dinner cruises around the Lake Erie Islands. From Sandusky, foot of Columbus Ave (June-Oct, daily). 101 E Shoreline Dr. For schedule phone 419/626-5557. Ferry ¢¢¢; Lunch & dinner cruises ¢¢¢¢¢

    MV *City of Sandusky.* 300-passenger excursion boat from downtown. (Memorial Day-Labor Day, daily; Sept, wkends) 226 W Shorline Dr. Phone 419/627-0198 or 800/426-6286.

Cedar Point. Swimming beach; marina; RV campground; resort hotels on Lake Erie. Amusement park has more than 50 rides, live shows, crafts area, marine-life show and aquarium, restaurants, concessions. Also here is Challenge Park, including Soak City water park, Challenge Golf miniature golf course and the Cedar Point Grand Prix go-kart race track (addl fee). (Early May-Labor Day, daily; after Labor Day-early Oct, wkends only) Price includes unlimited rides and attractions exc Challenge Park. SE on US 6 to Causeway Dr, then N over Causeway (look for Cedar Point signs in town). Phone 419/627-2350.   ¢¢¢¢¢

Merry-Go-Round Museum. Houses restored, working carousel, exhibits. Tours. (Wed-Sun; closed major hols) W Washington & Jackson Sts. Phone 419/626-6111.   ¢¢

Old Woman Creek National Estuarine Research Reserve. Old Woman Creek is protected as a Natl Estuarine Research Reserve and State Nature Preserve. It is one of Ohio's best remaining examples of a natural estuary and serves as a field laboratory for the study of estuarine ecology. Ohio Center for Coastal Wetlands Studies has a visitor center and reference library. Trails (daily). Visitor center (Apr-Dec, Wed-Sun afternoons; rest of yr, Mon-Fri; closed major hols). Approx 12 mi E on US 6 (2 mi E of Huron). Phone 419/433-4601.   **Free.**

Annual Events

Erie County Fair. Fairgrounds. Livestock show, rides, entertainment. Early Aug.

Tour of homes. Tour historic homes decorated for the holidays. Early Dec.

Motels

    ★ ★ ★ **BEST WESTERN-CEDAR POINT.** *1530 Cleveland Rd. 419/625-9234; FAX 419/625-9971.* 105 rms, 2 story. Early May-Labor Day: S $99-$175; D $99-$179; each addl $10; suites $150-$350; kit. units $200-$350; lower rates rest of yr; under 12 free. Crib $8. TV; cable (premium). Heated pool. Restaurant 7 am-midnight. Ck-out 11 am. Coin lndry. Sundries. Game rm. Microwaves avail. Cr cds: A, C, D, DS, MC, V.

    D ≈ ⊁ 🐾 SC

    ★ **FAIRFIELD INN BY MARRIOTT.** *6220 Milan Rd, 6 mi S on OH 250. 419/621-9500.* 63 rms, 2 story. May-Aug: S $40-$155; D $50-$170; each addl $6; under 18 free; lower rates rest of yr. Crib free. TV; cable (premium). Complimentary continental bkfst. Restaurant nearby. Business servs avail. Sundries. Coin lndry. Sauna. Indoor pool. Some in-rm whirlpools. Cr cds: A, D, DS, MC, V.

    D ≈ ⊁ 🐾 SC

Motor Hotels

    ★ ★ **CLARION INN-TWINE HOUSE.** *(132 N Main St, Huron 44839) 10 mi E on US 6. 419/433-8000; FAX 419/433-8552.* 65 rms, 3 story. May-Sept: S $49-$219; D $59-$219; each addl $10; suites $84-$259; under 18 free; lower rates rest of yr. Crib free. TV; cable (premium). Complimentary coffee in rms. Restaurant 7 am-midnight. Rm serv. Bar 11-2:30 am; entertainment. Ck-out 11 am. Meeting rms. Business servs avail. Bellhops. Sundries. Coin lndry. Golf privileges. Exercise equipt; bicycle, treadmill. Indoor pool; whirlpool, poolside serv. Game rm. Some in-rm whirlpools; microwaves avail. Picnic tables. On beach. Cr cds: A, C, D, DS, JCB, MC, V.

    D 🐾 ≈ ⊁ 🐾 SC

    ★ ★ ★ **FOUR POINTS BY SHERATON.** *1119 Sandusky Mall Blvd. 419/625-6280; FAX 419/625-9080.* 143 rms, 2 story. May-Sept: S, D $75-$140; suites $80-$200; under 18 free; lower rates rest of yr. Crib free. Pet accepted. TV; cable (premium). Indoor pool; whirlpool, poolside serv. Restaurant 7 am-10 pm. Rm serv. Bar 5 pm-2 am; entertainment Wed-Sat. Ck-out 11 am. Meeting rms. Business servs avail. In-rm modem link. Sundries. Game rm. Exercise equipt; bicycles, treadmills, sauna. Atrium. Cr cds: A, C, D, DS, MC, V.

    🐾 ≈ ⊁ 🐾 SC

    ★ ★ **HOLIDAY INN.** *5513 Milan Rd. 419/626-6671; FAX 419/626-9780.* 175 rms, 2 story, 15 suites. Late May-early Sept: S, D $100-$225; under 18 free; lower rates rest of yr. Crib free. TV; cable (premium). 2 pools, 1 indoor; whirlpools. Restaurant 6 am-2 pm, 5-10 pm. Rm serv. Bar 11-2 am. Ck-out 11 am. Free guest lndry. Meeting rm. Business servs avail. In-rm modem link. Valet serv. Sundries. Miniature golf. Exercise equipt; weights, bicycles, sauna. Game rm. Rec rm. Tennis adj. Some in-rm whirlpools. Cr cds: A, C, D, DS, JCB, MC, V.

    D ≈ ⊁ 🐾 SC

    ★ ★ ★ **RADISSON HARBOUR INN.** *2001 Cleveland Rd, at Cedar Point Causeway. 419/627-2500; FAX 419/627-0745.* 237 rms, 4 story, 49 suites. May-mid-Sept: S, D $99-$239; suites $109-$359; under 18 free; lower rates rest of yr. Crib free. Pet accepted, some restrictions. TV; cable (premium), VCR avail. Indoor pool; whirlpool, poolside serv. Supervised child's activities (May-mid-Sept); ages 4-13. Restaurant 6:30 am-11 pm. Rm serv. Bars 11-2 am; entertainment wkends. Ck-out noon. Coin lndry. Meeting rms. Business center. In-rm modem link. Bellhops. Valet serv. Gift shop. Airport, RR station, bus depot transportation. Exercise equipt; weights, bicycles. Game rm. Rec rm. Some refrigerators; microwaves avail. Private patios, balconies. Waterfront views of Sandusky Bay. Cr cds: A, C, D, DS, ER, JCB, MC, V.

    D 🐾 ≈ ⊁ 🐾 SC 🏂

Restaurant

    ★ ★ **BAY HARBOR INN.** *2 mi N of US 6, just outside of Cedar Point Park on Causeway Dr. 419/625-6373.* Hrs: 5-10 pm. Closed major hols; also Sun Oct-Apr. Res accepted Sun-Thur (summer), Mon-Fri (rest of yr). Bar from 4 pm. Semi-a la carte: dinner $12.95-$42.50. Child's meals. Specializes in fresh seafood, prime rib. Own pasta. View of Sandusky Bay and marina. Cr cds: A, DS, MC, V.

Serpent Mound State Memorial (F-3)

(For accommodations see Chillicothe, Portsmouth)

(4 mi NW of Locust Grove on OH 73)

The largest and most remarkable serpent effigy earthworks in North America. Built between 800 B.C. and A.D. 100 of stone and yellow clay, it curls like an enormous snake for 1,335 feet. An oval earthwall represents the serpent's open mouth. In the 61-acre area are an observation tower, a scenic gorge, a museum and picnicking facilities. Site (all yr); museum (Memorial Day-Labor Day, Wed-Sun; Sept-Oct, wkends; hrs vary, phone ahead). Phone 513/587-2796. Parking ¢¢

Sidney (D-2)

(See also Bellefontaine, Piqua, Wapakoneta)

Pop 18,710 **Elev** 956 ft **Area code** 513 **Zip** 45365
Information Sidney-Shelby County Chamber of Commerce, 100 S Main, Ste 201; 513/492-9122.

Annual Event

Country Concert at Hickory Hill Lakes. Phone 513/295-3000. July 11-13.

Motels

★ ★ **COMFORT INN.** *1959 W Michigan St, at jct I-75 & OH 47 exit 92.* 513/492-3001; FAX 513/497-8150. 72 rms, 2 story, 16 suites. S $53-$65; D $59-$70; each addl $5; suites $95-$110; family rates; higher rates special events. Crib free. TV; cable, VCR avail (movies). Heated pool. Complimentary continental bkfst. Restaurant adj 6 am-11 pm. Ck-out 11 am. Meeting rms. Business servs avail. Sundries. Refrigerator, microwave in suites. Cr cds: A, C, D, DS, JCB, MC, V.

D ≈ ≈ 🐾 SC

★ ★ **HOLIDAY INN.** *400 Folkerth Ave, OH 47 & I-75 exit 92.* 513/492-1131; FAX 513/498-4655. 134 rms, 2 story. S $65-$67; D $70-$77; each addl $5; suites $75-$77; under 19 free; package plans. Crib free. Pet accepted, some restrictions. TV; cable (premium), VCR avail. Pool. Restaurant 6:30 am-10 pm; Sat from 7 am; Sun to 9 pm. Rm serv. Bar 11 am-midnight, Fri, Sat to 1 am. Ck-out noon. Coin lndry. Meeting rms. Business servs avail. In-rm modem link. Valet serv. Sundries. Exercise equipt; weights, bicycles, sauna. Game rm. Microwaves in suites. Cr cds: A, C, D, DS, JCB, MC, V.

D 🐾 ≈ 🏋 ≈ 🐾 SC

Restaurant

★ ★ **FAIRINGTON.** *1103 Fairington Dr, I-75 exit 90.* 513/492-6186. Hrs: 11 am-2 pm, 4:30-10 pm; Sat from 5 pm. Closed Sun; most major hols. Res accepted. Bar. Semi-a la carte: lunch $4.99-$8.95, dinner $9.95-$17.95. Child's meals. Specializes in steak, seafood, pasta. Pianist Fri, Sat. Overlooks wooded area. Cr cds: A, D, DS, MC, V.

D SC 🔙

Springfield (E-2)

(See also Bellefontaine, Columbus, Dayton)

Founded 1801 **Pop** 70,487 **Elev** 980 ft **Area code** 937
Information Convention & Visitors Bureau, 333 N Limestone St, Ste 201, 45503; 937/325-7621.

Indian Scout Simon Kenton, an early settler, set up a gristmill and sawmill on the present site of the Navistar International plant. His wife gave the village its name. When the National Pike came in 1839, Springfield came to be known as the "town at the end of the National Pike."

Agricultural machinery gave Springfield its next boost. A farm journal, *Farm and Fireside,* published in the 1880s by P.J. Mast, a cultivator-manufacturer, was the start of the Crowell-Collier Publishing Co. The 4-H

movement was started here in 1902 by A. B. Graham, and hybrid corn grown by George H. Shull had its beginning in Springfield. A center for some 200 diversified industries, Springfield is in the rich agricultural valley of west-central Ohio.

What to See and Do

Antioch College (1852). (800 students) Liberal arts and sciences. Horace Mann, first president, aimed to establish a school free of sectarianism. Known for the cooperative education plan under which students alternate periods of study and work. 9 1/2 mi S on US 68, East Center College St in Yellow Springs. Phone 937/767-7331. Also has 1,000-acre Glen Helen nature preserve, phone 937/767-7375.

Buck Creek State Park. A 4,030-acre park with swimming, lifeguard, bathhouse (Memorial Day-Labor Day); fishing; boating (launch, ramp). Hiking. Snowmobile trails. Picnicking, concession. Camping; cabins. Standard fees. (Daily) 4 mi NE on OH 4; exit 62 off OH 70. Phone 937/322-5284. **Free.** On grounds is

David Crabill House (1826). Built by Clark County pioneer David Crabill; restored. Period rms; log barn; smokehouse. Maintained by Clark County Historical Society. (Tues-Fri) 818 N Fountain Ave. Phone 937/324-0657 for schedule. ¢

John Bryan State Park. A 750-acre park with fishing. Hiking. Picnic area. Camping. Standard fees. (Daily) 9 1/2 mi S of I-70 on US 68, then 3 mi SE via OH 343, 370, near Yellow Springs. Phone 937/767-1274. **Free.**

Pennsylvania House (1824). Built as tavern and stagecoach stop on National Pike; period furnishings, pioneer artifacts; button, quilt and doll collections. (1st Sun afternoon of each month; also by appt; closed Easter & late Dec-Feb) 1311 W Main St. Phone 937/322-7668. ¢¢

Springfield Museum of Art. Loaned exhibits change monthly; permanent collection includes 19th- and 20th-century American and French art; fine arts school; library; docent tours. (Daily exc Mon; closed hols, also wk of Christmas) 107 Cliff Park Rd. Phone 937/325-4673. **Free.**

Annual Event

Clark County Fair. Fairgrounds. Horse shows, rodeos, tractor pulls. Mid-July.

Seasonal Event

Springfield Arts Festival. Veteran's Memorial Park amphitheater, area auditoriums. Six-wk series of free performances; music, dance, visual arts, drama. Phone 937/324-2712. June-mid-July.

Motel

★ ★ **FAIRFIELD INN BY MARRIOTT.** *1870 W 1st St (45504), I-70 exit 52 B.* 937/323-9554. 63 rms, 3 story. Mar-Oct: S, D $60-$75; each addl $6; suites $70-$85; under 18 free; higher rates special events; lower rates rest of yr. Crib free. TV; cable (premium), VCR avail. Indoor pool; whirlpool. Complimentary continental bkfst. Restaurant adj 6 am-10 pm. Ck-out 11 am. Business servs avail. Health club privileges. Game rm. Some refrigerators. Microwave in suites. Cr cds: A, C, D, DS, MC, V.

D ≈ ≈ 🐾 SC

Hotel

★ ★ ★ **SPRINGFIELD INN.** *100 S Fountain Ave (45502).* 937/322-3600; FAX 937/322-0462; res: 800/234-3611. 124 rms, 6 story. S, D $78-$99; each addl $10; under 18 free; wkend rates. Crib free. TV; cable (premium), VCR avail. Complimentary coffee in rms. Restaurant 6 am-10 pm. Bar 11 am-midnight, wkends to 1 am. Ck-out noon. Meeting rms. Business servs avail. Health club privileges. Refrigerators avail. Balconies. Luxury level. Cr cds: A, C, D, DS, MC, V.

D ≈ 🐾 SC

Restaurants

★ ★ **CASEY'S.** *2205 Park Rd, I-70 to OH 68 N exit US 40 E. 937/322-0397.* Hrs: 11:30 am-2 pm, 5-10 pm; Sat from 5 pm. Closed Sun; major hols. Res accepted. Bar. Semi-a la carte: lunch $4.95-$7.95, dinner $8.95-$16.95. Specializes in steak, prime rib, fresh seafood. Own pasta. Cr cds: A, D, MC, V.

★ ★ **KLOSTERMAN'S DERR ROAD INN.** *4343 Derr Rd (45504), US 68N to Moorefield Rd E, then S on Derr Rd. 937/399-0822.* Hrs: 11 am-2 pm, 4 pm-close; Fri 11 am-2 pm, 5 pm-close; Sat from 5 pm; Sun 4-8 pm. Closed major hols. Res accepted. Continental menu. Bar. Semi-a la carte: lunch $4.50-$6.95, dinner $10.95-$18.95. Child's meals. Specializes in steaks, prime rib, fresh seafood. Own desserts. 1860s manor house with large windows overlooking property. Cr cds: A, C, D, DS, MC, V.

★ ★ **THE MILL.** *3404 W National Rd (OH 40). 937/324-4045.* Hrs: 11 am-10 pm; Fri, Sat to 11 pm; early-bird dinner Mon-Fri 4-6 pm. Closed Sun; major hols. Bar. Semi-a la carte: lunch $4.95-$6.95, dinner $6.50-$19.95. Child's meals. Specializes in steak, seafood. Former gristmill (1825). Cr cds: A, C, D, DS, MC, V.

Steubenville (D-6)

(See also East Liverpool)

Settled 1797 **Pop** 22,125 **Elev** 715 ft **Area code** 614 **Zip** 43952
Information Jefferson County Chamber of Commerce, 630 Market St, PO Box 278; 614/282-6226.

Although its early industries were pottery, coal, woolen cloth, glass and shipbuilding, the rolling mills of Wheeling-Pittsburgh Steel and Weirton Steel started Steubenville's economic growth.

The town's location was selected by the government as a fort in 1786. Fort Steuben (which was destroyed by fire in 1790) and the town were named for the Prussian Baron Frederick William von Steuben, who aided the colonies in the Revolutionary War. It is the seat of Jefferson County.

What to See and Do

Creegan Company. Country's largest designer and manufacturer of animations, costume characters and decor offers guided tours (approx 1 hr) through its 3-story factory and showroom. (Mon-Sat; Sun by appt) 510 Washington St. Phone 614/283-3708. **Free.**

Jefferson County Courthouse. Contains first county deed record, signed by George Washington, and portraits of Steubenville personalities. Statue of Edwin Stanton, Lincoln's secretary of war, is on the lawn. (Mon-Fri; closed major hols) 301 Market St. Phone 614/283-4111. **Free.**

Jefferson County Historical Association Museum and Genealogical Library. Tudor-style mansion with collection of historic memorabilia and genealogical materials; guided tours. (Mid-Apr-Dec, Tues-Sat; closed hols) 426 Franklin Ave. Phone 614/283-1133. **¢**

Union Cemetery. Contains many Civil War graves, including the "fighting McCook" plot, where members of a family that sent 13 men to fight in the Union Army are buried. (Daily) 1720 W Sunset Blvd. Phone 614/283-3384.

Motor Hotel

★ ★ ★ **HOLIDAY INN.** *1401 University Blvd, ³/₄ mi W of OH 7. 614/282-0901; FAX 614/282-9540.* 120 rms, 2 story. No elvtr. S, D $65; each addl $5; under 18 free. Pet accepted, some restrictions. TV; cable (premium), VCR avail. Heated pool. Restaurant 6 am-midnight. Rm serv.

Bar 7 am-10 pm. Ck-out noon. Coin lndry. Business servs avail. In-rm modem link. Bellhops. Valet serv. Cr cds: A, C, D, DS, JCB, MC, V.

Strongsville (B-5)

(For accommodations see Cleveland, Elyria)

Pop 35,308 **Elev** 932 ft **Area code** 440 **Zip** 44136
Information Chamber of Commerce, 18829 Royalton Rd; 440/238-3366.

First settled in 1816, Strongsville is the largest suburban community in Cuyahoga County.

What to See and Do

Gardenview Horticultural Park. English-style cottage gardens devoted to collecting uncommon and unusual plants. 16 acres include 6 acres of gardens with seasonal plantings, and a 10-acre arboretum; 2,000 flowering crabapples bloom first 2 wks May. (Early Apr-mid-Oct, Sat & Sun only) On US 42, 1¹/₂ mi S of US 82. Phone 440/238-6653. **¢¢**

Tiffin (C-3)

(See also Bellevue, Findlay, Fremont)

Founded 1817 **Pop** 18,604 **Elev** 758 ft **Area code** 419 **Zip** 44883 **E-mail** sccvb@bpsom.com **Web** www.bpsom.com/sccvb/visitor.html
Information Seneca County Convention & Visitors Bureau, 84 Jefferson St; 419/447-5866 or 888/736-3221.

Tiffin is a quiet, tree-shaded town on the Sandusky River; it has diversified industries that include pottery, glassware, electric motor, heavy machinery and conveyor manufacturing.

What to See and Do

Glass Heritage Gallery. Museum houses a collection of glass made in Fostoria plants from 1887 to 1920; examples include lamps, crystal bowls, mosaic art glass, novelty glass. (Tues-Sat; closed hols) 14 mi W via OH 18, at 109 N Main St in Fostoria. Phone 419/435-5077. **Free.**

Industrial tours.

Ballreich's Potato Chips. 30-min guided tours by appt (May-Dec, Mon, Tues, Thurs & Fri mornings; closed hols) 186 Ohio Ave. Phone 419/447-1814 or 800/323-2447. **Free.**

King's Glass Engraving. Demonstrations. (Daily exc Sun; closed hols) 181 S Washington St. Phone 419/447-0232. **Free.**

Crystal Traditions. Glassblowing and glass engraving. Free guided tours by appt (Mon-Fri; closed hols). Gift shop (daily exc Sun; closed hols). 145 Madison St. For tour information phone 419/448-4286.

Seneca County Museum. Historic house (ca 1853) museum contains extensive collection of Tiffin glass; drawing room furnished with early Victorian pieces; porcelain collection; research library; kitchen with original built-in stove; second floor has music room with a pianola and a 200-yr-old harp, and bedrooms with a rope bed and trundle bed. The third floor has collection of Native American artifacts, and toy and doll collection. Tours (June-Aug, Tues-Thurs & Sun afternoons; rest of yr, Wed & Sun afternoons; also by appt). 28 Clay St. Phone 419/447-5955. **Donation.**

Annual Events

Glass Heritage Festival. Glass festival features glass shows, tours, entertainment, arts & crafts. Fostoria. Phone 419/435-0486. 2nd wkend July.

Tiffin-Seneca Heritage Festival. Entertainment, crafts, living history village; ethnic foods, parade. 3rd wkend Sept.

Restaurant

★ **BLACK CAT.** (820 Sandusky St, Fostoria) 1/2 mi E on OH 12. 419/435-2685. Hrs: 11:30 am-10 pm; Sat from 4:30 pm; Sun 11:30 am-3 pm; early-bird dinner Mon-Fri 4:30-6:30 pm. Closed major hols; also mid-June-Labor Day Sun. Res accepted. Bar. Semi-a la carte: lunch $3.50-$4.50, dinner $7-$24.50. Child's meals. Specializes in steak, seafood. Over 575 black cat figurines on display. Cr cds: DS, MC, V.

Toledo (B-2)

(See also Bowling Green, Port Clinton)

Settled 1817 **Pop** 332,943 **Elev** 587 ft **Area code** 419 **E-mail** info@meettoledo.org **Web** www.meettoledo.org
Information Greater Toledo Convention & Visitors Bureau, 401 Jefferson, 43604; 419/321-6404 or 800/243-4667.

The French first explored the Toledo area, situated at the mouth of the Maumee River on Lake Erie, in 1615. Probably named after Toledo, Spain, the present city began as a group of small villages along the river. During 1835-1836 it was claimed by both Michigan and Ohio in the Toledo War, which resulted in Toledo becoming part of Ohio and the Northern Peninsula going to Michigan.

Toledo's large, excellent natural harbor makes it an important port. Numerous railroads move coal and ore to the south, east and north, grain from the southwest, steel from Cleveland and Pittsburgh and automobile parts and accessories to and from Detroit.

Edward Libbey introduced the glass industry to Toledo in 1888 with high-grade crystal and lamp globes. Michael Owens, a glassblower, joined him and invented a machine that turned molten glass into bottles by the thousands. Today Owens-Illinois, Inc, Libbey-Owens-Ford Co, Owens-Corning Fiberglas Corp and Johns-Manville Fiber Glass, Inc manufacture a variety of glass products. Metropolitan Toledo has more than 1,000 manufacturing plants producing jeeps, spark plugs, chemicals and other products.

What to See and Do

COSI Toledo. First-hand science learning is available here through hands-on experiments, demonstrations and eight Exhibition Worlds. These include Kidspace, Babyspace and an outdoors Science Park. Restaurant. (Mon-Sat, Sun afternoons; closed major hols) 1 Discovery Way, at the corner of Summit and Adams Sts. Phone 419/244-COSI.

Crane Creek State Park. A 79-acre park with swimming (lifeguard; Memorial Day-Labor Day). Fishing. Hiking. Picnicking. Ice fishing. Trail for birdwatching. (Daily) 18 mi E off OH 2, SE of Bono. Phone 419/898-2495. **Free.**

Fort Meigs State Memorial. Reconstruction of fort built under supervision of William Henry Harrison in 1813; used during War of 1812. Blockhouses with exhibits; demonstrations of military life. (Memorial Day-Labor Day, Wed-Sun; after Labor Day-Oct, wkends & hols) Picnicking in area. On W River Rd (OH 65). Take I-475 to exit 2, turn N onto OH 65. Phone 419/874-4121. ¢¢

Maumee Bay State Park. The wet woods and marshes of this 1,860-acre shoreline park are havens to wildlife and are good for birdwatching. Beaches; fishing; boat rentals. Hiking; 18-hole golf. Lodge. Camping (tent rentals avail), 20 cabins. Amphitheater. Nature center. Standard fees. (Daily) 8 mi E on OH 2, then N on Curtice Rd, in Oregon. Phone 419/836-7758 (park admin), 419/836-1466 (resort) or 800/282-7275 (lodge & cabin reservations). **Free.**

Parks.

Detwiler/Bay View Park. Pool (early May-Sept); boating (launch; fee), marina; picnicking, concessions; playgrounds on 219 acres; two golf courses (fee), tennis. Lighted ball field; view of port. (Daily) 4001 N Summit St at Manhattan Blvd. Phone 419/726-9353. **Free.**

Ottawa Park. Picnicking on 305 acres, concessions; playgrounds; 18-hole golf course (fee), tennis; jogging & nature trails; nature center; artificial skating rink (fee); cross-country ski trails (fee). Bancroft at Parkside St. Phone 419/472-2059.

Toledo Botanical Garden. Seasonal floral displays; herb, rhododendron and azalea gardens, perennial garden, rose garden, fragrance garden for the visually and physically impaired. 1837 Pioneer Homestead; art galleries, glassblowing studios. Gift shops. Special musical and craft programs throughout yr. Arts festival (fee). (Daily) 5403 Elmer Dr, 6 mi W near I-475 W Central exit. Phone 419/936-2986. **Free.**

Port of Toledo. In total tonnage, this is one of the 25 largest ports in the US and one of the world's largest shippers of soft coal and grain. More than 1,000 vessels call at the port each yr. Lower 7 mi of Maumee River. Phone 419/243-8251.

SS *Willis B. Boyer* Museum Ship. This 600-ft freighter, launched in 1911, has been authentically restored and houses memoribilia, photos and nautical artifacts. Tours (45 min-1 hr). (May-Sept, daily; rest of yr, Tues-Sat) Moored across from downtown, on the E side of the Maumee River at 26 Main St, in International Park. Phone 419/936-3070. ¢¢

The Toledo Museum of Art. Considered to be one of the finest art museums in the country; collections range from ancient Egypt, Greece, and Rome through the Middle Ages and the Renaissance to European and American arts of the present; includes glass collections, paintings, sculpture, decorative and graphic arts; Egyptian mummy, medieval cloister, French chateau room, African sculpture, Oriental art, and Southeast Asian and Native American art. Art reference library; cafe; museum store. (Daily exc Mon; closed major hols) 2445 Monroe St at Scottwood, 1 blk off I-75. Phone 419/255-8000. **Free.**

The Toledo Symphony. Presents classics, pops, music today, casual, chamber and Mozart concerts. Performances at different locations. (Mid-Sept-May) Facilities for hearing and visually impaired. 2 Maritime Plaza. For schedule phone 419/241-1272.

The Toledo Zoo. On exhibit are nearly 2,000 specimens of 400 species. On its 30 acres are fresh and saltwater aquariums, large mammal collection, reptiles, birds, a Children's Zoo, botanical gardens and greenhouse, Museum of Science and the Diversity of Life hands-on exhibit; "Hippoquarium," offering filtered underwater viewing of hippopotamus. (Daily; closed Jan 1, Thanksgiving, Dec 25) 2700 Broadway, 3 mi S of downtown on US 25. Phone 419/385-5721 or 419/385-4040. ¢¢

University of Toledo (1872). (25,000 students) The 250-acre main campus has 8 colleges, continuing education division, graduate school; 2-yr community and technical college on 160-acre campus at Nebraska Ave & Parkside Blvd; 47-acre arboretum, Sylvania Ave & Corey Rd; downtown at Jefferson Ave at Seagate Centre. Campus tours. Planetarium presents several shows (Oct-June). Savage Hall has frequent concerts and sports events. Music and theater departments have concerts and shows. Obtain free parking permit at information booth. W Bancroft St, 4 mi W. Phone 419/530-2675.

Wolcott Museum Complex. Museum complex includes early 19-century home, log house, Greek-revival village house, saltbox farmhouse and depot furnished with period artifacts. (Apr-Dec, Wed-Sun; closed hols) 1031 River Rd, SW via I-75, I-475 Anthony Wayne Trail exit in Maumee. Phone 419/893-9602. ¢¢

Annual Events

Crosby Festival of the Arts. At Toledo Botanical Garden. Fine arts and crafts, music, dance and drama. Phone 419/536-8365. Last full wkend June.

Northwest Ohio Rib-Off. Riverfront. Restaurants compete in rib cooking contest and offer samples and full slabs at nominal prices; bands, children's events, special events. 1st wkend Aug.

Seasonal Event

Horse racing. Toledo Raceway Park. 5700 Telegraph Rd, 5 mi N on US 24 or 2 mi W of I-75, exit Alexis Rd. Harness racing. Phone 419/476-7751. Wed & Fri-Sun. Late Mar-late Nov.

Motels

★ ★ **COMFORT INN.** *3560 Secor Rd (43606), at I-475 exit 17.* 419/531-2666; FAX 419/531-4757. 70 rms, 2 story. S, D $60-$65. Crib free. Pet accepted, some restrictions. TV; cable (premium). Complimentary continental bkfst. Restaurant adj. Ck-out noon. Health club privileges. Picnic tables. Cr cds: A, C, D, DS, JCB, MC, V.

D ⚡ ✕ ≈ ⚒ SC

★ ★ **COURTYARD BY MARRIOTT.** *(1435 E Mall Dr, Holland 43528) jct I-475 and OH 2.* 419/866-1001; FAX 419/866-9869. 149 units, 3 story, 12 suites. S $95; D $105; suites $115-$125; under 18 free; wkend rates. Crib free. TV; cable (premium). Indoor pool; whirlpool. Restaurant 6:30-10 am; wkend hrs vary. Bar 4-11 pm, closed Sun. Ck-out noon. Coin lndry. Meeting rms. In-rm modem link. Valet serv. Sundries. Free airport transportation. Exercise equipt; weights, bicycles. Refrigerator in suites. Private patios, balconies. Cr cds: A, C, D, DS, MC, V.

D ≈ ✕ ≈ ⚒ SC

✔★ **CROWN INN.** *1727 W Alexis Rd (43613).* 419/473-1485. 40 rms. S, D $44.99-$49.99; each addl $6; suites $87.99-$109.99; kits. $51.99-$56.99; under 16 free. Crib $6. TV; cable, VCR avail. Pool. Complimentary continental bkfst. Restaurant nearby. Ck-out noon. Sundries. Some refrigerators. Cr cds: A, C, D, DS, MC, V.

D ≈ ✕ ≈ ⚒ SC

✔★ ★ **DAYS INN.** *(150 Dussel Dr, Maumee 43537) 1 mi S off I-80/90 exit 4.* 419/893-9960; FAX 419/893-9559. 120 units, 2 story, 6 suites, 4 kits. S $34-$47; D $49-$68; each addl $6; suites, kit. units $47-$68; under 18 free; wkly rates. Crib free. Pet accepted. TV; cable (premium). Pool. Complimentary continental bkfst. Restaurant adj 6 am-11 pm. Ck-out noon. Business servs avail. Valet serv. Some refrigerators; microwaves avail. Cr cds: A, C, D, DS, JCB, MC, V.

D ⚡ ≈ ≈ ⚒ SC

★ ★ **HAMPTON INN-SOUTH.** *(1409 Reynolds Rd, Maumee 43537) 1/4 mi S off I-80/90 exit 4.* 419/893-1004; FAX 419/893-4613. Web www.hampton-inn.com. 129 rms, 4 story. S $56-$60; D $64-$72; under 18 free. Crib free. TV; cable (premium), VCR avail. Heated pool. Complimentary continental bkfst. Restaurant adj open 24 hrs. Ck-out noon. Meeting rms. Valet serv. Sundries. Free airport transportation. Exercise equipt; weight machine, stair machine. Cr cds: A, C, D, DS, JCB, MC, V.

D ≈ ✕ ≈ ⚒ SC

Motor Hotels

★ ★ ★ **CLARION-WESTGATE.** *3536 Secor Rd (43606).* 419/535-7070; FAX 419/536-4836. 305 rms, 3 story. S, D $79-$99; suites $99-$275; under 18 free. Crib free. Pet accepted, some restrictions. TV; cable. Indoor pool; whirlpool. Restaurant 6:30 am-2:30 pm, 6-11 pm. Rm serv. Bar. Ck-out noon. Convention facilities. Business center. In-rm modem link. Valet serv. Sundries. Gift shop. Exercise equipt; treadmill, stair machines. Game rm. Landscaped enclosed courtyard. Cr cds: A, C, D, DS, MC, V.

D ⚡ ≈ ✕ ⚑ ≈ ⚒ SC ⚒

★ ★ **HOLIDAY INN.** *2340 S Reynolds Rd (43614).* 419/865-1361; FAX 419/865-6177. 218 rms, 11 story. S, D $99; each addl $10; suites $109-$119; under 18 free; family, wkend rates. Crib free. Pet accepted. TV; cable (premium). Indoor pool. Restaurant 6:30 am-2 pm, 5-10 pm; Sat, Sun from 7 am. Rm serv. Bar 4:30 pm-midnight, Sat from 4 pm, closed Sun. Ck-out noon. Meeting rms. Business servs avail. In-rm

modem link. Bellhops. Gift shop. Beauty shop. Free airport transportation. Exercise equipt; bicycles, rowers. Cr cds: A, C, D, DS, JCB, MC, V.

D ⚡ ≈ ✕ ≈ ⚒ SC

★ ★ **RAMADA.** *2429 S Reynolds Rd (43614).* 419/381-8765; FAX 419/381-0129. 264 rms, 6 story. S $59-$78; D $63-$86; each addl $8; under 18 free; wkend rates. Crib free. Pet accepted, some restrictions. TV; cable (premium), VCR avail. Indoor pool; whirlpool, poolside serv. Playground. Restaurant 6 am-2 pm, 5-10 pm. Rm serv. Bar 11-2:30 am, Sun to 11 pm. Ck-out 11 am. Convention facilities. In-rm modem link. Bellhops. Valet serv. Sundries. Gift shop. Free airport transportation. Microwaves avail. Cr cds: A, C, D, DS, JCB, MC, V.

D ⚡ ≈ ≈ ⚒ SC

Hotels

★ ★ ★ **CROWNE PLAZA.** *2 Seagate (43604).* 419/241-1411; FAX 419/241-8161. Web www.meettoledo.org/crownehtml. 241 rms, 14 story. S, D $139; suites $149; under 18 free; wkend rates. Crib free. Pet accepted. Garage parking $10, valet. TV; cable (premium). Indoor pool; whirlpool. Restaurant 6:30 am-11 pm; Sat from 7 am. Bar from 11 am; Sun from 1 pm. Ck-out noon. Meeting rms. Business center. In-rm modem link. Gift shop. Exercise equipt; weights, bicycles, sauna. On river. Cr cds: A, C, D, DS, MC, V.

D ⚡ ≈ ✕ ≈ ⚒ SC ⚒

★ ★ **HILTON.** *3100 Glendale Ave (43614).* 419/381-6800; FAX 419/389-9716. 213 rms, 6 story. S, D $104-$144; each addl $10. Crib free. TV; cable (premium). Indoor pool; whirlpool. Complimentary coffee in rm. Restaurant 6:30 am-2 pm, 5-10 pm; Fri, Sat to 11 pm, Sun to 9 pm. Bar 4 pm-midnight. Ck-out noon. Meeting rms. Business servs avail. In-rm modem link. Free airport transportation. Lighted tennis. Sauna. Health club privileges. Refrigerators avail. Cr cds: A, C, D, DS, MC, V.

D ⚡ ≈ ✕ ≈ ⚒ SC

Restaurants

★ ★ ★ **FIFI'S.** *1423 Bernath Pkwy (43615), at Airport Hwy.* 419/866-6777. Hrs: 5-11 pm; wkends to midnight. Closed Sun; major hols. Res accepted. French, continental menu. Bar. Wine cellar. Semi-a la carte: dinner $16.95-$24.95. Specializes in seafood, veal, tableside cooking. Pianist Fri, Sat. Cr cds: A, D, DS, MC, V.

D ⚒

★ ★ **MANCY'S.** *953 Phillips Ave (43612).* 419/476-4154. Web www.mancys.com. Hrs: 11 am-2 pm, 5-9:30 pm; Fri to 10:30 pm; Sat 5-10:30 pm. Closed Sun; major hols. Res accepted. Bar. Semi-a la carte: lunch $4.95-$11.95, dinner $10.95-$22.95. Child's meals. Specializes in steak, fresh seafood. Tiffany lamps, antiques. Family-owned since 1921. Cr cds: A, C, D, DS, MC, V.

D ⚒

★ ★ **SMEDLAP'S SMITHY.** *(205 Farmsworth Rd, Waterville 43566) Just off US 24, 64.* 419/878-0261. Hrs: 11:30 am-10 pm; Fri, Sat to 11 pm. Closed Sun; major hols. Res accepted. Bar. Semi-a la carte: lunch $3.95-$8, dinner $7.95-$22.95. Child's meals. Specializes in prime rib. Old blacksmith shop with circular slide from second-floor loft. Cr cds: A, DS, MC, V.

SC ⚒

✔★ **TONY PACKO'S CAFE.** *1902 Front St (43605), I-280 exit 9.* 419/691-6054. E-mail eat@tonypacko.com; web www.tonypacko.com. Hrs: 11 am-11 pm; Fri to midnight; Sat 11 am-midnight; Sun noon-9 pm. Closed major hols. Res accepted. Hungarian menu. Bar. Semi-a la carte: lunch $4-$8, dinner $6.50-$10. Child's meals. Specializes in chili, stuffed cabbage, Hungarian hot dogs. Jazz band Fri, Sat evenings; Big Band last Tues of month. Family-owned. Cr cds: A, DS, MC, V.

Vandalia (E-2)

(See also Dayton, Springfield)

Settled 1838 **Pop** 13,882 **Elev** 994 ft **Area code** 937 **Zip** 45377 **E-mail** chamber@coax.net **Web** coax.net/vandalia
Information Chamber of Commerce, 76 Fordway Dr, PO Box 224; 937/898-5351.

What to See and Do

Trapshooting Hall of Fame and Museum. Exhibits depict highlights of this sport. (Mon-Fri; closed most hols) 601 W National Rd. Phone 937/898-1945 or 937/898-4638.   **Free.**

Annual Events

US Air & Trade Show. Dayton International Airport. Features approximately 100 outdoor exhibits; flight teams. Phone 937/898-5901. Late July.

Grand American World Trapshooting Tournament of the Amateur Trapshooting Assn of America. Trapshooting Hall of Fame Museum (see). Grand American Shoot; membership and shooting fee. Phone 937/898-4638. 10 days mid-Aug.

Motel

✔★ ★ **CROSS COUNTRY INN.** *550 E National Rd (OH 40), at I-75 exit 63. 937/898-7636; FAX 937/898-0630; res: 800/621-1429.* 94 rms, 3 story. S $35.99-$40.99; D $42.99-$47.99. Crib free. TV; cable (premium). Pool. Complimentary coffee in lobby. Restaurant adj 6 am-11 pm. Ck-out noon. Meeting rm. Business servs avail. Cr cds: A, C, D, DS, MC, V.

D ⚊ ⚊ ⚊ SC

Van Wert (C-1)

(For accommodations see Celina, Lima, Wapakoneta)

Founded 1835 **Pop** 10,891 **Elev** 780 ft **Area code** 419 **Zip** 45891
Information Chamber of Commerce, 118 W Main St; 419/238-4390.

What to See and Do

Van Wert County Historical Society Museum. Restored Victorian mansion (1890) houses the farm rm, fabric rm, children's rm; early town artifacts; research center. Annex built in 1985 houses war memorabilia; country store, cobbler's shop and barbershop. One-rm school building and caboose also on grounds. (Sun afternoons; also by appt; closed hols & last wk Dec) 602 N Washington St at 3rd St. Phone 419/238-5297.   **Free.**

Annual Event

Van Wert County Fair. Fairgrounds, Fox Rd off S Washington St. Begins Wed before Labor Day.

Vermilion (B-4)

(For accommodations see Elyria, Milan, Oberlin, Sandusky; also see Lorain)

Settled 1808 **Pop** 11,127 **Elev** 600 ft **Area code** 216 **Zip** 44089
Information Chamber of Commerce, 5495 Liberty Ave; 216/967-4477.

What to See and Do

Inland Seas Maritime Museum. Maritime museum containing Great Lakes ship models, paintings, photographs, artifacts. Audio-visual displays. (Daily; closed Dec 25) 480 Main St (US 6), on lakeshore. Phone 216/967-3467.   ¢¢

Annual Events

Festival of the Fish. Entertainment, exhibits, sports events, parade, contests, crazy craft race, lighted boat parade. Father's Day wkend.

Boat Regatta. More than 200 sailboats race from Put-In-Bay to Vermilion Boat Club. 1st wkend Aug.

Woolly Bear Festival. Races, children's games, crafts, entertainment. Phone 216/967-4477. Late Sept or early Oct.

Restaurant

★ ★ ★ **CHEZ FRANCOIS.** *555 Main St. 216/967-0630.* Hrs: 5-9 pm; Fri, Sat to 10 pm; Sun 4-9 pm. Closed Mon; also Jan-mid-Mar. Res accepted. French menu. Wine list. Semi-a la carte: dinner $14.95-$28.95. Specialties: beef Wellington, lobster Thermadore. Outdoor dining. Overlooks Vermilion River. Jacket. Cr cds: A, MC, V.

Wapakoneta (D-2)

(See also Bellefontaine, Celina, Lima)

Pop 9,214 **Elev** 895 ft **Area code** 419 **Zip** 45895

What to See and Do

Neil Armstrong Museum. Variety of aircraft, from balloons to spacecraft, showing aerospace accomplishments; audiovisual presentation, other exhibits. (Mar-Nov, daily) 500 S Apollo Dr. Phone 419/738-8811.   ¢¢

Motel

✔ ★ **BUDGET HOST INN.** *(505 State St, Botkins 45306) 7 mi S on I-75 exit 104. 937/693-6911; FAX 937/693-8200.* 50 rms, 4 kit. units. S $28.95-$39; D $35-$41; each addl $3; kit. units $35-$41; under 12 free; wkly rates. Crib $6. TV; cable (premium). Complimentary continental bkfst. Restaurant 5-10 pm. Bar 5 pm-2:30 am. Ck-out 11 am. Meeting rms. Business servs avail. Coin lndry. Tennis. Pool. Microwave in kit. units. Cr cds: A, DS, MC, V.

⚊ ⚊ ⚊ ⚊ SC

Motor Hotel

★ ★ **HOLIDAY INN.** *1510 Saturn Dr. 419/738-8181; FAX 419/738-6478.* 100 rms, 4 story. S, D $59; each addl $5; suites $69; under 18 free. Crib free. Pet accepted. TV; cable (premium), VCR avail. Pool. Complimentary continental bkfst. Complimentary coffee in rms. Restaurant 6 am-9 pm; Sat from 7 am; Sun 7 am-8 pm. Rm serv. Bar 11-1 am; Sat 5 pm-1 am. Ck-out noon. Coin lndry. Meeting rms. Business servs avail. In-rm modem link. Valet serv. Sundries. Exercise equipt; treadmill, stair machine. Neil Armstrong Museum adj. Cr cds: A, C, D, DS, JCB, MC, V.

Warren (B-6)

(See also Aurora, Kent, Youngstown)

Founded 1799 **Pop** 50,793 **Elev** 893 ft **Area code** 330

Information Youngstown/Warren Regional Chamber, 160 E Market, Ste 225, 44481; 330/393-2565.

In 1800 Warren became the seat of the Western Reserve and then the seat of newly formed Trumbull County. At one of its stagecoach inns, the Austin House, Stephen Collins Foster is said to have begun writing "Jeannie with the Light Brown Hair," and, according to local history, while walking along the Mahoning River he found the inspiration for "My Old Kentucky Home."

What to See and Do

John Stark Edwards House (1807). Oldest house in the Western Reserve, now maintained by Trumbull County Historical Society. (Sun afternoons, limited hrs; closed hols) Children must be accompanied by adult. 303 Monroe St NW. Phone 330/394-4653. ¢

Mosquito Lake State Park. A 11,811-acre park with 7,850-acre lake and 40 miles of lakeshore. Swimming; fishing, hunting; boating (launch, rentals). Hiking, bridle trails. Picnicking. Snowmobiling. Camping (showers; no electric hookup). Standard fees. (Daily) 7 mi NE on OH 5, then 1 mi W on OH 305 to park entrance. Phone 330/637-2856. **Free.**

Motel

★ ★ **BEST WESTERN-DOWNTOWN.** *777 Mahoning Ave (44483), just off OH 45.* 330/392-2515; FAX 330/392-7099. 73 rms, 2 story. S $50-$60; D $62-$72; each addl $3; under 16 free. Pet accepted. TV; cable (premium). Pool. Complimentary continental bkfst. Restaurant 3-11 pm. Bar to 2 am. Ck-out 11 am. Business servs avail. Valet serv. Some refrigerators. Cr cds: A, C, D, DS, ER, MC, V.

Motor Hotel

★ ★ ★ **AVALON INN.** *9519 E Market St (44484), at Warren-Sharon Rd.* 330/856-1900; FAX 330/856-2248; res: 800/221-1549 (exc OH), 800/828-2566 (OH). 144 rms, 2 story. S $72; D $85-$95; each addl $10; suites $95-$150; under 16 free. Crib free. TV. Indoor pool; whirlpool, lifeguard. Restaurant 6:30 am-10 pm; Fri, Sat to 11 pm. Snack bar. Rm serv. Bar 10:30-2:30 am. Ck-out noon. Meeting rms. Bellhops. Indoor, outdoor lighted tennis. Two 18-hole golf courses, greens fee $27-$45, pro, putting green, driving range. Exercise equipt; weight machines, bicycles, saunas. Lawn games. Many refrigerators. Some patios. Resort-type motor hotel. Cr cds: A, D, DS, MC, V.

Hotel

★ ★ **PARK.** *136 N Park Ave (44481).* 330/393-1200; FAX 330/399-2875; res: 800/397-7275. 55 rms, 4 story, 11 suites. S $60; D $70; each addl $10; suites $77; under 16 free. Crib free. Pet accepted. TV. Restaurant 6:30 am-10 pm. Bars. Ck-out noon. Meeting rms. Business servs avail. Airport transportation. Health club privileges. Restored brick hotel (1887). Cr cds: A, C, D, DS, MC, V.

Restaurant

★ ★ **ABRUZZI'S CAFE 422.** *4422 Youngstown Rd.* 330/369-2422. Hrs: 11 am-10 pm; Fri, Sat to 11 pm. Closed Dec 25. Res accepted. Bar. Semi-a la carte: lunch $4.95-$6.95, dinner $7.75-$20. Child's meals. Specializes in homemade Italian entrees, desserts. Family-owned. Cr cds: A, D, DS, MC, V.

Wauseon (B-2)

(See also Bowling Green, Toledo)

Pop 6,322 **Elev** 757 ft **Area code** 419 **Zip** 43567

What to See and Do

Sauder Farm & Craft Village. Three areas: farmstead has furnished 1860 farmhouse with summer kitchen and barnyard; pioneer village has craft demonstrations; museum building has antique implements and household items; costumed guides. (Mid-Apr-Oct, daily) 9 mi W via OH 2, near Archbold. Phone 419/446-2541. ¢¢¢

Motel

★ ★ **BEST WESTERN DEL-MAR.** *8319 SH 108, OH Tpke exit 3.* 419/335-1565; FAX 419/335-1828. 40 rms. June-Sept: S $52-$66; D $54-$66; each addl $10; suites $99-$109; under 18 free; lower rates rest of yr. Crib $6. Pet accepted. TV; cable (premium). Heated pool. Playground. Complimentary continental bkfst. Restaurant nearby. Ck-out 11 am. Cr cds: A, C, D, DS, ER, MC, V.

Wilmington (F-2)

(See also Dayton, Lebanon, Mason)

Pop 11,199 **Elev** 1,022 ft **Area code** 937 **Zip** 45177

Information Wilmington-Clinton County Chamber of Commerce, 40 N South St; 937/382-2737.

What to See and Do

Caesar Creek State Park. A 10,771-acre park. Crystal-blue lake waters have smallmouth and largemouth bass, crappie, catfish, bluegill and walleye. Swimming; fishing; boating (ramps). Hiking, bridle trails. Picnic areas. Snowmobiling, ice-skating. Campground has 287 sites (35 open in winter), 30 site horsemen's camp. Nature preserve, visitor center and complex near dam. A focal point of the park is Pioneer Village with many restored examples of early log architecture. (Daily) 11 mi NW on OH 73. Phone 937/897-3055. Visitor center **Free.**

Cowan Lake State Park. A 1,775-acre park with swimming; fishing; boating (launch, rentals) on 700-acre lake. Hiking. Picnicking, concession. Camping. Cabins. Standard fees. (Daily) 6 mi S via US 68, then W on OH 350. Phone 937/289-2105. **Free.**

Fort Ancient State Memorial (see). 11 mi SW on US 22, then 5 mi W on OH 350.

Little Miami Scenic State Park. This 452-acre park offers 45 mi of hiking and bridle trails, 22 mi of paved bicycle trails. Canoeing, access points at Corwin, Morrow and Loveland. (Daily) 15 mi NW on OH 73. Phone 937/897-3055. **Free.**

Rombach Place—Museum of Clinton Co Historical Society. Home of General James W. Denver, for whom Denver, CO was named. Antique furniture, Quaker clothing, tools, implements and kitchenware of pioneer days. Bronze animal sculptures and paintings by Eli Harvey, Quaker artist from Ohio. Photographs of Native American chieftains made in early 1900s by Karl Moon, a native of Wilmington. (Mar-Dec, Wed-Fri afternoons; closed hols) 149 E Locust St. Phone 937/382-4684.   •Donation.

Wilmington College (1870). (1,000 students) Liberal arts school. On campus is the Simon Goodman Memorial Carillon. Training camp in summer for Cincinnati Bengals (pro football). Campus tours. E on US 22. Phone 937/382-6661.

Motels

✔ ★ ★ **AMERIHOST INN.** *201 Carrie Dr. 937/383-3950; FAX 937/383-1693.* 61 rms, 2 story. S, D $65-$75; each addl $5; suites $99-$110; under 18 free. Crib free. TV; cable (premium). Complimentary continental bkfst. Coffee in rms. Restaurant nearby. Ck-out noon. Meeting rms. Business servs avail. In-rm modem link. Valet serv (Mon-Fri). Exercise equipt; weight machine, bicycle, sauna. Indoor pool; whirlpool. In-rm whirlpool, refrigerator, microwave in suites. Cr cds: A, C, D, DS, ER, JCB, MC, V.

[D] [≋] [🏋] [⛷] [⊠] [🐾] [SC]

★ **WILMINGTON INN.** *909 Fife Ave. 937/382-6000; FAX 937/382-6655.* 51 rms, 2 story. S $60-$125; D $65-$135; each addl $5; under 16 free. Crib $5. TV; cable (premium). Complimentary continental bkfst. Complimentary coffee in rms. Restaurant adj 6 am-10 pm. Ck-out 11 am. Meeting rms. Business servs avail. Cr cds: A, C, D, MC, V.

[D] [⊠] [🐾] [SC]

Restaurant

✔ ★ **DAMON'S.** *1045 Eastside Dr, E on OH 22/23. 937/383-1400.* Hrs: 11 am-11 pm; Fri, Sat to midnight; Sun to 10 pm. Closed Thanksgiving, Dec 25. Res accepted. Bar. Semi-a la carte: lunch $5-$6, dinner $10-$13. Child's meals. Specializes in ribs, steak, seafood. Contemporary sports bar atmosphere. Cr cds: A, C, D, DS, MC, V.

[D] [SC] [🍷]

Wooster (C-4)

(See also Akron, Canton, Mansfield, Massillon)

Settled 1807 **Pop** 22,191 **Elev** 897 ft **Area code** 330 **Zip** 44691 **E-mail** 103525.267@compuserve.com **Web** wooster-wayne.com/wccvb

Information Wayne County Convention & Visitor Bureau, 377 W Liberty St; 330/264-1800 or 800/362-6474.

Wooster claims to have had one of the first Christmas trees in America, introduced in 1847 by August Imgard, a young German immigrant. Disappointed with American Christmas, he cut down and decorated a spruce tree, which so pleased his neighbors that the custom spread throughout Ohio and the nation.

The town is in very productive farm country with wheat, corn, potatoes and many dairy farms. It also produces brass, paper, aluminum, roller bearings, brushes, rubber products, furniture and other products.

What to See and Do

College of Wooster (1866). (1,865 students) Liberal arts, sciences. Campus tours; art museum. Home of **Ohio Light Opera Company,** performing Gilbert & Sullivan and light opera classics with orchestra. (Mid-June-mid-Aug) E University St & Beall Ave, 1 mi N. Phone 216/263-2000 or 216/263-2345.

Ohio Agricultural Research and Development Center (1882). Research on livestock, fruits, vegetables, ornamentals, field crops, environmental and energy conservation, pesticides; greenhouses, orchards,

Secrest Arboretum, rhododendron and rose gardens. (Mon-Fri; closed hols; grounds open daily, tours by appt) Ohio State University. 1 mi S on Madison Ave. Phone 216/263-3779.   **Free.**

Wayne County Historical Society Museum. Pioneer relics, paintings, lusterware, Native American artifacts, mounted animals and birds; log cabin and country schoolhouse on grounds. Kister Bldg has carriage house, blacksmith and carpenter shops. (Daily exc Mon, also by appt; closed hols, also Dec 24-26 & Dec 31-Jan 2) 546 E Bowman St. Phone 216/264-8856 ¢¢

Annual Event

Wayne County Fair. Fairgrounds. W on US 30A. 5 days, beginning wkend after Labor Day.

Motel

✔ ★ **ECONO LODGE.** *2137 Lincoln Way E. 330/264-8883; FAX 330/264-8883, ext. 301; res: 800/248-8341.* 98 rms, 2 story. Apr-Oct: S $36.95-$39.95; D $40.95-$50; each addl $4; under 18 free; lower rates rest of yr. Crib free. Pet accepted. TV; cable. Indoor pool; whirlpool. Continental bkfst. Complimentary coffee in lobby. Restaurant adj 7 am-9 pm; closed Sun. Ck-out 11 am. Coin lndry. Meeting rm. Business center. Sundries. Airport transportation. Picnic tables. Cr cds: A, D, DS, MC, V.

[D] [🐾] [≋] [⊠] [🐾] [SC] [🏃]

Motor Hotel

★ ★ **BEST WESTERN WOOSTER PLAZA.** *243 E Liberty St, 4 blks N of US 30 Bypass. 330/264-7750; FAX 330/262-5840.* 100 rms, 3 story. S $62; D $68; each addl $6; suites $97; under 18 free. TV; cable (premium), VCR (movies). Outdoor pool. Restaurant 6 am-2 pm, 5-10 pm; Sun 7 am-2 pm, 5-9 pm. Rm serv. Bar 11-2 am. Ck-out noon. Meeting rms. Business servs avail. Valet serv. Beauty shop. Cr cds: A, C, D, DS, ER, JCB, MC, V.

[≋] [⊠] [🐾] [SC]

Inn

★ ★ ★ **WOOSTER INN.** *801 E Wayne Ave. 330/264-2341; FAX 330/264-9951.* 16 rms, 2 story. S, D $70-$95; each addl $15; suite $95-$130; 3-12 yrs, $5. Closed Jan 2-9, Dec 25, 26. Crib free. Pet accepted, some restrictions. TV; cable. Restaurant (see WOOSTER INN). Ck-out noon. Meeting rms. Business servs avail. Tennis privileges. 9-hole golf, greens fee $8-$9, putting green, driving range. Picnic tables. Colonial decor. Owned, operated by College of Wooster; on campus. Cr cds: A, C, D, DS, MC, V.

[D] [🐾] [🏋] [🎿] [🏌] [🎣] [⊠] [🐾]

Restaurants

★ ★ **TJ'S.** *359 W Liberty St. 330/264-6263.* Hrs: 11 am-10 pm; Fri to 10 pm; Sat 4:30-10 pm; early-bird dinner 4:30-6 pm. Closed Sun; major hols. Res accepted. Semi-a la carte: lunch $4.15-$7.50, dinner $6.95-$18.95. Child's meals. Specializes in prime rib, fresh seafood, cheesecake. Family-owned. Cr cds: A, D, DS, MC, V.

[D] [SC] [♥]

★ ★ **WOOSTER INN.** *(See Wooster Inn) 330/264-2341.* Hrs: 7 am-2 pm, 6-8:30 pm; Sun 7-11 am, 11:30 am-7 pm. Closed Jan 2-9, Dec 25, 26. Res accepted. Wine list. Bkfst $3-$8, lunch $6.50-$16, dinner $10-$21. Specializes in fresh seafood, local produce. Own baking. Totally nonsmoking. Cr cds: A, C, D, DS, MC, V.

[D]

Youngstown (C-6)

(See also Warren)

Settled 1797 **Pop** 95,732 **Elev** 861 ft **Area code** 330 **E-mail** tlyden@youngstowncvb.com **Web** www.youngstowncvb.com

Information Youngstown/Mahoning County Convention & Visitors Bureau, 101 City Centre One, 44503; 330/747-8200 or 800/447-8201.

Youngstown, five miles from the Pennsylvania line, covers an area of 35 square miles in the eastern coal province, which has nine-tenths of the country's high-grade coal. It is the seat of Mahoning County.

Youngstown's steel history started in 1803 with a crude iron smelter; the first coal mine began operating in the valley in 1826; in 1892 the first valley steel plant opened, Union Iron and Steel Company. Youngstown industry has become more diversified in recent years, with such products as rubber goods, electric light bulbs, aluminum and paper goods, office equipment, clothes, rolling-mill equipment, vans, automobiles and parts, paint, electronic equipment and plastics.

What to See and Do

Mill Creek Park. Park has more than 3,200 acres of gorges, ravines and rolling hills from the Mahoning River to S of US 224. A Western Reserve pioneer woolen mill (1821) is now the Pioneer Pavilion used for picnics and dancing. Lanterman's Mill (ca 1846), a working gristmill; tours. (May-Oct, daily exc Mon; Apr & Nov, wkends) Located in the SW part of city, bounded by Mahoning Ave, US 224, Lockwood & Mill Creek Blvd. Phone 330/740-7115. The Fellows Riverside Gardens has six acres of formal gardens including rose, chrysanthemum, lily, tulip and annual flower displays. Area includes Garden Center and a large stone terrace overlooking the city. The James L. Wick Jr Recreation Area has lighted tennis, horseshoe courts and par 3 golf course; supervised playground, ball diamonds, volleyball court, picnic facilities, ice-skating, and shelter house; on Old Furnace Rd is Ford Nature Education Center (daily; closed Jan 1, Thanksgiving, Dec 25; phone 330/740-7107). Walter Scholl Recreation Area and Volney Rogers Field have supervised playgrounds, picnic facilities, softball diamonds, tennis courts, shelter house. Two of the lakes provide fishing (May-Nov). Boat rides and rentals available at Newport and Glacier lakes. Park (daily); facilities (in season, fees for some). Phone 330/743-7275.

Stambaugh Auditorium. Seats 2,800. Local events, concerts and Monday Musical Club. 1000 5th Ave. Phone 330/747-5175.

The Arms Family Museum of Local History. Major arts & crafts house with original furnishings; local historical items; B.F. Wirt Collection of paintings, books and antiques; period costumes; pioneer and Native American artifacts. Guided tours. (Tues-Sun afternoons; closed hols) 648 Wick Ave. Phone 330/743-2589. ¢

The Butler Institute of American Art. Specializes in American art; collections include works on Native Americans, clipper ships; antique glass bells. (Daily exc Mon; closed some major hols) 524 Wick Ave. Phone 330/743-1107 or 330/743-1711. **Free.**

Youngstown Historical Center of Industry & Labor. Chronicles the rise and fall of the steel industry in Youngstown and its region; exhibit combines artifacts, videotaped interviews with steelworkers and executives, and full scale re-creation of the places the steelworkers lived and labored. (Wed-Sat, also Sun afternoon; closed Jan 1, Thanksgiving, Dec 25) 151 W Wood St. Phone 330/743-5934. ¢¢

Youngstown Playhouse. (Sept-June, wkends; addl summer productions) Off 2000 blk of Glenwood Ave, 1½ mi S of I-680. For reservations, phone box office 330/788-8739.

Youngstown State University (1908). (15,000 students) Planetarium on campus (by reservation only, phone 330/742-3616); also here is McDonough Museum of Art (phone 330/742-1400). Campus tours. 410 Wick Ave. Phone 330/742-3000.

Youngstown Symphony Center. Seats 2,350. Presents concerts, symphony, ballet and other cultural events. 260 Federal Plaza W. Phone 330/744-0246.

Motels

★ ★ **BEST WESTERN MEANDER INN.** *870 N Canfield-Niles Rd (44515). 330/544-2378; FAX 330/544-7926.* 57 rms, 2 story. S $54-$62; D $68-$74; each addl $4; suites $85-$95; under 18 free. Crib free. Pet accepted. TV; cable. Pool. Complimentary continental bkfst. Restaurant 3-10 pm. Rm serv. Bar. Ck-out noon. Coin lndry. Meeting rm. Cr cds: A, C, D, DS, MC, V.

D ✔ ⩲ ✕ 🐾 SC

✔ ★ **KNIGHTS INN.** *5431 Seventy-Six Dr (44515), 8 mi W on I-80 at OH 46 exit 223. 330/793-9305; FAX 330/793-2584.* 127 rms, 10 kit. units. S $41.95; D $43.95; each addl $6; kit. units $49.95; under 18 free; wkly, monthly rates. Crib free. TV; cable. Pool. Restaurant adj open 24 hrs. Ck-out noon. Business servs avail. Some refrigerators. Cr cds: A, DS, MC, V.

⩲ ✕ 🔥 SC

★ ★ **RAMADA INN.** *4255 Belmont Ave (44505). 330/759-7850; FAX 330/759-8147.* 140 rms, 2 story. June-Sept: S $64; D $69; each addl $7; suites $110-$150; under 18 free; lower rates rest of yr. Crib free. TV; cable (premium), VCR avail. Indoor pool. Restaurant 7 am-10 pm; Sun to 8 pm. Rm serv 7-10 pm. Bar 11 am-midnight; Fri, Sat to 2:30 am; entertainment Fri, Sat. Ck-out noon. Meeting rms. Business servs avail. Sundries. Barber, beauty shop. Cr cds: A, C, D, DS, MC, V.

D ⩲ ✕ 🔥 SC

Motor Hotels

★ ★ **COMFORT INN.** *4055 Belmont Ave (44505). 330/759-3180; FAX 330/759-7713.* 144 rms, 6 story. S $69; D $82; suites $125-$150; each addl $10; under 18 free. Crib free. TV; cable. Indoor pool. Complimentary continental bkfst. Restaurant 11:30 am-11 pm. Rm serv. Bar from 5 pm. Ck-out noon. Meeting rms. Business servs avail. In-rm modem link. Free airport transportation 8 am-11 pm. Game rm. Some refrigerators. Private balconies. Cr cds: A, C, D, DS, MC, V.

D ⩲ ✕ 🐾 SC

★ ★ ★ **HOLIDAY INN.** *(7410 South Ave, Boardman 44512) 7 mi S on I-680, W on US 224. 330/726-1611; FAX 330/726-0717.* 117 rms, 6 story. S, D $85; under 19 free. Crib free. TV; cable. Heated pool. Coffee in rms. Restaurant 6:30 am-10 pm. Rm serv. Bar. Ck-out noon. Coin lndry. Meeting rms. Business servs avail. In-rm modem link. Bellhops. Valet serv. Sundries. Health club privileges. Some refrigerators. Cr cds: A, C, D, DS, JCB, MC, V.

D ⩲ ✕ 🐾 SC

★ ★ **HOLIDAY INN METROPLEX.** *(1620 Motor Inn Dr, Girard 44420) 12 mi N on I-80, exit 229. 330/759-0606; FAX 330/759-7632.* 153 rms, 4 story. May-Sept: S $75-$85; D $82-$92; each addl $7; under 18 free; wkend rates; lower rates rest of yr. Crib free. TV; cable (premium). Heated pool. Complimentary coffee in rms. Restaurant 6:30 am-10 pm. Rm serv. Bar 5 pm-2 am. Ck-out noon. Meeting rms. Business servs avail. Bellhops. Free airport transportation. Exercise equipt; weight machine, stair machine. Cr cds: A, C, D, DS, JCB, MC, V.

D ⩲ 🏋 ✕ 🔥 SC

Hotel

★ ★ **WICK-POLLOCK INN.** *603 Wick Ave (44502). 330/746-1200; FAX 330/746-5800; res: 800/837-9425.* 80 rms, 5 story, 29 suites. S $70; D $80; each addl $10; suites $80-$125; under 18 free; wkend rates. Crib free. TV; cable (premium), VCR avail. Restaurant 6:30 am-10 pm. Bar. Ck-out noon. Meeting rms. Business servs avail. Airport transportation. Health club privileges. Mansion built as private residence in 1893; ashlar stone circular corner tower. Formal terraced garden. Cr cds: A, C, D, DS, MC, V.

D 🐾 SC

Restaurants

★ ★ ★ **ALBERINI'S.** *1201 Youngstown Warren Rd (44446), on US 422. 330/652-5895.* Hrs: 11:30 am-11 pm. Closed Sun; most major hols. Res accepted. Italian menu. Bar. Wine cellar. Semi-a la carte: lunch $5.95-$8, dinner $10.95-$22.95. Child's meals. Specializes in classic and nouvelle Italian cuisine, fresh seafood. Formal dining. Oil murals. Family-owned. Cr cds: A, C, D, DS, MC, V.

[D]

★ ★ ★ **MOONRAKER.** *(1275 Boardman-Poland Rd, Boardman) 7 mi S on I-680 exit 11A. 330/726-8841.* Hrs: 11 am-2:30 pm, 4-10 pm; Fri till midnight. Sat 4 pm-midnight; Sun brunch 11 am-3 pm. Closed major hols. Res accepted. Continental menu. Bar. Semi-a la carte: lunch, dinner $13.50-$22. Sun brunch $10.95. Child's meals. Specialties: veal Queen Victoria, veal Moonraker, steak. Own baking. Entertainment Fri-Sat. Valet parking. Multilevel dining areas; view of lake. Cr cds: A, D, DS, MC, V.

[D]

Zanesville (E-4)

(See also Cambridge, Coshocton, Newark)

Settled 1797 **Pop** 26,778 **Elev** 705 ft **Area code** 614 **Zip** 43701
Information Visitors and Convention Bureau, 205 N 5th St; 614/453-5004 or 800/743-2303.

Ebenezer Zane, surveyor of Zane's Trace through the dense Ohio forests and great-great-grandfather of Zane Grey, writer of Western novels, selected the Zanesville site because the valley was at the junction of the Muskingum and Licking rivers. First called Westbourne, it was the state capital from 1810 to 1812.

Today beautiful pottery is made here, as well as transformers, electrical steel sheets and automobile components. The "Y" Bridge, which a person can cross and still remain on the same side of the river from which he started, divides the city into three parts.

What to See and Do

Blue Rock State Park. A 350-acre park with swimming; fishing, hunting; boating (launch, electric motors only). Hiking, bridle trails. Picnicking, concession. Camping. Standard fees. (Daily) 12 mi SE off OH 60, adj Blue Rock State Forest. Phone 614/674-4794. **Free.**

Dillon State Park. A 7,690-acre park with swimming; boating (ramps, rentals). Picnicking (shelter), concession. Camping, cabins (by res). (Daily) 8 mi NW on OH 146. Phone 614/453-4377 (daytime). **Free.**

National Road-Zane Grey Museum. A 136-ft diorama traces history of Old National Rd (Cumberland, MD, to Vandalia, IL); display of vehicles that once traveled the road; Zane Grey memorabilia, reconstructed craft shops, antique art pottery exhibit. (Mar-Apr & Oct-Nov, Wed-Sun; May-Sept, daily) On US 22/40, 10 mi E via I-70 exit 164, near Norwich. Phone 614/872-3143. ¢¢

Ohio Ceramic Center. Extensive displays of pottery housed in five buildings. Exhibits include primitive stoneware; also area pottery. (Early May-mid-Oct, Wed-Sat, also Sun afternoon) Demonstrations of pottery making during pottery festival (wkend in mid-July). On OH 93, 12 mi S via US 22, near Roseville. Phone 614/697-7021. ¢

Robinson-Ransbottom Pottery Co. A 15-20-min self-guided tour of pottery factory; inquire for hrs. (Mon-Fri; closed hols) 12 mi S via US 22, OH 93, in Roseville. Phone 614/697-7355. **Free.**

Stern-wheeler *The Lorena,* named for the Civil War love song. One-hour trips on the Muskingum River. (May-Oct) For schedule or dinner reservations phone 614/455-8883 or 800/246-6303. ¢¢

Zane Grey Birthplace. The author's first story was written here. (Private residence) 705 Convers Ave.

Zanesville Art Center. American, European and Oriental art; children's art; early midwestern glass and ceramics; photographs; special programs; gallery tours. (Daily exc Mon; closed major hols) 620 Military Rd, 2 mi N on OH 60. Phone 614/452-0741. **Free.**

Annual Event

Zane's Trace Commemoration. Commemorates Pioneer Heritage. Fine arts, crafts, parades, flea market. 3 days mid-June.

Motels

★ ★ **COMFORT INN.** *500 Monroe St, I-70 exit 155. 614/454-4144.* 81 rms, 2 story. June-Aug: S, D $100-$139; under 18 free; lower rates rest of yr. Crib free. TV; VCR avail (movies). Indoor pool; whirlpool. Complimentary continental bkfst. Restaurant adj 6 am-11 pm. Ck-out noon. Business servs avail. Coin lndry. Meeting rms. Valet serv. Exercise equipt; treadmill, stair machine, sauna. Cr cds: A, C, D, DS, JCB, MC, V.

[D] [symbols] SC

★ **DAYS INN.** *4925 E Pike. 614/453-3400; FAX 614/453-9715.* 60 rms, 2 story. June-Sept: S, D $85-$100; under 12 free; lower rates rest of yr. Crib free. TV; cable (premium). Indoor pool. Complimentary continental bkfst. Restaurant adj 6 am-10 pm. Ck-out noon. Cr cds: A, C, D, DS, MC, V.

[symbols] SC

★ ★ **FAIRFIELD INN BY MARRIOTT.** *725 Zane St. 614/453-8770.* 63 rms, 3 story. June-Oct: S, D $66.95-$76.95; each addl $5; under 18 free; lower rates rest of yr. Crib free. TV; cable (premium). Complimentary continental bkfst. Restaurant nearby. Ck-out noon. Business servs avail. Valet servs. Game rm. Some refrigerators. Cr cds: A, C, D, DS, MC, V.

[D] [symbols] SC

★ ★ **HOLIDAY INN.** *4645 E Pike, off I-70 exit 160. 614/453-0771.* 130 rms, 2 story. S $69-$77; D $71-$99; each addl $5; under 19 free. Crib free. Pet accepted. TV; cable (premium). Indoor pool; whirlpool, poolside serv. Playground. Complimentary coffee in rms. Restaurant 6 am-2 pm, 5-10 pm; Sat, Sun 6:30 am-10 pm. Rm serv. Bars 2 pm-midnight. Ck-out noon. Coin lndry. Meeting rms. Business servs avail. In-rm modem link. Bellhops. Sundries. Exercise equipt; bicycles, stair machine, sauna. Cr cds: A, C, D, DS, ER, JCB, MC, V.

[D] [symbols] SC

Restaurants

★ ★ **MARIA ADORNETTO.** *953 Market St. 614/453-0643.* Hrs: 11 am-10 pm, Fri to 11 pm; Sat 4-11 pm; early-bird dinner 4-6:30 pm. Closed Sun; major hols. Res accepted. Italian menu. Bar. A la carte entrees: lunch $4.25-$8.50, dinner $6.95-$17.50. Specializes in pasta, fish, Italian dishes. Contemporary dining rm in converted home. Family-owned since 1937. Cr cds: A, C, D, DS, MC, V.

★ ★ **OLD MARKET HOUSE INN.** *424 Market St. 614/454-2555.* Hrs: 5-10 pm; Fri, Sat to 11 pm. Closed Sun; major hols. Italian, Amer menu. Bar. Semi-a la carte: dinner $7-$33. Specializes in shrimp, fresh fish, pasta. Old English decor. Cr cds: A, C, D, DS, MC, V.

Wisconsin

Population: 4,891,769
Land area: 54,424 square miles
Elevation: 581-1,951 feet
Highest point: Timms Hill (Price County)
Entered Union: May 29, 1848 (30th state)
Capital: Madison
Motto: Forward
Nickname: Badger State
State flower: Wood violet
State bird: Robin
State tree: Sugar maple
State fair: August 6-16, 1998, in Milwaukee
Time zone: Central
Web: tourism.state.wi.us

V irgin forests blotted out the sky over Wisconsin when the first French voyageurs arrived more than three centuries ago. Rich in natural resources, modern conservation concepts took strong root here; Wisconsin's 15,000 lakes and 2,200 streams are teeming with fish, and millions of acres of its publicly owned forest are abundant with game.

People of many heritages have contributed to the state's colorful past, busy industries and productive farms. Wisconsin is famous for the breweries of Milwaukee, great universities, forests, paper mills, dairy products and diverse vacation attractions.

Wisconsin is the birthplace of the statewide primary election law, workmen's compensation law, unemployment compensation and many other reforms that have since been widely adopted. It produced Senator Robert M. La Follette, one of the 20th century's foremost progressives, and many other honored citizens.

The Badger State acquired its nickname during the lead rush of 1827, when miners built their homes by digging into the hillsides like badgers. It is "America's dairyland," producing much of the nation's milk and over 30 percent of all cheese consumed in the US. It is a leader in the production of hay, cranberries and ginseng and harvests huge crops of peas, beans, carrots, corn and oats. It is the leading canner of fresh vegetables and an important source of cherries, apples, maple syrup and wood pulp. A great part of the nation's paper products, agricultural implements and nonferrous metal products and alloys are manufactured here.

The Wisconsin summer is balmy, and the winter offers an abundance of activities, making the state a year-round vacationland that lures millions of visitors annually. They find a land of many contrasts: rounded hills and narrow valleys to the southwest, a huge central plain, rolling prairie in the southeast, and the north, majestic with forests, marshes and lakes.

Native Americans called this land *Ouisconsin* ("where the waters gather"). French explorer Jean Nicolet, seeking the Northwest Passage to the Orient, landed near Green Bay in 1634 and greeted what he thought were Orientals. These Winnebago made a treaty of alliance with the French, and for the next 125 years a brisk trade in furs developed. The British won Wisconsin from the French in 1760 and lost it to the United States after the American Revolution.

Shortly before Wisconsin became a state it was a battleground in the Black Hawk War. After the campaign, word spread of the state's beauty and fertile land in the East, and opened the doors to a flood of settlers.

The rich lead mines brought another wave of settlers, and the forests attracted lumbermen—both groups remained to till the soil or work in the factories.

Diversified industry, enhanced recreational facilities, the trade opportunities opened by the St Lawrence Seaway and enlightened agricultural techniques promise continuing prosperity for Wisconsin.

When to Go/Climate

Cool forests and lake breezes make northern Wisconsin summers pleasant and comfortable, while the southern farmland is often uncomfortably hot. Temperatures from northern to southern Wisconsin can vary as much as 20°F. Winters are often snowy and harsh statewide. Fall is the best time to visit, with brilliant foliage, harvests and festivals.

AVERAGE HIGH/LOW TEMPERATURES (°F)

GREEN BAY

Jan 23/6	May 67/44	Sept 69/49
Feb 27/10	June 76/54	Oct 57/39
Mar 39/21	July 81/59	Nov 42/27
Apr 54/34	Aug 78/57	Dec 28/13

MILWAUKEE

Jan 26/12	May 64/45	Sept 71/53
Feb 30/16	June 75/55	Oct 59/42
Mar 40/26	July 80/62	Nov 45/31
Apr 53/36	Aug 78/61	Dec 31/18

CALENDAR HIGHLIGHTS

JANUARY

World Championship Snowmobile Derby (Eagle River). More than 300 professional racers fight for the championship. Phone 800/359-6315.

FEBRUARY

Winter Festival (Cedarburg). Cedar Creek Winery. Ice carving and snow sculpture contests, bed and barrel races across ice, winter softball and volleyball, Alaskan malamute weight pull, snow goose egg hunt; torchlight parade, horse-drawn sleigh rides. Phone 414/377-9620 or 800/827-8020.

American Birkebeiner (Cable). Cross-country ski race. More than 6,000 participants from 40 states and 15 countries. Phone 800/872-2753.

MAY

Festival of Blossoms (Door County). Month-long celebration of spring, with a million daffodils and blooming cherry and apple trees. Phone 414/743-4456 or 800/527-3529.

Great Wisconsin Dells Balloon Rally (Wisconsin Dells). More than 90 hot-air balloons participate in contests and mass liftoffs. Phone 800/22-DELLS.

JUNE

Walleye Weekend Festival and Mercury Marine National Walleye Tournament (Fond du Lac). Lakeside Park. Fish fry, food, entertainment, sports competitions. Phone 800/937-9123.

Summerfest (Milwaukee). Eleven different music stages; food. Phone 414/273-FEST or 800/837-FEST.

JULY

Art Fair on the Square (Madison). Capitol Concourse. Exhibits by 500 artists and craftspersons; food, entertainment. Contact Madison Art Center, 608/257-0158.

AUGUST

EAA (Experimental Aircraft Association) International Fly-In Convention (Oshkosh). Wittman Regional Airport. One of the nation's largest aviation events. More than 500 educational forums, workshops and seminars; daily air shows; exhibits; more than 12,000 aircraft. Phone 920/235-3007 for air show lodging information; 920/426-4800 for general information.

Wisconsin State Fair (Milwaukee). State Fair Park in West Allis. Entertainment, 12 stages, auto races, exhibits, contests, demonstrations, fireworks. Phone 414/266-7000.

Parks and Recreation Finder

Directions to and information about the parks and recreation areas below are given under their respective town/city sections. Please refer to those sections for details.

Key to abbreviations: I.P. = Interstate Park; N.B.C. = National Battlefield & Cemetery; N.B.P. = National Battlefield Park; N.F. = National Forest; N.G. = National Grassland; N.H. = National Historical Park; N.H.S. = National Historic Site; N.M. = National Monument; N.Mem. = National Memorial; N.M.P. = National Military Park; N.P. = National Park; N.Pres. = National Preserve; N.R. = National Recreational Area; N.R.R. = National Recreational River; N.S. = National Seashore; N.S.T. = National Scenic Trail; N.V.M. = National Volcanic Monument; S.B. = State Beach; S.C.P. = State Conservation Park; S.G. = State Garden; S.H.A. = State Historic Area; S.H.P. = State Historic Park; S.N.A. = State Natural Area; S.P. = State Park; S.R. = State Reserve; S.R.A. = State Recreation Area; S.Res.P. = State Resort Park; S.R.P. = State Rustic Park.

NATIONAL PARK AND RECREATION AREAS

Place Name	Listed Under
Apostle Islands National Lakeshore	BAYFIELD
Chequamegon N.F.	PARK FALLS
Ice Age National Scientific Reserve	DEVIL'S LAKE STATE PARK
Nicolet N.F.	THREE LAKES
St Croix National Scenic Riverway	ST CROIX FALLS

STATE RECREATION AREAS

Place Name	Listed Under
Amnicon Falls S.P.	SUPERIOR
Big Foot Beach S.P.	LAKE GENEVA
Black River Falls State Forest	BLACK RIVER FALLS
Blue Mound S.P.	MT HOREB
Bong S.R.A.	KENOSHA
Brule River State Forest	SUPERIOR
Brunet Island S.P.	CHIPPEWA FALLS
Buckhorn S.P.	MAUSTON
Copper Falls S.P.	ASHLAND
Devil's Lake S.P.	same
Flambeau River State Forest	LADYSMITH
Governor Dodge S.P.	DODGEVILLE
Governor Knowles State Forest	ST CROIX FALLS
Hartman Creek S.P.	WAUPACA
High Cliff S.P.	NEENAH-MENASHA
Interstate S.P.	ST CROIX FALLS
Kettle Moraine State Forest (North Unit)	FOND DU LAC
Kettle Moraine State Forest (South Unit)	WAUKESHA
Kohler-Andrae S.P.	SHEBOYGAN
Lake Kegonsa S.P.	MADISON
Lake Wissota S.P.	CHIPPEWA FALLS
Merrick S.P.	GALESVILLE
Mill Bluff S.P.	TOMAH
Mirror Lake S.P.	BARABOO
Nelson Dewey S.P.	PRAIRIE DU CHIEN
New Glarus Woods S.P.	NEW GLARUS
Newport S.P.	ELLISON BAY
Northern Highland-American Legion State Forest	BOULDER JUNCTION
Pattison S.P.	SUPERIOR
Peninsula S.P.	FISH CREEK
Perrot S.P.	GALESVILLE
Point Beach State Forest	TWO RIVERS
Potawatomi S.P.	STURGEON BAY
Rock Island S.P.	WASHINGTON ISLAND
Rib Mountain S.P.	WAUSAU
Tower Hill S.P.	SPRING GREEN
Wildcat Mountain S.P.	TOMAH
Willow River S.P.	HUDSON
Wyalusing S.P.	PRAIRIE DU CHIEN
Yellowstone Lake S.P.	MONROE

Water-related activities, hiking, bicycling, riding, various other sports, picnicking and visitor centers, as well as camping, are available in many of these areas. From May-Oct, camping is limited to three weeks; fee is $7-$12/unit/night; electricity $3. Camps can be taken down or set up between 6 am and 11 pm. Motor vehicle sticker for nonresidents: daily $7;

annual $25; residents: daily $5; annual $18. For additional information contact Wisconsin Department of Natural Resources, Bureau of Parks & Recreation, PO Box 7921, Madison 53707; 608/266-2181.

SKI AREAS

Place Name	Listed Under
Alpine Valley Ski Resort	ELKHORN
Cascade Mt Ski Area	PORTAGE
Christmas Mountain Village	WISCONSIN DELLS
Devil's Head Lodge Ski Area	BARABOO
Grand Geneva Resort	LAKE GENEVA
Hidden Valley Ski Area	MANITOWOC
Highlands Ski Hill	OCONOMOWOC
Little Switzerland Ski Area	MENOMONEE FALLS
Minocqua Winter Park Nordic Center	MINOCQUA
Mt Ashwabay Ski Area	BAYFIELD
Mt La Crosse Ski Area	LA CROSSE
Mt Telemark Ski Area	CABLE
Nordic Mountain Ski Area	WAUTOMA
Rib Mt Ski Area	WAUSAU
Sky Line Ski Area	WISCONSIN DELLS
Trollhaugen Ski Resort	ST CROIX FALLS
Whitecap Mountain Ski Area	HURLEY
Wilmot Mt	LAKE GENEVA
Wintergreen Cross-Country Ski Area	SPRING GREEN

FISHING & HUNTING

Wisconsin, eager to have visitors share the abundance of fish in the lakes and streams, posts few barriers. The state is very conservation-minded; regulations have been developed to ensure equally good fishing in the future. Fishing licenses: nonresident over 16, 4-day $15; 15-day $20; annual $34; family 15-day, $30; annual family $52; licenses expire Mar 31. Two-day Great Lakes, $10. A trout stamp must be purchased by all licensed anglers in order to fish for trout in inland waters, $7.25. A salmon and trout stamp is required, except those having a two-day license, to fish the Great Lakes, $7.25. For further information contact the Wisconsin Department of Natural Resources, Customer Service and Licensing, PO Box 7924, Madison 53707; 608/266-2621.

Wisconsin waters boast trout, muskellunge, northern pike, walleye, large and smallmouth bass and panfish throughout the state; salmon is primarily found in the Lake Superior/Michigan area; lake sturgeon in Winnebago waters/St Croix/Wisconsin, Chippewa, Flambeau & Menominee rivers; and catfish in Wolf, Mississippi and Wisconsin rivers. Inquire for seasons and bag limits.

The Department of Natural Resources issues separate pamphlets on trapping big game, pheasant and waterfowl hunting regulations. Hunting licenses: nonresident, furbearer $150; small game $75; archery $135; deer $135; 5-day small game $43. Hunting migratory birds requires a special federal stamp ($15), obtainable at any post office, as well as a state stamp, $7. A pheasant stamp ($7.25) is also required. Special hunting regulations apply to minors; contact Dept of Natural Resources for further information. **Note:** License fees subject to change.

Driving Information

Safety belts are mandatory for all persons in designated seating spaces within the vehicle. Children under 4 years of age must be in an approved safety seat anywhere in vehicle. Children ages 4-8 years may use a regulation safety belt. For further information phone 608/266-3212.

INTERSTATE HIGHWAY SYSTEM

The following alphabetical listing of Wisconsin towns in the *Mobil Travel Guide* shows that these cities are within 10 miles of the indicated Interstate highways. A highway map should, however, be checked for the nearest exit.

Highway Number	Cities/Towns within 10 miles
INTERSTATE 43	Cedarburg, Green Bay, Manitowoc, Milwaukee, Port Washington, Sheboygan.
INTERSTATE 90	Baraboo, Beloit, Janesville, La Crosse, Madison, Mauston, Portage, Sparta, Tomah, Wisconsin Dells.
INTERSTATE 94	Baraboo, Black River Falls, Eau Claire, Hudson, Kenosha, Madison, Mauston, Menomonie, Milwaukee, Oconomowoc, Portage, Racine, Tomah, Watertown, Waukesha, Wauwatosa, Wisconsin Dells.

Additional Visitor Information

The Wisconsin Department Tourism, PO Box 7606, Madison 53707; 608/266-2161, 800/372-2437 (northern IL, IA, MI, MN, WI only) or 800/432-TRIP (anywhere in US), produces and distributes a variety of publications covering sports, attractions, events and recreation. When requesting information, ask for *Adventure Guide, Events/Recreation Guide, Heritage Guide, Where to Stay in Wisconsin, Guide to State Golf Courses, Campground Directory* and/or state highway map.

There are several tourist information centers in Wisconsin. Visitors who stop will find helpful information and brochures. They are located in Beloit (I-90); Genoa City (US 12), (seasonal); Grant County (US 151/61), (seasonal); Hudson (I-94); Hurley (US 51); Kenosha (I-94); La Crosse (I-90); Madison (123 W Washington Ave); Prairie du Chien (211 Main St), (seasonal); Superior (305 E 2nd St), (seasonal). There is also an information center in Chicago, IL (342 N Michigan Ave).

Wisconsin offers a fabulous system of bicycle routes. To order a free guide to bicycling in Wisconsin contact the Department of Tourism, PO Box 7606, Madison 53707; 608/266-2161 or 800/432-TRIP.

Algoma (E-6)

(See also Green Bay, Sturgeon Bay)

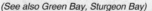

Settled 1818 **Pop** 3,353 **Elev** 600 ft **Area code** 920 **Zip** 54201 **E-mail** aacofc@itol.com **Web** www.algoma.org

Information Algoma Area Chamber of Commerce, 1226 Lake St; 920/487-2041 or 800/498-4888.

What to See and Do

Ahnapee State Trail. More than 15 mi of hiking and biking along the Ahnapee River. Snowmobiling. (Daily) Phone 920/487-2041 or 800/498-4888. **Free.**

Kewaunee County Historical Museum. Century-old building; displays include a letter written by George Washington, wood carvings, child's playroom with toys of 1890-1910 period, sheriff's office, ship models, old farm tools & artifacts. (Memorial Day-Labor Day, daily; rest of yr, by appt) 10 mi S via WI 42. Court House Square, 613 Dodge St in Kewaunee. Phone 920/388-4410. ¢

von Stiehl Winery. Housed in 140-yr-old brewery. Wine, cheese and jelly tasting at end of tour. Under 21 only with adult (wine tasting); no smoking. Gift shop; candy shop features homemade fudge. (May-Oct, daily; rest of yr, Fri-Sun) 115 Navarino St. Phone 920/487-5208 or 800/955-5208. ¢

Motel

✔★ **RIVER HILLS.** 820 N Water St (WI 42N). 920/487-3451; FAX 920/487-2031; res: 800/236-3451. E-mail rhmotel@itol.com. 30 rms. D $40-$60. Crib $3. Pet accepted, some restrictions; $3. TV; cable (premium). Ck-out 11 am. Business servs avail. Some refrigerators. Boat dock, ramps nearby. Cr cds: MC, V.

Restaurant

★ **CAPTAIN'S TABLE.** *133 N Water St (WI 42N). 920/487-5304.* Hrs: 5 am-9 pm; Nov-May hrs vary. Closed Thanksgiving, Dec 25. Res accepted. Semi-a la carte: bkfst $1.79-$5.95, lunch $1.50-$4.50, dinner $4.95-$9.95. Child's meals. Specializes in fresh fish. Salad bar. Nautical motif. No cr cds accepted.

Antigo (D-4)

(See also Wausau)

Settled 1876 **Pop** 8,276 **Elev** 1,498 ft **Area code** 715 **Zip** 54409 **E-mail** antigocc@newnorth.net **Web** www.newnorth.net/antigo.chamber
Information Chamber of Commerce, 329 Superior St, PO Box 339; 715/623-4134 or 888/526-4523.

What to See and Do

F. A. Deleglise Cabin (1878). First home of city's founder. (May-Sept, Tues, Thurs & Sun) 7th & Superior Sts, on grounds of public library. Phone 715/627-4464 or 715/623-3038. **Donation.**

Annual Event

North American Snowmobile Championship. 4th wkend Feb.

Motel

★ **CUTLASS MOTOR LODGE.** *915 S Superior St (US 45/WI 47/WI 52). 715/623-4185; FAX 715/623-6096; res: 800/CUTLASS.* 49 rms. S $44; D $54; each addl $8; suites $99-$159; under 18 free. Crib free. TV. Indoor pool. Restaurant 6:30-9:30 am, 4:30-9:30 pm. Bar 4:30 pm-2 am. Ck-out 11 am. Meeting rms. Business servs avail. Valet serv. Sundries. Downhill ski 15 mi; x-country ski 5 mi. Game rm. Whirlpool in suites. Cr cds: A, C, D, DS, MC, V.

Restaurant

★ **BLACKJACK STEAK HOUSE.** *800 S Superior St (US 45, WI 47/52). 715/623-2514.* Hrs: 11 am-2 pm, 5-11 pm. Closed Dec 24-25. Res accepted. Bar. Semi-a la carte: lunch $3.50-$5.50; dinner $5.50-$18. Friday fish fry $4.95-$8.50. Sun buffet 11 am-7 pm, $7.95. Chinese menu Mon, Tues, $3.50-$9.50. Child's meals. Specializes in seafood, prime rib. Salad bar. Family-owned. Cr cds: A, MC, V.

Apostle Islands National Lakeshore

(see Bayfield)

Appleton (E-5)

(See also Green Bay, Neenah-Menasha, Oshkosh)

Settled 1848 **Pop** 65,695 **Elev** 780 ft **Area code** 920 **E-mail** tourism@foxcities.org **Web** www.foxcities.org
Information Fox Cities Convention & Visitors Bureau, 3433 W College Ave, 54914; 920/734-3358 or 800/236-6673.

Located astride the Fox River, Appleton's economy centers around the manufacture of paper and paper products and insurance and service industries.

What to See and Do

⬛ **Charles A. Grignon Mansion** (1837). First deeded property in Wisconsin (1793); restored Greek-revival house of one of the area's early French-Canadian settlers; period furnishings; displays; summer events. Picnic area. Tours. (June-Aug, daily; rest of yr, by appt) 1313 Augustine St, 8 mi E off US 41 in Kaukauna. Phone 920/766-3122. ¢¢

Lawrence University (1847). (1,230 students) Merged in 1964 with Milwaukee-Downer College. Main Hall (1854), College Ave. 706 E College Ave at Lawe St. For campus tours contact Admissions Office, phone 920/832-6500. On campus is

Wriston Art Center. Traveling exhibits, lectures and art shows. (Sept-May, daily exc Mon; schedule may vary; closed hols) S Lawe & Alton Sts. Phone 920/832-6621. **Free.**

Music-Drama Center (1959). Quarters for Conservatory of Music, concert hall, practice rooms, classrooms; Cloak Theater, an experimental arena playhouse; Stansbury Theater. Concerts and plays (academic yr), phone 920/832-6611. Summer theater (mid-June-Aug), phone 920/734-8797.

New London Public Museum. Native American and African artifacts; mineral, rock and shell collection; mounted birds; local historical exhibits. (Daily exc Sun; closed hols) 20 mi NW via US 10, 45 at 412 S Pearl St in New London. Phone 920/982-8520. **Free.**

Outagamie Museum. Features local technology and industrial accomplishments. Major exhibit themes include electricity, papermaking, agriculture, transportation, communications. Also an extensive exhibit devoted to Appleton native Harry Houdini. (Sept-May, daily exc Mon; rest of yr, daily; closed major hols) 330 E College Ave. Phone 920/735-9370 or 920/733-8445. ¢¢

Motels

★ ★ **BEST WESTERN MIDWAY HOTEL.** *3033 W College Ave (WI 125) (54914). 414/731-4141; FAX 414/731-6343.* 105 rms, 2 story. S $67-$86; D $78-$98; each addl $12; under 18 free; wkend rates. Crib free. Pet accepted, some restrictions; $10. TV; cable. Indoor pool; whirlpool. Complimentary full bkfst (Mon-Fri). Coffee in rms. Restaurant 6:30 am-11 pm. Rm serv. Bar 11-1 am. Ck-out 11 am. Meeting rms. Business servs avail. In-rm modem link. Bellhops. Sundries. Free airport, bus depot transportation. Exercise equipt; bicycles, weights, sauna. Health club privileges. Rec rm. Cr cds: A, C, D, DS, MC, V.

🗸★ **EXEL INN.** *210 N Westhill Blvd (54914), off College Ave (WI 125). 414/733-5551; FAX 414/733-7199.* 105 rms, 2 story. S $37.99; D $45.99-$105; each addl $4; under 18 free. Crib free. Pet accepted, some restrictions. TV; cable (premium). Complimentary continental bkfst. Restaurant adj 6 am-11 pm. Ck-out noon. Business servs avail. In-rm modem link. Health club privileges. Refrigerator, microwave, in-rm whirlpool avail. Cr cds: A, C, D, DS, MC, V.

★ ★ **RAMADA INN.** *200 N Perkins St (54914). 920/735-2733; FAX 920/735-5588.* 91 units, 2 story. S $60-$80; D $70-$90; each addl $5;

suites $80-$100; under 18 free. Crib free. Pet accepted, some restrictions. TV; cable (premium), VCR avail (movies). Indoor pool; whirlpool. Complimentary bkfst buffet 6-10 am. Restaurant adj. Bar 11-1 am. Ck-out noon. Coin lndry. Meeting rms. Business servs avail. Valet serv. Sundries. Free airport, bus depot transportation. Exercise equipt; bicycle, stair machine. Some refrigerators. Cr cds: A, C, D, DS, JCB, MC, V.

 D ⊁ ≋ ⅋ ⊠ ⊠ SC

✔ ★ **ROAD STAR INN.** 3623 W College Ave (WI 125) (54914). 414/731-5271; FAX 414/731-0227; res: 800/445-4667. 102 rms, 2 story. S $35; D $41; each addl $5; suites $42.95-$44.95; under 15 free; higher rates special events. Pet accepted. TV; cable (premium). Complimentary continental bkfst. Restaurant adj 7 am-9 pm. Ck-out noon. Sundries. Cr cds: A, C, D, DS, MC, V.

D ⊁ ⚓ ⊠ ⊠ SC

★ ★ **WOODFIELD SUITES.** 3730 W College Ave (WI 125) (54914), E of jct US 41. 414/734-7777; FAX 414/734-0049; res: 800/338-0008. 98 rms, 2 story. S $69.95-$115; D $79.95-$115; each addl $10; under 19 free. Crib free. TV; cable (premium), VCR avail. 2 pools, 1 indoor; whirlpool. Complimentary continental bkfst. Coffee in rms. Restaurant adj 6 am-11 pm. Bar from 11 am. Ck-out noon. Meeting rm. Business servs avail. In-rm modem link. Valet serv. Free airport transportation. Sundries. Tennis. Sauna. Bowling. Game rm. Rec rm. Lawn games. Refrigerators. Cr cds: A, C, D, DS, MC, V.

D ⚓ ≋ ⊠ ⊠

Hotels

★ ★ ★ **HOLIDAY INN.** 150 Nicolet Rd (54914), near Outagamie County Airport. 920/735-9955; FAX 920/735-0309. 228 units, 8 story. S $79-$95; D $79-$105; each addl $10; suites $139-$189; under 19 free; wkend rates; higher rates Packer games, EAA Fly-In. Crib free. TV; cable (premium), VCR avail. Indoor pool; whirlpool, poolside serv. Complimentary coffee in rms. Restaurant 6 am-2 pm, 5-10 pm. Bar 3 pm-1 am, wkends 11-2 am. Ck-out noon. Coin lndry. Meeting rms. Business center. In-rm modem link. Gift shop. Free airport transportation. X-country ski 4 mi. Massage. Exercise rm; instructor, weights, bicycles, sauna. Refrigerator, microwave in suites. Cr cds: A, C, D, DS, JCB, MC, V.

D ⊁ ≋ ⅋ ✈ ⊠ ⚓ SC ⅋

★ ★ ★ **PAPER VALLEY HOTEL & CONFERENCE CENTER.** 333 W College Ave (WI 125) (54911). 920/733-8000; FAX 920/733-9220; res: 800/242-3499 (WI). 394 rms, 7 story. S $92.99; D $99; each addl $10; suites $129; under 18 free; wkend packages. Crib free. TV; cable (premium), VCR avail. Indoor pool; whirlpool, poolside serv. Complimentary coffee. Restaurant 6:30 am-11 pm. Bar 11-1 am; entertainment. Ck-out noon. Convention facilities. Business center. In-rm modem link. Shopping arcade. Barber, beauty shop. Free airport, bus depot transportation. Miniature golf. Exercise equipt; weights, bicycles, sauna. Game rm. Rec rm. Some refrigerators, microwaves. Cr cds: A, C, D, DS, MC, V.

D ≋ ⅋ ⊠ ⚓ SC ⅋

Restaurant

★ ★ **GEORGE'S STEAK HOUSE.** 2208 S Memorial Dr (54914). 920/733-4939. Hrs: 11 am-2 pm, 5-10:30 pm; Sat from 5 pm. Closed Sun; major hols. Res accepted. Bar to 1 am. Semi-a la carte: lunch $4-$7, dinner $9-$17.50. Child's meals. Specializes in steak, seafood. Piano bar. Cr cds: A, C, D, DS, MC, V.

D ⊷

Ashland (B-3)

(See also Bayfield)

Founded 1854 **Pop** 8,695 **Elev** 671 ft **Area code** 715 **Zip** 54806
Information Ashland Area Chamber of Commerce, 320 4th Ave W, PO Box 746; 715/682-2500 or 800/284-9484.

Located on Chequamegon Bay, which legend says is the "shining big sea water" of Longfellow's *Hiawatha,* Ashland is a port for Great Lakes ships delivering coal for the Midwest. It is also a gateway to the Apostle Islands. Papermaking machinery, fabricated steel and other industrial products provide a diversified economy.

What to See and Do

Copper Falls State Park. This 2,500-acre park has more than 8 mi of river; nature & hiking trails provide spectacular views of the river gorge and the falls. Swimming; fishing; canoeing. Backpacking. Cross-country skiing. Picnicking, playground, concession. Primitive & improved camping (hookups, dump station). Standard fees. (Daily) S off WI 13, 169 in Mellen. Phone 715/274-5123. Per vehicle ¢¢

Fishing. In Chequamegon Bay and in 65 trout streams and inland lakes (license & stamp required). Ice fishing is a popular winter sport. Also spring smelting & deep sea trolling in Lake Superior. Public boat landing at Sunset Park; RV park adj to Sunset Park (hookups, dump station).

Northland College (1892). (750 students) Founded to bring higher education to the people of the isolated logging camps and farm communities of northern Wisconsin. On campus are Sigurd Olson Environmental Institute, in an earth-sheltered, solar-heated building, and historic Wheeler Hall (1892), constructed of brownstone from the nearby Apostle Islands. Ellis Ave, on WI 13. Phone 715/682-1699.

Annual Events

Bay Days Festival. Sailboat regatta, art fair, bicycle & foot races, ethnic food booths, entertainment, dancing. 3rd wkend July.

Croation Day. Labor Day wkend.

Motels

★ ★ **BEST WESTERN HOLIDAY HOUSE.** Rte 3, Box 24, Lakeshore Dr (US 2/63/WI 13). 715/682-5235; FAX 715/682-4730. 65 rms, 2 story. Mid-May-early Oct: S $44-$56; D $48-$90; each addl $5; winter wkend packages; lower rates rest of yr. Crib free. Pet accepted, some restrictions. TV; cable (premium). Sauna. Indoor pool; whirlpool. Coffee in rms. Restaurants 6 am-2 pm, 4:30-10 pm. Bar. Ck-out 11 am. Business servs avail. Downhill ski 15 mi; x-country ski opp. Many balconies. Overlooks Chequamegon Bay. Cr cds: A, C, D, DS, ER, MC, V.

D ⊁ ⚓ ≋ ⊠ ⚓ SC

✔ ★ **SUPER 8.** 1610 Lake Shore Dr. 715/682-9377; FAX 715/682-5593. 70 rms, 2 story. Mid-June-Sept: S $58.88-$65.88; D $59.88-$74.88; each addl $5; under 12 free; lower rates rest of yr. Crib free. Pet accepted, some restrictions. TV; cable (premium), VCR avail. Indoor pool; whirlpool. Complimentary coffee in lobby. Ck-out 11 am. Coin lndry. Business servs avail. In-rm modem link. X-country ski 10 mi. Microwaves avail. Opp Lake Superior. Cr cds: A, C, D, DS, MC, V.

D ⊁ ⚓ ≋ ⊠ ⚓ SC

Hotel

★ ★ **HOTEL CHEQUAMEGON.** 101 Lake Shore Dr. 715/682-9095; FAX 715/682-9410; res: 800/946-5555. E-mail hotel@win.bright.net; web www.dockernet.com/~hotelc/. 65 units, 3 story, 6 kit. units. June-mid-Oct: S, D $85-$95; each addl $10; suites $95-$140; kit. units $95; under 12 free; lower rates rest of yr. Crib free. TV; cable (premium). Sauna. Indoor pool; whirlpool. Restaurant 6 am-9 pm; dining rm 4:30-10 pm. Bar 11:30-1 am. Ck-out 11 am. Meeting rms. Business servs avail. Some refrigerators, in-rm whirlpools. On Lake Superior. Large veranda overlooks marina. Cr cds: A, D, DS, MC, V.

Baileys Harbor (Door Co) (D-6)

(See also Door County)

Settled 1851 **Pop** 780 **Elev** 595 ft **Area code** 414 **Zip** 54202 **E-mail** lyons@mail.wiscnet.net **Web** doorcountyvacations.com

Information Door County Chamber of Commerce, 1015 Green Bay Rd, PO Box 406, Sturgeon Bay 54235; 414/743-4456 or 800/527-3529.

Bailey's Harbor is the oldest village in Door County (see), with one of the best harbors on the east shore. Range lights, built in 1870 to guide ships into the harbor, still operate. Its waters feature charter fishing for trout and salmon.

What to See and Do

Bjorklunden. A 325-acre estate, owned by Lawrence University (Appleton), with a replica of a Norwegian wooden chapel (stavkirke). The chapel was handcrafted by the original owners, the Boynton family, during the summers of 1939-1947. Seminars in the humanities are held on the estate each summer. Tours of chapel. (Mid-June-Aug, Mon & Wed) Phone 414/839-2216. ¢

Kangaroo Lake. Swimming; fishing; boating. Picnicking. S on WI 57.

Annual Event

Baileys Harbor Brown Trout Tournament. Late Apr.

Motel

★ **PETRY PLACE.** *8040 WI 57. 920/839-2345; res: 800/503-5959.* 39 rms, 7 A/C, 2 story. No rm phones. July-Aug: D $89-$95; each addl $7; suites $95-$109; lower rates Apr-June, Sept-Oct. Closed rest of yr. Crib avail. TV. Indoor pool. Complimentary coffee in lobby. Restaurant nearby. Ck-out 10 am. Sauna. Some refrigerators. On lake, beach. Cr cds: DS, MC, V.

Resorts

★ ★ **GORDON LODGE.** *1420 Pine Dr, on North Bay, 1/2 mi N on WI 57, then 6 1/2 mi NE on County Q. 920/839-2331; FAX 920/839-2450; res: 800/830-6235.* Web www.gordonlodge.com. 20 rms in lodge, 11 villas (1-2 bedrm). Late June-mid-Oct: S, D $100-$212; each addl $29; suites $212; 3-day min wkends July-Labor Day, Columbus Day; lower rates mid-May-mid-June. Closed rest of yr. TV; cable (premium). Heated pool. Complimentary full bkfst (in season). Complimentary coffee in rms. Dining rm (hrs vary). Box lunches. Bar noon-midnight; entertainment. Ck-out noon, ck-in 4 pm. Business servs avail. Lighted tennis. Putting green. Private sand beach. Row boats. Bicycles. Exercise equipt; bicycle, rower. Refrigerators; some microwaves, fireplaces. Some private patios. Spacious grounds; scenic lake view. Cr cds: A, DS, MC, V.

Restaurants

★ ★ **COMMON HOUSE.** *8041 Main St. 920/839-2708.* Hrs: 11:30 am-2 pm, 5:30-10 pm. Res accepted. No A/C. Bar. Semi-a la carte:

lunch $4.95-$9.95, dinner $10-$26.95. Child's meals. Own desserts. Old-fashioned wood stove in dining rm. Cr cds: DS, MC, V.

D

★ ★ **FLORIAN II.** *on WI 57. 920/839-2361.* Hrs: 5-9 pm; Sat, Sun 8 am-2:30 pm, 5-9 pm. Closed Nov-Mar. Res accepted. Bar. Buffet: bkfst $5.95. Semi-a la carte: lunch $5.95, dinner $9.95-$19.95. Child's meals. Specializes in prime rib, roast duck, barbecued ribs. Salad bar. Entertainment Fri, Sat. Solarium dining; overlooks Lake Michigan. Dock. Family-owned. Cr cds: MC, V.

D SC

✔★ **SANDPIPER.** *8166 WI 57. 920/839-2528.* Hrs: 7 am-9 pm; hrs vary off-season. Closed Nov-Mar. Wine, beer. Semi-a la carte: bkfst $2.95-$5.95, lunch $1.25-$6.95, dinner $6.95-$12.95. Fish boil mid-May-Oct (days vary): $9.95. Child's meals. Specializes in chicken, fish. Own soups. Outdoor dining. Cr cds: DS, MC, V.

D SC

Baraboo (F-4)

(See also Portage, Prairie du Sac, Reedsburg, Wisconsin Dells)

Founded 1830 **Pop** 9,203 **Elev** 894 ft **Area code** 608 **Zip** 53913
Information Chamber of Commerce, PO Box 442; 608/356-8333 or 800/BARABOO.

A center for the distribution of dairy products, Baraboo is a neatly ordered town of lawns, gardens, parks, homes and factories. The city is the original home of the Ringling Brothers and Gollmar circuses and still holds memories of its circus-town days. It was founded by Jean Baribeau as a trading post for the Hudson's Bay Company. Beautiful spring-fed Devil's Lake is three miles south of town.

What to See and Do

⭐ **Circus World Museum.** Has 50 acres and 8 buildings of circus lore; original winter quarters of Ringling Brothers Circus. Live circus acts under "Big Top"; daily circus parade; display of circus parade wagons; steam calliope concerts; P.T. Barnum sideshow; wild animal menagerie; merry-go-round, band organ. Unloading circus train with Percheron horses; picnic facilities. (Early May-mid-Sept, daily) Exhibit Hall open year-round. 426 Water St. Phone 608/356-8341 for schedule of events. ¢¢¢¢

Devil's Head Lodge Ski Area. Area has triple, 6 double, 3 quad chairlifts, 3 rope tows; patrol, school, rentals; snowmaking; lodge; restaurants, cafeteria, bars. Longest run 1 mi; vertical drop 500 ft. (Dec-Mar, daily) Night skiing; cross-country trails. 12 mi SE via WI 113, 78 in Merrimac. Phone 608/493-2251. ¢¢¢¢¢

Devil's Lake State Park (see). 3 mi S on WI 123. Phone 608/356-6618.

Ho-Chunk Casino & Bingo. Gaming casino featuring 48 blackjack tables, 1,200 slot machines, video poker and keno. (Daily, 24 hrs) 53214A US 12. Phone 800/746-2486.

International Crane Foundation. A nonprofit organization promoting the study and preservation of cranes. Features cranes and their chicks from all over the world. Movies, displays, nature trails. (May-Oct, daily) Guided tours (Memorial Day-Labor Day, daily; Sept-Oct, wkends) E11376 Shady Lane Rd. Phone 608/356-9462. ¢¢

Mid-Continent Railway Museum. Restored 1894 depot, complete 1900 rail environment; steam locomotives, coaches, steam wrecker, snowplows; artifacts and historical exhibits. Picnic area, gift shop. (Mid-May-Labor Day, daily; after Labor Day-mid-Oct, wkends only) One-hr steam train round trip on a branch of C & NW Railroad line, which once served early iron mines and rock quarries. Leaves North Freedom (same dates as museum; four departures daily). 5 mi W via WI 136, then 2 mi S to North Freedom. Phone 608/522-4261. **Free.** Train ride ¢¢¢

Mirror Lake State Park. A 2,050-acre park with swimming; fishing; boating, canoeing. Hiking. Cross-country skiing, picnicking, playground. Camping (fee; electric hookups, dump station). Standard fees. (Daily) 2 mi W off US 12. Phone 608/254-2333. Per vehicle ¢¢¢

Sauk County Historical Museum. Houses 19th-century household goods, textiles, toys, china, military items, pioneer collection, Native American artifacts, circus memorabilia, natural history display, photos; research library. (May-Oct, daily exc Mon) 531 4th Ave. Phone 608/356-1001. ¢

Motels

★ ★ **QUALITY INN.** 630 W Pine St, on US 12W. 608/356-6422; FAX 608/356-6422. 84 rms, 5 story, 12 suites. Memorial Day-Labor Day: S $70-$150; D $75-$150; each addl $5; suites $125-$150; under 17 free; ski, golf plans; lower rates rest of yr. Crib $4. TV; cable. Indoor pool; whirlpool. Complimentary coffee in rms. Restaurant 7 am-10 pm. Rm serv. Bar 10-1 am. Ck-out 11 am. Coin lndry. Meeting rms. Business servs avail. Valet serv. Sundries. Downhill ski 12 mi. Exercise equipt; weight machine, stair machine, sauna. Game rm. Refrigerator, wet bar, whirlpool in suites. Cr cds: A, C, D, DS, JCB, MC, V.

⊡ ⇆ ☇ ✕ ⊠ ⌖ SC

✔★ **SPINNING WHEEL.** 809 8th St, 2 mi E of US 12 on WI 33. 608/356-3933. 25 rms. S $33-$53; D $35-$63; each addl $6; under 12 free. Crib $6. Pet accepted. TV; cable (premium). Restaurant nearby. Downhill ski 10 mi; x-country ski 5 mi. Cr cds: A, DS, MC, V.

⊡ ⇝ ☇ ⊠ ⌖ SC

Bayfield (A-3)

(See also Ashland)

Pop 686 **Elev** 700 ft **Area code** 715 **Zip** 54814
Information Chamber of Commerce, 42 S Broad St, PO Box 138; 715/779-3335 or 800/447-4094.

What to See and Do

Apostle Islands National Lakeshore. 11 mi of mainland shoreline and 21 islands of varying size. The lakeshore area features hiking, boating, fishing; primitive campsites on 18 islands. Two visitor centers, in Bayfield (all yr) and at Little Sand Bay (Memorial Day-Sept), 13 mi NW of Bayfield. National Lakeshore Headquarters/Visitor Center (daily; free). N & E off Bayfield Peninsula. Phone 715/779-3397. Boat trips provided by

Apostle Islands Cruise Service. Lake Superior cruises to Apostle Islands on the *Island Princess* (May-early Oct, departures daily); also Stockton Island shuttle with Raspberry Island Lighthouse Adventure: two-hr layover & naturalist hike. City Dock. Reservations advised, inquire for schedule; phone 715/779-3925. ¢¢¢¢¢ Charter boats also in the area for island camping, deep-water fishing or diving.

Madeline Island. Part of island group but not under federal jurisdiction. 14 mi long, has 45 mi of roads; off the dock at La Pointe is

Madeline Island Historical Museum, located near the site of an American Fur Co post and housed in a single building combining four pioneer log structures. (Late May-early Oct, daily; fee) There are motels, housekeeping cottages and restaurants on the island. Guided bus tours. Camping in two parks. Cross-country skiing. Marina. Phone 715/747-2801. Bus tours ¢¢-¢¢¢

Madeline Island Ferry Line. The *Island Queen, Nichevo II* and the *Madeline* make frequent trips. (Apr-Dec, daily) Phone 715/747-2051. Per passenger, one-way ¢¢

Mt Ashwabay Ski Area. T-bar, 4 rope tows; patrol, school, rentals; restaurant, cafeteria, concession, bar. Longest run 3,200 ft; vertical drop 317 ft. (Dec-Mar, Wed, Sat-Sun; Christmas wk, daily) Half-day rates; night skiing (Wed & Sat). Also cross-country skiing (daily exc Mon), 24 mi of trails. 3 mi S on WI 13. Phone 715/779-3227. ¢¢¢¢

Annual Events

Sailboat Race Week. 1st wk of July.

Great Schooner Race. Last wkend in Sept.

Apple Festival. 1st full wkend Oct.

Motel

★ **BAYFIELD INN.** 20 Rittenhouse Ave. 715/779-3363. E-mail bayinn@win.bright.net; web www.travelreservations.com/wi/bayfield.htm. 21 rms, 2 story. No A/C. Memorial Day wkend-early Oct: S $50-$70; D $70-$85; each addl $15; under 12 free; wkends 2-day min (July-Aug); higher rates Apple Festival; lower rates rest of yr. Crib free. TV; cable, VCR avail (movies). Complimentary continental bkfst. Restaurant 11:30 am-9 pm. Rm serv. Ck-out 11 am. Business servs avail. Downhill ski 5 mi; x-country ski on-site. Sauna. Game rm. On lake. Cr cds: DS, MC, V.

⇆ ☇ ⊠ ⌖

★ **SUPER 8.** (Harbor View Dr, Washburn 54891) 12 mi S on WI 13. 715/373-5671; FAX 715/373-5674. 35 rms, 2 story. July-Sept: S $69.98-$75.98; D $79.98-$84.98; each addl $5; suite $89.98-$99.98; under 12 free; wkly & hol rates; higher rates Apple Fest; lower rates rest of yr. Crib free. Pet accepted, some restrictions; $25. TV; cable. Complimentary continental bkfst. Restaurant adj 4-10 pm. Ck-out 11 am. Business servs avail. Downhill/x-country ski 8 mi. Sauna. Whirlpool. Game rm. On lake. Cr cds: A, D, DS, MC, V.

⊡ ⇆ ⇝ ☇ ⊠ ⌖ SC

✔★ **WINFIELD INN.** Rte 1, Box 33, 4 blks N on WI 13. 715/779-3252; FAX 715/779-5180. 31 rms, 26 A/C, 1-2 story, 6 kit. apts (1-2 bedrm). June-Oct: S, D $66; kit. apts $95-$125; lower rates rest of yr. Crib free. Pet accepted. TV; cable. Complimentary coffee in rms. Restaurant nearby. Ck-out 11 am. Downhill/x-country ski 8 mi. Some balconies. Sun deck. Overlooks Lake Superior. Cr cds: A, DS, MC, V.

⊡ ⇆ ☇ ⊠ ⌖

Inn

★ ★ ★ **OLD RITTENHOUSE.** 301 Rittenhouse Ave (WI 13). 715/779-5111. 21 units in 4 guest houses, 2-3 story. No rm phones. D $99-$149; each addl $15; suites $149-$249; winter wkend plans. Crib avail. Complimentary continental bkfst in main house. Restaurant (see OLD RITTENHOUSE INN). Rm serv. Ck-out noon, ck-in 3:30 pm. Downhill ski 3 mi; x-country ski 1 mi. Some in-rm whirlpools. Fireplaces. Individually decorated rms in 4 restored Victorian houses; antique furnishings. Totally nonsmoking. Cr cds: MC, V.

⊡ ☇ ⊠ ⌖

Restaurant

★ ★ ★ **OLD RITTENHOUSE INN.** (See Old Rittenhouse Inn) 715/779-5111. Hrs: 11:15 am-1:30 pm, 5-9 pm; Oct-May dinner only; Nov-Apr wkends only; Sun brunch 11:15 am-1:30 pm. Res accepted. Wine. Complete meals: dinner $39.50. Sun brunch $15.50. Serv charge 16%. Child's meals. Specializes in fresh Lake Superior whitefish & trout, regional dishes. Own baking. In restored summer mansion (1890). Cr cds: MC, V.

Beaver Dam (F-5)

(See also Watertown, Waupun)

Settled 1841 **Pop** 14,196 **Elev** 879 ft **Area code** 414 **Zip** 53916 **E-mail** info@beaverdamchamber.com **Web** www.beaverdamchamber.com
Information Chamber of Commerce, 127 S Spring St; 414/887-8879.

What to See and Do

Beaver Dam Lake. 14 mi long; fishing for bullhead, perch, crappie, walleye & northern pike, ice fishing; waterfowl hunting; boating (docks, ramps), waterskiing. (Daily) W edge of town. Phone 414/885-6766.   **Free.**

Dodge County Historical Museum. In 1890 Romanesque building; china, Native American artifacts, spinning wheels, dolls. (Wed-Sat; closed hols) 105 Park Ave. Phone 414/887-1266.   **Free.**

Annual Events

Swan City Car Show. Swan City Park. Phone 414/887-7111. Father's Day.

Dodge County Fair. Fairgrounds, 3 mi E on WI 33. Phone 414/885-3586. 5 days mid-late Aug.

Motels

★ ★ **BEST WESTERN CAMPUS INN.** *815 Park Ave, jct WI 33 & US 151.* 414/887-7171; *res:* 800/572-4891. 94 rms, 4 story. S, D $66-$80; each addl $5; suites $80-$110; under 12 free. Crib $4. TV; cable (premium), VCR avail. Indoor pool; whirlpool. Restaurant 6 am-11 pm. Rm serv. Bar 4 pm-2 am. Ck-out 11 am. Coin lndry. Meeting rms. In-rm modem link. Valet serv. Sundries. Putting green. Game rm. Cr cds: A, C, D, DS, MC, V.

✔ ★ **GRAND VIEW.** *1510 N Center.* 414/885-9208; FAX 414/887-8706. 22 rms. S $26-$29; D $35-$39; each addl $4. Crib $3. Pet accepted, some restrictions. TV; cable (premium). Ck-out 11 am. Cr cds: DS, MC, V.

✔ ★ **MAYVILLE INN.** *(701 S Mountain Dr, Mayville 53050)* 14 mi E on WI 33, then 4 mi N on WI 67. 414/387-1234. 29 rms, 2 story. S, D $38-$75; each addl $5; under 12 free. Crib free. Complimentary continental bkfst. Restaurant nearby. Bar. Ck-out 11 am. Meeting rm. Business servs avail. In-rm modem link. Gift shop. X-country ski 5 mi. Whirlpool. Some refrigerators, wet bars. Cr cds: A, DS, MC, V.

Beloit (H-4)

(See also Delavan, Janesville; also see Rockford, IL)

Settled 1836 **Pop** 35,573 **Elev** 750 ft **Area code** 608 **Zip** 53511 **E-mail** bcvb@bossnt.com
Information Convention and Visitors Bureau, 1003 Pleasant St; 608/365-4838 or 800/4-BELOIT.

In 1837, the town of Colebrook, New Hampshire, moved almost en masse to this point at the confluence of Turtle Creek and Rock River. The community, successively known as Turtle, Blodgett's Settlement and New Albany, was finally named Beloit in 1857. The New Englanders, determined to sustain standards of Eastern culture and education, founded Beloit Seminary soon after settling; this small coeducational school be-

came Beloit College. Today the city's economy centers around the college, food processing and the production of heavy machinery.

What to See and Do

Beloit College (1846). (1,100 students) Noted for Theodore Lyman Wright Museum of Art (academic yr, daily). Logan Museum of Anthropology has changing displays of Native American and Stone Age artifacts. Campus contains prehistoric mounds. Campus tours (by appt). On US 51. Phone 608/363-2000.

Hanchett-Bartlett Homestead (1857). Restored historic limestone homestead on 15 acres is built in the transitional Greek-revival style, with Italianate details; restored in period colors. House contains furnishings of the mid-19th century; limestone barn houses collection of farm implements. On the grounds is a one-room schoolhouse (1880); picnic area. (June-Sept, Wed-Sun afternoons; also by appt) 2149 St Lawrence Ave. Phone 608/365-7835.   ¢

Annual Event

Riverfest. Riverside Dr, Riverside Park. Music festival with top-name performers; more than 50 bands feature variety of music. Food, carnival rides, children's entertainment. Phone 608/365-4838. Mid-July.

Motels

★ ★ **COMFORT INN.** *2786 Milwaukee Rd.* 608/362-2666. 56 rms, 2 story, 16 suites. June-Sept: S $45-$65; D $50-$70; each addl $5; suites $55-$75; under 18 free; wkly rates; higher rates special events; lower rates rest of yr. Crib free. Pet accepted. TV; cable (premium), VCR avail (movies). Indoor pool; whirlpool. Complimentary continental bkfst. Restaurant nearby. Ck-out 11 am. Business servs avail. Game rm. Refrigerator in suites. Cr cds: A, C, D, DS, JCB, MC, V.

☐ 🐾 🏊 ⛷ 🔥 SC

★ ★ **HOLIDAY INN.** *(200 Dearborn, South Beloit 61080)* 2 mi S at jct US 51, IL 75, 1/2 mi W of I-90 South Beloit exit. 815/389-3481; FAX 815/389-3481, ext. 519. 166 rms, 2 story. S $59-$85; D $67-$97; each addl $8; under 18 free. Crib free. TV; cable. Heated pool; whirlpool. Restaurant 6 am-10 pm. Rm serv. Bar 11 am-midnight. Ck-out noon. Meeting rms. Business center. Valet serv (Mon-Fri). X-country ski 5 mi. Exercise equipt; weight machine, treadmill. Sun deck. Cr cds: A, C, D, DS, JCB, MC, V.

☐ ⛷ 🏊 🏋 ⛷ 🔥 SC 🚶

✔ ★ **HOLIDAY INN EXPRESS.** *2790 Milwaukee Rd.* 608/365-6000; FAX 608/365-1974. 73 rms, 2 story. S $49-$65; D $60-$70; each addl $6; under 18 free. Crib free. TV; cable (premium). Complimentary bkfst. Coffee in rms. Ck-out noon. Meeting rm. Business servs avail. Valet serv. Cr cds: A, C, D, DS, JCB, MC, V.

☐ ⛷ 🔥 SC

Restaurant

★ ★ **BUTTERFLY CLUB.** *5246 E County Rd X, I-90 to WI 43 N, exit Hart Rd.* 608/362-8577. Hrs: 5-9:30 pm; Sun noon-8 pm. Closed Mon; Jan 1, Dec 24-25. Res accepted Tues-Thurs, Sat-Sun. Bar. Semi-a la carte: dinner $7-$35. Child's meals. Specializes in prime rib, chicken, fish. Own baking. Entertainment Fri, Sat. Outdoor dining. Cr cds: A, C, D, DS, MC, V.

Black River Falls (E-3)

(See also Sparta, Tomah)

Pop 3,490 **Elev** 796 ft **Area code** 715 **Zip** 54615
Information Black River Falls Area Chamber of Commerce, 336 N Water St; 715/284-4658.

In 1819, when the Black River countryside was a wilderness of pine, one of the first sawmills in Wisconsin was built here. Among the early settlers were a group of Mormons from Nauvoo, Illinois (see). Conflict developed with local landowners, and the the Mormons soon returned to Nauvoo. The seat of Jackson County, Black River Falls is situated on the Black River, which offers boating and canoeing. The area is also noted for deer hunting and winter sports.

What to See and Do

Black River Falls State Forest. A 66,000-acre forest. Swimming; fishing; boating, canoeing. Hiking, cross-country skiing, snowmobiling. Bridle trail. Picnicking, playground. Camping (fee). Lookout tower; abundant wildlife. Self-guided auto trail. All motor vehicles must have park sticker. (Daily) Standard fees. 6 mi E on WI 54. Phone 715/284-1400. Per vehicle ¢¢

Thunderbird Museum. Exhibits include Native American artifacts dating back to paleolithic man, weapons, minerals, dolls, coins, stamps, art. (May, by appt; Memorial Day-Labor Day, daily; Sept, wkends or by appt) In Hatfield, 10 mi NE via US 12, County K exit at Merrillan. Phone 715/333-5841. ¢¢

Annual Event

Winnebago Pow-Wow. 3 mi NE via WI 54, at Red Cloud Memorial Pow-Wow Grounds. Dancing. Held twice annually: Sun & Mon, Memorial Day wkend & Labor Day wkend.

Motels

✔★★ **AMERICAN HERITAGE INN.** *919 WI 54E, at jct I-94 exit 116.* 715/284-4333; FAX 715/284-9068; res: 800/356-8018. 86 rms, 2 story. S $36.99-$61.99; D $47.99-$63.99; suites $75-$110; under 12 free. Crib free. Pet accepted. TV; cable, VCR avail. Sauna. Indoor pool; whirlpool. Complimentary continental bkfst. Restaurant adj 6 am-11 pm. Ck-out noon. Coin lndry. Meeting rm. Business servs avail. In-rm modem link. Downhill ski 15 mi; x-country ski 1 mi. Game rm. Cr cds: A, C, D, DS, MC, V.

D ⚫ ⚫ ⚫ ⚫ ⚫ SC

★★★ **BEST WESTERN ARROWHEAD LODGE.** *600 Oasis Rd, 1 mi E on WI 54 at I-94.* 715/284-9471; FAX 715/284-9664; res: 800/284-9471. 144 rms, 3 story, 30 suites. S $43-$64.50; D $53-$74.95; each addl $5; suites $59.95-$149.95; under 12 free. Crib $3. Pet accepted. TV; cable, VCR avail. Sauna. Indoor pool; whirlpool. Playground. Restaurant 6:30 am-2 pm, 5-10 pm. Bar; entertainment Sat. Ck-out noon. Meeting rms. Business servs avail. In-rm modem link. Sundries. Snowmobile trails. Nature/fitness trail. Cr cds: A, C, D, DS, MC, V.

D ⚫ ⚫ ⚫ ⚫ ⚫ ⚫ SC

Boulder Junction (B-4)

(See also Eagle River, Land O'Lakes, Manitowish Waters, Minocqua, Sayner, Woodruff)

Pop 1,000 (est) **Elev** 1,640 ft **Area code** 715 **Zip** 54512
Information Chamber of Commerce, PO Box 286; 715/385-2400.

This secluded, little village within the Northern Highland-American Legion State Forest is the gateway to a vast recreational area with woodlands, scenic drives, streams and several hundred lakes where fishing for muskellunge is excellent. Indeed, "Musky Capital of the World" is its registered trademark. Boulder Junction also offers various winter activities, including snowmobiling, cross-country skiing and ice fishing. In nearby state nurseries, millions of young pine trees are raised and shipped all over the state for forest planting.

What to See and Do

Northern Highland-American Legion State Forest. A 225,000-acre forest with swimming beaches, waterskiing; fishing; boating, canoeing. Hiking. Cross-country skiing, snowmobiling. Picnicking. Improved and primitive camping (896 sites on lakes; dump station; fee), sites also along water trails. Standard fees. (Daily) Phone 715/356-5211. Per vehicle ¢¢

Annual Event

Musky Jamboree/Arts & Crafts Fair. Early Aug.

Cottage Colonies

★★ **WHITE BIRCH VILLAGE.** *1½ mi S on County M, then 6 mi E on County K.* 715/385-2182; FAX 715/385-2537. 11 kit. cottages (1-4 bedrm), 1-2 story. No A/C. Late May-early Oct: $550-$875/wk. Closed rest of yr. Crib free. Pet accepted. TV in sitting rm. Playground. Ck-out 9 am, ck-in 2 pm. Grocery. Coin lndry. Package store 8 mi. Business servs avail. Sand beach; dock, launching ramp, boats, canoes, sailboats, paddleboats. Lawn games. Tandem bicycles. Rec rm. Fishing guides, clean & store area. Library. Fireplaces. Private decks. Grills. Woodland setting on White Birch Lake. No cr cds accepted.

D ⚫ ⚫ ⚫ ⚫

★ **ZASTROW'S LYNX LAKE LODGE.** *4 mi N on County M, then 4 mi W on County B.* 715/686-2249; FAX 715/686-2257; res: 800/882-5969. 11 cottages (1-4 bedrm), 7 with kit. No A/C. MAP, May-Oct: $279/wk/person; family rates; EP off-season; 3-day min some wkends; lower rates Dec-Feb. Closed Mar-Apr & late Oct-Dec 26. Crib avail. Pet accepted. TV; cable. Playground. Dining rm 8-9:30 am, 5-9:30 pm. Box lunches. Bar 4:30 pm-2 am. Ck-out 10 am, ck-in 2 pm. Business servs avail. Grocery 4 mi. Coin lndry 8 mi. Package store. Gift shop. Free airport, bus depot transportation. Private beach, swimming; boats, rowboats, canoes, sailboats, paddleboats, motors. X-country ski on site. Snowmobiles. Bicycles. Lawn games. Movies. Rec rm. Fish/game clean & store area. Some fireplaces. No cr cds accepted.

D ⚫ ⚫ ⚫ ⚫ ⚫ ⚫

Restaurants

★ **GEORGE'S STEAK HOUSE.** *Main St.* 715/385-2350. Hrs: 11:30 am-2 pm, 5-10 pm. Closed Mon; Dec 24, 25. Res accepted. Bar 11-2 am. Semi-a la carte: lunch $2.75-$12.50, dinner $6.50-$29.95. Child's meals. Specializes in ribs, steak, lobster. Informal dining in North woods atmosphere; fireplace, pine boards. Cr cds: MC, V.

D SC ♥

★★ **GUIDE'S INN.** *On County M, in town.* 715/385-2233. Hrs: 5-10 pm. Closed Easter, Dec 25. Continental menu. Bar. Semi-a la carte:

dinner $6.50-$19.95. Child's meals. Specialties: beef Wellington, Black Forest schnitzel. Own ice cream, desserts. Cr cds: DS, MC, V.

Burlington (G-5)

(See also Delavan, Elkhorn, Fontana, Lake Geneva)

Settled 1835 **Pop** 8,855 **Elev** 766 ft **Area code** 414 **Zip** 53105
Information Chamber of Commerce, 112 E Chesnut St, PO Box 156; 414/763-6044.

Originally called Foxville, Burlington was renamed for the city in Vermont by a group of settlers arriving in 1835. It is the home of the Liar's Club, an organization dedicated to the preservation of the art of telling tall tales. A prize is awarded each year to the contributor who submits the most incredible "stretcher."

What to See and Do

Green Meadows Farm. Operating farm offers daily guided tours; pony rides, tractor-drawn hayrides; more than 20 "hands-on" animal areas; picnic areas. (May-June, Tues-Sat; July-Labor Day, Oct, daily; closed Sept) Pumpkin picking in Oct. 33603 High Dr, 5 mi N via WI 36, 3 mi W of Waterford on WI 20. Phone 414/534-2891. ¢¢¢

Spinning Top Exploratory Museum. Exhibits and displays dealing with tops, yo-yos, gyroscopes; top games, demonstrations; 35 tops for hands-on experiments. Video presentations. 533 Milwaukee Ave. For schedule phone 414/763-3946 or 414/728-5623. ¢¢

Annual Event

Chocolate City Festival. Two-day, city-wide celebration includes arts & crafts fair (fee), parade, entertainment. Phone 414/763-6044. Wkend after Mother's Day.

Seasonal Event

Aquaducks Water Ski Show. Fischer Park on Browns Lake. Performance each Sat evening; rain date Sun. June-Labor Day.

Motel

★ **AMERICINN INN.** 205 S Browns Lake Rd. 414/534-2125. 37 rms, 2 story. May-Oct: S, D $62.95-$81.87; each addl $6; suites $80.82-$99.44; under 14 free; lower rates rest of yr. Crib free. TV; cable (premium). Sauna. Indoor pool; whirlpool. Complimentary continental bkfst. Restaurant opp 11:30 am-10:30 pm. Ck-out 11 pm. Meeting rm. Cr cds: A, D, DS, MC, V.

D 🏊 ✕ 🐾 SC

Cable (B-2)

(For accommodations see Hayward)

Pop 817 **Elev** 1,370 ft **Area code** 715 **Zip** 54821
Information Mt Telemark, PO Box 277; 715/798-3811.

What to See and Do

Mt Telemark Ski Area. Area has 2 chairlifts, 2 T-bars, rope tow; alpine & nordic ski schools, rentals, patrol; snowmaking; nursery; restaurants, cafeteria, bar, lodge. Longest run one-half mi; vertical drop 370 ft. (Thanksgiving-Mar, daily) Cross-country trails (Dec-Mar, daily; rentals), more than 40 mi of trails. Hiking, bridle & bicycle trails rest of yr; also 18-hole golf, 8

tennis courts (4 indoor). 3 mi E on County M. Phone 715/798-3811. ¢¢¢¢

Annual Event

American Birkebeiner. Cross-country ski race. More than 6,000 participants from 40 states and 15 countries. 55 km. Late Feb.

Cedarburg (F-5)

(See also Milwaukee, Port Washington)

Pop 9,895 **Elev** 780 ft **Area code** 414 **Zip** 53012 **E-mail** CEDRBRG @aol.com
Information Chamber of Commerce, PO Box 104; 414/377-9620 or 800/CDR-BURG.

Cedarburg, surrounded by rich farmlands and protected forests and wetlands, has many beautiful old homes built in the 1800s. Many buildings in the historic downtown area have been restored.

What to See and Do

Cedar Creek Settlement and Winery. Stone woolen mill (1864) converted into a winery; houses shops, art studios & restaurants. Winery makes strawberry, cranberry and grape wines; museum of antique winemaking tools. (Daily; closed some hols) (See ANNUAL EVENTS) W6340 Bridge Rd, at N Washington. For tour information phone 414/377-8020 or 800/827-8020. Tours ¢

Annual Events

Winter Festival. Cedar Creek Winery. Ice carving & snow sculpture contests, bed & barrel races across ice, winter softball and volleyball, Alaskan malamute weight pull, snow goose egg hunt; torchlight parade, horse-drawn sleigh rides. 1st full wkend Feb.

Stone & Century House Tour. Tour of historic homes in the area. 1st full wkend June.

Ozaukee County Fair. W65 N796 Washington Ave (Firemen's Park & County Grounds). Educational and commercial exhibits, carnival, entertainment. Late July-early Aug.

Wine & Harvest Festival. Cedar Creek Winery. Grape-stomping contests; entertainment; farmers market; arts & crafts fair; scarecrow contest; food. 3rd wkend Sept.

Motels

★ ★ **BEST WESTERN QUIET HOUSE SUITES.** (10330 N Port Washington Rd, Mequon 53092) 6 mi S on I-43, exit 85. 414/241-3677; FAX 414/241-3707. 54 rms, 2 story. S $81-$150; D $91-$160; each addl $10; suites, kit. units $140-$160. Pet accepted; $15. TV; cable (premium). Indoor/outdoor pool; whirlpool. Complimentary continental bkfst. Restaurant adj 11 am-11 pm. Ck-out 11 am. Business servs avail. In-rm modem link. Exercise equipt; stair machine, treadmill. Cr cds: A, C, D, DS, MC, V.

D 🐾 🏊 🏃 ✕ 🐾

★ **BREEZE INN TO THE CHALET.** (10401 N Port Washington Rd, Mequon 53092) 6 mi S on I-43. 414/241-4510; FAX 414/241-5542; res: 800/343-4510. 41 rms, 2 story. May-Oct: S $40-$67; D $47-$67; each addl $7; suites $85-$125; under 12 free; wkly rates; higher rates special events, hols; lower rates rest of yr. Crib free. Pet accepted, some restrictions. TV; cable (premium). Restaurant 6 am-2 pm; Fri to 9:30 pm; Sat, Sun from 7 am. Bar. Ck-out 11 am. Meeting rm. Business servs avail. Many refrigerators. Cr cds: A, C, D, DS, MC, V.

 🐾 ✕ 🐾 SC

Inns

★ **STAGECOACH.** *W61 N520 Washington Ave. 414/375-0208; FAX 414/375-6170; 800 888/375-0208.* 12 rms, 3 story, 6 suites. Phone avail. S $55-$70; D $70-$85; each addl $10; suites $105. TV in suites. Complimentary continental bkfst. Restaurant nearby. Bar. Ck-out 11 am, ck-in 4 pm. Business servs avail. X-country ski 3 mi. Restored stagecoach inn (1853); antiques. In-rm whirlpool in suites. Totally non-smoking. Cr cds: A, D, DS, MC, V.

★ ★ **WASHINGTON HOUSE.** *W62 N573 Washington Ave at Center St. 414/375-3550; FAX 414/375-9422; res: 800/554-4717.* 34 rms, 3 story. S, D $59-$179; each addl $10. TV; cable (premium), VCR avail. Complimentary continental bkfst buffet. Restaurant opp. Ck-out noon, ck-in 3 pm. Meeting rm. Business center. X-country ski 5 mi. Sauna. Many in-rm whirlpools; some fireplaces. In a Victorian Cream City Brick Building (1886); antiques, historic memorabilia. Rms named after city's pioneers. Cr cds: A, C, D, DS, ER, MC, V.

Restaurants

★ ★ **BODER'S ON-THE-RIVER.** *(11919 N River Rd, Mequon 53092)* S on I-43 to exit 85 (Mequon Rd), W 3 mi to Ceduburg Rd, N 1½ mi to Friestadt Rd, E 1 mi to River Rd. *414/242-0335.* Hrs: 11:30 am-2 pm, 5:30-8:30 pm; Fri 5-9 pm; Sat 5:30-9 pm; Sun 11:30 am-2 pm, 4-7 pm; Sun brunch to 2 pm. Closed Mon; some major hols. Res accepted. Bar. Wine list. Complete meals: lunch $6.50-$10.95, dinner $12.95-$23.95. Sun brunch $14.95. Child's meals. Specializes in roast duck, sautéed fresh chicken livers. Own baking. Country inn (1840); fireplaces. Family-owned. Cr cds: A, C, D, DS, MC, V.

★ ★ **CLUB FOREST.** *(4200 W County Line Rd, Mequon 53092)* 6 mi S on I-43. *414/238-0876.* Hrs: 11:30 am-2 pm, 5-9 pm; Fri to 10 pm; Sat 5-10 pm; Sun 5-9 pm. Closed some major hols. Res accepted. Bar. A la carte entrees: lunch $6-$12, dinner $15-$30. Child's meals. Specializes in steak, prime rib, seafood. Own baking. Guitarist Fri, Sat. Outdoor dining. Casual, country atmosphere with large photo collection on walls. Cr cds: A, DS, MC, V.

★ **KOWLOON.** *W63 N145 Washington Ave. 414/375-3030.* Hrs: 11:30 am-9 pm; Fri to 10 pm; Sat 4:30-10 pm; Sun 4-9 pm. Closed Mon. Chinese menu. Bar. Semi-a la carte: lunch $2.50-$4.35, dinner $4.75-$7.75. Buffet: lunch $4.35, dinner $6.50. Specializes in Szechuan dishes. Chinese lanterns & fans. Cr cds: A, C, D, DS, MC, V.

★ ★ **THE RIVERSITE.** *(11120 N Cedarburg Rd, Mequon 53092)* 6 mi S on I-43. *414/242-6050.* Hrs: 5-10 pm. Closed Sun; major hols. Res accepted. Bar. Semi-a la carte: dinner $14.95-$26.95. Specializes in seafood, steak. Overlooking Milwaukee River. Cr cds: A, MC, V.

Chippewa Falls (D-2)

(See also Eau Claire, Menomonie)

Settled 1836 **Pop** 12,727 **Elev** 902 ft **Area code** 715 **Zip** 54729
Information Chamber of Commerce, 811 North Bridge St; 715/723-0331.

Water has replaced lumber as the prime natural resource of this city on the Chippewa River. Jean Brunet, a pioneer settler, built a sawmill and then a dam here. Soon the area was populated by lumberjacks. Today, hydro-electric power is channeled to the industries of Chippewa Falls, which has water noted for its purity.

What to See and Do

Brunet Island State Park. A 1,032-acre river island park. Swimming; fishing (pier); boating, canoeing. Nature & hiking trails. Cross-country skiing. Picnicking, playground, Camping (electric hookups, dump station). Naturalist programs. Standard fees. (Daily) N via US 53, then E on WI 64 in Cornell. Phone 715/239-6888. Per vehicle ¢¢

Chippewa Falls Zoo. Concentrates on native animals. Also picnic tables, playground, tennis courts, pool, camping. Fee for some activities. (May-Oct, daily) Irvine Park, N on WI 124. Phone 715/723-3890.   **Free.**

Cook-Rutledge Mansion (1870s). Restored Victorian mansion. Guided tours (June-Aug, Thurs-Sun; rest of yr, by appt). 505 W Grand Ave. Phone 715/723-7181.   ¢

Lake Wissota State Park. A 1,062-acre park with swimming, waterskiing; fishing; boating, canoeing. Hiking; fitness course. Cross-country skiing. Picnicking, playground, concession. Camping (dump station, hookups; reservations accepted). Observation points. Standard fees. (Daily) 5 mi E on WI 29. Phone 715/382-4574. Per vehicle   ¢¢

Annual Events

Northern Wisconsin State Fair. Fairgrounds. Phone 715/723-2861. Early or mid-July.

Pure Water Days. Downtown. Canoe paddling, sport competitions, contests, parade, dances, beer garden, food. 3rd wkend Aug.

Motels

✓★ **AMERICINN.** *11 W South Ave, 1 mi S on US 53. 715/723-5711; FAX 715/723-5254.* 62 rms, 2 story. S $49.90-$69.90; D $56.90-$69.90; suites $58.90-$104.90. Pet accepted; $25 deposit. TV; cable (premium). Complimentary coffee in lobby. Ck-out 11 am. Business servs avail. In-rm modem link. Indoor pool; whirlpool. Some refrigerators. Cr cds: A, C, D, DS, MC, V.

★ **COUNTRY INN.** *1021 W Park Ave. 715/720-1414.* 62 rms, 2 story. May-Sept: S $54.90-$98.90; D $62.90-$106.90; each addl $8; under 18 free; lower rates rest of yr. Crib avail. TV; cable (premium). Complimentary continental bkfst. Coffee in rms. Restaurant nearby. Ck-out 11 am. Business servs avail. In-rm modem link. Indoor pool; whirlpool. Some refrigerators. Cr cds: A, C, D, DS, MC, V.

★ **GLEN LOCH.** *1225 Jefferson Ave. 715/723-9121.* 19 rms. S $26; D $36-$44; each addl $4. TV; cable (premium). Complimentary coffee in lobby. Ck-out 11 am. Picnic tables. Cr cds: A, MC, V.

✓★ **INDIANHEAD.** *501 Summit Ave (WI 29/124). 715/723-9171; FAX 715/723-6142; res: 800/341-8000.* 27 rms. S, D $42-$47.25; each addl $5. Crib avail. Pet accepted. TV; cable (premium), VCR avail. Complimentary coffee in lobby. Restaurant adj. Ck-out 11 am. Valet serv. Some refrigerators. On bluff overlooking city. Cr cds: A, C, D, DS, MC, V.

★ ★ **PARK INN INTERNATIONAL.** *1009 W Park Ave (County J),* 1 blk N of WI 124. *715/723-2281; FAX 715/723-2283; res: 800/446-9320.* 67 rms. S $50-$57; D $57-$64; each addl $7. Crib avail. Pet accepted, some restrictions. TV; cable. Indoor pool; whirlpool. Restaurants 6:30 am-1:30 pm, 5-9:30 pm. Rm serv. Bar. Ck-out noon. Meeting rms. Business servs avail. Valet serv. Sundries. Some wet bars. Cr cds: A, C, D, DS, MC, V.

Restaurants

✔★ ★ **EDELWEISS.** *8988 WI 124N, 2 mi N on WI 124.* 715/723-7881. Hrs: 4:30-9:30 pm; Sun 10:30 am-2 pm, 4:30-9:30 pm. Closed Mon; Dec 24, 25. Res accepted. Bar to 1 am. Semi-a la carte: dinner $4.25-$12.95. Bavarian decor; beamed ceiling; loft dining area. Cr cds: DS, MC, V.

✔★ **LINDSAY'S ON GRAND.** *24 W Grand Ave.* 715/723-4025. Hrs: 6 am-9 pm. Closed Jan 1, Thanksgiving, Dec 25. Semi-a la carte: bkfst $2.75-$4.85, lunch, dinner $4.55-$7.95. Child's meals. Specialties: cod fillet, glazed ham steak. Own pasta. Casual family restaurant. No cr cds accepted.

Crandon (C-4)

(See also Rhinelander, Three Lakes)

Pop 1,958 **Elev** 1,629 ft **Area code** 715 **Zip** 54520

What to See and Do

Camp Five Museum and "Lumberjack Special" Steam Train Tour. Old steam train ride to Camp Five complex; harness and an active blacksmith shop; 1900 country store; logging museum with audiovisual presentation; nature center with diorama featuring area wildlife, 30-min guided forest tour; hayrack/pontoon boat trip (fee); country store; children's playground; concession. (Mid-June-late Aug, four departures daily) 11 mi E on US 8 & WI 32 in Laona. Phone 715/674-3414 or 800/774-3414. ¢¢¢¢

Motel

✔★ **FOUR SEASONS.** *304 W Glen St.* 715/478-3377; FAX 715/478-3785; res: 800/341-8000. 20 rms. S $34-$38; D $40-$46; under 6 free. Crib free. TV; cable. Ck-out 11 am. Business servs avail. Some refrigerators. Cr cds: A, DS, MC, V.

Delavan (G-5)

(See also Beloit, Burlington, Elkhorn, Fontana, Lake Geneva)

Settled 1836 **Pop** 6,073 **Elev** 940 ft **Area code** 414 **Zip** 53115

Between 1847 and 1894, Delavan was the headquarters of 28 different circuses. The original P.T. Barnum circus was organized here during the winter of 1870-1871 by William C. Coup. Spring Grove and St Andrew's cemeteries are "last lot" resting places for more than 100 members of the 19th-century circus colony. Today many flowering crabapple trees grace the town, blooming usually in mid-May.

Inn

★ **LAKESIDE MANOR.** *1809 S Shore Dr.* 414/728-5354; FAX 414/728-2043. 8 rms, 3 shared bath, 2 story. No rm phone. May-Oct: S, D $99-$125; suites $149; lower rates rest of yr. Children over 14 yrs only. TV; cable, VCR (movies). Complimentary continental bkfst. Restaurant nearby. Ck-out 11 am, ck-in 3 pm. Concierge. Downhill ski 15 mi; x-country on site. Built in 1897; antiques. Totally nonsmoking. Cr cds: MC, V.

Restaurant

✔★ ★ **MILLIE'S.** *N 2484 County O, 1 mi N of US 14.* 414/728-2434. Hrs: 8 am-4 pm. Closed Mon (exc July-Aug); Thanksgiving, Dec 25; also Tues-Fri Jan-Feb. Bar. Semi-a la carte: bkfst $2.50-$6.95, lunch, dinner $4.95-$10.95. Specializes in Pennsylvania Dutch-style cooking. Own pancakes. Antique furniture. On 80-acre farm; English gardens, gazebo. No cr cds accepted.

Devil's Lake State Park (F-4)

(For accommodations see Baraboo, Portage, Prairie du Sac, Wisconsin Dells)

(3 mi S of Baraboo on WI 123)

These 11,050 acres, with spring-fed Devil's Lake as the greatest single attraction, form Wisconsin's most beautiful state park. Remnants of an ancient mountain range surround the lake, providing unique scenery. The lake, 1¼ miles long, is in the midst of sheer cliffs of quartzite that rise as high as 500 feet above the water. Unusual rock formations may be found at the top of the bluffs. The park has a naturalist in residence who may be contacted for information concerning year-round nature hikes and programs. Sandy swimming beaches with bathhouses, concessions and boat landings are at either end. No motorboats permitted. The park provides hiking and cross-country skiing trails, picnic grounds, improved tent & trailer facilities (electric hookups, dump station); nature center. The lake is restocked yearly. Native American mounds include the Eagle, Bear and Lynx mounds. General tourist supplies are available at north and south shores. Standard fees. (Daily) Contact Park Superintendent, S5975 Park Rd, Baraboo 53913; 608/356-8301. Per vehicle ¢¢

Ice Age National Scientific Reserve. Naturalists explain evidence of Wisconsin glaciation; exhibits of local Ice Age features; trails; under development. Also included in the Reserve are Northern Unit Kettle Moraine State Forest (see FOND DU LAC) and two state parks, Mill Bluff (see TOMAH) and Interstate (see ST CROIX FALLS). Per vehicle ¢¢

Dodgeville (G-3)

(See also Mineral Point, Mt Horeb, New Glarus, Platteville)

Settled 1827 **Pop** 3,882 **Elev** 1,222 ft **Area code** 608 **Zip** 53533

What to See and Do

Governor Dodge State Park. A 5,029-acre park with 95-acre and 150-acre lakes. Rock formations, white pine. Swimming, bathhouse; fishing; boating (electric motors only; ramps), canoeing (rentals). Bicycle, hiking and bridle trails. Cross-country skiing, snowmobiling. Picnicking, playgrounds, concession. Camping (electric hookups, dump station), backpack campsites, horse campground. Nature programs (June-Aug). Standard fees. (Daily) 3 mi N via US 151, WI 23. Phone 608/935-2315. Per vehicle ¢¢

Motel

★ ★ **DON Q INN.** *1½ mi N of US 18 on WI 23.* 608/935-2321; FAX 608/935-2416; res: 800/666-7848. 61 rms, 3 story. Mid-May-Oct: S, D $69-$89; each addl $8; specialty rms $79-$255; under 18 free; lower rates rest of yr. Crib $8. TV. Indoor/outdoor pool; whirlpool. Coffee in lobby. Complimentary continental bkfst. Restaurant 5-8:30 pm. Ck-out noon.

Meeting rms. X-country ski 1½ mi. Some in-rm whirlpools. Game rm. Imaginatively furnished; rustic decor. Cr cds: A, C, D, DS, MC, V.

SC

★ ★ **NEW CONCORD INN.** *3637 WI 23N. 608/935-3770; FAX 608/935-9605; res: 800/348-9310.* 64 rms, 3 story. May-Oct: S, D $74; each addl $6; suites $82; under 12 free; lower rates rest of yr. Crib $6. TV; cable (premium). Indoor pool; whirlpool. Complimentary continental bkfst. Restaurant nearby. Ck-out 11 am. X-country ski 2 mi. Game rm. Some refrigerators. Cr cds: A, DS, MC, V.

D SC

Door County (D-6)

Famous for its fish boils, foliage and 250 miles of shoreline, Door County is a peninsula with Green Bay on the west and Lake Michigan on the east. Its picturesque villages, rolling woodlands, limestone bluffs and beautiful vistas are the reason the area is often referred to as the Cape Cod of the Midwest.

Door County offers year-round recreational opportunities. Spring and summer bring fishing, sailing, beachcombing, camping, hiking, biking and horseback riding. Thousands of acres of apple and cherry blossoms color the landscape in late May. There is excellent scuba diving in the *Portes des Mortes* (Death's Door) Straits at the tip of the peninsula, where hundreds of shipwrecks lie in the shifting freshwater sands. Fall colors can be viewed from the endless miles of trails and country roads, which become cross-country ski routes in winter.

Many artists reside here, as is evidenced by the towns' shops, galleries and boutiques. Summertime theater and concerts also attract tourists.

The taste of the peninsula is unquestionably the legendary fish boil. Trout or whitefish and potatoes & onions are cooked in a cauldron over an open fire. When the fish has almost finished cooking, kerosene is thrown onto the fire, creating a huge flame and causing the unwanted oils to boil out and over the pot. (See restaurant listings in individual towns.)

Door County Chamber of Commerce, 1015 Green Bay Rd, PO Box 406, Sturgeon Bay, 54235, 414/743-4456 or 800/52-RELAX, has winter and summer schedules of events, maps and details on recreational facilities. For a free vacation guide, phone 800/52-RELAX.

The following towns in Door County are included in the *Mobil Travel Guide.* For full information on any one of them, see the individual alphabetical listing. (See map) Baileys Harbor, Egg Harbor, Ellison Bay, Ephraim, Fish Creek, Sister Bay, Sturgeon Bay and Washington Island.

Annual Event

Festival of Blossoms. Phone 414/743-4456. Month of May.

Eagle River (C-4)

(See also Land O'Lakes, Rhinelander, St Germain, Three Lakes)

Pop 1,374 **Elev** 1,647 ft **Area code** 715 **Zip** 54521 **E-mail** info@eagle-river.com **Web** www.eagle-river.com

Information Eagle River Area Chamber of Commerce, PO Box 1917; 715/479-6400 or 800/359-6315.

The bald eagles that gave this town its name are still occasionally seen, and the Eagle chain of 28 lakes, the largest inland chain of freshwater lakes in the world, is an outstanding tourist attraction. Eagle River has developed as a center of winter sports. The result is lake vacationers in summer and ski fans, both cross-country and downhill, and snowmobilers in winter. There are more than 11 miles of cross-country ski trails on Anvil Lake trail and miles of snowmobile trails and several hiking areas are in the Nicolet National Forest. A Ranger District office of the Nicolet National Forest (see THREE LAKES) is located here.

What to See and Do

Trees For Tomorrow Natural Resources Education Center. Demonstration forests, nature trail; "talking tree." (Daily) Outdoor skills and natural resource programs with emphasis on forest ecology and conservation. Cross-country skiing. Orienteering. Natural resources workshops (fee). Guided tours (Tues & Thurs, summer). 611 Sheridan St. Phone 715/479-6456. **Free.**

Annual Events

World Championship Snowmobile Derby. 1½ mi N on US 45. 3rd wkend Jan.

Klondike Days. Oval sled dog races, winter events. Last wkend Feb.

Cranberry Fest. Cranberry bog tours, events. 1st wkend Oct.

Motels

★ ★ **AMERICAN HERITAGE INN.** *844 Railroad St N. 715/479-5151; FAX 715/479-8259; res: 800/356-8018.* 93 rms, 2 story. June-Oct: S $49-$74; D $59-$79.99; each addl $5; under 18 free; 2-day min wkends; higher rates for special events; lower rates rest of yr. Crib free. Pet accepted. TV; cable, VCR (movies). Sauna. Indoor pool; whirlpool. Complimentary coffee in lobby. Complimentary continental bkfst. Restaurant adj 5 am-9 pm. Ck-out 11 am. Coin lndry. Meeting rm. Business servs avail. X-country ski ½ mi. Game rm. Some in-rm whirlpools. Some refrigerators. Cr cds: A, C, D, DS, MC, V.

D SC

★ ★ **EAGLE RIVER INN.** *5260 WI 70W. 715/479-2000; FAX 715/479-2000.* 36 units, 2 story, 7 suites, 8 kits. Late June-Aug, Christmas wk, wkends Jan-Feb: S, D $89-$99; each addl $10; suites $149-$169; kit. units $109-$119; under 12 free; wkly rates; ski, golf plans; lower rates rest of yr. Crib $5. TV; cable, VCR avail (movies). Indoor pool; whirlpool. Playground. Restaurant 4-9 pm. Rm serv. Bar. Ck-out 11 am. Meeting rms. Business servs avail. Gift shop. X-country ski 2 mi. Exercise equipt; weight machine, bicycle, sauna. Miniature golf. Boats. In-rm whirlpool in some suites. Balconies. Picnic tables. On lake; dock. Cr cds: C, D, DS, MC, V.

D

✔★ **WHITE EAGLE.** *4948 WI 70W. 715/479-4426; res: 800/782-6488.* 22 rms. No A/C. Mid-June-mid-Oct: S, D $37-$71; lower rates rest of yr. Crib free. Pet accepted; $5. TV; cable. Sauna. Heated pool; whirlpool. Complimentary coffee. Restaurant nearby. Ck-out 10:30 am. X-country ski 3 mi. Snowmobile trails. Paddleboat. Picnic tables. On Eagle River; private piers. Driving range, miniature golf opp. Cr cds: DS, MC, V.

D

Resorts

★ ★ **CHANTICLEER INN.** *1458 E Dollar Lake Rd. 715/479-4486; FAX 715/479-0004; res: 800/752-9193.* 13 motel rms, 2 story, 8 kit. villas, 50 units (1-3 bedrm) in 20 town houses, 20 with kit., most A/C. S $49-$125; D $63-$220; each addl $10; under 16 free; ski, golf, package plans; higher rates: winter hols, snowmobile derby. Crib $10. TV. Playground. Complimentary coffee in motel rms. Dining rm 8-10 am, 5:30-9:30 pm. Box lunches, snacks. Bar from 8 am. Ck-out 10:30 am, ck-in 3 pm. Grocery, package store 2½ mi. Coin lndry. Meeting rms. Business servs avail. Gift shop. Free local airport transportation. 2 tennis courts, 1 lighted. 9-hole golf adj, daily greens fee. 2 sand beaches; boats, motors, canoes, pontoon boats. X-country ski on site. Rec rm. Fishing guides, clean & store area. Fireplace in villas/condos. Private patios or balconies in town houses & suites. Cr cds: A, D, DS, MC, V.

D

★ GYPSY VILLA. *950 Circle Dr. 715/479-8644; FAX 715/479-8644; res: 800/232-9714.* 21 kit. cottages (1-4-bedrm), 4 A/C. Phone avail. Kit. cottages $345-$1,681/wk (2-6 persons); daily rates; MAP avail. Crib free. Maid serv $20/day. Pet accepted. TV; VCR avail. Wading pool; whirlpool. Playground. Free supervised child's activities (June-Aug). Ck-out noon, ck-in 3 pm. Coin lndry. Meeting rms. Business servs avail. Grocery, package store 2 mi. Garage parking avail (fee). Tennis. Private swimming beach. Boats, waterskiing. Bicycles. Lawn games. Soc dir. Game rm. Exercise equipt; bicycles, rower, sauna. Fish/hunt guides. Fireplaces; some in-rm whirlpools. Private patios. Picnic tables, grills. Most cottages on Cranberry Island. Cr cds: A, DS, MC, V.

😾 🐾 🏃 ≈ 🕴 🔥 SC

Restaurant

✔★ PINE GABLES SUPPER CLUB. *5009 WI 70W. 715/479-7689.* Hrs: 4:30-closing. Closed Tues. German, Amer menu. Bar. Semi-a la carte: dinner $6.95-$15.95. Own soups, dressings. Rustic decor. Cr cds: MC, V.

East Troy

(see Elkhorn)

Eau Claire (D-2)

(See also Chippewa Falls, Menomonie)

Settled 1844 **Pop** 56,856 **Elev** 796 ft **Area code** 715 **E-mail** comments@eauclaire-info.com **Web** www.eauclaire-info.com

Information Eau Claire Convention Bureau, 3625 Gateway Dr, Suite F, 54701; 800/344-3866.

Once a wild and robust lumber camp and sawmill on the shores of the Eau Claire and Chippewa rivers, the city has turned to diversified industry. The name is French for "clear water."

What to See and Do

Chippewa Valley Museum. "Paths of the People" Ojibwe exhibit, "Settlement and Survival" 1850-1925 history of Chippewa Valley. Street scene, 21-rm doll house, agricultural wing, old-fashioned ice cream parlor, research library. Log house (1860); Sunnyview School (1880). Gift shop. (Daily exc Mon) Carson Park. Phone 715/834-7871. ¢¢

Dells Mills Museum (1864). Historic five-story water-powered flour and grist mill (1864) built of hand-hewn timbers; wooden pegged. One-room schoolhouse museum. Gun shop, antique shop. (May-Oct, daily) 20 mi SE via WI 12, 3 mi N of Augusta via WI 27 on County V. Phone 715/286-2714. ¢¢¢

⭐ **Paul Bunyan Logging Camp.** Restored 1890s logging camp with bunkhouse, cook shack, blacksmith shop, dingle, filers shack, barn; heavy equipment display. Artifacts, film at interpretive center. (Mid-Apr-Labor Day, daily; rest of Sept, Sat-Sun, also Tues-Fri afternoons) Carson Park, Clairemont Ave to Menomonie St, E to Carson Park Dr. Phone 715/835-6200. ¢¢

University of Wisconsin-Eau Claire (1916). (10,500 students) Planetarium; bird museum; greenhouses, dramatic productions, musical events; art gallery (free). Putnam Park arboretum, a 230-acre tract of forest land kept in its natural state, has self-guided nature trails. Park & Garfield Aves. Phone 715/836-2637.

Motels

✔★ ANTLERS. *2245 S Hastings Way (54701), 2 mi N of I-94, exit 70. 715/834-5313; res: 800/423-4526.* 33 rms, 1-2 story. S $38-$45; D $46-$52; each addl $5. Crib free. TV; cable (premium). Playground. Restaurant adj open 24 hrs. Ck-out 11 am. Cr cds: A, DS, MC, V.

D ≈ ≥ 🔥 SC

★ ★ BEST WESTERN MIDWAY MOTOR LODGE. *2851 Hendrickson Dr (54701), WI 37 at Craig Rd. 715/835-2242; FAX 715/835-1027.* 109 rms, 2 story. S $59-$68; D $71-$79; each addl $12; under 18 free. Crib free. TV; cable (premium), VCR avail. Indoor pool; whirlpool. Complimentary full bkfst Mon-Fri. Coffee in rms. Restaurant 6:30 am-2 pm, 5-9 pm; Sat, Sun 7 am-2 pm, 5-9 pm. Rm serv. Bar 4 pm-1 am, Sun noon-9 pm; entertainment. Ck-out 11 am. Meeting rms. Business servs avail. In-rm modem link. Valet serv. Sundries. Free airport, bus depot transportation. Sauna. Domed recreation area. Game rm. Cr cds: A, C, D, DS, MC, V.

D ≈ ≥ 🔥 SC

★ ★ BEST WESTERN WHITE HOUSE. *1828 S Hastings Way (US 53) (54701). 715/832-8356; FAX 715/836-9686.* 66 rms, 1-2 story. S $38-$48; D $55-$65; each addl $5. Crib $3. TV; cable (premium). Indoor pool; whirlpool. Complimentary afternoon refreshments. Restaurant 4:30-11 pm. Ck-out 11 am. Business servs avail. In-rm modem link. Valet serv. Sauna. Game rm. Refrigerators; some in-rm whirlpools. Some balconies. Sun deck. Cr cds: A, C, D, DS, ER, JCB, MC, V.

D ≈ ≥ 🔥 SC

★ ★ COMFORT INN. *3117 Craig Rd (54701). 715/833-9798.* 56 rms, 2 story. June-Aug: S $62.95-$70.95; D $67.95-$75.95; each addl $5; under 18 free; lower rates rest of yr. Crib avail. Pet accepted. TV; cable (premium). Indoor pool. Complimentary continental bkfst. Restaurant nearby. Ck-out 11 am. Business servs avail. In-rm modem link. X-country ski 2 mi. Cr cds: A, C, D, DS, ER, JCB, MC, V.

D 🐾 ≈ ≥ 🔥 SC

✔★ EXEL INN. *2305 Craig Rd (54701). 715/834-3193; FAX 715/839-9905.* 101 rms, 2 story. S $31.99-$43.99; D $42.99-$49.99; each addl $4. Crib free. Pet accepted. TV; cable (premium). Complimentary continental bkfst. Restaurant adj open 24 hrs. Ck-out noon. Business servs avail. Cr cds: A, C, D, DS, MC, V.

D 🐾 ≈ 🔥 SC

★ ★ HAMPTON INN. *2622 Craig Rd (54701). 715/833-0003; FAX 715/833-0915.* 106 rms, 3 story. S $59-$70; D $64-$70; under 19 free; wkend rates. TV; cable (premium). Indoor pool; whirlpool. Complimentary coffee in lobby. Restaurant opp 6 am-11 pm. Ck-out noon. Meeting rms. Business servs avail. In-rm modem link. X-country ski 2 mi. Exercise equipt; bicycles, treadmill. Cr cds: A, C, D, DS, MC, V.

D ≈ ≥ 🕴 ≈ 🔥 SC

★ HEARTLAND INN. *4075 Commonwealth Ave (54701). 715/839-7100; FAX 715/839-7050; res: 800/334-3277, ext. 40.* 88 rms, 2 story. S $44-$51; D $52-$59; each addl $5; under 17 free. Crib avail. Pet accepted. TV; cable (premium), VCR avail. Indoor pool; whirlpool. Complimentary continental bkfst. Restaurant nearby. Ck-out noon. Meeting rms. Business servs avail. In-rm modem link. Sundries. X-country ski 5 mi. Sauna. Cr cds: A, C, D, DS, MC, V.

D 🐾 ≈ ≥ 🔥 SC

✔★ MAPLE MANOR. *2507 S Hastings Way (US 53) (54701). 715/834-2618; FAX 715/834-1148; res: 800/624-3763.* 36 rms. S $29.95; D $39.95-$49.95; each addl $5; wkly rates. Crib $3. Pet accepted. TV; cable (premium). Complimentary full bkfst. Restaurant 6:30 am-1:30 pm. Bar to 11 pm. Ck-out 11:30 am. Sundries. Many refrigerators. Picnic tables. Cr cds: A, C, D, DS, MC, V.

🐾 ≥ 🔥 SC

★ ★ QUALITY INN. *809 W Clairemont (54702), US 12. 715/834-6611.* 120 rms, 2 story. S $52-$75; D $60-$75; suites $69-$139; under 18 free; Sun rates. Crib free. Pet accepted. TV; cable (premium), VCR avail. 2 pools, 1 indoor; whirlpool. Complimentary full bkfst Mon-Fri. Restaurant 6 am-10 pm; Fri, Sat to 10:30 pm. Rm serv. Bar 11-2 am; entertainment Tues-Sat. Ck-out noon. Meeting rms. Business servs avail. In-rm modem link. Valet serv. Sundries. Sauna. Rec rm. Private patios, balconies. Cr cds: A, C, D, DS, ER, JCB, MC, V.

✔★ **ROAD STAR INN.** *1151 W MacArthur Ave (54701). 715/832-9731; FAX 715/832-0690; res: 800/445-4667.* 62 rms, 2 story. S $30-$33; D $37-$40; each addl $3; under 16 free. TV; cable (premium). Complimentary continental bkfst. Restaurant nearby. Ck-out 11 am. Some refrigerators. Cr cds: A, C, D, DS, MC, V.

D ⬡ 🏊 🏃 SC

Motor Hotel

★★★ **RAMADA INN & CONFERENCE CENTER.** *1202 W Clairemont (54702), US 12. 715/834-3181; FAX 715/834-1630.* 238 rms, 2-5 story. S, D $62-$79; each addl $10. Crib free. TV; cable (premium). 2 indoor pools; poolside serv. Restaurant 6 am-10 pm. Rm serv. Bar 11-1 am; Sun from noon. Ck-out 11 am. Meeting rms. Business servs avail. In-rm modem link. Bellhops. Valet serv. Free airport transportation. Sundries. X-country ski 1 mi. Sauna. Rec rm. Cr cds: A, C, D, DS, JCB, MC, V.

D 🏊 🏊 🏃 🏃 SC

Inn

★★★ **FANNY HILL.** *3919 Crescent Ave (54703), 3 mi SW on Crescent Ave and County EE. 715/836-8184; FAX 715/836-8180; res: 800/292-8026.* 11 rms. S, D $79-$165; package plans. TV; cable (premium). Complimentary full bkfst. Restaurant (see FANNY HILL INN & DINNER THEATRE). Ck-out 11 am, ck-in 2:30 pm. Business servs avail. X-country ski adj. Dinner theater on premises. Victorian garden overlooking Chippewa River. Totally nonsmoking. Cr cds: A, C, D, DS, MC, V.

D 🏊 🏊 🏃

Restaurant

★★ **FANNY HILL INN & DINNER THEATRE.** *(See Fanny Hill Inn)* 715/836-8184. Hrs: 5-9 pm; Sun brunch 10 am-1:30 pm. Closed Mon, Tues (summer only); Dec 24-25. Res accepted; required for dinner theatre. Continental menu. Bar. A la carte entrees: dinner $12.95-$25.95. Sun brunch $9.95. Specializes in steak, seafood. Dinner theater Thurs-Sun. Family-owned. Cr cds: A, C, D, DS, MC, V.

D

Egg Harbor (Door Co) (D-6)

(See also Door County)

Pop 183 **Elev** 600 ft **Area code** 414 **Zip** 54209 **E-mail** lyons@mail.wisnet.net **Web** doorcountyvacations.com

Information Door County Chamber of Commerce, 1015 Green Bay Rd, PO Box 406, Sturgeon Bay 54235; 414/743-4456 or 800/52-RELAX.

This town in Door County (see) is on the shores of Green Bay.

Seasonal Event

Birch Creek Music Center. 3 mi E via County E. Concert series in unique barn concert hall. Early-mid-July: percussion series; mid-July-mid-Aug: big band series. Phone 414/868-3763. Other concerts and events through Labor Day.

Motels

★★ **ALPINE RESORT.** *3/4 mi SW on County G. 920/868-3000.* 52 motel rms, 3 story, 5 suites; 30 kit. cottages. No elvtr. No rm phones. Mid-June-Labor Day: S $59-$79; D $69-$93; each addl $10; suites $93; kit. cottages $101-$265 or $605-$1,115/wk; MAP avail; family, wkly rates; golf plan; lower rates Memorial Day-mid-June, Labor Day-mid-Oct. Closed rest of yr. Crib $5. Pet accepted, some restrictions. TV. Heated pool. Playground. Supervised child's activities (July & Aug); ages 3-8. Restaurant 7:30-11 am, 5:45-8:30 pm. Bar to midnight. Ck-out 10 am. Meeting rms. Business servs avail. Bellhops. Gift shop. Tennis. 27-hole golf, greens fee, putting green. Game rm. Rec rm. Some refrigerators; microwaves avail; wet bar in cottages. Picnic tables, grills. Swimming beach. Cr cds: A, DS, MC, V.

D 🏌 ⛳ 🏃 🏊 🏃

★★★ **ASHBROOKE.** *7942 Egg Harbor Rd. 920/868-3113; FAX 920/868-2837.* 36 rms, 2 story. Late June-mid-Oct (2-day min): S, D $99-$182; lower rates Dec-late June. Closed Dec; also wkdays Nov-Apr. Children over 13 only. TV; cable (premium). Indoor pool; whirlpool. Complimentary continental bkfst. Complimentary coffee in rms. Restaurant adj 7 am-9 pm. Ck-out 11 am. Business servs avail. X-country ski 5 mi. Exercise equipt; weights, bicycles, sauna. Refrigerators, microwaves. Some in-rm whirlpools, fireplaces. Totally nonsmoking. Cr cds: A, MC, V.

D 🏊 🏊 🍴 🏃 🏃

★★ **BAY POINT INN.** *N edge of town, on WI 42. 920/868-3297; FAX 920/868-2876; res: 800/707-6660.* E-mail lodgeminium@mail.doorcounty-wi.com; web www.lodge.minium.com. 10 kit. suites, 2 story. June-Sept: kit. suites $145-$179; each addl $12; wkly rates; lower rates rest of yr. Crib $5. TV; VCR (free movies). Heated pool; whirlpool. Complimentary continental bkfst (winter only). Restaurant nearby. Ck-out 11 am. Business center. X-country ski 6 mi. Microwaves; some fireplaces; whirlpool in suites. Balconies. Picnic tables, grills. Cr cds: A, D, DS, MC, V.

🏊 🏊 🏃 🏃 🏃

★★★ **EGG HARBOR LODGE.** *1 mi N on WI 42. 920/868-3115.* 25 rms, 3 story. July-Aug: S, D $82-$250; each addl $25; wkend rates vary; studio rms $135-$250; lower rates May-June, Sept-Oct. Closed rest of yr. Children over 17 yrs only. TV. Heated pool; whirlpool. Complimentary coffee in rms. Restaurant nearby. Ck-out 11 am. Tennis. Putting green. Refrigerators; some wet bars, in-rm whirlpools; microwaves avail. Private patios, balconies. Cr cds: A, MC, V.

D 🏃 🏊 🏃 🏃

★★ **LANDING.** *7741 Egg Harbor Rd (WI 42). 920/868-3282; FAX 920/868-2689; res: 800/851-8919.* 60 kit. units, 2 story. June-Aug: S $107-$125; D $129-$198; each addl $10; under 7 free; wkly rates; lower rates rest of yr. Crib $3. TV; cable (premium), VCR (movies $3). 2 pools, 1 indoor; whirlpool. Playground. Restaurant nearby. Ck-out 11 am. Business servs avail. Tennis. Game rm. Microwaves. Private patios. Picnic tables, grills. On 5 wooded acres. Cr cds: DS, MC, V.

D 🏃 🏊 🏃 🏃

★ **LULL-ABI.** *7928 Egg Harbor Rd (WI 42), 1/2 mi N on WI 42. 920/868-3135.* 23 rms, 2 story, 5 suites. July-Oct: D $69-$92; each addl $12; suites $76-$99; lower rates rest of yr. TV; cable (premium). Complimentary coffee in lobby. Restaurant nearby. Ck-out 11 am. Whirlpool. Refrigerator, microwave, minibar in suites. Cr cds: A, DS, MC, V.

D 🏃

Restaurants

✔★ **GRANT'S OLDE STAGE STATION.** *On WI 42. 920/868-3247.* Hrs: 8-2 am. Closed Dec 25. Italian, Amer menu. Bar. Semi-a la carte: lunch $3.95-$9.95, dinner $4.50-$14. Child's meals. Specializes in broasted chicken, chicken pot pie. Own desserts, bakery. Former stagecoach stop (1889). Outdoor dining. Cr cds: MC, V.

D SC

★ VILLAGE CAFE. *N on WI 42. 920/868-3342.* Hrs: 7 am-2 pm. Closed Nov-May. Wine, beer. Semi-a la carte: bkfst $2.55-$6.15, lunch $4.95-$6.25. Specializes in bkfst entrees. Outdoor dining on screened-in deck. Cr cds: MC, V.

D

Elkhart Lake (F-5)

(See also Fond du Lac, Sheboygan)

Pop 1,019 **Elev** 945 ft **Area code** 414 **Zip** 53020
Information Chamber of Commerce, 41 E Rhine St, PO Box 425; 414/876-2922.

This lake resort, famous for its good beaches, is one of the state's oldest vacation spots.

What to See and Do

Broughton-Sheboygan County Marsh. A 14,000-acre wildlife area. Duck hunting, fishing; boating, canoeing. Camping (53 sites; hookups), lodge, restaurant. Standard fees. 1 mi NE on County J. Phone 414/876-2535. **Free.**

Little Elkhart Lake. A 131-acre lake with heavy concentrations of pike, walleye, bass and panfish.

Old Wade House Historic Site. Restored Old Wade House (1850), early stagecoach inn. Nearby are smokehouse, blacksmith shop, mill dam site and Robinson House, a pre-Civil War residence and Jung Carriage Museum housing more than 100 restored horse and hand-drawn vehicles. Picnicking, concession. Horse-drawn carriage rides (fee). (May-Oct, daily) 2 mi N on County P, then SW via County P & A in Greenbush. Phone 414/526-3271. ¢¢¢

Timm House (1892). Ten-room, Victorian-style house contains period furniture; guided tours. (June-Sept, Sun; rest of yr, by appt) Approx 15 mi N via WI 32, NW via WI 57 in New Holstein at 1600 Wisconsin Ave. Phone 414/898-9006 or 414/898-5205. ¢ Admission includes

Pioneer Corner Museum. Exhibits of early German immigrant furniture; extensive button collection; general store & post office; Panama Canal memorabilia. (June-Sept, Sun; rest of yr, by appt) Main St. Phone 414/898-9006.

Seasonal Event

Road America. 1¹⁄₂ mi S on WI 67. Located on 525 rolling, wooded acres; a closed-circuit 4-mi sports car racecourse with 14 turns. One of the most popular events of the season is the CART Indy race, which draws top-name race teams. Phone 414/892-4576. Mon-Fri, June-Sept.

Inn

★ ★ ★ **52 STAFFORD.** *(PO Box 217, Plymouth 53073) 12 mi S on WI 67, S of jct WI 23. 920/893-0552; res: 800/421-4667.* 19 rms, 3 story, 4 suites. No elvtr. S, D $79.50-$119.50; suites $119.50. Crib free. TV; cable. Complimentary continental bkfst. Dining rm 5-9 pm; Fri, Sat to 10 pm. Ck-out 10:30 am, ck-in 3 pm. Business servs avail. X-country ski 12 mi. Many in-rm whirlpools. Four-poster beds. Built 1892; restored and furnished as an Irish guest house. Cr cds: A, D, DS, MC, V.

⊠ ⊿ 🐾

Resort

★ **BAREFOOT BAY.** *279 Lake St. 920/876-3323; FAX 920/876-3484; res: 800/345-7784.* 150 units, 49 in main building. MAP, May-Sept: D $100-$130/person; children $14.95-$19.95; wkly rates; EP avail; wkend packages; lower rates rest of yr. Crib free. TV; VCR avail. 2 pools, 1 indoor. Free supervised child's activities (May-Sept); ages 3-17.

Dining rm 8-10 am, 6:30-8 pm. Box lunches, snack bar, picnics. Bar 8-1 am. Ck-out 11:30 am, ck-in 4 pm. Convention facilities. Business servs avail. In-rm modem link. Bellhops. Valet serv. Sports dir. Miniature golf. Private beach; swimming, waterskiing; boats, motors, rowboats, canoes, sailboats, paddleboats, pontoons, jet skis. Hiking trails. Lawn games. Soc dir; entertainment. Game rm. Rec rm. Balconies. Picnic tables. Dock. Cr cds: A, DS, MC, V.

D 🛶 ≋ 🐾

Restaurant

★ **MARSH LODGE.** *W7039 Hwy SR, in Broughton Sheboygan Marsh Park. 920/876-2535.* Hrs: 7 am-9 pm. Closed Mon; some major hols. Bar. Semi-a la carte: bkfst $1.25-$6.95, lunch $2-$5.95, dinner $5.95-$11.95. Specializes in home-cooked food, soup, chili. Log building. No cr cds accepted.

D

Elkhorn (G-5)

(For accommodations see Burlington, Fort Atkinson, Janesville, Lake Geneva, Waukesha)

Settled 1837 **Pop** 5,337 **Elev** 1,033 ft **Area code** 414 **Zip** 53121 **E-mail** elkchamber@elknet.net
Information Chamber of Commerce, 9 S Broad St, PO Box 41; 414/723-5788.

What to See and Do

Alpine Valley Ski Resort. Resort has 6 triple, 5 double chairlifts, 5 rope tows; patrol, school, rentals; snowmaking; restaurant, cafeteria, bar. Longest run 3,300 ft; vertical drop 388 ft. (Dec-mid-Mar, daily; closed Dec 24 afternoon) Night skiing. Cross-country trails. Also motel; indoor/outdoor pools, sauna, whirlpool; golf, tennis. 1¹⁄₂ mi S off I-43 on County D & Townline Rd near East Troy. Phone 414/642-7374. ¢¢¢¢

Watson's Wild West Museum. Re-creation of general store. (Mid-Apr-Oct, daily exc Mon) W 4865 Potter Road. Phone 414/723-7505. Early or mid-July. ¢¢

Webster House. Restored 19th-century home of Joseph Philbrick Webster, composer of "Sweet Bye and Bye" and "Lorena." Mounted game bird collection. (Memorial Day-mid-Oct, Wed-Sun afternoons; Apr, by appt) 9 E Rockwell St. Phone 414/723-4248. ¢

Annual Event

Walworth County Fair. NE via WI 11 E to city limits. One of the largest in the state. Agricultural fair, grandstand entertainment and harness racing. Phone 414/723-3228. 6 days ending Labor Day.

Ellison Bay (Door Co) (D-6)

(See also Door County)

Pop 250 (est) **Elev** 610 ft **Area code** 414 **Zip** 54210 **E-mail** lyons@mail.wiscnet.net **Web** doorcountyvacations.com
Information Door County Chamber of Commerce, 1015 Green Bay Rd, PO Box 406, Sturgeon Bay 54235; 414/743-4456 or 800/527-3529.

This resort area is near the northern end of Door County (see). Fishing and boating are popular here; public launching ramps and charter boats are available. This is also considered a good area for scuba diving.

What to See and Do

Death's Door Bluff. Near top of peninsula between the mainland and Washington Island (see). According to legend, 300 Native Americans, attempting a surprise attack, were betrayed and dashed to death against the rocks. Also named because of the large number of ships lost here.

Door County Maritime Museum. Artifacts of fishing and shipbuilding industries; fishing tug open to public; Great Lakes sailing and US Coast Guard; nautical painting; also film on history of commercial fishing. (July-mid-Oct, days vary; closed rest of yr) 5 mi E & N on WI 42 in Gills Rock. Phone 414/854-2860. ¢

Ferry to Washington Island (see). Enclosed cabin plus open deck seating. 30-min trip. (Yr round) Also accommodates cars & bicycles (fees vary). (Daily) 8 mi E & N on WI 42 to Northport Pier, in Gills Rock. Contact Washington Island Ferry Line, phone 414/847-2546. One way, per pedestrian passenger ¢¢

Newport State Park. A 2,370-acre wilderness park with 11 mi of Lake Michigan shoreline. Beach. Hiking, cross-country ski trails. Picnicking. Backpack and winter camping. Standard fees. NE of town on County Hwy NP. Phone 414/854-2500. Per vehicle ¢¢

Annual Event

Old Ellison Bay Days. Parade, fishing contests, fish boil, bazaars, fireworks. Late June.

Motels

★ ★ **GRANDVIEW.** *1 mi S on WI 42.* 920/854-5150; res: 800/258-8208. 30 units, 2 story. Late June-mid-Oct: S, D $76; each addl $7; under 14, $3; lower rates early Apr-late June, mid-late Oct. Closed rest of yr. TV; VCR avail. Complimentary continental bkfst. Ck-out 11 am. Bellhops. Sundries. Bicycles. Rec rm. Refrigerators; some in-rm whirlpools, fireplaces. Private patios, balconies. Totally nonsmoking. Cr cds: A, DS, MC, V.

★ **SHORELINE RESORT.** *12747 WI 42.* 920/854-2606; FAX 920/854-5971. 16 rms, 2 story. July-Aug: S, D $89; kit. unit $99; lower rates May-June, Sept-Oct. Closed rest of yr. Crib free. TV. Restaurant adj 7 am-9 pm. Wine, beer. Ck-out 10 am. Business servs avail. Gift shop. Refrigerators, microwaves. Balconies. Picnic tables, grills. Overlooks Green Bay; dockage. Totally nonsmoking. Cr cds: DS, MC, V.

Inns

★ **GRIFFIN.** *11976 Mink River Rd.* 920/854-4306. 10 rms in inn, all share bath, 2 story, 4 cottages. No rm phones. S $75; D $79; each addl $10; cottages $86; winter wkend plans. Cottages closed Nov-Apr. Children over 5 yrs only (inn). TV in cottages. Complimentary full bkfst (inn); continental bkfst (cottages). Restaurant nearby. Ck-out 10:30 am, ck-in 2 pm. Business servs avail. X-country ski on site. Picnic tables, grills. Gazebo. Built 1910; antique furnishings, fireplace. Totally nonsmoking. No cr cds accepted.

★ ★ **HARBOR HOUSE.** *(12666 WI 42, Ellison Bay)* at Gills Rock. 920/854-5196; FAX 920/854-9717. 14 units, 8 with shower only, 13 with A/C, 2 story. No rm phones. July-Aug: S, D $55-$95; each addl $15; cabins $105-$110; wkly rates; 3-day min wkends; some lower rates May-June, Sept-Oct. Closed rest of yr. Pet accepted, some restrictions. TV. Playground. Complimentary continental bkfst. Restaurant nearby. Ck-out 10 am, ck-in 2 pm. Sauna. Whirlpool. Refrigerators; microwaves avail. Balconies. Picnic tables, grills. Lake view, beach access. Victorian-style house built 1904; many antiques. Totally nonsmoking. Cr cds: A, MC, V.

Resort

★ ★ **WAGON TRAIL.** *1041 County ZZ.* 920/854-2385; FAX 920/854-5278; res: 800/999-2466. 72 rms in 2-story lodge, 8 suites, 16 kits; 30 houses, 8 kit. cottages. May-Oct: S, D $109-$159; each addl $10; suites $159-$239; kit. cottages $175-$250; houses $175-$260; under 18 free in lodge; lower rates rest of yr. Crib free. TV. Indoor pool; whirlpool. Playground. Supervised child's activities; ages 2-9 yrs. Restaurant (see GRANDMA'S SWEDISH). Box lunches. Ck-out 10 am, ck-in 3 pm. Coin lndry. Meeting rms. Business servs avail. Package store 1 mi. Gift shop. Bakery shop. Tennis. Private beach, marina. Boats; motors. X-country ski on site; rentals. Sauna. Bicycle rentals. Lawn games. Movies. Game rm. Some refrigerators, in-rm whirlpools; microwaves avail. Some patios, fireplaces in cottages. Picnic tables, grills. On the shores of Rowleys Bay; extensive wooded grounds. Cr cds: DS, MC, V.

Restaurants

✔ ★ ★ **GRANDMA'S SWEDISH.** *(See Wagon Trail Resort)* 920/854-2385, ext. 831. Hrs: 7:30 am-2 pm, 5-8 pm; Fri, Sat to 9 pm. Swedish menu. Buffet: bkfst $6.95-$9.95, lunch $3.25-$7.95. Semi-a la carte: dinner $5.95-$14.95. Sun brunch $6.95-$9.95. Specialties: fish boil, pecan rolls. Salad bar. View of bay. Totally nonsmoking. Cr cds: MC, V.

✔ ★ **SHORELINE.** *12747 WI 42, at Gills Rock.* 920/854-2950. Hrs: 7 am-9 pm. Closed Nov-Apr. Wine, beer. Semi-a la carte: bkfst $1.95-$5.95, lunch $1.75-$7.25, dinner $4.95-$13.95. Child's meals. Specializes in white fish, perch. View of the bay. Cr cds: MC, V.

★ **VIKING.** *On WI 42.* 920/854-2998. E-mail fishboil@aol .com; web doorcounty.org/rest/vik.html. Hrs: 6 am-9 pm; to 7 pm in winter. Closed Easter, Thanksgiving, Dec 25. Wine, beer. Semi-a la carte: bkfst $1.99-$8.95, lunch $2.60-$7.95, dinner $7.25-$14.95. Fish boil $11.25. Child's meals. Specializes in fresh fish, white fish chowder. Outdoor dining. Cr cds: A, DS, MC, V.

★ ★ **VOIGHTS SUPPER CLUB.** *12010 WI 42.* 920/854-2250. Hrs: 5-10 pm; Sun brunch 10 am-2 pm. Closed Nov-Dec; also Sun-Wed Jan-Apr. Res accepted. Bar 3 pm-midnight. Semi-a la carte: dinner $8.95-$17.95. Sun brunch $8.95. Child's meals. Specializes in seafood, prime rib, duck. Cr cds: A, C, D, DS, MC, V.

Ephraim (Door Co) (D-6)

(See also Door County)

Founded 1853 **Pop** 261 **Elev** 600 ft **Area code** 414 **Zip** 54211 **E-mail** lyons@mail.wiscnet.net **Web** doorcountyvacations.com

Information Door County Chamber of Commerce, 1015 Green Bay Rd, PO Box 406, Sturgeon Bay 54235; 414/743-4456 or 800/52-RELAX.

Moravian colonists founded the second Ephraim here after leaving the first town of that name, now a part of Green Bay; a monument at the harbor commemorates the landing of Moravians in 1853. The village is now a quaint resort community and a center for exploration of the north and west shores of Door County (see).

Annual Event

Fyr-Bal Fest. Scandinavian welcome to summer. Fish boil, Blessing of the Fleet, art fair, lighting of the bonfires on the beach at dusk, coronation of Viking Chieftain. 3 days mid-June.

Motels

★ ★ **EDGEWATER.** 10040 WI 42. 920/854-2734. 40 units, 2 story. July-Aug, Sept-Oct (wknds): S, D $90-$146; lower rates May-June. Closed Nov-Apr. Crib free. TV; cable (premium). Heated pool. Restaurant (see EDGEWATER DINING ROOM). Ck-out 11 am. Refrigerators. On Green Bay. Cr cds: DS, MC, V.

🐕 🏊 🔥

★ **EPHRAIM.** 10407 WI 42N. 920/854-5959; res: 800/451-5995. 28 rms, 2 story. No rm phones. July-mid-Aug, Oct: S, D $78-$88 each addl $10; under 6 free; lower rates May-June, Sept. Closed rest of yr. Crib free. TV; cable, VCR. Heated pool. Complimentary continental bkfst. Restaurants nearby. Ck-out 11 am. Meeting rm. Refrigerators, microwaves. Balconies. Cr cds: MC, V.

D 🏊 🔥

★ ★ **EPHRAIM GUEST HOUSE.** 38 Cedar St. 920/854-2319; res: 800/589-8423. 16 kit. suites, 2 story. Late June-late Aug: S, D $125-$250; each addl $10; wkly rates; lower rates rest of yr. TV; cable (premium), VCR. Restaurant nearby. Ck-out 11 am. Coin lndry. X-country ski 3 mi. Some in-rm whirlpools, fireplaces. Private patios, balconies. Picnic tables, grills. Bay 1 blk. Cr cds: A, DS, MC, V.

D 🐕 🔥

★ ★ **EPHRAIM SHORES.** 10018 Water St, on WI 42, downtown. 920/854-2371; FAX 920/854-4926. 46 rms, 2 story. D $77-$115; each addl $10; suites $100-$175; under 12, $4; 12-18, $8; under 4 free. Crib $3. TV; cable. Indoor pool; whirlpool. Playground. Coffee in rms. Restaurant 8 am-8 pm. Ck-out 10:30 am. Business servs avail. Sundries. Game rm. Exercise equipt; weight machine, bicycle. Rec rm. Bicycle rentals. Refrigerators; some in-rm whirlpools. Sun deck. On Green Bay, overlooking Eagle Harbor. Totally nonsmoking. Cr cds: MC, V.

D 🐕 🏊 🏃 🍽 🔥

★ ★ **EVERGREEN BEACH.** at jct WI 42, German Rd. 920/854-2831; FAX 920/854-9222; res: 800/420-8130. 30 rms, 1-2 story. Memorial Day wkend-Labor Day: D $96-$110; each addl $6-$10; family rates; lower rates June, after Labor Day-late Oct. Closed rest of yr. Crib $5. TV; cable (premium). Heated pool. Playground. Complimentary continental bkfst. Restaurant nearby. Ck-out 10:30 am. Business servs avail. Lawn games. Refrigerators; many microwaves. Many balconies. On Eagle Harbor; private beach. Totally nonsmoking. Cr cds: A, DS, MC, V.

D 🐕 🏊 🍽 🔥

★ ★ **PINE GROVE.** on WI 42 in town. 920/854-2321; res: 800/292-9494. 44 rms, 2 story. May-Oct: S, D $79-$99; each addl $12; suites $165; wkly rates. Closed rest of yr. Crib free. TV; cable (premium). Indoor pool; whirlpool. Complimentary coffee. Ck-out 11 am. Coin lndry. Business servs avail. Sundries. Game rm. Exercise equipt; weight machine, stair machine. Refrigerators; some in-rm whirlpools. Balconies. On bay; gazebo, private sand beach. Cr cds: DS, MC, V.

D 🐕 🏊 🏃 🔥

✓★ ★ **SOMERSET INN.** N Water St, WI 42. 920/854-1819; FAX 920/854-9087; res: 800/809-1819. 20 rms, 2 story, 18 suites. Late June-Aug, wknds in fall: S, D $88; each addl $12; suites $119-$145; lower rates rest of yr. Crib $5. TV; cable (premium). 2 pools, 1 indoor; whirlpools. Playground. Complimentary coffee in rms. Restaurant nearby. Ck-out 11 am. X-country ski 1 mi. Refrigerators, microwaves; some in-rm whirlpools. Balconies. Picnic tables, grills. Totally nonsmoking. Cr cds: DS, MC, V.

D 🐕 🏊 🍽 🔥

★ **TROLLHAUGEN LODGE.** 10176 WI 42. 920/854-2713; res: 800/854-4118. 14 rms, showers only. July-Aug, 3 wknds in Oct: S, D $79; kit. cottage $115; under 2 free; wkly rates; wknds (2-day min); higher rates special events; lower rates Sept-Oct, mid-Apr-June. Closed rest of yr. TV; cable, VCR avail. Complimentary continental bkfst. Restaurant nearby. Ck-out 10 am. Refrigerators; many microwaves; some fireplaces. Some balconies. Picnic tables, grills. Cr cds: A, DS, MC, V.

🍽 🔥 SC

Inns

★ ★ ★ **EAGLE HARBOR.** 9914 Water St. 920/854-2121; res: 800/324-5427. E-mail nnedders@mail.wiscnet.net; web www.eagleharbor.com. 9 inn rms, 1-2 story, 32 suites. Inn: S, D $79-$139; suites, July-Aug: $159-$189; lower rates rest of yr. TV; cable (premium), VCR. Indoor pool. Playground. Full bkfst for inn guests. Restaurant nearby. Ck-out 10 am, ck-in 3 pm. Meeting rm. Business servs avail. In-rm modem link. X-country ski 1 mi. Exercise equipt; stair machine, bicycle, sauna. Massage. Microwaves avail. In-rm whirlpool, fireplace in suites. Picnic tables, grills. Opp beach. Decorated with turn-of-the-century antiques. Cr cds: MC, V.

D 🐕 🏊 🏃 🔥 🍽

★ ★ **EPHRAIM INN.** 9994 Pioneer Lane, WI 42. 920/854-4515; res: 800/622-2193. E-mail tchristo@mail.wisnet.net. 17 rms, 2 story. S, D $89-$160. Closed Nov-Apr (Mon-Thurs). Children over 12 yrs only. TV. Complimentary full bkfst. Ck-out 11 am, ck-in 3 pm. Opp beach. Overlooks Green Bay. Each rm has different theme. Cr cds: DS, MC, V.

D 🐕 🏊 🍽 🔥

✓★ **FRENCH COUNTRY INN.** 3052 Spruce Lane. 920/854-4001. 7 rms in main building, 5 share bath, 2 story, 1 kit. cottage. No A/C. May-Oct: S, D $60-$89; kit. cottage $87-$105; wkly rates; lower rates rest of yr. Children over 12 yrs only in main building. Crib free. TV in cottage. Complimentary continental bkfst. Restaurant nearby. Ck-out 11 am, ck-in 3 pm. X-country ski 1 mi. 2 sitting rms; antiques. Built 1912. Near bay. Totally nonsmoking. No cr cds accepted.

🏊 🍽 🔥

★ **HILLSIDE.** 9980 WI 42. 920/854-2417; FAX 920/854-4604; res: 800/423-7023. E-mail ksmcneil@juno.com. 11 rms, 3 share bath, 2 story, 2 kit. cottages. No A/C in inn. No rm phones. S, D $84-$89; kit. cottages $140-$180; wkly rates. Crib free. TV in sitting rm; cable. Complimentary full bkfst (rms only); afternoon refreshments. Restaurant nearby. Ck-out 10:30 am, ck-in 2 pm. Business servs avail. X-country ski 1 mi. In-rm whirlpool, fireplace in cottages. Grills. Built 1854; veranda, rocking chairs, antiques. On Eagle Harbor; private beach. Totally nonsmoking. Cr cds: DS, MC, V.

🐕 🏊 🍽 🔥 🍽

Restaurants

✓★ **EDGEWATER DINING ROOM.** (See Edgewater Motel) 920/854-4034. Hrs: 7:30-11 am, 5:30-8 pm. Closed Nov-Apr. Res accepted. Semi-a la carte: bkfst $2.50-$7.50. Fish boil $12.95. Child's meals. Overlooks bay. No cr cds accepted.

★ ★ **PAULSON'S OLD ORCHARD INN.** 10341 WI 42. 920/854-5717. Hrs: 8 am-8 pm; winter hrs vary. Semi-a la carte: bkfst, lunch $5-$8, dinner $9-$15. Specialties: Swedish meatballs, eggs Benedict. Own desserts. Fireplace, cathedral ceiling. Victorian gift shop. English country gardens in summer. Cr cds: DS, MC, V.

D

★ **SUMMER KITCHEN.** WI 42N. 920/854-2131. E-mail 414-5030.com. Hrs: 8 am-9 pm. Closed Nov-Apr. Semi-a la carte: bkfst $2.15-$6.95, lunch $2.15-$7.95, dinner $2.15-$18.95. Specializes in barbecued dishes. Own soups, desserts. Patio dining. Gazebo. No cr cds accepted.

D

Fish Creek (Door Co) (D-6)

(See also Door County)

Pop 200 (est) **Elev** 583 ft **Area code** 414 **Zip** 54212 **E-mail** lyons@mail.wiscnet.net **Web** www.doorcountyvacations.com

Information Door County Chamber of Commerce, 1015 Green Bay Rd, PO Box 406, Sturgeon Bay 54235; 414/743-4456 or 800/52-RELAX.

This picturesque Green Bay resort village, with its many interesting shops, is in Door County (see).

What to See and Do

Peninsula State Park. A 3,763-acre park with 9 mi of waterfront including sandy and cobblestone beaches; caves, cliffs; observation tower. Swimming, waterskiing; fishing; boating. Hiking, bicycle trails. Cross-country skiing, snowmobiling. Picnic grounds, playground, concession. Camping (471 sites, hookups, dump station). Naturalist programs. 18-hole golf course (mid-May-mid-Oct). Standard fees. N off WI 42. Phone 414/868-3258. Per vehicle ¢¢

Seasonal Events

Peninsula Players. 3 mi S on WI 42. Professional resident company performs in "theater in a garden." Phone 414/868-3287. Nightly exc Mon. Late June-mid Oct.

American Folklore Theatre. Peninsula State Park Amphitheater (see). Original folk musical productions based on American lore and literature. For reservations and information on limited fall season phone 414/839-2329. Nightly exc Sun. July-Aug.

Motels

★ **BEOWULF LODGE.** *3775 WI 42. 920/868-2046; FAX 920/868-2381; res: 800/433-7592.* 60 rms, 2 story, 9 suites, 26 kits. May-Oct: S, D $85; suites $110; kit. units $92; lower rates rest of yr. Crib $10. TV; cable, VCR avail. Indoor pool; whirlpool. Complimentary coffee in lobby. Restaurant nearby. Ck-out 11 am. Coin lndry. Business servs avail. Gift shop. Tennis. Downhill ski 20 mi; x-country ski on site. Bikes. Game rm. Microwaves avail. Picnic tables, grills. Cr cds: MC, V.

★ **BY-THE-BAY.** *WI 42, 2 blks N. 920/868-3456; FAX 920/868-1604.* 15 rms, 2 story. Mid-June-Labor Day & Oct: S, D $81-$115; each addl $8; some lower rates off-season. Closed Nov-Apr. Crib $5. TV; cable (premium). Restaurant adj 7 am-9 pm. Ck-out 10:30 am. Business servs avail. Public beach opp. Totally nonsmoking. Cr cds: DS, MC, V.

★ **CEDAR COURT.** *9429 Cedar St. 920/868-3361; FAX 920/868-2541.* Web www.doorcounty.com. 11 rms, 2 story, 9 kit. cottages. No rm phones in motel rms. Late June-Aug: S, D $75; suites $115; cottages $115-$235; each addl $5; under 12 free; wkly, 3-day wkend rates; ski plan; honeymoon package; lower rates rest of yr. Crib free. TV; cable, VCR avail. Heated pool. Complimentary coffee in rms. Restaurant nearby. Ck-out 11 am. Business servs avail. Downhill ski 20 mi; x-country ski 1 mi. Refrigerators; some in-rm whirlpools; microwaves avail. Balconies. Picnic tables, grills. Cr cds: MC, V.

★★ **HOMESTEAD.** *4006 Main St (WI 42). 920/868-3748; FAX 920/868-2874; res: 800/686-6621.* 33 units in 2 bldgs, 2 story, 23 suites. July-Aug: S, D $94; each addl $10; suites $129-$169; under 12 free; package plans; lower rates rest of yr. TV; cable (premium), VCR avail (movies $4). Indoor pool; whirlpool. Complimentary continental bkfst. Res-

taurant nearby. Ck-out 11 am. Business servs avail. In-rm modem link. Sundries. X-country ski adj. Bike trail adj. Exercise equipt; weight machine, bicycles, sauna. Refrigerators; many wet bars; microwaves in suites. Balconies. Picnic tables. Adj to Peninsula State Park. Cr cds: DS, MC, V.

★ **PENINSULA.** *4020 WI 42, adj to Peninsula State Park. 920/868-3281.* 12 units. Late-June-late Aug: S, D $72-$78; higher rates wkends; lower rates rest of yr. Crib free. TV; cable (premium). Restaurant 5:30-10 pm. Ck-out 10 am. X-country ski adj. Gazebo. Totally nonsmoking. Cr cds: DS, MC, V.

Inns

★★ **HARBOR GUEST HOUSE.** *2 blks off WI 42, on Fish Creek Harbor. 920/868-2284; FAX 920/868-1535.* Web doorcounty.org/lodging/hgh.html. 7 kit. suites (1-2-bedrm). 2 story. July-mid-Oct: suites $160-$220; family rates; lower rates rest of yr. Crib $5. TV; cable (premium). Complimentary coffee in rms. Restaurant nearby. Ck-out 10:30 am, ck-in 2 pm. X-country ski on site. Boat slips avail. Microwaves, fireplaces. Some balconies. Grills. View of Green Bay. Cr cds: MC, V.

✔★★ **SETTLEMENT COURTYARD.** *9126 WI 42, 1 mi S. 920/868-3524; FAX 920/868-3048.* 32 kit units, 2 story. July-Oct: S $98; D $103; each addl $5-$10; suites $124-$169; under 4 free; wkly rates; lower rates rest of yr. Crib free. TV; VCR avail. Continental bkfst in season. Restaurant nearby. Ck-out 10:30 am, ck-in 3 pm. Business servs avail. X-country ski on site. Fireplaces; microwaves avail. Hiking trails. Cr cds: A, DS, MC, V.

★★ **THORP HOUSE.** *4135 Bluff Rd. 920/868-2444; FAX 920/868-2141.* 4 inn rms, 3 suites, 6 kit. cottages. No A/C in cottages. July-Aug: S, D $75-$135; suites $155-$175; kit. cottages $80-$135; wkend, wkly rates; lower rates rest of yr. Adults only (inn). Crib free. TV; cable (premium), VCR. Complimentary continental bkfst (inn guests). Restaurants nearby. Ck-out 11 am, ck-in 3 pm. Downhill ski 20 mi; x-country ski 5 blks. Some in-rm whirlpools, fireplaces; microwaves avail. Picnic tables, grills. Built 1902; many antiques, library. Set atop hill; overlooks harbor. Bikes. Totally nonsmoking (inn). No cr cds accepted.

★★★ **WHISTLING SWAN.** *4192 Main St. 920/868-3442; FAX 920/868-1703.* Web www.doorcounty.org/lodging/wswan.html. 7 units, 2 story, 2 suites. D, suites $99-$138. Crib free. TV avail; cable (premium). Complimentary full bkfst. Restaurant adj 7:30 am-8 pm. Ck-out 11 am, ck-in 3 pm. Business servs avail. Renovated country inn (1887); antique furnishings. Near lake, swimming beach. Totally nonsmoking. Cr cds: A, DS, MC, V.

✔★★ **WHITE GULL.** *4225 Main St, 3 blks W of WI 42. 920/868-3517; FAX 920/868-2367.* Web www.innline.com. 9 rms, 1-2 story, 5 cottages. S, D $96-$185; cottages $157-$231; winter mid-wk packages. Crib free. TV in cottages; cable (premium), VCR (free movies). Restaurant (see WHITE GULL INN). Ck-out 11 am, ck-in 3 pm. Business servs avail. Free airport transportation. X-country ski 1 mi. Fireplaces. Balconies. Built 1896; library, antiques. Cr cds: A, C, D, DS, MC, V.

Restaurants

★★ **C & C SUPPER CLUB.** *on WI 42. 920/868-3412.* Hrs: 4:45-10 pm; Nov-Apr Thurs-Sun only, to 9:30 pm. Res accepted. Bar 11-2 am. Semi-a la carte: dinner $8.99-$21.99. Child's meals. Specializes in steak, seafood, pasta. Salad bar. Entertainment Fri, Sat. Parking. Cr cds: D, DS, MC, V.

D

✔★ **COOKERY.** *On WI 42.* 920/868-3634. Hrs: 7 am-9 pm; Nov-Apr, wkends only. Wine, beer. Semi-a la carte: bkfst $2.65-$7.25, lunch $2.59-$8.49, dinner $4.99-$11.99. Child's meals. Bakery & deli. Parking. Gift shop. Totally nonsmoking. Cr cds: MC, V.

D ♥

★★★ **KORTES' ENGLISH INN.** *Rte 1, 1¹/₂ mi N on WI 42.* 920/868-3076. Hrs: 5:30-9 pm. Closed Nov-Apr. Continental menu. Bar 4 pm-2 am. Extensive wine list. Complete meals: dinner $9.50-$26. Child's meals. Specializes in lamb, veal, seafood. Seafood buffet Fri. Own baking. Entertainment. Extensive dessert list. Parking. Old World decor; stained glass, wooden beams, local artwork. Cr cds: D, MC, V.

D

✔★ **PELLETIER'S.** *4199 Main St, at Founder's Square.* 920/868-3313. Hrs: 7:30 am-8 pm. Closed Nov-mid-May. Res accepted. Wine, beer. Semi-a la carte: bkfst $2.25-$6.25, lunch $3.25-$9.95. Fish boil dinner: $10.50. Specializes in crêpes, fish boil. Parking. Patio dining. Nautical decor. Family-owned. No cr cds accepted.

D ♥

★★ **SUMMERTIME.** *1 N Spruce St.* 920/868-3738. E-mail thol land@wiscnet.net; web www.doorcty.net. Hrs: 7:30 am-10 pm; Fri, Sat to 11 pm. Wine, beer. Semi-a la carte: bkfst $1.95-$6.95, lunch $2.75-$6.95, dinner $3.95-$16.95. Specializes in South African-style barbecue ribs, Italian & Greek cuisine. Own baking. Outdoor dining. Cr cds: A, MC, V.

D SC

★★ **WHITE GULL INN.** *(See White Gull Inn)* 920/868-3517. Web www.innline.com. Hrs: 7:30 am-2:30 pm, 5-8 pm. Closed Thanksgiving, Dec 25. Res accepted. Wine, beer. Semi-a la carte: bkfst $4-$8, lunch $4-$7, dinner $14.95-$19. Fish boil Wed, Fri-Sun evenings: $14.95. Child's meals. Classical guitarist. Parking. Turn-of-the-century decor. Family-owned. Cr cds: A, C, D, DS, MC, V.

D

Fond du Lac (F-5)

(See also Green Lake, Oshkosh, Waupun)

Settled 1835 **Pop** 37,757 **Elev** 760 ft **Area code** 414 **E-mail** fdlcvb@visitwisconsin.com **Web** www.visitwisconsin.com/fdl
Information Convention & Visitors Bureau, 19 W Scott St; 800/937-9123, ext 35.

Located at the foot of Lake Winnebago and named by French explorers in the 1600s, Fond du Lac, "foot of the lake," was an early outpost for fur trading, later achieving prominence as a lumbering center and railroad city.

What to See and Do

Galloway House and Village. Restored 30-rm Victorian mansion with 4 fireplaces, carved woodwork and stenciled ceilings; village of late 1800s; 22 buildings include one-room schoolhouse, print shop, general store, operating gristmill, museum with collection of Native American artifacts; war displays; other area artifacts. (Memorial Day-Labor Day, daily; rest of Sept, Sat & Sun) 336 Old Pioneer Rd. Phone 414/922-6390. ¢¢

Kettle Moraine State Forest, Northern Unit. The forest's 27,277 acres include Long and Mauthe Lake Recreation Areas, Scenic Kettle Moraine Dr. Swimming, waterskiing; fishing; boating, canoeing. There are 58 mi of hiking trails and bridle trails. Snowmobiling, cross-country skiing. Picnicking. Camping is avail (338 sites, hookups, dump station), including primitive and winter camping. Observation tower. Forest Supervisor is in

Campbellsport. Standard fees. (Daily) 17 mi SE on US 45 to Waucousta, then E on County F.Phone 414/626-2116. The forest is being developed as part of Ice Age National Scientific Reserve (see DEVIL'S LAKE STATE PARK). Nonresident admission per vehicle ¢¢¢¢ Also here is

Ice Age Visitors Center. Films, slides and panorama show visitors how glaciers molded Wisconsin's terrain; naturalists answer questions. (Daily; closed Jan 1, Dec 25) Phone 414/533-8322. **Free.**

Lake Winnebago. Swimming, sailing, windsurfing, waterskiing; fishing, ice-fishing, sturgeon spearing (last 2 wks Feb); boating, ice-boating. Snowmobiling.

Lakeside Park. A 400-acre park on Lake Winnebago. Petting zoo, playground, rides; picnic area; boating (ramps, canoe rentals); lighthouse. (June-Aug, daily) (See ANNUAL EVENTS) N end of Main St. Phone 414/929-2950. **Free.**

★ **Octagon House.** A 12-rm octagonal house built in 1856 by Isaac Brown and designed by Orson Fowler has hidden room, secret passageways and an underground tunnel. Period antiques, dolls, clothing. Native American display; ship collection; spinning wheel demonstrations. Carriage house has pony carriages. 90-min guided tours by appt only. 276 Linden St. Phone 414/922-1608. ¢¢¢

Silver Wheel Manor. A 30-rm mansion that was once part of 400-acre farm established 1860; antique furnishings; collection of more than 1,200 dolls & accessories; model trains; circus rm; horse-drawn vehicles; trick horse show; photography rm. (Memorial Day-Labor Day, daily exc Sun by appt) N6221 County K; E on WI 23, S on County K. Phone 414/922-1608. ¢¢¢

St Paul's Cathedral (Episcopal). English Gothic limestone structure with wood carvings from Oberammergau, Germany, rare ecclesiastical artifacts and a variety of stained-glass windows; cloister garden. Self-guided tours (daily). 51 W Division at Sophia St. Phone 414/921-3363. **Donation.**

Annual Events

Walleye Weekend Festival & Mercury Marine National Walleye Tournament. Lakeside Park. Fish fry, food, entertainment, sports competions. Phone 800/937-9123. 2nd wkend June.

International Aerobatic Championship. Airport. Aerobatic pilots from all over the world compete. Early Aug.

Motels

✔★ **DAYS INN.** *107 N Pioneer Rd (54935),* on US 41 at jct WI 23. 414/923-6790; FAX 414/923-6790. 59 rms, 2 story. S $39.95-$45.95; D $55.95-$60.95; each addl $6; under 17 free. Crib free. Pet accepted; $3. TV; cable (premium). Complimentary continental bkfst. Ck-out noon. Business servs avail. In-rm modem link. Cr cds: A, D, DS, MC, V.

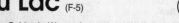

★ **ECONO LODGE.** *649 W Johnson St (WI 23) (54935).* 414/923-2020; FAX 414/929-9352. 48 rms, 2 story. S $44-$59; D $49-$64; each addl $5; higher rates special events. Crib $3. TV; cable (premium). Indoor pool; whirlpool. Complimentary continental bkfst. Restaurant nearby. Ck-out 11 am. Business servs avail. Refrigerators. Cr cds: A, C, D, DS, ER, MC, V.

≋ ⊠ 🔥 SC

★★ **HOLIDAY INN.** *625 W Rolling Meadows Dr (54937),* at jct US 41 & 151. 414/923-1440; FAX 414/923-1366. 141 rms, 2 story. S $69-$109; D $79-$119; under 19 free. Crib free. Pet accepted. TV; cable (premium). VCR avail. Indoor pool; whirlpool. Coffee in rms. Restaurant 6:30 am-10 pm. Rm serv. Bar 11-1 am. Ck-out 11 am. Coin lndry. Meeting rms. In-rm modem link. Bellhops. Valet serv. Sundries. Free airport transportation. Putting green. Exercise equipt; bicycle, treadmill, sauna. Rec rm. Golf course opp. Microwaves avail. Cr cds: A, C, D, DS, JCB, MC, V.

D ⊬ ≋ 🏋 ⊠ 🔥 SC

★ **NORTHWAY.** *301 North Pioneer Rd (54935),* off WI 41. 414/921-7975; FAX 414/921-7983. E-mail folcvv@visitwisconsin.com; web www.visitwisconsin.com/fondulac. 19 rms. June-Oct: S $30-$35; D

$49-$55; each addl $5; under 12 free; wkly rates; higher rates special events; lower rates rest of yr. Crib $4. Pet accepted; $7. TV; cable. Complimentary continental bkfst. Coffee in rms. Ck-out 11 am. X-country ski 10 mi. Refrigerators, microwaves avail. Picnic tables, grills. Cr cds: A, DS, MC, V.

Restaurants

✔★ **SALTY'S SEAFOOD & SPIRITS.** 503 N Park Ave (54935). 414/922-9940. Hrs: 11 am-10 pm; wkends to 11 pm. Closed some major hols. Bar. Semi-a la carte: lunch, dinner $3.95-$12.95. Specializes in seafood, prime rib, steak. Salad bar. Nautical decor. Cr cds: A, DS, MC, V.

★★ **SCHREINER'S.** 168 N Pioneer Rd (US 41) (54935), at jct WI 23. 920/922-0590. Hrs: 6:30 am-9 pm; summer to 10 pm. Closed Thanksgiving; Dec 24 evening, 25. Serv bar. Semi-a la carte: bkfst $3.50-$6, lunch, dinner $4.50-$10. Child's meals. Specializes in New England clam chowder, fresh baked goods. Colonial decor. Family-owned. Cr cds: A, DS, MC, V.

Fontana (H-5)

(See also Beloit, Burlington, Delavan, Elkhorn, Lake Geneva)

Pop 1,635 **Elev** 900 ft **Area code** 414 **Zip** 53125

Located on the western shore of Geneva Lake in territory once occupied by the Potawatomi, this town was named for its many springs.

Resort

★★★ **THE ABBEY.** 2 blks E, just off WI 67. 414/275-6811; FAX 414/275-3264; res: 800/558-2405. 334 rms, 2 story, 20 condos. S, D $95-$175; each addl $12; under 12 free; suites $175-$280; kit. units $280; package plans. Crib free. TV; cable, VCR. 5 pools, 2 indoor; whirlpool, poolside serv. Supervised child's activites (wkends); ages 4-12. Dining rms 7 am-10 pm. Snack bar. Rm serv. Bars 11-2 am. Ck-out noon, ck-in 4 pm. Convention facilities. Business center. In-rm modem link. Valet serv. Concierge. Gift shop. Barber, beauty shop. Airport transportation. Tennis. Waterskiing, marina, boats. Downhill ski 10 mi; x-country ski 2 mi. Bicycles. Lawn games. Rec dir. Rec rm. Game rm. Exercise equipt; weights, bicycles, sauna. Massage. Full service spa. Private patios & balconies (condos). On Geneva Lake. Cr cds: A, C, D, DS, MC, V.

Fort Atkinson (G-5)

(See also Elkhorn, Janesville, Madison, Watertown)

Settled 1836 **Pop** 10,227 **Elev** 790 ft **Area code** 920 **Zip** 53538 **E-mail** fortcham@idcnet.com **Web** www.idcnet.com/~fortcham/home.htm

Information Chamber of Commerce, 244 N Main St; 920/563-3210 or 888/SEE-FORT.

In 1872, William Dempster Hoard, later governor of Wisconsin, organized the Wisconsin State Dairyman's Association here. He toured the area, drumming up support by preaching the virtues of the cow, "the foster mother of the human race." More than any other man, Hoard was responsible for Wisconsin's development as a leading dairy state. Nearby are Lake Koshkonong, a popular recreation area, and Lake Ripley, where Ole Evinrude invented the outboard motor in 1908.

What to See and Do

Hoard Historical Museum. Housed in historic home (1864), museum features pioneer history and archaeology of the area; period rms, antique quilt, bird rm, old costumes and clothing, antique firearms; reference library; permanent and changing displays. (June-Aug, daily exc Mon; rest of yr, Tues-Sat; closed Thanksgiving, Dec 25) 407 Merchants Ave. Phone 920/563-7769. **Free.** Also here is

Dwight Foster House (1841). Historic home of city's founder; 5-room, 2-story Greek-revival frame house is furnished in the period, with many original pieces. (June-Aug, daily exc Mon; rest of yr, Tues-Sat; closed Thanksgiving, Dec 25) Phone 920/563-7769. **Free.**

National Dairy Shrine Museum. Traces development of the dairy industry for past 100 yrs. Collection of memorabilia; exhibits include old creamery, replica of early dairy farm kitchen, old barn and milk-hauling equipment. Multimedia presentation. (June-Aug, daily exc Mon; rest of yr, Tues-Sat; closed Thanksgiving, Dec 25) **Free.**

Panther Intaglio. Panther-shaped prehistoric earthwork; dates to A.D. 1000. Discovered by Increase Lapham in 1850. 1236 Riverside Dr.

Motel

★ **SUPER 8.** 225 S Water St E. 414/563-8444. 40 rms, 3 story. S $47-$49; D $50-$55; each addl $10; suites $75; under 12 free. Crib $5. TV; cable. Complimentary continental bkfst. Restaurant nearby. Bar 4 pm-midnight; Fri, Sat to 1 am; entertainment. Ck-out 11 am. Meeting rms. Sundries. Downhill/x-country ski 5 mi. Overlooks Rock River. Patio & deck chairs on riverbank. Cr cds: A, C, D, DS, MC, V.

Galesville (E-2)

(See also La Crosse)

Pop 1,278 **Elev** 712 ft **Area code** 608 **Zip** 54630

What to See and Do

State parks. Fishing; boating, canoeing. Hiking. Picnicking, playgrounds. Camping (electric hookups, dump stations). Standard fees.

Perrot State Park. Trempealeau Mt, a beacon for voyageurs for more than 300 yrs, is in this 1,425-acre park. Nicolas Perrot set up winter quarters here in 1686; a French fort was built on the site in 1731. Also cross-country skiing. Vistas, bluffs. Standard fees. (Daily) 11 mi SW via WI 35/54 & WI 93 to Trempealeau. Phone 608/534-6409. Per vehicle ¢¢

Merrick State Park. A 324-acre park along Mississippi River. Also swimming, waterskiing, canoeing. Camping. (Daily) 22 mi NW on WI 35. Phone 608/687-4936. Per vehicle ¢¢

Motel

✔★ **SONIC.** Rte 2, 1 mi W on WI 93, 54. 608/582-2281. 24 rms, 2 kits. S $36.95; D $40.95-$48.95. Crib free. TV; cable (premium). Complimentary coffee in rms. Ck-out 11 am. Gift shop. X-country ski 5 mi. Cr cds: MC, V.

Green Bay (E-5)

(See also Appleton)

Pop 96,466 **Elev** 594 ft **Area code** 920 **E-mail** tourism@dct.com **Web** www.greenbay.com

Information Visitors & Convention Bureau, PO Box 10596, 54307-0576; 920/494-9507 or 888/867-3342.

The strategic location that made Green Bay a trading center as far back as 1669 today enables this port city to handle nearly 1.8 million tons of cargo a year. Railroads and trucking firms converge on the harbor. The region was claimed for the King of France in 1634, and was named La Baye in 1669, when it became the site of the mission of St Francis. It then saw the rise of fur trading, a series of Native American wars, and French, British and US conflicts. Although it became part of the United States in 1783, Green Bay did not yield to American influence until after the War of 1812, when agents of John Jacob Astor gained control of the fur trade. Oldest settlement in the state, Green Bay is a paper and cheese producing center as well as a hub for health care. It is also famous for its professional football team, the Green Bay Packers.

What to See and Do

Green Bay Packer Hall of Fame. History of team from 1919 to present; a unique collection of multimedia presentations, memorabilia, hands-on activites, NFL films. (Daily; closed Dec 25) Brown County Expo Centre, 855 Lombardi Ave; 4 mi SW on US 41 Business. Phone 920/499-4281. ¢¢¢

Hazelwood (1837-1838). Greek-revival house where state constitution was drafted. (Memorial Day-Labor Day, Fri-Sun afternoons; rest of yr, by appt) 1008 S Monroe Ave. Phone 920/437-1840. ¢

Heritage Hill State Park. 40-acre living history museum; complex of 26 historical buildings illustrate the development of NE Wisconsin. (June-Aug, daily exc Mon; May & Sept, Sat-Sun) Christmas festival (Fri after Thanksgiving-2nd wknd Dec, daily). 2640 S Webster. Phone 920/448-5150. ¢¢¢

⭐ **National Railroad Museum.** Has 75 steam locomotives, diesels and cars; train rides; exhibit building; theater; gift shop. (May-mid-Oct, daily) 2285 S Broadway. Phone 920/437-7623. ¢¢-¢¢¢

Neville Public Museum. Science, history and art collections and exhibits. (Daily; closed major hols) 210 Museum Place. Phone 920/448-4460. **Donation.**

Oneida Nation Museum. Permanent and "hands-on" exhibits tell story of Oneida Nation. (Tues-Fri, limited hrs Sat & Sun; closed hols) 866 EE Rd, 7 mi SW on US 41 to County Rd EE. Phone 920/869-2768. ¢

Professional sports.

NFL (Green Bay Packers). 1265 Lombardi Ave. Phone 920/496-5700.

University of Wisconsin-Green Bay (1965). (5,000 students) Campus built on 700 acres. Weidner Center for the Performing Arts. Also here is Cofrin Memorial Arboretum; 9-hole golf course (fee); Bayshore picnic area. Tours of campus (by appt). N Nicolet Dr, 4 mi NE on WI 54, 57. Phone 920/465-2000.

Seasonal Event

Waterboard Warriors. Brown County Fairgrounds. Waterski shows performed by skiers from the area. Thurs (evenings). Memorial Day-Labor Day.

Motels

(Rates may be higher for special football wkends)

⭐ **BUDGETEL INN.** 2840 S Onieda (54304). 920/494-7887; FAX 920/494-3370. Web www.budgetel.com. 80 rms, 2 story. S $55.95-$66.95; D $55.95-$73.95; under 18 free; higher rates: wkends, special events, football games. Crib free. Pet accepted, some restrictions. TV;

cable (premium), VCR avail (movies). Complimentary continental bkfst. Complimentary coffee in rms. Restaurant adj. Ck-out noon. Meeting rms. Business center. X-country ski 10 mi. Health club privileges. Microwaves avail. Cr cds: A, C, D, DS, MC, V.

⭐ **COMFORT INN.** 2841 Ramada Way (54304). 920/498-2060; FAX 920/498-2060; res: 800/228-5150. Web www.comfortinn.com. 60 rms, 2 story. S $46.95-$64.95; D $52.95-$74.95; each addl $5; under 18 free; higher rates: Packers football games, EAA Fly-in, Dec 31; lower rates wkdays. Crib free. Pet accepted, some restrictions. TV; cable (premium). Indoor pool; whirlpool. Complimentary continental bkfst. Restaurant nearby. Ck-out 11 am. Business servs avail. In-rm modem link. Valet serv. X-country ski 5 mi. Health club privileges. Cr cds: A, C, D, DS, ER, JCB, MC, V.

✔⭐ **EXEL INN.** 2870 Ramada Way (54304), US 41 Oneida St exit. 920/499-3599; FAX 920/498-4055. 105 rms, 2 story. S $38-$41; D $44-$51; each addl $5; under 18 free. Crib free. Pet accepted, some restrictions. TV; cable. Complimentary continental bkfst. Restaurant adj open 24 hrs. Ck-out noon. Business servs avail. In-rm modem link. Health club privileges. Cr cds: A, C, D, DS, MC, V.

⭐ **FAIRFIELD INN BY MARRIOTT.** 2850 S Oneida (54304). 920/497-1010; FAX 920/497-3098. 63 rms, 3 story. May-Sept: S, D $58.95-$73; each addl $6; under 18 free; higher rates special events; lower rates rest of yr. TV; cable (premium), VCR avail. Complimentary continental bkfst. Restaurant adj open 24 hrs. Ck-out noon. Business servs avail. X-country ski 3 mi. Indoor pool; whirlpool. Microwaves avail. Cr cds: A, D, DS, MC, V.

⭐⭐ **HOLIDAY INN-AIRPORT.** 2580 S Ashland (54304). 920/499-5121; FAX 920/499-6777. 147 rms, 2 story. June-Aug: S $80-$90; D $90-$100; each addl $10; suites $110; under 18 free; lower rates rest of yr. Crib free. TV; cable (premium). Indoor pool; whirlpool. Complimentary coffee in rms. Restaurant 6:30 am-1:30 pm, 5:30-10 pm. Rm serv. Ck-out 11 am. Meeting rms. Business center. Bellhops. Free airport transportation. Health club privileges. Game rm. Some refrigerators. Cr cds: A, C, D, DS, JCB, MC, V.

⭐ **MARINER.** 2222 Riverside Dr (WI 57) (54301). 920/437-7107. 23 rms, 2 story. S $37.95-$50; D $42.50-$68; each addl $5; under 18 free; higher rates special events. Crib $5. TV; cable. Complimentary continental bkfst. Restaurant 11:30 am-2 pm, 5-9 pm; Fri, Sat to 10 pm. Rm serv. Ck-out 11 am. Meeting rms. Beauty shop. X-country ski 10 mi. Health club privileges. Lawn games. Refrigerators; microwaves avail. Patios. Gazebo. On the Fox River; dock. Cr cds: A, C, D, DS, MC, V.

✔⭐ **ROAD STAR INN.** 1941 True Lane (54304), ¼ mi E of US 41 Lombardi exit. 920/497-2666; FAX 920/497-4754; res: 800/445-4667. 63 rms, 2 story. July-Oct: S $34; D $40; each addl $3; under 15 free; higher rates: special events, wkends; lower rates rest of yr. Pet accepted. TV; cable. Complimentary continental bkfst. Restaurant nearby. Ck-out 11 am. Some refrigerators, wet bars. Cr cds: A, C, D, DS, MC, V.

✔⭐ **SKY-LIT.** 2120 S Ashland Ave (US 41 Business/WI 32) (54304). 920/494-5641; FAX 920/494-4032. 23 rms, some kits. S $29.50-$35; D $39.50-$56; under 12 free. Crib $5. Pet accepted, some restrictions. TV; cable (premium). Restaurant nearby. Ck-out 11 am. Coin lndry. Sundries. Microwaves avail. Picnic tables. Cr cds: DS, MC, V.

⭐ **SUPER 8.** 2868 S Oneida St (54304). 920/494-2042; FAX 920/494-6959. 84 rms, 2 story. Mid-June-Oct: S $53.88-$57.88; D $63.88-$67.88; lower rates rest of yr. Crib free. Pet accepted. TV; cable, VCR avail. Complimentary continental bkfst. Restaurant nearby. Ck-out 11 am. Coin lndry. Meeting rm. Business servs avail. Sauna. Whirlpool. Microwaves avail. Cr cds: A, D, DS, MC, V.

D ⚡ ⋈ ⋈ ⋈ SC

Motor Hotels

★ ★ **BEST WESTERN MIDWAY HOTEL.** *780 Packer Dr (54304). 920/499-3161; FAX 920/499-9401.* 145 rms, 2 story. S $65-$71; D $76-$82; each addl $7; under 12 free. Crib free. TV. Indoor pool; whirlpool. Restaurant 7 am-10 pm. Rm serv. Bar 11-1 am. Ck-out 11 am. Meeting rms. Business servs avail. In-rm modem link. Bellhops. Valet serv. Sundries. Free airport transportation. Downhill ski 10 mi; x-country ski 15 mi. Exercise equipt; rower, bicycle, sauna. Health club privileges. Game rm. Lambeau Field adj. Cr cds: A, C, D, DS, JCB, MC, V.

⋈ ⋈ ≬ ⋈ ⋈ SC

★ ★ **DAYS INN.** *406 N Washington St (54301), at Main St, adj to Port Plaza. 920/435-4484; FAX 920/435-3120.* 98 rms, 3 story. S $55-$85; D $65-$95; suites $70-$100; each addl $5; under 18 free. Crib free. Pet accepted. TV. Indoor pool. Restaurant 6:30 am-2 pm, 5-9 pm. Rm serv. Bar 3 pm-midnight. Ck-out noon. Meeting rms. Business servs avail. In-rm modem link. Valet serv. Sundries. Health club privileges. Microwaves avail. Overlooks Fox River. Cr cds: A, C, D, DS, ER, MC, V.

D ⚡ ⋈ ⋈ ⋈ SC

★ ★ **HOLIDAY INN-CITY CENTRE.** *200 Main St (US 141/WI 29) (54301). 920/437-5900; FAX 920/437-1199.* 149 rms, 7 story. S, D $89; family rates. Crib free. Pet accepted, some restrictions. TV; cable (premium). Indoor pool; whirlpool. Coffee in rms. Restaurant 6 am-10 pm. Rm serv. Bar 10-1 am; entertainment. Ck-out noon. Coin lndry. Meeting rms. Business servs avail. Bellhops. Valet serv. Sundries. Sauna. Health club privileges. On Fox River; marina. Luxury level. Cr cds: A, C, D, DS, JCB, MC, V.

D ⚡ ⋈ ⋈ ⋈ SC

★ ★ ★ **RADISSON INN.** *2040 Airport Dr (54313), near Austin Straubel Field Airport. 920/494-7300; FAX 920/494-9599.* Web www.radisson.com. 301 rms, 3, 6 story. S $99; D $119; each addl $10; suites $159-$279; under 18 free; wkend rates. TV; cable. Indoor pool; whirlpool. Restaurant 6 am-10 pm, wkends 7 am-11 pm. Rm serv. Bar 11-1:30 am; entertainment. Meeting rms. Business servs avail. In-rm modem link. Bellhops. Valet serv. Free airport transportation. Exercise equipt; stair machine, bicycles, sauna. Some bathrm phones, in-rm whirlpools, refrigerators, fireplaces. Cr cds: A, C, D, DS, ER, JCB, MC, V.

D ⋈ ≬ ⋈ ⋈ ⋈ SC

★ ★ ★ **RAMADA INN.** *2750 Ramada Way (54304), 1/2 mi E of US 41, Oneida St exit. 920/499-0631; FAX 920/499-5476.* 156 rms, 5 story. S $60-$95; D $73-$105; each addl $10; under 19 free. Crib free. TV; cable. Indoor pool; whirlpool. Restaurant 6 am-10 pm. Rm serv. Bar noon-1 am; entertainment Fri-Sat. Ck-out noon. Meeting rms. Business servs avail. Bellhops. Valet serv. Sundries. Free airport transportation. Putting green. Exercise equipt; bicycle, stair machine, sauna. Health club privileges. Game rm. Some balconies. Cr cds: A, C, D, DS, JCB, MC, V.

D ⋈ ≬ ⋈ ⋈ SC

Inns

★ ★ **ASTOR HOUSE.** *637 S Monroe Ave (54301). 920/432-3585; FAX 920/436-3145; res: 800/303-6370.* E-mail astor@execpc.com; web www.bestinns/usa/wi/astor.html. 5 rms, 4 with shower only, 3 story. S, D $79-$99; $109-$149 wkends. TV; cable, VCR (movies). Complimentary continental bkfst. Restaurant nearby. Ck-out 11 am, ck-in 4-6 pm. In-rm modem link. Luggage handling. X-country ski 10 mi. Some in-rm whirlpools, fireplaces. Built in 1888; antiques. Totally nonsmoking. Cr cds: A, DS, MC, V.

 ⋈ ⋈ ⋈

★ ★ ★ **JAMES STREET INN.** *(201 James St, DePere 54115) 920/337-0111; FAX 920/337-6135; res: 800/897-8483.* 30 rms, 4 story. S $69-$119; D $79-$129; each addl $5; suites $89-$129; under 12 free. Crib free. TV; cable (premium), VCR avail (movies). Complimentary continental bkfst. Restaurant nearby. Ck-out noon, ck-in 3 pm. Business servs avail. X-country ski 2 mi. Some in-rm whirlpools, microwaves. Old flour mill built in 1858. Cr cds: A, DS, MC, V.

D ⚡ ⋈ ⋈ ⋈ SC

Restaurants

★ ★ **EVE'S SUPPER CLUB.** *2020 Riverside Dr (WI 57) (54301). 920/435-1571.* Hrs: 11 am-2 pm, 5-10 pm; Sat from 5 pm. Closed Sun; Thanksgiving, Dec 24, 25. Res accepted Mon-Thurs. Bar. Semi-a la carte: lunch $2.50-$10.95, dinner $5.95-$35. Specializes in steak, seafood. View of Fox River. Cr cds: A, C, D, DS, MC, V.

★ ★ **LA BONNE FEMME.** *123 S Washington St (54301). 920/432-2897.* Hrs: 5-9 pm. Closed Sun; most major hols. Res accepted. Contemporary French menu. Serv bar. A la carte entrees: lunch $5.25-$8.75, dinner $18-$24. Specialties: sautéed veal with morel mushroom sauce, grilled salmon steak au saffron. Country French atmosphere. Totally nonsmoking. Cr cds: MC, V.

★ ★ **RIVERS BEND SUPPER CLUB.** *(792 Riverview Dr, Howard 54303) US 41, Velp Ave exit. 920/434-1383.* Hrs: 11:30 am-2 pm, 5-10 pm; Fri to 10:30 pm; Sat 5-10:30 pm; Sun 4:30-9 pm. Closed some major hols. Res accepted. Bar to 1 am. Semi-a la carte: lunch $3.95-$8, dinner $6-$29. Child's meals. Specializes in prime rib, steak, seafood. Salad bar. Local artwork on display. Overlooks Duck Creek. Cr cds: A, C, D, DS, MC, V.

D

★ ★ **THE WELLINGTON.** *1060 Hansen Rd (54304). 920/499-2000.* Hrs: 11:30 am-2 pm, 5-10 pm; Sat from 5 pm. Closed Sun; some major hols. Res accepted Mon-Fri. Semi-a la carte: lunch $6-$9.50, dinner $15.50-$19.50. Child's meals. Specializes in beef Wellington, fresh seafood. Outdoor patio dining. Cr cds: A, D, MC, V.

D

Green Lake (F-4)

(See also Fond du Lac, Waupun)

Pop 1,064 **Elev** 828 ft **Area code** 414 **Zip** 54941
Information Chamber of Commerce, 550 Mill St, PO Box 386; 414/294-3231.

This county seat, known as the oldest resort community west of Niagara Falls, is a popular four-season recreational area. Green Lake, 7,325 acres, is the deepest natural lake in the state and affords good fishing, including lake trout, swimming, sailing, powerboating and iceboating.

What to See and Do

Green Lake Conference Center/American Baptist Assembly. A 1,000-acre all-yr vacation-conference center. Activities include cross-country skiing (rentals), tobogganing, ice-skating; also camping (fee), fishing, hiking, biking, indoor swimming, tennis, 36-hole golf. (Daily) Phone 414/294-3323. ¢

Lake Cruises. 1¼-hr narrated cruise. (June-Aug, daily; May, Sept-Oct, Sat-Sun) Also dinner, brunch cruises; private charters. At Heidel House, Illinois Ave. For reservations phone 414/294-3344 or 800/444-2812. Narrated cruise ¢¢¢

Motel

★ **BAY VIEW.** *439 Lake St, off WI 23.* 414/294-6504. 17 rms, 2 story, 7 kits. May-Oct: S, D $78-$88; each addl $6; suites $180; golf plans; lower rates rest of yr. Crib $6. TV; cable. Coffee in rms. Restaurant nearby. Ck-out 10 am. X-country ski 5 mi. Pontoon, fishing boats; motors, launching ramp, dockage, boat-trailer parking. Freezer facilities. Picnic tables, grills. On lake. Cr cds: MC, V.

Inns

★ ★ **CARVERS ON THE LAKE.** *N5529 County Rd A.* 920/294-6931. 9 rms, 2 with shower only, 2 story. Some rm phones. Memorial Day-Sept: S, D $65-$150; kit. units $165; wkly rates; 2-day min wkends; lower rates rest of yr. TV; cable. Complimentary continental bkfst. Restaurant (see CARVERS ON THE LAKE). Rm serv. Ck-out 11 am, ck-in 3 pm. 18-hole golf privileges. X-country ski adj. Some microwaves, in-rm whirlpools, fireplaces. Picnic tables. On lake. Built 1925; antiques. Totally nonsmoking. Cr cds: MC, V.

★ **OAKWOOD LODGE.** *365 Lake St.* 920/294-6580; *res:* 800/498-8087. 12 rms, 2 story. No A/C. No rm phones. May-Sept: S, D $82-$108; each addl $20; golf plans; lower rates rest of yr. Crib free. TV in sitting rm; cable (premium), VCR avail. Complimentary full bkfst. Ck-out 11 am, ck-in 3 pm. X-country ski 5 mi. Microwaves avail. In-rm whirlpool. Some balconies. Grills. Built 1866; antique furnishings. On Green Lake; swimming. Totally nonsmoking. Cr cds: MC, V.

Resort

★ ★ ★ **HEIDEL HOUSE RESORT & CONFERENCE CENTER.** *643 Illinois Ave, 2 mi SE off WI 23.* 414/294-3344; *FAX* 414/294-6128; *res:* 800/444-2812 (WI). 200 rms, 1-5 story. June-Aug: S, D $129-$475; each addl $15; under 16 free; wkend, mid-wk rates; lower rates rest of yr. Crib free. TV; cable (premium), VCR avail (movies). 2 pools, 1 indoor; 2 whirlpools. Supervised child's activities (late May-early Sept); ages 4-12. Coffee in rms. Dining rm 6:30 am-10 pm. Rm serv. Bar 10:30-1:30 am; entertainment. Ck-out 11 am, ck-in 3 pm. Meeting rms. Business center. Valet serv. Gift shop. Airport transportation. Tennis. Dock; yacht cruises, charter fishing boats. Ice fishing. Exercise equipt; bicycles, treadmill, sauna. Game rm. Lawn games. Some microwaves, in-rm whirlpools, refrigerators. Picnic tables. 20-acre estate on Green Lake. Golf course adj. Cr cds: A, DS, MC, V.

Restaurants

★ ★ **ALFRED'S SUPPER CLUB.** *506 Hill St.* 920/294-3631. Hrs: 5-11 pm. Closed Mon in winter. Res accepted. Italian, Amer menu. Bar. Semi-a la carte: dinner $9-$25. Child's meals. Specializes in steak, pasta. Salad bar. Cr cds: DS, MC, V.

★ ★ **CARVERS ON THE LAKE.** *(See Carvers On The Lake Inn)* 920/294-6931. Hrs: 5 pm to closing. Closed Mon. Res accepted. Bar. Wine list. Semi-a la carte: dinner $16-$23.75. Child's meals. Specializes in fresh seafood, regional dishes, pasta. Own baking. Dining in old English country house; antiques. Cr cds: MC, V.

★ ★ **NORTON'S MARINE DINING ROOM.** *380 S Lawson Dr.* 920/294-6577. Hrs: 11 am-3 pm, 5-10 pm. Closed Dec 24, 25. Bar to 2 am. Semi-a la carte: lunch $3.25-$11.95, dinner $8.50-$39.95. Specializes in steak, seafood. Outdoor dining. Overlooks Green Lake. Cr cds: A, MC, V.

Hales Corners

(see Milwaukee)

Hayward (C-2)

(See also Cable, Spooner)

Settled 1881 **Pop** 1,897 **Elev** 1,198 ft **Area code** 715 **Zip** 54843

A Ranger District office of the Chequamegon National Forest (see PARK FALLS) is located here.

What to See and Do

Historyland. Logging camp. Walk-through tours; Native American museum. (Memorial Day-Labor Day, daily) 1 mi E on County B, off WI 27. Phone 715/634-4801. **Free.**

National Fresh Water Fishing Hall of Fame. A 143-ft long and 4^{1}/$_{2}$-story high walk-thru "muskie"; the mouth serves as an observation deck. Museum and educational complex contains more than 400 mounts representing many world species; world records and record photo gallery and library; thousands of angling artifacts; 350 outboard motor relics. Project covers 6 acres and includes 4 other museum display buildings. (Mid-Apr-Nov, daily) Snack shop, gift shop, playground with fish theme. 1 Hall of Fame Dr, off WI 27. Phone 715/634-4440. ¢¢

Annual Event

Lumberjack World Championship. On County B. Logrolling, tree chopping, climbing and sawing. Late July.

Motels

★ ★ **AMERICINN.** *620 E First St.* 715/634-2700; *res:* 800/634-3444; *FAX* 715/634-3958. 41 rms, 2 story. S $58.90-$68.90; each addl $71.90-$81.90; each addl $6; suites $81.90-$99.90; under 11 free; higher rates special events. Crib free. Pet accepted, some restrictions; $6. TV; cable (premium), VCR avail. Complimentary continental bkfst. Restaurant nearby. Ck-out 11 am. Meeting rms. Business servs avail. Downhill ski 20 mi; x-country ski adj. Sauna. Indoor pool; whirlpool. Game rm. Rec rm. Some in-rm whirlpools, refrigerators, microwaves. Picnic tables. Cr cds: A, C, D, DS, MC, V.

★ **CEDAR INN.** *WI 63 & 77.* 715/634-5332; *FAX* 715/634-1343; *res:* 800/776-2478. 22 rms. Memorial Day-early Oct: S $46-$56; D $51-$71; each addl $5; suites $100-$130; under 5 free; higher rates Birkebeiner Ski Race; lower rates rest of yr. Crib $5. TV; cable (premium). Complimentary continental bkfst. Restaurant nearby. Ck-out 10:30 am. Business servs avail. In-rm modem link. X-country ski 3 mi. Sauna. Whirlpool. Refrigerators; microwaves avail. Cr cds: A, DS, MC, V.

★ ★ **COUNTRY INN & SUITES.** *WI 27S.* 715/634-4100; *FAX* 715/634-2403. 66 rms, 2 story, 8 suites. June-Sept: S, D $68-$78; each addl $6; suites $78-$113; under 18 free; wkend rates; higher rates special events; lower rates rest of yr. Crib free. Pet accepted, some restrictions. TV; cable (premium). Complimentary continental bkfst. Coffee in rms. Restaurant 11 am-10:30 pm; closed Sun. Rm serv. Bar 11 am-midnight. Ck-out noon. Meeting rms. Business servs avail. In-rm modem link. X-country ski 4 mi. Indoor pool; whirlpool. Game rm. Bathrm phones, refrigerators, microwaves, wet bars; some in-rm whirlpools. Cr cds: A, C, D, DS, MC, V.

★ **NORTHERN PINE INTERNATIONAL INN.** *Rte 6, Box 6489, 1^{1}/$_{4}$ mi S on WI 27.* 715/634-4959; *FAX* 715/634-8999; *res:* 800/777-

7996. 39 rms. June-mid-Sept, mid-Dec-Feb: S, D $59-$69; each addl $5; suites $89-$99; under 12 free; lower rates rest of yr. Crib avail. TV; cable. Pool; whirlpool. Playground. Complimentary continental bkfst. Ck-out 11 am. Meeting rms. Business servs avail. Downhill ski 20 mi; x-country ski 1 mi. Sauna. Game rm. Some refrigerators, in-rm whirlpools; microwaves avail. Some patios. Picnic tables. Cr cds: A, DS, MC, V.

★ **NORTHWOODS.** *Rte 6, Box 6453, 1¹/₂ mi S on WI 27.* 715/634-8088; res: 800/232-9202. 9 rms. S $41; D $46; each addl $5; kit. suite $65; family rates; higher rates special events (3-day min). Crib free. Pet accepted. TV; cable. Complimentary coffee in lobby. Ck-out 10 am. Downhill ski 19 mi; x-country ski 3 mi. Cr cds: A, C, D, DS, MC, V.

★ **SUPER 8.** *317 South Dakota Ave, On WI 27.* 715/634-2646; FAX 715/634-6482. 46 rms, 1-2 story. Apr-Sept: S $49.88; D $55.88-$58.88; each addl $5; under 12 free; higher rates special events; lower rates rest of yr. Crib $5. Pet accepted. TV; cable (premium). Indoor pool; whirlpool. Complimentary coffee in lobby. Restaurant adj 5:30 am-9 pm. Ck-out 11 am. X-country ski 2 mi. Game rm. Cr cds: A, C, D, DS, MC, V.

Restaurant

★ **KARIBALIS.** *212 Main St.* 715/634-2462. Hrs: Memorial Day-Labor Day: 11 am-10 pm; Sun to 9 pm. Closed Easter, Thanksgiving, Dec 25. Res accepted. Bar to midnight. Semi-a la carte: lunch $5.50-$7.95, dinner $5.95-$13.50. Child's meals. Specializes in steak, seafood, pasta. Salad bar. Outdoor dining. Family-owned. Cr cds: A, DS, MC, V.

Hudson (D-1)

Pop 6,378 **Elev** 780 ft **Area code** 715 **Zip** 54016
Information Hudson Area Chamber of Commerce, 502 2nd St; 715/386-8411 or 800/657-6775.

What to See and Do

Octagon House (1855). Octagonal home furnished in the style of gracious living of the 1800s; garden house museum with country store and lumbering and farming implements; carriage house museum with blacksmith shop and special display areas. (May-Oct, daily exc Mon; 1st 3 wks Dec; closed hols) 1004 3rd St. Phone 715/386-2654. ¢¢

Willow River State Park. A 2,800-acre park with swimming; fishing; boating, canoeing. Cross-country skiing. Picnicking. Camping (hookups, dump station). Naturalist programs (summer only). River scenery with two dams. Standard fees. (Daily) 5 mi N on County A. Phone 715/386-5931. Per vehicle ¢¢

Motels

★ ★ **BEST WESTERN HUDSON HOUSE INN.** *1616 Crest View Dr.* 715/386-2394; FAX 715/386-3167. 102 rms, 1-2 story. S $49-$54; D $57-$64; each addl $6; studio rm $81-$160; under 13 free. Crib free. TV; cable (premium). Indoor pool. Restaurant 5-9 pm. Rm serv from 9 am. Bar 11:30-1 am; entertainment Fri, Sat. Ck-out 11 am. Meeting rms. Business servs avail. In-rm modem link. Valet serv. Sundries. Beauty shop. Downhill ski 8 mi. Cr cds: A, C, D, DS, MC, V.

★ ★ **COMFORT INN.** *811 Dominion Dr, 1 mi SE, just off I-94 exit 2.* 715/386-6355; FAX 715/386-9778. 60 rms, 2 story. S $44.95-$62.95; D $47.95-$72.95; each addl $5; under 18 free. Crib free. Pet accepted, some restrictions; $50. TV; cable (premium), VCR avail. Indoor pool; whirlpool.

Complimentary continental bkfst. Restaurant nearby. Ck-out 11 am. Guest lndry. Business servs avail. Cr cds: A, C, D, DS, ER, JCB, MC, V.

Inn

★ ★ ★ **PHIPPS.** *1005 3rd St.* 715/386-0800; FAX 715/386-0509. 6 rms, 3 story, 3 suites. No rm phones. S, D $89-$179. Complimentary full bkfst; afternoon refreshments. Ck-out 11 am, ck-in 4-6 pm. Downhill ski 8 mi; x-country ski 1 mi. In-rm whirlpools. Restored Queen Anne-style Victorian mansion (1884); formal music rm with baby grand piano, two parlors, 3 porches. Totally nonsmoking. Cr cds: MC, V.

Hurley (B-3)

(See also Manitowish Waters; also see Ironwood, MI)

Founded 1885 **Pop** 1,782 **Elev** 1,493 ft **Area code** 715 **Zip** 54534
E-mail hurley@mail.gogebic.cc.mi.us **Web** visit-usa.com/wi/hurley
Information Chamber of Commerce, 207 Silver St; 715/561-4334.

Originally a lumberjack and mining town, Hurley is now a winter sports center.

What to See and Do

Iron County Historical Museum. Exhibits of county's iron mining past; local artifacts; photo gallery. (Daily; closed Dec 25) Iron St at 3rd Ave S. Phone 715/561-2244. **Free.**

Whitecap Mountain Ski Area. Area has 6 chairlifts, rope tow; patrol, school, rentals; nursery; restaurant, cafeteria, concession area. Longest run 5,000 ft; vertical drop 400 ft. (Nov-Mar, daily) Half-day rates. 8 mi W on WI 77 to Iron Belt, then 3 mi W on County E. Phone 715/561-2227. ¢¢¢¢

Annual Events

Paavo Nurmi Marathon. Begins in Upson, SW via WI 77. Oldest marathon in state. Phone 715/561-4334. Related activities Fri-Sat. 2nd wkend Aug.

Red Light Snowmobile Rally. Phone 715/561-4334. 2nd wkend Dec.

Motel

★ ★ **HOLIDAY INN.** *1000 10th Ave, S of jct US 2, 51.* 715/561-3030; FAX 715/561-4280. 100 rms, 2 story. S $48-$65; D $62-$77; each addl $6; under 19 free; higher rates some winter hol wks & winter wkends. Crib free. Pet accepted. TV; cable. Indoor pool; whirlpool. Restaurant 7 am-2 pm, 5:30-10 pm. Rm serv. Bar 11-1 am. Ck-out noon. Coin lndry. Meeting rms. Business servs avail. Valet serv. Downhill/x-country ski 15 mi. Snowmobile trails. Game rm. Cr cds: A, C, D, DS, JCB, MC, V.

Janesville (G-4)

(See also Beloit, Fort Atkinson, Madison)

Founded 1836 **Pop** 52,133 **Elev** 858 ft **Area code** 608
Information Janesville Area Convention & Visitors Bureau, 51 S Jackson St, 53545; 608/757-3160 or 800/487-2757.

In 1836, pioneer Henry F. Janes carved his initials into a tree on the bank of the Rock River. The site is now the intersection of the two main streets of industrial Janesville. Janes went on to found other Janesvilles in Iowa and in Minnesota. Wisconsin's Janesville has a truck and bus assembly plant that offers tours. Because of its 1,900 acres of parkland, Janesville has been called "Wisconsin's Park Place."

What to See and Do

General Motors Corp. Guided tours (Mon-Thurs; closed hols). No cameras. 1000 Industrial Ave. Phone 608/756-7681.   **Free.**

Lincoln-Tallman Restorations. Tallman House (1855-1857), 26-rm antebellum mansion of Italianate design considered among the top 10 mid-19th-century structures for the study of American culture at the time of the Civil War. Restored Greek-revival Stone House (1842). Horse Barn (1855-1857) serves as visitors center and museum shop. Tours (daily). 440 N Jackson St, 4 blks N on US 14 Business. Phone 608/752-4519. Tours ¢¢

Milton House Museum (1844). Hexagonal building constructed of grout; underground railroad tunnel connects it with original log cabin; country store; guided tours. (Memorial Day-Labor Day, daily; May, Sept-mid-Oct, wkends, also Mon-Fri by appt) 18 S Janesville St in Milton, 8 mi NE at jct WI 26, 59. Phone 608/868-7772.   ¢¢

Municipal parks. Riverside. Boat launching, picnicking, fishing, wading pool; hiking; cross-country skiing, tennis courts; 18-hole golf; concession. N Washington St, N on US 14 Business. **Palmer.** Picnicking, wading pool; tennis courts, swimming beach, exercise course, 9-hole golf, concession. E Racine St, E on US 14 Business, exit WI 11. **Traxler.** Boat launching ramps for Rock River, fishing; ice-skating; waterski shows; rose gardens; children's fishing pond; picnicking. (Daily, May-Sept) N Parker Dr, ½ mi N on US 51. **Rockport.** Swimming pool, bathhouse; cross-country skiing, hiking. 2800 Rockport Rd.   **Free.**

Rotary Gardens. 12-acre botanical garden (Daily) 1455 Palmer Dr. Phone 608/752-3885. Guided tour ¢¢

Annual Event

Rock County 4-H Fair. Rock County 4-H Fairgrounds. One of largest 4-H fairs in country. Exhibits, competitions, carnival, grandstand shows, concerts. Phone 608/755-1470. Last wk July.

Seasonal Event

Waterski show. Traxler Park. Wed & Sun, Memorial Day-Labor Day.

Motels

✔★ **BEST WESTERN JANESVILLE MOTOR LODGE.** *3900 Milton Ave (53546), jct I-90, WI 26.* 608/756-4511. 106 rms, 3 story. May-Sept: S, D $65-$80; each addl $5; suites $95-$140; under 12 free; lower rates rest of yr. Crib free. Pet accepted. TV; cable. Indoor pool; whirlpool. Complimentary coffee in rms. Restaurant 6-9 pm; wkends 7 am-10 pm. Rm serv. Bar 4 pm-1 am. Ck-out noon. Meeting rms. Business servs avail. Airport transportation. Exercise equipt; treadmill, weight machine. Game rm. Cr cds: A, C, D, DS, JCB, MC, V.

D ✦ ≈ ✕ 🐾 SC

★★ **RAMADA INN.** *3431 Milton Ave (53545).* 608/756-2341; FAX 608/756-4183. 189 rms, 2 story. S $56-$62; D $62-$70; suites $125-$150; each addl $6; under 18 free. Crib free. TV; cable (premium). Complimentary continental bkfst (Mon-Fri). Indoor pool; whirlpool. Restaurant 6 am-1:30 pm, 5-10 pm. Rm serv. Bar 11-1 am. Ck-out noon. Meeting rms. Business servs avail. Sundries. Gift shop. Putting green. Exercise equipt; bicycle, stair machine, sauna. Game rm. Cr cds: A, C, D, DS, JCB, MC, V.

D ≈ ✕ ≋ 🐾 SC

Kenosha (G-6)

(See also Lake Geneva, Milwaukee, Racine; also see Waukegan, IL)

Settled 1835 **Pop** 80,352 **Elev** 610 ft **Area code** 414 **E-mail** KReiche@visit.kenoshal.com **Web** visit.kenoshal.com

Information Kenosha Area Convention & Visitors Bureau, 800 55th St, 53140; 414/654-7307 or 800/654-7309.

A major industrial city, port and transportation center, Kenosha was settled by New Englanders. The city owns 84 percent of its Lake Michigan frontage, most of it developed as parks.

What to See and Do

Bong State Recreation Area. A 4,515-acre area. Swimming; fishing; boating. Hiking, bridle, off-road motorcycle trails. Cross-country skiing, snowmobiling. Picnicking. Guided nature hikes; nature center; special events area. Family, group camping (fee). 17 mi W via WI 142; 9 mi W of I-94. Phone 414/878-5600 or 414/652-0377. Non-residents ¢¢¢

Carthage College (1847). (2,100 students) Civil War Museum in Johnson Art Center (Mon-Fri; closed hols). 2001 Alford Park Dr, WI 32, N edge of city on lakeside.Phone 414/551-8500.   **Free.**

Factory outlet stores. More than 170 outlet stores can be found at **Factory Outlet Center,** 7700 120th Ave; 414/857-7961 and **Lakeside Marketplace,** 11211 120th Ave; 414/857-2101. (Daily)

Kemper Center. Approx 11 acres. Several buildings including Italianate Victorian mansion (1860); complex has more than 100 different trees, rose collection; mosiac mural; outdoor tennis courts; picnic area; also Anderson Art Gallery (Thurs-Sun afternoons). Guided tours by appt. (Office, Mon-Fri; grounds, daily) 6501 3rd Ave. Phone 414/657-6005.   **Free.**

Kenosha County Historical Society and Museum. Items & settings of local & Wisconsin history, Native American material, folk and decorative art. Research library. (Tues-Sun afternoons; closed hols) 6300 3rd Ave. Phone 414/654-5770.   **Free.**

Kenosha Public Museum. Lorado Taft dioramas of famous art studios; Native American, Oceanic and African arts; Oriental ivory and porcelain; Wisconsin folk pottery; mammals exhibit; dinosaur exhibit. Changing art, natural history exhibits. (Daily; closed hols) Civic Center. 5608 10th Ave. Phone 414/653-4140.   **Free.**

Southport Marina. 2-mi walkway on Lake Michigan; playground. (Daily) From 97th to 57th Sts. Phone 414/657-5565.   **Free.**

University of Wisconsin-Parkside (1968). (5,100 students) A 700-acre campus. Buildings are connected by glass-walled interior corridors that radiate from $8-million tri-level Wyllie Library Learning Center. Nature, cross-country ski trails. Tours. Wood Rd. Phone 414/595-2355.

Seasonal Event

Bristol Renaissance Fair. 6 mi SW via I-94, Russell Rd exit, just N of the IL/WI state line. Re-creation of a 16th-century European marketplace featuring royal knights and swordsmen, master jousters, musicians, mimes, dancers and hundreds of craftsmen and food peddlers. Richly gowned ladies, tattered beggars, barbarians and soldiers stroll the grounds. Procession is heralded by trumpets and the royal drum corps. Phone 414/396-4320, 847/395-7773 or 800/52-FAIRE. Nine wkends beginning last wkend June.

Motels

✔★ **BUDGETEL INN.** *7540 118th Ave (53142), at jct I-94, WI 50.* 414/857-7911; FAX 414/857-2370. 95 rms, 2 story. S $43.95; D $46.95-$48.95; each addl $7; higher rates wkends; under 18 free. Crib free. Pet accepted. TV; cable (premium). Complimentary continental bkfst. Complimentary coffee in rms. Restaurant adj open 24 hrs. Ck-out noon.

Business servs avail. In-rm modem link. Valet serv. Downhill ski 15 mi. Cr cds: A, C, D, DS, MC, V.

★ **KNIGHTS INN.** 7221 122nd Ave (53142), off I-94 exit 344 (WI 50). 414/857-2622; FAX 414/857-2375. 113 rms, 14 kits. June-Oct: S, D $47.95-$69.95; each addl $5; kit. units $62.95-$68.95; under 18 free; higher rates wkends; lower rates rest of yr. Crib free. Pet accepted. TV. Complimentary coffee in lobby. Restaurant nearby. Ck-out noon. Business servs avail. Cr cds: A, C, D, DS, MC, V.

Motor Hotel

★ ★ **HOLIDAY INN EXPRESS.** 5125 6th Ave (53140). 414/658-3281; FAX 414/658-3420. 111 rms, 5 story. S, D 69-$89; under 19 free. Crib free. TV; cable (premium). Sauna. Indoor pool; whirlpool. Ck-out 11 am. Meeting rms. Business servs avail. On Lake Michigan. Cr cds: A, C, D, DS, JCB, MC, V.

Inn

★ ★ ★ **MANOR HOUSE.** 6536 3rd Ave (53143). 414/658-0014; FAX 414/653-9876. 6 rms, 3 story. S, D $100-$199. TV; VCR avail. Complimentary full bkfst. Ck-out 11 am, ck-in 2 pm. Meeting rms. Business servs avail. Tennis privileges. Downhill ski 20 mi; x-country ski 5 mi. Bicycles. Overlooking Lake Michigan. Restored mansion (1920); antique furnishings. Cr cds: A, MC, V.

Restaurants

★ ★ **HOUSE OF GERHARD.** 3927 75th St (53142). 414/694-5212. Hrs: 11:30 am-10 pm. Closed Sun; Dec 24-25; also 1 wk early July. Res accepted. German/Amer menu. Bar. Semi-a la carte: lunch $4.50-$11.95, dinner $8.95-$16. Child's meals. Specialties: schnitzel, rouladen, Cajun dishes. German decor. Family-owned. Cr cds: A, DS, MC, V.

★ ★ **MANGIA TRATTORIA.** 5717 Sheridan Rd. 414/652-4285. Hrs: 11:30 am-2 pm, 5-9 pm; Fri to 10 pm; Sat 5-10 pm; Sun 11 am-2 pm brunch, 4-9 pm. Closed some major hols. Res accepted. Italian menu. Bar. Semi-a la carte: lunch, dinner $9-$20. Specializes in pasta, fresh seafood, wood-burning oven pizza. Outdoor dining. Cr cds: A, D, DS, MC, V.

★ ★ ★ **RAY RADIGAN'S.** 11712 S Sheridan Rd (11712). 414/694-0455. Hrs: 11 am-10 pm; Fri, Sat to 11 pm; Sun from noon. Closed Mon; Dec 24-25. Res accepted. Bar. Semi-a la carte: lunch $5-$10, dinner $11.95-$30. Specializes in fresh seafood, steak. Own baking. Family-owned. Cr cds: A, C, D, DS, MC, V.

Lac du Flambeau (C-4)

(See also Manitowish Waters, Minocqua, Woodruff)

Pop 1,423 **Elev** 1,635 ft **Area code** 715 **Zip** 54538
Information Chamber of Commerce, PO Box 158; 715/588-3346.

The French gave this village the name "Lake of the Torch" because of the Chippewa practice of fishing and canoeing at night by the light of birch bark torches. Located in the center of the Lac du Flambeau Reservation, the village is tribal headquarters for more than 1,200 Chippewa still living in the area. It is also the center for a popular, lake-filled north woods recreation area. The reservation boasts 126 spring-fed lakes and its own fish hatchery.

What to See and Do

Chequamegon National Forest. S on County D, then W on WI 70. (See PARK FALLS)

Lac du Flambeau Chippewa Museum & Cultural Center. Displays of Native American artifacts, fur trading and historical items. Chippewa craft workshops (May-Oct). (Daily exc Sun; also by appt) Downtown. Phone 715/588-3333. ¢

Waswagoning Ojibwe Village. 20 acres of Ojibwe culture with guided tours. (Memorial Day-Labor Day). 1 mi N on County H. Phone 715/588-3560. ¢¢¢

Annual Event

Colorama. Last Sat Sept.

Seasonal Event

Powwows. At Indian Bowl, fronting on Lake Interlaken. Dancing by Waswa-gon Dancers. Tues evenings. July-mid-Aug.

Resort

★ ★ **DILLMAN'S SAND LAKE LODGE.** 3½ mi NE on County D. 715/588-3143; FAX 715/588-3110. 17 units, 18 cottages. No A/C. EP, mid-May-mid-Oct: daily, from $68/person; wkly, from $455/person; MAP avail; family rates. Closed rest of yr. Crib free. Pet accepted. TV in lobby, some rms. Playground. Dining rm (public by res) 8-9:30 am. Box lunches, cookouts. Serv bar. Ck-out 10 am, ck-in 2 pm. Package store. Meeting rms. Sports dir in summer. Tennis. Practice fairway. Sand beaches; water-skiing; windsurfing; scuba diving; boats, motors, kayaks, sailboats, canoes; private launch, covered boathouse. Archery. Bicycles. Lawn games. Hiking trails. Soc dir; wine & cheese party Sun. Nature study, photography, painting workshops. Rec rm. Fishing clean & store area. Some fireplaces; refrigerator in suites & cottages. On 250 acres. No cr cds accepted.

La Crosse (F-2)

(See also Galesville, Sparta)

Settled 1842 **Pop** 51,003 **Elev** 669 ft **Area code** 608 **E-mail** lacvb@century.net **Web** www.wi.centuryinter.net/lacvb
Information La Crosse Area Convention and Visitor Bureau, 410 E Veterans Memorial Dr, 54601; 608/782-2366 or 800/658-9424.

An agricultural, commercial and industrial city, La Crosse is washed by the waters of the Mississippi, the Black and La Crosse rivers. Once a trading post, it was named by the French for the native game the French called lacrosse. More than 200 businesses and industries operate here today.

What to See and Do

Goose Island County Park. Beach; fishing; boat ramps. Hiking trails. Picnicking. Camping (electric hookups). (Mid-Apr-mid-Oct, daily) 7 mi S on WI 35, then 2 mi W on County GI. Phone 608/788-7018. Camping ¢¢¢

Granddad Bluff. Tallest (1,172 ft) of the crags that overlook the city; it provides a panoramic view of the winding Mississippi, the tree-shaded city, and the Minnesota and Iowa bluffs. Picnic area. (May-late Oct, daily) Surfaced path to shelter house & top of bluff for the disabled. Bliss Rd, 2 mi E. Phone 608/789-7533. **Free.**

Hixon House (ca 1860). 15-rm home; Victorian and Oriental furnishings. Visitor information center and gift shop in building that once served as wash house. (Memorial Day-Labor Day, daily) 429 N 7th St. Phone 608/782-1980. ¢¢

Industrial tour, G. Heileman Brewing Co, Inc. One-hr guided tours. Gift shop. (Daily exc Sun; closed exc hols) 1111 S 3rd St. Phone 608/782-2337 or 800/433-BEER. **Free.**

La Crosse Queen **Cruises.** Sightseeing cruise on the Mississippi River aboard 150-passenger, double-deck paddlewheeler (early May-mid-Oct), daily). Also dinner cruise (Fri night, Sat & Sun). Charters (approx Apr-Oct). Boat Dock, Riverside Park, W end of State St. For schedule and additional fee information phone ticket office, 608/784-2893 or 608/784-8523. ¢¢¢

Mt La Crosse Ski Area. Area has 3 chairlifts, rope tow; patrol, rentals, school; snowmaking; night skiing; cafeteria, bar. Longest run 5,300 ft; vertical drop 516 ft. (Thanksgiving-mid-Mar, daily; closed Dec 25) Half-day rates on weekends, holidays. Cross-country trails (Dec-mid-Mar, daily). 2 mi S on WI 35. Phone 608/788-0044 or 800/426-3665. ¢¢¢¢¢

Pump House (Western Wisconsin Regional Arts). Regional art exhibits; performing arts (wkends). (Daily exc Sun; closed hols) 119 King St. Phone 608/785-1434. **Free.**

Swarthout Museum. Changing historical exhibits ranging from prehistoric times to the 20th century. (Memorial Day-Labor Day, Tues-Sat; rest of yr, daily exc Mon; closed hols) 112 S 9th St. Phone 608/782-1980. **Free.**

Annual Events

La Crosse Interstate Fair. 11 mi E on I-90 in West Salem. Stock car racing, farm exhibits; carnival, entertainment. Mid-June.

Riverfest. Riverside Park. Five-day festival with river events, music, food, entertainment, fireworks, children's events. Early July.

Oktoberfest. Oktoberfest Strasse, S side of town. Six days beginning last wkend Sept or 1st wkend Oct.

Motels

(Rates may be higher during Oktoberfest)

★ ★ ★ **BEST WESTERN MIDWAY.** *1835 Rose St (54603). 608/781-7000; FAX 608/781-3195.* 121 rms, 2 story. S $54-$76; D $68-$95; each addl $10; under 18 free. Crib free. TV; cable (premium), VCR. Indoor pool; whirlpool. Complimentary coffee in rms. Restaurant 6:30 am-10 pm. Rm serv to 9 pm. Bar 11:30-1 am; entertainment Tues-Sat. Ck-out noon. Meeting rms. Business servs avail. In-rm modem link. Valet serv. Sundries. Downhill/x-country ski 10 mi. Exercise equipt; weights, bicycles, sauna. Rec rm. On river; dockage. Private beach. Cr cds: A, C, D, DS, JCB, MC, V.

⧉

★ ★ **DAYS INN.** *101 Sky Harbor Dr (54603), I-90 exit 2. 608/783-1000; FAX 608/783-2948.* 148 rms, 2 story. S $55-$85; D $60-$85; each addl $5; under 18 free. Crib free. TV; cable. Sauna. Indoor pool; whirlpool. Complimentary coffee in rms. Restaurant 6:30 am-2 pm, 5-9 pm. Rm serv. Bar 4:30 pm-1 am. Ck-out 11 am. Meeting rms. Business servs avail. Valet serv. Sundries. Downhill/x-country ski 10 mi. Game rm. Cr cds: A, C, D, DS, JCB, MC, V.

⧉

★ **EXEL INN.** *2150 Rose St (54603). 608/781-0400; FAX 608/781-1216.* 102 rms, 2 story. S $31.99-$47.99; D $38.99-$54.99; each addl $4; suite $80-$100; under 19 free. Crib free. TV. Complimentary continental bkfst. Restaurant nearby. Ck-out noon. Coin lndry. Downhill/x-country ski 10 mi. Game rm. Cr cds: A, C, D, DS, MC, V.

⧉

★ ★ **HAMPTON INN.** *2110 Rose St (54603). 608/781-5100; FAX 608/781-3574.* 101 rms, 2 story. S $59-$69; D $67-$77; under 19 free. Crib free. TV; cable. Complimentary continental bkfst. Restaurant adj open 24 hrs. Ck-out noon. Meeting rms. Whirlpool. Cr cds: A, C, D, DS, MC, V.

⧉

★ **NIGHT SAVER INN.** *1906 Rose St (54603). 608/781-0200; FAX 608/781-0200; res: 800/658-9497.* 73 rms, 2 story. Mid-May-Oct: S $38-$44; D $46-$54; under 12 free; lower rates rest of yr. Crib avail. TV; cable (premium), VCR avail. Complimentary continental bkfst. Restaurant opp 6 am-11 pm. Ck-out 11 am. Business servs avail. In-rm modem link. Downhill ski 8 mi; x-country ski 1 mi. Exercise equipt; bicycles, stair machine. Whirlpool. Cr cds: A, C, D, DS, MC, V.

⧉

★ **ROAD STAR INN.** *2622 Rose St (54603), US 53 (WI 35) at I-90. 608/781-3070; FAX 608/781-5114; res: 800/445-4667.* 110 rms, 2 story. S $34.50-$46.50; D $40.50-$51.50; each addl $5; under 15 free; higher rates special events. TV; cable (premium). Complimentary continental bkfst. Restaurant adj open 24 hrs. Ck-out noon. Downhill/x-country ski 8 mi. Some refrigerators, wet bars. Cr cds: A, C, D, DS, MC, V.

⧉

★ **SUPER 8.** *1625 Rose St (54603). 608/781-8880; FAX 608/781-4366.* 82 rms, 2 story. S $52-$61.88; D $58-$69.88; each addl $5; under 18 free. Crib free. TV. Indoor pool; whirlpool. Complimentary continental bkfst. Restaurant nearby. Ck-out 11 am. Coin lndry. Meeting rms. Sundries. Downhill/x-country ski 10 mi. Some in-rm whirlpools. Cr cds: A, C, D, DS, MC, V.

⧉

Hotel

★ ★ ★ **RADISSON.** *200 Harborview Plaza (54601). 608/784-6680; FAX 608/784-6694, ext. 490.* 170 units, 8 story. S $89-$99; D $99-$109; each addl $10; suites $185-$420; under 18 free. Pet accepted. TV; cable. Indoor pool; whirlpool. Restaurant 6:30 am-11 pm. Bar 11-1 am; entertainment Fri-Sat. Ck-out noon. Meeting rms. Business servs avail. Free airport, bus depot transportation. Downhill/x-country ski 8 mi. Exercise equipt; weights, bicycles. Overlooks Mississippi River. Cr cds: A, C, D, DS, ER, JCB, MC, V.

⧉

Restaurants

★ ★ **FREIGHTHOUSE.** *107 Vine St. 608/784-6211.* Hrs: 4:30-10 pm; Fri, Sat 5-10:30 pm. Closed Easter, Thanksgiving, Dec 24-25. Bar to 1 am. Semi-a la carte: dinner $11.95-$35.95. Specialties: Alaskan king crab, prime rib. Outdoor dining overlooking river. Former freight house of the Chicago, Milwaukee and St Paul Railroad (1880). Cr cds: A, C, D, DS, MC, V.

★ ★ **PIGGY'S.** *328 S Front St. 608/784-4877.* Hrs: 11 am-10 pm; Fri, Sat to 11 pm; Sun from noon. Closed Memorial Day, Labor Day, Dec 24-25. Res accepted. Bar. Semi-a la carte: lunch $3.45-$9.95, dinner $6.95-$28.95. Child's meals. Specializes in ribs, pork chops. View of Mississippi River. Cr cds: A, C, D, DS, MC, V.

D

Ladysmith (C-2)

Pop 3,938 **Elev** 1,144 ft **Area code** 715 **Zip** 54848

Information Rusk County Information Center, 817 W Miner Ave; 715/532-2642 or 800/535-7875.

Ladysmith, county seat of Rusk County, is located along the Flambeau River. The economy is based on processing lumber and marketing dairy and farm produce. There are fishing and canoeing facilities in the area.

What to See and Do

Flambeau River State Forest. A 91,000-acre forest. Outstanding canoeing river; swimming, fishing, boating. Backpacking, nature & hiking trails, mountain biking. Cross-country skiing, snowmobiling. Picnicking; camping (dump station). Standard fees. (Daily) E on US 8 to Hawkins, then N on County M to County W, near Winter. Phone 715/332-5271. Per vehicle ¢¢

Annual Events

Northland Mardi Gras. Memorial Park. 3rd wkend July.

Rusk County Fair. 4 days mid-Aug.

Motels

★ ★ **BEST WESTERN EL RANCHO.** *8500 W Flambeau Ave. 715/532-6666; FAX 715/532-7551.* 27 rms. S $44-$48; D $52-$60; each addl $4; under 12 free. Crib $9. Pet accepted. TV; cable (premium). Restaurant 11 am-2 pm, 4:30-9:30 pm. Bar to 1 am. Ck-out 11 am. Business servs avail. Downhill ski 15 mi; x-country ski on site. Cr cds: A, C, D, DS, MC, V.

✔★ **EVERGREEN.** *On US 8, 2 blks W of WI 27. 715/532-5611.* 20 rms. S $34; D $38-$42; each addl $4. Crib $4. Pet accepted, some restrictions. TV; cable (premium). Complimentary coffee in rms. Restaurant nearby. Ck-out 11 am. Downhill/x-country ski 7 mi. Picnic tables. Cr cds: A, DS, MC, V.

[icons]

Lake Geneva (G-5)

(See also Burlington, Elkhorn, Fontana, Kenosha)

Settled 1840 **Pop** 5,979 **Elev** 880 ft **Area code** 414 **Zip** 53147 **Web** www.piiweb.com/lakegeneva

Information Geneva Lake Area Chamber of Commerce, 201 Wrigley Dr; 414/248-4416 or 800/345-1020.

This is a popular and attractive four-season resort area. Recreational activities include boating, fishing, swimming, horseback riding, camping, hiking, biking, golf, tennis, skiing, cross-country skiing, ice fishing, snowmobiling and ice boating.

What to See and Do

Big Foot Beach State Park. A 272-acre beach park on Geneva Lake. Swimming (lifeguard on duty mid-June-Labor Day); fishing. Picnicking, playground. Winter sports. Camping. Standard fees. (Daily) 1 mi S on WI 120. Phone 414/248-2528. Per vehicle ¢¢

Excursion boats. Two-hr round trip & one-hr rides; also lunch, Sun brunch, dinner cruises. (May-Oct, daily) Reservations required. Mail boat (mid-June-mid-Sept, once daily). Riviera Docks. Phone 414/248-6206 or 800/558-5911. ¢¢¢¢

Geneva Lake. This 5,230-acre lake provides a variety of game fish in clear waters. The surrounding hills are heavily wooded with elm, maple and oak trees.

Skiing.

Wilmot Mt. Quad, 3 triple, 4 double chairlifts, 6 rope tows; patrol, school, rentals; snowmaking; restaurant, cafeteria, bar. Longest run 2,500 ft; vertical drop 230 ft. (Day after Thanksgiving-Mar, daily; closed Dec 24 eve) 3 mi N of Antioch, IL on IL 83, then W on WI County C; 1 mi S of Wilmot, WI on Illinois state line. Phone 414/862-2301. ¢¢¢¢¢

Grand Geneva Resort. Area has 3 chairlifts, 2 rope tows; patrol, school, rentals; snowmaking; lodging (see RESORT); restaurant, cafeteria, con-

cession, bar. Longest run one-quarter mi; vertical drop 211 ft (Dec-Mar, daily) Cross-country trails. 2 mi E at jct US 12 & WI 50. Phone 414/248-8811. ¢¢¢¢

Annual Events

Winterfest. Riviera Park at the lakefront. Host of 1998 US Snow Sculpting Championships. Feb 6-8.

Venetian Festival. Flatiron Park. Rides, games, food; lighted boat parade & fireworks. 3rd wkend Aug.

Motels

✔★ ★ **AMBASSADOR.** *415 Wells St. 414/248-3452; FAX 414/248-0605.* 18 rms. Late May-mid-Sept: S $65-$135; lower rates rest of yr. TV. Indoor pool; whirlpool, sauna. Complimentary continental bkfst. Restaurant nearby. Ck-out 11 am. Meeting rms. Business servs avail. Tennis. Downhill/x-country ski 2 mi. Miniature golf adj. Some refrigerator, whirlpools. Totally nonsmoking. Cr cds: A, DS, MC, V.

★ **BUDGET HOST DIPLOMAT.** *1060 Wells St. 414/248-1809.* 23 rms, 2 story. Apr-Oct: S $41-$71; D $51-$101; under 12 free; ski plan; higher rates some hols; lower rates rest of yr. Crib free. TV; cable (premium), VCR avail. Pool. Complimentary coffee in lobby. Ck-out 11 am. Business servs avail. Downhill/x-country ski 2 mi. Balconies. Picnic tables. Cr cds: A, DS, MC, V.

[icons]

Motor Hotel

★ ★ ★ **INTERLAKEN.** *W 4240 WI 50, 4 mi W of Lake Geneva. 414/248-9121; FAX 414/245-5016; res: 800/225-5558.* 144 rms in 3-story lodge, 100 kit. villas. Lodge: S, D $49-$150; each addl $10; villas for 1-6, $140-$260; under 12 free; package plans avail. Crib free. TV; VCR (movies). 3 pools, 1 indoor; wading pool, whirlpool, poolside serv. Free supervised child's activites (June-Labor Day; also hols). Restaurant 7 am-10 pm. Rm serv. Bar 11-1 am; wkend entertainment. Ck-out noon. Meeting rms. Business servs avail. Valet serv. Concierge (seasonal). Sundries. Gift shop. Barber, beauty shop. Tennis. Downhill ski 5 mi; x-country ski on site. Snowmobiles; ice skates. Exercise equipt; weight machine, bicycles, sauna, steam rm. Game rm. Boats, waterskiing, windsurfing. Cr cds: A, C, D, DS, MC, V.

[icons]

Inns

★ ★ **FRENCH COUNTRY INN.** *W 4190 West End Rd, WI 50W. 414/245-5220; FAX 414/245-9060.* 24 rms, 2 story. May-Oct: S, D $105-$155; suites $115-$155; lower rates rest of yr. Crib free. TV; cable (premium). Pool. Dining rm 5-10 pm; Fri, Sat to 10:30 pm. Complimentary full bkfst; afternoon refreshments. Ck-out noon, ck-in 3 pm. Business servs avail. Golf privileges. Downhill ski 12 mi; x-country ski 1 mi. On lake; beach. Portions of guest house built in Denmark and shipped to US for the Danish exhibit at the 1893 Columbian Exposition in Chicago. Cr cds: A, MC, V.

[icons]

★ **THE OAKS.** *421 Baker St. 414/248-9711.* 6 rms, 2 story, 3 suites. No rm phones. S, D, suites $135-$275; lower rates rest of yr. TV; cable (premium), VCR. Restaurant. Bar. Ck-out 11 am, ck-in 3 pm. Concierge. Some in-rm whirlpools, fireplaces. Balconies. Grills. Built 1856; antiques, Victrola phonograph. Cr cds: A, MC, V.

[icons]

Resort

★ ★ **GRAND GENEVA.** *7036 Grand Geneva Way, 1 mi E at jct US 12 & WI 50. 414/248-8811; FAX 414/248-3192; res: 800/558-3417.* 355

rms, 3 story. S, D $99-$205; each addl $10; under 18 free. Crib free. TV; cable (premium), VCR (movies). 3 pools, 2 indoor; whirlpool. Playground. Supervised child's activities; ages 4-12. Complimentary coffee in rms. Restaurants 6:30 am-10 pm; Fri, Sat to 11 pm (also see RISTORANTÉ BRISSAGO). Bar 11:30-2 am; entertainment. Ck-out noon, ck-in 4 pm. Convention facilities. Business center. In-rm modem link. Valet serv. Gift shop. Airport transportation. Indoor, outdoor tennis, pro. 36-hole golf, pro, driving range, putting green. Paddleboats, hydrobikes. Downhill/x-country ski on site. Bicycle rentals. Exercise rm; instructor, weights, bicycles, sauna, steam rm. Spa center. Private patios, balconies. 1,300 acres of wooded, meadow land with private lake. Cr cds: A, C, D, DS, MC, V.

Restaurants

✔★ **POPEYE'S.** 811 Wrigley Dr. 414/248-4381. Hrs: 11 am-10 pm; Fri & Sat to 11 pm; winter 11:30 am-9 pm; Fri, Sat to 10 pm. Closed Dec 25. Bar. Semi-a la carte: lunch, dinner $5.95-$15.95. Child's meals. Parking. Nautical decor. Glass-enclosed deck with view of Geneva Lake. Cr cds: DS, MC, V.

★★ **RED GERANIUM.** Hwy 50E, at jct US 12. 414/248-3637. Hrs: 11:30 am-10 pm; Fri, Sat to 10:30 pm; Sun to 9 pm; winter to 9 pm. Closed Thanksgiving, Dec 25. Res accepted. Bar. Semi-a la carte: lunch $7.95-$12.95, dinner $12.95-$34.95. Child's meals. Specializes in seafood, steak, chicken. Own desserts. Parking. Gazebo motif. Overlooks garden, patio. Cr cds: A, DS, MC, V.

★★★ **RISTORANTÉ BRISSAGO.** (See Grand Geneva Resort) 414/248-8811. Hrs: 5:30-10 pm; Fri, Sat to 11 pm. Closed Mon. Res accepted. Italian menu. Bar. Wine list. A la carte entrees: dinner $9.75-$27. Specialties: osso buco Milanese, gamberi Mediterraneo, antipasto. Valet parking. Views of lake and wooded hills. Cr cds: A, C, D, DS, MC, V.

★★★ **ST MORITZ.** 327 Wrigley Dr. 414/248-6680. Hrs: 5:30-10 pm. Closed Mon. Res accepted. Continental menu. Bar. Wine cellar. Semi-a la carte: dinner $14.95-$24.95. Child's meals. Specializes in veal, fresh fish. Own baking. Parking. Historic Queen Anne house (1885); ornately decorated; 12 fireplaces. Cr cds: A, DS, MC, V.

Unrated Dining Spot

ANNIE'S ICE CREAM PARLOR. 712 Main St. 414/248-1933. Hrs: 6 am-10 pm; Fri, Sat to midnight; summer 10 am-11 pm. Closed some major hols. Semi-a la carte: bkfst, lunch, dinner $4.95-$7.95. Parking. Antique ice cream parlor back bar. No cr cds accepted.

Land O' Lakes (B-4)

(See also Boulder Junction, Eagle River)

Pop 700 (est) **Elev** 1,700 ft **Area code** 715 **Zip** 54540
Information Chamber of Commerce, US 45, PO Box 599; 715/547-3432 or 800/236-3432.

This lovely village, on the Michigan border amid more than 100 lakes, serves as a center for tourist traffic. Fishing and boating in the area are exceptional. East of town is Lac Vieux Desert, source of the Wisconsin River.

Motel

★ **PINEAIRE.** 1 mi N on US 45. 906/544-2313. 9 cottages (7 with shower only). No A/C, rm phones. Cottages $35-$45; each addl $3; under 8 free. Crib free. Pet accepted. TV. Restaurant nearby. Ck-out 10 am. X-country ski on site. Picnic tables. No cr cds accepted.

Resort

★★ **SUNRISE LODGE.** 5894 W Shore Dr, N off County E. 715/547-3684; FAX 715/547-6110; res: 800/221-9689. 22 units in 21 cottages, 18 kits. No A/C in cottages. May-Oct, AP: S $80; D $150; EP: S $49; D $59; wkly, family rates; fall plan; Nov-Apr, EP only: D $55-$125. Crib avail. Pet accepted. Playground. Dining rm 7:30-10 am, 11:30 am-2 pm, 5-7:30 pm; Sun 7:30-11 am, noon-3 pm; wkends only in winter. Box lunches. Meeting rm. Business servs avail. Airport, bus depot transportation. Tennis. Miniature golf. Private beach; boats, motors, canoes. X-country ski on site. Lawn games. Exercise trail. Nature trail. Bicycles. Rec rm. Fish/hunt guides; clean & store area. Refrigerators. Picnic tables, grills. Spacious grounds. On Lac Vieux Desert. Cr cds: DS, MC, V.

Madison (G-4)

(See also Mt Horeb, New Glarus, Prairie du Sac)

Settled 1837 **Pop** 191,262 **Elev** 863 ft **Area code** 608 **E-mail** gmcvb@visitmadison.com **Web** www.visitmadison.com
Information Greater Madison Convention & Visitors Bureau, 615 E Washington Ave, 53703; 608/255-2537 or 800/373-6376.

Madison was a virgin wilderness in 1836 when the territorial legislature selected the spot for the capital and the state university. Today this "City of Four Lakes," located on an isthmus between Lake Mendota and Lake Monona, is a recreational, cultural and manufacturing center. Both the university and state government play important roles in the community.

Madison has a rich architectural heritage left by Frank Lloyd Wright and the Prairie School movement. There are a number of Wright buildings here; many are private homes and not open to the public but may be viewed from the outside.

What to See and Do

Dane County Farmers' Market. Festive open-air market selling Wisconsin produce and agricultural products. Capitol Square (May-Oct, Sat); Martin Luther King, Jr Blvd (May-Oct, Wed). (2 locations) Capitol Square and 200 Martin Luther King, Jr Blvd. Phone 414/563-5037.

Edgewood College (1927). (1,725 students) A 55-acre campus on Lake Wingra; Native American burial mounds. 855 Woodrow St. Phone 608/257-4861.

Frank Lloyd Wright architecture.

First Unitarian Society. A classic example of Wright's Prairie School work. (May-Sept, Mon-Fri afternoons, also Sat mornings; closed hols & 2 wks Aug) 900 University Bay Dr. Phone 608/233-9774. ¢¢

Self-driving tour. These are private homes and not open to the public. However, they may be viewed from the outside. **Airplane House** (1908), 120 Ely Place; **Dr Arnold Jackson House** (1957), 3515 W Beltline Hwy; **Lamp House** (1899), 22 N Butler St; **J.C. Pew House** (1939), 3650 Lake Mendota Dr; **Louis Sullivan's Bradley House,** 106 N Prospect; **"Jacobs I" House** (1937), 441 Toepfer Ave.

Henry Vilas Park Zoo. World-famous for successful orangutan, Siberian tiger, spectacle bear, penguin, and camel breeding programs. Zoo exhibits include 750 specimens consisting of 180 species. Petting zoo; picnic area on an island in Lake Wingra's lagoon; camel rides (June-Sept, Sun only);

bathing beach, tennis courts. (Daily) 702 S Randall Ave on Lake Wingra. Phone 608/266-4732. **Free.**

Lake Kegonsa State Park. A 343-acre park. Swimming, waterskiing; fishing, boating. Hiking, nature trails. Picnicking, playground. Camping (May-mid-Oct, dump station). Standard fees. (Daily) 13 mi SE via I-90, then S on County N. Phone 608/873-9695. Per vehicle ¢¢

Madison Art Center. Features modern and contemporary art by international, national, regional and local artists; permanent collection. Tours (by appt, fee). (Daily exc Mon; closed hols) 211 State St in Civic Center. Phone 608/257-0158. ¢¢

Olbrich Botanical Gardens. Contains 14 acres of horticultural displays including annuals, perennials, shrubs, hybrid roses, lilies, dahlias, spring bulbs, rock and herb gardens. All-American Rose Selection Demonstration Garden. Garden building has a tropical conservatory housed inside a 50-ft high glass pryamid; tropical ferns, palms, flowering plants; waterfall, stream. (Daily; closed Dec 25) 3330 Atwood Ave. Phone 608/246-4551. Outdoor gardens **Free.** Conservatory ¢

State Capitol. Dominates the center of the city. The white granite building has a classic dome topped by Daniel Chester French's gilded bronze statue *Wisconsin*. Tours (daily; closed major hols). Capitol Square. Phone 608/266-0382. **Free.**

State Historical Museum. Permanent exhibits explore the history of Native American life in Wisconsin; gallery with changing Wisconsin, US history exhibits. Theater. (Daily exc Mon) 30 N Carroll St, located on Capitol Sq, jct State, Mifflin & Carroll Sts. Phone 608/264-6555. **Free.**

USDA Forest Products Laboratory. Devoted to scientific and technical research on properties, processing and uses of wood and wood products. Guided tour (one departure, Mon-Thurs afternoons; closed hols). 1 Gifford Pinchot Dr off N Walnut St. Phone 608/231-9200. **Free.**

University of Wisconsin-Madison (1849). (41,948 students) 929-acre campus extends for more than 2 mi along S shore of Lake Mendota. 7 blks W of Capitol. Maps and general information at Visitor & Information Place, N Park & Langdon Sts; or at Campus Assistance Center, 420 N Lake St, 608/263-2400. On campus are

  Carillon Tower. 56 bells; afternoon concerts (Sun).

  Observatory and Willow drives. Scenic drives along shore of Lake Mendota.

  Memorial Library. More than 5 million volumes; collection of rare books. Langdon & Lake Sts.

  Elvehjem Museum of Art. Paintings, sculpture, decorative arts, prints, Japanese woodcuts, other artworks from 2300 B.C. to present day; changing exhibits; 80,000-volume Kohler Art Library. (Daily; closed Jan 1, Thanksgiving, Dec 25) 800 University Ave. Phone 608/263-2246. **Free.**

  Washburn Observatory. Public viewing 1st & 3rd Wed evenings of each month (weather permitting). 1401 Observatory Dr. Phone 608/262-WASH. **Free.**

Wisconsin Veterans Museum. Dioramas, exhibits of events from Civil War to Persian Gulf War. (Apr-Sept, daily exc Mon; rest of yr, Tues-Sat; closed hols) 30 W Mifflin St. Phone 608/266-1680. **Free.**

Annual Events

Paddle & Portage Canoe Race. Downtown isthmus. July.

Art Fair on the Square. Capitol Concourse. Exhibits by 500 artists and craftspersons; food, entertainment. Contact Madison Art Center. Mid-July.

Dane County Fair. Dane County Exposition Center and Fairgrounds, 76 Fairgrounds Dr, N of US 12, 18. Late July.

Seasonal Event

Concerts on the Square. Six-week series; Wed evenings. Late June-early Aug.

Motels

★★ **BEST WESTERN WEST TOWNE SUITES.** *650 Grand Canyon Dr (53719). 608/833-4200; FAX 608/833-5614.* 101 suites, 2 story. Suites $60-$80; each addl $5; under 19 free. Crib free. Pet accepted. TV; cable. Complimentary full bkfst. Ck-out noon. Coin lndry. Meeting rms. Business servs avail. In-rm modem link. Exercise equipt; bicycles, treadmills. Health club privileges. Refrigerators, wet bars; microwaves avail. Cr cds: A, C, D, DS, JCB, MC, V.

🅳 ✦ ✕ ⬇ 🔥 SC

★★ **BUDGETEL INN.** *8102 Excelsior Dr (53717). 608/831-7711; FAX 608/831-1942.* 129 rms, 2 story, 14 suites. S, D $65.95; each addl $7; suites $70.95-$114.95; under 18 free; higher rates special events. Crib free. Pet accepted, some restrictions. TV; cable. Indoor pool; whirlpool. Complimentary continental bkfst. Complimentary coffee in rms. Bar from 5 pm. Coin lndry. Meeting rms. Business servs avail. Bellhops. Valet serv. Free airport transportation. Exercise equipt; rower, bicycles, sauna. Game rm. Refrigerator, wet bar in suites. Cr cds: A, C, D, DS, MC, V.

🅳 ✦ ≋ ✕ ⬇ 🔥 SC

✔★ **ECONO LODGE.** *4726 E Washington Ave (53704). 608/241-4171.* 98 rms, 2 story. S $37.95-$41.95; D $45.95-$57.95; each addl $4; theme rms $50.95-$62.95; under 18 free. Crib $3. TV; cable. Complimentary continental bkfst. Restaurant nearby. Ck-out noon. Business servs avail. Sundries. Some microwaves. Cr cds: A, C, D, DS, MC, V.

🅳 ⬇ 🔥 SC

✔★ **EXEL INN.** *4202 E Towne Blvd (53764). 608/241-3861; FAX 608/241-9752.* 102 rms, 2 story. May-Sept: S $39.99-$54; D $48.99-$63; each addl $4; under 18 free; wkly rates; higher rates special events; lower rates rest of yr. Crib free. Pet accepted, some restrictions. TV; cable (premium). Complimentary continental bkfst. Coffee in rms. Restaurant nearby. Ck-out noon. Business servs avail. In-rm modem link. Sundries. Coin lndry. X-country ski 3 mi. Exercise equipt; bicycle, treadmill. Health club privileges. Game rm. Some refrigerators; microwaves avail. Cr cds: A, C, D, DS, MC, V.

🅳 ✦ ✕ ✕ ⬇ 🔥 SC

✔★★ **FAIRFIELD INN BY MARRIOTT.** *4765 Hayes Rd (53704), off I-90/94 exit 135A, S on US 151, then right on frontage. 608/249-5300.* 134 rms, 3 story. S, D $44-$62; under 18 free. Crib free. TV; cable (premium). Heated pool. Complimentary continental bkfst. Restaurants nearby. Ck-out noon. Meeting rms. Business servs avail. Health club privileges. Cr cds: A, C, D, DS, MC, V.

🅳 ≋ ✕ 🔥 SC

★★ **HAMPTON INN-EAST.** *4820 Hayes Rd (53704), I-90/94 exit 135A. 608/244-9400; FAX 608/244-7177.* 116 rms, 4 story. S $69; D $79; under 19 free; higher rates special events. Crib free. TV; cable. Indoor pool; whirlpool. Complimentary continental bkfst. Restaurant nearby. Ck-out noon. Meeting rms. Business servs avail. X-country ski 10 mi. Exercise equipt; bicycles, treadmill. Microwaves avail. Cr cds: A, C, D, DS, MC, V.

🅳 ✕ ≋ ✕ ⬇ 🔥

★★ **IVY INN.** *2355 University Ave (53705). 608/233-9717; FAX 608/233-2660.* 57 rms, 2 story. S $60-$70; D $70-$75; each addl $7; under 13 free. Crib free. TV; cable. Restaurant 7 am-2 pm, 5-8 pm. Bar 4-11:30 pm. Ck-out noon. Business servs avail. Valet serv. Sundries. Cr cds: A, C, D, MC, V.

🅳 ✕ 🔥 SC

★★ **RAMADA CAPITAL CONFERENCE CENTER.** *3902 Evan Acres Rd (53704), at I-90 East Cambridge exit 142B. 608/222-9121; FAX 608/222-5332.* 186 rms, 2 story. S, D $59-$69; each addl $8; suites $95-$125; under 19 free. Crib free. Pet accepted, some restrictions. TV; cable. Indoor pool; poolside serv. Restaurant 6 am-1:30 pm, 5-9:30 pm. Rm serv. Bar 11-1 am. Ck-out noon. Meeting rms. Business center. Free airport transportation. Sauna. Game rm. 36-hole golf course adj. Some in-rm whirlpools; microwaves avail. Cr cds: A, C, D, DS, JCB, MC, V.

[D] [icons]

★ ★ **RAMADA LIMITED.** *3841 E Washington (53704). 608/244-2481; FAX 608/244-0383.* 194 rms, 2 story. Mid-May-Oct: S $59-$79; D $69-$89; each addl $10; suites $89-$163; under 18 free; lower rates rest of yr. Crib free. Pet accepted; $10. TV; cable (premium). Indoor pool; whirlpool. Complimentary bkfst. Ck-out noon. Meeting rms. Business servs avail. Valet serv. Airport transportation. Cr cds: A, C, D, DS, MC, V.

[D] [icons]

★ ★ **RESIDENCE INN BY MARRIOTT.** *501 D'Onofrio Dr (53719). 608/833-8333; FAX 608/833-2693.* 80 kit. suites, 2 story. Kit. suites $110-$140; higher rates special events. Crib free. Pet accepted, some restrictions. TV; cable, VCR. Heated pool; whirlpool. Complimentary continental bkfst. Restaurant nearby. Ck-out noon. Coin lndry. Meeting rms. Valet serv. Exercise equipt; bicycle, treadmill. Health club privileges. Microwaves. Private patios, balconies. Picnic tables, grills. Cr cds: A, C, D, DS, JCB, MC, V.

[D] [icons]

★ **SELECT INN.** *4845 Hayes Rd (53704), I-90/94 exit 151S. 608/249-1815; res: 800/641-1000.* Web www.selectinn.com. 96 rms, 2 story. June-mid-Sept: S $33.90-$53.90; D $41.90-$53.90; each addl $4; under 13 free. Pet accepted; $25 deposit. TV; cable. Complimentary continental bkfst. Restaurant nearby. Ck-out 11 am. Business servs avail. Sundries. Whirlpool. Some refrigerators, minibars. Cr cds: A, C, D, DS, MC, V.

[D] [icons]

Motor Hotels

★ ★ ★ **EDGEWATER.** *666 Wisconsin Ave (53701). 608/256-9071; FAX 608/256-0910.* 116 rms, 8 story. S, D $79-$160; suites $189-$389. Crib free. Pet accepted, some restrictions. TV; cable (premium). Restaurant (see ADMIRALTY). Rm serv 6:30 am-10:30 pm. Bar 11-12:30 am. Ck-out noon. Meeting rms. Business servs avail. Bellhops. Valet serv. Free garage. Free airport transportation. Massage. Health club privileges. Some microwaves. On Lake Mendota; swimming beach. Cr cds: A, C, D, MC, V.

[D] [icons]

★ ★ **HOWARD JOHNSON PLAZA HOTEL.** *525 W Johnson (53703), on university campus. 608/251-5511; FAX 608/251-4824.* 163 rms, 7 story. S $82-$135; D $92-$145; each addl $10; studio rms $92-$145; suite $125-$150; under 18 free. Crib free. TV; cable. Indoor pool; whirlpool. Coffee in rms. Restaurant 6 am-10 pm. Rm serv 4:30 pm-12:45 am. Ck-out noon. Meeting rms. Business servs avail. Valet serv. Sundries. Free airport transportation. X-country ski 1 mi. Health club privileges. Refrigerators avail. Cr cds: A, C, D, DS, ER, JCB, MC, V.

[D] [icons]

Hotels

★ ★ **BEST WESTERN INN ON THE PARK.** *22 S Carroll (53703), downtown. 608/257-8811; FAX 608/257-5995.* 213 rms, 9 story. S $82-$98; D $94-$108; each addl $10; suites $126-$136; under 12 free; higher rates special events. Crib free. Pet accepted. TV; cable (premium). Heated pool; whirlpool. Restaurants 6 am-9 pm. Bar 11 am-midnight. Ck-out noon. Meeting rms. Business servs avail. In-rm modem link. Gift shop. Free covered parking; valet. Free airport transportation. Exercise equipt; weights, bicycles. Some in-rm whirlpools. Cr cds: A, C, D, DS, MC, V.

[D] [icons]

★ ★ **CONCOURSE HOTEL & GOVERNOR'S CLUB-MADI-SON.** *1 W Dayton St (53703), just N of Capitol Square. 608/257-6000; FAX 608/257-5280; res: 800/356-8293.* E-mail slsnctr@madison.tds.net; web www.concoursehotel.com. 357 rms, 13 story. S $89-$175; D $99-$200;

each addl $10; suites $200-$350; under 13 free. Crib free. TV; cable. Pool; whirlpool. Restaurant 6:30 am-10 pm. Bar 11-1 am; entertainment. Ck-out noon. Convention facilities. Business center. Barber, beauty shop. Gift shop. Free garage. Airport transportation. X-country ski 3 mi. Exercise equipt; weights, bicycles, sauna, steam rm. Health club privileges. Some in-rm whirlpools, microwaves. Luxury level. Cr cds: A, C, D, DS, MC, V.

[D] [icons]

★ ★ ★ **SHERATON.** *706 John Nolen Dr (53713), at jct US 12 & 18. 608/251-2300; FAX 608/251-1189.* 236 rms. S $135; D $145; each addl $10; under 18 free; wkend rates. Crib free. TV; cable. Indoor pool; whirlpool. Restaurant 6:30 am-11 am, 11:30 am-2 pm, 5-10 pm. Bar 5 pm-1 am. Ck-out noon. Meeting rms. Gift shop. Exercise equipt; weight machine, bicycles, sauna. Game rm. Luxury level. Cr cds: A, C, D, DS, MC, V.

[D] [icons]

Inns

★ ★ ★ **ANNIE'S B & B.** *2117 Sheridan Dr (53704). 608/244-2224; FAX 608/242-9611.* 2 suites, 2 story. Suites $124; each addl $20; 2-day min. Adults only. TV; VCR avail (free movies). Complimentary full bkfst. Complimentary coffee in library. Ck-out noon, ck-in 4-6 pm. Business servs avail. In-rm modem link. X-country ski adj. Health club privileges. Whirlpool. Refrigerators. Picnic tables. Rustic cedar shake and stucco house; extensive gardens, gazebo, lily pond. Overlooks park. Near Lake Mendota. Cr cds: A, MC, V.

[icons]

★ ★ **COLLINS HOUSE.** *704 E Gorham St (53703). 608/255-4230; FAX 608/255-0830.* E-mail inncollin@aol.com. 5 rms, 3 story. S $75-$130; D $85-$140. Crib free. TV in sitting rm; VCR (free movies). Complimentary full bkfst. Restaurant nearby. Ck-out noon, ck-in 4 pm. X-country ski 3 mi. Some in-rm whirlpools; microwaves avail. Former residence of lumber industry executive (1911); example of Prairie School style of architecture. View of Lake Mendota. Totallly nonsmoking. Cr cds: DS, MC, V.

[icons]

★ ★ ★ **MANSION HILL.** *424 N Pinckney St (53703). 608/255-3999; FAX 608/255-2217; res: 800/798-9070.* 11 rms, 4 story. S $90-$250; D $110-$270; each addl $20; higher rates wkends. Children over 12 yrs only. TV; VCR avail. Complimentary continental bkfst. Ck-out noon, ck-in 4 pm. Business servs avail. In-rm modem link. Valet parking. Health club privileges. Minibars; many in-rm whirlpools. Some balconies. Italianate-Victorian mansion (1858) with 4-story spiral staircase; individually decorated rms including Turkish and Oriental themes. Totally nonsmoking. Cr cds: A, MC, V.

[icons]

Restaurants

★ ★ ★ **ADMIRALTY.** *(See Edgewater Motor Hotel) 608/256-9071.* Hrs: 6:30-10 am, 11 am-2 pm, 5:30-10 pm; Sun brunch 11 am-2 pm. Res accepted. Continental menu. Bar. Wine cellar. Semi-a la carte: bkfst $4.75-$12.95, lunch $7.95-$18.95, dinner $16-$30. Sun buffet $14.95. Specializes in fresh fish. Tableside cooking. Entertainment Fri, Sat (summer, fall). Parking. Outdoor dining. Overlooks Lake Mendota. Family-owned. Cr cds: A, C, D, MC, V.

[D]

✔ ★ ★ **CHINA HOUSE.** *1256 S Park St. 608/257-1079.* Hrs: 11:30 am-10 pm; Fri, Sat to 11 pm. Res accepted. Chinese menu. Bar. A la carte entrees: lunch $3.75-$4.75, dinner $5.95-$9.25. Specializes in Szechwan & Hunan cuisine. Parking. Chinese decor. Cr cds: A, MC, V.

[D]

★ ★ **COACHMAN'S. INN.** *(984 County Trunk A, Edgerton 53534) at I-90 & US 51 exit 156. 608/884-8484.* Web www.coachman.com. Hrs: 11 am-9 pm; Fri, Sat to 10 pm; Sun brunch 9 am-2 pm. Closed Dec

24 evening, Dec 25. Res accepted. Bar. Semi-a la carte: lunch $4-$7, dinner $7.75-$16.95. Sun brunch $10.50. Specializes in roast duck, char-coal-grilled steak. Salad bar. Parking. English country inn atmosphere. Guest rms avail. Cr cds: A, DS, MC, V.

D

✔★ **ESSEN HAUS.** *514 E Wilson St.* 608/255-4674. Hrs: 5-10 pm; Fri to 11 pm; Sat 4-11 pm; Sun 3-9 pm. Closed Mon; most major hols. Res accepted. German, Amer menu. Bar. Semi-a la carte: dinner $5.45-$14.95. Specializes in authentic German cuisine, prime rib, fresh fish. Live music nightly. Parking. Old World atmosphere; extensive stein collection. Cr cds: MC, V.

D

★★ **GRANITA.** *5518 University Ave (53705).* 608/233-2200. Hrs: 5-10 pm. Closed Sun; major hols. Res accepted. Italian menu. Bar. Semi-a la carte: dinner $8.45-$16.95. Specializes in pasta, fresh fish, veal. Parking. Mediterranean atmosphere. Cr cds: A, D, MC, V.

D

★★★ **L'ETOILE.** *25 N Pinckney (53703),* on Capitol Sq. 608/251-0500. Hrs: 5:30 pm-closing; Fri, Sat from 5 pm. Closed Sun; major hols. Res accepted. French, Amer menu. Bar. Semi-a la carte: dinner $18.50-$27.50. Specializes in seasonal & regional dishes. Menu changes daily. Contemporary decor; original artwork. View of capitol. Cr cds: D, MC, V.

★★ **MARINER'S INN.** *5339 Lighthouse Bay Dr,* on N shore of Lake Mendota. 608/246-3120. Hrs: 4:30-9:30 pm; Fri, Sat to 10 pm; early-bird dinner Sun-Fri 4:30-6 pm. Closed some major hols. Bar. Semi-a la carte: dinner $13.99-$21. Specializes in steak, seafood. Own cheese-cake. Parking. Nautical decor. View of lake; dockage. Family-owned. Cr cds: MC, V.

★ **NAU-TI-GAL.** *5360 Westport Rd (53704).* 608/244-4464. Hrs: 11:30 am-10 pm; Fri, Sat to 10:30 pm (summer); Sun 10 am-9 pm; Sun brunch to 2 pm. Closed Jan 1, Thanksgiving, Dec 25; also Super Bowl Sun, Mon Nov-Feb. Bar. Semi-a la carte: lunch $3.50-$8, dinner $7.99-$18. Sun brunch $12.99. Specializes in seafood. Outdoor dining. Nautical decor. Cr cds: MC, V.

D

★★ **QUIVEY'S GROVE.** *6261 Nesbitt Rd (53719).* 608/273-4900. Hrs: 11 am-10 pm. Closed some major hols. Res accepted. Bar. Semi-a la carte: lunch $5.75-$7.50, dinner $7.75-$22.50. Child's meals. Specializes in regional Wisconsin dishes, turtle pie. Parking. Converted historic mansion & stables (1855); many antiques. Cr cds: MC, V.

D

✔★ **SA-BAI THONG.** *2840 University Ave (53705),* at University Station Shopping Center. 608/238-3100. Hrs: 11 am-10 pm; Sun from 5 pm. Closed Jan 1, Thanksgiving, Dec 25. Res accepted. Thai menu. Wine, beer. A la carte entrees: lunch $4.95-$5.95, dinner $6.95-$11.95. Specializes in seafood, curry dishes. Contemporary Thai decor. Totally nonsmoking. Cr cds: MC, V.

D

Unrated Dining Spot

ELLA'S DELI. *2902 E Washington Ave.* 608/241-5291. Hrs: 10 am-11 pm; Fri, Sat to midnight. Closed Thanksgiving, Dec 24-25. Kosher-style deli menu. Semi-a la carte: bkfst $2.50-$5, lunch $3.50-$5.50, dinner $3.50-$6.50. Specializes in deli sandwiches, ice cream sundaes. Parking. Numerous cartoon character & clown decorations throughout dining area. Outdoor carousel. Cr cds: MC, V.

D

Manitowish Waters (B-3)

(See also Boulder Junction, Lac du Flambeau, Minocqua, Woodruff)

Pop 686 **Elev** 1,611 ft **Area code** 715 **Zip** 54545
Information Chamber of Commerce, PO Box 251, 54545; 715/543-8488.

Manitowish Waters is in Northern Highland-American Legion State Forest (see BOULDER JUNCTION), which abounds in small and medium-size lakes linked by streams. Ten of the 14 lakes are navigable without portaging, making them ideal for canoeing. There are 16 campgrounds on lakes in the forest (standard fees) and 135 overnight campsites on water trails. Canoe trips, fishing, swimming, boating, waterskiing and snowmobiling are popular here.

What to See and Do

Cranberry bog tours. Tours begin with a video and samples then follow guides in own vehicle. (Late July-early Oct, Fri) Community Center. Phone 715/543-8488 for fees and further information.

Seasonal Event

Waterski shows. July-Aug.

Motel

✔★ **GREAT NORTHERN.** *(US 51 S, Mercer 54547)* 715/476-2440; FAX 715/476-2205. 80 rms, 2 story. No A/C. S, D $49-$59; each addl $10; higher winter rates; under 10 free. Pet accepted. TV; cable (premium). Sauna. Indoor pool; whirlpool. Complimentary continental bkfst. Restaurant. Bar 5 pm-2 am. Ck-out 11 am. Meeting rms. Business servs avail. Gift shop. X-country ski 1 mi. Game rm. On lake; swimming beach. Cr cds: DS, MC, V.

Resort

★★ **VOSS' BIRCHWOOD LODGE.** *3 mi SE on US 51.* 715/543-8441. 2 rms, 4 suites in 2-story lodge, 12 kits, 20 cottages (1-3 bedrm). Memorial Day-Oct: D $65-$85; cottages $525-$850/wk; monthly rates. Closed rest of yr. Crib avail. Pet accepted. TV in some cottages. Playground. Dining rm (public by res) 8-10 am, 5:30-8 pm. Serv bar. Ck-out 10 am, ck-in 2 pm. Grocery, coin lndry, package store 1½ mi. Airport, bus depot transportation. Marina. Private beach; waterskiing. Bicycles avail. Fishing guides, store area. Many fireplaces, refrigerators. Sun deck. Tea room 11 am-4 pm. Art gallery; antiques. Spacious grounds on Spider Lake. No cr cds accepted.

D 🖈 🖻 🏊 🔥

Restaurants

★★ **LITTLE BOHEMIA.** *2 mi S on US 51.* 715/543-8433. Hrs: 4-11 pm; June-Aug expanded hrs. Closed Wed; Feb & Mar. Res accepted. No A/C. Bar. Semi-a la carte: dinner $8.95-$20. Child's meals. Specializes in ribs, steak, roast duck. Rustic decor. Site of a 1930s shoot-out between John Dillinger and the FBI; musuem. Cr cds: DS, MC, V.

★ **SWANBERG'S BAVARIAN INN.** *On County W, ¼ mi off US 51.* 715/543-2122. Hrs: 11:30 am-9 pm. Closed Sun, Tues. Res accepted. Continental menu. Bar. Semi-a la carte: lunch $3.50-$7.50, dinner $6.95-$25. Child's meals. Specialties: beef rouladen, Wienerschnitzel, seafood. Cr cds: DS, MC, V.

D

Manitowoc (E-6)

(See also Green Bay, Sheboygan, Two Rivers)

Settled 1836 **Pop** 32,520 **Elev** 606 ft **Area code** 414 **Zip** 54220
Information Manitowoc-Two Rivers Area Chamber of Commerce, 1515 Memorial Dr, PO Box 903, 54221-0903; 414/684-5575 or 800/262-7892.

A shipping, shopping and industrial center, Manitowoc has an excellent harbor and a geographical position improved by the completion of the St Lawrence Seaway. Shipbuilding has been an important industry since the earliest days. During World War II Manitowoc shipyards produced nearly 100 vessels for the United States Navy including landing craft, wooden minesweepers, sub chasers and 28 submarines. Manitowoc is the home of one of the largest manufacturers of aluminum ware and is a leader in the state's canning industry. Nearby lakes and streams provide excellent fishing.

What to See and Do

Hidden Valley Ski Area. Area has chairlift, 4 rope tows; patrol, school, rentals; snowmaking; snack bar, bar. Longest run 2,600 ft; vertical drop 200 ft. (Dec-Mar, Tues, Thurs, Sat & Sun; night skiing Tues-Fri). 13 mi N via I-43, exit 164, 1/2 mi S on County R to E Hidden Valley Rd. Phone 414/682-5475, 414/863-2713 (snow report). ¢¢¢¢- ¢¢¢¢¢

Lake Michigan Carferry. Departs from dock at S Lakeview Dr. (Early May-Oct, daily; advance reservations strongly recommended) Trips to Ludington, MI. For fees and reservations phone 414/684-0888 or 800/841-4243.

Lincoln Park Zoo. Array of animals in attractive settings; picnic, recreational facilities. (Daily) 1200 N 8th St. Phone 414/683-4537.   **Free.**

Pinecrest Historical Village. Site of 22 historic buildings depicting a typical turn-of-the-century Manitowoc county village. (May-Labor Day, daily; Sept-mid-Oct, Fri-Sun; also 2 wknds late Nov-early Dec) I-43 exit 152, then 3 mi W on County JJ, then left on Pine Crest Lane. Phone 414/684-5110. ¢¢

Rahr-West Art Museum. Victorian house with period rms; American art; collection of Chinese ivory carvings. Modern art wing featuring changing exhibits. (Daily; closed hols) 610 N 8th St at Park St. Phone 414/683-4501. **Free.**

Wisconsin Maritime Museum. Exhibits depict 150 yrs of maritime history including model ship gallery; narrated tours through the USS *COBIA*, a 312-ft World War II submarine. (Daily; closed major hols) 75 Maritime Dr. Phone 414/684-0218. ¢¢¢

Zunker's Antique Car Museum. More than 40 antique cars, motorbikes and cycles; antique gas station, automobile memorabilia. (May-Sept, daily) 3722 MacArthur Dr. Phone 414/684-4005.   ¢¢

Motor Hotels

★ ★ **HOLIDAY INN.** *4601 Calumet, at jct I-43 & US 151. 920/682-6000; FAX 920/682-6140.* 203 rms, 3 story. S $90-$120; D $100-$135; suites $150-$165; under 18 free. TV; cable (premium), VCR avail. Indoor pool; whirlpool. Coffee in rm. Restaurant 6:30 am-2 pm, 5-10 pm. Rm serv. Bar 4 pm-2 am; entertainment Fri, Sat. Ck-out noon. Meeting rms. Business servs avail. Bellhops. Valet serv. Airport, bus depot transportation. Downhill ski 20 mi; x-country ski 15 mi. Exercise equipt; weight machine, stair machines, sauna. Game rm. Some refrigerators; microwaves avail. Private patios, balconies. Picnic tables. Cr cds: A, C, D, DS, JCB, MC, V.

D 🐾 🏊 🎾 🍴 🧖 🐾 SC

★ ★ ★ **INN ON MARITIME BAY.** *101 Maritime Dr. 920/682-7000; FAX 920/682-7013; res: 800/654-5353.* 107 rms, 3 story. S, D $96; each addl $10; suites $119-$140; under 18 free; package plans. Crib free. Pet accepted, some restrictions; $25. TV; cable. Indoor pool; whirlpool, poolside serv. Coffee in rms. Restaurant 6 am-10 pm; Fri, Sat from 7 am. Rm

serv. Bar 11-1 am. Ck-out 11 am. Meeting rms. Business servs avail. In-rm modem link. Valet serv. Free airport transportation. Downhill ski 10 mi; x-country ski 5 mi. Sauna. Game rm. Refrigerators, microwaves avail. On lake. Cr cds: A, C, D, DS, MC, V.

D 🐾 🚲 🏊 🛟 🧖 🐾 🐾

Restaurant

★ **COLONIAL INN.** *1001 S Eighth St. 920/684-6495.* Hrs: 6:30 am-10 pm; wkends to 11 pm. Res accepted. Mexican, Amer menu. Bar. Semi-a la carte: bkfst $1.35-$5.25, lunch $2.95-$6.95, dinner $4.50-$22.50. Child's meals. Specializes in potato pancakes, stuffed tenderloin, veal. Colonial atmosphere. Cr cds: A, MC, V.

D

Marinette (D-6)

(See also Oconto, Peshtigo; also see Menominee, MI)

Settled 1795 **Pop** 11,843 **Elev** 598 ft **Area code** 715 **Zip** 54143 **E-mail** Marinette@mrnet.com **Web** www.mrnet.com/marinette
Information Chamber of Commerce, 601 Marinette Ave, PO Box 512; 715/735-6681 or 800/236-6681.

Located along the south bank of the Menominee River, Marinette is named for Queen Marinette, daughter of a Menominee chief. An industrial and port city, it is also the retail trade center for the surrounding recreational area.

What to See and Do

City Park. Picnicking. Camping (electric hookups, dump station; May-Sept). Carney Ave. Phone 715/732-0558. Camping   ¢¢¢

Fishing, whitewater rafting, canoeing. Trout streams, lakes and the Peshtigo River nearby. Inquire at Chamber of Commerce.

Marinette County Historical Museum. Features logging history of area; miniature wood carvings of logging camp; Native American artifacts. Tours by appt. (Memorial Day-Sept, daily) On Stephenson Island, US 41 at state border. Phone 715/732-0831. **Donation.**

Seasonal Event

Theatre On The Bay. 750 W Bay Shore St, University of Wisconsin Center/Marinette County. Comedies, dramas, musicals. Phone 715/735-4313 or -4300. June-Aug.

Motel

✔★ **SUPER 8.** *1508 Marinette Ave. 715/735-7887; FAX 715/735-7455.* 68 rms, 2 story. May 16-Sept 30: S $44; D $49; under 12 free; lower rates rest of yr. Crib free. Pet accepted, some restrictions. TV; cable (premium). Complimentary continental bkfst. Ck-out 11 am. Meeting rms. Business servs avail. X-country ski 5 mi. Sauna. Whirlpool. Cr cds: A, C, D, DS, MC, V.

D 🐾 🏊 🛟 🐾 SC

Motor Hotel

★ ★ **BEST WESTERN-RIVERFRONT INN.** *1821 Riverside Ave, on US 41. 715/732-0111; FAX 715/732-0800.* 117 rms, 6 story. S $49-$63; D $55-$70; each addl $6; under 18 free. Crib free. TV; cable; VCR avail (movies). Indoor pool. Coffee in rms. Restaurant 6 am-2 pm, 5-10 pm. Rm serv. Bar noon-1 am, Sat from 3 pm. Ck-out noon. Meeting rm. Business servs avail. Valet serv. Sundries. X-country ski 1 mi. Game rm. Cr cds: A, C, D, DS, MC, V.

D 🏊 🛟 🐾 🐾 SC

Inn

★★ **LAUERMAN GUEST HOUSE.** *1975 Riverside Ave.* 715/732-7800. 7 rms, 3 story. S $50; D $70; each addl $10. Complimentary full bkfst. Ck-out 11 am, ck-in 2 pm. Free airport, bus depot transportation. X-country ski 1 mi. Some in-rm whirlpools. Balcony. House (1910) across from Menominee River; antiques. Lake, swimming nearby. Cr cds: A, DS, MC, V.

🏊 🎿 SC

Marshfield (E-3)

(For accommodations see Stevens Point, Wisconsin Rapids)

Settled 1872 **Pop** 19,291 **Elev** 1,262 ft **Area code** 715 **Zip** 54449 **E-mail** macci@tznet.com **Web** mtecnserv.com/mtwp/macci

Information Visitors & Promotion Bureau, 700 S Central St, PO Box 868; 715/384-3454 or 800/422-4541.

Marshfield, a city that once boasted one sawmill and 19 taverns, was almost destroyed by fire in 1887. It was rebuilt on a more substantial structural and industrial basis. This is a busy northern dairy center, noted for its large medical clinic, manufactured housing wood products and steel fabrication industries.

What to See and Do

Upham Mansion (1880). Italianate, mid-Victorian house built entirely of wood. Some original furniture, custom-made in the factory of the owner. (Wed & Sun afternoons) 212 W Third St. Phone 715/387-3322 or 800/422-4541. **Free.**

Wildwood Park and Zoo. Zoo houses a variety of animals and birds, mostly native to Wisconsin. (Mid-May-late Sept, daily; rest of yr, Mon-Fri) Off WI 13 (Roddis Ave), S of business district or off 17th St from Central Ave S. Phone 715/384-4642 or 800/422-4541. **Free.**

Annual Events

Dairyfest. Salute to the dairy industry. 1st wkend June.

Central Wisconsin State Fair. Fair Park. Vine Ave & 14th St. Phone 800/422-4541. 6 days ending Labor Day.

Fall Festival. Phone 800/422-4541. Mid-Sept.

Mauston (F-3)

(See also Wisconsin Dells)

Settled 1840 **Pop** 3,439 **Elev** 883 ft **Area code** 608 **Zip** 53948

Information Greater Mauston Area Chamber of Commerce, 503 WI 82, PO Box 171; 608/847-4142.

What to See and Do

Buckhorn State Park. A 2,504-acre park with facilities for swimming, waterskiing; fishing, hunting; boating, canoeing. Hiking, nature trails. Picnicking, playground. Backpack and canoe camping. (Apr-Nov, daily) Standard fees. 11 mi N via County Rds Q & G, near Necedah. Phone 608/565-2789. Per vehicle ¢¢

Windsound Castle. Musical laser light show. (Memorial Day-Labor Day, daily) 209 William St. Phone 608/847-2225. ¢¢¢¢

Motels

✔★ **RAFTERS MOTOR INN.** *(New Lisbon 53950)* 9 mi NW, at jct WI 80, I-90/94 exit 61. 608/562-5141; FAX 608/562-5361; res: 800/341-8000. 72 rms. S $30-$49; D $42-$59; each addl $5; studio rms $49-$59. Crib free. TV; cable. Playground. Restaurant 6:30 am-9 pm. Bar 11:30-1 am. Ck-out 11 am. Meeting rm. Rec rm. Cr cds: A, C, D, DS, MC, V.

D 🎿 🔥 SC

★ **WALSH'S K & K.** *(Rte 2, Camp Douglas 54618)* 1/2 mi E on US 12/16 at I-90/94 exit 55. 608/427-3100; FAX 608/427-3824. 14 rms. S $30-$32.95; D $37.95-$46.95; each addl $5; higher rates special events. Crib free. TV; cable, VCR avail (movies $5). Coffee in lobby. Restaurant opp 11 am-10 pm. Ck-out 10 am. Coin lndry. Business servs avail. Refrigerators. Cr cds: A, C, D, DS, MC, V.

D 🛏 🎿 🔥 SC

Guest Ranch

★★ **WOODSIDE RANCH.** *W 4015 WI 82,* 41/2 mi E. 608/847-4275; res: 800/626-4275. 14 rms in 2-story lodge, 23 cottages (1-, 2- & 3-bedrm). No rm phones. AP, late June-late Sept, late Dec-late Feb: S $210-$545/wk; D $370-$980/wk; each addl $175-$420/wk; lower rates rest of yr. Crib free. Pet accepted. TV in lobby. Pool; wading pool; poolside serv. Playground. Free supervised child's activities. Complimentary coffee in lobby. Dining rm; sittings at 8 am, 12:30 & 5:30 pm. Snack bar, picnics. Bar 8-2 am; entertainment Tues, Sat. Ck-out 10 am, ck-in 1:30 pm. Coin lndry. Grocery, package store 5 mi. Gift shop. Sports dir. Tennis. Swimming. Boats. Downhill/x-country ski on site. Sleighing, sledding. Hiking. Soc dir. Rec rm. Game rm. Fireplace in cottages. On 1,400 acres. Cr cds: DS, MC, V.

D 🛏 🎿 🎿 🏊 🎿 🔥 SC

Menasha

(see Neenah-Menasha)

Menomonee Falls (G-5)

(See also Milwaukee, Wauwatosa)

Settled 1843 **Pop** 26,840 **Elev** 840 ft **Area code** 414 **Zip** 53051

Information Menomonee Falls Chamber of Commerce, N 88 W 16621 Appleton Ave, PO Box 73, 53052; 414/251-6565 or 800/801-6565.

What to See and Do

Little Switzerland Ski Area. 5 chairlifts, 2 rope tows; patrol, school, rentals; snowmaking; cafeteria, restaurant, bar. (Nov-Mar, daily; limited hrs Dec 24-25) Night skiing. 20 mi N via US 41, on WI AA in Slinger. Phone 414/644-5020 or 800/358-SNOW. ¢¢¢¢

Old Falls Village. Miller-Davidson farmhouse (1858) of Greek-revival style; decorative arts museum; 1851 schoolhouse; carriage house; barn museum; 1890 railroad depot; two restored log cabins; 1873 Victorian cottage; extensive grounds, picnic area. (May-Sept, Sun; also by appt) 1/2 mi N on County Line Rd. Phone 414/255-8346. ¢

Sub-Continental Divide. Water falling west of this crest of land goes into the Fox River Watershed and eventually into the Gulf of Mexico via the Mississippi River. Water falling on the E side goes into the Menomonee River watershed and enters the St Lawrence Seaway by flowing through the Great Lakes. Main St, 1 blk W of Town Line Rd. Phone 414/251-6565 or 800/801-6565.

Motel

★ **SUPER 8.** *(N 96 W 17490 County Line Rd, Germantown 53022)* US 41/45 at County Q. 414/255-0880; FAX 414/255-7741. 81 rms, 2 story. June-Sept: S $55; D $62-$72; each addl $5; suites $60-$65; under 12 free; lower rates rest of yr. Crib free. Pet accepted; $50 refundable. TV; cable (premium). Complimentary continental bkfst. Restaurant adj open 24 hrs. Ck-out 11 am. Coin lndry. Business servs avail. Cr cds: A, C, D, DS, MC, V.

D 🐾 ⛷ 🏄 SC

Restaurants

★ ★ ★ **FOX AND HOUNDS.** *(1298 Friess Lake Rd, Hubertus)* 6 mi NW on US 41 to Richfield, then 6 mi W on WI 167, then 1 mi S. 414/251-4100. Hrs: 5-10 pm; Sun 3-9 pm. Closed Mon; Jan 1, Dec 24. Res accepted. Bar. Semi-a la carte: dinner $14.50-$28. Child's meals. Specialties: braised lamb shanks, stuffed pork chops, duck. Own baking. Extensive wine & beer selection. Early American atmosphere in rambling stone and timber building (1843). Fireplaces. Family-owned. Cr cds: A, C, D, DS, MC, V.

D

★ ★ **JERRY'S OLD TOWN INN.** *(N 116 W 15841 Main St, Germantown 53022)* N on WI 41. 414/251-4455. Hrs: 4-10 pm; Fri, Sat to 10:30 pm; Sun to 9 pm. Res accepted. Bar. Semi-a la carte: dinner $12.95-$24.95. Child's meals. Specializes in barbecue ribs, steak tenderloin. Own baking. Casual dining; pig theme throughout. Cr cds: MC, V.

D

★ ★ **LOHMANN'S STEAK HOUSE.** *(W183 N9609 Appleton Ave, Germantown)* 1 mi W of US 41, at jct WI 175 & County Q. 414/251-8430. Hrs: 11:30 am-2 pm, 5-10 pm. Closed Sun; major hols. Res accepted. Bar. Semi-a la carte: lunch $4.50-$10.25, dinner $10.50-$42. Child's meals. Specializes in prime rib, steak, seafood. Fireplace. Family-owned. Cr cds: A, C, D, DS, MC, V.

D

Menomonie (D-2)

(See also Chippewa Falls, Eau Claire)

Settled 1859 **Pop** 13,547 **Elev** 877 ft **Area code** 715 **Zip** 54751
Information Chamber of Commerce, 700 Wolske Bay Rd, Suite 200, PO Box 246; 715/235-9087 or 800/283-1862.

Located on the banks of the Red Cedar River, Menomonie is home of the University of Wisconsin-Stout and was once headquarters for one of the largest lumber corporations in the country. The decline of the lumber industry diverted the economy to dairy products. Recently several new industries have located here, giving the city a more diversified economic base.

What to See and Do

Caddie Woodlawn Park. Two century-old houses and log smokehouse in five-acre park; memorial to pioneer girl Caddie Woodlawn. Picnicking. (Daily) 10 mi S on WI 25. Phone 715/235-2070. **Free.**

Empire in Pine Lumber Museum. Lumbering artifacts, slides of life in lumber camps; primitive furniture, displays including original pay office. (Early May-Oct, daily; mid-Apr-early May, by appt) 7 mi S on WI 25 in Downsville. Phone 715/235-2070. **Free.**

Mabel Tainter Memorial Building. Hand-stenciled and ornately carved cultural center constructed in 1889 by lumber baron Andrew Tainter in memory of his daughter Mabel. Theater with performing arts season;

reading room, pipe organ. Gift shop. Guided tours (daily). 205 Main St. Phone 715/235-9726 or 800/236-7675. ¢¢

Wilson Place Museum. Victorian mansion (1846); former residence of Senator James H. Stout, founder of Univ of Wisconsin. Almost all original furnishings. Guided tours (Memorial Day-Labor Day, daily; closed Jan 1, Thanksgiving, Dec 25) Wilson Circle. Phone 715/235-2283. ¢¢

Annual Events

Winter Carnival. Wakanda Park. 1st wkend Feb.

Victorian Christmas. Wilson Place Museum. Daily, mid-Nov-Dec.

Motels

✔★ ★ **BEST WESTERN HOLIDAY MANOR MOTOR LODGE.** 1815 N Broadway, at jct WI 25 & I-94. 715/235-9651; FAX 715/235-6568. 138 rms. S $53-$58; D $50-$109; each addl $4; under 12 free; higher rates special events. Crib $4. TV; cable (premium). Restaurant opp open 24 hrs. Bar 4 pm-2 am. Ck-out 11 am. Meeting rms. Business servs avail. Valet serv. Sundries. X-country ski 2 mi. Cr cds: A, C, D, DS, ER, MC, V.

D ⛷ 🏄 SC

★ **BOLO COUNTRY INN.** 207 Pine Ave, just S of I-94, Memomonie exit 41A. 715/235-5596. 25 rms. S $45-$60; D $60-$80. Pet accepted. TV; cable (premium). Complimentary bkfst. Restaurant 11:30 am-10 pm. Bar 11-1 am. Ck-out noon. Meeting rms. Picnic tables. Cr cds: C, D, MC, V.

D 🐾 ⛷ 🏄 SC

Milwaukee (G-6)

Settled 1822 **Pop** 628,088 **Elev** 634 ft **Area code** 414 **Web** www.milwaukee.com

Information Greater Milwaukee Convention & Visitors Bureau, 510 Kilbourn Ave, 53203; 414/273-3950 or 800/231-0903.

Suburbs Menomonee Falls, Port Washington, Waukesha, Wauwatosa. (See individual alphabetical listings.)

Thriving and progressive, Milwaukee has retained its *Gemütlichkeit*—though today's lively conviviality is as likely to be expressed at a soccer game or at a symphony concert as at the beer garden. This is not to say that raising beer steins has noticeably declined as a popular local form of exercise. While Milwaukee is still the beer capital of the nation, its leading single industry is not brewing but the manufacture of X-ray apparatus and tubes.

Long a French trading post and an early campsite between Chicago and Green Bay, the city was founded by Solomon Juneau, who settled on the east side of the Milwaukee River. English settlement began in significant numbers in 1833, and was followed by an influx of Germans, Scandinavians, Dutch, Bohemians, Irish, Austrians and large numbers of Poles. By 1846, Milwaukee was big and prosperous enough to be incorporated as a city. In its recent history perhaps the most colorful period was from 1916-1940 when Daniel Webster Hoan, its Socialist mayor, held the reins of government.

The city's Teutonic personality has dimmed, becoming only a part of the local color of a city long famous for good government, a low crime rate and high standards of civic performance.

With a history going back to the days when the Native Americans called this area Millioki, "gathering place by the waters," Milwaukee has undergone tremendous development since World War II. The skyline changed with new building, an expressway system was constructed, the St Lawrence Seaway opened new markets, new cultural activities were introduced and 44 square miles were tacked onto the city's girth.

Today a city of 96.5 square miles on the west shore of Lake Michigan, where the Milwaukee, Menomonee and Kinnickinnic rivers meet, Milwau-

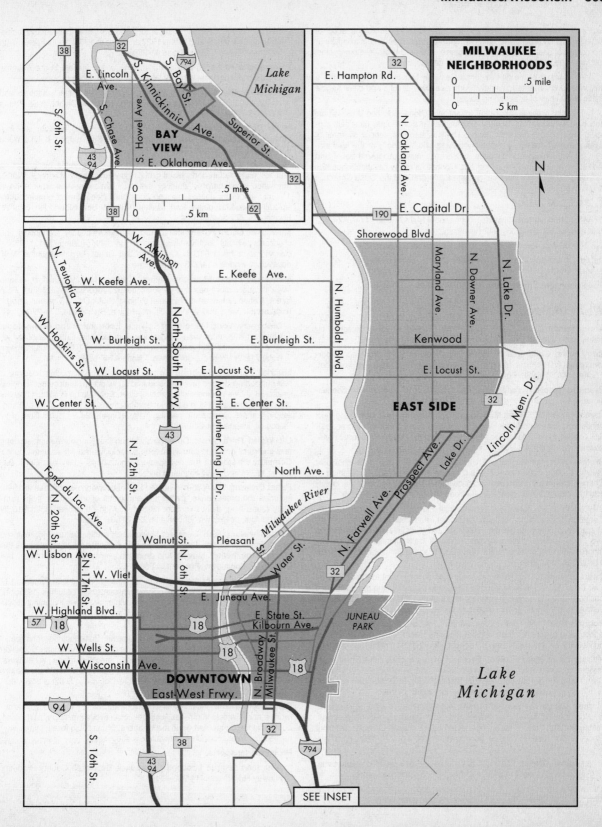

MILWAUKEE
NEIGHBORHOODS

0   .5 mile

0   .5 km

E. Hampton Rd.

BAY
VIEW

E. Lincoln Ave.

S. 6th St.

S. Chase Ave.

S. Howell Ave.

S. Kinnickinnic Ave.

S. Bay St.

Superior St.

E. Oklahoma Ave.

Lake Michigan

0   .5 mile

0   .5 km

N

E. Capital Dr.

Shorewood Blvd.

N. Oakland Ave.

Maryland Ave.

N. Downer Ave.

N. Lake Dr.

Kenwood

EAST SIDE

N. Teutonia Ave.

W. Atkinson Ave.

W. Keefe Ave.

E. Keefe Ave.

N. Humboldt Blvd.

Lincoln Mem. Dr.

W. Hopkins St.

North-South Frwy.

W. Burleigh St.

E. Burleigh St.

W. Locust St.

E. Locust St.

E. Locust St.

Martin Luther King Jr. Dr.

W. Center St.

E. Center St.

North Ave.

Prospect Ave.

Lake Dr.

Fond du Lac Ave.

N. 12th St.

Milwaukee River

N. Farwell Ave.

N. 20th St.

Walnut St.

Pleasant St.

Water St.

W. Lisbon Ave.

N. 6th St.

N. 17th St.

W. Vliet

E. Juneau Ave.

W. Highland Blvd.

E. State St.

Kilbourn Ave.

JUNEAU PARK

W. Wells St.

N. Broadway

Milwaukee St.

W. Wisconsin Ave.

DOWNTOWN

East-West Frwy.

Lake Michigan

S. 16th St.

SEE INSET

kee is the metropolitan center of five counties. "The machine shop of America" ranks among the nation's top industrial cities and is a leader in the output of diesel and gasoline engines, outboard motors, motorcycles, tractors, wheelbarrows, padlocks and, of course, beer.

As a result of the St Lawrence Seaway, Milwaukee has become a major seaport on America's new fourth seacoast. Docks and piers handle traffic of 10 lines of oceangoing ships.

The city provides abundant tourist attractions including professional and college basketball, hockey and football, major league baseball, top-rated polo, soccer and auto racing. There is also golf, tennis, swimming, sailing, fishing, hiking, skiing, tobogganing and skating. For the less athletic, Milwaukee has art exhibits, museums, music programs ballet and theater including the Performing Arts Center. Its many beautiful churches include St Josaphat's Basilica, St John Cathedral and the Gesu Church.

Transportation

General Mitchell Intl Airport: Information 414/747-5300; 414/747-5362 (lost and found); 414/936-1212 (weather).

Car Rental Agencies: See IMPORTANT TOLL-FREE NUMBERS.

Public Transportation: Milwaukee County Transit System, phone 414/344-6711.

Rail Passenger Service: Amtrak 800/872-7245.

What to See and Do

Annunciation Greek Orthodox Church. Domed structure designed by Frank Lloyd Wright. 9400 W Congress St. Phone 414/461-9400.

Betty Brinn Children's Museum. Hands-on exhibits; workshops; performances. (Daily exc Mon) 929 E Wisconsin Ave, near the lakefront. Phone 414/291-0888. Per vehicle ¢¢

Bradford Beach. The city's finest bathing beach, with bathhouse, concessions.

Captain Frederick Pabst Mansion (1893). Magnificent house of the beer baron; exquisite woodwork, wrought iron and stained glass; restored interior. Guided tours. (Daily; closed some major hols) 2000 W Wisconsin Ave, downtown. Phone 414/931-0808. ¢¢¢

Charles Allis Art Museum. Art treasures from the US, Near East, Far East & Europe dating from 600 B.C. to the 1900s; personal collection of Charles Allis in his preserved Tudor-style mansion. (Wed-Sun afternoons) 1801 N Prospect Ave, near the lakefront. Phone 414/278-8295. ¢

City Hall (1895). Milwaukee landmark of Flemish Renaissance design. Common Council Chamber and Anteroom retain their turn-of-the-century character; ornately carved woodwork, leaded glass, stenciled ceilings and two large stained glass windows; ironwork balconies surround 8-story atrium. (Mon-Fri; closed major hols) 200 E Wells St, downtown. Phone 414/286-3285. **Free.**

Court of Honor. Three-blk area serving as a monument to the city's Civil War dead. Bounded by Marquette University on the W and the downtown business district on the E, it contains an 18-story YMCA building, the Public Library, many towering churches and statues of historic figures.

Iroquois Boat Line Tours. View lakefront, harbor, lighthouse, breakwater & foreign ships in port. (Late June-Aug, daily) Board at Clybourn St Bridge on W bank of Milwaukee River. Phone 414/332-4194. ¢¢¢

Kilbourntown House (1844). Excellent example of Greek-revival architecture; restored and furnished in the 1844-1864 period. (Late June-Labor Day, Tues, Thurs, Sat-Sun) 4400 W Estabrook Dr, in Estabrook Park, 5 mi N on I-43, Capitol Dr E exit. Phone 414/273-8288. **Free.**

Marcus Center for the Performing Arts. Strikingly beautiful structure, overlooking the Milwaukee River, with four theaters, reception areas, restaurant and parking facility connected by a skywalk. Outdoor riverfront Peck Pavilion. 929 N Water St, downtown. Phone 414/273-7206. Also here is

Milwaukee Ballet. Classical and contemporary ballet presentations. (Sept-May) Phone 414/643-7677 or 414/273-7206 (box office).

Marquette University (1881). (11,000 students) Wisconsin Ave & 11th-17th Sts, downtown. Phone 414/288-3178. On campus are

St Joan of Arc Chapel (15th century). Brought from France and reconstructed on Long Island, NY in 1927 and here in 1964. Tours (daily). 14th St and Wisconsin Ave. Phone 414/288-6873.

Marquette Hall's 48-bell carillon. One of the largest in the country. Occasional concerts. 1217 W Wisconsin Ave. **Free.**

Haggerty Museum of Art. Paintings, prints, drawings, sculpture and decorative arts; changing exhibits. (Daily) 13th and Clybourn St. Phone 414/288-7290. **Free.**

Miller Brewing Co. One-hour guided tour, includes outdoor walking. (May-Sept, daily exc Sun; rest of yr, Tues-Sat; closed hols) Phone 414/931-BEER. 4251 W State St. **Free.**

Milwaukee County Zoo. On 194 wooded-acres. Mammals, birds, reptiles and fish exhibited in continental groupings with native backdrops. World-renowned predator/prey outdoor exhibits. Miniature train travels on a 1¼-mi track (fee); guided tours on Zoomobile (fee). 2 mi of cross-country ski trails (Dec-Mar, daily). Park (daily). 10001 W Blue Mound Rd, 6 mi W. Phone 414/771-3040. ¢¢¢

Milwaukee County Historical Center. Milwaukee history, firefighting, and children's exhibits, archive library housed in bank building (1913). (Daily; closed major hols) 910 N Old World 3rd St at Pere Marquette Park, downtown. Phone 414/273-8288. **Free.**

Milwaukee Public Museum. Natural & human history museum; unique "walk-through" dioramas and exhibits; life-size replicas of dinosaurs. Rain forest, Native American and special exhibits. IMAX Dome Theater. Shops; restaurant. (Daily) 800 W Wells St, downtown. Phone 414/278-2700. ¢¢

Discovery World Museum of Science, Economics and Technology. Museum with more than 140 participatory exhibits. Entrepreneurial village, stock wall and Into Einstein's Brain show. (Daily; closed major hols) 712 W Wells St, downtown. Phone 414/765-0777. ¢¢

Mitchell Park Horticultural Conservatory. Superb modern design, 3 self-supporting domes (tropical, arid and show dome) feature outstanding seasonal shows and beautiful exhibits all yr. Each dome is almost half the length of a football field in diameter and nearly as tall as a 7-story building. Also gift shop, picnic area; parking (free). (Daily) 524 S Layton Blvd at W Pierce St. Phone 414/649-9800. ¢¢

Old World Third Street. Downtown walking tour for gourmets, historians and lovers of antiques and atmosphere. Includes the *Milwaukee Journal* Company's history of the newspaper. Most shops (daily exc Sun). Between W Wells St & W Highland Blvd.

Pabst Brewing Co. A 35-min guided tour of brewery, established in 1844, includes the brew house, packaging and distribution centers; beer samples. (June-Aug, daily exc Sun; rest of yr, Mon-Fri; closed hols) 915 W Juneau Ave, downtown. Phone 414/223-3709. **Free.**

Pabst Theater (1895). Center of Milwaukee's earlier cultural life; restored to its original elegance. Lavish decor and excellent acoustics enhance the charm of the theater. Musical and dramatic events. Tours (Sat; free). 144 E Wells St, downtown. Phone 414/286-3663.

Park system. One of the largest in the nation, with 14,681 acres; 137 parks and parkways, senior and community centers, 5 beaches, 19 pools, 16 golf courses, 134 tennis courts and winter activities including cross-country skiing, skating, sledding. Fees vary. Phone 414/257-6100. Of special interest is

Whitnall Park. A 640-acre park with Boerner Botanical Gardens (parking fee) featuring the Rose Garden, one of the All American Selection Gardens; also nature trails, woodlands, formal gardens, wildflowers, shrubs, test gardens, fruit trees, rock, & herb gardens; Wehr Nature Center. 18-hole golf (fee). (Early Apr-mid-Oct, daily) S 92nd St & Whitnall Park Dr. Phone 414/425-1130. **Free.**

Port of Milwaukee. Includes Inner Harbor, formed by Milwaukee, Menomonee and Kinnickinnic rivers, and the commercial municipal port development in the Outer Harbor on the lakefront. Ships flying foreign flags may be seen at Jones Island on Milwaukee's south side.

Professional sports.

American League baseball (Milwaukee Brewers). County Stadium, Hawley Rd. Phone 414/933-4114.

IHL (Milwaukee Admirals). Bradley Center, 1001 N Fourth St. Phone 414/227-0550.

NBA (Milwaukee Bucks). Bradley Center, 1001 N Fourth St. Phone 414/227-0500.

Schlitz Audubon Center. Center has 225 acres of shoreline, grassland, bluff, ravine and woodland habitats with a variety of plants and wildlife including fox, deer, skunk and opossum; self-guided trails; some guided programs. (Daily exc Mon) 1111 E Brown Deer Rd. Phone 414/352-2880. ¢

University of Wisconsin-Milwaukee (1956). (25,400 students) The Manfred Olson Planetarium (fee) offers programs Fri & Sat evenings during academic yr; phone 414/229-4961. Also an art museum and three art galleries are open to the public. 3203 N Downer Ave, 4 mi NE. Phone 414/229-1122. For information on campus events phone 414/229-5900 (24 hrs).

Villa Terrace Decorative Arts Museum. Built in 1923, this Italian Renaissance-style house serves as a museum for decorative arts. Guided tours (reservations required). (Wed-Sun; closed Jan 1, Dec 25) 2220 N Terrace Ave, near the lakefront. Phone 414/271-3656. ¢

⭐ **War Memorial Center.** An imposing modern monument to honor the dead by serving the living; designed by Eero Saarinen. Provides facilities for civic groups and houses the

Milwaukee Art Museum. Permanent collection of American and European masters; folk, decorative and contemporary art. Special exhibits; films and tours. (Daily exc Mon; closed Jan 1, Thanksgiving, Dec 25) 750 N Lincoln Memorial Dr, near the lakefront. Phone 414/224-3200. ¢¢

Annual Events

Summerfest. Lakefront, E of downtown area. Eleven different music stages; food. Phone 414/273-FEST or 800/837-FEST. Late June-early July.

Great Circus Parade. Downtown. This re-creation of an old-time circus parade includes bands, costumed units, animals and unusual collection of horsedrawn wagons from the Circus World Museum. Mid-July.

Ethnic Festivals including German, Italian, Irish, Asian, Mexican and Polish, take place throughout the summer. Convention and Visitors Bureau has information.

Wisconsin State Fair. State Fair Park in West Allis, bounded by I-94, Greenfield Ave, 76th & 84th Sts. Entertainment, 12 stages, auto races, exhibits, contests, demonstrations, fireworks. Phone 414/266-7000. Aug 6-16.

Holiday Folk Fair. The Wisconsin Center. Continuous ethnic entertainment, 300 types of food from around the world, cultural exhibits, workshops. Phone 414/225-6225. Wkend before Thanksgiving.

Additional Visitor Information

The Greater Milwaukee Convention & Visitors Bureau, 510 W Kilbourn Ave, 53203; 414/273-3950 or 800/231-0903 has two other visitor centers: General Mitchell Airport (daily); Grand Ave Shopping Center, Wisconsin St entrance (daily). The Fun Line, phone 414/799-1177, provides information on daily events.

City Neighborhoods

Many of the restaurants, unrated dining establishments and some lodgings listed under Milwaukee include neighborhoods as well as exact street addresses. Geographic descriptions of these areas are given, followed by a table of restaurants arranged by neighborhood.

Bay View: Area south of Downtown; south of E Lincoln Ave, west of Lake Michigan, north of E Oklahoma Ave and east of S Chase Ave.

Downtown: South of Juneau Ave, west of Lake Michigan, north of I-794 and east of the North-South Frwy. **North of Downtown:** North of E Juneau Ave. **South of Downtown:** South of I-794. **West of Downtown:** West of I-43.

East Side: Area northeast of Downtown; south of Shorewood Dr., west of Lake Michigan, McKinley and Juneau parks, north of Juneau Ave and east of the Milwaukee River.

MILWAUKEE RESTAURANTS BY NEIGHBORHOOD AREAS
(For full description, see alphabetical listings under Restaurants)

BAY VIEW
Three Brothers. 2414 S St Clair

DOWNTOWN
Au Bon Appétit. 1016 E Brady St
Boulevard Inn. 925 E Wells St
Cafe Knickerbocker. 1030 E Juneau Ave
County Clare. 1234 N Astor St
Eagan's. 1030 N Water St
English Room (Pfister Hotel). 424 E Wisconsin Ave
Grenadier's. 747 N Broadway Ave at Mason
John Ernst's. 600 E Ogden Ave
Karl Ratzsch's. 320 E Mason St
King And I. 823 N 2nd St
Mader's. 1037 N Old World Third St
Mimma's Cafe. 1307 E Brady St
Osteria Del Mondo. 1028 E Juneau Ave
Polaris (Hyatt Regency Hotel). 333 W Kilbourn Ave
Safe House. 779 N Front St
Sanford. 1547 N Jackson St
Weissgerber's Third Street Pier. 1110 N Old World Third St
West Bank Cafe. 732 E Burleigh St

NORTH OF DOWNTOWN
Bavarian Inn. 700 W Lexington Blvd
Dos Bandidos. 5932 N Green Bay Ave
Pandl's In Bayside. 8825 N Lake Dr
Red Rock Cafe. 4022 N Oakland Ave
Yen Ching. 7630 W Good Hope Rd

SOUTH OF DOWNTOWN
Club Tres Hermanos. 1332 W Lincoln Ave
Mike & Anna's. 2000 S Eighth St
Old Town Serbian Gourmet House. 522 W Lincoln Ave
Porterhouse. 800 W Layton Ave
Royal India. 3400 S 27th St

WEST OF DOWNTOWN
Balistreri's Bluemound Inn. 6501 W Bluemound Rd
Pleasant Valley Inn. 9801 W Dakota St
Saz's State House. 5539 W State St

EAST SIDE
Bartolotta's Lake Park Bistro. 3133 E Newberry Blvd
Izumi's. 2178 N Prospect Ave

Note: When a listing is located in a town that does not have its own city heading, it will appear under the city nearest to its location. In these cases, the address and town appear in parenthesis immediately following the name of the establishment.

Motels

(Rates may be higher during state fair)

⭐ **BUDGETEL INN.** 5442 N Lovers Lane Rd (53225), just E of I-45 Silver Spring Dr exit E, north of downtown. 414/535-1300; FAX 414/535-1724. 140 rms, 3 story. S $45-$52; D $51-$58; each addl $7; suites $57.95-$67; under 18 free. Pet accepted, some restrictions. TV; cable (premium), VCR avail. Complimentary continental bkfst. Complimentary coffee in rms. Restaurant nearby. Ck-out noon. Meeting rm. Business servs avail. In-rm modem link. Valet serv. Microwaves avail. Cr cds: A, C, D, DS, MC, V.

D 🐾 ✈ 🎿 **SC**

★★ **CLARION HOTEL & CONFERENCE CENTER.** *5311 S Howell Ave (53207), opp General Mitchell Intl Airport, south of downtown.* 414/481-2400; FAX 414/481-4471. 180 rms, 3 story. S, D $70-$99; suites $89-$150; each addl $5; under 18 free. Crib $7. TV; cable (premium). Indoor pool. Complimentary continental bkfst. Restaurant 7 am-10 pm; Sun 9 am-9 pm. Rm serv. Bar 11 am-11 pm. Ck-out 11 am. Coin lndry. Meeting rms. Business servs avail. Bellhops. Free airport transportation. Exercise equipt; weights, treadmills. Cr cds: A, C, D, DS, ER, JCB, MC, V.

D ≈ 🏋 ✈ 🚫 🛒 SC

★ **EXEL INN-NORTHEAST.** *(5485 N Port Washington Rd, Glendale 53217) N on I-43, exit Silver Spring Dr.* 414/961-7272; FAX 414/961-1721. 125 rms, 3 story. S $39.99-$63.99; D $49.99-$76.99; each addl $7; under 17 free; wkend rates; higher rates special events. Crib free. Pet accepted, some restrictions. TV; cable (premium). Complimentary continental bkfst. Restaurant adj open 24 hrs. Ck-out noon. Coin lndry. Business servs avail. In-rm modem link. Sundries. Game rm. Some in-rm whirlpools; microwaves avail. Cr cds: A, C, D, DS, MC, V.

D 🐾 🚫 🛒 SC

✔★ **EXEL INN-SOUTH.** *1201 W College Ave (53154), just E of I-94 College Ave exit E, south of downtown.* 414/764-1776; FAX 414/762-8009. 110 rms, 2 story. S $33.99-$59.99; D $34.99-$69.99; each addl $4; under 18 free. Crib free. Pet accepted. TV; cable (premium). Complimentary continental bkfst. Complimentary coffee in lobby. Restaurant opp 6 am-noon. Ck-out noon. Coin lndry. Business servs avail. In-rm modem link. Free airport transportation. Microwaves avail. Cr cds: A, C, D, DS, MC, V.

D 🐾 🚫 🛒 SC

★★ **HAMPTON INN-NORTHWEST.** *5601 N Lovers Lane Rd (53225), north of downtown.* 414/466-8881; FAX 414/466-3840. 107 rms, 4 story. S, D $69-$99; under 18 free; higher rates: special events, summer wkends. Crib free. TV; cable. Indoor pool; whirlpool. Complimentary continental bkfst. Restaurant adj. Ck-out noon. Meeting rm. Business servs avail. In-rm modem link. Valet serv. Exercise equipt; treadmill, stair machine. Microwaves avail. Cr cds: A, C, D, DS, MC, V.

D ≈ 🏋 🚫 🛒 SC

✔★★ **HOSPITALITY INN.** *4400 S 27th St (53221), just N of I-894 27th St exit N, near General Mitchell Intl Airport, south of downtown.* 414/282-8800; FAX 414/282-7713; res: 800/825-8466. 167 rms in 2 bldgs, 81 suites. S, D $60-$200; each addl $10. TV; cable (premium). 2 indoor pools; whirlpool. Complimentary continental bkfst. Restaurant. Rm serv. Ck-out noon. Meeting rms. Valet serv. Free airport transportation. Exercise equipt; weight machine, stair machine. Many refrigerators; some in-rm whirlpools. Cr cds: A, C, D, DS, MC, V.

D ≈ 🏋 ✈ 🚫 🛒 SC

★★ **MANCHESTER SUITES-AIRPORT.** *200 W Grange Ave (53207), near General Mitchell Intl Airport, south of downtown.* 414/744-3600; FAX 414/744-4188; res: 800/723-8280. 100 suites, 4 story. S $64-$74; D $72-$82; each addl $8; under 14 free. Crib free. TV; cable (premium). Complimentary full bkfst. Coffee in rms. Ck-out noon. Meeting rm. Business servs avail. In-rm modem link. Valet serv. Sundries. Free airport transportation. Health Club Privileges. Refrigerators, microwaves, wet bars. Cr cds: A, C, D, DS, MC, V.

D ✈ 🚫 🛒 SC

✔★ **RED ROOF INN.** *(6360 S 13th St, Oak Creek 53154) At jct College Ave, I-94 exit 319 E.* 414/764-3500; FAX 414/764-5138. 108 rms, 2 story. S $36.99-$58.99; D $41.99-$69.99; under 18 free. Crib free. Pet accepted. TV; cable (premium). Complimentary coffee in lobby. Ck-out noon. Business servs avail. Cr cds: A, C, D, DS, MC, V.

D 🐾 🚫 🛒

Motor Hotels

★★★ **HOLIDAY INN AIRPORT.** *6331 S 13th St (53221), I-94 exit 319, south of downtown.* 414/764-1500; FAX 414/764-6531. 159 rms, 3 story. S $69-$90; D $79-$110; each addl $10; under 18 free. Crib free. Pet accepted. TV. Indoor pool. Playground. Restaurant 6 am-1 pm, 5-10 pm; Sat, Sun from 7 am. Rm serv. Bar. Ck-out 11 am. Coin lndry. Business servs avail. Bellhops. Sundries. Free airport transportation. Exercise equipt; weight machine, treadmill, saunas. Game rm. Balconies. Cr cds: A, C, D, DS, JCB, MC, V.

D 🏋 ≈ ✈ 🚫 🛒 SC

★★ **MANCHESTER SUITES NORTHWEST.** *11777 W Silver Spring Dr (53225), I-45 and Silver Spring, west of downtown.* 414/462-3500; FAX 414/462-8166; res: 800/723-8280. 123 suites, 4 story. Suites $62-$80; under 14 free. Crib free. TV; cable. Complimentary full bkfst. Coffee in rms. Restaurant nearby. Ck-out noon. Meeting rms. Business servs avail. In-rm modem link. Valet serv. Exercise equipt; treadmill, bicycle. Sundries. Refrigerators, microwaves, wet bars. Cr cds: A, C, D, DS, MC, V.

D 🏋 🚫 🛒 SC

★★ **RAMADA INN DOWNTOWN.** *633 W Michigan St (53203), downtown.* 414/272-8410; FAX 414/272-4651. E-mail ramadadt@execpc.com; web www.execpc.com/ramadadt. 155 rms, 7 story. S $70-$90; D $78-$101; each addl $10; suites $105-$145; under 18 free; wkend rates. Crib free. TV; cable (premium), VCR avail (movies). Heated pool. Restaurant 6 am-10 pm. Rm serv. Bar 11-2 am. Ck-out noon. Meeting rms. Business servs avail. In-rm modem link. Valet serv. Downhill ski 15 mi; x-country ski 7 mi. Exercise equipt; bicycles, treadmill. Cr cds: A, C, D, DS, JCB, MC, V.

D ≈ 🏋 ✈ 🚫 🛒 SC

★★ **RAMADA INN-WEST.** *201 N Mayfair Rd (53226), just N of I-94 Mayfair Rd (WI 100) exit, west of downtown.* 414/771-4400; FAX 414/771-4517. 230 rms, 3 story. May-Sept: S $84; D $99; under 18 free; lower rates rest of yr. Crib free. Pet accepted, some restrictions. TV; cable (premium). Indoor pool; whirlpool. Playground. Restaurant 6 am-1 pm, 5-9 pm. Rm serv. Bar 3 pm-1 am; Fri, Sat to 2 am. Ck-out noon. Coin lndry. Meeting rms. Business servs avail. Valet serv. Exercise equipt; weights, bicycles, sauna. Picnic tables. Cr cds: A, C, D, DS, ER, JCB, MC, V.

D 🐾 ≈ 🏋 ✈ 🚫 🛒 SC

★★★ **SHERATON INN-NORTH.** *(8900 N Kildeer Ct, Brown Deer 53209) 10 mi N via I-43 exit 82B Brown Deer Rd W.* 414/355-8585; FAX 414/355-3566. 149 rms, 6 story. S, D $96-$144; each addl $10; suites $141-$225; under 18 free; wkend rates. Crib free. TV; cable (premium), VCR avail. Indoor/outdoor pool; whirlpool, poolside serv. Coffee in rms. Restaurant 6:30 am-10:30 pm. Rm serv. Bar 10-2 am. Ck-out noon. Meeting rms. Business servs avail. In-rm modem link. Bellhops. Valet serv. Barber. Airport transportation. X-country ski 3 mi. Sauna. Health club privileges. Some refrigerators; microwaves avail. Cr cds: A, C, D, DS, JCB, MC, V.

D 🏋 ≈ 🚫 🛒

Hotels

★★★ **EMBASSY SUITES-WEST.** *(1200 S Moorland Rd, Brookfield 53008) 10 mi W via I-94, Moorland Rd S exit.* 414/782-2900; FAX 414/796-9159. 203 suites, 5 story. S, D, suites $99-$500; each addl $20; under 12 free; wkend rates; package plans. Crib free. Pet accepted, some restrictions. TV; cable (premium). Indoor pool; whirlpool. Complimentary full bkfst. Complimentary coffee in rms. Restaurant 11 am-11 pm. Bar to 1 am. Ck-out noon. Meeting rms. Business center. In-rm modem link. Concierge. Free airport transportation. Tennis privileges. Golf privileges. Exercise equipt; weight machine, bicycles, sauna, steam rm. Game rm. Refrigerators, microwaves, wet bars. Cr cds: A, C, D, DS, ER, JCB, MC, V.

D 🐾 🏋 ⛷ ≈ ✈ 🚫 🛒 SC 🏌

★★★ **THE GRAND MILWAUKEE.** *4747 S Howell Ave (53207), I-94 Airport E exit, near General Mitchell Airport, south of downtown.* 414/481-8000; FAX 414/481-8065; res: 800/558-3862. 510 rms, 6 story. S, D $64-$175; each addl $10; suites $225-$295; under 17 free; package plans. Crib free. TV; cable (premium). 2 heated pools, 1 indoor; whirlpool. Restaurants 6 am-10 pm. Bar 11-2 am. Ck-out noon. Meeting rms. Business center. In-rm modem link. Gift shop. Barber, beauty shop. Free airport transportation. Indoor tennis. Exercise equipt; weight machines, bicycles, sauna. Game rm. Some refrigerators. Cr cds: A, C, D, DS, MC, V.

★ ★ HILTON. 509 W Wisconsin Ave (53203), I-43 Civic Center exit, downtown. 414/271-7250; FAX 414/271-1039. 500 rms, 25 story. S, D $159-$179; each addl $20; suites $190-$1,000; under 18 free; wkend plan. Crib free. TV; cable (premium). Indoor pool. Restaurant 6:30 am-10 pm. Bar 11 am-1 am. Ck-out noon. Convention facilities. Business servs avail. In-rm modem link. Concierge. Gift shop. Barber, beauty shop. Exercise equipt; bicycle, treadmill, sauna. Cr cds: A, C, D, DS, ER, JCB, MC, V.

★ ★ HILTON INN MILWAUKEE RIVER. 4700 N Port Washington Rd (53212), I-43 exit Hampton Ave E, north of downtown. 414/962-6040; FAX 414/962-6166. Web www.hilton.com. 163 rms, 5 story. S $97-$111; D $112-$121; each addl $15; suites $180-$370; studio rms $114-$129; family rates. TV; cable (premium). Indoor pool. Coffee in rms. Restaurant 6:30 am-10 pm. Bar 11 am-midnight. Ck-out noon. Meeting rms. Business servs avail. In-rm modem link. Exercise equipt; weight machine, stair machine. Some refrigerators. Overlooks river. Cr cds: A, C, D, DS, ER, JCB, MC, V.

★ ★ HOLIDAY INN CITY CENTRE. 611 W Wisconsin Ave (53203), downtown. 414/273-2950; FAX 414/273-7662. 245 rms, 10 story. S $66-$119; D $76-$129; each addl $10; suites $119-$199; under 18 free; higher rates special events. Crib free. TV; cable (premium). Pool. Coffee in rms. Restaurant 6 am-10 pm. Rm serv. Bar from 4 pm. Ck-out noon. Meeting rms. Business center. In-rm modem link. Bellhops. Valet serv. Free valet parking. Health club privileges. Microwaves avail. Cr cds: A, C, D, DS, ER, JCB, MC, V.

★ ★ HOTEL WISCONSIN. 720 N Old World 3rd St (53203), downtown. 414/271-4900; FAX 414/271-9998. 234 rms, 11 story. Mid-June-Sept: S, D $69-$76; each addl $8; suites $85; kit. units $69-$82; under 17 free; lower rates rest of yr. Crib free. Pet accepted. TV; cable (premium), VCR avail. Restaurant 6 am-10 pm. Ck-out 11 am. Meeting rm. Business servs avail. Concierge. Sundries. Valet serv. Coin lndry. Game rm. Health club privileges. Some refrigerators; microwaves avail. Cr cds: A, C, D, DS, ER, JCB, MC, V.

★ ★ HYATT REGENCY. 333 W Kilbourn Ave (53203), downtown. 414/276-1234; FAX 414/276-6338. 484 rms, 22 story. S $99-$149; D $99-$174; each addl $25; parlor rms $95-$150; suites $175-$750; under 18 free; wkend rates; package plans. TV; cable (premium), VCR avail (movies). Restaurants 6:30 am-midnight (also see POLARIS). Bar from 11 am, Fri, Sat to 2 am. Ck-out noon. Convention facilities. Business center. Concierge. Gift shop. Exercise equipt; weight machine, bicycles. Health club privileges. Microwaves avail. Cr cds: A, C, D, DS, ER, JCB, MC, V.

★ ★ PARK EAST. 916 E State St (53202), downtown. 414/276-8800; FAX 414/765-1919; res: 800/328-7275. 159 rms, 5 story. S $81-$110; D $91-$120; each addl $10; suites $91-$250; under 18 free; wkend rates; package plans. Crib $5. TV; cable (premium), VCR (movies). Complimentary continental bkfst. Restaurant 6:30-10 am, 4:30-10 pm; wkends to 11 pm. Bar. Ck-out noon. Meeting rms. Business servs avail. In-rm modem link. Health club privileges. Some in-rm whirlpools, refrigerators, wet bars; microwaves avail. Cr cds: A, C, D, DS, MC, V.

★ ★ ★ PFISTER. 424 E Wisconsin Ave (53202), I-794 Van Buren exit, downtown. 414/273-8222; FAX 414/273-5025; res: 800/558-8222. 307 rms, 23 story. S, D $205-$225; each addl $20; suites $245-$650; under 18 free; wkend rates. Crib free. Parking $8; valet avail. TV; cable, VCR avail (movies). Indoor pool. Restaurant 6:30 am-11 pm (also see ENGLISH ROOM). Rm serv 24 hrs. Bars 11-2 am; entertainment. Ck-out noon. Convention facilities. Business servs avail. In-rm modem link. Con-

cierge. Gift shop. Barber, beauty shop. Airport transportation. Exercise equipt; weight machine, bicycle. Health club privileges. Bathrm phones. Cr cds: A, C, D, DS, JCB, MC, V.

★ ★ ★ WYNDHAM MILWAUKEE CENTER. 139 E Kilbourn Ave (53202), downtown. 414/276-8686; FAX 414/276-8007. 221 rms, 10 story, 77 suites. S, D $155-$199; each addl $20; suites $250-$520; under 12 free; wkend rates. Crib free. Garage $9. TV; cable, VCR avail. Complimentary coffee in rms. Restaurant 6:30 am-11 pm. Bar 11-2 am; entertainment Fri-Sat. Ck-out noon. Meeting rms. Business servs avail. Gift shop. Exercise equipt; weight machines, bicycles, sauna, steam rm. Whirlpool. Microwaves avail. Cr cds: A, C, D, DS, ER, JCB, MC, V.

Restaurants

✔★ AU BON APPÉTIT. 1016 E Brady St (53202), downtown. 414/278-1233. E-mail 107705,2212@compuserve.com. Hrs: 5-9 pm; Fri, Sat to 10 pm. Closed Sun, Mon; major hols. Res accepted. Mediterranean menu. Wine. Semi-a la carte: dinner $6.95-$11.95. Specializes in Lebanese dishes, hummos, tabouleh. Own baking. Street parking. Casual, intimate restaurant; Mediterranean decor. Cr cds: MC, V.

★ BALISTRERI'S BLUEMOUND INN. 6501 W Bluemound Rd (53213), west of downtown. 414/258-9881. Hrs: 11-1 am; Fri to 2 am; Sat 4 pm-2 am; Sun 4 pm-1 am. Closed Thanksgiving, Dec 24, 25. Res accepted. Italian, Amer menu. Bar. Semi-a la carte: lunch, dinner $6-$20. Specialties: veal Balistreri, pollo carcioffi, whitefish Frangelico. Own pasta. Casual, contemporary decor. Cr cds: A, C, D, DS, MC, V.

★ ★ BARTOLOTTA'S LAKE PARK BISTRO. 3133 E Newberry Blvd (53211), East Side. 414/962-6300. Hrs: 11:30 am-2 pm, 5:30-9 pm; Fri to 10 pm; Sat 5-10 pm; Sun 10:30 am-2 pm (brunch), 5-8:30 pm. Closed some major hols. Res accepted. French menu. Bar. Semi-a la carte: lunch $7-$15, dinner $12-$22. Sun brunch $18.95. Child's meals. Specializes in New York strip, Atlantic salmon, homemade desserts. Own baking. Former park pavilion; overlooks Lake Michigan. Cr cds: A, D, DS, MC, V.

★ ★ BAVARIAN INN. 700 W Lexington Blvd, exit I-43 at W Silver Spring Rd, north of downtown. 414/964-0300. Hrs: 11:30 am-2:30 pm, 5-9 pm; Fri to 10 pm; Sat 5-9 pm; Sun brunch 10:30 am-2 pm. Closed Mon; Jan 1, July 4, Dec 24, 25. Res accepted. German, Amer menu. Bar. Semi-a la carte: lunch $4.95-$9.95, dinner $7.95-$14.95. Sun brunch $12.95. Child's meals. Specializes in schnitzel. Accordionist Fri-Sun. Parking. Chalet-style building; large fireplace, timbered ceilings, stein and alpine bell collections. Cr cds: A, C, D, DS, MC, V.

★ ★ ★ BOULEVARD INN. 925 E Wells St (53202), in Cudahy Tower, downtown. 414/765-1166. E-mail blvdin@execpc.com; web www.execpc.com/homepage/~blvdin. Hrs: 11:30 am-9 pm; Fri, Sat to 10 pm; Sun from 10:30 am; Sun brunch to 2 pm. Closed some major hols. Res accepted. Bar. Wine list. Semi-a la carte: lunch $7.50-$11.50, dinner $16.95-$35.95. Sun brunch $10.45. Child's meals. Specializes in fresh fish, veal, German dishes. Own baking. Pianist. Valet parking. Some tableside preparation. Overlooks Lake Michigan. Family-owned. Smoking at bar only. Cr cds: A, C, D, DS, MC, V.

★ CAFE KNICKERBOCKER. 1030 E Juneau Ave (53202), downtown. 414/272-0011. Hrs: 6:30 am-10 pm; Fri, Sat to 11 pm; Sun 9 am-10 pm. Sun brunch 9 am-3 pm. Closed Thanksgiving, Dec 25. Res accepted. Bar. Semi-a la carte: bkfst $3.95-$7.95, lunch $3.95-$7.95, dinner $10.95-19.95. Sun brunch $3.95-$7.95. Specializes in seafood, pasta. Outdoor dining. Casual decor. Totally nonsmoking. Cr cds: A, MC, V.

✔★ **CLUB TRES HERMANOS.** *1332 W Lincoln Ave (53215), south of downtown.* 414/384-9050. Hrs: 11 am-midnight. Closed Thanksgiving, Dec 25. Res accepted. Mexican menu. Bar. Semi-a la carte: lunch $1.75-$5.99, dinner $1.75-$15. Child's meals. Specializes in seafood, burrito, taco. Salad bar. Entertainment Fri, Sat. Mexican decor. Totally nonsmoking. Cr cds: A, C, MC, V.

[D]

✔★ **COUNTY CLARE.** *1234 N Astor St (53202), downtown.* 888/942-5273. Hrs: 11:30 am-10 pm; Sun to 9 pm. Closed major hols. Irish menu. Bar to 1 am. Semi-a la carte: lunch $3.50-$9.50, dinner $3.50-$10.95. Specialties: Irish smoked salmon, corned beef and cabbage, Irish root soup. Traditional Irish music Sun. Irish pub decor with cut glass and dark woods. Cr cds: A, C, D, DS, MC, V.

[D]

✔★ **DOS BANDIDOS.** *5932 N Green Bay Ave (53209), I-43 to Silver Spring exit W, north of downtown.* 414/228-1911. Hrs: 11 am-10:30 pm; Fri to 11:30 pm; Sat noon-11:30 pm; Sun 4-9 pm. Closed major hols. Mexican, Amer menu. Bar. Semi-a la carte: lunch $3.95-$6.50, dinner $7.25-$11.95. Specializes in steak & chicken fajitas, spinach enchiladas, vegetarian dishes. Parking. Patio dining. Mexican cantina decor. Cr cds: A, DS, MC, V.

[D]

✔★ ★ **EAGAN'S.** *1030 N Water St (53202), downtown.* 414/271-6900. Hrs: 11 am-11 pm; Fri, Sat to 1 am; Sun brunch 11 am-2 pm. Closed most major hols. Bar. Semi-a la carte: lunch, dinner $6.95-$15.95. Sun brunch $6.95-$14.95. Specializes in seafood. Outdoor dining. Contemporary decor. Totally nonsmoking. Cr cds: A, D, DS, MC, V.

[D]

★ ★ **ELM GROVE INN.** *(13275 Watertown Plank Rd, Elm Grove 53122) W on I-94, N on Moorland Rd to Watertown Plank Rd.* 414/782-7090. Hrs: 11:30 am-2 pm, 5-9:30 pm; Sat from 5 pm. Closed Sun; major hols. Res accepted. Continental menu. Bar to midnight. Semi-a la carte: lunch $7.50-$13, dinner $17-$27. Specializes in fresh fish, veal, beef. Own baking. 1850s bldg has high-backed chairs, stained glass and large fireplace. Cr cds: A, DS, MC, V.

[D]

★ ★ ★ **ENGLISH ROOM.** *(See Pfister Hotel)* 414/390-3832. Hrs: 11:30 am-2 pm, 5:30-10 pm; Sat 5:30-11 pm; Sun from 5 pm. Res accepted. Bar. Extensive wine list. Semi-a la carte: lunch $7.75-$12. A la carte entrees: dinner $12-$25. Valet parking. Established 1893; past patrons include Teddy Roosevelt, Enrico Caruso. Cr cds: A, C, D, DS, MC, V.

[image]

★ ★ ★ ★ **GRENADIER'S.** *747 N Broadway Ave at Mason (53202), just N of I-794 Jackson-Van Buren exit, downtown.* 414/276-0747. Classic yet imaginative European-style cuisine is served on elegantly set tables in four unique and well-appointed dining rooms. French, continental menu. Specialties: Dover sole, lamb curry Calcutta, fresh seared tuna on ocean salad. Own pastries. Hrs: 11:30 am-2:30 pm, 5:30-10:30 pm; Sat from 5:30 pm. Closed Sun; major hols. Res accepted. Bar. Wine cellar. Semi-a la carte: lunch $8.95-$14.95. A la carte entrees: dinner $17.95-$24.95. Dégustation menu: dinner $31.95. Pianist. Valet parking (dinner). Chef-owned. Jacket. Cr cds: A, C, D, DS, MC, V.

[D] [image]

★ **IZUMI'S.** *2178 N Prospect Ave (53209), on the East Side.* 414/271-5278. Hrs: 11:30 am-2 pm, 5-10 pm; Fri, Sat 5-10:30 pm; Sun 4-9 pm. Closed major hols. Res accepted. Japanese menu. Wine, beer. Semi-a la carte: lunch $4.95-$12.95, dinner $9-$23. Specializes in sushi, sukiyaki, teriyaki dishes. Parking. Contemporary Japanese decor. Cr cds: A, D, MC, V.

[image]

★ ★ **JACK PANDL'S WHITEFISH BAY INN.** *(1319 E Henry Clay St, Whitefish Bay 53217) 6 mi N on WI 32, 2 mi NE of I-43 Hampton Ave exit E.* 414/964-3800. Hrs: 11:30 am-2:30 pm, 5-9 pm; Fri, Sat to 10:30 pm; Sun 10:30 am-2:30 pm, 4-8 pm. Res accepted. Bar. Semi-a la carte: lunch $5.95-$9.95, dinner $7.95-$21.95. Child's meals. Specializes in whitefish, German pancakes, Schaum torte. Parking. Established in 1915; antique beer stein collection. Family-owned. Cr cds: A, C, D, DS, MC, V.

★ ★ ★ **JOHN ERNST'S.** *600 E Ogden Ave (53202), at Jackson St, downtown.* 414/273-1878. E-mail jernst@execpc.com; web www.execpc.com/~jernst. Hrs: 11:30 am-10 pm; Sun 11 am-9:30 pm; Sun brunch to 2 pm. Closed Mon. Res accepted. Continental, Amer menu. Bar. Semi-a la carte: lunch $7.50-$10.75, dinner $13.50-$28.95. Child's meals. Specialties: prime steak, Kassler rippchen, jaegerschnitzel. Own pastries. Entertainment. Parking. Old World decor; stained glass, fireplace. Collection of steins. Established in 1878; oldest in city. Family-owned. Cr cds: A, C, D, DS, MC, V.

[D] [image]

★ **JUDY'S KITCHEN.** *(600 W Brown Deer Rd, Bayside 53217) 12 mi N on I-43.* 414/352-9998. Hrs: 11 am-2 pm, 5-9 pm; Fri to 11 pm; Sat 5-11 pm. Closed Sun; major hols. Bar 3:30 pm-2 am; Sat from 6 pm. Semi-a la carte: lunch $4.50-$10, dinner $8.95-$19.95. Spcializes in steak, fresh fish, homemade desserts. Own baking. Outdoor dining. Casual atmosphere; large aquarium at one wall. Totally nonsmoking. Cr cds: A, MC, V.

★ ★ **KARL RATZSCH'S.** *320 E Mason St (53202), I-794 Van Buren St exit, downtown.* 414/276-2720. Hrs: 4-9:30 pm; Sat to 10:30 pm; Sun to 9 pm. Closed major hols. Res accepted. German, Amer menu. Bar. Semi-a la carte: dinner $12.95-$24. Child's meals. Specializes in planked whitefish, roast goose shank, aged prime steak. Pianist evenings. Valet parking. Collection of rare steins, glassware. Old World Austrian atmosphere. Family-owned. Cr cds: A, C, D, DS, MC, V.

[image]

★ ★ **KING AND I.** *823 N 2nd St (53203), downtown.* 414/276-4181. Hrs: 11:30 am-10 pm; Sat 5-11 pm; Sun 4-9 pm. Closed major hols. Res accepted. Thai menu. Bar. Semi-a la carte: lunch $5-$8, dinner $9-$18. Specialties: volcano chicken, fresh red snapper, crispy duck. Southeast Asian decor; enameled wood chairs, hand-carved teakwood, native artwork. Cr cds: A, D, DS, MC, V.

[D] [image]

★ ★ **MADER'S.** *1037 N Old World Third St (53203), downtown.* 414/271-3377. Hrs: 11:30 am-10 pm; Fri, Sat to 11:30 pm; Sun 10:30 am-9 pm; Sun brunch to 2 pm. Res accepted. German, continental menu. Bar. Semi-a la carte: lunch $4.95-$8.95, dinner $13.95-$23.95. Sun Viennese brunch $14.95. Child's meals. Specialties: Rheinischer sauerbraten, Wienerschnitzel, roast pork shank. Valet parking. Old World German decor; antiques. Gift shop. Family-owned. Cr cds: A, C, D, DS, MC, V.

[D] [image]

★ ★ ★ **MANIACI'S CAFE SICILIANO.** *(6904 N Santa Monica Blvd, Fox Point 53217) 10 mi N on WI 32.* 414/352-5757. Hrs: 4-10 pm. Closed Sun; major hols; also wk of July 4. Res accepted. Continental menu. Serv bar. Wine cellar. Semi-a la carte: dinner $17.50-$32.95. Child's meals. Specializes in veal, fish, pasta. Own pasta. Sicilian decor with brick columns, tile floors. Family-owned. Cr cds: A, MC, V.

[image]

★ ★ **MIKE & ANNA'S.** *2000 S Eighth St (53204), south of downtown.* 414/643-0072. Hrs: 5:30-8:45 pm; Fri, Sat to 9:45 pm. Closed Mon; major hols. Res accepted. Bar. Semi-a la carte: dinner $19-$26.95. Specializes in salmon, rack of lamb. Menu changes daily. Restored corner tavern in residential setting; contemporary atmosphere. Cr cds: A, MC, V.

[D]

★ ★ ★ **MIMMA'S CAFE.** *1307 E Brady St (53202), downtown.* 414/271-7337. E-mail mimma89@jadetec.com. Hrs: 11:30 am-2:30 pm, 5-10 pm; Fri, Sat to midnight; Sun from 5 pm. Closed major hols. Res accepted. Italian menu. Bar. A la carte entrees: lunch $6-$12, dinner $8-$30. Specializes in pasta, seafood, veal. Contemporary decor. Cr cds: A, C, D, DS, MC, V.

[D]

★ ★ **NORTH SHORE BISTRO.** *(8649 N Port Washington Rd, Fox Point 53217) 10 mi N on WI 32.* 414/351-6100. Hrs: 11 am-10 pm; Sat to 11 pm; Sun from 4 pm. Closed most major hols. Res accepted. Bar. Semi-a la carte: lunch $6-$9.25, dinner $6-$24.95. Specializes in seafood, steak, pasta. Outdoor dining. Casual bistro atmosphere. Cr cds: A, MC, V.

[D]

✓ ★ OLD TOWN SERBIAN GOURMET HOUSE. *522 W Lincoln Ave (53207), south of downtown.* 414/672-0206; FAX 414/672-0810. Hrs: 11:30 am-2:30 pm, 5-11 pm; Sat, Sun from 5 pm. Closed Mon; some major hols. Res accepted. Serbian, Amer menu. Bar. Semi-a la carte: lunch $5-$9, dinner $12-$20. Child's meals. Entertainment (wkends). Parking. Family-owned. Cr cds: A, D, DS, MC, V.

[D] [⌐]

★ ★ ★ OSTERIA DEL MONDO. *1028 E Juneau Ave (53202), downtown.* 414/291-3770. Web www.osteria.com. Hrs: 11 am-2:30 pm, 5-10:30 pm; Sat 5-11 pm. Closed most major hols. Res accepted. Italian menu. Bar. Semi-a la carte: lunch $5.95-$11.95, dinner $9.95-$24.95. Sun brunch $6.95-$16.95. Specializes in seafood, pasta. Outdoor dining. Italian decor. Totally nonsmoking. Cr cds: A, D, MC, V.

[D]

★ ★ ★ PANDL'S IN BAYSIDE. *8825 N Lake Dr (53217), 10 mi N on WI 32, 1 mi E of I-43 Brown Deer Rd (E) exit, north of downtown.* 414/352-7300. Web www.pandl.com. Hrs: 11:30 am-10 pm; Fri-Sat to 11:30 pm; Sun 10 am-9 pm; Sun brunch to 2 pm. Closed Labor Day, Dec 25. Res accepted. Bar. Semi-a la carte: lunch, dinner $7.50-$19. Sun brunch $18.50. Child's meals. Specializes in fresh fish, prime meats. Salad bar (dinner). Own pastries. Parking. Family-owned. Cr cds: A, C, D, DS, MC, V.

★ PLEASANT VALLEY INN. *9801 W Dakota St (53227), west of downtown.* 414/321-4321. Hrs: 5-9 pm; Fri, Sat to 10 pm; Sun 4-8 pm. Closed Mon; major hols. Res accepted. Bar. Semi-a la carte: dinner $14-$22. Child's meals. Specializes in steak, seafood. Casual decor. Cr cds: A, DS, MC, V.

[D]

★ ★ POLARIS. *(See Hyatt Regency Hotel)* 414/276-1234. Hrs: 11:30 am-2 pm, 5-11 pm; Sat, Sun from 5 pm. Closed Jan 1, Thanksgiving, Dec 25. Res accepted. Bar. A la carte entrees: lunch $5.95-$8.95, dinner $13.95-$25. Specializes in prime rib au jus, grilled veal chops, chicken tortellini. Parking. Revolving restaurant on 22nd floor. Cr cds: A, C, D, DS, MC, V.

[D]

★ ★ PORTERHOUSE. *800 W Layton Ave (53221), south of downtown.* 414/744-1750. Hrs: 11 am-2:30 pm, 5-10 pm; Fri, Sat to 11 pm; Sun 4-9 pm. Closed Mon. Res accepted. Bar. Semi-a la carte: lunch $6.25-$11.95, dinner $9.95-$49.95. Child's meals. Specializes in charbroiled steak, ribs, seafood. Parking. Cr cds: A, C, D, DS, MC, V.

[D] [⌐]

✓ ★ RED ROCK CAFE. *4022 N Oakland Ave (53211), north of downtown.* 414/962-4545. Hrs: 11 am-2 pm, 5-9 pm; Fri, Sat to 10 pm; Sun from 5 pm. Closed Mon; major hols. Bar. Semi-a la carte: lunch $6.95-$11.95, dinner $8.25-$22.50. Child's meals. Specializes in seafood. Nautical decor. Totally nonsmoking. Cr cds: MC, V.

[D] [SC]

★ ★ RIVER LANE INN. *(4313 W River Lane, Brown Deer 53223)* 414/354-1975. Hrs: 11:30 am-2:30 pm, 5-10 pm. Closed Sun; most major hols. Bar. Semi-a la carte: lunch $6.75-$10.95, dinner $15.95-$20.95. Specializes in seafood. Casual decor. Cr cds: A, MC, V.

[D]

✓ ★ ROYAL INDIA. *3400 S 27th St (53215), south of downtown.* 414/647-2050. Hrs: 11 am-3 pm, 5-10 pm; Fri, Sat to 10:30 pm. Res accepted. Indian menu. Wine, beer. Buffet: lunch $6.95. Semi-a la carte: dinner $5.95-$11.95. Specializes in tandoori dishes, seafood, lamb. Own baking. Casual Indian decor. Totally nonsmoking. Cr cds: MC, V.

[D]

★ ★ ★ ★ SANFORD. *1547 N Jackson St (53202), downtown.* 414/276-9608. This is an elegant restaurant set in a remodeled grocery store and named for the chef, Sanford D'Amato. The cuisine is a mix of Western and Asian influences and has won national acclaim. Specialties: seared sea scallops; grilled breast of duck; cumin wafers with grilled, marinated tuna. Hrs: 5:30-9 pm; Fri, Sat to 10 pm. Closed Sun; major hols. Res accepted. Serv bar. Wine cellar. Semi-a la carte: dinner $23.95-$29.95. Tasting menu (changes monthly): $35. Valet parking. Totally nonsmoking. Cr cds: A, C, D, DS, MC, V.

[D]

★ SAZ'S STATE HOUSE. *5539 W State St, west of downtown.* 414/453-2410. Hrs: 11 am-midnight; Sun to 10 pm; Sun brunch 10:30 am-2:30 pm. Closed Dec 24, 25. Bar. Semi-a la carte: lunch $4.25-$7.95, dinner $7.50-$19.95. Specializes in barbecued ribs, fresh fish, chicken. Parking. Outdoor dining. 1905 roadhouse. Cr cds: A, MC, V.

[D] [⌐]

✓★ ★ SELENSKY'S GRAND CHAMPION GRILL. *(4395 S 76th St, Greenfield 53220)* 414/327-9100. Hrs: 3:30-11 pm; Sun 2:30-9 pm. Closed Mon; Jan 1, July 4, Dec 25. Bar. Semi-a la carte: dinner $8.95-$18.95. Child's meals. Specializes in prime rib, steak, fresh seafood. Casual decor. Cr cds: MC, V.

[D]

✓★ ★ SINGHA THAI. *(2237 S 108th St, West Allis 53227)* 414/541-1234. Hrs: 11 am-9 pm; Fri, Sat to 10 pm. Closed most major hols. Res accepted. Thai menu. Semi-a la carte: lunch $5-$10, dinner $6-$15. Specializes in noodle dishes, curry dishes. Casual atmosphere. Cr cds: MC, V.

[D]

★ ★ ★ STEVEN WADE'S CAFE. *(17001 Greenfield Ave, New Berlin 53151)* 414/784-0774; FAX 414/784-7311. Web www.foodspot.com. Hrs: 11:30 am-2 pm, 5:30-10 pm; Mon, Sat from 5:30 pm. Closed Sun; major hols. Res accepted. Contemporary Amer menu. Semi-a la carte: lunch $8-$14, dinner $16-$25. Specializes in wild game, pasta, seafood. Intimate atmosphere. Totally nonsmoking. Cr cds: A, C, D, DS, ER, MC, V.

[D] [SC]

✓★ THREE BROTHERS. *2414 S St Clair (53207), in Bay View.* 414/481-7530. Hrs: 5-10 pm; Fri, Sat 4-11 pm; Sun 4-10 pm. Closed Mon; some major hols. Res accepted. Serbian menu. Serv bar. Semi-a la carte: dinner $10.95-$14.95. Specialties: burek, roast lamb, gulash. Serbian artwork on display. No cr cds accepted.

[⌐]

★ ★ WEISSGERBER'S THIRD STREET PIER. *1110 N Old World Third St (53203), downtown.* 414/272-0330. Hrs: 11:30 am-2 pm, 5-10 pm; Sat from 5 pm; Sun 4-9 pm. Res accepted. Bar 11 am-. Semi-a la carte: lunch $6-$10, dinner $15.95-$34.95. Child's meals. Specializes in seafood, steak. Own desserts. Pianist Thurs-Sat. Valet parking. Outdoor dining. Lunch, dinner cruises on Lake Michigan avail. In restored landmark building on Milwaukee River. Cr cds: A, DS, MC, V.

[D] [⌐]

✓★ ★ WEST BANK CAFE. *732 E Burleigh St (53212), downtown.* 414/562-5555. Hrs: 5:30-9:30 pm; Fri, Sat to 10 pm. Closed most major hols. Chinese, Vietnamese menu. Serv bar. Semi-a la carte: dinner $7-$16. Specializes in Vietnamese dishes. Own baking. Street parking. Contemporary Oriental decor. Totally nonsmoking. Cr cds: A, MC, V.

✓★ YEN CHING. *7630 W Good Hope Rd (53223), north of downtown.* 414/353-6677. Hrs: 11:30 am-2 pm, 4:30-9:30 pm; Fri, Sat 4:30-10 pm; Sun 11:30 am-2:30 pm, 4:30-9 pm. Mandarin menu. Serv bar. Semi-a la carte: lunch $4.25-$5.50, dinner $6.50-$12. Specializes in beef, chicken, seafood. Parking. Oriental decor. Cr cds: A, C, D, DS, MC, V.

[D] [⌐]

Unrated Dining Spots

THE CHOCOLATE SWAN. *(890 Elm Grove Rd, Elm Grove) 2 mi W on Bluemound Rd to N Elm Grove Rd, at Elm Grove Village Court shopping center.* 414/784-7926. Hrs: 11 am-6 pm; Fri to 8:30 pm; Sat from 10 am. Closed Sun; most major hols. Dessert menu only. Desserts $1.75-$5.75. Specialties: Mary's chocolate interlude, yellow strawberry log. Tea room ambiance. Totally nonsmoking. Cr cds: MC, V.

SAFE HOUSE. *779 N Front St, entrance at International Exports, Ltd, downtown.* 414/271-2007. Hrs: 11:30-2 am; Fri, Sat to 2:30 am; Sun 4 pm-midnight. Res accepted. Bar. Semi-a la carte: lunch, dinner $4.25-$12.95. Specializes in sandwiches, specialty drinks. DJ Fri & Sat, magician Sun-Thurs. Spy theme decor. Cr cds: A, MC, V.

Mineral Point (G-3)

(See also Dodgeville, New Glarus, Platteville)

Settled 1827 **Pop** 2,428 **Elev** 1,135 ft **Area code** 608 **Zip** 53565 **E-mail** minpt@mhtc.net **Web** www.mhtc.net/~minpt

Information Chamber of Commerce, 225 High St, PO Box 78; 608/987-3201 or 888/764-6894.

The first settlers were New Englanders and Southerners attracted by the lead (galena) deposits. In the 1830s miners from Cornwall, England settled here. These "Cousin Jacks," as they were called, introduced superior mining methods and also built the first permanent homes, duplicating the rock houses they had left in Cornwall. Since the mines were in sight of their homes their wives called them to meals by stepping to the door and shaking a rag—so the town was first called "Shake Rag."

What to See and Do

Pendarvis, Cornish Restoration. Guided tour of 6 restored log and limestone homes of Cornish miners (ca 1845). Also 40-acre nature walk in old mining area (free) which has mine shafts, wildflowers and abandoned "badger holes." (May-Oct, daily) 114 Shake Rag St. Phone 608/987-2122. Tours ¢¢

Motel

✔★ REDWOOD. *RR 3, Box 43, 1 mi NE on US 151.* 608/987-2317; res: 800/321-1958. 28 rms, 2 story. May-Oct: S $34-$50; D $43-$55; each addl $5; lower rates rest of yr. TV; cable. Restaurant adj 6 am-8 pm. Ck-out 11 am. Business servs avail. Free airport transportation. X-country ski 17 mi. Miniature golf. Cr cds: DS, MC, V.

D 🐾 🎿 SC

Minocqua (C-4)

(See also Boulder Junction, Eagle River, Lac du Flambeau, Rhinelander, St Germain, Woodruff)

Pop 3,522 **Elev** 1,603 ft **Area code** 715 **Zip** 54548 **E-mail** mavwacc@minocqua.org **Web** www.minocqua.org

Information Minocqua-Arbor Vitae-Woodruff Area Chamber of Commerce, 8216 US 51, PO Box 1006; 715/356-5266 or 800/44-NORTH.

Minocqua, the "Island City," is surrounded by the 2,000 acres of Lake Minocqua. Summer homes, youth camps and resorts are along the lakeshore. This has become a popular four-season resort area.

What to See and Do

Area has 2,000 lakes with every major type of freshwater fish found in Wisconsin. Also clear water for diving. The Min-Aqua-Bat waterski shows are held mid-June-mid-Aug on Wed, Fri & Sun eves. For winter sports enthusiasts there are hundreds of miles of groomed snowmobile and cross-country ski trails. Inquire at Chamber of Commerce.

Circle M Corral Family Fun Park. Horseback riding, bumper boats, go-carts; train ride with robbery aboard replica C.P. Huntington; water slide; miniature golf; children's rides. Picnic area, snack bar. (Mid-May-mid-Oct, daily) 2½ mi W of US 51 on WI 70 W. Phone 715/356-4441. ¢¢¢¢-¢¢¢¢¢

Jim Peck's Wildwood. A wildlife park featuring hundreds of tame animals and birds native to the area; many can be petted at baby animal nursery; walk among tame deer; trout and musky ponds. Picnic area; nature walk; adventure boat rides; gift shop, snack wagon. (May-mid-Oct, daily) US 51 to WI 70, then 2 mi W. Phone 715/356-5588. ¢¢¢

Minocqua Winter Park Nordic Center. Center has over 35 mi of groomed and tracked cross-country trails; 2 groomed telemarking slopes; more than one mi of lighted trails for night skiing (Thurs-Fri only). School, shop, rentals. Heated chalet, concessions. (Dec-Mar, daily) 6 mi W on WI 70 to Squirrel Lake Rd, then approx 6 mi S, follow the signs. Phone 715/356-3309. ¢¢¢

Wilderness Cruise. Two-hr cruise on the Willow Flowage aboard the *Wilderness Queen.* Also brunch, dinner and fall foliage cruises. (Mid-May-Oct, daily; res required) 7 mi S on US 51, then 7 mi on County Y to Willow Dam Rd in Hazelhurst. Phone 715/453-3310 or 800/472-1516. Sightseeing cruise ¢¢¢

Seasonal Event

Northern Lights Playhouse. 10 mi S on US 51 in Hazelhurst. Professional repertory theater presents Broadway plays, musicals & comedies; also Children's Theatre. Phone 715/356-7173. Memorial Day-early Oct.

Motels

★ AQUA AIRE. *806 US 51 N.* 715/356-3433; FAX 715/356-3433. 10 rms (with shower only), 1 story. June-Aug: S $32-$59; D $59-$79; each addl $5; under 3 free; wkly rates; higher rates special events; lower rates rest of yr. Crib free. Pet accepted, some restrictions. TV; cable (premium). Restaurant opp 7 am-2:30 pm. Ck-out 11 am. Business servs avail. X-country ski 7 mi. Refrigerators. Picnic tables. Cr cds: MC, V.

🐾 🐾 🎿 🛶 SC

★ ★ BEST WESTERN LAKEVIEW MOTOR LODGE. *3 blks S on US 51.* 715/356-5208; FAX 715/356-1412. 41 rms, 2 story. June-Sept, also hols: S $73-$103; D $79-$109; each addl $6; 2-story chalet units avail; lower rates rest of yr. Pet accepted; $6. TV; cable (premium). Continental bkfst. Restaurant nearby. Ck-out 11 am. Business servs avail. X-country ski 10 mi. Snowmobiling. Some in-rm whirlpools. Some balconies. Picnic tables. On Lake Minocqua; dock. Cr cds: A, C, D, DS, MC, V.

🐾 🐾 🎿 ≈ 🛶 🎿 SC

★ CROSS TRAILS. *8644 US 51N.* 715/356-5202; FAX 715/356-1104; res: 800/842-5261. 17 rms. Mid-June-mid-Aug: S, D $59-$69; each addl $4-$5; lower rates rest of yr. Crib $4. Pet accepted. TV; cable (premium). Restaurant 6 am-8 pm; off-season to 7 pm. Ck-out 11 am. Business servs avail. In-rm modem link. X-country ski 8 mi. Snowmobiling. Small wildlife refuge. Cr cds: A, C, D, DS, MC, V.

D 🐾 🐾 🎿

★ ★ NEW CONCORD INN. *US 51.* 715/356-1800; FAX 715/356-6955. 53 rms, 3 story. July-Sept, Dec-Feb: S, D $83-$115; each addl $7; suites $115; under 13 free; lower rates rest of yr. Crib $5. TV; cable (premium), VCR avail. Indoor pool; whirlpool. Complimentary continental bkfst. Restaurant nearby. Ck-out 11 am. Meeting rms. Business servs avail. Sundries. Game rm. Some refrigerators. Cr cds: A, D, DS, MC, V.

Restaurants

★ ★ **NORWOOD PINES.** *10171 US 70W. 715/356-3666.* Hrs: 5 pm-closing. Closed Sun, Dec 24-25. Semi-a la carte: dinner $8.95-$18.25. Friday fish fry $6.95. Child's meals. Specializes in veal, steak, seafood. Pianist, sing-along. Cr cds: C, D, MC, V.

✔★ **PAUL BUNYAN LOGGING CAMP.** *8653 US 51N, 1 mi N, between Minocqua & Woodruff. 715/356-6270.* Hrs: 7 am-9 pm. Closed Oct-Apr. Bar. Complete meals: bkfst $5.95, lunch $4.50-$9.95, dinner $9.95. Fri fish fry $6.95. Child's meals. Specializes in lumberjack-style meals. 2 entrees daily; family-style serv. Replica of typical 1890 logging camp. Family-owned. Cr cds: MC, V.

★ **RED STEER.** *8230 WI 51S. 715/356-6332.* Hrs: 4:30 pm-closing. Closed Tues; also Thanksgiving, Dec 24. Res accepted. Bar. Semi-a la carte: dinner $7.95-$18.95. Child's meals. Specializes in charcoal-broiled steak, ice-cream drinks. Rustic decor. Cr cds: A, D, DS, MC, V.

★ **SPANG'S.** *318 Milwaukee St. 715/356-4401.* Hrs: 5-10 pm. Closed Easter, Thanksgiving, Dec 24-25. Italian menu. Bar. Semi-a la carte: dinner $6.25-$13.95. Child's meals. Specializes in pasta, pizza. Cr cds: A, DS, MC, V.

Monroe (H-4)

(See also Janesville, New Glarus)

Pop 10,241 **Elev** 1,099 ft **Area code** 608 **Zip** 53566
Information Chamber of Commerce, 1505 9th St; 608/325-7648.

A well-known community of Swiss heritage in an area of abundant dairy production, Monroe is the site of a unique courthouse with a 120-foot tall clock tower.

What to See and Do

Alp and Dell Cheesery, Deli and Country Cafe. Watch cheese making process (Mon-Fri). Self-guided tours. Retail store (daily). 657 2nd St. Phone 608/328-3355. **Free.**

Yellowstone Lake State Park. A 785-acre park on Yellowstone Lake. Swimming, waterskiing; fishing; boating (rentals). Hiking. Cross-country skiing, snowmobiling. Picnicking, playground, concession. Camping (electric, dump station; res accepted by dept form only), winter camping. Standard fees. (Daily) 16 mi NW on WI 81 to Argyle, then N on County N, then W on Lake Rd. Phone 608/523-4427. Per vehicle ¢¢

Annual Event

Balloon Rally. Phone 608/325-7648. Late July.

Motel

✔★ **ALPHORN INN.** *250 N 18th Ave, WI 81 exit 18th Ave. 608/325-4138; res: 800/448-1805.* 63 rms, 2 story. S $30-$40; D $40-$50; each addl $4; under 13 free. Crib free. TV; cable. Complimentary coffee in lobby. Restaurant nearby. Ck-out 11 am. Business servs avail. In-rm modem link. Cr cds: A, C, D, DS, MC, V.

Mt Horeb (G-4)

(See also Dodgeville, Madison, New Glarus)

Pop 4,182 **Elev** 1,230 ft **Area code** 608 **Zip** 53572
Information Chamber of Commerce, PO Box 84; 608/437-5914 or 888/765-5929.

What to See and Do

Blue Mound State Park. A 1,150-acre park with scenic views and lookout towers. Swimming pool. Nature, hiking and cross-country ski trails. Picnicking, playgrounds. Camping (dump station). Standard fees. (Daily) W on US 18, 1 mi NW of Blue Mounds. Phone 608/437-5711. Per vehicle ¢¢¢

Cave of the Mounds. Colorful onyx formations in limestone cavern, rooms on 2 levels. Registered National Natural Landmark. 1-hr guided tours. (Mid-Mar-mid-Nov, daily; rest of yr, wkends) Also picnic grounds, gardens, snack bar and gift shops. 4 mi W on US 18/151, then follow signs to Cave of the Mounds. Phone 608/437-3038. ¢¢¢

★ **Little Norway.** Norwegian pioneer farmstead built in 1856; museum of Norse antiques. Guided tours (45 min). (May-late Oct, daily) W via US 18/151 to Cave of the Mounds Rd, then follow signs to County JG. Phone 608/437-8211. ¢¢¢

Mt Horeb Mustard Museum. Large collection of mustards, mustard memorabilia and samplings. (Daily) 109 E Main. Phone 608/437-3986. **Free.**

Motel

★ ★ **BEST WESTERN KARAKAHL INN.** *1405 US 18 Business/151 E. 608/437-5545; FAX 608/437-5908.* 75 rms, 1-2 story. Mid-May-mid-Oct: S $59-$64; D $69-$174; each addl $5; suites $119; under 12 free; lower rates rest of yr; Crib $4. Pet accepted, some restrictions; $5. TV; cable. Saunas. Indoor pool. Complimentary coffee in lobby. Restaurant 7 am-2 pm, 5-8 pm; Fri, Sat to 10 pm; closed Sun eve. Bar 5 pm-1 am. Ck-out noon. Business servs avail. X-country ski 2 blks. Cr cds: A, C, D, DS, MC, V.

Neenah-Menasha (E-5)

(See also Appleton, Green Bay, Oshkosh)

Settled 1843 **Pop** Neenah, 23,219; Menasha, 14,711 **Elev** 750 ft **Area code** 920 **Zip** Neenah, 54956; Menasha, 54952 **E-mail** tourism @foxcities.org **Web** www.foxcities.org
Information Fox Cities Convention & Visitor Bureau, 3433 W College Ave, Appleton, 54914; 414/734-3358 or 800/236-6673.

Wisconsin's great paper industry started in Neenah and its twin city, Menasha. The two cities, located on Lake Winnebago, are still among the nation's leaders in dollar volume of paper products. Many paper product factories are located here in addition to large wood product plants, printing and publishing houses, foundries and machine shops.

What to See and Do

Bergstrom-Mahler Museum. More than 1,800 glass paperweights; antique German glass; American regional paintings; changing exhibits. (Daily exc Mon; closed hols exc Easter) Museum shop, specializing in glass. 165 N Park Ave, Neenah. Phone 920/751-4658. **Free.**

Doty Cabin. Home of Wisconsin's second territorial governor, James Duane Doty. Boating (ramp). Tennis courts. Picnic facilities, playgrounds.

Park (daily). Cabin (Mid-June-mid-Aug, Sun-Thurs afternoons). Doty Park, Webster & Lincoln Sts, Neenah. Phone 920/751-4614. **Donation.**

High Cliff State Park. A 1,139-acre park with beautiful wooded bluffs. Swimming, bathhouse, waterskiing; fishing; boating (marina). Nature, hiking, snowmobile and cross-country ski trails. Picnicking, playgrounds, concession. Camping (dump station). Naturalist program. Standard fees. (Daily) 9 mi E, off WI 114, on opposite shore of Lake Winnebago. Phone 920/989-1106. Per vehicle ¢¢ In the park is

High Cliff General Store. Museum depicts life in the area from 1850 to the early 1900s. Store was once the center of activity of the lime kiln community and housed the post and telegraph offices. Relic of old lime kiln oven nearby. (Mid-May-Sept, Sat-Sun & hols) **Free.**

Smith Park. Monument to Jean Nicolet, who came in 1634 to arrange peace between Native American tribes. Tennis courts. Cross-country skiing. Picnic areas, pavilion, playground. Native American effigy mounds; formal gardens; historic railroad caboose representing birthplace of Central Wisconsin Railroad. (Daily) Keyes St, Menasha. Phone 920/751-5106. **Free.**

Motel

★ **PARKWAY.** (1181 Gillingham Rd, Neenah 54956) 2 mi N on WI 47, across bridge. 920/725-3244. 19 rms, 8 with shower only, 1-2 story. June-Sept: S $27-$30; D $32-$34; each addl $5; under 5 free; wkly rates; higher rates special events; lower rates rest of yr. Crib $3. Pet accepted, some restrictions. TV; cable. Complimentary continental bkfst. Restaurant adj 11 am-10:30 pm. Ck-out 11 am. Heated pool. Playground. Picnic tables, grills. Cr cds: A, DS, MC, V.

🐾 🌊 🎿 🐾 SC

New Glarus (G-4)

(See also Madison, Monroe, Mt Horeb)

Settled 1845 **Pop** 1,899 **Elev** 900 ft **Area code** 608 **Zip** 53574
Information New Glarus Tourism, PO Box 713; 608/527-2095 or 800/527-6838.

When bad times struck the Swiss canton of Glarus in 1844, a group of 193 set out for the New World and settled New Glarus. Their knowledge of dairying brought prosperity. The town is still predominantly Swiss in character and ancestry.

What to See and Do

Chalet of the Golden Fleece. Replica of Swiss chalet, with more than 3,000 Swiss items. Guided tours. (May-Oct, daily) 618 2nd St at 7th Ave. Phone 608/527-2614. ¢¢

New Glarus Woods State Park. Park has 34 campsites in 360 acres of wooded valleys. Picnicking, playgrounds. Standard fees. (Apr-Oct, daily) 1 mi S on WI 69. Phone 608/527-2335. Per vehicle ¢¢

Sugar River State Trail. A 23-mi trail follows abandoned railroad bed between New Glarus and Brodhead to the SE. Hiking, biking, snowmobiling, and cross-country skiing. (Daily) Phone 608/527-2334. ¢¢

⭐ **Swiss Historical Village.** Replicas of first buildings erected by settlers, including blacksmith shops, cheese factory, schoolhouse, and print shop; original furnishings and tools; guided tours. (May-Oct, daily) 612 7th Ave. Phone 608/527-2317. ¢¢

Annual Events

Heidi Festival. Phone 800/527-6838. Last full wkend June.

Swiss Volksfest. Wilhelm Tell Shooting Park, 1/2 mi N on County O. Singing, yodeling, dancing. Honors birth of Swiss confederation in 1291. 1st Sun Aug.

Wilhelm Tell Festival. Alpine Festival, Swiss entertainment, Sat; Schiller's drama, *Wilhelm Tell*, in German, Sun; in English, Sat, Mon; Tell Amphitheater, 1 1/4 mi E on County W. Also fine arts show, Village Park, Sun. Phone 608/527-2921. Labor Day wkend.

Motels

★ ★ **CHALET LANDHAUS.** at jct WI 69, 39. 608/527-5234; FAX 608/527-2365. 67 rms, 3-4 story. May-Oct: S $49-$60; D $68-$75; each addl $12; suites $130; family rms $100; under 8 free; lower rates rest of yr. Crib $12. Pet accepted. TV; cable. Restaurant 7-11 am, 5:30-9 pm; Sun, Mon to 11 am. Ck-out 11 am. Meeting rms. Business servs avail. X-country ski 2 mi. Whirlpool in suites. Some balconies. Cr cds: A, MC, V.

D 🐾 🎿 🐾 SC

✔★ **SWISS-AIRE.** 1200 WI 69. 608/527-2138; res: 800/798-4391. 26 rms. May-Oct: S $45-$49; D $45-$65; each addl $6; under 5 free; lower rates rest of yr. Crib free. Pet accepted. TV; cable. Heated pool. Complimentary continental bkfst. Ck-out 11 am. Meeting rms. Picnic tables. Cr cds: DS, MC, V.

🐾 🌊 🐾 🔥

Inn

★ ★ **COUNTRY HOUSE.** 180 WI 69. 608/527-5399. 4 rms, 2 story. S, D $65-$110. Complimentary full bkfst. Ck-out 11 am, ck-in 4-7 pm. Built in 1892; antiques. Totally nonsmoking. Cr cds: MC, V.

🖼 🔥

Restaurant

✔★ ★ **NEW GLARUS HOTEL.** 100 6th Ave, just W of jct WI 39, 69. 608/527-5244. Hrs: 11 am-9 pm; Fri, Sat to 10 pm; Sun brunch 10:30 am-3 pm. Closed Thanksgiving, Dec 24-25; also Tues in Nov-Apr. Res accepted. Swiss, Amer menu. Bar. Semi-a la carte: lunch $3.50-$9, dinner $5-$15. Sun brunch $10.50. Child's meals. Specialties: beef & cheese fondues, piccata schnitzel, three filet (pork, veal, beef). Own baking. Polka Fri, Sat; yodeling (summer). Cr cds: A, DS, MC, V.

D

Oconomowoc (G-5)

(See also Milwaukee, Watertown)

Pop 10,993 **Elev** 873 ft **Area code** 414 **Zip** 53066 **E-mail** oconcham@mail.cedar.net **Web** www.oconomowoc.org
Information Greater Oconomowoc Area Chamber of Commerce, 152 E Wisconsin Ave; 414/567-2666.

Native Americans called this place "the gathering of waters," because of its location between Fowler Lake and Lac La Belle. Once an exclusive vacation spot for wealthy southern families, Oconomowoc today is an all-season sports center.

What to See and Do

Highlands Ski Hill. Area has 2 chairlifts, rope tow; patrol, school, rentals; snowmaking; bar. Longest run 2,200 ft; vertical drop 196 ft. (Nov-Mar, daily) Cross-country ski trails. WI 67 & I-94. Phone 414/567-2577. ¢¢¢¢

Honey of a Museum. Bee Tree provides a close-up view of bee activities; pollination & beeswax exhibits; multimedia show about beekeeping yesterday, today & around the world; nature walk, honey tasting. (Mid-May-Oct, daily; rest of yr, Mon-Fri; closed hols) Honey Acres, 10 mi N, on WI 67 just N of Ashippun. Phone 414/474-4411. **Free.**

Motel

★★ **COUNTRY PRIDE INN.** (2412 Milwaukee St, Delafield 53018) 3 mi E on I-94, exit 287. 414/646-3300; FAX 414/646-3491. 56 rms, 2 story. May-Sept: S $52; D $62; suites $85-$125; each addl $5; lower rates rest of yr. Crib $5. TV; cable (premium). Indoor pool; whirlpool, sauna. Complimentary coffee in lobby. Restaurant adj 6 am-11 pm. Ck-out 11 am. Meeting rm. Business servs avail. Sundries. Downhill ski 6 mi; x-country ski ¼ mi. Some in-rm whirlpools. Cr cds: A, C, D, DS, MC, V.

Inn

★★ **INN AT PINE TERRACE.** 351 E Lisbon Rd. 414/567-7463; res: 800/421-4667. 13 rms, 3 story. S, D $60-$120; each addl $15. Pet accepted, some restrictions. TV; cable (premium). Heated pool. Complimentary continental bkfst. Restaurant nearby. Ck-out 10:30 am, ck-in 3 pm. Restored mansion (1879); antique furnishings. Cr cds: A, C, D, DS, MC, V.

Resort

★★★ **HOLIDAY INN SUNSPREE.** 1350 Royale Mile Rd, I-94 exit 282. 414/567-0311; FAX 414/567-5934; res: 800/558-9573 (exc WI). 253 units, 3-4 story. S, D $89-$129; each addl $20; suites $189-$249; family, ski & golf plans. TV; cable (premium). Supervised child's activities. Coffee in rms. Dining rm 6:30 am-10 pm. Rm serv 7 am-10 pm. Bars 11-2 am. Ck-out noon, ck-in 4 pm. Meeting rms. Business servs avail. Grocery 1 blk. Deli. Valet serv. Barber, beauty shop. Indoor, outdoor tennis. 18-hole golf, greens fee, pro, driving range. Downhill ski. Entertainment Fri & Sat; movies. Game rm. Exercise rm; instructor, weights, sauna, steam rm. Some refrigerators. Fireplaces in suites. Cr cds: A, C, D, DS, ER, JCB, MC, V.

Restaurants

★★★ **GOLDEN MAST INN.** (1270 Lacy Lane, Okauchee) 3 mi E on WI 16. 414/567-7047. Hrs: 5-11 pm; Sun 11 am-9; Sun brunch 11 am-2 pm. Closed Mon in Oct-Apr. Res accepted. German, Amer menu. Bar. Wine cellar. Semi-a la carte: dinner $15.95-$34.95. Sun brunch $9.50-$13.95. Child's meals. Specializes in Wienerschnitzel, Kasseler Rippchen, seafood. Outdoor dining in beer garden. German decor; antiques, fireplace. View of lake and landscaped grounds. Family-owned. Cr cds: A, MC, V.

D

★ **RED CIRCLE INN.** (33013 Watertown Plank Rd, Nashotah 53058) E on WI 16, exit Hwy C. 414/367-4883. Hrs: 5-9:30 pm. Closed Sun & Mon; most major hols. Res accepted. Bar from 4 pm. Semi-a la carte: dinner $17.95-$25. Specializes in veal, fresh fish, steak. Former stagecoach stop; one of oldest restaurants in state (est 1848). Cr cds: A, DS, MC, V.

D

Oconto (D-5)

(For accommodations see Green Bay, Marinette; also see Peshtigo, Menominee, MI)

Pop 4,474 **Elev** 591 ft **Area code** 414 **Zip** 54153

On Green Bay at the mouth of the Oconto River, Oconto was the home of Copper Culture people 4,500 years ago.

What to See and Do

Beyer Home (ca 1868). Victorian house with furnishings of 1880-1890s. Adj museum annex has exhibits of Copper Culture people and antique vehicles. (June-Labor Day, Mon-Sat, also Sun afternoons) 917 Park Ave. Phone 414/834-2260. ¢

North Bay Shore County Park. Swimming; fishing; boating. Tent & trailer sites. Fall Salmon Run. Camping (late May-late Sept; fee). (Daily) 9 mi N on County Y. Phone 414/834-6825 or 414/834-6820. **Free.**

Annual Event

Old Copper Festival. Parade, waterskiing shows, ice cream social, arts & crafts displays and sales. Phone 414/834-3246. 2nd wkend June.

Oshkosh (E-5)

Settled 1836 **Pop** 55,006 **Elev** 767 ft **Area code** 920

Information Oshkosh Convention & Visitors Bureau, 2 N Main St, 54901; 920/236-5250 or 800/876-5250.

Named for the Chief of the Menominee, Oshkosh is located on the west shore of Lake Winnebago, the largest freshwater lake within the state. The city is known for the many recreational activities offered by its lakes and rivers. This is the original home of the company that produces the famous overalls that help make Oshkosh a household word. The economy of the town, once called "Sawdust City," is centered on transportation equipment manufacturing, tourism and candle making.

What to See and Do

★ **EAA Air Adventure Museum.** More than 90 aircraft on display including home-built aircraft, antiques, classics, ultralights, aerobatic and rotary-winged planes. Special World War II collection. Extensive collections of aviation art and photography; special displays of engines, propellers and scale models. Five theaters. Antique airplanes fly on wkends (May-Oct). (Daily; closed major hols) 3000 Poberezny Rd. Phone 920/426-4818. ¢¢¢

Menominee Park. Swimming beach (lifeguard); fishing; sailing, paddleboats. Tennis courts. Picnic shelters, concession. Train rides. Children's zoo (late May-early Sept, daily). Fee for some activities. (Daily) On Lake Winnebago, enter off Hazel or Merritt Sts. Phone 920/236-5080.

Oshkosh Public Museum. Housed in turn-of-the-century, Tudor-style mansion with Tiffany stained-glass windows and interior; also occupies adj addition. Apostles Clock, china and glassware collection; life-sized dioramas depicting French exploration, British occupation, pioneer settlement and native wildlife; antique fire and train equipment; meteorites; Native American exhibits; fine and decorative art. (Daily exc Mon; closed hols) 1331 Algoma Blvd. Phone 920/424-4731. **Free.**

Paine Art Center and Arboretum. Tudor-revival house; period rooms, European and American paintings & sculpture, Oriental rugs, furniture and decorative arts; changing art exhibitions. Arboretum and display gardens. (Tues-Fri, also Sat-Sun afternoons; closed hols) 1410 Algoma Blvd, at jct WI 21, 110. Phone 920/235-6903. ¢¢

University of Wisconsin-Oshkosh (1871). (11,000 students) Priebe Art Gallery, Reeve Memorial Union, Kolf Sports and Recreation Center. Campus tours (Mon-Fri; Sat by appt). 800 Algoma Blvd. For tour information phone 920/424-0202 or 800/624-1466.

Annual Events

Sawdust Days. Commemorates lumbering era. Early July.

EAA International Fly-In Convention. (Experimental Aircraft Association). Held at Wittman Regional Airport.One of the nation's largest aviation events. More than 500 educational forums, workshops and seminars; daily air shows; exhibits; more than 12,000 aircraft. For air show lodging information, phone 920/235-3007; 920/426-4800 (general information). Late July-early Aug.

Motels

(Rates higher EAA Intl Fly-in Convention)

★ ★ **FAIRFIELD INN BY MARRIOTT.** *1800 S Koeller (54901).* *920/233-8504.* 57 rms, 3 story, 10 suites. June-Sept: S $51.95-$61.95; D $57.95-$77.95; each addl $6; suites $67.95-$74.95; under 18 free; lower rates rest of yr. Crib $5. TV; cable (premium). Indoor pool; whirlpool. Complimentary continental bkfst. Restaurant nearby. Ck-out noon. Meeting rms. Business servs avail. In-rm modem link. Game rm. Some refrigerators, microwaves. Cr cds: A, D, DS, MC, V.

 D ⛵ 🏊 🛷 🔥 SC

✔ ★ **HOWARD JOHNSON.** *1919 Omro Rd (54901), at jct US 41 & WI 21.* *920/233-1200; FAX 920/233-1135.* 100 rms, 2 story. May-Aug: S $45-$55; D $50-$80; each addl $5; under 18 free; lower rates rest of yr. Crib free. Pet accepted, some restrictions. TV; cable (premium). Indoor pool; whirlpool. Restaurant adj 6 am-10 pm. Bar 4 pm-1 am. Ck-out noon. Meeting rms. Business servs avail. Private patios, balconies. Cr cds: A, C, D, DS, ER, MC, V.

D ⛵ 🏊 🛷 🔥 SC

★ ★ **RAMADA INN.** *500 S Koeller St (54901), US 41 exit 9th St, near Whittman Airport.* *920/233-1511; FAX 920/233-1909.* 132 rms, 2 story. S $50-$70; D $55-$75; each addl $8; under 18 free; wkend rates. TV; cable (premium). Indoor pool; whirlpool, poolside serv. Restaurant 6 am-2 pm, 5-10 pm. Rm serv. Ck-out noon. Coin lndry. Meeting rms. Business center. Bellhops. Valet serv. Sundries. Free airport transportation. Exercise equipt; weight machine, bicycles, sauna. Microwave avail. Cr cds: A, C, D, DS, MC, V.

D 🏊 ✈ ✈ 🛷 🔥 SC 🎿

Hotels

★ ★ ★ **HILTON.** *1 N Main St (54901).* *920/231-5000; FAX 920/231-8383.* E-mail www.hiltonnet.com; web hilton, 8 story. S, D $65-$95; suites $125; under 18 free. Pet accepted, some restrictions. TV; cable (premium). VCR avail. Indoor pool; whirlpool, poolside serv. Restaurant 6:30 am-10 pm. Bar 11-1 am. Ck-out noon. Meeting rms. Business center. In-rm modem link. Concierge. Free covered parking. Free airport transportation. Exercise equipt; bicycles, treadmills. Health club privileges. Some refrigerators; microwaves avail. View of river. Luxury level. Cr cds: A, C, D, DS, MC, V.

D ⛵ 🏊 🏊 ✈ 🛷 🔥 SC 🎿

★ ★ ★ **PIONEER INN.** *1000 Pioneer Dr (54903), on Ki Ni Island.* *920/233-1980; FAX 920/426-2115; res: 800/683-1980 (WI).* 192 rms, 2-3 story. S $75-$149; D $85-$159; each addl $5; under 18 free; package plans. Crib free. TV; cable (premium). VCR avail. 2 pools, 1 indoor; wading pool, whirlpool. Supervised child's activities; ages 5-12. Restaurants 7 am-10 pm. Bar 10:30-1 am. Ck-out noon. Business servs avail. In-rm modem link. Free airport transportation. Tennis. Exercise equipt; bicycles, treadmill. Massage. Social dir. Miniature golf. Lawn games. Guest bicycles. Some in-rm whirlpools, microwaves. On lake; boat rentals, marina, sailing. Cr cds: A, C, D, DS, MC, V.

D ⛵ 🏃 🏊 🛷 🔥 SC

Restaurants

★ **FIN'N FEATHER SHOWBOATS.** *(22 W Main St, Winne-conne 54986)* 12 mi NW on WI 110 to WI 116, then W. *920/582-4305.* Hrs: 8 am-11 pm; winter months to 10 pm; Sun brunch 9 am-2 pm. Closed Dec 25. Res accepted. Bar to 2:30 am. Semi-a la carte: bkfst $1.95-$6.95, lunch, dinner $2.65-$24.95. Sun brunch buffet $8.95. Specializes in fish, Angus steak, pasta. Salad bar. Replica of riverboat; excursions avail on Showboat II. Family-owned. Cr cds: A, MC, V.

D SC

★ ★ **ROBBINS.** *1810 Omro Rd (WI 21) (54901).* *920/235-2840.* Hrs: 11 am-10 pm; Fri, Sat to 11 pm; Sun to 9 pm. Closed Dec 25. Res accepted. Continental menu. Bar to 2 am. Semi-a la carte: lunch $4.45-$6.45, dinner $6.45-$18.95. Child's meals. Specializes in prawns, shrimp,

tenderloin. Vocalist, pianist Fri, Sat. Semi-formal atmosphere; elaborate cut-glass panel at entrance. Cr cds: A, MC, V.

D ⤢

✔ ★ **WISCONSIN FARMS.** *2450 Washburn.* *920/233-7555.* Hrs: 5 am-9 pm. Closed Jan 1, Thanksgiving, Dec 25. Res accepted. Semi-a la carte: bkfst $1.35-$7.95, lunch $2.35-$15.99, dinner $2.95-$15.99. Child's meals. Specializes in beef, cheesecake. Country atmosphere. Cr cds: MC, V.

D

Park Falls (C-3)

(For accommodations see Lac du Flambeau, Manitowish Waters)

Pop 3,104 **Elev** 1,490 ft **Area code** 715 **Zip** 54552

Information Park Falls Area Chamber of Commerce, 400 S 4th Ave S, Suite 8; 715/762-2703 or 800/762-2709.

Park Falls has been proclaimed "ruffed grouse capital of the world," since more than 5,000 acres within this area have been used to create a natural habitat for the bird.

What to See and Do

Chequamegon National Forest. Aspen, maple, pine, spruce, balsam and birch on 855,000 acres. Rainbow Lake and Porcupine Lake Wilderness areas; Great Divide National Scenic Byway. Canoeing on south fork of Flambeau River, the North & South forks of the Chippewa River and Namekagon River; muskellunge, northern pike, walleye and bass fishing; hunting for deer, bear and small game; archery. Blueberry & raspberry picking. Swimming; boat launching. Ice Age and North Country National Scenic Trails, hiking, motorcycle, cross-country skiing, and snowmobile trails. Camping (May-Sept; some sites to Dec) on a first-come basis (fee). Pets must be leashed. Resorts and cabins are located in and near the forest. (Daily) E on WI 29, 70, or US 8 and 2; also NW on WI 13 and 63. A District Ranger office is located here, phone 715/762-2461. **Free.**

Concrete Park. Fred Smith's concrete and glass statues includes northwoods people, folklore, fantasies, historic personages, Native Americans, angels and animals. (Daily) 22 mi S via WI 13 in Phillips. **Free.**

Old Town Hall Museum. Artifacts of logging era (1876-1930); replica of turn-of-the-century living rm and kitchen; county historic display; old opera house. (June-Labor Day, Fri & Sun afternoons) W 7213 Pine St. Phone 715/762-4571. **Free.**

Post Office Lumberjack Mural. In 1938 the US Government provided artists the opportunity to submit artwork to be put into local post offices throughout the country. The Park Falls Post Office features one of the 2,200 that were finally selected. The restored mural, covering one entire wall, depicts the history of logging. (Daily exc Sun) 109 N 1st St. Phone 715/762-4575.

Annual Event

Flambeau Rama. Downtown. 4-day event including parades, arts & crafts show, Evergreen Road Run, games. 1st wkend Aug.

Peshtigo (D-6)

(For accommodations see Marinette, Oconto; also see Menominee, MI)

Pop 3,154 **Elev** 600 ft **Area code** 715 **Zip** 54157

Information City Clerk, City Hall, 331 French St, PO Box 100; 715/582-3041.

On October 8, 1871, the same day that the Chicago fire claimed 250 lives, 800 people died in Peshtigo, virtually unpublicized, when the entire town burned to the ground in a disastrous forest fire. A monument to those who died in the fire is located in the Peshtigo Fire Cemetery on Oconto Ave. The city is now a manufacturing center.

What to See and Do

Badger Paper Mills, Inc. 3/4-hr guided tours (June-Aug, Mon-Fri; also by appt; closed hols). No children under 12 yrs. (Daily) 200 W Front St. Phone 715/582-4551. **Free.**

Badger Park. Swimming; fishing (northern, bass, coho salmon). Tent & trailer sites (electric hookups); (May-Oct, daily) N Emery Ave on Peshtigo River. Phone 715/582-4321 or 715/582-3041. **Free.** Camping **¢¢¢**

Peshtigo Fire Museum. Local historical items. (Memorial Day-early Oct, daily) 400 Oconto Ave. Phone 715/582-3244. **Free.**

Platteville (G-3)

(See also Mineral Point)

Pop 9,708 **Elev** 994 ft **Area code** 608 **Zip** 53818 **Web** www.cybertown.net/wi/chamber

Information Chamber of Commerce, 275 US 151 W, PO Box 16; 608/348-8687.

Sport fishing is very popular in the many streams in the area as are ice fishing on the Mississippi River and hunting for upland game, waterfowl and deer. The world's largest letter "M" was built on Platteville Mound in 1936 by mining engineering students; it is lit twice each year for the University of Wisconsin-Platteville's homecoming and Miner's Ball.

What to See and Do

Mining Museum. Traces the development of lead and zinc mining in the area. Guided tour includes a walk down into Bevans Lead Mine and a mine train ride (May-Oct, daily). Changing exhibits (Nov-Apr, Mon-Fri). 385 E Main St. Phone 608/348-3301. **¢¢** Admission includes

Rollo Jamison Museum. Museum contains a large collection of everyday items collected by Jamison during his lifetime, including horse-drawn vehicles, tools and musical instruments. 405 Main St. Phone 608/348-3301.

Seasonal Events

Wisconsin Shakespeare Festival. In Center for the Arts on campus of University of Wisconsin-Platteville. Nightly exc Mon; matinees Wed, Sat & Sun. Phone 608/342-1298. Early July-early Aug.

Chicago Bears Summer Training Camp. University of Wisconsin-Platteville. Football team's summer residence. Mid-July-mid-Aug.

Motels

★ ★ **BEST WESTERN GOVERNOR DODGE MOTOR INN.** *West US 151, 5 blks S on US 151, 1/4 mi W of jct WI 80, 81. 608/348-2301; FAX 608/348-8579.* 74 rms, 2 story. S $45-$64; D $69-$75; each addl $5-$7; suites $105-$140; under 12 free. Crib $3. Pet accepted, some restrictions. TV; cable, VCR avail (movies). Indoor pool; whirlpool. Complimentary coffee in lobby. Restaurant 6 am-10 pm; Sun to 7 pm; winter to 9 pm. Ck-out noon. Meeting rms. Business servs avail. Exercise equipt; rower, stair machine, saunas. Game rm. State university 5 blks. Cr cds: A, C, D, DS, MC, V.

★ ★ **BEST WESTERN WELCOME INN.** *(420 W Maple, Lancaster 53813) 608/723-4162; FAX 608/723-4843.* 22 rms, 2 story. S $39; D $46; under 12 free. Crib $3. TV; cable (premium). Complimentary continental bkfst. Restaurant nearby. Ck-out 11 am. Coin lndry. Cr cds: A, C, D, DS, MC, V.

D ⊠ SC

✓★ **SUPER 8.** *100 WI 80/81S. 608/348-8800.* 73 rms, 2 story. S $34-$47; D $47-$64; each addl $5; suites $125. Crib $4. Pet accepted; $10. TV; cable (premium). Complimentary continental bkfst. Restaurant adj open 24 hrs. Ck-out 11 am. Coin lndry. Meeting rms. Sauna. Whirlpool. Some bathrm phones, refrigerators. Balconies. Overlooks stream. Gazebo. Cr cds: A, D, DS, MC, V.

D ➤ ⊠ ⌖

Inn

★ **WISCONSIN HOUSE.** *(2105 Main St, Hazel Green 53811) S on WI 80 to jct WI 11, then 1 blk E on County W. 608/854-2233.* 8 rms, 2 share bath, 3 story, 2 suites. No rm phones. S $55-$85; D $55-$95; each addl $15; suites $110; wkday rates. TV in sitting rm; cable, VCR avail. Complimentary full bkfst. Dinner avail Fri & Sat. Ck-out 10 am, ck-in 3 pm. X-country ski 5 mi. Balconies. Built 1846; former stagecoach stop. Smoking permitted in sitting rm only. Cr cds: DS, MC, V.

⌖ ⊠ SC

Restaurants

✓★ **GADZOOKS.** *300 McGregor Plaza. 608/348-7700.* Hrs: 6 am-9 pm; Fri to 10 pm; Sat 8 am-10 pm; Sun 8 am-3 pm. Closed most major hols. Semi-a la carte: bkfst $1.75-$5.25, lunch $2.75-$6.95, dinner $5.95-$11.95. Child's meals. Specializes in steak. Cr cds: DS, MC, V.

D SC

★ ★ **TIMBERS.** *670 Ellen St, jct US 151, WI 80/81. 608/348-2406.* Hrs: 11 am-1:30 pm, 5-10 pm; Sun 3-9 pm; Sun brunch 10:30 am-2 pm. Res accepted. Continental menu. Bar from 11 am. Semi-a la carte: lunch $3.75-$7.50, dinner $9.50-$19.95. Sun brunch $10.95. Child's meals. Specializes in steak, seafood. Pianist wkends, organist nightly. Large custom-built electronic theater pipe organ. Cr cds: A, C, D, DS, MC, V.

D

Portage (F-4)

(See also Baraboo, Prairie du Sac, Wisconsin Dells)

Settled 1835 **Pop** 8,640 **Elev** 800 ft **Area code** 608 **Zip** 53901

Information Chamber of Commerce, 301 W Wisconsin St; 608/742-6242or 800/474-2525.

Portage is built on a narrow strip of land separating the Fox and Wisconsin rivers. In the early flow of traffic, goods were hauled from one river to another, providing the name for the city. Before permanent settlement, Fort Winnebago occupied this site; several historic buildings remain. Modern Portage is the business center of Columbia County.

What to See and Do

Cascade Mt Ski Area. Double, 3 quad, 3 triple chairlifts, rope tow; patrol, school; snack bar, cafeteria, dining rm, bar. 26 runs; longest run 1 mi; vertical drop 460 ft. (Mid-Nov-Mar, daily) NW on I-90/94, then 1/4 mi W on WI 33 to Cascade Mt Rd. Phone 608/742-5588 or 800/992-2-SKI. **¢¢¢¢**

Fort Winnebago Surgeons' Quarters. Original log house (1828), surviving from Old Fort Winnebago, used by medical officers stationed at the fort. Restored; many original furnishings. Garrison school (1850-1960). (Mid-May-mid-Oct, daily) 1 mi E on WI 33. Phone 608/742-2949. **¢¢**

Home of Zona Gale. Greek-revival house built in 1906 for the Pulitzer Prize-winning novelist; some original furnishings. (Mon-Fri, by appt) 506 W Edgewater St. Phone 608/742-7744. **¢**

Old Indian Agency House (1832). Restored house of John Kinzie, US Indian Agent to the Winnebago and an important pioneer; his wife Juliette wrote *Wau-bun,* an early history of their voyages to Fort Winnebago.

Period furnishings. (May-Oct, daily; rest of yr, by appt) 1 mi E on WI 33 to Agency House Rd. Phone 608/742-6362 or 608/742-2739. ¢¢

Silver Lake. Swimming, beach, lifeguards, waterskiing; fishing (rainbow trout, largemouth bass, northern pike, panfish); boating (public landing). Picnic area (shelter), playground. Parking. (Early June-Labor Day, daily) N side of town. Phone 608/742-2176. **Free.**

Motel

✔★ ★ RIDGE MOTOR INN. *2900 New Pinery Rd, 2 mi N on US 51.* 608/742-5306. 113 rms, 3 story, 9 kit. suites. June-Aug: S $50-$75; D $70-$90; each addl $5; kit. suites $100-$125; under 12 free; wkend rates; package plans; lower rates rest of yr. Crib $4. Pet accepted. TV; cable (premium), VCR avail (movies). Indoor pool; whirlpool. Complimentary coffee in rms. Restaurant 6 am-10 pm. Rm serv. Bar. Ck-out 11 am. Coin lndry. Meeting rms. Business servs avail. Downhill ski 4 mi; x-country ski 16 mi. Exercise rm; instructor, weight machine, bicycles, sauna, steam rm. Massage. Health club privileges. Game rm. Cr cds: A, C, D, DS, MC, V.

D ⊱ ⚓ ≋ ⏃ ⇲ ⬡ SC

Port Washington (F-6)

(See also Cedarburg, Milwaukee, Sheboygan)

Settled 1830 **Pop** 9,338 **Elev** 612 ft **Area code** 414 **Zip** 53074 **E-mail** ptwashcc@execpc.com **Web** www.discoverusa.com/wi/ptwash

Information Tourist Center located in the Pebble House, 126 E Grand Ave, PO Box 153; 414/284-0900 or 800/719-4881.

Located along the shore of Lake Michigan, Port Washington has many pre-Civil War homes. The Port Washington Marina, one of the finest on Lake Michigan, provides exceptional facilities for boating and fishing.

What to See and Do

Eghart House. Built in 1872; Victorian furnishings from 1850-1900 in hall, parlor, dining-living rm, bedrm, kitchen and pantry. Tours. (Late May-late Sept, Sun afternoons; wkdays by appt) 316 Grand Ave. Phone 414/284-2897. ¢

Lizard Mound County Park. Features 31 outstanding examples of earthen effigy mounds in the shape of animals and birds, constructed by prehistoric Wisconsin natives. Nature trail, hiking. Picnicking. (Daily) 20 mi W on WI 33, then 1½ mi N on WI 144, then E on County Hwy A. Phone 414/335-4445. **Free.**

Motels

★ BEST WESTERN HARBORSIDE MOTOR INN. *135 E Grand Ave.* 414/284-9461; FAX 414/284-3169. 96 rms, 5 story. S $64-$107; D $74-$117; each addl $10; under 12 free. Crib free. Pet accepted. TV; cable (premium). Sauna. Indoor pool; whirlpool. Bkfst 7-10 am. Bar 4 pm-1 am. Ck-out noon. Meeting rms. Business servs avail. Valet serv. Game rm. On Lake Michigan; dock. Some whirlpools. Cr cds: A, C, D, DS, MC, V.

D ⚓ ⚓ ≋ ⇲ ⬡ SC

★ ★ WEST BEND INN. *(2520 W Washington, West Bend 53095)* 17 mi W on WI 33. 414/338-0636; FAX 414/338-4290; res: 800/727-9727. 86 rms, 2 story, 25 theme suites. S $59-$65; D $69-$75; each addl $8; suites $99-$179; under 18 free. Crib free. TV; cable (premium), VCR avail (movies). Sauna. Indoor/outdoor pool; whirlpool. Complimentary continental bkfst. Restaurant 11:30 am-2 pm, 5-9:30 pm; Sun from 9:30 am. Rm serv. Bar 5-10 pm. Ck-out noon. Meeting rms. Business servs avail. Valet serv. Game rm. Uniquely decorated suites with varying themes. Cr cds: A, C, D, DS, MC, V.

D ≋ ⇲ ⬡ SC

Restaurants

★ ★ BUCHEL'S COLONIAL HOUSE. *1000 S Spring St.* 414/284-2212. Hrs: 5-10 pm. Closed Sun-Mon; major hols. Res accepted. Continental menu. Bar. Semi-a la carte: dinner $11.50-$20. Child's meals. Specializes in homemade soup, veal. Colonial, nautical decor. Cr cds: MC, V.

D

★ ★ SMITH BROS "FISH SHANTY". *100 N Franklin St, off I-43, on WI 32 at Lake.* 414/284-5592. Hrs: 11 am-10 pm; Fri, Sat to 11 pm. Closed Thanksgiving, Dec 25. Res accepted. Bar. Semi-a la carte: lunch $4.95-$10.95, dinner $7.50-$15.50. Child's meals. Specialties: seafood, lemon meringue pie. Outdoor deck dining. Nautical decor. View of Port Washington harbor & marina. Cr cds: A, D, DS, MC, V.

D

Prairie du Chien (G-2)

Settled 1736 **Pop** 5,659 **Elev** 642 ft **Area code** 608 **Zip** 53821 **Web** www.prairieduchien.org

Information Chamber of Commerce, 211 S Main St, PO Box 326; 608/326-8555 or 800/732-1673.

This is the second oldest European settlement in Wisconsin, and dates to June 1673. Marquette and Jolliet discovered the Mississippi River just south of the prairie that the French adventurers then named Prairie du Chien ("prairie of the dog") for Chief Alim, whose name meant "dog." The site became a popular gathering place and trading post. The War of 1812 led to the construction of Fort Shelby and Fort Crawford on an ancient Native American burial ground in the village. Stationed here were Jefferson Davis, later president of the Confederacy, and Zachary Taylor, later president of the United States. In 1826, Hercules Dousman, an agent for John Jacob Astor's American Fur Company, came and built a personal fortune, becoming Wisconsin's first millionaire. When Fort Crawford was moved, Dousman bought the site and erected Villa Louis, the "House of the Mound," a palatial mansion.

What to See and Do

★ **Kickapoo Indian Caverns and Native American Museum.** Largest caverns in Wisconsin, used by Native Americans for centuries as a shelter. Sights include subterranean lake, Cathedral Room, Turquoise Room, Stalactite Chamber and Chamber of the Lost Waters. Guided tours. (Mid-May-Oct, daily) W 200 Rhein Hollow, 6 mi S on US 18, then 9 mi E on WI 60 in Wauzeka. Phone 608/875-7723. ¢¢¢

Nelson Dewey State Park This 756-acre park offers nature, hiking trails. Playground. Camping (hookups). Standard fees. (Daily) 35 mi S via US 18, WI 35 & 133 near Cassville. Phone 608/725-5374. Also here is

Stonefield. Named for a rock-studded, 2,000-acre farm that Dewey (first elected governor of WI) established on the bluffs of the Mississippi River. State Agricultural Museum contains display of farm machinery. Site also features re-creation of an 1890 Stonefield Village including blacksmithy, general store, print shop, school, church and 26 other buildings. Horse-drawn wagon rides (limited hrs; fee). (Memorial Day-early Oct, daily) Phone 608/725-5210. ¢¢

Prairie du Chien Museum at Fort Crawford. Relics of 19th-century medicine, Native American herbal remedies, drugstore, dentist & physicians' offices. Educational health exhibits; Dessloch Theater displays "transparent twins." Dedicated to Dr. William Beaumont, who did some of his famous digestive system studies at Ft Crawford. (May-Oct, daily) 717 S Beaumont Rd. Phone 608/326-6960. ¢¢

★ **Villa Louis** (1870). Built on site of Ft Crawford. Restored to its 19th-century splendor. Contains original furnishings, collection of Victorian decorative arts. Surrounded by extensive grounds, bounded by the Mississippi

River. Tours include Museum of Prairie du Chien and Fur Trade Museum. (May-Oct, daily) 521 Villa Louis Rd, off US 18. Phone 608/326-2721. ¢¢¢

Wyalusing State Park. A 2,654-acre park at the confluence of the Mississippi and Wisconsin rivers. Sentinel Ridge (500 ft) provides a commanding view of the area; valleys, caves, waterfalls, springs; Native American effigy mounds. Swimming beach nearby; fishing; boating (landing), canoeing. 18 mi of nature, hiking and cross-country ski trails. Picnicking, playground, concession. Camping (electric hookups, dump station). Nature center; naturalist programs (summer). Standard fees. (Daily) 7 mi SE on US 18, then W on County C, X. Phone 608/996-2261. Per vehicle ¢¢

Motels

★ ★ **BEST WESTERN-QUIET HOUSE SUITES.** *US 18S & WI 35/60.* 608/326-4777; FAX 608/326-4787. 42 suites, 2 story. S $63-$125; D $73-$135; each addl $10. Pet accepted. TV; cable (premium). Indoor pool; whirlpool. Restaurant opp 5 am-10 pm. Ck-out 11 am. Business servs avail. In-rm modem link. Sundries. Exercise equipt; bicycles, stair machine. Some in-rm whirlpools. Cr cds: A, C, D, DS, ER, MC, V.

★ **BRISBOIS MOTOR INN.** *533 N Marquette Rd.* 608/326-8404; res: 800/356-5850. 46 rms. S, D $34-$59; each addl $5; under 17 free. Crib free. TV; cable (premium). Heated pool. Playground. Complimentary coffee in rms. Restaurant adj 6 am-11 pm. Ck-out 11 am. Meeting rm. Free airport transportation. X-country ski 2 mi. Cr cds: A, D, DS, MC, V.

★ **HOLIDAY.** *1010 S Marquette Rd.* 608/326-2448; FAX 608/326-2413; res: 800/962-3883. 18 rms, 1-2 story. May-Oct: S $38-$45; D $50-$56; suite $70-$76; each addl $5; under 16 free; lower rates rest of yr. Crib free. Pet accepted, some restrictions. TV; cable (premium). Complimentary coffee. Restaurant nearby. Ck-out 11 am. Business servs avail. Cr cds: A, DS, MC, V.

✔★ **PRAIRIE.** *1616 S Marquette Rd.* 608/326-6461; res: 800/526-3776. 32 rms. May-Oct: S $35-$49; D $49-$59; family rates; lower rates rest of yr. Crib $3. Pet accepted. TV; cable (premium). Heated pool. Playground. Complimentary coffee in rms. Ck-out 11 am. X-country ski 2 mi. Miniature golf. Lawn games. Some refrigerators. Picnic tables, grills. Cr cds: A, D, DS, MC, V.

Prairie du Sac (F-4)

(For accommodations see Baraboo, Madison; also see Spring Green)

Pop 2,380 **Elev** 780 ft **Area code** 608 **Zip** 53578
Information Sauk Prairie Area Chamber of Commerce, 207 Water St, Sauk City 53583; 608/643-4168.

A favorite launching area for canoeists on the Wisconsin River. It is possible to see bald eagles south of the village at Ferry Bluff, where many of them winter. Watching them feed on fish in the open water is a favorite winter pastime.

What to See and Do

Wollersheim Winery (1857). Guided tours, wine tasting, cheese, gift shop. (Daily; closed major hols) 7876 WI 188. Phone 608/643-6515 or 800/VIP-WINE. Tours ¢¢

Annual Event

Harvest Festival. Wollersheim Winery. Grape stompers competition; music; cork toss; grape spitting contest; foods. 1st wkend Oct.

Racine (G-6)

(See also Burlington, Kenosha, Milwaukee)

Founded 1834 **Pop** 84,298 **Elev** 626 ft **Area code** 414 **Web** www.racine.org
Information Racine County Convention and Visitors Bureau, 345 Main St, 53403; 414/634-3293 or 800/C-RACINE.

Racine is situated on a thumb of land jutting into Lake Michigan. The largest concentration of people of Danish descent in the US can be found here; in fact, West Racine is known as "Kringleville" because of its Danish pastry. There are more than 300 manufacturing firms located here.

What to See and Do

Architectural tour. A 30-min tour of SC Johnson Wax world headquarters designed by Frank Lloyd Wright (Tues-Fri; closed hols). 1525 Howe St. Reservations required; phone 414/631-2154. **Free.**

Charles A. Wustum Museum of Fine Arts. Painting, photography, graphics, crafts and sculpture displays; works of local, regional and nationally known artists are featured. Permanent and changing exhibits. Also park and formal gardens. (Daily; closed hols) 2519 Northwestern Ave. Phone 414/636-9177. **Free.**

Golden Rondelle Theater. Features three films (Tues-Fri; closed hols; reservations required). SC Johnson Wax Guest Relations Center, 1525 Howe St. For schedule information phone 414/631-2154. **Free.**

Racine County Heritage Museum. Cultural history of Racine County, including permanent and temporary exhibits, archive and photographic collection. (Tues-Fri, also Sat & Sun afternoons; closed major hols) 701 S Main St. Phone 414/636-3926. **Free.**

Racine Zoological Gardens. Extensive animal collection, picnic area, swimming (beach). (Daily) 2131 N Main St. Phone 414/636-9189. **Free.**

Annual Event

Salmon-A-Rama. Lakefront. Fishing contest. Mid-July.

Motels

✔★ **KNIGHTS INN.** *1149 Oakes Rd (53406).* 414/886-6667; FAX 414/886-1501; res: 800/843-5644. 107 rms, 1 story. June-Labor Day: S, D $48.95-$52.95; each addl $3; suites $51.95-$55.95; kit. units $58.95-$62.95; under 18 free; lower rates rest of yr. Crib free. Pet accepted. TV; cable (premium), VCR avail (movies). Complimentary continental bkfst. Restaurant adj 10 am-11 pm. Ck-out noon. Cr cds: A, C, D, DS, ER, MC, V.

★ ★ **QUALITY INN.** *3700 Northwestern Ave (53405), off Green Bay Rd.* 414/637-9311; FAX 414/637-4575. 112 rms, 2 story. S $54-$89; D $62-$99; each addl $6; under 18 free. Crib free. Pet accepted. TV; cable (premium). Heated pool. Complimentary coffee in rms. Restaurant 6 am-2 pm, 5:30-9 pm. Rm serv. Bar 4 pm-2 am. Ck-out noon. Coin lndry. Meeting rms. Business servs avail. In-rm modem link. Bellhops. Valet serv. Sundries. X-country ski 3 mi. Game rm. Lawn games. Picnic tables. On Root River. Cr cds: A, C, D, DS, JCB, MC, V.

Restaurants

★ **GREAT WALL.** *6025 Washington Ave.* 414/886-9700. Hrs: 11 am-8:30 pm; Fri to 9:30 pm; Sat 4-9:30 pm; Sun 11 am-2 pm. Closed Mon; major hols. Res accepted. Pan-Asian menu. Bar. Semi-a la carte: lunch $4.50-$5.25, dinner $6.75-$15.50. Buffet 11 am-2 pm: lunch $5.25, Sun $6.95. Specializes in Szechwan & Mandarin dishes. Chinese decor. Cr cds: A, DS, MC, V.

★ ★ **HOB NOB.** *277 S Sheridan Rd (53403). 414/552-8008.* Hrs: 5-10 pm; Sun from 4 pm. Closed Dec 24, 25; also Super Bowl Sun. Res accepted. Bar. Semi-a la carte: dinner $9.95-$19.95. Specializes in seafood, steak, duck. View of Lake Michigan. Cr cds: A, D, MC, V.

D

✔★ **SPINNING WHEEL.** *6025 Douglas Ave (53402), at 5 Mile Rd. 414/639-7005.* Hrs: 11:30 am-1:30 pm, 5-8:30 pm; Fri, Sat to 10 pm. Closed Sun, Mon; Jan 1, July 4, Dec 24-25. Res accepted. Bar. Semi-a la carte: lunch $3.95-$8.95, dinner $7.95-$14.95. Child's meals. Specializes in steak, seafood and Italian cuisine. Rustic decor. Cr cds: A, MC, V.

Reedsburg (F-3)

(For accommodations see Baraboo, Portage, Wisconsin Dells; also see Prairie du Sac)

Pop 5,834 **Elev** 926 ft **Area code** 608 **Zip** 53959
Information Chamber of Commerce, 240 Railroad St, PO Box 142; 608/524-2850 or 800/844-3507.

Self-proclaimed "butter capital of America," Reedsburg is the home of one of the largest butter producing plants in the world. The Wisconsin Dairies plant produces more than 50,000,000 pounds of butter here each year.

What to See and Do

Carr Valley Cheese Factory. Observation area for viewing production of cheddar cheese. (Daily exc Sun; closed Jan 1, Dec 25) 9 mi W on County K, G in La Valle. Phone 608/986-2781. **Free.**

Historical Society Log Village and Museum. Log cabin with loft, Oetzman log house (1876), log church and library, one-room schoolhouse, blacksmith shop; completely furnished kitchen, living room and bedroom; apothecary shop; Native American and army memorabilia. Located on 52 acres of pine forest and farm fields. (June-Sept, Sat-Sun) 3 mi E via WI 33. Phone 608/524-2807. **Donation.**

Museum of Norman Rockwell Art. One of the largest collections of Norman Rockwell memorabilia spans the artist's 65-yr career. Video. Gift shop. (Mid-May-Oct, daily; rest of yr, daily exc Mon; closed major hols) 227 S Park. Phone 608/524-2123. **¢¢**

Park Lane Model Railroad Museum. Features working model railroad layouts; hundreds of individual cars on display. (Mid-May-mid-Sept, daily) 8 mi E on WI 23 at Herwig Rd. Phone 608/254-8050. **¢¢**

Wisconsin Dairies. Viewing window for butter making process. (Mon-Fri) 501 S Pine. Phone 608/524-2351. **Free.**

Annual Event

Butter Festival. Nishan Park. Four-day festival with parade, tractor and horse pulls, carnival rides, events, arts & crafts, food. 3rd wkend June.

Rhinelander (C-4)

(See also Crandon, Eagle River, Minocqua, Three Lakes, Tomahawk)

Settled 1880 **Pop** 7,427 **Elev** 1,560 ft **Area code** 715 **Zip** 54501 **Web** www.bfm.org/rhinelanderinfo
Information Rhinelander Area Chamber of Commerce, 450 W Kemp St, PO Box 795; 715/365-7464 or 800/236-4386.

Rhinelander is the gateway to the "world's most concentrated lake region." It lies at the junction of the Wisconsin and Pelican rivers. 232 lakes, 11 trout streams and two rivers within a 12-mile radius make the city a thriving resort center. Fishing is good in lakes and streams, and there is hunting for upland game and deer. The logging industry, which built this area, still thrives and the many miles of old logging roads are excellent for hiking and mountain biking. Paved bicycle trails and cross-country skiing are also popular in this northwoods area.

Rhinelander is headquarters for the Nicolet National Forest (see THREE LAKES); phone 715/362-3415.

What to See and Do

Forest tour. Begins at Consolidated's Monico Timberlands Office. A 17-mi self-guided auto tour of Consolidated Papers' forest lands demonstrates forest management techniques. (May-mid-Sept, daily) 10 mi E near jct US 8 & 45. Cross-country ski booklet for nearby trail on company land avail at company offices in Rhinelander or by phone, 715/422-3789. **Free.**

⭐ **Rhinelander Logging Museum.** Most complete displays of old-time lumbering in Midwest. On grounds are "Five Spot," last narrow-gauge railroad locomotive to work Wisconsin's northwoods, and a restored depot dating from late 1800s. Also on premises is one-room schoolhouse. Museum houses the "hodag," called "the strangest animal known to man." Created as a hoax, it has become the symbol of the city. (Memorial Day-Labor Day, daily) In Pioneer Park, on US 8, WI 47. Phone 715/369-5004. **Donation.** Also on the grounds is

Civilian Conservation Corps Museum. Houses photographs, memorabilia, artifacts, tools and papers that record much of the history of the CCC. The manner of clothing worn, how the enrolee was housed and fed, the tools used in project work are on the display. (Last wk May-1st wk Sept, daily) **Free.**

Annual Events

Hodag Country Festival. Three-day country music festival featuring top-name entertainment. Phone 800/762-3803. Mid-July.

Oktoberfest. Downtown. Phone 800/236-4386. Mid-Oct.

Motels

★ ★ **AMERICINN.** *648 W Kemp (US 8W). 715/369-9600; FAX 715/369-9613.* 52 rms (3 with shower only), 2 story. Mid-June-Labor Day: S $56.90-$61.90; D $58.90-$63.90; each addl $6; suites $84.90-$98.90; under 12 free; lower rates rest of yr. Pet accepted. TV; cable (premium), VCR avail. Sauna. Indoor pool; whirlpool. Complimentary continental bkfst. Restaurant opp 6 am-11 pm. Ck-out 11 am. Meeting rm. Business servs avail. Sundries. Valet serv. Coin lndry. X-country ski 1 mi. Some refrigerators. Cr cds: A, C, D, DS, MC, V.

D 🐾 ⚲ ≋ ≋ 🔥 **SC**

★ ★ **BEST WESTERN CLARIDGE.** *70 N Stevens St. 715/362-7100; FAX 715/362-3883.* 81 rms, 2-4 story. S $49-$63; D $53-$73; each addl $8; under 18 free. Pet accepted. TV; cable. Indoor pool; whirlpool. Restaurant 6:30 am-2 pm, 5-10 pm; Sun, hols to 9 pm. Rm serv 5-9 pm. Bar 11 am-2 pm, 4 pm-midnight. Ck-out 11 am. Lndry facilities. Meeting rms. Business servs avail. Valet serv. Sundries. Free airport transportation. X-country ski 5 mi. Exercise equipt: stair machine, weight machine, treadmill. Cr cds: A, C, D, DS, MC, V.

D 🐾 ⚲ ≋ 🕴 ≋ 🔥 **SC**

★ ★ **HOLIDAY INN.** *1 mi W at jct US 8, WI 47. 715/369-3600; FAX 715/369-3600, ext. 276.* 101 rms, 2 story. S $55-$64; D $64-$79; each addl $8. Crib free. TV; cable, VCR avail (movies). Indoor pool; whirlpool. Restaurant 6:30 am-2 pm, 5-10 pm; Sun from 7 am. Rm serv. Bar 11:30 am-midnight; entertainment. Ck-out noon. Coin lndry. Meeting rms. Business servs avail. Sundries. Free airport transportation. Downhill ski 20 mi; x-country ski 5 mi. Exercise equipt; bicycles, treadmill, sauna. Game rm. Cr cds: A, C, D, DS, JCB, MC, V.

D ⚲ ≋ 🕴 ≋ 🔥 **SC**

Resorts

★ **HOLIDAY ACRES.** *Lake George Rd, 4 mi E on US 8, then 2 mi N on Lake George Rd.* 715/369-1500; FAX 715/369-3665; res: 800/261-1500. 28 rms in 2-story lodge, 28 kit. cottages (1-4 bedrm; boat incl; maid serv avail). Lodge, mid-June-late Aug, also Fri & Sat Dec 24-mid-Mar: S, D $85-$109; each addl $11.50; cottages for 2-8, $99-$239; winter wkend package; lower rates rest of yr. Pet accepted; $6. TV; cable, VCR avail (movies). Indoor pool. Playground. Coffee in rms. Dining rm 5 am-10 pm. Box lunches, coffee shop. Rm serv. Bar 4 pm-1 am. Ck-out 11 am (cottages in summer, 10 am). Meeting rms. Business servs avail. Grocery, package store 3 mi. Gift shop in season. Airport transportation. Tennis. Sand beach; boats, motors, rafts, canoes, sailboat, windsurfing. Downhill ski 20 mi; x-country ski on site. Snowmobile trails. Bicycles. Lawn games. Fireplace in 24 cottages, 2 lodge rms; some screened porches. 1000 acres on Lake Thompson. Cr cds: A, C, D, DS, MC, V.

★ **KAFKA'S.** *4281 W Lake George Rd, off US 8.* 715/369-2929; res: 800/426-6674. 10 kit. cottages (2-3 bedrm; boat incl). Mid-June-Aug: cottages for 2-6, $450-$690/wk; lower rates rest of yr. TV in lobby; avail in cottages; cable. Playground. Bar 1 pm-midnight. Ck-out 9 am, ck-in 2 pm. Grocery, package store 2 mi. No maid serv. Free airport transportation. Private beach, swimming; boats, motors, canoes. Downhill ski 20 mi; x-country ski 5 mi. Snowmobiling. Lawn games. Rec rm. Fishing guides, clean & store area. Picnic tables, grills. No cr cds accepted.

Restaurants

★★ **RHINELANDER CAFE.** *33 N Brown St.* 715/362-2918. Hrs: 7 am-11 pm. Closed Thanksgiving, Dec 25. Bar 10:30-1 am. Semi-a la carte: bkfst $1.50-$5.75, lunch $1.50-$8, dinner $4-$22. Child's meals. Specializes in prime rib, roast duck. Nautical decor. Family-owned. Cr cds: D, DS, MC, V.

✔★ **TULA'S.** *232 S Courtney, in Oneida Mall.* 715/369-5248. Hrs: 6 am-9 pm. Closed Dec 25. Res accepted. Bar 11 am-midnight. Semi-a la carte: bkfst $2.29-$6.95, lunch $2.79-$6.99, dinner $2.79-$14.95. Child's meals. Specializes in fish, Italian cuisine. Own soups. Outdoor dining. Cr cds: DS, MC, V.

Rice Lake (C-2)

(See also Spooner)

Pop 7,998 **Elev** 1,140 ft **Area code** 715 **Zip** 54868 **E-mail** rlkarcbr@bucky.win.bright.net **Web** chamber.rice-lake.wi.us

Information Rice Lake Area Chamber of Commerce, 37 S Main St; 715/234-2126 or 800/523-6318.

Formerly headquarters for the world's largest hardwood mills, Rice Lake has an economy based on industry and retail trade. The city and lake were named for nearby wild rice sloughs, which were an important Sioux and Chippewa food source. Surrounded by 84 lakes, the city is in a major recreation area.

Annual Events

Aquafest. June.

County Fair. July.

Motels

★ **AMERICINN.** *2906 Pioneer Ave S.* 715/234-9060; res: 800/634-3444. 43 rms, 2 story. June-Sept: S $52-$61; D $58-$79; each addl $6; under 13 free; lower rates rest of yr. Crib free. TV; cable (premium). Complimentary continental bkfst. Restaurant nearby. Ck-out 11 am. Business servs avail. In-rm modem link. Downhill ski 10 mi; x-country ski 1 mi. Indoor pool; whirlpool. Playground. Some refrigerators. Cr cds: A, C, D, DS, MC, V.

★★ **CURRIER'S LAKEVIEW.** *2010 E Sawyer, east shore of Rice Lake.* 715/234-7474; res: 800/433-5253. 19 rms, 2 story, 8 kits. Mid-May-mid-Sept: S, D $50-$98; kit. units for 2-8, $4 addl; lower rates rest of yr. Crib $2. Pet accepted. TV; cable (premium). Continental bkfst. Ck-out 11 am. Meeting rm. Free airport transportation. Downhill/x-country ski 18 mi. Snowmobile trails. Refrigerators. Private beach; boats, motors, dockage; paddle boats, sailboats, canoes, pontoons. Picnic tables, grill. Wooded grounds; on lake; park adj. Cr cds: A, DS, MC, V.

✔★ **EVERGREEN.** *1801 W Knapp.* 715/234-1088. 21 rms. S $35-$51; D $40-$55; each addl $5; under 12 free. Pet accepted. TV; cable (premium). Complimentary continental bkfst. Restaurant nearby. Ck-out 10:30 am. Business servs avail. Cr cds: MC, V.

✔★ **SUPER 8.** *(115 Second St, Chetek 54728) 24 mi S on US 53.* 715/924-4888; FAX 715/924-2538. 40 rms, 2 story. June-Sept: S $48-$55; D $48-$56; each addl $6; under 13 free; lower rates rest of yr. Crib free. TV; cable (premium). Complimentary continental bkfst. Restaurant nearby. Ck-out 11 am. Business servs avail. In-rm modem link. Indoor pool; whirlpool. Cr cds: A, C, D, DS, MC, V.

Inn

★★★ **CANOE BAY INN & COTTAGES.** *(W 16065 Hogback Rd, Chetek 54728) 16 mi S on US 53, exit Chetek.* 715/924-4594; FAX 715/924-2098; res: 800/568-1995. E-mail canoebay@discover.net; web www.discover.net/canoebay. This inn offers luxury and pampering in an unspoiled wilderness environment. The Frank Lloyd Wright-inspired architecture is the perfect complement to the tranquil, forested setting. Accommodations include any of a combination of whirlpools, fireplaces, private decks, convenience bars, video and audio systems and fabulous lake views. 17 units, 6 rms in inn, 4 rms in lodge, 7 cottages. Rm phone avail. S, D $215-$375. Adults only. TV; cable (premium), VCR (movies). Complimentary bkfst served in rms. Complimentary coffee in rms. Restaurant sitting 6-8 pm. Rm serv noon-8 pm. Ck-out 11 am, ck-in 3 pm. Luggage handling. Concierge serv. Business servs avail. 9-hole golf privileges. X-country ski on site. Ice skating. Spa. Refrigerators; microwaves avail. Picnic tables. On 2 lakes. Totally nonsmoking. Cr cds: DS, MC, V.

Restaurants

✔★ **MARK'S.** *2900 S Main, 6 blks S on County Rd O.* 715/234-3660. Hrs: 8 am-9 pm; Sat to 5:30 pm; Sun to 5 pm. Closed Thanksgiving, Dec 25. Res accepted. Semi-a la carte: bkfst $1.79-$5.29, lunch $3.95-$5.95, dinner $5.95-$7.95. Specializes in chicken, seafood. Informal family atmosphere. Cr cds: A, DS, MC, V.

✔★ **NORSKE NOOK.** *2900 Pioneer Ave.* 715/234-1733. Hrs: 5:30 am-10 pm; Sun 8 am-8 pm. Closed Thanksgiving, Dec 25. Res accepted. Semi-a la carte: bkfst, lunch, dinner $3.25-$12. Child's meals. Specialzies in hot sandwiches, pies. Own pasta. Old-style family restaurant. Cr cds: MC, V.

Richland Center (F-3)

(For accommodations see Reedsburg, Spring Green; also see Reedsburg)

Settled 1849 **Pop** 5,018 **Elev** 731 ft **Area code** 608 **Zip** 53581

Information Richland Chamber of Commerce, 174 S Central, PO Box 128; 608/647-6205 or 800/422-1318.

This is the birthplace of famed architect Frank Lloyd Wright (1867).

What to See and Do

Eagle Cave. Large onyx cavern contains stalactites, stalagmites, fossils. Camping (hookups; fee); marked trails, picnicking, deer farm; fishing, swimming, horseback riding; hay rides; game rm. 220 acres. Guided cave tours (Memorial Day-Labor Day, daily) 12 mi SW via WI 80 & 60. Phone 608/537-2988. Tours ¢¢

Annual Events

June Dairy Days. Contests, games. Early June.

Wisconsin High School State Rodeo Finals. Late June.

Centerfest. Tours of apple orchards, Ocooch Mountain Bike Tour, parade. Early Oct.

St Croix Falls (C-1)

Settled 1837 **Pop** 1,640 **Elev** 900 ft **Area code** 715 **Zip** 54024

Headquarters for the Interstate State Park, St Croix Falls has become a summer and winter resort area. The oldest community in Polk County, it depends on farming, industry, dairying and the tourist trade. Lions Park north of town has picnicking and boat launching, and there are many miles of groomed snowmobile trails in Polk County. Fishing for catfish, walleye, sturgeon and panfish is excellent in the St Croix River and the many area lakes.

What to See and Do

Crex Meadows Wildlife Area. This 30,000-acre state-owned wildlife area is a prairie-wetlands habitat; breeding wildlife species include giant Canada geese, 11 species of ducks, sharp-tailed grouse, prairie chickens, sandhill cranes, bald eagles, ospreys, trumpeter swans and loons. Wildlife observation and photography; guided (by appt) and self-guided tours. Hunting, trapping (fall); canoeing. Hiking. Picnicking. Camping (Sept-Dec). (Daily) N via WI 87, 1 mi N of Grantsburg. Phone 715/463-2896. **Free.**

Governor Knowles State Forest. A 33,000-acre forest extending N & S along the St Croix River. Fishing; boating, canoeing. Hiking, bridle, snowmobile and cross-country ski trails. Picnicking. Group camping. (Daily) Headquarters 23 mi N via WI 87, just N of Grantsburg on WI 70. Phone 715/463-2898. Per vehicle ¢¢

⭐ **Interstate State Park.** A 1,325-acre park; Wisconsin's oldest state park. Swimming; fishing; boating, canoeing. Nature, hiking and cross-country ski trails. Picnicking. Camping (dump station). Permanent naturalist; naturalist programs. Part of the Ice Age National Scientific Reserve. The Reserve operates a visitors center here. (Daily) Standard fees. 2 blks S of US 8 on WI 35. Phone 715/483-3747. Per car ¢¢   In the park is

The Gorge of the St Croix River. Forms the Dalles of the St Croix, with volcanic rock formation, sheer rock walls, some over 200 ft tall; series of potholes, wooded hills and valley; state trout hatchery is located just N of Interstate Park (daily). Phone 715/483-3535. **Free.**

St Croix National Scenic Riverway. Northern unit, 200 mi of scenic riverway in mixed pine and hardwood forest. Southern unit, 52 mi of scenic riverway in mixed pine and hardwood forests, high rocky bluffs. Information stations (Memorial Day-Labor Day, daily); headquarters information station (mid-May-Oct, daily; rest of yr, Mon-Fri; closed hols in winter) Phone 715/483-3284.   **Free.**

Trollhaugen Ski Resort. Resort has 3 chairlifts, 7 rope tows; patrol, school, rentals; snowmaking; bars, cafeterias, restaurant; entertainment. 22 runs. (Early Nov-Mar, daily) 3 mi S on WI 35 to Dresser, then 3/4 mi E on County F. Phone 715/755-2955 or 800/826-7166 (WI).   ¢¢¢¢¢

Motel

⭐⭐ **DALLES HOUSE.** Box 664, 3/4 mi S on WI 35, 1 blk S of jct US 8. 715/483-3206; FAX 715/483-3207; res: 800/341-8000. 50 rms, 2 story. S, D $39-$85; each addl $5. Crib $7. Pet accepted. TV; cable (premium). Sauna. Indoor pool; whirlpools. Restaurant 8 am-11 pm. Ck-out 11 am. Coin lndry. Meeting rm. Business servs avail. In-rm modem link. Downhill ski 3 mi; x-country ski 1/4 mi. Interstate State Park adj. Cr cds: A, C, D, DS, MC, V.

⛷ 🎣 ⛷ ⟆ 🔥

St Germain (C-4)

(See also Eagle River, Minocqua, Three Lakes, Woodruff)

Pop 1,100 (est) **Elev** 1,627 ft **Area code** 715 **Zip** 54558

Cottage Colony

⭐⭐ **ESCH'S SERENITY BAY.** 1276 Halberstadt Rd, 1 mi NE on WI 70. 715/479-8866. 9 kit. cottages (2-3 bedrm). No A/C. Mid-June-mid-Aug: wkly (with boat), 4-6 persons, $850-$1,095; each addl $75; daily rates; lower rates rest of yr. No maid serv. Linens rented. Crib $10. TV; cable (premium). VCR avail. Playground. Restaurant nearby. Ck-out 9 am, ck-in 3 pm. Grocery, coin lndry, package store 2 1/2 mi. Business servs avail. In-rm modem link. Tennis. 500-ft sand beach; waterskiing, equipt; boats, motors, paddleboat. X-country ski 1 mi. Lawn games. Fireplaces. Private porches, decks. Picnic tables, barbecue pits. Set in pines on shore of Little St Germain Lake. Cr cds: MC, V.

D 🎣 ⛷ ⟆ 🔥 SC

Restaurants

⭐ **ELIASON'S "SOME PLACE ELSE".** On WI 70 at WI 155. 715/542-3779. Hrs: 5-9 pm. Closed Mon; Dec 24-25; also Nov. Bar. Semi-a la carte: dinner $4.95-$19.95. Friday fish fry $6.95. Specializes in prime rib, lobster. Entertainment Fri, Sat. Country decor. Gift shop. Family-owned. Cr cds: MC, V.

D

✔⭐ **SPANG'S.** 1 mi E on WI 70. 715/479-9400. Hrs: 5-10 pm. Closed Easter, Thanksgiving, Dec 24-25. Italian, Amer menu. Bar. Semi-a la carte: dinner $6.95-$14.95. Child's meals. Specializes in pasta, pizza. Garden lounge. Old World atmosphere. Family-owned. Cr cds: A, C, D, DS, MC, V.

D

Sayner (C-4)

(See also Boulder Junction, Eagle River, Minocqua, Woodruff)

Pop 450 (est) **Elev** 1,675 ft **Area code** 715 **Zip** 54560

Centrally located in the Northern Highland-American Legion State Forest and boasting 42 sparkling lakes, the Sayner-Star Lake area offers camping, waterskiing, and excellent all-year fishing. Considered the birthplace of the snowmobile, Sayner is near miles of scenic well-groomed trails.

Resort

★ ★ **FROELICH'S SAYNER LODGE.** 1/2 mi NE of WI 155. 715/542-3261; res: 800/553-9695. 11 lodge rms, 2 story, 25 cottages (1-3 bedrm). No A/C exc public rms. Late May-Oct: S, D $40-$60; cabana: $70; cottage $70-$180; under 5, $26. Closed rest of yr. Pet accepted. TV; VCR avail. Heated pool. Playground. Bar 4 pm-1 am, closed Tues. Ck-out 10 am, ck-in 2 pm. Grocery, coin lndry, package store 3/4 mi. Airport transportation. Tennis. Boats, motors, canoe, pontoon boat; waterskiing. Lawn games. Hiking trails. Rec rm. Fishing guides. Library. Screened porch in most cottages; some fireplaces. On Plum Lake. Cr cds: MC, V.

Shawano (D-5)

Settled 1843 **Pop** 7,598 **Elev** 821 ft **Area code** 715 **Zip** 54166
Information Chamber of Commerce, 1404 E Green Bay St, PO Box 38; 715/524-2139 or 800/235-8528.

A city born of the lumber boom, Shawano is now a retail trade center for the small surrounding farms and produces dairy and wood products.

What to See and Do

Shawano Lake. Lake is four mi wide and seven mi long. Fishing, ice fishing, hunting; boating (ramps). 300 mi of snowmobile trails, 8 mi of cross-country ski trails. Camping (fee). 2 mi E on WI 22.

Wolf River Beach. Bathhouse, dock, rafts, lifeguards. (June-mid-Aug, daily) Beaches close if temperature is below 65°F. 5th St & Riverside Dr N. Phone 715/526-6171. **Free.**

Motels

✔★ ★ **AMERICINN.** 1330 E Green Bay St. 715/524-5111; FAX 715/526-3626. 47 rms, 2 story. S, D $54.90-$64.90; each addl $6; suites $69.90-$94.90; under 12 free. Crib free. TV; cable (premium), VCR avail. Sauna. Indoor pool; whirlpool. Complimentary continental bkfst. Restaurant nearby. Ck-out 11 am. Meeting rms. Business servs avail. In-rm modem link. X-country ski 1 mi. Refrigerator in suites. Cr cds: A, D, DS, MC, V.

★ ★ **BEST WESTERN VILLAGE HAUS MOTOR LODGE.** 201 Airport Rd. 715/526-9595; FAX 715/526-9826; res: 800/553-4479. 89 rms, 2 story. June-Aug: S $50-$65; D $65-$85; each addl $6; under 12 free. Crib free. TV; cable. Indoor pool; whirlpool. Restaurant 6 am-9 pm; Sun 7 am-2 pm. Bar 4:30 pm-2 am, closed Sun. Meeting rms. Business servs avail. Sundries. X-country ski 5 mi. Game rm. Near lake, river; beach swimming. Cr cds: A, C, D, DS, MC, V.

Restaurant

★ **ANELLO'S TORCH LIGHT.** 1276 E Green Bay St. 715/526-5680. Hrs: 11 am-2 pm, 5-10 pm; Fri, Sat 5-11 pm. Closed Sun; Thanksgiving, Dec 25. Res accepted. Italian, Amer menu. Bar. Semi-a la carte: lunch $4-$5.95. Complete meals: dinner $5.95-$26.95. Salad bar. Castle motif; full suit of armor. Cr cds: A, DS, MC, V.

Sheboygan (F-6)

(See also Manitowoc, Port Washington)

Settled 1818 **Pop** 49,676 **Elev** 633 ft **Area code** 920 **E-mail** sccc@tcbi.com **Web** sheboygan.org
Information Sheboygan County Convention & Visitors Bureau, 712 Riverfront Dr, 53081; 920/457-9495 or 800/457-9497, ext 800.

A harbor city on the west shore of Lake Michigan, Sheboygan is a major industrial city and a popular fishing port.

What to See and Do

John Michael Kohler Arts Center. Changing contemporary art exhibitions, galleries, shop, historic house; theater, dance & concert series. (Daily; closed hols) 608 New York Ave. Phone 920/458-6144. **Free.**

Kohler-Andrae State Park. Includes 1,000 acres of woods and sand dunes. Swimming, bathhouse. Nature and cross-country ski trails. Picnicking, playgrounds, concession. Camping (105 sites, electric hookups, dump station), winter camping. Nature center (closed winter). Standard fees. (Daily) S on I-43 exit 120, on Lake Michigan. Phone 920/451-4080. Per vehicle ¢¢

Lakeland College (1862). (2,500 students) On campus are Lakeland College Museum (Wed-Thurs, also by appt; free) and Bradley Fine Arts Gallery (Mon-Fri afternoon during school yr; free). 10 mi NW on County M off County A (access to County A from WI 42 and 57). Phone 920/565-2111.

Scenic drives along lakeshore on Broughton Dr, Riverfront Dr, Lakeshore Dr.

Sheboygan County Historical Museum. Exhibit center plus Judge David Taylor home (1850); two-story loghouse (1864) furnished with pioneer items; restored barn; 1867 cheese factory. (Apr-Oct, Tues-Sat, also Sun afternoons; closed Good Friday, Easter, July 4) 3110 Erie Ave. Phone 920/458-1103. ¢¢

Waelderhaus. Reproduction of Kohler family home in Austrian Alps. Guided tours (afternoons, 3 departures daily; closed hols). 1 mi S off County PP, on W Riverside Dr in Kohler. Phone 920/452-4079. **Free.**

Annual Events

Polar Bear Swim. Deland Park. More than 350 swimmers brave Lake Michigan's icy winter waters. Jan 1.

Great Cardboard Boat Regatta. Rotary Riverview Park. Human-powered cardboard craft compete in various classes for fun & prizes. Part of city-wide Independence Day festivities. July 4.

Outdoor Arts Festival. On the grounds of John Michael Kohler Arts Center. Multi-arts event features works by 125 juried artists; demonstrations, entertainment, refreshments. 3rd full wkend July.

Holland Festival. 1 mi W off I-43 via exit 113 in Cedar Grove. Dutch traditions: wooden-shoe dancing, street scrubbing, folk fair, food, music, art fair, parade. Phone 920/668-6118. Last Fri & Sat July.

Motels

✔★ **BUDGETEL INN.** 2932 Kohler Memorial Dr (53081), E of I-43 exit 126 N. 920/457-2321; FAX 920/457-0827. Web www.budgetel.com. 97 rms, 2 story. S $40.95-$51.95; D $43.95-$55.95; under 18 free. Crib free. Pet accepted, some restrictions. TV; cable. Complimentary continental bkfst. Complimentary coffee in rms. Restaurant adj 6 am-11 pm. Ck-out noon. Business servs avail. Cr cds: A, C, D, DS, MC, V.

★ **HARBOR INN.** 905 S 8th St (53081). 920/452-2424; FAX 920/452-0239. 29 rms, 2 story. May-Oct: S $51.95-$61.95; D $56.95-$66.95; each addl $5; suites $79.95-$175; under 12 free; lower rates rest of yr. Crib $5. TV; cable, VCR avail (movies $2). Complimentary coffee in lobby. Restaurant nearby. Ck-out 11 am. Meeting rm. Business servs avail. Valet serv. Sundries. Gift shop. Microwaves avail. View of river. Cr cds: A, C, D, DS, MC, V.

★ **PARKWAY.** 3900 Motel Rd (53081), 6 mi S on I-43 exit 120, at jct County OK, V. 920/458-8338; FAX 920/459-7470; res: 800/341-8000. Web www.imalodging.com. 32 rms. June-Sept: S, D $59.90-$81.90; each addl $3; higher rates special events; lower rates rest of yr. Crib $6. Pet accepted. TV, cable (premium). Complimentary coffee in rms. Restaurant nearby. Ck-out 11 am. Business servs avail. Sundries. X-country ski 2 mi. Refrigerators; microwaves avail. Picnic table, grill. Cr cds: A, C, D, DS, MC, V.

Hotels

★ ★ ★ **THE AMERICAN CLUB.** (Highland Dr, Kohler 53044) 3 mi SW off I-43 exit 126 to Kohler. 920/457-8000; FAX 920/457-0299; res: 800/344-2838. Web www.americanclub.com. The same people who make plumbing in a huge factory across the street have created a delightful resort hotel in a three-story, Tudor-style, rambling, red brick building that originally housed the plant's immigrant workers. In 1981 it was converted into the American Club, with tastefully furnished guest rooms; a large, cozy, book-lined lounge; a superb gourmet restaurant among several dining choices; many recreational and fitness opportunties nearby; and four elaborately planted courtyard gardens, each with a different theme. 236 rms, 3-story. S $175-$750; D $205-$750; each addl $15; under 16 free. Crib free. TV; cable (premium), VCR avail (movies). Heated pool; whirlpool. Supervised child's activities; ages 4-teens. Complimentary afternoon refreshments. Restaurants (see THE IMMIGRANT). Rm serv 24 hrs. Bar 11:30-1 am; entertainment. Ck-out noon. Airport, RR station, bus depot transportation. Meeting rms. Business center. In-rm modem link. Concierge. Gift shop. Indoor tennis, 2 pros. 36-hole golf, 3 pros, par course. X-country ski on site. Exercise rm; instructor, weight machines, bicycles, sauna, steam rm. Spa. Health club privileges. Trap shooting. In-rm whirlpools, minibars, wet bars; some bathrm phones, refrigerators. Carriage rides; bicycles; trolley. Cr cds: A, C, D, DS, MC, V.

★ ★ ★ **INN ON WOODLAKE.** (705 Woodlake Rd, Kohler 53044) 920/452-7800; FAX 920/452-6288; res: 800/919-3600. 60 rms, 3 story. May-Oct: S $109-$199; D $129-$209; each addl $10; under 16 free; lower rates rest of yr. Crib free. TV; cable (premium), VCR avail (movies). Indoor pool; whirlpool, sauna. Complimentary continental bkfst. Restaurant adj 11 am-10 pm. Ck-out noon. Tennis privileges. Golf privileges. Exercise equipt; weight machines, treadmills. Health club privileges. X-country ski on site. Some refrigerators. Cr cds: A, C, D, DS, MC, V.

Inns

★ ★ **ROCHESTER.** (504 Water St, Sheboygan Falls 53085) W on WI 23, then S on Hwy Y to Greenfield Dr then W on Monroe St to Water St. 920/467-3123. E-mail rochesterinn@excelnet; web www.classinns. 5 rms, 3 story, 4 suites. May-Sept: D $89.50; suites $149.50. TV; cable, VCR. Complimentary continental bkfst; full bkfst on wkends. Restaurant adj 11 am-10 pm. Ck-out 10:30 am, ck-in 3 pm. Health club privileges. X-country ski 5 mi. In-rm whirlpools, microwaves avail; wet bars in suites. Built 1848; former general store, post office. Totally nonsmoking. Cr cds: A, MC, V.

✔ ★ ★ **YANKEE HILL INN.** (315 & 405 Collins St, Plymouth 53073) 920/892-2222. E-mail yankee@excel.net; web www.excel.net /~yankee. 12 rms, 5 with A/C, 3 with shower only, 2 story. S, D $76-$102; each addl $15. TV in common rm; cable, VCR avail. Complimentary full bkfst. Restaurant nearby. Ck-out 11 am, ck-in 3 pm. Business servs avail. Luggage handling. Gift shop. Downhill/x-country ski 1 mi. Many in-rm

whirlpools; microwaves avail. Picnic tables, grills. 2 separate houses: Henry H. Huson house built in 1870; Gothic Italianate home. Gilbert L. Huson house built in 1891; Queen Anne home. Totally nonsmoking. Cr cds: DS, MC, V.

Restaurants

✔ ★ ★ **CITY STREETS RIVERSIDE.** 712 Riverfront Dr (53081). 920/457-9050. Hrs: 11 am-2 pm, 5-9 pm; Fri to 10 pm; Sat 5-10 pm. Closed Sun; some major hols. Res accepted. Bar to 2 am. Semi-a la carte: lunch $4-$8, dinner $5.95-$15.95. Specializes in prime rib, seafood. Beamed ceiling. Cr cds: A, C, D, MC, V.

★ ★ ★ **THE IMMIGRANT.** (See The American Club Hotel) 920/457-8000. Web www.americanclub.com. Hrs: 6-10 pm; Sat to 11 pm. Closed Sun, Mon. Res accepted. Bar. Wine cellar. Regional Amer menu. A la carte entrees: dinner $19-$30. Specializes in fresh fish, game, beef. Own baking. Entertainment Fri, Sat. Six elegant dining areas with distinct ethnic decor. Jacket. Cr cds: A, C, D, DS, MC, V.

★ ★ **RICHARD'S.** (501 Monroe St, Sheboygan Falls 53085) W on Indiana Ave. 920/467-6401. Hrs: 11 am-2 pm, 5-10 pm. Closed Sun. Res accepted. Bar 5 pm-2 am. Semi-a la carte: lunch $4-$10, dinner $10-$35. Specialties: oysters Rockefeller, veal chops. Former stagecoach inn (ca 1840s). Cr cds: MC, V.

Sister Bay (Door Co) (D-6)

(See also Door County)

Pop 675 **Elev** 587 ft **Area code** 414 **Zip** 54234 **E-mail** lyons@mail.wiscnet.net **Web** doorcountyvacations.com

Information Door County Chamber of Commerce, 1015 Green Bay Rd, PO Box 406, Sturgeon Bay 54235; 414/743-4456 or 800/527-3529.

This town is near the northern tip of Door County (see).

Annual Event

Sister Bay Fall Festival. Fish boil, fireworks, parade, street auction. Mid-Oct.

Motels

★ **BLUFFSIDE.** 403 Bluffside Lane, at jct WI 42 & 57. 920/854-2530; FAX 920/8542002. 18 units, 1-2 story. July-Labor Day, late Sept-Oct: D $66; each addl $6; lower rates May-June, wkdays after Labor Day-late Sept. Closed rest of yr. Crib free. TV; cable. Complimentary coffee in rms. Restaurant nearby. Ck-out 10 am. Free airport transportation. Refrigerators; microwaves avail. Picnic tables, grills. Cr cds: MC, V.

✔ ★ **COACHLITE INN & SUITES.** 830 S Bay Shore Dr, WI 42. 920/854-9462; res: 800/745-5031. 22 rms, 2 story, 2 suites. July-Oct: D $69; suites $99; each addl $7; lower rates rest of yr. Crib $3. TV; cable. Complimentary coffee in lobby. Restaurant nearby (open in season). Ck-out 10 am. X-country ski 3 mi. Some in-rm whirlpools, microwaves. Balconies. Picnic tables. Cr cds: MC, V.

★ ★ ★ **COUNTRY HOUSE.** 715 N Highland Rd, 1/4 mi S off WI 42. 920/854-4551; FAX 920/854-9809; res: 800/424-0041. E-mail country house@mail.doorcounty-wi.com; web www.country-house.com. 46 rms, 2 story. S, D $76-$151; each addl $22; suites $155-$250. Children over 13 yrs only. TV; cable (premium). Pool; whirlpool. Complimentary continental bkfst. Coffee in rms. Ck-out 11 am. Meeting rm. Business servs avail. Tennis. Row boats, dock facilities. Bicycles. Lawn games. Refrigerators; some in-rm whirlpools, microwaves. Private balconies overlook water. Picnic tables, grills. Green Bay shoreline, on 16 wooded acres. Cr cds: A, DS, MC, V.

★ **EDGE OF TOWN.** 11092 WI 42. 920/854-2012. 10 rms. No rm phones. Mid-June-Oct: S, D $62-$65; each addl $7; family rates; lower rates rest of yr. Crib free. Pet accepted, some restrictions; $7. TV; cable (premium). Complimentary coffee in lobby. Restaurant nearby. Ck-out 11 am. Refrigerators, microwaves. Cr cds: DS, MC, V.

★ ★ **HELM'S 4 SEASONS.** 414 Mill Rd, off WI 42. 920/854-2356. 41 rms, 2 story, 9 kit. apts. Mid-June-late Oct: D $92-$98; each addl $8-$10; kit. apts $115-$180; varied lower rates rest of yr. Crib free. TV; cable. Indoor pool; whirlpool. Complimentary continental bkfst (Labor Day-Memorial Day). Restaurant nearby. Ck-out 10 am. Coin lndry. Meeting rm. Gift shop. Sundries. Free airport transportation. X-country ski 5 mi. Snowmobiling. Sun deck. Refrigerators; some fireplaces. Many private patios, balconies. On Sister Bay, dock. Cr cds: MC, V.

★ ★ **HOTEL DU NORD.** 3/4 mi N on WI 42. 920/854-4221; FAX 920/854-2710. E-mail hoteldunord@doorcounty-wi.com. 56 rms, 2 story. S, D $83-$150. Crib free. TV; VCR avail (movies). Heated pool; whirlpool. Continental bkfst. Restaurant (see HOTEL DU NORD). Ck-out 11 am. Coin lndry. Business servs avail. Free airport transportation. Sundries. Some in-rm whirlpools. On Green Bay. Cr cds: A, DS, MC, V.

★ ★ **INN AT LITTLE SISTER HILL.** 2715 Little Sister Hill Rd. 920/854-2328; FAX 920/854-2696; res: 800/768-6317. 26 kit. suites, 2 story. June-Oct: kit. suites $109-$139; each addl $10; lower rates rest of yr. Crib $10. TV; cable, VCR (movies). Heated pool. Playground. Complimentary coffee in rms. Ck-out 11 am. Coin lndry. Meeting rm. Game rm. X-country ski 3 mi. Bicycle rentals. Refrigerators, microwaves. Some balconies. Picnic tables, grills. Cr cds: DS, MC, V.

★ ★ **NORDIC.** 2721 Nordic Dr, 1 mi S on WI 42. 920/854-5432; FAX 920/854-5974. 33 rms, 2 story. July-Oct: D $68-$88; each addl $5-$10; under 2 free; higher rates: Fall Festival, some hols; lower rates rest of yr. Crib free. TV; cable (premium). Indoor pool; whirlpool. Complimentary continental bkfst. Ck-out 11 am. Microwaves avail. Balconies. Picnic tables, grills. Golf course opp. Near Pebble Beach. Totally nonsmoking. Cr cds: DS, MC, V.

★ ★ **OPEN HEARTH LODGE.** 1109 S Bay Shore Dr. 920/854-4890. 32 rms, 2 story. July-Oct: D $74-$94; each addl $3-$10; family rates; lower rates rest of yr. Crib free. TV; cable. Indoor pool; whirlpool. Playground. Complimentary coffee. Restaurant nearby. Ck-out 11 am. Refrigerators; microwaves avail. Cr cds: A, DS, MC, V.

✔★ **SCANDIA.** 11062 Beach Rd. 920/854-2447. 6 kit. cottages. No rm phones. June-Oct, Dec-Feb: kit. cottages $65-$150; each addl $5-$10; family, wkly rates; ski plan; lower rates rest of yr. Crib $2. TV; cable. Restaurant nearby. Ck-out 10 am. X-country ski 4 mi. Picnic tables, grills. Bay nearby. Totally nonsmoking. Cr cds: MC, V.

★ **VOYAGER INN.** 232 WI 57. 920/854-4242; FAX 920/854-2670. 28 rms. July-Aug, wkends Sept-mid-Oct: D $72-$78; each addl $7;

lower rates May-June. Closed rest of yr. Crib $5. Heated pool; whirlpool. Restaurant nearby. Ck-out 11 am. Business servs avail. Sauna. Refrigerators; microwaves avail. Some balconies. Cr cds: DS, MC, V.

Motor Hotel

★ ★ ★ **CHURCH HILL INN.** 425 Gateway Dr. 920/854-4885; FAX 920/854-4634; res: 800/422-4906. 34 rms, 2 story. S, D $119-$164; each addl $19; higher rates wkends. Children over 8 yrs only. TV; cable. Heated pool; whirlpool. Complimentary full bkfst; afternoon refreshments. Ck-out 10:30 am. Meeting rms. Business servs avail. X-country ski 4 mi. Exercise equipt; weights, bicycles, sauna. Some refrigerators, in-rm whirlpools. Balconies. Common rms with fireplaces. Totally nonsmoking. Cr cds: A, MC, V.

Resort

★ **LITTLE SISTER.** 360 Little Sister Rd. 920/854-4013; FAX 920/854-5076. 6 chalets, 13 cottages (1-2-bedrm). MAP only, July-Aug: wkly, chalets, cottages $330-$440/person; family rates; lower rates rest of yr. Closed Nov-Apr. Crib $7. TV; cable (premium). Playground. Ck-out 10 am. Grocery store 2 mi. Coin lndry. Tennis. Hiking. Bicycles. Lawn games. Boat rentals. Balconies. Picnic tables. On swimming beach. Cr cds: MC, V.

Restaurants

★ **AL JOHNSON'S SWEDISH RESTAURANT.** 702 Bayshore Dr, on WI 42. 920/854-2626. Hrs: 6 am-9 pm; Nov-Apr to 8 pm. Closed Thanksgiving, Dec 25. Swedish, Amer menu. Semi-a la carte: bkfst (all day) $2.95-$8.25; lunch $3.50-$11.95. Complete meals: dinner $13.25-$17.50. Child's meals. Specializes in Swedish pancakes, meatballs. Swedish-style structure, decor. Gift shop. Goats graze on grass-covered roof. Family-owned. Cr cds: A, DS, MC, V.

★ **CHERRYWOOD INN.** 321 Country Walk Dr. 920/854-9590. Hrs: 5-9 pm. Closed Nov-mid-May. Res accepted. Bar. Semi-a la carte: dinner $6.75-$16.75. Child's meals. Specializes in fish boils, walleye pike, cajun chicken alfredo. Outdoor dining. Cr cds: DS, MC, V.

✔★ **DOOR DELI.** On WI 42. 920/854-4514. Hrs: 6 am-8 pm, Fri, Sat to 10 pm; mid-June-Aug 6 am-10 pm. Wine, beer. Semi-a la carte: bkfst $2-$4, lunch $2-$5, dinner $5-$10. Child's meals. Specializes in seafood, bratwurst, gourmet hamburgers. Ice cream fountain. Outdoor dining; fireplace. Cr cds: DS, MC, V.

★ ★ **HOTEL DU NORD.** (See Hotel Du Nord Motel) 920/854-4221. Hrs: 5:30-10 pm; Sun brunch 9:30 am-12:30 pm. Res accepted. Bar 4:30 pm-midnight. Semi-a la carte: bkfst $4-$8, lunch $6-$10, dinner $16.25-$22. Sun brunch $11.95. Child's meals. Overlooks Green Bay. Cr cds: A, DS, MC, V.

Sparta (F-3)

(See also Black River Falls, La Crosse, Tomah)

Settled 1849 **Pop** 7,788 **Elev** 793 ft **Area code** 608 **Zip** 54656
Information Chamber of Commerce, 111 Milwaukee St; 608/269-4123 or -2453.

Sparta is the home of several small industries manufacturing, among other items, dairy products, brushes and automobile parts. The area is also well-known for its biking trails. Fort McCoy, a US Army base, is five miles northeast on WI 21.

What to See and Do

Elroy-Sparta State Trail. Built on an old railroad bed, this 32-mi hard-sur-faced (limestone screenings) trail passes through 3 tunnels and over 23 trestles. Biking (fee). (Apr-Oct, daily) Phone 608/337-4775 or 608/463-7109. Trail pass ¢¢

Motels

✔★ **BEST NIGHTS INN.** *303 Wisconsin St. 608/269-3066; FAX 608/269-3175.* 28 rms. Mid-May-Oct: S $30-$69; D $35-$89; each addl $7; under 16 free; lower rates rest of yr. Crib avail. Pet accepted. TV; cable. Complimentary continental bkfst (wkends). Restaurant opp open 24 hrs. Ck-out 11 am. Refrigerators. Totally nonsmoking. Cr cds: A, C, D, DS, MC, V.

★★ **COUNTRY INN.** *737 Avon Rd. 608/269-3110; FAX 608/269-6726; res: 800/456-4000.* 61 rms, 2 story. S $50.95-$58.95; D $57.95-$67.95; suites $60.95-$112.90; under 18 free. Crib avail. Pet accepted. TV; cable (premium), VCR avail (movies). Indoor pool; whirlpool. Complimentary continental bkfst. Restaurant adj 6 am-11 pm. Bar from 4 pm. Ck-out noon. Coin lndry. Meeting rms. Business servs avail. Downhill ski 7 mi; x-country ski 1 mi. Some refrigerators. Cr cds: A, C, D, DS, MC, V.

✔★ **DOWNTOWN.** *509 S Water St. 608/269-3138.* 17 rms. S $32-$39.95; D $36-$45; each addl $3; under 12 free. Crib free. TV; cable (premium). Restaurant 6 am-1 pm. Ck-out 11 am. Cr cds: DS, MC, V.

★★ **HERITAGE.** *704 W Wisconsin St, at jct US 16 & WI 27. 608/269-6991; res: 800/658-9484.* 22 rms, 2 story. S $31; D $37-$45; each addl $3. Crib $5. Pet accepted. TV; cable (premium). Pool; whirlpool. Restaurant adj open 24 hrs. Ck-out 11 am. Cr cds: A, C, D, DS, MC, V.

Inn

★★ **JUST-N-TRAILS.** *Rte 1, Box 274, on County J. 608/269-4522; FAX 608/269-3280; res: 800/488-4521.* 5 rms, 3 with bath, 1-2 story, 4 cottages. S $65-$85; D $75-$95; cottages $145-$250; family rates. Crib free. Complimentary full bkfst. Ck-out noon, ck-in 3 pm. X-country ski on site. Library/sitting rm. Restored 1920s farmhouse; country decor. Cr cds: A, DS, MC, V.

Spooner (C-2)

(For accommodations see Hayward, Rice Lake)

Settled 1883 **Pop** 2,464 **Elev** 1,065 ft **Area code** 715 **Zip** 54801 **Web** www.spoonerwisconsin.com
Information Spooner Area Chamber of Commerce, 122 N River St; 715/635-2168 or 800/367-3306.

Once a busy railroad town, Spooner is now a popular destination for fishermen and nature lovers.

What to See and Do

Railroad Memories Museum. Memorabilia, model railroad in old Chicago & Northwestern depot. (Mid May-mid-Oct, daily) 400 Front St. Phone 715/635-3325. ¢¢

St Croix National Scenic Riverway. One of two in the US; excellent canoeing (Class #1 rapids) and tubing. (See ST CROIX FALLS) Contact Chamber of Commerce or National Park Service Information Station in Trego; 715/635-8346.

Trego Lake Park. Heavily wooded area on the Namekagon River (Wild River). Fishing; boating, canoeing, inner tubing. Hiking. Picnicking. Camping (electric hookups). (May-Sept) 1/4 mi N, jct US 53, 63 in Trego. Phone 715/635-9931 or 715/635-2091. Camping ¢¢¢

Annual Events

Badger Wheels Car Show. Early June.

Heart of the North Rodeo. PRCA approved. Country music. Mid-July.

Motels

✔★ **COUNTRY HOUSE.** *US 63S. 715/635-8721.* E-mail bjcrites@spacestar.net; web www.spoonerwisconsin.com/motel.html. 22 rms. June-Oct: S $32-$52; D $42-$55; each addl $4; under 6 free; lower rates rest of yr. Crib $3. TV; cable, VCR avail. Complimentary coffee in lobby. Restaurant adj 6:30 am-9 pm. Ck-out 11 am. Business servs avail. Microwaves avail. Cr cds: A, C, D, DS, MC, V.

★ **GREEN ACRES.** *N 4809 US 63S, 1 mi S on US 63. 715/635-2177; res: 800/373-5293; FAX 715/635-6305.* 21 rms. Late May-Aug: S, D $59; each addl $5; higher rates rodeo; lower rates rest of yr. Crib $5. Pet accepted, some restrictions; $5. TV; cable (premium). Complimentary coffee in lobby. Ck-out 10 am. Business servs avail. X-country ski 2 mi. Playground. Lawn games. Microwaves avail. Picnic tables, grills. Cr cds: A, C, D, DS, MC, V.

Restaurant

✔★ **CLUB 70.** *WI 70, 2 1/2 mi W on WI 70. 715/635-9300.* Hrs: 4-9 pm; Fri, Sat to 10 pm. Closed Sun-Tues; Jan 1, Dec 24, 25. Res accepted. Italian, Amer menu. Bar. Semi-a la carte: dinner $6.95-$14.95. Child's meals. Specializes in steak, seafood, pasta. Own pasta. Contemporary decor; ceiling fans, large windows. Cr cds: MC, V.

Spring Green (G-3)

(For accommodations see Dodgeville, Mineral Point; also see Prairie du Sac)

Pop 1,283 **Elev** 729 ft **Area code** 608 **Zip** 53588

Information Chamber of Commerce, PO Box 3; 608/588-2042 or 800/588-2042.

This is where Frank Lloyd Wright grew up, built his home (Taliesin East), and established the Taliesin Fellowship for the training of apprentice architects.

What to See and Do

⭐ **House on the Rock.** Designed and built by Alexander J. Jordan atop a chimney-like rock, 450 ft above valley. Waterfalls, trees throughout house; collections of antiques, Oriental objets d'art and automated music machines (many of the musical exhibits require addl money to activate the automation mechanism). Restaurant. (Mid-March-late Oct, daily) 9 mi S on WI 23. Phone 608/935-3639. ¢¢¢¢

⭐ **Taliesin.** Features Frank Lloyd Wright's home, studio, farm and school. (May-Oct, daily) 3 mi S on WI 23. Phone 608/588-7948. ¢¢¢-¢¢¢¢

Tower Hill State Park. Park has 77 acres of wooded hills and bluffs overlooking the Wisconsin River. Site of Civil War shot tower and early lead-mining village of Helena. Fishing; canoeing. Picnicking (shelter), playgrounds. Camping. Standard fees. (Daily) 3 mi E on US 14, then S on County Hwy C. Phone 608/588-2116. Per vehicle ¢¢

Wintergreen Cross Country Ski Area. Area has 20 mi of groomed trails; patrol, rentals; snack bar. (Dec-mid-Mar, daily) 3 mi S on WI 23, then 1 mi W on County C. Phone 608/588-7000. ¢¢-¢¢¢

Seasonal Event

American Players Theatre. Rte 3, Golf Course Rd. Theater arts center for the classics. Summer performances in outdoor amphitheater (Tues-Sun; also matinees Tues-Fri in Sept & Oct) Phone 608/588-2361. Mid-June-early Oct.

Motels

✔⭐ **PRAIRIE HOUSE.** E4884 US 14. 608/588-2088. 51 rms, 1 story. July-Aug: S $42-$62; D $52-$62; each addl $5; under 18 free; lower rates rest of yr. Crib $5. TV. Complimentary coffee in lobby. Restaurant nearby. Ck-out 11 am. Meeting rm. X-country ski 5 mi. Exercise equipt; bicycles, weight machine, sauna. Whirlpool. Some refrigerators. Cr cds: A, DS, MC, V.

🅳 ⚓ 🛁 ⛷

✔⭐ **ROUND BARN LODGE.** US 14/WI 23. 608/588-2568. 44 rms, 2 story. June-Aug: S, D $44.50-$79.50; each addl $5; suites $109.50; under 6 free; lower rates rest of yr. Crib free. TV; cable (premium), VCR avail. Indoor pool; whirlpool. Complimentary coffee in lobby. Restaurant 7 am-9 pm. Ck-out 11 am. Meeting rm. X-country ski 5 mi. Cr cds: A, C, D, DS, MC, V.

🅳 ⚓ ⛷

Restaurant

✔⭐ ⭐ **POST HOUSE.** 127 E Jefferson. 608/588-2595. Hrs: 11 am-2 pm, 5-9 pm; Fri, Sat to 10 pm; Sun 11 am-8 pm. Sun brunch 8-11 am (summer). Closed Mon, Tue (Nov-Apr); major hols. Res accepted. Bar. Semi-a la carte: lunch $5.75-$7, dinner $8.50-$14.50. Sun brunch $6.95. Child's meals. Specializes in prime rib, roast duck. Outdoor dining. Contemporary American decor. Cr cds: MC, V.

Stevens Point (E-4)

(See also Marshfield, Wisconsin Rapids)

Settled 1838 **Pop** 23,006 **Elev** 1,093 ft **Area code** 715 **Zip** 54481 **E-mail** spacvb@coredcs.com **Web** www.easy-axcess.com/spacvb

Information Stevens Point Area Convention and Visitors Bureau, 23 Park Ridge Dr; 715/344-2556 or 800/236-4636.

A diversified community on the Wisconsin River near the middle of the state, Stevens Point was established as a trading post by George Stevens, who bartered with the Potawatomi. Incorporated as a city in 1858, today it has a number of industries and markets the dairy produce and vegetable crops of Portage County.

What to See and Do

George W. Mead Wildlife Area. Preserved and managed for waterfowl, fur bearers, deer, prairie chickens, ruffed grouse and other game and nongame species. Bird watching; limited fishing; hunting. Hiking. (Mon-Fri) 15 mi NW on US 10 to Milladore, then 5 mi N on County S. Phone 715/457-6771. **Free.**

Stevens Point Brewery (1857). The brewery tour has been described as one of the most interesting in the country. (Daily exc Sun, reservations suggested) 2617 Water St, corner of Beer & Water Sts. Phone 715/344-9310.

University of Wisconsin-Stevens Point (1894). (8,500 students) Across the entire front of the four-story Natural Resources Building is the world's largest computer-assisted mosaic mural. Museum of Natural History has one of the most complete collections of preserved birds and bird eggs in the country (academic yr, daily). Planetarium show in Science Hall (academic yr, Sun). Fine Arts Center houses 1,300 American Pattern glass goblets. 2100 Main St. Phone 715/346-4242.

Motels

⭐ **BUDGETEL INN.** 4917 Main St, jct US 51 & US 10. 715/344-1900; FAX 715/344-1254. 80 rms, 3 story. S $39.95-$44.95; D $47.95-$51.95; under 19 free. Crib free. Pet accepted. TV; cable (premium). Complimentary continental bkfst. Complimentary coffee in rms. Restaurant adj open 24 hrs. Ck-out noon. Coin lndry. Meeting rms. Business servs avail. In-rm modem link. X-country ski 1 mi. Cr cds: A, C, D, DS, MC, V.

🅳 ⚓ ⛷ 🚫 🐾 SC

⭐ ⭐ **COMFORT SUITES.** 300 N Division St. 715/341-6000; FAX 715/341-8908. 105 suites, 3 story. S $69-$99; D $79-$99; each addl $10; under 18 free. Crib free. TV; VCR avail (movies). Indoor pool; whirlpool. Complimentary continental bkfst. Complimentary coffee in rms. Restaurant adj open 24 hrs. Ck-out noon. Coin lndry. Meeting rms. Business servs avail. In-rm modem link. Valet serv. Sundries. X-country ski 2 mi. Exercise equipt; weight machine, bicycles. Refrigerators; some in-rm whirlpools, wet bars. Cr cds: A, C, D, DS, ER, JCB, MC, V.

🅳 ⚓ ⛷ 🛁 🚫 🐾 SC

✔⭐ **POINT.** 209 Division St. 715/344-8312; res: 800/344-3093. 44 rms, 2 story. S $33; D $37-$42; each addl $4. Crib $4. Pet accepted. TV; cable, VCR avail. Coffee in lobby. Complimentary continental bkfst. Ck-out 11 am. Meeting rm. Cr cds: A, C, D, DS, MC, V.

🅳 ⚓ 🚫 🐾 SC

✔⭐ **TRAVELER.** 3350 Church (US Business 51). 715/344-6455; FAX 715/344-6455; res: 800/341-8000. 17 units. S $24.95-$36.95; D $28.95-$45.95; each addl $4; under 18 free. Crib $5. Pet accepted, some restrictions. TV; cable (premium). Complimentary coffee in rms. Ck-out 11 am. Downhill ski 12 mi. Cr cds: A, DS, MC, V.

Motor Hotel

★ ★ ★ **HOLIDAY INN.** *1501 N Point Dr, exit 161 on US 51.* 715/341-1340; FAX 715/341-9446. 295 rms, 2-6 story. S $79; D $89; each addl $10; suites $99-$168; under 18 free. Crib free. Pet accepted. TV; cable, VCR (movies). Indoor pool; whirlpool, poolside serv. Restaurant 6:30 am-10 pm; Fri, Sat to 11 pm. Rm serv. Bar 11-1 am; entertainment. Ck-out 11 am. Coin lndry. Convention facilities. Business servs avail. In-rm modem link. Valet serv. Sundries. Gift shop. Free airport transportation. Downhill ski 20 mi; x-country ski 1 mi. Exercise equipt; weight machine, bicycle, sauna. Cr cds: A, C, D, DS, JCB, MC, V.

Restaurants

★ **HOT FISH SHOP.** *1140 Clark St.* 715/344-4252. Hrs: 11 am to closing. Res accepted. Semi-a la carte: lunch $6-$12, dinner $7-$29. Child's meals. Specializes in fresh seafood, steak, sandwiches. Nautical motif. Cr cds: A, C, D, DS, MC, V.

★ ★ ★ **THE RESTAURANT.** *1800 N Point Dr.* 715/346-6010. Hrs: 5-9 pm; Fri, Sat to 10 pm. Closed Sun; major hols. Res accepted. Italian menu. Bar. Wine list. A la carte entrees: dinner $5-$17. Specializes in pasta, veal, seafood. Own baking. Outdoor dining. Cr cds: A, MC, V.

Sturgeon Bay (Door Co) (D-6)

(See also Algoma, Door County, Green Bay)

Settled 1870 **Pop** 9,176 **Elev** 588 ft **Area code** 414 **Zip** 54235 **E-mail** lyons@mail.wiscnet.net **Web** doorcountyvacations.com

Information Door County Chamber of Commerce, 1015 Green Bay Rd, PO Box 406; 414/743-4456 or 800/527-3529.

Sturgeon Bay, in Door County (see), sits at the farthest inland point of a bay where swarms of sturgeon were once caught and piled like cordwood along the shore. The historic portage from the bay to Lake Michigan, used for centuries by Native Americans and early explorers, began here. The Sturgeon Bay ship canal now makes the route a waterway used by lake freighters and pleasure craft. The city is the county seat and trading center. Two shipyards and a number of other industries are located here. Ten million pounds of cherries are processed every year in Door County.

What to See and Do

Cave Point County Park. Wave-worn grottoes and caves in limestone bluffs. Sand dunes, beautiful landscapes nearby. 10 mi NE via WI 57, Clark Lake Rd.

Door County Maritime Museum. Shipbuilding history and artifacts; boats on display; actual pilothouse of a Great Lakes ore carrier. (Memorial Day-mid-Oct, daily) 120 N Madison. Phone 414/743-5958. **Donation.**

✖ **Door County Museum.** Old-time stores; fire dept with antique trucks; county memorabilia & photographs. Slide presentation. Gift shop. (May-Oct, daily) 4th Ave & Michigan St. Phone 414/743-5809. **Donation.**

Potawatomi State Park. 1,200 acres of woodland along the shores of Sturgeon Bay. Limestone bluffs. Waterskiing; fishing; boating, canoeing. Nature, hiking, snowmobile and cross-country ski & bicycle trails; downhill skiing. Picnicking, playgrounds. Camping (125 sites, 23 hookups), winter camping. Standard fees. 2 mi NW. Phone 414/746-2890. Per vehicle ¢¢

Robert La Salle County Park. Site where La Salle and his band of explorers were rescued from starvation by friendly Native Americans. Monument marks location of La Salle's fortified camp. Picnicking. SE on Lake Michigan.

The Farm. Farm animals and fowl in natural surroundings; pioneer farmstead. (Memorial Day-Labor Day, daily) 4 mi N on WI 57. Phone 414/743-6666. ¢¢¢

US Coast Guard Canal Station. At entrance to ship canal on Lake Michigan. Coast Guard provides maritime law enforcement patrols, search and rescue duties, weather reports; lighthouse. Tours (by appt). 2501 Canal Rd. Phone 414/743-3367. **Free.**

Annual Events

Shipyards Tour. Early May.

Taste of Door County. Mid-June.

Maritime Days. Early Aug.

Motels

★ ★ **BAY SHORE INN.** *4205 Bay Shore Dr.* 920/743-4551; FAX 920/743-3299; res: 800/556-4551. 30 kit. suites, 3 story. Mid-July-Aug: S, D $165-$270; 2-3-night min wkends; lower rates rest of yr. Crib $5. TV; cable (premium). Indoor pool; 1 indoor; whirlpool. Playground. Complimentary coffee in rms. Ck-out 11 am. Coin lndry. Meeting rms. Business servs avail. Tennis. X-country ski 6 mi. Guest bicycles, paddle boats. Game rm. In-rm whirlpools, microwaves. Some balconies. Picnic tables. On swimming beach. Cr cds: A, DS, MC, V.

★ ★ **BEST WESTERN MARITIME INN.** *1001 N 14th Ave.* 920/743-7231; FAX 920/743-9341. 91 rms, 2 story. July-Oct: S $81-$90; D $88-$99; each addl $7; suites $145-$160; under 12 free; package plans; lower rates rest of yr. TV; cable (premium). Indoor pool; whirlpool. Complimentary continental bkfst. Restaurant nearby. Ck-out 11 am. Business servs avail. Sundries. Downhill/x-country ski 5 mi. Game rm. Refrigerators; microwaves avail. Cr cds: A, C, D, DS, MC, V.

✔★ **CHAL-A.** *3910 WI 42-57.* 920/743-6788. 20 rms. S $24-$44; D $29-$49; each addl $4. Crib $5. TV. Complimentary coffee in lobby. Ck-out 10:30 am. Downhill ski 7 mi. Museum on premises; features collections of cars, toys and dolls. Cr cds: MC, V.

★ ★ **THE CLIFF DWELLERS.** *3540 N Duluth Ave, S city limits on Bay.* 920/743-4260. 16 lodge rms, 1-2 story; 13 kit. cottages (1-2 bedrm). Mid-June-Oct: S, D $89-$110; each addl $15-$20; package plans; lower rates May-mid-June. Closed rest of yr. Crib avail. TV; cable. Heated pool; whirlpool. Bkfst tray in rms. Ck-out 11 am. Tennis. Sauna. Rowboats. Bicycles. Sun deck. Lawn games. Balconies. Grills. Overlooks Sturgeon Bay. Cr cds: A, DS, MC, V.

✔★ **HOLIDAY.** *(29 N Second Ave, Sturgeon Bay)* 920/743-5571; FAX 920/743-5395. 18 rms, 2 story. July-Aug: S $49; D $65; each addl $5; under 18 free; wkly rates; higher rates: wkends Sept, Oct; 2-day min wkends; lower rates rest of yr. Crib free. Pet accepted, some restrictions; $5. TV; cable, VCR avail (free movies). Complimentary continental bkfst. Restaurant nearby. Ck-out 11 am. Business servs avail. X-country ski 4 mi. Refrigerators; microwaves avail. Cr cds: A, D, DS, MC, V.

★ ★ **LEATHEM SMITH LODGE.** *1640 Memorial Dr.* 920/743-5555; FAX 920/743-5355; 800 888/DOOR-WIS. 63 rms, 2 story. 16 suites. June-Aug & late Dec-early Jan: S, D $79-$95; suites $119-$295; under 12 free; 2-day min hols (some higher rates); lower rates rest of yr. Crib $10. TV; cable, VCR avail (movies $3.75). Heated pool; poolside serv. Playground. Ck-out 11 am. Meeting rms. Business servs avail. Gift shop. Tennis. 9 hole par 3 golf; greens fee $6, putting green. Downhill/x-country ski 6 mi. Lawn games. Some refrigerators, microwaves. 48 slip marina with boat ramp. Cr cds: A, MC, V.

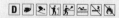

★ ★ **WHITE BIRCH INN.** *1009 S Oxford Ave. 920/743-3295.* 14 units, 2 story, 3 suites. May-mid-Oct: S, D $75-$95; each addl $10; lower rates rest of yr. Crib free. TV. Complimentary continental bkfst. Restaurant 11:30 am-1:30 pm, 5:30-9:30 pm; Sat from 5 pm. Rm serv. Ck-out 11:30 am. Gift shop. Free airport transportation. X-country ski 6 mi. Picnic tables. Southwestern decor; Native American artifacts. Cr cds: MC, V.

Lodge

★ ★ **CHERRY HILLS LODGE & GOLF RESORT.** *5905 Dunn Rd. 920/743-4222; res: 800/545-2307.* Web www.golfdoorcounty.com. 31 rms, 2 story. July-Aug & wkends in Sept: S, D $99-$139; each addl $15; golf plan; lower rates rest of yr. TV. Heated pool; whirlpool. Dining rm 6:30-10:30 am, 11 am-1:30 pm, 6-9 pm. Bar; entertainment. Ck-out 11 am. Meeting rms. Business servs avail. Gift shop. 18-hole golf, greens fee $15-$26. Downhill/x-country ski 7 mi. Refrigerators, minibars. Patios, balconies. Picnic tables. Cr cds: A, C, D, DS, MC, V.

Inns

★ ★ ★ **BARBICAN.** *132 N Second Ave. 414/743-4854.* 18 suites in 3 houses, 2 story. No rm phones. D $120-$185; package rates. TV; cable (premium), VCR. Complimentary continental bkfst. Restaurant nearby. Rm serv. Ck-out 11 am, ck-in 2 pm. Downhill/x-country ski 10 mi. In-rm whirlpools, refrigerators, fireplaces. Restored Victorian houses (1873); antiques. Former residence of local lumber baron. Cr cds: MC, V.

★ ★ **CHADWICK.** *25 N Eighth Ave. 920/743-2771; FAX 920/743-4386.* E-mail nrbreg@itol.com. 3 suites, 3 story. No rm phones. Apr-Oct: suites $100-$115; package plans; lower rates rest of yr. TV; cable (premium), VCR avail. Complimentary continental bkfst in rms. Restaurant nearby. Ck-out noon, ck-in 2 pm. Some street parking. Free airport transportation. Downhill/x-country ski 5 mi. In-rm whirlpools, fireplaces. Balconies. Built 1895; original woodwork, antique glassware, Chickering piano (1823). Cr cds: MC, V.

★ ★ ★ **CHANTICLEER GUEST HOUSE.** *4072 Cherry Rd (CO HH), WI 42 left on CO BB, right on CO HH (Cherry Rd). 920/746-0334.* 8 rms, 3 story. S, D $115-$175; wkly rates; 2-day min wkends, 3-day min hol wkends. Adults only. TV; VCR. Heated pool. Complimentary continental bkfst. Ck-out 11 am, ck-in 2 pm. Luggage handling, X-country ski on site. Sauna. Refrigerators, microwaves, in-rm whirlpools, fireplaces. Balconies. Picnic tables. Country house built 1916 on 30 acres; gazebo & sheep. Hiking trail. Cr cds: DS, MC, V.

★ ★ **INN AT CEDAR CROSSING.** *336 Louisiana St. 920/743-4200; FAX 920/743-4422.* 9 rms, 2 story. D $90-$150; each addl $15; suites $130-$165; package plans. TV in lobby; cable (premium), VCR (free movies). Complimentary bkfst. Restaurant (see INN AT CEDAR CROSSING). Ck-out 11 am, ck-in 2 pm. Business servs avail. Free airport transportation. Downhill/x-country ski 5 mi. Some in-rm whirlpools, fireplaces. Balconies. Built 1884. Antique furnishings. Totally nonsmoking. Cr cds: DS, MC, V.

★ ★ ★ **SCOFIELD HOUSE.** *908 Michigan St. 920/743-7727; 800 888/463-0204.* E-mail scofhse@mail.wiscnet.net; web www.scofieldhouse.com. 6 rms, 3 story. No rm phones. S, D $93-$196. TV; cable (premium), VCR (free movies). Complimentary full bkfst; afternoon refreshments. Restaurant nearby. Ck-out 11 am, ck-in 3 pm. Business servs avail. Downhill/x-country ski 6 mi. Many balconies. Many in-rm whirlpools. Many balconies. Former mayor's residence (1902); antiques, stained glass. Totally nonsmoking. No cr cds accepted.

★ ★ ★ **WHITE LACE.** *16 N Fifth Ave. 920/743-1105.* 18 rms, 2 story. D $98-$198; ski rates; lower rates Sun-Thurs Nov-Apr. Adults only. TV in most rms; VCR avail. Complimentary bkfst. Ck-out 11 am, ck-in 3 pm. Downhill/x-country ski 5 mi. Some in-rm whirlpools; microwaves avail. Balconies. Four buildings built 1880, 1900. White-columned front porch. Antiques; some fireplaces. Totally nonsmoking. Cr cds: A, DS, MC, V.

Restaurants

★ ★ **INN AT CEDAR CROSSING.** *(See Inn At Cedar Crossing) 920/743-4249.* Hrs: 7 am-9 pm; Fri, Sat to 9:30 pm. Closed Dec 25. Res accepted. Bar. Semi-a la carte: bkfst $1.95-$6.95, lunch $4.95-$8.95, dinner $8.95-$32. Specializes in poultry, fresh fish. Own desserts. Victorian storefront (1884); antique furnishings, fireplaces. Totally nonsmoking. Cr cds: DS, MC, V.

★ **MILL SUPPER CLUB.** *4128 WI 42/57. 920/743-5044.* Hrs: 4:30 pm-1 am. Closed Mon; Easter, Dec 24, 25. Bar. Semi-a la carte: dinner $7.50-$36.95. Child's meals. Specializes in family-style chicken, prime rib, seafood. Family-owned. Cr cds: A, DS, MC, V.

✔★ **PERRY'S CHERRY DINER.** *230 Michigan St. 920/743-9910.* Hrs: 6 am-9 pm; Sun 8 am-3 pm. Closed Dec 25. Greek, Amer menu. Semi-a la carte: bkfst $2-$6, lunch $2.50-$6, dinner $5-$7.79. Specializes in gyros, moussaka, old-fashioned malts. No cr cds accepted.

Superior (B-2)

Founded 1852 **Pop** 27,134 **Elev** 642 ft **Area code** 715 **Zip** 54880 **E-mail** superior.visitsuperior.com **Web** www.visitsuperior

Information Tourist Information Center, 305 Harborview Parkway; 800/942-5313.

At the head of Lake Superior, with the finest natural harbor on the Great Lakes, Superior-Duluth has been one of the leading ports in the country in volume of tonnage for many years. The Burlington Northern Docks and taconite pellet handling complex are the largest in the US. More than 200 million bushels of grain are shipped in and out of the area's elevators each year. Here is the largest coal-loading terminal in the US with 12 coal docks in the Superior-Duluth area, also a briquet plant, a shipyard, a refinery and a flour mill. Production of dairy products is also a major industry. Long before its founding date, the city was the site of a series of trading posts. The University of Wisconsin-Superior is located here.

What to See and Do

Amnicon Falls State Park. An 825-acre park with many small waterfalls and interesting rock formations. Hiking. Picnicking. Camping. Standard fees. (May-mid-Oct, daily) 10 mi E on US 2. Phone 715/398-3000 or 715/399-8073. Per vehicle ¢¢

Barker's Island. Boating (launching ramps, marina). Picnic facilities, lodging, dining. From E 2nd St & 6th Ave E, off US 2, 53, WI 13. Also here are

Duluth-Superior Excursions. A 1¾-hr narrated tour of Superior-Duluth Harbor and Lake Superior on the *Vista King* or *Vista Queen.* (Mid-May-mid-Oct, daily) Also lunch & dinner cruises. Phone 715/394-6846 or 218/722-6218. ¢¢¢-¢¢¢¢¢

The S.S. *Meteor* (1896), last remaining whaleback freighter, is moored here and is open to visitors as a maritime museum. (Memorial Day-Labor Day, daily) Phone 715/392-5742. ¢¢

Brule River State Forest. Contains 40,218 acres. Fishing; boating, canoeing. Nature, hiking, snowmobile and cross-country ski trails. Picnicking.

Camping. Standard fees. (Daily) 30 mi SE via US 2. Phone 715/372-4866. Nonresident camping ¢¢¢¢

Fairlawn Mansion and Museum. Restored 42-rm Victorian mansion overlooking Lake Superior. Collections and exhibits detail the economic, social and maritime history of the Lake Superior region. (Daily; closed some major hols) 906 E 2nd St. Phone 715/394-5712. ¢¢

Old Fire House and Police Museum. Firehouse (1898) serving as a museum devoted to the history of police and fire fighting. Historical vehicles, artifacts. (June-Aug; daily) 23rd Ave E & 4th St. Phone 715/398-7558. ¢¢

Pattison State Park. Has 1,370 acres of sand beach and woodlands. Swimming; fishing; canoeing. Nature, hiking, cross-country ski trails. Picnic grove, playgrounds. Primitive & improved camping (electric hookups, dump station). Nature center. Outstanding park attraction is Big Manitou Falls (165-ft drop), the highest waterfall in the state. Little Manitou Falls (31-ft drop) is located upstream of the main falls. Standard fees. (Daily) 15 mi S on WI 35. Phone 715/399-8073. Per vehicle ¢¢

Superior Municipal Forest. Has 4,500 acres of scenic woods bordering the shores of the St Louis River. Fishing; boating. Hiking, jogging, cross-country skiing. N 28th St & Billings Dr. **Free.**

Wisconsin Point. Popular for picnicking by light of driftwood fires. Swimming; fishing. Bird-watching. On shores of Lake Superior. **Free.**

Annual Event

Head-of-the-Lakes Fair. Fairgrounds, 48th & Tower Ave. Phone 715/394-7848. July.

Motels

★ ★ **BARKER'S ISLAND INN.** *300 Marina Dr. 715/392-7152; FAX 715/392-1180; res: 800/344-7515.* E-mail barkers@cp.duluth.mn.us; web www.bisitduluth.com/barkers. 114 rms, 2 story. Mid-June-mid-Oct: S, D $65-$95; suites $135; wkday rates; higher rates: Grandmas Marathon, Dec 31; lower rates rest of yr. Crib free. TV; cable. Sauna. Indoor pool; whirlpool. Restaurant 7 am-9 pm. Rm serv. Bar noon-1 am (summer), 4 pm-1 am (winter). Ck-out 11 am. Coin lndry. Meeting rms. Business servs avail. Sundries. Lighted tennis. Downhill ski 10 mi; x-country ski 5 mi. Game rm. On marina. Cr cds: A, C, D, DS, MC, V.

D ⚓ ✈ ⛷ ≋ 🏋 ⊠ 🐾 SC

★ ★ **BEST WESTERN BAY WALK INN.** *1405 Susquehanna. 715/392-7600; FAX 715/392-7680.* 50 rms, 2 story. June-Sept: S $50-$75; D $55-$81; each addl $6; suites $80-$125; under 16 free; higher rates special events; lower rates rest of yr. Crib free. Pet accepted, some restrictions. TV; cable (premium), VCR avail (movies). Sauna. Indoor pool; whirlpool. Complimentary continental bkfst. Restaurant adj 11 am-9 pm. Ck-out 11 am. Coin lndry. Business servs avail. Downhill ski 7 mi; x-country ski 1 mi. Game rm. Some refrigerators. Cr cds: A, C, D, DS, MC, V.

D 🐾 ✈ ≋ ⊠ 🐾 SC

★ ★ **BEST WESTERN BRIDGEVIEW MOTOR INN.** *415 Hammond Ave, at jct 5th St, near foot of Duluth-Superior Bridge. 715/392-8174; FAX 715/392-8487.* 96 rms, 2 story. Mid-June-Sept: S $50-$100; D $60-$100; each addl $5; under 18 free; lower rates rest of yr. Pet accepted. TV; cable (premium). Sauna. Indoor pool; whirlpool. Complimentary continental bkfst. Restaurant nearby. Bar 5-10:30 pm, to midnight wkends. Ck-out noon. Coin lndry. Meeting rm. Business servs avail. Sundries. Downhill/x-country ski 8 mi. Some refrigerators, microwaves. Cr cds: A, C, D, DS, ER, JCB, MC, V.

D 🐾 ✈ ≋ ⊠ 🐾 SC

★ ★ **DAYS INN.** *110 Harbor View Pkwy. 715/392-4783; FAX 715/392-2068.* 110 rms, 2 story. Mid-June-Aug: S, D $69-$109; each addl $5; under 18 free; higher rates special events; lower rates rest of yr. Crib free. TV; cable. Indoor pool; whirlpool. Ck-out noon. Coin lndry. Business servs avail. Downhill/x-country ski 15 mi. Sauna. Game rm. Cr cds: A, C, D, DS, MC, V.

D ✈ ≋ ⊠ 🐾 SC

✔★ **SUPER 8.** *4901 E 2nd St. 715/398-7686; FAX 715/398-7686.* 40 rms, 2 story. May-Sept: S $55; D $50-$65; under 12 free; lower rates rest of yr. Crib free. TV; cable (premium). Complimentary continental bkfst. Restaurant adj 7 am-11 pm. Ck-out 11 am. Business servs avail. Downhill ski 20 mi; x-country ski adj. Cr cds: A, C, D, DS, MC, V.

D ✈ ≋ ⊠ 🐾 SC

Restaurants

★ ★ **LIBRARY.** *1410 Tower Ave. 715/392-4821.* Hrs: 11 am-10 pm; Sun 10 am-9 pm; Sun brunch 11 am-3 pm. Closed Thanksgiving, Dec 25. Res accepted. Bar. Semi-a la carte: lunch $4.25-$9, dinner $5.99-$19. Sun brunch $14.99. Child's meals. Specializes in pasta, steak, fresh fish. Salad bar. Library motif; black mahogany wood paneling, book-lined shelves. Family-owned. Cr cds: A, C, D, DS, MC, V.

D

★ ★ **SHACK SMOKEHOUSE & GRILLE.** *3301 Belknap St. 715/392-9836.* Web www.shackonline.com. Hrs: 11 am-2:30 pm, 4:30-9 pm; Fri, Sat to 10 pm; Sun 11:30 am-8 pm. Closed Dec 24, 25. Res accepted. Bar 10 am-midnight. Semi-a la carte: lunch $4.99-$6.99, dinner $9.99-$17.99. Specializes in authentic hickory smoked barbeque, local seafood, prime rib. Own soups. Family-owned. Cr cds: D, DS, MC, V.

D ⊸

★ **ZONA ROSA.** *1410 Tower Ave. 715/392-4821.* Hrs: 11 am-10 pm; Sun to 9 pm; Sun brunch 11 am-3 pm. Closed Thanksgiving, Dec 25. Res accepted. Mexican, Amer menu. Bar. Semi-a la carte: lunch $3.50-$8, dinner $4-$12. Buffet lunch $6.49. Sun brunch $14.99. Specializes in Tex-Mex dishes, fajitas. Mexican decor. Cr cds: A, C, D, DS, MC, V.

D

Three Lakes (C-4)

(See also Crandon, Eagle River, Rhinelander, St Germain)

Pop 1,900 **Elev** 1,637 ft **Area code** 715 **Zip** 54562

Information Three Lakes Information Bureau, PO Box 268; 715/546-3344 or 800/972-6103.

Between Thunder Lake and the interlocking series of 28 lakes on the west boundary of Nicolet National Forest, Three Lakes is a provisioning point for parties exploring the forest and lake country.

What to See and Do

Fruit of the Woods Winery. Produces fruit wines. Winery tours (late May-mid-Oct, daily); wine tasting room (all yr; must be 21 or over to taste wine). Corner of WI 45 and County A. Phone 715/546-3080. **Free.**

Nicolet National Forest. Forest has 661,000 acres, and is 62 mi long and 36 mi wide; elevation ranges from 860 ft to 1,880 ft. Noted for scenic drives through pine, spruce, fir, sugar maple, oak and birch trees. More than 1,200 lakes and 1,100 mi of trout streams. Fishing for trout, pike, bass, muskellunge and walleye and hunting for deer, bear, grouse and waterfowl. Swimming; canoeing, boating, rafting. Interpretive nature trails. Hiking. More than 122 mi of cross-country ski trails, 520 mi of snowmobile trails, snowshoeing. Three wilderness areas and several non-motorized walk-in areas provide more than 33,000 acres for backpacking and primitive camping. Picnicking, camping and other outdoor recreational activities in general forest zone are unrestricted and no permits are required. Within developed areas, camping and picnicking are restricted to designated sites and most are on a first-come basis; reservations are available for selected campgrounds. Fees are charged at most developed campgrounds. (Daily) N on WI 32. Phone 715/362-1300. **Free.**

Motel

✔★ **ONEIDA VILLAGE INN.** *1785 Superior St. 715/546-3373; FAX 715/546-8060; res: 800/374-7443.* 47 rms, 2 story. June-Aug & mid-Dec-Feb: S $45; D $55; each addl $7; suites $65-$75; kits. $48; under 12 free; wkend, wkly rates; higher rates special events; lower rates rest of yr. Crib $5. Pet accepted; $10. TV; cable. Complimentary coffee in lobby. Restaurant 5-10 pm. Bar; entertainment (summer). Ck-out 11 am. Meeting rms. Business servs avail. X-country ski ½ mi. Game rm. Cr cds: DS, MC, V.

Resort

★ ★ **VAN KIRK'S LAKE BREEZE.** *¾ mi SE on WI 32, then 1 mi N on County X. 715/546-3616; FAX 715/546-3920.* 16 cottages (1-4 bedrm), 7 kits. No A/C. D $300-$650/wk (boat included). Crib avail. TV in lodge. Playground. Set ups. Ck-out 9:30 am, ck-in 1 pm. Grocery, coin lndry, package store 1½ mi. Meeting rm. Tennis. Boats, motors, paddleboats, canoes. Sailing. X-country ski 2 mi. Snowmobile trails. Lawn games. Rec rm. Fishing guides; clean/store area. Refrigerators. Screened porches. Sand beach on Town Line Lake. Cr cds: MC, V.

Tomah (F-3)

(See also Sparta)

Pop 7,570 **Elev** 960 ft **Area code** 608 **Zip** 54660

Information Greater Tomah Area Chamber of Commerce, 306 Arthur St, PO Box 625; 608/372-2166 or 800/94-TOMAH.

Tomah is Wisconsin's "Gateway to Cranberry Country." This was also the home of Frank King, the creator of the comic strip "Gasoline Alley"; the main street was named after him. Lake Tomah, on the west edge of town, has boating, waterskiing, fishing, ice-fishing and snowmobiling.

What to See and Do

Harris G. Allen Telecommunication Historical Museum. Collection of more than 100 telephones dating back to 1894. History walls, video and educational displays. (Daily exc Sun) 306 Arthur St. Phone 608/374-5000. **Free.**

Little Red Schoolhouse Museum. Built in 1864, in use until 1965; many original furnishings, books. (Memorial Day-Labor Day, afternoons) Superior Ave in Gillett Park. Phone 608/372-2166. **Free.**

Mill Bluff State Park. Has 1,258 acres with rock bluffs. Swimming. Picnicking. Camping. Being developed as part of Ice Age National Scientific Reserve. Standard fees. (Daily) 7 mi E, off US 12, 16. Phone 608/427-6692 or 608/337-4775. Per vehicle ¢¢

Necedah National Wildlife Refuge. Water birds may be seen during seasonal migrations; lesser numbers present during the summer. Resident wildlife include deer, wild turkey and ruffed grouse. Viewing via 11-mi self-guided auto tour or one-mi self-guided foot trail. (All yr, daily; office, Mon-Fri; foot trail, mid-Mar-mid-Nov only; auto tour is along township roads, which may close due to inclement weather) 6 mi E via WI 21 near Necedah. Phone 608/565-2551. **Free.**

Wildcat Mountain State Park. Has 3,470 acres of hills and valleys. Trout fishing in Kickapoo River, Billings and Cheyenne creeks; canoeing. Nature, hiking, bridle and cross-country ski trails. Picnicking, playgrounds. Camping. Observation points provide panoramic view of countryside. Standard fees. (Daily) 25 mi S via WI 131, 33, near Ontario. Phone 608/337-4775. Per vehicle ¢¢

Annual Event

Cranberry Festival. Main St in Warrens. Late Sept.

Motels

✔★ **BUDGET HOST DAYBREAK.** *215 E Clifton, WI 12, 16. 608/372-5946; FAX 608/372-5947; res: 800/999-7088.* 32 rms, 1-2 story. Mid-May-mid-Oct: S $36-$48; D $58-$63; each addl $7; lower rates rest of yr. Crib $4. Pet accepted. TV; cable (premium). Restaurant opp 10 am-midnight. Ck-out 10:30 am. Business servs avail. Downhill ski 10 mi; x-country ski 1 mi. Snowmobile trails. Business servs avail. Refrigerators. Municipal park, pool opp. Cr cds: A, C, D, DS, MC, V.

★ **COMFORT INN.** *305 Wittig Rd. 608/372-6600; FAX 608/372-6600.* 52 rms, 2 story. May-Aug: S, D $52.95-$79.95; each addl $5; under 18 free; lower rates rest of yr. Crib avail. Pet accepted. TV; cable (premium). Indoor pool; whirlpool. Complimentary continental bkfst. Restaurant adj. Ck-out 11 am. Business servs avail. Downhill ski 15 mi; x-country ½ mi. Some refrigerators. Cr cds: A, C, D, DS, MC, V.

★ ★ **HOLIDAY INN.** *3 mi N at jct WI 21, I-94. 608/372-3211; FAX 608/372-3243.* 100 rms, 2 story. Mid-May-Labor Day: S $72; D $78; each addl $6; family rates; lower rates rest of yr. Crib free. TV; in-rm movies avail. Sauna. Heated pool; whirlpool, poolside serv. Restaurant 6 am-2 pm, 5-10 pm. Rm serv. Bar. Ck-out noon. Coin lndry. Meeting rms. Business servs avail. In-rm modem link. Valet serv. Sundries. X-country ski ½ mi. Game rm. Rec rm. Some refrigerator. Cr cds: A, C, D, DS, JCB, MC, V.

★ **LARK INN.** *229 N Superior Ave. 608/372-5981; res: 800/447-LARK.* 25 rms, 1-2 story, 3 kits. S $45-$55; D $50-$60; each addl $5; kits. $60-$70; under 16 free. Crib $3. Pet accepted. TV; cable (premium), VCR avail (movies $2.50). Restaurant 6 am-11 pm. Rm serv. Ck-out 11 am. Coin lndry. Sundries. Downhill ski 10 mi; x-country ski 1 mi. Some refrigerators. Picnic tables. Cr cds: A, C, D, DS, MC, V.

✔★ **REST WELL.** *E on US 12 (WI 16). 608/372-2471.* 12 rms (10 with shower only). No rm phones. S $20-$36; D $30-$50. Pet accepted. TV. Ck-out 10 am. Downhill ski 10 mi; x-country 1 mi. Cr cds: MC, V.

★ **SUPER 8.** *I-94 & WI 21, exit 143. 608/372-3901; FAX 608/372-5792.* 64 rms, 2 story. Mid-June-late Sept: S, D $42.98-$104.98; each addl $5; under 19 free; lower rates rest of yr. Crib free. Pet accepted. TV; cable. Complimentary continental bkfst. Restaurant adj open 24 hrs. Ck-out 11 am. Coin lndry. Business servs avail. Downhill ski 12 mi; x-country ski 1 mi. Some refrigerators. Cr cds: A, C, D, DS, MC, V.

Restaurant

★ ★ **BURNSTAD'S.** *WI 12 & 16 E. 608/372-3277.* Hrs: 8 am-9 pm; Sun 7 am-9 pm. Closed most major hols. Res accepted. Continental menu. Semi-a la carte: bkfst $1.95-$4.25, lunch $4.75-$5.95, dinner $10.25-$14.95. Specialties: European pirozhki, shrimp de jonghe. Intimate dining in European village decor. Family-owned. Cr cds: A, C, D, DS, MC, V.

Two Rivers (E-6)

(For accommodations see Green Bay, Manitowoc, Sheboygan)

Pop 13,030 **Elev** 595 ft **Area code** 414 **Zip** 54241

Information Manitowoc-Two Rivers Area Chamber of Commerce, 1515 Memorial Dr, PO Box 903, Manitowoc 54221-0903; 414/684-5575 or 800/262-7892.

A fishing fleet in Lake Michigan and light industry support Two Rivers.

What to See and Do

Point Beach Energy Center. Center houses working models, including simulated nuclear reactor and solar and wind-energy systems. Also films, exhibits, computer games. Energy theme nature trail; observation tower. Picnicking. (Daily; closed major hols) 6600 Nuclear Dr, approx 10 mi N on WI 42, adj to Point Beach Nuclear Plant. Phone 414/755-4334. **Free.**

Point Beach State Forest. A 2,843-acre park with heavily wooded areas, sand dunes and beach along Lake Michigan. Nature, hiking, snowmobile and cross-country ski trails; ice skating. Picnicking, playgrounds, concession. Improved camping, winter camping. Nature center. Standard fees. (Daily) 5 mi N on County Trunk O. Phone 414/794-7480. Per vehicle **¢¢**

Rogers Street Fishing Village Museum. Artifacts of commercial fishing industry; 60-yr-old diesel engine; artifacts from sunken vessels; 1886 lighthouse; life-size woodcarvings. Art & craft galleries feature local area artists. (June-Aug, daily) 2102 Jackson St. Phone 414/793-5905. **¢**

Washington Island (Door Co) (C-6)

(See also Door County)

Settled 1869 **Pop** 623 **Elev** 600 ft **Area code** 414 **Zip** 54246 **E-mail** lyons@mail.wiscnet.net **Web** doorcountyvacations.com

Information Door County Chamber of Commerce, 1015 Green Bay Rd, PO Box 406, Sturgeon Bay 54235; 414/743-4456 or 800/527-3529.

Washington Island, six miles off the coast of Door County is one of the oldest Icelandic settlements in the United States. Many Scandinavian festivals are still celebrated. Surrounding waters offer excellent fishing. The island may be reached by ferry (see ELLISON BAY).

What to See and Do

Rock Island State Park. Reached by privately-operated ferry (June-Oct, daily; fee) from Jackson Harbor located at the NE corner of island. This 912-acre park was the summer home of electrical tycoon, C.H. Thordarson. Buildings in Icelandic architectural style. Potawatomi Lighthouse (1836) on northern point. Swimming; fishing; boating. Nature trail, more than 9 mi of hiking and snowmobile trails. Picnicking. Primitive camping; no supplies available. No vehicles permitted. Standard fees. (Daily) Phone 414/847-2235 (mid-Apr-mid-Nov); 414/847-2500 (rest of yr). Per vehicle **¢¢**

Washington Island Museum. Native Americans artifacts; antiques; rocks and fossils. (May-mid-Oct, daily) Little Lake Rd, NW corner of island. Phone 414/847-2213. **¢**

Annual Event

Scandinavian Dance Festival. Dance festival and Viking Games. Early Aug.

Motels

✔★ ★ **FINDLAY'S HOLIDAY INN.** *2 mi E of ferry dock, on Detroit Harbor.* 920/847-2526; FAX 920/847-2752. E-mail jfindlay@mail.wisenet.net; web www.holidayinn.net. 16 rms, some A/C. S $76-$85; D $83-$105; under 6 free; wkly rates. Crib free. TV. Restaurant (see FINDLAY'S HOLIDAY INN). Ck-out 10 am. Business servs avail. Gift shop. Health club privileges. Lawn games. On Lake Michigan; beach. Cr cds: MC, V.

D ⟋ ⟎ ⟍

★ **VIKING VILLAGE.** *2 mi NE of ferry dock.* 920/847-2551; res: 800/522-5469. E-mail jfindlay@mail.wisenet.net; web www.holidayinn.net. 12 kit units. No A/C. S $55-$75; D $66-$95; each addl $6; suites $85-$110; under 6 free; wkly rates. Crib free. Pet accepted. TV. Coffee in rms. Restaurant 7 am-1:30 pm, 5:30-7:30 pm. Ck-out 10 am. Health club privileges. Refrigerators; some microwaves, fireplaces. Cr cds: MC, V.

D ⟋ ⟋ ⟍

Restaurant

★ **FINDLAY'S HOLIDAY INN.** *(See Findlay's Holiday Inn Motel)* 414/847-2526. E-mail jfindlay@mail.wisenet.net; web www.holidayinn.net. Hrs: 7-10:30 am, 11:30 am-2 pm, 5:30-7:30 pm. Closed Nov-Apr. Res accepted. Wine, beer. Semi-a la carte: bkfst $2-$7, lunch $3.50-$10, dinner $5-$12. Specializes in seafood. Salad bar. Entertainment. Norwegian decor. Totally nonsmoking. Cr cds: MC, V.

D

Watertown (G-5)

(For accommodations see Beaver Dam, Fort Atkinson, Oconomowoc)

Settled 1836 **Pop** 19,142 **Elev** 823 ft **Area code** 414 **Zip** 53094

Information Chamber of Commerce, 519 E Main St; 414/261-6320.

Waterpower, created where the Rock River falls 20 feet in 2 miles, attracted the first New England settlers. A vast number of German immigrants followed, including Carl Schurz, who became Lincoln's minister to Spain and Secretary of the Interior under President Hayes. His wife, Margarethe Meyer Schurz, established the first kindergarten in the United States. Watertown, with diversified industries, is in the center of an important farming and dairy community.

What to See and Do

⊠ **Octagon House and First Kindergarten in USA.** Completed in 1854 by John Richards, the 57-rm mansion has 40-ft spiral cantilever hanging staircase; Victorian-style furnishings throughout, many original pieces. On grounds are restored kindergarten founded by Margarethe Meyer Schurz in 1856 and 100-yr-old barn with early farm implements. (May-Oct, daily) 919 Charles St. Phone 414/261-2796. **¢¢**

Annual Event

Riverfest. 4-day event; craft show, carnival, raft race, car show, entertainment. Early Aug.

Waukesha (G-5)

(See also Milwaukee)

Settled 1834 **Pop** 56,958 **Elev** 821 ft **Area code** 414 **E-mail** Visit@wauknet.com **Web** www.wauknet.com/visit

Information Waukesha Area Convention & Visitors Bureau, 223 Wisconsin Ave, 53186; 414/542-0330 or 800/366-8474.

Mineral springs found here by pioneer settlers made Waukesha famous as a health resort; in the latter half of the 19th century, it was one of the nation's most fashionable. Before that it was an important point on the Underground Railroad. The *American Freeman* (1844-1848) was published here. Today the city is enjoying important industrial growth. Carroll College lends the city a gracious academic atmosphere. The name "Waukesha" (by the little fox) comes from the river that runs through it. The river, along with the cities many parks and wooded areas adds to a beautiful atomosphere for leisure activities.

What to See and Do

Kettle Moraine State Forest, Southern Unit. Contains 20,000 acres of rough, wooded country includes Ottawa and Whitewater lakes. Swimming, waterskiing; fishing; boating, canoeing. Trails: hiking, 74 mi; bridle, 50 mi; snowmobile, 52 mi; cross-country ski, 40 mi; nature, 3 mi. Picnicking, playground. Primitive and improved camping (electric hookups, dump station), winter camping. Standard fees. (Daily) Camping reservations, phone 414/594-2135. 17 mi SW on WI 59. For other information phone 414/594-2135. Per vehicle ¢¢

⊠ Old World Wisconsin. A 576-acre outdoor museum with more than 50 historic structures (1840-1915) reflecting various ethnic backgrounds of Wisconsin history. Restored buildings include church, town hall, schoolhouse, stagecoach inn, blacksmith shop and 10 complete 19th-century farmsteads. All buildings furnished in period artifacts; staffed by costumed interpreters. Also 8 mi of groomed cross-country ski trails (Jan-Mar; fee). Tram system; restaurant. (May-Oct, daily) 14 mi SW on WI 67; 1 mi S of Eagle. Phone 414/594-6300. ¢¢¢

Waukesha County Museum. Historical exhibits (Tues-Sat, also Sun afternoons; closed hols). Research library (Tues-Sat; closed hols; fee). 101 W Main St at East Ave. Phone 414/548-7186. **Free.**

Annual Event

Waukesha County Fair. Includes performances by top-name Country & Western and rock artists. Phone 414/544-5922. Mid-July.

Motels

★ **ECONO LODGE.** 2111 E Moreland Blvd (53186). 414/547-7770; FAX 414/547-0688. 98 rms, 2 story. July-Aug: S, D $65-$89; each addl $6; under 19 free; higher rates special events; lower rates rest of yr. Crib avail. TV; cable (premium); VCR avail. Sauna. Whirlpool. Complimentary continental bkfst. Restaurant adj. Ck-out 11 am. Business servs avail. Some refrigerators. Cr cds: A, C, D, DS, ER, JCB, MC, V.

D ⊠ 🐾

✓★ ★ **FAIRFIELD INN BY MARRIOTT.** (20150 W Bluemound Rd, Brookfield 53045) off I-94 exit 297 (Bluemound Rd E), near jct Barker Rd. 414/785-0500; FAX 414/785-0500, ext. 709. 135 rms, 3 story. S $54.95-$95.95; D $64.95-$95.95; each addl $10; under 18 free. Crib free. TV; cable (premium). Pool. Complimentary continental bkfst, coffee in lobby. Restaurant adj 6-1 am. Ck-out noon. Business servs avail. In-rm modem link. Cr cds: A, C, D, DS, MC, V.

D ≋ ⊠ 🐾

★ ★ **HAMPTON INN BROOKFIELD.** (575 N Barker Rd, Brookfield 53045) off I-94 exit 297, at jct Barker Rd. 414/796-1500; FAX 414/796-0977. 120 rms, 4 story. S, D $79; under 18 free; higher rates special

events. Crib free. TV; cable (premium). Indoor pool; whirlpool. Complimentary continental bkfst. Restaurant adj 6 am-3 am. Ck-out noon. Meeting rm. Business servs avail. Sundries. Cr cds: A, C, D, DS, MC, V.

D ≋ ⊠ 🐾 SC

✓★ **SELECT INN.** 2510 Plaza Court (53186), at jct I-94 exit 297, County JJ. 414/786-6015; FAX 414/786-5784. 101 rms, 2-3 story. No elvtr. S, D $39-$51; under 12 free. Pet accepted; $25 refundable. TV; cable. Complimentary continental bkfst. Ck-out 11 am. Meeting rm. Business servs avail. X-country ski 5 mi. Some refrigerators. Cr cds: A, C, D, DS, MC, V.

D 🐾 ≋ ⊠ 🐾 SC

Motor Hotel

★ ★ **WYNDHAM GARDEN.** (18155 Bluemound Rd, Brookfield 53045) off I-94. 414/792-1212; FAX 414/792-1201. 178 rms, 3 story. S, D $59-$169; wkend rates; higher rates special events. Crib avail. TV; cable, VCR avail. Indoor pool; whirlpool. Complimentary coffee in rms. Restaurant 7 am-9 pm. Bar 4 pm-midnight. Ck-out noon. Meeting rms. Business servs avail. In-rm modem link. Sundries. Valet serv. Free Milwaukee airport transportation. Exercise equipt; weight machine, stair machine. Game rm. Balconies. Picnic tables. Cr cds: A, C, D, DS, JCB, MC, V.

D ≋ 🏃 🏋 ⊠ 🐾 SC

Restaurants

★ ★ **SEVEN SEAS.** (1807 Nagawicka Rd, Hartland 53029) just off WI 83. 414/367-3903. Hrs: 11:30 am-2 pm, 5-10 pm; Sat from 5 pm; Sun brunch from 11 am; Sun 4-9 pm. Closed Tues (Oct-Apr). Res accepted. German, Amer menu. Bar. Semi-a la carte: lunch $6.95-$8.95, dinner $14.95-$42. Sun brunch $13.95. Child's meals. Specializes in Wienerschnitzel, roast duck, seafood. Outdoor dining. Overlooks Lake Nagawicka; nautical decor. Cr cds: A, MC, V.

★ ★ ★ **WEISSGERBER'S GASTHAUS INN.** 2720 N Grandview Blvd. 414/544-4460. Hrs: 11:30 am-2:30 pm, 5-10 pm; Sat from 5 pm; Sun 4-9 pm. Res accepted. German, Amer menu. Bar. Semi-a la carte: lunch $6-$10, dinner $16-$22. Specialties: stuffed pork chops, pork shanks, Wienerschnitzel. Own desserts. Outdoor beer garden. Cathedral ceiling; fireplace. Cr cds: A, MC, V.

D

Waupaca (E-4)

(For accommodations see Stevens Point; also see Wautoma)

Pop 4,957 **Elev** 870 ft **Area code** 715 **Zip** 54981 **E-mail** discoverwaupaca@waupacaareachamber.com **Web** www.waupacaareachamber.com

Information Waupaca Area Chamber of Commerce, 221 S Main, PO Box 262; 715/258-7343 or 800/236-2222.

This community, near a chain of 22 lakes to the southwest, is a boating, fishing and tourist recreation area.

What to See and Do

Canoeing and tubing. Two- to three-hr trips. (May-Labor Day) Contact Chamber of Commerce. On the Crystal and Wolf rivers.

Covered Bridge. A 40-ft lattice design with 400 handmade oak pegs used in its construction. 3 mi S on Hwy K near the Red Mill Colonial Shop.

Hartman Creek State Park. A 1,400-acre park with 300-ft sand beach on Hartman Lake. Swimming; fishing; boating (no gasoline motors), canoeing. Nature, hiking, snowmobile & cross-country ski trails. Picnicking. Camping (dump station), winter camping. Standard fees. (Daily) 6 mi W via WI 54, then 1¹/₂ mi S on Hartman Creek Rd. Phone 715/258-2372. Per vehicle ¢¢¢

Scenic cruises. Sternwheeler *Chief Waupaca* offers 1¹/₂-hr cruises on 8 lakes of the Chain O' Lakes. Also cruises aboard motor yacht *Lady of the Lakes*. (Memorial Day-Sept, daily) Private evening charters arranged. 4 mi SW via WI 54 & County QQ at Clear Water Harbor. Phone 715/258-2866. ¢¢¢

South Park. Offers swimming beach, bathhouse; fishing dock; boat landing. Picknicking. Mirror & Shadow lakes, S end of Main St. Also in park is

> **Hutchinson House Museum.** Restored 12-rm Victorian pioneer home (1854); furnishings, artifacts; herb garden; Heritage House. For schedule, fees contact the Chamber of Commerce. End of Main St in South Park.

Annual Events

Strawberry Fest. 3rd wkend June.

Fall-O-Rama. Arts & crafts fair, entertainment, food, road rally. 3rd wkend Sept.

Waupun (F-5)

(See also Beaver Dam, Fond du Lac, Green Lake)

Founded 1839 **Pop** 8,207 **Elev** 904 ft **Area code** 920 **Zip** 53963
Information Chamber of Commerce, 434 E Main; 920/324-3491.

The city's Native American name means "Early Dawn of Day." Diversified crops, light industry and three state institutions contribute to this small city's economy.

What to See and Do

City of Sculpture. First bronze casting of famous sculpture by James Earl Frazer, designer of Indian head nickel. Also six other historical bronze statues. Madison St at Shaler Park.

Fond du Lac County Park. Park has 100 acres of virgin timber on Rock River. Swimming pool (mid-June-Aug, daily; fee). Picnic area (tables, fireplaces), playgrounds. Camping (mid-May-Nov, daily). Park (all yr). W on WI 49 to County Trunk MMM. Phone 920/324-2769. Camping per night ¢¢¢¢

Horicon National Wildlife Refuge. Large flocks of Canada geese and various species of ducks can be seen Oct, Nov, Mar, Apr. Many visitors stop during migratory seasons to watch the birds resting and feeding on the Horicon Marsh (daylight hrs). Limited hunting & fishing (inquire for dates); canoeing. Hiking trails. (Daily) Headquarters, 6¹/₂ mi E on WI 49, then 4 mi S on Dodge County Z. Phone 920/387-2658.   **Free.**

Motel

★ **INN TOWN.** *27 S State St, off WI 49. 414/324-4211; res: 800/433-6231.* 16 rms. S $31-$36; D $44-$47; each addl $3. Crib $3. TV; cable (premium). Coffee in rms. Restaurant nearby. Ck-out 10 am. Refrigerators; microwaves avail. Cr cds: A, DS, MC, V.

[D] [⊠] [🐾] [SC]

Wausau (D-4)

(See also Antigo, Stevens Point)

Settled 1839 **Pop** 37,060 **Elev** 1,195 ft **Area code** 715 **Zip** 54401 **E-mail** tourism@wausauchamber.com **Web** www.wausauchamber.com

Information Wausau Area Convention and Visitors Bureau, 300 3rd St, Suite 200, PO Box 6190, 54402-6190; 715/845-6231, ext 324 or 800/236-9728.

Known as Big Bull Falls when it was settled as a lumber camp, the town was renamed Wausau, Native American for "Faraway Place." When the big timber was gone, the lumber barons started paper mills; paper products are still one of the city's many industries.

What to See and Do

Leigh Yawkey Woodson Art Museum. Collection of wildlife art, porcelain and glass; changing exhibits. (Daily exc Mon; closed hols) 700 N 12th St. Phone 715/845-7010.   **Free.**

Marathon County Historical Museum. Former home of early lumberman Cyrus C. Yawkey. Victorian period rms; model railroad display; changing theme exhibits. (Tues-Thurs, Sat & Sun; closed hols) 403 McIndoe St. Phone 715/848-6143.   **Free.**

Rib Mountain State Park. A 860-acre park; summit of Rib Mountain is one of the highest points (1,940 ft) in the state; 60-ft observation tower. Hiking trails that wind past rocky ridges and natural oddities in quartzite rocks. View of miles of Wisconsin River Valley, the city and countryside. Picnicking, playgrounds, concession. Camping. Standard fees. (Daily) 4 mi SW on County N. Phone 715/842-2522 (summer months) or 715/359-4522 (winter months). Per vehicle   ¢¢ In park is

> **Rib Mountain Ski Area.** Area has 3 chairlifts, rope tow; patrol, school, rentals; snowmaking; cafeteria, bar. Longest run 3,800 ft; vertical drop 624 ft. (Late Nov-Mar, daily) 2 mi SW via WI 51 & 29, NN exit. Phone 715/845-2846.   ¢¢¢¢

Annual Events

The Great Wisconsin River Log Jam. 4th wkend June.

Wisconsin Valley Fair. Marathon Park. Early Aug.

Big Bull Falls Blues Festival. Mid-Aug.

Motels

★ ★ **BEST WESTERN MIDWAY HOTEL.** *2901 Martin Ave, on US 51 & WI 29 at exit 190. 715/842-1616; FAX 715/845-3726.* 98 rms, 2 story. S $75-$87; D $85-$97; each addl $12; under 18 free. Crib free. Pet accepted. TV; cable. Sauna. Indoor pool; whirlpool. Playground. Coffee in rms. Restaurant 6 am-10 pm. Rm serv. Bar; entertainment. Ck-out noon. Meeting rms. Business servs avail. In-rm modem link. Valet serv. Free airport, Rib Mt ski slope transportation. Downhill ski 1 mi; x-country ski 3 mi. Rec rm. Lawn games. Picnic tables. Cr cds: A, C, D, DS, MC, V.

[D] [⛄] [≋] [≈] [⛷] [🐾] [SC]

✔ ★ **BUDGETEL INN.** *1910 Stewart Ave. 715/842-0421; FAX 715/845-5096.* 96 rms, 2 story. S $43.95; D $50.95; under 18 free. Crib free. Pet accepted. TV; cable. Spa. Indoor pool. Continental bkfst. Coffee in rms. Restaurant nearby. Ck-out noon. Business servs avail. In-rm modem link. Downhill/x-country ski 2 mi. Cr cds: A, C, D, DS, MC, V.

[D] [⛄] [≋] [≈] [⛷] [🐾] [SC]

✔ ★ **EXEL INN.** *116 S 17th Ave. 715/842-0641; FAX 715/848-1356.* 123 rms, 2 story. S $35.99-$45.99; D $44.99-$51.99; each addl $4; under 18 free. Crib free. Pet accepted. TV. Complimentary continental bkfst. Restaurant nearby. Ck-out noon. Business servs avail. Lndry facilities. Downhill ski 3 mi; x-country ski 3 mi. Game rm. View of Rib Mt. Cr cds: A, C, D, DS, MC, V.

 SC

★ **RIB MOUNTAIN INN.** *2900 Rib Mountain Way. 715/848-2802; FAX 715/848-1908.* 16 rms, 2 story, 4 villas, 4 townhouses. S $48-$71; D $55-$78; villas $95-$155; townhouses $125-$155; wkly, monthly rates; ski plan; higher rates: ski season, wkends. Pet accepted. TV; cable (premium), VCR (movies). Continental bkfst. Ck-out 11 am. Business servs avail. Driving range. Downhill ski 1/4 mi; x-country ski 7 mi. Sauna. Lawn games. Refrigerators, fireplaces. Patios, balconies. Picnic tables, grills. On Rib Mountain. Adj to state park. Cr cds: A, C, D, DS, MC, V.

SC

★ **SUPER 8.** *2006 Stewart Ave. 715/848-2888; FAX 715/842-9578.* 88 rms, 2 story. S $44-$47; D $56-$59; each addl $5-10; under 18 free. Crib free. Pet accepted. TV; cable. Indoor pool; whirlpool. Complimentary continental bkfst. Ck-out noon. Business servs avail. Valet serv. Sundries. Cr cds: A, C, D, DS, MC, V.

SC

Inn

★ **ROSENBERRY INN.** *511 Franklin St (54403). 715/842-5733.* 9 rms, 3 rms. No rm phones. S $49-$135; D $65-$135; each addl $10; under 12 free. TV in sitting rm; cable. Complimentary full bkfst. Restaurant nearby. Ck-out 11 am, ck-in 2 pm. Downhill/x-country ski 5 mi. Some in-rm whirlpools. Built 1908; Prairie School-style architecture, antiques. Cr cds: MC, V.

Restaurants

★ **BILL'S FINE FOOD & LOUNGE.** *932 S 3rd Ave. 715/842-3669.* Hrs: 6 am-9:30 pm; Sun from 7 am. Closed July 4, Dec 25. Bar. Complete meals: lunch $4.75-$7.25, dinner $5.95-$16.50. Child's meals. Specializes in homemade soup, pies. Family-owned. Cr cds: MC, V.

✔★ **CARMELO'S.** *3605 N Mountain Rd. 715/845-5570.* Hrs: 5-10 pm; Sun, Mon to 9 pm. Closed some major hols. Res accepted Sat-Thurs. Italian menu. Bar. Semi-a la carte: dinner $5.50-$14.95. Specializes in pasta. Parking. Family-owned. Cr cds: A, DS, MC, V.

D

★★ **GULLIVER'S LANDING.** *2204 Rib Mountain Dr. 715/842-9098.* Hrs: 11 am-10 pm; wkends to 11 pm. Closed major hols. Res accepted. Bar. Semi-a la carte: dinner $7.95-$29.95. Child's meals. Specializes in steaks, seafood, cajun cooking. Own breads. Parking. Outdoor dining. Nautical decor; aquariums. Dockage. Cr cds: A, D, DS, MC, V.

★★ **MICHAEL'S.** *2901 Rib Mountain Dr. 715/842-9856.* Hrs: 5-10 pm. Closed Sun; major hols. Res accepted. Continental menu. Bar from 4 pm. Semi-a la carte: dinner $6.50-$19.95. Child's meals. Specializes in seafood, veal, beef. Parking. Wildlife pictures on walls. Cr cds: A, C, D, DS, MC, V.

D

★★ **WAGON WHEEL.** *3901 N 6th St (54403). 715/675-2263.* Hrs: 5-10 pm. Closed Sun. Res accepted Mon-Thurs. Bar. A la carte entrees: dinner $9.95-$33.50. Specializes in charcoal-broiled steak, barbecued ribs, seafood. Parking. Rustic atmosphere. Family-owned. Cr cds: DS, MC, V.

✔★ **WAUSAU MINE CO.** *3904 W Stewart Ave, at 39th Ave. 715/845-7304.* Hrs: 11 am-midnight. Closed Easter, Thanksgiving, Dec 24-25. Res accepted Sun-Thurs. Bar. Semi-a la carte: lunch, dinner $3.95-$14.75. Child's meals. Parking. Cr cds: C, D, DS, MC, V.

Wautoma (E-4)

(For accommodations see Green Lake; also see Waupaca)

Pop 1,784 **Elev** 867 ft **Area code** 414 **Zip** 54982

What to See and Do

Nordic Mountain Ski Area. Triple, double chairlifts, T-bar, pomalift, rope tow; patrol, school, rentals; snowmaking; restaurant, cafeteria, concession, bar. Longest run 1 mi; vertical drop 265 ft. (Dec-mid-Mar, daily, limited hrs Wed; closed Dec 25) 13 mi of cross-country trails (wkends only; free). 8 mi N via WI 152. Phone 414/787-3324 or 800/253-7266. ¢¢¢¢¢

Wild Rose Pioneer Museum. Historical complex of buildings includes Elisha Stewart House, containing furniture of the late 19th century; pioneer hall; outbuildings; carriage house; blacksmith shop, cobbler shop, replica of general store, one-room schoolhouse, apothecary; weaving room; gift shop. Tours. (Mid-June-Labor Day, Wed & Sat afternoons; also by appt during summer) 8 mi N on WI 22, Main St, in Wild Rose. Phone 414/622-3364. ¢

Wauwatosa (G-5)

(See also Menomonee Falls, Milwaukee)

Settled 1835 **Pop** 49,366 **Elev** 634 ft **Area code** 414
Information Chamber of Commerce, 7707 W State St, 53213; 414/453-2330.

What to See and Do

Lowell Damon House (1844). Community's oldest home is a classic example of colonial architecture; period furnishings. Tours (Sun, Wed; closed major hols). 2107 Wauwatosa Ave. Phone 414/273-8288. **Free.**

Motels

✔★ **EXEL INN-WEST.** *115 N Mayfair Rd (US 100) (53226). 414/257-0140; FAX 414/475-7875.* 123 rms, 2 story. S $35.99-$46.99; D $37.99-$56.99; suites $85-$125; each addl (up to 4) $4; under 17 free. Crib free. Pet accepted, some restrictions. TV; cable (premium). Complimentary continental bkfst in lobby. Restaurant adj 6 am-10 pm. Ck-out noon. Business servs avail. Cr cds: A, C, D, DS, MC, V.

D SC

★ **FORTY WINKS INN.** *11017 W Bluemound Rd (53226). 414/774-2800.* 31 rms (12 with shower only), 2 story. June-Aug: S $60-$75; each addl $6; kit. units $65-$85; lower rates rest of yr. Crib $5. TV; cable (premium). Complimentary coffee in lobby. Restaurant nearby. Ck-out 11 am. Sundries. X-country ski 1 mi. Some refrigerators. Cr cds: A, DS, MC, V.

D SC

★★ **HOLIDAY INN EXPRESS.** *11111 W North Ave (53226), 1 blk E of I-45. 414/778-0333; FAX 414/778-0331.* 122 rms, 3 story. S $65-$79; D $71-$85; each addl $6; suites $85-$95; under 18 free. Crib free. TV; cable (premium), VCR avail. Complimentary continental bkfst. Restaurant adj open 24 hrs. Ck-out noon. Meeting rms. Business servs avail. Valet serv. Heath club privileges. Some refrigerators. Some balconies. Cr cds: A, C, D, DS, ER, JCB, MC, V.

D SC

Motor Hotels

★ ★ **BEST WESTERN MIDWAY HOTEL.** *251 N Mayfair Rd (53226), I-94 exit US 100 N.* 414/774-3600; FAX 414/774-5015. 116 rms, 3 story. S $84-$109; D $94-$119; each addl $10. Crib free. TV; cable (premium). Indoor pool; whirlpool. Complimentary coffee in rms. Restaurant 6 am-10 pm. Rm serv. Bar 11-1:30 am. Ck-out noon. Coin lndry. Meeting rms. Business servs avail. In-rm modem link. Bellhops. Sundries. Valet serv. Free airport, RR station, bus depot transportation. Exercise equipt; bicycle, stair machine, sauna. Some refrigerators. Cr cds: A, D, DS, MC, V.

[D] [≈] [✕] [⊠] [⚒] [SC]

★ ★ ★ **RADISSON.** *2303 N Mayfair Rd (US 100) (53226).* 414/257-3400; FAX 414/257-0900. 150 rms, 8 story. S $79-$128; D $89-$138; each addl $10; under 18 free; lower rates wkends. Crib free. TV; cable (premium). Sauna. Indoor pool. Coffee in rms. Restaurant 6 am-2 pm, 5-10 pm. Rm serv. Bar 11-2 am. Ck-out noon. Meeting rms. Business servs avail. In-rm modem link. Bellhops. Sundries. Free airport transportation. X-country ski 2 mi. Cr cds: A, C, D, DS, MC, V.

[D] [≈] [≈] [⊠] [⚒] [SC]

Restaurants

★ ★ **ALIOTO'S.** *3041 N Mayfair Rd (Hwy 100).* 414/476-6900. Hrs: 11:30 am-9 pm; Fri to 10 pm; Sat 4-9:30 pm. Closed Sun (exc hols); also 1st wk July. Res accepted. Italian, Amer menu. Bar. Semi-a la carte: lunch $4.25-$7.95, dinner $7-$18. Child's meals. Specializes in veal, prime rib, breaded Sicilian steak. Family-owned. Cr cds: A, C, D, DS, MC, V.

[D] [SC] [⊸]

★ ★ **JAKE'S.** *6030 W North Ave (53213), at N 61st St.* 414/771-0550. Hrs: 5-10 pm; Sun to 9 pm. Closed some major hols; also Super Bowl Sun. Bar. Semi-a la carte: dinner $10.95-$23.95. Child's meals. Specializes in steak, fresh seafood, roast duck. Family-owned. Totally nonsmoking. Cr cds: A, C, D, MC, V.

[D]

★ ★ ★ **RISTORANTE BARTOLOTTA.** *7616 W State St (53213).* 414/771-7910. Hrs: 5:30-10 pm; Fri, Sat to 10:30 pm. Closed Sun; major hols. Res accepted. Italian menu. Bar. Semi-a la carte: $12.95-$21.95. Child's meals. Specialties: sautéed veal chop with marsella cream sauce, grilled seafood. Entertainment. Outdoor dining. Italian decor. Totally nonsmoking. Cr cds: A, D, DS, MC, V.

[D]

Wisconsin Dells (F-4)

(See also Baraboo, Mauston, Portage, Prairie du Sac)

Settled 1856 **Pop** 2,393 **Elev** 912 ft **Area code** 608 **Zip** 53965 **E-mail** wisdells@midplains.net **Web** www.wisdells.com

Information Wisconsin Dells Visitor & Convention Bureau, 701 Superior St, PO Box 390; 608/254-4636 or 800/22-DELLS.

Until 1931 this city was called Kilbourn, but it changed its name in the hope of attracting tourists to the nearby Dells. It seems to have worked—Wisconsin Dells has become the state's prime tourist attraction.

What to See and Do

Beaver Springs Fishing Park and Riding Stables. Guided 1-hr rides. Spring fed ponds stocked with trout, catfish, bass and other fish. Pay for fish caught. Pole rental. (Apr-Oct, daily) 600 Trout Rd, ½ mi S on WI 13. Phone 608/254-2735 (fishing) or 608/254-2707 (stable).

Dells Boat Tours. Guided sightseeing tours through the Dells Scenic Riverway. View of towering sandstone cliffs, narrow fern-filled canyons and unique rock formations. Upper Dells tour is two hrs with scenic shorelandings at Stand Rock and Witches Gulch; Lower Dells tour is one hr and features the Rocky Island region, caverns and cliffs; complete tour is Upper and Lower Dells combination. (Mid-Apr-Oct, daily, departures every 30 min in July & Aug) Phone 608/254-8336, 608/254-8500 or 608/253-1561. ¢¢¢¢

⊠ **Duck tours.**

Original Wisconsin Ducks. One-hr, 8½-mi land and water tours on the Original Wisconsin Ducks. (Apr-Oct, daily) 1 mi S on US 12. Phone 608/254-8751. ¢¢¢¢-¢¢¢¢

Dells Ducks. One-hr land/water tour of scenic rock formations along Wisconsin River. (Late May-late Oct, daily) 1½ mi S on US 12. Phone 608/254-6080. ¢¢¢¢

H.H. Bennett Foundation Museum (1865). Oldest photographic studio in the US. The landscape and nature photography of H.H. Bennett helped make the Dells area famous. The studio is still in operation and it is possible to purchase enlargements made from Bennett's original glass negatives. (Memorial Day-Labor Day, daily; rest of yr, by appt) 215 Broadway. Phone 608/253-2261. **Free.**

Riverview Park & Waterworld. Wave pool, speed slides, tube rides and kids pools. Grand Prix, go-carts, dune cat track. Park (late May-early Sept); admission free; fee for activities. Waterworld (late May-early Sept, daily). ¼ mi S on US 12. Phone 608/254-2608. Waterworld day pass ¢¢¢¢

Skiing.

Sky Line. Area has 2 chairlifts, rope tow; patrol; school; rentals; snowmaking; restaurant, cafeteria, bar. Longest run one-half mi; vertical drop 335 ft. (Dec-Mar, Fri-Sun) Cross-country trails. 25 mi N on WI 13, ½ mi W of Friendship. Phone 608/339-3421. ¢¢¢¢¢

Christmas Mountain Village. Area has 2 chairlifts, rope tow; patrol; rentals; snowmaking; restaurant, bar, snack bar. Lodge. Seven power-tilled runs; longest run one-half mi; vertical drop 250 ft. (Mid-Dec-mid-Mar, daily; closed Dec 24 eve) Cross-country trails. Night skiing. 4 mi W on County H. Phone 608/254-3971. ¢¢¢¢¢

Tommy Bartlett's Thrill Show. Water ski theme, "Ski Celebration," features juggling jokester, the Nerveless Knocks, "Mr Sound Effects" Wes Harrison and colorful entrancing waters; also laser light show (evening performances only). (Late May-early Sept, daily) 3 mi S on US 12, in Lake Delton. Phone 608/254-2525. ¢¢¢¢

Tommy Bartlett's Robot World & Exploratory. More than 90 hands-on exhibits, including the cosmic Electrostat, Tesla Coil and lightning tube. Principles of light, sound and motion are explored. Features robot-guided tour. (Daily) 3 mi S on US 12. Phone 608/254-2525. ¢¢

Wisconsin Deer Park. A 28-acre wildlife exhibit. (May-mid-Oct, daily) ½ mi S on US 12. Phone 608/253-2041. ¢¢

Annual Event

Great Wisconsin Dells Balloon Rally. I-90/94 at US 12, exit 92. More than 90 hot-air balloons participate in contests and mass liftoffs. Wkend after Memorial Day.

Motels

(Some motels may have a 2-day min in season; season dates are approximate.)

★ ★ **AMERICAN WORLD.** *400 County A & US 12.* 608/253-4451; FAX 608/254-4770; res: 800/433-3557. E-mail amworld@dellsnet .com; web www.dells.com/amworld.html. 160 rms, 3 bldgs, 2-3 story. Memorial Day-Labor Day: S, D $59-$119; each addl $7; suites $129-$179; wkly rates; higher rates hol wkends; lower rates rest of yr. TV; cable. 6 pools; 3 indoor, whirlpools. Restaurant nearby. Ck-out 10 am. Coin lndry. Business servs avail. Tennis. Downhill ski 7 mi; x-country ski 3 mi. Lawn games. Some refrigerators, in-rm whirlpools; microwaves avail. Balconies. Picnic tables. RV park. Cr cds: A, D, DS, MC, V.

[D] [≈] [⛷] [≈] [⊠] [⚒] [SC]

★ ★ BEST WESTERN AMBASSADOR INN. *610 Frontage Rd S, on WI 13, just off I-90/94 exit 87.* 608/254-4477; FAX 608/253-6662. 181 units, 3 story, 27 suites. Late June-mid-Oct: S, D $68-$98; each addl $6; suites $88-$198; under 17 free; lower rates rest of yr. Crib $5. TV; cable (premium), VCR avail (movies). 2 pools, 1 indoor; wading pool, whirlpool. Complimentary coffee. Restaurant nearby. Ck-out 11 am. Coin lndry. Meeting rms. Business servs avail. Sundries. Gift shop. Downhill/x-country ski 4 mi. Sauna. Game rm. Refrigerator, minibar in suites; microwaves avail. Picnic tables. Cr cds: A, C, D, DS, MC, V.

★ ★ BLACK HAWK. *720 Race St, at Broadway.* 608/254-7770; FAX 608/253-7333. Web www.dells.com/blackhawk.html. 75 motel rms, 1-2 story, 9 kit. cottages. Mid-June-Labor Day: S, D $55-$110; each addl $5; suites $100-$160; cottages for 2-7, $65-$170; lower rates Apr-mid-June, after Labor Day-Oct. Closed rest of yr. Crib $5. TV; cable (premium), VCR avail (movies). Indoor/outdoor pool; wading pool, whirlpools. Playground. Complimentary coffee in lobby. Restaurant nearby. Ck-out 11 am; off-season, noon. Coin lndry. Saunas. Game rm. Some in-rm whirlpools; microwaves avail. Cr cds: A, C, D, DS, MC, V.

★ ★ CAROUSEL INN & SUITES. *1031 Wisconsin Dells Pkwy.* 608/254-6554; res: 800/648-4765. E-mail winterg@tcs.itis.com; web www.dells.com/wintergrn.html. 102 rms, 16 with shower only, 2 story. July-Aug: S, D $130; suites $260; under 18 free; higher rates wknds, hols; lower rates May-June, Sept. Closed rest of yr. Crib $8. TV; cable (premium), VCR avail (movies $5). Indoor pool; whirlpool. Playground. Restaurant adj 7 am-7 pm. Ck-out 10:30 am. Business servs avail. Gift shop. Game rm. Refrigerators. Some in-rm whirlpools. Balconies. Outdoor waterpark. Picnic tables. Cr cds: A, DS, MC, V.

★ CHIPPEWA. *1114 E Broadway.* 608/253-3982; FAX 608/254-2577. 50 rms, 2 story. Mid-June-Labor Day: D $52-$95; suites $85-$150; family rates; lower rates rest of yr. Crib $4. TV; cable (premium). Indoor pool; whirlpool. Playground. Restaurant opp 7 am-10 pm. Ck-out 10 am. Coin lndry. Business servs avail. Sauna. Game rm. Some in-rm whirlpools; microwaves avail. Picnic tables. Cr cds: A, D, DS, MC, V.

✔★ ★ COMFORT INN. *703 Frontage Rd N.* 608/253-3711; FAX 608/254-2164. 75 rms, 3 story. Memorial Day-Labor Day: S $65-$104; D $73-$104; each addl $6; higher rates spring & fall wknds; lower rates rest of yr. Crib free. TV; cable (premium). Indoor pool; whirlpool. Complimentary continental bkfst. Restaurant adj 6:30 am-1 pm, 5-9 pm. Ck-out 11 am. Business servs avail. Game rm. Refrigerators, microwaves. Cr cds: A, C, D, DS, JCB, MC, V.

★ ★ DAYS INN. *944 US 12, 1 mi E of I-90/94 exit 87.* 608/254-6444. Web www.dells.com/daysinn.html. 100 rms, 2 story. Late June-Aug: S $85-$99; D $105-$135; each addl $5; suites $119-$152; under 12 free; lower rates rest of yr. Crib free. TV; cable (premium). Indoor/outdoor pool; whirlpool. Restaurant adj open 24 hrs. Ck-out 11 am. Business servs avail. Downhill/x-country ski 7 mi. Sauna. Microwaves avail. Cr cds: A, C, D, DS, MC, V.

★ ★ HOLIDAY INN AQUA DOME. *WI 13 & I-90/94 exit 87.* 608/254-8306. 228 rms, 2 story. July-Labor Day: S, D $139; family rates: winter, spring; lower rates rest of yr. Crib free. TV; cable (premium). 4 pools, 2 indoor; whirlpools, slides. Supervised child's activities (June-Aug); ages 2-12. Coffee in rms. Restaurant 6:30 am-1 pm, 5-9 pm. Rm serv. Bar; entertainment. Ck-out 10:30 am. Coin lndry. Meeting rms. Business servs avail. Gift shop. Downhill/x-country ski 8 mi. Sauna. Game rm. Microwaves avail. Cr cds: A, C, D, DS, JCB, MC, V.

✔★ ★ INDIAN TRAIL. *1013 E Broadway.* 608/253-2641. Web www.dells.com/indiantr.html. 45 rms. July-Labor Day: S $45-$80; D $60-$100; lower rates Apr-June, after Labor Day-Oct. Closed rest of yr. Crib $5. TV; cable (premium). 2 pools, 1 indoor; whirlpool. Playground. Restaurant

adj 7 am-10 pm. Ck-out 10 am. Lawn games. Refrigerators, in-rm whirlpools; microwaves avail. On 11 acres. Cr cds: A, DS, MC, V.

★ INTERNATIONAL. *1311 E Broadway.* 608/254-2431. 45 rms. July-Labor Day: S $55; D $80; lower rates May-June, after Labor Day-mid-Oct. Closed rest of yr. Crib $5. Pet accepted, some restrictions. TV; cable (premium). Heated pool; wading pool. Playground. Complimentary coffee in lobby. Restaurant adj 7 am-midnight. Ck-out 11 am. Game rm. Refrigerators avail. Balconies. Picnic tables on patio. Cr cds: A, C, D, DS, MC, V.

✔★ LUNA INN & SUITES. *1111 Wisconsin Dells Pkwy, 2 mi S on WI 23 & US 12.* 608/253-2661; res: 800/999-5862. 70 rms, 1-2 story. Mid-June-mid-Sept: S $45-$80; D $48-$99; each addl $6; lower rates mid-Sept-mid-Nov, mid-Apr-mid-June. Closed rest of yr. Crib $5. TV; cable (premium). 2 pools, 1 indoor; whirlpool. Coffee in lobby. Restaurant adj 7 am-10 pm. Ck-out 10:30 am. Some refrigerators, microwaves. Cr cds: A, DS, MC, V.

★ ★ MAYFLOWER I. *910 Wisconsin Dells Pkwy, 1 mi S on US 12, 2 mi N of I-90, 94 exit 92.* 608/253-6471; FAX 608/253-7617; res: 800/345-7407. 72 rms, 1-2 story. Mid-June-early Sept: S, D $78-$98; each addl $6; lower rates rest of yr. Crib $6. TV; cable (premium). 2 pools, 1 indoor; wading pool, whirlpool. Playground. Restaurant adj. Ck-out 11 am. Coin lndry. Business servs avail. Downhill ski 7 mi; x-country ski 3 mi. Sauna. Game rm. Refrigerators, microwaves; some in-rm whirlpools. Balconies. Picnic tables. Cr cds: A, C, D, DS, MC, V.

✔★ PARADISE. *1700 Wisconsin Dells Pkwy, 1 1/2 mi S on WI 23.* 608/254-7333. 47 rms. Mid-June-Labor Day: S, D $60-$95; suites $85-$155; family of 6-8, $85-$185; lower rates rest of yr. Crib $5. TV; cable (premium). Heated pool; wading pool, whirlpool. Playground. Restaurant nearby. Ck-out 11 am. Refrigerators; some in-rm whirlpools. Cr cds: A, DS, MC, V.

★ ★ RIVER INN. *1015 River Rd.* 608/253-1231; FAX 608/253-6145; res: 800/659-5395. Web www.dells.com/riverinn.html. 54 rms, 5 story. June-Sept: S, D $84-$159; suites $114-$159; lower rates rest of yr. TV; cable (premium). 2 pools, 1 indoor; whirlpool. Playground. Coffee in rms. Restaurant 8 am-10 pm (in season). Rm serv. Bar 4 pm-1 am. Ck-out 11 am. Business servs avail. Downhill/x-country ski 7 mi. Exercise equipt; weight machine, bicycles, sauna. Refrigerators; some microwaves. Some balconies, patios. Cr cds: A, C, D, DS, MC, V.

★ ★ RIVIERA. *811 Wisconsin Dells Pkwy, I-90/94 exit 92 (Lake Delton).* 608/253-1051; FAX 608/253-9038; res: 800/800-7109. 58 rms. July-Aug: D $89-$195; lower rates rest of yr. Crib $7. TV; cable (premium). 2 pools, 1 indoor; whirlpool. Restaurant nearby. Ck-out 10:30 am. Business servs avail. Sauna. Some in-rm whirlpools, microwaves, fireplaces. Picnic table, grill. Cr cds: DS, MC, V.

★ ★ SUNSET BAY RESORT. *921 Canyon Rd.* 608/254-8406; FAX 608/253-2062; res: 800/435-6515. E-mail sunsetbay@dellsnet.com; web www.dells.com/sunsetbay.html. 74 units, 21 suites, 16 mini-suites, 4 cottages, 1-2 story. July-Aug: S, D $95-$195; kit. cottages $650-$975/wk; lower rates Apr-June & late Aug-Nov. Closed rest of yr. Crib $7. TV; cable (premium). 4 pools, 2 indoor; wading pool. Playground. Complimentary continental bkfst (off season). Ck-out 10 am. Meeting rms. Business servs avail. Lawn games. Exercise equipt; weight machine, bicycle. Game rm. Some fireplaces, microwaves. Balconies. Picnic tables. On lake; swimming beach. Cr cds: DS, MC, V.

★ ★ WINTERGREEN RESORT & CONFERENCE CENTER. *(60 Gasser Rd, Lake Dalton 53940) exit 92 off I-90/94, 1/2 mi N.* 608/254-2285; FAX 608/253-6235; res: 800/648-4765. E-mail winterg@tcs.itis .com; web www.dells.com/wintergrn.html. 108 rms, 3 story. July-Aug: S, D $130-$160; each addl $8; suites $195-$325; under 18 free; wkly rates; package plans;

higher rates wkends (2-day min); lower rates rest of yr. Crib $10. TV; cable (premium). 2 pools, 1 indoor; wading pool, whirlpool. Playground. Restaurant 7 am-9 pm. Rm serv. Ck-out 11 am. Coin lndry. Meeting rms. Business servs avail. Sundries. Gift shop. Downhill ski 12 mi; x-country ski 2 mi. Sauna. Game rm. Refrigerators, microwaves, minibars; some in-rm whirlpools. Balconies. Picnic tables. Water park. Cr cds: A, DS, MC, V.

Resort

★ ★ ★ CHULA VISTA. 4031 N River Rd, 2¹/2 mi N on River Rd. 608/254-8366; FAX 608/254-7653; res: 800/388-4782. E-mail chula @dellsnet.com; web www.wisdells.com/chulavista. 260 rms. Memorial Day-Labor Day: S, D $105-$279; each addl $5; suites $179-$279; lower rates rest of yr. Crib $10. TV; cable (premium). 5 pools, 1 indoor; wading pool, whirlpool, poolside serv. Dining rm 7:30 am-11 pm. Rm serv. Bar. Ck-out 10:30 am, ck-in 3 pm. Convention facilities. Business servs avail. Gift shop. Package store. Airport, RR station, bus depot transportation. Tennis. Golf. Downhill ski 5 mi. Snowmobiling. Hiking trails. Exercise equipt; weights, bicycles, sauna, steam rm. Miniature golf. Microwaves; some in-rm whirlpools. Balconies. Cr cds: A, C, D, DS, MC, V.

Cottage Colony

✔★ ★ MEADOWBROOK RESORT. 1533 River Rd. 608/253-3201. 18 units, 2 story, 6 with kit., 14 cabins. No rm phones. Mid-June-Labor Day: S, D $79-$119; cabins for 4, $79-$119; kit. cabins $109-$199; family rates; lower rates May-mid-June, after Labor Day-Oct. Closed rest of yr. TV; cable (premium). Heated pool. Playground. Restaurant nearby. Ck-out 10 am, ck-in 3 pm. Grocery 1 mi. Package store 1 mi. Hiking. Lawn games. Refrigerators, microwaves. Some balconies. Picnic tables, grills. Extensive wooded grounds; fishing pond. Cr cds: A, DS, MC, V.

Restaurants

★ ★ DEL-BAR SUPPER CLUB. (800 Wisconsin Dells Pkwy, Lake Delton) 2¹/2 mi S of I 90/94 on US 12 in Lake Delton. 608/253-1861. E-mail dbarinc@aol.com. Hrs: 4:30-10 pm; June-Aug to 10:30 pm. Closed Thanksgiving, Dec 25. Bar. Semi-a la carte: dinner $12-$25. Friday fish fry $8.50. Specializes in custom-cut steak, pasta, fresh seafood. Parking. Family-owned. Cr cds: A, C, D, DS, MC, V.

D

★ ★ FISCHER'S. (441 Wisconsin Dells Pkwy S, Lake Delton) 3 mi S on US 12, 1 mi N of I-90/94 Lake Delton-Baraboo exit 92. 608/253-7531. Hrs: 4-11 pm. Closed Thanksgiving, Dec 24-25. Res accepted. Bar. Semi-a la carte: dinner $6-$18. Specializes in steak, barbecue ribs, fresh seafood. Child's meals. Parking. Family-owned. Cr cds: DS, MC, V.

D

★ ★ ISHNALA. (Ishnala Rd, Lake Delton) I-90 exit 92, left on Gasser to Ishnala Rd. 608/253-1771. Hrs: 5-10 pm; Sat 4-10:30 pm; Sun 4-9 pm; after Labor Day-mid-Sept wkends only. Closed mid-Sept-late May. Bar from 4 pm. Semi-a la carte: dinner $15-$25. Child's meals. Specializes in barbecued ribs, aged meats, fresh seafood. Rustic; Native American decor. Parking. On Mirror Lake. Totally nonsmoking. Cr cds: A, MC, V.

★ ★ WALLY'S HOUSE OF EMBERS. (935 Wisconsin Dells Pkwy, Lake Delton 53940) S on US 12. 608/253-6411. Web www.dells .com/embers.html. Hrs: 4:30 pm-midnight. Res accepted. Bar. Semi-a la carte: dinner $9.90-$22.90. Child's meals. Specializes in hickory-smoked ribs, steak, fresh seafood. Entertainment wkends. Outdoor gazebo; garden. Family-owned. Cr cds: A, MC, V.

D

★ WINTERGREEN GRILL. (60 A Gasser Rd, Lake Dalton 53940) 608/254-7686. Web www.dells.com/wintergrn.html. Hrs: 7 am-9

pm; Sun bkfst buffet 8-11:30 am. Closed Dec 25. Amer, Italian menu. Wine, beer. Semi-a la carte: bkfst $3.50-$7.95, lunch $4.75-$7.95, dinner $9.95-$17.95. Sun buffet $5.95. Child's meals. Specializes in ribs, pizza. Parking. Cr cds: D, DS, MC, V.

D

Wisconsin Rapids (E-4)

(For accommodations see Marshfield, Stevens Point)

Pop 18,245 Elev 1,028 ft Area code 715 Zip 54494 E-mail brogers@wctc.net Web www.wctc.net/chamber

Information Wisconsin Rapids Area Visitor & Convention Bureau, 1120 Lincoln St; 715/422-4856 or 800/554-4484.

A paper manufacturing and cranberry center, Wisconsin Rapids was formed in 1900 by consolidating the two towns of Grand Rapids and Centralia after the Wisconsin River had devastated large sections of both communities. At first the combined town was called Grand Rapids, but the name was changed when confusion with the Michigan city developed. Cranberry marshes here produce the largest inland cranberry crop in the world.

What to See and Do

Forest tour. Self-guided walking or cross-country skiing tour of site of Consolidated Papers' first tree nursery, now planted with various types of hard and soft woods; 27 marked points of special interest on 60 acres. (Daily) 5 mi NE on County U, on banks of Wisconsin River. Phone 715/422-3789. Free.

Grotto Gardens. A six-acre garden park with series of religious tableaux, statues and grottoes (daily). Picnic grounds. Gift shop/information center (Memorial Day-Labor Day, daily). 7 mi N via WI 34, County C in Rudolph. Phone 715/435-3120. ¢

Industrial tour. Consolidated Papers, Inc. Enamel printing papers. One-hr tour (Wed, Thurs & Sat mornings; closed most hols). Jackson St, just W of Wisconsin River. Phone 715/422-3789. Free.

South Wood County Historical Corporation Museum. Historical museum in town mansion. (June-Aug, Tues, Thurs & Sun, afternoons) 540 3rd St S. Phone 715/423-1580. Free.

Annual Event

River Cities Fun Fest. Tours, car show, arts & crafts fair, water ski shows. 1st wkend Aug.

Woodruff (C-4)

(For accommodations see Boulder Junction, Eagle River, Lac du Flambeau, Minocqua, Rhinelander, St Germain)

Pop 2,000 (est) Elev 1,610 ft Area code 715 Zip 54568
Information Minocqua-Arbor Vitae-Woodruff Area Chamber of Commerce, PO Box 1006, Minocqua, 54548; 715/356-5266 or 800/446-6784.

Woodruff is a four-seasons playground for families and sportsmen alike. It is also the headquarters for fishing excursions and exploration of the Northern Highland-American Legion State Forest. It is the nearest town for many summer camps.

What to See and Do

Woodruff State Fish Hatchery. Hatchery (mid-Apr-mid-June). Aquariums (Memorial Day-Labor Day). (Mon-Fri) 2¹/2 mi SE on County Trunk J. Phone 715/356-5211. Free.

Canada

Population: 28,114,000
Land area: 3,849,674 square miles (9,973,249 square kilometers)
Highest point: Mt Logan, Yukon Territory, 19,850 feet (5,951 meters)
Capital: Ottawa
Speed limit: 50 or 60 MPH (80 or 100 km/h), unless otherwise indicated

Just north of the United States, with which it shares the world's longest undefended border, lies Canada, the world's largest country in terms of land area. Extending from the North Pole to the northern border of the United States and including all the islands from Greenland to Alaska, Canada's area encompasses nearly 4 million square miles (10.4 million square kilometers). The northern reaches of the country consist mainly of the Yukon and Northwest territories, which make up the vast, sparsely populated Canadian frontier.

Jacques Cartier erected a cross at Gaspé in 1534 and declared the establishment of New France. Samuel de Champlain founded Port Royal in Nova Scotia in 1604. Until 1759 Canada was under French rule. In that year, British General Wolfe defeated French General Montcalm at Québec and British possession followed. In 1867 the British North America Act established the Confederation of Canada, with four provinces: New Brunswick, Nova Scotia, Ontario and Québec. The other provinces joined later. Canada was proclaimed a self-governing Dominion within the British Empire in 1931. The passage in 1981 of the Constitution Act severed Canada's final legislative link with Great Britain, which had until that time reserved the right to amend the Canadian Constitution.

Today, Canada is a sovereign nation—neither a colony nor a possession of Great Britain. Since Canada is a member of the Commonwealth of Nations, Queen Elizabeth II, through her representative, the Governor-General, is the nominal head of state. However, the Queen's functions are mostly ceremonial with no political power or authority. Instead, the nation's chief executive is the prime minister; the legislative branch consists of the Senate and the House of Commons.

Visitor Information

Currency. The American dollar is accepted throughout Canada, but it is advisable to exchange your money into Canadian currency upon arrival. Banks and currency exchange firms typically give the best rate of exchange, but hotels and stores will also convert it for you with purchases. The Canadian monetary system is based on dollars and cents, and rates in *Mobil Travel Guide* are given in Canadian currency. Generally, the credit cards you use at home are also honored in Canada.

Goods and Services Tax (GST). Most goods and services in Canada are subject to a 7% tax. Visitors to Canada may claim a rebate of the GST paid on *short-term accommodations* (hotel, motel or similar lodging) and on *most consumer goods* purchased to take home. Rebates may be claimed for cash at participating Canadian Duty Free shops or by mail. For further information and a brochure detailing rebate procedures and restrictions contact Revenue Canada, Customs and Excise, Visitors' Rebate Program, Ottawa, ON K1A 1J5; 613/991-3346 or 800/66-VISIT (in Canada).

Driving in Canada. Your American driver's license is valid in Canada; no special permit is required. In Canada the liter is the unit of measure for gasoline. One US gallon equals 3.78 liters. Traffic signs are clearly understood and in many cities are bilingual. All road speed limits and mileage signs have been posted in kilometers. A flashing green traffic light gives vehicles turning left the right-of-way, like a green left-turn arrow. The use of safety belts is generally mandatory in all provinces; consult the various provincial tourism bureaus for specific information.

Holidays. All Canada observes the following holidays, and these are indicated in text: New Year's Day, Good Friday, Easter Monday, Victoria Day (usually 3rd Mon May), Canada Day (July 1), Labour Day, Thanksgiving (2nd Mon Oct), Remembrance Day (Nov 11), Christmas and Boxing Day (Dec 26). See individual provinces for information on provincial holidays.

Liquor. The sale of liquor, wine, beer and cider varies from province to province. Restaurants must be licensed to serve liquor, and in some cases liquor may not be sold unless it accompanies a meal. Generally there are no package sales on holidays. Minimum legal drinking age also varies by province. **Note:** It is illegal to take children into bars or cocktail lounges.

Daylight Saving Time. Canada observes Daylight Saving Time beginning the first Sunday in April through the last Sunday in October, except for most of the province of Saskatchewan, where Standard Time is observed year-round.

Tourist information is available from individual provincial and territorial tourism offices (see Border Crossing Regulations in MAKING THE MOST OF YOUR TRIP).

Province of Ontario

Pop 9,101,690 **Land area** 412,582 sq mi (1,068,175 sq km) **Capital** Toronto **Web** www.ontario-canada.com

Information Ministry of Economic Development, Trade and Tourism, Queen's Park, Toronto M7A 2E1; 800/ONTARIO.

Although first explored by Samuel de Champlain in the 17th century, the Ontario region was not heavily settled until the 18th century by Loyalist refugees from the American Revolution. British settled in what was to become Ontario while French populated Québec. Two territories were formed following the battle of 1759; in 1867 they became provinces in the Dominion of Canada.

This vast province can be divided into northern and southern Ontario; the far northern wilderness dominated by lakes, forests and logging camps; the southern agricultural and industrial section inhabited by nine-tenths of the population. The province is easily accessible from many points across the United States, with each area offering exciting and beautiful sights for the traveler.

Certainly one of the most spectacular sights is Niagara Falls. Cosmopolitan Toronto, the provincial capital, and Ottawa, the country's capital, offer the tourist a wide spectrum of experiences including theater, fine restaurants, galleries, museums and recreational facilities. The Stratford Festival in Stratford, the Shaw Festival in Niagara-on-the-Lake and Upper Canada Village in Morrisburg are not to be missed.

Ontario is also known for its many recreational areas, such as Algonquin and Quetico provincial parks and St Lawrence Islands National Park. To the north lie Sudbury and Sault Ste Marie; to the northwest, Thunder Bay, Fort Frances and Kenora, offering a variety of wilderness activities including canoeing, fishing and hunting. Perhaps more appealing than any one attraction is the vast, unspoiled nature of the province itself. More than 400,000 lakes and magnificent forests form a huge vacationland just a few miles from the US border, stretching all the way to Hudson Bay.

Ontario lies mostly within the Eastern Time Zone. Travelers should note that fees are charged at international bridges, tunnels and ferries.

In addition to national holidays, Ontario observes Simcoe Day (1st Monday in August).

Safety belts are mandatory for all persons anywhere in vehicle. Children under 40 pounds in weight must be in an approved safety seat anywhere in vehicle.

Brantford (E-6)

(See also Hamilton, Stratford)

Founded 1784 **Pop** 81,290 **Elev** 815 ft (248 m) **Area code** 519 **E-mail** btourism@bfree.on.ca
Information Tourism Brantford, 1 Sherwood Dr, N3T 1N3; 519/751-9900 or 800/265-6299.

As compensation for their losses in the American Revolution and because of their loyalty to the British crown, Captain Joseph Brant and the Six Nations tribes were given land here by the British in 1784. The river crossing became known as Brant's Ford and even today retains many associations with the culture and heritage of the Six Nations people. Brantford is equally famous as the place where Alexander Graham Bell lived and invented the telephone. The first long-distance call was made from here to Paris, ON, in 1876.

What to See and Do

Bell Homestead. The house is furnished just as it was when Alexander Graham Bell lived here in the 1870s. Also located here are the first telephone office and artifacts housed in a display center. (Daily exc Mon; closed Tues following Mon hols) 94 Tutela Heights Rd. Phone 519/756-6220. ¢

Brant County Museum. Collection of Native American artifacts, life histories of Captain Joseph Brant and Pauline Johnson. Also displays of pioneer life in Brant County, including Brant Square & Brant Corners, where former businesses are depicted. (Wed-Sat; also Sun June-Aug; closed Jan 1, Thanksgiving, Dec 25) 57 Charlotte St. Phone 519/752-2483. ¢

Glenhyrst Art Gallery of Brant. Gallery with changing exhibits of paintings, sculpture, photography and crafts surrounded by 16-acre (7-hectare) estate overlooking the Grand River. Beautiful grounds and nature trail. (Daily exc Mon; closed major hols) 20 Ava Rd. Phone 519/756-5932. **Free.**

Her Majesty's Royal Chapel of the Mohawks (1785). The first Protestant church in Ontario, the "Mohawk Chapel" is the only Royal Native Chapel in the world belonging to Six Nations people. (May-June, Wed-Sun afternoons; July-Labour Day, daily; early Sept-mid-Oct, Sat & Sun afternoons) 190 Mohawk St. Phone 519/445-4528. ¢¢

Myrtleville House Museum (1837). Georgian-style house is one of the oldest in Brant County; original furniture of the Good family, who lived here for more than 150 yrs. On 5½ acres (2 hectares) of parkland. Picnicking. (Mid-Apr-mid-Sept, daily exc Mon; closed hols) 34 Myrtleville Dr. Phone 519/752-3216. ¢

Riverboat Cruises. Big Creek Boat Farm. Dinner cruises on the Grand River. (Mid-May-Sept; reservations required) ON 54, 4 mi (6.4 km) W of Caledonia. Phone 905/765-4107. ¢¢¢¢¢

Sanderson Centre for the Performing Arts. This 1919 vaudeville house has been restored and transformed to a theater featuring music, dance and dramatic performances. 88 Dalhousie St. Phone 519/758-8090 or 800/265-0710 for schedule and ticket information.

Woodland Cultural Centre. Preserves and promotes culture and heritage of First Nations of eastern woodland area. Education, research and museum programs; art shows, festivals. (Daily; closed major hols) 184 Mohawk St. Phone 519/759-2650. Museum ¢¢

Annual Events

Riverfest. Three-day festival celebrates the Grand River. Entertainment, fireworks, crafts. Children's activities. Phone 519/751-9900. Last wkend May.

International Villages Festival. Ethnic villages celebrate with ethnic folk dancing, pageantry and food. Early July.

Six Nations Native Pageant. Forest Theatre, Sour Springs Rd, at Six Nations reserve. Six Nations people reenact their history and culture in natural forest amphitheater. Phone 519/445-4528. Fri, Sat. First 3 wkends Aug.

Six Nations Native Fall Fair. Ohsweken Fairgrounds. Native dances, authentic craft and art exhibits. Phone 519/445-4528. Wkend after Labour Day.

Motels

★ ★ ★ **BEST WESTERN-BRANT PARK INN.** *(19 Holiday Dr, Brantford ON N3T 5W5)* Park Rd exit. 519/753-8651; FAX 519/753-2619. E-mail kbrown@bfree.on.ca. 115 rms, 2 story. June-Sept: S $64.95; D $71.95; each addl $7; under 12 free. Crib free. Pet accepted. TV; cable. Heated pool; wading pool, whirlpool, lifeguard. Playground. Restaurant 6:30 am-9:30 pm. Rm serv. Ck-out noon. Meeting rms. Business servs avail. In-rm modem link. Bellhops. Valet serv. Exercise equipt; stair machine, bicycle, sauna. Private patios; some balconies. Cr cds: A, D, DS, ER, MC, V.

D ✦ ≈ ✕ ⇘ ⋈ **SC**

✦ ★ ★ **DAYS INN.** *(460 Fairview Dr, Brantford ON N3R 7A9)* 519/759-2700; FAX 519/759-2089; res: 800/329-7466. Web www.daysinn .com/daysinn.html. 75 rms, 2 story. Apr-Oct: S $52.95; D $59.95-$76.95; each addl $7; under 12 free; wkly, wkend rates; lower rates rest of yr. Crib free. Pet accepted. TV; cable (premium). Pool privileges. Restaurant 7-1 am. Ck-out 11 am. Meeting rms. Business servs avail. In-rm modem link. Health club privileges. Cr cds: A, D, DS, ER, JCB, MC, V.

D ✦ ≈ ⋈ **SC**

Restaurants

★ **COLONIAL.** *(162 Colborne St, Brantford ON M3T 2G6)* 519/753-3297. Continental menu. Specializes in roast beef, seafood. Salad bar. Hrs: 8:30 am-9 pm. Closed Sun. Res accepted. Bar from 11 am. Semi-a la carte: bkfst $3.85-$5, lunch $3.95-$5, dinner $9.95-$12.95. Complete meals: lunch $5, dinner $10. Mediterranean decor. Family-owned. Cr cds: A, MC, V.

★ ★ **OLDE SCHOOLHOUSE.** *(Hwy 2W & Powerline Rd W, Brantford ON N3T 5M1)* 519/753-3131. International menu. Specializes in steak, seafood. Hrs: 11:30-1 am; Sat from 5 pm; Sun brunch 11 am-3 pm. Closed Dec 25. Res accepted; required Sat. Bar. Semi-a la carte: lunch $6.95-$12.95, dinner $16.95-$25.95. Complete meals: dinner (Mon-Fri) $12.95. Sun brunch $10.95. Piano lounge. Restored 1850s schoolhouse; antiques, pioneer and school memorabilia. Cr cds: A, D, ER, MC, V.

SC

Brockville (C-10)

(See also Alexandria Bay; also see Ogdensburg, NY)

Settled 1784 **Pop** 21,000 (est) **Elev** 300 ft (91 m) **Area code** 613 **E-mail** dpaul.brockville.com **Web** www.brockville.com

Information Tourism Office, 1 King St West, PO Box 5000, K6V 7A5; 613/342-8772.

Settled by United Empire Loyalists, the town was known as Elizabethtown until 1812 when it was named Brockville after Major General Sir Isaac Brock. It was incorporated as a town in 1832, the first in Ontario. Brockville is the eastern gateway to the Thousand Islands on the St Lawrence River. It is home to the oldest railway tunnel in Canada which runs one quarter of a mile under the city to the riverfront. The city features many Victorian homes along with a historic downtown business section with numerous buildings more than 100 years old.

What to See and Do

Thousand Island Cruises. Aboard the *General Brock*. Shallow-draft boat makes trips (1 hr) through heart of the region, including Millionaires Row and many smaller channels inaccessible to larger boats. (May-late Oct, daily) 14 mi (23 km) W via Hwy 401 to 1000 Islands Pkwy. Phone 613/659-3402 or 800/563-8687. ¢¢¢

Annual Events

Great Balloon Rodeo. Mid-June.

Riverfest. Waterfront. Mid-June-early July.

Motels

★ ★ **BEST WESTERN WHITE HOUSE.** *(RR1, Brockville ON K6V 5T1)* 1½ mi E on ON 2. 613/345-1622; FAX 613/345-4284. 56 rms. S $67; D $72-$77; each addl $5. Crib $5. TV. Heated pool. Complimentary coffee in rms. Restaurant 6:30 am-2 pm, 5-9 pm. Ck-out 11 am. Meeting rms. Business servs avail. In-rm modem link. Sundries. Picnic tables. Cr cds: A, C, D, DS, ER, MC, V.

⌂ ⊠ 🔥 SC

★ **DAYS INN.** *(160 Stewart Blvd, Brockville ON K6V 4W6)* Hwy 401 exit 696. 613/342-6613; FAX 613/345-3811. 56 rms, 2 story. Mid-June-mid-Oct: S $57-$64; D $72-$74; each addl $7; under 17 free; lower rates rest of yr. Crib free. TV; cable (premium). Pool. Complimentary coffee in rms. Restaurant 11 am-2 pm, 4:30-9 pm. Bar noon-1 am. Ck-out 11 am. Meeting rms. Business servs avail. Picnic tables. Cr cds: A, C, D, DS, ER, JCB, MC, V.

⌂ ⊠ 🔥 SC

Hotel

★ ★ ★ **ROYAL BROCK.** *(100 Stewart Blvd, Brockville ON K6V 4W3)* off OT 401 on OT 29S exit 696. 613/345-1400; FAX 613/345-5402; res: 800/267-4428. 72 rms, 5 story. S $108-$123; D $120-$135; each addl $12; suites $225-$237; studio rms $117-$129; under 16 free. Crib free. TV; cable (premium). Indoor pool; whirlpool, poolside serv. Supervised child's activities. Restaurant 6:30 am-11 pm. Bar 11:30-2 am; entertainment exc

Sun. Ck-out noon. Meeting rms. Business servs avail. In-rm modem link. Beauty shop. Tennis. Exercise equipt; weight machines, bicycles, sauna, steam rm. Massage. Cr cds: A, C, D, DS, ER, JCB, MC, V.

Cornwall (C-10)

(See also Morrisburg; also see Massena, NY)

Pop 46,144 **Elev** 200 ft (62 m) **Area code** 613 **Web** www.visit.cornwall.on.ca

Information Cornwall and Seaway Valley Tourism, 231 Augustas St, K6J 3W2; 800/937-4748.

Cornwall is a thriving community located on the banks of the St Lawrence River. It is connected to Massena, New York (see) by the Seaway International Toll Bridge. The Robert H. Saunders Generating Station, one of the largest international generating stations in the world, is here.

What to See and Do

Inverarden Regency Cottage Museum (1816). Retirement home of fur trader John McDonald of Garth. Collection of Canadian & English Georgian furniture; houses local picture archives. Tea rm (Sun in summer). (Apr-mid-Nov, daily; rest of yr by appt) Montreal & Boundary Rds. Phone 613/938-9585. **Free.**

Long Sault Parkway. Six-and-one-half-mi (10-km) causeway loop connects 11 islands in the St Lawrence River between Long Sault and Ingleside; 1,300 scenic acres (526 hectares) with beaches and campsites. Toll. 8 mi (13 km) W off ON 2.

United Counties Museum. Old stone house has displays showing early life of the United Empire Loyalists. (Apr-late Nov, daily) 731 Second St W. Phone 613/932-2381. **Free.**

Upper Canada Village. 25 mi (40 km) W on ON 2 in Morrisburg (see).

Annual Events

Raisin River Canoe Races. On Raisin River. Mid-Apr.

Worldfest/Festimonde. Cornwall Civic Complex. International folk festival; ethnic music, dancing, displays, costumes. 6 days early July.

Williamstown Fair. Mid-Aug.

"Awesome August" Festival. Balloon lift-off, Cornfest, performances. Mid-Aug.

Motel

★ ★ ★ **BEST WESTERN PARKWAY INN.** *(1515 Vincent Massey Dr (Hwy 2), Cornwall ON K6H 5R6)* 613/932-0451; FAX 613/938-5479. 91 rms, 2 story. S $86; D $110-$145; each addl $6; suites $200; under 18 free. Crib free. Pet accepted. TV; cable (premium). Pool; whirlpool. Coffee in rms. Restaurant 6:30 am-10 pm; Sun to 9 pm. Bar 11-2 am. Ck-out noon. Meeting rms. Business servs avail. In-rm modem link. Valet serv. X-country ski 2 mi. Exercise equipt; weights, bicycles, sauna. Refrigerators, some fireplaces. Cr cds: A, C, D, ER, MC, V.

🐾 ⊠ ≈ ⌂ ⊠ 🔥 SC

Fort Frances (F-1)

Pop 8,906 **Elev** 1,100 ft (335 m) **Area code** 807 **E-mail** thefort@ff. lakeheadu.ca

Information Chamber of Commerce, 474 Scott St, P9A 1H2; 807/274-5773 or 800/820-FORT.

Across the river from International Falls, Minnesota, Fort Frances is a prosperous paper town and an important border crossing point for visitors from the United States heading for northwestern Canadian destinations. "The Fort" is a popular summer resort town. It is also a major fly-in center for the vast wilderness areas to the north and east, a region of 40,000 lakes.

What to See and Do

Fort Frances Museum. This small museum has changing displays dealing with the indigenous era, the fur trade and later settlement. (Mid-June-Labour Day, daily; rest of yr, daily exc Sun; closed major hols) 259 Scott St. Phone 807/274-7891. Summer admission ¢

Industrial tour. Abitibi Consolidated. The paper manufacturing process is followed from debarking of the logs to the finished paper. (June-Aug, Mon-Fri by res only) Ages 12 yrs and over only; flat, closed-toe shoes required. 145 3rd St W. Phone 807/274-5311. **Free.**

Noden Causeway. Excellent island views may be seen from this network of bridges. E on ON 11.

Pither's Point Park. This beautiful park has a reconstructed fort, logging tug boat and a lookout tower with a pioneer logging museum at its base. Tower, fort and boat (mid-June-Labour Day, daily). Campground (fee) with swimming beach; fishing; boating (rentals adj to park). Playground; fitness trail; cafe. (Late June-Labour Day) On Rainy Lake. Phone 807/274-5087 or -5502. **Free.** Museum ¢

Annual Events

"Culturama" Festival. Mid-May.

"Fun in the Sun" Festival. Late June.

Motel

★ ★ **LA PLACE RENDEZ-VOUS.** (1201 Idylwild Dr, Fort Frances ON P9A 3N1) 1 mi E on Hwy 11, adj Pither's Point Park. 807/274-9811; FAX 807/274-9553; res: 800/544-9435. 54 units, 1-2 story. S $85-$90; D $92-$97; each addl $7; under 12 free. Crib free. TV; cable, VCR avail. Restaurant (see LA PLACE RENDEZ-VOUS). Rm serv. Bar 11-1 am. Ck-out 11 am. Meeting rms. Business servs avail. In-rm modem link. Whirlpool, sauna. Some balconies. Picnic tables. On Rainy Lake; swimming beach. Cr cds: A, MC, V.

Restaurant

★ ★ **LA PLACE RENDEZ-VOUS.** (See La Place Rendez-Vous Motel) 807/274-9811. Specializes in prime rib, walleye. Hrs: 6 am-10 pm; Fri, Sat to 11 pm. Closed Dec 25. Res accepted. Bar 11-1 am. Semi-a la carte: bkfst $2.95-$9.95, lunch $4.95-$10.95, dinner $10.50-$19.95. Child's meals. Outdoor dining. Overlooks Rainy Lake. Family-owned. Cr cds: A, MC, V.

Gananoque (D-9)

(See also Kingston; also see Alexandria Bay & Clayton, NY)

Pop 4,863 **Elev** 300 ft (91 m) **Area code** 613 **E-mail** gan@post.kosone. com **Web** www.gananoque.com

Information 1000 Islands Gananoque Chamber of Commerce, 2 King St E, K7G 1E6; 613/382-3250 or 800/561-1595.

What to See and Do

1000 Islands Camping Resort. Campground area with tent & trailer sites (hookups, showers, dump station). Pool, playground; nature trails; miniature golf (fee). Store, snack bar. Coin lndry. (Mid-May-mid-Oct, daily) 1000 Islands Pkwy, 5 mi (8 km) E. Phone 613/659-3058. Within the park is

Giant Waterslide. A 175-ft (53-m) water slide. (Mid-June-Labour Day, daily) Per hour ¢¢

1000 Islands Skydeck. Atop 350-ft (107-m) tower; elevator to three observation decks. (Early May-late Oct, daily) Between the spans of the Thousand Islands International Bridge, on Hill Island, Lansdowne. Phone 613/659-2335. ¢¢

Arthur Child Heritage Centre. Historical displays. Gift shop; clothing outlets. Overlooks St Lawrence River. 125 Water St. 613/382-2535. **Free.**

Gananoque Boat Line. Three-hr tours through the 1000 Islands with a stop at Boldt Castle; snack bar. (Mid-May-mid-Oct; 1-hr trips July-Aug) Water St. Phone 613/382-2146. ¢¢¢¢

Gananoque Historical Museum. Former Victoria Hotel (1863); parlour, dining rm, bedrm, kitchen furnished in Victorian style. Military and indigenous artifacts; china, glass, 19th- and 20th-century costumes. (June-Oct, daily) 10 King St E. Phone 613/382-4024. ¢

House of Haunts (1883). Ghost tour of 10 programmed and automated displays in "haunted" house. (Mid-May-mid-Oct, daily) Main & Water Sts. Phone 613/382-4154. ¢¢¢

St Lawrence Islands National Park (see). 9 mi (14.5 km) E.

Motels

★ ★ **BEST WESTERN PROVINCIAL.** (846 King St E (Hwy 2), Gananoque ON K7G 1H3) 613/382-2038; FAX 613/382-8663. 78 rms. July-Labour Day: S $68-$80; D $78-$98; each addl $6; lower rates Mar-June, after Labour Day-Oct. Closed rest of yr. Crib $6. TV; cable. Heated pool. Restaurant 7:30 am-9:30 pm; off-season to 9 pm. Bar noon-10 pm. Ck-out 11 am. Sundries. Gift shop. Lighted tennis. Some in-rm whirlpools. Cr cds: A, C, D, DS, ER, MC, V.

★ ★ **DAYS INN.** (650 King St E, Gananoque ON K7G 1H3) 613/382-7292; FAX 613/382-4387. 30 rms, 2 story. Late June-Labor Day: S, D $79-$119; suites $139-$179; under 18 free; lower rates rest of yr. Crib free. TV; cable, VCR avail (movies). Complimentary coffee in rms. Restaurant 8 am-10 pm; off season 11 am-9 pm. Serv bar. Ck-out 11 am. Meeting rms. Business servs avail. Cr cds: A, C, D, DS, ER, JCB, MC, V.

★ ★ ★ **GANANOQUE INN.** (550 Stone St S, Gananoque ON K7G 2A8) 613/382-2165; res: 800/465-3101; FAX 613/382-7912. 50 rms, 3 story. No elvtr. Early June-early Sept: S, D $87.50-$99; suites $120-$199; higher rates wkends; lower rates rest of yr. Crib free. TV; cable. Restaurant 7 am-11 pm. Rm serv. Bar 11:30-2 am, entertainment Thurs-Sat. Business servs avail. Ck-out 11 am. X-country ski 5 mi. Bicycle, boat rentals. Some in-rm whirlpools. Balconies. Old carriage works overlooking river. Cr cds: A, MC, V.

Inn

★ ★ ★ **TRINITY HOUSE.** *(90 Stone St S, Gananoque ON K7G 1Z8) 613/382-8383; FAX 613/382-1599; res: 800/265-4871 (CAN).* 8 rms, 3 story, 2 suites. No rm phones. S, D $75-$150; suites $135-$190; MAP avail. TV; cable, VCR avail. Complimentary continental bkfst. Dining rm (public by res) sittings from 5:30 pm. Rm serv. Bar. Ck-out 10 am, ck-in 2 pm. Business servs avail. Victorian mansion (1859) built with bricks imported from Scotland. Victorian gardens. Sundeck overlooking waterfalls. Sailing excursions on 10-m boat. Cr cds: MC, V.

Restaurant

★ ★ **GOLDEN APPLE.** *(45 King St W PB 83 (Hwy 2), Gananoque ON) 613/382-3300.* Specializes in prime rib, roast lamb, seafood. Hrs: 11 am-9 pm; Sun brunch to 3 pm. Closed Jan-Mar. Res accepted. Serv bar. A la carte entrees: lunch $5.95-$12.95. Complete meals: dinner $14.95-$29.95. Sun brunch $11.95. Child's meals. Patio dining. Converted 1830 mansion; antiques. Exposed stone walls. Cr cds: A, MC, V.

Hamilton (E-7)

(See also Brantford, Mississauga, St Catharines, Toronto)

Pop 306,434 **Elev** 776 ft (237 m) **Area code** 905
Information Greater Hamilton Visitor and Convention Services, 1 James St S, 3rd Floor, L8P 4R5; 905/546-2666.

Thriving both industrially and culturally, Hamilton is Canada's largest steel center. It is located on Hamilton Harbour, spanned by the majestic Skyway Bridge to Toronto, which offers excellent views of the city.

What to See and Do

African Lion Safari. Drive-through wildlife park; exotic animal and bird shows, demonstrations. Admission includes large game reserves, *African Queen* boat, shows, scenic railway; play areas. Camping (June-Sept, fee). Park (Apr-Oct, daily). W on Hwy 8 between Hamilton & Cambridge, on Safari Rd. Phone 519/623-2620. ¢¢¢¢

Andrés Wines. Escorted tours and tastings. (Apr-Dec, daily; rest of yr, by appt) Wine shop. 5 mi (8 km) W at Kelson Rd & S Service Rd, in Grimsby. Phone 905/643-TOUR. ¢

Art Gallery of Hamilton. Collection of more than 8,000 photographs, sculptures and photographs covering several centuries, by American, Canadian, British and European artists. Impressive building; many international, national and regional exhibitions. (Wed-Sun; closed statutory hols) Fee may be higher for some shows. 123 King St W. Phone 905/527-6610. ¢

Battlefield House and Monument. Devoted to the "Battle of Stoney Creek," this 1795 settler's home and monument honors one of the most significant encounters of the War of 1812. Some rms furnished as a farm home of the 1830s. Guides in period costumes. (Open for tours; mid-May-June & early Sept-mid-Oct, daily exc Sat; July-Labour Day, daily; rest of yr, by appt) QEW exit at Centennial Pkwy, 77 King St in Stoney Creek. Phone 905/662-8458. ¢

Ben Veldhuis Limited. More than 2 acres (1 hectare) of greenhouses; thousands of varieties of cacti, succulents, saintpaulias and hibiscus; flowering tropical plants. Hibisci bloom all yr. (Daily; closed Jan 1, Dec 25) 154 King St E, off ON 8, W in Dundas. Phone 905/628-6307. **Free.**

Canadian Football Hall of Fame and Museum. Sports museum and national shrine tracing 120 yrs of history of Canadian football. (Daily; closed Sun in winter & spring) 58 Jackson St W. Phone 905/528-7566. ¢

Children's Museum. Participatory learning center where children between the ages of 2-13 can expand their sensory awareness of the world. "Hands-on" exhibits; changing theme exhibits. (Daily exc Mon; closed Dec 25, 26, also Jan & Sept) 1072 Main St E. Phone 905/546-4848. Adults free with child. Per child ¢

Dundurn Castle. Home of Sir Allan Napier MacNab, Prime Minister of the United Provinces of Canada (1854-1856). The 35-rm mansion is restored to its former splendor. Exhibits, programs, special events featured all yr. Castle (late May-Labour Day & Dec, daily; rest of yr, daily exc Mon; closed Jan 1, Dec 25). York Blvd. Phone 905/546-2872. ¢¢

Hamilton Military Museum. Displays Canadian uniforms, equipment and weapons from ca 1800. (Late May-Labour Day & Dec, daily; rest of yr, daily exc Mon; closed Jan 1, Dec 25) Dundurn Park. Phone 905/546-4974. ¢

Flamboro Downs. Harness racing (all yr). Grandstand seats 3,000; restaurants, lounges. Confederation Cup race for top 3-yr-old pacers in North America held here (Aug). 967 Hwy 5, W in Flamborough. Phone 905/627-3561. ¢¢

Hamilton Place. Live theater and concerts featuring international artists in a spectacular cultural center. (All yr) Main St. Phone 905/546-3050.

Hamilton's Farmers' Market. Fresh produce, flowers, meat, poultry, fish, cheese and baked goods are brought from all over the Niagara garden belt. (Tues, Thurs-Sat) 55 York Blvd. Phone 905/546-2096.

Museum of Steam and Technology. An 1859 Pumping Station contains unique examples of 19th-century steam technology; gallery features permanent and temporary exhibits on modern technology; also special events. Guided tours (daily; closed Jan 1, Dec 25). 900 Woodward Ave. Phone 905/546-4797. ¢¢

Royal Botanical Gardens. Colorful gardens, natural areas and a wildlife sanctuary. Rock Garden with seasonal displays; Laking Garden (herbaceous perennials); Arboretum (world-famous lilacs in late May); Rose Garden; Teaching Garden; woodland, scented and medicinal gardens. At Cootes Paradise Sanctuary trails wind around more than 1,200 acres (486 hectares) of water, marsh and wooded ravines. Mediterranean Garden greenhouse wing has particularly interesting displays (fee). Guided tours (fee). Peak period for gardens: May-Sept. (All yr, daily) Information Centre. 680 Plains Rd W at ON 2, 6 & 403. Phone 905/527-1158. ¢¢

Whitehern. Former home of the McQuesten family; 19th-century Georgian-style mansion furnished with original family possessions. Landscaped gardens. (June-Labour Day, daily; rest of yr, Tues-Sun afternoons; closed Jan 1, Dec 25) Jackson St W & McNab Sts. Phone 905/522-2018. ¢¢

Annual Events

Around the Bay Road Race. Canada's oldest footrace (1894). Phone 905/624-0046. Late Mar.

Hamilton International Air Show. Hamilton Civic Airport. Large international air show. Phone 905/528-4425. Mid-June.

Festival of Friends. Musicians, artists, craftsmen, puppets, dance, mime, theater. Phone 905/525-6644. 2nd wkend Aug.

Festitalia. Opera, concerts, bicycle race, fashion shows, ethnic foods. Phone 905/546-5300. Mid-Sept.

Hamilton Mum Show. Gage Park, in greenhouses. More than 6,000 blooms. Phone 905/546-2866. 1st 2 wks Nov.

Motels

✔★ ★ **ADMIRAL INN.** *(3500 Billings Ct, Burlington ON L7N 3N6) N via Hwy 2/6 or QEW. 905/639-4780; FAX 905/639-1967.* 67 rms, 2 story. S $51.95; D $62.95; each addl $4; under 12 free. Crib free. TV; cable (premium), VCR avail. Restaurant 7 am-11 pm. Bar 11 am-11 pm. Ck-out 11 am. Meeting rms. Business servs avail. Valet serv. Cr cds: A, D, ER, MC, V.

✔★ ★ **ADMIRAL INN.** *(149 Dundurn St N, Hamilton ON L8R 3E7) 905/529-2311; FAX 905/529-9100.* 58 rms, 3 story. S $54.95; D $62.95;

each addl $4; suites $79.95; under 12 free. Crib free. TV; cable (premium), VCR avail. Restaurant 7 am-11 pm. Rm serv. Ck-out 11 am. Meeting rms. Business servs avail. Valet serv. Microwaves avail. Downhill/x-country ski 10 mi. Cr cds: A, D, MC, V.

★ **DAYS INN.** *(1187 Upper James St, Hamilton ON L9C 3B2)* 905/575-9666; FAX 905/575-1098. Web www.daysinn.ca. 30 rms, 2 story. Late May-late Sept: S $55-$65; D $65-$75; each addl $7; under 14 free; lower rates rest of yr. Crib free. TV; cable (premium), VCR avail. Complimentary coffee in lobby. Restaurant 24 hrs. Bar. Ck-out 11 am. Meeting rms. Business servs avail. In-rm modem link. Downhill ski 7 mi. Health club privileges. Some refrigerators; microwaves avail. Cr cds: A, D, DS, ER, MC, V.

★★ **QUALITY INN.** *(175 Main St W, Hamilton ON L8P 1J1)* 905/528-0611; FAX 905/528-1130. Web www.qualityinn.com. 57 rms, 2 story. Apr-Sept: S $49.95-$59.95; D $59.95-$69.95; each addl $8; suite $89.29; under 18 free; wkly, hol rates; higher rates wkends (2-day min); lower rates rest of yr. Crib free. TV. Restaurant 7 am-9 pm. Meeting rms. Business servs avail. In-rm modem link. Downhill/x-country ski 15 mi. Microwaves avail. Cr cds: A, C, D, ER, MC, V.

Motor Hotel

★★ **VENTURE INN-BURLINGTON.** *(2020 Lakeshore Rd, Burlington ON L7S 1Y2)* N via Hwy 2/6 or QEW. 905/681-0762; FAX 905/634-4398; res: 800/486-8873. Web www.jwg.com/ventureinns. 122 rms, 7 story. S $89; D $99; each addl $10; suites $150; under 19 free. Crib free. Pet accepted, some restrictions. TV. Indoor pool; whirlpool, sauna. Continental bkfst. Restaurant adj 7-2 am; Sat, Sun 9-2 am. Bar; live band. Meeting rms. Business servs avail. Valet serv. Sun deck. Picnic tables. Opp lake, beach. Cr cds: A, D, DS, ER, MC, V.

Hotels

★★ **HOWARD JOHNSON ROYAL CONNAUGHT.** *(112 King St E, Hamilton ON L8N 1A8)* 905/546-8111; FAX 905/546-8144. 206 rms, 11 story. S $89-$99, D $99-$109; each addl $10; suites from $139; under 18 free; wkend package. Crib free. Pet accepted. TV; cable (premium), VCR avail. Indoor pool; whirlpool. Coffee in rms. Restaurant 24 hrs. Rm serv 24 hrs. Bars 11-2 am. Ck-out noon. Meeting rms. Business servs avail. Barber, beauty shop. Exercise equipt; weight machine, bicycle, sauna. Some refrigerators, minibars; microwaves avail. 124-ft (38-m) pool slide. Cr cds: A, C, D, DS, ER, MC, V.

✔★★ **RAMADA.** *(150 King St E, Hamilton ON L8N 1B2)* 905/528-3451; FAX 905/522-2281. 215 rms, 12 story. S, D $69-$110; each addl $10; suites $195-$400; under 19 free. Crib free. Pet accepted. TV; cable, VCR avail. Heated pool; wading pool, whirlpool. Restaurant 7:30 am-10 pm. Bar Fri-Sat 5:30 pm- 2 am. Ck-out 11 am. Meeting rms. Business servs avail. Shopping arcade. Barber, beauty shop. Exercise equipt; weights, bicycles, sauna. Health club privileges. Cr cds: A, C, D, DS, ER, JCB, MC, V.

★★★ **SHERATON.** *(116 King St W, Hamilton ON L8P 4V3)* in Lloyd D Jackson Sq. 905/529-5515; FAX 905/529-8266. E-mail shsales@netaccess.on.ca. 299 units, 18 story. S, D $175-$195; each addl $18; suites from $225; under 17 free; wkend rates. Crib free. Pet accepted. Parking $7.99. TV; cable (premium). Indoor pool; whirlpool. Complimentary coffee in rms. Restaurant 6:30 am-10.30 pm. Rm serv to 1 am. Bar 11-2 am; entertainment. Ck-out noon. Convention facilities. Business center. In-rm modem link. Shopping arcade. Barber, beauty shop. Exercise equipt; weights, bicycles, sauna. Downhill/x-country ski 4 mi. Health club privileges. Bathrm phones; microwaves avail. Direct access to Convention Centre & Hamilton Place Concert Hall. Cr cds: A, C, D, DS, ER, JCB, MC, V.

Restaurants

★★★ **ANCASTER OLD MILL INN.** *(548 Old Dundas Rd, Ancaster ON L9G 3J4)* off ON 403 to Mohawk Rd, W, then ½ mi to Old Dundas Rd. 905/648-1827. Continental menu. Specializes in steak, prime rib, fresh seafood. Salad bar. Own baking. Hrs: 11:30 am-2:30 pm, 4:30-8:30 pm; Fri, Sat to 11 pm; Sun to 8 pm; Sun brunch 9 am-2 pm. Res accepted. Bar. Wine list. A la carte entrees: lunch $9.47-$12.97, dinner $12.95-$29.97. Sun brunch $22.97. Child's meals. Pianist wkends. Outdoor dining. Originally a gristmill (1792); tour. Gift shop, bakery. Cr cds: A, ER, MC, V.

★★ **L'ESCARGOT.** *(1375 King St E, Hamilton ON L8M 1H6)* 905/549-6212. French menu. Specializes in venison, salmon, breast of duck. Hrs: 11:30 am-2 pm, 5:30-10:30 pm. Closed Sun, Mon; most major hols. Res accepted. Serv bar. A la carte entrees: lunch $5.95-$10.95, dinner $16.50-$20.95. French Provincial decor. Cr cds: A, MC, V.

★★★ **SHAKESPEARE'S DINING LOUNGE.** *(181 Main St E, Hamilton ON L8N 1H2)* 905/528-0689. Continental menu. Specializes in steak, seafood, wild game. Hrs: noon-2:30 pm, 5-10:30 pm; Sat 5-11 pm. Closed Sun; Jan 1, Dec 25. Res accepted. Bar. A la carte entrees: lunch $6.50-$18.95, dinner $16.95-$38.95. Elizabethan decor; antique reproductions. Family-owned. Cr cds: A, C, D, ER, JCB, MC, V.

★★ **SIRLOIN CELLAR.** *(14½ James St N, Hamilton ON L8R 2J9)* 905/525-8620. Specializes in steak, lobster, fresh seafood. Hrs: 11 am-2:30 pm, 4:30-10 pm; Sat, Sun from 4:30 pm. Closed most major hols. Res accepted. Bar. Semi-a la carte: lunch $7.25-$15.95, dinner $10.95-$32.95. Cr cds: A, D, ER, MC, V.

★ **TOPS 24.** *(1187 Upper James St, Hamilton ON L9C 3B2)* 905/318-1414. Canadian, Greek menu. Specializes in moussaka, shish kebob. Hrs: 11 am-11 pm; Closed Dec 25. Bar. Semi-a la carte: lunch, dinner $3.95-$11.95. Child's meals. Parking. Outdoor dining. Bright, airy dining rm with Mediterranean murals. Cr cds: A, ER, MC, V.

Kenora (E-1)

Founded 1882 **Pop** 9,817 **Elev** 1,348 ft (411 m) **Area code** 807 **E-mail** info@lakeofthewoods.com **Web** www.lakeofthewoods.com

Information Lake of the Woods Visitor Services, 1500 Hwy 17E, P9N 1M3; 807/467-4637 or 800/535-4549.

An attractive and prosperous pulp and paper town, Kenora is also a popular resort center and gateway to both the Lake of the Woods area to the south and the wilderness country to the north. Fishing, hunting, boating, sailing and excellent resort accommodations may be found here, along with 14,500 islands and 65,000 miles (104,600 km) of shoreline on the lake. Winter activities include ice fishing, snowmobiling, downhill and cross-country skiing, curling and hockey. The Harbourfront in downtown Kenora hosts weekend summer festivals. There are many indigenous pictographs in the area. As fly-in capital of the country, many visitors pass through Kenora on the way to the wilderness of the north.

What to See and Do

Lake cruises. Lake Navigation, Ltd. The MS *Kenora* makes three 18-mi (29-km) cruises through the many islands and channels of Lake of the

Woods (daily). Included is Devil's Gap, with its "spirit rock" painting. Lunch, mid-afternoon and dinner cruises. Restaurant, bar. (Mid-May-early Oct, daily) Harbourfront Wharf. Phone 807/468-9124. ¢¢¢¢

Lake of the Woods Museum. Houses more than 15,000 articles reflecting local, native and pioneer history. (July-Aug, daily; Sept-June, Tues-Sat) 300 Main St. Phone 807/467-2105. ¢¢

Rushing River Provincial Park. Approx 400 acres (160 hectares). Beautiful natural setting with a long and photogenic cascade. Swimming; fishing; boating. Nature, cross-country skiing trails. Picnicking, playground. Camping (fee, reservations). Museum (summer, daily). Park (all yr). 12 mi (20 km) E on Hwy 17 & 4 mi (6 km) S on Hwy 71. Phone 807/468-2501 (winter) or 807/548-4351(summer). Per vehicle (summer) ¢¢¢

Stone Consolidated. Paper manufacturing process is followed from debarking of logs to the finished product. Ages 12 yrs and over only. Flat, closed-toe shoes required. (June-Sept, Mon & Wed-Fri, by res only) 504 9th St N. Phone 807/467-3000. **Free.**

Annual Events

ESCAPE (Exciting, Scenic, Canadian/American Powerboat Excursion). Lake of the Woods. Four-day event for powerboats to explore the many channels, islands and historic features of the lake. Canadian & US participants meet in vicinity of Flag Island, MN. Early July.

Kenora International Bass Fishing Tournament. 3-day competition. Early Aug.

Kenora Agricultural Fair. Kenora Recreation Centre Complex. Three days of competitions and cultural exhibitions including a midway show. Mid-Aug.

Motels

★ **COMFORT INN.** *(1230 Hwy 17E, Kenora ON P9N 1L9)* *807/468-8845; FAX 807/468-1588.* 77 rms, 2 story. Mid-June-mid-Sept: S $70-$90; D $75-$100; each addl $4; under 18 free; lower rates rest of yr. Crib free. Pet accepted. TV; cable (premium). Restaurant nearby. Ck-out 11 am. Business servs avail. Cr cds: A, D, DS, ER, MC, V.

D ⟵ ⋈ ⋈ SC

★ ★ **TRAVELODGE.** *(800 Hwy 17E, Kenora ON P9N 1L9)* *807/468-3155; FAX 807/468-4780.* 42 rms, 1-2 story, 5 kits. Mid-June-mid-Sept: S $75-$80; D $75-$104; lower rates rest of yr. Crib $6. Pet accepted. TV; cable (premium). 2 pools, 1 indoor; whirlpool. Playground. Restaurant 6 am-11 pm. Rm serv. Bar 11-1 am. Ck-out noon. Meeting rms. Business servs avail. Valet serv. Downhill/x-country ski 6 mi. Exercise equipt; bicycles, weight machine, sauna. Picnic tables. Cr cds: A, D, DS, ER, JCB, MC, V.

D ⟵ ⋈ ⋈ ⋔ ⋈ ⋈ SC

Hotel

★ ★ **BEST WESTERN LAKESIDE INN.** *(470 1st Ave S, Kenora ON P9N 1N5) just off Hwy 17 on Lake of the Woods.* 807/468-5521; FAX 807/468-4734. 94 rms, 9 story. S $93; D $103; each addl $10; suites $175-$225; under 14 free. Crib avail. Pet accepted. TV; cable (premium), VCR avail. Indoor pool. Complimentary coffee in rms. Restaurant 7 am-10 pm. Bar 11:30-1 am. Ck-out 11 am. Meeting rms. Business servs avail. Downhill/x-country ski 4 mi. Exercise rm; instructor, treadmills, stair machines, sauna. Game rm. Rec rm. Refrigerators avail. Minibar in suites. On lakeshore. Cr cds: A, C, D, DS, ER, JCB, MC, V.

D ⟵ ⋈ ⋈ ⋔ ⋈ ⋈ SC

Kingston (D-9)

(See also Gananoque; also see Alexandria Bay & Clayton, NY)

Founded 1673 **Pop** 55,051 **Elev** 305 ft (93 m) **Area code** 613 **E-mail** tourism@kingstonarea.on.ca **Web** www.kingstonarea.on.ca
Information Tourist Information Office, 209 Ontario St, K7L 2Z1; 613/548-4415 or 888/855-4555.

Kingston is a city rich in tradition, and Kingstonians are justly proud of their city's 300-year history. Since July of 1673, when Count Frontenac, Governor of New France, erected a fort on the site of present-day Kingston, the city has played an important part in Canadian history. It was here that the United Empire Loyalists relocated to begin their new life. Kingston also had the honor of being the capital of the United Provinces from 1841-1844. However, because Kingston was vulnerable to attack by water from the United States, the capital was moved to Montréal, and later to Ottawa. Although Kingston did not retain its position as the capital city, its citizens can boast that it was a Kingstonian, Sir John A. Macdonald, who was the first Prime Minister of Canada and who later became known as the Father of Confederation.

Since Fort Frontenac was built in 1673, Kingston has grown and prospered to become a flourishing city. Yet over the years, Kingston has not lost the charm and grace that are unique to the city. In honor of the centennial year a beautiful waterfront area was created in front of City Hall with a new yacht basin.

Located at the eastern end of Lake Ontario where it empties into the St Lawrence, Kingston is Canada's freshwater sailing capital.

What to See and Do

Bellevue House National Historic Site. Italianate villa (1840) was home of Sir John A. Macdonald, first Prime Minister of Canada. Restored and furnished with period pieces. Modern display and video presentation at Visitor Centre. (Apr-Oct, daily; rest of yr, by appt) 35 Centre St. Phone 613/545-8666. ¢¢

Boat trips.

Island Queen. Showboat of the 1,000 Islands. Offers 3-hr river cruises through the Islands. (May-Oct, daily) Departs from Kingston Harbour, downtown. For information and reservations contact Kingston & The Islands Boatline, 6 Princess St, K7L 1A2; 613/549-5544. ¢¢¢¢

Canadian Empress. This replica of a traditional steamship cruises St Lawrence and Ottawa rivers on 6 different routes; trips span 4 or 5 nights, some reaching Montréal and Québec City. (Mid-May-Nov) Ages 12 & up. Departs from front of City Hall. Contact St Lawrence Cruise Lines, 253 Ontario St, K7L 2Z4; 613/549-8091 or 800/267-7868 (reservations). ¢¢¢¢¢

Canadian Forces Communications & Electronics Museum. Displays history of Canadian Forces branch and aspects of military communications. Collection ranges from early radios to satellites and modern technology; excellent telephone collection. (Mid-May-Labour Day, daily; rest of yr, Mon-Fri; closed hols in winter) Vimy Barracks, 1 mi (1.6 km) E on ON 2. Phone 613/541-5395. **Free.**

City Hall. Built of limestone in 1843-44 while Kingston was the capital of the United Provinces of Canada. (Daily) 216 Ontario St. Phone 613/546-4291. **Free.**

Confederation Tour Trolley. 50-min, 10-mi (16-km) narrated tour of Kingston. (Victoria Day-Labour Day, daily on the hour; charters avail) Leaves from Confederation Park, 209 Ontario St. Phone 613/548-4453. ¢¢¢

Fort Henry. One of Ontario's most spectacular historic sites, the present fortification was built in the 1830s and restored during the 1930s. Guided tour; 19th-century British infantry & artillery drills; military pageantry; exhibits of military arms, uniforms, equipment; garrison life activities. Fort (mid-May-late Sept, daily; closed some hols). E at jct Hwys 2 & 15. Phone 613/542-7388. ¢¢¢

Grand Theatre. Century-old, renovated theater. Live theater, dance, symphonic and children's performances by professional companies and local groups; summer theater (See SEASONAL EVENT). (Daily) 218 Princess St. Phone 613/530-2050.

International Ice Hockey Federation Museum. Displays trace history of hockey from its beginning in Kingston in 1885 to present day. (Mid-June-Labour Day, daily; rest of yr, by appt) 303 York St. Phone 613/544-2355. ¢

MacLachlan Woodworking Museum (ca 1850). "Wood in the service of humanity" is theme of museum; highlights life of the pioneer farmer in both the field and kitchen, as well as workshops of a cooper, blacksmith, cabinetmaker. (Victoria Day-Labour Day, daily; Mar-mid-May, early Sept-Oct, Wed-Sun) 2993 Hwy 2, 10 mi (16 km) E in Grass Creek Park. Phone 613/542-0543. ¢¢

Marine Museum of the Great Lakes at Kingston. Ships have been built in Kingston since 1678. This museum explores the tales, adventures and enterprise of "Inland Seas" history. Ship Building Gallery, 1889 Engine Room, with dry dock engines & pumps; artifacts; changing exhibits. Library & archives. The **Museum Ship *Alexander Henry,*** a 3,000-ton icebreaker, is open for tours and bed & breakfast accommodations (Victoria Day-Thanksgiving). (Apr-Dec, daily; rest of yr, Mon-Fri; closed Dec 25) 55 Ontario St, on the waterfront. Phone 613/542-2261. Each museum   ¢¢ One blk away is

Pump House Steam Museum. Displays on steam technology, model trains, small engines. (June 1-Labour Day, daily) 23 Ontario St. Phone 613/542-2261. ¢¢

Murney Tower Museum (1846). Martello tower is now a museum with exhibits of the area's military and social history. Changing exhibits. (Mid-May-Labour Day, daily) King St at Barrie. Phone 613/544-9925. ¢¢

Queen's University (1841). (13,000 students) Between Barrie, Union, Collingwood & King Sts. For tours phone 613/545-2217. **Free.** On campus are

Agnes Etherington Art Centre. Changing exhibitions of contemporary and historical art. (Daily exc Mon; closed hols) University Ave & Queen's Crescent. Phone 613/545-2190. ¢

Geology Museum. Collection of minerals from around the world. (Mon-Fri; closed hols) Miller Hall on Union St. Phone 613/545-6767. **Free.**

Royal Military College of Canada (1876). (800 students) Canada's first military college and first institution of its kind to achieve university status. E of Kingston Harbour on Hwy 2. On grounds is

Fort Frederick & College Museum. Exhibits depict the history of the college and the earlier Royal Dockyard (1789-1853); Douglas Collection of small arms and weapons that once belonged to General Porfirio Díaz, president of Mexico from 1886-1912. (Late June-Labour Day, daily) In large Martello Tower. Phone 613/541-6664 , 613/541-6652 or 613/541-6000. **Free.**

St Lawrence Islands National Park (see).

Seasonal Event

Kingston Summer Festival. Grand Theatre. Phone 613/530-2050. Late June-Labour Day.

Motels

★ **BEAVER.** *(1488 Hwy 15, Kingston ON K7L 5H6) ¹/₂ mi S of ON 401 exit 623.* 613/546-6674. 22 rms. Mid-June-mid-Sept: S, D $60-$75; each addl $5; kit. units $10 addl; lower rates rest of yr. Crib $5. TV. Heated pool. Playground. Restaurant 7 am-7 pm. Ck-out 11 am. Sundries. Some refrigerators. Picnic tables, grills. Cr cds: MC, V.

⌦ 🏊

★ ★ **BEST WESTERN FIRESIDE INN.** *(1217 Princess St (Hwy 2), Kingston ON K7M 3E1)* 613/549-2211; FAX 613/549-4523. 75 rms, 2 story. S, D $96.50-$139; each addl $10; under 17 free; suites $179-$429. Crib free. TV; cable (premium). Heated pool. Restaurant 7 am-11 pm. Rm serv. Bar 11:30-1 am. Ck-out noon. Meeting rms. Business servs avail.

In-rm modem link. Valet serv. Sundries. Fireplaces; some in-rm whirlpools. Cr cds: A, C, D, DS, ER, MC, V.

🏊 🏖 SC

✔★ **ECONO LODGE.** *(2327 Princess St (Hwy 2), Kingston ON K7M 3G1)* 613/531-8929. 32 rms, 8 kits. May-Labour Day: S $48; D $58-$78; each addl $4; kit. units $4 addl; lower rates rest of yr. Crib $4. Pet accepted; $12/day. TV; cable. Heated pool. Playground. Complimentary coffee in lobby. Restaurant adj 7 am-9 pm. Ck-out 11 am. Refrigerators. Picnic tables. Grills. Cr cds: A, C, D, ER, MC, V.

D 🐾 🏊 🏖 SC

★ ★ **FIRST CANADA INN.** *(First Canada Court, Kingston ON K7K 6W2)* Hwy 401 exit 617 S. 613/541-1111; FAX 613/549-5735; res: 800/267-7899. 74 rms, 2 story. June-Oct 1: S $53.95-$69.95; D $60.95-$76.95; each addl $5; suites $85.95-$125.95; under 12 free; lower rates rest of yr. Crib free. Pet accepted. TV; cable, VCR avail (movies). Complimentary continental bkfst. Complimentary coffee in rms. Restaurant opp 10-2 am. Bar 4 pm-1 am. Coin lndry. Meeting rms. Business servs avail. Refrigerators. Cr cds: A, D, ER, MC, V.

D 🐾 🏊 🏖 SC

★ ★ **GREEN ACRES.** *(2480 Princess St (Hwy 2), Kingston ON K7M 3G4)* 613/546-1796; FAX 613/542-5521; res: 800/267-7889. 32 rms, 3 kits. July-Aug: S $74-$99; D $77-$109; each addl $6; kit. suites $175; lower rates rest of yr. Crib $6. TV; cable. Heated pool. Playground. Continental bkfst. Coffee in rms. Ck-out 11 am. Coin lndry. Meeting rm. Valet serv. X-country ski 10 mi. Lawn games. Refrigerators. Whirlpool in suites. Picnic tables, gas grill. Cr cds: A, MC, V.

🏊 🏊 🏖 SC

★ **SEVEN OAKES.** *(2331 Princess St (Hwy 2), Kingston ON K7M 3G1)* 613/546-3655; FAX 613/549-5677. 40 rms. June-Oct 1: S $64; D $68-$74; each addl $5; package plans; lower rates rest of yr. Crib free. Pet accepted. Heated pool; whirlpool. Sauna. Playground. Bar. Ck-out 11 am. Coin lndry. Sundries. Lighted tennis. Refrigerators; some in-rm whirlpools. Picnic tables, grills. Cr cds: A, D, DS, ER, MC, V.

🐾 🎿 🏊 🏖 SC

Lodge

★ ★ ★ **ISAIAH TUBBS RESORT.** *(RR 1, West Lake Rd, Picton ON K0K 2T0)* Approx 40 mi W on Hwy 33 and County Rd 12. 613/393-2090; FAX 613/393-1291; res: 800/267-0525. 60 rms in lodge, inn, many A/C, 12 kit. cabins. No phone in cabins. July-Labour Day: S $95-$200; D $150-$220; each addl $10; kit. suites $150-$200; cabins $650-$900/wk; under 5 free; MAP, conference plan avail; lower rates rest of yr. Crib free. TV. 2 pools, 1 indoor; whirlpool. Playground. Free supervised child's activities (July-Aug); ages 4-12. Dining rm 8-1 am. Bar. Ck-out 11 am, ck-in 4 pm. Coin lndry. Meeting rms. Business servs avail. Tennis. Swimming beach. X-country ski 1 mi. Lawn games. Exercise equipt; weights, treadmill, sauna. Some refrigerators. Picnic tables, grills. On West Lake, adj Sandbanks Provincial Park. Cr cds: A, D, ER, MC, V.

D 🐾 🎿 🏊 🏃 🏖 SC

Motor Hotels

★ ★ **HOWARD JOHNSON CONFEDERATION PLACE.** *(237 Ontario St, Kingston ON K7L 2Z4)* 613/549-6300; FAX 613/549-1508. 94 rms, 6 story. May-late Sept: S, D $99-$160; each addl $10; suites $225-$250; under 18 free; higher rates special events; lower rates rest of yr. Crib free. Pet accepted. TV; cable. Heated pool; whirlpool, poolside serv. Restaurant 7 am-10 pm. Rm serv. Ck-out 11 am. Meeting rms. Business servs avail. Underground free parking. Exercise equipt; weight machine, bicycles. X-country ski 3 mi. On waterfront. Cr cds: A, D, DS, ER, MC, V.

🐾 🏊 🏃 🏖 🏊 SC

✔★ ★ **TRAVELODGE HOTEL LA SALLE.** *(2360 Princess St (Hwy 2), Kingston ON K7M 3G4)* 613/546-4233. 69 rms, 4 story. May-mid-Sept: S, D $72-$90; under 12 free; lower rates rest of yr. Crib free. TV;

cable, VCR avail. Indoor pool. Playground. Restaurant 6 am-10 pm. Rm serv. Bar 11 am-11 pm. Ck-out noon. Meeting rms. Business servs avail. Sundries. Balconies. Cr cds: A, D, DS, ER, MC, V.

Inns

★ ★ ★ **HOCHELAGA.** (24 Sydenham St S, Kingston ON K7L 3G9) 613/549-5534; FAX 613/549-5534; res: 800/267-0525. 23 rms, 3 story. S, D $135-$145; each addl $10; under 5 free; lower rates rest of yr. Crib free. TV; cable (premium). Complimentary continental bkfst. Restaurant nearby. Ck-out 11 am, ck-in 3 pm. Business servs avail. Some balconies. Renovated house (1872); period antiques. Cr cds: A, D, ER, MC, V.

★ ★ **MERRILL.** (343 Main St E, Picton ON K0K 2T0) Approx 40 mi W on Hwy 33 to Hwy 49 (Main St). 613/476-7451; FAX 613/476-8283; res: 800/567-5969. 14 rms, 3 story, 2 suites. No elvtr. July-Sept: S, D $85-$125; each addl $10; suites $125; under 3 free; lower rates rest of yr. Crib free. TV; cable (premium). Complimentary continental bkfst. Restaurant 11 am-11 pm. Ck-out 11 am, ck-in 3 pm. Meeting rm. Lawn games. Rms individually decorated with period antiques. Brick Victorian house (ca 1878); built for Edwards Merrill, one of Canada's top barristers. Cr cds: A, D, ER, MC, V.

★ ★ ★ **ROSEMOUNT INN.** (46 Sydenham St S, Kingston ON K7L 3H1) 613/531-8844; FAX 613/531-9722. 8 rms, 2 story. No A/C. No rm phones. S, D $99-$159; each addl $30; wkends, hols (2-day min). Closed Mid-Dec-early Jan. Children over 13 yrs only. Complimentary full bkfst; afternoon refreshments. Ck-out 11 am, ck-in 4 pm. Business servs avail. Luggage handling. Valet serv. Concierge serv. Gift shop. Some street parking. X-country ski 5 mi. Massage. Fireplace. Built in 1850. Victorian decor; antiques. Totally nonsmoking. Cr cds: A, MC, V.

Restaurant

★ ★ **AUNT LUCY'S.** (1399 Princess St (Hwy 2), Kingston ON) 613/542-2729. Specializes in steak, seafood, pasta. Hrs: 11:30 am-11 pm. Bar. Semi-a la carte: lunch, dinner $5.95-$19.95. Sun brunch $10.99. Child's meals. Open-hearth grill. Family-owned. Cr cds: A, MC, V.

Kitchener-Waterloo (E-6)

Pop Kitchener, 139,734; Waterloo, 49,428 **Elev** Kitchener, 1,100 ft (335 m); Waterloo, 1,075 ft (328 m) **Area code** 519
Information Visitor & Convention Bureau, 2848 King St E, Kitchener N2A 1A5; 519/748-0800 or 800/265-6959.

The twin cities of Kitchener-Waterloo were settled in the early 1800s by Mennonites, Amish and Germans whose cultural heritage is still clearly visible. Not far to the north in Elmira is the heart of Ontario's Pennsylvania German country, with Maple Sugar Festival and tours of Mennonite country. Although Kitchener and Waterloo are separate cities, each takes pride in the achievements of the other. A vigorous spirit of youth and industry pervades both cities, making a visit to the Kitchener-Waterloo area a pleasure for any traveler.

What to See and Do

Bingeman Park. Recreation center on banks of Grand River; swimming (pool, wave pool), watersliding, bumper boats; go-cart track, arcade, roller skating, miniature golf, golf driving range; batting cages; cross-country skiing; picnicking, restaurant; playground; camping. Park (summer, daily; also spring & fall, weather permitting). Campgrounds & restaurant (all yr, daily). Fee for some activities. 1380 Victoria St N, Kitchener. Phone 519/744-1555.

Doon Heritage Crossroads. Re-creation of early 20th-century village (ca 1915) includes museum, grocery store, post office/tailor shop, blacksmith, church, two farms and several houses. (May-late Dec, daily; closed Dec 23) Hwy 401 exit 275, Homer Watson Blvd. Phone 519/748-1914 or 519/575-4530. ¢¢¢

Farmers' Market. More than 100 vendors sell fresh produce, meat, cheese and handicrafts. Mennonite specialties featured. (All yr, Sat; mid-May-mid-Oct, also Wed). Market Square, Frederick & Duke Sts, downtown Kitchener. Phone 519/741-2287. **Free.**

Glockenspiel. Canada's first glockenspiel tells fairy tale of Snow White. Twenty-three bells form the carillon. Performance lasts 15 min (4 times daily). King & Benton Sts.

Joseph Schneider Haus. Pennsylvania German Mennonite house (1820), one of area's oldest homesteads, restored and furnished; "living" museum with costumed interpreters; daily demonstrations. Adj Heritage Galleries, including Germanic folk art; exhibits change every 3 months. (Victoria Day-Labour Day, daily; rest of yr, daily exc Mon; closed Jan 1, Dec 25, 26) 466 Queen St S, Kitchener. Phone 519/742-7752. ¢

Kitchener-Waterloo Art Gallery. Six exhibition areas cover all aspects of the visual arts. Gift shop. (Daily exc Mon; closed major hols) 101 Queen St N, at The Centre in the Square. Phone 519/579-5860. **Free.**

Laurel Creek Conservation Area. Approx 750 acres (305 hectares) of multipurpose area. Dam, swimming beach, boating (no motors), hiking, sports fields, camping (fee), picnicking, reforested areas and bird-watching. (May-mid-Oct) NW corner of Waterloo, bounded by Westmount Rd, Conservation Dr & Beaver Creek Rd. Phone 519/884-6620. ¢¢

⭐ **Museum & Archive of Games.** Collection includes over 3,500 games. Many "hands-on" exhibits drawn from collection ranging from Inuit bone games to computer games. Exhibits change every 4 months. Archive contains documents pertaining to games and game-playing. (Tues-Thurs & Sun; closed univ hols) B.C. Matthews Hall, University of Waterloo. Phone 519/888-4424. **Free.**

The Seagram Museum. Complex is housed in century-old, renovated barrel warehouse and is devoted to history and technology of the wine and spirits industry; restaurant. (May-Dec, daily; rest of yr, daily exc Mon; closed Jan 1, Dec 25) 57 Erb St W, Waterloo. Phone 519/885-1857 or 800/465-8747. **Free.**

Waterloo Park. Log cabin schoolhouse built 1820 surrounded by picnic area and lake; playground. Small zoo and band concerts in summer (Sun). Central St, Waterloo. Phone 519/747-8733. (See ANNUAL EVENTS) **Free.**

Woodside National Historic Site. 528 Wellington St N, Kitchener. Boyhood home of William Lyon Mackenzie King, Canada's 10th prime minister. 1890s Victorian restoration. Interpretive center has theater and display on King's early life and career. Picnicking. (May-Dec, daily; closed winter hols) Phone 519/742-5273. **Free.** Nearby is

Pioneer Memorial Tower. Tribute to industrious spirit of pioneers who first settled Waterloo County. Cemetery on grounds includes graves of several original founders. Excellent view of Grand River. (May-Oct) **Free.**

Annual Events

Waterloo County Quilt Festival. Quilt exhibits, displays, workshops and demonstrations. Phone 800/265-6959. 9 days mid-May.

Sounds of Summer Music Festival. Waterloo Park. 3 days mid-June.

White Owl Culture Pow-Wow. Celebration of North American Aboriginal Culture in Waterloo Park. Phone 519/743-8635. Mid-June.

Busker Carnival Festival. International showcase of street performers. Phone 519/747-8738. Late Aug.

Wellesley Apple Butter & Cheese Festival. Pancake breakfast, farmers' market; free tours of farms, cider mill; horseshoe tournament, quilt auction, smorgasbord dinner, model boat regatta, antique cars & tractors. Phone 519/656-2222. Last Sat Sept.

Motels

★ **COMFORT INN.** (220 Holiday Inn Dr, Cambridge ON N3C 1Z4) ON 401 exit ON 24 N. 519/658-1100; FAX 519/658-6979; res: 800/228-5150. 84 rms, 2 story. S $59-$80; D $67-$95; each addl $4; under 18 free. Crib free. Pet accepted. TV; cable (premium), VCR avail. Complimentary coffee in lobby. Ck-out 11 am. Business servs avail. Sundries. Downhill/x-country ski 4 mi. Cr cds: A, C, D, DS, ER, JCB, MC, V.

⛵ ≋ ✕ 🔥 SC

★ **DAYS INN.** (650 Hespeler Rd, Cambridge ON N1R 6J8) S on ON 24, off Hwy 401. 519/622-1070; FAX 519/622-1512. 119 rms, 2 story. S $69.95; D $74.95; each addl $7; under 18 free. Crib free. Pet accepted. TV; cable (premium), VCR avail. Heated pool. Playground. Ck-out 11 am. Meeting rms. Business servs avail. Valet serv. Sundries. Microwaves avail. Cr cds: A, D, ER, MC, V.

⛵ ≋ ✕ 🔥 SC

★ **NEWBURG INN.** (Hwy 7 & 8 West, New Hamburg ON N0B 2G0) 10 mi W on ON 7, at ON 8. 519/662-3990. 12 rms. S $50; D $75; each addl $5; suite $75; monthly rates. TV; cable. Complimentary coffee in lobby. Restaurant nearby. Ck-out 11 am. Some refrigerators. Cr cds: A, MC, V.

🔥

Motor Hotels

★★ **CLARION INN.** (1333 Weber St E, Kitchener ON N2A 1C2) 519/893-1234; FAX 519/893-2100. 102 rms, 2-4 story. S $89-$109; D $99-$129; each addl $8; under 18 free; higher rates Oktoberfest. Crib free. Pet accepted, some restrictions; $50 refundable. TV; cable, VCR avail. Heated pool; whirlpool, sauna, poolside serv. Complimentary coffee in rms. Retaurant 7 am-9 pm. Rm serv. Bar 11-1 am; entertainment Thurs-Sat. Ck-out 11:30 am. Meeting rms. Business center. Sundries. Some refrigerators; microwaves avail. Balconies. Cr cds: A, C, D, DS, ER, MC, V.

D ⛵ ≋ ✕ 🔥 SC 🚶

★★ **HOLIDAY INN.** (30 Fairway Rd S, Kitchener ON N2A 2N2) 519/893-1211; FAX 519/894-8518. 182 rms, 2-6 story. S $119.95-$139.95, D $129.95-$149.95; each addl $10; suites $195.95-$295.95; under 19 free. Crib free. Pet accepted. TV; cable (premium). Indoor/outdoor pool; poolside serv. Supervised child's activities (July-Aug). Restaurant 6:30 am-10 pm. Bar 11-1 am. Ck-out noon. Meeting rms. Business center. In-rm modem link. Valet serv. Downhill/x-country ski 2 mi. Exercise equipt; weight machine, bicycles. Microwaves avail. Private patios, balconies. Cr cds: A, C, D, DS, ER, JCB, MC, V.

D ⛵ ≈ ≋ ✕ ✕ 🔥 SC 🚶

★★ **WATERLOO INN.** (475 King St N, Waterloo ON N2J 2Z5) 1 mi N on ON 86. 519/884-0220; FAX 519/884-0321; res: 800/361-4708. Web www.nrzone.com/waterlooinn/. 160 rms, 4 story. S $93; D $103; each addl $12; suites from $165; under 16 free. Crib free. Pet accepted. TV; cable. Indoor pool; whirlpool, poolside serv. Complimentary coffee in rms. Restaurant 7 am-10 pm. Rm serv. Bar 11-1 am. Convention facilities. Business servs avail. In-rm modem link. Valet serv. Sundries. Downhill ski 10 mi; x-country ski ½ mi. Exercise equipt; weights, bicycles, sauna. Game rm. Balconies. Landscaped courtyard. Cr cds: A, D, DS, ER, MC, V.

D ⛵ ≋ ≈ ✕ ✕ 🔥 SC

Hotels

★★★ **FOUR POINTS BY SHERATON.** (105 King St E, Kitchener ON N2G 2K8) at Benton. 519/744-4141; FAX 519/578-6889. 202 rms, 9 story. S, D $119-$139; each addl $10; suites $130-$269; studio rms $79; under 18 free. wkend package. Crib free. Pet accepted, some restrictions. TV; cable, VCR avail. Pool; whirlpool, poolside serv. Supervised child's activities; ages 6-16. Complimentary coffee in rms. Restaurant 6:30 am-2 pm, 5:30-10:30 pm. Bar 5 pm-1 am; entertainment. Ck-out noon. Meeting

rms. Business center. In-rm modem link. Free covered parking. Downhill/x-country ski 4 mi. Exercise rm; instructor, weights, treadmill, sauna. Game rm. Miniature golf. Rec rm. Minibars; microwaves avail. Some balconies. Cr cds: A, C, D, ER, MC, V.

D ⛵ ≋ ≈ ✕ ✕ 🔥 SC 🚶

★★★ **LANGDON HALL.** (RR 33, Cambridge ON N3H 4R8) E on Hwy 8 to Fountain St, turn right to Blair Rd then left to Langdon. 519/740-2100; FAX 519/740-8161; res: 800/268-1898. E-mail langdon@golden .net. 43 rms, 3 story. 2-day min: S, D $199-$269; suites $369. Crib $25. Pet accepted, some restrictions; $25. TV; cable (premium), VCR avail. Heated pool; whirlpool, poolside serv. Complimentary continental bkfst. Restaurant (see LANGDON HALL). Rm serv 24 hrs. Bar. Ck-out noon. Meeting rms. Business servs avail. In-rm modem link. Gift shop. Tennis. Downhill ski 4 mi; x-country ski on site. Hiking trail. Exercise equipt; weights, bicycles, sauna, steam rm. Massage. Rec rm. Lawn games. Balconies. Antebellum-style building in rural setting. Cr cds: A, D, ER, MC, V.

D ⛵ ≋ 🏃 ≈ ✕ ✕ 🔥

★★ **SUPER 8.** (730 Hespeler Rd, Cambridge ON N3H 5L8) S on Hwy 24, at Hwy 401. 519/623-4600; FAX 519/623-2688. 106 rms, 7 story, 11 suites. S $69.88; D $73.88; each addl $10; suites $83.88; under 12 free; wkly rates; higher rates Octoberfest. Crib free. TV; cable (premium). Indoor pool; whirlpool, sauna. Complimentary continental bkfst. Coffee in rms. Restaurant nearby. Ck-out 11 am. Coin lndry. Meeting rms. Business servs avail. In-rm modem link. Downhill/x-country ski 5 mi. Game rm. Refrigerators; microwaves avail. Cr cds: A, D, DS, ER, MC, V.

D ≋ ≈ ✕ 🔥 SC

★★ **WALPER TERRACE.** (1 King St W, Kitchener ON N2G 1A1) At Queen St. 519/745-4321; res: 800/265-8749; FAX 519/745-3625. 59 rms, 5 story, 20 suites. S, D $99; each addl $10; suites $99-$210; under 13 free; wkend rates. Crib free. TV; cable (premium), VCR avail. Complimentary coffee in rms. Restaurant 7:30-1 am. Bar from 11:30 am. Ck-out noon. Business servs avail. Concierge. Barber, beauty shop. Free valet parking. Health club privileges. Microwaves avail. Restored landmark hotel in the heart of downtown; retains air of old-fashioned elegance. Cr cds: A, D, ER, MC, V.

✕ ✕ SC

Inn

★★★ **ELORA MILL.** (77 Mill St W, Elora ON N0B 1S0) 12 mi N. 519/846-5356; FAX 519/846-9180. 32 rms, 5 story, 5 suites. S, D $135-$150; each addl $50; suites $200; under 13, $25. TV; cable. Complimentary full bkfst. Restaurant (see ELORA MILL). Bar 4:30 pm-1 am. Ck-out 11:30 am, ck-in 4 pm. Meeting rm. Business center. Valet serv. X-country ski 1 mi. Health club privileges. Some refrigerators, fireplaces. Located in historic pre-Confederation village. Cr cds: A, ER, MC, V.

≈ ✕ 🚶

Restaurants

★ **BARRELS.** (95 Queen St S, Kitchener ON N2G 1W1) 519/745-4451. Portuguese, Thai menu. Specialties: mussels, piglet, pepper steak. Hrs: 11:30 am-2 pm, 5-10:30 pm. Closed Mon; Dec 24, 25. Res accepted. Bar. A la carte entrees: lunch $6.50-$7.95, dinner $10.95-$18. Cr cds: A, D, ER, MC, V.

★★ **BENJAMIN'S.** (17 King St, St Jacobs ON N0B 2N0) N on Hwy 86. 519/664-3731. Continental menu. Specializes in beef, pasta, seafood. Hrs: 11:30 am-3 pm, 3-5 pm (tea), 5-9 pm; Fri, Sat to 10 pm. Closed Jan 1, Dec 25, 26. Res accepted. Bar. A la carte entrees: lunch $5.95-$8.95, dinner $10.95-$18. Re-creation of 1850s country inn; fireplace, artifacts. Cr cds: A, D, ER, MC, V.

★ ★ ★ **CHARCOAL STEAK HOUSE.** *(2980 King St E, Kitchener ON N2A 1A9) 519/893-6570.* Specializes in steak, spareribs, pigtails. Own baking. Hrs: 11:30-1 am; Sat from noon; Sun 10 am-11 pm. Res accepted. Bar. Wine list. A la carte entrees: lunch $4.95-$16.95, dinner $10.99-$29.99. Child's meals. Parking. Cr cds: A, C, D, ER, MC, V.

★ ★ **ELORA MILL.** *(See Elora Mill Inn) 519/846-5356.* Regional menu. Own baking. Hrs: 8-10 am, 11:30 am-2 pm, 5-8 pm; Fri, Sat to 9 pm. Res accepted. Bar. A la carte entrees: bkfst $7.95, lunch $8.95-$13.95, dinner $18-$28.50. Parking. Restored gristmill (1859). Cr cds: A, MC, V.

✔★ ★ **KNOTTY PINE.** *(115 Fountain St, Cambridge ON) 519/653-5709.* Web www.knottypine.on.ca. Specialty: roast prime rib of beef. Hrs: 7:30 am-11 pm; Sun 10 am-10 pm. Closed Dec 25, 26. Res accepted. Bar. A la carte entrees: lunch $4.50-$9, dinner $6.75-$11.99. Child's meals. Parking. Rustic; overlooks park and Speed River. Family-owned. Cr cds: A, MC, V.

D **SC** 🛳

★ ★ **LANGDON HALL.** *(See Langdon Hall Hotel) 519/740-2100.* E-mail langdon@golden.net. Specialties: goat cheeze quenelle, roasted veal with tarragon, twice-cooked duck. Hrs: 7-10 am, noon-2 pm, 6-9 pm. Res required. Bar noon-1 am. Wine cellar. A la carte entrees: bkfst $4.75-$7.25, lunch $12.50-$18.50, dinner $12.50-$34. Parking. Outdoor dining. Elegant dining rm overlooking park. Gardens. Cr cds: A, D, ER, MC, V.

D

★ ★ **STONE CROCK.** *(59 Church St W, Elmira ON N3B 1M8) 9 mi N on Hwy 86. 519/669-1521.* Specializes in spareribs, turkey, cabbage rolls. Salad bar. Hrs: 7 am-8:30 pm; Sun from 11 am. Closed Dec 25. Semi-a la carte: bkfst $1.75-$5.75, lunch $5-$9.50, dinner $10.15-$15.25. Buffet: dinner $13.25. Sat, Sun brunch $10.95. Child's meals. Parking. Country atmosphere. Gift shop. Cr cds: MC, V.

★ ★ **SWISS CASTLE INN.** *(1508 King St E, Kitchener ON N2G 2P1) 519/744-2391.* Web www.cyberdineout.com. Swiss, continental menu. Specializes in Wienerschnitzel, lobster tail. Own baking. Hrs: 11:30 am-2:30 pm, 4:30-9:30 pm; Sat from 5 pm; Sun 4:30-8 pm; early-bird dinner 4:30-6 pm. Closed major hols. Res accepted. Bar. Wine list. Semi-a la carte: lunch $5.99-$9.95, dinner $9.95-$19.95. Child's meals. Parking. Fireplace. Swiss bell collection. Cr cds: A, D, ER, MC, V.

SC 🛳

★ ★ ★ **WATERLOT.** *(17 Huron St, New Hamburg ON N0B 2G0) 11 mi W via ON 8, behind Royal Bank. 519/662-2020.* French menu. Specializes in crab crêpes, duckling. Own baking. Hrs: 11:30 am-2 pm, 5-8:30 pm; Sun 5-7:30 pm; Sun brunch (2 sittings) 11:30 am, 1:30 pm. Closed Mon; Good Friday, Dec 25. Res accepted. Bar. Wine list. A la carte entrees: lunch $6.95-$8.95, dinner $15.50-$24.95. Complete meals: dinner (Sun-Fri) $24. Sun brunch $16.95. Child's meals. Victorian house (1845); guest rms avail. Cr cds: A, D, ER, MC, V.

D 🛳

London (E-5)

Pop 300,000 (est) **Elev** 912 ft (278 m) **Area code** 519

Information Visitors and Convention Services, 300 Dufferin Ave, N6B 1Z2; 519/661-5000 or 800/265-2602.

Called the "Forest City," London is a busy modern city with charming small-town atmosphere. Located on the Thames River, its street names are similar to those of the other London. A contrast of Victorian architecture and contemporary skyscrapers is prevalent here.

What to See and Do

Double-decker Bus Tour of London. Two-hr guided tour aboard authentic double-decker English bus with stop at Storybook Gardens in Springbank Park and Regional Art Museum. Departs City Hall (Wellington St and Dufferin Ave). (July-Labour Day, daily) Reservations suggested. Phone 519/661-5000. ¢¢¢

Eldon House (1834). Oldest house in town; occupied by same family until donated to the city. Furnished much as it was in the 19th century with many antiques from abroad. Spacious grounds, lawns, brick paths, gardens, conservatory-greenhouse. Guided tours (by appt). (Daily exc Mon; closed Dec 25) 481 Ridout St N. Phone 519/661-5169. ¢¢

Fanshawe Pioneer Village. Living history museum of 24 buildings moved to this site to display artifacts & re-create the life of a typical 19th-century crossroads community in southwestern Ontario. Log cabin, barns and stable; blacksmith, weaver, harness, gun, woodworking and barbershops; general store, church, fire hall, school and sawmill; costumed interpreters. (May-Dec, daily) Also at Fanshawe Conservation Area is Ontario's largest flood-control structure; swimming, sailing, fishing (walleye), camping, various sports activities and nature trails. NE edge of town; E end of Fanshawe Park Rd. Phone 519/457-1296. ¢¢

Grand Theatre. Contemporary facade houses 1901 theater, built by Colonel Whitney of Detroit and Ambrose Small of Toronto. Restored interior, proscenium arch, murals and cast plasterwork. Professional stock theater (Oct-May). 471 Richmond St. Phone 519/672-8800.

Guy Lombardo Music Centre. Institution housing artifacts belonging to world-famous London-born musician. Exhibits on other big-band era greats. (Mid-May-early Sept, daily) 205 Wonderland Rd S, in Springbank Park. Phone 519/473-9003. ¢

London Museum of Archaeology. Traces prehistory of southwestern Ontario; more than 40,000 artifacts show how indigenous people lived thousands of yrs before Columbus was born; archaeological and ethnographic exhibits from southwestern Ontario. Gallery, theater and native gift shop. (Daily; closed Good Friday, Dec 25) 1600 Attawandaron Rd. Phone 519/473-1360. ¢¢   Also here is

Indian Village. Ongoing excavation and reconstruction of authentic 500-yr-old Neutral village located on original site. (Admission included in Museum fee; May-Oct, daily)

London Regional Art and Historical Museums. Changing exhibits on art, history and culture of the London area; regional, national and international art. (Daily exc Mon; closed Dec 25) 421 Ridout St N. Phone 519/672-4580. **Free.**

London Regional Children's Museum. Hands-on galleries allow children to explore, touch and discover. There are artifacts to touch, costumes to put on, and crafts to make. Children learn about their world, past, present and future; also special events. (Daily; closed Jan 1, Dec 25) 21 Wharncliffe Rd S. Phone 519/434-5726. ¢¢

Ska Nah Doht Indian Village. Re-created Iroquoian village depicting native culture in southwestern Ontario 800-1,000 yrs ago. Guided tours; slide shows, displays; nature trails; picnicking, group camping. Park (daily). Resource Centre & Village (Victoria Day-Labour Day, daily; rest of yr, Mon-Fri). 20 mi (32 km) W via ON 2 in the Longwoods Road Conservation Area. Phone 519/264-2420. Per vehicle ¢¢¢

Storybook Gardens. Family-oriented theme park, children's playworld and zoo, 8 acres (3 hectares) within London's largest park of 281 acres (114 hectares). (Early May-mid-Oct, daily) Springbank Park, Thames River Valley. Phone 519/661-5770. ¢¢

The Royal Canadian Regiment Museum. Displays include artifacts, battle scenes from 1883 to present, weapons and uniforms. (Daily exc Mon; closed hols) Wolseley Hall, Canadian Forces Base. Phone 519/660-5102 or 519/660-5173. **Free.**

Annual Events

London International Air Show. Airport. Flying exhibitions (2-hr show); ground displays. 1st wkend June.

Home County Folk Festival. Victoria Park. 3-day outdoor music fest. Mid-July.

Western Fair. Western Fairgrounds. Entertainment and educational extravaganza; horse shows, musicians, exhibits, livestock shows. 10 days early Sept.

Panorama Ethnic Festival. Throughout city. Open house of ethnic clubs; music, dance, food, crafts. 3 days late Sept.

Motels

★ ★ **BEST WESTERN LAMPLIGHTER INN.** *(591 Wellington Rd, London ON N6C 4R3)* 519/681-7151; FAX 519/681-3271. 126 rms, 2 story. S $67-$150; D $78-$150; each addl $8; suites $85-$200; under 12 free. Pet accepted, some restrictions. TV; cable. Pool. Complimentary coffee in rms. Restaurant 6:30 am-9 pm; Sun to 8 pm. Bar 4 pm-midnight. Ck-out 11 am. Meeting rms. Business servs avail. Some in-rm whirlpools. Private patios, balconies. Picnic tables. Cr cds: A, D, DS, ER, MC, V.

D ⮌ ≋ ✕ 🛇 SC

✔★ **HOLIDAY INN EXPRESS.** *(800 Exeter Rd, London ON N6E 1L5)* exit ON 401 at Wellington Rd N. 519/681-1200; FAX 519/681-6988. 125 rms, 2-3 story, 32 suites. S, D $72-$84; each addl $5; under 19 free; suites $91. Crib free. TV; cable (premium), VCR. Complimentary bkfst. Restaurant adj 7 am-midnight. Ck-out 11 am. Meeting rms. Business servs avail. Microwaves avail. Cr cds: A, D, DS, ER, MC, V.

D ✕ 🛇 SC

★ ★ **RAMADA INN-401.** *(817 Exeter Rd, London ON N6E 1W1)* at ON 401 interchange 186 N. 519/681-4900; FAX 519/681-5065. 124 rms, 2 story. S, D $95-$105; each addl $10; suites $175-$225; under 18 free. Crib free. TV; cable. Indoor pool; sauna, lifeguard in summer. Complimentary coffee in rms. Restaurant 6:30 am-11 pm; Sat, Sun from 7 am. Rm serv. Bar 11-1 am. Ck-out 1 pm. Meeting rms. Business servs avail. Valet serv. Sundries. Health club privileges. Microwaves avail. Cr cds: A, C, D, DS, ER, JCB, MC, V.

D ≋ ✕ 🛇 SC

Hotels

★ ★ ★ **DELTA LONDON ARMOURIES.** *(325 Dundas St, London ON N6B 1T9)* 519/679-6111; FAX 519/679-3957. 250 rms, 20 story. S $155-$175; D $165-$185; each addl $10; suites $250-$450; under 18 free; wkend rates. Crib free. Pet accepted. TV; cable (premium), VCR avail (movies). Indoor pool; whirlpool, wading pool. Supervised child's activities (July & Aug, daily; rest of yr, Sat, Sun); ages 5-12. Coffee in rms. Restaurant 6:30 am-10 pm. Bar to 1 am. Ck-out noon. Meeting rms. Business center. Concierge. Valet parking. Putting green. Exercise equipt; weights, bicycles, sauna. Health club privileges. Rec rm. Minibars. Some balconies. Luxury level. Cr cds: A, C, D, DS, ER, MC, V.

D ⮌ ≋ 🏋 ✕ 🛇 SC ⮌

★ ★ ★ **WESTIN.** *(300 King St, London ON N6B 1S2)* 519/439-1661; FAX 519/439-9672. Web www.westin.com. 322 rms, 22 story. S, D $110-$130; suites $240; under 18 free; wkend rates. Crib free. Pet accepted. TV; cable, VCR avail. Heated pool; wading pool, whirlpool, poolside serv. Restaurant 7 am-11 pm. Bar 11:30-1 am; entertainment. Ck-out 1 pm. Convention facilities. Business servs avail. In-rm modem link. Concierge. Gift shop. Exercise equipt; weights, bicycles, sauna. Health club privileges. Minibars. Luxury level. Cr cds: A, C, D, DS, ER, JCB, MC, V.

D ⮌ ≋ 🏋 ✕ 🛇 SC

Inn

★ ★ ★ **IDLEWYLD.** *(36 Grand Ave, London ON N6C 1K8)* 519/433-2891; res: 800/267-0525. 27 rms, 8 suites. S, D $89-$110; each addl $10; suites $119-$169; under 8 free; wkly rates. Crib free. TV; cable (premium). Complimentary continental bkfst. Ck-out noon, ck-in 3 pm. Business servs avail. In-rm modem link. X-country ski 3 mi. Some balconies. Picnic tables. Victorian mansion (1878); some original decor. Cr cds: A, D, ER, MC, V.

D 🕿 ✕ 🛇 SC

Restaurants

✔★ **FELLINI KOOLINI'S.** *(153 Albert St, London ON N6A 1L9)* 519/642-2300. Italian menu. Specializes in pizza, pasta. Hrs: 11 am-10 pm; Fri, Sat to midnight; Sun 4:30-10:30 pm. Closed Jan 1, Dec 25, 26. Bar to 1 am. Semi-a la carte: lunch, dinner $7.95-$16.95. Child's meals. Outdoor dining. Italian country inn decor. Cr cds: A, D, ER, MC, V.

★ ★ **MARIENBAD.** *(122 Carling St, London ON N6A 1H6)* 519/679-9940. Continental menu. Specialties: Wienerschnitzel, beef tartar. Hrs: 11:30 am-midnight. Closed Jan 1, Dec 25. Res accepted. Bar 11:30-1 am. A la carte entrees: lunch $5.25-$9.95, dinner $9.95-$17.95. Child's meals. Atrium dining. Original and reproduction 19th-century furnishings. Murder mystery & dinner 3rd Fri each month. Cr cds: A, MC, V.

D

★ ★ **MARLA JANE'S.** *(460 King St E, London ON)* 519/858-8669. Specializes in Cajun dishes. 11:30 am-11 pm; Sun 11 am-10 pm. Closed Mon; Dec 25. Res accepted (dinner). A la carte entrees: lunch $6.25-$12.95, dinner $11.95-$18.95. Herb garden; terrace. Former embassy (ca 1900), Victorian architecture. Stained glass; changing art displays. Cr cds: A, D, ER, MC, V.

★ ★ **MICHAEL'S-ON-THE-THAMES.** *(1 York St, London ON N6A 1A1)* 519/672-0111. Continental menu. Specializes in table-side cooking, châteaubriand, fresh seafood. Hrs: 11:30 am-11 pm; Thurs, Fri to midnight; Sat 5 pm-midnight; Sun, hols 5-9 pm. Closed Jan 1, Labour Day, Dec 25. Res accepted. Bar. A la carte entrees: lunch $6.95-$9.95, dinner $9.95-$22.95. Child's meals. Pianist Sat-Sun. Cr cds: A, D, ER, MC, V.

D ⮌

Mississauga (D-7)

(See also Hamilton, Toronto)

Pop 430,000 **Elev** 569 ft (173 m) **Area code** 905
Information City of Mississauga, 300 City Centre Dr, L5B 3C1; 905/896-5058 or 905/896-5000.

One of the fastest-growing areas in southern Ontario, Mississauga is a part of the greater Toronto area, bordering Lester B. Pearson International Airport.

Motels

✔★ **DAYS INN.** *(4635 Tomken Rd, Mississauga ON L4W 1J9)* 905/238-5480; FAX 905/238-1031. 61 rms, 3 story. No elvtr. S, D $60-$80; each addl $5; suites $135; under 18 free; wkly rates. Crib free. Pet accepted. TV; cable, VCR (movies). Complimentary continental bkfst. Restaurant opp 11:30 am-midnight. Ck-out 11:30 am. Business servs avail. Some refrigerators. Cr cds: A, C, D, DS, ER, JCB, MC, V.

D 🕿 ✕ 🛇 SC

★ **HOWARD JOHNSON.** *(2420 Surveyor Rd, Mississauga ON L5N 4E6)* 905/858-8600; FAX 905/858-8574. 117 rms, 2 story. June-Sept: S $64-$69; D $69-$79; each addl $5; under 18 free; wkly, wkend, hol rates; lower rates rest of yr. Crib free. Pet accepted, some restrictions. TV; cable (premium). Complimentary continental bkfst. Complimentary coffee in rms. Restaurant opp open 24 hrs. Ck-out 1 pm. Coin lndry. Meeting rms. Business servs avail. Downhill/x-country ski 15 mi. Game rm. Some refrigerators. Picnic tables. Cr cds: A, D, DS, ER, MC, V.

🕿 ✕ 🛇 SC

★ ★ **QUALITY INN-AIRPORT WEST.** *(50 Britannia Rd E, Mississauga ON L4Z 2G2)* 905/890-1200; FAX 905/890-5183. 108 rms, 2 story. S, D $68-$86; each addl $7; suites $119-$145; under 18 free; monthly rates. Crib free. TV; cable (premium). Restaurant 7 am-10 pm. Rm serv. Serv bar 11-1 am. Ck-out noon. Meeting rms. Business servs avail. Exercise equipt; weight machine, bicycles, sauna. Refrigerators avail. Cr cds: A, C, D, DS, ER, MC, V.

D 🏃 ⤢ SC

✔ ★ **TRAVELODGE-TORONTO   SOUTHWEST/CARRIAGE INN.** *(1767 Dundas St E, Mississauga ON L4X 1L5)* off Hwy 427. 905/238-3400; FAX 905/238-9457. 85 rms, 2 story; 1 suite. June-Sept: S $70; D $75; each addl $5; suites $125-$150; under 12 free; wkly rates; lower rates rest of yr. Crib $5. TV; cable (premium). Complimentary continental bkfst. Restaurant nearby. Ck-out 11 am. Meeting rms. Health club privileges. Some refrigerators. Cr cds: A, D, DS, ER, MC, V.

D ⤢ 🔥 SC

Motor Hotels

★ ★ **DAYS INN-TORONTO AIRPORT.** *(6257 Airport Rd, Mississauga ON L4V 1E4)* near Lester B. Pearson Intl Airport. 905/678-1400; FAX 905/678-9130. Web www.vsamotas@cara.com. 202 rms, 7 story. S $140; D $150; each addl $10; suites $150; under 18 free; wknd rates. Crib free. Pet accepted, some restrictions; $10. TV; cable (premium). Indoor pool; whirlpool. Coffee in rms. Restaurant 6:30 am-11 pm. Rm serv. Bar noon-1 am. Ck-out noon. Meeting rms. Business servs avail. Bellhops. Gift shop. Barber, beauty shop. Valet serv. Airport transportation. 18-hole golf privileges. Downhill/x-country ski 20 mi. Exercise equipt; weight machine, stair machine, sauna. Balconies. Cr cds: A, C, D, DS, ER, JCB, MC, V.

D ✔ 🏃 🏌 ⤢ 🏃 ⤢ 🔥 SC

★ ★ **HOLIDAY INN.** *(2125 North Sheridan Way, Mississauga ON L5K 1A3)* QEW exit Erin Mills Pkwy. 905/855-2000; FAX 905/855-1433. E-mail sholinn.miss.qew@sympat.on.cat. 151 rms, 6 story, 80 suites. S, D $120-$155; each addl $10; suites $120-$155; under 19 free. Crib free. TV; cable (premium), VCR avail. Heated pool; poolside serv. Coffee in rms. Restaurant 6:30 am-10 pm. Rm serv 7 am-midnight. Bar 11-1 am. Ck-out 1 pm. Meeting rms. Bellhops. Valet serv. Sundries. Airport transportation. Health club privileges. Wet bars; some in-rm whirlpools. Refrigerators, microwaves avail. Cr cds: A, C, D, DS, ER, JCB, MC, V.

D ⤢ 🔥 SC

★ ★ **HOLIDAY INN-TORONTO WEST.** *(100 Britannia Rd, Mississauga ON L4Z 2G1)* 905/890-5700; FAX 905/568-0868. Web www.holiday-inn.com. 132 air-cooled rms, 6 story. S, D $125; each addl $8; under 20 free. Crib free. Pet accepted, some restrictions. TV; cable (premium), VCR avail. Complimentary bkfst buffet. Coffee in rms. Restaurant from 6:30 am. Rm serv. Bar. Ck-out noon. Meeting rms. Business servs avail. In-rm modem link. Valet serv. Free airport transportation. Exercise equipt; weight machine, bicycles, sauna. Whirlpool. Refrigerators avail. Cr cds: A, D, DS, ER, JCB, MC, V.

D ✔ 🏃 ⤢ 🔥 SC

★ ★ ★ **RADISSON-TORONTO/MISSISSAUGA.** *(2501 Argentia Rd, Mississauga ON L5N 4G8)* 905/858-2424; FAX 905/821-1592. 207 rms, 8 story. S, D $135-$145; each addl $10; suites $165; under 18 free; wknd rates. Crib free. TV; cable (premium). Indoor pool; whirlpool. Coffee in rms. Restaurant. Rm serv. Bar 11-1 am. Ck-out noon. Coin lndry. Meeting rms. Business servs avail. Bellhops. Valet serv. Sundries. Gift shop. Free airport transportation. Exercise equipt; weights, bicycles, sauna. Refrigerators; bathrm phone in suites. Microwaves avail. Picnic tables. Cr cds: A, D, DS, ER, JCB, MC, V.

D ⤢ 🏃 ⤢ 🔥 SC

★ **TRAVELODGE-TORONTO WEST.** *(5599 Ambler Dr, Mississauga ON L4W 3Z1)* SW of jct ON 401, Dixie Rd. 905/624-9500; FAX 905/624-1382. 225 rms, 6 story. S $59; D $68; under 18 free; suites $86.95. Crib free. Pet accepted. TV; cable. Indoor pool; whirlpool. Complimentary coffee in rms. Restaurant 7-1 am. Bar from noon. Ck-out 11 am.

Guest lndry. Meeting rms. Business servs avail. Valet serv. Sundries. Cr cds: A, D, DS, ER, JCB, MC, V.

D ✔ ⤢ ⤢ 🔥 SC

Hotels

★ ★ ★ **DELTA MEADOWVALE RESORT & CONFERENCE CENTER.** *(6750 Mississauga Rd, Mississauga ON L5N 2L3)* in Meadowvale Business Park. 905/821-1981; FAX 905/542-4036; res: 800/268-1133 (CAN), 800/877-1133 (US). 374 rms, 15 story. S $195-$205; D $205-$220; each addl $15; suites $150-$300; under 18 free. Crib free. Pet accepted. TV; cable (premium), VCR avail. 2 pools, 1 indoor; whirlpool, poolside serv. Supervised child's activities; ages 2-14. Restaurant 6:30 am-10:30 pm. Rm serv 24 hrs. Bar 11-2 am; entertainment. Ck-out noon. Meeting rms. Business servs avail. Barber, beauty shop. Free airport transportation. Indoor tennis, pro shop. Golf privileges. Exercise rm; instructor, weight machine, bicycles. Lawn games. Minibars; some fireplaces. Microwaves avail. Balconies. Extensive grounds. Cr cds: A, D, DS, JCB, MC, V.

D ✔ 🏃 🏌 ⤢ 🏃 ⤢ 🔥 SC

★ ★ ★ **FOUR POINTS BY SHERATON.** *(5444 Dixie Rd, Mississauga ON L4W 2L2)* ¼ mi S of ON 401 Dixie Rd S exit. 905/624-1144; FAX 905/624-9477. Web www.sheraton.com/863. 296 rms, 10 story. S, D $89-$178; each addl $10; suites $225-$395; under 18 free; wknd package plans. Crib free. Pet accepted, some restrictions. TV; cable (premium), VCR avail. Heated pool. Supervised child's activities; ages 2-12. Complimentary coffee in rms. Restaurant 6:30 am-10 pm; Sat, Sun from 7 am. Bars 11:30-1 am. Ck-out 1 pm. Meeting rms. Business center. In-rm modem link. Gift shop. Beauty shop. Garage parking. Free airport transportation. Exercise equipt; weights, bicycles, sauna. Game rm. Refrigerators, minibars. Cr cds: A, C, D, DS, ER, JCB, MC, V.

D ✔ ⤢ 🏃 ⤢ 🔥 SC 🏃

★ ★ ★ **HILTON INTERNATIONAL-TORONTO AIRPORT.** *(5875 Airport Rd, Mississauga ON L4V 1N1)* 1 mi W of jct ON 427, Dixon Rd, near Lester B. Pearson Intl Airport. 905/677-9900; FAX 905/677-5073. Web www.hilton.com. 413 rms, 11 story. S, D $139-$179; each addl $20; suites $159-$189; family rates; wknd packages. Crib free. Pet accepted, some restrictions. TV; cable (premium). Heated pool; poolside serv. Coffee in rms. Restaurant 6:30 am-11 pm. Bars 11-2 am; entertainment. Ck-out noon. Meeting rms. Business center. Barber. Free garage parking. Free airport transportation. Exercise equipt; weights, bicycle, sauna. Minibars; many bathrm phones. Cr cds: A, D, DS, ER, JCB, MC, V.

D ✔ ⤢ 🏃 🏃 ⤢ 🔥 SC 🏃

★ ★ **NOVOTEL.** *(3670 Hurontario St, Mississauga ON L5B 1P3)* jct ON 10 & Burnhamthorpe Rd. 905/896-1000; res: 800/668-6835; FAX 905/896-2521. E-mail missmail@aol.com; web novojack -cooled rms, 14 story. S, D $160; each addl $15; suite $250; under 16 free; wknd rates. Crib free. Pet accepted. TV; cable (premium). Indoor pool. Restaurant 6 am-midnight. Bar 11-1 am. Ck-out 1 pm. Meeting rms. Business servs avail. In-rm modem link. Shopping arcade. Beauty shop. Covered parking. Free airport transportation. Health club privileges. Minibars; some bathrm phones. Shopping center opp. Cr cds: A, C, D, DS, ER, JCB, MC, V.

D ✔ ⤢ ⤢ 🔥 SC

★ ★ ★ **STAGE WEST.** *(5400 Dixie Rd, Mississauga ON L4W 4T4)* 905/238-0159; FAX 905/238-9820; res: 800/668-9887. Web www.missis saloga.com/stage_west.htm. 224 suites, 16 story. Suites $129; family, wkly rates; package plans. Crib free. Pet accepted. TV; cable (premium), VCR avail. Indoor pool; whirlpool, lifeguard, water slide. Supervised child's activities; ages 1-12. Restaurant 6:30 am-midnight. Bar 11-1 am. Ck-out noon. Meeting rms. Business center. In-rm modem link. Concierge. Shopping arcade. Barber, beauty shop. Valet parking $5/day. Free airport transportation. Downhill/x-country ski 20 mi. Exercise equipt; weights, rower. Health club privileges. Microwaves avail. Complex includes Stage West Dinner Theatre. Cr cds: A, D, ER, MC, V.

D ✔ ⤢ 🏃 ⤢ 🔥 SC 🏃

Inn

★ ★ ★ **GLENERIN.** *(1695 The Collegeway, Mississauga ON L5L 3S7)* off Mississauga Rd. 905/828-6103; res: 800/267-0525. 39 rms, 2½ story, 13 suites. S $89-$129; D $99-$139; each addl $10; suites $159-$369; under 3 free; wkly rates; wkend packages. Crib free. TV; cable (premium), VCR avail. Complimentary bkfst. Dining rm 7 am-11 pm. Rm serv. Ck-out 11 am, ck-in 4 pm. Meeting rms. Business servs avail. Downhill/x-country ski 10 mi. Health club privileges. Some fireplaces. English-style manor house (1927); antique and modern furnishings. Rms vary in size and style. Cr cds: A, D, ER, MC, V.

D ⊁ ⋈ ⋏ SC

Restaurants

★ ★ **CHERRINGTONS.** *(7355 Torbram Rd, Mississauga ON L4T 3W3)* 905/672-0605. Continental menu. Specializes in fresh fish, steak, pasta. Hrs: 11:30 am-3 pm, 5-10:30 pm; Sat from 5 pm. Closed Sun; Easter, Dec 25. Res accepted. Bar to 1 am. Semi-a la carte: lunch $6.95-$12.95, dinner $15.95-$29.95. Child's meals. Entertainment Fri, Sat. Parking. Elegant dining rm divided by bar. Cr cds: A, D, ER, MC, V.

D ⌐

★ ★ **CHERRY HILL HOUSE.** *(680 Silvercreek Blvd, Mississauga ON L5A 3Z1)* in Silvercreek Mall. 905/275-9300. French, continental menu. Hrs: 11:30 am-2:30 pm, 5-8:30 pm; Sat from 5:30 pm. Closed Sun; statutory hols. Res accepted. Bar. A la carte entrees: lunch $8.75-$13.25, dinner $13.50-$19.75. Converted house (ca 1850) is a designated historic site. Cr cds: A, C, D, DS, ER, MC, V.

⌐

★ **DECKER-TEN.** *(1170 Burnhamthorpe Rd W, Mississauga ON L5C 4E6)* 905/276-7419. Japanese menu. Specialties: sashimi, beef teriyaki. Sushi bar. Hrs: 11:45 am-2:15 pm, 5:30-10 pm; Sat from 5:30 pm; Sun 5-9:30 pm. Closed Jan 1, July 1, Dec 24, 25. Res accepted. Bar. A la carte entrees: lunch $7-$15, dinner $12-$20. Complete meal: dinner $17-$25. Child's meals. Japanese art. Cr cds: A, MC, V.

⌐

★ ★ **LA CASTILE.** *(2179 Dundas St E, Mississauga ON L4X 1M3)* 905/625-1137. Steak and seafood menu. Specializes in shrimp cocktail, prime rib, barbecued ribs. Hrs: 11:30 am-2:30 pm, 5 pm-midnight; Mon, Tues to 11 pm. Closed Sun; Dec 25. Res accepted. Bar to 2 am. Semi-a la carte: lunch $9.95-$18.95, dinner $16.95-$36.95. Child's meals. Pianist Wed-Sat. Parking. 16th-century castle decor; cathedral ceiling, tapestries, original oil painting. Cr cds: A, D, ER, MC, V.

★ ★ ★ **MOLINARO.** *(50 Burnhamthorpe Rd W, Mississauga ON L5B 3C2)* 905/566-1330. Italian menu. Specializes in pasta. Hrs: 11:30 am-2:30 pm, 5:30-10 pm; Thurs, Fri to 11 pm; Sat 5:30-11 pm. Closed Sun; major hols. Res accepted; required Fri, Sat (dinner). Bar. Wine list. A la carte entrees: lunch $8.95-$14.95, dinner $9.50-$25.95. Entertainment Thurs-Sat. Large windows; city views. Cr cds: A, D, DS, ER, MC, V.

D ⌐

★ ★ ★ **MON RÊVE.** *(1011 Eglinton Ave E, Mississauga ON L4W 1K4)* 905/238-8483. French, continental menu. Specializes in seafood, steak, veal. Hrs: noon-11 pm; Sat from 5 pm. Closed Sun; Jan 1, Dec 25. Res accepted. Bar. Wine list. Semi-a la carte: lunch $7.95-$13.95, dinner $16.95-$36.95. Parking. Old French Provincial decor. Cr cds: A, D, ER, MC, V.

D ⌐

★ ★ **MUSKY SUPPER HOUSE.** *(261 Lakeshore Rd E, Mississauga ON L5H 1G8)* 905/271-9727. Continental menu. Specialty: hickory smoked pork with sour cherries. Hrs: 5:30-10 pm; Fri, Sat to 11 pm. Closed Sun, Mon; some major hols. Res accepted. Bar. A la carte entrees: dinner $15-$23. Guitarist. Original art and carvings. Totally nonsmoking. Cr cds: MC, V.

D

★ ★ ★ **OLD BARBER HOUSE.** *(5155 Mississauga Rd, Mississauga ON L5M 2L9)* 905/858-7570. Specializes in veal, pasta, rack of lamb. Own pastries. Hrs: 11:30 am-3 pm, 5-11 pm; Sat from 5 pm. Closed Sun; Jan 1, Dec 25. Res accepted. Bar 11-1 am. A la carte entrees: lunch $9.95-$13.95, dinner $12.95-$34.95. Parking. Victorian house (1862). Cr cds: A, ER, MC, V.

⌐

★ ★ **OUTRIGGER STEAK & SEAFOOD.** *(2539 Dixie Rd, Mississauga ON L4Y 2A1)* 905/275-7000. Specializes in steak, seafood. Salad bar. Own baking. Hrs: noon-11 pm; Sat, Sun from 4 pm. Closed Dec 25. Res accepted. Bar 4 pm-1 am. A la carte entrees: lunch $6.95-$12.95, dinner $13.79-$39.99. Child's meals. Cr cds: MC, V.

D ⌐

★ ★ **SNUG HARBOUR.** *(14 Stavebank Rd S, Mississauga ON L5G 2T1)* 905/274-5000. E-mail cvm.portcredit@city.mississauga.on.ca. Continental menu. Specializes in fresh seafood, pasta. Hrs: 11:30 am-11 pm. Closed Jan 1, Dec 24-26. Res accepted. Bar. Semi-a la carte: lunch, dinner $6.95-$19.95. Child's meals. Jazz Fri, Sat. Outdoor dining. On Lake Ontario. Cr cds: A, MC, V.

D ⌐

✔★ **W.D. CLUTTERBUCKS.** *(1970 Dundas St E, Mississauga ON L4X 2W7)* 905/896-4944. Specialties: roast beef, chicken brochette, souvlaki deluxe. Hrs: 8 am-10 pm; Fri, Sat 7am-11 pm. Res accepted. Bar. Semi-a la carte: bkfst $3.25-$7.50, lunch $5-$10, dinner $7.50-$13.75. Child's meals. Parking. Garden decor with village atmosphere. Cr cds: A, MC, V.

D

Morrisburg (C-10)

(See also Cornwall; also see Massena & Ogdensburg, NY)

Pop 2,308 **Elev** 250 ft (76 m) **Area code** 613
Information Chamber of Commerce, PO Box 288, K0C 1X0; 613/543-3443.

Rising waters of the St Lawrence Seaway forced the removal of Morrisburg and many other towns to higher ground. This was one of the earliest settled parts of Canada, and homes, churches and buildings of historic note were moved and reconstructed on the Crysler Farm located in the Upper Canada Village, itself a historic spot.

What to See and Do

Crysler Farm Battlefield Park. Scene of a decisive battle of the War of 1812, where 800 British and Canadians defeated 4,000 American troops. Also here are Crysler Park Marina, Upper Canada Golf Course, Crysler Beach (fee), Battle of Crysler's Farm Visitor Centre and Memorial Mound, Pioneer Memorial, Loyalist Memorial, Air Strip and Queen Elizabeth Gardens. Varying fees. 7 mi (11 km) E on ON 2. Nearby is

Upper Canada Village. An authentic recreation of a rural 1860s riverfront village. Demonstrations by staff in period costumes. Historic buildings include an operating woolen mill, sawmill, gristmill; Willard's Hotel; blacksmith's, tinsmith's, dressmaker's, shoemaker's and cabinetmaker's shops; tavern, churches, school, bakery, working farms, canal. May be seen on foot, by carryall or *bateau*. (Mid-May-mid-Oct, daily; closed some hols) Phone 613/543-3704. ¢¢¢

Fort Wellington National Historic Site. Original British fort first built in 1813, rebuilt in 1838 after Canadian Rebellions of 1837-1838. Restored blockhouse, officers' quarters, latrine; guides in period costume depict life at the fort circa 1846. Underground stone tunnel designed to defend the flank of the fort. Large military pageant with mock battles (3rd wkend July). (Mid-May-Sept, daily; rest of yr, by appt) 33 mi (53 km) SW via Hwy 401, in Prescott. Phone 613/925-2896. **Free.**

Prehistoric World. Life-size reproductions of prehistoric animals along a 3/4-mi (1-km) nature trail. More than 40 exhibits completed, including Brontosaurus and Tyrannosaurus Rex; others in various stages of construction. (Late May-Labour Day, daily) 5 mi (7 km) E via Hwy 401, exit 758. Phone 613/543-2503. ¢¢

Motel

★ **LOYALIST HOTEL.** *(Hwy 2 & 31, Morrisburg ON K0C 1X0) 613/543-2932; FAX 613/543-3316.* 31 rms, 1-2 story. S $39-$49; D $49-$69; wkend rates. Pet accepted. TV; cable. Heated pool. Restaurant 11:30 am-2 pm, 5-9:30 pm. Bar noon-1 am. Ck-out 11 am. Cr cds: A, MC, V.

Niagara Falls (E-7)

(See Niagara-on-the-Lake, St Catharines; also see Buffalo & Niagara Falls, NY)

Pop 70,960 **Elev** 589 ft (180 m) **Area code** 905 **E-mail** nfcvcb@niagara.com **Web** tourismniagara.com/nfcvcb

Information Visitor & Convention Bureau, 5433 Victoria Ave, L2G 3L1; 905/356-6061 or 800/563-2557.

The Canadian side of Niagara Falls offers some viewpoints different from, and in many ways superior to, those on the American side. Center of a beautiful 35-mile (60-kilometer) stretch of parks and home of a tremendous range of man-made attractions, this area is popular all year with tourists from all over the world.

What to See and Do

Boat ride. *Maid of the Mist* leaves from foot of Clifton Hill on Niagara River Pkwy near Rainbow Bridge (see NIAGARA FALLS, NY). Phone 716/284-4233 (NY) or 905/358-0311 (CAN). ¢¢¢

Historic Fort Erie. Site of some of the fiercest fighting of the War of 1812; restored to period. Guided tours by interpreters dressed in uniform of the Glengarry Light Infantry. (Mid-May-mid-Sept) 21 mi (34 km) S via QEW, at 4330 River Rd in Fort Erie. Phone 905/356-2241. ¢¢

Great Gorge Adventure. Niagara River at its narrowest point. Elevator and 240-ft (73-m) tunnel takes visitors to the boardwalk at edge of whirlpool rapids. (Apr-Oct, daily) 2 mi (3 km) N at 4330 River Rd. Contact PO Box 150, L2E 6T2; 905/356-2241. ¢¢

Guinness World of Records Museum. Based on the popular book of records; hundreds of original exhibits, artifacts; laser video galleries; recreations of many of the world's greatest accomplishments. (Daily) 4943 Clifton Hill. Phone 905/356-2299. ¢¢¢

Journey Behind the Falls. Elevator descends to point about 25 ft (8 m) above river, offering excellent view of Falls from below and behind; waterproof garments are supplied. (Daily; closed Dec 25) 1 mi S of Rainbow Bridge on Niagara Pkwy in Queen Victoria Park. Phone 905/354-1551. ¢¢¢   Also in park is

Greenhouse. Tropical and native plants; animated fountain, garden shop. (Daily) Phone 905/354-1721. **Free.**

Louis Tussaud's Waxworks. Life-size, historically costumed wax figures of the past and present; Chamber of Horrors. (Daily; closed Dec 25) 4915 Clifton Hill. Phone 905/374-6601 or 905/374-4534. ¢¢¢

Lundy's Lane Historical Museum (1874). On the site of the Battle of Lundy's Lane (1814). Interprets early settlement and tourism of Niagara Falls; 1812 war militaria; Victorian parlor, early kitchen, toys, dolls, photographs; galleries and exhibits. (May-Nov, daily; rest of yr, Mon-Fri; closed Jan 1, Dec 25) 5810 Ferry St. Phone 905/358-5082. ¢

Marineland. Performing killer whales, dolphins, sea lions; wildlife displays with deer, bears, buffalo and elk; thrill rides, including one of the world's largest steel roller coasters; restaurants, picnic areas. Park (Mar-mid-Dec, daily); rides (mid-May-early Oct). 7657 Portage Rd. Phone 905/356-8250. ¢¢¢¢

Niagara Falls Museum. One of North America's oldest museums, founded in 1827. Twenty-six galleries of rare, worldwide artifacts, including "Niagara's Original Daredevil Hall of Fame"; Egyptian mummy collection; dinosaur exhibit. (Summer, daily; winter, schedule varies) 5651 River Rd. Phone 905/356-2151 or 716/285-4898 (US). ¢¢¢

Niagara Parks Botanical Gardens. Nearly 100 acres of horticultural exhibits. Nature shop. (Daily) Niagara Pkwy North. Phone 905/356-8554. **Free.**   On grounds is the

Niagara Parks Butterfly Conservatory. Approx 2,000 butterflies make their home in this 11,000-sq-ft (1,022-sq-m), climate-controlled conservatory filled with exotic greenery and flowing water. Nearly 50 species of butterflies can be viewed from a 600-ft (180-m) network of walking paths. Outdoor butterfly garden (seasonal). Gift shop. (Daily) Phone 905/356-8119. ¢¢¢

Niagara Spanish Aero Car. The 1,800-ft (549-m) cables support a car that crosses the whirlpool and rapids of the Niagara River. Five-min trip each way. (Mid-Apr-mid-Oct, daily) 3 1/2 mi (5 km) N on Niagara Parkway. Phone 905/354-5711. ¢¢

★ **Observation towers.**

Minolta Tower Centre. This awesome 325-ft (99.06-m) tower offers a magnificent 360° view of the Falls and surrounding areas. Eight levels at top; specially designed glass for ideal photography; Minolta exhibit floor; "Waltzing Waters" water & light spectacle (free; seasonal); gift shops; incline railway to Falls (fee; free parking); "Top of the Rainbow" dining rms overlooking Falls (reservations suggested). (Daily; closed Dec 24, 25) 6732 Oakes Dr. For addl information contact 6732 Oakes Dr, Niagara Falls L2G 3W6; 905/356-1501. ¢¢¢

Skylon Tower. Stands 775 ft (236 m) above base of Falls. Three-level dome contains an indoor/outdoor observation deck and revolving and stationary dining rooms served by three external, glass-enclosed "Yellow Bug" elevators. Specialty shops at base of tower. (Daily) 5200 Robinson St. Phone 905/356-2651. ¢¢¢   Adj is

IMAX Theatre and Daredevil Adventure. Six-story-high movie screen shows *Niagara: Miracles, Myths and Magic,* a film highlighting the falls. Daredevil Adventure has displays, exhibits and some of the actual barrels used to traverse the falls. (Daily; closed Dec 25) 6170 Buchanan Ave. Phone 905/374-IMAX (recording) or 905/358-3611. ¢¢¢

Typhoon Lagoon. Family water park featuring waterslides, pools, hot tubs; arcade, restaurant, gift shop. (June-mid-Sept, daily) 7430 Lundy's Lane. Phone 905/357-3380. ¢¢¢¢

Motels

(Rates are usually higher on holiday wkends)

★ ★ **CARRIAGE HOUSE.** *(8004 Lundy's Lane (ON 20), Niagara Falls ON L2H 1H1)* 1/2 mi W of QEW. *905/356-7799; res: 800/267-9887.* 120 rms, 2 story. July-Aug: S, D $65-$105; suites $100-$130; family rates; higher rates special events; lower rates rest of yr. Crib free. TV. 2 pools, 1 indoor; whirlpool. Restaurant 7 am-noon. Ck-out 11 am. Business servs avail. Sundries. X-country ski 4 mi. Some in-rm whirlpools. Some balconies. Cr cds: A, C, D, DS, ER, MC, V.

★ **CAVALIER.** *(5100 Centre St, Niagara Falls ON L2G 3P2)* 3 blks W of Falls. *905/358-3288.* 39 rms, 2 story. July-Aug: S, D $60-$85; under 5 free; lower rates rest of yr. Crib free. TV; cable. Heated pool. Restaurant opp from 7 am. Ck-out 11 am. French provincial decor. Cr cds: A, MC, V.

★ **CRYSTAL.** *(4249 River Rd (Niagara River Pkwy), Niagara Falls ON L2E 3E7)* 905/354-0460; FAX 905/374-4972.* 38 rms, 2 story. Mid-June-mid-Sept: S, D $68-$95; each addl $8; lower rates rest of yr. Crib $4. TV; cable (premium). Heated pool. Restaurant nearby. Ck-out 11 am.

Refrigerators; some in-rm whirlpools. Some balconies. 1 blk N of Whirlpool Rapids Bridge. Cr cds: A, MC, V.

⚋ ⚋ ⚋ SC

✔★ ECONO LODGE. (7514 Lundy's Lane (ON 20), Niagara Falls ON L2H 1G8) 2³/₄ mi W of Falls at QEW. 905/354-1849. 45 rms. Late June-mid-Sept: S, D $38-$96; each addl $8; higher rates hol wkends; lower rates rest of yr. Crib free. TV. Heated pool. Playground. Restaurant nearby. Ck-out 11 am. X-country ski 3 mi. Picnic tables. On landscaped grounds; back from highway. Cr cds: A, C, D, DS, MC, V.

⚋ ⚋ ⚋ ⚋ SC

★ ECONO LODGE. (5781 Victoria Ave, Niagara Falls ON L2G 3L6) at Lundy's Lane. 905/356-2034. 57 rms, 2 story. Late June-Sept: S, D $79.95-$149.95; each addl $10; suites $149.95-$199.95; under 18 free; lower rates rest of yr. Crib free. TV; cable. Indoor pool; whirlpool. Restaurant adj open 24 hrs. Ck-out 11 am. X-country ski 2 mi. Cr cds: A, D, DS, MC, V.

⚋ ⚋ ⚋ ⚋ SC

✔★ ★ FLAMINGO MOTOR INN. (7701 Lundy's Lane (ON 20), Niagara Falls ON L2H 1H3) 1¹/₂ mi W of Falls. 905/356-4646. 95 rms, 2 story. Mid-June-Labour Day: S, D $52-$84; each addl $8; suite $80-$200; lower rates rest of yr. Crib free. Pet accepted, some restrictions. TV; cable. Heated pool. Restaurant adj 7 am-10 pm. Ck-out 11 am. Gift shop. Picnic tables. Cr cds: A, C, D, DS, MC, V.

⚋ ⚋ ⚋ ⚋ SC

★ ★ HONEYMOON CITY. (4943 Clifton Hill, Niagara Falls ON L2G 3N5) 905/357-4330; FAX 905/357-0423; res: 800/668-8840. Web www.niagara.com/falls. 77 rms, 2 story. Mid-June-early Sept: S, D $49.50-$149.50; suites, kits. $79.50-$269.50; under 12 free; wkend, hol rates; lower rates rest of yr. Crib free. Pet accepted, some restrictions. TV; cable, VCR avail (movies). Heated pool. Restaurant 7 am-11 pm. Ck-out 11 am. Business servs avail. Shopping arcade. X-country ski 2 mi. Some balconies. Cr cds: A, DS, MC, V.

⚋ ⚋ ⚋ ⚋ SC

★ LIBERTY INNS. (6408 Stanley Ave, Niagara Falls ON L2G 3Y5) 2 blks W of Falls. 905/356-5877; FAX 905/356-9452; res: 800/263-2522. 102 rms, 3 story, 4 suites. June-Sept: S, D $79-$95; each addl $7.50; suites $130-$160; under 15 free; lower rates rest of yr. Crib $7.50. TV. Indoor pool. Restaurant 7-1 am; hrs vary rest of yr. Rm serv. Bar from noon. Ck-out 11 am. X-country ski 5 mi. Sauna. Balconies. Picnic tables. Cr cds: A, D, ER, JCB, MC, V.

⚋ ⚋ ⚋ SC

★ ★ OLD STONE INN. (5425 Robinson St, Niagara Falls ON L2G 7L6) 905/357-1234; FAX 905/357-9299. 114 rms, 3 story. May-Oct: S, D $105-$185; each addl $10; suites $195-$295; under 12 free; wkend rates; higher rates hols; lower rates rest of yr. Crib free. TV; cable, VCR avail. 2 pools, 1 indoor; whirlpool, poolside serv. Restaurant (see THE MILLERY). Rm serv. Bar 11-1 am. Ck-out 11 am. Meeting rms. Business servs avail. Bellhops. Gift shop. Valet serv. X-country ski 2 mi. Main bldg former flour mill built 1904. Cr cds: A, D, DS, ER, JCB, MC, V.

D ⚋ ⚋ ⚋ ⚋

★ PILGRIM MOTOR INN. (4955 Clifton Hill, Niagara Falls ON L2G 3N5) 905/357-4330. 40 rms, 3 story, no ground-floor rms. Mid-June-mid-Sept: S, D $48.50-$78.50; each addl $5; honeymoon rms $99-$129.50; higher rates: hols, wkends; lower rates rest of yr. Crib free. TV; cable. Ck-out noon. Balconies. Sun deck. Cr cds: A, MC, V.

⚋ ⚋ SC

★ SURFSIDE INN. (3665 Macklem St (Niagara River Pkwy), Niagara Falls ON L2G 6C8) 905/295-4354; FAX 905/295-4374; res: 800/263-0713. 31 rms. Mid-April-mid-Nov: D $55-$125; each addl $6; suites $99-$185; lower rates rest of yr. Crib free. TV. Pool. Coffee in rms. Restaurant nearby. Ck-out 11 am. Many refrigerators; microwaves avail. Some whirlpools in suites. Bicycle trail. Cr cds: A, D, DS, ER, MC, V.

D ⚋ ⚋ ⚋ SC

★ ★ TRAVELODGE BONAVENTURE. (7737 Lundys Lane, Niagara Falls ON L2H 1H3) 905/374-7171; FAX 905/374-1151. 115 rms, 3 story, 16 suites. Mid-June-Sept: S, D $54.50-$159; each addl $8; suites $154-$169; under 17 free; 2-day min wkends; lower rates rest of yr. Crib free. TV; cable (premium). 2 pools, 1 indoor. Complimentary coffee in lobby. Restaurant opp 7-1 am. Ck-out 11 am. X-country ski 4 mi. Whirlpool in suites. Cr cds: A, D, ER, MC, V.

D ⚋ ⚋ ⚋ ⚋ SC

★ VILLAGE INN. (5685 Falls Ave, Niagara Falls ON L2E 6W7) just off QEW Spur at Rainbow Bridge, in Maple Leaf Village Complex. 905/374-4444; FAX 905/374-0800; res: 800/263-7135. Web www.falls.net/skyline. 206 rms, 2 story. Late July-Aug: S, D $119.99; lower rates June, Sept. Crib free. TV; cable. Playground. Complimentary continental bkfst. Restaurant 6:30-11 am. Business servs avail. Health club privileges. Microwaves avail. Cr cds: A, D, DS, ER, JCB, MC, V.

⚋ ⚋ SC

Motor Hotels

★ ★ ★ BEST WESTERN CAIRN CROFT. (6400 Lundy's Lane (ON 20), Niagara Falls ON L2H 1T6) 1¹/₄ mi W of Falls. 905/356-1161; FAX 905/356-8664. E-mail bestwestern@niagara.net; web niagara .net/cairncroft. 165 rms, 5 story. Late June-Aug: S, D $99.50-$149.50; each addl $10; suites $150-$199; under 18 free; lower rates rest of yr. Crib free. TV. Playground. Indoor pool. Restaurant 7 am-2 pm, 5-8 pm. Rm serv. Bar 4 pm-1 am; entertainment Tues-Sat. Ck-out 11 am. Meeting rms. Business servs avail. Bellhops. Valet serv. X-country ski 3 mi. Enclosed courtyard. Cr cds: A, C, D, DS, ER, MC, V.

⚋ ⚋ ⚋ ⚋ SC

★ ★ BEST WESTERN FALLSVIEW. (5551 Murray St, Niagara Falls ON L2G 2J4) 1 blk to Falls. 905/356-0551; FAX 905/356-7773. 244 rms, 4-6 story. June-Sept: S, D $79-$169; each addl $10; lower rates rest of yr. Crib $5. Pet accepted. TV; cable. Indoor pool; whirlpool. Sauna. Restaurant 6 am-10 pm. Bar 11-1 am. Ck-out 11 am. Coin lndry. Meeting rms. Business center. Bellhops. Gift shop. Sundries. Game rm. Some in-rm whirlpools. Cr cds: A, C, D, DS, ER, JCB, MC, V.

D ⚋ ⚋ ⚋ ⚋ SC ⚋

★ CASCADE INN. (5305 Murray St, Niagara Falls ON L2G 2J3) 1 blk W of Falls. 905/354-2796; FAX 905/354-2797; res: 800/663-3301. 65 rms, 3-6 story. Mid-May-Labour Day: D $84-$118; lower rates rest of yr. Crib free. TV. Pool. Restaurant 6-11 am. Ck-out 11 am. Gift shop, money exchange. X-country ski 2 mi. Near Skylon Tower. Cr cds: A, DS, MC, V.

⚋ ⚋ ⚋ ⚋ SC

★ ★ COMFORT SUITES IMPERIAL. (5851 Victoria St, Niagara Falls ON L2G 3L6) 905/356-2648; FAX 905/356-4068. 104 suites, 3 story. July-Aug: S, D $99-$159; each addl $15; under 16 free; lower rates rest of yr. Crib $10. TV; cable, VCR avail. Indoor pool; whirlpool. Restaurant adj 7 am-10 pm. Bar 11-2 am. Ck-out noon. Coin lndry. Meeting rms. Business servs avail. Gift shop. X-country ski 2 mi. Game rm. Refrigerators; microwaves avail. Cr cds: A, D, DS, MC, V.

D ⚋ ⚋ ⚋ ⚋ SC

★ ★ HAMPTON INN AT THE FALLS. (5591 Victoria Ave, Niagara Falls ON L2G 3L4) 905/357-1626; FAX 905/357-5869. 127 units, 3-6 story. Mid-June-Labour Day: S, D $85-$169; suites $139-$249; under 18 free; lower rates rest of yr. Crib free. TV; cable (premium). Indoor pool; whirlpool. Sauna. Complimentary continental bkfst. Bar 4 pm-1 am (in season). Ck-out 11 am. Meeting rms. Business servs avail. In-rm modem link. Sundries. Game rm. Balconies. Cr cds: A, D, DS, ER, MC, V.

D ⚋ ⚋ ⚋ SC

★ ★ HOLIDAY INN BY THE FALLS. (5339 Murray St, Niagara Falls ON L2G 2J3) 2 blks W of Falls. 905/356-1333; FAX 905/356-7128. E-mail res@holidayinn.com; web www.holidayinn.com. 122 rms, 6 story. Mid-June-mid-Sept: S, D $95-$195; each addl $10; bridal suite $175-$225; lower rates rest of yr. Crib $5. Pet accepted. TV. 2 pools, 1 indoor;

whirlpool. Restaurant 7 am-10 pm; winter from 8 am. Rm serv. Bar noon-2 am. Ck-out noon. Meeting rm. Business servs avail. Sundries. Sauna. Some in-rm whirlpools. Balconies. Cr cds: A, C, D, DS, ER, JCB, MC, V.

D ✔ ≋ ⊠ 🔥 SC

✔ ★ ★ **HOWARD JOHNSON BY THE FALLS.** (5905 Victoria Ave, Niagara Falls ON L2G 3L8) 905/357-4040; FAX 905/357-6202. 196 rms, 6-7 story. S, D $59-$299; each addl $10; suites $69-$349; under 18 free. Crib free. TV; cable, VCR avail. Indoor/outdoor pool; whirlpool. Restaurant open 24 hrs. Ck-out noon. Meeting rms. Business servs avail. Gift shop. X-country ski 2 mi. Sauna. Game rm. Some in-rm whirlpools. Some balconies. Cr cds: A, C, D, DS, ER, JCB, MC, V.

D ≋ ≋ ⊠ 🔥 SC

★ ★ **MICHAEL'S INN.** (5599 River Rd, Niagara Falls ON L2E 3H3) just N of Rainbow Bridge. 905/354-2727; FAX 905/374-7706; res: 800/263-9390 (US). E-mail michaels@michaelsinn.com; web www.com putan.on.ca/corp/michaels. 130 rms, 4 story. May-Oct: S, D $59-$189; suites $125-$375; lower rates rest of yr. Crib $5. TV; cable (premium). Indoor pool; wading pool, whirlpool, lifeguard in season. Restaurant 7 am-11:30 pm. Rm serv. Bar. Ck-out 11 am. Meeting rms. Business servs avail. Bellhops. Valet serv. Sauna. Some refrigerators. Overlooks the Falls. Cr cds: A, C, D, ER, JCB, MC, V.

D ≋ ≋ 🔥 SC

★ ★ **RAMADA-CORAL INN RESORT.** (7429 Lundy's Lane (ON 20), Niagara Falls ON L2H 1G9) 2 mi W of Falls. 905/356-6116; FAX 905/356-7204. E-mail ramada.niagara@sympatico.ca; web ourismnia gara.com/ramcoral. 130 units, 2-4 story. Mid-June-early Sept: S, D $79-$129.50; each addl $8; suites, studio rms $119.50-$159; under 18 free; package plans; higher rates: Sat in season, hols, special events; lower rates rest of yr. Crib free. Pet accepted, some restrictions; $8. TV. 2 heated pools, 1 indoor; whirlpool. Restaurant 7 am-10 pm. Ck-out 11 am. Meeting rms. Business center. Valet serv. Gift shop. 9-hole golf privileges. Sauna. Health club privileges. Playground. Game rm. Refrigerators, in-rm whirlpools; fireplace in suites. Cr cds: A, C, D, DS, ER, JCB, MC, V.

✔ 🏂 ≋ ≋ 🔥 SC 🚶

★ ★ **TRAVELODGE-NEAR THE FALLS.** (5234 Ferry St, Niagara Falls ON L2G 1R5) 905/374-7771. 81 rms, 4 story, 22 suites. July-Aug: S, D $99-$149; each addl $10; suites $129-$199; family, wkly rates; higher rates hol wkends, lower rates rest of yr. Crib free. TV; cable (premium). Indoor pool; whirlpool. Sauna. Complimentary coffee in lobby. Restaurant 7 am-10 pm. Ck-out 11 am. X-country ski 2 mi. Cr cds: A, D, MC, V.

D ≋ ≋ 🔥 SC

Hotels

★ **DAYS INN.** (6361 Buchanan Ave, Niagara Falls ON L2G 3V9) 905/357-7377; FAX 905/357-9300. Web www.daysinn.com /daysinn.html. 193 rms, 15 story. Late June-early Sept: S, D $99-$399; each addl $10; under 12 free; lower rates rest of yr. Crib free. TV. Indoor pool; whirlpool. Complimentary coffee in rms. Restaurant adj open 24 hrs. No rm serv. Bar. Ck-out 11 am. Meeting rms. Business servs avail. No bellhops. Gift shop. X-country ski 2 mi. Sauna. Game rm. Cr cds: A, D, DS, ER, MC, V.

≋ ≋ ⊠ 🔥 SC

✔ ★ **DAYS INN NEAR THE FALLS.** (5943 Victoria Ave, Niagara Falls ON L2G 3L8) 905/374-3333. 117 rms, 7 story. S, D $99-$199; each addl $10; under 12 free. Crib free. TV; cable. Indoor pool; whirlpool. Restaurant adj open 24 hrs. No rm serv. Ck-out noon. No bellhops. Gift shop. X-country ski 2 mi. Sauna. Game rm. Cr cds: A, D, DS, ER, MC, V.

≋ ≋ ⊠ 🔥 SC

★ ★ **OAKES INN.** (6546 Buchanan Ave, Niagara Falls ON L2G 3W2) 2 blks S of Falls. 905/356-4514; FAX 905/356-3651; res: 800/263-2577 (exc ON & PQ). 800/263-7134 (ON & PQ). 167 units, 12 story. Mid-June-mid-Sept: S, D $87-$299; each addl $5; suites $202-$349; family units; lower rates rest of yr. Crib $10. TV; cable. 2 heated pools, 1 indoor; whirlpool. Restaurants 7 am-midnight; off-season 8 am-9 pm. Bar noon-1

am. Ck-out 11 am. Meeting rms. Business servs avail. Gift shop. X-country ski 2 mi. Exercise equipt; bicycles, weight machine, sauna. Some in-rm whirlpools. Some rms with view of Falls. Enclosed observation deck. Minolta Tower 1/2 blk. Cr cds: A, C, D, DS, ER, JCB, MC, V.

🏂 ≋ 🍴 ⊠ 🔥 SC

✔ ★ ★ **QUALITY.** (5257 Ferry St, Niagara Falls ON L2G 1R6) 905/356-2842; FAX 905/356-6629. 80 rms, 8 story. Mid-June-mid-Sept: S, D $89.99-$249.99; each addl $10; lower rates rest of yr. Crib free. TV; cable. Indoor pool; whirlpool. Restaurant 7 am-noon. No rm serv. Ck-out noon. Meeting rms. Business servs avail. No bellhops. Gift shop. X-country ski 2 mi. Sauna. Cr cds: A, C, D, DS, ER, JCB, MC, V.

D 🏂 ≋ ⊠ 🔥 SC

★ ★ ★ **RAMADA SUITES-NIAGARA.** (7389 Lundy's Lane, Niagara Falls ON L2H 2W9) 905/356-6119; FAX 905/356-7204. 73 suites, 7 story. Mid-June-early Sept: S, D $89.50-$149.50; each addl $8; under 18 free; suites $119.50-$159.50; family rates; higher rates: hol wkends, Sat in season; lower rates rest of yr. Crib free. TV. Indoor pool; whirlpool. Restaurant 7 am-midnight. No rm serv. Bar 11:30 am-midnight. Ck-out 11 am. Meeting rms. Business center. In-rm modem link. Exercise equipt; weights, bicycles, sauna. Refrigerators; whirlpool in suites. Cr cds: A, C, D, DS, ER, JCB, MC, V.

D ≋ 🍴 ⊠ 🔥 SC 🚶

★ ★ ★ **RENAISSANCE FALLSVIEW.** (6455 Buchanan Ave, Niagara Falls ON L2G 3V9) 905/357-5200; FAX 905/357-3422. Web www .niagara.com/nf-renais sance. 262 rms, 19 story. Late May-early Oct: S, D $149-$319; each addl $20; under 18 free; lower rates rest of yr. Crib free. TV; cable, VCR avail. Indoor pool. Restaurants 7 am-11 pm (also see MULBERRY'S). Bar 11-1 am. Ck-out 11 am. Meeting rms. Business servs avail. Exercise equipt; weights, bicycles, sauna. Cr cds: A, D, DS, ER, JCB, MC, V.

D ≋ 🍴 ⊠ 🔥 SC

★ ★ **SHERATON INN.** (6045 Stanley Ave, Niagara Falls ON L2G 3Y3) 905/374-4142; FAX 905/358-3430. 112 rms, 8 story. Late June-mid-Sept: S, D $129-$229; each addl $10; under 14 free; 2-day min wkends; higher rates hol wkends; lower rates rest of yr. Crib free. TV; cable. Indoor pool; whirlpool, poolside serv. Restaurant 7 am-2 pm, 5-10 pm. Bar from 5 pm. Ck-out 11 am. Meeting rms. Business center. Gift shop. X-country ski 2 mi. Cr cds: A, D, DS, ER, JCB, MC, V.

D 🏂 ≋ ⊠ 🔥 🚶

★ ★ **SKYLINE BROCK.** (5685 Falls Ave, Niagara Falls ON L2E 6W7) just off QEW Spur at Rainbow Bridge, in Maple Leaf Village Complex. 905/374-4445; FAX 905/357-4804; res: 800/263-7135. Web www.falls.net/skyline. 233 rms, 12 story. June-Sept: S, D $119-$359; each addl $10; suites $249-$429; under 18 free; lower rates rest of yr. Crib free. TV; cable. Parking $5-$8 (in season). Restaurant 7 am-11 pm. Bar in season 11-1 am. Ck-out 11 am. Meeting rms. Business servs avail. Health club privileges. Microwaves avail. Most rms overlook Falls. Cr cds: A, C, D, DS, ER, JCB, MC, V.

⊠ 🔥 SC

★ ★ **SKYLINE FOXHEAD.** (5875 Falls Ave, Niagara Falls ON L2E 6W7) in Maple Leaf Village complex. 905/374-4444; res: 800/263-7135; FAX 905/357-4804. Web www.falls.net/skyline. 399 rms, 14 story. June-Sept: S, D $119-$269; each addl $10; under 18 free; lower rates rest of yr. Crib free. Valet parking $12/day in season. TV; cable (premium). Pool. Restaurant 6:30 am-10 pm. Bar from 11 am. Ck-out 11 am. Meeting rms. Business center. Concierge. Shopping arcade. X-country ski 2 mi. Exercise equipt; weight machine, rowers. Some balconies overlooking Falls. Cr cds: A, C, D, DS, ER, JCB, MC, V.

D 🏂 🍴 ⊠ 🔥 SC 🚶

Restaurants

★ ★ **CAPRI.** (5438 Ferry St, Niagara Falls ON L2G 1S1) 905/354-7519. Italian menu. Specializes in seafood, steak, pasta. Hrs: 11 am-11 pm. Closed Dec 24-26. Res accepted. Bar. A la carte entrees: lunch

$5.75-$12.50, dinner $8.95-$13.25. Complete meals: dinner $11.95-$34.95. Child's meals. Parking. Family-owned. Cr cds: A, C, D, ER, JCB, MC, V.

D ⊡

★ FOUR BROTHERS. *(5283 Ferry St, Niagara Falls ON L2E 1R6)* 905/358-6951. Italian menu. Specializes in steak, seafood, gourmet pasta dishes. Hrs: 11 am-11 pm; summer 7-1 am. Closed Dec 24, 25. Res accepted. Bar. A la carte entrees: bkfst $1.99-$5.50, lunch $1.95-$10.95, dinner $7.95-$19.95. Child's meals. Parking. Old World decor. Family-owned. Cr cds: A, D, DS, ER, MC, V.

D ⊡

★ ★ THE MILLERY. *(See Old Stone Inn Motel)* 905/357-1234. Continental menu. Specialties: prime rib, rack of lamb. Hrs: 7 am-3 pm, 5-10 pm; early-bird dinner 5-6 pm. Res accepted (dinner). Bar 11-1 am. Semi-a la carte: bkfst $1.95-$7.95, lunch $4.25-$7.95, dinner $12.95-$44.95. Child's meals. Outdoor dining. In historic mill. Cr cds: A, D, DS, ER, JCB, MC, V.

D ⊡

★ ★ MULBERRY'S. *(See Renaissance Fallsview Hotel)* 905/357-5200. Specializes in prime rib. Hrs: 6:30 am-2 pm, 5-9:30 pm; Sun brunch noon-3 pm. Res required (dinner). Wine cellar. A la carte entrees: bkfst $5.50-$9.25, lunch, dinner $3.25-$7.95. Dinner buffet $21.95. Sun brunch $10.95. Child's meals. Pianist exc Mon. Garden atmosphere. Cr cds: A, C, D, DS, ER, JCB, MC, V.

D ⊡

★ ★ QUEENSTON HEIGHTS. *(14184 Niagara Pkwy, Niagara Falls ON L2E 6T2)* 6 mi N of falls. 905/262-4274. Specializes in prime rib, rack of lamb, steak. Hrs: noon-3 pm, 5-9 pm; Sat to 10 pm; high tea 3-5 pm; mid-June-Labour Day to 9:30 pm; Sun brunch 11 am-3 pm. Closed Jan 5-wk before Easter. Res accepted. Bar. A la carte entrees: lunch $8.85-$11.95, dinner $15.95-$24.95. Sun brunch $15.95. Child's meals. Parking. Enclosed balcony dining overlooks river, orchards. Patio. War of 1812 battle site. Cr cds: A, D, ER, MC, V.

D ⊡

★ ★ VICTORIA PARK. *(S on Niagara Pkwy, Niagara Falls ON)* in Queen Victoria Park. 905/356-2217. Canadian, Amer menu. Specializes in prime rib. Menu changes seasonally. Hrs: 11:30 am-9 pm; early-bird dinner 4-6:30 pm; late June-Aug to 10 pm; Sun brunch 11:30 am-3 pm. Closed mid-Oct-Apr. Res accepted. No A/C. Bar. Semi-a la carte: lunch $8.99-$10.49, dinner $15.99-$21.99. Sun brunch $13.95. Child's meals. Victorian decor. Parking. Outdoor patio with view of Falls. Also cafeteria. Cr cds: A, D, MC, V.

D

Niagara-on-the-Lake (E-7)

(See also Niagara Falls, St Catharines; also see Niagara Falls, NY)

Settled 1776 **Pop** 12,186 **Elev** 262 ft (80 m) **Area code** 905
Information Chamber of Commerce, 153 King St, PO Box 1043, L0S 1J0; 905/468-4263.

Often called the loveliest in Ontario, this picturesque town has a long and distinguished history which parallels the growth of the province. Originally the Neutral village of Onghiara, it attracted Loyalist settlers after the American Revolution, many of whom were members of the feared Butler's Rangers. Pioneers followed from many European countries, and after a succession of names including Newark, the town finally received its present name. In 1792 it became the first capital of Upper Canada and remained so until 1796. Governor John Greaves Simcoe, considering the proximity to the United States in case of war, moved the seat of government to York, near Toronto. The town played a significant role in the War of 1812, was occupied and eventually burned along with Fort George in 1813.

Once a busy shipping, shipbuilding and active commercial center, the beautiful old homes lining the tree-shaded streets testify to the prosperity of the area. The town's attractions now include major theater events, historic sites, beautiful gardens and Queen St with its shops, hotels and restaurants. Delightful in any season, this is one of the best-preserved and prettiest remnants of the Georgian era.

What to See and Do

Brock's Monument. Massive, 185-ft (56-m) memorial to Sir Isaac Brock, who was felled by a sharpshooter while leading his troops against American forces at the Battle of Queenston Heights in Oct 1812. Narrow, winding staircase leads to tiny observation deck inside monument. Other memorial plaques in park; walking tour of important points on the Queenston Heights Battlefield begins at the Brock Monument; brochure available here. Brock and his aide-de-camp, Lieutenant-Colonel Macdonell, are buried here. (Mid-May-Labour Day, daily) 7 mi (11 km) S in Queenston Heights Park. Phone 905/468-4257. **Free.**

Court House (1847). Built on site of original government house, 3-story building is now the home of the Court House Theatre. First home of the Shaw Festival (see SEASONAL EVENT). Queen St. Opp is

Clock Tower (1921). Erected in memory of those who died in world wars. Set in center of the road surrounded by floral displays.

Fort George National Historic Site (1797). Once the principal British post on the frontier, the fort saw much action during the War of 1812. 11 restored, refurnished buildings and massive ramparts. (Mid-May-Oct, daily; rest of yr, by appt; living history mid-May-Labour Day) Guided tours by appt. On Niagara Pkwy. Phone 905/468-3938. ¢¢

Laura Secord Homestead. Restored home of Canadian heroine is furnished with early Upper Canada furniture. After overhearing the plans of the Americans billeted in her home, Laura Secord made an exhausting and difficult 19-mi (30-km) walk to warn British troops, which resulted in a victory over the Americans at Beaverdams in 1813. (Victoria Day-Labour Day, daily) Partition St, 5 mi (8 km) S in Queenston. Phone 905/262-4851 or 905/357-4020. Tours ¢

McFarland House (1800). Georgian brick home used as a hospital in the War of 1812; furnished in the Loyalist tradition, 1835-1845. (July-Labour Day, daily; mid-May-June & after Labour Day-Sept, wkends only) McFarland Point Park, Niagara Pkwy, 1 mi (1.6 km) S. Phone 905/356-2241. ¢

Niagara Apothecary (ca 1820). Restoration of pharmacy which operated on the premises from 1866-1964. Has large golden mortar and pestle over the door; original walnut and butternut fixtures, apothecary glass & interesting remedies of the past. (May-Labour Day, daily) Queen & King Sts. Phone 905/468-3845. **Free.**

Niagara Historical Society Museum. Opened in 1907, the earliest museum building in Ontario. Items from the time of the United Empire Loyalists, War of 1812, early Upper Canada and the Victorian era. (Mar-Dec, daily; rest of yr, wkends or by appt; closed Jan 1, Good Friday, Dec 25-26) 43 Castlereagh St. Contact the Niagara Historical Society, PO Box 208, L0S 1J0; 905/468-3912. ¢¢

St Mark's Anglican Church (1805, 1843). Original church damaged by fire after being used as a hospital and barracks during the War of 1812. Rebuilt in 1822 and enlarged in 1843. Unusual 3-layer stained-glass window. Churchyard dates from earliest British settlement. (July-Aug, daily; rest of yr, by appt) 41 Byron St, opp Simcoe Park. Phone 905/468-3123.

St Vincent de Paul Roman Catholic Church (1835). First Roman Catholic parish in Upper Canada. Excellent example of Gothic-revival architecture; enlarged in 1965; older part largely preserved. Picton & Wellington Sts.

Seasonal Event

Shaw Festival. Shaw Festival Theatre, specializing in the works of George Bernard Shaw and his contemporaries, presents ten plays each yr in repertory. Housed in three theaters, including Court House Theatre. Staged by an internationally acclaimed ensemble company. Also lunchtime theater featuring one-act plays by Shaw. Queen's Parade &

Wellington St. Contact PO Box 774, L0S 1J0; 800/724-2934 (US) or 800/267-4759 (Canada). Mid-Apr-Oct.

Motor Hotel

★ ★ ★ **WHITE OAKS INN & RACQUET CLUB.** (RR 4, Niagara-on-the-Lake ON L0S 1J0) Taylor Rd (L0S 1J0), 10 mi NW on QEW, Glendale Ave exit. 905/688-2550; FAX 905/688-2220; res: 800/263-5766. E-mail hotel@whiteoaks.on.ca; web www.whiteoaks.on.ca/corp/whiteoak. 90 rms, 3 story. S $104-$109; D $114-$119; each addl $10; suites $140-$180; under 13 free; wkend rates. TV; cable, VCR avail. Indoor pool; poolside serv. Playground. Supervised child's activities; to age 10. Complimentary coffee in rms. Restaurant 7 am-11 pm. Rm serv. Bar 11-1 am. Ck-out noon. Meeting rms. Business center. In-rm modem link. Concierge. Valet serv. Indoor, outdoor tennis, pro. Putting green. Exercise equipt: weight machine, rower. Rec rm. Bathrm phones. Private patios, balconies. Extensive grounds. Cr cds: A, D, ER, MC, V.

Hotel

★ ★ **PRINCE OF WALES.** (6 Picton St, Niagara-on-the-Lake ON L0S 1J0) 905/468-3246; FAX 905/468-1310; res: 800/263-2452. 101 rms. May-Oct: S, D $129-$225; each addl $20; suites $275; wkend rates (winter); lower rates rest of yr. Crib free. TV; cable (premium). Indoor pool; whirlpool. Restaurant 7 am-midnight (also see PRINCE OF WALES). Bar 11:30-1 am. Ck-out 11 am. Meeting rms. Business center. In-rm modem link. Exercise equipt; weights, bicycles, sauna. Health club privileges. Sun deck. Victorian building (1864). Cr cds: A, D, DS, ER, MC, V.

Inns

★ ★ **GATE HOUSE HOTEL.** (142 Queen St, Niagara-on-the-Lake ON L0S 1J0) 905/468-3263; FAX 905/468-7900. 10 rms, 2 story. June-Sept: S, D $150-$170; each addl $10; under 12 free; lower rates Mar-May, Oct-Dec. Closed rest of yr. Crib free. TV; cable (premium). Complimentary continental bkfst. Dining rm noon-2:30 pm, 5-10 pm. Bar 11:30-2 am. Ck-out 11 am. X-country ski 2 mi. Minibars. Modern decor. Cr cds: A, D, ER, JCB, MC, V.

★ ★ **KIELY HOUSE HERITAGE INN.** (209 Queen St, Niagara-on-the-Lake ON L0S 1J0) 905/468-4588; FAX 905/468-2194. 11 rms, 2 story, 4 suites. No A/C. Mid-Apr-Oct: S $75; D $119; suites $145-$175; under 12 free; lower rates rest of yr. Crib free. Complimentary bkfst buffet. Restaurant 11:30 am-9 pm. Ck-out 11 am, ck-in 1 pm. Lighted tennis privileges, pro. X-country ski 1 mi. Balconies. Built 1832 as private summer residence; several screened porches. Cr cds: A, MC, V.

★ ★ **MOFFAT INN.** (60 Picton St, Niagara-on-the-Lake ON L0S 1J0) QEW via ON 55. 905/468-4116; FAX 905/468-4747. Web www.com.is.on.ca/moffatinn. 22 rms, 2 story. May-Oct: S, D $79-$119; each addl $10; lower rates rest of yr. TV. Complimentary coffee in rms. Dining rm 8 am-midnight. Bar. Ck-out 11 am, ck-in 2 pm. Business servs avail. In-rm modem link. Some private patios. Historic inn (1835); individually decorated rms, many with brass bed; some with fireplace. Totally nonsmoking. Cr cds: A, MC, V.

★ ★ **PILLAR & POST.** (48 John St, Niagara-on-the-Lake ON L0S 1J0) King & John Sts. 905/468-2123; res: 800/361-6788; FAX 905/468-3551. Web www.pillarandpost.com. 123 rms. S, D $160; each addl $20; suites $195-$350; under 12 free; winter packages. TV; cable (premium). Heated pool; whirlpool. Restaurant (see THE CARRIAGES). Rm serv. Bar 11-1:30 am. Ck-in 3 pm. Meeting rm. Business center. In-rm modem link. Luggage handling. Gift shop. Tennis privileges. Golf privileges. Bicycle rentals. Exercise rm; instructor, weights, bicycles,

sauna. Spa. Minibars; some fireplaces. Turn-of-the-century fruit canning factory. Cr cds: A, D, DS, ER, MC, V.

★ ★ ★ **QUEEN'S LANDING.** (155 Byron St, Niagara-on-the-Lake ON L0S 1J0) at Melville. 905/468-2195; FAX 905/468-2227; res: 800/361-6645. 138 rms, 3 story. S, D $195-$255; each addl $20; suites $395; under 18 free (max 2); some lower rates off-season. Crib free. TV; cable (premium), VCR avail. Indoor pool; whirlpool. Dining rm 7 am-10 pm. Rm serv to 1 am. Bar 11-2 am. Ck-out 11 am, ck-in 3 pm. Meeting rms. Business servs avail. In-rm modem link. Bellhops. Valet serv. Concierge. Tennis privileges. 18-hole golf privileges. X-country ski 6 mi. Exercise equipt; weight machine, bicycles, sauna. Health club privileges. Minibars. Antique furnishings; distinctive appointments. Many rms have fireplace, canopy bed, in-rm whirlpool. Located at the mouth of the Niagara River, opp historic Fort Niagara. Bicycle rentals avail. Cr cds: A, D, DS, ER, MC, V.

Restaurants

★ ★ **BUTTERY THEATRE.** (19 Queen St, Niagara-on-the-Lake ON L0S 1J0) 905/468-2564. Continental menu. Specialties: spare ribs, roast leg of lamb, lobster Newburg. Hrs: 9:30 am-10 pm; Fri, Sat to midnight. Closed Dec 25. Res accepted. Bar. A la carte entrees: lunch $7.50-$15.50, dinner $14.95-$19.50. Child's meals. Medieval feast Fri, Sat. Patio dining. Family-owned. Cr cds: A, MC, V.

★ ★ ★ **THE CARRIAGES.** (See Pillar & Post Inn) 905/468-2123. E-mail www.pillarandpost.com. Continental menu. Specializes in rack of lamb. Hrs: 7:30-10:30 am, noon-2 pm, 5-9 pm. Res required. Bar 11-1:30 am. Wine list. Semi-a la carte: bkfst $1.95-$7.25, lunch $9.95-$14.50, dinner $15.95-$25.95. Bkfst buffet $10.50. Child's meals. Intimate dining. Cr cds: A, DS, ER, MC, V.

★ **FANS COURT.** (135 Queen St, Niagara-on-the-Lake ON L0S 1J0) 905/468-4511. Chinese menu. Hrs: noon-10 pm. Res accepted. Bar. A la carte entrees: lunch $5-$7.50, dinner $8-$15.80. Outdoor dining. Large display of antique Chinese vases, jade & figurines. Cr cds: A, D, JCB, MC, V.

★ ★ ★ **PRINCE OF WALES.** (See Prince Of Wales Hotel) 905/468-3246. Continental menu. Specializes in rack of lamb, fresh salmon. Own pastries. Hrs: 7-10:30 am, 11:30 am-2 pm, 5-10 pm; winter 6-9 pm, Fri, Sat to 10 pm; Sun brunch 11 am-2:30 pm. Res accepted. Bar. A la carte entrees: bkfst $2-$9.50, lunch $7.95-$16.95, dinner $19.50-$27.50. Sun brunch $19.97. Child's meals. Greenhouse dining. Victorian decor. Built 1864. Cr cds: A, D, DS, ER, MC, V.

Ottawa (C-9)

Founded 1827 **Pop** 295,163 **Elev** 374 ft (114 m) **Area code** 613 **Web** www.tourottawa.org

Information Tourism & Convention Authority, 130 Albert St, Suite 1800, K1P 5G4; 613/237-5150.

The capital city of Canada, Ottawa is situated at the confluence of the Ottawa, Gatineau and Rideau rivers. A camp established by Champlain in 1615 served as headquarters for explorations from Québec to Lake Huron. For nearly two centuries, fur traders and missionaries used the Ottawa River—their only transportation route—for travel to the interior.

The first European settlement in the area was Hull, Québec, founded across the Ottawa River in 1800. In 1823 the Earl of Dalhousie secured ground for the crown on what is now Parliament Hill. Shortly after, two settlements bordered this: Upper Town and Lower Town.

The area was named Bytown in 1827, after Colonel John By, an engineer in charge of construction of the Rideau Canal, which bisects the city and connects the Ottawa River to Lake Ontario. In 1854 Bytown was renamed Ottawa. About this time four cities were rivals for capital of the United Provinces of Upper and Lower Canada: Montréal, Québec City, Kingston and Toronto. Queen Victoria, in anticipation of confederation, unexpectedly selected Ottawa as capital in 1857, because the city was a meeting point of French and English cultures. Ten years later confederation took place, and Ottawa became capital of Canada.

Today Ottawa is an important cultural center with few heavy industries. With its parks full of flowers and its universities, museums and diplomatic embassies, Ottawa is one of Canada's most beautiful cities.

What to See and Do

By Ward Market. Traditional farmers' market; building houses boutiques and art galleries; outdoor cafés. Exterior market (daily); interior market (Apr-Dec, daily; rest of yr, daily exc Mon). Bounded by Dalhousie & Sussex Dr, George & Clarence Sts. Phone 613/562-3325. **Free.**

Bytown Museum. Artifacts, documents and pictures relating to Colonel By, Bytown, and the history and social life of the region. Tours (by appt). (Early May-mid-Oct, daily; rest of yr, Mon-Fri or by appt) Commissariat Building, 50 Canal Lane, beside the Ottawa Locks, Rideau Canal. Phone 613/234-4570. ¢¢

★ **Canadian Museum of Civilization.** This vast facility employs state-of-the-art exhibition technology to illustrate Canada's history and heritage over 1,000 yrs of settlement. Permanent attractions include **The Children's Museum,** offering a variety of hands-on displays, workshops and activities; **CINÉPLUS,** the world's first convertible IMAX/Omnimax theater; **History Hall,** a setting for many life-size reconstructions of various buildings and environments in Canada's past; and **The Grand Hall,** an expansive space housing six Pacific Coast indigenous houses as well as demonstrations, native ceremonies and participatory activities. Large galleries with changing exhibits; theater. Tours. (May-mid-Oct, daily; rest of yr, daily exc Mon; closed Jan 1, Dec 25) Free admission to museum Sun mornings. 100 Laurier St, Hull, PQ. Phone 819/776-7000. Museum ¢¢; CINÉPLUS ¢¢¢-¢¢¢¢

Canadian Parliament Buildings. Neo-Gothic architecture dominates this part of the city. House of Commons and Senate meet here; visitors may request tickets (free) to both chambers when Parliament is in session. 45-min guided tour includes House of Commons, Senate Chamber, Parliamentary Library. (Daily; closed Jan 1, July 1, Dec 25) (See SEASONAL EVENTS) Wellington St on Parliament Hill. Phone 613/996-0896. **Free.** Also here are the **Centennial Flame,** lit in 1967 as a symbol of Canada's 100th birthday, and **Memorial Chapel,** dedicated to Canadian servicemen who lost their lives in the Boer War, World Wars I & II and the Korean War. **Observation Deck** atop the Peace Tower.

Canadian Ski Museum. History of skiing; collection of old skis & ski equipment from Canada and around the world. (Daily exc Mon; closed some hols) 457A Sussex Dr. Phone 613/241-5832. ¢

Canadian War Museum. Exhibits tracing Canada's military history include arms, aircraft, military vehicles, uniforms and action displays. (May-mid-Oct, daily; rest of yr, daily exc Mon; closed Dec 25) 330 Sussex Dr. Phone 819/776-8627. ¢¢

Central Experimental Farm. Approx 1,200 acres (486 hectares) of field crops, ornamental gardens, arboretum; showcase herds of beef and dairy cattle, sheep, swine, horses. Tropical greenhouse (daily). Agricultural museum (daily; closed Jan 1, Dec 25). Clydesdale horse-drawn wagon or sleigh rides. Picnicking. (May-mid-Oct) Grounds (daily). Some fees. Prince of Wales Drive. Phone 613/991-3044.

City Hall. Situated on Green Island, on the Rideau River. View of city and surrounding area from 8th floor. Guided tours (Mon-Fri, by appt; closed hols). 111 Sussex Dr. Phone 613/244-5464. Opp are the Rideau Falls. **Free.**

Currency Museum. Artifacts, maps and exhibits tell the story of money and its use throughout the world. (May-Labour Day, daily; rest of yr, daily exc Mon) 245 Sparks St. Phone 613/782-8914. ¢

Laurier House. Former residence of two prime ministers: Sir Wilfrid Laurier and W.L. Mackenzie King. Re-created study of Prime Minister Lester B. Pearson. Books, furnishings and memorabilia. (Daily exc Mon; closed Jan 1, Good Fri, Dec 25) 335 Laurier Ave E. Phone 613/992-8142. ¢¢

Museum of Canadian Scouting. Depicts the history of Canadian Scouting; exhibits on the life of Lord R.S.S. Baden-Powell, founder of the Boy Scouts; pertinent documents, photographs and artifacts. (Mon-Fri; closed hols) 1345 Base Line Rd, 8 mi (13 km) SW. Phone 613/224-5131. **Free.**

National Archives of Canada. Collections of all types of material relating to Canadian history. Changing exhibits. (Daily) 395 Wellington St. Phone 613/995-5183. **Free.** Opp is **Garden of the Provinces.** Flags representing all Canadian provinces and territories; fountain illuminated at night. (May-Nov)

National Arts Centre. Center for the performing arts that houses a concert hall and two theaters for music, dance, variety and drama; home of the National Arts Centre Orchestra; more than 800 performances each yr; canal-side cafe (see RESTAURANTS). Landscaped terraces with panoramic view of Ottawa. Guided tours (free). 53 Elgin St at Confederation Square. Phone 613/996-5051 or 613/755-1111 (Ticketmaster).

★ **National Gallery of Canada.** Permanent exhibits include European paintings from 14th century to present; Canadian art from 17th century to present; contemporary and decorative arts, prints, drawings, photos and Inuit art; video and film. Reconstructed 19th-century Rideau convent chapel with Neo-Gothic fan vaulted ceiling, only known example of its kind in North America. Changing exhibits (fee), gallery talks, films; restaurants, bookstore. Guided tours (daily). (May-mid-Sept, daily; rest of yr, Wed-Sun; closed statutory hols) 380 Sussex Dr, at St Patrick St. Phone 613/990-1985. **Free.**

National Museum of Science and Technology. More than 400 exhibits with many do-it-yourself experiments; Canada's role in science and technology is shown through displays on Canada in space, transportation, agriculture, computers, communications, physics and astronomy. Unusual open restoration bay allows viewing of various stages of artifact repair & refurbishment. Cafeteria. (May-Labour Day, daily; rest of yr, daily exc Mon; closed Dec 25) 1867 St Laurent Blvd. Phone 613/991-3044. ¢¢ The museum also maintains

National Aviation Museum. More than 100 historic aircraft, 49 on display in a "Walkway of Time." Displays demonstrate the development of aircraft in peace and war, emphasizing Canadian aviation. (Daily) Rockcliffe Airport, NE end of city. Phone 613/993-2010 or 800/463-2038. ¢¢

Nepean Point. Lovely view of the area; Astrolabe Theatre, a 700-seat amphitheater, is the scene of musical, variety and dramatic shows in summer. Just W of Sussex Dr & St Patrick. Phone 613/239-5000. **Free.**

Professional sports.

NHL (Ottawa Senators). Corel Center, 1000 Palladium Dr, in Kanata. Phone 613/721-0115.

Recreational facilities. For information on canoes, rowboats, docking and launching, swimming at outdoor beaches and pools, phone 613/239-5000. Gatineau Park, across the Ottawa River in Québec, offers swimming, fishing, bicycling, cross-country skiing, picnicking and camping. There are more than 87 mi (140 km) of recreational trails and approximately 50 golf courses in the area. Boats can be rented on the Rideau Canal at Dow's Lake, Queen Elizabeth Driveway & Preston St. Contact the National Capital Commission, 90 Wellington St, opposite Parliament Hill, phone 613/239-5000. Fishing licenses (required in Québec for nonresidents) may be obtained at the Québec Dept of Tourism, Fish & Game, 13 rue Buteau, J8Z 1V4 in Hull, PQ (wkdays, exc summer hols); 613/771-4840.

★ **Rideau Canal.** Constructed under the direction of Lieutenant-Colonel John By of the Royal Engineers between 1826-32 as a safe supply route to Upper Canada. The purpose was to bypass the St Lawrence River in case of an American attack. There are 24 lock stations where visitors can picnic, watch boats pass through the hand-operated locks and see wooden lock gates, cut-stone walls and many historic structures. During summer there are interpretive programs and exhibits at various locations. Areas of special interest include Kingston Mills Locks, Jones Falls Locks (off ON 15), Smith Falls Museum (off ON 15), Merrickville Locks (on ON 43) and

Ottawa Locks. Boating is popular (mid-May-mid-Oct, daily) and ice-skating is available on portions of the canal (mid-Dec-late Jan, daily). Runs 125 mi (202 km) between Kingston and Ottawa. Phone 613/283-5170. **Free.**

Royal Canadian Mint. Production of coins; collection of coins and medals. Guided tours and film; detailed process of minting coins and printing bank notes is shown. (Daily; tours by appt) 320 Sussex Dr. Phone 613/991-5853. ¢

Sightseeing tours.

Paul's Boat Lines, Ltd. Rideau Canal sightseeing cruises depart from Conference Centre (mid-May-mid-Oct, daily). Ottawa River sightseeing cruises depart from foot of Rideau Canal Locks (mid-May-mid-Oct, daily). Phone 613/225-6781. ¢¢¢

Ottawa Riverboat Company. Two-hr cruises on Ottawa River. Boats depart from Hull & Ottawa docks (daily). Also evening dinner/dance cruises (Wed-Fri). Phone 613/562-4888. ¢¢¢-¢¢¢¢

Gray Line bus tours. (May-Oct, daily) Phone 613/725-1441.

Double-Decker bus tours. Capital Trolley Tours. Buses seen in service in Britain visit various highlights of the city. (Mid-Apr-mid-Nov, daily) Phone 613/729-6888. ¢¢¢¢

Victoria Memorial Museum Building. Castle-like structure houses museum that interrelates man and his natural environment. Houses the **Canadian Museum of Nature.** Natural history exhibits from dinosaurs to present day plants and animals. Outstanding collection of minerals and gems. (Daily; closed Dec 25) Metcalfe & McLeod Sts. Phone 613/566-4700. ¢¢

Annual Events

Winterlude. Ten-day extravaganza devoted to outdoor concerts, fireworks, skating contests, dances, music, ice sculptures. 3 wkends Feb.

Canadian Tulip Festival. Part of a month-long celebration, culminated by the blooming of more than one million tulips presented to Ottawa by Queen Juliana of the Netherlands after she sought refuge here during World War II. Tours of flower beds; craft market and demonstrations, kite flying, beer gardens, boat parade, fireworks. Phone 613/567-5757. May.

Canada Day. Celebration of Canada's birthday with many varied events throughout the city including canoe and sailing regattas, concerts, music and dance, art and craft demonstrations, children's entertainment. Phone 613/239-5000. July 1.

Ottawa International Jazz Festival. Phone 613/594-3580. 10 days July.

Seasonal Events

Sound & Light Show on Parliament Hill. Phone 613/239-5000. Mid-May-Labour Day.

Changing the Guard. Parliament Hill. Phone 613/239-5000. Late June-late Aug.

Motor Hotel

★ ★ **SUPER 8.** (480 Metcalfe St, Ottawa ON K1S 3N6) Hwy 417 exit Metcalfe St. 613/237-5500; FAX 613/237-6705. 157 rms, 9 story. S, D $70.88; each addl $10; suites $110; under 19 free; wkend rates. Crib free. TV; cable. Indoor pool. Complimentary coffee in rms. Restaurant 7 am-2 pm, 5-10 pm; Sun to 2 pm. Ck-out noon. Meeting rms. Business servs avail. In-rm modem link. Valet serv. Downhill/x-country ski 10 mi. Cr cds: A, D, DS, ER, MC, V.

Hotels

★ ★ ★ **ALBERT AT BAY.** (435 Albert St, Ottawa ON K1R 7X4) 613/238-8858; FAX 613/238-1433; res: 800/267-6644. 189 kit. suites, 12 story. S, D $124-$144; under 16 free; wkend, monthly rates. Crib free. Garage $8. TV; cable. Restaurant 6:30 am-midnight; Sat, Sun from 11 am. Ck-out noon. Coin lndry. Meeting rms. Business servs avail. In-rm modem link. Downhill ski 8 mi; x-country ski 5 mi. Exercise equipt; weight machine,

bicycles, sauna. Whirlpool. Microwaves. Balconies. Renovated apartment building. Roof-top garden with picnic tables, lawn chairs. Cr cds: A, C, D, DS, ER, JCB, MC, V.

✔ ★ **BEST WESTERN HOTEL JACQUES CARTIER.** (131 Laurier St, Hull (Québec) ON J8X 3W3) On N side of Alexandria Bridge (to Ottawa). 819/770-8550; FAX 819/770-9705. 130 rms, 9 story. Mid-May-mid-Oct: S, D $86-$125; each addl $10; kit. units $100-$125; under 18 free; lower rates rest of yr. Crib free. TV; cable. Indoor pool; lifeguard. Restaurant 7 am-2 pm, 5-10 pm; wkend hrs vary. Bar 11-3 am; entertainment. Ck-out noon. Meeting rms. Business servs avail. Many refrigerators. Some balconies. Opp Museum of Civilization. Cr cds: A, C, D, DS, ER, MC, V.

★ ★ **BEST WESTERN VICTORIA PARK SUITES.** (377 O'Connor St, Ottawa ON K2P 2M2) 613/567-7275; FAX 613/567-1161. E-mail steph@vpsuites.com; web www.vpsuites.com. 100 kit. units, 8 story. May-Oct: S $90-$135; D $100-$145; wkend rates; lower rates rest of yr. Crib free. Garage parking $7. TV; cable. Complimentary continental bkfst. Restaurant nearby. Ck-out noon. Coin lndry. Meeting rms. Business servs avail. Exercise equipt; weight machine, stair machine. Microwaves. Cr cds: A, D, DS, ER, MC, V.

★ ★ ★ **CHÂTEAU LAURIER.** (1 Rideau St, Ottawa ON K1N 8S7) opp Rideau Canal from Parliament Hill. 613/241-1414; FAX 613/592-7030; res: 800/441-1414. 425 rms, 8 story. S, D $131-$231; each addl $25; suites $290-$470; under 18 free. Crib free. Garage parking (fee). TV; cable (premium). Indoor pool; lifeguard. Supervised child's activites (summer). Restaurant 6:30 am-11 pm; dining rm (summer) 11:30 am-11 pm. Rm serv 24 hrs. Bar noon-1 am. Ck-out noon. Convention facilities. Business center. In-rm modem link. Concierge. Shopping arcade. Downhill/x-country ski 12 mi. Exercise rm; instructor, weights, stair machine, sauna. Massage. Rec rm. Minibars. Built in1912. Luxury level. Cr cds: A, C, D, DS, ER, JCB, MC, V.

★ ★ ★ **CITADEL-OTTAWA HOTEL AND CONVENTION CENTRE.** (101 Lyon St, Ottawa ON K1R 5T9) 613/237-3600; FAX 613/237-2351; res: 800/567-3600. 411 rms, 26 story. May-Oct: S $85-$98; D $95-$105; each addl $10; suites $150-$450; under 18 free; package plans; lower rates rest of yr. Crib free. Garage (fee). TV; cable. Heated indoor pool. Complimentary continental bkfst. Restaurant 6:30 am-10 pm. Bar 11-1 am. Ck-out 1 pm. Meeting rms. Business servs avail. Concierge. Gift shop. Downhill/x-country ski 12 mi. Exercise rm; instructor, weights, bicycles, sauna. Minibars. Underground shopping mall adj. Cr cds: A, C, D, DS, ER, MC, V.

★ ★ ★ **DELTA.** (361 Queen St, Ottawa ON K1R 7S9) off Lyon St. 613/238-6000; FAX 613/238-2290; res: 800/268-1133. Web www.delta hotels.com. 328 units, 18 story. May-June, Sept-Oct: S $140-$155; D $155-$175; each addl $15; suites $175-$190; under 18 free; wkend rates; special summer rates; lower rates rest of yr. Crib free. Pet accepted. Garage $11.50. TV; cable. Indoor pool; whirlpool. Restaurant 6:30 am-10 pm; dining rm 5-10 pm. Rm serv 6 am-11 pm. Bars 11-2 am. Ck-out noon. Meeting rms. Business center. In-rm modem link. Barber, beauty shop. Downhill/x-country ski 12 mi. Exercise rm; instructor, weights, bicycles, saunas. Minibars. Some balconies. Cr cds: A, D, ER, MC, V.

★ ★ **LORD ELGIN.** (100 Elgin St, Ottawa ON K1P 5K8) at Laurier Ave. 613/235-3333; FAX 613/235-3223; res: 800/267-4298. 311 rms, 11 story. S $109-$135; D $115-$141; each addl $5; suites $225-$300; under 18 free; wkend rates. Crib free. Pet accepted, some restrictions. Garage; valet, in/out $11. TV; cable. Coffee in rms. Restaurant 7 am-11 pm. Bar 11:30-1 am. Ck-out 1 pm. Meeting rms. Business servs avail. In-rm modem link. Gift shop. Downhill/x-country ski 12 mi. Exercise equipt;

weight machines, treadmill. Originally opened 1941; completely renovated. Cr cds: A, C, D, ER, JCB, MC, V.

★ ★ ★ **RADISSON-OTTAWA CENTRE.** (100 Kent St, Ottawa ON K1P 5R7) 613/238-1122; FAX 613/783-4229. 478 rms, 26 story. S, D $125-$155; each addl $10; suites $300-$400; under 19 free; wkend rates. Crib free. Pet accepted. Garage (fee). TV; cable (premium). Indoor pool; whirlpool. Restaurant 6:30 am-11 pm; revolving rooftop dining rm 11:30 am-2:30 pm, 6-11 pm; Sat from 6 pm. Bar 11-1 am. Ck-out 1 pm. Meeting rms. Business servs avail. In-rm modem link. Downhill ski 15 mi. Exercise rm; instructor, weights, bicycles, sauna. Minibars. Many balconies. Adj underground shopping mall. Luxury level. Cr cds: A, C, D, DS, ER, JCB, MC, V.

★ ★ ★ **SHERATON.** (150 Albert St, Ottawa ON K1P 5G2) 613/238-1500; FAX 613/235-2723. 236 rms, 18 story. S $175; D $185; each addl $20; suites $180-$390; family rates; wkend package plan. Crib free. Garage (fee). Pet accepted. TV; cable. Indoor pool; whirlpool; poolside serv. Coffee in rms. Restaurant 6:30 am-11 pm. Ck-out noon. Meeting rms. Business center. In-rm modem link. Downhill/x-country ski 12 mi. Exercise equipt; weights, bicycles, sauna. Minibars. Luxury level. Cr cds: A, D, DS, ER, JCB, MC, V.

★ ★ ★ **THE WESTIN.** (11 Colonel By Dr, Ottawa ON K1N 9H4) connects with Ottawa Congress Center, Rideau Center. 613/560-7000; FAX 613/560-7359. 484 rms, 24 story. Mid-Apr-June, mid-Sept-mid-Nov: S, D $175-$195; each addl $20; suites $265-$700; under 18 free; wkend rates; lower rates rest of yr. Crib free. Pet accepted, some restrictions. TV; cable. Indoor pool; whirlpool. Restaurants 6:30 am-11 pm. Rm serv 24 hrs. Bar 11:30-2 am. Ck-out 1 pm. Convention facilities. Business center. Concierge. Shopping arcade adj. Barber, beauty shop. Valet parking. Downhill/x-country ski 12 mi. Exercise rm; instructor, weights, bicycles, sauna. Massage. Minibars; some bathrm phones. Opp Rideau Canal; near Parliament Hill. Cr cds: A, C, D, DS, ER, JCB, MC, V.

Inns

★ ★ ★ **GASTHAUS SWITZERLAND INN.** (89 Daly Ave, Ottawa ON K1N 6E6) 613/237-0335; FAX 613/594-3327; res: 800/267-8788. E-mail switzinn@magi.com; web infoweb.magi.com/~switzinn/. 22 rms, 3 story. May-Oct: S $68-$98; D $78-$108; each addl $20; suites $158-$188; lower rates rest of yr. Children over 12 yrs only. TV; cable. Complimentary full bkfst. Restaurant nearby. Ck-out 11 am, ck-in 3 pm. In-rm modem link. Some in-rm whirlpools. Picnic tables, grills. In restored 1872 house. Totally nonsmoking. Cr cds: A, C, D, ER, MC, V.

✔★ **VOYAGEUR'S GUEST HOUSE.** (95 Arlington Ave, Ottawa ON K1R 5S4) 613/238-6445; FAX 613/236-5551. 4 rms, 2 share bath, 2 story. No rm phones. S $34; D $44; each addl $10; higher rates Canada Day. TV; cable (premium). Complimentary full bkfst. Restaurant nearby. Ck-put 11 am, ck-in 1 pm. Downhill 20 mi/x-country ski 3 mi. Cr cds: V.

Resort

★ ★ ★ **LE CHÂTEAU MONTEBELLO.** (392 Rue Notre Dame, Montebello, Quebec QE J0V 1L0) 40 mi E on Hwy 148. 819/423-6341; FAX 819/423-5283; res: 800/441-1414. 210 rms, 3 story. Mid-May-mid-Oct, MAP: S $176.50; D $228; each addl $71.50; under 4 free; lower rates rest of yr. Crib free. Pet accepted. TV; cable. 2 pools, 1 indoor; whirlpool, lifeguard. Playground. Supervised child's activities (mid-June-early Sept); ages 3-12. Dining rm (see AUX CHANTIGNOLES). Rm serv 7 am-11 pm. Bar 11-1 am; entertainment Fri-Sat. Ck-out noon, ck-in 3 pm. Meeting rms. Business center. In-rm modem link. Bellhops. Valet serv. Gift shop. Sports dir. Indoor & outdoor tennis. 18-hole golf, greens fee (incl cart) $54, pro,

putting green. X-country ski on site (rentals). Sleighing. Curling. Bicycles. Horseback riding. Lawn games. Soc dir. Rec rm. Game rm. Squash courts. Exercise rm; instructor, weight machines, bicycles, sauna, steam rm. Massage. Fishing, hunting guides. Minibars. Marina. On 65,000 acres. Cr cds: A, C, D, DS, JCB, MC, V.

Restaurants

★ **AL'S STEAK HOUSE.** (3817 Richmond Rd, Ottawa ON) 613/828-8349. Specializes in steak, fresh seafood, chicken. Hrs: 11 am-11 pm; Sun, Mon to 10 pm. Closed Dec 25. Res accepted. Bar. Semi-a la carte: lunch $7.75-$9.95, dinner $10.95-$35.95. Child's meals. Parking. Family-owned. Cr cds: A, D, ER, MC, V.

★ ★ ★ **AUX CHANTIGNOLES.** (See Le Château Montebello Resort) 819/423-6341. French, continental menu. Specializes in seafood, veal, game. Own baking. Hrs: 7 am-3 pm, 5:30-10 pm; Sun brunch 11 am-3 pm. Res accepted. Serv bar. Wine list. Buffet: bkfst $14. Complete meals: lunch $19.50. A la carte entrees: dinner $24.50-$29.50. Sun brunch $27.75. Child's meals. Parking. Outdoor dining. Rustic decor; fireplace. Cr cds: A, C, D, DS, ER, JCB, MC, V.

★ ★ **CHEZ BUNTHA.** (64 Queen St, Ottawa ON K1P 5C6) off Elgin St. 613/234-0064. Continental menu. Specialties: lamb with fine herbs, sirloin flambé, seafood. Hrs: 11:30 am-midnight; Sat from 5 pm. Res accepted. Wine list. A la carte entrees: lunch $7.50-$12, dinner $12.95-$19.95. Child's meals. Formal, contemporary decor. Cr cds: A, C, D, ER, MC, V.

★ **FULIWAH.** (691 Somerset St W, Ottawa ON K2A 2C2) in Chinatown area. 613/233-2552. Chinese menu. Specializes in Cantonese, Szechwan cuisine. Hrs: 11 am-midnight; Sat, Sun from 10 am. Res accepted. Bar. Semi-a la carte: lunch, dinner $6.50-$24. Dim sum $2.25-$3.25. Parking. Cr cds: A, D, MC, V.

★ ★ **LA GONDOLA.** (188 Bank St, Ottawa ON K2P 1W8) 613/235-3733. Continental, Italian menu. Specializes in veal, pasta. Hrs: 11:30 am-11:30 pm; Sun 10 am-10 pm; Sat, Sun brunch 10 am-3 pm. Closed Dec 25. Res accepted. Bar. A la carte entrees: lunch $5.95-$10.95, dinner $8.95-$22. Sat, Sun brunch $3.25-$7. Child's meals. Outdoor dining. Cr cds: A, C, D, ER, MC, V.

✔★ **LAS PALMAS MEXICAN RESTAURANT.** (111 Parent Ave, Ottawa ON K1N 7B3) 613/241-3738. Mexican, Brazilian menu. Specializes in fajitas, enchiladas, South American (Gaucho) grill. Hrs: 11:30 am-11 pm. Bar. A la carte entrees: lunch, dinner $6-$13.95. Sun brunch $12.95. Mexican village setting. Outdoor dining. Cr cds: A, C, D, ER, JCB, MC, V.

★ ★ **LE CAFÉ.** (53 Elgin St (National Arts Centre), Ottawa ON K1P 5W1) Confederation Sq. 613/594-5127. Nouvelle Canadian menu. Own pastries. Hrs: noon-11 pm. Closed Jan 1, Dec 24, 25; also Sun Sept-May. Res accepted. Bar. A la carte entrees: lunch $7.95-$13.95, dinner $12.95-$22.95. Child's meals. Parking. Outdoor dining on terrace overlooking Rideau Canal. Totally nonsmoking. Cr cds: A, D, ER, MC, V.

★ ★ **MARBLE WORKS.** (14 Waller St, Ottawa ON K2N 9C4) 613/241-6764. Specializes in steak, seafood, pasta. Hrs: 11:30 am-2 pm, 5-10 pm; Sat from 5 pm; Sun from 10:30 am. Closed Dec 25. Res accepted. Bar to 2 am. A la carte entrees: lunch $5-$9, dinner $12-$18.

Sun brunch $11.95. Child's meals. Sat murder mysteries. Parking. Outdoor dining. In renovated 1866 building. Cr cds: A, C, D, ER, MC, V.

★ ★ **THE MILL.** *(555 Ottawa River Pkwy, Ottawa ON K1P 5R4) Wellington Ave and Portage bridge.* 613/237-1311. Continental menu. Specializes in prime rib, fish, chicken. Hrs: 11:30 am-2:30 pm, 4:30-11 pm; wkends from 4:30 pm; Sun brunch 10:30 am-1:30 pm. Closed July 1. Bar. A la carte entrees: lunch $5.95-$7.95, dinner $9.95-$15.95. Complete meals: dinner $15.95-$20.95. Sun brunch $4.95-$9.95. Child's meals. Parking. Outdoor dining. Former mill (1850); mill structure visible through glass wall. Cr cds: A, C, D, ER, MC, V.

✔★ ★ **SITAR.** *(417A Rideau St, Ottawa ON K1N 5Y9)* 613/789-7979. Indian menu. Specializes in tandoori-prepared dishes, vegetarian dishes. Own breads. Hrs: 11:45 am-2 pm, 5-10:30 pm; Sun 5-10:30 pm. Closed Jan 1, Dec 25. Complete meals: lunch $7.95, dinner $13.75-$15.95. Cr cds: A, C, D, ER, MC, V.

Quetico Provincial Park (F-2)

(For accommodations see Fort Frances, Thunder Bay)

Information Superintendent, Ministry of Natural Resources, 108 Saturn Ave, Atikokan P0T 1C0; 807/597-2735.

(On Minnesota-Ontario border)

Quetico is a wilderness park and as such is composed largely of rugged landscape. There are no roads in the park, but its vast network of connecting waterways allows for some of the best canoeing in North America. More than 900 miles (1,450 kilometers) of canoe routes are within Quetico's 1,832-square-mile (4,622-square-kilometer) area. Canoeing (no motor-powered craft allowed), fishing and swimming are primary activities in the park. Appropriate fishing licenses are required. Interior fee/person/night ¢¢

Car camping is permitted at 106 sites in two areas of the Dawson Trail Campgrounds. Permits can be obtained at Park Ranger Stations. Payments may be made in Canadian or US currency (no personal checks). For reservations phone 807/597-2737 (Canadian residents) or 807/597-2735(nonresidents). Camping ¢¢¢¢-¢¢¢¢¢

Picnic facilities, trails and a large assortment of pictographs may be enjoyed. In winter the vacationer can ice-fish and cross-country ski, although there are no maintained facilities. Park (Victoria Day wkend-Thanksgiving wkend, daily). Day-use fee/vehicle ¢¢¢

St Catharines (E-7)

(See also Hamilton, Niagara-on-the-Lake, Niagara Falls, NY & ON)

Pop 124,018 **Elev** 321 ft (98 m) **Area code** 905 **Web** www.st.catharines.com
Information Tourism Marketing Coordinator, City Hall, 50 Church St, PO Box 3012, L2R 7C2; 905/688-5601, ext 1999.

St Catharines, "The Garden City of Canada," is located in the heart of the wine country and the Niagara fruit belt, which produces half of the province's entire output of fresh fruit. A historic city, originally a Loyalist settlement, it was also a depot of the Underground Railway. Located on the Welland Ship Canal, and the site of the first canal, St Catharines was also the home of the first electric streetcar system in North America.

What to See and Do

Brock University (1964). (6,000 students) A 540-acre (219-hectare) campus encompasses some of the finest woods and countryside in the Niagara region. Named in honor of General Sir Isaac Brock, commander of the British forces at the Battle of Queenston Heights in 1812. Tours (Mon-Fri, by appt). Glenridge Ave/Merrittville Hwy, at St David's Rd. Phone 905/688-5550, ext 3245.

Happy Rolph Bird Sanctuary & Children's Farm. Feeding station for native fowl and farm animals; three ponds; nature trail; picnicking; playground. (Victoria Day-Thanksgiving, daily; ponds all yr) Queen Elizabeth Way, Lake St exit N to Lakeshore Rd E, cross ship canal, then N on Read Rd. Phone 905/937-7210.   **Free.**

Morningstar Mill. Waterpowered, fine old mill containing rollers and millstones for grinding flour and feed. Picnic area. (Victoria Day wkend-Thanksgiving wkend, daily; rest of yr, Sat, Sun) De Cew Rd, at De Cew Falls. Phone 905/937-7210.   **Free.**

Old Port Dalhousie. An 18th century harborfront village, once the northern terminus of the first three Welland Ship Canals; now part of a larger recreation area with handcrafted wooden carousel, restaurants and shops. Ontario St, N of QEW to Lakeport Rd. Phone 905/935-7555.

Prudhomme's Wet "N" Wild Water Park. Park features wave pool, water and tube slides; rides, arcades. Roller rink; miniature golf; playground; beach; picnicking, snack bar, restaurant (June-Labour Day). 8 mi (13 km) W off Queen Elizabeth Way, Victoria Ave exit 57, near Vineland. Phone 905/562-7304 or 905/562-7121. Day pass ¢¢¢¢

Rodman Hall Arts Centre. Art exhibitions, films, concerts, children's theater. (Daily exc Mon; closed hols) 109 St Paul Crescent. Phone 905/684-2925.   **Free.**

The Farmers' Market. Large variety of fruit and vegetables from the fruit belt farms of the surrounding area. (Tues, Thurs & Sat) Church & James Sts, behind City Hall. Phone 905/688-5601, ext 1999.

Welland Canal Viewing Complex at Lock III. Via Queen Elizabeth Way exit at Glendale Ave to Canal Rd then N. Unique view of lock operations from an elevated platform. Ships from over 50 countries can be seen as they pass through the canal. Arrival times are posted. Large information center; picnicking, restaurant. Phone 905/688-5601, ext 1999. Also here is

St Catharines Museum. Illustrates development, construction and significance of the Welland Canal; working scale model lock; displays on history of St Catharines. Exhibitions on loan from major museums. (Daily; closed Jan 1, Dec 25-26) 1932 Government Rd. Phone 905/984-8880. ¢¢

Annual Events

Salmon Derby. Open season on Lake Ontario for coho & chinook salmon; rainbow, brown & lake trout. Prizes for all categories. Phone 905/935-6700. Mid-Apr-mid-May.

Folk Arts Festival. Folk Art Multicultural Centre, 85 Church St. Open houses at ethnic clubs, concerts, ethnic dancing and singing. Art and craft exhibits; big parade. Phone 905/685-6589. 2 wks late May.

Can-Am Soapbox Derby. Jaycee Park, QEW N, exit Ontario St. More than 100 competitors from US and Canada. June.

Niagara Grape and Wine Festival. Wine and cheese parties, athletic events, grape stomping, arts & crafts, ethnic concerts and a parade with bands and floats to honor the ripening of the grapes. Grand Parade last Sat of festival. Phone 905/688-2570. 10 days late Sept.

Seasonal Event

Royal Canadian Henley Regatta. Henley Rowing Course. Champion rowers from all parts of the world. Second in size only to the famous English regatta. Several nation- and continent-wide regattas take place on this world-famous course from Apr to Oct. Phone 905/935-9771.

Motels

✔★★ **HIGHWAYMAN MOTOR INN.** *(420 Ontario St, St Catharines ON L2R 5M1)* 905/688-1646. Web www.ont.net/highway man/owerche. 52 rms, 2 story. Mid-May-Sept: S $49.95; D $69-$89; each addl $5; under 12 free; lower rates rest of yr. Crib $5. TV; cable (premium). Heated pool. Restaurant 7 am-2 pm. Ck-out noon. Meeting rms. Business servs avail. In-rm modem link. Valet serv. Sundries. Cr cds: A, C, D, DS, ER, MC, V.

[≈] [✕] [🐾] [SC]

★★★ **HOLIDAY INN.** *(2 N Service Rd, St Catharines ON L2N 4G9)* at QEW Lake St exit. 905/934-8000; FAX 905/934-9117. E-mail holiday@niagra.com. 140 rms, 2 story. July-Sept: S $99-$129; D $109-$139; each addl $10; under 18 free; lower rates rest of yr. Crib free. Pet accepted. TV; cable (premium) VCR avail (movies). Indoor/outdoor pool; poolside serv, lifeguard. Playground. Restaurant 7 am-11 pm. Rm serv. Bar noon-1 am. Ck-out 1 pm. Business servs avail. In-rm modem link. Bellhops. Valet serv. Gift shop. Exercise rm; instructor, weights, rower, sauna. Balconies. Cr cds: A, C, D, DS, ER, JCB, MC, V.

[D] [🐾] [≈] [✕] [✕] [🐾] [SC]

Motor Hotels

★★★ **EMBASSY SUITES.** *(3530 Schmon Pkwy, Thorold ON L2V 4Y6)* 905/984-8484; FAX 905/984-6691. Web www.embassy-suites.com. 128 kit. suites, 4 story. S, D $94-$200; each addl $10; under 18 free. Crib free. Pet accepted. TV; cable, VCR avail. Indoor pool. Complimentary full bkfst. Restaurant 11 am-11 pm. Rm serv. Bar. Ck-out noon. Meeting rms. Business center. In-rm modem link. Valet serv. Sundries. Exercise equipt; weights, rowers, sauna. Lawn games. Microwaves. Cr cds: A, D, DS, ER, MC, V.

[D] [🐾] [≈] [✕] [✕] [🐾] [SC] [✕]

✔★★ **HOWARD JOHNSON.** *(89 Meadowvale Dr, St Catharines ON L2N 3Z8)* just off QEW Lake St N exit. 905/934-5400; FAX 905/646-8700. 96 rms, 5 story. S $59-$89; D $69-$99; each addl $10; under 18 free. Crib free. Pet accepted. TV. Indoor pool; sauna. Coffee in rms. Restaurant open 24 hrs. Bar 11-2 am. Ck-out noon. Coin lndry. Meeting rm. Business servs avail. In-rm modem link. X-country ski 10 mi. Exercise equipt; weights, rower. Microwaves avail. Cr cds: A, C, D, DS, ER, MC, V.

[D] [🐾] [≈] [✕] [✕] [🐾] [SC]

★★ **RAMADA PARKWAY INN.** *(327 Ontario St, St Catharines ON L2R 5L3)* QEW exit 47 S. 905/688-2324; FAX 905/684-6432. 124 rms, 5 story. Late June-Labor Day: S $85-$95; D $95-$105; each addl $10; under 18 free; wkend plan off-season; lower rates rest of yr. Crib free. TV; cable. Indoor pool; whirlpool, sauna. Restaurant 6:30 am-11 pm. Bar from 11 am. Ck-out 11 am. Meeting rms. Business servs. Bowling alley. Refrigerators. Plaza adj. Cr cds: A, C, D, DS, ER, MC, V.

[D] [≈] [✕] [🐾] [SC]

Restaurant

★★ **CELLAR BENCH.** *(81 James St, St Catharines ON L2R 3H6)* 905/641-1922. Continental menu. Specializes in regional wine-country cuisine. Hrs: 11 am-11 pm; Mon to 9 pm; Fri, Sat to midnight; Sun 3-10 pm; early-bird dinner Mon-Fri 4-6 pm. Closed some major hols. Res accepted. Bar. A la carte entrees: lunch $6.50-$11.95, dinner $11.50-$16.95. Child's meals. Jazz Fri. Outdoor dining. Intimate atmosphere. Cr cds: A, D, ER, MC, V.

[D] [✕]

St Lawrence Islands National Park (D-9)

(For accommodations see Gananoque, Kingston; also see Alexandria Bay & Clayton, NY)

Information Superintendent, 2 County Rd 5, RR 3, Mallorytown, ON, K0E 1R0; 613/923-5261.

Established in 1904, this park lies on a 50 mile (80 kilometer) stretch of the St Lawrence River between Kingston and Brockville. It consists of 21 island areas and a mainland headquarters at Mallorytown Landing. The park offers boat launching facilities, beaches, natural and historic interpretive programs, island camping, picnicking, hiking and boating. A visitor reception center and the remains of an 1817 British gunboat at Mallorytown Landing (mid-May-mid-Oct, daily; rest of yr, by appt).

The islands can be accessed by water taxi or by boat rentals at numerous marinas along both the Canadian and American sides.

Sarnia (E-5)

(See also London)

Founded 1856 **Pop** 50,892 **Elev** 610 ft (186 m) **Area code** 519

Information Convention and Visitors Bureau of Sarnia-Lambton, 224 N Vidal St, N7T 5Y3; 519/336-3232 or 800/265-0316.

Sarnia was originally known as "The Rapids" and was renamed Port Sarnia in 1836. The town grew because of timber stands in the area, the discovery of oil and the arrival of the Great Western Railway in 1858. Today it is Canada's most important petrochemical center.

Sarnia is located in the center of one of Canada's most popular recreation areas. Lake Huron offers beaches from Canatara Park to nearby Lambton County beaches; the St Clair River flows south of Sarnia into Lake St Clair. Facilities for water sports and boating are excellent. The city and surrounding area has many golf courses, campsites and trailer parks. Easy access to the United States is provided by the International Blue Water Bridge (toll) spanning the St Clair River between Sarnia and Port Huron, Michigan (see Border Crossing Regulations in MAKING THE MOST OF YOUR TRIP).

What to See and Do

Canatara Park. Information center housed in reconstructed 19th-century log cabin (Victoria Day wkend-Labour Day wkend, Mon-Fri afternoons; rest of yr, wkends). Facilities for swimming, picnicking, barbecuing. Also refreshments, beach and bathhouse; lookout tower; fitness trail, natural area, toboggan hill, playground equipment and ball diamond. (Daily) At Cathcart Blvd, off N Christina St. Phone 800/265-0316. **Free.** Also in the park are

Children's Animal Farm. Farm buildings; animals, poultry and waterfowl. (Daily) **Free.**

Log Cabin. Two-floor cabin with natural wooden peg flooring, two fireplaces; interpretive programs featured in summer. Adj are carriage shed, with farm implement artifacts from 1850, and a smokehouse. (Open for special events) **Free.**

Lambton Heritage Museum. Features more than 400 Currier & Ives prints, Canada's largest collection of antique pressed-glass water pitchers; two farm machinery barns; slaughterhouse, chapel and main exhibit center with a chronological natural & human history of Lambton County. (Mar-Oct, daily; rest of yr, Mon-Fri; closed Dec 25-Jan 1) Picnicking. 45 mi (72 km) NE via ON 21, Grand Bend, opp Pinery Provincial Park. Phone 519/243-2600. ¢¢

Moore Museum. Country store, early switchboard, late-1800s church organ in main building; Victorian cottage; log cabin; farm implements;

one-rm schoolhouse; 1890 lighthouse. (Mar-June, Wed-Sun; July & Aug, daily; Sept-mid Dec, Mon-Fri) 12 mi (19 km) S in Mooretown, 94 Moore Line, 2 blks E of St Clair Pkwy (County Rd 33). Phone 519/867-2020. ¢

Oil Museum of Canada. On site of first commercialized oil well in North America; historic items and data regarding the discovery. Six acres (2¹/₂ hectares) of landscaped grounds with blacksmith shop, pioneer home & post office, railroad station, working oil field using 1860 methods; picnic pavilion. Guided tours. (May-Oct, daily; rest of yr, Mon-Fri) 30 mi SE in Oil Springs on Kelly Rd. Phone 519/834-2840. ¢¢

Sombra Township Museum. Pioneer home with displays of household goods, clothes, books & deeds, marine artifacts, indigenous and military items, music boxes, photographic equipment and farming tools. (June-Sept, afternoons; May, wkends; also by appt) 3470 St Clair Pkwy, S in Sombra. Phone 519/892-3982. ¢

The Gardens. Wide variety of plant life. The park also offers facilities for tennis, lawn bowling, swimming (fee), horseshoes, baseball and soccer. Germain Park, East St. Phone 519/332-0330.

Annual Event

Sarnia Highland Games. Centennial Park. Caber & hammer tossing; stone throwing; haggis-hurling; clan village, bands, dancers. Phone 519/336-5054. Mid-Aug.

Seasonal Events

Sarnia Waterfront Festival. Centennial Park. More than 80 events including singers, dancers; children's shows. Phone 800/265-0316. Late Apr-Labour Day wkend.

Celebration of Lights. Seven-wk festive season featuring 60,000 lights in waterfront park. Residential, commercial displays. Phone 800/265-0316. Late Nov-Dec.

Motels

★ ★ **COMFORT INN.** *(751 N Christina St, Sarnia ON N7V 1X5) ON 402 Exit Front St.* 519/383-6767; FAX 519/383-8710. 100 rms, 3 story. S $55-$75; D $65-$85; each addl $5; family rates. Crib free. TV; cable. Complimentary continental bkfst. Complimentary coffee in lobby. Restaurant adj 6:30 am-midnight. Ck-out noon. Meeting rms. Business center. In-rm modem link. Exercise equipt; weights, bicycles. Refrigerators avail. Cr cds: A, D, DS, ER, MC, V.

[D] [symbols] SC

★ ★ **DRAWBRIDGE INN.** *(283 N Christina St, Sarnia ON N7T 5V4)* 519/337-7571; FAX 519/332-8181; res: 800/663-0376. 97 rms, 3 story. S, D $82; each addl $9; suites $115-$135; under 12 free; wkend rates. Crib free. Pet accepted. TV; cable. Indoor pool; sauna. Restaurant 7 am-2 pm, 5-9 pm; Fri-Sun 8 am-2 pm, 5-9 pm. Rm serv. Bar noon-11 pm. Ck-out noon. Meeting rms. Business center. In-rm modem link. Bellhops. Valet serv. Health club privileges. Cr cds: A, D, DS, ER, MC, V.

[symbols] SC

✔ ★ ★ **HARBOURFRONT INN.** *(505 Harbour Rd, Sarnia ON N7T 5R8) 1/2 mi SW of Bluewater Bridge.* 519/337-5434; FAX 519/332-5882; res: 800/787-5010. 105 rms, 2 story. S $51-$58; D $59-$67; each addl $4; under 16 free. Crib free. Pet accepted, some restrictions. TV; cable, VCR avail. Restaurant adj 11-1 am. Ck-out 11 am. Valet serv. Picnic tables. On river. Cr cds: A, D, ER, JCB, MC, V.

[D] [symbols] SC

★ ★ **HOLIDAY INN.** *(1498 Venetian Blvd, Sarnia ON N7T 7W6)* 519/336-4130; FAX 519/332-3326. 151 rms, 2 story. S, D $69-$89; suites $180-$240; under 19 free; wkend rates. Crib free. Pet accepted. TV; cable (premium). 2 pools, 1 indoor; whirlpool. Playground. Restaurant 6:30 am-10:30 pm. Rm serv. Bar 11-1 am. Ck-out 1 pm. Meeting rms. Bellhops. Valet serv. Golf privileges, greens fee $10, putting green. Exercise equipt; weight machine, treadmill, sauna. Lawn games. Balconies. Cr cds: A, C, D, DS, ER, JCB, MC, V.

[D] [symbols] SC

Sault Ste Marie (B-3)

Pop 83,300 (est) **Elev** 580 ft (177 m) **Area code** 705 **E-mail** ssmcoc@age.net **Web** www.sault-canada.com

Information Chamber of Commerce, 334 Bay St, P6A 1X1; 705/949-7152.

Founded and built on steel, Sault Ste Marie is separated from its sister city in Michigan by the St Mary's River. Lake and ocean freighters traverse the river, which links Lake Huron and Lake Superior—locally known as "the Soo."

What to See and Do

Agawa Canyon Train Excursion. A scenic day trip by Algoma Central Railway through a wilderness of hills and fjord-like ravines. Two-hr stop-over at the canyon. Dining car on train. (June-mid-Oct, daily; Jan-Mar, wkends only) Advance ticket orders avail by phone; over the counter ticket pickup recommended one day in advance. 129 Bay St. Contact Passenger Sales, Algoma Central Railway, PO Box 7000, P6A 1W7; 705/946-7300 or 800/242-9287. ¢¢¢¢¢

Bellevue Park. Features animal, bird and floral displays; greenhouse; playground, concessions (summer), bandshell, view of lake and boats; cross-country skiing; home of Algoma Sailing Club. (Daily) Queen St, E end of city. Phone 705/759-5223. **Free.**

Boat cruises. Two-hr boat cruises from Norgoma dock, next to Holiday Inn on MV *Chief Shingwauk* and MV *Bon Soo* through American locks; also three-hr dinner cruises. (June-mid-Oct) Contact Lock Tours Canada, PO Box 424, P6A 5M1; 705/253-9850. ¢¢¢¢

Double-Decker bus tours. Day and evening city tours. Wilderness excursions; also Aubrey Falls; St Joseph Island; Lake Superior Wawa Tour and Twin Sault Tour. Foster Dr. Contact Hiawathaland Tours, PO Box 185, P6B 5L6; 705/759-6200 or 800/387-6200. ¢¢¢-¢¢¢¢¢

Sault Ste Marie Museum. Local and national exhibits in a building originally built as a post office. Skylight Gallery traces history of the region dating back 9,000 yrs; includes prehistoric artifacts, displays of early industries, re-creation of 1912 Queen St house interiors. Durham Gallery displays traveling exhibits from the Royal Ontario Museum and locally curated displays. Discovery Gallery for children features hands-on exhibits. (Daily exc Mon; closed statutory hols) 690 Queen St E. Phone 705/759-7278. **Donation.**

Annual Events

Ontario Winter Carnival Bon Soo. Features more than 100 events: fireworks, fiddle contest, winter sports, polar bear swim, winter playground sculptured from snow. Last wkend Jan-1st wkend Feb.

Algoma Fall Festival. Visual and performing arts presentations by Canadian and international artists. Late Sept-late Oct.

Motel

★ ★ **QUALITY INN-BAY FRONT.** *(180 Bay St, Sault Ste Marie ON P6A 6S2)* 705/945-9264; FAX 705/945-9766. 109 rms, 7 story. Sept-mid-Oct: S $102-$165; D $112-$165; each addl $10; family rates; ski; package plans; lower rates rest of yr. Crib free. TV; cable (premium), VCR avail. Indoor pool; whirlpool. Restaurant 7 am-midnight. Rm serv. Bar from 11:30 am. Ck-out 1 pm. Meeting rms. Bellhops. Valet serv. Downhill/x-country ski 8 mi. Exercise equipt; weight machine, bicycles, sauna. Some refrigerators. Cr cds: A, C, D, DS, ER, JCB, MC, V.

[D] [symbols] SC

Motor Hotels

★ ★ ★ **ALGOMA'S WATER TOWER INN.** *(360 Great Northern Rd, Sault Ste Marie ON P6A 5N3)* 705/949-8111; FAX 705/949-1912.

E-mail awtinn@age.net; web watertowerinn.com. 180 rms, 5 story. S, D $79-$99; each addl $7; suites $130-$290; under 18 free; ski plans. Crib free. Pet accepted. TV; cable (premium), VCR avail. Heated pool; whirlpool. Restaurant 7 am-11 pm. Rm serv 7-11 am, 5-10 pm. Bar noon-1 am, dancing. Ck-out noon. Meeting rms. Bellhops. Valet serv. Airport transportation. Sundries. X-country ski 5 mi. Exercise equipt; weights, treadmill. Some refrigerators, microwaves; whirlpool in suites. Cr cds: A, C, D, DS, ER, JCB, MC, V.

⚹⚹ **HOLIDAY INN.** *(208 St Mary's River Dr, Sault Ste Marie ON P6A 5V4)* 705/949-0611; FAX 705/945-6972. 195 rms, 9 story. June-mid-Oct: S $89-$115; D $99-$120; each addl $10; suites $175-$275; under 12 free; wkend rates; lower rates rest of yr. Crib free. Pet accepted. TV; cable (premium). Indoor pool; whirlpool, poolside serv in season. Supervised child's activities (June-Aug). Restaurant 6 am-11 pm; off-season from 7 am. Rm serv. Bars noon-1 am. Ck-out 1 pm. Meeting rms. Business center. In-rm modem link. Bellhops. Valet serv. Sundries. Gift shop. Airport transportation. Downhill ski 20 mi; x-country ski 10 mi. Exercise equipt; weight machine, rowers, sauna. Game rm. Refrigerator in some suites. Cr cds: A, C, D, DS, ER, JCB, MC, V.

⚹⚹ **RAMADA INN & CONVENTION CENTRE.** *(229 Great Northern Rd (Hwy 17 N), Sault Ste Marie ON P6B 4Z2)* 705/942-2500; FAX 705/942-2570. 210 units, 2-7 story. S $70-$92; D $80-$112; each addl $10; suites $84-$250; studio rms $90; under 18 free; ski, package plans. Crib free. Pet accepted. TV; cable, VCR avail. 2 pools, 1 indoor; whirlpool. Restaurant 7 am-11 pm. Rm serv. Bar 11-1 am. Ck-out noon. Meeting rms. Business servs avail. Bellhops. Valet serv (Mon-Fri). Sundries. Downhill ski 20 mi; x-country ski 3 mi. Exercise equipt; weight machine, treadmill. Miniature golf; water slide. Carousel. Bowling. Game rms. Some refrigerators. Cr cds: A, C, D, ER, MC, V.

Restaurants

⮕⚹ **GIOVANNI'S.** *(516 Great Northern Rd, Sault Ste Marie ON P6B 4Z9)* 705/942-3050. Italian menu. Specializes in family-style dinners. Hrs: 11:30 am-midnight; Sun to 11 pm. Closed Jan 1, Labor Day, Dec 25. Res accepted. Bar. Semi-a la carte: lunch $5-$8, dinner $7-$15. Child's meals. Cr cds: A, MC, V.

⚹⚹ **NEW MARCONI.** *(480 Albert St W, Sault Ste Marie ON P6A 1C3)* 705/759-8250. Italian, Amer menu. Specialties: barbecued ribs, veal parmigiana, chicken cacciatore. Own pasta. Hrs: noon-11 pm. Closed Sun; Jan 1, Dec 25. Res accepted. Serv bar. Semi-a la carte: lunch $4.25-$8.50, dinner $7.45-$27.45. Complete meals: dinner $15.95. Family-owned. Cr cds: A, MC, V.

Stratford (E-6)

(See also Brantford, Kitchener-Waterloo)

Pop 27,500 (est) **Elev** 119 ft (36 m) **Area code** 519
Information Tourism Stratford, 88 Wellington St, N5A 2L2; 519/271-5140 or 800/561-SWAN.

The names Stratford and Avon River can conjure up only one name in most travelers' minds—Shakespeare. And that is exactly what you will find in this lovely city. World-renowned, the festival of fine theater takes place in this city every year.

What to See and Do

⚁ **Shakespearean Gardens.** Fragrant herbs, shrubs and flowering plants common to William Shakespeare's time. Huron St. Phone 519/271-5140. Free.

The Gallery/Stratford. Public gallery in parkland setting; historical and contemporary works. Guided tours on request. (Daily) 54 Romeo St N. Phone 519/271-5271. Admission (June-mid-Nov) ¢¢ Adj is

Confederation Park. Features rock hill, waterfall, fountain, Japanese garden and commemorative court.

Annual Event

Kinsmen Antique Show. Stratford Arena. Late July-Aug.

Seasonal Event

Stratford Festival. Contemporary, classical and Shakespearean dramas and modern musicals. Performances at Festival, Avon and Tom Patterson theaters. Contact Box Office, Stratford Festival, PO Box 520, N5A 6V2; 519/273-1600, 416/363-4471 (Toronto) or 800/567-1600. May-Nov, matinees & evenings.

Motels

⚹⚹⚹ **FESTIVAL INN.** *(1144 Ontario St, Stratford ON N5A 6W1)* 519/273-1150; FAX 519/273-2111; res: 800/463-3581. 183 rms, 1-2 story. May-mid-Nov: S $74-$105; D $80-$125; suites $135; under 12 free; lower rates rest of yr. Crib free. TV; cable (premium), VCR avail. Indoor pool; whirlpool, sauna. Restaurant 7 am-9 pm; Sat from 7:30 am; Sun 7:30 am-9 pm. Bar 11:30-1 am. Ck-out 11 am. Meeting rms. Business servs avail. Exercise equipt; bicycle, treadmill. Lawn games. Many refrigerators. Cr cds: A, D, ER, MC, V.

⮕⚹ **MAJER'S.** *(2970 Ontario St E, Stratford ON N5A 6S5)* 1¼ mi E on Ontario St (ON 7/8). 519/271-2010; FAX 519/273-7951; res: 800/561-4483. 31 rms. May-Oct: S $57-$65; D $70-$75; each addl $10; lower rates rest of yr. Crib free. TV; cable (premium). Heated pool. Playground. Complimentary coffee in lobby. Restaurant adj 11 am-11 pm. Ck-out 10:30 am. Refrigerators. Picnic tables. Cr cds: A, MC, V.

⚹⚹ **STRATFORD SUBURBAN.** *(2808 Ontario St E, Stratford ON N5A 6S5)* 2½ mi E on Ontario St (ON 7/8). 519/271-9650; FAX 519/271-0193; res: 800/387-1070. 25 rms. S $58-$67; D $68-$78; each addl $8. TV; cable. Heated pool. Restaurant nearby. Ck-out 11 am. Tennis. Refrigerators. Cr cds: MC, V.

Motor Hotel

⚹⚹ **VICTORIAN INN.** *(10 Romeo St N, Stratford ON N5A 5M7)* 519/271-4650; FAX 519/271-2030. E-mail victorian-inn@orc.ca; web www.victorian-inn.on.ca. 115 rms, 4 story. Mid-May-mid-Nov: S, D $79-$159; each addl $10; under 12 free; lower rates rest of yr. Crib $10. TV; cable (premium), VCR avail. Heated pool; poolside serv. Complimentary coffee in rms. Dining rm 7 am-2 pm, 5-9 pm. Ck-out noon. Meeting rms. Business servs avail. In-rm modem link. Valet serv. Sundries. Exercise equipt; weights, rowers. Game rm. Balconies. On Lake Victoria. Cr cds: A, D, DS, ER, JCB, MC, V.

Inn

⚹⚹⚹ **QUEEN'S INN.** *(161 Ontario St, Stratford ON N5A 3H3)* 519/271-1400; res: 800/461-6450; FAX 519/271-7373. 32 rms, 3 story, 7 suites. May-Oct: S $75-$110; D $85-$120; each addl $25; suites $130-$200; kit. units $190-$200; under 12 free; ski plans; lower rates rest of yr.

Crib free. Pet accepted, some restrictions. TV; cable, VCR avail (movies). Restaurant 7 am-10 pm. Rm serv. Ck-out 11 am, ck-in 2 pm. Business servs avail. Luggage handling. Valet serv. Concierge serv. Downhill ski 20 mi; x-country ski 10 mi. Exercise equipt; weights, bicycle. Microwaves avail. Built in 1850. Cr cds: A, D, ER, MC, V.

Restaurants

★ ★ ★ **THE CHURCH RESTAURANT & THE BELFRY.** *(70 Brunswick St, Stratford ON N5A 6V6)* at Waterloo St. 519/273-3424. French menu. Specialties: salmon monette, filet mignon, loin of lamb. Own baking. Hrs: 11:30 am-2 pm, 5-10:30 pm; after-theater menu Tues-Sat to 1 am. Closed Mon; Jan 1, Dec 25. Res accepted. Serv bar. Wine cellar. A la carte entrees: lunch $10.95-$13, dinner $14.95-$24.25. Complete meals: lunch $10-$20, dinner $42.25-$53.25. Child's meals. Parking. In 1870 Gothic church. Cr cds: A, D, ER, MC, V.

✔ ★ **GENE'S.** *(81 Ontario St, Stratford ON)* 519/271-9678. Chinese, Canadian menu. Specializes in Cantonese, Szechwan dishes. Own pies. Hrs: 11 am-midnight; Thurs to 11 pm; Fri, Sat to 2:30 am; Sun noon-9 pm. Closed Dec 25, 26. Res accepted. Bar. A la carte entrees: lunch $6-$7.50, dinner $8.25-$11.25. Child's meals. Oriental decor. Family-owned. Cr cds: A, D, ER, MC, V.

★ ★ **HOUSE OF GENE.** *(108 Downie St, Stratford ON)* 519/271-3080. Chinese, Szechwan, Canadian menu. Specializes in Cantonese dishes. Hrs: 11 am-8 pm; Fri, Sat to 9 pm; Sun from noon. Closed Dec 25, 26. Res accepted. Bar. A la carte entrees: lunch $6.25-$7.95, dinner $9.25-$12.50. Buffet: lunch $6.95, dinner $8.95. Child's meals. Modern Oriental decor. Cr cds: A, D, ER, MC, V.

★ ★ **KEYSTONE ALLEY CAFE.** *(34 Brunswick St, Stradford ON N5A 3L8)* 519/271-5645. Continental menu. Specializes in pasta, fresh fish. Hrs: 11:30 am-3 pm, 5-9 pm; Mon to 3 pm. Closed Sun; most major hols. Res accepted. Bar. A la carte entrees: lunch $5.95-$7.50, dinner $7.95-$17.95. Child's meals. Open kitchen. Cr cds: A, D, ER, MC, V.

✔ ★ **MADELYN'S DINER.** *(377 Huron St, Stratford ON)* 519/273-5296. Specialties: English fish & chips, homemade pies. Hrs: 7 am-8 pm; Sun 8:30 am-1:30 pm. Closed Mon; Dec 25. Res accepted. Bar from 11 am. Semi-a la carte: bkfst $2.50-$7.95, lunch $2.75-$7.25, dinner $6.95-$10.45. Parking. Cr cds: A, MC.

★ ★ **OLD PRUNE.** *(151 Albert St, Stratford ON N5A 3K5)* 519/271-5052. Web www.cyg.net/~oldprune. Specializes in seafood, lamb. Hrs: 11:30 am-1:30 pm, 5-10 pm; Tues from 5 pm. Closed Mon; also Nov-Apr. Res accepted. Bar. A la carte entrees: lunch $7.50-$14.50, dinner $26-$35. Complete meals: dinner $51.50. Child's meals. Parking. Restored Edwardian residence; enclosed garden terrace. Cr cds: A, MC, V.

★ ★ **RUNDLES.** *(9 Cobourg St, Stratford ON N5A 3E4)* 519/271-6442. Hrs: 5-8:30 pm; Wed, Sat, Sun 11:30 am-1:30 pm, 5-8:30 pm. Closed Nov-May. Res accepted. Bar. Complete meals: lunch $14-$26, dinner $52.50-$62.50. Theatrical decor. Overlooks Lake Victoria. Cr cds: A, D, ER, MC, V.

Thunder Bay (F-3)

Pop 112,486 **Elev** 616 ft (188 m) **Area code** 807 **E-mail** toursim@city.thunderbay.on.ca **Web** www.tourism@city.thunderbay.on.ca

Information Tourism Thunder Bay, 500 Donald St E, P7E 5V3; 800/667-8386 or 807/983-2041.

Thunder Bay was formed with the joining of the twin cities of Fort William and Port Arthur. It is located on Lake Superior and is a major grain shipping port. The history of Thunder Bay is tied very closely to the fur trade in North America. In the early 19th century, the North West Company had acquired most of the fur trade. Fort William became the inland headquarters for the company, and today much of the activity and spirit of those days can be relived at the fort.

Thunder Bay offers the vacationer outdoor recreation including skiing, parks, and historical attractions and serves as a starting point for a drive around Lake Superior.

What to See and Do

Amethyst Centre. Full lapidary shop and gem cutting operation; retail, gift and jewelry shop. Tours. (Daily exc Sun; closed hols) 400 E Victoria Ave. Phone 807/622-6908. **Free.**

Amethyst Mine Panorama. Open-pit quarry adj to Elbow Lake. The quarrying operation, geological faults, Canadian Pre-Cambrian shield and sample gem pockets are readily visible. Gem picking; tours. (Mid-May-mid-Oct, daily) 35 mi (56 km) NE, 5 mi (8 km) off Hwy 11/17 on East Loon Rd. Phone 807/622-6908. **¢**

Centennial Conservatory. Wide variety of plant life including banana plants, palm trees, cacti. (Daily; closed Jan 1, Good Friday, Dec 24-26) Balmoral & Dease Sts. Phone 807/622-7036. **Free.**

Centennial Park. Summer features include a reconstructed 1910 logging camp; logging camp museum. Playground. Cross-country skiing; sleigh rides (by appt; fee) in winter. (Daily) Near Boulevard Lake, at Centennial Park Rd. Phone 807/683-6511. **Free.**

⭐ **International Friendship Gardens.** Park is composed of individual gardens designed and constructed by various ethnic groups including Slovakian, Polish, German, Italian, Finnish, Danish, Ukranian, Hungarian and Chinese. (Daily) 2000 Victoria Ave. Phone 807/625-3166. **Free.**

Kakabeka Falls Provincial Park. Spectacular waterfall on the historic Kaministiquia River, formerly a voyageur route from Montréal to the West. The 128-ft (39-km) high falls may be seen from highway stop. Waterflow is best in spring and on wkends—flow is reduced during the wk. Sand beach in the park, hiking, interpretive trails. Camping (day-use, electrical hook-ups; fee). Playground; visitor service center. 20 mi (32 km) W via ON 11/17. Phone 807/475-1535 (Oct-Apr) or 807/473-9231 (May-Sept). Per vehicle **¢¢¢**

Old Fort William. Authentic reconstruction of the original Fort William as it was from 1803 to 1821. Visitors experience the adventure of the Nor'westers convergence for the Rendezvous (re-creation staged 10 days mid-July). Costumed staff populate 42 buildings on the site, featuring trademen's shops, farm, apothecary, fur stores, warehouses, Great Hall, voyageur encampment, indigenous encampment; historic restaurant. Gift shop. Walking tours (exc winter). (May-Oct, daily) 1 King Rd, off Hwy 61S. Phone 807/577-8461. **¢¢¢**

Quetico Provincial Park (see). 27 mi W on ON 11/17.

Thunder Bay Art Gallery. Changing exhibitions from major national and international museums; regional art; contemporary native art. Tours, films, lectures, concerts. Gift shop. (Daily exc Mon; closed some hols) On Confederation College Campus; use Harbour Expy from Hwy 11/17. Phone 807/577-6427. **Free.**

Motels

✔★ COMFORT INN. *(660 W Arthur St, Thunder Bay ON P7E 5R8) near Thunder Bay Airport.* 807/475-3155; FAX 807/475-3816. 80 rms, 2 story. S $70-$85; D $75-$93; each addl $8; under 19 free. Crib free. Pet accepted. TV; cable. Complimentary coffee in lobby. Restaurant adj 7 am-11 pm. Ck-out 11 am. Business servs avail. In-rm modem link. Cr cds: A, D, DS, ER, MC, V.

[D] [✈] [⌁] [⌁] [SC]

★★★ VICTORIA INN. *(555 W Arthur St, Thunder Bay ON P7E 5R5) near airport.* 807/577-8481; res: 800/387-3331; FAX 807/475-8961. E-mail vicinn@tbaytel.net. 182 rms, 3 story. S $76.95-$155; D $86.95-$155; each addl $10; suites $179-$229; under 16 free. Crib free. Pet accepted; $15. TV; cable, VCR avail (movies). Complimentary coffee in rms. Restaurant 7 am-11 pm. Rm serv. Bar 11:30-1 am. Ck-out noon. Meeting rms. Business servs avail. In-rm modem link. Valet serv. Sundries. Coin lndry. Free airport transportation. Downhill ski 8 mi; x-country ski 5 mi. Exercise equipt; treadmill, stair machine, sauna. Indoor pool; wading pool, whirlpool, poolside serv, lifeguard. Some refrigerators. Cr cds: A, C, D, DS, ER, MC, V.

[D] [✈] [⌁] [⌁] [🏋] [✈] [⌁] [⌁] [SC]

Motor Hotels

★★★ AIRLANE HOTEL. *(698 W Arthur St, Thunder Bay ON P7C 5R8) at jct ON 11/17 & ON 61, near Thunder Bay Airport.* 807/577-1181; FAX 807/475-4852; res: 800/465-5003. E-mail inquire@airline.com; web www.airline.com. 160 rms, 2-3 story. S $79-$105; D $85-$110; each addl $5; wkend rates. Crib free. Pet accepted. TV; cable (premium), VCR avail. Indoor pool; whirlpool. Restaurants 7 am-11 pm. Rm serv. Bar 4 pm-1 am, closed Sun; entertainment. Ck-out 11 am. Meeting rms. Business center. In-rm modem link. Bellhops. Valet serv. Sundries. Free airport transportation. Exercise equipt; weights, stair machine, sauna. Minibars. Cr cds: A, C, D, ER, MC, V.

[D] [✈] [⌁] [🏋] [✈] [⌁] [SC] [⛷]

★ BEST WESTERN CROSSROADS. *(655 W Arthur St, Thunder Bay ON P7E 5R6) at jct ON 11/17 & ON 61, near Thunder Bay Airport.* 807/577-4241; FAX 807/475-7059. 60 rms, 2 story. May-Oct: S $73; D $78; under 12 free; lower rates rest of yr. Crib free. Pet accepted. TV; cable. Complimentary coffee. Restaurant opp 7 am-midnight. Ck-out 11 am. Business servs avail. In-rm modem link. Valet serv. Free airport transportation. Some refrigerators. Cr cds: A, C, D, DS, ER, MC, V.

[✈] [✈] [⌁] [⌁] [SC]

★★ LANDMARK INN. *(1010 Dawson Rd, Thunder Bay ON P7B 5J4) jct Hwy 11/17 & 102, County Fair Plaza.* 807/767-1681; FAX 807/767-1439; res: 800/465-3950 (CAN & MI, WI, IN). 106 rms, 4 story. S $80; D $86; each addl $8; under 12 free. Crib free. Pet accepted; $50. TV; cable. Indoor pool; whirlpool, sauna, water slide, poolside serv. Complimentary continental bkfst. Coffee in rms. Restaurant 7-1 am. Rm serv. Bar 11-1 am. Ck-out 11 am. Meeting rms. Business servs avail. In-rm modem link. Valet serv. Sundries. Free airport transportation. Downhill ski 20 mi. Cr cds: A, DS, ER, MC, V.

[D] [✈] [⌁] [⌁] [⌁] [⌁] [SC]

✔★★ PRINCE ARTHUR. *(17 N Cumberland, Thunder Bay ON P7A 4K8)* 807/345-5411; FAX 807/345-8565; res: 800/267-2675. E-mail pahotel@tbaytel.net; web www.tradenet.ca/prince_arthur. 121 rms, 6 story. S $59-$75; D $65-$79; each addl $8; suites $105-$135; under 16 free. Crib free. Pet accepted. TV; cable. Indoor pool; wading pool, whirlpool, saunas. Coffee in rms. Restaurant 6:30 am-10 pm. Bar 11-1 am. Rm serv. Ck-out noon. Meeting rms. Business servs avail. In-rm modem link. Valet serv. Sundries. Free airport transportation. Health club privileges. Some refrigerators; microwaves avail. Downhill ski 10 mi. Overlooks harbor. Shopping mall opp. Cr cds: A, C, D, ER, MC, V.

[D] [✈] [⌁] [⌁] [⌁] [⌁] [SC]

★★★ VALHALLA INN. *(1 Valhalla Inn Rd, Thunder Bay ON P7E 6J1) at jct ON 11/17 & ON 61, near Thunder Bay Airport.* 807/577-1121; res: 800/964-1121; FAX 807/475-4723. E-mail valvay@baynet.net; web www.valhallainn.com. 267 rms, 5 story. S $175-$190; D $185-$200; each addl $10; suites $295-$305; under 18 free; ski, wkend plans. Crib free. Pet accepted; $10. TV. Indoor pool; whirlpool. Complimentary coffee in rms. Restaurant 6:30 am-11:30 pm. Rm serv. Bar 4:30 pm-2 am. Ck-out 1 pm. Meeting rms. Business servs avail. In-rm modem link. Bellhops. Valet serv. Sundries. Free airport transportation. Downhill ski 3 mi; x-country ski 4 mi. Exercise equipt; weights, bicycles, sauna. Bicycle rentals. Game rm. Some bathrm phones, minibars; microwaves avail. Luxury level. Cr cds: A, C, D, DS, ER, MC, V.

[D] [✈] [⌁] [⌁] [🏋] [✈] [⌁] [⌁] [SC]

★★ VENTURE INN. *(450 Memorial Ave, Thunder Bay ON P7B 3Y7) adj to auditorium.* 807/345-2343; FAX 807/345-3246; 800 888/483-6887. Web www.jwg.com/ventureinns/. 93 rms, 3 story. S $75; D $85; each addl $10; under 20 free. Crib free. Pet accepted. TV; cable. Indoor pool; sauna. Complimentary continental bkfst. Restaurant adj 11-1 am. Ck-out 1 pm. Meeting rms. Business servs avail. In-rm modem link. Sun deck. Downhill ski 15 mi. Cr cds: A, C, D, DS, ER, MC, V.

[✈] [⌁] [⌁] [⌁] [⌁] [SC]

Restaurant

★★ THE KEG. *(735 Hewitson Ave, Thunder Bay ON) Balmoral at Harbour Expy.* 807/623-1960. Specializes in steak, seafood. Salad bar. Own cheesecake. Hrs: 4 pm-1 am. Closed Dec 24, 25. Bar. Semi-a la carte: dinner $11.99-$22.99. Child's meals. Pub atmosphere; open-hearth mesquite grill. Cr cds: A, D, ER, MC, V.

[D]

Toronto (D-7)

(See also Hamilton, Mississauga)

Founded 1793 **Pop** 3,400,000 (metro) **Elev** 569 ft (173 m) **Area code** 416

Information Tourism Toronto, Queens Quay Terminal at Harbourfront, 207 Queens Quay W, M5J 1A7; 416/203-2500 or 800/363-1990.

Toronto is one of Canada's leading industrial, commercial and cultural centers. From its location on the shores of Lake Ontario, it has performed essential communications and transportation services throughout Canadian history. Its name derives from the native word for meeting place, as the area was called by the Hurons who led the first European, Etienne Brule, to the spot. In the mid-1800s, the Grand Trunk and Great Western Railroad and the Northern Railway connected Toronto with the upper St Lawrence, Portland, Maine and Chicago, Illinois.

After French fur traders from Québec established Fort Rouille in 1749, Toronto became a base for further Canadian settlement. Its population of Scottish, English and United States emigrants was subject to frequent armed attacks, especially during the War of 1812 and immediately thereafter. From within the United States, the attackers aimed at annexation; from within Canada, they aimed at emancipation from England. One result of these unsuccessful threats was the protective confederation of Lower Canada, which later separated again as the province of Québec, and Upper Canada, which still later became the province of Ontario with Toronto as its capital.

Toronto today is a cosmopolitan city with many intriguing features. Once predominantly British, the population is now exceedingly multicultural—the United Nations deemed Toronto the world's most ethnically diverse city in 1989. A major theater center with many professional playhouses, including the Royal Alexandra Theatre, Toronto is also a major banking center, with several architecturally significant banks. Good shopping can be found throughout the city, but Torontonians are most proud of their "Underground City," a series of subterranean malls linking

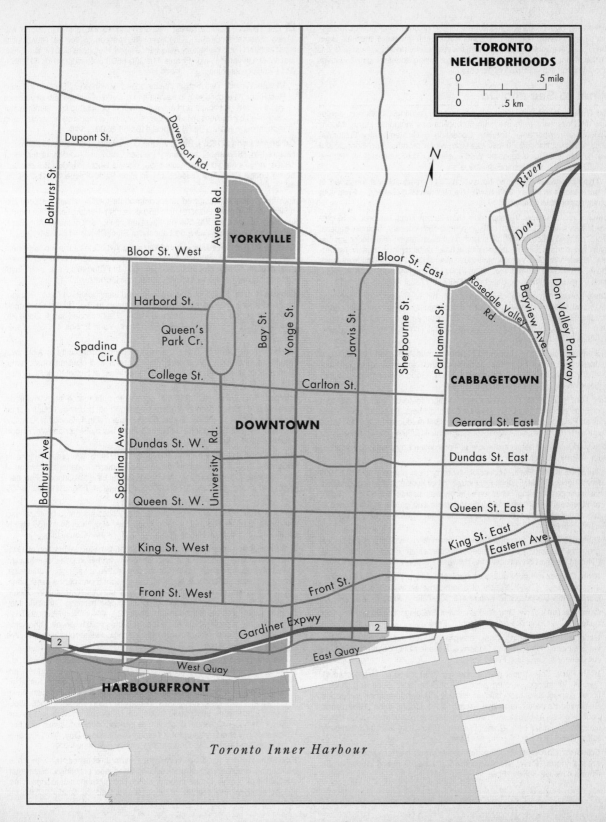

TORONTO
NEIGHBORHOODS

0   .5 mile
0   .5 km

Dupont St.

Davenport Rd.

Bathurst St.

Avenue Rd.

River

Don

YORKVILLE

Bloor St. West

Bloor St. East

Rosedale Valley Rd.

Bayview Ave.

Don Valley Parkway

Harbord St.

Queen's
Park Cr.

Bay St.

Yonge St.

Jarvis St.

Sherbourne St.

Parliament St.

Spadina
Cir.

College St.

Carlton St.

CABBAGETOWN

DOWNTOWN

Gerrard St. East

Spadina Ave.

Dundas St. W.

University Rd.

Dundas St. East

Bathurst Ave.

Queen St. W.

Queen St. East

King St. West

King St. East

Eastern Ave.

Front St. West

Front St.

Gardiner Expwy

2

West Quay

East Quay

2

HARBOURFRONT

Toronto Inner Harbour

more than 300 shops and restaurants in the downtown area. For professional sports fans, Toronto offers the Maple Leafs (hockey), the Blue Jays (baseball), Raptors (basketball), and the Argonauts (football). A visit to the Harbourfront, a boat tour to the islands or enjoying an evening on the town should round out your stay in Toronto.

What to See and Do

Art Gallery of Ontario. Changing exhibits of paintings, drawings, sculpture and graphics from the 14th-20th centuries including Henry Moore Collection; permanent Canadian Collection & Contemporary Galleries; films, lectures, concerts. (Daily exc Mon; winter months Wed-Sun; closed Jan 1, Dec 25) Free admission Wed evenings. 317 Dundas St W. Phone 416/977-0414. ¢¢ Behind gallery is

The Grange. A Georgian house (ca 1817) restored and furnished in early Victorian style (1835-1840). (Same hrs as Art Gallery) **Free** with admission to Art Gallery.

Black Creek Pioneer Village. More than 30 buildings, restored to re-create life in a rural Canadian village of mid-19th-century, include general store, printing office, town hall, church, firehouse, blacksmith shop; special events wkends. Visitor reception centre has exhibit gallery, theater, restaurant. (Early Mar-Dec, variable schedule; closed Dec 25) 1000 Murray Ross Pkwy. Jane St & Steeles Ave, 2 mi (3 km) N on Hwy 400, E on Steeles, then 1/2 mi (1 km) to Jane St. Phone 416/736-1733. ¢¢¢

Casa Loma. A medieval-style castle built by Sir Henry Pellatt between 1911 and 1914. Furnished rms, secret passages, underground tunnel and stables. Restored gardens (May-Oct). Gift shop; cafe. (Daily; closed Jan 1, Dec 25) One Austin Terrace, 1½ mi (2 km) NW of downtown. Phone 416/923-1171. ¢¢¢ Adj is

Spadina (ca 1865). Home of financier James Austin and his descendants; Victorian & Edwardian furnishings and fine art; restored gardens. (Daily exc Mon, afternoons; closed Jan 1, Good Fri, Dec 25, 26) 285 Spadina Rd. Phone 416/392-6910. ¢¢

City Hall (1965). Distinctive modern design features twin towers that appear to support round, elevated council chambers. Exhibits, concerts in Nathan Phillips Square in front of building. Self-guided tours; guided tours (summer). (Mon-Fri) 100 Queen St W. Phone 416/392-7341. **Free.**

City parks. Listed below are some of Toronto's many parks. Contact the Dept of Parks & Recreation, 416/392-1111.

Toronto Island Park. Accessible by ferry (fee; phone 416/392-8193) from foot of Bay St. Historic lighthouse, other buildings. Fishing, boating, swimming, bicycling; children's farmyard; scenic tram ride (free); amusement area (fee); mall with fountains and gardens; fine views of city and lake. (May-Oct, daily) S across Inner Harbour. Phone 416/392-8186. **Free.**

Riverdale Park. Summer: tennis, swimming, wading pools, playgrounds, picnicking, band concerts. Winter: skating; 19th-century farm. (Daily) W side of Broadview Ave, between Danforth Ave & Gerrard St E.

Allan Gardens. Indoor/outdoor botanical displays, wading pool, picnicking, concerts. (Daily) W side of Sherbourne St to Jarvis St between Carlton St & Gerrard St E. Phone 416/392-7288. **Free.**

Queen's Park. The Ontario Parliament Buildings are located in this park. (Daily) Queen's Park Crescent. **Free.**

Grange Park. Wading pool, playground. Natural ice rink (winter, weather permitting). (Daily) Dundas & Beverley Sts, located behind the Art Gallery of Ontario. **Free.**

High Park. The largest park in the city (399 acres or 161 hectares). Tennis, swimming, wading pool and playgrounds, picnicking, hiking, floral display and rock falls in Hillside Gardens, animal paddocks. Shakespeare performances at Dream Site outdoor theater. Restaurant, concessions; trackless tour train. Ice-skating. Also here is Colborne Lodge (S end of park). (Daily) Between Bloor St W & The Queensway at Parkside Dr, near lakeshore. **Free.**

Edwards Gardens. Civic garden center; rock gardens, pools, pond, rustic bridges. (Daily) NE of downtown, at Leslie Ave E & Lawrence St. Phone 416/392-8186. **Free.**

★ **CN Tower.** World's tallest free-standing structure (1,815 ft/553 m). Three observation decks (daily), revolving restaurant (see 360 REVOLVING RESTAURANT) and nightclub. Also various activities (fees). 301 Front St W, just W of University Ave. Phone 416/360-8500 (information) or 416/362-5411 (dining reservations). ¢¢¢¢ Here is

Virtual World. Two virtual reality-based adventures, Battletech® and Red Planet®, allow users to navigate in a world of fantasy. Strap yourself into a high-tech cockpit and enter a universe populated by machines but controlled by humans; or sit at the controls of a modified hovercraft and race through Mars. (Daily) Phone 416/360-8500. ¢¢¢

Colborne Lodge (1837). Built by John G. Howard, architect and surveyor; restored to 1870 style; art gallery houses changing exhibits; artifacts of 1830s; artist's studio. (Daily exc Mon; closed Good Fri, Dec 25-26) Colborne Lodge Dr & The Queensway in High Park. Phone 416/392-6916. ¢¢

Exhibition Place. Designed to accommodate the Canadian National Exhibition (see ANNUAL EVENTS), this 350-acre (141-hectare) park has events yr-round, as well as the Marine Museum of Upper Canada. (Aug-Sept, daily) S off Gardener Expy, on Lakeshore Blvd. Phone 416/393-6000.

George R. Gardiner Museum of Ceramic Art. One of the world's finest collections of Italian majolica, English delftware and 18th-century continental porcelain. (Daily; closed Jan 1, Dec 25) 111 Queen's Park, opp Royal Ontario Museum. Phone 416/586-8080. **Donation.**

Gibson House. Home of land surveyor and local politician David Gibson; restored and furnished as it would have been in the 1850s. Costumed interpreters conduct demonstrations. Tours. (Daily; closed Jan 1, Good Fri, Dec 24-26) 5172 Yonge St (ON 11), in North York. Phone 416/395-7432. ¢¢

Harbourfront Centre. This 10-acre waterfront community is alive with theater, dance, films, art shows, music, crafts and children's programs. Most events free. (Daily) 235 Queens Quay West at foot of York St. Phone 416/973-3000.

Historic Fort York. Restored War of 1812 fort and battle site. Costumed staff provide military demonstrations; eight original buildings house period environments and exhibits. Tours. (Daily; closed Jan 1, Good Fri, Dec 25, 26) Garrison Rd, SE near jct Bathurst & Fleet Sts by Strachan Ave. Phone 416/392-6907. ¢¢

Hummingbird Centre for the Performing Arts. Stage presentations of Broadway musicals, dramas and concerts by international artists. Home of the Canadian Opera Company and the National Ballet of Canada. Pre-performance dining; gift shop. 1 Front St E at Yonge St. Phone 416/393-7469 or 416/872-2262 (tickets).

Huronia Historical Parks. Two living history sites animated by costumed interpreters. (Daily) 63 mi (101 km) N via Hwy 400, then 34 mi (55 km) N to Midland on Hwy 93. Phone 705/526-7838. ¢¢¢ Consists of

Sainte-Marie among the Hurons (1639-1649). Reconstruction of 17th-century Jesuit mission that was Ontario's first European community. Twenty-two furnished buildings include native dwellings, workshops, barn, church, cookhouse, hospital. Candlelight tours, canoe excursions. Cafe features period-inspired meals and snacks. Orientation center, interpretive museum. Free parking and picnic facilities. (Victoria Day wkend-Oct, daily) E of Midland on Hwy 12. ¢¢¢ World-famous Martyrs' Shrine (site of Papal visit) is located across the highway. Other area highlights include pioneer museum, replica indigenous village, Wye Marsh Wildlife Centre.

Discovery Harbour. Marine heritage center and reconstructed 19th-century British Naval dockyard. Established in 1817, site includes 19th-century military base. Now rebuilt, the site features eight furnished buildings and orientation center. Replica of 49-ft (15-m) British naval schooner HMS *Bee;* also HMS *Tecumseth* and *Perseverance.* Costumed interpreters bring base to life, ca 1830. Sail-training and excursions (daily). Audiovisual display; free parking, docking, picnic facilities. Theater; gift shop, restaurant. (Victoria Day-Labour Day, Mon-Fri; after Labour Day-Sept, daily) Church St, Penetanguishene. ¢¢¢

Kortright Centre for Conservation. Environmental center with trails, beehouse, maple syrup shack, wildlife pond and plantings. Naturalist-guided hikes (daily). Cross-country skiing (no rentals); picnic area, cafe; indoor exhibits and theater. (Daily; closed Dec 24 & 25) 9550 Pine

Valley Dr, Klienberg; 12 mi (19.3 km) NW via Hwy 400, Major MacKenzie Dr exit, then 2 mi (3 km) W, then S on Pine Valley Dr. Phone 905/832-2289. ¢¢

Mackenzie House. Restored 19th-century home of William Lyon Mackenzie, first mayor of Toronto; furnishings and artifacts of the 1850s; 1840s print shop. Group tours (by appt). (Daily exc Mon, afternoons; closed Jan 1, Good Fri, Dec 25, 26) 82 Bond St. Phone 416/392-6915. ¢¢

Marine Museum of Upper Canada. Contains exhibits depicting waterways of central Canada, the Great Lakes-St Lawrence System; shipping memorabilia; marine artifacts; wireless rm; fur trade exhibit. Adj is 80-ft (24-m) steam tugboat preserved in dry berth; 12-ft (4-m) tall operating marine triple-expansion steam engine is also on display. (Daily exc Mon; closed Jan 1, Good Fri, Dec 25, 26) Exhibition Place. Phone 416/392-1765. ¢¢

McMichael Canadian Art Collection. Works by Canada's most famous artists—the Group of Seven, Tom Thomson, Emily Carr, David Milne, Clarence Gagnon and others. Also Inuit (Eskimo) and contemporary indigenous art and sculpture. Restaurant, book, gift shop. Constructed from hand-hewn timbers and native stone, the gallery stands in 100 acres (40 hectares) on the crest of the Humber Valley; nature trail. (June-early Nov, daily; rest of yr, daily exc Mon; closed Dec 25) N via ON 400 or 427, 10365 Islington Ave in Kleinburg. Phone 905/893-1121. ¢¢

⭐ **Metro Toronto Zoo.** Approx 710 acres (287 hectares) of native and exotic plants and animals in six geographic regions: Indo-Malaya, Africa, North and South America, Eurasia and Australia. The North American Domain can be seen on a 3-mi (5-km) A/C vehicle ride. The Zoomobile takes visitors on half-hr drive through Eurasian, South American, and African areas. Parking fee. (Daily; closed Dec 25) 10 mi (16 km) E of Don Valley Pkwy on Hwy 401, then N on Meadowvale Rd in Scarborough. Phone 416/392-5900. ¢¢¢¢

Ontario Parliament Buildings. Guided tours of the Legislature Bldg and walking tour of grounds. Gardens; art collection; historic displays. (Victoria Day-Labour Day, daily; rest of yr, Mon-Fri; closed some hols) Queen's Park. Phone 416/325-7500. **Free.**

Ontario Place. A 96-acre (39-hectare) cultural, recreational and entertainment complex on three man-made islands in Lake Ontario. Includes outdoor amphitheater for concerts, two pavilions with multimedia presentations, Cinesphere theater with IMAX films (yr-round; fee); children's village. Three villages of snack bars, restaurants and pubs; miniature golf; lagoons, canals, two marinas; 370-ft (113-m) water slide, showboat, pedal & bumper boats; Wilderness Adventure Ride. (Mid-May-early Sept; daily) Parking fee. 955 Lakeshore Blvd W. Phone 416/314-9900 (recording) or 416/314-9811. ¢¢¢¢

Ontario Science Centre. Hundreds of hands-on exhibits in the fields of space, technology, communications, food, chemistry and earth science. Demonstrations on electricity, papermaking, metal casting, lasers, cryogenics. OmniMax theater (fee). Special exhibitions. (Daily; closed Dec 25) 770 Don Mills Rd, at Eglinton Ave E, 6 mi (10 km) NE via Don Valley Pkwy, in Don Mills. Phone 416/429-4100 (recording). Per person ¢¢¢; Parking ¢¢

Paramount Canada's Wonderland. More than 125 attractions in 8 themed areas offer 11 live stage shows and 50 rides, including Vortex & Top Gun (suspended roller coasters). Splash Works, a 10-acre area offers 15 water-related rides and attractions (mid-June-Labour Day, weather permitting; free with Pay-One Price admission). Special events, fireworks displays, top-name entertainment. (May & Sept-, wkends; June-Aug, daily) 9580 Jane St, 18 mi (29 km) N on Hwy 400. Phone 905/832-7000. Pay-One-Price Passport ¢¢¢¢¢

Professional sports.

American League baseball (Toronto Blue Jays). SkyDome, 1 Blue Jays Way. Phone 416/341-1000.

NBA (Toronto Raptors). SkyDome, 1 Blue Jays Way. Phone 416/214-2255.

NHL (Toronto Maple Leafs). Maple Leaf Gardens, 60 Carlton St. Phone 416/977-1641.

Royal Ontario Museum (ROM). Extensive permanent displays of fine and decorative art, archaeology and earth and life sciences. The collection includes Chinese temple wall paintings; 12 dinosaur skeletons; the Ming

Tomb Gallery; the hands-on Discovery Gallery; Greek, Etruscan, Chinese, European and Egypt and Nubia galleries; special programs. (Daily; closed Jan 1, Dec 25) 100 Queen's Park. Phone 416/586-5549 or -5736. ¢¢¢

Scarborough Civic Centre. Houses offices of municipal government. Guided tours (daily; closed Dec 25). Concert Sun afternoons. 150 Borough Dr in Scarborough. Phone 416/396-7216. **Free.**

Sightseeing tours.

Gray Line bus tours. Contact 184 Front St E, Ste 601, M5A 4N3; 416/594-3310 for schedule and fees.

Toronto Tours Ltd. Four different boat tours of Toronto Harbour. Phone 416/869-1372. ¢¢¢-¢¢¢¢¢

SkyDome. State of the art sports stadium with a fully retractable roof; contains a hotel (see HOTELS), a Hard Rock Cafe and North America's largest McDonald's restaurant. Guided tours (1 hr) begin with 15-min film *The Inside Story* and include visits to a skybox, media center, locker room and the playing field (all subject to availability). Tour (daily, schedule permitting). 1 Blue Jays Way, adj CN Tower. Phone 416/341-2770. ¢¢¢

St Lawrence Centre for the Arts. Performing arts complex features theater, music, dance, films and other public events. 27 Front St E. Phone 416/366-7723 (box office).

The Market Gallery. Exhibition center for Toronto Archives; displays on city's historical, social and cultural heritage; art, photographs, maps, documents and artifacts. (Wed-Sat, also Sun afternoons; closed hols) 95 Front St E. Phone 416/392-7604. **Free.**

Todmorden Mills Heritage Museum & Arts Centre. Restored historic houses; Parshall Terry House (1797) and William Helliwell House (1820). Also museum; restored 1899 train station. Picnicking. (May-Sept, daily exc Mon; Oct-Dec, Mon-Fri) 67 Pottery Rd, 2¼ mi (4 km) N, off Don Valley Pkwy in East York. Phone 416/396-2819. Museum **Free;** Tours ¢¢

Toronto Stock Exchange. Stock Market Place visitor center has multimedia displays, interactive games and archival exhibits to aid visitors in understanding the market. The Exchange Tower, 2 First Canadian Pl (King & York Sts). For schedule phone 416/947-4676. **Free.**

Toronto Symphony. Classical, pops and children's programs; Great Performers series. Wheelchair seating, audio enhancement for hearing-impaired. Roy Thomson Hall, 60 Simcoe St. For schedule, information phone 416/593-4828.

University of Toronto (1827). (55,000 students) Largest university in Canada. Guided walking tours of magnificent Gothic buildings begin at Hart House and include account of campus ghost (June-Aug, Mon-Fri; free). Downtown, W of Queen's Park. Phone 416/978-5000 for tour information.

Woodbine Racetrack. Thoroughbred racing (late Apr-Oct, Wed-Sun afternoons; Queen's Plate race in mid-July). 15 mi (24 km) N via Hwy 427 in Etobicoke. Phone 416/675-RACE. ¢¢

Young People's Theatre. Local professional productions for the entire family. (Sept-May, daily; Aug, wkends only) 165 Front St E. Phone 416/862-2222.

Annual Events

International Caravan. Fifty pavilions scattered throughout the city present ethnic food, dancing, crafts. Phone 416/977-0466. 3rd wk June.

Chin International Picnic. At Paramount Canada's Wonderland. Contests, sports, picnicking. Phone 416/531-9991. 1st wkend July.

Outdoor Art Show. Nathan Phillips Sq. Phone 416/408-2754. Mid-July.

Caribana. Caribbean music, grand parade, floating nightclubs, dancing, costumes, food at various locations throughout city. Phone 416/465-4884. Late July-early Aug.

Canadian National Exhibition. Exhibition Place on the lakefront. This gala celebration originated in 1879 as the Toronto Industrial Exhibition for the encouragement of agriculture, industry and the arts, although agricultural events dominated the show. Today sports, industry, labor and the arts are of equal importance to CNE. The "Ex," as it is locally known, is so inclusive of the nation's activities that it is a condensed Canada. A special 350-acre (141-hectare) park has been built to accommodate the exhibition.

Hundreds of events include animal shows, parades, exhibits, a midway, water and air shows. Virtually every kind of sporting event is represented, from frisbee-throwing to the National Horse Show. Phone 416/393-6000. Mid-Aug-Labour Day.

Toronto International Film Festival. Celebration of world cinema in downtown theaters; Canadian and foreign films, international movie makers and stars. Phone 416/967-7371. Early Sept.

Canadian International. Woodbine Racetrack. World-class Thoroughbreds compete in one of Canada's most important races. Mid-late Oct.

Royal Agricultural Winter Fair. Coliseum Bldg, Exhibition Place. World's largest indoor agricultural fair exhibits the finest livestock. Food shows; Royal Horse Show features international competitions in several catergories. Phone 416/393-6400. Nov 5-14.

Additional Visitor Information

For further information contact Tourism Toronto, Queens Quay Terminal at Harbourfront, 207 Queens Quay W, M5J 1A7; 416/203-2500 or 800/363-1990 (US & Canada). Toronto's public transportation system is extensive and includes buses, subways, streetcars and trolley buses; for maps phone 416/393-4636.

City Neighborhoods

Many of the restaurants, unrated dining establishments and some lodgings listed under Toronto include neighborhoods as well as exact street addresses. Geographic descriptions of these areas are given, followed by a table of restaurants arranged by neighborhood.

Cabbagetown: North of Gerrard St, east of Parliament St, south of Rosedale Valley Rd and west of the Don River.

Downtown: North of Inner Harbour, east of Spadina Ave, south of Bloor St and west of Sherbourne St. **North of Downtown:** North of Bloor St. **East of Downtown:** East of Sherbourne St. **West of Downtown:** West of Spadina Ave.

Harbourfront: North of Inner Harbour, east of Bathurst St, south of Gardiner Expy and west of Yonge St.

Yorkville: North of Bloor St, east of Avenue Rd, south of Davenport Rd and west of Yonge St.

TORONTO RESTAURANTS BY NEIGHBORHOOD AREAS
(For full description, see alphabetical listings under Restaurants)

CABBAGETOWN
Provence. 12 Amelia St

DOWNTOWN
360 Revolving Restaurant. 301 Front St W
Accents (Sutton Place Grande Hotel). 955 Bay St
Avalon. 270 Adelaide St W
Bangkok Garden. 18 Elm St
Barootes. 220 King St W
Bistro 990. 990 Bay St
Bumpkins. 21 Gloucester St
Cafe Victoria (King Edward Hotel). 37 King St E
Canoe. 66 Wellington St W
Carman's Club. 26 Alexander St
Chanterelles (Crowne Plaza Toronto Centre Hotel). 225 Front St W
Chez Max. 166 Wellington St W
Chiaro's (King Edward Hotel). 37 King St E
Ed's Warehouse. 270 King St W
La Fenice. 319 King St W
Lai Wah Heen (Metropolitan Hotel). 108 Chestnut St
Le Papillion. 16 Church St
Lichee Garden. 595 Bay St
Matienon. 51 Ste Nicholas St
Mövenpick Of Switzerland. 165 York St
Old Spaghetti Factory. 54 The Esplanade
Pawnbrokers Daughter. 1115 Bay St
Rivoli Cafe. 332 Queen St W

Senator. 253 Victoria St
Shopsy's Delicatessen. 33 Yonge St
Splendido. 88 Harbord St
Sushi Bistro. 204 Queen St W
Tiger Lily's Noodle House. 257 Queen St W
Truffles (Four Seasons Hotel). 21 Avenue Rd at Bloor St
Wayne Gretzky's. 99 Blue Jays Way
Xango. 106 John St
Yamase. 317 King St W

NORTH OF DOWNTOWN
Arlequin. 134 Avenue Rd
Centro Grill. 2472 Yonge St
Dimaggio's. 1423 Yonge St
Grano. 2035 Yonge St
Grazie. 2373 Yonge St
Harvest Cafe (Inn On The Park Hotel). 1100 Eglinton Ave E
Jerusalem. 955 Eglinton Ave W
Kally's. 430 Nugget Ave
North 44 Degrees. 2537 Yonge St
Pronto. 692 Mount Pleasant Rd
Scaramouche. 1 Benvenuto Place
Thai Flavour. 1554 Avenue Rd
United Bakers Dairy Restaurant. 506 Lawrence Ave W
Vanipha Lanna. 471 Eglinton Ave W
Zucca Trattoria. 2150 Yonge St

EAST OF DOWNTOWN
Ellas. 702 Pape Ave
Rosewater Supper Club. 19 Toronto St

WEST OF DOWNTOWN
Chiado. 864 College St
Old Mill. 21 Old Mill Rd
Oxford Steak House & Tavern. 1130 Martin Grove Rd
Ukrainian Caravan. 5245 Dundas St W
Villa Borghese. 2995 Bloor St W
Zachary's (Wyndham Bristol Place Hotel). 950 Dixon Rd

HARBOURFRONT
Pier 4 Storehouse. 245 Queen's Quay W

YORKVILLE
Boba. 90 Avenue Rd
Chicqry. 14 Prince Arthur Ave
Corner House. 501 Davenport Rd
Il Posto. 148 Yorkville Ave
Joso's. 202 Davenport Rd
Lovelock's. 838 Yonge St
Marketta. 138 Avenue Rd
Opus. 37 Prince Arthur Ave
Patachou. 1095 Yonge St

    Note: When a listing is located in a town that does not have its own city heading, it will appear under the city nearest to its location. In these cases, the address and town appear in parenthesis immediately following the name of the establishment.

Motel

(Rates will be higher during Canadian National Exhibition)

    ✔★ **SEA HORSE INN.** *(2095 Lakeshore Blvd W (ON 2), Toronto ON M8V 1A1)* jct QEW, west of downtown. 416/255-4433; FAX 416/251-5121; res: 800/663-1123. 74 rms, 1-3 story. S $57-$67; D $57-$85; each addl $5; suites $75-$170; under 18 free. TV; cable (premium). Pool; whirlpool. Playground. Complimentary continental bkfst. Ck-out 11 am. Meeting rms. Lighted tennis. Sauna. Refrigerators. Picnic tables, grills. On Lake Ontario. Cr cds: A, C, D, DS, ER, MC, V.

Motor Hotels

✔★ ★ **HOLIDAY INN EXPRESS.** *(50 Estates Dr, Scarborough ON M1H 2Z1) at jct Hwys 48 & 401.* 416/439-9666; FAX 416/439-4295. 136 rms, 2-3 story. No elvtrs. S $56-$79; D $62-$79; each addl $10; under 19 free; wkend rates. Crib free. TV; cable (premium). Complimentary continental bkfst. Restaurant adj 11:30-1 am, Sat, Sun from 4:30 pm. Ck-out 11 am. Meeting rms. Business servs avail. Health club privileges. Cr cds: A, C, D, DS, ER, JCB, MC, V.

⊡ ⇌ 🔥 SC

★ ★ **HOWARD JOHNSON-EAST.** *(940 Progress Ave, Scarborough ON M1G 3T5)* 416/439-6200; FAX 416/439-5689. 186 rms, 6 story. S $99; D $109; each addl $10; under 18 free; wkend package plan. Crib free. Pet accepted. TV; cable (premium). Heated pool; whirlpool. Restaurant 6:30 am-2 pm, 5-10 pm. Rm serv. Bar 4:30 pm-1 am. Ck-out noon. Coin lndry. Meeting rms. Business servs avail. Valet serv. Sundries. Gift shop. Exercise equipt; weight machine, bicycle, sauna. Health club privileges. Microwaves avail. Cr cds: A, C, D, DS, ER, JCB, MC, V.

⊡ ✔ ⇌ ✕ ⇌ 🔥 SC

✔★ **INN ON THE LAKE.** *(1926 Lakeshore Blvd W, Toronto ON M6S 1A1) west of downtown.* 416/766-4392; res: 800/463-9926; FAX 416/766-1278. 110 rms, 4 story. June-early Sept: S $79-$110; D $79-$125; each addl $10; under 12 free; wkly rates; lower rates rest of yr. Crib free. TV; cable (premium). Restaurant nearby. Ck-out 11 am. Meeting rms. Sundries. Many balconies. Opp park; pool, beach. Cr cds: A, MC, V.

⊡ ⇌ 🔥 SC

★ ★ **RAMADA HOTEL-TORONTO AIRPORT.** *(2 Holiday Dr, Etobicoke ON M9C 2Z7) near Lester B Pearson Intl Airport.* 416/621-2121; FAX 416/621-9840. 179 rms, 2-6 story. June-Aug: S, D $140-$150; each addl $10; suites $250-$350; under 19 free; wkly, wkend rates; lower rates rest of yr. Crib free. Pet accepted. TV; cable (premium). Indoor/outdoor pool; whirlpool, lifeguard. Complimentary coffee in rms. Restaurant 6 am-11 pm. Rm serv. Bar 11:30-1 am. Ck-out noon. Business servs avail. In-rm modem link. Bellhops. Valet serv. Free airport transportation. Exercise equipt; weights, sauna. Some minibars; microwaves avail. Cr cds: A, C, D, DS, ER, JCB, MC, V.

⊡ ✔ ⇌ ✕ ✈ ⇌ 🔥 SC

★ ★ **TRAVELODGE-NORTH.** *(50 Norfinch Dr, North York ON M3N 1X1) N on Hwy 400 to Finch Ave, then E to Norfinch Dr.* 416/663-9500; FAX 416/663-8480. Web www.travelodge.com. 184 rms, 6 story. S $76; D $84; each addl $8; under 17 free. Crib free. Pet accepted, some restrictions. TV; cable (premium). Indoor pool; whirlpool. Coffee in rms. Restaurant 7-1 am. Rm serv. Bar. Ck-out 11 am. Meeting rms. Business servs avail. Sundries. Cr cds: A, D, DS, ER, MC, V.

⊡ ✔ ⇌ ⇌ 🔥 SC

★ ★ **TRAVELODGE-TORONTO EAST.** *(20 Milner Business Ct, Scarborough ON M1B 3C6)* 416/299-9500; FAX 416/299-6172. Web www.travelodge.com. 156 rms, 6 story. S, D $66-$76; each addl $6; suites $75-$81; under 17 free. Pet accepted. TV; cable (premium). VCR. Indoor pool; whirlpool. Complimentary coffee in rms. Restaurant 11-2 am. Rm serv noon-11 pm. Ck-out 11 am. Meeting rms. Business servs avail. Sundries. Health club privileges. Microwaves avail. Cr cds: A, D, DS, ER, JCB, MC, V.

⊡ ✔ ⇌ ⇌ SC

★ ★ ★ **VALHALLA INN.** *(1 Valhalla Inn Rd, Etobicoke ON M9B 1S9)* 416/239-2391; FAX 416/239-8764; res: 800/268-2500. 236 rms, 2-12 story. S $140; D $150; each addl $10; suites $189-230; under 18 free; AP avail; wkend packages. Crib free. Pet accepted. TV; cable (premium). Heated pool. Coffee in rms. Restaurant 6 am-11 pm; dining rm noon-2:30 pm, 5:30-10 pm. Rm serv 6 am-11 pm. Bars 11-1 am; entertainment. Ck-out 1 pm. Meeting rms. Business servs avail. In-rm modem link. Bellhops. Valet serv. Sundries. Free airport transportation. Health club privileges. Some bathrm phones. Private patios, balconies. Grills. Cr cds: A, C, D, DS, ER, MC, V.

✔ ⇌ ⇌ ⇌ 🔥 SC

★ **VENTURE INN-YORKVILLE.** *(89 Avenue Rd, Toronto ON M5R 2G3) downtown.* 416/964-1220; FAX 416/964-8692; res: 800/387-3933. 71 rms, 8 story. S $124; D $134; each addl $10; under 19 free; wkend rates off-season. Crib free. Pet accepted, some restrictions. Parking $6.50/day. TV; cable (premium), VCR avail. Complimentary continental bkfst. Ck-out 1 pm. Meeting rms. Business servs avail. Health club privileges. Cr cds: A, D, DS, ER, MC, V.

✔ ⇌ 🔥 SC

Hotels

★ ★ ★ **BEST WESTERN CARLTON PLACE.** *(33 Carlson Court, Etobicoke ON M9W 6H5) near Lester B. Pearson Intl Airport.* 416/675-1234; FAX 416/675-3436. 524 rms, 12 story. S $160-175; D $175-$190; each addl $15; suites $250-$350; under 18 free; wkend, mid-wk rates. Crib free. Parking in/out $4/day. Pet accepted. TV; cable (premium). Indoor pool; whirlpool. Complimentary coffee in rms. Restaurant 6:30-1 am. Rm serv 24 hrs. Bar 11-1 am. Ck-out 1 pm. Meeting rms. Business center. Gift shop. Airport transportation. Exercise equipt; bicycles, treadmill, sauna. Health club privileges. Minibars. Cr cds: A, D, DS, ER, JCB, MC, V.

⊡ ✔ ⇌ ✕ ⇌ 🔥 SC ⛷

★ ★ **BEST WESTERN PRIMROSE.** *(111 Carlton St, Toronto ON M5B 2G3) at Jarvis St, downtown.* 416/977-8000; FAX 416/977-6323. 338 rms, 23 story. S, D $149; each addl $10; suites $275; under 18 free. Crib free. Garage $12.50. TV; cable. Pool; sauna. Complimentary coffee in rms. Restaurant 6:30 am-10 pm. Bar 11-1 am. Ck-out 11 am. Meeting rms. Business servs avail. Exercise equipt; treadmill, bicycle. Cr cds: A, C, D, DS, ER, JCB, MC, V.

⊡ ⇌ ✕ ⇌ 🔥 SC

★ **BOND PLACE.** *(65 Dundas St E, Toronto ON M5B 2G8) east of downtown.* 416/362-6061; FAX 416/360-6406; res: 800/268-9390. 286 rms, 18 story, 51 suites. May-Oct: S, D $89-$109; each addl $15; suites $104-$134; under 15 free; lower rates rest of yr. Crib free. Parking, in/out $11. TV; cable (premium), VCR avail. Restaurant 7 am-11 pm. Rm serv 11 am-10 pm. Bar 11-1 am. Ck-out 11 am. Meeting rms. Business servs avail. Cr cds: A, C, D, DS, ER, MC, V.

⊡ ⇌ SC

★ ★ ★ **THE CAMBERLEY CLUB HOTEL.** *(40 King St W, Toronto ON M5H 3Y2) at Bay St, in the Scotia Plaza Bldg, downtown.* 416/947-9025; FAX 416/947-0622; res: 800/555-8000. 54 suites on 28th & 29th floors of 68-story bldg. Suites $210-$300; under 16 free; monthly rates. Crib free. Garage parking $20 in/out. TV; cable (premium), VCR (free movies). Complimentary continental bkfst. Restaurant 6:30-1 am. Rm serv 24 hrs. Bar from 11 am. Ck-out noon. Meeting rms. Business center. In-rm modem link. Concierge. Shopping arcade. Barber, beauty shop. Health club privileges. Bathrm phones, in-rm whirlpools. Cr cds: A, D, ER, MC, V.

⊡ ⇌ 🔥 ⛷

★ ★ ★ **CLARION ESSEX PARK.** *(300 Jarvis St, Toronto ON M5B 2C5) downtown.* 416/977-4823; FAX 416/977-4830. E-mail clarion@net.com.ca; web www.hotelchoice.com. 102 rms, 10 story, 44 suites. S $140; D $155; each addl $15; suites $170-$250; under 18 free. Crib free. Garage parking $15. TV; cable (premium). Indoor pool; whirlpool. Complimentary coffee in lobby. Restaurant 7 am-2 pm, 5-9 pm. Bar from 11 am. Ck-out 11 am. Meeting rms. Business servs avail. Concierge. Downhill/x-country ski 10 mi. Exercise equipt; weights, bicycle, sauna. Rec rm. Refrigerators. Cr cds: A, C, D, DS, ER, JCB, MC, V.

⇌ ⇌ ✕ ⇌ 🔥 SC

✔★ ★ **COMFORT HOTEL-DOWNTOWN.** *(15 Charles St E, Toronto ON M4Y 1S1) downtown.* 416/924-1222; FAX 416/927-1369. 108 rms, 10 story. S $89; D $99; each addl $10; suites $109-$119; under 18 free; wkend rates. Crib $10. Parking $9. TV; cable (premium), VCR avail. Restaurant noon-10 pm. Piano bar. Ck-out 11 am. Meeting rms. Business servs avail. Health club privileges. Refrigerators; microwaves avail. Cr cds: A, C, D, DS, ER, MC, V.

⇌ 🔥 SC

★ ★ ★ **CROWNE PLAZA-TORONTO CENTRE.** (225 Front St W, Toronto ON M5V 2X3) downtown. 416/597-1400; FAX 416/597-8128. Web crowneplaza.com. 587 rms, 25 story. S, D $219-$234; each addl $15; suites $335-$435; under 18 free; wkend rates. Crib free. TV; cable (premium), VCR avail. Indoor pool; wading pool, whirlpool, poolside serv. Coffee in rms. Restaurant 6-2 am (also see CHANTERELLES). Bar 11:30-2 am; entertainment. Ck-out noon. Meeting rms. Business center. In-rm modem link. Concierge. Valet parking. Exercise rm; instructor, weights, bicycles, sauna. Massage. Minibars; microwaves avail. Formal decor. Cr cds: A, C, D, DS, ER, JCB, MC, V.

★ **DAYS INN-DOWNTOWN.** (30 Carlton St, Toronto ON M5B 2E9) adj to Maple Leaf Gardens, between Yonge & Church Sts, downtown. 416/977-6655; FAX 416/977-0502. Web www.daysinn.com/daysinn.html. 536 rms, 23 story. S, D $89-$129; each addl $15; under 16 free. Crib free. Pet accepted, some restrictions. Covered parking $13/day. TV; cable. Indoor pool; sauna. Restaurant 7 am-10 pm. Bar 11:30-2 am. Ck-out 11 am. Coin lndry. Meeting rms. Business servs avail. Sundries. Barber, beauty shop. Some refrigerators. Sun deck. Cr cds: A, D, DS, ER, JCB, MC, V.

★ ★ ★ **DELTA CHELSEA INN.** (33 Gerrard St W, Toronto ON M5G 1Z4) between Bay & Yonge Sts, downtown. 416/595-1975; FAX 416/585-4362; res: 800/268-1133. E-mail reservations@deltachelsea .com; web www.deltahotels.com. 1,594 rms, 26 story. S $225-$235; D $240-$250; each addl $15; suites, kit. units $240-$345; under 18 free; wkend rates. Crib free. Pet accepted, some restrictions. Valet parking $21 in/out. TV; cable, VCR avail. 2 heated pools; whirlpool. Supervised child's activities; ages 2-13. Restaurant 6:30-1 am. Rm serv 24 hrs. Bar 11-1 am; entertainment. Ck-out 11 am. Convention facilities. Business center. Gift shop. Exercise equipt; weights, bicycles, sauna. Health club privileges. Game rm. Refrigerator in some suites. Microwaves avail. Many balconies. Cr cds: A, C, D, DS, ER, JCB, MC, V.

★ ★ ★ **DELTA-TORONTO AIRPORT.** (801 Dixon Rd, Etobicoke ON M9W 1J5) near Lester B. Pearson Intl Airport. 416/675-6100; FAX 416/675-4022; res: 800/668-1444. E-mail delta@nbnet.nb.ca; web www. deltahotels.com. 251 rms, 8 story. S, D $105-$155; each addl $15; suites $155-$205; under 18 free; wkend package plan. Crib free. Pet accepted, some restrictions. TV; cable (premium). Indoor pool; sauna. Supervised child's activities (June-Aug). Restaurant 6 am-11 pm. Rm serv 24 hrs. Bar 11:30-2 am. Ck-out 1 pm. Convention facilities. Business center. Valet serv. Gift shops. Exercise equipt; bicycles, treadmill. Health club privileges. Minibars. Microwave avail. Cr cds: A, C, D, DS, ER, JCB, MC, V.

★ ★ ★ **EMBASSY SUITES.** (8500 Warden Ave, Markham ON L6G 1A5) 905/470-8500; FAX 905/477-8611. 332 suites, 10 story. S, D $152-$172; each addl $20; wkend packages; under 18 free. Crib free. Valet parking $3. TV; cable (premium). Indoor pool; whirlpool. Complimentary full bkfst. Coffee in rms. Restaurant 6:30 am-midnight. Bar 11-2 am. Ck-out noon. Convention facilities. Business center. Shopping arcade. Barber, beauty shop. Exercise rm; instructor, weights, bicycles, sauna, steam rm. Minibars; microwaves avail. Extensive grounds; elaborate landscaping. Elegant atmosphere. Cr cds: A, C, D, ER, MC, V.

★ ★ ★ ★ **FOUR SEASONS.** (21 Avenue Rd at Bloor St, Toronto ON M5R 2G1) downtown. 416/964-0411; FAX 416/964-2302; res: 800/332-6282 (CAN & NY). Web www.fshr.com. This fashionable, elegant hotel has a prime location in Toronto. 380 rms, 32 story. S $250-$280; D $280-$315; each addl $25; suites $375-$2,400; under 18 free; wkend rates. Crib free. Pet accepted. Garage $18.75/day. TV; cable (premium), VCR avail (movies). Indoor/outdoor pool; whirlpool, poolside serv, lifeguard. Restaurants 6:30 am-11 pm (also see TRUFFLES). Rm serv 24 hrs. Bar 11:30-2 am; entertainment exc Sun. Ck-out 1 pm. Convention facilities. Business center. In-rm modem link. Concierge. Barber, beauty shop. Valet parking. Exercise rm; instructor, weights, bicycles, sauna. Massage. Bathrm

phones, minibars; microwaves avail. Some balconies. Cr cds: A, C, D, ER, JCB, MC, V.

★ ★ ★ **HILTON.** (145 Richmond St W, Toronto ON M5H 2L2) at University Ave, downtown. 416/869-3456; FAX 416/869-1478. Web www.hilton.com. 601 rms, 32 story. Apr-Nov: S, D $239-$259; each addl $20; suites $249-$1,600; family rates; wkend package plans; lower rates rest of yr. Crib free. Garage $17.50. TV; cable (premium). Indoor/outdoor pool; whirlpool, poolside serv in summer. Restaurant 6:30 am-11 pm. Rm serv 24 hrs. Bar 11:30-2 am. Ck-out noon. Convention facilities. Business center. Exercise equipt; weights, bicycles, sauna. Massage. Minibars. Luxury level. Cr cds: A, C, D, DS, ER, JCB, MC, V.

★ ★ ★ **HOLIDAY INN.** (1100 Eglinton Ave E, Toronto ON M3C 1H8) north of downtown. 416/446-3700; FAX 416/446-3701. 298 rms, 14 story. S $75-$115; D $85-$125; each addl $10; suites $175-$325; family, wkend, wkly rates. Crib free. Pet accepted, some restrictions. TV; cable (premium), VCR avail (movies). Complimentary coffee in lobby. Restaurant 6:30 am-11 pm. Rm serv from 5 pm. Bar 11:30-1 am; entertainment Thurs-Sat. Ck-out noon. Convention facilities. Business servs avail. In-rm modem link. Concierge. Shopping arcade. Barber, beauty shop. Free valet parking. Airport, RR station transportation. Indoor tennis, pro. X-country ski 1/4 mi. Exercise equipt; weights, stair machine, sauna. Indoor/outdoor pool; whirlpool, poolside serv, lifeguard. Playground. Supervised child's activities (May-Sept); ages 5-12. Game rm. Lawn games. Bathrm phones, refrigerators. Many balconies. Cr cds: A, C, D, DS, ER, JCB, MC, V.

★ ★ **HOLIDAY INN.** (970 Dixon Rd, Etobicoke ON M9W 1J9) near Lester B. Pearson Intl Airport. 416/675-7611; FAX 416/674-4364. 444 rms, 12 story. S, D $160-$175; suites $230-$430; wkend rates. Crib free. Pet accepted. TV; cable (premium). 2 heated pools, 1 indoor; whirlpool. Playground. Coffee in rms. Restaurant 6 am-10:30 pm. Rm serv to 1 am. Bar 11-2 am; Sun noon-11 pm. Ck-out 1 pm. Meeting rms. Business center. Concierge. Barber, beauty shop. Free airport transportation. Exercise equipt; weights, bicycles, sauna. Rec rm. Minibars. Cr cds: A, C, D, DS, ER, JCB, MC, V.

★ ★ ★ **HOLIDAY INN ON KING.** (370 King St W, Toronto ON M5V 1J9) downtown. 416/599-4000; FAX 416/599-7394. E-mail 104664.3505@compuserve.com; web www.hick.com. 425 rms, 20 story. S $169; D $189; each addl $15; suites $209-$239; family, monthly rates. Crib free. Garage $16. TV; cable, VCR avail. Heated rooftop pool; poolside serv, lifeguard. Complimentary coffee in rms. Restaurant 6:30-2 am. Bar from 11 am. Ck-out noon. Convention facilities. Business center. Concierge. Gift shop. Exercise equipt; weight machine, treadmill, sauna. Massage. Wet bars. Cr cds: A, C, D, DS, ER, JCB, MC, V.

★ ★ **HOLIDAY INN-YORKDALE.** (3450 Dufferin St, Toronto ON M6A 2V1) 1 blk S of ON 401 Dufferin St exit, north of downtown. 416/789-5161; FAX 416/785-6845. 365 rms, 12 story. S $134.95; D $149.95; each addl $15; suites $299.95-$499.95; under 19 free; wkend rates. Crib free. TV; cable (premium). Heated pool; whirlpool. Supervised child's activities. Complimentary coffee in rms. Restaurant 6 am-11 pm. Bar 11-1 am. Ck-out noon. Meeting rms. Business center. Exercise equipt; weights, bicycles, sauna. Rec rm. Minibars. Some balconies. Cr cds: A, C, D, DS, ER, JCB, MC, V.

★ ★ **HOWARD JOHNSON PLAZA.** (600 Dixon Rd, Etobicoke ON M9W 1J1) 416/240-7511; FAX 416/240-7519. 172 rms, 2-5 story. S, D $89-$109; each addl $10; suites $129-$149; under 18 free. Crib free. TV; cable, VCR avail. Heated pool; wading pool, poolside serv. Coffee in rms. Restaurant 24 hrs. Ck-out 1 pm. Meeting rms. Business servs avail. Exercise equipt: stair machine, weights. Cr cds: A, C, D, DS, ER, MC, V.

★ ★ ★ **HOWARD JOHNSON PLAZA.** *(2737 Keele St, North York ON M3M 2E9) N on Hwy 401, exit Keele St, then 1 blk N. 416/636-4656; FAX 416/633-5637.* Web www.hojo.com. 367 rms, most A/C, 10 story, 27 suites. S, D $129-$179; each addl $10; suites $175-$375; family, wkly, wkend, hol rates. Crib free. Pet accepted. TV; cable (premium), VCR avail. Indoor pool. Supervised child's activities (June-Sept); ages 4-12. Complimentary coffee in rms. Restaurant 6:30 am-11 pm, Sun to 10 pm. Bar 11-1 am; entertainment. Ck-out 1 pm. Meeting rms. Business servs avail. Free garage parking. Downhill/x-country ski 10 mi. Exercise equipt; weight machine, treadmill, sauna. Game rm. Rec rm. Some minibars; microwaves avail. Cr cds: A, C, D, DS, ER, JCB, MC, V.

D ⚑ ⚓ ≈ 🕍 ↟ SC

★ ★ ★ **INN ON THE PARK.** *(1100 Eglinton Ave E, Toronto ON M3C 1H8) at Leslie St, north of downtown. 416/444-2561; FAX 416/446-3308; res: 800/268-6282 (CAN).* This hotel is set in a 600-acre park just 15 minutes from downtown Toronto. Guest rooms are bright and inviting, with all the amenities for relaxation or business. 270 rms, 23 story. S $120-$175; D $135-$195; each addl $20; suites $225-$750; under 18 free; wkend rates. Crib free. TV; cable (premium), VCR avail. 2 heated pools, 1 indoor; whirlpool, lifeguards. Free supervised child's activities (May-Sept); ages 5-12. Restaurants 6:30 am-midnight (also see HARVEST CAFE). Bar 11:30-1 am; vocalist exc Sun. Ck-out noon. Business servs avail. In-rm modem link. Concierge. Barber, beauty shop. Valet parking. Lighted tennis, pro. X-country ski 1/4 mi. Exercise equipt; weights, bicycles, sauna, steam rm. Rec rm. Lawn games. Some minibars. Some private patios, balconies. Cr cds: A, C, D, ER, JCB, MC, V.

D ⚑ ⚓ ≈ 🕍 ⛷ ↟ SC

★ ★ ★ ★ **INTER-CONTINENTAL.** *(220 Bloor St W, Toronto ON M5S 1T8) downtown. 416/960-5200; FAX 416/960-8269.* Web www.interconti.com. Edwardian and art-deco touches embellish public spaces and guest rooms of this post-modern structure. 209 rms, 8 story. S $235-$315; D $255-$335; suites $400-$1,400. Crib free. Valet parking $21.40. TV; cable (premium), VCR avail (movies). Indoor pool. Restaurants 7 am-11 pm. Rm serv 24 hrs. Bar noon-1 am. Ck-out 1 pm. Meeting rms. Business center. In-rm modem link. Concierge. Gift shop. Exercise equipt; weights, treadmill, sauna. Massage. Bathrm phones, minibars. Cr cds: A, C, D, ER, JCB, MC, V.

D ≈ 🕍 🛬 ↟ SC ↟

★ ★ ★ **INTERNATIONAL PLAZA.** *(655 Dixon Rd, Toronto ON M9W 1J4) near Lester B. Pearson Intl Airport, west of downtown. 416/244-1711; FAX 416/244-8031; res: 800/668-3656.* 415 rms, 12 story. S, D $150; each addl $10; suites $250-$450; under 18 free; wkly, wkend, hol rates. Crib free. Pet accepted. Valet parking $6. TV; cable (premium). Indoor pool; wading pool, poolside serv, lifeguard. Supervised child's activities; ages 3-12. Restaurant 6:30 am-11 pm. Rm serv 24 hrs. Bar 11-2 am. Ck-out noon. Convention facilities. Business center. Concierge. Gift shop. Beauty, barber shop. Exercise equipt; weight machine, treadmill, sauna. Massages. Game rm. Refrigerators. Minibars in suites. Cr cds: A, D, DS, ER, MC, V.

D ⚑ ≈ 🕍 🛬 ↟ SC ↟

★ ★ ★ ★ **KING EDWARD.** *(37 King St E, Toronto ON M5C 1E9) downtown. 416/863-9700; FAX 416/367-5515; res: 800/225-5843.* E-mail 104665.3516@compuserve.com. Built in 1903 and remodelled in the early 1980s, this stately and attractive hotel has a vaulted ceiling, marble pillars and palm trees in its lobby. 299 rms, 9 & 16 story. S $229-$289; D $249-$309; suites $300-$500; under 17 free; wkend rates. Crib free. Covered parking, valet $24. TV; cable (premium), VCR avail. Restaurants 6:30 am-2:30 pm, 5-11 pm (see CHIARO'S, also see CAFE VICTORIA, Unrated Dining). Rm serv 24 hrs. Bars noon-1 am. Ck-out noon. Convention facilities. Business center. In-rm modem link. Concierge. Shopping arcade. Beauty shop. Exercise equipt; weights, bicycles, whirlpools, sauna. Massage. Health club privileges. Bathrm phones, minibars; microwaves avail. Cr cds: A, C, D, ER, JCB, MC, V.

D 🕍 🛬 ↟ SC ↟

★ ★ ★ **MARRIOTT-EATON CENTRE.** *(525 Bay St, Toronto ON M5G 2L2) downtown. 416/597-9200; FAX 416/597-9211.* 459 rms, 18 story. May-Oct: S, D $250; suites $600-$1800; family rates; wkly, wkend,

hol rates; higher rates special events; lower rates rest of yr. Crib free. Garage parking $14, valet $18. TV; cable (premium), VCR avail. Indoor pool; whirlpool, poolside serv. Restaurant 6:30 am-10 pm. Rm serv 24 hrs. Bar 11-1 am. Ck-out noon. Convention facilities. Business center. Concierge. Shopping arcade. Drug store. Barber, beauty shop. Exercise equipt; weight machine, stair machines, sauna. Cr cds: A, D, JCB, MC, V.

D ≈ 🕍 🛬 ↟ SC ↟

★ ★ ★ **MARRIOTT-AIRPORT.** *(901 Dixon Rd, Etobicoke ON M9W 1J5) near Lester B. Pearson Intl Airport. 416/674-9400; FAX 416/674-8292.* 424 rms, 9 story. S, D $240; suites $300-$1,000; under 18 free; wkend rates. Crib free. TV; cable (premium). Indoor pool; whirlpool. Restaurants 6 am-11 pm. Bar noon-2 am. Ck-out noon. Convention facilities. Business center. Gift shop. Covered parking. Free airport transportation. Exercise rm; instructor, weights, bicycles, sauna. Luxury level. Cr cds: A, C, D, ER, JCB, MC, V.

D ≈ 🕍 🛬 ↟ SC ↟

★ ★ ★ **METROPOLITAN.** *(108 Chestnut St, Toronto ON M5G 1R3) downtown. 416/977-5000; res: 800/668-6600; FAX 416/977-9513.* E-mail reservations@metropolitan.com; web www.metropolitan.com. 480 rms, 26 story. S $160; D $180; each addl $20; suites $195-$850; wkend rates. Crib free. Parking, in/out $15.87. Pet accepted, some restrictions. TV; cable (premium), VCR avail (free movies). Indoor pool; whirlpool. Restaurant 6:30 am-midnight (see also LAI WAH HEEN). Rm serv 24 hrs. Bar 11-1 am. Ck-out noon. Meeting rms. Business center. In-rm modem link. Concierge. Gift shop. Exercise equipt; treadmill, bicycles, sauna. Bathrm phones, minibars. Adj to City Hall. Eatons Centre 2 blks. Cr cds: A, C, D, DS, ER, JCB, MC, V.

D ≈ 🕍 🛬 ↟ SC ↟

★ ★ **NOVOTEL-AIRPORT.** *(135 Carlingview Dr, Etobicoke ON M9W 5E7) near Lester B. Pearson Intl Airport. 416/798-9800; FAX 416/798-1237; res: 800/668-6835.* E-mail tairmail@aol.com. 192 rms, 7 story. S $165; D $175; suites $175; family, wkly, wkend rates. Crib free. Pet accepted. TV; cable (premium), VCR avail. Indoor pool; whirlpool. Restaurant 6 am-11 pm. Bar 11-1 am. Ck-out 1 pm. Meeting rms. Business center. In-rm modem link. Gift shop. Free garage parking. Free airport transportation. Downhill/x-country ski 20 mi. Exercise equipt; weights, treadmill, sauna. Minibars. Cr cds: A, D, DS, ER, JCB, MC, V.

D ⚑ ⚓ ≈ 🕍 🛬 ↟ SC

★ ★ ★ **NOVOTEL-TORONTO CENTRE.** *(45 The Esplanade, Toronto ON M5E 1W2) downtown. 416/367-8900; FAX 416/360-8285; res: 800/668-6835.* Web novotel-northamerica.com/welcome. 262 rms, 9 story. S, D $135-$185; each addl $15; suites $215; under 16 free; wkend rates. Crib free. Pet accepted. Garage (fee). TV; cable (premium). Indoor pool; whirlpool. Restaurant 6 am-midnight. Bar 11-1 am. Ck-out 1 pm. Meeting rms. Business servs avail. Exercise equipt; weights, rowers, sauna. Minibars. Cr cds: A, D, DS, ER, JCB, MC, V.

D ⚑ ≈ 🕍 ↟ SC

★ ★ ★ **PARK PLAZA.** *(4 Avenue Rd, Toronto ON M5R 2E8) at Bloor St, downtown. 416/924-5471; FAX 416/924-6693; res: 800/977-4197.* 261 rms, 12-18 story; 40 suites. S, D $225-$260; each addl $15; suites $350-$750; family, wkend rates. Crib free. Pet accepted. Garage in/out $18. TV; cable (premium), VCR avail. Restaurant 7 am-10:30 pm. Bar 11:30-2 am. Ck-out noon. Meeting rms. Business center. Concierge. Health club privileges. Minibars. Many antique furnishings in public areas. Royal Ontario Museum opp. Cr cds: A, C, D, DS, ER, JCB, MC, V.

D ⚑ ↟ ↟ SC ↟

★ **QUALITY.** *(111 Lombard St, Toronto ON M5C 2T9) downtown. 416/367-5555; FAX 416/367-3470; res: 800/228-5151.* 196 rms, 16 story. S $129; D $139; each addl $10; under 18 free. Crib free. Pet accepted. Garage $11.75/day. TV; cable. Ck-out 11 am. Business servs avail. Health club privileges. Cr cds: A, D, DS, JCB, MC, V.

D ⚑ ↟ ↟ SC

★ **QUALITY.** *(280 Bloor St W, Toronto ON M5S 1V8) downtown. 416/968-0010; FAX 416/968-7765.* 210 rms, 14 story. Mid-Mar-Oct: S $115-$130; D $127-$152; under 18 free; wkend rates; higher rates special events; lower rates rest of yr. Crib free. Pet accepted, some restrictions. Garage in/out $11.50. TV; cable. Restaurant 7 am-11 pm. Bar 11 am-11 pm. Ck-out 11 am. Meeting rms. Business servs avail. No bellhops. Health club privileges. Cr cds: A, D, DS, JCB, MC, V.

D ⟵ ⊠ ⧖ SC

✔★★ **QUALITY SUITES.** (262 Carlingview Dr, Etobicoke ON M9W 5G1) near Lester B. Pearson Intl Airport. 416/674-8442; FAX 416/674-3088. Web hotelchoice.com. 254 suites, 12 story. S, D $120-$145; each addl $5; under 18 free; wkend, hol rates. Crib free. Pet accepted. TV; cable (premium), VCR avail (movies). Complimentary coffee in rms. Restaurant 6:30-1 am. Bar. Ck-out 11 am. Meeting rms. Business servs avail. No bellhops. Gift shop. Downhill/x-country ski 15 mi. Exercise equipt; bicycles, stair machine. Health club privileges. Game rm. Minibars; microwaves avail. Cr cds: A, D, DS, ER, JCB, MC, V.

D ⟵ ⊠ ⧖ ✈ ⊠ ⧖ SC

★ **QUALITY-AIRPORT EAST.** (2180 Islington Ave, Toronto ON M9T 3P1) west of downtown. 416/240-9090; FAX 416/240-9944. Web www.qualityinn.com. 214 rms, 12 story. S, D $85-135; each addl $5; under 18 free; wkly, wkend rates; higher rates special events. Crib free. Pet accepted. TV; cable (premium). Restaurant 7 am-10 pm. Bar from 11 am. Ck-out 11 am. Meeting rms. In-rm modem link. Microwaves avail. Near airport. Cr cds: A, D, DS, ER, JCB, MC, V.

D ⟵ ⊠ ⧖ SC

★★★ **RADISSON.** (50 E Valhalla Dr, Markham ON L3R 0A3) N on Hwy 404, at jct Hwy 7. 905/477-2010; FAX 905/477-2026. Web www.radisson.com/toronto/markham. 202 rms, 15 story, 26 suites. S, D $210; each addl $15; suites $250; under 19 free; wkly, wkend rates; golf plans; higher rates Dec 31. Crib free. Indoor pool; whirlpool. Complimentary continental bkfst. Complimentary coffee in rms. Restaurant 6:30 am-11 pm. Bar 11-2 am. Ck-out noon. Meeting rms. Business servs avail. Gift shop. Tennis privileges. 18-hole golf privileges. Downhill/x-country ski 12 mi. Exercise equipt; weights, bicycle, sauna. Rec rm. Minibars; microwaves avail. Picnic tables. Cr cds: A, C, D, DS, ER, JCB, MC, V.

D ⊠ ⧖ ✈ ⊠ ⊠ ⧖ SC

★★★ **RADISSON PLAZA.** (90 Bloor St E, Toronto ON M4W 1A7) at Yonge St, downtown. 416/961-8000; FAX 416/961-4635; res: 800/267-6116. Web www.radisson.com. 256 rms, 6 story. S $225; D $240; each addl $15; under 18 free. Crib $15. Garage parking, valet $18.50. TV; cable (premium), VCR avail. Coffee in rms. Restaurant 6:30 am-11:30 pm. Bar 11:30-1 am. Ck-out 1 pm. Meeting rms. Business center. Health club privileges. Minibars; bathrm phone in suites, microwaves avail. Luxury level. Cr cds: A, C, D, DS, ER, JCB, MC, V.

D ⊠ ⧖ SC ⛷

★★★ **RADISSON PLAZA-HOTEL ADMIRAL.** (249 Queens Quay W, Toronto ON M5J 2N5) downtown. 416/203-3333; FAX 416/203-3100. 157 air-cooled rms, 8 story, 17 suites. Early-May-mid-Nov: S, D $205-$255; each addl $20; suites from $450; family, wkend rates. Crib free. Parking $15/day. TV; cable (premium). Heated pool; whirlpool, poolside serv. Restaurant 7 am-11 pm. Rm serv 24 hrs. Bar 11:30-1 am. Ck-out noon. Meeting rms. Business servs avail. Concierge. Gift shop. Health club privileges. Bathrm phones, minibars. On waterfront; nautical theme throughout. View of Harbour. Cr cds: A, C, D, DS, ER, JCB, MC, V.

D ⊠ ⊠ ⧖ SC ⛷

★★★ **RADISSON SUITE-TORONTO AIRPORT.** (640 Dixon Rd, Etobicoke ON M9W 1J1) near Lester B. Pearson Intl Airport. 416/242-7400; FAX 416/242-9888. Web www.radisson.com. 215 suites, 14 story. S, D $204-216; under 18 free. Crib free. Pet accepted, some restrictions. TV; cable, VCR avail. Complimentary continental bkfst. Restaurant 6:30 am-11 pm. Bar 11-1 am. Ck-out noon. Meeting rms. Business center. In-rm modem link. Concierge. Gift shop. Free valet parking. Exercise equipt; weights, bicycles. Minibars; microwaves avail. Cr cds: A, C, D, DS, ER, JCB, MC, V.

D ⟵ ✈ ✈ ⊠ ⧖ SC ⛷

★★ **RAMADA-DON VALLEY.** (185 Yorkland Blvd, Toronto ON M2J 4R2) at jct ON 401, Don Valley Pkwy. 416/493-9000; FAX 416/493-5729. 281 rms, 10 story. S, D $105-$165; each addl $15; suites $175-$300; under 18 free; wkend rates. Crib free. TV; cable (premium), VCR avail (movies). Indoor pool; sauna. Coffee in rms. Restaurant 6:30 am-10:30 pm; Sat from 7 am. Bar 11-2 am; Sun to 11 pm. Ck-out noon. Meeting rms. Business servs avail. In-rm modem link. Exercise equipt; bicycles, weight machine. Health club privileges. Game rm. Rec rm. Some in-rm whirlpools. Luxury level. Cr cds: A, C, D, DS, ER, JCB, MC, V.

D ⊠ ✈ ✈ ⊠ ⧖ SC

★★★ **REGAL CONSTELLATION.** (900 Dixon Rd, Etobicoke ON M9W 1J7) near Lester B. Pearson Intl Airport. 416/675-1500; FAX 416/675-1737; res: 800/268-4838. Web www.dms-destination.com/regal/regal.htm. 710 rms, 8-16 story. S, D $95-$165; each addl $15; suites from $275; under 18 free; wkend package plan. Crib free. Pet accepted, some restrictions. Valet parking $7.50/day. TV; cable (premium), VCR avail. 2 heated pools, 1 indoor/outdoor; whirlpool, poolside serv in season. Restaurant 6:30 am-11 pm; dining rm 11 am-2 pm, 5:30-10 pm. Rm serv 24 hrs. Bar 11-2 am; entertainment Thurs-Sat. Ck-out noon. Concierge. Convention facilities. Business center. Gift shop. Barber, beauty shop. Airport transportation. Exercise equipt; weights, bicycles, sauna. Some balconies. Cr cds: A, C, D, DS, ER, MC, V.

D ⟵ ⊠ ✈ ✈ ⊠ ⧖ SC ⛷

★★★ **ROYAL YORK.** (100 Front St W, Toronto ON M5J 1E3) opp Union Station, downtown. 416/368-2511; FAX 416/368-2884; res: 800/828-7447 (US). E-mail reserve@ryh.mhs.compuserve.com; web www.cphotels.ca. 1,365 rms, 22 story. S, D $189-$289; each addl $20; suites $295-$1,750; under 18 free; wkend packages. Crib free. Pet accepted. Garage (fee). TV; cable. Pool; wading pool, whirlpool. Restaurant 6:30 am-10:30 pm. Rm serv 24 hrs. Bars noon-2 am; entertainment. Ck-out noon. Convention facilities. Business center. Concierge. Shopping arcade. Barber, beauty shop. Exercise rm; instructor, weight machines, rower, sauna. Massage. Health club privileges. Minibars; refrigerators, microwaves avail. Luxury level. Cr cds: A, C, D, DS, ER, JCB, MC, V.

D ⟵ ⊠ ✈ ⧖ SC ⛷

★★★ **SHERATON CENTRE.** (123 Queen St W, Toronto ON M5H 2M9) opp City Hall, downtown. 416/361-1000; FAX 416/947-4854. Web www.sheratonctr.toronto.on.ca. 1,382 rms, 43 story. Late June-Dec: S $250; D $285; each addl $20; suites $405-$780; under 18 free; wkend rates; lower rates rest of yr. Covered parking, valet $22/day. TV; cable (premium), VCR avail. Indoor/outdoor pool; whirlpool, sauna, poolside serv (summer), lifeguard. Supervised child's activities (daily July-mid-Sept; wkends rest of yr). Complimentary coffee in rms. Restaurant 6 am-11 pm. Rm serv 24 hrs. Bars. Ck-out noon. Convention facilities. Business center. Concierge. Shopping arcade. Barber, beauty shop. Exercise equipt; weights, treadmills. Massage. Health club privileges. Rec rm. Minibars; microwaves avail. Private patios, balconies. Waterfall in lobby; pond with live ducks. Cr cds: A, C, D, DS, ER, JCB, MC, V.

D ⊠ ✈ ✈ ⧖ SC ⛷

★★★ **SHERATON GATEWAY.** (PO Box 3000, Toronto ON L5P 1C4) at Lester B. Pearson Intl Airport, west of downtown. 905/672-7000; FAX 905/672-7100. 474 rms, 8 story. S, D $180-$210; each addl $15; suites $270-$695; under 18 free; wkly, wkend rates. Crib free. Pet accepted. Garage parking $8; valet $18. TV; cable (premium), VCR avail. Indoor pool; whirlpool. Restaurant 6 am-11 pm. Rm serv 24 hrs. Bar 11-1 am. Ck-out noon. Convention facilities. Business center. Concierge. Shopping arcade. Barber, beauty shop. Free airport transportation. Exercise equipt; weights, rowers, sauna. Massage. Minibars. Modern facility connected by climate-controlled walkway to Terminal 3. Cr cds: A, C, D, DS, ER, JCB, MC, V.

D ⟵ ⊠ ✈ ✈ ⊠ ⧖ SC ⛷

★★★ **SHERATON-TORONTO EAST.** (2035 Kennedy Rd, Scarborough ON M1T 3G2) 416/299-1500; FAX 416/299-8959. E-mail sheraton@maple.net; web www.sheraton.com/toronto. 371 rms, 13 story. S, D $198; each addl $15; suites $350-$595; under 18 free; wkend rates. Crib free. Pet accepted. TV; cable. Indoor pool; wading pool; whirlpool. Free supervised child's activities (mid-Mar & mid-June-Aug, daily; rest of yr, Sat,

Sun & hols); ages 3-15. Restaurants 6:30-2 am. Rm serv 24 hrs. Bar 11-2 am. Ck-out noon. Convention facilities. Business servs avail. In-rm modem link. Concierge. Gift shop. Barber, beauty shop. Covered valet parking. Putting green. Exercise rm; instructor, weights, bicycles, sauna. Game rm. Microwaves avail. Luxury level. Cr cds: A, C, D, DS, ER, JCB, MC, V.

D ⊠ ≋ ⅀ ⚡ SC

★ ★ ★ **SKYDOME.** *(1 Blue Jays Way, Toronto ON M5V 1J4) adj CN Tower, downtown.* 416/341-7100; FAX 416/341-5090; res: 800/441-1414. E-mail mgeorge@sky.mhs.compuserv.com; web www.cphotels.ca. 346 rms, 11 story, 70 suites. Apr-Oct: S, D $139-$179; each addl $30; suites from $300; under 18 free; wknd rates; package plans. Crib avail. Pet accepted. Garage parking $16; valet $22. TV; cable, VCR avail. Indoor pool. Complimentary coffee in rms. Supervised child's activities (June-Sept). Restaurant 7-1 am. Rm serv 24 hrs. Bar. Ck-out 9:30 am-noon. Convention facilities. Business center. Concierge. Gift shop. Health club privileges. Massage. Minibars. Modern facility within SkyDome complex; lobby and some rms overlook playing field. Cr cds: A, C, D, DS, ER, JCB, MC, V.

D ⊠ ≋ ⅀ ⚡ SC ⚒

★ ★ ★ **SUTTON PLACE GRANDE.** *(955 Bay St, Toronto ON M5S 2A2) downtown.* 416/924-9221; res: 800/268-3790; FAX 416/924-1778. E-mail gm@tor.suttonplace.com; web www.travelweb.com/sutton.html. 292 rms, 33 story, 62 suites. S $260; D $280; each addl $20; suites $380-$1,500; under 18 free; wknd rates. Crib free. Garage parking $17, valet $19. TV; cable (premium), VCR avail (movies). Indoor pool; poolside serv. Restaurant (see ACCENTS). Rm serv 24 hrs. Bar 11-2 am; entertainment. Ck-out noon. Convention facilities. Business center. Concierge. Gift shop. Barber, beauty shop. Exercise equipt; weight machine, treadmill, sauna. Massage. Minibars. Cr cds: A, C, D, DS, ER, MC, V.

D ⊠ ≋ ⅀ ⚡ SC ⚒

★ ★ **TOWN INN.** *(620 Church St, Toronto ON M4Y 2G2) downtown.* 416/964-3311; FAX 416/924-9466; res: 800/387-2755. E-mail mitch@towninn.com; web towninn.com/. 200 kit. units (1-2 bedrm), 29 story. June-Dec: S $95-$125; D $110-$135; each addl $15; under 12 free; monthly rates; lower rates rest of yr. Crib free. Pet accepted. Garage $13. TV; cable (premium). Heated pool; saunas. Complimentary continental bkfst. Restaurant 7-10 am. Ck-out noon. Meeting rms. Business servs avail. Tennis. Exercise equipt; bicycles. Health club privileges. Refrigerators, microwaves. Balconies. Cr cds: A, C, D, ER, MC, V.

D ⚡ ≋ ⅀ ⚡ SC

✔ ★ ★ **TRAVELODGE.** *(55 Hallcrown Pl, North York ON M2J 4R1) ON 401 exit 376, then N on Victoria Park Ave, off Consumer Rd.* 416/493-7000; FAX 416/493-6577. 228 rms, 9 story. S, D $95-$100; each addl $10; suites $150-$225; under 17 free; wknd rates. Crib free. TV; cable (premium), VCR avail. Indoor pool; whirlpool. Complimentary coffee in rms. Restaurant 7 am-10 pm. Bar. Ck-out noon. Meeting rms. Business servs avail. Sauna. Cr cds: A, C, D, DS, ER, MC, V.

D ≋ ⅀ ⚡ SC

★ ★ **VENTURE INN-AIRPORT.** *(925 Dixon Rd, Etobicoke ON M9W 1J8) near Lester B. Pearson Intl Airport.* 416/674-2222; FAX 416/674-5757; res: 888/4-VENTURE. Web www.jwg.com/ventureinns/. 283 rms, 17 story. S $95; D $105; each addl $10; suites $140-$275; under 19 free; wknd rates. Crib free. Pet accepted. TV, cable (premium). Indoor pool; whirlpool. Complimentary continental bkfst. Restaurant 11-2 am. Bar. Ck-out 1 pm. Convention facilities. Business servs avail. In-rm modem link. Airport transportation. Sauna. Health club privileges. Gift shop. Cr cds: A, D, DS, ER, MC, V.

D ⚡ ≋ ⅀ ⚡ SC

★ ★ ★ **WESTIN PRINCE.** *(900 York Mills Rd, North York ON M3B 3H2) N on Don Valley Pkwy, W on York Mills Rd.* 416/444-2511; FAX 416/444-9597. E-mail toprince@idirect.com; web www.princehotels.co.jp. 381 rms, 22 story. S $190-$225; D $210-$245; each addl $20; suites $340-$1,800; under 18 free; wknd rates. Crib free. TV; cable (premium), VCR avail (movies). Pool; whirlpool, poolside serv. Playground. Restaurant 6:30 am-10 pm. Rm serv 24 hrs. Bar 11:30-2 am; entertainment Mon-Sat. Ck-out 1 pm. Convention facilities. Business center. In-rm mo-

dem link. Concierge. Shopping arcade. Barber, beauty shop. Tennis. 18-hole golf privileges. Exercise equipt; weights, bicycle, sauna. Game rm. Refrigerators. Balconies. Cr cds: A, C, D, DS, ER, JCB, MC, V.

D ⚡ ⛷ ≋ ⅀ ⚡ SC ⚒

★ ★ ★ ★ **WYNDHAM BRISTOL PLACE HOTEL.** *(950 Dixon Rd, Etobicoke ON M9W 5N4) near Lester B. Pearson Intl Airport.* 416/675-9444; FAX 416/675-4426; res: 800/268-4927. E-mail bristol@interlog.com. This traditional hotel has a small waterfall in the main lobby, and guest rooms are individually decorated. 287 rms, 15 story. S, D $189-$225; each addl $15; suites from $275; under 18 free; wknd rates; package plans. Crib free. TV; cable (premium). Indoor/outdoor pool; poolside serv. Playground. Supervised child's activities; ages 2-16. Restaurant 7 am-midnight (also see ZACHARY'S). Rm serv 24 hrs. Bars 11-2 am; entertainment. Ck-out 1 pm. Convention facilities. Business center. In-rm modem link. Concierge. Valet parking. Free airport transportation. Exercise equipt; weight machine, bicycle, sauna. Minibars; bathrm phone, whirlpool in some suites; microwaves avail. Some private patios. Cr cds: A, C, D, DS, ER, JCB, MC, V.

D ≋ ⅀ ⚡ ⚡ SC ⚒

Inns

✔ ★ ★ **GUILD.** *(201 Guildwood Pkwy, Scarborough ON M1E 1P6)* 416/261-3331; FAX 416/261-5675. 95 rms, 3-6 story. Apr-Dec: S, D $75; each addl $10; suites $125; under 18 free; AP, MAP; wkly rates; lower rates rest of yr. Crib free. TV; cable (premium); VCR (movies). Pool. Restaurant (see GUILD INN). Ck-out noon, ck-in 3 pm. Business servs avail. Tennis. Exercise equipt; weight machine, bicycles. Balconies. Opened in 1923 as art community. On 90-acres overlooking Lake Ontario. Log cabin (1805) on grounds. Cr cds: A, C, D, DS, ER, MC, V.

D ⛷ ≋ ⅀ ⚡ SC

★ ★ ★ **MILLCROFT.** *(55 John St, Alton ON L0N 1A0) Hwy 10 to Hwy 24, W to Hwy 136, then N to John St.* 519/941-8111; FAX 519/941-9192; res: 800/383-3976 (ON only). E-mail wstich@auracom.com. 52 rms, 2 story, 20 chalets. S, D $175-$225. Crib free. Heated pool; whirlpool, poolside serv. Complimentary continental bkfst. Restaurant (see MILL-CROFT INN). Bar. Ck-out noon, ck-in 4 pm. Guest lndry. Meeting rm. Business servs avail. Valet serv. Tennis. Golf privileges. X-country ski on site. Exercise equipt; weights, bicycles, sauna. Volleyball. Game rm. Some private patios. 100 acres on Credit River. Former knitting mill (1881). Cr cds: A, D, ER, MC, V.

D ⛷ ⚡ ⛷ ≋ ⅀ ⚡ SC

Restaurants

★ ★ ★ **360 REVOLVING RESTAURANT.** *(301 Front St W, Toronto ON M5V 2T6) in CN Tower, downtown.* 416/362-5411. Web www.cntower.ca. Continental menu. Specializes in fresh rack of lamb, prime rib, corn-fed free-range chicken. Own baking. Hrs: 10:30 am-2:30 pm, 4:30-9:30 pm; Sat, Sun 10:30 am-2:30 pm, 4:30-10:30 pm; July, Aug hrs vary. Res accepted. Bar. Wine cellar. A la carte entrees: lunch $22-$34, dinner $25-$36. Sun brunch from $25. Revolving restaurant; view of harbor and city. Cr cds: A, D, ER, MC, V.

D

★ ★ ★ **ACCENTS.** *(See Sutton Place Grande Hotel)* 416/324-5633. Continental menu. Specializes in market fresh cuisine. Hrs: 6:30 am-11:30 pm. Res accepted. Bar. Wine cellar. A la carte entrees: bkfst $2.95-$10.50, lunch $8.50-$14.50, dinner $14.50-$32. Pianist Thurs-Sat. Parking. Continental atmosphere. Cr cds: A, C, D, DS, ER, JCB, MC, V.

D ⚡

★ ★ **ARKADIA HOUSE.** *(2007 Eglinton Ave E, Scarborough ON M1L 2M9) Approx 10 mi E on Hwy 2.* 416/752-5685. Greek menu. Specializes in roast lamb, fresh fish, souvlaki. Hrs: 11:30 am-3 pm, 4 pm-midnight. Closed Dec 24. Res accepted. Bar. Wine list. A la carte entrees: lunch $5.95-$11.95, dinner $10.95-$19.95. Child's meals. Parking. Garden cafe atmosphere. Cr cds: A, D, ER, MC, V.

☒

★ **ARLEQUIN.** (134 Avenue Rd, Toronto ON M5R 2H6) north of downtown. 416/928-9521. French, Mediterranean menu. Hrs: 8:30 am-10 pm; Fri, Sat to 11 pm. Closed most major hols. Res accepted. Bar. A la carte entrees: lunch $7.95-$10, dinner $12.95-$18.95. Complete meals (Mon-Thurs): dinner $22.95. Small bistro with harlequin motif. Cr cds: A, D, ER, MC, V.

★ ★ ★ **AVALON.** (270 Adelaide St W, Toronto ON M5H 1X6) downtown. 416/979-9918. Specialties: wood-roasted cornish hen, yellow fin tuna steak, grilled dry-aged rib steak. Hrs: noon-2:30 pm, 5:30-10 pm; Mon, Tues from 5:30 pm; Fri to 11 pm; Sat 5:30-11 pm. Closed Sun; most major hols. Res accepted. Bar. Wine list. A la carte entrees: lunch $13-$22, dinner $20-$30. Artwork by local artists. Cr cds: A, D, ER, MC, V.

☒

★ ★ ★ **BANGKOK GARDEN.** (18 Elm St, Toronto ON M5G 1G7) downtown. 416/977-6748. Thai menu. Specializes in lemon shrimp soup, curry dishes, seafood. Hrs: 11:30 am-2 pm, 5-10 pm; Sat, Sun from 5 pm. Res accepted. Bar. A la carte entrees: lunch $7.95-$14.95, dinner $14.95-$19.25. Complete meals: dinner $25.95-$39.95. Buffet (Mon, Fri): lunch $9.95. Child's meals. Thai decor; indoor garden. Cr cds: A, C, D, ER, MC, V.

☒

✔★ ★ **BAROOTES.** (220 King St W, Toronto ON M5H 1K4) downtown. 416/979-7717. International menu. Specialties: fresh stir-fry, Thai satay combination, grilled marinated lamb tenderloin. Hrs: 11:30 am-2:30 pm, 5-11 pm. Closed Sun; Jan 1, Dec 25. Res accepted. Bar. A la carte entrees: lunch $8.95-$21.95, dinner $11.50-$24.95. Traditional dining rm; fine wood paneling throughout. Cr cds: A, D, ER, MC, V.

☒

★ ★ **BISTRO 990.** (990 Bay St, Toronto ON M5S 2A5) downtown. 416/921-9990. Specializes in lamb, fresh fish. Hrs: noon-10:30 pm; Sat from 5:30 pm. Closed Sun. Res accepted. Bar. A la carte entrees: lunch $14-$19, dinner $13.50-$29.50. Prix fixe: lunch, dinner $19.90. Outdoor dining. French bistro decor. Cr cds: A, D, ER, MC, V.

☒ ☒

★ ★ **BOBA.** (90 Avenue Rd, Toronto ON M5R 2H2) in Yorkville. 416/961-2622. Specializes in vegetarian dishes, desserts. Hrs: 5:30-10 pm. Closed Sun; Jan 1, Dec 25, 26. Res required. Bar. A la carte entrees: dinner $19.50-$26.95. Patio dining. Intimate dining rm; bistro atmosphere. Totally nonsmoking. Cr cds: A, D, ER, MC, V.

☒

★ ★ **BOY ON A DOLPHIN.** (1911 Eglinton Ave E, Scarborough ON M1L 2L6) 416/759-4448. Specializes in steak, seafood. Salad bar. Hrs: 11 am-midnight; Sat from 4 pm; Sun 4-10 pm; Sun brunch 11 am-2:30 pm. Res accepted. Bar to 1 am. Semi-a la carte: lunch $7.95-$12.95, dinner $14.95-$29.95. Sun brunch $9.95. Child's meals. Parking. Mediterranean decor. Cr cds: A, D, ER, MC, V.

☒ ☒

★ ★ **BUMPKINS.** (21 Gloucester St, Toronto ON M4Y 1L8) between Church & Yonge Sts, downtown. 416/922-8655. Web www.wheremags.com. French, Amer menu. Specialty: shrimp Bumpkins. Hrs: noon-2:30 pm, 5-11 pm; Sat from 5 pm. Closed Sun. A la carte entrees: lunch $3.95-$8.50, dinner $8.75-$22.95. Child's meals. Outdoor dining. Cr cds: A, ER, MC, V.

☒

★ ★ ★ **CANOE.** (66 Wellington St W, Toronto ON M5K 1H6) downtown. 416/364-0054. Specialties: Québec foie gras, Yukon caribou, roast sea scallops. Hrs: 11:30 am-2:30 pm, 5-10:30 pm. Closed Sat, Sun; major hols. Res accepted. Bar to 2 am. Wine cellar. Semi-a la carte: lunch

$17-$24, dinner $21-$32. View of harbor and islands. Totally nonsmoking. Cr cds: A, D, ER, MC, V.

☒ ♥

★ ★ ★ **CARMAN'S CLUB.** (26 Alexander St, Toronto ON) downtown. 416/924-8558. Web www.dine.net/visit/carmans. Specializes in steak, rack of lamb, Dover sole. Own pastries. Hrs: 5:30 pm-midnight. Closed Good Friday, Dec 25. Res accepted. Serv bar. Wine cellar. Complete meals: dinner $31.95-$35.95. Child's meals. In pre-1900 house; fireplaces. Family-owned. Cr cds: A, MC, V.

☒

★ ★ ★ **CENTRO GRILL.** (2472 Yonge St, Toronto ON M4P 2H5) north of downtown. 416/483-2211. The facade of etched glass, granite and marble may seem hard-edged, but the interior is as warm as the folksy town of Asolo. Massive columns that seem to hold up a bright blue ceiling and salmon-colored walls lined with comfortable banquettes help to create an intimate setting. Italian, Amer menu. Specialty: rack of lamb with tomato, garlic, Spanish capers, eggplant and salsa. Own baking. Hrs: 5 pm-1 am. Closed Sun. Res accepted. Bar. A la carte entrees: dinner $18.50-$30.95. Pianist. Cr cds: A, D, ER, MC, V.

★ ★ ★ **CHANTERELLES.** (See Crowne Plaza Toronto Centre Hotel) 416/597-1400. Web crowneplaza.com. Continental menu. Specialty: aiguilettes of duck. Own baking. Hrs: 11:45 am-2 pm, 5:45-10 pm; Sat, Sun from 6 pm. Res accepted. Bar to 1 am. Semi a la carte: lunch $11.95-$21.95, dinner $15.50-$26. Table d'hôte: lunch $21.95-$28. Valet parking. Cr cds: A, C, D, DS, ER, JCB, MC, V.

☒

★ ★ ★ **CHEZ MAX.** (166 Wellington St W, Toronto ON) downtown. 416/599-9633. French menu. Specialties: filet mignon with red wine sauce, shrimp with pink peppercorn and vegetables. Hrs: noon-2:30 pm, 5:30-10 pm; Sat from 5:30 pm. Closed Sun; Jan 1, Dec 25. Res accepted. Bar. A la carte entrees: lunch $8.95-$17.25, dinner $16.50-$28.95. Patio dining. Modern decor. Jacket. Cr cds: A, D, ER, MC, V.

★ ★ ★ **CHIADO.** (864 College St, Toronto ON M6H 1A3) west of downtown. 416/538-1910. Portuguese menu. Specializes in Portuguese classical cuisine. Hrs: noon-midnight; early-bird dinner 5-7 pm. Closed Sun; Dec 24-26. Res accepted. Wine cellar. A la carte entrees: lunch $9.50-$14, dinner $16-$27. Child's meals. Oil paintings. Cr cds: A, C, D, ER, MC, V.

☒

★ ★ ★ **CHIARO'S.** (See King Edward Hotel) 416/863-9700. Web toprestaurants.com/toronto/chiaros.htm. Located in the opulent King Edward Hotel, this softly lit, plush dining room in shades of gray serves superior French-and-other-inspired cuisine. Continental menu. Specializes in rack of lamb, Dover sole, New York steak. Hrs: 6-10 pm. Closed Sun. Res accepted. Bar to 1 am. Wine cellar. Semi-a la carte: dinner $23-$38. Child's meals. Valet parking. Cr cds: A, C, D, ER, JCB, MC, V.

☒ ☒

★ ★ ★ **CHICQRY.** (14 Prince Arthur Ave, Toronto ON M5R 1A6) in Yorkville. 416/922-2988. Mediterranean menu. Specializes in pasta, seafood, beef. Hrs: 11 am-11 pm. Closed Sun; Dec 25. Res accepted. Wine cellar. A la carte entrees: lunch $7.50-$9.95, dinner $14.95-$20.95. Outdoor dining. Glassed cathedral entrance. Cr cds: A, D, DS, ER, MC, V.

☒

★ ★ **CORNER HOUSE.** (501 Davenport Rd, Toronto ON M4V 1B8) in Yorkville. 416/923-2604. French menu. Specializes in rack of lamb, poached salmon. Hrs: 6-10 pm. Closed Sun; major hols, also 1st Mon Aug. Res accepted; required lunch. Bar. Prix fixe: dinner $23.75. Four intimate dining rms in old house. Family-owned. Cr cds: A, D, ER, MC, V.

☒

★ ★ ★ **DAVID DUNCAN HOUSE.** (125 Moatfield Dr, North York ON) 1 mi S of ON 401, Leslie St exit. 416/391-1424. Specializes in steak, seafood, rack of lamb. Hrs: 11:30 am-3 pm, 5-11 pm; Sat, Sun from 5 pm. Res accepted. Bar. Wine list. Semi-a la carte entrees: lunch $8.95-$13.95, dinner $16.95-$41.95. Valet parking. In restored, Gothic-revival house (1865) with elaborate gingerbread & millwork, antiques, stained-glass skylight. Jacket. Cr cds: A, D, ER, MC, V.

D

★ ★ ★ **DIMAGGIO'S.** (1423 Yonge St, Toronto ON M4T 1Y7) north of downtown. 416/924-3288. Mediterranean menu. Specialties: honey pecan rack of lamb, maple-marinated salmon. Hrs: 11:30 am-3 pm, 5-10 pm; Fri to 11 pm; Sat 5-11 pm. Closed Sun; most major hols. Res accepted. Bar. Wine cellar. A la carte entrees: lunch $8.95-$14.95, dinner $15.95-$21.95. Original artwork throughout restaurant, including on tables. Cr cds: A, D, ER, MC, V.

D

★ ★ ★ **THE DOCTOR'S HOUSE.** (21 Nashville Rd, Kleinberg ON L0J 1C0) 20 mi N on Hwy 27/427 to Kleinburg, turn right on Nashville Rd to top of hill. 905/893-1615. Continental menu. Hrs: 11-1 am; Sun brunch 10:30 am-3 pm. Res accepted; required Sun brunch. Bar. Semi-a la carte: lunch $12-$16; dinner $16-$34. Sun brunch $28.50. Child's meals. Pianist Fri, Sat. Parking. Outdoor dining. Early Canadian atmosphere; antique cabinets with artifacts. Cr cds: A, MC, V.

D

★ ★ ★ **ED'S WAREHOUSE.** (270 King St W, Toronto ON M5V 1H8) downtown. 416/593-6676. English, Amer menu. Specializes in roast beef, steak. Own baking. Hrs: 4:30-8 pm; Sat to 9 pm. Closed Dec 24, 25. Serv bar. Wine list. A la carte entrees: dinner $10.95-$16.95. Unusual theatrical decor; many French antiques & statues, Tiffany lamps. Family-owned. Cr cds: A, D, MC, V.

★ ★ ★ **ELLAS.** (702 Pape Ave, Toronto ON) east of downtown. 416/463-0334. E-mail eria@ellas.com; web www.ellas.com. Greek menu. Specializes in lamb, shish kebab, seafood. Own pastries. Hrs: 11-1 am; Sun to 11 pm. Closed Dec 25. Res accepted. Bar. Semi-a la carte: lunch $7.95-$9.95, dinner $10.95-$32.95. Ancient Athenian decor; sculptures. Family-owned. Cr cds: A, D, ER, MC, V.

✔ ★ ★ **GRANO.** (2035 Yonge St, Toronto ON M4S 2A2) north of downtown. 416/440-1986. Italian menu. Specializes in pasta. Hrs: 10 am-11 pm. Closed Sun; major hols. Res accepted. Bar. Semi-a la carte: lunch $7.95-$13.95, dinner $8.95-$18.95. Outdoor dining. Italian street cafe ambience. Cr cds: A, D, ER, MC, V.

★ ★ **GRAZIE.** (2373 Yonge St, Toronto ON M4P 2C8) north of downtown. 416/488-0822. Italian menu. Specializes in pizza, pasta. Hrs: noon-11 pm; Fri, Sat to midnight. Closed some major hols. Res accepted. Bar. A la carte entrees: lunch, dinner $9-$14. Child's meals. Bistro atmosphere. Cr cds: A, MC, V.

D

★ ★ ★ **GUILD INN.** (See Guild Inn) 416/261-3331. Continental menu. Specialties: smoked Atlantic salmon, prime rib. Salad bar. Own baking. Hrs: 7 am-10 pm; Sun brunch 10:30 am-2:30 pm. Res accepted. Bar. Wine list. Semi-a la carte: bkfst $2.75-$8.50, lunch $6.50-$15.95, dinner $14-$29.50. Sun brunch $17.95. Child's meals. Garden setting in former artist colony. Cr cds: A, C, D, DS, ER, MC, V.

★ ★ ★ **HARVEST CAFE.** (See Inn On The Park Hotel) 416/444-2561. Continental menu. Own baking. Hrs: 6:30 am-11:30 pm. Res accepted. Wine list. A la carte entrees: bkfst $3.95-$11.95, lunch, dinner $8.50-$18.95. Child's meals. Valet parking. Cr cds: A, C, D, DS, ER, JCB, MC, V.

D

★ ★ **IL POSTO.** (148 Yorkville Ave, Toronto ON M5R 1C2) in Yorkville. 416/968-0469. Northern Italian menu. Specializes in liver & veal chops, pasta with lobster, carpaccio. Hrs: noon-2:30 pm, 6-10:30 pm. Closed Sun; hols. Res accepted. A la carte entrees: $11.75-$16, dinner $13.50-$29. Outdoor dining. Cr cds: A, D, ER, MC, V.

★ ★ **JERUSALEM.** (955 Eglinton Ave W, Toronto ON M6C 2C4) north of downtown. 416/783-6494. Middle Eastern menu. Specialties: shish tawoo, siniyeh bitaheena, falafel plate. Hrs: 11:30 am-10:30 pm; Fri to 11:30 pm; Sat noon-11:30 pm; Sun noon-10 pm. Closed Jan 1, Dec 25. Res accepted. A la carte entrees: lunch $5.95-$6.50, dinner $8.95-$13.95. Child's meals. Outdoor dining. Old-world decor. Family-owned. Cr cds: A, MC, V.

★ ★ ★ **JOSO'S.** (202 Davenport Rd, Toronto ON M5R 1J2) in Yorkville. 416/925-1903. Mediterranean menu. Specializes in Italian dishes, seafood. Hrs: 11:30 am-2:30 pm, 5:30-11 pm; Sat from 5:30 pm. Closed Sun; some major hols. Res accepted. A la carte entrees: lunch $7-$19, dinner $9-$27. Child's meals. Outdoor dining. Wine cellar. Cr cds: A, D, ER, MC, V.

D

★ ★ **KALLY'S.** (430 Nugget Ave, Toronto ON M1S 4A4) north of downtown. 416/293-9292. Specializes in steak, ribs. Salad bar. Hrs: 11:30 am-10 pm; Sun 4-9 pm. Closed hols; also 1st Mon in Aug. Serv bar. A la carte entrees: lunch $4.45-$11.95, dinner $6.95-$13.45. Child's meals. Parking. Pyramid-shaped skylights. Cr cds: A, MC, V.

D

★ ★ ★ **LA FENICE.** (319 King St W, Toronto ON M5V 1J5) downtown. 416/585-2377. Italian menu. Specializes in fresh seafood, pasta. Hrs: 11:30 am-2:30 pm, 5:30-10:30 pm; Sat from 5:30 pm. Closed Sun; major hols. Res accepted. Bar to 1 am. Extensive wine list. A la carte entrees: lunch $10.50-$24, dinner $14.50-$26. Sleek Milan-style trattoria. Near theater district. Cr cds: A, D, ER, JCB, MC, V.

★ ★ **LAI WAH HEEN.** (See Metropolitan Hotel) 416/977-9899. E-mail lwh@metropolitan.com. Specializes in Cantonese dishes. Hrs: 11:30 am-3 pm, 5-11:30 pm. Res accepted. Wine cellar. A la carte entrees: lunch $12-$25, dinner $18-$48. Complete meal: lunch $16-$32, dinner $58. Chinese decor. Cr cds: A, D, DS, ER, JCB, MC, V.

D

✔ ★ ★ **LE PAPILLION.** (16 Church St, Toronto ON M5E 1M1) downtown. 416/363-0838. French menu. Specialties: crêpes Bretonne, French onion soup. Hrs: noon-2:30 pm, 5-10 pm; Fri, Sat to midnight; Sun brunch to 3 pm. Closed Mon. Res accepted. Bar. Semi-a la carte: lunch, dinner $7.75-$18.95. Sun brunch $16.95. Child's meals. Parking. Patio dining. French country kitchen decor. Braille menu. Cr cds: A, D, ER, MC, V.

D

★ ★ ★ **LICHEE GARDEN.** (595 Bay St, Toronto ON M5G 2C2) opp Eaton's Centre, downtown. 416/977-3481. Cantonese, Szechwan menu. Specialties: Peking duck, steak kew, kung po chicken. Own pastries. Hrs: 11:30 am-midnight; Fri, Sat to 1 am; Sun to 11 pm. Closed Dec 25. Res accepted. Bar. A la carte: lunch $4-$10.50, dinner $9.95-$17.50. Entertainment exc Sun. Parking. Oriental decor. Cr cds: A, D, ER, MC, V.

D

✔ ★ **LOVELOCK'S.** (838 Yonge St, Toronto ON M4W 2H1) in Yorkville. 416/968-0063. Continental menu. Specialties: grilled calamari, rack of lamb. Hrs: 11:30 am-10 pm; Thurs-Sat to 11 pm. Closed Sun; Jan 1, Dec 25. Res accepted. Bar to 2 am. Wine list. A la carte entrees: lunch $6.95-$10.50, dinner $10.95-$19.95. Outdoor dining. French bistro atmosphere. Cr cds: A, MC, V.

★ ★ **MARKETTA.** (138 Avenue Rd, Toronto ON M5R 2H7) in Yorkville. 416/924-4447. Mediterranean menu. Specialties: grilled sirloin burger, brick-grilled chicken. Hrs: 11:30 am-3 pm, 5-10:30 pm; Thurs-Sat to 11 pm; Sun 11 am-3 pm (brunch), 5-10 pm. Closed Mon; most major hols. Res accepted. Bar. A la carte entrees: lunch $9.95-$16.95, dinner

$10.95-$16.95. Sun brunch $9.95-$16.95. French bistro ambience. Cr cds: A, D, ER, MC, V.

★ ★ **MATIENON.** *(51 Ste Nicholas St, Toronto ON M4Y 1W6) downtown.* 416/921-9226. Specializes in rack of lamb, duck breast, la darne de saumon aux câpres. Hrs: 11:30 am-2:30 pm, 5-10 pm. Res accepted. Bar. A la carte entrees: lunch $8.95-$15.95, dinner $13.50-$17.95. French atmosphere. Cr cds: A, D, ER, MC, V.

★ ★ ★ **MILLCROFT INN.** *(See Millcroft Inn)* 519/941-8111. Continental menu. Specializes in game meat. Hrs: 7:30-10 am, noon-2 pm, 6-9 pm; Sat, Sun 8-10:30 am; Sun brunch 11:30 am-2 pm. Res accepted. Bar from 11 am. A la carte entrees: bkfst $6.95-$9.95, lunch $16-$18.95, dinner $26-$35.98. Sun brunch $26.95. Valet parking. Restored knitting mill (1881) on the Credit River. Cr cds: A, D, ER, MC, V.

✔★ **MILLER'S COUNTRY FARE.** *(5140 Dundas St W, Etobicoke ON M9A 1C2)* 416/234-5050. Specializes in ribs, chicken, beef stew. Hrs: 11 am-10 pm; Fri to 11 pm; Sat 10 am-11 pm; Sat, Sun brunch to 2:30 pm. Closed Dec 25. Bar from 11 am. Semi-a la carte: lunch, dinner $6.25-$13.95. Sat, Sun brunch $3.95-$10.95. Child's meals. Parking. Country decor. Cr cds: A, D, ER, MC, V.

★ ★ **MÖVENPICK OF SWITZERLAND.** *(165 York St, Toronto ON M5H 3R8) downtown.* 416/366-5234. Continental menu. Specializes in Swiss dishes. Salad bar. Hrs: 7:30 am-midnight; Fri to 1 am; Sat 9-1 am; Sun 9 am-midnight. Res accepted. Bar. Semi-a la carte: bkfst $2.50-$13.80, lunch $6.50-$16.90, dinner $9.25-$16.80. Buffet: dinner (exc Sun) $16.80-$27.50. Sun brunch $21.80. Child's meals. Parking. Outdoor dining. European decor. Cr cds: A, D, ER, MC, V.

★ ★ ★ **NORTH 44 DEGREES.** *(2537 Yonge St, Toronto ON M4P 2H9) north of downtown.* 416/487-4897. North 44, Toronto's latitude, is the restaurant's logo and an oft-repeated visual refrain. The trendy atmosphere is fostered by a metallic, modern look, but chef Mark McEwan's dishes more than hold their own in this singular decor. Specializes in mixed appetizer platters, angel hair pasta, rack of lamb. Hrs: 5 pm-1 am. Closed Sun; some major hols. Res accepted. Bar. A la carte entrees: dinner $12.95-$31.95. Child's meals. Entertainment Wed-Sat. Cr cds: A, D, ER, MC, V.

★ ★ ★ **OLD MILL.** *(21 Old Mill Rd, Toronto ON M8X 1G5) west of downtown.* 416/236-2641. Continental menu. Specializes in roast beef, roast duck. Own baking. Hrs: noon-2:30 pm, 3-5 pm (afternoon tea), 5:30-10 pm; Sat 5:30-11 pm; Sun 5:30-9 pm; Sun brunch 10:30 am-2 pm. Closed Dec 24. Res accepted. Bar. A la carte entrees: lunch $10.95-$16.95, dinner $24.50-$33. Buffet: lunch (Mon-Fri) $19.95, dinner (Sun) $24.95. Sun brunch $22.95. Cover charge (Fri, Sat from 8 pm) $3.50. Child's meals. Parking. Old English castle motif. Jacket (dinner). Cr cds: A, D, ER, MC, V.

✔★ **OLD SPAGHETTI FACTORY.** *(54 The Esplanade, Toronto ON M5E 1A6) downtown.* 416/864-9761. Italian menu. Specialties: fettucine with seafood, chicken parmigiana. Hrs: 11:30 am-11 pm; Fri, Sat to midnight. Closed Dec 24. Bar. Semi-a la carte: lunch $3.95-$7.50, dinner $6.99-$14.25. Child's meals. Outdoor dining. Bright decor; carousel effect. Family-owned. Cr cds: A, D, DS, ER, MC, V.

★ ★ ★ **OPUS.** *(37 Prince Arthur Ave, Toronto ON) in Yorkville.* 416/921-3105. Web www.cook-book.com\opus. Continental menu. Hrs: 5:30-11:30 pm. Res accepted. Bar to 2 am. Wine list. Semi-a la carte: dinner $12.95-$29.95. Cr cds: A, ER, MC, V.

★ **OXFORD STEAK HOUSE & TAVERN.** *(1130 Martin Grove Rd, Etobicoke ON M9N 4W1)* 416/249-1516. Specializes in steak, pasta. Hrs: 7-1 am. Closed Good Friday, Dec 25; other hols for dinner. Bar from 11 am. Semi-a la carte: bkfst $2.50-$7.95, lunch $3.95-$12.95 dinner $7-$15.95. Child's meals. Entertainment Wed-Sat. Parking. English-style dining rm; prints. Cr cds: A, D, ER, MC, V.

★ **PAWNBROKERS DAUGHTER.** *(1115 Bay St, Toronto ON M5S 2B3) downtown.* 416/920-9078. Hrs: 11-2 am. Res accepted. Bar. A la carte entrees: lunch, dinner $4-$14.95. Pub atmosphere; pool table, video games. Cr cds: A, MC, V.

★ ★ **PIER 4 STOREHOUSE.** *(245 Queen's Quay W, Toronto ON M5J 2K9) Harbourfront.* 416/203-1440. Specializes pepper steak Peru, red snapper. Pasta bar. Hrs: noon-2:30 pm; 4:30 pm-midnight; Sun 11:30 am-2:30 pm, 4:30-10 pm. Closed Dec 25. Res accepted. Bar. Semi-a la carte: lunch $7-$11, dinner $12.75-$34.95. Child's meals. Patio dining. Located at water end of a quay on Toronto Bay. Cr cds: A, D, DS, ER, JCB, MC, V.

★ ★ **PREGO.** *(15474 Yonge St, Aurora ON L4G 1P2) approx 30 mi (48 km) N of downtown Toronto.* 905/727-5100. Italian menu. Specializes in baked rack of lamb, pasta. Hrs: 11:30 am-2:30 pm, 5:30-10:30 pm; Sat from 5:30 pm; Sun 5-9:30 pm. Closed Mon; Jan 1, Good Friday, Dec 25, 26. Res accepted. Bar. A la carte entrees: lunch $7.95-$11.95, dinner $8.95-$19. Parking. Casual atmosphere. Cr cds: A, D, ER, MC, V.

★ ★ ★ **PRONTO.** *(692 Mount Pleasant Rd, Toronto ON) north of downtown.* 416/486-1111. Italian, continental menu. Hrs: 5-11:30 pm; Sun to 10:30 pm. Closed Jan 1, Dec 24, 25. Res accepted. Bar. A la carte entrees: dinner $12.95-$28.95. Valet parking. Elegant modern decor; local artwork. Cr cds: A, C, D, ER, MC, V.

✔★ ★ **PROVENCE.** *(12 Amelia St, Toronto ON M4X 1A1) in Cabbagetown.* 416/924-9901. French menu. Specialties: rack of lamb, duck confit, steak. Hrs: 11:30-1 am; Sat, Sun brunch 11:30 am-3 pm. Closed Dec 25. Res accepted. Bar to 1 am. Semi-a la carte: lunch, dinner $14.95-$21. Sat, Sun brunch $12.95. French country cottage decor; original artwork. Cr cds: A, MC, V.

✔★ **RIVOLI CAFE.** *(332 Queen St W, Toronto ON M5V 2A2) downtown.* 416/596-1908. Web home.1star.cia/~rivoli. Asian, Caribbean menu. Specialties: Sri Malay Bombay, Laotian spring rolls. Hrs: 11:30-2 am. Closed most major hols. Bar. A la carte entrees: lunch $5.95-$9.50, dinner $7.50-$12.95. Patio dining. Adj club offers comedy/variety shows evenings. Totally nonsmoking. Cr cds: A, MC, V.

★ ★ ★ **ROSEWATER SUPPER CLUB.** *(19 Toronto St, Toronto ON M5C 2R1) east of downtown.* 416/214-5888. Continental menu. Own baking. Hrs: noon-2:30 pm, 5:30-11 pm; Sat from 5:30 pm. Closed Sun; major hols; July 1, Dec 26. Res required. Bar 11:30-2 am. Wine cellar. A la carte entrees: lunch $13-$19, dinner $19-$31. Pianist evenings. Early 20th-century atmosphere; elaborate Victorian crown moldings and cathedral-style windows. Totally nonsmoking. Cr cds: A, D, ER, MC, V.

★ ★ ★ ★ **SCARAMOUCHE.** *(1 Benvenuto Place, Toronto ON M4V 2L1) north of downtown.* 416/961-8011. This is Toronto's most luxurious French restaurant. Superb service and delicious food are served up in an atmosphere of understated elegance. Continental, French menu. Specialties: grilled Atlantic salmon, roasted rack of lamb. Own baking. Hrs: 6-10 pm; Sat to 11 pm. Closed Sun; major hols. Res accepted. Bar to midnight. A la carte entrees: dinner $24.75-$29.75. Pasta bar $13.75-$22.75. Valet parking. Cr cds: A, D, ER, MC, V.

★ **SEA SHACK.** *(2130 Lawrence Ave E, Scarborough ON M1R 3A6)* 416/288-1866. Continental menu. Specializes in seafood, steak. Hrs: 11 am-11 pm; Sat 4-11 pm; Sun noon-10 pm. Closed Jan 1, Dec 25. Res accepted. Bar. Semi-a la carte: lunch $5.50-$9.95, dinner $7.95-$26.95. Child's meals. Parking. Nautical theme. Cr cds: A, MC, V.

★ ★ **SENATOR.** *(253 Victoria St, Toronto ON M5B 1T8)* downtown. 416/364-7517. Specializes in steak, seafood. Hrs: 11:30 am-2:30 pm, 5 pm-midnight. Closed Mon; some major hols. Res accepted. Bar. A la carte entrees: lunch $9.95-$14.95, dinner $19.95-$33.95. Parking. 1920s decor; in heart of theatre district. Cr cds: A, D, ER, JCB, MC, V.

★ ★ ★ **SPLENDIDO.** *(88 Harbord St, Toronto ON M5S 1G5)* downtown. 416/929-7788. Continental menu. Specialties: rack of veal with grilled tomatoes, grilled peppered beef tenderloin with crispy fries. Hrs: 5-11 pm. Closed Sun. Res accepted. Bar. Semi-a la carte: dinner $19.95-$28.95. Valet parking. Fashionable trattoria with inviting atmosphere. Cr cds: A, D, ER, MC, V.

✔ ★ **SUSHI BISTRO.** *(204 Queen St W, Toronto ON M5V 1Z2)* downtown. 416/971-5315. Japanese menu. Specializes: shrimp and mushrooms, sushi rolls, sashimi. Hrs: noon-2:45 pm, 5-10 pm; Fri, Sat noon-midnight. Closed Sun; major hols. Res accepted. Bar. A la carte entrees: lunch $7-$11, dinner $8.50-$18. Child's meals. Traditional Japanese food in modern setting. Cr cds: A, D, JCB, MC, V.

★ **THAI FLAVOUR.** *(1554 Avenue Rd, Toronto ON M5M 3X5)* north of downtown. 416/782-3288. Thai menu. Specialties: cashew nut chicken, pad Thai, basil shrimp. Hrs: 11 am-3 pm, 5-11 pm; Sun 5-10 pm. Closed Jan 1, Dec 25. Res accepted. Serv bar. A la carte entrees: lunch, dinner $7.45-$9.50. Cr cds: A, MC, V.

★ ★ **TIGER LILY'S NOODLE HOUSE.** *(257 Queen St W, Toronto ON M5V 1Z4)* downtown. 416/977-5499. Pan-Asian menu. Specializes in home-style egg roll. Hrs: 11:30 am-9 pm; Wed to 10 pm; Thurs-Sat to 11 pm. Closed most major hols. A la carte entrees: lunch, dinner $5.95-$10.95. Totally nonsmoking. Cr cds: A, MC, V.

★ ★ **TRAPPER'S.** *(3479 Yonge St, North York ON M4N 2N3)* 416/482-6211. Web www.yongestreet.com. Continental menu. Specializes in fresh fish, steak, pasta. Hrs: 11:30 am-2:30 pm, 5-10:30 pm; Sat from 5 pm; Sun 5-9:30 pm. Closed Dec 25. Res accepted. Bar. A la carte entrees: lunch $8.50-$11.95, dinner $12.95-$25.95. Child's meals. Casual dining. Cr cds: A, D, ER, MC, V.

★ ★ ★ ★ **TRUFFLES.** *(See Four Seasons Hotel)* 416/964-0411. The wine list offers rare European and North American vintages in this formal, contemporary restaurant with bay windows and a high ceiling. Murals and ceramics by local artists decorate the room. Provençale cuisine. Specialties: Québec duck, rack of lamb with mustard seed sauce. Own pastries. Hrs: 6-11 pm. Res accepted. Wine cellar. Semi-a la carte: dinner $26-$39. Table d'hôte: dinner $75. Child's meals. Valet parking. Jacket. Cr cds: A, C, D, ER, JCB, MC, V.

★ **UKRAINIAN CARAVAN.** *(5245 Dundas St W, Toronto ON M9B 1A5)* west of downtown. 416/231-7447. Ukrainian, Amer menu. Specializes in pierogies, meat-on-a-stick. Own coffees. Hrs: 11-2 am; Sun 10 am-10 pm. Res accepted. Bar. Semi-a la carte: lunch $3.99-$11.95, dinner Mon-Fri (nonshow nights) $10-$20, Sat (show nights) $21.95-$30.95. Cossack cabaret Sat. Cr cds: A, D, ER, MC, V.

★ ★ **UNIONVILLE HOUSE.** *(187 Main St, Unionville ON L3R 2G8)* N on Don Valley Pkwy, E on Hwy 7 to Kennedy Rd, then N. 905/477-4866. Continental menu. Specializes in pasta, fish. Hrs: 11:30

am-2:30 pm, 5:30-10 pm; Sun to 9 pm. Res accepted. Semi-a la carte: lunch $6.95-$8.95, dinner $9.95-$23.95. Outdoor dining. Authentic pioneer-style cottage (1840); antique furnishings, decor. Cr cds: A, D, ER, MC, V.

★ ★ **VANIPHA LANNA.** *(471 Eglinton Ave W, Toronto ON M5N 1A7)* north of downtown. 416/484-0895. Thai menu. Specializes in northern Thai dishes. Hrs: noon-11 pm; Sat to midnight. Closed Sun; most major hols. Res accepted Fri, Sat. A la carte entrees: lunch $6.25-$9.95; dinner $8.25-$12.50. Thai decor. Totally nonsmoking. Cr cds: A, MC, V.

★ ★ **VILLA BORGHESE.** *(2995 Bloor St W, Etobicoke ON M8X 1C1)* 416/239-1286. Italian menu. Specializes in fresh fish, veal, pepper steak. Own pasta. Hrs: noon-midnight; Sat, Sun from 4 pm. Closed Mon; Easter, Dec 25. Res accepted. Bar. Semi-a la carte: lunch $8-$15, dinner $12.95-$23.95. Entertainment. Italian villa decor. Cr cds: A, D, MC, V.

✔ ★ **WAYNE GRETZKY'S.** *(99 Blue Jays Way, Toronto ON M5V 9G9)* downtown. 416/979-7825. Specializes in pasta, grilled meats. Hrs: 11:30-1 am. Closed Dec 25. Res accepted. Bar. Semi-a la carte: lunch, dinner $6.99-$24.99. Rooftop patio dining. Display of Gretzky memorabilia. Cr cds: A, D, ER, MC, V.

★ ★ **XANGO.** *(106 John St, Toronto ON M5V 2E1)* downtown. 416/593-4407. South Amer menu. Specialty: raw fish marinated in lime juice. Hrs: 5 pm-2 am. Closed Dec 24-26. Res accepted. Bar. A la carte entrees: dinner $21-$28. Complete meal: dinner $18-$48. Outdoor dining. Converted house with veranda. Cr cds: A, D, MC, V.

★ **YAMASE.** *(317 King St W, Toronto ON M5V 1J5)* downtown. 416/598-1562. Japanese menu. Specializes in sushi, teriyaki, tempura dishes. Hrs: noon-2:30 pm, 5:30-11 pm; Sat from 5 pm. Sun 5-10 pm. Closed Jan 1. Res accepted. Bar. A la carte entrees: lunch $5.50-$14.50, dinner $7.50-$24.50. Complete meals: dinner $15-$50. Intimate atmosphere; Japanese decor, artwork. Cr cds: A, D, ER, MC, V.

★ ★ ★ **ZACHARY'S.** *(See Wyndham Bristol Place Hotel)* 416/675-9444. E-mail bristol@interlog.com. Continental menu. Specialty: rack of lamb. Own baking. Hrs: noon-2:30 pm, 6-10 pm; Sat from 6 pm; Sun brunch 11 am-2:30 pm. Res accepted. Bar 11-1 am. Wine list. A la carte entrees: lunch $13.25-$18.50, dinner $22.50-$32.50. Complete meals: lunch $19.75, dinner $29.50. Sun brunch $23.50. Valet parking. Modern decor with Chinese prints. Cr cds: A, C, D, DS, ER, JCB, MC, V.

✔ ★ **ZUCCA TRATTORIA.** *(2150 Yonge St, Toronto ON M4S 2A8)* north of downtown. 416/488-5774. Web www.yongestreet.com/food/zucca. Italian menu. Specializes in whole grilled fish, pasta. Hrs: noon-2:30 pm, 6-10:30 pm. Closed Sun; major hols. Res accepted. Bar. A la carte entrees: lunch $7.50-$12.95, dinner $11-$17. Totally non smoking. Cr cds: A, MC, V.

Unrated Dining Spots

CAFE VICTORIA. *(See King Edward Hotel)* 416/863-9700. Continental menu. Specializes in scones, pastries, sandwiches. Own baking. Hrs: 6:30 am-2:30 pm, 5-9 pm; Fri to 11 pm; Sat, Sun 7:30 am-2:30 pm, 5-11 pm. Traditional English tea service $13.95. Valet parking. Cr cds: A, D, MC, V.

PATACHOU. *(1095 Yonge St, Toronto ON)* in Yorkville. 416/927-1105. French menu. Specialties: cafe au lait, croque Monsieur. Own baking. Hrs: 8:30 am-6 pm; Sun from 10:30 am. Closed statutory hols. Pastries, croissants, desserts, sandwiches, quiche $5-$10. Patio dining. No cr cds accepted.

SHOPSY'S DELICATESSEN. *(33 Yonge St, Toronto ON) downtown.* 416/365-3333. Delicatessen, all-day bkfst menu. Hrs: 7-1 am. Bar 11-1 am. A la carte entrees: bkfst $2.10-$6.75, lunch $3.95-$8.95, dinner $3.75-$11.75. Outdoor dining. Cr cds: A, MC, V.

D

UNITED BAKERS DAIRY RESTAURANT. *(506 Lawrence Ave W, Toronto ON) in the Lawrence Plaza, north of downtown.* 416/789-0519. Jewish menu. Specializes in cheese blintzes, soups, gefilte fish. Hrs: 7 am-10 pm; Fri to 8 pm; Sat, Sun to 9 pm. A la carte entrees: lunch $5-$10, dinner to $12. Parking. Bakery on premises. Family-owned. Cr cds: MC, V.

Windsor (F-4)

Pop 192,083 **Elev** 622 ft (190 m) **Area code** 519 **E-mail** cvb@city.windsor.on.ca **Web** www.city.windsor.on.ca/cvb

Information Convention & Visitors Bureau of Windsor, Essex County and Pelee Island, 333 Riverside Dr W, City Centre Mall, Suite 103, N9A 5K4; 519/255-6530 or 800/265-3633.

Windsor is located at the tip of a peninsula and is linked to Detroit, Michigan by the Ambassador Bridge and the Detroit-Windsor Tunnel. Because of its proximity to the United States, it is often referred to as the Ambassador City. Because of its many beautiful parks, Windsor is also known as the City of Roses. The Sunken Gardens and Rose Gardens in Jackson Park boast more than 500 varieties of roses. Coventry Garden & Peace Fountain has the only fountain floating in international waters. Whatever the nickname, for many people traveling from the United States, Canada begins here.

Windsor is a cosmopolitan city, designated a bilingual-bicultural area because of the French influence so much in evidence. Windsor also has a symphony orchestra, theaters, a light opera company, art galleries, nightlife and all the amenities of a large city. Within its boundaries are 900 acres (364 hectares) of parks giving the city the charm of a rural environment. With easy access to lakes Erie and St Clair, and such pleasure troves as Pelee Island, it is also the major city in Canada's "Sun Parlor," Essex County. Because of mild climate and beautiful beaches, it is an excellent place to visit all year.

What to See and Do

Casino Windsor & Northern Belle Casino. Games include Baccarat, Blackjack, Roulette and more than 1,700 slot machines. The casino overlooks the Detroit skyline and is easily accessible from a number of hotels. (Daily) Riverside Dr in City Centre. Phone 519/258-7878 or 800/991-7777.

Colasanti Farms, Ltd. "A tropical paradise under glass." Over 20 greenhouses with acres of exotic plants; large collection of cacti; farm animals, parrots and tropical birds; restaurant. (Daily; closed Jan 1, Dec 25) 28 mi (45 km) SE, on Hwy 3 near Ruthven. Phone 519/322-2301. **Free.**

★ **Coventry Gardens and Peace Fountain.** Riverfront park & floral gardens with 75-ft-high (23-m) floating fountain; a myriad of three-dimensional water displays with spectacular night illumination (May-Sept, daily). Concessions. (Daily) Riverside Dr E & Pillette Rd. Phone 519/253-2300. **Free.**

Fort Malden National Historic Park. Ten-acre (four-hectare) park with remains of fortification, original 1838 barracks and 1851 pensioner's cottage; visitor and interpretation centers with exhibits. (Daily) 100 Laird Ave, 18 mi (29 km) S via Hwy 18, in Amherstburg. Contact PO Box 38, 100 Laird Ave, N9V 2Z2; 519/736-5416. ¢¢

Heritage Village. Historical artifacts and structures on 54 acres (22 hectares). Log cabins (1826 & 1835), railway station (1854), house (1869), church (1885), schoolhouse (1907), barber shop (ca 1920), general store (1847); transportation museum. Special events. Picnic facilities. 20 mi (32 km) SE via ON 3, then 5 mi (8 km) S of Essex on County Rd 23. Phone 519/776-6909. ¢¢

Jack Miner Bird Sanctuary. Features Canada geese and other migratory waterfowl; ponds; picnicking; museum. Canada geese "air shows" during peak season (Mar and late Oct-Nov; daily). (Daily exc Sun) 27 mi (44 km) SE via ON 3 & 29S, 2 mi (3 km) N of Kingsville. Phone 519/733-4034. **Free.**

North American Black Historical Museum. Chronicles achievements of black North Americans, many of whom fled the US for freedom in Canada. Permanent exhibits on Underground Railroad; artifacts, archives, genealogical library. (Apr-Nov, Wed-Fri, also Sat & Sun afternoons) 18 mi (29 km) S on Hwy 18, exit Richmond St E, at 227 King St in Amherstburg. Phone 519/736-5433. ¢¢

Park House Museum. Solid log, clapboard-sided house (ca 1795), considered to be oldest house in area. Built in Detroit, moved here in 1799. Restored & furnished as in the 1850s. Demonstrations of tinsmithing; pieces for sale. (June-Aug, daily; rest of yr, Tues-Fri & Sun) 219 Dalhousie St, 18 mi (29 km) S via ON 18, on the King's Naval Yard, near Ft Malden in Amherstburg. Phone 519/736-2511. ¢

Point Pelee National Park. The park is a 6-sq-mi (16-sq-km) tip of the Point Pelee peninsula. Combination dry land and marshland, the park also has a deciduous forest and is situated on two major bird migration flyways. More than 350 species have been sighted in the park. A boardwalk winds through the 2,500 acres (1,011 hectares) of marshland. Fishing, swimming, picnicking, trails and interpretive center. Canoeing and biking (rentals), transit ride (free). (Daily) 30 mi (48 km) SE via ON 3, near Leamington. Contact Chief of Visitor Services, RR 1, Leamington, N8H 3V4; 519/322-2365. Entrance fee/vehicle/day ¢¢-¢¢¢

The Art Gallery of Windsor. Collections consist of Canadian art, including Inuit prints and carvings, with emphasis on Canadian artists from the late 18th century to the present. Children's gallery; gift shop. (Daily exc Mon; closed major hols) 3100 Howard Ave. Phone 519/969-4494. **Free.**

University of Windsor. (16,000 students) On campus is Essex Hall Theatre, featuring seven productions/season (Sept-Mar, fee; box office phone 519/253-4565). 401 Sunset Ave. Phone 519/253-4232, ext 3240.

Willistead Manor. (1906). Restored English Tudor mansion built for Edward Chandler Walker, son of famous distiller Hiram Walker, on 15 acres (6 hectares) of wooded parkland; elegant interiors with hand-carved woodwork; furnished in turn-of-the-century style. (July-Aug, Sun & Wed; Sept-June, 1st & 3rd Sun of each month) 1899 Niagara St, at Kildare Rd. Phone 519/253-2365. ¢¢

Windsor Reptile World. One of Canada's largest displays of reptiles and amphibians; houses over 100 exhibits and 400 animals, including the world's largest snakes. Feedings can be viewed Wed evenings. (Daily; closed Dec 25) 853 Division Rd. Phone 519/966-1762. ¢¢¢

Windsor's Community Museum. Exhibits and collections interpret the history of Windsor and southwestern Ontario. (Tues-Sat, also Sun afternoons; closed hols) Located in the historic Francois Baby House. 254 Pitt St W. Phone 519/253-1812. **Free.**

Annual Event

International Freedom Festival. Two-wk joint celebration by Detroit and Windsor with many events, culminating in fireworks display over the river. Phone 519/252-7264. Late June-1st wk July.

Motels

★ ★ **BEST WESTERN CONTINENTAL INN.** *(3345 Huron Church Rd, Windsor ON N9E 4H5)* 519/966-5541; FAX 519/972-3384. 71 rms, 2 story. S $66-$76; D $70-$80; each addl $6-$10; under 12 free. TV; cable (premium), VCR avail. Heated pool. Restaurant 7 am-10 pm. Rm serv. Ck-out 11 am. Meeting rms. Cr cds: A, D, DS, MC, V.

⊠ ⊠ ⊠ SC

★ ★ **COMFORT INN.** *(1100 Richmond St, Chatham ON N7M 5J5)* E on HWY 401 to exit 81. 519/352-5500; FAX 519/352-2520. 81 rms, 2 story. May-Sept: S $57-$95; D $65-$105; each addl $4; under 19 free; wkend rates; lower rates rest of yr. Crib free. Pet accepted. TV; cable.

Complimentary coffee in lobby. Restaurant adj 9 am-10 pm. Ck-out 11 am. Cr cds: A, C, D, DS, ER, JCB, MC, V.

D ↩ ⤢ 🕊 SC

✔★ ★ MARQUIS PLAZA. *(2530 Ouellette Ave, Windsor ON N8X 1L7)* 519/966-1860; FAX 519/966-6619; res: 800/265-5021. 97 rms, 2 story. S $48-$150; D $60; each addl $5; suites $90-$150. Crib $5. Pet accepted, some restrictions; $10. TV; cable (premium), VCR avail. Ck-out noon. Meeting rms. Cr cds: A, D, ER, MC, V.

D ↩ ⤢ 🕊 SC

★ ★ ROYAL MARQUIS. *(590 Grand Marais E, Windsor ON N8X 3H4)* near Intl Airport. 519/966-1900; FAX 519/966-4689. 99 rms, 5 story, 14 suites. S $70; D $80; each addl $5; suites $90-$175; under 12 free; wkend rates; higher rates prom. Crib $5. Pet accepted, some restrictions; $10. TV; cable (premium), VCR avail. Indoor pool; whirlpool. Supervised child's activities; ages 5-10. Restaurant 6:30 am-10 pm. Rm serv. Bar; entertainment Thurs-Sun. Ck-out noon. Meeting rms. Valet serv. Concierge. Barber. Beauty shop. X-country ski 5 mi. Exercise equipt; stair machine, treadmill, sauna. Luxurious furnishings, atmosphere. Cr cds: A, D, ER, MC, V.

D ↩ ⤢ ≈ 🕊 🕊

Motor Hotel

★ ★ BEST WESTERN WHEELS INN. *(615 Richmond St, Chatham ON N7M 5K8)* NE on Hwy 2, at Keil Dr. 519/351-1100; FAX 519/436-5541. 350 rms, 2-10 story. S, D $96.88-$151.88; each addl $5; suites $188.88-$208.88; under 18 free; lower rates mid-wk. Crib free. TV; cable. 2 pools, 1 indoor/outdoor; whirlpools, poolside serv (summer); lifeguard. Supervised child's activities; ages 3-12. Restaurant 7-1 am. Rm serv 7-11 am, 5 pm-midnight. Bar noon-1 am; entertainment exc Sun. Ck-out 11:30 am. Convention facilities. Business center. Gift shop. Free airport transportation. Indoor tennis. Miniature golf. Exercise rm; instructor, weights, bicycles, saunas, steam rm. Bowling. Game rm. Rec rm. Some balconies. Resort atmosphere; more than 7 acres of indoor facilities. Atrium with waterfalls, water slides. Cr cds: A, C, D, DS, ER, JCB, MC, V.

D ↩ ⤢ ≈ 🕊 🕊 SC 🕊

Hotels

★ COMPRI. *(333 Riverside Dr W, Windsor ON N9A 5K4)* 519/977-9777; FAX 519/977-1411. 207 rms, 19 story. S, D $95; under 12 free. Crib free. Pet accepted, some restrictions. Garage avail. TV; cable (premium). Indoor pool; whirlpool. Complimentary full bkfst. Restaurant nearby. Ck-out noon. Meeting rms. In-rm modem link. Exercise equipt; weight machine, bicycle, saunas. Minibars. Cr cds: A, D, DS, ER, MC, V.

D ↩ ≈ 🕊 🕊 🕊 SC

★ ★ HILTON. *(277 Riverside Dr W, Windsor ON N9A 5K4)* 519/973-5555; FAX 519/973-1600. 303 units, 22 story, 10 suites. S $115-$165; D $125-$175; each addl $15; suites $350-$700; family, wkend rates. Crib free. Parking $10, valet $21. TV; cable (premium), VCR avail. Indoor

pool. Restaurant 6:30 am-10:30 pm. Rm serv 24 hrs. Bar 4:30 pm-1 am; entertainment. Ck-out noon. Convention facilities. Business center. In-rm modem link. Concierge. Gift shop. Exercise equipt; treadmill, rower. Refrigerators, minibars. Opp river. Cr cds: A, C, D, DS, ER, JCB, MC, V.

D ≈ 🕊 🕊 🕊 SC 🕊

Restaurants

★ ★ CHATHAM STREET GRILL. *(149 Chatham St W, Windsor ON N9A 5M7)* 519/256-2555. Specializes in fresh seafood, certified Angus beef. Hrs: 11:30 am-midnight; Sat from noon; Sun 5-11 pm. Closed major hols; Good Friday. Res accepted. Bar. Semi-a la carte: lunch $5.95-$10, dinner $10.95-$18.95. Cr cds: A, MC, V.

✔★ ★ COOK SHOP. *(683 Ouellette Ave, Windsor ON N9A 4J4)* 519/254-3377. Italian, continental menu. Specializes in pasta, steak, rack of lamb. Hrs: 5-10 pm; Fri, Sat to midnight. Closed Mon; Dec 24, 25; also Aug. Res required. Serv bar. Semi-a la carte: dinner $7.65-$15.85. Parking. Cr cds: A, MC, V.

✔★ ★ PASTA SHOP. *(683 Ouellette Ave, Windsor ON N9A 4J4)* 519/254-1300. Italian, continental menu. Specialties: pasta, steak Diane, veal scaloppini. Hrs: 5-10 pm; Fri, Sat to midnight. Closed Mon; Dec 24, 25; also Aug. Res required. Serv bar. Semi-a la carte: dinner $11.50-$15.85. Parking. Open kitchen; intimate dining. Cr cds: A, MC, V.

★ ★ TOP HAT SUPPER CLUB. *(73 University Ave E, Windsor ON N9A 2Y6)* 519/253-4644. Specializes in steak, seafood, barbequed baby back ribs. Hrs: 11 am-midnight; Fri, Sat to 2 am. Res accepted. Bar. Semi-a la carte: lunch $4-$10, dinner $6.50-$25. Child's meals. Entertainment Fri, Sat. Parking. Fireplace. Family-owned. Cr cds: A, DS, MC, V.

★ ★ TUNNEL BAR-B-Q. *(58 Park St E, Windsor ON N9A 3A7)* at tunnel exit. 519/258-3663. Specializes in barbecued ribs, chicken, steak. Hrs: 8-2 am; Fri, Sat to 4 am. Closed Dec 25. Wine, beer. Semi-a la carte: bkfst $3.25-$5.95, lunch $4.25-$7.95, dinner $7.45-$18.95. Child's meals. Old English decor. Family-owned. Cr cds: D, MC, V.

D

★ ★ TUNNEL BAR-B-Q'S OTHER PLACE. *(3067 Dougall Ave, Windsor ON)* 519/969-6011. Specializes in steak, seafood, veal. Salad bar (lunch). Hrs: 11 am-11 pm; Sat to 1 am; Sun to 10 pm; Sun brunch to 2:30 pm. Closed some major hols. Res accepted. Bar. Semi-a la carte: lunch $4.95-$10.95, dinner $9.95-$27.95. Sun brunch $15.95. Child's meals. Dinner music Fri, Sat. Valet parking. Old English-style banquet area. Cr cds: A, D, ER, MC, V.

D SC ⤢

★ ★ YE OLDE STEAK HOUSE. *(46 Chatham St W, Windsor ON N9A 5M6)* 519/256-0222. Specializes in French Canadian onion soup, charcoal-broiled steak, fresh seafood. Hrs: 11:30 am-10 pm; Fri to 11 pm; Sat 4-11 pm: Sun from 4 pm. Closed Good Friday, Dec 25. Res accepted. Bar to 1 am. Semi-a la carte: lunch $3.75-$12, dinner $11-$24. Child's meals. Old English decor. Family-owned. Cr cds: A, D, ER, MC, V.

Index

Establishment names are listed in alphabetical order followed by a symbol identifying their classification, and then city, state and page number. Establishments affiliated with a chain appear alphabetically under their chain name, followed by the state, city and page number. The symbols for classification are: [H] for hotel; [I] for inns; [M] for motels; [L] for lodges; [MH] for motor hotels; [R] for restaurants; [RO] for resorts, guest ranches, and cottage colonies; [U] for unrated dining spots.

ROSCOE VILLAGE INN [M] *Coshocton OH,* 239

ROSEMONT INN BED & BREAKFAST [I] *Saugatuck MI,* 196

ROSEMONT SUITES O'HARE [H] *Chicago O'Hare Airport Area IL,* 33

ROSEMOUNT INN [I] *Kingston CAN,* 351

ROSENBERRY INN [I] *Wausau WI,* 339

ROSEWATER SUPPER CLUB [R] *Toronto CAN,* 382

ROSEWOOD [R] *Chicago O'Hare Airport Area IL,* 34

ROUND BARN LODGE [M] *Spring Green WI,* 331

ROWE INN [R] *Charlevoix MI,* 141

ROYAL BROCK [H] *Brockville CAN,* 345

ROYAL INDIA [R] *Milwaukee WI,* 315

ROYAL MARQUIS [M] *Windsor CAN,* 385

ROYAL PONTALUNA [I] *Grand Haven MI,* 158

ROYAL YORK [H] *Toronto CAN,* 378

RUGBY GRILLE [R] *Birmingham MI,* 139

RUNDLES [R] *Stratford CAN,* 369

RUSSIAN TEA CAFE [R] *Chicago IL,* 30

RUSTY'S [R] *Edwardsville IL,* 39

RUTH'S CHRIS STEAK HOUSE [R] *Indianapolis IN,* 108

SA-BAI THONG [R] *Madison WI,* 305

SAFE HOUSE [U] *Milwaukee WI,* 316

SAGE'S SAGES [R] *Arlington Heights IL,* 6

SAIL INN [R] *Beulah MI,* 138

THE SALOON [R] *Chicago IL,* 30

SALPICON [R] *Chicago IL,* 30

SALT CREEK INN [M] *Nashville IN,* 118

SALT FORK RESORT & CONFERENCE CENTER [M] *Cambridge OH,* 216

SALTY'S SEAFOOD & SPIRITS [R] *Fond du Lac WI,* 293

SAM'S JOINT [R] *Battle Creek MI,* 136

SAMMY'S [R] *Cleveland OH,* 233

SAMURAI JAPANESE STEAK HOUSE [R] *Beachwood OH,* 214

SANCTUARY AT WILDWOOD [I] *Three Rivers MI,* 200

SANDPIPER [R] *Holland MI,* 164

SANDPIPER [R] *Baileys Harbor (Door Co) WI,* 278

SANFORD [R] *Milwaukee WI,* 315

SANS SOUCI [R] *Cleveland OH,* 233

SANTORINI [R] *Chicago IL,* 30

SARAH'S [R] *Portsmouth OH,* 262

SAYAT NOVA [R] *Chicago IL,* 30

SAYAT NOVA [R] *Chicago O'Hare Airport Area IL,* 34

SAYFEE'S [R] *Grand Rapids MI,* 161

SAZ'S STATE HOUSE [R] *Milwaukee WI,* 315

SCANDIA [M] *Sister Bay (Door Co) WI,* 329

SCARAMOUCHE [R] *Toronto CAN,* 382

SCHELDE'S [R] *Traverse City MI,* 203

SCHLANG'S BAVARIAN INN [R] *Gaylord MI,* 157

SCHMIDT'S SAUSAGE HAUS [R] *Columbus OH,* 238

SCHNITZELBANK [R] *Jasper IN,* 109

SCHNITZELBANK [R] *Grand Rapids MI,* 161

SCHREINER'S [R] *Fond du Lac WI,* 293

SCHULER'S OF MARSHALL [R] *Marshall MI,* 182

SCHULER'S OF STEVENSVILLE [R] *St Joseph MI,* 195

SCHULIEN'S [R] *Chicago IL,* 30

SCOFIELD HOUSE [I] *Sturgeon Bay (Door Co) WI,* 333

SCOOZI [R] *Chicago IL,* 30

SCOTTY'S [R] *Ludington MI,* 175

SEA HORSE INN [M] *Toronto CAN,* 374

SEA SHACK [R] *Toronto CAN,* 383

SEAFOOD 32 [R] *Cincinnati OH,* 226

SEASONS [R] *Chicago IL,* 30

SEASONS LODGE [M] *Nashville IN,* 118

SEAWAY [M] *Sault Ste Marie MI,* 197

SECRETS [R] *Joliet IL,* 54

SELECT INN
Wisconsin
Madison, [M] 304; *Waukesha,* [M] 337

SELENSKY'S GRAND CHAMPION GRILL [R] *Milwaukee WI,* 315

SENATOR [R] *Toronto CAN,* 383

THE SENECA [H] *Chicago IL,* 24

SETTLEMENT COURTYARD [I] *Fish Creek (Door Co) WI,* 291

SEVEN OAKES [M] *Kingston CAN,* 350

SEVEN SAUCES [R] *Athens OH,* 212

SEVEN SEAS [R] *Waukesha WI,* 337

SEVEN STARS DINING ROOM [R] *Columbus OH,* 238

SHACK SMOKEHOUSE & GRILLE [R] *Superior WI,* 334

SHAKER INN [M] *Lebanon OH,* 250

SHAKESPEARE'S DINING LOUNGE [R] *Hamilton CAN,* 348

SHANGHAI GARDEN [R] *Grand Rapids MI,* 161

SHANGRAI-LA [M] *Saugatuck MI,* 195

SHANTY CREEK [RO] *Bellaire MI,* 137

SHAW'S CRAB HOUSE [R] *Chicago IL,* 30

SHAW'S INN [R] *Lancaster OH,* 249

SHERATON
Canada
Hamilton, [H] 348; *Kitchener-Waterloo,* [H] 352; *Mississauga,* [H] 355; *Niagara Falls,* [H] 359; *Ottawa,* [H] 364; *Toronto,* [H] 378
Illinois
Chicago, [H] 24; *Chicago O'Hare Airport Area,* [H] 34; *Northbrook,* [H] 65
Michigan
Ann Arbor, [MH] 135; *Lansing & East Lansing,* [MH] 173; *Saginaw,* [MH] 192
Ohio
Canton, [MH] 217; *Cincinnati,* [H] 224; *Cleveland,* [H] 231; *Columbus,* [H] 237; *Sandusky,* [MH] 263
Wisconsin
Madison, [H] 304; *Milwaukee,* [MH] 312

SHERMAN HOUSE [I] *Batesville IN,* 90

SHERMAN HOUSE [R] *Batesville IN,* 90

Notes

Notes

Notes

Notes

Notes

Mobil Travel Guide

Looking for the Mobil Guides . . . ?

**Call toll-free 800/533-6478 around the clock
or use the order form below.**

Please check the guides you would like to order:

☐ 0-679-03506-0
America's Best Hotels & Restaurants
$11.00 (Can $14.95)

☐ 0-679-03498-6
California and the West (Arizona, California, Nevada, Utah)
$15.95 (Can $21.95)

☐ 0-679-03500-1
Great Lakes (Illinois, Indiana, Michigan, Ohio, Wisconsin, Canada: Ontario)
$15.95 (Can $21.95)

☐ 0-679-03501-X
Mid-Atlantic (Delaware, District of Columbia, Maryland, New Jersey, North Carolina, Pennsylvania, South Carolina, Virginia, West Virginia)
$15.95 (Can $21.95)

☐ 0-679-03502-8
Northeast (Connecticut, Maine, Massachusetts, New Hampshire, New York, Rhode Island, Vermont, Canada: New Brunswick, Nova Scotia, Ontario, Prince Edward Island, Québec)
$15.95 (Can $21.95)

☐ 0-679-03503-6
Northwest and Great Plains (Idaho, Iowa, Minnesota, Montana, Nebraska, North Dakota, Oregon, South Dakota, Washington, Wyoming, Canada: Alberta, British Columbia, Manitoba)
$15.95 (Can $21.95)

☐ 0-679-03504-4
Southeast (Alabama, Florida, Georgia, Kentucky, Mississippi, Tennessee)
$15.95 (Can $21.95)

☐ 0-679-03505-2
Southwest & South Central (Arkansas, Colorado, Kansas, Louisiana, Missouri, New Mexico, Oklahoma, Texas)
$15.95 (Can $21.95)

☐ 0-679-03499-4
Major Cities (Detailed coverage of 45 major U.S. cities)
$17.95 (Can $25.00)

☐ 0-679-00047-X
Southern California (Includes California south of Lompoc, with Tijuana and Ensenada, Mexico)
$12.00 (Can $16.95)

☐ 0-679-00048-8
Florida
$12.00 (Can $16.95)

☐ 0-679-03548-6
On the Road with Your Pet (More than 3,000 Mobil-rated Lodgings that Welcome Travelers with Pets)
$12.00 (Can $16.95)

☐ My check is enclosed.

☐ Please charge my credit card

☐ VISA ☐ MasterCard ☐ American Express

Total cost of book(s) ordered $ _____

Shipping & Handling (please add $2 for first book, $.50 for each additional book) $ _____

Add applicable sales tax (In Canada and in CA, CT, FL, IL, NJ, NY, TN and WA.) $ _____

TOTAL AMOUNT ENCLOSED $ _____

Credit Card # _____

Expiration _____

Signature _____

Please ship the books checked above to:

Name _____

Address _____

City _____ State _____ Zip _____

Please mail this form to: Mobil Travel Guides, Random House, 400 Hahn Rd., Westminster, MD 21157

Mobil Travel Guide

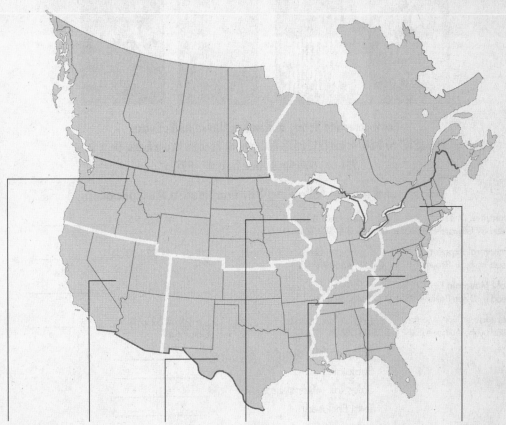

**Northwest &
Great Plains**

Idaho
Iowa
Minnesota
Montana
Nebraska
North Dakota
Oregon
South Dakota
Washington
Wyoming

Canada:
Alberta
British Columbia
Manitoba

**California
& the West**

Arizona
California
Nevada
Utah

**Southwest &
South Central**

Arkansas
Colorado
Kansas
Louisiana
Missouri
New Mexico
Oklahoma
Texas

**Great
Lakes**

Illinois
Indiana
Michigan
Ohio
Wisconsin

Canada:
Ontario

Southeast

Alabama
Florida
Georgia
Kentucky
Mississippi
Tennessee

Mid–Atlantic

Delaware
District of Columbia
Maryland
New Jersey
North Carolina
Pennsylvania
South Carolina
Virginia
West Virginia

Northeast

Connecticut
Maine
Massachusetts
New Hampshire
New York
Rhode Island
Vermont

Canada:
New Brunswick
Nova Scotia
Ontario
Prince Edward Island
Quebec

MAKE THE MOST OF YOUR TRAVELING TIME . . .

with Random House AudioBooks.

WITH MORE THAN 500 TITLES TO CHOOSE FROM, LISTEN TO GREAT BOOKS WHILE STILL ADMIRING THE SCENERY . . . YOU'LL REACH YOUR DESTINATION IN NO TIME.

  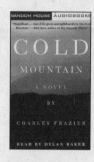 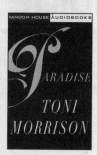

For a complete listing of Random House AudioBooks,
Fax: (212) 572-6074; call (212) 572-6004; write: Random House Audio, Dept. CC,
201 East 50th Street, New York, NY 10022

Please send me the following Random House AudioBooks:

Executive Orders by Tom Clancy (abridged, 6 hours)   _____ @ $25.95 = _____
Read by Edward Herrmann • ISBN: 0-679-43696-0

Unnatural Exposure by Patricia Cornwell (abridged, 4 hours)   _____ @ $24.00 = _____
Read by Blair Brown • ISBN: 0-679-44509-9

Cold Mountain by Charles Frazier (abridged, 3 hours)   _____ @ $18.00 = _____
Read by Dylan Baker • ISBN: 0-679-46069-1

Paradise by Toni Morrison (abridged, 6 1/2 hours)   _____ @ $25.95 = _____
Read by the Author • ISBN: 0-375-40179-2   (Quantity)

Shipping/Handling*   = _____

Subtotal   = _____

Sales Tax (where applicable)   = _____

Total Enclosed   = _____

*Please enclose $4.00 to cover shipping and handling (or $6.00 if total order is more than $30.00).
☐ If you wish to pay by check or money order, please make it payable to Random House Audio Publishing.
☐ To charge your order to a major credit card, please fill in the information below.

Charge to   ☐ American Express   ☐ Visa   ☐ MasterCard

Account No._____ Expiration Date_____

Signature_____

Name_____

Address_____

City_____State_____Zip_____

Also available wherever books are sold.

Send your payment with the order form above to:
Random House Audio Publishing, Dept. CC, 23-2, 201 East 50th Street, New York, NY 10022.
Prices subject to change without notice. Please allow 4-6 weeks for delivery.

HELP US GET TO KNOW YOU AND RECEIVE A FREE KEY CHAIN!

Please complete and return this postage paid card to Mobil Travel Guide. The information on you and your travel habits will help us improve the Guide to better serve you in the future. The first 500 respondents who successfully complete and return this questionnaire will receive a free Mobil key chain with our thanks and appreciation. The information supplied herein will be treated in confidence; names and addresses will not be released to mailing list houses or any other associations or organizations.

Please circle the appropriate letter or number, or fill in the blank, as necessary.

1. 1.__Mr.   2.__Mrs.   3.__Ms.   4.__Miss

_____

First Name   Initial   Last Name

_____

Street   Apt. No.

_____

City   State   Zip Code

2. Date of Purchase: Month___ Date___ Year___

3. How many round trips of 200 miles or more via any method of transportation have you taken in the last year?
a) How many of these were for leisure/pleasure? _____
b) How many of these were for business? _____

4. What is the duration of your average trip?
a) Leisure/pleasure travel? _____
b) Business travel? _____

5. How many of these trips were by car?
a) Leisure/pleasure travel? _____
b) Business travel? _____

6. Do you use the Mobil Travel Guide in your car?
a) Yes   b) No

7. What cities/towns/states or regions were your destinations for your last three (3) leisure/pleasure trips?
_____ _____ _____

8. What cities/towns/states or regions were your destinations for your last three (3) business trips?
_____ _____ _____

9. What kinds of activities do you prefer when you travel for leisure/pleasure? Circle all that apply.
a) Sightseeing-Historical
b) Sightseeing-Scenic
c) Camping/hiking
d) Sports and recreation
e) Shopping
f) Rest and relaxation
g) Visiting museums/galleries
h) Fine dining
i) Going to the beach

10. How much do you typically spend (on a per-night basis) for your accommodations when you travel for leisure/pleasure?
$_____ per night

11. How much do you typically spend (on a per-night basis) for your accommodations when you travel for business?
$_____ per night

12. What are your restaurant preferences when you travel for leisure/pleasure?
a) 4 or 5 Star   c) Family
b) Moderately priced   d) Fast food chain

13. What are your restaurant preferences when you travel for business?
a) 4 or 5 Star   c) Family
b) Moderately priced   d) Fast food chain

14. What kind of resources are used to plan your trips?
a) Leisure/pleasure travel?
 i) Travel books/guides
 ii) Magazines
 iii) Internet
 iv) Friends/family recommendations
 v) Travel agent
 vi) Other _____
b) Business travel?
 i) Travel books/guides
 ii) Magazines
 iii) Internet
 iv) Friends/family recommendations
 v) Travel agent
 vi) Other _____

15. If your vacation/business travel requires you to rent an automobile, how likely would you be to buy a travel guide of the area if offered (1: Not likely 5: Very likely)
1 2 3 4 5

16. Did you purchase the Mobil Travel Guide primarily for (choose one)?
a) Leisure/pleasure travel
b) Business travel
c) Maps
d) Coupons
e) Other _____

17. How did you hear about the Mobil Travel Guide?
a) Advertisement
b) Friends and family
c) Colleague
d) Point of sale (bookstore, service station)
e) Other _____

18. Where did you purchase the Mobil Travel Guide?
a) Furnished by employer
b) It was a gift
c) Chain bookstore Which? _____
d) Independent bookstore Which? _____
e) Travel store Which? _____
f) Department store
g) Drug store
h) Gift shop
i) Newsstand
j) Service station
k) Other _____

19. When was the last time you purchased a Mobil Travel Guide?
a) Never   d) Three to five years ago
b) Last year   e) More than five years ago
c) Two years ago

20. Why did you choose the Mobil Travel Guide in lieu of other options (choose three)?
a) Price
b) Quality ratings of accommodations
c) Quality ratings of restaurants
d) Factual information on accommodations
e) Factual information on restaurants
f) Information on things to see and do in the area
g) Maps
h) Discount coupons
i) Background information on states, cities and towns
j) Other _____

002

FOLD AND TAPE (OR SEAL) FOR MAILING—PLEASE DO NOT STAPLE

CUT ALONG DOTTED LINE

21. What three (3) features would you like to see more of?
   a) Accommodation choices
   b) Details/comments on accommodations
   c) Restaurant choices
   d) Details/comments on restaurants
   e) Things to see and do in the area
   f) State/city background information
   g) Maps
   h) Icons/Easy-to-use symbols
   i) Discount Coupons
   j) Other _____

22. In your opinion, does the Mobil Travel Guide improve Mobil Corporation's image?
   a) Yes
   b) No
   c) Not sure

23. You are:
   a) Female
   b) Male

24. Your age is:
   a) 18-24
   b) 25-34
   c) 35-44
   d) 45-54
   e) 55-64
   f) 65+

25. You are:
   a) Single/never married
   b) Married
   c) Separated/divorced
   d) Widowed

26. The ethnic group that best describes you is:
   a) African-American
   b) Asian
   c) Other _____
   d) Caucasian/White
   e) Hispanic

27. Highest level of education:
   a) Some High School
   b) High School Graduate
   c) Some College
   d) Technical Certification
   e) College Degree (2- or 4-Year)
   f) Some Post College Study
   g) Advanced Degree

28. Your occupation is:
   a) Professional
   b) Executive, Managerial, Administrative
   c) Military
   d) Clerical, Sales, Technical
   e) Precision, Crafts, Repair
   f) Retired
   g) Other

29. Your spouse/significant other's occupation is:
   a) Professional
   b) Executive, Managerial, Administrative
   c) Military
   d) Clerical, Sales, Technical
   e) Precision, Crafts, Repair
   f) Retired
   g) Other

30. How many children do you have living at home in the following age groups?
   a) None
   b) < 1 Year
   c) 1-2 Years
   d) 3-5 Years
   e) 6-9 Years
   f) 10-11 Years
   g) 12-14 Years
   h) 15-18 Years
   i) Over 18

31. Which choice best describes your household income level?
   a) Under $10,000
   b) $10,000-$19,999
   c) $20,000-$29,999
   d) $30,000-$39,999
   e) $40,000-$49,999
   f) $50,000-$59,999
   g) $60,000-$69,999
   h) $70,000-$79,999
   i) $80,000-$89,999
   j) $90,000-$99,999
   k) > $100,000

32. Which types of credit cards do you use most for travel?
   a) American Express, Diners Club, Discover, Carte Blanche
   b) Bank Card (Mastercard, Visa)
   c) Gas, Department Store
   d) None of the Above

33. What type of vehicle do you drive on your trips?
   a) Luxury
   b) Mid Size
   c) Compact
   d) Mini Van
   e) Sport Utility
   f) RV

34. Do you belong to an automobile club?
   a) Yes Which? _____
   b) No

35. What other products/services do you purchase specifically for travel?
   a) Tire/Auto Service
   b) Luggage
   c) Travel Store Items
   d) Maps
   e) Other _____

YOU CAN HELP MAKE THE *MOBIL TRAVEL GUIDE* MORE ACCURATE AND USEFUL

ALL INFORMATION WILL BE KEPT CONFIDENTIAL

Your Name_____
(Please Print)

Street_____

City, State, Zip_____

Were children with you on trip? ☐ Yes ☐ No

Number of people in your party _____

Your occupation_____

1.

Establishment name_____

Hotel ☐ Resort ☐ Other ☐
Motel ☐ Inn ☐ Restaurant ☐

Street_____ City_____ State _____

Do you agree with our description? ☐ Yes ☐ No; if not, give reason _____

Please give us your opinion of the following:

DECOR	CLEANLINESS	SERVICE	FOOD
☐ Excellent	☐ Spotless	☐ Excellent	☐ Excellent
☐ Good	☐ Clean	☐ Good	☐ Good
☐ Fair	☐ Unclean	☐ Fair	☐ Fair
☐ Poor	☐ Dirty	☐ Poor	☐ Poor

1998 *GUIDE* RATING _____ ★

CHECK YOUR SUGGESTED RATING BELOW:
☐ ★ good, satisfactory ☐ ★★★★ outstanding
☐ ★★ very good ☐ ★★★★★ one of best
☐ ★★★ excellent in country
☐ ✓ unusually good value

Comments:_____

Date of visit_____   First ☐ Yes visit? ☐ No

2.

Establishment name_____

Hotel ☐ Resort ☐ Other ☐
Motel ☐ Inn ☐ Restaurant ☐

Street_____ City_____ State _____

Do you agree with our description? ☐ Yes ☐ No; if not, give reason _____

Please give us your opinion of the following:

DECOR	CLEANLINESS	SERVICE	FOOD
☐ Excellent	☐ Spotless	☐ Excellent	☐ Excellent
☐ Good	☐ Clean	☐ Good	☐ Good
☐ Fair	☐ Unclean	☐ Fair	☐ Fair
☐ Poor	☐ Dirty	☐ Poor	☐ Poor

1998 *GUIDE* RATING _____ ★

CHECK YOUR SUGGESTED RATING BELOW:
☐ ★ good, satisfactory ☐ ★★★★ outstanding
☐ ★★ very good ☐ ★★★★★ one of best
☐ ★★★ excellent in country
☐ ✓ unusually good value

Comments:_____

Date of visit_____   First ☐ Yes visit? ☐ No

3.

Establishment name_____

Hotel ☐ Resort ☐ Other ☐
Motel ☐ Inn ☐ Restaurant ☐

Street_____ City_____ State _____

Do you agree with our description? ☐ Yes ☐ No; if not, give reason _____

Please give us your opinion of the following:

DECOR	CLEANLINESS	SERVICE	FOOD
☐ Excellent	☐ Spotless	☐ Excellent	☐ Excellent
☐ Good	☐ Clean	☐ Good	☐ Good
☐ Fair	☐ Unclean	☐ Fair	☐ Fair
☐ Poor	☐ Dirty	☐ Poor	☐ Poor

1998 *GUIDE* RATING _____ ★

CHECK YOUR SUGGESTED RATING BELOW:
☐ ★ good, satisfactory ☐ ★★★★ outstanding
☐ ★★ very good ☐ ★★★★★ one of best
☐ ★★★ excellent in country
☐ ✓ unusually good value

Comments:_____

Date of visit_____   First ☐ Yes visit? ☐ No

FOLD AND TAPE (OR SEAL) FOR MAILING—PLEASE DO NOT STAPLE

CUT ALONG DOTTED LINE

Mobil Travel Guide®

Las Vegas TRAVEL

UP TO 20% OFF

ENJOY 20% OFF, PLUS FREE FUN BOOKS, MEAL AND SHOW DISCOUNTS.

Call Las Vegas Travel for a 20% discount for most major casino hotels in Las Vegas.

Mention this coupon to receive free fun books, free meals and discounts on Las Vegas shows. Call **800-449-4697** for more information. For golf reservations call **800-627-4465**.

OFFER EXPIRES JUNE 30, 1999

≋ National Car Rental.

ONE CAR CLASS UPGRADE

PRESENT THIS CERTIFICATE AT A NATIONAL RENTAL COUNTER TO RECEIVE A ONE CAR-CLASS UPGRADE ON A COMPACT THROUGH FULL-SIZE 2-DOOR CAR. VALID AT PARTICIPATING NATIONAL LOCATIONS IN THE U.S.

Reservations recommended. Contact your Travel Agent or National at **800-CAR RENT®**. Subject to terms and conditions on reverse side.

Discount #5130876   PC #013354-5   Type 7

OFFER EXPIRES JUNE 30, 1999

ASTROLAND AMUSEMENT PARK
"Home of the World Famous CYCLONE"

1000 Surf Ave. • Brooklyn, NY
718-265-2100

FREE BAND

ENJOY ONE COMPLIMENTARY PAY-ONE-PRICE BAND.

Valid for one complimentary Pay-One-Price Band when a second Pay-One-Price Band of equal or greater value is purchased. Not valid on kiddie rides. Offer valid June 21 thru September 7, 1998.

VALID DURING THE 1998 OPERATING SEASON

ONE HOUR MOTOPHOTO®

50% OFF FILM DEVELOPING

ONE HOUR MOTOPHOTO INVITES YOU TO ENJOY 50% OFF THE REGULAR PRICE OF PROCESSING AND PRINTING 35MM COLOR PRINT FILM.

Limit one roll; standard size prints only. Not valid with other coupons or extra set promotions. Coupon may not be combined with any other discount or coupon. Club members take an additional 10% off coupon price. *Participating stores only.*

ZZ70101

OFFER EXPIRES JUNE 30, 1999

 Alamo

ONE FREE UPGRADE

CERTIFICATE IS VALID FOR ONE FREE UPGRADE TO THE NEXT CAR CATEGORY (WITH SAME TRANSMISSION IN EUROPE).

Just reserve a compact through a premium 4-door car in the United States or Canada, or a Group B through F in Europe or Mexico. Valid on rentals of at least 3 days. For reservations, contact your travel agent or call Alamo at **1-800-354-2322**. Be sure to request **ID Number 422325, Rate Code BY** and coupon code **UM5B** at time of reservation. For interactive reservations, **UM5B** access us at **www.goalamo.com**. See terms, conditions and blackout dates on reverse side of this coupon.

OFFER EXPIRES JUNE 15, 1999

 SUPER 8 MOTELS

10% OFF

RECEIVE A 10% DISCOUNT AT ALL SUPER 8 MOTEL LOCATIONS, OVER 1,600 MOTELS.

Mention 8800/10185 when calling Super 8 Motels at 1-800-800-8000 to make reservations.
E-Mail Address: **http://www.super8motels.com**

OFFER EXPIRES JUNE 30, 1999

CRUISE AMERICA   CRUISE CANADA

10% OFF

RECEIVE A 10% DISCOUNT OFF ALL TIME AND MILEAGE CHARGES ON CRUISE AMERICA OR CRUISE CANADA VEHICLES ONLY.

For reservations call: **800-327-7799** US and Canada.

OFFER EXPIRES JUNE 30, 1999

Please note: All offers may not be available in Canada. Call
(410) 825–3463 if you are unable to use an 800 number
listed on the coupon.

TERMS AND CONDITIONS. *National Car Rental.*

Valid for car classes indicated on front at participating National locations in the U.S. (Not valid in Manhattan, NY.) • Subject to availability and blackout dates. • Rate and time parameters, local rental and minimum rental day requirements apply. • Cannot be used in multiples or with any other certificate, special discount or promotion. • Standard rental qualifications apply. • Minimum rental age at most locations is 25.

In addition to rental charges, where applicable, renter is responsible for: Optional loss Damage Waiver, up to $15.99 per day; a per mile charge in excess of mileage allowance; taxes; surcharges; additional charges if car is not returned within a prescribed rental period; drop charge and additional driver fee; optional refueling charge; optional insurance benefits.

RENTAL AGENT INSTRUCTIONS. 1. Rental Screen 1: • Key Promo Coup # from the front side. **2.** Rental Screen 3: Key Discount # from the front side in "RATE RECAP #" field. • Key applicable rate in "RATE RECAP #" field. • Change rate for one car class lower than class of car actually rented. **3.** Write RA# and rental date below. **4.** Retain certificate at rental. Send certificate to Headquarters, Attn: Travel Industry Billing. RA#_____ Rental Date __/__/__

TASTE PUBLICATIONS INTERNATIONAL

Las Vegas TRAVEL

Advance reservations required. For show, wedding, or casino information call 900-RESORT CITY. Valid Sunday thru Thursday only, except holidays and during city-wide conventions. May not be used in conjunction with any other discount or promotion.

800-449-4697 – One Toll-Free Call Gives You All These:

Luxor • Monte Carlo • Tropicana • Circus Circus • Caesar's Palace
New York-New York • Bally's • The Orleans • Rio Suite Hotel • Plaza
Stardust • Stratosphere • Boomtown • Sahara • Westward Ho
Holiday Inn Board • Excalibur • Flamingo Hilton • Las Vegas Hilton
Lucky Lady • The Plaza • San Remo • And so many more.

TASTE PUBLICATIONS INTERNATIONAL

ONE HOUR MOTOPHOTO®

TASTE PUBLICATIONS INTERNATIONAL

CONEY ISLAND ASTROLAND AMUSEMENT PARK
"Home of the World Famous CYCLONE"

Not valid with other discount offers or on holidays.
Valid Monday-Friday in season.

TASTE PUBLICATIONS INTERNATIONAL

 SUPER 8 MOTELS

Not valid in conjunction with other discounts or promotions.
Each Super 8 Motel is independently owned and operated.

TASTE PUBLICATIONS INTERNATIONAL

 Alamo

TERMS AND CONDITIONS.

• Upgrade is subject to availability at time of rental, as certain car categories may be sold out. Valid on self-drive rentals only.
• Only one certificate per rental; not to be used in conjunction with any other discounted or promotional rate. Cannot be used with any Alamo Express Plus(SM) or a Quicksilver(SM) rental.
• Please make your reservations at least 24 hours before arrival. Travel agents please include /SI-C-UM5B in the car sell. Valid only on Association Rate Codes.
• You must present this certificate at the Alamo counter on arrival. It is void once redeemed.
• Certificate has no cash value and does not include taxes (including in California, VLF taxes ranging up to $1.89 per day), registration fee/tax reimbursements, airport concession recoupment charges, fuel, other optional items, or airport access fees, if any.
• Any used portion is non-refundable.
• Reproductions will not be accepted and expired or lost certificates cannot be replaced.
• Offer valid through March 1, 1998 through June 15, 1999. The following blackout dates apply: In the United States and Canada: 4/09-4/11/98, 5/21-5/23/98, 7/02-7/04/98, 7/16-8/15/98, 9/03-09/05/98, 10/08-10/10/98, 11/25-11/27/98, 12/17-12/31/98, 2/11-2/13/99 and 4/1-4/3/99. In the United Kingdom, Germany, Belgium, The Netherlands and Switzerland: 6/15-7/31/98 and 12/20-12/31/98. In Ireland, Greece, Portugal, the Czech Republic, and Malta: 7/15-9/30/98 and 12/20-12/31/98. In Mexico: 7/15-8/31/98 and 12/15/98-1/31/99.
• Offer is valid at airport and airport serving locations and at participating European or Mexican locations operating under the name of Alamo. Coupon not valid on plan code A1.

TASTE PUBLICATIONS INTERNATIONAL

CRUISE AMERICA MOTORHOME RENTAL & SALES
CRUISE CANADA MOTORHOME RENTAL & SALES

Offer not available in conjunction with other discount offers or promotional rates. Excludes other rental charges, deposits, sales tax, and fuels. Normal rental conditions and customer qualification procedures apply. Members must reserve vehicle through Central Reservations only, at least one week in advance of pick up and mention membership affiliation at time of reservation.

TASTE PUBLICATIONS INTERNATIONAL

Mobil Travel Guide®

The Guide That Saves You Money When You Travel!

 Audio Diversions

$25.00 VALUE

FREE 1ST YEAR MEMBERSHIP IN THE "LITERATURE FOR LISTENING CLUB™."

Membership gives you 10% off on all purchases and rentals. When renting you get twice as long (30 days) to listen to your selections with over 2,600 titles to choose from. You will never run out of choices. Call **800-628-6145**.

OFFER EXPIRES JUNE 30, 1999

 Budget All The Difference In The World.™

15% OFF

TAKE 15% OFF WEEKLY OR WEEKEND STANDARD RATES.

Valid on Economy through Full-Size Cars. For reservations call: **800-455-2848**. Be sure to mention **BCD#: T445311**.

OFFER EXPIRES JUNE 30, 1999

 Empire State Building Observatories

UP TO FOUR ADMISSIONS

ENJOY $1.00 OFF ADULT ADMISSIONS AND $1.00 OFF CHILDREN ADMISSIONS.

Offer good for up to four admissions upon presentation of coupon at ticket office. Open daily 9:30 am - midnight. Last elevator to the top at 11:30 pm.

OFFER EXPIRES JUNE 30, 1999

 DAYS INN Follow the Sun™

10% SPECIAL DISCOUNT

FOLLOW THE SUN TO DAYS INNS.

Now you can save even more at any of our more than 1,700 Days Inns throughout the United States and internationally. Just present this coupon upon check-in and we'll take 10% off our regular room rate for your entire length of stay! Advance reservations recommended so call now! For reservations and location information call **800-DAYS-INN**.

OFFER EXPIRES JUNE 30, 1999

FREE CAMPING STAY

CAMP FREE WHEN YOU RENT A KOA DEAL MOTOR HOME FROM CRUISE AMERICA.

Call **800-327-7778** and request a KOA DEAL Motor Home rental and learn how to camp free at participating KOA Kampgrounds.

OFFER EXPIRES JUNE 30, 1999

 **BUSCH GARDENS** AND **WATER COUNTRY USA** WILLIAMSBURG, VA. Anheuser-Busch Theme Parks.

UP TO $21.00 OFF

BUSCH GARDENS WILLIAMSBURG AND WATER COUNTRY USA INVITE YOU TO ENJOY $3.50 OFF THE ONE-DAY REGULAR OR CHILD'S ADMISSION PRICE.

For information on opening schedule call **800-343-SWIM**. See reverse for details.

OFFER EXPIRES JUNE 30, 1999

 AVIS We try harder.®

UP TO $20.00 OFF

SAVE FROM $10.00 TO $20.00 ON A WEEKEND RENTAL.

Rent an Intermediate through Full Size 4-Door car for a minimum of two consecutive weekend days and you can save $5.00 per day, up to a total of $20.00 off for four weekend rental days, when you present this coupon at a participating Avis location in the U.S. Subject to complete Terms and Conditions on back. For information and reservations, call the special Avis reservation number: **800-831-8000**. Be sure to mention the special Avis Worldwide Discount (AWD) number for this offer A291814. Avis features GM cars. Offer cannot be used in conjunction with any other coupon, promotion or offer.

Coupon #MUGD717 for a 2 day rental • Coupon #MUGD718 for a 3 day rental • Coupon #MUGD719 for a 4 day rental

OFFER EXPIRES JUNE 30, 1999

Taste Publications International, The Mobil Travel Guide, and Fodor's Travel Publications, Inc., will not be responsible if any establishment breaches its contract or refuses to accept coupons. However, Taste Publications International will attempt to secure compliance. If you encounter any difficulty, please contact Taste Publications International. We will do our best to rectify the situation to your satisfaction. ©1998 Taste Publications International

TASTE PUBLICATIONS INTERNATIONAL • 1031 CROMWELL BRIDGE ROAD • BALTIMORE, MD 21286

Budget
All The Difference In The World.

TERMS AND CONDITIONS

Be sure to mention BCD# T445311 when reserving an economy through full-size car and present this certificate at participating U.S. Budget locations (except in the New York metro area) to receive your member savings discount. This offer requires a one-day advance reservation, and is subject to vehicle availability. Vehicle must be returned to the original renting location except where intra-inter metro area drop-offs are permitted. Local age and rental requirements apply. Locations that rent to drivers under 25 may impose an age surcharge. Offer is not available with CorpRate, government or tour/wholesale rates, or with any other promotion. Refueling services, taxes, surcharges, and optional items are extra. Blackout dates may apply. Limit one certificate per rental.

TASTE PUBLICATIONS INTERNATIONAL

Audio Diversions

Good Books are for listening too!

More than 2,600 titles carefully drawn from among the best in travelbooks, adventure, biographies, business, children's, classics, education, how to's, foreign language, inspirational, literature, motivational, mystery, and self help books, Audio Diversions is sure to have what you need. Rentals are 10% off plus come with addressed and stamped packages for easy return.
10 % off everything.

TASTE PUBLICATIONS INTERNATIONAL

Available at participating properties. This coupon cannot be combined with any other special discount offer. Limit one coupon per room, per stay. Not valid during blackout periods or special events. Void where prohibited. No reproductions accepted.

TASTE PUBLICATIONS INTERNATIONAL

Empire State Building Observatories
Managed by:
Helmsley Spear, Inc.

Built in 1931, this 1,454 foot high skyscraper was climbed by King Kong in the movie classic. View Manhattan from the 86th floor observatory with outdoor promenade. Also enjoy the enclosed 102nd floor and exhibits of the eight wonders of the world.

TASTE PUBLICATIONS INTERNATIONAL

Present this coupon when purchasing your ticket at any Busch Gardens Williamsburg or Water Country USA General admission price. Children two and under are admitted FREE. Admission price includes all regularly scheduled rides, shows and attractions. This coupon has no cash value and cannot be used in conjunction with any other discount. Prices and schedule subject to change without notice. Busch Gardens Williamsburg and Water Country USA have a "no solicitation" policy. Limit six tickets per coupon.

1   2   3   4   5   6

PLU #R364 C365   Please circle number of admissions.

TASTE PUBLICATIONS INTERNATIONAL

KOA has over 550 locations throughout the U.S. and Canada. Cruise America and Cruise Canada have over 100 rental centers.

TASTE PUBLICATIONS INTERNATIONAL

AVIS
We try harder.

TERMS AND CONDITIONS (Save up to $20.00 on a Weekend Rental)

Offer valid on an Intermediate (Group C) through a Full Size 4-door (Group E) car for a 2-day minimum rental. Coupon must be surrendered at time of rental; one per rental. Coupon valid at Avis corporate and participating licensee locations in the continental U.S. Weekend rental period begins Thursday noon, and car must be returned by Monday 11:59 p.m. or a higher rate will apply. Offer not available during holiday and other blackout periods. Offer may not be available on all rates at all times. An advance reservation is required. Cars subject to availability. Taxes, local government surcharges and optional items, such as LDW, additional driver fee and refueling, are extra. Renter must meet Avis age, driver and credit requirements. Minimum age is 25. Offer expires June 30, 1999.

RENTAL SALES AGENT INSTRUCTION AT CHECKOUT: **1.** In AWD, enter A291814. **2.** For a 2 day rental, enter MUGD717 in CPN. **3.** For a 3 day rental, enter MUGD718 in CPN. **4.** For a 4 day rental, enter MUGD719 in CPN. **5.** Complete this information:

RA#_____ Rental Date __/__/__ **6.** Attach to COUPON tape.

TASTE PUBLICATIONS INTERNATIONAL

Mobil Travel Guide ®

The Guide That Saves You Money When You Travel!

FREE FANNY PACK

YOURS FREE WHEN YOU JOIN NPCA NOW!

Join NPCA and save our national treasures! We are offering a special one-year introductory membership for only $15.00! Enjoy the many benefits of a NPCA membership and receive: a free National Parks and Conservation Association Fanny Pack, a free PARK-PAK, travel information kit, an annual subscription to the award-winning National Parks magazine, the NPCA discount photo service, car rental discounts and more.

See reverse for order form.

MTG98

OFFER EXPIRES JUNE 30, 1999

Ripley's Believe It or Not! ®

BUY ONE GET ONE FREE!*
(Limit 6 people)

*****Receive one complimentary admission with purchase of an equal value ticket.**

Not valid with any other offers. Not for resale.
Valid only at locations listed. Coupon non-relinquishable.

Ripley's and Believe It or Not! are registered trademarks of Ripley Entertainment Inc.

PLU-MOBIL

OFFER EXPIRES JUNE 30, 1999

ADVENTURE WORLD THE GREAT ESCAPE.

$7.00 OFF

SAVE $7.00 OFF EACH REGULAR ADMISSION (UP TO 6 PEOPLE) WHEN YOU PRESENT THIS COUPON AT ANY ADVENTURE WORLD TICKET WINDOW.

One (1) coupon good for up to six people and cannot be combined with any other discount, sold, or be redistributed, and not valid with Junior or Senior admission. Valid 1998/1999 season. Call for details **301-249-1500**, for dates and time.

Code: 1017

OFFER EXPIRES JUNE 30, 1999

CHOICE HOTELS INTERNATIONAL
Sleep Comfort Quality Clarion
Friendship Econo Lodge Rodeway

10% OFF

ENJOY A 10% DISCOUNT AT PARTICIPATING COMFORT, QUALITY, CLARION, SLEEP, ECONO LODGE AND RODEWAY INN HOTELS AND SUITES.

The next time you're traveling call **800-4-CHOICE** and request Mobil discount #00052333. Advance reservations required. Kids 18 and under stay free and 1,400 hotels will provide free continental breakfast.

OFFER EXPIRES JUNE 30, 1999

Travel Discounters

UP TO $100.00 OFF

RECEIVE UP TO $100.00 OFF WHEN YOU BUY AN AIRLINE TICKET FROM TRAVEL DISCOUNTERS. CALL 800-355-1065 AND MENTION CODE MTG IN ORDER TO RECEIVE THE DISCOUNT.

Savings are subject to certain restrictions and availability. Valid for flights on most major airlines. See reverse for discount chart.

OFFER EXPIRES JUNE 30, 1999

General Cinema · LOEWS THEATRES SONY THEATRES · UNITED ARTISTS

THEATER DISCOUNT

Valid at all participating theatres.

Please send me:

_____ Sony/Loews at $4.50 each = _____
_____ United Artists at $4.50 each = _____
_____ General Cinema at $5.00 each = _____

Add $1.00 for handling. Allow 2-3 weeks for delivery. Orders over $75.00 will be sent via certified mail and may require additional processing time.

Limit 20 tickets per order.

OFFER EXPIRES JUNE 30, 1999

American Tourister · Samsonite COMPANY STORE

SAVE 20% OFF

SHOPPING SPREE!

20% off selected merchandise when you visit any American Tourister or Samsonite Company Store. All stores carry first quality luggage, accessories and gifts to fit all your travel needs at 35%-50% off comparable prices.

Call 1-800-547-BAGS for a location nearest you.

OFFER EXPIRES JUNE 30, 1999

Read each coupon carefully before using. Discounts only apply to the items and terms specified in the offer at participating locations. Remove the coupon you wish to use.

Ripley's Believe It or Not!®

Atlantic City, NJ	Myrtle Beach, SC
Branson, MO	Newport, OR
Buena Park, CA	Niagara Falls, Canada
Cavendish, P.E.I.	Orlando, FL
Grand Prairie, TX	San Antonio, TX
Hollywood, CA	San Francisco, CA
Jackson Hole, WY	St. Augustine, FL
Key West, FL	Wisconsin Dells, WI

TASTE PUBLICATIONS INTERNATIONAL

❑ **YES!** I want to preserve and protect our National Parks by becoming a National Parks and Conservation Association Member.

❑ I have enclosed a check in the amount of $15.00 for my one-year membership.

❑ Charge my annual dues to my ❑ Visa ❑ MasterCard ❑ Amex

Acct. #: _____ Exp. Date: _____

Signature: _____

Name: _____

Address: _____

City: _____ State: _____ Zip: _____

Phone: _____
Please allow 6-8 weeks for delivery of your fanny pack and first issue of National Parks Magazine.

Make checks payable and mail to: NPCA, 1776 Massachusetts Ave. NW, Washington, DC 20036-1904

TASTE PUBLICATIONS INTERNATIONAL

CHOICE HOTELS INTERNATIONAL

Sleep · Comfort · Quality · Clarion

Friendship · Econo Lodge · Rodeway

Discount is limited to availability at participating hotels and cannot be used with any other discount. Kids stay free in same room as parents. Advance reservations through **1-800-4-CHOICE** required.

TASTE PUBLICATIONS INTERNATIONAL

ADVENTURE WORLD THE GREAT ESCAPE

13710 Central Ave. · Largo, MD

301-249-1500

From Washington, DC metro area,
take I-495/I-95 to exit 15A (Rt. 214 east, Central Ave.).
Adventure World located 5 miles on left.

From Baltimore metro area,
take I-695 to I-97 south to Exit 7, Rt. 3/301 south, to Rt. 214/Central Ave. west.
Adventure World located 3 miles on right.

TASTE PUBLICATIONS INTERNATIONAL

General Cinema · **LOEWS THEATRES** SONY THEATRES · **UNITED ARTISTS**

Prices are subject to change. A self-addressed stamped envelope must be enclosed to process your order. No refunds or exchanges. Mail order only, not redeemable at box office. Passes have expiration dates, generally one year from purchase. In some cases, tickets cannot be used during the first two weeks of a first-run movie.

Name: _____

Address: _____

City: _____ State: _____ Zip: _____

Make check payable to:
Taste Publications International, 1031 Cromwell Bridge Road, Baltimore, MD 21286.

TASTE PUBLICATIONS INTERNATIONAL

Travel Discounters

Minimum ticket price	Save
$200.00	$25.00
$250.00	$50.00
$350.00	$75.00
$450.00	$100.00

TASTE PUBLICATIONS INTERNATIONAL

 COMPANY STORE
American Tourister · Samsonite

20% Off Selected Merchandise.

SHOPPING SPREE!
Call 1-800-547-BAGS

Not valid with any other promotional offer. Not valid on sale or previously purchased merchandise. Not valid on Kodak, Hasbro, Safety 1st or Ex Officio Products.

TASTE PUBLICATIONS INTERNATIONAL

Mobil Travel Guide.

When You Travel!

Coupons may not be used in conjunction with any other promotion or discount offers. **Example:** special promotional pricing.
If in doubt, please check with the establishment.